PENGUIN REFERENCE

The Penguin Dictionary of British History

Juliet Gardiner read history at University College, London. Her post-graduate research was on post-war French history and she was a Research Fellow at the Institute of Historical Research. From 1980 to 1985 she was the editor of *History Today* and subsequently an academic and trade publisher before returning to teach Communication, Cultural and Media Studies at Middlesex University in 1993.

She is the author of eight books and the editor of four on cultural and social history. These include *Over Here: GIs in Britain 1942–4* (1992), *The History Debate* (1993), *Picture Post Women* (1994), *Queen Victoria* (1998), *From the Bomb to the Beatles: The Changing Face of Post-War Britain 1945–65* (1999, in conjunction with an exhibition at the Imperial War Museum) and *Who's Who in 2000 Years of British History* (2000).

List of Contributors

55BC–AD1068
Professor David Bates, *University of Glasgow*

1068–1485
Professor John Gillingham, *London School of Economics*

1485–1660
Professor Diarmaid MacCulloch, *St Cross College, Oxford*

1660–1801
Joanna Innes, *Somerville College, Oxford*

1801–1914
Dr David Englander†, *Open University*

1914–1979
Dr John Stevenson, *Worcester College, Oxford*

The Penguin Dictionary of

British History

Edited by Juliet Gardiner

PENGUIN BOOKS

PENGUIN BOOKS

Published by the Penguin Group
Penguin Books Ltd, 27 Wrights Lane, London W8 5TZ, England
Penguin Putnam Inc., 375 Hudson Street, New York, New York 10014, USA
Penguin Books Australia Ltd, Ringwood, Victoria, Australia
Penguin Books Canada Ltd, 10 Alcorn Avenue, Toronto, Ontario, Canada M4V 3B2
Penguin Books (NZ) Ltd, Private Bag 102902, NSMC Auckland, New Zealand

Penguin Books Ltd, Registered Offices: Harmondsworth, Middlesex, England

Originally published in 1995 as *The History Today Companion to British History* by Collins & Brown Ltd
This revised and updated edition published by Penguin in agreement with Collins & Brown Ltd 2000

Typeset in Great Britain by Saxon Graphics, Derby
Printed and bound in Great Britain by Clays Ltd, St Ives plc

Preface

If no statement is value-free, few can escape their history. The film *The Madness of King George III* had overseas audiences wondering if they had missed parts one and two; the predicate of 'New Labour' is that there was (or is) an old Labour; news items about Zimbabwe offer explanation by reference to the country's colonial identity as Rhodesia; the most recent cinema version of Jane Austen's *Mansfield Park* anchors the gracious houses and rolling grounds to wealth culled from slavery and, to (grossly) paraphrase Sir William Harcourt, 'devolution has made historians of us all'.

To visit a National Trust stately home, to join in a political debate, to hold views on the role of the monarchy, the need for judicial review or the power of state, to ponder the name for a two-wheeled horse-drawn cab, or to call your computer-hostile colleague a 'Luddite', all these are moments of engagement with British history just as is research into historical documents, the careful retrieval of pottery shards or sitting a history exam.

The Penguin Dictionary of British History aims to be a guide for all those moments: its coverage is comprehensive from the first Roman invasion of Britain in AD 43 to the activities of the G8 nations in 2000, encompassing the history of all parts of the British Isles: England, Ireland, Scotland and Wales. It has been written by six distinguished historians, each an expert in his or her particular period. In addition specialists in business, colonial, constitutional, diplomatic, economic, legal, military, naval history and the history of science have contributed entries and part entries. Each entry reflects the complexity of the period, and the diversity – even sometimes the inconsistency across entries – of these approaches complements the diversity and richness of Britain's history. Since history is concerned both with what happened in the past and how the past is recounted, the entries are both factual and interpretative, covering events, processes and debates. Many of the headings will be familiar and predictable: many will not.

There are entries on political, economic, social, religious and cultural history but in a single volume reflecting such longevity and breadth, choices have had to be made and there is much that has had to be left out. Some entries are period-specific, many are not and entries like Blasphemy, Divorce, Homosexuality, Missionaries, for example, straddle several centuries. There is a strong historiographical strand and for some subjects where the sequence of events is complex, chronologies have been included: there are also maps and a list of monarchs and prime ministers, and there is a web of cross references throughout the *Dictionary* so that an entry may be informed by a nexus of other entries.

What, therefore were the criteria for inclusion and reluctant exclusion? As this is a dictionary of British History that is what informs the entries. People and events have entries if they are salient to the course of British history. There is a concentration on events and processes while biographical entries are limited to a representative range of major figures in the narrative of Britain, and historians whose chronicles are a primary source of historical information are also included.

In biographical entries, life dates immediately follow the name: regnant dates or other dates of office follow the position or office to which they relate. Biographical entries are restricted to a single forename except for persons widely known by two forenames (e.g., Brunel, Isambard Kingdom) or initials (e.g. Smith, F(rederick) E(dwin), or because it is necessary to distinguish between two or more persons with the same surname, who also share a forename (e.g., Cecil, Robert and Cecil, Robert Gascoyne). All kings, queens and royal princes and princesses are listed under their forenames (e.g. Anne Boleyn). More controversially, all peers are listed under their family names (e.g. Wellesley, Arthur rather than Wellington, 1st Duke of), but all are cross referenced from title to family name. Given the various systems for numbering peerages G.E. Cockayne's *Complete Peerage of England, Scotland, Ireland etc.* (revised edition V. Gibbs, 13 volumes, London 1910–1914) was followed as the standard source for the forms of titles. Saints appear under their names, while towns or institutions named after saints appear under St (thus Alban, St but St Albans). The names of Romans are given in their familiar form (e.g. Agricola, Julius Ceasar) with their full name given in brackets. Cross references are indicated by small capitals in the text: given the large number of cross references and the desire not to overload the text, the references do not always match the exact wording of the entry (e.g. Luther cross references to Lutherism).

I am grateful to the six main contributors to the *Penguin Dictionary of British History* namely Professor David Bates, Professor John Gillingham, Professor Diarmaid MacCulloch, Joanna Innes, Dr John Stevenson, and Dr David Englander who tragically died before this book was published. In addition I would like to acknowledge the work of Dr David Souden, Dr Stephen Badsey, Royal Military Academy, Sandhurst, Professor Theo Barker, Professor Emeritus, London School of Economics, Professor Clive Emsley, Open University, Dr Bernard Foley, University of Liverpool, Professor Henry Horwitz, University of Iowa, Professor Pat Hudson, University of Cardiff, David Lyon, National Maritime Museum, Dr Ian MacBride, Corpus Christi College, Cambridge. Thanks are also due to Susanne Atkin, Mark Collins, Alexander Gardiner, Kate Kirby, Ulla Weinberg, Neil Wenborn and Nigel Wilcockson.

In a work of this ambition there will be inevitable omissions, excesses and idiosyncrasies and for any of these which grate, as editor, I apologise.

Juliet Gardiner

List of Maps

A

Aachen, Treaty of, *see* AIX-LA-CHAPELLE, TREATY OF, 1748

Abadan Crisis, Anglo-Iranian crisis provoked when the Mussadeq government nationalized the Iranian oil industry in 1951, and seized the main oil production and refinery installations of the Anglo-Iranian Oil Company (later British Petroleum) at Abadan on the Gulf without offering compensation. The incident became the most serious post-war dispute between an oil-producing country and major international oil corporations. Britain considered military action and appealed to the International Court at The Hague. Pressure on Iran from the American and British governments and domestic disquiet at the lack of any oil revenues led in 1953 to a military coup which toppled Mussadeq. The dispute was then settled by a treaty under which Iran retained ownership of its oil but sold it to a consortium of eight international oil companies, including BP, and shared profits with them.

Abbot, George (1562–1633), Archbishop of Canterbury (1611–33). After a distinguished Oxford career, he became dean of Westminster in 1600. Favour from JAMES I resulted in appointments to bishoprics, culminating in CANTERBURY in 1611. A strong CALVINIST and supporter of the alliance with the Dutch United Provinces, he was detested by LAUD and the ARMINIANS; his influence with James therefore declined. In 1621, his reputation as a churchman was damaged when he accidentally killed a gamekeeper while hunting with a crossbow. CHARLES I never favoured him, and in Abbot's last years, Laud was archbishop in all but name.

Abdication Crisis, 1936, political dilemma that led to the abdication on 11 Dec. 1936 of EDWARD VIII in favour of his brother, the Duke of York, who became GEORGE VI. It resulted from Edward's desire to marry the twice-divorced American woman Wallis Simpson, which he announced to Prime Minister BALDWIN in Nov. and made public on 3 Dec. Baldwin, with the support of the opposition, the Church of England and the DOMINIONS regarded such a marriage as inconsistent with the king's status as head of the Church of England. When his proposal of a MORGANATIC MARRIAGE proved unacceptable to the government, the king was forced to choose between his prospective bride and the throne. There was much sympathy for Edward, and a popular 'King's Party' was briefly mooted. Faced, however, with virtual unanimity of opinion against the marriage within the establishment, Edward chose to abdicate. He married Mrs Simpson in France in June 1937.

Aberdeen The third largest city in Scotland and royal BURGH with its charter from DAVID I, Aberdeen was burned by EDWARD III in 1337, and the town and its cathedral were subsequently rebuilt. The two UNIVERSITIES, King's College, founded 1494, and Marischal College, founded 1593, were united in 1860. Aberdeen is Scotland's largest fishing port, and the harbour was constructed in two phases in the 19th century. Its principal appearance is of grey, Victorian solidity, most of its building stone being granite. The city had a considerable new lease of life and injection of wealth from the late 1970s with the NORTH SEA OIL boom.

Aberdeen, 4th Earl of, *see* GORDON, GEORGE

Abhorrers, 1680, LOYALISTS who counter-petitioned against those demanding the exclusion of the Catholic Duke of York (the future JAMES II) from the succession, in the EXCLUSION CRISIS of 1679–81.

Abingdon Abbey, Oxon. (formerly Berks.), founded in the latter part of the 7th century, but achieved eminence after the derelict site was granted to St Ethelwold in *c.*954. As one of the first monasteries to be restored by the TENTH-CENTURY REFORM, it was the source from which many other new foundations, such as ELY, PETERBOROUGH and THORNEY, were colonized. It was dissolved in 1537.

Abortion Induced abortion through human intervention was illegal in the United Kingdom until the passing of the Abortion Act 1967, which permitted the termination of pregnancy in certain circumstances up to 28 weeks (subsequently reduced to 24 weeks).

It is impossible to estimate how far abortion was practised in the past. Until the advance of modern clinical techniques, abortions were procured through the administration of herbs, spirits or other treatments, or by physical intervention, all of which carried considerable hazards for the mother. Most evidence – in the form of prosecutions, memoirs or ORAL HISTORY – for abortion being practised comes from the 20th century, when women were more likely to limit fertility within marriage than in previous centuries. (*See* BIRTH CONTROL; DEMOGRAPHIC TRANSITION; FERTILITY.)

Abortion is a contentious ethical issue. The Roman Catholic Church and Islam forbid it, the law technically regards it as acceptable only when the health of mother or child are at some risk, whereas many, especially feminists, regard the issue as entirely a woman's choice.

Aboukir Bay, Battle of, *see* NILE, BATTLE OF THE

Abyssinian Crisis, *see* APPEASEMENT; HOARE-LAVAL PACT

Accession Day Tilts, Elizabethan court TOURNAMENTS held on the Queen's accession day (17 Nov.), a national holiday by the 1570s. Masterminded by Sir Henry Lee, they revived the cult of CHIVALRY in the interests of Protestant patriotism, and became theatrical shows full of contemporary allusion, much of it now obscure.

Acts of Parliament are all listed under their titles: e.g. for Act in Restraint of Appeals, *see* RESTRAINT OF APPEALS, ACT IN.

Adam of Usk (*c.*1352–1430), historian. After taking his doctorate at Oxford, he became a lawyer on the staff of Archbishop Thomas ARUNDEL and was thus an eyewitness to the turbulent events at the end of RICHARD II's reign. After some adventurous years in Rome and on the fringes of the opposition to HENRY IV, in 1411 he was allowed to return to England and to a quieter life. In his *Chronicon* – a continuation of HIGDEN's *Polychronicon* – he covered the period 1377–1421. His work closes with comments on the costs of HENRY V's wars, which that monarch's admirers have always found disquieting.

Adams, Gerald (Gerry) (1948–), politician From a Republican background, Adams has been politically active since the 1960s. When the IRISH REPUBLICAN ARMY (IRA) split from SINN FÉIN (1969–70) Adams sided with the Provisional IRA but the extent of his involvement with the IRA is a matter of dispute. In the late 1970s he emerged as the leader of a group urging the development of community politics as an auxiliary to military action, and in 1980 was elected MP for West Belfast (1983–92, 1997–). With John Hume (1937–) he entered into negotiations in the 1990s which led to the IRA ceasefire and the involvement of Sinn Féin in the peace process, after its isolation during the violence of the 1980s. Sinn Féin endorsed the Good Friday Agreement in April 1998 (*see* ULSTER) and Adams was crucial in gaining acceptance for the Northern Ireland Assembly, but progress has been fragile due to the continued refusal of the IRA to start the process of decommissioning arms. Adams has played a significant part in the political evolution of Sinn Féin, but it remains unclear how far he can reconcile Sinn Féin's role as an anti-system party with the exercise of political power.

Addington, Henry (1st Viscount Sidmouth) (1757–1844), Tory politician and Prime Minister (1801–4). A Tory SPEAKER of the House of Commons from 1789 to 1801, and prime minister thereafter, Addington was committed to a policy of peace abroad and retrenchment at home. These seem to have been achieved with the Treaty of AMIENS in 1802 and the abolition of the wartime necessity of INCOME TAX. However, the treaty turned out to be little more than a truce and Addington was finally forced to resign. Whereas he had been an uninspiringly mediocre prime minister and regarded as a placeman, Addington (who was created Viscount Sidmouth in 1805) was a harsh secretary of state for home affairs (1812–22) with but a single response to manifestations of 'distress' in his treatment of LUDDITE activities and popular radicalism, particularly with the introduction of the repressive SIX ACTS in 1819 after the PETERLOO MASSACRE.

Addled Parliament, nickname of the Parliament called in April 1614 to solve the crown's financial problems. The Earls of Somerset and Suffolk stirred up trouble, probably to harass William Herbert, Earl of Pembroke, who had been urging the calling of Parliament. Suspicions of royal intentions in the COMMONS culminated in a fierce dispute about privileges with the LORDS. When JAMES I abruptly dissolved the Parliament in June, nothing had been achieved.

Adela of Louvain (?–1151), Queen of England. The daughter of Godfrey, Duke of Lotharingia and Count of Louvain, Adela (or Adeliza) was married to HENRY I in Jan. 1121, a few weeks after the death of Henry's only legitimate son in the wreck of the WHITE SHIP. Consequently, she was under enormous pressure to produce a male heir. To make this more likely, she was required to stay at Henry's side and, as a result, had no opportunity to act (as did most queens of the ANGLO-NORMAN REALM) as regent in her husband's absence. No child was born, and the succession dispute between STEPHEN and the Empress MATILDA followed Henry's death in 1135. Adela then married William de Albini, Earl of Arundel, and provided an heir before retiring to a nunnery. She was an important patron of ANGLO-NORMAN literature.

Aden, one of the former British imperial bases in the Middle East sphere, now in the Republic of Yemen. The port city was acquired in 1839 and became a coaling port on the route between the SUEZ CANAL and INDIA. With the collapse of British influence in the region after the SUEZ CRISIS, Aden was accorded a strategic importance out of all proportion to its real status. Britain made a bold attempt to forge a South Arabian Federation of Aden and the princely Yemeni states, but this was short-lived as by the mid-1960s Aden had become the focus of Arab nationalist unrest. British troops were involved in frontier fighting with the Yemen from 1964 and were faced by internal disorders, which erupted into serious riots and terrorism in early 1967. Following a UNITED NATIONS mission, Britain granted Aden independence in Nov. 1967 as the People's Republic of South Yemen, and completed a military withdrawal.

Adler, Nathan (1803–90), Chief Rabbi of the British Empire (1844–79). German-born, he created the centralized ecclesiastical hierarchy that was a distinctive feature of Anglo-Jewry. He monopolized ecclesiastical and rabbinical authority and was legally recognized as the arbiter on all religious issues within the United Synagogue. The father of the Anglo-Jewish pulpit, he created Jews' College, London (1855) to develop a Jewish variant of the Anglican ministry. *See also* JEWS IN BRITAIN.

Admiralty, department of state controlling the NAVY. A board of lords commissioners evolved from the office of lord admiral (later lord high admiral) during the 17th century, the crucial developments apparently happening during the CIVIL WAR and Commonwealth (*see* INTERREGNUM). This board was placed over the older Navy board, and other and lesser boards (victualling, sick & hurt, etc.) which controlled this most complex and expensive of government departments. The Admiralty board was the main policy-forming body. Recent research has tended to show that, despite legends to the contrary, it was reasonably efficient and often forward-looking, whilst the degree of corruption was exaggerated by the reformers of the late 18th and early 19th centuries. The first lord might be a sailor or a politician, by the 19th century normally the latter. In 1832 the navy board was abolished as part of a programme of WHIG reforms. The result was to overload the Admiralty with administrative work at the expense of intelligent policy-making, a defect which would only begin to be remedied by the creation of a proper naval staff just before the beginning of WORLD WAR I. The naval officers on the board were the sea lords, the first being the professional head of the service, and in the 1900s also the navy's representative on the chiefs of staff committee. The creation of a unified ministry of defence in 1964 ended its existence.

Admonitions to Parliament, controversial pamphlets. The first *Admonition* (1572), ostensibly an open letter to Parliament, was an unprecedentedly bitter PURITAN attack on the Church hierarchy of the ELIZABETHAN SETTLEMENT and medieval liturgical survivals. Its probable authors, John Field and Thomas Wilcox, were imprisoned.

The second *Admonition* (also 1572), probably written by Christopher Goodman, and a *Reply* (1573) by Thomas Cartwright, were responses to a reply by the bishops, and provoked angry literary exchanges (1573–7) between Cartwright and John WHITGIFT.

Adrian IV (*c.*1100–59), Pope (1154–9). Born near St Albans, after studying in Paris Nicholas Breakspear became a CANON and then Abbot of St Rufus in Avignon. He was made a cardinal in 1149, and as papal legate to Scandinavia in 1152–3, he carried through an important reorganization of the churches there. In Dec. 1154, he was elected pope – the only English-born one so far – taking the name Adrian IV (or Hadrian IV). From 1156 until the end of his pontificate, he was at odds with the Emperor Frederick Barbarossa; his grant of Ireland to HENRY II (*see* LAUDABILITER) was less controversial at the time but the cause of endless controversy since.

Adullamites, a phrase coined by John BRIGHT in 1866 to describe the WHIG dissidents led by Robert Lowe against the Liberal government's proposals for FRANCHISE reform, whose opposition brought about the fall of the RUSSELL ministry. The name – derived from 'Adullam', the cave to which David escaped from Saul and gathered followers (1 Samuel 22) – underscores how often biblical references featured in Victorian political discourse.

Advowson, the right to present a clergyman to the bishop for appointment to a BENEFICE within his DIOCESE. It is considered a property right, and therefore disputes about advowsons have always been triable in royal courts rather than CHURCH COURTS.

Ælfgar (?–*c.*1062), Earl of Mercia. The son of Earl LEOFRIC of Mercia and an important participant in English politics on the eve of the NORMAN CONQUEST. He was twice exiled from England, probably because of his opposition to the apparently inexorable rise to power of HAROLD, TOSTIG and other sons of Earl GODWINE of Wessex. He was able to maintain his status and pass his earldom on to his son EDWIN because he could rely on Welsh military support to secure his reinstatement in MERCIA.

Ælfheah, St, Archbishop of Canterbury (1005–12). The drafter, with Archbishop WULFSTAN of York, of some of the important legislation of ETHELRED II THE UNREADY's reign. He was taken prisoner by the Danish army of THORKELL THE TALL in 1011, and was murdered by the latter's followers in 1012 when he protested against a ransom that the Danes were demanding for his release.

Ælfhere, Ealdorman of Mercia (956–83). One of the most powerful magnates of the reigns of EADWIG and EDGAR, he was particularly notable for his part in the anti-monastic reaction that followed Edgar's death, and in the TENTH-CENTURY REFORM. The so-called anti-monastic reaction in the reign of EDWARD THE MARTYR and at the start of the reign of ETHELRED II THE UNREADY is generally seen as being more concerned with property and power than as springing from any anti-religious feeling. Ælfhere was one of a group who exploited the disorders of the period to attack the power of politically influential churchmen such as Bishop ETHELWOLD of Winchester.

Ælfthryth (?–*c.* 1000) Queen of England. Second wife of King EDGAR and mother of King ETHELRED II THE UNREADY, her notoriety rests on sources from the late 11th century onwards, which suggest her complicity in the murder of her stepson, EDWARD THE MARTYR, in 978. Some scholars accept her innocence because of the absence of contemporary testimony, while others point to the fact that the murderers were never punished. Although influential until her death, she disappeared from court between 984 and 993, a period when the weak-willed Ethelred allowed Church lands to be plundered.

Ælle (?–*c.* 491), King of the South Saxons. The first of the seven kings named by BEDE as exercising *imperium* over the English peoples south of the Humber (*see* BRETWALDA). Later sources credit him with the establishment of the kingdom of the South Saxons (i.e. SUSSEX) in the late 5th century, but all specific details of his activities are open to doubt.

Ælthelfryth, St (?–679), Queen of Northumbria. The daughter of Anna, King of EAST ANGLIA, and founder of the double monastery of ELY in 673, she is an example of the women of high social standing who played a major part in the development of English MONASTICISM. Prior to becoming an abbess, she had apparently remained a virgin through two marriages (one to ECGFRITH, King of NORTHUMBRIA). An example, like that of St Hilda (614–80), a Northumbrian princess, abbess of Whitby, of the major role which aristocratic women played in the development of Christianity in England (*see* CONVERSION).

Affinity, the relationship between two people created by marriage or sexual intercourse within or outside marriage. In CANON LAW, a pre-existing affinity renders a MARRIAGE null within certain degrees of relationship (for instance sister- and brother-in-law), although the computation of these degrees has varied over time; it achieved particular complexity in the later Middle Ages. *See also* CONSANGUINITY.

Afghan Wars, a series of wars waged by the British in Afghanistan, north-west of INDIA, to establish control and contain the encroaching power of Russia. In the first war (1838–42) Britain failed to install a puppet ruler in the face of Russian confrontation, provoking a major rebellion in the capital, Kabul, in 1841. The British army was forced into a humiliating surrender, and almost 20,000 retreating soldiers died.

Sher Ali secured victory in the Afghan civil war of 1863–6, and sought defensive alliances with Britain, and then with Russia. In 1876, however, when the Afghans refused the British envoy but accepted a Russian one, the British invaded. Although Britain and Russia had already made peace, fighting continued in Afghanistan in the second Afghan war (1878–80). Soon after the treaty of Gandamak was signed in 1879, there was a rising in Kabul. The British, under General ROBERTS, retaliated with considerable force, and an accommodation was again reached.

The third and final conflict occurred in 1919 when the Afghans, feeling Britain's strength had been sapped by WORLD WAR I, sought to rid themselves of Britain and British India. They were however no match for the superior forces and firepower of the British, but Britain finally recognized Afghanistan as a separate sovereign state.

Africa Britain had had connections with the Mediterranean areas of North Africa since the prehistoric trade with the Phoenicians, but it was in the 17th century that contact with the continent flourished, especially with SLAVE TRADING posts in the James River on the GAMBIA, Sierra Leone and the GOLD COAST, the latter under the ROYAL AFRICAN COMPANY by 1676. English settlement in the Dutch colony at the Cape of Good Hope in the south finally resulted in its seizure by Britain in 1806 during the NAPOLEONIC WARS. The creation of the African Association in 1788 and the foundation of MISSIONARY SOCIETIES had meanwhile paved the way for the exploration of the interior, in a series of heroic expeditions including Mungo Park's up the Niger in 1805–6, LIVINGSTONE's three expeditions between 1841 and 1873, and STANLEY's of 1871–7, the first east–west crossings of the continent.

Africa was generally regarded by Britain as an unexploited reserve resource and became the principal object of European IMPERIAL ambitions in the late 19th century. Rebellions from the 1880s, notably the ZULU WARS, and the incursions into Africa by other European powers – France, Germany, and the Belgian king – led to the SCRAMBLE FOR AFRICA when large areas of the continent were claimed as British colonies. By 1910 conquest had given way to administrative control, with the process complete by 1924, and to economic exploitation, as settlers arrived and many of the indigenous population became migrant workers. SOUTH AFRICA, the principal white colony, increasingly went its own way, notably with the institutionalized racial discrimination of the apartheid system. The steady growth of independence movements, with notable outbursts of violence like the MAU MAU troubles in KENYA, and the economic instability of the exploitation of tropical cash crops, meant that African colonies were short-lived. The WIND OF CHANGE foretold by MACMILLAN blew swiftly through the continent in the 1960s, as nation after nation gained its independence from the colonial power. *See also* BASUTOLAND; BECHUANALAND; BOER WARS; BRITISH EMPIRE; EGYPT; NIGERIA; NYASALAND; RHODES, CECIL; RHODESIA; SUDAN; SWAZILAND; TANGANYIKA; UGANDA; ZANZIBAR.

Agadir Crisis, 1911. One of the incidents that heightened the tensions which were to erupt in WORLD WAR I, the crisis arose out of the opposition of Germany to the possible French annexation of Morocco – ostensibly to assist the sultan in crushing a local rebellion – and the dispatch of the warship *Panther* to defend German interests. The British, fearing the construction of a German naval base at Agadir on the Moroccan coast, threatened war. The international conference that resolved the issue compensated the Germans with territory in the Congo; French control in Morocco remained undisturbed. As a consequence, the British drew closer to the French, and in the series of naval talks that followed, it was agreed that, in the event of a war involving either country, the French fleet would be deployed in the Mediterranean while the British fleet would guard France's north coast. The defence of France had, in effect, become the central tenet of British foreign policy. *See also* ANGLO-GERMAN RIVALRY.

Agincourt, Battle of, 25 Oct. (St Crispin's Day) 1415, one of the key engagements of the HUNDRED YEARS WAR, fought between the French and an English army commanded by HENRY V. Having captured Harfleur, Henry marched across Normandy towards Calais, and was intercepted by a larger French force near the village of Azincourt (the modern French spelling conventionally anglicized to 'Agincourt'). The overconfident French launched a frontal assault on the English position and suffered appalling losses at the hands of Henry's archers. The victory opened the way for the English king's conquest of Normandy, and made him into a hero overnight. As represented by SHAKESPEARE in his history play *Henry V*, Agincourt became the archetypal patriotic victory of the 'few' fighting in a just cause against a foreign foe, a view accentuated in the wartime (1944) film of the play directed by and starring Laurence Olivier.

Agitators, *see* PUTNEY DEBATES

Agrarian Revolution, *see* AGRICULTURAL REVOLUTION

Agricola (Gnaeus Julius Agricola) (40–93), Roman soldier and governor (78–84). A wealth of information about him is contained in the laudatory biography written in 97–8 by his son-in-law TACITUS. During Agricola's governorship, he was the capable agent of the Romans' imperial policy of continuing military advance in Britain. He first crushed the ORDOVICES and annexed Anglesey, then carried out a series of campaigns that took Roman power northwards to the Forth–Clyde line and culminated even further north in the victory against the CALEDONII at the battle of MONS GRAUPIUS. As a result, a LEGIONARY FORTRESS was begun at INCHTUTHIL in Tayside.

Agricola's achievements were many and significant, including the establishment of Roman bases at Carlisle and CORBRIDGE and the building of forts and roads up to and along the Forth–Clyde line. Consolidation of his advance into northern Scotland became impossible when, shortly after his recall, an entire legion was removed from Britain to deal with a crisis on the Danube frontier. *See also* ROMAN CONQUEST; DUMNONII; NOVANTAE; SELGOVAE; VOTADINI.

Agricultural Holdings Acts 1875, 1883, 1906 These addressed the long-standing grievance whereby all agricultural improvements – temporary and permanent – passed to the landlord at the end of the tenancy without any compensation being payable. Provisions for payment of compensation were loosely drawn and easily evaded in the early attempts at legislation. The Agricultural Holdings Act 1906, which was more effective than its predecessors, conferred on tenants the rights to freedom of cropping, disposal of produce, and compensation for damage done by game and for unreasonable disturbance.

Agricultural Rates Act 1896 A response to the agricultural DEPRESSION, it devoted about £1 million to the relief of rates with reduced assessment for land. As land alone was affected, it was condemned as a blatant piece of class legislation.

Agricultural Revolution, historians' term, classically evoking an agricultural counterpart of the INDUSTRIAL REVOLUTION. The century 1750–1850 saw both a restructuring of rural social relations – with the passage of hundreds of parliamentary ENCLOSURE acts reducing common rights and promoting the consolidation of individual holdings, and increases in farm size expanding the numbers of very substantial tenant farmers – and increases in output and (to a lesser extent) in productivity, stimulated by the need to feed the growing population, and achieved by an extension of the cultivated area, exploitation of economies of scale, and the diffusion of new crops and farming methods (traditionally associated with such men as Robert Bakewell, Coke 'of Norfolk', 'Turnip' (2nd Viscount) TOWNSHEND, and Jethro Tull and Arthur Young). Historiographical debate surrounds not only the character of these changes, but the place of agricultural change in relation to the broader process of industrialization, and whether it preceded, reinforced or arose from the British INDUSTRIAL REVOLUTION. Some historians have wanted to extend the term back to the 17th century, or even to appropriate it for that period. By 1750, most English farm land was already enclosed; much land was held on lease, and especially in the south there was a large agricultural labouring class. Most of the innovations which were to be diffused in the following century had been pioneered; regional specialization was well advanced; and the rise of an export trade in grain in the early 18th century suggests growing productivity. Other historians have stressed that there were continuing and arguably more important changes after 1850: it was only from *c.* 1840 that the absolute size of the rural population and agricultural labour force began its long decline; the scale of investment in farm machinery rose significantly; new techniques and technologies – especially improved drainage – made possible changes in the regional pattern of production; and new – sometimes artificial – fertilizers helped enhance productivity.

Whether, when and how the agricultural revolution was an important force in industrialization is also hotly debated. Growing landlessness was clearly vital in generating a supply of proletarianized workers for the industrial sector, whilst agriculture was also important in supplying food, raw materials and capital. Contemporaries such as MALTHUS and Ricardo saw agriculture as a brake on the economy and historians currently stress that the food supply only just kept pace with the growing population of the late 18th and early 19th centuries, whilst agriculture also absorbed considerable capital during the NAPOLEONIC WAR period, just when the industrial economy needed it most.

CHRONOLOGY

1733 *Horse-hoeing Husbandry* published by Jethro Tull, its emphasis on clean farming and reductions in seed and drilling points towards important principles of cultivation.

1764 Joseph Elkington of Warwicks. develops use of deep trench for underdrainage of sloping land that was flooded by the bursting of springs.

1778 Thomas Coke holds first of his annual gatherings that were to diffuse agricultural knowledge widely.

1784 Threshing machine invented by Andrew Meikle.

1800 Hay-tossing machine invented by Salmon of Woburn.

1827 Reaper invented by the Revd Patrick Bell of Carmyllic.

1830–40 Substitution of iron tools for wood; iron ploughs and harrows come into general use.

1835 James Smith of Deanston, Perths., institutes system of shallow drains filled with stones and covered over.

1843 Cylindrical clay pipe invented by John Read, a signal advance in artificial drainage systems; Rothamsted experimental station in Herts. founded to promote application of agricultural chemistry to manure and fertilizers.

1845 Machine-made clay pipes produced by Thomas Scruggy.

1848 State loans for drain pipes, repayable over 22 years, made available by PEEL.

Agricultural Societies Originating in the 18th century, these aimed to promote agricultural improvement by testing and publicizing new methods, crops and machinery. The Scottish Society of Improvers (founded in 1723) and the Irish DUBLIN SOCIETY (1731) were early examples; both offered prizes to encourage innovation. The English Society of Arts (1754) shared these concerns. In the later 18th century, English regional societies appeared – e.g. the Bath Agricultural Society (1777). Agricultural shows were held under their auspices. The longevity of these societies – some of which still survive – suggests that they were felt to perform a useful function.

Agriculture

ROMAN AND ANGLO-SAXON

Knowledge of agriculture in the Roman and early medieval periods depends heavily on the evidence of archaeology and aerial photography, and, subsequently, on trying to generalize from findings which are, by their very nature, local and, therefore, quite probably, untypical. The agriculture of Roman Britain was in broad terms organized either around the VILLA, an imposed economic unit farmed mostly by slaves, or the small fields of a multitude of British farmers. The Roman villa system usually failed to survive the ANGLO-SAXON SETTLEMENTS. These settlements are also generally associated with a shift to farming in the valleys in regions of relatively dense settlement and to the cultivation of the arable, and away from the more upland, pastoral emphasis of British farming. The extent of change should not, however, be exaggerated even in areas of relatively dense settlement, since the OPEN FIELDS typical of English farming have on occasion been shown to overlay a British field system. It is also doubtful whether the Anglo-Saxons brought in any major technological improvements; the heavy plough, fundamental to any improvement in crop yields, was probably used in parts of Britain in Roman times. The livestock, especially cattle and sheep, which were basic to the British pastoral economy, remained of great importance to farming throughout the Anglo-Saxon period.

MEDIEVAL

The greatest changes of the medieval period are primarily associated with the continued clearing of moorland and forest and the creation of nucleated villages; the latter should probably be seen as representing an increasingly communal exploitation of local lands organized by a lord, and involving organized and defined labour services (*see* MANOR). The increasingly frequent references to markets in the sources from the 10th century onwards shows that agricultural production was not – and probably never had been – merely to satisfy local needs. Even in the earliest historical periods, the agrarian economy of the more populous regions of Britain was far from being a localized subsistence economy.

During the middle ages mixed farming was the rule throughout the British Isles. In Ireland and in the Highland zone of Britain farmers tended to grow oats and barley rather than wheat, and keep more cattle than sheep; in lowland Britain these proportions were often reversed. In England DOMESDAY BOOK reveals that as much land was under the plough in 1086 as in 1900. Although the absence of records means that peasant farming largely escapes the view of historians, the agricultural productivity of great estates can be investigated thanks to the survival of thousands of sets of manorial accounts for the period *c*.1250 to *c*.1450 – themselves the products of the adoption of new management techniques after *c*.1200. In the 13th century – a period of HIGH FARMING – rising population and rising demand for cereals meant that lords were principally interested in the profits of arable farming. Since the long-term effect of cropping was to lower yields through the continuous depletion of soil nitrogen, in maintaining cereal yields per acre that were not significantly surpassed until the 18th century, farmers showed both ingenuity and innovation. They achieved this by growing legumes which converted air nitrogen into soil nitrogen, and through an integrated regime of arable and pastoral husbandry (i.e. using dung, both animal and human, to recycle nitrogen). Indeed until *c*.1310 cereal yields per acre tended to improve as high grain prices and relatively low wages enabled more labour-intensive methods of preparing the soil, weeding and harvesting to be adopted. Moreover on land newly taken into cultivation crops benefited for a few decades from the reserves of soil nitrogen. Even so by 1300 productivity in terms of labour was probably falling, and living standards falling.

Whether or not the economy could have coped with a population which continued to grow is a moot point. As it happened, natural disasters caused population levels to drop dramatically – first, 'the great famine' of 1315–17, the result of harvest failures caused by bad weather; then the BLACK DEATH and subsequent outbreaks of BUBONIC PLAGUE in the later 14th century. From the 1370s grain prices fell and labour costs rose, so yields per acre probably dropped slightly, but demand for meat and dairy produce remained relatively buoyant. Increasingly lords expanded their pasture and turned to animal husbandry to produce meat, milk and wool – a switch in emphasis that continued until the early 16th century.

EARLY MODERN

Following the pioneering work of R. H. Tawney, historians saw the period 1500–1650 as crucial for English agriculture. Stimulated by POPULATION growth, farming turned from subsistence towards the market, and the area of cultivable land was expanded for the first time since the contraction of the early 14th century. Traditional forms of tenure were eroded by LEASEHOLD, small farmers lost out to larger landowners, and ENCLOSURES greatly eroded the OPEN FIELD system. Productivity rose and new crops were introduced, including winter feed for livestock, while pastoral farming, particularly of sheep, gained in profitability against arable.

Inevitably, subsequent historians have proposed substantial modifications to this picture. Many of the innovations were not Tudor but late medieval; the market, for instance, was more important in medieval production than previously realized. The enclosure movement was already active in the 15th century, while the open field system had long been of minor importance in wooded regions. Conversely, it was the mid- or late 17th century before output was much affected by wider cultivation and new crops; diversification may, in any case, have been a response to slackening demand after 1650. It is difficult to generalize between different agricultural regions, but nationwide, the number of small cultivators was actually rising simultaneously with the number of large farms.

Nevertheless the distinctiveness of the period 1500–1650, between two eras of population stagnation, remains undeniable: England's population more than doubled – from 2.5 million to 5.2 million – and the growth of industry, particularly CLOTH, also stimulated demand for agricultural produce. Boom prices in the WOOL industry collapsed after the 1520s, so more land came into food production, with increasing regional specialization between cattle and arable produce. FAMINE was still possible in the early 17th century, causing constant government worry about grain supply, but surviving evidence of late 16th-century farmhouses and other buildings suggests new agricultural prosperity.

1650–1870

In the late 17th and early 18th centuries English agriculture entered a phase of rising output stimulated by increasing labour productivity. Estimates suggest that each worker in agriculture was producing food for 1.5 non-agricultural workers in 1650, 2.5 by 1800 and 6.0 by 1911. These improvements, which set England aside from continental experiences, were propelled by technological changes (new crops, rotations and more investment in buildings, drainage, etc.), and by institutional change: the growth of large estates and larger farms, enclosure, and changing employment relations. Before population growth and urbanization accelerated after the mid-18th century, the sector produced a significant grain surplus which was exported to southern and northern Europe. Grain was important to the balance of payments in the first half of the 18th century at a time when European demand for English manufactures was sluggish. Innovations, initiated in the 16th and early 17th centuries, were significantly if patchily extended: manuring, stock-breeding and convertible husbandry (the use of grass leys, sheep folding and nitrogen-fixing fodder crops). The light sandy soils of the south and east adapted most easily to the new crops and rotations and they became the major grain-producing areas of England, whilst areas like the clay regions of the Midlands were forced to change to grass, and to turn to manufacturing BY-EMPLOYMENTS to combat unemployment. Specialist crops for local urban markets were developed: hops, vegetables, fruit, dyestuffs, commercial pig and poultry rearing, cattle raising and fattening. Guano and coprolite were used as fertilizers from the late 18th century, but as with farm machinery, their spread and impact was slight before the 1830s and 1840s. Innovations were pioneered as much by tenant farmers, smallholders and labourers as by aristocrats like Bakewell, TOWNSHEND and Coke, or leisured cranks like Jethro Tull, who have usually been depicted as the heroes of development. The use of rotational techniques accelerated in the early 19th century as a response to rising prices, especially during the NAPOLEONIC WARS, but the spread of innovations, especially the threshing machine in the 1830s and 1840s was slowed by bitter labour resistance, including arson, animal maiming and the Captain SWING RIOTS. Labourers feared further erosion of their wages (low by national standards throughout the 19th century) and unemployment.

In many areas of the country, small owner-occupied farms were squeezed out by the process of enclosure, and a three-tier structure of large estates with tenant farmers employing landless labourers became dominant. This was not, however, the case in all areas: the pastoral north and west and the market gardening areas near to towns tended to retain a large share of small owner-occupied units, and very small farmers (owner occupiers and tenants together) remained much more common than is usually thought. Institutional changes together with increasing labour productivity and rising prices of foodstuffs led to changes in employment relations. The employment of live-in farm servants for year-long periods declined in favour of wage labour, although the old system was retained through the 19th century in some areas, notably east Yorks. Also, many fewer women were employed resulting in serious losses to family earnings in rural areas.

Most debate about agriculture during this period revolved around the concept of an AGRICULTURAL REVOLUTION, the role of agriculture in the INDUSTRIAL REVOLUTION, and the developments, such as HIGH FARMING, which occurred in the mid-19th century in response to the repeal of the Corn Laws which had protected English agriculture from grain imports in the early 19th century.

1870–1980

In the late 1870s agriculture suffered, along with the rest of the economy, from the onset of economic depression. For arable farming in particular the effects of the domestic recession were severe but in addition a new phenomenon was in play: since 1873 imports of grain from the United States had been rising, and by 1879 the price of grain actually fell. The US effectively became the 'swing producer', filling shortfalls in domestic production and thereby keeping prices down: by 1895 the price of wheat was less than half of its average price between 1867 and 1877. The acreage given over to wheat production fell by nearly 40 per cent, from 2.9 million in 1880 to 1.8 million by 1900. The gross value of all cereals was less than half of what it had been 20 years before. Livestock producers were also under pressure: from the 1870s imports of beef, mutton, pigmeat, etc., reached 300,000 tons per annum coming mainly from Europe and the Midwest of the USA. By 1885 improvements in refrigeration made it feasible to freeze meat almost indefinitely, thereby increasing competition from NEW ZEALAND, AUSTRALIA and Argentina. By 1895 imports of meat reached 500,000 tons – over 30 per cent of domestic consumption.

The contribution of agriculture to national output fell from approximately 17 per cent in 1870 to 10 per cent in 1890, and was down to 6 per cent in 1911–13. At the same time the labour force continued its inexorable decline, so that by 1901 it accounted for only 8 per cent of total employment in Great Britain. Not all of the decline reflected agricultural depression however: younger people were attracted to other forms of employment, and as transport improved so too did access to nearby towns, thereby increasing occupational mobility.

The depression at the end of the 19th century was a result of various factors, some of which were national and local, but British agriculture was also subjected to significant technological and structural changes in the world economy. In particular transport and refrigeration improvements extended the competitive reach of grain and livestock producers in distant parts of the globe.

Nevertheless the decade before World War I saw a gradual amelioration in the position of British farming. Not only was this period marked by generally rising prices compared with the years of the Great Depression, but it was also characterized by considerable improvements in agricultural education and the application of scientific methods drawn from plant physiology, agricultural zoology, animal nutrition, etc. This had long-term beneficial effects on farming productivity.

WORLD WAR I changed the market for agricultural output in the UK but initially the reactions of both farmers and government were sluggish. However, the German submarine campaign in 1916 made it clear that reliance on imports could not be taken for granted and that it was necessary to increase domestic production. For the first time a policy for food could be discerned. Thus in 1917 the Corn Production Act guaranteed wheat and oat prices until 1922. The existence of a guaranteed minimum gave farmers confidence and the acreage ploughed increased sharply. The price guarantees were an open-ended commitment of the public purse, however, which was apparent within a year: grain prices dropped sharply in 1921 and the government found itself faced with very substantial outlays. By Aug. 1921 the government abandoned its scheme; the farmers were embittered by what they perceived as 'betrayal' and agriculture faced a further prolonged spell of falling prices and contracting employment.

The slump of the 1930s was particularly severe for agriculture as the sector lacked any form of protection. Whilst other countries closed their markets, the UK became a target for exporters. Protection was unavoidable and in 1932 the NATIONAL GOVERNMENT introduced the Import Duties Act, the essential instrument by which Britain administered its tariff arrangements. However, the position of agriculture in the UK was complicated because Britain was the head of an Empire much of which produced agricultural commodities; hence an indiscriminate tariff was not feasible. This problem was tackled at the OTTAWA CONFERENCE of 1932 which established the regime of IMPERIAL PREFERENCE. Its essential principle was that domestic producers enjoyed protection but that Empire producers faced lower duties than 'foreigners'. The reciprocal outcome of course was that British exports received preferential treatment and there were guarantees that protection against British goods would not be 'excessive'. Unfortunately this agreement was of little benefit to agriculture in the UK because, while European farmers enjoyed the benefit of import barriers, British farmers faced aggressive competition from the Empire.

This is not to say that government did nothing to aid agriculture: subsidies, marketing schemes and sporadic import restrictions were used. Marketing schemes were generally viewed favourably and were based on the Agricultural Marketing Acts of 1931 and 1933. Schemes could set minimum and maximum prices and a variety of other regulations, e.g. the quantities sold by members could be restricted. The Milk Marketing Boards were established under this legislation and were regarded as highly successful. In effect the scheme enhanced the bargaining power of the producer vis-à-vis the distributors; all milk was sold through the Boards who had the power to negotiate with the distributors and to choose the highest prices. In addition, there was a tiered system of prices, so that the price of milk for liquid use was higher than the prices charged to wholesalers using milk for dairy products – cheese and butter producers. The Milk Marketing Boards were swiftly followed by marketing schemes for potatoes, bacon and pigs.

In the context of the 1930s, however, these measures were at best palliative: in 1933 the overall index for agricultural prices was 76 per cent of its average for 1927–29, while by 1938 it had risen to some 88 per cent. Farmers' incomes of course reflected this problem, and the numbers of people employed in farming dropped from nearly 860,000 in 1930 to 697,000 by 1938.

Britain entered WORLD WAR II with a much clearer plan for food supply than in 1914: the ministry of food was the only purchaser of food and immediately took control of existing stocks; RATIONING was introduced and price controls were imposed at various stages of distribution. Farmers were effectively guaranteed a market at fixed prices and were in addition offered incentives to stimulate production of potatoes, wheat and milk. By the autumn of 1940 the government guaranteed these arrangements until the end of hostilities and for a further year thereafter. Home production rose sharply, as it had to given the problems in keeping Atlantic shipping routes open. In 1944 the price of sheep, cattle and milk was guaranteed until 1948; in addition an annual review of farm prices was agreed.

After World War II the emphasis was on expanding food production to meet prevailing shortages and to economize on scarce foreign exchange. State intervention in agriculture became a feature of the UK economy: not only were prices guaranteed, but farmers were given subsidies, extensive aid with investment and cheap credit facilities. The main support for domestic agriculture was now effected by a system of deficiency payments: the government maintained price guarantees to farmers and allowed markets to operate freely. Thus consumers were able to buy agricultural commodities at world prices which were generally lower than UK prices as they were determined by the most efficient producers. Domestic farmers who could not produce profitably at the world price would receive a higher guaranteed amount determined at the annual review. This had the merits of being reasonably efficient and transparent. Consumers were able to enjoy the benefits of cheap food; producers could sell as much as they wished; the degree of subsidy extended to the industry was clear; and finally, as the deficiency payments came from general taxation, to which the better off contributed more than the poor, the scheme even tilted towards greater equality of incomes.

Entry into the EEC (*see* EUROPEAN UNION) involved considerable difficulty for agricultural policy in Britain. The system of support for farmers in Europe was one of high market prices and protection from international sources of supply via tariffs, which was enshrined by the Common Agricultural Policy. The switch to a scheme based on protection would clearly increase food prices, and the burden of support would now fall on consumers. This change from a traditional policy of cheap food posed domestic political problems, but in addition there were international difficulties. The effect of the CAP on the *pattern* of British imports would be considerable. Most of the UK's agricultural imports came from non-European areas and over half from the Commonwealth: the CAP involved the imposition of trade barriers on the larger part of UK imports and relaxing them on only a small proportion. A staged adjustment process – so-called transitional arrangements – of 4–5 years was agreed before the full CAP regime was to apply to the UK. Nevertheless this inefficient 'trade diversion' was part of the price the UK (and non-European producers) were required to pay to enjoy the industrial/commercial and political advantages of EU membership. Unfortunately the overall demand for food was not rising as rapidly as supply; hence overproduction in a number of products came to be the norm. In addition, Britain's entry into the EU in 1973 coincided with the end of the post-war boom. The rise in unemployment in other sectors of the economy limited the opportunities for farmers to move out of agriculture. The increase in oil prices also drove up inflation, which increased further the financial outlays on the CAP; by 1980 it was absorbing nearly three-quarters of the total EU budget, leaving that much less for other policies. The British government as one of the major net contributors to the EU was obviously concerned to stabilize these commitments, and reforming the CAP became a major objective of policy in the 1980s. Whilst the productivity of British agriculture has risen over 40 per cent since 1973 (largely due to declining labour input), it is an industry in crisis due to a number of factors: the oversupply of commodity markets, cheap food imports, a declining market for exports, reduction in EU subsidies, and the strength of sterling all leading to a sharp fall in prices over the last few years. The price producers received for sheep fell 37 per cent between 1996 and 1998 and 54 per cent for pigs. In March 1996 the government announced a possible link between BSE (Bovine Spongiform Encephalopathy) or 'mad cow disease' in cattle and a new variant of Creutzfeldt–Jakob disease (CJD) in humans. This led to an EU world-wide ban on exports from the UK of all bovine animals, beef and beef products. Various safeguards were put in place, cattle slaughtered etc., and by 1999 the incidence of BSE had fallen from around 1,000 cases a week in 1993 to 55, but the ban was not lifted until July 1999, and the take up has not been enthusiastic. It is estimated that the total cost of the BSE crisis in eradication measures and lost exports was around £5 billion.

EU regulated tests of genetically modified (GM) crops in the UK have met with intense consumer resistance whilst organic agriculture (produced without artificial feed, fertilizers or pesticides) is growing in popularity, but at present prices make it a choice for the better off.

Agriculture, Golden Age of British, 1850–73, a term describing the period of exceptional prosperity following the repeal of the CORN LAWS, and created by the inability of foreign competitors to take advantage of Britain's FREE TRADE policy. Urbanization and POPULATION growth extended the market for British farmers and improvements in livestock breeding, drainage and farm buildings, together with more businesslike management, specialization and the economies derived from mixed (livestock and arable) farming, enabled widespread prosperity for landowners and tenant farmers, if not for their labourers whose wages remained amongst the lowest in the economy.

Aid, a payment that medieval kings and lords expected from their tenants at times of special need. According to MAGNA CARTA, tenants were obliged to aid their lord to meet the costs of ransoming him (if necessary) and knighting his eldest son, as well as financing his eldest daughter's first marriage. During the 13th and 14th centuries, English kings ordinarily levied aids on these occasions, and the practice was revived by the Tudors. Meanwhile, in the 13th century, the summoning of assemblies to discuss whether or not an extraordinary aid should be paid to the crown – e.g. to meet the costs of war – played an important role in the development of PARLIAMENT.

Aircraft and Air Transport Both the NAVY and the ARMY had been interested in the possibilities of aviation some time before the first aircraft flew in Britain (1908). By 1914 there were naval and military arms of the ROYAL FLYING CORPS (the former to split off as the Royal Naval Air Service – only to be merged again in the RAF in 1918) and an embryonic aircraft industry. WORLD WAR I caused an immense expansion of all of these and forced the pace of technical development. After the war bombers were adapted as pioneer airliners, and in 1924 Imperial Airways was founded by amalgamating a number of small airlines. In 1940 this became British Overseas Airways Corporation (BOAC), specializing at first in 'Empire' routes, and British European Airways (BEA). These two were merged in 1969 to form British Airways, which is now one of the biggest airlines in the world. Between the wars aircraft performance increased by leaps and bounds, with metal construction, better streamlining, engine developments and improved fuel technology, and by 1945 after further wartime development supersonic flight was in sight and the availability of concrete runways built for military purposes meant that the foundation for the post-war explosion of air travel was laid. One set of figures can stand for this incredible growth: in 1936 6 million passenger kilometres were flown by British airlines, in 1979 the figure was 47 billion. In 1998 UK airlines flew a record 1.3 billion aircraft kilometres, 71% more than in 1988 and carried 62 million passengers on scheduled services and 31 million on charter flights. If planning permission is granted, a fifth terminal could be operational by 2006 catering for 30 million passengers a year, and there are improvements planned for Stanstead, Gatwick, Edinburgh, Manchester, Bristol and Belfast too. Meanwhile the large number of aircraft manufacturers in 1945 (including Avro, Bristol, De Havilland, Fairey, Handley-Page, Hawker, Short, and Vickers-Supermarine) were reduced by failures and government-encouraged mergers by the 1980s to two, and then one (British Aerospace), main firms, with a helicopter manufacturer (Westlands) and Shorts in Northern Ireland. The expense of starting new projects has made most of the more recent military and large airline projects into joint ones with European partners to share the burdens of research and development, and to compete with the American aerospace giants in the vitally important escort markets. *See also* WARFARE, AIR.

Some of the more important and successful British aircraft were: (fighters) Sopwith Camel, Hawker Fury and Hurricane, Supermarine Spitfire, Hawker Hunter and Harrier; (bombers) Handley Page 0/400, Avro Lancaster, English Electric Canberra; (general purpose military) Bristol Fighter, De Havilland Mosquito; (trainers) Avro 504C and Tutor, De Havilland Tiger Moth, Br. Ae. (Hawker) Hawk; (airliners) Handley-Page Heracles, De Havilland Comet, BAe (De Havilland) 146. Notable firsts include the first cabin aircraft, the first all-metal aircraft, the development of jet propulsion, the first jet airliner, the first commercial supersonic airliner (together with the French) and the introduction of the 'jump jet' fighter.

Air Raid Precautions (ARP) Extensive air raid precautions were begun to deal with ZEPPELIN raids during WORLD WAR I. Growing fear of aerial bombardment, possibly using gas, led to the implementation of precautions in peacetime in 1935, including the distribution of gas masks and leaflets on protecting civilians from blast and incendiary bombs. On the eve of WORLD WAR

II, air raid precautions involved the organization of the hospital services into a unified national scheme to deal with casualties and the increasing provision of both area and domestic shelters. ARP wardens were responsible for enforcing the 'blackout' and assisting in maintaining services after raids.

Aix-la-Chapelle, Congress of, 1818. This was preoccupied with the rehabilitation of post-Napoleonic France. Once France's debts had been paid, it was agreed to withdraw the army of occupation from its soil and invite France to join Britain, Russia, Austria and Prussia in the maintenance of international stability. A Russian proposal for a league of great powers to guarantee to all sovereigns their thrones and territories was unacceptable to a British public sceptical of diplomacy by conference and unwilling to police Europe on behalf of monarchical reaction.

Aix-la-Chapelle, Treaty of, 1668, *see* TRIPLE ALLIANCE, 1668

Aix-la-Chapelle (or Aachen), Treaty of, Oct. 1748. This ended the war of the AUSTRIAN SUCCESSION, providing for the restoration of all conquests, except Prussia's of Silesia. France was victorious on the Continent, but Britain had control of the seas. Louisbourg on Cape Breton Island was returned to France in return for the surrender of French conquests in the Low Countries and INDIA. DOMINICA, TOBAGO, ST LUCIA and ST VINCENT were to be 'neutral islands', settled by no European power, though this did not take effect. The Pragmatic Sanction (assuring Maria Theresa's position in Austria) and the British PROTESTANT SUCCESSION were guaranteed, and Charles Edward STUART, the Young Pretender, excluded from France. Territorial disputes in Italy, which had raged since the Peace of UTRECHT, were settled in Spain's favour: Parma and Piacenza were given to a Spanish Bourbon. The ASIENTO between Spain and Britain was extended for four years. Most powers were dissatisfied with the slightness of their gains; within eight years, conflict was again joined with the outbreak of the SEVEN YEARS WAR.

***Alabama* Claims,** demands for compensation made by the United States against Britain for damage done to American shipping by the commerce raider *Alabama*, built by Lairds of Birkenhead for the Confederate Navy. The ship had been finally sunk off Cherbourg by the US Navy in 1864. The US government charged Britain with breach of neutrality, and made a formal claim which GLADSTONE settled by arbitration at Geneva in 1872; Britain agreed to pay the US $3,160,000. Anglo-American relations were much improved in consequence.

Alanbrooke, 1st Viscount, *see* BROOKE, ALAN

Alban, St (?3rd–4th century AD), Christian martyr. A Roman soldier residing in the town of VERULAMIUM, he reputedly sheltered a Christian during a persecution, was himself converted to Christianity and preferred to die rather than hand over the man to whom he had given refuge. The story is first told in an early 5th-century source and, because of its early date, can probably be accepted, despite the relatively slight evidence for persecution in Roman Britain. The martyrdom supposedly took place on what is now the site of the high altar of the abbey church of St Albans, founded by OFFA.

Albemarle, 1st Duke of, *see* MONCK, GEORGE

Albert, Prince (1819–61), Prince Consort of Queen Victoria. The younger son of the Duke and Duchess of Saxe-Coburg-Gotha, he was serious, studious, conscientious and capable. He married VICTORIA, his first cousin, in 1840 and was given the title Prince Consort in 1857. Because his German connections made him suspect in the eyes of the British public, his direct influence on politics was limited, though he replaced Lord Melbourne (*see* LAMB, WILLIAM) as his wife's political adviser and mentor, and thus she gradually shed her anti-Tory inclinations. However, he found greater scope for his energies in philanthropic activity and the promotion of the arts and sciences. He organized the GREAT EXHIBITION of 1851 and was instrumental in the development of the South Kensington museums in London. His premature death from typhoid led to the partial withdrawal of the queen from public life and a temporary weakening of the monarchy as a result.

Alchemy Strictly, the term applies to the search for methods of creating gold and silver out of other substances, but in a wider sense to the whole practice of experimental and theoretical chemistry in the medieval world. Its principles were derived from Greek science mediated through Arab civilization, a history reflected in the uncertain derivation of the word itself, which may be either Greek, Ancient Egyptian or Arabic. *See also* HERMETICISM.

Alcuin of York (*c*.737–804), scholar. Northumbrian, educated at YORK, who became Charlemagne's leading adviser on intellectual and educational matters, Alcuin was one of a number of Englishmen who found employment in the Frankish kingdoms, and was the most influential Englishman abroad since the time of St BONIFACE. He was a poet and voluminous letter writer as well as a great organizer, and was richly rewarded by Charlemagne for his considerable services.

Alderman, a term derived from the Anglo-Saxon EALDORMAN. In origin, aldermen were officials chosen by BOROUGHS to keep order within a certain area or WARD, but the term was soon used more generally and vaguely for those holding senior civic office, either within GUILDS or on the governing councils of towns: in imitation of LONDON city organization, they often formed a court of aldermen. They became part of the standardized structure of boroughs created in 1835, being elected for six years by the members of the borough council, and this was extended in 1888 to the new county councils by the LOCAL GOVERNMENT ACT. The office was abolished after 1974, and aldermen now survive only in the anomalous government of the City of London, which retains its Court of Aldermen.

Aldfrith, King of the Northumbrians (685–705). Although responsible for restoring stability to NORTHUMBRIA after the turbulent reign of King ECGFRITH, he is most important for his extensive patronage of learning, which gave great encouragement to the development of the so-called NORTHUMBRIAN RENAISSANCE of the age of BEDE.

Aldhelm, St (*c*.640–709), Abbot of MALMESBURY from *c*.674 and Bishop of SHERBORNE from 705. A man whose range of contacts and writings shed much light on the early English CHURCH, like his great contemporary BEDE Aldhelm was a master of all branches of learning, having studied under both Roman and Irish scholars. Malmesbury certainly became the most important southern English abbey during his lifetime.

Ale and Alehouses Ale, now a description applied to certain types of modern beer, was originally the general name for the drink brewed by fermentation with an infusion of malt; brewing is a sensible strategy for drinks when water supplies are often polluted. Hops for brewing beer were introduced to England by the 15th century, and beer gradually replaced ale as a standard drink. Alehouses may have existed as early as the Anglo-Saxon period. Late medieval drinking-places became socially stratified: inns provided meals and high-class accommodation; 'respectable' drinking (wine and beer) was done in taverns; but alehouses were more common – in both senses of the word. They became central to the world of ordinary folk when 16th-century Protestantism curbed church-centred social drinking (e.g. CHURCH ALES); figures indicate that, by 1577, throughout England there was one alehouse for every 150 inhabitants. Their popularity never flagged down the years to the emergence of the modern public house in the 19th century, despite frequent attacks by magistrates and clergy on what one JP called these 'nurseries of naughtiness', beginning with statutory licensing in 1552. Establishment hostility was especially strong during the REFORMATION, the INDUSTRIAL REVOLUTION and the FRENCH REVOLUTION. *See also* TEETOTALLERS; TEMPERANCE SOCIETIES.

Alexander I (*c*.1077–1124), King of Scots (1107–24). The son of MALCOLM CANMORE and St MARGARET, he married Sybilla, illegitimate daughter of HENRY I. Upon succeeding his brother EDGAR on the throne, he continued his parents' policy of 'reforming' the Scottish Church, bringing in monks and canons from England – e.g. to his new priory at SCONE. He died childless and was buried at Dunfermline.

Alexander II (1198–1249), King of Scots (1214–49). The son of WILLIAM I THE LION, he successfully overcame challenges for the throne from the MACWILLIAM dynasty. Although promised the northern counties of England for his support of the MAGNA CARTA rebellion (1215–17), in the end the Anglo-Scottish agreement of 1217 (which effectively allowed the English king to retain the northern shires) ushered in a peace between the two kingdoms that lasted 80 years. This was formalized by Alexander's marriage to HENRY III's sister Joan in 1221, and then by the treaty of York (1237) by which Alexander renounced the ancestral claim to NORTHUMBRIA. Thus the Tweed-Solway line was finally established as the Anglo-Scottish border. He pursued an active western policy, campaigning in ARGYLL in 1221–2, and putting an end to GALLOWAY's status as kingdom in 1234. He was on the verge of annexing the Western Isles when he died in 1249 on the island of Kerrera in Oban Bay.

Alexander III (1241–86), King of Scots (1249–86). The son of ALEXANDER II, he was married to HENRY III's daughter Margaret in 1251. Ten years later, as soon as he was able to take personal control of government, he resumed his father's policy of annexing the Western Isles. King Haakon of Norway reacted vigorously, but the drawn battle of LARGS in Oct. 1263 and Haakon's death two months later ensured that the western highlands and islands would be won for the Scottish crown. In 1264, the Kingdom of MAN surrendered to Alexander, and in 1266, the Norwegians agreed to the treaty of PERTH. In 1284, following the deaths of his sons, Alexander secured the recognition of his granddaughter MARGARET, MAID OF NORWAY as his heir-presumptive, but still hoping for a son, he married a second wife, Yolande of Dreux. Five months later, on 18 March 1286, during a night ride to see her, he fell from his horse and was killed.

Alexander, Harold (1st Earl Alexander of Tunis) (1891–1969), soldier. Having served in WORLD WAR I and later in India, he fought with the BRITISH EXPEDITIONARY FORCE in France in WORLD WAR II and was evacuated at DUNKIRK on 3 June 1940. Appointed commander-in-chief of the British forces in the Middle East in Aug. 1942, he framed the strategies that underlay MONTGOMERY'S victories in the Western Desert (*see* EL ALAMEIN) leading to the final surrender of the Axis forces in Tunisia in May 1943. The invasion of Sicily in July 1943 was carried out under Alexander's overall command on the ground, and in Dec. 1943 he was promoted to field marshal and appointed supreme Allied commander in the Mediterranean, overseeing the bitter fighting of the Italian Campaign to its conclusion in May 1945.

After the war, Alexander served as governor-general of CANADA (1946–52), then as minister of defence (1952–4).

Alfred the Great (849–99), King of Wessex (871–99). Alfred ruled during what was undoubtedly one of the decisive periods in England's history. He became king at a time when the GREAT ARMY was threatening to overrun all the English kingdoms, and until 878 his reign was largely one of desperate defence and, finally, of apparent despair when he was driven to take refuge in ATHELNEY. His emergence to win the battle of EDINGTON and make the peace of WEDMORE with GUTHRUM seems miraculous, but was probably the result of better preparations than historical sources admit.

The 880s were a period of consolidation. For example, it was during that decade that the *BURHS* were constructed that enabled Alfred to resist the renewed VIKING attacks of the 890s without too much difficulty. Although Alfred was not able to expand the frontiers of WESSEX much during his lifetime, he conclusively contained the Viking threat and laid the basis for the military advances of his 10th-century successors.

Most of the contemporary sources – such as ASSER's *Life* and the *ANGLO-SAXON CHRONICLE* – were written close to Alfred's court. Because of their inevitable bias, the impression they give of a moral and justified ruler is unlikely to be a true one. Someone who achieved as much as Alfred must have been extremely ruthless. The seizure of LONDON, a MERCIAN town, the proclamation that he was king of all the English not under Danish rule (thereby denying the rights of other ruling dynasties – *see* UNIFICATION), the seizure of monastic lands and the massive scheme of public works involved in building the *burhs* – all demonstrate that Alfred was a man willing to override existing property rights and push through massive projects when it suited him.

None the less, Alfred's range of activities is exceptionally impressive. This is above all true of his educational and literary reforms; not only did he bring scholars to his court, he also himself translated key texts from the Latin, such as Gregory the Great's *CURA PASTORALIS*. His purpose in doing this was partly to make his people pleasing in the eyes of God and partly to make available literature that would encourage in times of adversity.

Alien Priories, priories in medieval England belonging to foreign churches, usually French abbeys. Most were the result of benefactions made by newly rich Normans after the conquest of 1066. Anti-French feeling during the HUNDRED YEARS WAR led to their suppression in 1414.

Allegiance, *see* OATHS

Allen, William (1532–94), Cardinal. His promising Oxford career cut short by the ELIZABETHAN SETTLEMENT, he was at Louvain University in 1561–2 and then returned to England, but in 1565 he fled once more to avoid punishment for his Catholic activism. He inspired the foundation of an English college at Douai (Flanders), pioneering the training of priests to win England back to Roman Catholicism (politics forced a move to Rheims in 1578). Resident at Rome from 1582, he was drawn into intrigue against the English government and backed the Spanish ARMADA. He was made a cardinal in 1587. His death was a blow to the English Catholic community, left without effective leadership to heal serious divisions (*see also* APPELLANTS, ROMAN CATHOLIC).

Alliance Party, Northern Irish political party founded in April 1970 as a non-sectarian grouping seeking support across denominational boundaries. It is committed to power-sharing and the devolution of responsibility to the parties of Northern Ireland. It has so far failed to have any MPs elected to Westminster but secured 6 per cent of the votes cast at the Northern Irish Assembly elections and 6 seats on the Assembly set up under the terms of the 'Good Friday Agreement' (1998) for which elections were held in June 1998.

Almanacs, annual publications containing astrological prognostications. Almanacs were among the vast output of ephemeral printed material from the late 16th century onwards which attests to the growth in READING (nearly 0.5 million were being sold annually in the 1660s), and they were an important part of many publishers' stock in trade. Although they turned into journals and their foretelling character gradually diminished, they never quite lost that element, and it occasionally survives to this day.

Almshouse, communal house or separate housing funded by private charity for the reception and support of the poor, usually the aged. Their endowment was a conspicuous and common act of philanthropy in the 16th and 17th centuries, persisting to the 19th century. Inmates were usually subject to a form of discipline in dress and behaviour so as to be seen as worthy recipients of charity. *See also* POOR RELIEF.

Alney, Peace of, 1016. This treaty, made on an island in the Severn near Deerhurst, Glos., between EDMUND IRONSIDE and CNUT, was an attempt to reach a settlement in the warfare between the two men, which was a continuation of the events of the reign of ETHELRED II THE UNREADY. It gave WESSEX to Edmund and the rest of England to Cnut.

Alternative Service Book, *see* PRAYER BOOKS

Amboina Massacre, 1623, an incident in the East Indies which symbolized increasing tension between the overseas enterprises of England and the newly independent United Provinces of the NETHERLANDS. Ten English settlers were tortured and executed on the island of Molucca by the Dutch governor on charges (probably false) of conspiring with the Japanese against Dutch rule. In the short term, the English EAST INDIA COMPANY took the hint and abandoned its attempts at major competition in the spice trade of the East Indies; however, the affair left a legacy of bitterness which was to have major symbolic value in the DUTCH WARS and into the early 18th century.

Ambrosius Aurelianus (5th century AD), Romano-British chieftain. Mentioned by GILDAS as a British leader who gained victories – including his greatest at the battle of Mount BADON – against the Anglo-Saxons after they had overthrown the British ruler later named by BEDE and NENNIUS as VORTIGERN. All that can realistically be said of Ambrosius – whose name suggests Roman descent – is that he was a chieftain who stemmed the tide of the English advance for some considerable time (*see* ANGLO-SAXON SETTLEMENT).

American Independence, War of, 1775–83. Initially an attempt to reassert British power over rebellious American colonies, this escalated eventually into a world war when the French also declared war on Britain in 1778, followed by the Spanish in 1779 and the Dutch in 1780. Differences between Britain and her American colonies spiralled into conflict from 1763, when GRENVILLE'S STAMP ACT – designed to secure an American contribution to the costs of colonial defence of the SEVEN YEARS WAR – encountered concerted resistance. The first Rockingham ministry (*see* WENTWORTH, CHARLES) repealed the Stamp Act in 1766, but by passing a DECLARATORY ACT insisting on Britain's right to tax the colonies, it encouraged discussion of constitutional issues. The Townshend duties (*see* TOWNSHEND ACT 1767) added more fuel to the fire. In 1770, Lord NORTH repealed all duties except that on TEA; though this concession slowed the deterioration of relations, the tea duty became the focus of protest in the 1773 BOSTON TEA PARTY. Parliament, pinning its hopes on the possibility of splitting the colonies, as it was to do repeatedly, attempted to address the near collapse of imperial control over MASSACHUSETTS by the INTOLERABLE ACTS of 1774, which focused on that colony. However, in April a Continental Congress met at Philadelphia, displaying colonial solidarity, and insisting that the British seek American consent for legislation affecting them. The Intolerable Acts failed to subdue Massachusetts, and in Jan. 1775 the colony was declared to be in a state of rebellion. Lord North's offer to treat the colonies individually but not collectively on fiscal matters evoked a favourable response only from NOVA SCOTIA. British and American forces clashed at Lexington and Concord in April, opening the war; in May, the second Continental Congress met. The rebels were harassed from the sea, but began an increasingly successful PRIVATEERing campaign. In Aug. a general proclamation of rebellion in America was issued. In Dec. American forces invaded CANADA and captured Montreal. They were driven back in the summer of 1776, but meanwhile British forces had evacuated Boston. The Declaration of Independence was signed on 4 July. In Sept., in a major amphibious assault, British forces under the HOWE brothers captured NEW YORK City. In 1777 General Howe moved south to Philadelphia, defeating, but failing to eliminate, the Continental Army under WASHINGTON at the Battle of Brandywine in Sept. The British had simultaneously attempted to divide New England from the other colonies by sending forces under General Burgoyne down from Canada to meet others coming north from New York City. However, Burgoyne's forces were surrounded and surrendered at Saratoga in Oct.

This defeat induced the British to send a peace commission, under the Earl of Carlisle, offering to repeal all offensive acts passed since 1763 and to recognize the Continental Congress. But French offers of assistance had arrived earlier: a Franco-American treaty of commerce and alliance was signed in Feb. 1778. General Howe returned to New York, and France declared war on Britain in June. The American naval raider John Paul Jones had meanwhile brought war to the British coast, attacking Whitehaven in Cumberland in April 1778, and shipping in the Irish Sea: this sparked the formation of VOLUNTEER forces in Ireland. In July, French and English fleets fought an inconclusive naval battle off Ushant; the subsequent court-martial of Admiral Keppel split the Royal Navy. A French fleet was also sent to North America – and from then on there were a series of more or less indecisive actions there and in the WEST INDIES between the French and British navies. In Dec. 1778, a new campaign was opened in the south; British forces under Campbell subdued GEORGIA, and moved into South CAROLINA. In June 1779, Spain entered the war and a combined Franco-Spanish fleet threatened the invasion of Britain – it was the ravages of disease aboard that fleet which saved the country from this potential disaster. The Royal Navy was in an inferior, defensive position, a position worsened by the Dutch entrance into the war a year later, so Britain was fighting all the other major naval powers. GIBRALTAR was besieged and most of Campbell's troops were withdrawn to protect Florida, acquired from the Spanish at the close of the Seven Years War. It became clear that the French and Spanish were keen, above all, to make gains in the West Indies; they succeeded in seizing several British islands from 1778–80, though their preoccupation with this task did leave the British relatively free to pursue the war in the south.

The Rockinghamite and Chathamite oppositions had opposed the war from its inception, advancing peace proposals in Jan. 1775 and 1776. In May 1778, Chatham (*see* PITT THE ELDER) collapsed in the Lords and died. By 1779, North was facing serious divisions within ministerial ranks: Gower and Weymouth, erstwhile followers of the Duke of Bedford, resigned in the autumn. Exploiting public discontent, both with the apparent mismanagement of the war and with its mounting cost, BURKE announced his intention of bringing in a bill for ECONOMICAL REFORM; Christopher Wyvill launched the ASSOCIATION MOVEMENT to support the measure. Meanwhile, Irish discontent with the wartime collapse of trade had mounted; 1780 saw Irish counties petitioning for Irish LEGISLATIVE INDEPENDENCE. In April, the ministry was defeated over DUNNING'S MOTION bewailing the increasing 'influence of the Crown'; North offered to resign, but was dissuaded by the king. In June, London was devastated by the anti-Catholic GORDON RIOTS. The king again sounded out the Rockinghamites, as he had after Pitt's death, about joining the ministry, but found them now inclined to lay down policy conditions.

In Aug., Russia, Sweden and Denmark inaugurated the League of ARMED NEUTRALITY. North's position received a much-needed boost with the arrival of news of the capture of Charleston, South Carolina, which had followed the transfer of the main British army from New York to the south at the beginning of the year. A general election held against this background brought him back to power, but with a reduced majority. In June, war had broken out in southern INDIA, where Hyder Ali gained ascendancy over British troops; in 1782, Sir Eyre Coote succeeded in reversing the position, despite the arrival of French forces. Cornwallis, who had been attempting to subdue South Carolina since the previous year, captured Yorktown in Aug., but was surprised and trapped there by combined French and American forces. The French fleet held off a British one at the battle of Chesapeake and Cornwallis was forced to surrender.

In Feb. 1782 a motion that no further attempt be made to subdue the Americans by force was carried in Parliament. North resigned in March. The king reluctantly called on Rockingham to form an administration, but following the latter's death in July, Shelburne (*see* PETTY, WILLIAM) was appointed. War against France and Spain continued: a spectacular naval victory at the Battle of the SAINTES in April secured British control of the West Indies; in the summer, the French succeeded in landing reinforcements for Hyder Ali and in challenging British sea power off India. In the autumn, a Spanish assault on Gibraltar was repulsed. Peace preliminaries with the Americans were agreed in Nov. and with France and Spain in Jan. 1783. The Peace of VERSAILLES was signed in Sept.

The war badly dented British confidence, but the worst fears of its critics were not realized. Britain retained many of the territorial gains she had made over the past century; by the late 1780s, it was already clear that American independence was compatible with booming North Atlantic trade. The experience of the war strengthened the cause of reform in Britain: power passed from North's hands into those of somewhat variously inclined reform-minded ministers: Rockingham, Shelburne, FOX and PITT THE YOUNGER. The Rockingham ministry's concession of Irish legislative independence resulted indirectly from the war. But conservative forces regrouped in the war's aftermath. The loss of America placed a large hole in the centre of the system built up under the NAVIGATION ACTS, but proposals partly to dismantle the traditional system of protection were successfully opposed. The more conservatively inclined did not forget that opposition politicians and reform-minded religious DISSENTERS had questioned the justice of the British cause, and openly sympathized with American rebels. Antipathy seeded in this conflict came to flower following the FRENCH REVOLUTION.

The war was an enormous strain on Britain. The effort of supporting and supplying an entire army across an ocean whilst fighting all the other major naval powers could have been sustained by no other country at that time. In the end Britain survived and it was France that succumbed to the economic strains induced by the war.

American War of 1812, *see* ANGLO-AMERICAN WAR

Amicable Grant, 1525, misnamed effort by WOLSEY to raise money for the Anglo-French war (1522–5). He demanded one-sixth of laymen's goods and one-third of the clergy's without parliamentary sanction. Widespread national unrest in May culminated in massive demonstrations in south Suffolk, pacified by the Dukes of Norfolk and Suffolk, who nevertheless pressurized Wolsey into abandoning the tax. Potentially a full-scale rising, it was one of very few successful acts of resistance to Tudor central government.

Amiens, Battle of, northern France, 8–12 Aug. 1918. 'The black day of the German Army', the decisive defeat of the Germans by British and DOMINION forces under HAIG, it convinced Germany to sue for peace and began the 'Hundred Days' campaign of victories through to the end of WORLD WAR I. It was the only time in the war other than CAMBRAI that TANKS were used *en masse*.

Amiens, Mise of, Jan. 1264, the arbitration settlement ('mise') of the dispute between HENRY III and Simon de MONTFORT, which was pronounced at Amiens by Louis IX (St Louis) of France. Simon's refusal to accept the settlement led to the outbreak of the BARONS' WAR.

Amiens, Treaty of, 1802, treaty between Britain and France, ending the FRENCH REVOLUTIONARY WAR. Under ADDINGTON's unimpressive leadership, Britain conceded a great deal for relatively small gains. She was to return all maritime conquests except TRINIDAD (taken from Spain) and CEYLON (taken from the Dutch); the Cape of Good Hope was returned to the Dutch. France agreed to evacuate southern Italy, MALTA – which was handed over to a Neapolitan garrison – and Egypt – which was returned to the Ottoman Empire. Britain was left with no base but GIBRALTAR to support its power in the Mediterranean, nor did the treaty incorporate any guarantees of the boundaries of existing European states – such as had been incorporated in France's 1801 treaty of Luneville with Austria.

The British hope seems to have been that the treaty would provide the basis for real peace, but the French intended it to set the scene for their own complete dominance of the continent – nor had they renounced hope of further expansion in the eastern Mediterranean and America.

Amritsar Massacre, incident in April 1919 at the Sikh holy city of Amritsar in northern INDIA. Troops under Brigadier-General R. E. H. Dyer opened fire on a crowd of demonstrators who refused to disperse. In the shooting and subsequent stampede 379 were killed and over 1,200 injured, including women and children. The army had been called in by the police after several days of protest riots against new security laws in which some Europeans had been killed. A subsequent official inquiry censured Dyer, who was forced to resign his commission. The incident seriously undermined the legitimacy of British rule in India and became a milestone in the history of INDIAN INDEPENDENCE.

Anabaptists, technically 'rebaptizers' – i.e. continental REFORMATION radicals who rebaptized as adults those who had received traditional infant baptism. The name is applied to various groups descended from 16th-century Anabaptist activists (e.g. Hutterites, Mennonites, Moravians), who should be distinguished from BAPTISTS. However, the label was rather loosely used by both Catholics and Magisterial Protestants to refer to a variety of radical groups and individuals holding such assorted ideas as pacifism, community of goods and UNITARIANISM. English Anabaptists were never numerous, though continental refugees, including the FAMILY OF LOVE, inspired some native religious radicals. Anabaptists were scarcer still in Scotland. All English monarchs from HENRY VIII to JAMES I were ready to burn them as HERETICS.

Anatomy Act 1832, legislation designed to curb the activities of RESURRECTIONISTS who were illicitly acquiring bodies for dissection in medical schools, by requisitioning the corpses of paupers for that purpose. The Act, the working of which survived into the 20th century, was one element in the Victorian fear of the WORKHOUSE, and it has been argued that its emotive influence still remains.

Ancrum Moor, Battle of, 27 Feb. 1545. After a destructive English invasion in 1544, a Scots force under Angus, defeated the English border captain, Sir Ralph Evers, near Jedburgh, encouraging the Scots to undertake an invasion of England which proved a fiasco.

Andover Scandal, scandal of 1845–6 in the WORKHOUSE at Andover, Hants. The outcry was caused by a miserly Board of Guardians who drove the starving inmates to eat rotting bone marrow. It proved fatal to the POOR LAW COMMISSION, the unpopular administrative agency run from London.

Andrew of Wyntoun (*c*.1350–*c*.1425), poet. Prior of St Serf's Isle, he was the author of the *Orygynal Cronykil of Scotland*, a narrative poem in Scots verse retelling the story of Scotland from its legendary beginnings until 1408. When it reaches the year 1286, the poem becomes a heroic saga of the wars of SCOTTISH INDEPENDENCE against the English.

Angel, an English gold COIN first minted in 1464 and worth 6 shillings 8 pence (6s 8d), i.e. one-third of a £, the original value of the NOBLE, which it replaced. Its name derived from the design on the obverse: the archangel Michael standing on a dragon. The minting of angels and half-angels continued into the early Stuart period.

Angevin Empire, a term invented by historians to refer to the dominions held by the family of the counts of Anjou – the Angevins, often known as the PLANTAGENETS – during the years they ruled England, NORMANDY and AQUITAINE as well as Anjou, Maine and Touraine.

The first ruler of this empire was HENRY II, heir to Anjou, Normandy and England and ruler of Aquitaine by virtue of his marriage to ELEANOR. His aggressive policies led to the assertion of rights over Toulouse, Brittany and Wales and to the invasion of Ireland. He and RICHARD I were able to give important financial and military help to the kingdom of Jerusalem – held by a junior branch of the house of Anjou. In this period, the Plantagenets were the most powerful dynasty in Europe.

Although England, as the only kingdom, ranked first among the Angevin dominions, the empire's centre lay in France. Henry was born at Le Mans, died at Chinon and was buried at Fontevrault; he and Richard I – and JOHN for as long as he could – spent most of their reigns on the Continent. The communities of the valleys of the Seine, Loire and Garonne were prosperous and culturally creative, and Plantagenet France produced two vital commodities: WINE and SALT. Its great ports – Rouen, Nantes, La Rochelle, Bordeaux and Bayonne – traded with LONDON, SOUTHAMPTON, BRISTOL and DUBLIN; in economic terms, this was a seaborne empire. Both merchants and the empire's ruler gained enormously from the political and commercial ties that linked together a number of complementary and increasingly interdependent regional economies.

When John lost Anjou, Normandy and much of Aquitaine in 1202–5, the heart was torn out of the empire. Thereafter the Plantagenets became Kings of England who occasionally visited their dominions across the sea, which, after the loss of La Rochelle in 1224, were limited to Gascony and the Channel Islands. Defeat for John and HENRY III meant victory for the Capetian kings of France.

Many historians have taken for granted that a political structure that cut across the supposedly predestined frontiers of the national monarchies of England and France was doomed from the start. They argue that it was peculiarly vulnerable because the Plantagenets owed homage to the king of France for all their continental dominions and because the empire was always likely to be partitioned between heirs.

In both respects, this empire was a continuation of the ANGLO-NORMAN REALM – the Norman empire. In the event, however, although the Plantagenets at times – and especially during Henry II's reign – quarrelled among themselves, their empire remained undivided. This meant that Richard and John, like Henry II, had greater resources at their disposal than their Capetian overlord. The collapse of the empire in 1202–5 was not due to its feudal dependence but to John's incompetence in the face of one of the most successful kings of France, the shrewd and determined Philip II Augustus.

CHRONOLOGY

1128 Geoffrey PLANTAGENET marries Empress MATILDA at Le Mans.

1136–44 Geoffrey conquers NORMANDY.

1152 HENRY II marries ELEANOR OF AQUITAINE.

1153 Treaty of Winchester: Henry recognized as STEPHEN's heir.

1156 Henry's brother Geoffrey resigns his claim to Anjou.

THE ANGEVIN EMPIRE c.1200
0 km 200
0 miles 100
SCOTLAND
KINGDOM OF MAN
(to Norway)
St Andrews
Glasgow
Edinburgh
NORTH SEA
Newcastle
IRELAND
(English conquest in progress)
York
R. Shannon
Dublin
Nottingham
R. Trent
Limerick
Norwich
Waterford
WELSH STATES
(Vassals of Henry II)
R. Severn
ENGLAND
R. Rhine
R. Thames
London
Cardiff
Bristol
Winchester
Dover
Southampton
FLANDERS
Exeter
Bouvines
1214
English Channel
HOLY
ROMAN
EMPIRE
Dieppe
Rouen
ATLANTIC OCEAN
Andely
Bayeux
Caen
Paris
NORMANDY
R. Seine
FRANCE
MAINE
Rennes
Le Mans
BRITTANY
Angers
Tours
ANJOU
Chinon
TOURAINE
R. Loire
1202
Mirebeau
BERRI
Poitiers
POITOU
Bay of Biscay
La Rochelle
LA MARCHE
Limoges
SAINTONGE
LIMOUSIN
Angoulême
AUVERGNE
Battle
Eastern limit of English possessions in France, 1180
Lost by the English in France by 1200
Frontiers in 1180
R. Rhône
PÉRIGORD
Bordeaux
R. Garonne
AGENAIS
TOULOUSE
GASCONY
Bayonne
Toulouse
BÉARN
MEDITERRANEAN
SEA
LEÓN
CASTILLE
NAVARRE
ARAGON

1157 Henry recovers Northumbria from the king of Scots.
1157–65 Henry's four invasions of Wales.
1159 Toulouse expedition: Henry captures Cahors.
1166–8 Henry invades Brittany; installs his son Geoffrey as count.
1171–2 Henry invades Ireland.
1173–4 Eleanor and sons rebel against Henry.
1177 Henry creates JOHN 'lord of Ireland'.
1183 Rebellion and death of HENRY THE YOUNG KING.
1189 Henry defeated by RICHARD I and Philip II Augustus and dies soon afterwards.
1193–4 Philip II Augustus invades Normandy and Anjou.
1199 Richard killed at Chalus; John and ARTHUR OF BRITTANY dispute succession.
1200 Treaty of Le Goulet: Philip recognizes John as heir to Angevin Empire.
1201 Revolt of the LUSIGNANS.
1202 Philip declares confiscation of all fiefs held of the crown of France.
1202–5 Philip conquers Normandy and Anjou.
1204 Eleanor dies; Poitou recognizes Philip; Alfonso of Castile invades Gascony.
1206 John recovers Gascony and the Saintonge.
1214 Defeats for John and his allies at Roche-au-Moine and BOUVINES.
1216–17 Louis of France (later LOUIS VIII) invades England.
1224 Louis VIII captures La Rochelle.
1242 Taillebourg campaign: Louis IX defeats HENRY III.
1259 Treaty of PARIS: Henry III resigns claims to Normandy, Anjou and Poitou.

Angles, one of the three peoples identified by BEDE as taking part in the migration of Germanic peoples which supposedly overwhelmed Britain in the 5th century. The Angles came from the southern part of the Danish peninsula and neighbouring islands and, according to Bede, took over MERCIA, NORTHUMBRIA, EAST ANGLIA and ESSEX. The results of extensive archaeological work have confirmed this statement in its broad outline, but suggest that Angles and SAXONS were more intermingled than he believed.

Anglicanism In a medieval context, '*Anglicana*' was simply a Latin word, meaning English, as in '*Ecclesia Anglicana*', 'the Church in England'. From the early 17th century, 'Anglican' was occasionally used as an English adjective to describe the Church *of* England, and this passed into common use in the 19th century. Historians use it for the attitudes of those who strongly supported the established Church of England after the RESTORATION of CHARLES II against attempts to favour DISSENTERS (*see* CHURCH AND KING; CHURCH IN DANGER). Theologically, Anglicanism is the religious outlook gradually developed in the post-Reformation Church of England and Church of Ireland. Its proponents seek to form a synthesis of the theology of the Western Church up to the 5th century with that of the 16th century REFORMATION. The mixture is variable: the ANGLO-CATHOLIC extreme has developed a taste for medieval Catholicism (*see* HIGH CHURCHMANSHIP), the EVANGELICAL extreme emphasizes the Church's PROTESTANT purity (*see* LOW CHURCHMANSHIP), while the middle ground deplores extremism of any sort (*see* BROAD CHURCH). As a result of English colonial adventuring, there is a worldwide Anglican Communion of Churches, which share an informal relationship to the archbishopric of CANTERBURY and are conscious of a common heritage (*see* PRAYER BOOKS). *See also* CHURCH: ENGLAND.

Anglo-American Mutual Aid Agreement, *see* LEND-LEASE

Anglo-American War, 1812–15, also known as the War of 1812. The last time Britain and the United States went to war with one another, it arose out of the pressing of allegedly British seamen from American ships by the Royal NAVY which also seized US ships attempting to break the British blockade of France during the NAPOLEONIC WARS, as well as American ambitions and border disputes concerning CANADA.

The land war focused on the Great Lakes, Washington DC and New Orleans. In 1812, an American attempt to attack upper Canada from both ends of Lake Erie was repulsed at Detroit (Aug.) and Queenstown (Oct.). In 1813, the Americans won control of Lake Erie and raided Toronto which they burnt, but their attack on Montreal failed. The last American attempt in Canada ended in July 1814, with a British victory at Lundy's Lane, near Niagara whilst a British attempt to invade southwards was stopped by an American naval victory on Lake Champlain.

At sea the small but efficient American Navy used its very powerful frigates to humble the pride of the hitherto almost always victorious Royal Navy in a series of actions between single ships. American PRIVATEERS took 1,607 British merchant ships. However neither of these facts, though causing much public alarm at the time, made any serious difference to the slow accumulation of British maritime strength off the American Coast. American commerce was strangled, the American Navy confined to its bases or captured. The war became very unpopular in New England and separatist tendencies there were very powerful.

A British amphibious force under Admiral Cockburn and General Ross landed in Maryland and defeated a scratch lot of defenders at the battle of Bladensburg. Washington was captured and its public buildings burnt – in retaliation for the burning of Toronto. Ross was killed in an unsuccessful attack on Baltimore, but the American coast and its cities were vulnerable to more attacks of this kind. The final battle of the war happened over a month after peace was signed at Ghent at the end of 1814. A Brtitish invading force was turned back before New Orleans. The peace treaty settled neither the shipping issue nor the disputed frontier though the former was rendered less pressing by the fall of Napoleon and peace in Europe. The argument over the frontier was not settled until 1846, when the 49th parallel was accepted as the boundary line between Canada and the United States (*see also* ASHBURTON TREATY; OREGON TREATY).

Anglo-Catholicism With its origins in the 19th century – the word was first used in 1838 – this concept describes those in the Anglican communion who adopt a 'high' view of the Church and its institutions, sacraments, doctrines and orders, and who stress the place of ANGLICANISM within the universal Church and downplay the importance of the Protestant tradition. Its early leaders were John Keble, NEWMAN and Augustus Pusey, founders of the OXFORD MOVEMENT. *See also* CHURCH: ENGLAND; HIGH CHURCHMANSHIP; RITUALISM.

Anglo-Dutch Wars, *see* DUTCH WAR, FIRST, SECOND, THIRD

Anglo-Egyptian Treaty, 1936. The treaty formally ended British occupation of EGYPT, though Britain retained a garrison in the country and control over the SUEZ CANAL Zone. In the event of war, Britain had the right of reoccupation and unrestricted use of Egyptian roads, ports and airports. The treaty legitimized the use of Egypt as a pivot of operations in the Middle East during WORLD WAR II.

A further treaty signed in October 1954 relinquished British control of the Canal Zone. However, in October 1956, fears by the EDEN government that Egyptian president Nasser was a dangerous aggressor, following his announcement of the nationalization of the Suez Canal, led to a joint Anglo-French invasion of the Canal Zone, in breach of the treaty (*see* SUEZ CRISIS).

Anglo-French *Entente,* 1904. The death of the pro-German Queen VICTORIA, Germany's challenge to British naval supremacy (*see* ANGLO-GERMAN RIVALRY) and Britain's dangerous isolation as revealed by the BOER WAR all prompted a shift in foreign policy towards an accommodation with France.

Anglo-French colonial rivalries were peacefully resolved; France looked for British support against Germany while the British hoped that France and her Russian ally might act as a moderating influence on a dynamic and dangerous Germany. EDWARD VII's visit to Paris in 1903 paved the way for the accord of the following year.

Anglo-German Naval Agreement, June 1935. This agreement permitted the German navy to build up to 35 per cent of the tonnage of British capital ships and up to 45 per cent in submarines. The treaty recognized Germany's breach of the restrictions imposed on her by the treaty of VERSAILLES (1919) and was part of the process of piecemeal APPEASEMENT by which Britain sought agreements to limit the threats posed by potentially hostile powers. Germany used the agreement to build up a major surface fleet based on battleships, including the *Bismarck* and the *Tirpitz*, though she did not take full advantage of the submarine clauses before war broke out.

Anglo-German Rivalry, 1895–1914. Considered by many historians to have been a key factor in the origins of WORLD WAR I, it arose partly from the growth of German industrial power and the British experience of relative economic decline; was fuelled by colonial and commercial competition between the two nations; and was sharpened by German determination to challenge British naval supremacy. The hitherto small German navy was rapidly built up to being second only to the Royal Navy. The Germans were heavily influenced by the writings of the American theorist of the importance of seapower, Admiral Mahan, but seem never to have quite decided whether they were making an outright challenge for first position or merely blackmailing Britain into giving them their 'place in the sun'. This was a mistake as the British saw their naval strength as the basis of their position in the world. At the beginning of the 1890s both nations had reasonable expectations of a friendly alliance. The Germans overplaying their hand caused the naval threat to backfire and eventually caused Britain to ally with Germany's enemies.

CHRONOLOGY

1895, June Kiel Canal opens, allowing passage of German battleships between Baltic and North Sea.

1896, Jan. KRUGER TELEGRAM designed to persuade British to join the German-led TRIPLE ALLIANCE. It angers British public opinion and underscores the need to escape from diplomatic isolation.

1898 Abortive attempt by Joseph CHAMBERLAIN to negotiate Anglo-German alliance to defend British interests in Far East; Germany refuses to be drawn into possible war with Russia on behalf of the British. German Navy Bill lays foundation for German battle fleet. Wilhelm II, in speech on proposed Berlin–Baghdad railway, presents himself as protector of Muslim peoples; both project and speech regarded as challenge to British interests.

1900 German Navy Bill enlarges provision for battle fleet.

1901 German miscalculation leads to rejection of final British offer of alliance and eventually drives British into arms of French.

1906 Britain launches first DREADNOUGHT.

1907 New ambitious naval programme introduced in Germany by Tirpitz.

1909–12 Britain builds 18 battleships to Germany's 9.

1911 AGADIR CRISIS strengthens ANGLO-FRENCH *ENTENTE* after French–German rivalry in Morocco.

1913 British request for a halt to naval construction programmes ignored; widening of the Kiel Canal for passage of Dreadnought-class German battleships is accelerated.

1914 Anglo-German discussions about Africa and agreement on southern Persia give false hope for peaceful resolution of international difficulties.

Anglo-Irish, *see* NEW ENGLISH IN IRELAND

Anglo-Irish Treaty, 1921, treaty between Britain and plenipotentiaries of the Irish government ending the ANGLO-IRISH WAR. Narrowly ratified by the Irish parliament in January 1922, the treaty set up an IRISH FREE STATE with Dominion status, allowing the six counties comprising modern ULSTER the opportunity to opt out, which they exercised. Bitterness on the part of extreme nationalists at having surrendered a united Ireland and at the acceptance of an oath of allegiance to the British crown precipitated the IRISH CIVIL WAR between pro- and anti-treaty forces.

Anglo-Irish war, 1919–21. The final fight, in what became known as the Irish War of Independence, began on 21 Jan. 1919 with the ambush and murder of two Royal Irish Constabulary officers in Tipperary, and the first meeting on the same day of the DÁIL and its declaration of independence. Following this lead, the rest of the year was marked by lightning raids by volunteers, and the formation of the IRISH REPUBLICAN ARMY in Aug. Partition between north and south was engineered under the 1920 Government of Ireland Act, which came into force in 1921, but meanwhile LLOYD GEORGE had refused to recognize the Dáil and its independence. The unofficial war in Ireland was waged by the RIC and the notorious BLACK AND TANS, recently demobbed soldiers transformed into a fighting force noted for the viciousness of their reprisals. By mid-1920 questions were being asked in Westminster about the wisdom of using these tactics; meanwhile, on 3–4 April all tax offices in Ireland had been destroyed, a general strike had been called, and nationalist prisoners went on hunger strike. Amid the increasing violence, the British government began to feel its way towards peace. The Dáil formally declared war on 11 March 1921, and the two sides engineered a truce on 11 July. Finally, under the ANGLO-IRISH TREATY of 6 Dec. that year, the IRISH FREE STATE was born.

Anglo-Japanese Alliance, 1902. A departure in British foreign policy, it arose out of the Russian challenge to British influence in China and marked the first significant break with the principle of splendid isolation. It was agreed with Japan that, if either party was involved in a war with another country, the other allied power would remain neutral, but in the event of one ally being attacked by two or more powers, the other partner would come to its assistance.

Anglo-Jewry, *see* JEWS IN BRITAIN

Anglo-Norman, the name given by language scholars to the dialect of Old French that was spoken within the territories of the ANGLO-NORMAN REALM until 1204, and thereafter in England, until it was increasingly replaced by English in the later Middle Ages. The earliest extant works written in Anglo-Norman date from *c.*1120. Since the majority of the population in England never learned Anglo-Norman, it remained the language of the ruling élite, of government and polite society. It survived longest in the form of 'law French' (*see* YEAR BOOKS).

Anglo-Norman Realm, a term that usually refers to England and Normandy between 1066 (when WILLIAM I THE CONQUEROR became king of England) and 1144 (when King STEPHEN lost control of Normandy), but which sometimes includes the years 1154–1204, when these two lands were part of the ANGEVIN EMPIRE. Although, throughout this period, England and Normandy were generally held by a single ruler, the word 'realm' is somewhat misleading since the two lands never became part of a single kingdom. Normandy remained a French duchy; the duke of Normandy, even when he was also king of England, always owed homage to the king of France.

None the less, there was a real sense in which England and Normandy constituted a single political community. The NORMAN CONQUEST resulted in the dispossession of the Anglo-Saxon aristocracy and its replacement by a single French-speaking élite holding estates on both sides of the Channel. These aristocrats had a powerful vested interest in the union of the two lands under a single ruler: the king-duke. For instance, discussion at an assembly held in Normandy in 1136 to consider the succession to HENRY I ended abruptly when the participants learned that Stephen had already obtained control of England. That settled the matter: Stephen must become Duke of Normandy, too. Thus, although Normandy and England could be separated – as when William the Conqueror bequeathed the former to ROBERT II (Robert Curthose) and the latter to WILLIAM II RUFUS – such periods (1087–96, 1100–6, 1144–54) tended to be turbulent and brief.

The families of the Anglo-Norman élite gradually divided into Norman and English branches, but the very richest landowners retained estates on both sides of the Channel. In 1204, there were still more than 100 Norman TENANTS-IN-CHIEF who also held land in England. In other ways, too, the Anglo-Norman community survived. Some clerics moved effortlessly between the two Churches. Walter of Coutances, for example, was simultaneously archdeacon of Oxford and treasurer of Rouen cathedral, was then promoted to bishop of Lincoln and finally became archbishop of Rouen. The system of cross-Channel ferries, with horses carried much as cars are today, reflected the high degree of economic, as well as political, integration of England and Normandy. Moreover, although the two lands always had their own legal, administrative and monetary systems, the differences between them slowly became less obvious as the result of parallel developments on both sides of the Channel.

Some variations remained. In Normandy, French was the language of the whole population, not just of the ruling élite as in England; and Normandy remained a fief of France. In 1202, when Philip II Augustus of France declared Normandy forfeit and his armies invaded, these differences counted – all the more so when the duke of Normandy was a ruler as incompetent as King JOHN.

Anglo-Polish Alliance In March 1939 Britain reluctantly abandoned her APPEASEMENT policy with a joint Franco-British pledge to support Poland if threatened by armed aggression. The guarantee was an attempt finally to stop Hitler's expansion following his seizure of the rest of Czechoslovakia in breach of the MUNICH AGREEMENT. Hitler's increasingly belligerent demands for the reincorporation of Danzig (now Gdansk) and the Polish Corridor (the strip of land through Prussia linking Poland with Danzig) into the German Reich led to a formalization of the pledge into an Anglo-Polish Alliance on 25 Aug. When Hitler invaded Poland on 1 Sept. 1939, the Alliance provided the basis of Britain's declaration of war on 3 Sept.

Anglo-Russian Treaty, March 1915, secret treaty by which Britain agreed that Russia would obtain control of Constantinople and the Straits after the conclusion of WORLD WAR I, while Britain would be given concessions in Persia and Asiatic Turkey. An important agreement which extended Allied war aims to a partition of the Turkish Empire, it was one of the 'secret treaties' implicitly condemned in Woodrow Wilson's Fourteen Points. However, it never had to be honoured because of the Russian Revolution and the consequent breach in Anglo-Russian relations.

Anglo-Saxon, the adjective generally (and not entirely accurately) used to describe the period of English history between the departure of the Romans and 1066, the people who lived in England during that time, and their language (also more commonly called 'Old English') (*see* ENGLISH LANGUAGE, DEVELOPMENT OF).

Anglo-Saxon Architecture, name given to the architectural style of the late 10th and 11th centuries until the NORMAN CONQUEST and the advent of ROMANESQUE architecture. Notably surviving in churches, it is marked by solidity, narrow proportions, round-headed arches, and the characteristic 'long and short work' of corner-stones set alternately on their long and short edges. The links with continental styles were marked, and especially so in the reign of EDWARD THE CONFESSOR. Intact survivals are few and precious.

Anglo-Saxon Chronicle, the main source for the events and chronology of the English peoples from the 5th to the 11th centuries. The *Chronicle* is, in fact, a compilation of factual year-by-year entries, first brought together in the late 9th century during the reign of ALFRED THE GREAT, and continued thereafter in various interdependent versions written at different monasteries. One version of the *Chronicle* was continued at the abbey of PETERBOROUGH until 1154. Unravelling the relationship of the separate texts is a complex scholarly operation.

The information it supplies is uneven in quality. It is, for example, particularly expansive on the triumphs of Alfred the Great's reign and on the disasters of ETHELRED II THE UNREADY'S.

Anglo-Saxon Settlement The process by which the Anglo-Saxon tribes took over eastern and southern Britain after the departure of the Romans is one of the most complex of all historical problems. The quantity of written evidence is extremely limited, and other forms of evidence – namely, archaeological and PLACE-NAME – are difficult to interpret.

The one contemporary written source, GILDAS, tells of a process whereby Germanic tribesmen were used by the Romans and their British successors to combat other enemies, such as the PICTS and SCOTS. These mercenaries eventually rebelled against their employers and immigrated in greater numbers, finally securing political domination.

Archaeological evidence suggests that the process began in the later 4th century and continued into the early years of the 6th, and that (as Gildas suggested) there were periods of effective British resistance – associated with, for example, the victory at Mount BADON and with the career of the mythical ARTHUR. This type of evidence also supports BEDE's notion that the colonizers were ANGLES, SAXONS and JUTES, although archaeology has also revealed that these peoples were much more intermingled in Britain than he believed, and that they associated with others, such as Frisians.

Work on place names and ESTATE boundaries has largely led to the rejection of the idea that the Britons were either exterminated or driven west (*see* BRITISH SURVIVAL). Instead the newcomers are seen as taking over and assimilating with an existing, primarily agricultural society. However, they were sufficiently numerous and forceful to impose both their language and their form of Germanic PAGANISM on to the natives.

The immigrants often organized their settlements within established estate bound-

ANGLO-SAXON BRITAIN
(Principal Early Kingdoms)
▲ Battle
MORAY
R. Tay
ALBA
DALRIADA
Edinburgh
R. Clyde
BERNICIA
Lindisfarne
Bamburgh
NORTH SEA
STRATHCLYDE
NORTHUMBRIA
Bewcastle
Roman Wall
Jarrow
ULSTER
Whitby
R. Ouse
Catterick
600
DEIRA
York
MEATH
IRISH SEA
R. Trent
GWYNEDD
Offa's Dyke 784
MERCIA
LEINSTER
Lichfield
Tettenhall
910
R. Severn
R. Ouse
EAST ANGLIA
POWYS
Worcester
ESSEX
991
Maldon
Cirencester
577
628
Oxford
DYFED
Dyrham
Wantage
London
R. Thames
Bath
Ellandune
825
Canterbury
0 km 150
0 miles 80
KENT
WESSEX
Glastonbury
Winchester
SUSSEX
Corfe
CORNWALL (DUMNONIA)
English Channel

aries. Place-name forms such as '*-ingas*' and '*ham*' suggest a tribal or family settlement within a defined area (sometimes called a '*regio*'). These groupings – or rather their amalgamation – must often have been the basis of the earliest kingdoms, whose existence is frequently attested in the late 5th century.

The survival of some of these early units can still be perceived in the (probably) 7th-century document known as the TRIBAL HIDEAGE. Others among the early kingdoms, such as Kent or Essex, may have been based on existing Roman political units. After a long and obscure development, the 7th century witnessed the emergence, from this early phase, of the kingdoms of the HEPTARCHY.

Anglo-Soviet Pact, 1942, treaty between the USSR and Britain, signed by Soviet foreign minister Molotov and British foreign secretary EDEN. Eden had initiated negotiations on a visit to Moscow in December 1941, but these proved inconclusive due to the Soviets' insistence on a western 'Second Front' against Germany and Stalin's determination to retain the territorial gains he had made under the Hitler–Stalin pact. The 20-year treaty signed the following year contained no details of a post-war settlement, but committed the two countries to pursue the war against Germany and the rest of the Axis, and to resist any renewal of German aggression once victory was won. A similar treaty was signed between France and the USSR in December 1944. Both treaties were cancelled by the USSR in 1955 when Britain and France agreed to German rearmament.

Anguilla, British crown colony in the Leeward Islands with a population of about 7,000. Colonized by Britain in 1650, it was subjected to frequent invasion attempts by native Caribs and the French until 1796. It was associated with ST KITTS AND NEVIS from 1816, thereafter within the wider LEEWARD ISLANDS FEDERATION. Forced for administrative convenience to be part of a federation of St Kitts-Nevis-Anguilla, which was given independence in 1967, it staged a non-violent rebellion in 1969, throwing out the St Kitts police force and expelling a British official negotiator. At the request of the St Kitts' authorities, in March 1969 the WILSON government dispatched two frigates, carrying a detachment of the Parachute Regiment and a group of officers from the Metropolitan Police, to 'invade' the island and restore the status quo. The episode attracted much international mirth. By the end of the month Anguilla's secessionist wishes were granted and it reverted to full colonial status.

Annales Cambriae One of the chief sources for early Welsh history, these annals provide a sparse, year-by-year record of events from the 5th to the 13th centuries. It is generally thought that they were compiled at ST DAVID'S from the late 8th century onwards, and that the earlier texts, which contain little about Wales, derive from Irish and northern British material. One of the earliest sources to mention the enigmatic and probably legendary King ARTHUR, they contain the statement (unlikely to be true) that he died in AD 537.

Annals of Ulster, a major source for early medieval Irish history, which provide a year-by-year record of events starting in the 5th century. The accuracy of the early entries is a subject of scholarly controversy. It is likely that the annals, which were written in several different monasteries, are contemporary with events only from the 7th century.

Annates, *see* FIRST FRUITS AND TENTHS

Anne (1665–1714), Queen of England, Ireland and Scotland (1702–14). The second of the two children (both daughters) surviving to adulthood of James, Duke of York (JAMES II), and his first wife Anne Hyde, Anne received a strictly Protestant education. In 1683 she married Prince George of Denmark; all their children died young. When William of Orange (the future WILLIAM III) invaded in 1688, Anne fled to Nottingham. Under pressure from William and advised by Sarah and John CHURCHILL (the former a childhood friend), she eventually acquiesced in the settlement of the throne on William and MARY for their joint lives, thus postponing her own right to that of the Prince. Subsequently, when Churchill (now Earl of Marlborough) was deprived of his military and other offices on suspicion of JACOBITISM, Anne stood by him and his wife. In 1701, after the death of her only surviving child, Anne agreed to the Act of SETTLEMENT, designed to ensure a PROTESTANT SUCCES-

SION. She succeeded William in March 1702. Prince George, who did not become joint monarch, died in 1708.

Anne took an active part in government, and frequently attended debates in the House of LORDS. She was particularly concerned with church affairs, taking personal control of the crown's ecclesiastical patronage, and in 1704 establishing QUEEN ANNE'S BOUNTY. The politics of Anne's reign were remarkable for the 'rage of party': partisan struggle between WHIGS and TORIES. She did not expect her government to become the prisoner of any one party, but relied on court-oriented ministers to manage Parliament. Foreign affairs were dominated by the War of the SPANISH SUCCESSION (1702–3). Though happy to accept the HANOVERIAN SUCCESSION, she wanted no rival close to home, and would not allow any claimant to settle in the kingdom in her lifetime.

Anne Boleyn (?1501–36), Queen of England. Daughter of Sir Thomas Boleyn (1477–1539, a courtier from a leading Norfolk family), she spent her teenage years at the Netherlands and French courts, coming to the English court in 1521. Her charm, intelligence and strong personality won her many ardent admirers. From 1526, these included HENRY VIII, tiring of CATHERINE OF ARAGON and beginning to think of divorce. By 1527, they were probably informally betrothed; by Aug. of that year, Henry was approaching the Pope about an annulment of his marriage. Events moved tortuously slowly, and Anne began living openly with Henry during 1531; when, in 1532, the king determined to secure an annulment unilaterally, she was created Marchioness of Pembroke in her own right, and became pregnant towards the end of the year.

A secret marriage took place, perhaps on 24 or 25 Jan. 1533, and in May, after CRANMER had pronounced Catherine's divorce, Anne was crowned queen, to widespread public disgust. Her first child, born in Sept. 1533, was not the looked-for son but ELIZABETH, yet Anne's position with Henry did not become dangerous until after a stillbirth in Jan. 1536. Henry found a new love in JANE SEYMOUR, and began to listen to conservative intrigue against Anne, which Thomas CROMWELL joined out of political opportunism. During April, Anne was accused of treasonous adultery and divorced, and on 19 May 1536 she was executed on absurd charges, her supposed lovers having already suffered the same fate.

Quite apart from her importance in precipitating the divorce crisis, Anne played a major role during her brief 'reign' in promoting religious reform and advancing reformers to positions of power in the Church. Historians are revising previous jaundiced opinions about her, promulgated by certain Catholic commentators, particularly Ambassador Chapuys, a passionate supporter of Catherine of Aragon.

Anne Neville (1454–85), Queen of England. Younger daughter and co-heiress of Warwick the Kingmaker (*see* NEVILLE, RICHARD), in 1470 she was betrothed to HENRY VI's son, EDWARD, Prince of Wales. However, by 1474, she was married to Richard of Gloucester, and was crowned queen in 1483 when he took the throne as RICHARD III. She died in March 1485, a year after the death of their only son; widespread rumours that Richard had plotted her death forced the king to issue a public denial.

Anne of Bohemia (1367–94), Queen of England. Sister of King Wenceslas of Bohemia, she married RICHARD II in 1382. She was granted a generous dower, and since she was small and plain, this led to the allegation that the king had paid too high a price 'for a tiny bit of flesh'. But on her death in 1394, Richard, apparently inconsolable, ordered the demolition of Sheen, the manor house in which she had died.

Anne of Cleves (1515–57), Queen of England. The strategic importance of the Duchy of Cleves, lying between the Low Countries and the German imperial territories, and the Protestant inclinations of John, Duke of Cleves which suited Thomas CROMWELL's reformist religious policies, made the Duke's second daughter, Anne, the choice for the fourth wife of HENRY VIII. Henry was delighted with Holbein's portrait of Anne, but their first meeting on New Year's Day, 1540, was a disaster. Cromwell held the king to the marriage, which duly took place on 6 Jan. 1540; however, not only did Henry continue to detest Anne, but the diplomatic value of Cleves declined. By July, Henry had insisted on an annulment of the marriage, so

Anne took a handsome settlement of English lands and retired to discreet and comfortable grass widowhood. The affair was the main reason for Cromwell's fall. Anne is often seen through Henry's eyes as a dull and lumpish 'Flanders mare', but her skilful reaction to the crisis, and her acquisition of tolerable English from scratch within a few weeks, suggests that she was no fool.

Anne of Denmark (1574–1619), Queen of England, Ireland and Scotland, daughter of Frederick II of Denmark and Norway. Marriage negotiations with JAMES VI began in 1585, but were obstructed by ELIZABETH I. Determined pressure from the Scots nobility led to a proxy wedding in Copenhagen in Aug. 1589, and with uncharacteristic drama, James collected his bride from Norway in person, in Nov. 1589. James did not share Anne's sympathy for Catholicism, although he consistently sought her tacit approval for his homosexual favourites. After he became King of England as James I, she encouraged English court extravagance in building, art and entertainment, especially MASQUES.

Annesley v. Sherlock, 1719, *see* DECLARATORY ACT, 1720

Annulment, *see* DIVORCE

Anonimalle Chronicle, an anonymous (hence its name) French chronicle compiled at St Mary's Abbey, York. Mostly based on the French prose work *BRUT* and its continuations, the section on the years 1369 to 1381 – for which the compiler had a London source, probably a chancery clerk – contains important accounts of the PEASANTS' REVOLT and the GOOD PARLIAMENT, by far the best surviving description of a medieval Parliament.

Anselm, St (1033–1109), Archbishop of Canterbury (1093–1109). Born at Aosta in the Italian Alps, he entered the Norman abbey of Bec in 1059 and studied under LANFRANC. In 1078, Anselm became Abbot of Bec and, subsequently, a prolific author of theological and philosophical works. In 1093, WILLIAM II RUFUS invested him as Lanfranc's successor as Archbishop of Canterbury, where he met his biographer, the English monk EADMER.

Anselm's insistence on the rights of his Church rapidly led to quarrels with William Rufus. When the king tried to discipline him, the archbishop caused consternation by arguing that he could not be judged in a secular court and appealing to the Pope. In 1097, Anselm went into exile, but three years later, after Rufus's death, he was invited back by the much more conciliatory HENRY I.

While in exile, Anselm had attended papal councils in Italy and had become acquainted with some of the principal tenets of the papal reform programme: the decrees banning lay investiture and ordering churchmen not to do homage to laymen. The fundamental issues of church–state relations which these decrees raised inevitably led to further quarrels, and in 1103, Anselm went into exile again. Not until 1107 was a compromise reached that allowed him to return to his see.

Anselm's scholarship, the simplicity of his life-style, his promotion of reform movements within the Church and, above all, his insistence that his loyalty to God and to the Vicar of St Peter overrode his duty to the king, led Thomas BECKET, in the 1160s, to press for his canonization. Ironically, Becket's own 'martyrdom' meant that, after 1170, Canterbury's saintly requirements were more than adequately satisfied; not until the 18th century was Anselm's status as a saint of the Roman Catholic Church put on a more formal basis.

Anti-Catholicism, perhaps the most consistent political idea in England and Scotland from 1580 to 1780. Its roots lie in John FOXE's 'Book of Martyrs', the St Bartholomew massacre of Protestants in France in 1572, the late 16th-century war with Spain, the 1605 GUNPOWDER PLOT and the constant fear of Irish rebellion. It appeared in every major British political upheaval, notably the EXCLUSION CRISIS, and was confirmed by the reign of JAMES II and the subsequent JACOBITE threat. The GORDON RIOTS in 1780 were a major manifestation, but the French revolution produced new sympathy for continental Catholic suffering. However, anti-Catholicism revived in the 19th century, fuelled by opposition to Irish nationalism, English Roman Catholic expansion and ANGLO-CATHOLICISM. Except in ULSTER, it has ceased to be a major political force, even in such late strongholds as Glasgow and Liverpool. *See also* RECUSANCY; REFORMATION.

Anti-Clericalism, distrust of clergy, their power and pretensions, which has tended to be used by historians to account for or portray religious discontent at a variety of periods. In medieval England, it was certainly displayed by the LOLLARDS and, on the eve of the REFORMATION, by special-interest groups such as lawyers, but the wider extent of feeling is dubious. Equally questionable is the suggestion that the Reformation gave anti-clericalism fresh impetus because of the increased education and social prestige of the ANGLICAN clergy. In modern times, anti-clericalism has not been a major feature of politics in Britain, unlike in Catholic European countries where the polarization caused by the French revolution and its aftermath left ugly scars. However, interdenominational rivalry between the Church of England and the FREE CHURCHES affected party politics in the Victorian and Edwardian periods, and there were calls for church disestablishment, particularly in Wales. *See also* CHURCH: ENGLAND.

Anti-Corn Law League, 1838–46. Manchester-based, it became a nationwide organization led by manufacturers, which campaigned against the PROTECTIONISM embodied in the CORN LAWS on the grounds that it impeded economic growth and political and moral progress. In particular it was argued that manufactured EXPORTS were suffering because trading partners were not able to gain currency by selling foodstuffs to Britain: i.e. the corn laws protected the landed interest at the expense of the manufacturers and industrial workers who had to pay high prices for their bread. Its spokesmen raised the issue in Parliament, but it was the efficiency of its nationwide extra-parliamentary campaign that struck the public imagination. The League organized lectures and petitions, held mass meetings and issued tracts, pamphlets and other publications. The net effect was to create a climate of opinion in favour of reform which resulted in the repeal of the corn laws. The Anti-Corn Law League was a model pressure group that was to be much imitated in the years that followed.

Anti-Jacobin and ***Anti-Jacobin Review,*** *see* JACOBINS

Anti-Poor Law Riots Provoked by the attempt to enforce the POOR LAW AMENDMENT ACT 1834, they were largely confined to the North of England and were caused by the confluence of trade depression, the decision to expedite the WORKHOUSE construction programme and the perceived harshness of the New POOR LAW towards the able-bodied unemployed.

Anti-Poor Law committees, formed in the textile towns of Lancs. and Yorks. and led by such TORY radicals as Richard Oastler, John Fielden and the CHARTIST Joseph Stephens, generated a large, if localized, popular following and were evidence of the depth of feeling that Poor Law policy aroused. A rash of riots in Todmorden, Preston, Stockport and elsewhere at the close of the 1830s was sufficient to prevent the effective establishment of the New Poor Law in the North until the 1860s.

The riots were a reminder that the reform of the Poor Law had been prompted by conditions in the agricultural South of England and were considered inappropriate to the industrial North.

Antigua, Caribbean island colonized by Britain in 1632. Large SUGAR estates and natural harbours made Antigua an important possession and the principal 18th-century naval base in the eastern Caribbean. The Codrington family had the largest sugar-planting enterprise, leasing neighbouring Barbuda as well as owning the most extensive Antiguan estates. Sugar production ceased in 1974. A member of the LEEWARD ISLANDS FEDERATION until 1959, Antigua and Barbuda became an independent nation in 1981.

Antiquaries and Antiquarianism When research in English history began to proliferate in the 16th century, one powerful impulse was a consciousness of the loss of antiquities associated with the destruction caused by the REFORMATION, especially the DISSOLUTION OF THE MONASTERIES. Historians owe much, therefore, to the passion for identifying and listing ancient objects which is the heart of antiquarian enthusiasm. Early interest concentrated on the recording of family pedigrees, funeral monuments and HERALDRY, naturally enough since most of those involved were gentlemen and clergy; from William Lambarde (1536–1601), the author of the popular *Perambulations of Kent* (1570), on, there was also a concern to write county history, reflecting the ethos of the COUNTY COMMUNITY. A national English society, the Society of Antiquaries of London, was first founded in 1707 and chartered in 1717, as a refoundation of an earlier body associated with Sir Robert Cotton (1571–1631), and it has offices in Burlington House, Piccadilly; the earliest local history society, the Spalding Gentleman's Society, was founded in 1710. The Society of Antiquaries of Scotland was founded in 1780, and the Royal Society of Antiquaries of Ireland in 1849 (it was chartered in 1912). Historical study remained largely the preserve of amateurs until the foundation of university history departments in the 19th century; after this, the word 'antiquarian' acquired a slightly condescending nuance, encouraged by the affectionate but parodic portrait of an enthusiast in Sir Walter Scott's *The Antiquary* (1816). It was the mid-20th century before academic historians generally rediscovered the value of LOCAL HISTORY both as an academic discipline and as a valuable means of firing interest in history among the wider public.

Anti-Slavery Anti-slavery sentiments, fuelled by the high value attached to 'liberty', were frequently expressed from the late 17th century, paralleling but initially having little effect upon the growth of the SLAVE TRADE and employment of slave labour in British America and the West Indies. Granville Sharp, inspired by his success in the SOMERSET CASE, tried to convert sentiment into reforming activism from the 1770s; support from QUAKERS and EVANGELICALS provided an organizational base for a major public campaign in 1787–8, which placed the abolition of the slave trade and need for radical reform, if not outright abolition of slavery, on the political agenda. Opposition from the West Indies interest and fears prompted by the French Revolution and a slave insurrection in St-Domingue (Haiti) mobilized opposition; however, pressure from the WHIGS, backed by continuing public agitation, brought about a parliamentary ban on the slave trade in 1807. Reformers, notably William WILBERFORCE and the CLAPHAM SECT, then refocused attention on slavery itself. After extensive agitation, an Emancipation Act was passed in 1833.

Antonine Itinerary, an early 3rd century description of the roads of the Roman Empire, which also lists the places found along the roads and the distances between them. Thought to have been a guide for government officials, it is now an invaluable source for Roman settlement in Britain as well as throughout other parts of Europe (*see* ROADS).

Antonine Wall, Strathclyde. This was constructed in the early 140s AD after Roman forces had again taken over the SCOTTISH LOWLANDS on the orders of the emperor Antoninus Pius (138–61). Intended to replace the earlier HADRIAN'S WALL as the northernmost limit of Roman power, it was approximately 37 miles long and ran roughly from Bo'ness to Old Kilpatrick, connecting the rivers Forth and Clyde. Constructed of turf on a stone base approximately 4 m (13 ft) wide, it was fronted by a ditch about 12 m (39 ft) wide and 3 m (10 ft) deep. Forts and intermediate stations were built on the same pattern as Hadrian's Wall.

The Antonine Wall was only briefly occupied. Probably by the early 160s, the Romans had decided that the task of holding down Lowland Scotland was too demanding in terms both of men and resources. *See also* ROMAN CONQUEST.

Anzio, Battle of, Italy, 22 Jan.–23 May 1944, Allied amphibious landing in WORLD WAR II at Anzio, 40 miles behind German lines and 30 miles south of Rome, in an attempt to break the stalemate on the 'Gustav Line' (*see* MONTE CASSINO). Despite minimal German opposition at first the advance inland did not begin in earnest until 30 Jan., by which time German reinforcements had arrived. The Allies were penned into their beach-head and took heavy casualties.

Apology of the Commons, 1604. A document produced by a committee of the House of COMMONS during a dispute with JAMES I about parliamentary obstruction of his proposals, it asserted parliamentary privilege against PRIVY COUNCIL interference. However, James became conciliatory, so it was never presented to him. Traditional views of it as an opening shot in a constitutional clash have been exaggerated.

Apostles, The Founded in CAMBRIDGE in 1820, its proper name was 'The Cambridge Conversazione Society' and its aim was friendship, the articulation of feelings and formal discussion. The poet Alfred, Lord Tennyson was among the 19th-century members; largely under the influence of the philosopher George Moore it became an intense intellectual and social hothouse in the early 20th century with members like John Maynard KEYNES, the writers Leonard Woolf, E. M. Forster and, later, the art historian Anthony Blunt.

Apostolic Succession, a view of church ministry which stresses the continuity of a line of EPISCOPAL succession from the twelve Apostles, and hence to Jesus Christ himself; so that bishops, successors of the apostles, have a right to pronounce on what is correct Christian doctrine. Apostolic succession is essential to the claims for authority made by the Roman Catholic and Eastern Orthodox Churches, and is also claimed by the episcopal succession of the Anglican Communion, where HIGH CHURCHMEN lay especial stress on it.

Appeasement, the term, now used pejoratively, applied to the foreign policy principally of British governments in the 1930s, which endeavoured, by the granting of concessions, to contain the aggression of Hitler and Mussolini.

Associated principally with the leadership of Stanley BALDWIN and Neville CHAMBERLAIN, appeasement was subsequently condemned as a craven policy of sacrificing smaller and weaker powers in an unsuccessful bid to prevent war. Combined with the failure to rearm, it led to the indictment of pre-war leaders for bringing Britain to the brink of defeat in 1940.

An alternative view of appeasement suggests that it was a genuine and principled attempt to come to terms with the dictators, to settle outstanding grievances left over from WORLD WAR I, and to establish an orderly framework of negotiated settlements that would avoid a repetition of the horrors of the Great War.

Appeasement had its origins in Britain's concern throughout the inter-war years to avoid international conflict and minimize defence costs. Widespread agreement that the treaty of Versailles required revision, strong anti-war feeling, and domestic economic difficulties (*see* DEPRESSION) undermined any attempt to take a firm stand against such acts of aggression as Mussolini's conquest of Ethiopia and Germany's remilitarization of the Rhineland.

The accession of Chamberlain as prime minister in 1937 saw appeasement elevated to a positive policy aimed at bringing about a general settlement of outstanding issues. Hitler's absorption of Austria in the *Anschluss* was tolerated, but his claims on the German-speaking Sudetenland provoked the policy's most serious test. Chamberlain's determined attempts to resolve the crisis in his meetings with Hitler produced the MUNICH AGREEMENT, which forestalled war at the cost of dismembering Czechoslovakia and provoked intense debate about the morality and effectiveness of appeasement.

Within the CONSERVATIVE PARTY, CHURCHILL led calls for rearmament, while the LABOUR PARTY's earlier distrust of rearmament policies was giving way to alarm at the progress of Fascism, emotively demonstrated by the imminent fall of the Spanish Republic. Hitler's overthrow of the Czech government in March 1939 forced a reappraisal, including a crash defence programme and guarantees to Poland and Romania against Hitler's territorial demands.

CHRONOLOGY

1931 Japanese conquest of Manchuria shows ineffectiveness of LEAGUE OF NATIONS in containing aggression.

1933 Hitler comes to power in Germany. 'KING AND COUNTRY' DEBATE at Oxford Union widely interpreted abroad as evidence of anti-war sentiment among younger generation in Britain.

1935 Ethiopian crisis: Italian troops invade Ethiopia. Subsequent HOARE–LAVAL PACT shows British government's readiness to accede to Italian aggression. Hitler repudiates military restrictions of treaty of Versailles. Britain signs ANGLO-GERMAN NAVAL AGREEMENT, allowing Germans to build fleet up to one-third of British naval strength. BALDWIN fights and wins general election on policy of 'no big armaments'.

1936 German troops reoccupy demilitarized Rhineland in defiance of Versailles treaty.

Outbreak of Spanish Civil War; Britain adopts policy of non-intervention despite the extensive involvement of German and Italian forces.
1937 CHAMBERLAIN becomes prime minister.
1938 Germany absorbs Austria into Reich during *Anschluss*, contrary to Versailles settlement. Germany's claims on Sudetenland of Czechoslovakia bring Europe close to war. Chamberlain flies to meet Hitler, eventually signing MUNICH AGREEMENT that surrenders Sudetenland to Germany.
1939 Germany occupies Prague. Britain introduces peacetime CONSCRIPTION and offers guarantees to Poland (*see* ANGLO-POLISH ALLIANCE) and Romania. Hitler demands adjustment of German–Polish frontier in Germany's favour. German forces invade Poland (1 Sept.). Britain issues ultimatum to Germany to withdraw (2 Sept.); non-compliance leads Britain to declare war on Germany (3 Sept.).

Appellants (Lords Appellant), opponents of RICHARD II – Thomas of Woodstock and the Earls of Arundel, Warwick, Derby (the future HENRY IV) and Nottingham – who, in an unprecedented procedure, brought an 'appeal' (i.e. accusation) of treason against a group of the king's friends in the Parliament of Nov. 1387. The accused raised an army against them, but victory at the battle of Radcot Bridge enabled the Appellants to take control of the government and proceed with their appeal in the MERCILESS PARLIAMENT of Feb. 1388. Richard's leading supporters either fled abroad or were executed. In 1397, Richard turned this same procedure against the Appellants themselves.

Appellants, Roman Catholic Following Cardinal ALLEN's death in 1594, English Catholics were left leaderless, with disputes between SECULAR and REGULAR clergy, especially concerning the JESUITS, whom seculars saw as undermining Catholicism by disloyalty to the crown. Rather than appoint a bishop, Rome chose George Blackwell as archpriest; he was a secular, but was seen as Jesuit-dominated. Between 1598 and 1602, a group of seculars appealed to Rome against his jurisdiction – hence their name: the Appellants. Following negotiations with the English government, a royal proclamation in 1602 offered personal protection against persecution to secular priests who submitted; the following year, 13 seculars supporting the Appellants swore loyalty to the crown and repudiated any claim to political power by the pope. The deal, short-lived and highly circumscribed though it was, represented the first move towards religious toleration in England.

Apprentices at Law, *see* BARRISTERS

Apprenticeship, period of training, in a trade or craft. Apprenticeship was historically one of the most important means of acquiring skills, especially in towns; many incorporated towns until the 18th century would only permit those who were freemen – that is men who had served an apprenticeship and become masters in their own right – to ply their trade. Apprenticeships were for a term of years, usually seven, and a premium was paid to the master to take the boy on; the higher-class the trade, the higher the premium. The system was regulated by the Statute of ARTIFICERS of 1563, and in incorporated towns controlled by the craft GUILDS. Apprenticeship was in sharp decline by the late 18th century, although it remained into the 20th century in some handicraft and engineering trades. Old controls proved inadequate in the face of rising demand for British manufacturers and competition increased the need for cheap labour. Most trades could be learnt in less than seven years and the old justification for apprenticeship – that it controlled entry to a trade, hence wage levels and standards of workmanship – was swept away by the rise of new trades and the expansion of markets.

Parish apprentices were pauper children whose labour was allocated to local farmers or tradesmen under the Old POOR LAW; some of the early FACTORY owners used pauper apprentice labour until the imposition of CHILD LABOUR legislation. Serving an apprenticeship, like a spell in SERVICE, was a step on the way to adulthood for many young people in pre-industrial and early industrial Britain; both also conferred rights to settlement under the SETTLEMENT laws before 1834.

Appropriation, provision in a finance bill that monies raised might be used ('appropriated') only for a specified purpose. In the 1660s and 1670s, MPs critical of the government struggled to insert such clauses in numerous bills. From the 1690s, such provisions became routine.

Appropriations, *see* FEOFFEES FOR IMPROPRIATIONS

Aquitaine Originally an administrative region in the south-west of Roman Gaul, from the 9th century it was a more or less independent duchy within the kingdom of France. In 1152, upon the marriage of ELEANOR OF AQUITAINE and HENRY II, it was incorporated into the ANGEVIN EMPIRE. From then until EDWARD III's reign, the kings of England (as dukes of Aquitaine) owed HOMAGE to the kings of France. This made them vulnerable to judicial actions such as that taken in 1202 when Philip II Augustus pronounced the confiscation of all of JOHN's fiefs in France. While Eleanor lived, this had little effect in Aquitaine, but after her death in 1204, most of the lords and towns of Poitou transferred their allegiance to Philip. John retained only GASCONY and south-west Poitou (Angoulême, Aunis and Saintonge).

In 1224, while the siege of Bedford held the attention of the government of HENRY III's minority, Louis VIII of France conquered La Rochelle and the rest of Plantagenet Poitou. This left a duchy of Aquitaine comprising little more than Gascony, and from then on, the two names were used interchangeably. When Philip IV of France pronounced Aquitaine forfeit in 1294, the English crown countered with the novel argument that Gascony had never been a French fief – a claim that has convinced some 20th-century historians, but was certainly not accepted by the French crown. Continuing disagreement over the status of Aquitaine contributed to the outbreak of the HUNDRED YEARS WAR. Under the treaty of BRÉTIGNY (1360), Poitou was transferred to Edward III, and in this way EDWARD THE BLACK PRINCE was briefly prince of a greater Aquitaine. However, with the renewal of war in 1369, the French armies soon restored the *status quo ante*. From then until the final collapse in 1453, the history of 'English' Aquitaine was essentially the history of Gascony.

Arbroath, Declaration of, 1320, a letter sent to Pope John XXII by Scottish barons seeking papal diplomatic support in the War of SCOTTISH INDEPENDENCE. It was probably drafted in Robert BRUCE's chancery, yet concluded with the statement that, were Bruce to submit to the English, they would make another king, 'for so long as a hundred men remain alive we will never in any way be bowed beneath the yoke of English domination; for it is not for glory, riches or honours that we fight, but for freedom alone, that which no man of worth yields up, save with his life'.

Archaeology, study of the past conducted from the material remains of the past, especially from prehistoric and early historical periods. ANTIQUARIANS like John Aubrey (1626–97) and William Stukeley (1687–1765), treasure seekers, and 18th-century travellers to Greece and Rome, were among the first to investigate material remains and to dig to find what had been lost, and to display their finds in cabinets of curiosities and MUSEUMS. Developments in geology and Britain's imperial expansion in the 19th century both gave further impetus to an emerging and increasingly professionalized science, with the organized 'dig' becoming the main form of investigation. Spectacular successes like Schliemann's discovery of Troy between 1871 and 1890, Sir Arthur Evans' (1851–1941) excavation of Knossos 1883–90, and Howard Carter's (1874–1939) opening of the tomb of Tutankhamun in 1923, added glamour to the subject, while General A. H. Pitt-Rivers (1827–1900) in the late 19th century transformed excavation from a hobby into an arduous scientific endeavour. Experts like Sir Mortimer Wheeler (1890–1976), with his excavations in India and at MAIDEN CASTLE, Dorset, caught the popular imagination. Archaeological techniques, with a methodology including painstaking physical analysis and careful recording, have been used increasingly to study more recent times, with the growth of medieval and post-medieval archaeology, notably in the history of LONDON and other towns. *See also* ASHMOLEAN MUSEUM; BRITISH MUSEUM.

Archenfield (Ergyng) The predominantly Welsh district of Archenfield appears in DOMESDAY BOOK as part of Herefords. (as it is now). Briefly a kingdom in the 6th century, it probably became part of England only after the death of GRUFFUDD AP LLYWELYN in 1063. Its local customs, as recorded in 1086, reveal the system by which food was taken from different localities to support early Welsh KINGSHIP. They also show that, during the time it was a region of Wales, Archenfield had sent representatives to the SHIRE-COURT of Hereford – a sign of cross-border co-operation despite the frequent outbreaks of hostilities between English and Welsh rulers.

Architectural Styles, *see* ANGLO-SAXON ARCHITECTURE; ARTISAN MANNERISM; ARTS AND CRAFTS; BAROQUE; DECORATED; EARLY ENGLISH; GOTHIC; GOTHICK; MODERN MOVEMENT; NEO-CLASSICISM; NORMAN ARCHITECTURE; PALLADIANISM; PERPENDICULAR; ROCOCO; ROMANESQUE; TRANSITIONAL; VERNACULAR BUILDINGS.

Arcos Raid, search in May 1927 of the London headquarters of the Soviet trading company, Arcos, and part of the anti-COMMUNIST reaction of the CONSERVATIVE government following the GENERAL STRIKE. The government alleged that the Soviet government was using the company to front subversion and used the raid as the pretext for ending the Anglo-Soviet trade agreement concluded by the LABOUR government three years earlier and for breaking off diplomatic relations.

Arctic Convoys, convoys carrying munitions to Russia during WORLD WAR II, using the route round the north of German-occupied Norway to the Arctic seaports of Murmansk and Archangel. This was done in the teeth of fierce attack from German aircraft, submarines and capital ships, and in some of the worst weather in the world. Between Sept. 1941 and 1945 a total of 4 million tons of supplies including 5,000 tanks and 7,000 planes were carried, though even more went by the less spectacular route via the Persian Gulf and Iran. British and Allied losses were heavy in both merchantmen and escorts, but a price to be paid to keep Russia in the war. One convoy (PQ17) was prematurely dispersed on ADMIRALTY order and lost 21 out of 34 ships. The next one (PQ18) was fought through in the equivalent of a major naval battle. The successful defence of a later convoy by a weak escort caused Hitler to abandon any faith in his heavy warships.

Argyll, island and highland region in Scotland that, in the 12th century under the rule of SOMERLED, became a distinct political entity with its own kings. Although, formally, these monarchs held the islands from the king of Norway and the mainland from the king of Scotland, in practice they remained independent powers until the 13th century. Thereafter, as 'Lords of the Isles', Somerled's descendants continued to play a major role in Scottish politics until the abolition of the lordship in 1492.

Argyll, 2nd Duke of, *see* CAMPBELL, JOHN

Argyll, 9th Earl of, *see* CAMPBELL, ARCHIBALD

Aristocracy, literally government by the best: a concept derived from classical Greece, 'best' commonly being interpreted to mean well-born. Political analysts of the classical world, the most articulate and influential of whom was Aristotle, analysed their political history as an interplay between government by sole ruler (monarchy), government by the nobility (aristocracy) and government by the entire citizen body (democracy); a favourite cliché of debate was to argue about which form of government was best. The categories, and the debate, became an active part of political discourse once more during the RENAISSANCE. From the 17th century, the House of LORDS was identified as forming the aristocratic element in an English system of government somewhat complacently described by its admirers as possessing a balance between monarchic, aristocratic and democratic components.

However, the word has taken on further meanings in the modern world. In the 18th century, the terms 'aristocracy' and 'aristocratic' were sometimes pejoratively applied to those thought to favour concentration of power in the hands of a minority of great families: ROCKINGHAMITE and FOXite WHIGS especially came under attack for supposedly preferring the claims of aristocracy to those of either king or people. During the era of the FRENCH REVOLUTION 'aristocrat' was employed, as in France, as a term of abuse for supporters of the political status quo. In the 19th century, the word was increasingly commonly used to designate a social group rather than a system of government: the PEERAGE and great landowners.

In this sense of class or social, rather than political, description the word has now become much used by historians as a simple synonym for noblemen, peers or major landowners, being freely used in discussion of the 16th and 17th centuries and even in medieval history. One must, however, realize the problems of using the word in these earlier contexts, particularly in relation to medieval FEUDAL society where terminology and concepts of politics from the classical world had no living currency. One Latin word for the well-born élite, '*nobilitas*' ('nobility'), did survive in medieval Europe; by the 16th century, political analysts gave it a twofold meaning in relationship to the titled parliamentary peerage, '*nobilitas maior*' (or greater nobility), and the ARMIGEROUS gentry, '*nobilitas minor*' (or lesser nobility). Lawrence Stone's influential book *The Crisis of the Aristocracy* (1965) was an attempt to analyse the decline of the 16th- and early 17th-century English peerage relative to the GENTRY, and as such was a contribution to the debate about the origins of the CIVIL WARS and to the 'gentry controversy'. His title provides an illustration of the difficulties caused by the term 'aristocracy' in describing early modern society; one could argue that Stone's peerage and his gentry both belonged to the aristocracy, rendering his main thesis of aristocratic decline meaningless.

Armadas, Spanish, 1588, 1596, 1597. The 1588 Armada is one of the best-known events in popular history, but this encounter was only the first in a series of attempts by Spain to strike a decisive blow at England, in an undeclared world war which raged from the mid-1580s to 1604 (*see also* NETHERLANDS, REVOLT OF). Although the English government quickly moved to establish the 1588 defeat as a national event of major significance commemorated with an annual celebration, much insecurity remained, which can only be said to have been overcome with the defeat of the Spanish expeditionary force at KINSALE (1601).

One of the curious features of the 1588 events is that they are much better documented in eyewitness accounts from Spanish participants than from the English side; of course, the Spaniards had more to explain. The Spanish plan was to sail a fleet under the command of the Duke of Medina Sidonia from Spain to the Straits of Dover, to cover the Spanish army (possibly 26,000 men) in the Low Countries (Belgium) commanded by the Duke of Parma, which was intended to cross the Channel in barges and invade south-east England, supported by guns, soldiers and munitions carried in the fleet.

There was a basic flaw in this plan: the Dutch 'rebels' had a force of shallow-draft craft in the shallow waters off the invasion force which would have cut that army to pieces before it had a chance to reach the protection of the deep-draft ships of the Spanish fleet – even if the latter had beaten the English fleet, and even if both forces could have concerted their efforts. In the event communications between fleet and army were, as might be expected at that period, totally inadequate, whilst Parma was deeply unwilling to divert his soldiers from the defeat of the Dutch.

Both sides assembled fleets which mainly consisted of merchant ships impressed for the purpose. The English had more warships than the Spanish, and had more ships suited for fighting and to northern waters than their opponents. There was also a considerable advantage in numbers and power of guns, in the way they were mounted and the way they were fought. However, no one had realized, before the experience of this action, just how much ammunition was needed, and in any case there was little chance that the impecunious Elizabethan NAVY could have assembled anything like the quantities of powder and shot that would have been required.

After initially being driven back to Corunna by storms, the Armada reached English waters in good formation, and all the way up the Channel the Spanish contrived to hold that formation against not very effective English attacks. The English problem was how to break that formation, and they finally had their chance when the Spaniards anchored off Gravelines. Fireships were hastily improvised and sent in by night. They did not destroy any of the enemy but the threat was enough to cause the cutting of cables and the abandonment of the formation. At last the English ships came to close quarters with the Spaniards, who were lucky to escape being driven onto the sands and retreated northwards up the North Sea. The English fleet, now almost out of ammunition, shadowed them north, until it was clear that they could not return. The English ships returned to harbour, where they lost a horrifying proportion of their crews to disease and want. Their opponents also lost many aboard the ships that finally came back to Spain, but many more still were lost in the ships wrecked off Scotland and Ireland through a combination of battle damage and bad weather. Numbers of these wrecks have been excavated by divers in recent years. Ultimately, the reason for failure must lie in the sheer scale of the operation; in the primitive logistical conditions of the 16th century, even the Spanish empire could not get it right, and the consistent advantage was with the English defenders. One strong piece of evidence for this is the lack of English success when England in turn went on the offensive after the 1588 deliverance. A conscientious commander of an overstretched and undersupplied enterprise, Medina Sidonia did very well against the English commander, Howard of Effingham (*see* HOWARD, CHARLES), and his subordinates, HAWKINS and DRAKE. Both sides were fighting a naval battle of a type and scale not hitherto seen. It was seen as a protestant success in a war against Roman CATHOLICISM, which had reverberations throughout Europe. The English fleet had scored a defensive success which the elements had turned into a crushing defeat for Spain. It was to be bad weather alone which destroyed the two subsequent armadas.

CHRONOLOGY

(*Dates are given according to the Julian calendar and are thus 10 days behind those used on the Continent – see* GREGORIAN CALENDAR)

1584, Jan. Expulsion of Spanish ambassador from London for plotting pushes England and Spain further towards undeclared war.

1585 Francis DRAKE provokes Spain by Atlantic-wide attacks; Philip II agrees to invasion of England.

1587, April–May Drake's raid on Cadiz 'singeing the king of Spain's beard' delays Spanish preparations of the Armada fleet.

1588, Feb. Following the death of the Marquis of Santa Cruz, Medina Sidonia reluctantly takes command of Armada.

1588, 18 May Armada sets sail from Lisbon; delays and storm disruption follow.

1588, 19 July English make first sighting of Armada.

1588, 21 July First engagement of the fleets off Eddystone Rock, Devon.

1588, 28 July Armada arrives off Calais substantially intact after indecisive engagements: English cause panic by sending in fireships.

1588, 29 July Main battle at Gravelines, northern France: the Spaniards flee north.

1588, 3 Aug. Spanish commanders decide to keep a northward course, rounding Scotland to return home.

1588, 9–10 Aug. Inspection of troops at Tilbury, Essex, by ELIZABETH I: she makes a key speech, although probably not the familiar version.

1588, 21 Aug. Duke of Parma stands down his Flanders fleet, recognizing that liaison with the Armada is now impossible.

1588, Autumn Much of the Armada wrecked off Scottish and Irish coasts.

1588, 20 Nov. Parma forced to abandon the siege of Bergen-op-Zoom: first substantial Anglo-Dutch military success.

1588, 24 Nov. London celebratory service at St Paul's cathedral: culmination of a series of thanksgiving events and the date observed nationwide in later years.

1589, April–July English launch counterattack on Iberian coast: a disaster, principally because of epidemics on board ships.

1596, Spring Spaniards prepare second Armada; driven back by storms.

1597 Third Spanish Armada repelled by bad weather.

1601 Spanish defeat at KINSALE.

Armagh, city in county of the same name, and a place of great importance in the early religious and political history of the Irish kingdoms (*see* KINGSHIP; MONASTICISM). Supposedly founded in 444, it subsequently acquired a reputation as having been the base for St PATRICK's missionary activities. As a result, it gained superior status among the Irish churches, a primacy in rank that was formally recognized in 737. The Archbishop of Armagh is the Primate of All Ireland. The county of Armagh, and especially the border between Northern Ireland and the Republic, has become notorious since the 1960s as an arena of violent political activity.

Armed Neutrality, League of, 1780, 1800–1, associations of states which set, and pledged to defend by force of arms, limits to the powers of belligerents to search and seize neutral shipping. These leagues chiefly aimed to constrain Britain as the leading naval power in the 18th and 19th centuries. The first league was inaugurated by Russia, Sweden and Denmark in 1780, against the background of the War of AMERICAN INDEPENDENCE; Britain had been attempting to secure Russia as an ally. The Russian decision instead first to declare neutrality in April, and then to found the league in Aug., represented major setbacks for British diplomacy. It also led to a decisive breach in the traditional alliance between Britain and Holland. When it appeared likely that the Dutch would adhere to the league, the British insisted that they stick by treaty obligations and come to Britain's aid; in Dec. 1780, to pre-empt the Dutch joining the league and gaining the support of other members, Britain declared war. A second league, with Russia, Sweden, Denmark and Prussia as members, was formed in 1800, in the context of the FRENCH REVOLUTIONARY WAR. This collapsed in the spring of 1801 when Tsar Paul was murdered by court conspirators, and the British fleet attacked and destroyed the Danish fleet in harbour at Copenhagen.

Arminianism, religious movement in the Church of England, taking its name from the Dutch theologian Jacobus Arminius (Jakob Hermandszoon, 1560–1609). He denied that God's grace could not be resisted, so human beings could be damned because they resisted divine grace; he thus challenged the CALVINIST doctrine of predestination.

Arminius' Dutch followers were condemned at the ultra-Calvinist synod of DORT (Dordrecht, 1618–19). At the same time in England, the hostile nickname 'Arminian' was given to a group of clergy similarly opposing the Calvinist theological consensus in the Church of England. However, this group had formed in the 1580s before Arminius was heard of, and they were not so much interested in predestination as in reviving CATHOLIC ceremony and a sense of continuity within the Church.

The Arminians remained a small university clique until the reign of JAMES I; he began advancing them in the Church, and under CHARLES I, they became powerful, particularly when William LAUD became Archbishop of Canterbury in 1633. They aroused great hostility for their energetic changes to Church ceremony and furnishings, and for advocating obedience to royal power. Mostly clergy, they never built up a mass following, and were a primary target when Charles's regime collapsed in 1640. However, after the RESTORATION, their Catholic theology continued to influence the Church of England, and it was later revived by the OXFORD MOVEMENT (*see* ANGLO-CATHOLICISM).

Some 17th-century religious radicals also emphasized the importance of free will in salvation, and have been labelled Arminian (*see* BAPTISTS). John WESLEY later applied the Arminian label to his METHODIST societies, because of his hostility to Calvinism. *See also* DURHAM HOUSE SET.

Armistice Day, annual commemoration on 11 Nov. of the dead of both World Wars, marking the end of WORLD WAR I at 11 a.m., 11 Nov. 1918. The main commemoration has now moved to the nearest Sunday, known as Remembrance Sunday, with ceremonies at war memorials, the principal one being at the CENOTAPH.

Army The provision of military service was one of the most fundamental of all obligations required by the earliest kingdoms in Britain (*see* WARFARE, LAND). Long before the NORMAN CONQUEST this obligation had taken two basic forms: a requirement for common service in times of trouble (*see* COMMON BURDENS; *FYRD*), which had developed into the MILITIA by the Assize of Arms of 1181; and a small permanent force of warriors under royal control (*see* HOUSECARLS). Medieval armies were raised by a mixture of these methods together with feudal obligation (*see* TENANT-IN-CHIEF) and mercenaries. By Tudor times armies consisted almost entirely of paid troops raised temporarily for war, and the granting of money for them was an important privilege of PARLIAMENT. A STANDING ARMY was considered a potential instrument of royal despotism, and the only permanent force was a small royal bodyguard, the Yeoman of the Guard, founded by HENRY VII in 1485.

The issue came to a head in 1639–40 with Parliament's refusal to grant money to CHARLES I to repel a Scots invasion, an incident which was one immediate cause of the English CIVIL WARS. The NEW MODEL ARMY created by parliament in 1645 is considered the chief ancestor of the British army, but its role in enforcing the rule of the Protectorate (*see* INTERREGNUM) left a strong anti-military prejudice which lasted into the 20th century. The first permanent standing army was created under CHARLES II in 1661 as 'His Majesty's GUARDS AND GARRISONS'. Unlike the Royal Navy, neither the existence nor the purpose of the army was enshrined by statute, and a contest developed between crown and Parliament for its control. After JAMES II's expansion of the army by royal prerogative, the 1689 DECLARATION OF RIGHTS set out that its existence was illegal without parliamentary approval, which was provided by the annual MUTINY ACT until 1955, when it was replaced by the five-yearly Armed Forces Act. In 1751 a permanent nucleus of guards, infantry and cavalry (together with the Royal Regiment of Artillery, founded 1716) was given official acknowledgement by a Royal Warrant. Thereafter the issue largely died away. The last king to lead his army personally into battle was GEORGE II at DETTINGEN in 1743.

England's main defence against invasion was its NAVY, and particularly after the UNION with Scotland (1707) a large army at home was not required. The British army developed both in itself and in relation to its society in a way utterly unlike the armies of continental Europe (particularly Prussia). Old relics of the mercenary system, such as officers purchasing their commissions and regiments having considerable autonomy from central authority, persisted well into the 19th century. Parliamentary fears led to rigid control of the army budget, a divided system of command and responsibility, and a general military and social conservatism including a tradition of non-involvement in politics. Officers were drawn largely from the lesser GENTRY, while recruitment of soldiers hardly touched the bulk of the population, being largely confined to the poorest classes. The army served almost entirely overseas, and the establishment of military barracks at home in 1792 to prevent subversion by revolutionary ideas completed its isolation from the population.

The army's major roles, although only first officially defined in 1888, existed from its creation. It acted against internal dissent or revolt, a role which diminished with the introduction of POLICE forces in the 19th century, and defended Britain against invasion. More importantly, it acted as a garrison and field army for the Empire, starting with Scotland and Ireland and gradually expanding throughout the globe. The main commitment was to INDIA, particularly after the loss of America in the War of AMERICAN INDEPENDENCE and the crown's take-over of the EAST INDIA COMPANY army as the Indian Army in 1858, following the INDIAN MUTINY. Lastly, the army frequently provided an intervention force to maintain the 'balance of power in Europe', the traditional British strategy of opposing the dominant European power by creating a coalition against it. This produced a pattern of rapid expansion of the army in times of war, including the employment of mercenaries and the subsidizing of the armies of other states, followed immediately on peace with an equally rapid reduction. The 'British' armies which won BLENHEIM (1704) or WATERLOO (1815) or EL ALAMEIN (1942) were multinational armies under a British commander with a core of British troops.

A pattern of 18th-century wars fought both in Europe and outside culminated in the FRENCH REVOLUTIONARY and NAPOLEONIC WARS, for the army an almost unbroken succession of fighting in Europe from 1793 to 1815 which resulted in its increased professionalization and a more than tenfold increase in its size. In the century between Waterloo and WORLD WAR I, however, the army was involved almost entirely in Imperial campaigns, fighting in Europe on a large scale just once in the CRIMEAN WAR (1853–6). A series of 19th-century reforms created a predominantly infantry army to garrison the Empire and did away with many of the older abuses, reaching a high point with the abolition of purchase under Edward Cardwell in 1871, and the creation of the 'county' regimental system in 1881.

Britain was the only European power without CONSCRIPTION, which was seen as a threat to British liberties. Its inability to create an effective intervention force during the Franco-Prussian War (1870–1) and problems revealed by the second BOER WAR (1899–1902) led to further widespread reforms associated with Richard Haldane before World War I which laid the foundations of the modern army and created the BRITISH EXPEDITIONARY FORCE (BEF). During World War I another massive expansion of the army was achieved entirely by voluntary means until Jan. 1916, when conscription was introduced and maintained until the end of the war. By 1922 the army had been reduced to a voluntary long-service Imperial garrison force once more.

In March 1939 conscription in peacetime was introduced for the first time in British history and used to expand the army again for WORLD WAR II. Conscription was maintained after the war (*see* NATIONAL SERVICE), and the army's two main roles changed to covering the retreat from empire and maintaining forces in Europe as part of NATO. The army returned once more to an all-volunteer force as a result of the Duncan Sandys 1957 Defence Review, which also combined the three services into a single ministry of defence and led to a general modernization. In 1995 the most fundamental reorganization of the British army since 1945 brought the regular and part time soldiers under a single Land Command. The total number had declined from 3,007,300 in 1945 to approximately 140,000 soldiers. In the 1980s and 1990s British troops served in the Falklands (1982), Iraq (1990), Bosnia (1993) and Northern Ireland. In 1994 the 25,000-strong British Army of the Rhine (BAOR) was renamed the United Kingdom Support Command, a force designed to serve as a multinational rapid reaction force. Over the past decade recruitment to the army has been falling and the situation is now acute.

Arnhem, Battle of, Netherlands, 17–26 Sept. 1944. It was a small but important battle of WORLD WAR II, the largest airborne battle in history and MONTGOMERY's only major defeat. Codenamed Operation 'Market-Garden', it was Montgomery's attempt to gain a bridgehead over the Rhine by dropping three divisions of paratroops and gliders (two American and one British) deep behind German lines in the belief that the war was almost over and resistance would be slight. A poor plan and strong German counter-attacks meant that only a few airborne troops reached the key objectives including Arnhem bridge, and delayed the advance of the ground forces. Surviving British troops (including a Polish contingent) were evacuated from Arnhem at the end of the battle.

Arras, Battle of, north-eastern France, 9–24 April 1917, a major WORLD WAR I battle by British and DOMINION troops under Sir Edmund Allenby against the Germans. Fought in almost winter weather, it achieved limited success with the capture of Vimy Ridge by the Canadians, but weakened the Army for the delayed offensive at YPRES later that year.

Arras, Congress of, 1435, peace conference that marked an important turning point in the HUNDRED YEARS WAR. Charles VII of France offered concessions, but the English insisted that the terms of the treaty of TROYES be implemented. The main effect of English intransigence was to accelerate the further development of Franco-Burgundian understanding. Since the earlier strong English position in northern France had depended heavily on the alliance with BURGUNDY, this was a serious setback.

Art mac Murrough (Mor mac Murchadha) (?–*c*.1416), King of Leinster (1375–1416). In 1391, the English government's confiscation of his Anglo-Irish wife's inheritance – he had married her in contravention of the statute of KILKENNY – was a source of grievance. He posed a threat sufficient to draw RICHARD II to Ireland in 1394. Although Art was forced to submit, relations with the English soon broke down again, and by 1399 not only was he claiming to be king of Ireland, but this time Richard was unable to break his resistance. Indeed Art, an outstanding military leader, remained a potent thorn in the flesh of the Lancastrian government until shortly before his death.

Arthur (1486–1502), Prince of Wales. Eldest son of HENRY VII, he was created Prince, with a COUNCIL IN THE MARCHES OF WALES, in 1489. In March 1488, negotiations had begun for his marriage to CATHERINE OF ARAGON; the wedding, on 14 Nov. 1501, was accompanied by spectacular pageantry – a pioneering venture in Tudor court display inspired by the court ceremony of BURGUNDY. Arthur's early death at Ludlow (perhaps from plague) led to Catherine's remarriage to his younger brother, the future HENRY VIII; the papal dispensations for this second marriage caused much dispute in Henry's first divorce. The question of whether Arthur's marriage had been consummated (central to the divorce disputes) remains difficult. Against Catherine's firm insistence that she had remained a virgin, we can only range hearsay and reports of Arthur's adolescent sexual boasting.

Arthur, King, one of the most famous characters in British history, even though he may never have existed. Even if he did, his exploits are unlikely to have resembled those attributed to him by later legends.

The earliest reference to a historic Arthur – the name is Roman – is contained in a Welsh poem of *c.*600, which states that another named warrior was 'no Arthur'. An early 7th-century text lists 12 battles that Arthur is supposed to have won as leader of the native British. (In the 10th-century *ANNALES CAMBRIAE*, two of these battles are assigned dates in the first half of the 6th century.) The earliest evidence of the development of the idea of a legendary British champion on which the subsequent stories were constructed is found in the early 9th-century history attributed to NENNIUS. There have been interesting excavations designed to discover Arthur's court at such places as South CADBURY or TINTAGEL, but all that can be proved is that these sites were inhabited by a British prince who wielded local power in the immediate aftermath of the departure of the Romans, not by *the* Arthur. Ultimately, the only thing that can be said of the historic Arthur is that there may have existed a great soldier who temporarily halted the Anglo-Saxon assault, but it is doubtful whether he was able to unite the British against the invaders.

In subsequent history there are two very different *legendary* King Arthurs. One is the warrior champion who led the Britons in numerous battles against the invading Saxons – a distinctly Celtic hero. The other presided over a magnificent court, CAMELOT, and his deeds tended to be outshone by those of his followers, the Knights of the Round Table. This Arthur is quite simply, an ideal king – a model for any monarch of Britain, not necessarily one who was a Briton or a Celt. Any king who claimed lordship over the British Isles would be perfectly happy to look upon him as his predecessor.

By the early 12th century, Arthur's story was clearly well known in Wales, Cornwall and Brittany, and one of its salient features was already established: the oppressed Britons dreamed of the day when King Arthur (like Cynan and Cadwaladr before him) would return and restore to his people their rightful dominion over the island of Britain.

This was the figure of Celtic legend whom GEOFFREY OF MONMOUTH transformed in the 1130s into the dominating personality of his historical fantasy, the *History of the Kings of Britain*. In Geoffrey's hands, Arthur remained the British champion, but he also became much more. As conqueror of Scotland, Ireland, Iceland, Norway, Denmark and Gaul, he was the equal of Alexander and Charlemagne, and his court was a spectacular centre of international CHIVALRY, love, courtliness and high fashion. When Geoffrey was translated into ANGLO-NORMAN – e.g. by WACE – these new elements rapidly became more prominent. On the one hand, this provided a courtly setting for the Arthurian romances of authors from Chrétien de Troyes on. On the other, it made it easier to overlook the specifically Celtic Arthur. The politically inspired 'discovery' of Arthur's body – still bearing terrible wounds – at GLASTONBURY in *c.*1190 may also have helped to push into the background the image of a king being healed at Avalon so that he might return and drive out the English.

This cleared the way for the reconstruction of Arthur as an English king, a process that was aided by the habit, common already in the 12th century, of treating 'Britain' and 'England' as virtually interchangeable terms. Thus it seems that the earliest king of England to identify himself with King Arthur was RICHARD I, a ruler who set off on crusade brandishing Excalibur; by the 14th century, EDWARD III was described as 'unmatched since the days of Arthur, one-time king of England'.

Thanks to the genius of Sir Thomas Malory (*c.*?1416–?1471) in his romance *Morte d'Arthur* completed *c.* 1470, the cult of King Arthur survived into modern times, to be taken up and reworked in an extraordinary multiplicity of ways. Doubtless the Welsh blood of the Tudors allowed the poet Edmund Spenser (?1552–99) to tell ELIZABETH I that her name, realm and race were all derived from 'this renowned prince'. But without any such association, Sir Richard Blackmore could make his Arthur represent William of Orange (the future WILLIAM III), while Alfred Tennyson could equally well imagine ALBERT, VICTORIA's Prince Consort, finding in King Arthur 'some image of himself'. As for the British champion who would return to liberate his oppressed people, the Welsh found in Owain GLYN DWR some compensation for the loss of their Arthur to the international world of art and letters.

Artificers, Statute of, 1563, legal initiative which set up procedures for fixing maximum wages by JUSTICES OF THE PEACE and regulating the system of APPRENTICESHIP and entry into trade crafts. The statute was a response to POPULATION growth and INFLATION. It remained in force as the defining measure for apprenticeship until 1814.

Artisans' and Labourers' Dwellings Act 1875, legislation passed under DISRAELI's government which, although assuming that urban HOUSING was best left to private provision, provided that, in exceptional circumstances, municipal action might be required to remove impediments to the smooth operation of market forces. It therefore gave local authorities powers of compulsory purchase for slum clearance and rebuilding. It was permissive rather than mandatory and largely irrelevant to the problem of poverty that lay at the heart of the housing crisis.

Arts and Crafts, architectural style and artistic movement of the period *c.*1870–1920 which was a reaction to the machine age of Victorian Britain and its products. Special emphasis was placed upon traditional techniques and hand-craft production, following the writings of John Ruskin and William Morris which often invoked medieval and socialist communitarian ideals. The architectural style fostered by Philip Webb and Morris was continued through the work of C. F. Voysey, Edwin Lutyens and others to the applied art and craft of Eric Gill, while the furniture, fabrics and other products were sold through Morris's own company and Liberty's. Arts and Crafts art and architecture were characterized by a strong feeling for nature and stylized two-dimensional forms.

Arundel, Thomas (1353–1414), Chancellor and Archbishop of Canterbury (1396–7). The combination of a high aristocratic birth (he was the third son of Richard Fitzalan, Earl of Arundel) and high ambition made him one of the most powerful of all English prelates. Beginning his ecclesiastical career as a youthful bishop of Ely in 1374, he became archbishop of York in 1388, then of Canterbury in 1396. His political connections led to his banishment by RICHARD II in 1397 and restoration by HENRY IV two years later. He had no fewer than five terms of office as chancellor – 1386–9, 1391–6, 1399, 1407–10, 1412–13 – but his vigorous opposition to the LOLLARDS showed that he cared about religious as well as secular affairs.

Ascension Island, a mid-Atlantic volcanic island, and a British possession since 1815. Since 1922 the island has been a dependency of ST HELENA, 700 miles away; from 1899 it was a principal mid-ocean imperial TELECOMMUNICATIONS station. Ascension saw its most active service as a mid-way station in the Falklands War of 1982.

Ashburton Treaty, 1842. A significant step in the settlement of the long-running frontier dispute between CANADA and the United States, it decided the boundary line on the eastern seaboard. The western boundary was later settled by the OREGON TREATY. *See also* ANGLO-AMERICAN WAR.

Ashby v. White, one of the most controversial and constitutionally important election cases of the 18th century. Conflict between the WHIG-dominated LORDS and TORY-dominated COMMONS came to a head in 1701 over a disputed election at Aylesbury, Bucks., when votes of almshouse inhabitants subject to Thomas Wharton's (1648–1715) influence were disallowed. One of the voters sued; a verdict favouring him was overturned in the court of Queen's Bench in 1703, the judges ruling that the Commons only could judge in election cases. Wharton appealed to the Lords, who ruled that voters might sue for damages. The ensuing dispute between the two Houses produced a major pamphlet controversy. When five more voters brought actions, the Commons committed them and their attorney for a breach of privilege. In March 1705, Parliament was prorogued and the 'Aylesbury men' released. The right of the Commons to determine the qualification of electors was not challenged again.

Ashdown, Jeremy ('Paddy') (1941–), politician. A former member of the Royal Marines who served as a commando in Northern Ireland, Ashdown was elected Liberal MP for Yeovil (Som.) in 1982. Leader of the LIBERAL DEMOCRATS from 1988 his policy of 'equidistant' between the two main parties

– 'neither left, nor right, but centre' – built the party into a significant election force both at by-elections and the 1992 General Election. In the run up to the 1997 Election, he replaced the centrist position with the commitment that the LibDems would only form a coalition with Labour. In the event this was not required: though Ashdown's party won 46 seats, the highest number since 1929 when it won 59 seats as the LIBERAL PARTY, LABOUR's 178-seat overall majority meant that dialogue about participation in government came to nothing and indeed alienated some LibDem activists who consider that the party must remain an *independent* 'third way' in British politics. Ashdown was succeeded as party leader by Charles Kennedy in 1999.

Ashley Cooper, Anthony, *see* COOPER, ANTHONY ASHLEY

Ashmolean Museum, Oxford. Established in 1683, it has been called the first public museum in Britain – though the TRADESCANT collection in Lambeth had been open to paying visitors in the 1650s. The ANTIQUARIAN and astrologer Elias Ashmole (1617–92), who had acquired the Tradescants' Cabinet of Curiosities, presented it to the University of OXFORD, with a new building containing a lecture room and a chemical laboratory. His primary object was to revitalize the teaching of the natural sciences. Robert Plot, first keeper of the Museum, was also the first professor of chemistry. After 1860, scientific holdings were relocated in the new University Museum; the Ashmolean became and remains an art museum.

Asiento, the contract that granted a monopoly in the supply of slaves to Spain's American colonies, first agreed between Spain and France in 1702. It was transferred to Britain for a 33-year term by the peace of UTRECHT (1713): Britain was to provide 4,800 slaves a year. Disagreements over payments played a part in bringing about the War of JENKINS' EAR (1739), upon which the monopoly lapsed. The Asiento was renewed for four years by the treaty of AIX-LA-CHAPELLE (1748), but rights were sold out in 1750. The monopoly trade was managed by the SOUTH SEA COMPANY. *See also* SLAVE TRADE.

Asquith, H(erbert) H(enry) (1st Earl of Oxford and Asquith) (1852–1928), Liberal politician and Prime Minister (1908–16). An orphan, educated at Oxford and called to the Bar, Asquith first entered Parliament in 1886 as a Gladstonian Liberal sitting for East Fife, and soon established a reputation for debate, political craftsmanship and the potential for high office. In 1892 he was appointed home secretary in GLADSTONE's final administration, a post he retained under Rosebery (*see* PRIMROSE, ARCHIBALD). His first wife died in 1891 and three years later Asquith married Margot Tennant, the clever, sharp-tongued daughter of a wealthy Glasgow industrialist, whose restless and forceful intelligence bought him both a wider intellectual and social circle, and, on occasions, considerable political and financial handicaps and personal exhaustion.

Although clearly the most able candidate, Asquith declined for financial reasons to lead the LIBERAL PARTY when Sir William Harcourt retired in Dec. 1898, and he was soon in conflict with the new leader, CAMPBELL-BANNERMAN, and a large section of the party over their opposition to the BOER WAR. His chance to reassert both traditional Liberal values and his own supremacy came in May 1903 when he led the opposition to Joseph CHAMBERLAIN on the issue of TARIFF REFORM. Whilst his defence of FREE TRADE was masterly, the 'Relugas compact' between Asquith, Edward GREY and R. B. Haldane, to push Campbell-Bannerman to the Lords, was not. However, Asquith's appointment in Dec. 1905 as chancellor of the Exchequer and deputy leader of the COMMONS meant that, after the 1906 Liberal landslide, he was seen as the natural successor to Campbell-Bannerman, becoming leader of the Liberal Party and prime minister in 1908. He oversaw the dispute with the LORDS over LLOYD GEORGE'S PEOPLE'S BUDGET in 1909 and the passage of the PARLIAMENT ACT of 1911 which limited the powers of the Upper House. He instituted OLD AGE PENSIONS and national insurance as well as other reforms seen as forerunners of the WELFARE STATE.

Faced from 1910 with the campaign of the militant SUFFRAGETTES and major strikes, his parliamentary majority after 1910 was dependent upon the Irish Nationalist Party. His HOME RULE proposals in 1913–14 led to the threat of civil war in Ireland, though a Home Rule Act was passed on the eve of WORLD WAR I. He led the country into the war over the German invasion of Belgium, but was increasingly criticized for his less than energetic war policy. In May 1915 the SHELLS SCANDAL and other problems forced him to form a coalition government, but in Dec. 1916 he was removed in a political coup led by Lloyd George and the CONSERVATIVES.

He led his own faction of the Liberal Party, the 'WEE FREES', against the Lloyd George-led coalition in the COUPON ELECTION of 1918 but was badly defeated and lost his seat. His split with Lloyd George gravely weakened the party in the post-war years and, although the factions reunited in 1923–6 under his leadership, he was seen as presiding over the demise of the Liberals as a governing party. An upholder of traditional Liberal values, he was ill-suited to the problems of mass democracy and total war with which he had to deal. He was made an earl in 1925.

Asser (?-909 or 910), Welsh monk and author. Asser's *Life of Alfred* is thought by most scholars to have been composed in 893 during its subject's lifetime, though some believe it to be a late 10th- or early 11th-century forgery. He was a monk and priest at ST DAVID'S, who first went to ALFRED THE GREAT's court in the mid-880s, and was made bishop of SHERBORNE between the years 892 and 900. The *Life of Alfred* is modelled on Einhard's *Life of Charlemagne* and attempts to give a personal portrait of its subject. Some of its detail (if authentic) is fascinating, but its presentation of Alfred as a human and kingly paragon is the foundation of an often excessively uncritical approach to its subject.

Assisted Areas First defined under the SPECIAL AREAS ACT 1934, these were areas of the country where, during the inter-war DEPRESSION, there was a significant decline in heavy or textile industries. State support was introduced to counter the effects of unemployment and provide jobs in new industries, with a range of government incentives for investment. Incentives were first introduced under the Special Areas Act 1934 but the same sort of regional policy continued after the war. Although successive governments, especially CONSERVATIVE ones, have sought to decrease the money spent on assisting depressed areas, the human wastage involved and slow mobility of labour and capital have forced them into continuing assistance.

Assize Sermon, *see* OXFORD MOVEMENT

Assizes, system of royal justices which replaced the justices in EYRE during the 13th century, and survived until replaced by the crown courts in 1971; the Norman-French for 'sitting' produces 'assize'. Judges ('Justices') of the Westminster courts were sent out twice yearly to try cases in specified regional circuits. Their powers derived from various royal commissions: of assize, gaol delivery, or 'oyer and terminer' ('to hear and determine': especially useful for quick action in political crises and rebellions). They also heard cases *nisi prius* (from the Latin for 'unless previously'): civil cases which Westminster courts would try unless they were previously heard locally. *See also* JURY.

Association, a term used not only as synonym for league or society, but also specifically of large groups of subjects formally banded together for some major constitutional purpose. Bonds of Association were undertakings to protect the monarch, probably modelled on BONDS OF MANRENT. The Oct. 1584 Bond was designed by CECIL and WALSINGHAM to defend ELIZABETH I's life and pursue anyone who tried to harm her: MARY QUEEN OF SCOTS was the obvious target. Thousands joined this extra-legal vigilante group, which in modified form was given legality by Parliament. The experiment may have influenced the COVENANT, and was repeated when an Association to Preserve the Life and Estates of WILLIAM III was formed in 1696 after an assassination attempt upon him. Similarly, a Protestant Association was formed in 1745, in the face of Jacobite rebellion. When the ASSOCIATION MOVEMENT of 1780 invited people to associate to promote the cause of parliamentary reform, some questioned the constitutional propriety of the initiative. In the later 18th century the term was increasingly variously employed, but older usages were often evoked: e.g. by the PROTESTANT ASSOCIATION of 1779, and by John Reeves' Association for the Protection of Liberty and Property against Republicans and Levellers of 1792.

Association Movement, a late 18th-century movement for PARLIAMENTARY REFORM, through some combination of more frequent elections, extension of the franchise and redrawing of constituency boundaries.

The 'Association' was originally a notional group of all those who were determined to elect none but reformers in the 1780 election. Reformers organized themselves into city and county groupings, and some 'associated counties' sent representatives to a reform convention in 1781. The movement ran out of steam as key supporters fell out over tactics, and once the fall of NORTH and the ending of the War of AMERICAN INDEPENDENCE had removed the focuses of their discontent. Some of its leaders, notably the Yorkshireman Christopher Wyvill, then pinned their hopes on the younger PITT, who did float an unsuccessful reform motion in Parliament in 1785.

Astor, Nancy (née Langhorne; Viscountess Astor) (1879–1964), Conservative politician. American-born Nancy Astor became the first woman to sit in the British Parliament when she took over the seat of her second husband. Waldorf Astor had to relinquish his role as CONSERVATIVE MP for Plymouth Sutton when he inherited his father's viscountcy in 1919, but intended to resume his seat under a proposed bill to allow peers to sit in the COMMONS. However, this was never enacted, and Nancy Astor held the seat for the next 25 years. Until 1921 she was the only woman MP.

Lady Astor was outspoken on matters affecting the family, women and children, and also on the evils of drink; she became a convert to Christian Science in 1914. She was a leading member of the notoriously pro-APPEASEMENT CLIVEDEN SET, but by the outbreak of war in 1939 she was deeply critical of German policy.

Athelney, isle in the marshes around Bridgwater, Som., where ALFRED THE GREAT took refuge in 878 at the lowest point of his reign, emerging to win the battle of EDINGTON. Athelney is also where he is reputed to have burned the cakes, whose cooking an old woman had asked him to supervise. This famous (and probably legendary) story, first recorded in the late 10th century, undoubtedly owes its later renown to the picturesque image of a great king – having sunk to such depths that he no longer resembles a monarch and goes unrecognized by one of his subjects – so preoccupied with the calamitous fate of his kingdom that he fails to perform a simple domestic task correctly. Alfred later founded a monastery at Athelney to commemorate his escape.

Athelstan (*c*.895–939), King of the English (924–39). The eldest son of EDWARD THE ELDER, Athelstan was the first king to exercise control over all the English and have a quasi-IMPERIAL status among the British. He overthrew the Scandinavian kingdom of YORK in 927 and subsequently defeated an alliance of Scandinavians and Scots at the battle of BRUNANBURH in 937. A great law-giver with extensive political and family connections throughout Europe, his reign is important for the consolidation of WESSEX's authority over other parts of England (*see* COINS AND COINAGE; EALDORMAN; HUNDRED; SHIRES) and for the beginnings of the TENTH-CENTURY REFORM. Subsequent kings further consolidated his political achievements.

Athelstan 'Half-King' (?–956), one of the most powerful magnates of 10th-century England, as his nickname implies. He became EALDORMAN of EAST ANGLIA in 932 (two of his brothers were also ealdormen), and he was also guardian of the young King EDGAR. A supporter of the TENTH-CENTURY REFORM, he became a monk at St DUNSTAN's abbey of GLASTONBURY in 956.

Atlantic, Battle of the, name given by CHURCHILL in March 1941 to the struggle to protect the merchant ships bringing supplies to Britain in WORLD WAR II. The chief enemies were German submarines ('U-boats'), though surface raiders, bombers, mining and Italian submarines also played a less important part. As in WORLD WAR I Britain, heavily reliant on seaborne supplies, came near to defeat before mastering the submarine menace. Too much reliance had been put on the new 'ASDIC' (sonar) detection device, but the small German submarine force under Admiral Karl Doenitz was not a serious menace until the fall of Norway and then France falsified all pre-war calculations by giving Germany most of the Atlantic coast of Europe to operate from. The surfaced 'wolf pack' attacks by increasing numbers of submarines strained the new CONVOY escorts to near breaking point in late 1940 and early 1941. If U-boats continued to sink ships at this rate Britain would be forced out of the war. However, more and better-trained escorts, American help and successes in the technological and codebreaking fronts tilted the balance back in Britain's favour later in 1941. Early 1942 saw the U-boats winning an unnecessary success in American waters, thanks to the Americans' purblind failure to try the convoy. In early 1943 there was a crisis when it briefly seemed as if the U-boats had beaten the convoys, but simultaneous improvements in numbers of new merchantmen and escorts, in detection systems and training, combined with the breakthroughs in codebreaking and, perhaps most important of all, increases in air support, produced a very rapid reversal of fortunes. By late 1943 the battle had been won in the North Atlantic, though the struggle against the submarine went on till the end of the war, with the Germans developing new weapons and types of submarine, and being matched by the Allied scientists.

A major reason for Allied victory was the use made of science – the techniques of operational research were developed during the battle. The real heroes of the struggle were the Allied merchant seamen – over 30,000 British lost their lives, almost identical to the total of U-boat men who died.

Atlantic Charter, propagandist declaration issued by Roosevelt and CHURCHILL after they met, on board warships off Newfoundland, in Aug. 1941. It embraced eight principles, including the right of people to choose their own forms of government, with territorial changes only by consent, and freer trade. Essentially a statement of liberal-democratic principles, mixing Wilson's Fourteen Points with Roosevelt's own New Deal, it cast Roosevelt in a favourable light as a defender of democracy and defined the US's non-belligerent status while edging Americans closer to taking responsibility for the removal of Fascism. Churchill, on the other hand, made it clear that it was not intended to affect Britain's imperial position.

Atomic Energy Attempts to obtain peaceful nuclear power dated from the experiments with controlled nuclear fission, carried out under the auspices of the Allied Manhattan Project to build the atomic bomb during WORLD WAR II. By achieving a slowed-down nuclear reaction, the tremendous heat generated could be used to produce electricity.

Following the war, Britain's desire to obtain its own NUCLEAR WEAPONS went hand-in-hand with the generation of electricity as a by-product of the production of weapons-grade nuclear materials. As a result, the world's first industrial-scale production of electricity from nuclear power was inaugurated at CALDER HALL in Cumbria in 1956 from a reactor primarily designed to produce plutonium for bombs.

However, in 1955 a purely civil nuclear programme had already begun, trebling in size two years later under the impact of the SUEZ CRISIS. Under this programme, 18 'Magnox' reactors were built, the last completed in 1971, by which time 10 per cent of electricity production was nuclear and Britain was generating more nuclear electricity than any other country in the world. A new generation of Advanced Gas Cooled Reactors (AGRs) was ordered during the 1970s as nuclear power generation spread rapidly under the dual impact of growing energy needs and the increased price of oil. Long-term plans included much more efficient 'fast-breeder' reactors, while nuclear scientists anticipated the eventual harnessing of nuclear fusion to produce electricity in almost limitless quantities.

By the early 1980s, however, Britain's lead in atomic power had been lost, with her atomic energy programme suffering a series of technical setbacks. Growing concern about the environmental effects and safety of nuclear power were reinforced by belated recognition of the seriousness of the 1957 fire at WINDSCALE (Sellafield), Cumbria, the 1979 Three Mile Island accident and the Chernobyl disaster in 1986.

Eventually, the privatization of the electricity industry would reveal that the price of nuclear energy was much greater than had been suggested.

CHRONOLOGY

1942 Enrico Fermi's team at Chicago achieves the first controlled nuclear reaction.

1952 Britain explodes its first atom bomb.

1955 Britain orders the first generation of 'Magnox' nuclear reactors.

1956 Calder Hall is the first nuclear reactor in the world to feed into a national supply network.

1957 Fire at Windscale releases radioactive materials into the atmosphere.
1959 Dounreay experimental 'fast-breeder' reactor set up.
1971 Completion of 'Magnox' programme and Advance Gas Cooled Reactor programme begun.
1973 Arab oil boycott stimulates increased nuclear programmes worldwide.
1979 Three Mile Island incident in USA stimulates fear of nuclear accidents.
1984 Britain opts for four American Pressurized Water Reactors.
1986 Chernobyl nuclear accident triggers worldwide concern about future of nuclear power.
1990 Privatization of electricity generation forces full recognition of costs of nuclear power, and virtual end to further expansion.

Atrebates, one of the tribes that dominated Britain immediately before the Roman invasions. The territory of the Atrebates lay in the modern counties of Hants., Berks. and parts of Surrey, Sussex and Wilts. The tribe had close associations with the Atrebates of Gaul, whose king, Commius, came as an ambassador with JULIUS CAESAR. It is possible that a request for help against the CATUVELLAUNI made by Verica, king of the British Atrebates, encouraged the invasion organized by the emperor CLAUDIUS. The Atrebatan kingdom was one of the earliest CLIENT KINGDOMS, and may have been ruled at one stage by COGIDUBNUS. Soon after his death, it was divided into *CIVITATES* around the urban centres of SILCHESTER, WINCHESTER and CHICHESTER (*see* ROMAN CONQUEST).

Attainder, Act of, an Act of Parliament used to convict political opponents of treason without having to go through the bother of putting them on trial; the word is derived from the Anglo-Norman *attaindre*, to convict. Those named in the Act were 'attainted' (declared guilty): they lost all civil rights and their property was forfeited to the crown; their blood was held to be 'corrupted', and in consequence, their descendants were disinherited. Despite this, most attainders were reversed in subsequent Parliaments.

Attainders were originally used to supplement conviction of a capital offence in a court of law, but in 1459 the process was used on its own – at the so-called 'Parliament of Devils' – when MARGARET OF ANJOU and the LANCASTRIANS were determined to destroy the YORKIST faction. During the WARS OF THE ROSES and their aftermath, both Yorkist and Tudor kings found attainder an irresistibly convenient weapon, and by 1504, some 400 people had been attainted. Although the rate then declined, both HENRY VIII and ELIZABETH I continued to use attainder to punish rebels.

Fewer attainders were passed after 1660, although the JACOBITE rebellions produced a crop; the last was of Lord Edward Fitzgerald, the Irish rebel, in 1798. The procedure was abolished in 1870.

Atterbury Plot, 1722, a JACOBITE conspiracy by which Francis Atterbury, Bishop of Rochester, and his four fellow-conspirators were to enlist 5,000 men to seize the BANK OF ENGLAND. The conspirators asked the French regent for support, but he informed the British government. The plot was exploited by the WHIGS to discredit their opponents and strengthen their own hold on power.

Attlee, Clement (1st Earl Attlee) (1883–1967), Labour politician and Prime Minister (1945–51). Coming from a conventional upper middle-class professional background, he was called to the Bar in 1906, and for the next 14 years (apart from active service in WORLD WAR I) lived and spent his spare time in the East End of London. Influenced by the WEBBS, he joined the FABIAN SOCIETY and the INDEPENDENT LABOUR PARTY. He became the first LABOUR mayor of Stepney in 1920 and Labour MP for Limehouse in 1922.

He was parliamentary private secretary to Ramsay MACDONALD (1922–4), under-secretary of state for war (1924), chancellor of the Duchy of Lancaster (1930–1) and postmaster-general (1931). He succeeded LANSBURY as leader of a much depleted and demoralized Labour Party in 1935. After leading the Labour opposition to the successive NATIONAL GOVERNMENTS (1935–40), he joined CHURCHILL's all-party coalition Cabinet and was designated deputy prime minister in 1940, serving also as lord Privy Seal (1940–2), secretary of state for dominion affairs (1942–3) and lord president of the Council (1943–5).

Following Labour's sweeping victory in 1945, Attlee led the first Labour government to have its own parliamentary majority.

Despite massive post-war economic problems, it consolidated the work of the wartime coalition by instituting a massive programme of public ownership and social reform, including the NATIONALIZATION of the COAL INDUSTRY and RAILWAYS and the completion of a comprehensive WELFARE STATE. It also decided to grant INDIAN INDEPENDENCE as rapidly as possible. With BEVIN at the Foreign Office, Attlee aligned Britain with the US, as the COLD WAR developed, over the founding of NATO, the Berlin airlift and later the KOREAN WAR. Without informing Parliament or his Cabinet as a whole, he took the decision that led to the building of a British atomic bomb.

Attlee led Labour to victory in the general election of February 1950, but with a majority reduced to 10. His government was destabilized by the ill-health of CRIPPS, the death of Bevin and the resignation in April 1951 of BEVAN and WILSON in protest against the increase in defence spending because of Korea and the imposition of charges for some health services. Attlee lost the election of Oct. 1951 and a Conservative government was returned under Churchill. Attlee remained Labour leader for a further four years of increasingly bitter infighting between the party's left and right wings, delaying his final retirement to steer the succession toward GAITSKELL.

Attlee was a punctilious, thoughtful man, frequently underestimated by his contemporaries. On his election to Parliament in 1922 *The Times* described him as 'the type that would construct a new heaven on earth on violently geometric principles'. He brought a rectitude to his embattled party and did more than any other individual to prepare Labour for office after the war. He used his six years in power to put through a domestic reform programme of historic proportions.

Attorney Attorneys at law were in origin (*c.*1200) representatives for aggrieved parties in lawsuits. The Court of COMMON PLEAS developed a staff of attorneys, and their work was concentrated there; they were excluded from the INNS OF COURT, which became reserved for BARRISTERS. The office was abolished with common pleas in 1873, although it survives in the legal system of the United States. A letter of attorney is a written grant of temporary powers by one person to another to act on his or her behalf. *See also* SOLICITOR.

Attorney-General, the crown's senior law officer. Various ATTORNEYS acted for the CROWN in the medieval COMMON LAW courts, but during the 15th century, one attorney was given seniority there by the king. Shortsighted snobbery led the SERJEANTS AT LAW to consider the office too unimportant for them, so attorneys-general were appointed from among BARRISTERS by the late 16th century, frequently thereafter rising to be lord chancellor or chief justice in COMMON PLEAS or KING'S BENCH. From the 1530s, the normal practice became to appoint the previous SOLICITOR-GENERAL as attorney-general. Together, these two officers remain the senior legal advisers of the government.

Aughrim, Battle of, 12 July 1691. Fought in Co. Galway, this was the last major battle in the final campaign between WILLIAM III and the Irish armies of JAMES II. The JACOBITE army under Charles Chalmont, Marquis de St Ruth, appeared to be winning when St Ruth was killed and his forces lost their nerve and fled; 7,000 may have been killed, including many leading Catholic Irish gentlemen. Although the earlier battle of the BOYNE (1690) has remained more celebrated, this was the most decisive battle in the war: the remaining Catholic strongholds capitulated over the next few months.

Augsburg, League of, 1686, defensive league against France, formed in July 1686 by the Holy Roman Emperor, the King of Spain as Duke of Burgundy, and several German princes. The French responded in 1688 by occupying the Rhineland and invading the Palatinate, giving William of Orange (the future WILLIAM III) both cause and opportunity to exploit his father-in-law JAMES II's difficulties with his subjects in the hope of rallying England to the alliance.

Augsburg, War of the League of, *see* KING WILLIAM'S WAR

Augustine, St (?– between 604 and 609), missionary and first Archbishop of Canterbury (597–604/9). Sent in 597 as leader of the Roman mission to convert the English by Pope Gregory the Great, he successfully converted the kings of KENT and ESSEX and many of their people, thus establishing a foothold for the Roman Church in England. His career also demonstrates the considerable gap in understanding and ritual that separated Rome from the native British Christians, since his encounters with Britons were invariably unsuccessful. Augustine relied on an approach to a royal court and the conversion of a king and queen, in the expectation that their subjects would follow. His achievement was to begin the CONVERSION of a small part of England, and to establish a connection with Rome, which ultimately played a crucial part in the development of the English Church.

Augustinian Rule, a simple rule for monastic life attributed (now generally thought correctly) to the great North African theologian and bishop St Augustine of Hippo (354–430). Simpler than the BENEDICTINE rule, it was revived in the 12th century after long neglect, because of widespread dissatisfaction with Benedictine monasticism, and thereafter until the DISSOLUTION OF THE MONASTERIES Augustinian monasteries were very common; their monks were known as CANONS Regular, or informally as 'Austin Canons', and were more actively involved in the life of PARISHes than Benedictine monks. Various groupings or 'congregations' of Augustinian monasteries developed, including the PREMONSTRATENSIANS and Victorines, and the Augustinian rule was officially adopted in 1256 by one order of FRIARS, informally known as the Austin Friars.

Auld Alliance, the alliance with France that was the main plank of Scottish foreign policy between 1295 and 1560. For most of this period, it was a defensive response to English aggression, beginning with EDWARD I's attempt to conquer Scotland in 1295 and continuing, from 1340, with the claims of EDWARD III and his successors to the throne of France. After the REFORMATION, with both Scotland and England becoming Protestant while France remained Catholic, the traditional alliance made less sense. However, nearly three centuries of co-operation against the 'auld enemy' had strengthened cultural and commercial ties, which survived for much longer and may even now be contributing to the concept of an 'independent Scotland in Europe' promoted by the SCOTTISH NATIONAL PARTY.

Aulus Plautius (*fl.* AD 40s), Roman general. Commander of the successful invasion of much of lowland Britain, which began in 43 in the time of the emperor CLAUDIUS, he was subsequently the first Roman governor of Britain until 47. He began his campaign by defeating British armies under the leadership of CARATACUS and Togodumnus and, by the end of his term of office, appears to have extended Roman power roughly to the line of the FOSSE WAY. On his return to Rome, he received the rare tribute of a triumphal ovation. *See also* ROMAN CONQUEST; MEDWAY, BATTLE ON THE.

Austerity, a policy of severe retrenchment and rationing associated with the 1945–51 ATTLEE governments, especially the period 1947–50 and the chancellorship of CRIPPS. Faced with low gold and hard currency reserves following WORLD WAR II, and the consequent need to cut imports and increase exports from wartime levels in order to reduce the trade deficit, the policy involved higher taxation, even stricter rationing than wartime, and the diversion of domestic production to exports. Under Cripps's stern guidance the policy, assisted by MARSHALL PLAN aid, proved remarkably successful in restoring economic stability, but at the price of the loss of public support which contributed to LABOUR'S general election defeat in 1951.

Austin Canons and Friars, *see* AUGUSTINIAN RULE; FRIARS

Australia, continental land mass and Commonwealth state with a federal constitution, based upon white settlement since the late 18th century. Australia, 'the southern land', was discovered by the Dutch in the early 17th century, but had few contacts from Europe until the voyage of James COOK in 1770, who explored the eastern coast and named it NEW SOUTH WALES. In the wake of the War of AMERICAN INDEPENDENCE, it was chosen in 1786 as the destination for convicts sentenced to TRANSPORTATION.

Want of labour and British government neglect were the principal obstacles to Australia's internal development in the early 19th century. Convict labour was employed until free settlers were sufficient in number to manage without them; 53,000 convicts had arrived by 1830, but convicts were excluded from New South Wales in 1840, and finally from WESTERN AUSTRALIA in 1867.

Extensive land grants, sheep-rearing, and then in the 1850s the discovery of gold, opened up Australia. The separate colonies were formed by process of division from New South Wales – TASMANIA in 1812, VICTORIA in 1851, QUEENSLAND in 1858 – and by exploration and settlement: Western Australia in 1827, South Australia in 1834. Apart from Western Australia, which did not secure independence until 1890, the other colonies were able under the AUSTRALIAN COLONIES ACT 1850 to select their own form of government. The idea of federalism grew slowly but eventually resulted in the Australian Commonwealth Act 1900, creating a federal parliament in a new capital, Canberra, and a governor-general to represent the sovereign.

The new nation contributed considerably to imperial forces in the BOER WAR and both WORLD WARS, while immigration continued at high levels. The proportion of British emigrants has fallen steadily, increasing Australia's sense of separateness from Britain and the crown, though a referendum to end allegiance to the British monarchy in favour of a republic was rejected in 1999. In recent decades, Australia has also begun to recognize the extent of the marginalization and destruction of its indigenous aboriginal population. *See also* BRITISH EMPIRE; COMMONWEALTH; MIGRATION.

Austrian Succession, War of the, 1740–8, precipitated by Frederick the Great of Prussia's seizure of Silesia from Maria Theresa when both succeeded their fathers in 1740. Maria Theresa asked for help from the powers who had guaranteed the Pragmatic Sanction by the Treaty of VIENNA in 1731. Britain and the United Provinces came to her aid, the British promising both subsidies and mercenary troops. In practice this arrayed them against not merely Prussia but also her allies Bavaria and France, who were also supporting Spain against Britain in the War of JENKIN'S EAR, though technically Britain and France were not initially at war. In Sept. 1741 GEORGE II as Elector of Hanover negotiated Hanoverian neutrality, promising support for the Franco-Bavarian candidate for Holy Roman Emperor – to the consternation of his British ministers. Less concerned to contain Prussian than French power, the British helped secure an Austro-Prussian truce at Klein Schnellendorf in Oct. 1741, freeing Austrian forces to campaign against France and Bavaria.

The 1741 election had left WALPOLE's government precariously placed. Criticism of the ministry's foreign policy helped bring about his fall in Feb. 1742. John Carteret (1690–1763), who dominated foreign policy from 1742–4, was to attract even more opprobrium, above all for his supposed subservience to the king's Hanoverian inclinations – though in fact his main aim was to construct a new grand alliance against France, akin to those formed in KING WILLIAM'S WAR and the War of the SPANISH SUCCESSION. In Jan. 1742 French interests were advanced by the election of the Bavarian Charles Albert as Holy Roman Emperor. After a Prussian victory at Chotusitz in May 1742, Carteret pressed Austria to cede Silesia to them as the price of peace. On this basis the 'First Silesian War' was ended in June. Austrian forces then pushed back the French, and occupied Bavaria. Hanover, having abandoned its neutral stance, formed a 'Pragmatic Army' with Hanoverian and Hessian troops under the personal command of George II. Striving to drive a wedge between French and Bavarian forces, the army was trapped in June 1743, but George II managed to extricate it from danger at the battle of DETTINGEN.

Carteret's policy of alliance-building scored a significant gain in Sept. when Sardinia, by the Treaty of Worms, pledged to defend Habsburg power in Italy. However, this backfired. The strengthening of the Habsburg position alarmed the Prussians, who in April 1744 renewed their alliance with France, and invaded Bohemia. The 'Second Silesian War' was declared. In Oct., the French formed an alliance with Spain, and declared war on Britain (a battle had already been fought in Feb. off Toulon between a combined Franco-Spanish fleet and a British one). The scale of Britain's continental commitment caused alarm at home, and sharpened criticism of Carteret; in Nov. 1744 PELHAM and Newcastle (*see* PELHAM-HOLLES, THOMAS) persuaded the king to dismiss him.

New opportunities opened up with the death of the recently-elected emperor in Jan. 1745. The war was driven into Prussia, but British forces had to withdraw to cope with the JACOBITE rising at home. Following a series of Prussian victories, the Treaty of

Dresden was signed in Dec.: the Prussians accepted Maria Theresa's husband as the new emperor, but in return the Austrians had to recognize Silesia as Prussian. The French meanwhile pressed hard on the Austrian Netherlands, forcing the Pragmatic Army to retreat after defeat at Fontenoy in May 1745, and attacking major fortresses between 1746 and 1748, but their position was weakened by famine and fiscal crisis in 1747. Peace, concluded at AIX-LA-CHAPELLE in Oct. 1748, left Silesia in Prussian hands, but otherwise largely confirmed the *status quo ante*.

The war demonstrated the difficulty of holding together a grand alliance against the French, given the growing strength of central European rivalries. Austria, feeling that Britain had required her to sacrifice too much, was to look to France for future help: the 'old alliance' between the Holy Roman Empire and Britain, a feature of the two previous major wars, was sundered by this one. The first major war fought under a Hanoverian monarch underlined the scope for conflict between Hanoverian and British interests, and the British public's sensitivity to this. Widespread hostility to all forms of continental entanglement was also revealed: some would have preferred more emphasis on the BLUEWATER POLICY which entailed assaults on European powers in extra-European settings. The French fortress of Louisbourg on Cape Breton Island had surrendered to the Navy and colonial forces after a long siege in June 1745 (offsetting despondency induced by defeat at Fontenoy). In INDIA, French forces had captured the British settlement of Madras in 1746. The British surrendered Louisbourg at the peace, as the price of regaining Madras, but the episode helped to focus attention on the scope for territorial gain in North America, the more so since lack of success in the parallel War of Jenkin's Ear had reduced hopes of reining back Spanish power in the South.

Avebury, Wilts. Avebury and its neighbour STONEHENGE are the most important prehistoric stone circles in Britain, each the focus of a huge ceremonial and burial area. The Avebury monument covers an area of 28 acres, with the present-day village largely built within it, and was constructed in the 3rd and 2nd millennia BC.

Avon, 1st Earl of, *see* EDEN, SIR ANTHONY

B

'B' Specials, the largest of three branches of the Ulster Special Constabulary, established by LLOYD GEORGE in 1920. (The Royal Ulster Constabulary was formed in 1922.) The Specials had their origins in Protestant vigilante groups which emerged as Ireland began to split; exclusively Protestant in composition and strongly LOYALIST in their outlook, they were viewed at the time and subsequently as perpetuating the lack of civil rights for the Catholic population in ULSTER. After their controversial role in BELFAST and LONDONDERRY at the start of the TROUBLES, they were disbanded in 1969.

Bacon, Francis (1st Baron Verulam, 1st Viscount St Albans) (1561–1626), royal servant and philosopher. One of two brilliant younger sons of Sir Nicholas Bacon, his ambition was encouraged by his meagre inheritance. He combined law and politics, becoming MP for a variety of constituencies from 1584. The Earl of Essex's patronage (*see* DEVEREUX, ROBERT) during the 1590s did him little good and brought fierce rivalry with Edward COKE; by 1600, Bacon had jettisoned Essex, and he testified against him after the 1601 rebellion. Preferment came more readily from his fellow-homosexual and intellectual, JAMES I; despite Robert CECIL's dislike, Bacon became solicitor-general in 1607, attorney-general in 1617 and lord chancellor in 1618, gaining his barony in 1618. However, in 1621, the same year as he achieved his viscountcy, a combination of enemies brought his IMPEACHMENT on bribery charges (only marginally justified), and although he was only briefly imprisoned, his career was ruined.

Bacon wrote prolifically on science, philosophy, history and education, and his political disgrace increased his output. His *Advancement of Learning* (1605) was to be an inspiration to the ROYAL SOCIETY, while the scientific method discussed in his *Novum Organum* (1620), which decisively detached scientific investigation from theological concerns, was to be of importance throughout Europe. He was, in effect, the patron saint of the early Royal Society, and – along with NEWTON and LOCKE – of the Enlightenment. His *Essays* (successive enlargements from 1597) contributed to English prose style, compensating for the certainty that he did not write the plays of SHAKESPEARE. His research led to his death – from a chill caught while investigating how to refrigerate a chicken.

Baden-Powell, Robert (1st Baron Baden-Powell of Gilwell) (1857–1941), *see* SCOUT MOVEMENT

Badon, Mount, Battle of, ?*c.*500, an engagement recorded by GILDAS, the site of which cannot now be located, in which the British under AMBROSIUS AURELIANUS are said to have gained a great victory over the invading ANGLES and SAXONS. Gildas suggests that the victory gave the British a respite from attack of almost half a century. Some later sources (rightly or wrongly) identify King ARTHUR as the Britons' leader.

Baedeker Raids, a stage in the escalation of the bombing offensive of WORLD WAR II. Raids by the *Luftwaffe* in reprisal for Allied raids on old German cities like Lübeck in March and April 1942, targeted EXETER on 23 April and then BATH, NORWICH and CANTERBURY. German propaganda dubbed these 'Baedeker Raids' and intimated that the *Luftwaffe* planned to attack every English city to which the well-known German tourist guidebook had awarded three stars.

Bagehot, Walter (1826–77), journalist. Son of a banker, he was educated at University College, London, and became editor of *The*

Economist in 1860. A prolific author, his best-known book was *The English Constitution* (1867). In it, Bagehot tried to penetrate beyond the façade of the system of government – CROWN, LORDS and COMMONS – to explain how power operated and where it lay. His observations on the growing power of the CABINET, his definition of the rights of the monarch – 'the right to be consulted, the right to encourage, the right to warn' – and his account of the place of ceremonial and deference in the political culture of the nation, supply valuable insights into the workings of the mid-Victorian constitution. Indeed GLADSTONE referred to Bagehot as his 'spare chancellor'.

Baghdad Pact, February 1955. The pact provided for mutual defence and economic co-operation between Britain, Iran, Iraq, PAKISTAN and Turkey. It was opposed by the Soviet Union which saw it as a threat to its southern flank. Renamed the Central Treaty Organization (CENTO) when Iraq withdrew in 1959, it was further disrupted by the fall of the Shah of Iran in 1979.

Bahamas, Caribbean archipelago, settled by England in 1629 from BERMUDA. It long had a history as a centre for PIRACY, smuggling and, during the American Civil War, blockade-running. Becoming independent in 1973, it has very close ties to the nearby USA.

Bailiff, general medieval term for an officer, used very commonly also for the presiding officer or officers for a jurisdiction under a lord, including BOROUGHS (*see also* MAYOR). The term survives in England mainly for the debt-collectors of the COUNTY COURT. In Scotland, in the form 'bailie', the term describes a senior officer or councillor within a BURGH corporation.

Baker, Geoffrey (*fl.* 1350), chronicler. Author of a lively chronicle of the years 1303 to 1356, written for the Oxon. knight, Sir Thomas de la More, who was also one of his informants, it includes the most dramatic version of EDWARD II's death, as well as a patriotic account of the early stages of the HUNDRED YEARS WAR.

Balaclava, Battle of, *see* CRIMEAN WAR

Balance of Power, term first given general European diplomatic sanction in the treaty of UTRECHT (1713), and widely employed in Britain to 1914. It assumed that peace was most likely to be preserved by preventing the dominance of the continent of Europe by a single power. Adjustment to restore equilibrium constituted the basis of foreign policy from 1814 to 1914.

Baldwin, Stanley (1st Earl Baldwin of Bewdley) (1867–1947), Conservative politician and Prime Minister (1923–4, 1924–9, 1935–7). An MP from 1908, he was a surprise choice as premier when Bonar LAW resigned because of ill health in 1923, having only had short spells in office as president of the Board of Trade (1921–2) and as a not very successful chancellor of the Exchequer (1922–3). But the avuncular, pipe-smoking image that he cultivated – 'the man you can trust' – masked a tough-minded party politician. He had already led the CONSERVATIVE anti-Coalition revolt that brought down LLOYD GEORGE in Oct. 1922. Though failing to win general elections in 1924 and 1929, and not particularly effective in opposition, Baldwin dominated the Conservative party for 12 years, making it appear the 'sensible party' after years of political division. During this time he was three times prime minister for a total of over seven years, and also, as lord president of the Council, the leading Tory in the MACDONALD NATIONAL GOVERNMENT of 1931–5.

As prime minister, in 1925 he took Britain back onto the GOLD STANDARD. His political standing was enhanced by the way in which he orchestrated the defeat of the TUC in the GENERAL STRIKE of 1926 and by his skill in handling the ABDICATION CRISIS in 1936. When he retired in the immediate afterglow of GEORGE VI's Coronation and took an earldom in 1937, his reputation for political honesty and sagacity was intact, and enhanced by the fact that the new media of radio and newsreels had made him the first prime minister familiar to the electorate. Subsequently, he came to be criticized for his foreign policy after 1935 – named as one of the 'guilty men' for his support of APPEASEMENT and his failure to re-arm early and fast enough – and for his highly orthodox economic policies, which prolonged the DEPRESSION and created social division.

Balfour, A(rthur) J(ames) (1st Earl of Balfour) (1848–1930), Conservative politician and Prime Minister (1902–5). He entered Parliament in 1874, and from 1878 to 1880 served his political apprenticeship as private secretary to his uncle Lord Salisbury (*see* CECIL, ROBERT GASCOYNE), under whom he subsequently held high office, including chief secretary for Ireland (1887–91) where he earned the sobriquet 'Bloody' Balfour.

Balfour's own premiership was notable for the passing of the EDUCATION ACT 1902, and the creation of the Committee of Imperial Defence which aimed to defuse the question of TARIFF REFORM which was threatening to destroy the CONSERVATIVE PARTY and was a crucial factor in their landslide defeat in the 1906 election. His aristocratically aloof style – languid is the other epithet most commonly bestowed on Balfour – was not, however, suited to the rough and tumble of pre-war politics, and he resigned as party leader in 1911. He returned to office as foreign secretary during WORLD WAR I, and it was in this capacity that he made the famous BALFOUR DECLARATION in 1917. A thinker of distinction and subtlety, his *Defence of Philosophic Doubt* (1879) made a powerful case for intellectual liberty in the face of a dogmatic scientism. Balfour's political career has been seen as one that epitomized the transition from the closed circle of late-Victorian politics to the realities of mass democracy.

Balfour Declaration, a crucial document in the development of the Jewish state of Israel. In a letter of 2 Nov. 1917 to the British Zionist leader, Lord Rothschild, Arthur BALFOUR, then foreign secretary, stated Britain's support for the establishment of a Jewish 'national home' in Palestine. The letter included the provision that nothing should be done to prejudice the civil and religious rights of the non-Jewish communities in the area. Its terms were incorporated into Britain's MANDATE for Palestine under the LEAGUE OF NATIONS. Often seen as a wartime concession to secure influential American Jewish support for the Allied cause during WORLD WAR I, the Declaration's guarded commitment was crucially important in allowing Palestine to become the focus of Jewish refugee settlement from Europe between the wars.

Balliol, Edward (*c.*1283–1364), King of Scots (1332–56). On the death of Robert BRUCE in 1328, Edward, son of John BALLIOL, was encouraged by the DISINHERITED to claim the Scottish throne. In Sept. 1332, after the victory at DUPPLIN MOOR, he was crowned at SCONE. But his hold on his kingdom was always precarious, and his dependence on English arms led him to do HOMAGE to EDWARD III in 1333. Three years later, he was forced to retire to the English court, and in 1356, he surrendered all claim to the Scottish crown to Edward III.

Balliol, John (*c.*1250–1313), King of Scots (1292–6). Following the death of MARGARET, MAID OF NORWAY in 1290, no one held the undisputed title to the kingdom of Scotland. In the GREAT CAUSE, John Balliol was awarded the crown by EDWARD I, and he was enthroned in Nov. 1292. Edward's subsequent overbearing treatment left him in an impossible position, but when he rebelled, the English king declared his throne forfeit and invaded. After being defeated at the battle of DUNBAR, John Balliol was captured (July 1296) and imprisoned in the Tower of London; in 1299, he was released into papal custody and was later handed over to the French. While others took over leadership in the wars of SCOTTISH INDEPENDENCE, he spent the last decade of his life in exile as a political pawn in French hands.

Ballot Act 1872 Designed to curb the illegitimate influence of landlords and employers on voters and diminish bribery and disturbance at elections, it provided for voting by secret ballot in place of nomination on the hustings, a public platform. However, indirect bribery through subscriptions by candidates to local institutions still continued.

Bancroft, Richard (1544–1610), Archbishop of Canterbury (1604–10). Cambridge-educated, he developed a lifelong detestation of PURITANS, probably while chaplain to Bishop Cox of Ely. Later devoted to Archbishop WHITGIFT and Sir Christopher Hatton, he made his name exposing Puritan activity, culminating in the prosecution of CLASSICAL MOVEMENT leaders in 1591 (*see* PRESBYTERIANISM); two years earlier, he had preached a sensational PAUL'S CROSS sermon, attacking Puritans and Presbyterians. Appointed bishop of London in 1597, he continued Whitgift's drive for conformity, revising CANON LAW in 1604, the year he became Archbishop of Canterbury.

Bangladesh, *see* PAKISTAN

Bangorian Controversy, 1717–20. This was precipitated by the Bishop of Bangor Benjamin Hoadly's (1676–1761) pamphlet, *A Preservative against the Principles and Practices of the Non-Jurors, both in Church and State* (1716), and sermon the following year in which he denied that Jesus had conferred special authority on any vicegerents, interpreters or judges. Although Hoadly argued for state power over the Church, the anti-authoritarian tendency of his ideas caused alarm. A committee appointed by CONVOCATION reported that such concepts threatened all government and discipline in the Church, as well as ROYAL SUPREMACY in ecclesiastical matters. The ministry, fearing his doctrine might be formally condemned, had Convocation prorogued in Nov. 1717. The issue generated a voluminous pamphlet debate. *See also* NON-JURORS.

Bank Charter Act 1833 This gave the BANK OF ENGLAND the authority to ignore the usury laws when fixing the rate of interest. The ancient usury laws – which set a 5 per cent limit on the rate of interest chargeable on loans – were considered a hindrance to economic growth, albeit one that was frequently evaded. They were finally repealed in 1854. *See also* BANK NOTES.

Bank Charter Act 1844 A measure intended to develop the financial infrastructure of an increasingly industrial market economy. It made the BANK OF ENGLAND responsible for managing the currency on behalf of the state, as well as serving as a 'lender of last resort'. The Act sought to remove the danger of inflation by limiting to a small sum (£14 million) the Bank's power to increase the money supply by printing notes in excess of those backed by gold. The Act however left the Bank's deposit and discount business uncontrolled and separate. This meant that the level of private Bank business could still exacerbate the trade and investment cycles. In the crises of 1847 and 1857 the separation of the two departments of the Bank's business had to be suspended and the later evolution of central Bank responsibility in line with the Act emerged gradually and without further legislation. *See also* BANK NOTES; BANK OF ENGLAND; BANKS.

Bank Notes, paper notes issued by a BANK which circulate as money, technically payable to the bearer on demand. Originating in the 17th century (and earlier) as receipts issued by goldsmiths for deposits, which then circulated as quasi-money, the ability of the new BANK OF ENGLAND to issue bank notes was converted into a near-monopoly in 1708. The separate banking system of Scotland saw a much wider circulation of banks' notes. English provincial joint-stock banks were given the opportunity to issue notes in 1826 (following the failure of many country banks). The BANK CHARTER ACT 1833 made Bank of England notes legal tender, and the Bank's dominant position in note-issuing was confirmed. Debate as to what proportion of a bank's notes should be backed by gold, in contrast to other forms of securities, was resolved largely in favour of gold in the BANK CHARTER ACT of 1844; meanwhile new banks formed by mergers could no longer issue their own notes. (The last of these English note-issuing banks survived until 1921; the practice continues in Scotland.) In the series of 19th-century banking crises the necessity to back with gold was usually suspended, and the provision was removed in 1914.

Bank of England, the national reserve bank, founded in 1694 to support the public debt in the expensive wars of WILLIAM III. It bought heavily in government stock, and issued notes on this security; the Bank also accepted private deposits. In 1697, Parliament forbade the opening of any other JOINT-STOCK bank in England, a condition not relaxed until 1826, although Scottish joint-stock banks began to flourish in the 18th century. The Bank of England's notes began to circulate as tender, although with a minimum value of £10 they were rare items. During the 18th century, private BANKS in London and country banks in the localities began to grow, oiling the wheels of trade, especially from the 1780s. After 1797 the Bank of England was released from its obligation to exchange its notes on demand for gold, while lower-denomination notes were issued, making it the bedrock of the banking system until 1821 when convertibility was reimposed.

The Bank Charter Acts of 1825–6, which followed crises in the financial world, legalized other joint-stock banks, which boomed, first outside London and then in and near

London. Further banking crises of 1836 and 1839 resulted in legislation under PEEL in 1844 which restricted the issue of bank notes: ultimately the Bank of England was to have the sole right, placing it at the head of the financial structure and increasing its control over the money supply. The Bank, although it remained a private institution until NATIONALIZATION in 1946, acted increasingly from the mid-19th century with the motives and policies of a central bank, steering the City of LONDON through such crises as that at BARINGS in 1890, and maintaining the currency against the GOLD STANDARD. In addition the Bank manages the government's borrowing programme and the National Debt. The Bank has always tended to err on the side of conservative caution, earning itself the nickname 'The Old Lady of Threadneedle Street', its City of London location.

Banks, institutions for deposit, loans, or exchange of money. Many early banks, especially in LONDON, developed from the business activities of goldsmiths, who had both the means of keeping securities and the most precious medium of trade, gold. By the late 17th century, there were private bankers in London, EDINBURGH and GLASGOW, all dealing with the financing both of trade and of landownership. The foundation of the BANK OF ENGLAND in 1694, the Bank of Scotland in 1695 and the Royal Bank of Scotland in 1727 marked the beginning of public banks. All of these became issuers of BANK NOTES, whereas the private banks did not; the Bank of England also became the government's bankers. In addition, particularly in London, a number of new private banks were founded, those in the City of London dealing with commercial clients, stockbrokers and country clients, those in the West End and WESTMINSTER with the GENTRY and lawyers.

The financing of the industrial expansion of the 18th century was conducted in large part by the new provincial private banks, many with NONCONFORMIST and especially QUAKER backing – growing in England from about 12 in 1750 to 120 by 1784 and 280 by 1793. Their numbers continued to rise – in both industrial regions and the agricultural counties of the south and west – until savagely cut down by the banking crisis of 1825–6, which reverberated throughout the whole financial system. Scottish banking was already the most developed in Europe, and remained ahead of England's until the 1820s. The banking expansion was fuelled not only by industrial and commercial growth, with banks providing credit through the use of their deposits, but also by the issuing of bank notes, since the Mint and Bank of England were slow to put ready money into circulation. After 1825 the country banks were only allowed to issue notes of under £5 (although exceptions were allowed in Scotland after 1829), JOINT-STOCK banks were permitted to operate, and the Bank of England started its own provincial network. The gradual cessation of provincial bank note issue was completed by the BANK CHARTER ACT 1844.

The growth of joint-stock banking saw the very slow establishment of branch networks and bank mergers. The joint-stock banks were the fastest-growing part of the banking network from the 1840s to the 1870s, interrupted by periodic crises (in 1847 and 1866), and fuelled by the booms of the 1860s and early 1870s. The later years of the 19th century saw banks across the spectrum benefiting from greater foreign investment and finance (but *see* BARING CRISIS). Meanwhile, the principal banks had embarked upon the sequence of mergers and takeovers which continues to the present day; the Midland Bank, for example, which had begun in and around BIRMINGHAM, began to make vigorous expansionist moves from the 1890s, achieving a national presence (except in the south-west) by 1918.

Meanwhile, as the Bank of England retreated from its private banking role to its present status (consolidated in the 1920s) as note-issuer and central bank, the influence of the banking system was reaching ever further, as an ever-higher proportion of the general population made use of banks and their services. The banks have not kept all that increase to themselves, a function of the growth of non-bank financial intermediaries, especially BUILDING SOCIETIES. A few private banks have survived, but most were in their turn taken over by the big banking combines; some of the City banks which had begun to prosper in the 18th century retained their function as mobilizers of financial capital rather than individuals' private deposits, resulting in the distinction between the MERCHANT BANKS of London and other principal centres, and the clearing banks with their systems for dealing with cheques and other personal transactions. In May 1997 the power to set the base rate was transferred from the TREASURY to the Bank of England; the government still sets the inflation target, and it is the Bank's responsibility to set interest rates to meet that target. The responsibility for supervising banks was transferred from the Bank to the new Financial Services Authority (FSA), a regulatory agency which was established in 1997 largely as the result of the alleged widespread mis-selling of PENSIONS by previously unregulated financial advisers acting on commission.

Banneret, a title with strong implications of military office. In England from the 13th to the 17th centuries, it was used to distinguish higher-ranking knights holding military command from ordinary knights bachelor. Like peers, bannerets were entitled to display their arms on a square banner (rather than the triangular pennon of the knight bachelor).

Bannockburn, Battle of, 24 June 1314. By marching to the relief of Stirling castle, EDWARD II issued a challenge that, reluctantly, Robert BRUCE felt bound to accept. On the day, Bruce's tactical superiority and the fighting spirit of the Scottish infantry proved more than a match for the larger, but incompetently led, English army. As the only occasion when an army led personally by a king of England was defeated by Scots, the battle, which was fought near Stirling, has obtained heroic proportions in the eyes of Scottish nationalists. *See also* SCOTTISH INDEPENDENCE, WARS OF.

Baptists, advocates of believers' (i.e. adult) baptism as the only scriptural form. The former Cambridge don and CHURCH OF ENGLAND minister John Smyth (?1570–1612) is often known as 'the Se-Baptist' (i.e. 'Self-Baptist'), because he rebaptized himself and then rebaptized members of an English separatist congregation exiled in Amsterdam. Controversy about his relation to earlier Continental ANABAPTISM is still unresolved. Numbers began growing during the British CIVIL WARS, and some Baptists formed communities in North America; especially noteworthy was that of Roger Williams at Rhode Island, which particularly in its early years upheld ideals of wide religious toleration and kept friendly relations with the native Americans. A division developed between Baptists who retained CALVINIST views on salvation (the Particular Baptists), and those who held views similar to the ARMINIANS (General Baptists); both set up co-ordinating organizations during the INTERREGNUM. Some General congregations became UNITARIAN during the 18th century; others backed the Baptist Missionary Society 1792, a pioneer in overseas missionary work. A new co-ordinating body formed in 1813 developed into the Baptist Union of Great Britain and Ireland, but many congregations (especially Strict Particular Baptists) have always held aloof, let alone participated in wider ecumenical schemes.

Barbados, Caribbean island and former British colony. First discovered by the Portuguese, English settlers under the Earl of Carlisle colonized the uninhabited island in 1627, along with other nearby islands during renewed war with Spain. It was intended as a TOBACCO colony; INDENTURED SERVANTS formed the bulk of the initial labour force. From the 1640s, when opportunity arose during the DUTCH WARS and Brazilian SUGAR exports to Europe were interrupted, Barbadian planters switched to sugar production. The island rapidly became a monoculture, with Negro SLAVERY substituted for white workers; sugar continued to be its mainstay. Barbados gained independence from Britain in 1966.

Barbuda, *see* ANTIGUA

Bardi and Peruzzi, two Florentine banking houses which dominated European high finance in the early 14th century. Their cash advances to EDWARD III in the early stages of the HUNDRED YEARS WAR – totalling roughly 1.5 million gold florins – enabled him to pay his armies and build up a grand coalition against France. His failure to repay the banks precipitated the great crash of the 1340s, and meant that his successors were never again able to borrow on this scale from foreign bankers.

Barebones Parliament, 1653, assembly replacing the RUMP PARLIAMENT. More properly known as the 'Nominated Parliament', it was nicknamed after one of its members:

Praise-God Barbon (or Bare bones), a London trader and INDEPENDENT. The membership – nominated by the COUNCIL OF OFFICERS – for the first time represented (theoretically) the whole of the British Isles, and although there was a significant MILLENARIAN group, it was not the fanatical rabble of Royalist legend. The assembly made a start on sweeping reforms, but disagreements led to one faction suddenly handing power back to Oliver CROMWELL in Dec. 1653.

Baring Crisis The MERCHANT BANK Baring Bros. considerably overextended itself in lending to the great variety of new capital schemes in Argentina, which had been attracting new investment since a stable government had come to power in 1865. The repayments suddenly ceased in 1890. Many of the projects into which Barings had put money were unsound and untested, and the extent of their commitment shook the City of LONDON money markets very severely. The government secretly agreed with the BANK OF ENGLAND to stand half the loss involved in propping up and restructuring the bank, thereby averting what would otherwise have been a catastrophic banking crash. The crisis had a marked effect, since overseas lending was severely reduced in the ensuing decade until confidence began to return, particularly as loans for mineral exploitation, especially in SOUTH AFRICA, bore spectacularly profitable fruit.

Barings Bank was finally bought to collapse in 1995 by the activities of a 'rogue trader', Nick Leeson, an employee who committed the bank to unrepayable debts.

Barnet, Battle of, 14 April (Easter Sunday) 1471, a Yorkist victory in the WARS OF THE ROSES. In the early morning mist, north of London, EDWARD IV's aggressive tactics defeated a force commanded by the NEVILLE brothers (Warwick and Montagu), both of whom were killed in the fighting, before they could be joined by MARGARET OF ANJOU. The battle was a vital step in Edward's recovery of the throne.

Baron, lowest rank in the hereditary PEERAGE. Originally barons held military or honourable service from the king or some other great lord. The word came to refer exclusively to the king's barons, and then particularly to the great barons who attended the king's GREAT COUNCIL or, from the time of HENRY III, were summoned to PARLIAMENT. Thus the term came to mean a peer, or lord of Parliament. The creation of barons by patent, and the establishment of the title in the status order, began under RICHARD II.

Baronetcy, hereditary title ranking above knighthood and below the younger sons of barons. It was invented by a needy JAMES I in 1611, supposedly to finance defence for the Ulster PLANTATIONS; a further colonial venture was the inauguration of the NOVA SCOTIA baronetcies in 1624–5. Initially the scheme attracted eager buyers, but the Stuarts' greed overreached itself in a general 'inflation of honours', devaluing the creations and causing ill will. However, this has not stopped the prominent from being gratified by fresh baronetcies ever since.

Barons' War, 1264–8. Civil war between HENRY III and those barons led by Simon de MONTFORT who were determined that the king should accept the limitations on royal power set out in the PROVISIONS OF OXFORD (1258) and the PROVISIONS OF WESTMINSTER (1259). De Montfort won the battle of LEWES in 1264 and captured the king, but was himself defeated and killed at EVESHAM the following year. The last of the Montfortians submitted in 1268.

Baroque, artistic style, usually dated to 1680–1720 in Britain. Continental baroque architecture, characterized by massive grandeur and flamboyant handling of classical motifs, was influential from the late 17th century. William Talman's Chatsworth (1686), Sir Christopher Wren's Greenwich Hospital, and Sir John Vanbrugh's Blenheim (1705) have all been termed baroque, as has Edward Lovet Pearce's Parliament House, Dublin, now the Bank of Ireland. When Neo-PALLADIANISM became the fashion, baroque furniture, designed by William Kent amongst others, remained popular. The Flemish sculptors Roubiliac, Rysbrack and Scheemakers, who arrived in England in the second quarter of the 18th century, sustained a fashion for baroque sculpture. Later in the 18th century, Joshua Reynolds and Robert Adam were influenced by aspects of baroque style.

Barri, Gerald de (1146–1223), writer, often referred to as Gerald of Wales or Giraldus Cambrensis. A lively, opinionated author of numerous Latin works of history, religion, ethnography and autobiography. Born into a MARCHER family with kinship ties to the Welsh princes, and educated at Paris, he looked to the English court for patronage and promotion until the mid-1190s. His best-known writings – *The Topography of Ireland, The Journey through Wales* and *The Description of Wales* – belong to this stage of his career. His ambition disappointed, he accepted election as bishop of St David's in 1199; his attempts to make this see the archbishopric of Wales led him to espouse the cause of Welsh independence. Thwarted in this well, he turned to Louis VIII of France, writing in praise of the Capetian monarchy.

Barrier Treaties, 1709–15. Broached following the Treaty of RYSWICK, these developed the idea that the Dutch were entitled to maintain a barrier against French aggression. The first treaty in 1709 was an agreement between Britain and Holland to provide the Dutch with a barrier against French attack by means of a line of frontier fortresses, including Ypres, Lille, Tournai, Valenciennes and Namur. In return, the Dutch agreed to supply Britain with 6,000 troops in the event of a JACOBITE invasion. In 1713 the Dutch renewed this promise, which they made good in the face of the Jacobite rising of 1715. Under the third treaty (1715), the Dutch were to hold seven fortresses in what were now the Austrian Netherlands; Britain was to supply men and warships if the barrier was attacked.

Barristers, lawyers who have the right to plead (present cases) at the bar of the COMMON LAW courts. These practitioners were from the 13th century known as apprentices at law; the term barrister-at-law, not found before the 15th century, at first related to their status within the INNS OF COURT, but during the 16th century this status came to be seen as conferring exclusive rights to plead within the courts. Certain practitioners were called on to help the ATTORNEY-GENERAL and SOLICITOR-GENERAL with royal legal business, and were known as 'King's Counsel learned in the law'. The title 'King's Counsel' (KC) or 'Queen's Counsel' (QC) became a largely honorary distinction for senior barristers during the 18th century.

Barton, Elizabeth (?1506–34), Nun of Kent. A Kentish servant girl who began uttering prophecies in 1525, she was declared a genuine visionary after a diocesan investigation. She was installed in St Sepulchre's nunnery, CANTERBURY, under the care of leading monks of Canterbury cathedral, and as 'the Nun [or Maid] of Kent', she much impressed such leading Catholics as WOLSEY, FISHER, WARHAM and MORE. Her prophecies quickly developed a political slant amid HENRY VIII's divorce crisis and break with Rome, ending with, in 1533, a declaration that the king would be deposed; she and her clerical backers, led by Edward Bocking, were arrested. Under interrogation, she was forced to say that her trances were faked, and she was executed with her associates on 20 April 1534.

Bastard Feudalism, a term coined by Charles Plummer in the late 19th century, and now widely applied to English political society between the 13th and 16th centuries, thanks to its adoption in the 1940s by the influential late-medievalist K. B. McFarlane. It usually denotes a type of society in which lords tended to obtain services and support not by granting land to tenants to hold for life (or by hereditary right) – as in supposedly 'pure' FEUDALISM – but by paying annual retaining fees and daily wages. Surviving documents recording such contracts are known as 'INDENTURES of retainer'.

According to some historians, the 'typical' lord paid retaining fees to royal judges to encourage these 'public' servants to bow to 'private' interests. Thus bastard feudalism is seen as the mechanism by which the aristocracy retained its dominance in the face of the challenges posed by a money economy and an expanding system of royal justice. However, since McFarlane's analysis it is no longer simply assumed that the increasing use of the cash nexus was automatically associated with a decline in political morals, even though 'loyalty unto death' was (supposedly) replaced by 'loyalty for as long as it pays'.

Basutoland, southern African territory and former British colony. The territory that became Basutoland, and subsequently Lesotho (which lies completely surrounded by modern SOUTH AFRICA), was first penetrated by British and French MISSIONARIES from 1833. They were followed by Boer settlers on the Great Trek (*see* BOER WARS). The establishment of the Orange Free State in 1854 prompted the Basotho people into a series of wars and uneasy peaces, until a final peace and formal annexation of the territory of Basutoland in 1868. From 1871 its government was subordinate to the CAPE COLONY administration. The diamond rush promoted local agriculture and migrant labour; with the proceeds the Basotho bought guns, using them in war against the Cape in 1880–1. The natives won partial victory, and from 1884–1966 the country was governed from Britain. Enclosed by South Africa, which left the COMMONWEALTH over its apartheid policy, Basutoland was a perennial logistical problem to both. Independence was granted in 1966, when Lesotho became a member of the Commonwealth, and an uneasy relationship with South Africa persisted.

Bate's Case, legal case of 1606 involving John Bate in the EXCHEQUER court. The decision, which went against Bate, stated that duties regulating commerce were an unchallengeable part of the royal prerogative. This victory for JAMES I, secured from a pliant judge, was immediately exploited by Robert CECIL to impose new tariffs.

Bath (*Aquae Sulis*). The great complex of Roman baths here was begun during the 60s or 70s AD near the FOSSE WAY. Built around a spring, it became a healing centre dedicated to the Celtic god Sulis and the Roman goddess Minerva. Greatly extended during the years of Roman occupation, the baths fell into disuse in the 5th century. However, archaeological excavation has revealed their size and splendour and that of the neighbouring temple.

Recovery from probable virtual abandonment is witnessed by the presence in the 8th century of a major church served by CANONS, which was refounded as a monastery by DUNSTAN and was the setting for EDGAR's 'second coronation' (973). In 1093 Bishop John de Villula of Wells made Bath Abbey his CATHEDRAL, and although his successors quickly returned to Wells, the diocese is still known as Bath and Wells. The present Abbey church represents a complete rebuilding begun in 1499 and not finished until the early 17th century.

During the medieval period, Bath regained its prosperity as a cloth-manufacturing town, and new baths were built. Their fashionable status was well established by 1600, but the Georgian age was Bath's modern heyday, the SPA waters attracting both fashionable society and quacks. The PALLADIAN architectural splendours of the housing built by John Wood (*c.*1700–54) and his son, also John (1728–81), set the style for the genteel development which followed. Much survives of Georgian Bath, despite the action of German bombers in the so-called BAEDEKER RAIDS of WORLD WAR II and post-war redevelopment which prompted outcry from the CONSERVATION movement.

Battle, *see* TRIAL BY BATTLE

Battle Abbey, Sussex. The abbey was founded by WILLIAM I THE CONQUEROR as a thank-offering for his victory at the battle of HASTINGS (hence the name). At William's insistence, the altar was sited to mark the spot where King HAROLD II fell. The abbey was dissolved in 1538, but ruins remain.

Battle of Britain, *see* BRITAIN, BATTLE OF

Battleship From the middle of the 17th century naval battles under sail were normally fought in line ahead. From this came the concept that only the most powerful warships were fit to be 'line of battle ships' or 'ships of the line'. The word 'battleship' for the most powerful type of ship in a fleet did not come into general use until the late 19th century, with steam warships superseding ironclads as steel armour replaced iron. Only ships with the heaviest guns and the most powerful armour could be called battleships, and the Royal NAVY tried to maintain the position of having as many as the next two biggest navies combined (the 'two-power standard') until the intensity of German rivalry made it impracticable. In 1906 a new type of battleship appeared with the all-big-gun DREADNOUGHT, but within a decade increases in size, guns and armour produced the 'Super-Dreadnought'.

Battleships became increasingly expensive, whilst their vulnerability to new forms of attack – mines, torpedoes and bombs – grew. During WORLD WAR II the aircraft carrier became increasingly the new type of 'capital ship' and the last British battleship was scrapped in 1960. *See also* WARFARE, NAVAL.

Bayeux Tapestry, misnomer for what is, in fact, an embroidered strip of linen – in its present state, roughly 68 m (223 ft) long and 0.5 m (1.5 ft) wide – depicting events leading up to and now culminating (the end is missing) in the battle of HASTINGS. It was probably commissioned for ODO OF BAYEUX, conceivably for the dedication of his rebuilt cathedral in 1077, and designed by an English artist, perhaps using a workshop at St Augustine's Abbey, CANTERBURY. It was presumably intended as a wall-hanging celebrating the NORMAN CONQUEST, but partly because it is such an extraordinary survival – wall-hangings were certainly common, but nothing else on this scale survives from before the 14th century – almost everything about it remains controversial.

BBC (British Broadcasting Corporation). In 1922, the British Broadcasting Company was founded by radio companies. Five years later, in 1927, a royal charter valid for 70 years established the 'Corporation' as a broadcasting monopoly operated by a board of governors and director-general. It was the world's first public-service broadcasting organization, and was paid for by licence fees from owners of radios and, later, televisions. Imperial and then World Service broadcasts began in 1932 with government support.

Under the domination of its first director-general, John Reith (1889–1971), the BBC developed a reputation for serious, 'highbrow' programming, as well as light entertainment and sport, which soon made it a national institution. The world's first regular television service was launched in 1936 from Alexandra Palace in London. Interrupted by the war, the service resumed in 1946, and with the boom in sales of television sets in the 1950s, notably at the Coronation of Queen ELIZABETH II in 1953, it became the dominant part of the Corporation's activities.

The BBC's broadcasting monopoly was broken by the introduction of commercial television (*see* ITV) under the Independent Television Authority (ITA) in 1954 and the licensing of commercial radio stations in 1972. Despite recurrent inquiries into the future of broadcasting (Pilkington Committee, 1962; Annan Committee, 1977; Peacock Committee, 1986) the government has so far left the BBC's non-commercial, public service element intact, but has extended the range of services and further opened up broadcasting to commercial entrepreneurs. In 1996 the BBC was granted a 10-year renewal of its Charter.

The government has agreed that the license fee will remain the chief source of finance for the BBC (£2.155 billion in 1998–9) until at least 2002: this has fuelled continuing debate about the role and privileged position of public service broadcasting in a highly competitive market, where the Corporation is seen to be in direct competition in such areas as digital television, sport, 24-hour news provision etc.

Beaconsfield, 1st Earl of, *see* DISRAELI, BENJAMIN

Beatty, David (1st Earl Beatty) (1871–1936), Admiral of the Fleet. Selected in 1913 by CHURCHILL as first lord of the Admiralty to take command of the fast but vulnerable Battlecruiser Squadron. He was a dashing, popular but sometimes slapdash leader, and his partial successes at the Heligoland Bight (Aug. 1914) and Dogger Bank (Jan. 1915) were marred by communications failures. His role at JUTLAND is even more controversial: the battlecruisers were worsted by their German opposite numbers in the opening phase of the battle, and though he did lure the German fleet onto JELLICOE's force, he failed to keep him informed. He replaced Jellicoe as commander of the Grand Fleet later in 1916, and did well in keeping up its morale till the German fleet surrendered. His period as first sea lord (1919–27) was probably his greatest triumph; he proved very effective in difficult circumstances.

Beaufort, Edmund (2nd Duke of Somerset) (*c*.1406–55). Earl from 1444 and duke from 1448, his feud with RICHARD OF YORK precipitated the outbreak of the WARS OF THE ROSES.

After 20 years of military experience and high command in France, his supine conduct of the defence of Normandy in 1449 came as a shock. The surrender of Rouen, widely held to be dishonourable, led to York launching a series of personal attacks on him from late 1450 onwards. Yet he retained HENRY VI's confidence, was appointed captain of CALAIS in 1451, and continued to accumulate the crown offices and pensions he wanted to supplement a relatively small landed inheritance in England. Inevitably this exploitation of his dominance over a feeble king, combined with the catastrophic ending of the HUNDRED YEARS WAR, made him intensely unpopular.

Arrested when York became PROTECTOR in 1454, he was released as soon as the king recovered his sanity. In May 1455, York and his allies took up arms and, at the first battle of ST ALBANS, made sure that Somerset was killed.

Beaufort, Henry (1377–1447), royal servant and Cardinal. Son of JOHN OF GAUNT and Katherine Swynford, he became bishop of Lincoln in 1398 and was translated to Winchester in 1404, but his influence in Church matters extended well beyond England. In 1417, in recognition of his services at the Council of Constance, Pope Martin V wanted to make him a cardinal; in 1427, he led an unsuccessful crusade against the Hussites of Bohemia. Ultimately, however, his interests and loyalties were English. Thus, he bowed to HENRY V's refusal to allow him to accept the cardinal's hat (he finally achieved it in 1426), and in 1429, after preaching another anti-Hussite crusade, he used the resulting army to prop up the English cause in France.

His ability, his great wealth – which he used to make substantial loans to the crown – and his royal connections enabled him to play a prominent political role during the reigns of his kinsmen, not only Henry V but also HENRY IV and HENRY VI. Three times he served as chancellor (1403–5, 1413–17, 1424–6). In later years, his more conciliatory attitude towards France added fuel to the flames of his long-standing rivalry with his nephew Duke HUMPHREY OF GLOUCESTER.

Beaufort, Lady Margaret (Countess of Richmond and Countess of Derby) (1443–1509) and mother of HENRY VII by her marriage to Edmund TUDOR, Earl of Richmond, in 1455. She remarried twice more, for the last time to Thomas Stanley, Earl of Derby. Able and resourceful, she sent Henry to Brittany and France for safety, and later played leading roles in planning his marriage to Elizabeth of York and in the rebellions of 1483 and 1485. During Henry's reign, she was given extensive power, backed large-scale FEN DRAINAGE schemes, and became a patron of the printers CAXTON and Wynkyn de Worde. Persuaded by her confessor John FISHER to extend her pious energy to finance humanist learning, she endowed professorships of divinity at OXFORD and CAMBRIDGE as well as the Cambridge colleges of St John's and Christ's.

Bechuanaland, southern African nation now known as Botswana, and a former British protectorate. The country is dominated by the Kalahari desert. After a series of cattle raids by native peoples, in the 1850s an attempted invasion was prevented, but in subsequent decades the Bechuanaland territories became a refuge for those fleeing the path of white conquest in South and southern AFRICA. The Warren expedition of 1885 took the territory under British protection. The threat to turn it over to the British South African Company in 1895 was never carried out; nor was the plan to integrate it with SOUTH AFRICA in 1909. The protectorate was neglected by Britain until the 1930s, and remained considerably underdeveloped until the 1950s; its economic mainstay was providing migrant labour to South Africa and other neighbouring countries. Independence was granted in 1966, and an uneasy accommodation was necessarily reached with South Africa. The discovery of diamonds in 1967 was a considerable boost to the new nation's economy.

Becket, Thomas (?1120–70), Archbishop of Canterbury (1162–70) and saint. Born of Norman parents settled in London, he attracted HENRY II's attention while in the service of Archbishop Theobald of Canterbury, and was appointed CHANCELLOR in 1155. In this office, he displayed a wide range of talents – administrative, diplomatic, military – and such a zealous concern for the king's interests, even where they seemed to conflict with the Church's, that when Theobald died, Henry decided to make Thomas his successor. On 2 June 1162, he was ordained priest, and the next day was consecrated archbishop.

At once, Becket began to oppose the king. Many more or less creative attempts have been made by historians to explain his mysterious volte-face, but in the absence of good evidence for his state of mind in 1162–3, they remain highly speculative. The earliest lives of Becket – by JOHN OF SALISBURY, for example – do little to unravel the puzzle; as part of the campaign to secure his canonization, they present him as a martyred saint.

Whatever Becket's motives, Henry felt bewildered and betrayed. King and archbishop were soon quarrelling over a number of issues, among them the question of BENEFIT OF CLERGY. In Jan. 1164, Becket reluctantly but publicly accepted the Constitutions of CLARENDON, but then infuriated the king and confused his fellow bishops by trying to wriggle out of this commitment. Henry brought him to trial at the Council of Northampton (Oct. 1164); Becket, seeing that the king was determined to break him, fled in disguise to France, where he remained in exile until 1170, studying CANON LAW, leading an ascetic life and claiming to be defending not only the rights of the archbishop of Canterbury but also those of the Church.

The coronation of HENRY THE YOUNG KING in June 1170 by the archbishop of York brought matters to a head: in Becket's eyes, crowning the king was one of the privileges of Canterbury. He swiftly agreed terms with Henry. This enabled him to return to England with the intention of punishing those who had infringed that privilege. In Nov., he excommunicated the archbishop of York and the bishops of London and Salisbury; they complained to the king, then in Normandy. Henry's angry words prompted four knights to cross the Channel and kill Becket in Canterbury cathedral on 29 Dec. 1170 – a murder that shocked Christendom. In Feb. 1173, he was formally canonized by Pope Alexander III.

During his lifetime, few churchmen believed that Becket's truculence did much to help the cause of the English Church; probably none thought him saintly. But his murder put the king in the wrong, and forced him to make concessions, though none of lasting significance. Only CANTERBURY undeniably gained: for centuries, until it was destroyed in 1538, Becket's tomb in the cathedral was the greatest pilgrimage shrine in England. HENRY VIII declared Becket a traitor and took particular care to eliminate his cult.

Bede, St (672 or 673–735), monk and scholar. A product of the so-called NORTHUMBRIAN RENAISSANCE, Bede spent almost his entire life as a monk in the community of MONKWEARMOUTH and JARROW, using the library assembled by Benedict Biscop (?628–89) to become, in his day, the most learned man in Europe. His greatest and best-known work – *The Ecclesiastical History of the English Church and People*, completed in 731 – is by far the best source of information for the CONVERSION of the English to Christianity, not only because of the record of events it supplies, but also because of the care that Bede took to recount particular incidents in detail.

For him, the *Ecclesiastical History* was the culmination of a life's work devoted to a moral and didactic purpose – to educate his fellow men in how a good Christian life should be led. Yet because of his profound interest in humanity, it is lively and provocative. Bede's other works include the writing of Latin grammars for the benefit of his fellow monks, biblical commentary, and the study of chronology (he popularized the system of division of time into BC and AD; *see COMPOTUS*). All his works have his personal imprint on them; all reflect a man whose purpose was to leave the world a better place than he had found it.

Bede's range of learning was prodigious and his scholarship rigorous, even if his biases are also obvious. His writings were immensely popular and influential. For instance, both OFFA and ALFRED THE GREAT adopted to great effect the idea that Bede had first expressed – that the English were a single people (*see* UNIFICATION). As a result, his impact on the medieval centuries (and indeed beyond) was enormous. His tomb is now in Durham cathedral.

Bedford, 1st Duke of, *see* JOHN OF LANCASTER

Bedlam A corruption of 'Bethlehem', and a shorthand for the Bethlehem Royal Hospital, this was a priory in Bishopsgate, London, that was converted into an asylum for lunatics in 1547. In 1675–6 it was moved to a building in Moorfields. By then it had become a considerable tourist attraction, with visitors paying to see chained patients writhing in their cells and galleries like animals in a menagerie. The hospital was transferred to St George's Fields, Lambeth, in 1815. The term 'bedlamite' came to be applied to any person behaving like a madman, and 'bedlam' is still used as a signifier of chaos. The site of the old hospital in Lambeth is now occupied by the Imperial War Museum.

Beeching Report, 1963, notorious plan for rapid reduction in the rail network by the chairman of the British Railways Board, Lord Beeching (1913–90). It recommended major cuts in unprofitable lines and the introduction of inter-city express trains to compete with road. 'Beeching's axe' was wielded between 1965 and 1970, and it reduced passenger railway lines by one-fifth and the number of stations by one-third causing continuing problems of rural mobility.

Beerage and Racketeerage, pejorative term for the raising to the PEERAGE in the later 19th century of 'new money' – brewers, merchants, and the social set around the Prince of Wales, later EDWARD VII.

Belach Lechta, Battle of, Co. Cork, 978. An important event in the rise to power of BRIAN BORU, enabling him to overcome a rival for the kingship of MUNSTER and establish his authority. He subsequently used his base in Munster to attack and temporarily overcome the other Irish kingdoms.

Belach Mugna, Battle of, Co. Carlow, 908. A significant victory gained by the UÍ NÉILL and their allies over the Eóganacht king of MUNSTER. His defeat began a long period of weakness for that kingdom, from which it emerged in the later 10th century with the rise of the DÁL CAIS and the career of BRIAN BORU.

Belfast, capital of Northern Ireland since the partition of Ireland, and long the principal manufacturing centre in Ireland. A CASTLE was established in 1178, subsidiary to nearby Carrickfergus; this was given in 1603 to Sir Arthur Chichester, subsequently the lord justice of Ireland, who planned a new town there. Partly destroyed in the sieges of the CIVIL WAR, Belfast was rebuilt and enjoyed a growing prosperity, mainly through international trade. A population of 8,500 in 1750 had swollen to 20,000 by 1800, and mushroomed to reach 350,000 by 1900. The Donegalls, successors to the Chichesters, oversaw Belfast's building explosion and its industrial transformation, with COTTON, linen and notably, after 1850, SHIPBUILDING. Its growth rate was unmatched anywhere else in the British Isles, and Belfast remains visually a late Victorian and Edwardian city. The later 20th century has seen the emergence of the ULSTER troubles as the dominant force in Belfast's recent history, both with housing improvements in the wake of civil rights activism and with the destruction of life and property in the continuing terrorism since 1969. During the first seven, most destructive, years, over 25,000 houses and 200 pubs were damaged or destroyed. Over the past decade investment in the reconstruction of Belfast both from the British government and the EU has been considerable.

Belize, *see* BRITISH HONDURAS

Benedictine Monasticism Benedictine monks follow the Rule originally compiled in the 6th century by St Benedict of Nursia. Its chief characteristic is that it enables monks to live as a community (as opposed to as hermits, commonly found in Egyptian and Irish MONASTICISM) and to spend their days in a regular round of prayer and services.

The Rule's pre-eminence in western Europe dates from its adoption within the CAROLINGIAN Empire in the 9th century. Its imposition in all new monastic foundations was one of the great aims of the TENTH-CENTURY REFORM, and its stricter interpretation was one of the objectives of the 12th-century CISTERCIANS. Its status in England was eventually challenged by the foundation of AUGUSTINIAN communities in the 12th century and the emergence of the FRIARS in the 13th. *See also* CARTHUSIANS; CLUNIACS; GILBERTINES; TIRONENSIANS.

Benefice Originally a life grant of land as a reward (*beneficium*) for service, it is now used in the English context for a Church office carrying oversight of a PARISH (as RECTOR vicar or perpetual curate), or (loosely) for the parish itself.

Benefit of Clergy From the 12th century, the Church claimed that the clergy belonged to a privileged order exempt from the jurisdiction or sentence of ordinary courts of law – i.e. they should be tried only in ecclesiastical courts. Since these Church courts could not impose the death penalty, this certainly benefited clerics accused of serious crimes. HENRY II tried to deal with the problem of 'criminous clerks' – the conventional term for such clerics – in the Constitutions of CLARENDON, which became one of the issues at stake in his quarrel with BECKET. The upshot of this was that, although the king's courts recognized 'benefit of clergy', they would only hear a plea of exemption on grounds of 'clergy' *after* a jury in an ordinary court had delivered its verdict; only then would the accused be handed over to the Church courts. Initially this was done in response to a formal demand made by a bishop's officer; from the 14th century any man who could prove that he knew Latin by reading the so-called 'neck verse' (Psalm 51.1) could 'save his neck' by claiming benefit of clergy.

In 1489 and 1512 Parliament passed laws stating that those convicted of particularly heinous crimes (e.g. murder, rape and highway robbery) were ineligible for benefit of clergy; from this point, the system increasingly operated to differentiate not people but crimes (historians speak of 'clergyable' and 'non-clergyable' offences). From 1576, clergied offenders were no longer passed to ecclesiastical authorities for purgation, but discharged. Exemption from punishment was extended to women in some cases from 1624. In 1706, the reading test was abolished, and henceforth anyone committing a clergyable offence was safe from the gallows. The privilege was finally abolished in 1827.

Benevolence, a euphemism for a forced loan made to the English crown. Although forbidden by statute in 1484, this 15th-century expedient for raising revenue was still occasionally used by the Tudors and Stuarts.

Bentham, Jeremy (1748–1832), philosopher and jurist. Trained as a barrister, he devoted most of his life to voluminous schemes for the rationalization of English law, paralleling the work of the law reformers of the continental ENLIGHTENMENT. His works include: *A Fragment on Government* (1776), questioning BLACKSTONE's celebration of the English legal system; *Introduction to the Principles of Morals and Legislation* (1789); and *Constitutional Code* (1827–30). He advocated the 'greatest happiness' principle – i.e. government should promote the greatest good of the greatest number – and is seen as one of the progenitors of UTILITARIANISM. In the 1790s, he made strenuous efforts to interest government in his plans for a new model prison, the 'Panopticon'; disappointment in this and other things helped to persuade him of the need for PARLIAMENTARY REFORM. His thought was disseminated by a small circle of disciples, including RICARDO and James and John Stuart MILL. Numerous reforming administrators, most notably Sir Edwin Chadwick, sought to put his ideas into practice, and they also attracted enthusiastic interest in the newly independent South American states. University College London was founded under the influence of his educational ideas.

Bentinck, William Cavendish (3rd Duke of Portland) (1738–1809), politician and Prime Minister (1783, 1807–9). Occupying a key place within the kinship network of WHIG magnates, and loyal to the Whig dissidents who formed a distinct grouping under Rockingham (*see* WENTWORTH, CHARLES) in the 1760s, Portland was assigned a variety of senior posts. Made lord chamberlain when the ROCKINGHAMITE WHIGS took office in 1765, he resigned with them in 1766; he was appointed lord lieutenant of Ireland in 1782, and in 1783 became first lord of the Treasury and as such nominal head of the FOX–NORTH administration. Selectively supportive of the younger PITT's government from 1792, he led a group of Whigs into formal alliance with Pitt in 1794. He became home secretary, and lord president of the Council under ADDINGTON in 1802. In 1807, though largely incapacitated by age, he became nominal head of a Pittite ministry effectively dominated by CANNING and Castlereagh (*see* STEWART, ROBERT), resigning in their wake in 1809 and dying the same year.

Beowulf, a remarkable epic poem in Old English, comprising more than 3,000 lines. Its date is uncertain, although most authorities suggest that it was written during the 8th century. It is set in the 5th and 6th centuries and tells the story of the hero Beowulf who rid the court of Hrothgar, King of the Danes, of two monsters, became a king himself and was eventually killed in a conflict with a dragon. Its form is one found elsewhere in the early medieval West – for example in the well-known *Nibelungenlied* epic (later immortalized by Wagner).

Beowulf is invaluable for historians for its picture of successful kings surrounded by troops of young warriors, and for its portrayal of the extravagant generosity expected of all early medieval rulers. The poem – which exhibits the heroic tone expected by an aristocratic audience – also demonstrates the close and enduring connections that existed between England and Scandinavia long before the VIKING invasions.

Berlin, Congress of, 1878. It was held at the conclusion of the Russo-Turkish War of 1877–8, in which Russia was victorious. All the European powers were represented at the Congress, and DISRAELI himself led the British delegation. The Austrians were anxious to check Russian dominance in the Balkans and the British to safeguard their interests in EGYPT and the SUEZ CANAL, while Bismarck, who wished to prevent war between his allies Russia and Austria, played honest broker.

Russia lost at the negotiating table all that it had gained on the battlefield: it did not gain Constantinople; Greater Bulgaria, created earlier by the treaty of San Stefano, was cut down in size, leaving Turkish territory unbroken from the Adriatic to the Black Sea. Britain secured Cyprus as a Mediterranean base for further assistance to the Turks if required, and thus an unimpeded passage to the Black Sea, and the ability to monitor Russia to the north and the Suez Canal to the south. Disraeli returned in triumph proclaiming 'peace with honour'.

Bermuda British crown colony in the Caribbean, and one of the few remaining dependent territories, Bermuda consists of some 150 small islands. Inhabited from 1609, when it was claimed after a VIRGINIA ship had foundered there, the island was chartered to the Virginia Company in 1612, becoming a royal colony in 1684. It was a major naval base during the 19th century. Its principal income today comes from offshore business.

Bernicia, Kingdom of, one of the two chief constituent kingdoms of the later kingdom of NORTHUMBRIA. It stretched from (roughly) the River Tees to the Scottish Lowlands. Archaeological evidence shows that its first king, Ida (whose reign began in 547, according to BEDE), and his successors were ANGLES who ruled over a largely British population. The Bernician king ETHELFRITH absorbed the southerly kingdom of DEIRA in the early 7th century, although the two were afterwards separated on several occasions.

Bertha (died after 601), Queen of Kent. A Christian Frankish princess, she was married to King ETHELBERT of KENT. Although, like most medieval women, she remained very much in the background, her religion and contacts with the already-Christian Franks are likely to have proved extremely important in enabling the acceptance of St AUGUSTINE's mission of CONVERSION.

Berwick-upon-Tweed, border town between Scotland and England, now in Northumb. Berwick has always had a curiously anomalous position, and was often listed separately in official documents (although the story that it was omitted from the treaty of VERSAILLES in 1919 and hence is technically still at war with Germany is apocryphal).

Berwick's town defences, which remain more or less intact, were begun in 1555, and are the only British example of the continental system of fortification by bastions – designed to keep out the Scots, with whom the English were soon to be united. Berwick's other remarkable features are the three great bridges over the River Tweed, of which Robert STEPHENSON's railway bridge of 1847 is the most magnificent.

Bessemer Process, a metallurgic process invented by Sir Henry Bessemer (1813–98), an autodidact inventor who learned metallurgy in his father's type foundry. The process superseded PUDDLING for certain kinds of cast-iron and was used for the general manufacture of steel iron. First demonstrated in 1856, it consisted in the forcing of atmospheric air into molten pig iron in a converter to remove impurities. The process, subsequently improved, gave a tremendous boost to the development of the IRON AND STEEL INDUSTRY. However, whereas North American steelmakers made a fortune with it, their British competitors were slower to adopt it.

Bevan, Aneurin ('Nye') (1897–1960), Labour politician. Son of a Welsh miner, at the age of 13 he became one himself, then rose through the South Wales Miners' Federation to become MP for Ebbw Vale in 1929. A passionate left-wing socialist and a brilliant orator, he was responsible, as minister of health in the ATTLEE government, for the founding of the NATIONAL HEALTH SERVICE in 1946, steering the Bill through Parliament and conducting the difficult negotiations with doctors and consultants which secured the creation of the world's first free-at-delivery health service.

Appointed minister of labour in January 1951, he resigned from the Cabinet in April in protest at the introduction of prescription charges, and led the 'Bevanite' left in opposition to GAITSKELL, who defeated him for the LABOUR leadership in 1955. As chief spokesman for foreign affairs, he ultimately turned against the UNILATERALISM with which he had been associated, uttering the famous declaration that no British minister should be sent 'naked into the conference chamber'. He became deputy leader of the party in 1959, and his early death deprived it of one of its most charismatic figures, who still retains an almost mythic place in its history.

Beveridge Report, report on Social Insurance and Allied Services by Sir William (later Lord) Beveridge, published in 1942, which became the blueprint for the post-war WELFARE STATE. Beveridge was invited to chair an inter-departmental committee of officials to recommend administrative rationalization of the various existing social insurance schemes; instead he asked for the committee's technical advice on his personal proposal that after the war there should be a comprehensive programme of future social security 'from the cradle to the grave'. He proposed that social insurance, by attacking 'want', should be part of a 'comprehensive policy of social progress' designed to attack the other four 'giants on the road of reconstruction': disease, ignorance, squalor and idleness. His aim was to bring the entire adult population into a compulsory scheme covering sickness, unemployment, retirement and family support. Individual and employers' contributions to the scheme were to be at a flat rate, with benefits to be paid as of right without a MEANS TEST and the balance of funding to come from the Exchequer.

The report, coming out in the month after the victory at EL ALAMEIN, captured the public imagination. The government's cagey initial response disappointed Beveridge, who spent much of the following year campaigning for his vision. His compromise to defer the introduction of the full pension won KEYNES's influential support for the plan and persuaded the Treasury that the costs were supportable. The proposals were broadly accepted in a government White Paper in 1944 and mostly implemented by the ATTLEE government in the NATIONAL INSURANCE ACT 1946.

The radical gloss Beveridge gave to the report masked its foundation on the existing principle of insurance contributions from employees, employers and the state, as well as the assumption that full employment would be possible after the war.

Bevin, Ernest (1881–1951), trade unionist and Labour politician. With only a primary school education, he worked as a carter in Bristol before becoming, in 1911, a full-time official in the dockers' union. A leading figure in the National Transport Workers' Federation (NTWF), he achieved prominence for his presentation of the workers' case before the 1920 Shaw Inquiry into dock labour, where he earned the nickname 'The Dockers' KC'. The following year, he urged his union to take a moderate stand over BLACK FRIDAY, and was opposed to the TRIPLE ALLIANCE with the miners and railwaymen. In 1922, he was one of the founders of the Transport and General Workers' Union (TGWU), soon to become Britain's largest TRADE UNION, and was its general secretary from 1922 to 1940.

Following the GENERAL STRIKE, he played a leading part – with CITRINE – in strengthening links between the unions and the LABOUR PARTY and, through the latter's General Council, increasingly influenced the direction of Labour policy, especially after the 1931 election débâcle. A fierce anti-Communist, he maintained the TGWU's pro-Labour stance throughout the DEPRESSION and, as minister of labour (1940–5) in CHURCHILL's coalition, ensured organized labour's co-operation with the war effort. As foreign secretary in the ATTLEE government, he supported NATO and the development of NUCLEAR WEAPONS – an issue that was to divide the party for years to come – and firmly aligned Britain with the US in the COLD WAR.

Bible Christians, *see* METHODISM

Bible in English and Celtic Languages Only partial attempts at Anglo-Saxon or Middle English biblical translations survive. About 1390, LOLLARDS began a complete translation from the Latin, probably directed by Nicholas of Hereford and John Purvey –

not, as is sometimes said, by the Lollard leader John WYCLIF. The results of their endeavours were banned by a provincial Church council at Oxford in 1407, and no official substitute was provided: this ban was almost unique in medieval Europe.

New translations were begun in the 1520s, first with the incomplete but vital work of William TYNDALE. In the next decade HENRY VIII authorized the English Bible, and even MARY I did not ban this. After publication of the Authorized Version in the early 17th century, significant new English translation work only began again in the late 19th century, producing a flood of new versions. Translations by Protestants for Celtic-language speakers were provided only gradually.

CHRONOLOGY TO 1900

***c*.1523–35** William TYNDALE produces a nearly complete version.
1535 Miles Coverdale revises Tyndale.
1537 'Matthew's Bible': first to be officially authorized, but mainly the Tyndale/Coverdale text.
1539 Great Bible. A Coverdale revision under Thomas CROMWELL's patronage; in 1540, given preface by CRANMER.
1557–60 Geneva Bible (nicknamed 'Breeches Bible' from translation of Genesis 3:7).
1563–7 Welsh New Testament by William SALESBURY and Richard Davies.
1566–72 Bishops' Bible, official rival to Geneva.
1573 Irish Gaelic New Testament by Nicholas Walsh, printed in 1602.
1582–1610 Douai or Rheims Bible, by exiled Roman Catholics.
1588 Welsh Bible by William Morgan.
1604–11 Authorized Version backed by JAMES I.
1767 Scots Gaelic New Testament by James Stuart.
1810 Complete Irish Gaelic Bible.
1881–5 Revised Version.

Bible Societies, associations intended to propagate the Christian Bible. The first was established in 1719, and they expanded rapidly in the early 19th century following the formation of MISSIONARY SOCIETIES established between 1792 and 1800. The BRITISH AND FOREIGN BIBLE SOCIETY was one of the most prolific, publishing biblical texts in 700 languages and dialects and distributing 550 million copies of the Bible. The National Bible Society of Scotland was scarcely less energetic: in a single year before WORLD WAR II, it distributed 11 million Bibles. The influence of these societies in spreading cultural values may well have been greater than their spiritual influence.

Bill of Exchange, Origins of, method of payment, developed in the 16th century: the intended recipient of goods issued a 'bill' promising to pay an agreed sum at an agreed date. The recipient of the bill might treat it as currency, by endorsing it and assigning it to a third party. 'Outland' and 'inland' bills were generated by foreign and domestic trade respectively. The delay in promise to pay represented a credit element. In inland trade 3 months was common, in overseas trade the due date could be much later. Banks would often cash bills which had not yet matured at a discounted value and specialist brokers developed who paid cash for bills. By the late 18th century there existed a specialized bill market.

Bill of Middlesex, *see* KING'S BENCH; LEGAL FICTIONS

Bill of Rights 1689, an act of the CONVENTION PARLIAMENT of 1689 giving statutory form to the DECLARATION OF RIGHTS. It also provided that only a Protestant heir might succeed to the throne. Although in the end the Bill closely echoed the Declaration, both additions and removals were proposed and debated, revealing the continuingly controversial character of the REVOLUTION SETTLEMENT.

Bills of Mortality, a term used in the 17th and 18th centuries to designate the London metropolitan region (the name 'London' strictly applied only to the City). 'Bills of mortality', compiled by PARISH clerks, listed births and numbers and causes of deaths in metropolitan parishes and are thus of considerable value in HISTORICAL DEMOGRAPHY, especially in charting the EPIDEMICS to which London was prone.

Birinus, St (died *c*.648), a missionary from Rome and the first to undertake the CONVERSION of the kingdom of WESSEX. He baptized King Cynegils (611–43) and was given DORCHESTER-ON-THAMES for the seat of his bishopric.

Birmingham Now Britain's second city, its considerable growth from the later 16th century derived from its position in the centre of the West Midlands metalworking trades, both as a manufacturing base (specializing early in small arms) and as a merchants' centre. With the growth of full-time industrial working in the region rather than BY-EMPLOYMENT, Birmingham grew ever faster. Its 24,000 people in 1751 had trebled by 1800, and its population and extent have continued to grow ever since. Few buildings survive from before the 18th century, and although there are gracious NEO-CLASSICAL civic buildings of the early 19th century, and Victorian GOTHIC structures of the mid- and late 19th century, much of the modern impression of the city is of large-scale post-war reconstruction, for which plans were being laid even before WORLD WAR II, using the considerable local rate revenues. Birmingham today is a central point on the national motorway system, as in the late 18th and early 19th centuries it was a principal node on the CANAL network. Under Joseph CHAMBERLAIN'S control, Birmingham became one of the most forward-thinking municipal authorities of the late 19th century, with pioneering reforms in public amenities, sanitation and transport; the establishment of BOURNVILLE by the QUAKER chocolate firm of Cadbury Bros was another example of Birmingham enlightenment.

Birmingham Political Union Founded in 1830 by Thomas Attwood (1783–1856) an economist and advocate of currency reform, to agitate for parliamentary reform in order to alleviate economic distress. The height of the Union's activities came with mass demonstrations in support of the 1832 REFORM ACT. After the passing of the Act, it went into decline and was largely absorbed by the CHARTIST movement.

Birmingham Pub Bombings, Nov. 1974, the most serious IRA bombing incident on the British mainland, when bombs planted in two pubs in Birmingham killed 21 people. Together with a similar attack in Guildford it caused a huge outcry, leading the government to pass the PREVENTION OF TERRORISM ACT. After a long campaign the men found guilty of the bombing ('the Birmingham Six') had their convictions quashed in the Appeal Court in March 1991. On the day of their release, the government appointed a Royal Commission to look at the functioning of the criminal justice system.

Birth Control Demographic evidence suggests that forms of 'natural' family limitation were practised from the earliest times, including delayed marriage, abstinence, the prolongation of breast-feeding to inhibit conception, the use of *coitus interruptus*, and resort to ABORTION, although it also points to little use of contraceptive devices within marriage until the 19th century, and especially the onset of the DEMOGRAPHIC TRANSITION. Artificial means of birth control such as sheaths and sponges were only available to the more affluent urban population before the end of the 19th century, when vulcanization of rubber made cheaper and more reliable condoms available and knowledge of contraceptive pessaries for women became more widespread. Contraceptive knowledge was greatly extended during WORLD WAR I, with the issue of condoms to troops to prevent VENEREAL DISEASE. In the 20th century, new methods of birth control have been developed aimed mainly at women, including the 'Dutch cap' and intra-uterine devices such as the coil. The most significant breakthrough in female contraception came with the development of the contraceptive pill in the early 1960s, although there is still concern over possible harmful side effects. Safe and simple forms of male and female sterilization have become increasingly available.

Although birth control was supported by some early reformers such as Francis PLACE, open advocacy remained taboo. In 1877 Charles Bradlaugh and Annie Besant were fined for publishing a book which gave details of birth-control methods. In 1918 Marie Stopes published *Wise Parenthood*, her much acclaimed book supporting birth control, opening the first birth-control clinic three years later. The post-war period saw the increasing use of contraceptives, the emergence of more relaxed attitudes and the almost universal spread of birth-control information, though significant groups within the population – notably the Roman Catholic Church – remained opposed to artificial forms of birth control.

Birth Rate, the annual number of live births calculated per 1,000 of the total POPULATION, estimated at midway through a calendar year.

Bishoprics, English The organization of the bishoprics of medieval England was basically the work of THEODORE OF TARSUS, Archbishop of Canterbury, after the synod of HERTFORD in 672. He began the process of dividing up the existing five bishoprics as the opportunity presented itself, following the principle that each of the new ones should have an episcopal centre and that they should conform to existing territorial divisions – thus, for example, the Magonsaetan and the HWICCE received their own bishoprics at Hereford and Worcester. By the mid 9th century, 16 bishoprics had come into existence.

Theodore's achievement fell far short of Gregory the Great's plan for two archbishoprics at LONDON and YORK, each with 12 SUFFRAGANS. Theodore had, however, accepted the political realities of the 7th century and established a pattern that, in broad terms, endured until the REFORMATION: the southern archbishop took his title from the KENTish capital at CANTERBURY. The existence of some dioceses in northern and eastern England was disrupted by the VIKINGS, but most were afterwards revived. Subsequently, major changes included the creation of the enormous diocese of DORCHESTER-ON-THAMES/ LINCOLN after the Viking invasions, and the creation of ELY and Carlisle in the 12th century. Thereafter, the next major alterations and increases in numbers were made by HENRY VIII, as a by-product of the DISSOLUTION OF THE MONASTERIES; Henry showed genuine enthusiasm for the reforming potential of his scheme, but he was probably also aware of its value for conciliating both dispossessed abbots and conservative religious opinion in general. Six monasteries – BRISTOL, CHESTER, GLOUCESTER, Oseney (soon moved to OXFORD), PETERBOROUGH and WESTMINSTER – were made into secular cathedrals, while all the former monastic cathedrals except Coventry (which was demolished) also became secular COLLEGIATE BODIES, with DEANS. By Act of Parliament in 1542 Sodor and MAN, which had had a succession of English bishops in the Isle of Man from the 14th century, was recognized as a diocese within the province of YORK. Westminster diocese was reabsorbed into LONDON in 1550, but other changes in bishoprics then contemplated or put into operation did not survive the death of EDWARD VI. Altogether these Henrician foundations represented the most substantial structural change brought about in the Church of England during the REFORMATION; they were revived without alteration after the INTERREGNUM at the RESTORATION of CHARLES II.

During the 19th century, shifts in population, particularly those caused by the INDUSTRIAL REVOLUTION, brought a need for reorganization and for more dioceses, beginning with Ripon in 1836. These new foundations have continued in the 20th century, the most recent being DERBY and PORTSMOUTH (1927). The Roman Catholic church did not re-create territorial structure for its work until 1688, but these areas long remained only vicariates apostolic (areas served by bishops given nominal titles from overseas); twelve Roman Catholic dioceses with titles derived from English towns were created in 1850, causing an uproar from PROTESTANTS, who characterized it as 'the Papal Aggression'. *See also* CHURCH: ENGLAND, IRELAND, SCOTLAND, WALES; EPISCOPACY.

Bishops' Book, 1537. This statement of the doctrine of HENRY VIII's Church, officially entitled *The Institution of a Christian Man*, was a compromise between religious conservatives and reformers, setting forth moderate reformist theology, and it was produced with difficulty by a diverse committee of bishops. Henry had it published, but did not give it royal authorization, and he soon set about revising it, which eventually led to the *KING'S BOOK* of 1543.

Bishops' Wars, 1639, 1640. CHARLES I's imposition of the 1637 PRAYER BOOK on Scotland provoked the COVENANT in Feb. 1638, and led to the identification of EPISCOPACY with the king's folly; as a result, the General Assembly of the KIRK declared episcopacy abolished. Charles sent an English expeditionary force so obviously inadequate that he did not risk a battle but negotiated the treaty of Berwick in June 1639, ending the first Bishops' War.

Encouraged to take revenge by Strafford (see WENTWORTH, THOMAS), newly returned from Ireland, Charles launched a new army, but this was humiliated by the Scots in the second Bishops' War in Aug. 1640. A treaty signed at Ripon left the Scots occupying NEWCASTLE UPON TYNE and exacting a massive indemnity from the English government. Charles's credibility in England was shattered. However, good evidence has now emerged of collusion between the Scots nobility and the English aristocratic opposition to Charles.

Black Act 1723, an unusually loosely focused capital statute (i.e. one bearing the death penalty), chiefly concerned with deer stealing and poaching, but also with the cutting down of trees, the sending of anonymous letters and arson. It was so worded as to make certain activities felonies if perpetrators had blackened their faces. Sometimes employed in controversial circumstances – for example, against rioting coal-heavers in 1768 – by the late 18th century it was cited by critics of the status quo as exemplifying the rigours of the BLOODY CODE. Its initial targets were deer-stealers in Waltham Chase, near Bishop's Waltham, Hants., who were suspected of links with JACOBITE conspirators. It was repealed in 1823.

Black Acts 1584, the nickname given to the Acts forced through the Scottish Parliament in May 1584 by a victorious JAMES VI in revenge for his humiliation by the RUTHVEN RAIDERS. The Acts affirmed EPISCOPACY and the jurisdiction of Parliament and king in the Church, and denounced presbyteries. *See also* GOLDEN ACT.

Black and Tans The nickname – which derived from their hybrid uniform of dark green and khaki – given to the additional recruits, mainly ex-soldiers, to the Royal Irish Constabulary during the ANGLO-IRISH WAR. Recruited by the British government from January 1920, their participation in reprisals and atrocities – including the burning of property at Balbriggan, near Dublin, and in the centre of Cork – as well as ill-treatment of suspected members of the IRA, left an enduring legacy of bitterness. The force was disbanded on 18 Feb. 1922 following the signing of the ANGLO-IRISH TREATY.

Black Ball Line, sailing ship company founded by James Baines of Liverpool in 1852 at the height of the Australian gold rush to convey emigrants to Melbourne (appropriating the name of a famous American company which in 1813 had been the first to operate a scheduled service, or 'line', across the Atlantic). It was immensely successful in the early years, but suffered in the depression that ended the decade. A revival in the numbers of emigrants helped the company to recover, but the collapse of Barned's Bank in 1866 took it to bankruptcy. The Line was re-formed but failed again.

Black Death, the name commonly given (since the 18th century) to the medieval pandemic of PLAGUE that began in central Asia and spread throughout the rest of Asia, North Africa and Europe. It reached England through Dorset ports in June 1348 and, by December 1349, had spread more or less throughout the British Isles, although it did not reach the more remote Gaelic-speaking areas of western Ireland until 1357.

During the initial outbreak, plague raged during winter as well as summer, so it presumably involved the particularly deadly pneumonic, as well as bubonic, form of the disease. Reliable statistics for the number of deaths do not exist, but most historical demographers believe that the population of England was 5 or 6 million in 1347, plunged to about 3 million, then drifted downwards for at least another century as a result either of the cumulative effect of further (though much less virulent) eruptions or of depressed levels of fertility.

This was the greatest demographic disaster in European history: the economic and social consequences were therefore immense. In the immediate years afterwards, old patterns of society were swiftly re-created, but over decades much land went out of use as people decided to seek better conditions. Although, contrary to popular modern belief, few communities were completely wiped out by the plague itself, many suffered a steady decline in numbers – mostly those with previously poor economic prospects. Geographical and social mobility were thus much encouraged; attempts to enforce the Statute of LABOURERS – the government's attempt to prevent the rise of real wage levels resulting from the shortage of labour – contributed to the resentment that led to the PEASANTS' REVOLT.

Black Friday, 15 April 1921, the name given by trade unionists to the day when the TRIPLE ALLIANCE broke down over the refusal of transport workers and railwaymen to come out in sympathy with the miners in a strike to begin the following day. The miners struck alone, but were forced to return to work in June. The decision of two of the major industrial workforces not to join the strike marked a watershed in immediate post-WORLD WAR I industrial relations, and ended temporarily the threat of co-ordinated action by the most powerful unions.

Black Prince, *see* EDWARD THE BLACK PRINCE

Blackstone, Sir William (1723–80), judge and jurist. His Oxford and Middle Temple education led to a fellowship of All Souls, and in 1758 he became the first Vinerian professor of English law at OXFORD (previously English law had not been taught there). He became an MP in 1761, but was never a successful politician. Becoming SOLICITOR-GENERAL to Queen Charlotte in 1763, from 1770 he was a justice of COMMON PLEAS, then briefly of KING'S BENCH before returning to Common Pleas. His greatest and lasting achievement was his publication of his Oxford lectures as *Commentaries on the Laws of England* (1765–9); the admiring picture which it promulgated of the English constitution as a carefully regulated system of checks and balances was disseminated throughout Europe in translations of his works, and influenced the creators of the constitution of the United States of America.

Blair, Anthony (Tony) (1953–), politician and Prime Minister. A public-school educated barrister, Blair was elected Labour MP for Sedgefield (Co. Durham) in 1983 and leader of the party on the death of John SMITH in 1994. His 'project' to continue Neil KINNOCK'S work of making Labour electable after 18 years in opposition by recasting it as a party with appeal to all classes and interests (including big business) through the politics of the 'third way' neither socialism nor unfettered capitalism, paid off handsomely in 1997 when the party returned 418 MPs in the general election, an overall majority of 178 seats. 'New Labour' enjoyed a remarkable 'honeymoon' period in the country with Blair reaching unprecedented heights of personal popularity until two years into the life of the government when rumblings of lack of substance, a stifling of debate and a neglect of 'old Labour' heartlands in favour of middle England, inevitably began to surface, though the Labour Party remained generally unitedly 'on message' behind their successful leader.

Blake, William (1757–1827), artist and poet. Son of a prosperous London hosier, he was sent to drawing school and apprenticed to an engraver. Later he studied at the ROYAL ACADEMY and, in 1774, opened a print shop. He wrote poetry from boyhood, and developed a unique style of intaglio (relief etching) to illustrate his verse. Although his *Songs of Innocence* (1789) and *Songs of Experience* (1794) employ simple verse forms, they offer serious moral comment. *The Book of Thel* (1789–94) was the first of a series of visionary and prophetic works, challenging conventional morality. Blake became openly critical of the established order, but was acquitted of a 'seditious words' charge in 1800. Blake's engravings, and the profundity of his warnings against a mechanized, inhuman post-industrial world, have ensured his growing reputation into the 20th century.

Blanketeers, Lancs. weavers, so named because of the blankets they carried on their attempted march on London in March 1817. Their aim was to petition the Prince Regent (the future GEORGE IV) to relieve the severe economic distress caused by the contraction of industry and employment after the defeat of Napoleon; however, they were stopped by the military.

Blasphemy The offence of blasphemy – reviling God – found in both Greek and Jewish traditions seems to have been the offence for which Jesus Christ died. As a crime against Christian belief, it was normally subsumed into HERESY until the 16th century, when PROTESTANTS, accused of heresy themselves, were often too embarrassed to persecute others as heretics and revived the blasphemy offence to achieve the same end. The first English secular legislation, enacting imprisonment, came in 1547. An Act of 1677 abolished the medieval heresy laws, but authorized CHURCH COURTS to continue trying for blasphemy. The Blasphemy Act 1698 laid down statutory penalties (modified in 1813 to benefit UNITARIANS), and the common law also recognizes the offence. The last British execution was under Scots law in 1697; prosecutions have been occasional during the 19th and 20th centuries, though George Holyoake (1817–1906), the founder of the magazine SECULARISM, was the last person to be imprisoned in England (1842) on a charge of atheism. The British law only protects the doctrines of the established CHURCHES of England and Scotland.

From its foundation, Islam absorbed earlier Judaeo-Christian and Persian ideas about blasphemy, and treated blasphemy against God, Muhammad or any part of divine revelation as an offence in Islamic law. This has affected Britain: in 1989, the death sentence was pronounced *in absentia* by Iranian theologians on the British writer Salman Rushdie for alleged blasphemies in his novel *The Satanic Verses*.

Blast Furnaces, furnaces in which a blast of air is used for smelting iron. Developed by Abraham DARBY to use coke, they had a significant influence on the development of the IRON AND STEEL INDUSTRY, raised the level of output and served to bring COAL into general use as a furnace fuel, especially when converted into coke (*see* CORT), so replacing wood.

Bleddyn Ap Cynfyn (?–1075), King. One of the kings installed in Wales by Earl Harold of WESSEX (the future HAROLD II) and EDWARD THE CONFESSOR after the defeat of GRUFFUDD AP LLYWELYN in 1063. He is normally associated with the kingdom of POWYS, but may also have ruled in GWYNEDD. Despite his early client status, he was well regarded by Welsh chroniclers, and followed the traditional policy of his predecessors: assisting Earl EDWIN of Mercia in a fruitless rebellion against WILLIAM I THE CONQUEROR. *See also* KINGSHIP.

Blenheim, Battle of, 2/13 Aug. 1704, a British and German Imperial victory during the War of the SPANISH SUCCESSION. Marlborough (*see* CHURCHILL, JOHN) dramatically moved his troops 250 miles from the Netherlands to Bavaria to block an assault on Habsburg lands. A French and Bavarian attempt to attack Vienna was stopped by Marlborough and the Imperial forces under Prince Eugene at the village of Blenheim, north of Augsburg. Tens of thousands were killed or captured on both sides. This decisive battle saved Vienna, drove the surviving French forces back across the Rhine, and took Bavaria out of the war. Marlborough's 'palace' outside Oxford took its name from this victory.

Bligh, William (1754–1817), naval officer. Bligh served as master of HMS *Resolution* in COOK's last voyage of exploration (1775–9). In 1787 he was given command of the armed transport *Bounty*, for a voyage to transport breadfruit plants from Tahiti to the WEST INDIES. The crew mutinied, led by Bligh's second-in-command Fletcher Christian, and Bligh and 18 men were set adrift in an open boat. By outstanding seamanship, he reached the Dutch colony of Coupang, 4,000 miles distant. After service at Camperdown and COPENHAGEN, he was sent as governor to NEW SOUTH WALES. His reputation for sadism is undeserved, being promoted by Christian's friends in a bid to clear the mutineer's name.

Blitz, the, the name – derived from the German *Blitzkrieg* ('lightning war') – given to the bombing of British cities and towns in WORLD WAR II. It was at its heaviest between September 1940 and May 1941, but continued sporadically thereafter. LONDON had the largest share of the raids, which destroyed a third of the City and caused extensive damage to the East End. However, almost all major ports and industrial areas suffered attacks, particularly PLYMOUTH, LIVERPOOL, MANCHESTER and SHEFFIELD. The raid on COVENTRY on 14 November 1940 destroyed the heart of the city and killed over 600 people. Further BAEDEKER RAIDS in 1942 also seriously damaged a number of historic cities. The last phase of the Blitz, from 1944, was carried out by V WEAPONS.

The first sustained attack by a modern air force on a civilian population, the Blitz was a military failure for the Germans. Hitler's diverting of his air force to bomb London from September 1940 crucially eased pressure on the RAF in the Battle of BRITAIN, while the raids failed either seriously to impede the war effort or to force Britain to sue for peace. Their effects were limited by effective AIR RAID PRECAUTIONS and the Germans' lack of heavy bombers. Increasingly effective use of RADAR-equipped night fighters by the RAF began to master the night raiders at the stage when the growing demands of other campaigns drained off the German bombers' strength.

Blockade, the weapon, much used by Britain, of the dominant naval power against the fleets, the trade and the economy of its enemies. Hawke's patrol off Brest during the SEVEN YEARS WAR was the first major use of continuous blockade against an invasion fleet. It required an excellent supply organization, and this policy of 'close blockade' was taken to its extreme against Napoleon's attempts to rebuild his fleet after TRAFALGAR. At the same time blockade of the entire enemy coast became the major weapon of economic warfare. While Napoleon's CONTINENTAL SYSTEM, enforced by his armies, attempted to exclude British goods from the continent, Britain's ORDERS IN COUNCIL and the ships of the Royal NAVY kept European trade from the rest of the world.

Torpedoes and mines made close blockade over-dangerous by 1914. During WORLD WAR I the British practised a distant blockade, both against German warships and against German trade, by patrolling the exits of the North Sea. The trade war, using diplomacy and finance as much as patrols, played a major but unquantifiable part in producing the German collapse. Meanwhile the German attempt to blockade Britain by submarine attack failed by a narrow margin, as it was to do in WORLD WAR II.

Blood Feud, a central feature of all early western European societies. Anglo-Saxon England provides a number of spectacular examples of individuals and kindred seeking revenge for the murder of a member of their family, some of which escalated into the wars fought between families for the domination of the early kingdoms (*see* NORTHUMBRIA; WESSEX).

By the 7th century, however, references to *WERGELDS* in law codes show that society was already attempting to moderate violence through a system of monetary compensation. Tenth-century kings legislated against the blood feud, but they could still take place, as the sequence of events that began with the death of Uhtred Earl of Northumbria in *c.* 1016 reveals. CONVERSION to Christianity, too, had little impact on the blood feud: the Church insisted on penance, but it also acknowledged social convention to the extent that priests were assigned *wergelds*.

Blood Libel, *see* JEWS IN BRITAIN

Bloody Assizes, 1685, the summer ASSIZES: of the western circuit following Monmouth's (*see* SCOTT, JAMES) rebellion. They became notorious because, during them, Chief Justice JEFFREYS sentenced to death more than 300 of those who had been involved. The hangings and quarterings continued for several months, and many hundreds of others were transported to the West Indies.

Bloody Code, a term applied by historians to the series of criminal statutes enacted by 18th-century British parliaments, many of which prescribed the death penalty (*see* CAPITAL PUNISHMENT). Sir William Meredith, who began campaigning for a reduction in the number of capital statutes in the 1770s, was the first to attempt to count such Acts in order to demonstrate the scale of 18th-century innovation in criminal law-making; subsequent penal reformers continued the tally. The claim that hanging laws were mainly innovations was probably designed to counter conservative objections to reform; in fact, murder and certain forms of aggravated theft – the crimes for which people were most commonly hanged – had long been capital crimes; new 18th-century laws were, by contrast, relatively rarely invoked.

Bloody Sunday (1), 13 Nov. 1887. A demonstration against unemployment, organized by radicals and socialists, was held in London's Trafalgar Square – in defiance of the authorities – as the culmination of a campaign in support of the rights to freedom of speech and free assembly. It was bloodily suppressed, with many injuries and one fatality. The efficiency of the police and military served to convince many activists that the path to socialism lay through the ballot rather than the bullet.

Bloody Sunday (2), 30 Jan. 1972. A symbolic event in recent Irish history, when a banned civil rights march in Londonderry led to an incident in which 13 were killed and 17 wounded by the British army. The incident provoked a rapid increase in sectarian violence, in the light of which the HEATH government imposed DIRECT RULE in March. Bloody Sunday marked the end of any support by the Catholic community for the deployment of troops in ULSTER, which it had generally welcomed in 1969.

Bloomsbury Gang, name applied to the group of politicians associated with John Russell, 4th Duke of Bedford, who owned much property in Bloomsbury. They included notably his son-in-law Earl Gower and the Earl of Weymouth. Richard Rigby was 'man of business' to the group. Brought into the Grafton (*see* FITZROY, AUGUSTUS) ministry without their ageing patron in 1767, the group remained important throughout the 1770s. Initially distinguished by their hard-line anti-American stance, they deserted NORTH in 1779, significantly weakening his position.

Bloomsbury Group, the name given to a group of writers, painters and intellectuals who gathered around the home of Virginia and Vanessa Stephen (daughters of Sir Leslie Stephen) in the area of London around the BRITISH MUSEUM known as Bloomsbury. The group originated around 1905 when Thoby Stephen brought CAMBRIDGE friends to his sisters' Thursday evenings at 46 Gordon Square, and soon a regular – if loosely-knit – group emerged, which continued after Vanessa married the writer Clive Bell in 1907 and Virginia married the ex-civil servant and writer Leonard Woolf in 1912. The 'Bloomsberries' were to include at various times the economist and writer J. M. KEYNES, the writers E. M. Forster, Lytton Strachey and Desmond MacCarthy, the philosopher and author of *Principia Ethica*, G. E. Moore, the painters Dora Carrington and Duncan Grant, the art critic Roger Fry, and later the writer David Garnett. Its members' combined artistic and literary production was considerable – novels, biographies, art criticism, economic and political theory, paintings and decorative domestic arts, and Leonard and Virginia Woolf set up the Hogarth Press in 1917 which published many fine books, including T. S. Eliot's *The Waste Land* in 1923. The members of the Bloomsbury Group were critical and mocking of what they regarded as Victorian vulgarity and narrowness of vision. They were élitist in their attitudes, yet generally if rather unspecifically left-wing in their politics, agnostic, avant-garde in literary, artistic, personal and sexual matters, and collectively – and in most cases individually too – continue to have a seemingly unceasing fascination.

Blue Books, name commonly given to Parliamentary Papers, especially the Reports of Select Committees, from the original colour of their cover. The great series of social reforms instigated in the 19th century in, e.g. FACTORY or CHILD LABOUR legislation were usually prefaced by official investigations recorded in Blue Books.

Blue Funnel, shipping company, founded as the Ocean Steam Ship Company in 1865 by Alfred Holt. Named for the heroes of the Iliad, the Blue Funnel ships traded first to China, initially round the Cape and from 1869 through the newly-opened SUEZ CANAL. New routes were continually added, until by 1915 with the opening of the Panama Canal they encircled the globe. After WORLD WAR I the fleet, always built to the highest standards, was modernized and its losses replaced; but almost half of its 88 ships were lost in WORLD WAR II. Thereafter, the company suffered from increasing competition from other nations and the loss of passenger traffic to the airlines. A series of restructurings from the 1950s on failed to halt the decline, and the last two ships were sold in 1988.

Bluestockings The original 'bluestocking' was a man: the scholar and botanist Benjamin Stillingfleet, who was noted for his unusual preference for blue stockings. He was one of a number of men sympathetic to the serious reading and discussion practised by a group of women friends – from both the gentry and the aristocracy – who clustered around Elizabeth Montagu from the 1750s. By the 1770s, the term was already commonly applied to women of intellectual bent.

Bluewater Policy, a term used by historians for an 18th-century maritime strategy involving the concentration of effort on the navy, colonial conquest and overseas trade, and avoidance of continental military commitments. Continental allies might be subsidized to carry on land warfare.

Boadicea, *see* BOUDICCA

Board of Agriculture, semi-official body established in 1793 to make a county-by-county survey with a view to the general improvement of British agriculture. Its secretary was Arthur Young (1741–1820), its president the Scottish agricultural improver and publicist Sir John Sinclair (1754–1835). Eccentrically combining features of a government department and a private club, the Board also sponsored research and took an interest in legislation, lobbying for a bill to facilitate ENCLOSURES. During the agricultural depression which followed the NAPOLEONIC WARS, it challenged the government's FREE TRADE policies, arguing for agricultural protection. In 1821 LIVERPOOL therefore stopped its grant and, after attempting to continue as a voluntary body, it folded in 1822. Re-formed in 1893, it became the Ministry of Agriculture and Fisheries, absorbing the Ministry of Food in 1954.

Board of Control Established under PITT THE YOUNGER'S INDIA ACT of 1784, its role was to superintend the EAST INDIA COMPANY'S government of India in all matters relating to revenue, administration, war and diplomacy. Trade and patronage were to be left to the Company. When India was brought under direct crown control after the INDIAN MUTINY, responsibility for Indian affairs passed to a secretary of state for India.

Board of Education Act 1899, *see* BRYCE COMMISSION

Board of Trade The PRIVY COUNCILS of the 17th century spawned numerous committees charged with responsibility for trade and PLANTATIONS. In 1696, under pressure from Parliament to make better provision for commerce, WILLIAM III established a Board of Trade to advise the Privy Council; its work in relation to American colonial government has received much attention from historians. It was abolished in 1782 in the context of the ROCKINGHAMITE campaign for ECONOMICAL REFORM, but was effectively revived four years later as a committee of the Privy Council. Its powers grew considerably as a Department of State in the 19th and 20th centuries, with the burgeoning, and increasing central direction, of the economy. In the inter-war period, with the growth of protectionism following the collapse of the international economy, the administration of trade controls such as tariffs and quotas and the IMPERIAL PREFERENCE Scheme were part of its remit. Furthermore during and immediately after WORLD WAR II, the Board was responsible for controlling the allocation of a wide range of raw materials – issuing import licences and permits to manufacturers. In the 1950s, the Board played a key role in the dismantling of controls and the liberalization of international trade. The emergence of the European Common Market (*see* EUROPEAN UNION) in the late 1950s was initially treated as a matter for commercial policy and hence relations between the Six and the UK were seen as the province of the Board of Trade. The earliest negotiations for UK entry were conducted by the then president of the Board of Trade, Edward HEATH, but as the wider political issues loomed larger the Foreign Office and the Treasury played a more significant role. The Board's functions were not confined to trade relations however: in the 1950s and 60s it played an important part in managing the contraction of the COTTON INDUSTRY and overseeing industrial restructuring in general. In the 1970s this wider remit was eventually recognized and the Board of Trade became the Department of Trade and Industry.

Board Schools, schools under local elected boards created in W. E. Forster's EDUCATION ACT 1870 in England and Wales. Any area which voted for it could have a new elected school board; in areas where a deficiency of school provision was proved, a school board was imposed. The board schools were designed to provide schooling where it was needed most – compromises over grants for education negotiated in the 1830s and 1840s had given funds to localities where the National Society for Promoting the Education of the Poor or a similar denominational body (*see* MONITORIAL SYSTEM) was already taking an initiative, so grants were not reaching areas of 'educational destitution' – and to instil a proper sense of discipline in the future working population. Both voluntary and board schools were eligible for government grants, and both charged fees; but board schools could draw on the rates. The Education Act (Scotland) of 1872 brought universal board schools north of the border. The LONDON School Board was a national pacemaker in the rash of new board school building of the 1870s and 1880s, introducing separate classrooms for each age group, a central hall for whole-school activities, and later adding specialist rooms for practical activities. School boards were abolished under BALFOUR'S EDUCATION ACT 1902. *See also* ELEMENTARY SCHOOLS.

Boer Wars The conflict between Britain and the Boers (1899–1902), widely known as the Boer War, was preceded by the first Boer War (1880–1). This arose from the British annexation in 1877 of the bankrupt Transvaal Republic. Following British expansion northward in the ZULU WAR, the Boers (literally 'farmers' or settlers) of the Transvaal rose in revolt in Dec. 1880. A small British force under Major-General Sir George Pomeroy-Colley was decisively defeated at Majuba Hill on 27 Feb. 1881, and GLADSTONE's government decided on withdrawal. By the Convention of Pretoria of 5 April 1881 the Transvaal regained its independence under nominal British suzerainty.

This episode failed to resolve the underlying problems of British expansion and the isolationism of the Boers, descendants of Dutch colonists who had moved north from CAPE COLONY in the 'great trek' of 1836 to found the Transvaal and Orange Free State. The discovery of gold in the Transvaal in 1886 produced an influx of non-Boers from Cape Colony, and in 1896 Cecil RHODES backed the abortive JAMESON RAID, an attempt to overthrow the Transvaal government. The failure of Governor Alfred Milner to agree the rights of British citizens in the Transvaal with President Paul Kruger was the immediate excuse for the second Boer War.

At first the Boers were successful, invading Cape Colony and NATAL and besieging MAFEKING, Kimberley and Ladysmith, and inflicting three defeats on the British in 'Black Week', 10–15 Dec. 1899. Receiving massive reinforcements including DOMINION troops the following year, the British under Frederick Roberts occupied and annexed both Boer republics. The relief of Mafeking (defended by Colonel Baden-Powell) on 18 May 1900 produced widespread celebrations in Britain. Many Boers fought on as guerrillas 'to the bitter end', and to contain their families KITCHENER (who had replaced Roberts) used settlements called 'concentration camps' in which deaths from disease provoked a scandal. (The later Nazi use of the term was deliberate anti-British propaganda.)

The Peace of Vereeniging of May 1902 absorbed the Boer republics into the BRITISH EMPIRE in return for a promise of self-government honoured in 1907, followed by their joining Cape Colony and Natal in the Union of SOUTH AFRICA in 1910. In Britain the war produced ARMY reforms (*see* WORLD WAR I) and an end to splendid isolation (*see* KRUGER TELEGRAM).

Boethius, Alfred's Translation of Boethius, a 6th-century Roman, wrote the treatise *Consolation of Philosophy* while awaiting execution in prison. Four centuries later, the book was personally translated into Anglo-Saxon by ALFRED THE GREAT. One of the most influential works of the Middle Ages, its theme – the influence of providence on human existence – was seen by Alfred as relevant to the tribulations of his own times.

Boleyn, Anne, *see* ANNE BOLEYN

Bolingbroke, 1st Viscount, *see* ST JOHN, HENRY

Bolingbroke, Henry, *see* HENRY IV

Bombing Offensive, sustained and controversial bombing of Germany, other Axis countries and parts of occupied Europe during WORLD WAR II by the ROYAL AIR FORCE (RAF) and, after 1941, by the US Army Air Force (*see* WARFARE, AIR). RAF daylight raids on German military installations early in the war proved very costly and from Sept. 1940 attacks on German cities were mounted. This remained the only direct method of attacking Germany's war effort for almost four years, tying down German resources in air defence. From 1942 commander-in-chief Arthur Harris vigorously pursued an area bombing campaign against industrial cities which rapidly increased in intensity, with the first 1,000-bomber raid on Cologne on 30 May. The USAAF pursued a policy of precision bombing by daylight which in practice was no more discriminate. Harris's campaign culminated in the Battle of Berlin over winter 1943–4, a controversial and unsuccessful attempt to knock Germany out of the war before the D-DAY landings. On two occasions bombing of cities produced a freak firestorm with massive loss of life: Hamburg (24–29 July 1943) and Dresden (13–14 Feb. 1945). The bombing offensive has been criticized both for waging indiscriminate war against civilians (*see* HOME FRONT) and for being ineffective since despite the devastation German morale did not crack. About 600,000 German civilians and 50,000 British aircrew died in the campaign.

Bonar Law, Andrew, *see* LAW ANDREW BONAR

Bond, a legal document engaging to observe some condition, usually with a note of the penalty for non-compliance. In commercial practice, the penalty was generally a specified sum of money. In England, bonds were enforceable from the end of the

12th century at COMMON LAW, generally in the Court of COMMON PLEAS in matters of debt, subsequently, relief from the penalties of bonds became available in the Court of CHANCERY.

Bondfield, Margaret (1873–1953), trade unionist and Labour politician. She began work as a shop assistant, aged 11, and in 1898 became an official in the Shop Assistants Union. At the TUC conference the following year, she supported the setting up of the LABOUR REPRESENTATION COMMITTEE, the forerunner of the LABOUR PARTY, to ensure parliamentary representation for smaller unions. She was national officer of the National Union of General and Municipal Workers 1908–38 and served on the TUC General Council 1918–24 (chair, 1923) and 1926–9. The most prominent woman in the Labour movement in the inter-war years, she became an MP (1923–4, 1926–31), and was the first woman to take a seat in Cabinet as minister of labour (1929–31). She was also active in the National Council of Social Service and in women's training and employment.

Bonds of Association, *see* ASSOCIATION

Bonds of Manrent, Scots written instruments granting protection in return for a period of service, which originated in the 14th century and were common from 1450 to 1600. Bonds were frequently used to combat the course of justice, and today they provide invaluable information about Scottish political alliances during the period.

Boniface, St (*c*.675–754), the greatest of the 8th-century Anglo-Saxon MISSIONARIES to the Continent and a notable religious reformer within the kingdom of the Franks. His wide-ranging activities from 719 onwards made an important contribution to the Christianization of what we now call Germany and its incorporation into the CAROLINGIAN Empire; this, in turn, had massive consequences for the future history of Europe. His connections with the papacy greatly strengthened its relationship with the Franks and helped create the circumstances that were ultimately responsible for Charlemagne's imperial coronation in 800. He may also have anointed the first Carolingian king, Pepin the Short, in 751 when the latter's family displaced the Merovingians. Boniface and his followers were also responsible for the dissemination on the Continent of the works of BEDE and other NORTHUMBRIAN scholars. Because of this, he can be seen as one of the founders of the court-sponsored Carolingian Renaissance and a precursor of other Englishmen at the Carolingian court, of whom the most notable was ALCUIN.

Book of Discipline 'Discipline' – the structuring of the Church and regulation of its members' lives – was a central preoccupation of CALVINIST churches. Two books were prepared for the Scottish Church in 1560 and 1578–81, respectively by KNOX and MELVILLE. English PURITANS, chief among them Walter Travers (who had written his own scheme in 1574), prepared one (known as the '*Directory*') between 1583 and 1587, in a vain attempt to have it adopted by the 1586–7 Parliament.

Book of Kells, an 8th- or early 9th-century Gospel book, now preserved in the library of Trinity College, DUBLIN. Its superb illuminations have made it the most famous of all the manuscripts produced by the Irish and Celtic churches. It shows a mixture of stylistic influences, including Irish and Northumbrian; it may well have been produced at IONA, with its wide-ranging international contacts, before being transferred to Kells in Ireland when the Iona community migrated there.

Book of Llandaff, *see* LIBER LANDAVENSIS

Book of Sports Issued by JAMES I in 1618 to authorize certain Sunday pastimes and reissued by CHARLES I in 1633, it proved bitterly divisive, offending widespread SABBATARIANISM. Opposition to it became a symbol of opposition to ARMINIANISM.

Bookland, an Anglo-Saxon legal term used to describe land held by charter or 'book'. Such land would normally have been permanently transferred to its holder and his family, who was usually also given the right to alienate it (transfer ownership) out of the family's possession or into another man's or woman's lordship. Rights of jurisdiction might also be granted, but the holder and his heirs remained obliged to perform the COMMON BURDENS of the kingdom.

Books of Orders Regulations issued to JUSTICES OF THE PEACE by early modern governments in times of economic difficulty, most famously by CHARLES I in 1630–1, instructing JPs to make regular reports about their localities. The relatively traditional provisions and limited effectiveness of these Books indicate the limitations of Charles's personal rule.

Books of Rates, valuations used for levying customs dues. Rates on a range of exports and imports were laid down in 1275, 1303 and 1347, were reformed under MARY I in 1558 and left static at unrealistic levels thereafter. Revisions in 1608 (after BATE'S CASE) and in 1634–5 showed how much revenue could be raised in this way, but this also raised fears about crown PREROGATIVE. *See also* EXCISE.

Booth, Catherine (1829–90) and **Booth, William** (1829–1912), *see* SALVATION ARMY

Booth, Charles (1840–1916), social reformer. A wealthy businessman drawn into social research, he was responsible for the first scientific estimates of poverty and the development of survey methods in social investigation. His magnum opus, *Life and Labour of the People in London*, with its memorable series of coloured maps of poverty, was begun in 1886 and completed 17 years later. Among other factors, he identified old age as a major source of poverty, and campaigned for old age pensions with some success. *See* OLD AGE PENSIONS ACT 1908.

Bordar, a word deriving from the French *borde* that was imported into England at the time of the NORMAN CONQUEST. For a few generations, it remained the standard term for the smallholder, a tenant who held a few acres of farm land, or even just a cottage garden (the Anglo-Saxon word for this class was 'cottar'). Of the households recorded in *DOMESDAY BOOK*, 30 per cent were those of bordars or cottars.

Border Wardens, medieval and Tudor officials appointed to supervise the border with Scotland. Normally there were three separate English wardens for the East, West and Middle Marches, and corresponding appointments on the Scots side of the border.

Borough Derived from the late Latin 'burgus' (as is the Anglo-Saxon *BURH*), it was a term applied from the 11th century to a settlement with urban characteristics, such as a regular market, and perhaps defensive fortifications. TOWNS led the burst of economic prosperity in the 12th century and sought privileges and exemptions from outside interference by CHARTERS, formal grants from FEUDAL lords or from the king; often records of these grants only survive in a later confirmation or *INSPEXIMUS*. Many boroughs were created in England and Wales by lords in an effort to promote economic development, and not all flourished; up to the 19th century boroughs were extraordinarily varied in their constitutions and privileges, let alone their size, ranging from a city, LONDON, to a totally deserted earthwork at Old Sarum, Wilts. Cities (from the Latin *civitas*) were towns of exceptional status, usually those in which the CATHEDRAL of a bishop was situated. The exceptionally prosperous and powerful borough of BRISTOL led the way in 1373 in being granted county status, with its own SHERIFF as well as JUSTICES OF THE PEACE, and this became the aim (rarely achieved) of larger towns and cities in England thereafter. An important gain was made by Hull in 1440 when it was the first borough to achieve the right of incorporation in law; henceforth it could sue and be sued and generally act as a corporate person, and this became the characteristic of a corporate borough.

From the reign of EDWARD I most English cities and many (but not all) boroughs sent representatives to the House of COMMONS, generally in pairs: these were known as 'burgesses of Parliament' and were reckoned as secondary in status to the county representatives (KNIGHTS OF THE SHIRE). Welsh boroughs were added to the Commons from 1542 (*see* UNION OF WALES AND ENGLAND). New English and Welsh boroughs were created up to *c.*1640, and old ones decayed, but there was remarkably little institutional reform between the 15th and 19th centuries, apart from the politically inspired *QUO WARRANTO* campaigns of CHARLES II and JAMES II.

The situation became absurd in the INDUSTRIAL REVOLUTION when many of the newly rich and populous towns of northern

England did not have chartered borough status, and pressure grew for reform and rationalization. The 1830s WHIG government undertook drastic reforms by the MUNICIPAL CORPORATIONS ACT of 1835; borough corporations were left with fewer powers than at any time in their history. New towns were given powers to set up IMPROVEMENT Commissions, and some old corporations followed suit; it was necessary to consolidate this rash of new enterprise into a uniform borough system by the Municipal Corporations Act 1882, which also tackled the organization of the remaining smaller traditional borough corporations. In the District and Parish Councils Act 1894, urban district councils (UDCs) were created, rather than further proliferating boroughs.

All these arrangements were swept away by the LOCAL GOVERNMENT REORGANIZATION ACT 1972, although this allowed district councils to assume the title 'borough' if there was traditional justification, and also left intact the system of boroughs set up for London in 1963.

Boroughs in Ireland were mostly associated with medieval Anglo-Norman and English settlement, and their fortunes waxed and waned with those of Anglo-Irish culture; they were rare on the west coast and virtually absent in the north-west. The more significant boroughs and cities were represented in the Irish PARLIAMENT. Their pattern of 19th-century reform followed English legislation. For Scotland, *see* BURGH. *See also* POCKET BOROUGHS.

Borough-English, the name given in English law to the custom of ultimogeniture – the right of the youngest son to inherit his father's estate. The term derives from a court case heard in 1327 when it was shown to be the custom of the old English borough of Nottingham – whereas primogeniture was the practice in the neighbouring French suburb (*burgh Francoys*) that had grown up after the NORMAN CONQUEST. Despite its apparently 'bourgeois' name, the custom of ultimogeniture was more commonly found in the English countryside.

Boroughbridge, Battle of, 16 March 1322. The dwindling forces of the rebel THOMAS OF LANCASTER were intercepted and defeated at the crossing of the River Ure in Yorks. by an army loyal to EDWARD II, commanded by Andrew Harclay. Afterwards, Edward ordered the execution of more than 20 of the leading rebels – an unprecedented judicial bloodbath that shocked contemporaries.

Boston Tea Party, 1773, landmark event in the period immediately before the War of AMERICAN INDEPENDENCE. Following attempts by the British government to impose stamp duty (*see* STAMP ACTS) upon the American colonists in 1765, and then other indirect taxes in 1767, both of which were withdrawn after concerted opposition on the grounds of 'no taxation without representation', Lord NORTH's government permitted the EAST INDIA COMPANY to ship tea directly to America. The small duty still payable on the tea – North described it as a 'peppercorn of principle' – caused a furore on the grounds that Britain was still trying to tax its colonies arbitrarily. At the end of 1773 determined opponents of the tax boarded ships at Boston, Mass., throwing 342 chests of tea into the harbour. Penalties were imposed on the colonists until the tea was paid for, a move which finally turned opposition into outright war in 1774.

Bosworth, Battle of, 22 Aug. 1485. A victory over RICHARD III, it secured the English throne for the returning exile, Henry Tudor (*see* HENRY VII). With French naval and military support, Henry landed at Milford Haven (Pembrokes.) and then marched into England. Many of those who received Richard's summons to arms did nothing, like the Earl of Northumberland, or chose to fight against him, like the Stanleys. Richard himself was killed launching a despairing attack against his rival. It has recently been suggested that the battle took place not at the traditional site (the slope of Ambien Hill in Leics.) but at nearby Dadlington. *See also* WARS OF THE ROSES.

Botany Bay, penal colony in NEW SOUTH WALES, AUSTRALIA, five miles south of present day Sydney, where the first convicts to be transported to Australia were landed in 1788. James COOK so named it in 1770 because of the large variety of hitherto unknown plants found there. *See also* TRANSPORTATION.

Bothwell Bridge, Battle of, 22 June 1679. Following the revolt of the Scottish COVENANTERS against the policies of John MAITLAND, Duke of Lauderdale, the royal army under Monmouth (*see* SCOTT, JAMES) attacked them at Bothwell Bridge, on the Clyde near Hamilton, Lanarks., inflicting heavy losses. But victory brought no resolution to the problems of Scottish government.

Botswana, *see* BECHUANALAND

Boudicca (*fl.* AD 60s), Queen of the Iceni. Boudicca (also Boadicea, a Victorian corruption normally rejected by the specialists) was the widow of Prasutagus, King of the ICENI, and led a famous unsuccessful rebellion against the Romans in AD 61. The Iceni had been a Roman CLIENT KINGDOM since soon after 43, but, following Prasutagus's death in 60, Boudicca and her daughters and many of their people were brutally treated by the Romans. The rebellion that followed attracted massive support not only from the Iceni, but also from other tribes, suggesting widespread British discontent with Roman rule. The TRINOVANTES, for example, appear to have been aggrieved by the conversion of COLCHESTER into a Roman colony in 49. The uprising's early successes also owed a great deal to the fact that the Roman governor of Britain, SUETONIUS PAULINUS, was away campaigning in North Wales.

The rebels sacked Colchester, LONDON and VERULAMIUM and defeated part of the 9th Legion before suffering the same fate at the hands of Suetonius Paulinus at an unidentified site in the Midlands. Boudicca died shortly afterwards, possibly from taking poison. The revolt, which caused massive casualties and considerable destruction, was followed by a more conciliatory approach by the governors who succeeded Suetonius Paulinus (*see* ROMAN CONQUEST).

Boundary Commission In 1924 a tripartite Commission was set up under the terms of the ANGLO-IRISH TREATY to fix the boundary between the IRISH FREE STATE and ULSTER, with representatives for Ulster and the Irish Free State under a neutral chairman. An agreement settling the border was signed on 3 Dec. 1925 between the British and Irish governments.

Each country of the UK has a Boundary Commission with the responsibility, every 10–15 years, of drawing fresh PARLIAMENTary CONSTITUENCY boundaries as fairly as possible, while at the same time having regard for local ties and convenience. Constituency sizes vary, with smaller numbers of electors in Scotland, Wales and Northern Ireland. The redrawing of boundaries has frequently been at the expense of inner-city constituencies with the move of the population to the suburbs and rural fringe.

Bournville, model industrial estate in south-west BIRMINGHAM, instituted by the chocolate-making company Cadbury Brothers in 1879. The firm, founded by QUAKER John Cadbury in 1831, had occupied premises in central Birmingham, but moved out to the countryside to obtain hygienic surroundings and improved conditions. In 1893 Alexander Harvey was commissioned to design a model village for the workforce, of which 313 houses had been built by 1900; by 1955 there were 3,500 houses in Bournville. The influence of Bournville was immense. It was a built expression of the GARDEN CITY idea which was circulating at the end of the 19th century, being less exclusive than PORT SUNLIGHT, which provided only for Lever employees.

Bouvines, Battle of, 27 July 1214. Fought near Lille, France, between Philip II Augustus of France and a combined Anglo-Flemish-German army, it was a defeat for the allies and marked the end of King JOHN's 'grand strategy' of invading France on two fronts in the hope of recovering the ANGEVIN lands he had lost in 1203–5. This new humiliation brought the MAGNA CARTA rebellion significantly nearer.

Bow Street Runners, a force of law-enforcement agents first established by Henry Fielding in 1750, when he was serving as a JUSTICE OF THE PEACE for WESTMINSTER in an office in Bow Street. Initially composed in part of former freelance 'thieftakers', the team of runners investigated crimes and arrested offenders under Fielding's direction. Similar teams were attached to the offices of the stipendiary magistrates established by the Middlesex Justices Act of 1792. They were ultimately integrated into the new Metropolitan POLICE.

Bowdlerization, *see* SHAKESPEARE

Bower, Walter (*c*.1385–1449), Abbot of Inchholm. He was the author of the *Scotichronicon*, a long narrative amplifying and continuing FORDUN, which offers an intensely patriotic account of Scottish history from its legendary beginnings until 1437.

Boxer Rebellion, anti-foreign rising in northern China in 1900, in the wake of Britain's territorial acquisition of Wei-hai-wei in 1898, Germany's of Kiaochow, and Russia's of Port Arthur, which caused widespread resentment. Young Chinese, with the connivance of the Dowager Empress, enrolled in a secret society of 'Harmonious Fists', hence Boxers. Attacks on Westerners and Western-influenced Chinese made the powers decide to take action to safeguard their nationals, and a military expedition was met with force. A Boxer rising in Peking led to the assassination of the German minister there and to the foreign embassies being besieged. The six-nation force which relieved them looted Peking (just as the British and French had done in 1860), and a German force which followed took reprisals to avenge the minister's murder. Boxer risings in other provinces provoked the Russians to occupy them. The West's military effort only served to intensify anti-foreign feeling, driving many young Chinese into the nationalist, anti-imperial movement which resulted in the Revolution of 1911.

Boy Scouts, *see* SCOUTING MOVEMENT

Boycott, On 13 Dec. 1880, the *Daily Mail* coined the word to describe the tactics of the IRISH LAND LEAGUE in their anti-eviction campaign of 1880. Charles Boycott (1832–97) was the agent for a large Co. Mayo landowner who was punished for breaking the League's code by a campaign of social and commercial ostracism and his crops were only saved by a specially recruited workforce of Orangemen, working under the protection of a force of more than 1,000 troops. The term entered general usage thereafter in English and other languages.

Boyle, Robert (1627–91), natural philosopher. Son of Richard BOYLE, 2nd Earl of Cork (1566–1643), he travelled on the Continent with a tutor, then went to OXFORD in 1654, where he became a leading member of the 'Invisible College' that preceded the ROYAL SOCIETY, and played an important part in rethinking the objects and procedures of scientific study. With his assistant Robert Hooke, he devised an improved air pump, and established experimentally the relationship between the pressure and volume of gases: 'Boyle's law' gives abstract expression to his findings. Gases formed the subject of several of his published books; he also wrote treatises on ALCHEMY, to which he applied experimental methods. A pious Christian, he founded the Boyle Lectures for the defence of Christianity against atheists, Jews and Muslims, and used his position as a director of the EAST INDIA COMPANY to encourage missionary activity in the East.

Boyne, Battle of the 1 July 1690. After the GLORIOUS REVOLUTION, JAMES II's position in Ireland remained strong. WILLIAM III's army was able to force a passage across the river Boyne near Drogheda in Co. Louth, outflanking the Jacobite army. The victory was followed by James's flight to France, and DUBLIN and Waterford soon capitulated. Limerick held out longer, but by the end of 1691, John CHURCHILL (the future Duke of Marlborough) had subdued all of southern Ireland. Symbolizing as it did the frustration of Irish Catholic hopes, and preparing the way for a triumphalist PROTESTANT ASCENDANCY, the battle continues to be both reviled and celebrated (on 12 July) as a key event in Ireland's history and one that continues to exacerbate tension between Northern Ireland's catholic and protestant communities.

Brackley, 1st Viscount, *see* EGERTON, SIR THOMAS

Bracton, the name by which a massive treatise officially entitled *On the Laws and Customs of England*, the early 'bible' of the COMMON LAW, is still commonly and conveniently known. It is a misnomer derived from an early attribution to Henry Bracton, a royal judge active in the mid-13th century. It was, in fact, very largely written by a judge, or judge's clerk, from the generation before Bracton, though he may well have made some additions of his own.

Breakspear, Nicholas, *see* ADRIAN IV

Breda, Declaration of, 1660. A manifesto issued by CHARLES II in exile, it offered a general pardon and an amnesty for all offences committed during the CIVIL WARS and INTERREGNUM. He undertook to rely on the advice of a free Parliament, and promised a degree of religious liberty. The declaration paved the way for what was in the event the more conservative RESTORATION settlement.

Breda, Treaty of, July 1667, agreement ending the second DUTCH WAR, by which England retained NEW YORK and New Jersey, and regained the Caribbean islands captured by the French. Holland retained Surinam and gained recognition for her claims in West Africa and the East Indies. Acadia (NOVA SCOTIA) was restored to France. The NAVIGATION ACT was modified in favour of the Dutch.

Breedon-on-the-Hill Monastery Situated in Leics., it was one of the great MERCIAN monasteries of the 7th century. Although virtually no record of it remains, the survival of some fine sculpture and its recorded role in the education of Tatwine, Archbishop of Canterbury (731–4), indicate its once great importance.

Brehon, term derived from the Irish word *breithemain*, meaning 'judge', and used in English in the early modern period to refer to a man learned in customary Irish law. Thus 'brehon law' has become the conventional term for native Irish law as declared by brehons. It remained basic to Irish society until the 17th century, but outside Ireland it came to be widely regarded, from the 12th century, as primitive and immoral, particularly in the areas of family and marriage.

Brethren A protestant NONCONFORMIST group founded in Ireland by J. N. Darby (1800–82), they are also known as 'Plymouth Brethren' after the name of the first English centre established in 1830. CALVINISTIC in belief, puritanical in conduct, only admitting occupations that were deemed compatible with New Testament standards, they were CONGREGATIONALISTS in ethos and organization and prone to division. The major split occurred in 1849 between the 'Open Brethren' and the 'Exclusive Brethren'.

Brétigny, Treaty of, May 1360, a treaty between England and France in which it was agreed that a ransom of 3 million écus would be paid for King John II of France, captured at POITIERS, and that CALAIS, Guines and Ponthieu as well as all of AQUITAINE, including Poitou, would be ceded to EDWARD III. In return, Edward, having besieged and failed to take Rheims (Dec. 1359–Jan. 1360), promised to renounce the French crown when John renounced French sovereignty over Aquitaine. In the event, these renunciations were never carried through, and the way was left open for the resumption of the HUNDRED YEARS WAR in 1369.

Bretton Woods, monetary and financial conference held at Bretton Woods, New Hampshire, USA, July 1944. Called by President Roosevelt to establish a post-war monetary system that would avoid the international economic crises and consequent political instability of the inter-war period, the conference was attended by some 1,300 experts from 44 countries and largely dominated by Harry Dexter White of the US Treasury and J. M. KEYNES. Its recommendations led to the establishment in Dec. 1945 of two new international institutions as agencies of the UNITED NATIONS: the International Monetary Fund (IMF) to administer a loan fund for stabilizing national currencies, and the International Bank for Reconstruction and Development (World Bank) to channel investment funds to projects in less developed countries. A third proposal to establish a World Trade Organization failed because of US opposition and instead the GENERAL AGREEMENT ON TARIFFS AND TRADE (GATT) – a weaker organization – was established.

The conference also established a system of exchange rates officially fixed in terms of US dollars. Known as 'Bretton Woods', this system became the basis for almost a quarter-century of relative stability between major currencies and unprecedented growth of industrial economies and world trade. However, in the late 1970s the large deficits run by the US economy and the political effects of the Vietnam war combined to undermine the general acceptance of the dollar as the standard international currency on which Bretton Woods depended, and led to increasing use of floating exchange rates.

Bretwalda, collective term used in the 9th century *ANGLO-SAXON CHRONICLE* to describe the seven kings said by BEDE to have exercised *imperium* over the English peoples south of the Humber. The kings were: ÆLLE of SUSSEX, CEALWIN of WESSEX, ETHELBERT of KENT, REDWALD of EAST ANGLIA, and EDWIN, OSWALD and OSWY of NORTHUMBRIA. *Imperium* is now translated as 'overlordship', implying no more than a general pre-eminence over other kings and kingdoms, which at most would have involved leadership in war against the Britons and the receipt of tribute. Its significance for the eventual UNIFICATION of the English is now thought to be minimal. *See also* KINGSHIP.

Brian Boru (?–1014), King of Munster (975–1014) and Irish high-king. He emerged from the dynastic politics of MUNSTER during the 960s (*see* DAL CAIS; MATHGAMAIN) to dominate that kingdom, and over the next 30 years gradually asserted his control over the coastal VIKING settlements (*see* DUBLIN) and over other Irish kings. Notable landmarks in his rise to power include: the battle of BELACH LECHTA (978), which established his power in Munster; the submission of LEINSTER in 983; the capture of Dublin in 999; and the submission of the UÍ NÉILL high-king MÁEL SECHNAILL II in 1002.

Brian's successes always rested on a fragile military basis, and in 1014 he was killed fighting against an alliance of Vikings and Irish at the battle of CLONTARF. His achievements were somewhat misleadingly elevated to heroic status by the 12th-century biography *Wars of the Gaedhil against the Gaill.*

Bridewell, a house of correction or prison. The name derives from HENRY VIII's Bridewell Palace in Blackfriars, London, erected near the site of the holy well of St Bridget (St Bride; *c.* 450–523) to house the Emperor Charles V on a royal visit. In 1553, EDWARD VI gave this to the City of LONDON as a WORKHOUSE for unruly apprentices and vagrants. It also administered a facility for the insane – Bethlehem Royal Hospital, commonly known as BEDLAM – and was linked with Christ's Hospital for destitute children and St Thomas's and St Bartholomew's for the sick. The scheme was widely admired, and HOUSES OF CORRECTION, often termed 'bridewells', were set up by town and county MAGISTRATES throughout the country over the next century, though they were often not so much workhouses as gaols for the poor. *See also* POOR RELIEF.

Bridewell was reconstructed in 1676 after the Great Fire of London with facilities for the public to spectate at punishments, and in the 17th and 18th centuries visitors flocked to see a good whipping. The Bridewell in London was closed in 1855 and demolished eight years later.

Bridge-Work In Anglo-Saxon England, the construction and repair of bridges by landholders was one of the three fundamental elements of the COMMON BURDENS that were the basis of the kingdom's defence system.

Bridgettines, *see* SYON ABBEY

Bridgwater Canal Built by Francis Egerton, 3rd Duke of Bridgwater (1756–1803), to transport the large coal deposits from his Worsley estate, near Wigan, to Manchester, the project was directed by James Brindley and completed in 1761. Although not the first canal to be built in Britain, it was one of the most successful, lowering transport costs and thus reducing the price of coal to local consumers. It made a handsome profit for the Bridgwater Canal Co. and encouraged others to invest in similar ventures. *See also* CANALS.

Brigantes, one of the most important tribes that dominated pre-Roman Britain. They controlled a territory roughly approximate to modern England north of the Humber, although there were certainly sub-tribes settled within the same region (*see* CARVETII and PARISI). The Brigantes appear to have entered into an alliance with the Romans very soon after the latter arrived in AD 43 (*see* CLIENT KINGDOMS) – the Brigante queen CARTIMANDUA handed over the British resistance leader CARATACUS in 51. There were, none the less, tensions within the Brigantes, which culminated in the driving out of Cartimandua in 69 and the subsequent military conquest by PETILLIUS CERIALIS between 71 and 74.

The Brigantes appear never to have become fully reconciled to Roman rule. Although a *CIVITAS* was established around YORK and Aldbrough in the time of the Emperor HADRIAN, much of the rest of the region between the Humber and HADRIAN'S WALL continued to be controlled by garrison forts during the remaining centuries of Roman domination. There are also references to native rebellions, such as the one that took place in 154–5, which caused the Romans to pull back from the ANTONINE WALL.

Bright, John (1811–89), radical politician. Son of a QUAKER carpet manufacturer from Rochdale, Lancs., he was an ardent FREE TRADER, a leader of the ANTI-CORN LAW LEAGUE and a member of the Peace Society. He entered Parliament in 1843, where he attacked aristocracy and privilege, and opposed the CRIMEAN WAR and the Confederacy during the American Civil War. A supporter of progress and democracy and a powerful orator, he was an advocate of temperance reform, spoke in favour of the abolition of CAPITAL PUNISHMENT, and introduced a bill for the repeal of the GAME LAWS. He favoured the removal of civil and political disabilities from British Jews, and supported PARLIAMENTARY REFORM, an extension of the FRANCHISE and BRADLAUGH'S request for permission to affirm in place of the oath of allegiance. He attained Cabinet rank but broke with GLADSTONE over Irish HOME RULE.

Brighton, Sussex seaside town which became popular from the mid-18th century. The advocacy of sea bathing by Dr Russell from 1750 and his development of local SPA waters brought the fashionable to the former fishing village, among them GEORGE IV when Prince Regent. The fantastical Indian-Moorish-style Royal Pavilion, built by the architect John Nash in 1815–22, was the last in a sequence of seaside houses built there for the Prince. Meanwhile, Brighton was growing as a place of genteel resort, with its crescents, villas and terraces built to accommodate residents and visitors; with the RAILWAYS it became a town of general holiday-making and now conference-holding. Its proximity to London and rather louche air gave Brighton a degree of notoriety on which it still trades.

Bristol In the late Saxon period a commercial centre developed at the lowest possible road-crossing of the Som./Glos. River Avon ('Bridge-stow', i.e. the place of the bridge); the town was important enough for a major royal castle to be built there from *c.* 1120. During the Middle Ages and into the early 18th century Bristol was second as a city only to LONDON; it was made a county of itself in 1373. St Augustine's Abbey was converted into a CATHEDRAL in 1542. Bristol's prosperity was much bolstered in the 17th and 18th centuries by the growth of trade with America, including the SLAVE TRADE, and it developed its own SPA at Hotwells. However, massive expenditure attempting to solve the problems of the dock facilities made its harbour dues less competitive than newer ports like LIVERPOOL, leading to relative decline; henceforward its prosperity was based on manufacture, notably in the 19th and 20th centuries TOBACCO and chocolate, and in the 20th century, armaments.

Bristol, Treaty of, 28 Aug. 1574, a treaty between England and Spain, which sought to end trading disputes. It failed to bring lasting peace.

Britain, Battle of, 1940, decisive aerial conflict in WORLD WAR II between the ROYAL AIR FORCE and the German *Luftwaffe*. Following the fall of France in June 1940 the Germans sought to win air superiority over the English Channel and southern England in order to mount their invasion, Operation SEALION, or force Britain to come to peace terms. From July to September 1940 under Air Chief Marshal Hugh Dowding's (1882–1970) leadership RAF Fighter Command (heavily outnumbered but benefiting from effective use of RADAR and ground control and, in the front line, of Spitfire and Hurricane fighter planes) engaged enemy formations, inflicting sufficiently severe losses to convince the Germans that they had failed to secure air supremacy while greatly stiffening British morale. On 20 Aug. CHURCHILL proclaimed the 'battle' won and praised 'the few', though heavy air battles continued. A switch in German tactics to the BLITZ on British cities rather than attacks on RAF airfields in early Sept. finally eased the pressure. Each side at the time greatly exaggerated the other's losses, but the Germans are estimated to have lost over 1,700 aircraft compared with over 900 British.

Britannia, the name given to the two provinces of the Roman Empire comprising roughly half what is now England and Wales: Britannia Inferior and Britannia Superior. *See also* ROMAN CONQUEST OF BRITAIN.

British and Foreign Bible Society The largest of the BIBLE SOCIETIES, it was an interdenominational lay body founded in London in 1804 to print and distribute the Bible at home and abroad. *See also* MISSIONARY SOCIETIES.

British Association for the Advancement of Science Founded in 1831 to stimulate scientific inquiry and promote the diffusion of scientific knowledge, it still holds an annual week-long session in one of the major provincial centres, publishes its proceedings and remains the principal pressure group concerned with science education.

British Columbia Settlement in the westernmost province of CANADA began largely with the GOLD RUSH of the 1860s, although Spain had ceded her interests in the early 19th century and Fort Victoria was established on Vancouver Island in 1843. Linked to the rest of Canada by the transcontinental Canadian Pacific RAILWAY, but separated physically and psychologically by the Rocky Mountains, British Columbia joined the Canadian Federation in 1871.

British Commonwealth, *see* COMMONWEALTH, BRITISH

British Empire At its height at the beginning of the 20th century, it covered more than one-fifth of the land mass of the globe and was the largest empire the world had ever known. GEORGE V reigned over 11,400,000 sq. miles of territory and a population of 410 million. Moreover, the British Empire differed from its predecessors in that its territory was not continuous, or even relatively continuous. Its ramifications embraced every continent; its interests were paramount on every sea.

The expanse of its territory was matched only by the complexity of its organization. The empire included:

— self-governing DOMINIONS – AUSTRALIA, CANADA, NEW ZEALAND and the Union of SOUTH AFRICA

— crown colonies not possessing responsible government – some with an elected house of assembly, some with a partly legislative council, some with a legislative council nominated by the crown, and some without any such provision

— a number of dependencies indirectly controlled by the secretary of state for the colonies, and a miscellaneous collection of territories administered by the India Office, the Foreign Office (EGYPT), the Admiralty (ASCENSION ISLAND, technically a 'man-of-war' under the Admiralty) and the Home Office (CHANNEL ISLANDS).

This complexity reflected the haphazard manner in which imperial power had been built up – by settlement, conquest and annexation, sometimes in response to the fortunes of war, or the exigencies of strategy, or the need to secure order in outlying territories. The foundations were laid in the century 1750–1850, during which Britain acquired INDIA, Australia, Canada, New Zealand, CAPE COLONY, GIBRALTAR, HONG KONG, BRITISH GUIANA, BRITISH HONDURAS, sundry islands, and various colonies on the African coast. The imperial upsurge of the late 19th century saw the acquisition of new territories as INFORMAL EMPIRE gave way to more direct controls during the SCRAMBLE FOR AFRICA. The zenith of empire came at the end of WORLD WAR I with the acquisition of new mandates for the territories of the defunct Turkish Empire in the Middle East and German colonies in Africa. By then, nationalism was becoming as disruptive to the British as it had been to their predecessors, and it served to accelerate the transfer of power which, in respect of the Dominions, had been a gradual and peaceful affair, but which was undertaken with unseemly haste after WORLD WAR II (*see* DECOLONIZATION).

The British Empire deeply influenced –

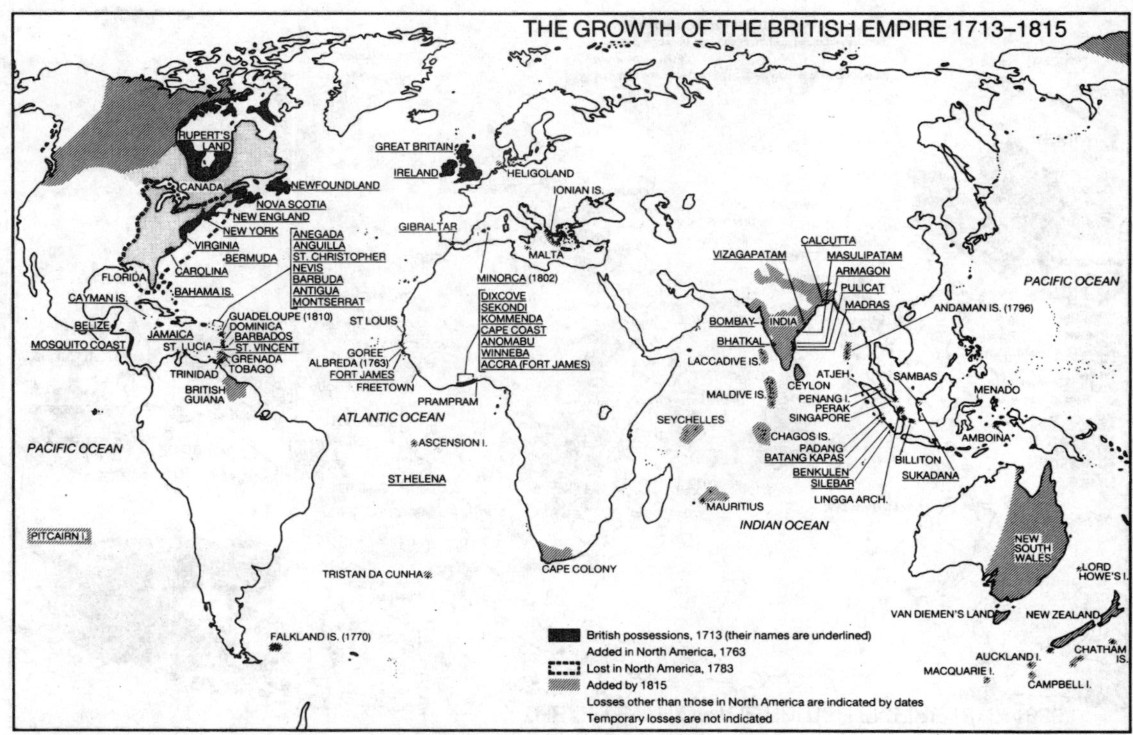
THE GROWTH OF THE BRITISH EMPIRE 1713–1815
RUPERT'S LAND
CANADA
GREAT BRITAIN
IRELAND
HELIGOLAND
NEWFOUNDLAND
NOVA SCOTIA
NEW ENGLAND
NEW YORK
VIRGINIA
BERMUDA
CAROLINA
FLORIDA
BAHAMA IS.
CAYMAN IS.
BELIZE
JAMAICA
MOSQUITO COAST
ANEGADA
ANGUILLA
ST. CHRISTOPHER
NEVIS
BARBUDA
ANTIGUA
MONTSERRAT
GUADELOUPE (1810)
DOMINICA
BARBADOS
ST. LUCIA
ST. VINCENT
GRENADA
TOBAGO
TRINIDAD
BRITISH GUIANA
IONIAN IS.
GIBRALTAR
MALTA
MINORCA (1802)
ST LOUIS
GOREE
ALBREDA (1763)
FORT JAMES
FREETOWN
DIXCOVE
SEKONDI
KOMMENDA
CAPE COAST
ANOMABU
WINNEBA
ACCRA (FORT JAMES)
PRAMPRAM
ATLANTIC OCEAN
ASCENSION I.
PACIFIC OCEAN
ST HELENA
PITCAIRN I.
TRISTAN DA CUNHA
CAPE COLONY
FALKLAND IS. (1770)
CALCUTTA
VIZAGAPATAM
MASULIPATAM
ARMAGON
PULICAT
MADRAS
PACIFIC OCEAN
ANDAMAN IS. (1796)
BOMBAY
INDIA
BHATKAL
LACCADIVE IS.
ATJEH
SAMBAS
CEYLON
MENADO
MALDIVE IS.
PENANG I.
PERAK
SINGAPORE
SEYCHELLES
CHAGOS IS.
AMBOINA
PADANG
BATANG KAPAS
BILLITON
BENKULEN
SUKADANA
SILEBAR
LINGGA ARCH.
MAURITIUS
INDIAN OCEAN
NEW SOUTH WALES
LORD HOWE'S I.
VAN DIEMEN'S LAND
NEW ZEALAND
British possessions, 1713 (their names are underlined)
Added in North America, 1763
Lost in North America, 1783
Added by 1815
Losses other than those in North America are indicated by dates
Temporary losses are not indicated
AUCKLAND I.
CHATHAM IS.
MACQUARIE I.
CAMPBELL I.

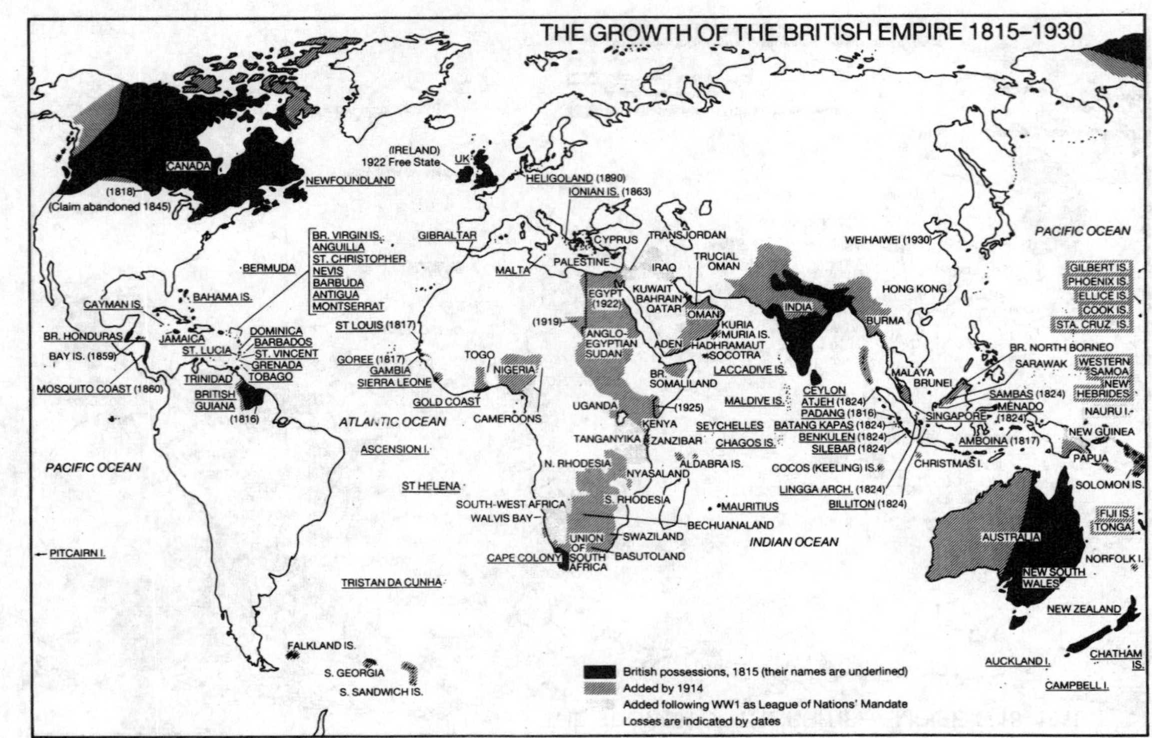
THE GROWTH OF THE BRITISH EMPIRE 1815–1930
PACIFIC OCEAN
ATLANTIC OCEAN
INDIAN OCEAN
CANADA
(1818)
(Claim abandoned 1845)
NEWFOUNDLAND
(IRELAND)
1922 Free State
UK
HELIGOLAND (1890)
IONIAN IS. (1863)
GIBRALTAR
MALTA
CYPRUS
PALESTINE
TRANSJORDAN
IRAQ
KUWAIT
BAHRAIN
QATAR
TRUCIAL
OMAN
EGYPT
(1922)
(1919)
ANGLO-
EGYPTIAN
SUDAN
ADEN
HADHRAMAUT
SOCOTRA
KURIA
MURIA IS.
BR.
SOMALILAND
(1925)
KENYA
UGANDA
TANGANYIKA
ZANZIBAR
ALDABRA IS.
SEYCHELLES
NYASALAND
N. RHODESIA
S. RHODESIA
BECHUANALAND
SWAZILAND
BASUTOLAND
UNION
OF
SOUTH
AFRICA
CAPE COLONY
SOUTH-WEST AFRICA
WALVIS BAY
MAURITIUS
CHAGOS IS.
MALDIVE IS.
LACCADIVE IS.
INDIA
CEYLON
BURMA
HONG KONG
WEIHAIWEI (1930)
MALAYA
BRUNEI
SARAWAK
BR. NORTH BORNEO
SINGAPORE
ATJEH (1824)
PADANG (1816)
BATANG KAPAS (1824)
BENKULEN (1824)
SILEBAR (1824)
COCOS (KEELING) IS.
LINGGA ARCH. (1824)
BILLITON (1824)
CHRISTMAS I.
SAMBAS (1824)
MENADO
(1824)
AMBOINA (1817)
NAURU I.
NEW GUINEA
PAPUA
SOLOMON IS.
GILBERT IS.
PHOENIX IS.
ELLICE IS.
COOK IS.
STA. CRUZ IS.
WESTERN SAMOA
NEW HEBRIDES
FIJI IS.
TONGA
NORFOLK I.
AUSTRALIA
NEW SOUTH WALES
NEW ZEALAND
CHATHAM IS.
AUCKLAND I.
CAMPBELL I.
BERMUDA
BAHAMA IS.
CAYMAN IS.
JAMAICA
BR. HONDURAS
BAY IS. (1859)
MOSQUITO COAST (1860)
BR. VIRGIN IS.
ANGUILLA
ST. CHRISTOPHER
NEVIS
BARBUDA
ANTIGUA
MONTSERRAT
DOMINICA
BARBADOS
ST. VINCENT
GRENADA
TOBAGO
ST. LUCIA
TRINIDAD
BRITISH GUIANA
(1816)
ST LOUIS (1817)
GOREE (1817)
GAMBIA
SIERRA LEONE
GOLD COAST
TOGO
NIGERIA
CAMEROONS
ASCENSION I.
ST HELENA
TRISTAN DA CUNHA
FALKLAND IS.
S. GEORGIA
S. SANDWICH IS.
PITCAIRN I.
British possessions, 1815 (their names are underlined)
Added by 1914
Added following WW1 as League of Nations' Mandate
Losses are indicated by dates

for good and ill – all who came into contact with it. Its passing, experienced as something of a trauma in the post-war period, was indicative not only of the nation's reduced circumstances, but also of the profound cultural influence exerted by the imperial experience upon the British people. *See also* ADEN; AFRICA; ALBERTA; AMERICAN INDEPENDENCE, WAR OF; ANGUILLA; ANTIGUA; AUSTRALIA; BAHAMAS; BARBADOS; BASUTOLAND; BECHUANALAND; BERMUDA; BOER WARS; BRITISH COLUMBIA; BRITISH EMPIRE, FIRST AND SECOND; BRITISH GUIANA; BRITISH HONDURAS; BRITISH INDIAN OCEAN TERRITORIES; BRITISH NORTH AMERICA ACT; BRITISH VIRGIN ISLANDS; BURMA; CANADA; CAPE COLONY; CAROLINA, NORTH & SOUTH; CAYMAN ISLANDS; CENTRAL AFRICAN FEDERATION; CEYLON; CLIVE, ROBERT; COMMONWEALTH; CYPRUS; DARIEN SCHEME; DECOLONIZATION; DELAWARE; DOMINICA, COMMONWEALTH OF; DOMINIONS; EGYPT; FALKLAND ISLANDS; FIJI; GAMBIA, THE; GEORGIA; GIBRALTAR; GOLD COAST; GRENADA; HONG KONG; INDIA; INDIAN INDEPENDENCE; INFORMAL EMPIRE; IRAQI MANDATE; IRISH QUESTION; JAMAICA; KENYA; LEEWARD ISLANDS FEDERATION; MAINE; MALAYA; MANITOBA; MARYLAND; MASSACHUSETTS; MAURITIUS; MONTSERRAT; NEW BRUNSWICK; NEW ENGLAND; NEW HAMPSHIRE; NEW SOUTH WALES; NEW WORLD, EARLY BRITISH INVOLVEMENT IN; NEW YORK; NEW ZEALAND; NEWFOUNDLAND; NIGERIA; NORTHERN TERRITORY; NORTHWEST TERRITORIES; NOVA SCOTIA; NYASALAND; ONTARIO; OTTAWA CONFERENCE; PAKISTAN; PALESTINE; PARIS, TREATY OF; PITCAIRN; PLANTATION ECONOMIES; PRINCE EDWARD ISLAND; QUEBEC; QUEENSLAND; RHODES, CECIL; RHODESIA, NORTHERN; RHODESIA, SOUTHERN; SASKATCHEWAN; SCRAMBLE FOR AFRICA; SINGAPORE; SLAVERY; SOLOMON ISLANDS; SOUTH AFRICA; ST HELENA; ST KITTS & NEVIS; ST LUCIA; STRAITS SETTLEMENTS; ST VINCENT & THE GRENADINES; SUGAR; SWAZILAND; TANGANYIKA; TASMANIA; TONGA; TRINIDAD & TOBAGO; TRISTAN DA CUNHA; TURKS & CAICOS ISLANDS; UGANDA; VANUATU; VICTORIA; VIRGINIA; WEST INDIES; WESTERN AUSTRALIA; 'WIND OF CHANGE' SPEECH; WINDWARD ISLANDS FEDERATION; ZANZIBAR.

British Empire, First and Second, terms used by historians to distinguish the primarily North American and WEST INDIAN empire built up by England, later Britain, between the 16th century and late 18th-century loss of the 13 American colonies on the one hand and, on the other hand, the more easterly-oriented empire which developed, with INDIA as the 'jewel in the crown', thereafter.

British Expeditionary Force (BEF) 1914, four divisions – later reinforced to six – and a cavalry division sent to France at the start of WORLD WAR I under Sir John FRENCH. Probably the best British Army in history, it was known as the 'Old Contemptibles' from the Kaiser's description of 'French's contemptibly little army'. Small compared to continental armies but of very high quality, it played an important role in checking the Germans at MONS and again at the MARNE. Throughout the war, the official title of the British Army on the Western Front remained the BEF.

1939–40 Much less well prepared than its World War I equivalent, the BEF sent to France under Lord Gort on the outbreak of WORLD WAR II in 1939 was reinforced by 1940 to 10 divisions (including Territorials) and a tank brigade. Although it performed competently, the general Allied collapse following the German attack of May 1940 led to its evacuation through DUNKIRK, losing most of its equipment.

British Guiana, former British colony in South America, renamed Guyana on becoming a republic. Associated with RALEIGH's fruitless search for Eldorado, it was settled by the Dutch from 1616. It and its island neighbours were held by the Dutch (in exchange for NEW YORK) from the 1667 Treaty of BREDA until captured by Britain in 1796. Restored to the Dutch in 1802, the colony was almost immediately retaken; British possession was secured in 1814. Coffee, COTTON and SUGAR became the staple crops. Independence in 1966 was followed by the formation of a socialist republic.

British Honduras, Central American

former colony, now Belize. English settlers came from JAMAICA in 1640, but Britain only claimed possession after neighbouring Guatemala and Mexico became independent from Spain in 1821. The borders were recognized in 1859, with Belize colony established in 1862 and the crown colony of British Honduras in 1871. Guatemala's claim to it has persisted since 1859, and a British military presence was maintained after independence in 1981.

British Indian Ocean Territories Formerly the Oil Islands, and once providing coconut oil for lamps, this collection of eleven small islands in the central Indian Ocean remains British territory. It was constituted as a separate territory in 1965 upon the independence of MAURITIUS and the Seychelles. One island, Diego Garcia, became a strategic American military base in clandestine deals subsequently made with the USA; and international scandal ensued when it was discovered that the 2,000 islanders had been forcibly evicted.

British Museum One of the world's great collections of antiquities, it was instituted in 1759, emulating the great continental collections. Initially it housed Sir John Cotton's library, preserved for public use by Parliament in 1700, Sir Hans Sloane's library and collection of curiosities and natural history, acquired by bequest in 1753, and the HARLEY collection of manuscripts, purchased in the same year. The Royal Library was added to the collection in 1822. Money was raised by lottery to buy Montagu House, Bloomsbury, London; admission was initially restricted, but in 1784 a bill to introduce admission charges was defeated. The collection was augmented by gifts and purchases from collectors: James COOK and Sir Joseph Banks, for example, sent specimens collected on their voyages, while the expansion of ARCHAEOLOGY and imperial gains in the 19th century considerably augmented the collections. Under successive Copyright Acts, the Museum's library became a national collection. The famous circular Reading Room was built in 1852–7 by Sidney Smirke, completing the new Museum buildings begun in 1823. In 1973 the library was separated from the Museum to form the British Library. There was a protracted struggle to provide it with a purpose-made building (eventually on a site beside St Pancras Station, to the designs of Colin St John Wilson). The new British Library finally opened in August 1998.

British North America Act 1867 A measure designed to improve the unity and cohesion of CANADA and enable it to resist possible aggression from the United States, it created a self-governing federation of four provinces (NEW BRUNSWICK, NOVA SCOTIA, ONTARIO and QUEBEC) along the lines sketched by Lord Durham. Each province was allowed to retain its own local government, parliament and ministry under a lieutenant-governor nominated by the governor-general. A DOMINION Parliament, with a nominated senate and representative assembly, met at Ottawa to decide questions affecting the Dominion. MANITOBA joined in 1870, BRITISH COLUMBIA in 1871, PRINCE EDWARD ISLAND in 1873, and ALBERTA and SASKATCHEWAN in 1905. The Dominion of Canada was independent of Britain apart from the link provided by the crown, and marked a significant stage in the development of the BRITISH EMPIRE towards RESPONSIBLE GOVERNMENT.

British Survival in England The near-total absence of documentary evidence for the period during which the ANGLES, SAXONS and JUTES settled in Britain (*see* ANGLO-SAXON SETTLEMENT) makes the survival of the indigenous British peoples within the territory that later became England one of the most complex of historical problems. It is particularly difficult to decide how far they survived in eastern and southern England, the areas of most intense settlement by the newcomers.

It was once thought that the domination of the (evolving) ENGLISH LANGUAGE everywhere by the 9th century – as well as, in the east and south, the near-complete absence of British PLACE NAMES – suggested that the British had been exterminated, but this view is nowadays rejected. Language is seen as a reflection of political domination, and an impressive range of evidence in such forms as estate boundaries, stray archaeological remains, river names and the relatively small number of graves in Anglo-Saxon CEMETERIES all suggest British survival everywhere, often as a majority of the local population.

British Union of Fascists, *see* FASCISTS, BRITISH UNION OF

British Virgin Islands, crown colony, comprising some 60 Caribbean islands. Originally settled by the Dutch, they were acquired by Britain in 1666. Administered in the LEEWARD ISLANDS FEDERATION between 1872 and 1956, they have since had separate administration.

Britons, *see* BRITISH SURVIVAL

Brittany, British Settlement in The migration of numerous Britons from the south-western regions of the British Isles during the period from the 4th to the early 7th century, well attested in early sources such as GILDAS and in saints' lives, profoundly changed the character of the former Roman province of Armorica, as well as providing it with both its modern name and the Breton language. The numerous CELTIC PLACE NAMES in northern and western Brittany show the direction of migration; however, its causes and scale are much debated.

The turbulence in western Britain resulting from the attacks of ANGLES, SAXONS, PICTS and SCOTS may have contributed to it, as must the long-standing religious connections typified by the careers of such Church figures as St SAMSON OF DOL and the dedication of Cornish churches to Breton saints and vice versa. However, no simple explanation of this notable movement of peoples is likely ever to emerge; the migrations were one among many that took place during this period.

Broad Bottom Ministry, 18th-century term for a broadly based, or non-partisan ministry. It was particularly applied to PELHAM's ministry of 1744–6, comprising the OLD CORPS WHIGS and 'New Allies', former opposition Whigs including John Russell, 7th Duke of Bedford, Chesterfield and PITT THE ELDER. A few TORIES were also given office. Cartoonists exploited the term's comic potential, particularly in the corpulent form of the Tory Sir John Hynde Cotton.

Broad Church, a term used in the 19th century to describe a loose aggregation of Anglicans who avoided the doctrinal and ecclesiastical issues that divided the HIGH CHURCH and EVANGELICAL movements. Broad Churchmen stressed the national, comprehensive character of the Church of England, and shared a common rejection of doctrines they considered morally indefensible (e.g. the punishment of eternal hell), an acceptance of the results of modern scientific and historical methods, and a toleration of theological and religious diversity (*see* LIBERALISM, THEOLOGICAL). The work of the Broad Churchmen culminated in *ESSAYS AND REVIEWS* (1860), an attack on biblical literalism. Major figures were F. D. Maurice, Charles Kingsley, the CHRISTIAN SOCIALISTS in general, and the biblical scholar Benjamin Jowett. The term has entered general usage to connote any organization that encompasses or claims to tolerate a wide spectrum of views among its members. *See also* CHURCH: ENGLAND.

Brooke, Sir Alan (1st Viscount Alanbrooke) (1883–1963), soldier. From a military family he was commissioned in the Royal Artillery in 1902 and went to France with the India Corps in 1914; by the end of WORLD WAR I he was a brigadier-general. During the inter-war years he was a student and instructor in several military colleges before being appointed director of military training at the war office in 1936; and in July 1938 he was promoted to lieutenant-general and charged with organizing the air defence of Britain in case of aerial attack. On the outbreak of WORLD WAR II he was given command of II Corps of the BRITISH EXPEDITIONARY FORCE; after its evacuation at DUNKIRK, which he had fought Winston CHURCHILL to authorize, Brooke was knighted and in July appointed commander-in-chief of home forces, responsible for the defence of Britain against the expected German invasion. In Nov. 1941 he succeeded Sir John Dill in the politically difficult position of chief of the imperial general staff, and by March 1942 was effectively professional head of the ARMY and, as such, the man responsible for representing the advice of the combined services to the prime minister and the war CABINET.

Brooke, who had been vetoed by the Americans to direct the Allied invasion of Normandy, was pessimistic about the success of Operation OVERLORD, and believed that the Axis forces should be defeated in North Africa and southern Europe before a cross-Channel assault was attempted. His long-sighted strategy won the day at the CASABLANCA CONFERENCE in Jan. 1943, but his battles both with the Americans – he was particularly opposed to Operation Anvil, the landing of allied troops in southern France – and Churchill (who at one time wanted British troops to engage the Japanese forces in Sumatra) were constant. Brooke was promoted to field marshal in Jan. 1944, and at the end of the war had the task of reorganizing the army for its peacetime role. He retired in 1946 after a distinguished career as a strategist, crucial in curbing the excesses of Churchill's imaginative military initiatives.

Brothels, *see* STEWS

Brougham, Henry (1st Baron Brougham and Vaux) (1778–1868), lawyer and social reformer. A man of wide intellectual interests and enormous energy, he was a founder and regular contributor to the *EDINBURGH REVIEW*, a fervent opponent of the SLAVE TRADE (*see also* ANTI-SLAVERY), a great educationalist, and an outstanding legal reformer. He held office as lord chancellor from 1830 to 1834 and played an important role in the REFORM ACT debates. But he is best remembered for his defence of Queen CAROLINE in 1820 and for the type of horse-drawn carriage that bears his name. His RADICALISM – practical rather than visionary – made a significant contribution to the campaign for a more humane and democratic society.

Bruce, Edward (?–1318), King of Ireland (1316–18). As younger brother of Robert BRUCE and heir-presumptive to the Scottish throne, he was a key figure in the Bruces' policy of uniting the Celtic peoples of the British Isles against English domination. In 1315, he led a Scottish army across the Irish Sea and was proclaimed King of Ireland by his Gaelic supporters. The great famine of 1315–17 made military operations difficult, however, and although there was one moment in Feb. 1317 when it looked as though DUBLIN might fall into his hands, his authority was rarely acknowledged outside ULSTER. In Oct. 1318, he was defeated and killed at the battle of Faughart (near Dundalk).

Bruce, Robert (Robert I) (1274–1329), King of Scots (1306–29). The story of the patriot king – who, by a mixture of patience and daring, recaptured nearly all the Scottish castles held by the English until he was at last strong enough to confront the challenge of a full-scale invasion personally led by the king of England – is one of the great heroic romances of British history, and was told as such in John Barbour's epic poem. *The Bruce*, composed in the 1370s. Yet initially Bruce's secret hopes of obtaining the Scottish crown, as grandson of one of the competitors in the GREAT CAUSE, meant that he could be no more than a lukewarm and occasional supporter of the wars of SCOTTISH INDEPENDENCE for as long as they were waged in the name of John BALLIOL.

However, by his sacrilegious murder of the Red COMYN in Greyfriars kirk at Dumfries in Feb. 1306, he simultaneously revealed the extent of his ambition and publicly committed himself to the path of war. Enthroned at SCONE in March, he was defeated at Methven in June and became a fugitive while EDWARD I hunted down his family and friends.

More than anything else, the succession of the inept EDWARD II to the English throne in 1307 saved Bruce's cause, but his active and shrewd leadership was also crucial. At Inverurie in 1308, he defeated the partisans of Comyn and Balliol and then used their confiscated estates to reward Thomas Randolph and James Douglas (who was to carry Bruce's heart into battle against the 'Saracens' of Granada). He dismantled castles captured from the English to deprive the occupying forces of potential strongpoints, and for as long as possible, he avoided battle against the main English army. However, when the unavoidable challenge came at BANNOCKBURN in 1314, he demonstrated both intelligence and prowess.

This victory enabled him to open up another front in the shape of his brother Edward BRUCE's invasion of Ireland (1315–18), appealing to pan-Gaelic patriotism. A series of raids on the north of

England further increased pressure on the English, and in 1318, Robert Bruce captured BERWICK. Despite the fine words of the Declaration of ARBROATH, his position in 1320 was still far from unassailable – as the ferociously suppressed conspiracy to put William de Soules on the throne attests. However, by the time of the Cambuskenneth Parliament (1326), an innovative grant of taxation and the settlement of the succession on his long-awaited legitimate son, the future DAVID II, all suggested that the new dynasty was firmly established. One more devastating attack across the border finally brought the recognition of Bruce's kingship from the English government, in the treaty of NORTHAMPTON of 1328.

Brude mac Bili, King of the Picts (*c.*672–93). Controversy surrounds the manner by which Brude acquired kingship over the southern PICTS. The latest theory suggests that his kingship represented a resurgence of the lordship of the STRATHCLYDE Britons over the southern Picts after the death of the previous overlord, OSWY of NORTHUMBRIA, in 670. Whatever the case, Brude's reign is especially important because his victory over ECGFRITH of Northumbria at NECHTANESMERE in 685 ensured that Northumbrian power was henceforth confined to south of the Forth.

Brunanburh, Battle of, 937, King ATHELSTAN's great victory against an army led by OLAF GUTHRICSSON, King of DUBLIN, and the Kings of the Scots and Strathclyde (*see* CONSTANTINE II). The conflict was the result of the alarm that Athelstan's military expansion had caused among his British and Scandinavian neighbours. The site of the battle is unknown; it may have been in the east Midlands.

Brunel, Isambard Kingdom (1806–59), engineer and inventor. Brunel was one of the greatest, and most self-publicizing, engineers of the Victorian age. His supreme surviving achievement is the former Great Western Railway, with its many tunnels and viaducts, constructed between 1835 and 1841, and the London terminus at Paddington station, built 1850–4. Its original 7-feet broad-gauge track eventually had to be altered under the GAUGE ACT. Brunel designed the *GREAT WESTERN* (1838), the first ocean-going screw-steamer GREAT BRITAIN (1845), and the *GREAT EASTERN* (1857). He also constructed suspension bridges, notably that at Clifton, Bristol, as well as docks.

Brunswick, House of, *see* HANOVERIAN SUCCESSION

Brussels, Treaty of, a fifty-year guarantee of mutual military assistance signed on 17 March 1948 between Great Britain, France, Belgium, the Netherlands and Luxembourg. Joined by West Germany and Italy in 1955, the organization set up under this treaty was known as the Western European Union (WEU). Of little significance following the formation of NATO under American leadership in the following year, the WEU emerged with the ending of the COLD WAR as a forum for military and other discussion concerning future peace and stability in Europe.

Brut, name by which the most popular of late medieval English chronicles was known. The name came from Brutus, the fictional Trojan prince whose claim as the first ruler of Britain had been given wide currency by GEOFFREY OF MONMOUTH. So popular was this anonymous work that in English and Welsh the word 'brut' came to mean 'chronicle'. The French prose original (which should be distinguished from Lawman's (*fl.* 1200) Middle English verse *Brut*) summarized Geoffrey's 'history', then added a more sober account of events up to the time of writing (EDWARD I's reign). Translated into English and Latin, and extended in various versions up to the 15th century, it survives in more than 200 manuscripts and, as CAXTON's *Chronicles of England*, was the first English history to be printed. *See also* WACE.

Brut y Tywysogion ('Chronicle of the Princes'), a set of annals written originally in Latin but surviving only in Welsh translation, which continued the history of the Britons from where GEOFFREY OF MONMOUTH left off. They cover Welsh history from 681 (the abdication of Cadwaladr) to 1282 (EDWARD I's conquest).

Bryce Commission, 1894–5. Appointed under the chairmanship of LIBERAL intellectual James Bryce to consider the creation of a coherent system of secondary EDUCATION in England, it recommended the unification of elementary and secondary education within a single department under the supervision of a minister of education. This was embodied in the Board of Education Act of 1899. Secondary education was thereafter regarded as part of an integrated national system of provision.

Brycheiniog Although there are references to a kingdom of Brycheiniog (Brecon) existing from the 8th to the early 10th centuries, the scarcity of sources for early Welsh history makes it unclear whether it had an earlier or later history. Frequently suffering the depredations of its more powerful neighbours – the kings of GWYNEDD and the English – it was apparently absorbed into Gwynedd in the 10th century and conquered by the Normans. *See also* KINGSHIP.

Bubble Act 1720, passed at the height of the South Sea speculative frenzy with the backing of the SOUTH SEA COMPANY as a means of sustaining the price of its shares against competitors in the stock market. The Act did not prevent the collapse of the Bubble but, until its repeal in 1825, it severely inhibited the formation of new JOINT STOCK companies with transferable stock. *See also* LIMITED LIABILITIES ACT 1855; STOCK EXCHANGE.

Bubonic Plague, highly infectious epidemic disease attacking the lymphatic system which probably first appeared in Europe as the BLACK DEATH pandemic of 1348–9, and returned to England at regular intervals thereafter until it disappeared in the 1660s in the wake of the GREAT PLAGUE. The pathogen, *pasteurella pestis*, has since been shown to be associated with fleas carried on rats, and may well have been endemic in some resident black rat populations; when infected fleas bit humans, plague resulted. Outbreaks came to be associated particularly with dense urban populations, notably LONDON; MORTALITY rates were high, and death came very quickly when the variant forms, septicaemic or pneumonic plague, developed. The reasons for the disappearance of the plague have been argued over vigorously, with the disappearance of the black rat and the rebuilding of London after the GREAT FIRE often advanced as causes. Historians now point more readily to the growing effectiveness of quarantine measures across Europe, and in England particularly, preventing the movement of traffic which probably carried infected fleas and rats.

Buckingham, 4th Duke of, *see* VILLIERS, GEORGE

Buckingham's Rebellion, Oct.–Nov. 1483. The name is conventionally given to a revolt, largely of the southern English counties, in the name of Henry Tudor (the future HENRY VII), which broke out in the wake of rumours that RICHARD III had murdered his nephews, the 'Princes in the Tower' (*see* EDWARD V). The rebellion was swiftly suppressed.

The principal rebels, mostly former members of EDWARD IV's household, must have been as astonished as historians have been ever since when Henry Stafford, Duke of Buckingham, joined the conspiracy. Since only a few months before he, much more than anyone else, had helped put Richard on the throne, his participation was disconcerting and very puzzling. This can have done little for the confidence and determination of the other rebels or to encourage others to take the huge – life-risking – gamble of revolt.

Buellt A kingdom of Buellt (Builth, Powys) is recorded in 8th- and 9th-century sources, but given the scarcity of written evidence for early Welsh history, it is unclear whether it existed before or after this. The latter is unlikely, since it would probably have been absorbed into the kingdom of GWYNEDD. The political fluidity and the ephemeral nature implied by its history are typical of early Welsh KINGSHIP.

Building Societies, mutual savings and loan organizations intended to provide for the purchase of houses. Emerging out of mutual societies in late Georgian northern England, and FRIENDLY SOCIETIES, and subject to increased regulation from 1836 onwards, they came to underpin the growing owner-occupation of HOUSING from the early 20th century to the present day. By 1940, after considerable expansion in the 1930s, there were 1.5 million borrowers from building societies, which had risen to 5.3 million by 1979. As building societies became more active financial institutions, so the process of consolidation and takeover also seen in BANKS occurred, and the MORTGAGE interest rate has become since WORLD WAR II a matter of public and political concern. Following the Building Societies Acts (1986 and 1997) which permitted societies to undertake an unrestricted range of activities in the financial services and housing markets, the sector has been contracting with a large number of societies abandoning their mutual status to become banks – a move often encouraged by investors, in some cases against the advice of the Society's boards – for the 'windfall' of shares these changes bring.

Bulgarian Agitation, 1876. A phase of the EASTERN QUESTION, it arose out of a series of conflicts between Turkey and her subject peoples, which culminated in a Bulgarian rising in 1875 that was met by massacres at the hands of ill-trained Turkish troops. The British government, fearing Russian intervention on behalf of Christian Slavs, treated the atrocities as a matter of power politics rather than a moral question. GLADSTONE thought otherwise: his pamphlet *The Bulgarian Horrors and the Question of the East* – published in Sept. 1876 and advocating the expulsion of the Turks 'bag and baggage' from Bulgaria – marked the end of his brief retirement from public life and the beginnings of the high-minded populism that brought him back to the premiership in 1880. His demand respecting the Turks was conceded in the treaty of San Stefano, 1878.

Bulge, Battle of the, Dec. 1944–Jan. 1945. Final German counter offensive of WORLD WAR II against the advancing Allied forces (predominantly the 1st US Army) in the Ardennes to split the Allied line, seize fuel supplies and communication links. The offensive, which was fought in a bitter winter, was repulsed with heavy German losses, and the Allied advance to the Rhine continued.

Bull, John, the archetypical Englishman represented as bluff, big and burly. The character is thought to have been invented by political pamphleteer John Arbuthnot (1667–1735) and first appeared in his *History of John Bull* (1712). It remained a symbol of continuing national significance until the end of WORLD WAR II.

Bullock Reports, reports from two government committees of inquiry chaired by the historian Alan (now Lord) Bullock. The 1975 report, *A Language for Life*, was a milestone in the introduction of progressive practices in the teaching of READING in schools.

The 1977 report, *Industrial Democracy*, sought to find the best means of introducing industrial democracy, advocating employee representation on boards of directors of all companies employing more than 2,000 workers. The committee itself was divided, with industrialist members rejecting the proposals, and there was considerable public debate. Government commitment to industrial democracy was ended by the defeat of the LABOUR government in the 1979 general election.

Bunyan, John (1628–88), religious writer. A Beds. tinsmith who served as a PARLIAMENTARIAN soldier (1644–6), he became fired by religious zeal through the influence of his wife and the FIFTH MONARCHISTS. In about 1653 he joined an INDEPENDENT congregation in Bedford, becoming a strict CALVINIST on predestination and an enthusiastic MILLENARIAN, and he began to preach and write, especially against the QUAKERS. Persecuted by PRESBYTERIAN clergy in 1658, he suffered more seriously after the RESTORATION, spending most of the period 1660–72 in prison for holding a CONVENTICLE. Thereafter he travelled, preaching and writing his masterpiece *Pilgrim's Progress* (1678, 2nd expanded ed. 1684). An immediately, outstandingly and enduringly successful work, it became a centrepiece of English Protestant literature, especially for EVANGELICALS and NONCONFORMISTS, and was said to be one of the few books commonly found in the cottages of the barely literate.

Burdett, Sir Francis (1770–1844), radical politician. Younger son of the 4th baronet, he lived in Paris during the early part of the

FRENCH REVOLUTION, returning to England in 1793. In 1796 he was elected an MP; he opposed the FRENCH REVOLUTIONARY WAR and supported PARLIAMENTARY REFORM. He campaigned successfully for an inquiry into the mismanagement of Coldbath Fields prison, a showpiece of PRISON REFORM, where several radicals were held.

In 1802, he was elected MP for Middlesex in the first of a series of hard-fought battles in popular constituencies. When this election was declared void, he fought again but lost; he won the seat in 1805, lost it in 1806, and then was elected for Westminster. He opposed corporal punishment in the army and, in 1809, campaigned for an inquiry into a scandal over the sale of army commissions, which implicated the duke of York. He was imprisoned in 1810 for breach of parliamentary privilege, and again in 1819 for criticizing repression at PETERLOO. In 1828, he successfully promoted CATHOLIC EMANCIPATION. He remained an MP until his death, latterly supporting PEEL.

Representing himself as a champion of 'traditional' English liberty rather than as an innovator, he interpreted this cause in radical ways, and won a devoted popular following. His secure social background gave him the opportunity to emerge as one of the most prominent and effective early 19th-century radical spokesmen. *See also* RADICALISM.

Burgage, a unit of property in BOROUGHS, generally consisting of a house with little land attached, held from the grantor by money rent (the system known as burgage tenure). Of the 31 parliamentary boroughs in which owners of the burgages monopolized the franchise in the century before 1832, Old Sarum was probably the most notorious.

Burgesses of Parliament, *see* BOROUGH

Burgh, the Scots form of BOROUGH. There were a number of urban centres in Scotland before the 12th century, but burghal status for a community was associated with royal grants of privilege, the first of which were made by DAVID I. The Scottish monarchs also allowed ecclesiastical and lay lords to found burghs (respectively 'burghs of barony' and 'burghs of regality'). Most burghs of barony assumed the status of royal burghs when the Scottish bishops lost their power and estates at the REFORMATION. As in England, burghs were characterized by BURGAGE tenure and they imitated English and continental varieties of self-government and law; as in Ireland, they were associated with those parts of the kingdom dominated by Anglo-Norman culture.

From the 1290s there is mention of a court to administer the law of four main burghs (Stirling, EDINBURGH, Roxburgh and BERWICK, the last two later replaced by Lanark and Linlithgow); it later included representatives of other burghs. It was replaced during the 16th century by informal meetings which in turn formalized into a Convention of Royal Burghs; this met annually from 1587 until its replacement by a Convention of Scottish local authorities in 1974. Representatives of the burghs also attended meetings of PARLIAMENT as a third estate from 1312, and 15 members were included in the UNION Parliament from 1707, their numbers increasing after 1832. From 1833, royal burghs underwent similar standardizing reforms to English boroughs, while the burghs of regality (mostly smaller and less important) were reformed by legislation of 1892.

Burgh, Hubert de (*c.*1175–1243), Earl of Kent. The younger son of a family of Norfolk gentry, he rose to govern England and become brother-in-law to the king of Scotland. In the 1190s, he entered JOHN's service, and made his name by his determined defence of Chinon in 1205. He was seneschal of Poitou from 1212 to 1215, and was then appointed JUSTICIAR at Runnymede (*see* MAGNA CARTA), remaining in that office, with overall responsibility for the administration of England, until 1232. He played a key role in the civil war of 1215–17, first as defender of Dover (1216–17), then as commander of the victorious fleet at the battle of SANDWICH. From 1219, he was the most influential figure in HENRY III's government, successfully presenting himself as a moderate and patriotic Englishman opposed to the arbitrary excesses of such foreigners as Falkes de Breauté and Peter des Roches. In 1221, he married, as his third wife, Margaret, sister of ALEXANDER II, and four years later, he was created Earl of Kent. In

1232, de Burgh's life-long rival des Roches finally persuaded the king to dismiss and imprison him. Although he made a dramatic escape in 1233 and was reconciled to Henry in 1234, he never recovered his former position.

Burghal Hideage, a document probably dating from the reign of EDWARD THE ELDER (899–924), which is crucial to the understanding of the defensive system inaugurated by ALFRED THE GREAT. It records the number of HIDES responsible for the defence of each *BURH*, then explains that each hide is responsible for providing one warrior, and that four warriors were necessary to defend a length of a *burh*'s rampart equivalent to 4.5 m (5.5 yd).

Burghley, 1st Baron, *see* CECIL, WILLIAM

Burgred, King of the Mercians (852–74). The last king of independent MERCIA, he was expelled by the VIKINGS. Little is known about him, but it appears that he attempted to defend his kingdom against the GREAT ARMY in alliance with successive kings of WESSEX (*see* ALFRED THE GREAT; ETHELWULF) before capitulating to overwhelming force.

Burgundy and England Late medieval Burgundy was a patchwork of dispersed territories cemented together by inheritance, scheming and marriage alliance. The reigns of Philip the Good (1419–67) and Charles the Bold (1467–77) supplemented the old French duchy of Burgundy with most of the Low Countries – what is now the Netherlands and Belgium (FLANDERS). Strong traditional links between England and the Low Countries ensured that Burgundy was drawn into a relationship with England. Rivalry between the Duke of Burgundy and his overlord, the King of France, lent added attraction to an alliance with France's old enemy, culminating in the marriage of EDWARD IV's sister MARGARET to Charles the Bold in 1468.

Burgundian influence was as much artistic as political, however. As part of their state-building, Philip and Charles made their court the most magnificent in Europe, and its ceremony, music and design were widely imitated, not least by the courts of Edward IV and the Tudors. After Charles's death, the duchy passed by marriage to the imperial Habsburg family (although Burgundy itself was lost to the French), and the Anglo-Burgundian political axis continued under the early Tudors, widening to include Spain when the Habsburgs inherited that kingdom. With occasional lapses, it remained the cornerstone of English foreign policy until the late 1560s and the gradual drift into war between Spain and ELIZABETH I's government. See also NETHERLANDS, REVOLT OF THE.

Burh The *burhs* of Anglo-Saxon England were fortified centres established in WESSEX by ALFRED THE GREAT and in MERCIA by his son EDWARD THE ELDER and his daughter ETHELFLÆD and her husband, to combat the Danish invasions and reconquer lost territory. A fundamental document for understanding this system of defence is the *BURGHAL HIDEAGE*. Aerial views of several English towns still show the line of their *burhs*' earthwork ramparts, and archaeology has revealed that the *burhs* all had near-identical street-plans. During the 10th century, royal legislation insisted on the central role of the *burhs* as markets and MINTS, which thereby became the basis of English urban development (*see* TOWNS).

Burke, Edmund (1729–97), politician and writer. The son of an Irish barrister, he himself read for the bar and became an MP. In his heyday an outstanding political rhetorician, from the 1760s to the early 1780s, Burke effectively served as ideologist to the ROCKINGHAMITE WHIGS; his *Thoughts on the Cause of the Present Discontents* (1770) expounds their paranoid view of recent political developments. In the 1770s, he denounced the misgovernment of the American colonies and, in the following decade, the rapacious exploitation of INDIA. He advocated religious toleration, especially (but by no means uniquely) in relation to Catholics, but also argued that religious establishments performed important social functions. His *Reflections on the Revolution in France* (1790), although composed during its early, moderate days, denounced revolutionary excess.

Although sometimes acclaimed as a father of CONSERVATIVE thought, Burke was a more complex figure than this might suggest, combining a consistent horror of oppressive and exploitative styles of government with an equally consistent distrust of the RADICAL language of rights.

Burma Annexed as a province of British INDIA in 1886, Burma was overrun by the Japanese in the early stages of WORLD WAR II. After bitter fighting, British armies reconquered the country, seizing Rangoon on 2 May 1945. Following INDIAN INDEPENDENCE in 1947, Burma became a sovereign state in 1948, declining to become a member of the COMMONWEALTH and setting up an isolationist, socialist state under General Ne Winh. It is now called Myanmar.

Burnet, Gilbert (1643–1715), cleric and historian. He took a master's degree at Aberdeen University at 14, then studied divinity, learning Hebrew at Amsterdam, where he was impressed by Dutch religious tolerance. His willingness to serve in an episcopal system, at a time when support for PRESBYTERIANISM was strong in Scotland, was influenced by his conviction that religion should be above party: this conviction worked unevenly in his favour in RESTORATION Britain.

Initially patronized by Lauderdale (*see* MAITLAND, JOHN), in 1669 he became (professor of divinity at Glasgow. He was active in negotiations for accommodation with the COVENANTERS, which earned him disfavour and he left for London; he was later a witness at Lauderdale's IMPEACHMENT. In 1679, he began to publish a *History of the Reformation*; the POPISH PLOT gave this subject special resonance.

After some of his friends were executed for complicity in the RYE HOUSE PLOT, Burnet left England for the Continent and, in 1686, he took up a post in the entourage of the Prince of Orange. He wrote the text of WILLIAM III's 1688 DECLARATION OF RIGHTS, and accompanied him to England. Appointed Bishop of Salisbury under the new regime, he favoured COMPREHENSION, and his sermons contributed to the popularization of a new, LATITUDINARIAN preaching style. His informative but partisan *History of My Own Time* was published posthumously (1723–34).

Burton Abbey The most northerly religious house affected by the TENTH-CENTURY REFORM, the abbey, at Burton-upon-Trent in Staffs., was founded in *c.*1004 by the MERCIAN noble WULFRIC and received monks from St Ethelwold's church at Winchester. It was dissolved in 1539.

Bury St Edmunds, Suffolk. The shrine of EDMUND, King of the East Angles, was built at the 10th-century religious community in what had originally been called Beodricsworth, where an earlier community had been destroyed by the VIKINGS. The major abbey established there by CNUT in *c.*1020 became one of the wealthiest of all English monasteries, its territory forming the later county of West Suffolk (abolished 1974). The chronicle of JOCELIN OF BRAKELOND, describing the abbey and its life (1173–1202), inspired Thomas Carlyle's historical vision in *Past and Present* (1843). The abbey, one of the largest in Western Christendom, became the object of discontent among the people of the town which grew up at its gates, notably in the PEASANTS' REVOLT, and was comprehensively destroyed at its DISSOLUTION in 1539. The town became a centre of the CLOTH INDUSTRY, and an important social centre of the 17th and 18th centuries (reflected in its surviving buildings), focused upon the annual Bury Fair.

Bushell's Case, 1670, established new conventions regarding the independence of JURIES. The QUAKERS William Penn and William Mead were tried for tumultuous assembly and acquitted; the jurors were fined by the Recorder of London and imprisoned until they paid. Edward Bushell, one of the jurors, obtained a writ of *HABEAS CORPUS* and was discharged by the Court of COMMON PLEAS. Chief Justice Vaughan declared that jurors were the sole judges of fact in a trial; the judge could advise a jury on matters of law, but not direct it to deliver a particular verdict. Although the judgment was overturned on the grounds that Common Pleas had no jurisdiction in Bushell's case, Vaughan's principle was maintained.

Business Cycle, *see* TRADE CYCLE

Bute, 3rd Earl of, *see* STUART, JOHN

Butler, Richard Austen (Rab) (Baron Butler of Saffron Walden) (1902–82), Conservative politician. CONSERVATIVE MP for Saffron Walden from 1929, he was a junior minister from 1932 until 1941. He then joined CHURCHILL's wartime Cabinet as minister of education, where he masterminded the 1944 EDUCATION ACT, establishing free secondary education for all up to the school-leaving age of 15. After the 1945 Tory election defeat he played a central role in moulding the party and its policies to post-war requirements.

Always on the liberal wing of the party, his consensus policies as chancellor of the Exchequer (1951–5) came to be dubbed BUTSKELLISM for their similarity to those of LABOUR's Hugh GAITSKELL. He remained a powerful though enigmatic *éminence grise* in all Conservative Cabinets from 1951 to 1964.

He was assumed to be the front runner to succeed as prime minister both in Jan. 1957 when EDEN resigned after the SUEZ CRISIS and in Oct. 1963 when MACMILLAN resigned through ill health on the eve of the party conference. Butler apparently had the backing of the majority of the Cabinet, but Macmillan regarded him as uninspiring and insufficiently ruthless for the premiership – 'he lacked the last six inches of steel'. In true Tory style, a previously unconsidered contender, the Earl of Home (*see* DOUGLAS-HOME, ALEC), the foreign secretary, 'emerged'. Butler nevertheless agreed to serve the new prime minister in the now vacant post of foreign secretary. He accepted a life peerage from Harold WILSON and the Mastership of Trinity College, Cambridge.

Butsecarls, an obscure term used to describe one of the various groups of warriors who appear in 11th-century ANGLO-SAXON sources. It probably refers to troops responsible for guarding coastal fortifications.

Butskellism, word used to describe the growing convergence in the 1950s of CONSERVATIVE and LABOUR policy over questions of the mixed economy, the WELFARE STATE and other social and economic issues. It elided parts of the surnames of BUTLER, Conservative chancellor of the Exchequer 1951–5 and then leader of the House of Commons, and GAITSKELL, Labour chancellor 1950–1 and leader of the opposition 1955–63.

Butt, Isaac (1813–79), Irish politician. Son of a Protestant rector, he was called to the Irish bar in 1835 and entered politics shortly afterwards. He opposed the revolutionary FENIANS and put forward a federal solution to the Irish demand for self-government. In 1870 he founded the Home Government Association, which he replaced with the Home Rule League in 1873. As MP for Limerick he led the 58-strong Irish HOME RULE group in the Commons in 1874, but he failed to convince Parliament of the need for serious consideration of the IRISH QUESTION. Three years later, he was replaced as leader by PARNELL, to whose policy of obstruction Butt was opposed.

Buttington, Battle of, 893. A Danish army on a raid across England was cornered and defeated in POWYS by a combined force of Wessex, Mercian and Welsh troops commanded by Ealdorman Ethelred of Mercia. The battle marks a significant moment in the development of the collaborative efforts of WESSEX and MERCIA to drive back the Scandinavian conquerors.

By-Employment, part-time employment, especially agricultural workers' part-time engagement in small-scale industrial production: for example, in knitting, weaving, lace-making; the making of pins, nails or cooking pots; starch, soap and vinegar. Such industrial employment increased considerably in the 16th to 18th centuries, playing a part in the process of PROTO-INDUSTRIALIZATION.

Byrhtferth (?–*c.*1015), monk of RAMSEY. Described by historian Sir Frank Stenton (1880–1967) as 'the most eminent man of science produced by the English Church since the death of BEDE', Byrhtferth's particular scientific interests lay in what we would now call mathematics and astronomy. His manual on the *COMPOTUS* is a typical product of the TENTH-CENTURY REFORM, since it was written in both Latin and English in order to educate parish priests. He also wrote historical works, such as a *Life* of St Oswald.

Byrhtnoth (?–991), Ealdorman of Essex. He achieved immortality because his death in battle against the Danes was recorded in the Old English poem describing the battle of MALDON. He became EALDORMAN of ESSEX in 956, was a strong supporter of the TENTH-CENTURY REFORM and had extensive power and land throughout eastern England.

C

Cabal, word in use from the mid-17th century to denote an intrigue or a secret meeting or group and still in use today to describe political intrigues. Derived from *Kabbala*, Jewish traditions of interpreting the Hebrew scripture, hence secret tradition generally, contemporaries noted that it was also an acronym of the names of some of the leading ministers in the government of 1667–73: Sir Thomas Clifford; Henry Bennet, Earl of Arlington; George Villiers, 5th Duke of Buckingham; Anthony Ashley Cooper, Earl of Shaftesbury; and John MAITLAND, Earl of Lauderdale. Although they all supported a third DUTCH WAR in alliance with France, this ministry broke up when a changing political climate made it increasingly difficult for those sympathetic either to Catholicism or to DISSENT to maintain a united front. Historians have found the term 'Cabal ministry' convenient shorthand for an administration that was not clearly dominated by any one figure. The name is, however, potentially misleading: the ministry was not marked by any great unity of purpose, and only some of its members were privy to its most conspiratorial initiative: the making of the secret treaty of DOVER.

Cabinet, usage in modern British politics for the small group of senior politicians chosen by the PRIME MINISTER, who direct the country's government and shape policy. The term was originally abusive; the origins of the institution were in the small group of ministers, the 'Cabinet Council', on whom late 17th-century monarchs relied, when the PRIVY COUNCIL grew too large to be an effective instrument of government. Already under WILLIAM III it was possible to list a recognized membership of the Cabinet Council; within it was an 'inner cabinet' to deal with particularly secret and important affairs. After 1717 the monarch virtually never sat with the cabinet, and during the 18th century it took more and more decisions on its own initiative and on that of the prime minister. The word remained an informal term until the Ministers of the Crown Act (1937) provided for a distinctive salary level for cabinet ministers. Modern British cabinet ministers are customarily appointed to the Privy Council, and are therefore given the title 'Right Honourable'. The convention of British cabinet government, imitated in countries affected by the British governmental system, is that all members are equally responsible for decisions taken after discussion (collective responsibility): failure to agree with the cabinet's policy is generally considered a matter on which to resign. A 'shadow cabinet' formed by the parliamentary opposition was originally composed of a group of politicians which gathered around the heir to the throne at certain stages in 18th-century politics; the term is now applied to the MPs of the main opposition party in Parliament who would hold ministerial office if their party were in power.

Cabinets of Curiosities, *see* MUSEUMS

Cable Street, Battle of, Nov. 1936. The clashes around Cable Street in the East End of London were between police and anti-Fascist demonstrators, who were attempting to prevent a march by MOSLEY'S British Union of FASCISTS through an area of Jewish settlement. The march was prevented but, coming as a culmination of violence caused by the provocative marches of the BUF, it led the government into the rapid passage of the PUBLIC ORDER ACT before the end of 1936.

Cadbury, South, Som. The refortification of the large Iron Age hillfort at South Cadbury during the 5th and 6th centuries AD is one of the most spectacular manifestations of British resistance to the invading ANGLES and SAXONS (*see* BRITISH SURVIVAL). The size of the enclosure and the presence of a large hall have led to the suggestion that this was the residence of a British chieftain. A connection – completely unverifiable – with King ARTHUR and a possible location for the legendary CAMELOT (based on an association first recorded by John Leland in the 1530s) have also been proposed.

Cade's Rebellion, 1450, a Kentish revolt – and prelude to the WARS OF THE ROSES – led by Jack Cade (about whom virtually nothing is known before the summer of 1450) against an inept government blamed for England's defeat in the HUNDRED YEARS WAR and high taxes. When HENRY VI's courtiers threatened reprisals against the people of Kent, whom they held responsible for the murder in May 1450 of William de la Pole, 1st Duke of Suffolk, Kent's response was to rebel.

The rebels' manifesto – the *Complaint of the Commons of Kent* – effectively caught the mood of the country, and for some weeks, the government seemed helpless in the face of a large army, including many gentry, drawn up on Blackheath outside London. When an advance guard of the king's army was ambushed, Henry retreated to Kenilworth, allowing Cade's men to enter the capital (4 July) and execute unpopular courtiers. When Cade proved unable to discipline his men, the Londoners turned against him; promised a free pardon, he disbanded his troops, but was then hunted down and killed (12 July). The rebels' critique of the LANCASTRIAN government was then taken up by RICHARD OF YORK.

Cadog, St (*fl.* 6th century), monk. One of the most renowned of the early Welsh saints. Details of his career and some relevant CHARTERS are preserved in a life written in the late 11th or early 12th century. He is believed to have lived in the 6th century, to have been abbot of LLANCARFAN in the Vale of Glamorgan, and to have presided over a monastic confederation that stretched throughout south-east Wales. He was also venerated as a saint in Ireland.

Cadwalla, King of Wessex (685–9). Notable for his conquest of the JUTES on the Isle of Wight and the establishment of a temporary hegemony over SUSSEX and Surrey, he occasionally called himself 'king of the SAXONS', indicating that his reign marked a significant stage in the evolution of his family's rule towards KINGSHIP over the larger region, which was eventually controlled by his successors – the 9th- and 10th-century kings of WESSEX. In 689, he resigned his kingdom and went to Rome on pilgrimage.

Cadwallon (?–634), King of Gwynedd (*c.*625–34). One of the most powerful of the early kings of GWYNEDD, he appears to have reacted violently to the advance of NORTHUMBRIA's power in northern Britain, and in 633, in alliance with PENDA of MERCIA, he defeated and killed King EDWIN. His career ended a year later with his death in battle against OSWALD of Northumbria. Cadwallon is the only British ruler known to have overthrown an English king. His life illustrates the violent and fluid politics of the period when the early kingdoms were formed, as well as the impossibility of separating its 'Welsh', 'English' and 'Scottish' elements. *See also* KINGSHIP.

Caer Caradog, Church Stretton, Salop, the reputed site of the British chieftain CARATACUS' last stand against the conquering armies of the Roman governor OSTORIUS SCAPULA in AD 47. The absence of archaeological finds in the vicinity has made the identification seem unlikely, and recent opinion favours the site of the hillfort at Llanymynech, Salop.

Caerleon (*Isca Silurum*), Gwent, along with CHESTER and YORK, one of the three great LEGIONARY FORTRESSES of Roman Britain. It was constructed in AD 74–5 as part of the subjugation of the Welsh tribes (*see* ROMAN CONQUEST). Archaeological excavations have revealed extensive buildings, including a great amphitheatre, and suggest that the site was probably abandoned in the later 3rd century. According to GEOFFREY OF MONMOUTH, King ARTHUR held court here.

Caerwent (*Venta Silurum*), Gwent. This was created by the Romans as the centre of the *CIVITAS* of the SILURES, probably during the governorship of JULIUS FRONTINUS (*c.*AD 75). Since the site was deserted soon after the 5th century, it has been possible to trace Caerwent's town plan with considerable accuracy. There is evidence of all the usual

Roman amenities, such as a forum and an amphitheatre, as well as of Celtic and Roman religious activity.

Caesar, Julius, *see* JULIUS CAESAR

Cairo Conference, Nov.–Dec. 1943, also known as the Sextant conference, held in Cairo during WORLD WAR II between CHURCHILL, Roosevelt and the Chinese Nationalist leader, Chiang Kai-shek. The conference discussed strategy in the Far East and determined on the expulsion of Japan from all conquered territories in China and Korea. While Roosevelt and Churchill journeyed on to meet Stalin in TEHRAN, Anglo-American staff talks in Cairo concluded arrangements for the Normandy landings (*see* D-DAY) in 1944.

Calais, the port in north-western France captured by EDWARD III in 1347 after a long siege and held by the English crown until 1558. During the HUNDRED YEARS WAR, their possession of it generally gave the English the upper hand against the French in the Channel. From 1363, the wool STAPLE was established there, making the London–Calais connection the main artery through which English WOOL was exported and coin imported. With the end of the Hundred Years War in 1453, Calais remained the only English possession in France, with a small surrounding territory – the PALE. A permanent garrison was stationed there, and the captain of Calais became the most important military officer in the kingdom, often playing a key role in the WARS OF THE ROSES. It was captured without difficulty by the French in 1558 after prolonged neglect of its defences. It sent MPs to the English Parliament between 1536 and 1558.

Calder Hall, Cumbria, site of Britain's first nuclear power station to produce commercial electricity, opened in 1956 with considerable publicity by Queen ELIZABETH II. The plant was, however, primarily designed to produce weapons grade plutonium, of which ATOMIC ENERGY was the by-product. Purely commercial atomic power stations only came on stream in the late 1950s.

Caledonii, said by the Roman geographer Ptolemy and the Emperor SEPTIMIUS SEVERUS to be the people inhabiting what would now be called the central Highland region of Scotland. Roman writers say little about their history beyond recording their seemingly frequent raids southwards, which contributed to the abandonment of the ANTONINE WALL and, at times, threatened HADRIAN'S WALL. The Roman governor AGRICOLA and Severus both launched campaigns against them with no long-term results. After the 4th century, these peoples are normally referred to by contemporaries as PICTS.

Calendar Customs, term used as general description of popular activities and festivities on particular HOLIDAYS, especially those of some antiquity. They were the object of considerable interest in the folklore revival of the later 19th century onwards, and have often been the subject of self-conscious revival since.

Callaghan, James (Baron Callaghan of Cardiff) (1912–), Labour politician and Prime Minister (1976–9). Elected as LABOUR MP for Cardiff South in 1945, he was a junior minister in the ATTLEE government (1947–51), and became chancellor of the Exchequer in the 1964 WILSON government. His economic policy, based on a fixed rate of exchange, was over-whelmed by the financial crisis that forced the government into DEVALUATION in Nov. 1967. He resigned as chancellor and became home secretary with two major issues to deal with: Northern Ireland and immigration. In 1969 he opposed proposals to control unofficial strikes, based on the White Paper *IN PLACE OF STRIFE*, which the Wilson government was forced to drop. He was also against British membership of the EEC (*see* EUROPEAN UNION). He became foreign secretary in the 1974 Wilson government and prime minister when Wilson unexpectedly resigned in 1976.

Callaghan inherited a difficult economic situation, with a weak balance of payments, industrial unrest and rising inflation. In Sept. 1976 he told the annual Labour Party conference that the option of solving economic problems by increasing taxes and higher government spending 'no longer exists', a speech which in many ways prefigured the policies of the THATCHER government. At the same time, his government had to apply for $3.9 billion in credits from the International Monetary Fund and in return was forced to accept a regime of public spending cuts.

During 1977 and 1978 the Callaghan government remained in office as a result of the LIB-LAB PACT. The voluntary SOCIAL CONTRACT with the TRADE UNIONS broke down in 1977, and mounting union hostility culminated in the WINTER OF DISCONTENT 1978–9. The government lost a vote of confidence by one vote in March 1979, resulting in a general election in May which returned the CONSERVATIVES under Thatcher. Callaghan resigned as party leader in Oct. 1980 and was replaced by Michael FOOT.

Calvinism, the theological system of John Calvin (1509–64). The French-born PROTESTANT theologian, who settled in Geneva between 1536–8 and 1541–64, came to dominate its REFORMATION and, from the 1550s, had a European-wide influence. His theology is expounded in his *Christianae Religionis Institutio* (the *Institutes*: successive editions from 1536). It was elaborated by his successor at Geneva, Theodore Beza, and others in Heidelberg, the Netherlands, CAMBRIDGE and elsewhere, particularly on predestination of souls either to salvation or damnation; Calvin also strongly argued for PRESBYTERIANISM as the biblical pattern of church government. Argument continues about his influence on the Church of England: Calvinism came too late to play much part in shaping its official doctrines (formulated under EDWARD VI), but was very important in the thinking of Elizabethan churchmen, and only gradually lost its hold during the 17th century. In Scotland, Calvinism shaped the thought and institutions of the Church. *See also* ARMINIANISM; CHURCH: ENGLAND, SCOTLAND; REFORMED CHURCHES.

Cambrai, Battle of, north-eastern France, 20–22 Nov. 1917, small WORLD WAR I battle which saw the first use of TANKS *en masse* by the British against the Germans (*see* AMIENS). It was followed by a German counter-attack on 30 Nov. which retook the ground gained in the original battle.

Cambrensis, Giraldus, *see* BARRI, GERALD DE

Cambridge Platonists, *see* PLATONISTS

Cambridge, Statute of, *see* POOR RELIEF

Cambridge University Medieval and Tudor rivalries with OXFORD UNIVERSITY led Cambridge's supporters to claim that it had been founded by an ancient Spanish prince called Cantaber, with a later charter from no less a figure than King ARTHUR. Oxford countered with a legend of foundation by the first Briton: the Trojan exile Brutus.

Cambridge's genuine origins lie in the early 13th century. A number of centres of higher education had emerged in England in the previous century, mostly around CATHEDRALS (LINCOLN, EXETER, Hereford, YORK, LONDON), but those that survived were in towns where there was no great Church corporation to interfere. In the late 12th century, Oxford became important, but then various troubles and disagreements led to migrations of scholars to Stamford, Northampton and Cambridge. Of these, only Cambridge developed permanent institutions, and a chancellor is first recorded in 1225. At both universities, colleges began to be established in the late 13th century, initially small, primarily CHANTRY foundations not intended for undergraduates. The relative importance of colleges and the central teaching and degree-awarding institutions of the universities has fluctuated to this day.

On the eve of the REFORMATION, Cambridge was dominated by its chancellor, John FISHER, but it produced many more Reformation leaders than Oxford – e.g. John Bale, William CECIL, John Cheke, Thomas CRANMER, Hugh Latimer, Matthew PARKER, Nicholas Ridley. During the 17th-century CIVIL WARS, Cambridge was not directly affected by the fighting, being under Parliamentary control.

Reforms in the 1850s transformed Cambridge from a small medieval university, characterized by ramshackle educational provision, into a modern centre of learning. Tripos exams in natural and moral sciences (begun in 1851), in law (1859) and in history (1870) modernized the syllabus. Intercollegiate lectures began in 1868, allowing the university to play an educational as well as a degree-awarding role. Colleges for women were also founded from 1869 and women were first allowed to sit examinations in 1881 (but were not permitted to gain university degrees until 1948). Religious tests were abolished in 1871, thus opening the university to non-Anglicans. The opening of the Cavendish laboratory in the 1870s heralded the expansion of modern scientific study. The annual admissions to the university tripled between the 1820s and 1890s, and the introduction of joint Oxford–Cambridge entrance examinations encouraged middle-class students from throughout Britain and the empire to compete for entry. The 20th century has seen further increase in collegiate foundations and teaching departments.

FOUNDATIONS OF COLLEGES

1284 Peterhouse.
1338 Clare (University Hall, 1326).
1347 Pembroke.
1350 Trinity Hall.
1352 Corpus Christi (or Bene't).
1441 King's.
1448 Queens' (St Bernard's, 1446).
1473 St Catharine's (or Catharine Hall).
1497 Jesus.
1505 Christ's (God's House, 1442).
1511 St John's.
1542 Magdalene (Buckingham, 1428).
1546 Trinity (Michaelhouse, 1324; King's Hall, 1337).
1557 Gonville & Caius (Gonville Hall, 1348).
1584 Emmanuel.
1594 Sidney Sussex.
1800 Downing.
1824 Homerton.
1869 Girton (moves to Cambridge from Hitchin 1873).
1870 Newnham.
1882 Selwyn.
1885 Hughes Hall.
1954 New Hall.
1960 Churchill.
1964 Darwin.
1965 Lucy Cavendish; Wolfson.
1966 Clare Hall; Fitzwilliam.
1977 Robinson.

Camden, William (1551–1623), historian and pioneer of documentary and archaeological research. Educated at Oxford, he was first usher, then headmaster of Westminster school from 1575, until appointed as Herald (Clarenceux King of Arms) in 1597 (*see* HERALDS AND HERALDRY). He was involved in the foundation of the first Society of ANTIQUARIES in *c.*1585. Encouraged by Dean Goodman of Westminster, from 1571 to 1600 he travelled throughout England gathering material on antiquity. The first version of his *Britannia* – a nationwide survey arranged ostensibly by classical tribes, but in reality by county – came out in 1586. He published many other historical collections, including (part-posthumously) the *Annals* of ELIZABETH I's reign.

Camelot, the legendary site of King ARTHUR's chivalric court. The search for the historical Arthur has produced several suggested identifications for Camelot, notably South CADBURY and TINTAGEL in Cornwall. Archaeological excavation has not discovered convincing evidence at any site.

Cameron Report, report in Sept. 1969 of a commission appointed by the Northern Ireland government and headed by a Scottish judge, Lord Cameron, on the disturbances arising from the civil rights protests in Northern Ireland in 1967–8. It confirmed and documented discrimination against Roman CATHOLICS in local politics and housing, criticized the behaviour of the Royal Ulster Constabulary, and condemned the 'B' SPECIALS as a 'partisan and paramilitary' force. Its conclusions were reinforced by those of the Hunt Report published a month later, which led to the replacement of the head of the RUC by an English policeman, the disarming of the RUC, and the disbandment of the 'B' Specials.

Cameronians, extremist COVENANTERS who, after being defeated by government troops at BOTHWELL BRIDGE, subscribed to Richard Cameron's Sanquhar Declaration of June 1680, declaring war on CHARLES II as an enemy of God. Their attacks and murders were met with savage repression, many dozens being summarily executed. When EPISCOPACY was abolished in 1690, some were not satisfied with the CALVINIST purity of the PRESBYTERIAN settlement, and remained separate; they formed a Reformed Presbytery in 1743, and a small Reformed Presbyterian Church has resisted all blandishments at reunion with the Church of Scotland since. *See* CHURCH: SCOTLAND.

Campaign for Homosexual Equality, *see* HOMOSEXUALITY AND BRITISH LAW

Campaign for Nuclear Disarmament (CND), British anti-nuclear movement, formed in 1958 by a committee which included Bertrand Russell, J. B. Priestley, Michael FOOT and Canon L. John Collins, to demand the UNILATERAL abandonment of NUCLEAR WEAPONS. The annual Easter 'Aldermaston' March, culminating in a demonstration in Trafalgar Square, London, drew large support in the years to 1964. In 1960–1 CND had thousands of active supporters, and in 1960 the LABOUR PARTY conference passed a resolution in favour of unilateral disarmament. However, between 1961 and 1979 CND's fortunes waned. In 1961 the Labour Party reversed its position in favour of MULTILATERALISM: the Labour government which took office in 1964 had no great sympathy towards CND, while the PARTIAL TEST BAN TREATY of 1963 appeared to have made the movement obsolescent.

CND revived from 1979, when NATO ministers agreed on a policy involving the siting of a new generation of nuclear missiles in Europe, its membership rising from 9,000 in 1980 to almost 100,000 at the height of its campaign against the siting of Cruise missiles at bases at Molesworth Heath (Cambs.), and Greenham Common (Berks.).

Campbell, Archibald (9th Earl of Argyll) (1629–85), politician. Unlike his father, executed in 1661, he fought on the Royalist side; in 1656–7, he refused to take a new oath for the Scottish nobility, and was imprisoned in Edinburgh castle. Favoured by Lauderdale (*see* MAITLAND, JOHN), he was made a member of the Scottish Privy Council in 1664, and employed in various capacities. His independent power in the Highlands – the Argylls had long been one of the most powerful Scottish families – combined with his staunch PROTESTANTISM worried the Duke of York (the future JAMES II); in 1681, he was prosecuted for expressing doubts about the consistency of the Scottish TEST ACT, and sentenced to death; his estates were confiscated. However, he escaped, and the fear of the political embarrassment that might result probably saved him from rearrest. He was implicated in the RYE HOUSE PLOT; fleeing to Holland, he plotted with Monmouth (*see* SCOTT, JAMES). He took a force to Scotland in 1685, and at Campbeltown in Argyll proclaimed Monmouth the rightful king. Invading the Lowlands, but unable to overcome royal troops, he was captured in June and executed at Edinburgh without trial, being still under sentence of death.

Campbell, John (2nd Duke of Argyll) (1678–1743), soldier and statesman. Head of the PRESBYTERIAN and therefore traditionally Whiggish Campbell clan, his social standing helped secure him high political office at an early age, and he remained a key figure for any government seeking influence in Scotland. As lord high commissioner for Scotland, he promoted the UNION of 1707. A successful general in the War of the SPANISH SUCCESSION, he was hostile to Marlborough (*see* CHURCHILL, JOHN), and therefore associated with HARLEY and the TORIES, who made him commander-in-chief in Spain in 1711 and, at the end of the war, commander of the forces in Scotland. His opposition to JACOBITISM won him the favour of GEORGE I, who retained him in post to repress the 1715 rebellion. Deprived of office for a few years during a period of WHIG backlash, he held a series of official positions from 1718. Made field marshal in 1736, he was responsible for repressing the PORTEOUS RIOTS. He used his electoral influence in Scotland to help topple WALPOLE, but retired from politics after the latter's fall.

Campbell-Bannerman, Sir Henry (1836–1908), Liberal politician and Prime Minister (1905–8). Born in Glasgow and educated at Cambridge, he worked for the family drapery firm before entering Parliament in 1868 as LIBERAL member for Stirling – a seat he represented for 40 years until his death. 'C-B' was a committed supporter of Irish HOME RULE and held office as chief secretary for Ireland during GLADSTONE's third administration (Jan.–June 1886) and then as secretary of state for war (1892–5). In June 1895 after a vote of censure was narrowly passed on him by the Commons for not having provided the army with sufficient cordite, a new, smokeless explosive, the Cabinet resigned and lost the ensuing general election.

When Rosebery (*see* PRIMROSE, ARCHIBALD) resigned as leader the following year the Liberal Party was in further disarray, particularly over social reform, the conduct of the BOER WAR and the tensions between liberalism and IMPERIALISM. In 1898 Sir William Harcourt, unable to contain the factions, also resigned and, almost by default, Campbell-Bannerman was elected to lead the Liberals in the Commons. His conciliatory temperament and steadfast insistence that the Liberal Party mattered more than a Liberal political agenda paid dividends: on BALFOUR's resignation in 1905 he was invited by EDWARD VII to form a government, and in the ensuing election, in 1906, the Liberals had a landslide victory and 'C–B' formed a new 'Ministry of All the Talents' which included ASQUITH, GREY, LLOYD GEORGE and Morley. It was to be a 'splendid sunset of his career' as a colleague put it, and laid the basis for the reform of the House of LORDS, the Union of SOUTH AFRICA and TRADE UNION recognition. 'C–B' died in office, a stalwart GLADSTONIAN LIBERAL to the end: he was respected by many as a practical, undidactic premier, and applauded by others for the idealism which led him to condemn the 'barbarities' of the Boer War, and for his belief in arbitration to settle international disputes.

Campion, Edmund (1540–81), writer and martyr. A London bookseller's son, Campion was set on a brilliant career at Oxford. He was ordained deacon in 1568, but then converted to Roman Catholicism, left for Dublin in 1569 and, after an interval in London, fled arrest to Douai in 1571. He joined the JESUITS in Rome in 1573 and, in June 1580, reached England with Robert PARSONS to begin a new Jesuit mission, causing great government alarm. He was arrested in Berks. in July 1581, was tortured and, on 1 Dec. 1581, was executed. During his lifetime, he also wrote poetry, a history of Ireland, and Catholic propaganda.

Canada England had had a stake in the northern regions of America since establishing cod fishing grounds in NEWFOUNDLAND, and this was increased by the subsequent exploration of the interior and the exploitation of the fur trade under the HUDSON'S BAY COMPANY, given its royal charter in 1670. The lead had been taken by the French, and Canada's history is dominated by the constant, and continuing, confrontation between English and French culture and language. Throughout the 18th century Canada was one of the principal battlegrounds in the wars between Britain and France, culminating in WOLFE's capture of Quebec in 1759 during the SEVEN YEARS WAR. *See also* QUEBEC ACT 1774.

During the War of AMERICAN INDEPENDENCE Canada remained aloof, and was the resort of many LOYALISTS who refused to support the American rebel cause: NEW BRUNSWICK was carved out of the existing colony of NOVA SCOTIA as a Loyalist enclave. PITT THE YOUNGER'S CANADA ACT 1791 also introduced representative government to the two newly created but antagonistic provinces of Upper and Lower Canada – ONTARIO and QUEBEC. The rebellions of 1837 reflected their deep divisions over language, religion, politics and economics. Lord Durham, sent to assess the situation, made a number of recommendations: the reunification of the provinces; responsible government in all but defence, foreign affairs and external trade; and the introduction of a federal system of government. His report influenced both the CANADA ACT 1840 and the policies pursued by Lord Elgin, governor-general 1847–54. The OREGON TREATY of 1854, which established the Canada–US boundary at the 49th parallel, and the BRITISH NORTH AMERICA ACT 1867, which conferred DOMINION status, helped to create a distinct Canadian identity and pointed towards the transformation of the BRITISH EMPIRE into the British COMMONWEALTH. *See also* BRITISH COLUMBIA; MANITOBA; NORTHWEST TERRITORIES; PRINCE EDWARD ISLAND; SASKATCHEWAN.

Canada Act 1791, legislation under PITT THE YOUNGER which placed responsibility for government in CANADA upon the ministry and Parliament in London, while creating representative assemblies, elected on a restricted franchise, for the two new Canadian provinces of Upper and Lower Canada. Upper Canada was largely British, and Lower Canada French. The system lasted until the CANADA ACT 1840.

Canada Act 1840, legislation embodying some of the proposals in the report by Lord Durham for the reform of government in CANADA, uniting Upper and Lower Canada, and instituting a bicameral legislature with a nominated legislative council and an elected assembly. Responsibility for Canadian affairs gradually passed from WESTMINSTER, and the 1867 BRITISH NORTH AMERICA ACT gave Canada federal and almost wholly self-governing DOMINION status.

Canals Until the later 18th century most British schemes to improve navigability involved river improvement rather than canals. Although overshadowed by the BRIDGWATER CANAL (1759–61), it is the Sankey Brook Navigation – which, on its opening in 1757, connected St Helens with the River Mersey and was used to carry COAL to LIVERPOOL – that marks the beginning of the canal era. The network grew piecemeal, with no overall plan apart from Brindley's concept of 'The Cross', the object of which was to connect the four major ports and rivers of England by a system of canals and navigable rivers: Liverpool (the Mersey), Hull (the Humber), BRISTOL (the Severn) and LONDON (the Thames) were thus to be linked by a waterway network that intersected at BIRMINGHAM in the Midlands. Despite this conception, the bulk of canal traffic remained short-haul and they acted as regional rather than national economic integrators. To an extent they were also used for export as with the transport of textiles from West Yorkshire and Lancashire via the Leeds–Liverpool canal.

By 1830, the some 4,000 miles of canals had become the arteries of early industrial Britain. Internal and export markets were the principal beneficiaries. Inland areas without navigable rivers – e.g. the Black Country, south Wales, Birmingham and the Potteries – owed much of their prosperity to the canals, as did such towns as Leicester, Stourport, Goole and Runcorn. Canal building also kept large numbers of NAVVIES in employment. The civil engineering expertise gained in the construction of canals was subsequently applied to the development of the RAILWAYS by which they were largely superseded from 1840, rapidly in passenger trade and more slowly in the transport of low-value bulk goods such as grain and coal.

CHRONOLOGY: CANAL DEVELOPMENT 1757–1894

1757 Sankey Brook Navigation, built by John Eye, links St Helens with Mersey.
1759–61 BRIDGWATER CANAL built to carry coal from Worsley to MANCHESTER.
1767 Bridgwater Canal extended from Manchester to Runcorn.
1772 Staffordshire & Worcester Canal opens, linking partially completed Grand Trunk Canal to Severn at Stourport. Birmingham Canal connects that city with Staffordshire & Worcester Canal.
1777 Grand Trunk Canal (Trent & Mersey Canal), started in 1766 by Brindley, further advances development of 'The Cross'.
1790 'The Grand Cross' completed with opening of Oxford and Coventry canals, which between them link Thames with Grand Trunk Canal.
1791–4 'Canal mania': more than 40 canals authorized and built.
1805 Grand Junction Canal creates direct link between BIRMINGHAM and LONDON; Ellesmere Canal also opened.
1810 Kennet & Avon Canal built.
1811 Huddersfield Canal built.
1814 Grand Union Canal opened.
1815 Worcester & Birmingham Canal opened.
1816 LEEDS–LIVERPOOL Canal.
1819 North Wiltshire and Sheffield canals.
1822 Caledonian Canal; Edinburgh and Glasgow Union canals.
1824 Thames & Medway Canal.
1826 Lancaster Canal.
1827 Harecastle New Tunnel Canal; Gloucester & Berkeley Canal.
1820 Hereford Union Canal.
1831 Liskeard & Lowe, Portsmouth & Arundel, and Macclesfield canals completed.
1833 Glastonbury Canal.
1835 Birmingham & Liverpool Canal.
1839 Manchester & Selfield Canal.
1853 Droitwich Junction Canal.
1894 Manchester Ship Canal.

Canning, George (1770–1827), Tory politician and Prime Minister (1827). After his father's death, his mother became an actress and then a linen-draper to support George and a growing brood of illegitimate children. He entered Parliament in 1794 and found preferment under the younger PITT, whom he served in various capacities. Marriage to an heiress in 1800 brought him financial security rather than serenity, and vanity and a consequent inability to work with colleagues kept him from obtaining early office.

A brilliant and controversial figure, he was twice foreign secretary (1807–9, 1822–7) and briefly prime minister (April–Aug. 1827). As a progressive TORY, he identified with liberal policies at home and overseas, and unlike Castlereagh (*see* STEWART, ROBERT), he declined to support the European autocracies in their attempt to suppress, through the CONGRESS SYSTEM, liberal and revolutionary movements. His liberalism, which suited

British commercial interests, and his dislike of restrictive permanent commitments were to shape British foreign policy until the end of the 19th century. For instance, he supported the movement of independence among the former Spanish colonies in Latin America principally because they had become an important market for British exports, and he welcomed the Monroe doctrine which gave them American protection. His intervention in the Greek War of Independence secured freedom for the Greeks and checked Russian advancement.

Canon, a member of a community of SECULAR clergy living under a rule (*canon*='rule' in Greek) in a CATHEDRAL or COLLEGIATE CHURCH (*see* CELIBACY). Traditionally, they were financed by a portion of land often styled a prebend (hence the equivalent term PREBENDARY). Before the DISSOLUTION OF THE MONASTERIES, monks in some religious orders – e.g. AUGUSTINIANS and PREMONSTRATENSIANS – were also known as canons, as are also (confusingly) items of CANON LAW.

Canon Law The legal system of the Church, which originated in rulings of early councils, was formalized mainly by the papal bureaucracy from the 12th century, but derives many principles from the law of the Roman Empire. Strenuous English REFORMATION efforts to replace it (*see REFORMATIO LEGUM*) came to nothing, though HENRY VIII abolished its study in the universities, and henceforth it could only be operated by CIVIL LAW practitioners. In 1604, Archbishop BANCROFT made a substantial revision for the CHURCH OF ENGLAND, but no further reforms followed until Archbishop Geoffrey Fisher supervised a wholesale revision in the 1950s.

Canterbury, Kent. The town of Canterbury has had an importance in British life out of all proportion to its size. It was the chief town of the CANTIACI before the advent of the Romans, and subsequently became the centre of a *CIVITAS*.

There are some signs of economic decline in the 5th century. However, in the 6th, it was the main residence of King ETHELBERT of KENT, and thus it was there that St AUGUSTINE established his Christian mission (*see* CONVERSION OF THE ENGLISH TO CHRISTIANITY).

Security and proximity to the Continent meant that it continued to be an important centre despite Gregory the Great's wish to make LONDON the seat of the southern English archbishopric. Its ecclesiastical pre-eminence was occasionally challenged – for example, by LICHFIELD in the 8th century and YORK in the 11th. However, its status was safeguarded by its special, distinguished place in the history of English Christianity and by events such as the martyrdom of Thomas BECKET, which made it a centre of pilgrimage. The town continued to be economically significant during most of the medieval period. However, with the DISSOLUTION of its monasteries and friaries, and the destruction of Becket's shrine in the cathedral (1538), it became a centre of merely regional importance.

The abbey of St Augustine's (*not* the cathedral church) was established outside the walls of Canterbury in the early 7th century by St Augustine's Roman mission – the only monastery known to have been founded by them. It was subsequently reformed by St DUNSTAN and placed under the BENEDICTINE Rule. It was the burial place of the early kings of Kent and of some of the Roman missionaries. It was dissolved in 1538.

Cantiaci JULIUS CAESAR's reference to the presence of four kings in KENT suggests the existence there of tribal groupings that are normally referred to as the Cantiaci. The region was the earliest to be conquered by the Romans after AD 43, and it was subsequently organized into a *CIVITAS* around the capital of CANTERBURY.

Cantref, a subdivision of the early Welsh kingdoms. Because of the scarcity of evidence for early medieval Wales, the origins of the cantrefi are obscure. At some stage, they may well have been estates (*see* SOKE) and lordships. In time, they came to be a unit for both the collection of the food supplies that sustained the itinerant courts of early Welsh kings, and the communal action of the people who lived within them. Their boundaries became fixed in the later Middle Ages, after the prevalence of what is thought to have been rather more flexible conditions in earlier centuries.

Canute, *see* CNUT

Cape Colony, principal British colony in southern Africa, centred upon Cape Town, and absorbed into the Union of SOUTH

AFRICA in 1910. The former Dutch colony was seized by the British in the war with France in 1795, restored in 1801, retaken in 1806, and ceded to Britain in 1814. The relations with the settlers of Dutch origin, the Boers, were continually fraught, especially because of their harsh attitudes towards the indigenous population and their expansionist land policies. In 1835 the Boers embarked on the Great Trek, first into NATAL and then, when the British took control there in 1843, into the Transvaal and into the area which would eventually in 1854 become the Orange Free State. Diamond discoveries of the late 1860s and the GOLD RUSH of the late 1880s provided the impetus for further white expansion into the Cape Colony's hinterland, as well as inroads into the Boer-controlled states. RHODES, Cape Colony's prime minister 1890–6, pursued a policy towards the Transvaal (*see* JAMESON RAID) which hastened the onset of the BOER WAR of 1899–1902, after which union of the South African provinces eventually followed.

Capital Punishment, judicial punishment prescribing death by hanging, beheading, burning or other form. One of the features commonly held to separate an enlightened society from a pre-modern unenlightened one is the abolition of 'cruel and unnecessary punishments', of which the death penalty is the most obvious.

For early applications of the death penalty to crime, *see* BLOOD FEUD. Anglo-Saxon LAW CODES also provided that certain crimes were not redeemable by a money payment and warranted the death penalty for the offender; this was associated with the crimes for which OUTLAWRY was imposed. As COMMON LAW developed, death became the punishment for treason and FELONIES (the deliberate causing of death, and major theft). The penalty of burning for HERESY, inherited from the Roman Empire, was also revived by the Western church on a major scale in the 12th century; in England, in response to the LOLLARD threat, this was imposed under common law by the statute *De Heretico Comburendo* (1401), as CHURCH COURTS did not impose capital sentences (*see* BENEFIT OF CLERGY). Other customary common law methods were hanging for ordinary criminals, beheading for noblemen and women, and for traitors the prolonged tortures of (partial) hanging, drawing (disembowelment and castration while alive) and quartering (hacking the body into quarters, for public display). HENRY VIII was particularly panicked by a case of poisoning, and encouraged Parliament to introduce boiling alive for this crime (1531); this was repealed in 1547. English law considered the continental penalties of crucifixion and breaking on the wheel as cruel and unusual punishments.

The actual incidence of capital punishment was, throughout the centuries, reduced by benefit of clergy (already extended to laymen in the 15th century), as limited by statute in 1489 and subsequently, judicial reprieves (culminating in royal pardons), and by trial jurors' reluctance to see the death sentence for property offences imposed when the defendant was neither a professional criminal nor guilty of using force or the threat of force. The incidence of executions was further reduced by the operation of the Transportation Act of 1718, allowing the bench the option instead of hanging to recommend TRANSPORTATION overseas, first to North America and later to AUSTRALIA. None the less, the number of capital crimes on the statute books rose in the century after 1688 (*see* BLOODY CODE), for deterrence by example was the logic of the unreformed criminal justice system; hence, the continuation of public hanging up to 1868.

The movement for the abolition of the death penalty gained momentum from the mid-19th century on the grounds of morality, the irreversibility of the act, and the sufferings inflicted on others. PEEL'S reforms reduced capital crimes to four for civilians: high treason, murder, piracy with violence, and destruction of public arsenals and dockyards. The Criminal Justice Act (1956) further diminished the grounds for capital punishment, and the LABOUR government abolished hanging in 1965 after the issue had been raised in a series of parliamentary debates and following a sequence of controversial judgments and miscarriages of justice. This measure was ostensibly for a trial period, but, despite periodic calls from the CONSERVATIVE right wing, its reintroduction has so far been resisted.

Caratacus (*fl.* AD 40s), British resistance leader. He has acquired semi-heroic status as the leader of British resistance to the ROMAN

CONQUEST that began in AD 43. The son of CUNOBELIN, King of the CATUVELLAUNI, he was defeated by AULUS PLAUTIUS during the initial invasion. He reappeared in 47 leading, first, the SILURES, then the ORDOVICES in unsuccessful resistance (*see* CAER CARADOG). He was handed over to the Romans by CARTIMANDUA, Queen of the BRIGANTES, in 51 and taken to Rome. There, according to TACITUS, he made a speech that so impressed the emperor CLAUDIUS that he was granted his freedom.

Carausius, Roman 'emperor' (287–93). A Menapian (i.e. a member of a tribe inhabiting what is now modern Belgium), he was given the responsibility – early in the reign of the emperor Diocletian (284–305) – of defending the English Channel against barbarian raids. In 287, he revolted and declared himself emperor, 'ruling' apparently successfully in Britain and parts of northern France until he was assassinated by one of his followers. His murderer, Allectus, subsequently maintained himself as emperor until 296, when he was defeated and killed by an invading Roman army led by CONSTANTIUS Chlorus. Britain was then rejoined to the Roman Empire.

The Britons' complacent acceptance of this brief secession is best explained in terms that also explain the Gallic empire. Having become one of the most peaceful provinces of the Roman Empire, the British were content with arrangements that removed them from direct involvement in the turbulence elsewhere.

Cardiff, capital city of Wales. There was a major Roman fort here from the 1st century AD, substantial remains of which survive as part of the CASTLE begun in the 12th century. Around this grew up a BOROUGH which gained a royal charter in 1324. However, the growth of Cardiff is of relatively recent origin, and is particularly associated with the influence of the Earls of Bute in the mid- and late 19th century and their IRON and COAL interests, Cardiff being developed as their main port. Many of the city's most important buildings date from the period *c.*1890–1920.

Carding Machine, *see* COTTON INDUSTRY

Carham, Battle of, ?1018, a victory for MALCOLM II, King of Scots, over the NORTHUMBRIANS at a ford over the Tweed. It does not appear to have been followed by Scottish territorial gains, except perhaps in STRATHCLYDE. Malcolm subsequently acknowledged the traditional English overlordship when CNUT led an army north in 1027.

Caribbean, *see* WEST INDIES

Carlton Club Meeting, a meeting on 19 Oct. 1922 at which the CONSERVATIVE leader, Austen CHAMBERLAIN, intended to spike the guns of the Tory opposition to the coalition government led by LLOYD GEORGE, which had been formed in May 1915 to win the war and had been in office ever since. The Cabinet intended to hold a general election on a coalition ticket and it was becoming clear that a number of CONSTITUENCIES (the Conservative chief whip estimated 184) would run an independent Conservative candidate against the official coalition candidate. The meeting, held in a private club, has frequently been portrayed as a cabal of conspirators; but it was only with reluctance that the former Conservative leader, Bonar LAW, convinced that his party was in danger of tearing itself apart, would consider heading the somewhat disparate group of Conservative anti-coalitionists in Parliament and the party. Supported by *The Times* and the Beaverbrook press, and of certain knowledge that Lloyd George – to whom he felt considerable loyalty – would not voluntarily dissolve the coalition, on the eve of the meeting Bonar Law decided to intervene. The next morning came news of the Newport by-election: the independent Conservative had won a resounding victory, with the coalition LIBERAL lagging a poor third after LABOUR. At the Carlton Club meeting Bonar Law evoked PEEL's splitting the Conservative Party over the repeal of the CORN LAWS in 1846 and declared that he would vote for ending the coalition; the vote was carried 187–87. That afternoon Lloyd George resigned, and on 23 Oct. Bonar Law was elected leader of the Conservative Party. That same day he was formally appointed prime minister. At the general election on 15 Nov., with their opponents so divided, the Conservatives won with a majority of 77: 344 seats to Labour's 138, the ASQUITH Liberals' 60 and the Lloyd George Liberals' 57.

Carmarthen By-Election, *see* PLAID CYMRU

Carmarthen, 1st Marquess of, *see* OSBORNE, THOMAS

Carmelites, *see* FRIARS

Carolina, North and South, states of the USA and British colonies before 1776. They were named after the restored CHARLES II, with North Carolina founded in 1660, South in 1670. The first attempted English colony in North America, ROANOKE, was briefly established on the Banks on the North Carolina coast in 1587. The Carolinas came to specialize in rice, tobacco and indigo production.

Caroline (1768–1821), Queen of Great Britain and Ireland. Daughter of Charles, Duke of Brunswick, she married her first cousin, George, then Prince of Wales, on 8 April 1795. The marriage was a disaster from the start and the couple separated in 1796, a few months after the birth of their daughter, Charlotte (who died in 1817). Caroline's subsequent behaviour at home and abroad was unconventional and indiscreet – though she was exonerated from charges of adultery by a 'Delicate Investigation' in 1806. When her husband succeeded to the throne as GEORGE IV in 1820, she determined to return to England and take her place as queen. She landed at Dover in June, having spurned a government annuity of £50,000 to relinquish her title and stay in exile. The next month, a Bill of Pains and Penalties was introduced by the government in the House of Lords to divorce her from the king and strip her of her queenship. The combination of her popularity in the country (she was taken up by RADICALS and WHIGS), and her incisive defence by BROUGHAM led to the withdrawal of the Bill. Nevertheless she was forcibly excluded from her husband's coronation in July 1821 and died at Hammersmith a few weeks later.

Caroline (or Carolingian) Minuscule, a style of script disseminated within the CAROLINGIAN Empire during the 8th and 9th centuries, whose letter-forms are essentially those we use today. It was brought to England in ALFRED THE GREAT's time and became more widely used during the TENTH-CENTURY REFORM, most notably in manuscripts produced at St Ethelwold's church at WINCHESTER.

Carolingian Influence on Anglo-Saxon England The empire created by Charlemagne (768–814) was the largest and most successful of the early medieval period. Scholars are currently observing how often the policies followed by English kings seem to have been influenced by Carolingian example. Obvious instances are ALFRED THE GREAT's educational policy and patronage of court scholars, and the 10th-century COINAGE reforms. There are also numerous indications of a profound Carolingian influence on the TENTH-CENTURY REFORM.

Carthusians, monastic ORDER which developed the BENEDICTINE RULE as a framework for creating communities of monks living as hermits. The first house was founded in France by St Bruno in 1084 at the Grande Chartreuse ('Carthusium' in Latin; corrupted into English as 'Charterhouse', which became the designation for English houses of the order). The Carthusians' austere lifestyle meant that they were never numerous, but it also saved them from the corruption of their original ideals, and so they retained widespread respect in late medieval England. Carthusians were one of the few orders which offered much resistance to HENRY VIII's monastic DISSOLUTIONS. The buildings of the London Charterhouse later became the site of a leading PUBLIC SCHOOL.

Cartimandua (*fl.* AD 50s), Queen of the Brigantes. She maintained the independence of the BRIGANTES during the early stages of the ROMAN CONQUEST by allying herself with the invaders. In this role, she handed over to them the British resistance leader CARATACUS in 51. After a quarrel with her husband Venutius, she had to be rescued by the Romans, an event that opened up northern England for conquest.

Carucage, tax assessed on *CARUCATES*. It was first levied by RICHARD I in 1198 and then only occasionally in the early 13th century.

Carucate, the equivalent of the HIDE in the counties of eastern and northern England in the Middle Ages, and the basis there of the assessment of service and taxation. Originally comprising as much land as one plough team could manage in a day, its origins were once thought to be Scandinavian, but it is now seen as a new unit imposed by the English kings in the 10th and 11th centuries.

Carvetii, one of the smaller tribes that controlled Britain before the arrival of the Romans. Their territory lay around Carlisle, and they presumably fell under Roman domination in AD 71–2, at the same time as their much more powerful neighbours, the BRIGANTES. A *CIVITAS* was created for them some time during the 2nd or 3rd century.

Casablanca Conference, Jan. 1943, meeting between CHURCHILL and Roosevelt during WORLD WAR II at which it was agreed to invade Sicily and Italy rather than France during 1943. The policy of Unconditional Surrender was formally endorsed to reassure Stalin of the western Allies' commitment to the final defeat of Germany.

Cassivellaunus (*fl.* 50s BC), British war leader. He was chosen in 54 BC by a confederacy of the tribes of southern Britain to head the resistance to the Roman invasion led by JULIUS CAESAR. Other than his military exploits and the fact that he may have been king of the CATUVELLAUNI, nothing is known about him. Although he lost a pitched battle, had his base camp captured and was eventually forced to make an apparently disadvantageous peace, his tenacious resistance obstructed Caesar's advance and contributed much to undermining the Romans' plans for conquest.

Castile, Eleanor of, *see* ELEANOR OF CASTILE

Castillon, Battle of, east of Bordeaux, 17 July 1453, the French victory that sealed the fate of English GASCONY, and which is generally regarded as marking the end of the HUNDRED YEARS WAR. The English commander, John Talbot, was killed.

Castle, heavily fortified residence generally held by a king or a lord, and especially associated with the three centuries following the NORMAN CONQUEST. Although the castle has now been shown to have had antecedents in the Anglo-Saxon era (*see* GOLTHO), the development of the castle fully began only after 1066. Early castles were built at strategic locations to dominate the population of an area; most of them were wooden structures on a mound or motte, usually with a moated earthwork enclosure or bailey, although a number of the important early castles – the TOWER OF LONDON, COLCHESTER, Essex, and Richmond, Yorks. – were of stone. From the 12th century, most English castles were built, or rebuilt, in stone, and often on an increasingly elaborate scale. (However, in the early stages of the invasion of Ireland, earthwork and timber castles again proliferated.) Among the largest and grandest castles were those built to subjugate Wales by EDWARD I, e.g. Caernarfon. As the threat of attack gradually subsided, so the large defensive structures were dismantled or lords chose to live in fortified manor houses, and then in houses without defences. Many castles indeed only ever saw military action in the CIVIL WARS of the 17th century. By the early 17th century castles were still occasionally being built as part of the romantic evocation of medieval tradition, e.g. Bolsover, Derbys., by the Smythsons, and that romanticism has continued, notably in the 19th century GOTHIC revival. The most recent castle to be built in Britain was Edwin Lutyens' Castle Drogo in Devon, 1910–30.

Castlereagh, 1st Viscount, *see* STEWART, ROBERT

'Cat and Mouse Act' 1913 Officially known as the Prisoner's Temporary Discharge for Ill-Health Act, this legislation was rushed through Parliament in 1913 by the LIBERAL government of ASQUITH as a response to public disquiet about the forcible feeding of SUFFRAGETTES on hunger strike. The Bill soon became known as 'The Cat and Mouse Act' since the prison authorities (the 'cat') were empowered to release hunger-strikers on a special licence, and then rearrest them (like mice) to finish their sentences. The Act did not succeed in its intention of breaking the suffragettes' morale and putting an end to hunger and thirst strikes, since the 'mice' often went missing on their release and evaded rearrest, while public disquiet was not much assuaged by the spectacle.

Cateau-Cambresis, Treaties of, 1559, two treaties between, respectively, England and France, and Spain and France, ending their war (1557–9). France retained CALAIS, theoretically for eight years, but renounced ambitions in Italy.

Catechisms, manuals of religious instruction, normally in question and answer form;

the PRAYER BOOK includes one of 1552. Historians are beginning to realize their educational importance in the REFORMATION, in realigning England and Wales towards PROTESTANTISM.

Cathal mac Finguine (?–742), King of Munster. Cathal mac Finguine was one of the few kings of MUNSTER before the reign of BRIAN BORU to cut a figure on a broader Irish stage. His career of military expansion, begun in 721, was characterized by a mixture of successes and failures. Later legend extravagantly suggested that he had been king of all Ireland (*see* KINGSHIP).

Cathedral, a church which is the principal seat, or *cathedra*, of a diocesan bishop. In non-episcopalian churches, notably in Scotland (*see* CHURCH: SCOTLAND), the title is retained by churches which were bishops' seats before the REFORMATION. In the 8th century there were 17 DIOCESES in what would become England, whereas in the troubles of the 9th century the number fell to 12. Reformism in the 10th century increased the number of diocesan seats, and the NORMAN CONQUEST brought their removal to larger centres of population. Cathedrals, both with secular clergy and – almost peculiar to England – with monks, were among the most important recipients of medieval benefactions, and cathedrals and abbeys sought to acquire a saint whose cult would improve their wealth and fame. Thus cathedrals were also among the most avant-garde centres of each new architectural style: notable examples are SALISBURY, Wells, GLOUCESTER, DURHAM, and the pre-eminent archiepiscopal cathedrals, CANTERBURY and YORK.

By the reign of HENRY I there were 17 English dioceses. At the DISSOLUTION OF THE MONASTERIES, five new dioceses were created – Chester, Gloucester, Peterborough, OXFORD, and BRISTOL – with WESTMINSTER ABBEY given a brief life as a diocesan cathedral before becoming a unique COLLEGIATE CHURCH. In the 17th and 18th centuries many cathedrals suffered considerable neglect, both as a result of deliberate depredation in the period of CIVIL WAR and INTERREGNUM and because of general lack of interest in the care and state of churches, the building of WREN's St Paul's in LONDON being one of the few exceptions to the rule. Further significant changes occurred only in the 19th century, as a result of the ecclesiastical revival and the efforts of the restorers, notably SCOTT, when many ancient buildings were transformed and re-edified, and with the formation of new dioceses – a total of 19 between 1836, when the ancient minster at Ripon was upgraded, and the post-1945 new building of Guildford, together with a further three additions in Wales. Basil Spence's rebuilding of COVENTRY cathedral became one of the great symbols of post-war reconstruction. The re-establishment of a Roman Catholic hierarchy likewise caused the formation of dioceses with cathedrals, the English archdiocese being based in J. F. Bentley's neo-Byzantine WESTMINSTER cathedral (1895–1903).

Catherine Howard (1521–42), Queen of England. Niece of Thomas HOWARD, Duke of Norfolk, she was promoted by the conservative faction at court to console HENRY VIII for the ANNE OF CLEVES disappointment. She was a racy young lady who did not have the sense to see the danger of continuing her amorous dalliances after her royal marriage in 1540. Unsurprisingly, it was a PROTESTANT courtier who uncovered the evidence of her indiscretions, and Archbishop CRANMER who passed it to the king. Henry, humiliated and grief-stricken, had her and her lovers executed.

Catherine of Aragon (1485–1536), Queen of England. Daughter of Ferdinand and Isabella of Aragon and Castile, she was married in her teens to Prince ARTHUR and, after his death, to his younger brother, HENRY VIII, on 24 June 1509. The marriage was at first successful, Catherine proving to be an able regent of England in Henry's absence in France in 1513. However, she produced only one child to survive infancy, Mary (the future MARY I) in 1516, and the relationship cooled. Henry, desperate for a male heir, had already, in 1514, mooted an annulment to secure a fertile wife; from 1526, with the incentive of his love for ANNE BOLEYN, he obsessively pursued this course, attacking the dispensations that had allowed his marriage to Catherine (which had been required because she was his brother's widow). In 1527 and 1529 – with the backing of her nephew Charles V, particularly in the form of pressure on Pope Clement VII – she put up a fierce resistance to successive attempts to declare her marriage invalid, but when the king embarked on a unilateral course in 1532–3, she could only refuse to recognize the annulment sentence (May 1533) and the declaration that her daughter was illegitimate. Attracting much public sympathy, especially from fellow religious conservatives, she lived her last years in dignified misery, although punctiliously surrounded by the comforts appropriate to a princess dowager. Her death delighted Henry who did not attend her funeral in Peterborough abbey.

Catherine of Valois (1401–37), Queen of England. Daughter of Charles VI of France, in 1420 she was married to HENRY V in accordance with the terms of the Treaty of TROYES, and bore him a son, the future HENRY VI. Widowed in 1422, she secretly (*c.*1431–2) married Owen ap Maredudd ap Tudor, and bore Edmund Tudor (later Earl of Richmond and father of HENRY VII) and Jasper Tudor. Buried in Westminster Abbey, her remains were there kissed by Samuel PEPYS on his 36th birthday (23 Feb. 1669) as a tribute to her legendary beauty.

Catherine Parr (1512–48), Queen of England. Daughter of Sir Thomas Parr, a royal official, she had been twice widowed when HENRY VIII chose to marry her in 1543. Her warmth and tact – and her openness to her assorted royal stepchildren – made the marriage a success. She developed PROTESTANT sympathies, promoting reformist interests at court, but conservative attempts to discredit her with Henry (and even destroy her) backfired. On the king's death, she married an earlier love, Lord Thomas Seymour; published a reformist pious tract, *The Lamentations of a Sinner*; and encouraged the publication of ERASMUS's *Paraphrases* in translation.

Catholic, from the Greek *katholikos*, 'universal'. An adjective applied with various religious nuances: (1) the doctrine accepted as basic by all mainstream Christians; (2) a self-designation for that part of the medieval Western Church remaining loyal to Rome in the 16th-century REFORMATION (otherwise 'Roman Catholics'; *see* CATHOLIC, ROMAN; COUNTER REFORMATION); and (3) a self-designation for the theological views of HIGH CHURCH ANGLICANS and like-minded groups within the FREE CHURCHES and the CHURCH OF SCOTLAND.

Catholic Apostolic Church, a Church founded after a REVIVALIST group gathered round a former TORY MP, Henry Drummond (1786–1860), and a charismatic CHURCH OF SCOTLAND minister, Edward Irving (1792–1834); outsiders often informally referred to the Church as 'Irvingite'. The members believed in the imminent Second Coming of Jesus Christ, and by 1835 Drummond gathered twelve Apostles to await this event. Rapidly, and surprisingly, they developed RITUALIST interest, eventually worshipping with the most elaborate liturgy ever devised for ordinary use in a Western Church. Their membership was largely middle-class, with a sprinkling of aristocrats, and their church buildings tended to be splendid in design, but unfinished. However, they made no provision for any postponement of the Second Coming, and after the death of the last Apostle in 1901, the Church diminished in numbers. It largely disintegrated in Britain in the 1960s and 1970s, but offshoots survive in North America and central Europe.

Catholic Committee, Irish, 1759–95, committee set up initially by DUBLIN Catholic merchants and professionals to coordinate Irish Catholic political activity during the period which saw the growth of agitation for CATHOLIC EMANCIPATION. The group petitioned the lord lieutenant expressing the hope that they might serve as useful members of the community, and coordinated a congratulatory address from the Catholics of Ireland on the accession of GEORGE III. An initial focus of agitation was resistance to Irish town guilds' efforts to collect 'quarterage' dues from Catholic merchants, despite their exclusion from civic and political power; support from sympathetic lords lieutenant helped the Catholic cause. The War of AMERICAN INDEPENDENCE provided a new opportunity for Catholics to proclaim loyalty and hope for government aid in return; the committee also appointed a resident agent in England and began to raise funds through PARISH collections. Relief Bills of 1778 and 1782 rewarded these efforts, and in 1789 the committee (now a nationally elected body) began to campaign for political rights. But internal tensions between liberals and radicals emerged and it became evident to the administration that there was a case for further conciliatory concessions. However, modest concessions in 1792 merely spurred the committee to further efforts, including the appointment of a full-time assistant secretary, PROTESTANT barrister Wolfe TONE. Electoral arrangements were refurbished, and a new committee of 230 delegates met in Dublin in Dec. Though 25 UNITED IRISHMEN were among their number, the committee maintained cool relations with radicals, calculating that an independent position would serve it best. A 1793 Bill went further to meet Catholic aspirations, admitting them to the franchise, removing restrictions on holding of all but the highest offices, and extending to propertied Catholics the right to bear arms. The committee subsequently divided as to the merits of pursuing PARLIAMENTARY REFORM. Legislation banning national representative bodies prompted its dissolution in 1793.

Catholic Emancipation, repeal of penal laws against Catholics. The term 'emancipation' came into favour in this context once the campaign against the SLAVE TRADE, which gathered force in the late 1780s, had given it special resonance. Modification of the laws – termed 'Catholic Relief' – began in 1774 in Ireland, and in 1778 in England. The English Act precipitated the GORDON RIOTS; demonstrating the strength of popular ANTI-CATHOLICISM, the riots impressed GEORGE III with the potential dangers of radical action. None the less, very restrictive Irish laws were further modified in 1782, to allow CATHOLIC purchase of FREEHOLD land. English Catholic protestations of loyalty, embodied most notably in a 'Protestation' of 1788 which denied papal temporal authority, and signed by the four Vicars Apostolic, 240 priests and 1,500 laymen, helped to secure further modification of English law in 1791, removing all religious, but not all civil disabilities: the TEST ACT continued to bar Catholics from parliament and other civil offices. In 1792 further modifications of the Irish laws allowed Irish Catholics to marry Protestants, to teach and to practise law; from 1793 they were also allowed to vote. Most remaining disabilities were removed by the CATHOLIC EMANCIPATION (RELIEF) ACT 1829, which applied to the whole of the United Kingdom. *See also* CATHOLIC COMMITTEE, IRISH.

Catholic Emancipation (Relief) Act 1829, proposal brought forward by PEEL to prevent civil war in the aftermath of Daniel O'CONNELL's success at the Co. Clare election. The Act enabled Roman Catholics to sit in Parliament and made them eligible for all public offices except regent, lord lieutenant and lord chancellor. For Peel and Wellington (*see* WELLESLEY, ARTHUR), previously staunch advocates of the PROTESTANT ASCENDANCY, this statesman-like measure represented a volte-face that destroyed their administration. Despite general repeal of anti-Catholic measures, it remains a requirement by the Act of SETTLEMENT 1701 that the monarch must not be a Roman Catholic or marry one. *See also* ANTI-CATHOLICISM.

Catholic, Roman Roman Catholicism in England was severely repressed during ELIZABETH I's reign, and the government was very successful in associating ANTI-CATHOLICISM with patriotism, aided by FOXE's *Book of Martyrs*, the Spanish ARMADA and the GUNPOWDER PLOT (*see also* COUNTER-REFORMATION). The Catholic community became a gentry-led minority, which played little role in politics, even when JAMES II briefly gave it the chance. During the 18th century, the enforcement of anti-Catholic legislation gradually lapsed, and CATHOLIC EMANCIPATION began to remove most civil disabilities. Extensive Irish immigration during the 19th century aided a steady institutional and demographic recovery, but only in the latter half of the 20th century has the Roman Catholic Church fully emerged into the mainstream of English life.

Catholicism, Liberal, term used to describe the views of those Roman Catholics and ANGLICANS who sought to preserve a traditional approach to doctrine while accommodating certain of the ideas associated with the historical and critical study of the Scriptures. The Anglican authors of *LUX MUNDI* (1889) embody this approach. *See also* MODERNISM, RELIGIOUS.

Cato Street Conspiracy, a plot hatched by Arthur Thistlewood and others to assassinate ministers of the crown at a dinner party at Lord Harrowby's house in Grosvenor Square, London, on 23 Feb. 1820. Thistlewood was betrayed and his gang arrested as they made their preparations at a house in Cato Street

TRIBAL BRITAIN
VACOMAGI
CALEDONII
TAEXALI
R Tay
VENICONES
R Clyde
DUMNONII
EPIDII
VOTADINI
SELGOVAE
NOVANTAE
BRIGANTES
NORTH SEA
IRISH SEA
R Ouse
PARISI
DECEANGLI
CORITANI
R Trent
ORDOVICES
CORNOVII
ICENI
R Ouse
R Severn
CATUVELLAUNI
TRINOVANTES
DEMETAE
DOBUNNI
SILURES
R Thames
CANTIUM
0 km 150
0 miles 80
ATREBATES
DUROTRIGES
DUMNONII
English Channel

near the Edgware Road, west London. English JACOBINISM died on the gallows with them.

Cattle Acts 1663, 1667, legislation restricting the importation of Irish and Scottish cattle into England, prompted by a desire to improve the balance of trade, and concern for the falling price of English grazing land. The Acts demonstrated the English Parliament's concern to promote English prosperity, if necessary at the expense of other parts of the British Isles. Restrictions on Scottish imports lapsed with the Act of UNION in 1707; those on Ireland remained in place till 1759. Whether Irish economic development was in practice retarded by such measures has been questioned: revisionists note that markets were found for alternative products, such as salt beef.

Catuvellauni, the most powerful of the British tribes of pre-Roman southern Britain. The centre of their power lay in what is now Herts., but the evidence suggests that, under the rule of CUNOBELIN and his sons in the first decades of the 1st century, they dominated most of south-eastern England, including their main rivals, the TRINOVANTES. It must have been a predominantly Catuvellaunan army that the Roman general AULUS PLAUTIUS defeated in AD 43 at the great battle on the River MEDWAY. After the Roman victory, Cunobelin's surviving son, CARATACUS, fled west to continue the resistance. The former tribal territory was formed into a *CIVITAS* with its capital at VERULAMIUM (St Albans).

Cavalier Parliament Lasting from May 1661 to Jan. 1679, it was so named because of the large proportion of loyalist MPs. Religiously more conservative than the CONVENTION PARLIAMENT of 1660 which preceded it, it enacted the repressive CLARENDON CODE. By-elections effected some change in its membership, but about half of the initial MPs remained throughout.

Cavaliers, *see* ROYALISTS

Cavalry, *see* WARFARE, LAND

Cavendish, William (4th Duke of Devonshire) (1720–64), politician and Prime Minister (1756–7). Entering the Commons as WHIG MP for Derbyshire in 1741, his marriage to Lord Burlington's daughter seven years later brought him further powerful Whig connections. These, together with his social position, were to make him an important political figure of the second rank. Appointed lord lieutenant of Ireland in 1754, he returned to serve as first lord of the Treasury upon Newcastle's (*see* PELHAM-HOLLES) resignation in 1756, in what was effectively PITT THE ELDER's administration. Resigning in the latter's wake in 1757, he became lord chamberlain of the household. Like other OLD CORPS WHIGS, he was both distrustful of and distrusted by GEORGE III; when he resigned office in 1762, the king struck his name from the list of PRIVY COUNCILLORS with his own hand.

Caxton, William (*c.*1420–91), printer and publisher. After seeing printed books in circulation in Bruges where he was in business, he visited Cologne to acquire the skill and the equipment and then, in 1476, returned to Bruges to set up his own printing shop. Two years later, he moved to Westminster, where he became the first English publisher of printed books. Frequently acting as his own translator and editor, he published over 100 titles covering a remarkably wide range of subjects: school books, law books, religious and philosophical works, poetry (including CHAUCER and John Lydgate (*c.*1370–*c.*1451), historical and chivalric literature and romances including Malory's *Morte d'Arthur. See also* PRINTING.

Cayman Islands, crown colony in the Caribbean, which was ceded to Britain under the Treaty of Madrid 1670. It became a dependency of JAMAICA, and in the 18th century was a major PRIVATEERING base. Becoming independent from Jamaica in 1962, the islands voted for crown colony status; offshore banking and business are their major earner.

Ceawlin (?–593), King of Wessex. The earliest king of WESSEX for whom there is certain historical information. One of the seven kings named by BEDE as exercising overlordship over the English peoples south of the Humber (*see* BRETWALDA), he is chiefly known as a war leader based on the upper Thames, who fought several battles, including DYRHAM (577), against his British and English neighbours. It appears that, during his time, there was a resumption in the English advance after the long peace following the battle of Mount BADON.

Cecil, Robert (1st Viscount Cranbourne, 15th [1st Cecil] Earl of Salisbury) (1563–1612), royal servant. Younger and much-cherished son of William CECIL, despite ill health he amply rewarded his careful nurture – studying law, travelling on the Continent and undertaking diplomatic missions. He gradually took over his father's role in late Elizabethan government, formalizing this as secretary of state, 1596–1608. A feud with the Earl of Essex (*see* DEVEREUX, ROBERT) was an almost inevitable result of their personality clash and, with almost equal inevitability, it was won by Cecil. He succeeded in securing a smooth succession for JAMES VI to the English throne in 1603; the following year, he also negotiated peace with Spain.

Thereafter, hostility – particularly that of the Howard family – gradually undermined his position, while his work was complicated by the crown's financial problems and the failure of his efforts to remedy them (*see* GREAT CONTRACT); his health broke down, and he died in serious debt. Writer and patron, he combined workaholism with broad and informed cultural interests, delighting in art, music, building (including Hatfield House) and garden design.

Cecil, Robert Gascoyne (3rd Marquess of Salisbury) (1830–1903), Conservative politician and Prime Minister (1885–6, 1886–92, 1895–1902). Sceptical of democracy and hostile to socialism, Salisbury upheld a traditional concept of Conservatism. Its core elements included resistance to HOME RULE, maintenance of law and order, support of the ANGLICAN establishment, safeguarding of property and a firm defence of British interests overseas. Foreign policy was his principal concern. But even here pessimism was pronounced. Statesmanship, in his view, lay principally in the containment of popular national feelings and the postponement of the international conflict he considered inevitable. Distrustful of the populism of DISRAELI or Lord Randolph CHURCHILL, he was nevertheless a shrewd politician, who created an effective Unionist alliance, based on modest social reforms and opposition to Home Rule, that secured the CONSERVATIVE PARTY's ascendancy between 1886 and 1906.

Cecil, William (1st Baron Burghley) (1520–98), royal servant. At CAMBRIDGE UNIVERSITY, he made lifelong friends who later proved very significant in promoting the REFORMATION. He entered the service of Edward SEYMOUR, Duke of Somerset but, after his fall, became secretary of state (1550); he also escaped serious consequences for his (hesitant) involvement in Lady JANE GREY's usurpation.

His career as principal secretary (1558–72) resumed on ELIZABETH I's accession, when he was the chief architect of the ELIZABETHAN SETTLEMENT with his brother-in-law Nicholas Bacon; he was later (1572–98) lord treasurer. During the 1560s, he faced aristocratic opposition, particularly from religious conservatives, which came to a head in 1568–9, but he emerged from this crisis with Elizabeth's confidence in him strengthened. From then on, his life was synonymous with the story of Elizabethan government at home and abroad, and is illuminated by his voluminous surviving papers. He was also active as chancellor of Cambridge University, and acquired a handsome fortune, building enormous houses at Burghley in Northants., and Theobalds, Herts.

Despite his efforts to avoid wars, he was unsuccessful in preventing such descents into foreign military adventuring as the disastrous expedition to France in 1562–3, and the drift into war with Spain in the 1580s. After a lifetime of gingerly patronage of moderate PURITANS, he and his son Robert CECIL turned towards the anti-CALVINISTS in the 1590s. In his last illness, Elizabeth nursed him personally.

A brilliant administrator, he can be criticized for running a decaying administrative system efficiently rather than finding bold solutions to problems left by early Tudor governmental reforms.

Celibacy of Clergy Abstention from marriage and/or sexual relations was always required of monks and nuns (except in some early Celtic CULDEE communities), and came to be expected of higher clergy. The basis for this was a belief that sexuality was a distraction from love for God, and an increasing association in Western Christian theology between the sexual act and sin. There was also a justified suspicion that married clergy would divert Church lands and revenues for the benefit of their children.

From the 11th century, the Western Church waged a determined campaign to extend compulsory celibacy to all clergy. This had just about succeeded by the 16th century, when all PROTESTANT Churches abolished the obligation in England in 1549. MARY I re-established it, and ELIZABETH I hankered after retaining it, but was prevented from doing so except for cathedral CANONS and fellows of OXFORD and CAMBRIDGE colleges (the Oxbridge prohibition lasted until the 19th century).

Celtic Revival, term used to describe the 18th- and 19th-century rediscovery of the Celtic past, especially in Scotland and Ireland, with the revival of Gaelic language and poetry, traditional (and frequently invented) forms of dress, and the study and publication of ancient stories and texts. A Celtic revival was also of increasing importance in 19th-century Wales, notably with the cultivation of the Welsh language and the revival of the poetry and cultural festivals, EISTEDDFODAU. The revival was intimately associated with a growing sense of nationalism in Ireland and the independence movement; it received institutional expression in the foundation of the Gaelic Athletic Association in 1884 to promote traditional games, and the Gaelic League in 1893 to promote the use of the Gaelic language. The poetry of W. B. Yeats (1865–1939) was perhaps the greatest artistic product inspired by the revival.

Celts, term established during the 18th and 19th centuries and used to refer to prehistoric and early historic peoples of Europe. Celtic peoples, divided into distinct tribal groupings, inhabited the British Isles from the Bronze Age, from at least the 5th century BC. They had a distinctive religion, led by DRUIDS, and were renowned for their warrior fearlessness and brutality. The Celts were subjugated by the invading Romans after AD 43, leaving only Ireland unscathed. In what became England, they thereafter lived under the political domination of the Romans and the mixture of peoples who came subsequently to be called the English (*see* BRITISH SURVIVAL IN ENGLAND). There was a resurgence of Celtic art and culture after the Roman era ended, and a vigorous native Celtic church (*see* COLUMBA; IONA; CHURCH: IRELAND), but the remaining independent Celtic peoples were under great pressure from the 11th century, and were gradually absorbed, conquered, and to varying extents assimilated into the prevailing English-based culture. The most important survival of the Celtic presence is in language. Many place names, including LONDON, have Celtic roots. Of the two branches of Celtic language which survived or survive in the British Isles, Irish GAELIC, Scottish Gaelic and Manx are known as Goidelic, and Welsh, Cornish and Breton as Brythonic. The self-conscious, and often nationalistic, CELTIC REVIVAL from the 18th century helped to preserve these languages and some of their attendant cultures.

Cemeteries, Early Anglo-Saxon Because Anglo-Saxon PAGANISM required that some of a dead person's most treasured belongings should be interred with the body, burials and cemeteries have become very important sources for our understanding of English history between the 5th and early 8th centuries. Around 1,500 cemeteries have now been excavated and the discoveries utilized to develop our knowledge of society at that time.

The different types of brooches and pots found can, for example, give clues to the pace and kind of settlement, and can help in analysing the distinctions between ANGLES, SAXONS and JUTES (*see* ANGLO-SAXON SETTLEMENT). A spectacular cemetery such as SUTTON HOO is but the tip of an iceberg, since the variety of treasures discovered elsewhere indicates an ECONOMY more prosperous and varied than might be suspected from the literary sources. The persistence of grave-goods burials into the 8th century also illustrates the relative slowness with which pagan practices were abandoned, despite the supposed CONVERSION of the people to Christianity.

Cenotaph, public monument to the dead of WORLD WAR I situated in WHITEHALL, and focus of the annual Remembrance Sunday commemoration (*see* ARMISTICE DAY). The memorial was designed by Sir Edwin Lutyens as a temporary structure in 1919, but it struck such a chord that the form was reproduced in stone and was the prototype for war memorials across the nation.

Censorship of the Press Most societies can rely on informal repression and public opinion to take care of any need for censorship, but they may also develop institutional forms. The medieval Church suppressed what it thought objectionable – notably, in England, the English BIBLE from 1407 – but early modern 'thought police' faced new problems: rising LITERACY and the sudden increase in book circulation through PRINTING. In the 1530s, HENRY VIII's government followed censorship moves throughout Europe by both Church and secular government. The torrent of publications after Somerset's (*see* SEYMOUR, EDWARD) abolition of censorship in 1547 frightened Northumberland's (*see* DUDLEY, JOHN) government into its reimposition after the 1549 rebellions. In 1556–7, MARY I imposed a registration system run by the Stationers' Company, which was supplemented in 1586 by requirements for licences from the archbishop of Canterbury or the bishop of London. A familiar pattern followed the collapse of this system in 1640: a free-for-all, then new controls from INTERREGNUM governments. Statutory licensing of the press was imposed at the RESTORATION, though the Act lapsed with the demise of the CAVALIER PARLIAMENT in 1678 so that the press proved one of the most effective weapons of the opponents of the future JAMES II in the EXCLUSION CRISIS. Re-enacted in 1685, the Licensing Act remained in force until parliament declined to renew it in 1695. The result was a print explosion and the birth of the NEWSPAPER industry, first in London and then in the provinces. None the less, 18th-century ministries still had some means at their disposal to hamper the press, especially stamp taxes on publications and prosecutions for seditious libel (*see* GENERAL WARRANTS). Efforts at censorship continued down to the 19th century, ending with the abolition of duties on newspapers and paper in 1855, 1861 and 1870. However, censorship was reimposed on private letters as well as printed material during the two world wars. *See also* LICENSING ACTS.

Census, enumeration of the POPULATION. Various European countries, especially in Scandinavia, had instituted censuses in the 18th century, but the first national census of the British population was taken in 1801, for better record-keeping, military preparedness and statistical inquiry. War provided the context in which the British government decided to act, an earlier attempt in 1753 having failed. The population of England and Wales was enumerated at 9,168,000, of Scotland at 1,608,000. (The first Irish census was taken in 1813–15.) Since 1801, censuses have been taken every 10 years, with the exception of 1941.

With the survival of the manuscript schedules from 1841, usually released to public scrutiny after 100 years, personal details on household members are available, of interest both to historians of the FAMILY and GENEALOGISTS. The census frequently elicits a wide range of personal information, from birthplace, and recently ethnicity, to household structure, age and occupation; the 1911 census asked women to provide detailed FERTILITY histories. The census and CIVIL REGISTRATION are both the responsibility of the registrar-general, now within the Office of Population and Census Surveys. John Rickman was in charge of the first three censuses. He surveyed 18th-century population growth by using a questionnaire sent to parish clergy (the details were published with the first census in 1801). Rickman designed the early census forms but their scope was considerably extended by his successors, John Lister and William Farr, increasing concerns about population density, public and occupational health. Suspicion, illiteracy and the engagement of unpaid enumerators, together with the prolonged gathering of census data, made the early censuses inaccurate. By the late 19th century, the census was more carefully and professionally administered and had evolved to a point of greater accuracy although some questions, such as those concerning women's work, elicited answers which continue to frustrate historians.

Central Treaty Organization (CENTO), *see* BAGHDAD PACT

Centralization, caught on as a pejorative term in the early 19th century, connoting especially the supposedly high degree of central control associated with the enlightened despots of 18th-century continental Europe, and with Napoleon. In fact, England, and later Britain, was in certain respects a highly centralized state far earlier than others in Europe. Its Anglo-Saxon central institutions for taxation and law were more sophisticated than elsewhere, and ANGLO-NORMAN monarchs built on this foundation, creating a unified system of royal law based on courts increasingly permanently based in WESTMINSTER (*see* COMMON LAW; EARLDOMS, ANGLO-SAXON). From the 14th century, a single PARLIAMENT represented most parts of England. The Tudor monarchs extended the effectiveness of central control, using especially the ASSIZES, JUSTICES OF THE PEACE and STAR CHAMBER, to assert their influence in the northern and western highland zone of England as effectively as medieval monarchs had generally done in the south-eastern lowland zone. They also integrated the government of Wales, and began the assault on Irish independence of Westminster which was completed by Oliver CROMWELL and by the defeat of Irish Catholic power in WILLIAM III's campaigns of 1690–1 (subsequently partly undone with the re-establishment of an independent Irish parliament). The assimilation of Scotland remained imperfect, despite the Act of UNION (1707) and the military defeats of the Scottish JACOBITES. Bureaucracy, especially for fiscal administration (*see* EXCISE), grew steadily from the late 17th century. True, municipal and parish authorities had acquired habits of independence over time, and it was in defence of the traditional character and powers of such bodies that the cry of 'centralization' was sounded. In practice, however, early 19th-century reforming efforts were directed rather towards the reconstitution than towards the destruction of local government. *See also* CIVIL SERVICE.

Cenwulf (?–821), King of Mercia (796–821). The last MERCIAN king to exercise supremacy over the southern English kingdoms, there are indications that he might not have been able to wield as much power as his predecessor OFFA had – e.g. his abandonment of Offa's campaign to have LICHFIELD made into an archbishopric. Cenwulf did, however, campaign successfully against the Welsh, and is the only English king before the 10th century to be referred to as an emperor (*see* IMPERIAL THEORY OF KINGSHIP).

Ceolwulf (?–764), King of NORTHUMBRIA (729–37). A patron of learning and the king to whom BEDE's *Ecclesiastical History* is dedicated. He seems not to have been a successful ruler, being temporarily deposed after two years of his reign in 731 and then retiring to the abbey of LINDISFARNE in 737.

Ceorl, an Anglo-Saxon term whose significance used to be much discussed in the context of whether English society originally comprised equal, free peasants. An acceptable translation is probably 'the head of a non-noble household' whose status was superior to that of a slave (*see* SLAVERY). The *ceorl* had much in common with later medieval peasants owing labour services. The various categories of *ceorl* are illustrated in *RECTITUDINES SINGULARUM PERSONARUM.*

Cerdic (died ? *c.*530), King of Wessex. Sources such as the late 9th-century *ANGLO-SAXON CHRONICLE* name Cerdic as the first king of WESSEX and state that he was a (possibly Saxon) warleader who landed in England in 495. He may well be a legendary figure, invented by later ages to impose a pattern on the obscure process whereby the English arrived in Britain.

Ceredigion, Welsh kingdom. The earliest existing reference to a king of Ceredigion dates to the early 9th century. However, given the scarcity of evidence for early Welsh history, it is possible that the kingdom dates back to the 5th or 6th century. It came to an end in 872 when it was absorbed into GWYNEDD. *See also* KINGSHIP.

Ceylon, large island territory off the southern tip of INDIA, ruled by Britain between 1796 and 1948. The Dutch had had control since 1638, with some areas having been under Portuguese rule between 1596 and 1658. The island was taken by the British EAST INDIA COMPANY in 1796 during the French wars, along with other Dutch possessions in south and south-east Asia (*see* e.g. MALAYA). The island was systematically developed by the British for commercial crops: first cinnamon and coconut, then TEA, coffee and rubber. Ceylon was thereby well tied into world markets, and large plantations were established under European ownership. Universal suffrage was granted in 1931, and the island's separatist political movements and growth of a Congress party paralleled those of India. Independence was granted in 1948, the year after India's. The country was renamed Sri Lanka in 1972.

Chamber, Royal, and Finance The Chamber was originally the king's private apartment, a magnificent bedsitting room. Naturally, the king kept stores of personal cash there. The chamber therefore doubled in the 11th and 12th centuries as the main financial office of the English royal household until in the 13th century its place was taken by another royal domestic department, the WARDROBE. The Chamber briefly revived in importance under EDWARD II. Chamber finance refers to this household system of managing the finance of the kingdom, either through the Chamber itself or through the Wardrobe, rather than through the formal procedures of the WESTMINSTER-based EXCHEQUER. While royal government was essentially itinerant, chamber finance remained at the centre of the royal financial system, and clerks of the Chamber like Walter of Coutances, or Chamberlains like Hubert de BURGH, went on to hold the highest office in the land. Since the Chamber was the chief spending department, the itinerant king was accompanied by his Chamber clerks and their carts loaded with silver pennies and Chamber records (nearly all of them no longer extant).

When royal government became more settled at Westminster in the 14th century, the Exchequer regained its financial dominance; however, EDWARD IV continued to rely after his seizure of the throne on the revenue-collection methods which he had used on his estates before his accession, which meant that his personal staff in the Chamber once more took over the main revenue role from the Exchequer. Contemporary aristocratic estate practice used receivers, auditors and surveyors to obtain the maximum revenue from estates, and to account to Chamber officials. This version of Chamber finance was not sophisticated, for it involved the direct receipt of cash and depended on intensive face-to-face supervision, but used conscientiously it proved very effective, and a brief return to Exchequer dominance in HENRY VII's first years proved temporary.

Under HENRY VIII, Chamber financial organization was recognized as a formal Court of GENERAL SURVEYORS (1515), but it was challenged by diversion of cash to what was now the real royal private suite – the PRIVY CHAMBER – and it became merely one revenue-raising department among several. During the 1540s, overhaul of financial departments began, spurred by grave revenue problems. Exchequer officials won a belated victory when General Surveyors was absorbed into the Exchequer in 1554, but it was an untidy compromise, with Chamber procedures continuing to function in the Exchequer alongside the older Exchequer 'course'. Thereafter, from *c.* 1600 both Chamber financial procedures and the Exchequer itself were sidelined by the growth of yet another informal financial system which became the TREASURY.

Chamberlain, Joseph (1836–1914), politician. A screw-manufacturing industrialist, Chamberlain built up his political fiefdom in BIRMINGHAM, where as mayor (1873–6) his acquisition of land and public utilities, 'gas and water socialism', transformed the city from an industrial slum into a model municipality. A dynamic, radical reformer, he had the reputation of 'talking pure undiluted politics at social functions'. From the local stage he moved to the national: elected to Parliament as LIBERAL MP in 1876, he was determined to do for the nation what he had done for the city. His 'unauthorized programme', proclaimed in 1885 whilst he was president of the BOARD OF TRADE in GLADSTONE's second ministry, called among other things for 'three acres and a cow' – smallholdings of their own – for agricultural workers. Committed to the principle of imperial unity and expansion, Chamberlain resigned in 1886 over Gladstone's conversion to HOME RULE for Ireland and led the LIBERAL UNIONISTS (including his son Austen Chamberlain, 1863–1937) into an alliance with the CONSERVATIVES.

As secretary for the Colonies (1895–1903) under Salisbury (*see* CECIL, ROBERT GASCOYNE), he was largely responsible for British policy over the BOER WAR. His belief that Britain should follow a policy of IMPERIAL PREFERENCE and abandon the tenets of FREE TRADE, led him to resign from the government in order to launch a campaign for TARIFF REFORM in 1903. This split the Conservatives and led to the Liberal landslide of 1906, the year of Chamberlain's stroke, which forced him out of public life.

When campaigning for his 'unauthorized programme', Chamberlain had declared, 'I am told that if I pursue this course I shall break up the Party...but I care little for party...except to promote the objects which I publicly avowed when I first entered Parliament'. The man who had operated such an effective party machine in Birmingham managed to focus political opposition to such an extent that in turn the two major national parties broke asunder.

Chamberlain, Neville (1869–1940), Conservative politician and Prime Minister (1937–40). From a distinguished BIRMINGHAM political dynasty (the son of Joseph CHAMBERLAIN and half-brother of Austen Chamberlain, 1863–1937), he entered political life relatively late, becoming the city's lord mayor in 1915. He briefly obeyed a summons from LLOYD GEORGE in 1917 to take up the post of director-general of National Service; but it was not until Dec. 1918 that he left local politics for the national arena as CONSERVATIVE MP for Birmingham Ladywood – a seat he held until 1929, when he moved to represent Birmingham Edgbaston. He held office as postmaster-general (1922–3), paymaster-general (1923), minister of health (1924–9, 1931) and chancellor of the Exchequer (1931–7). He proved an efficient domestic administrator, supervising the abolition of the poor law (*see* POOR RELIEF) in 1929, reorganizing UNEMPLOYMENT ASSISTANCE (1934–5) and maintaining the orthodox economic policies of the NATIONAL GOVERNMENT.

His premiership, which began when he succeeded BALDWIN in 1937, was dominated by the issue of APPEASEMENT. He immediately attempted to pursue a 'general settlement' of foreign policy issues, but was increasingly forced to address the crises brought about by Hitler's aggression. In 1938, he took the initiative in trying to avert war by flying to Germany to bargain with the dictator and eventually secured the MUNICH AGREEMENT. Although later accused of craven concessions to Hitler, he attached considerable importance to the 'piece of paper' he had induced the Führer to sign renouncing war between the two states (in return for Britain's recognition of his claims for the Czech Sudetenland); promising 'peace in our time', Chamberlain was received as a hero on his return to England. When Hitler revealed his disregard for the agreement by invading Czechoslovakia, Chamberlain gave guarantees to Poland and Romania (*see* ANGLO-POLISH ALLIANCE), and, with the invasion of Poland, was forced to declare war on 3 Sept. 1939.

He proved an uninspiring war leader. In May 1940 the débâcle of the NORWEGIAN CAMPAIGN led to a censure motion of no confidence in the House of Commons. Although Chamberlain won the vote, many Conservatives voted against him or abstained, and when LABOUR and LIBERALS refused to serve in a National Government under him, he resigned. He continued in office for a short time as lord president of the Council in CHURCHILL's war cabinet, but in Oct. retired from politics, a dying man.

Chambers of Commerce, local commercial associations set up by businessmen and manufacturers to increase co-operation and to provide a pressure-group for their interests. French exemplars began to spawn British imitations from the 1770s: a Glasgow Chamber of Commerce was incorporated in 1783. Further such foundations essentially gave new form to long-established habits of provincial commercial lobbying, and inter-provincial commercial co-operation. Their influence continues to the present day.

Chanak Crisis, crisis in Anglo-Turkish relations in autumn 1922 which brought about the fall of LLOYD GEORGE as prime minister. Faced by a revival of Turkish power under Atatürk which threatened the European territories allotted to Greece by the treaty of Sèvres, Lloyd George ordered the British garrison at Chanak on the Dardanelles to stand firm against the Turkish armies. Only an agreement reached by the local British commander with the Turks, subsequently ratified at the treaty of Lausanne, defused the crisis. The crisis brought to a head CONSERVATIVE opposition to the Lloyd George coalition for risking war with Turkey, leading on 19 October to a vote at the CARLTON CLUB by Conservative backbenchers to withdraw from the coalition (*see also* 1922 COMMITTEE). Lloyd George resigned as prime minister the same day.

Chancellor, originally an officer who sat protected from the public behind a screen (*cancella*, from which *cancellarius*), and hence a senior administrative and legal official in many European political systems – in England from the late Saxon period. Like most administrators he was a cleric, and often personal chaplain to the king. After the NORMAN CONQUEST the chancellor, as head of CHANCERY, was given custody of the GREAT SEAL; he remained a senior political figure (*see* WALTER, HUBERT). A similar development of the office took place in 12th-century Scotland. The English chancellor also presided in the EXCHEQUER during the 12th century; on his withdrawal, the clerk who then substituted for his administrative duties there was known as the CHANCELLOR OF THE EXCHEQUER. From time to time no one was appointed chancellor, and custody of the Great Seal was given to an official or team of officials known as keepers. Because of the legal jurisdiction which the chancellor developed in Chancery, he became the senior legal officer in the realm, and he presided in PARLIAMENT. Later, when separate meetings were held of PEERS and COMMONS, he continued to preside over the meetings of peers, and later over meetings of the formally-constituted House of LORDS. Thomas WOLSEY, who concentrated much of his administrative energy on the Court of Chancery and whose secular power derived from this office, was the first chancellor to be known as lord chancellor. Similarly, from the later Tudor period, when a lord chancellor was not appointed his lower-ranking substitute was known as lord keeper of the Great Seal, or if a team of officials were appointed, they were called lords commissioners of the Great Seal. The lord chancellor remains the one officer of the ANGLO-NORMAN monarchy to retain a genuine leading role in English government; his jurisdiction does not extend to the separate legal system of Scotland. The last chancellor of Scotland, James Ogilvy, 1st Earl of Seafield, appointed before the 1707 Act of UNION and then reappointed in 1708 for life, died in 1730. Analogous senior officials in non-royal (e.g. ducal or EPISCOPAL) administration were also called chancellors (e.g. chancellor of the Duchy of Lancaster), and ANGLICAN DIOCESES retain the office for legal work.

Chancellor of the Exchequer This was not an important post until modern times. The CHANCELLOR of England was one of the royal officials attending the EXCHEQUER in the 12th century, but when he withdrew to establish the separate administration of CHANCERY, he left behind a clerk to undertake certain of his administrative duties, and by the 13th century this official was known as chancellor of the Exchequer. He remained an assistant to the lord high treasurer and one of the officers hearing cases in the equity court of the Exchequer, but as the real financial functions of government passed to the TREASURY in the 17th century, he was also customarily one of the officials commissioned to sit at the Treasury Board. As the FIRST LORD OF THE TREASURY became more occupied with general political matters (*see* PRIME MINISTER), the chancellor took over his financial responsibilities, and by the late 19th century (surviving the abolition of the Exchequer's financial function in 1833), the chancellor had become a politician of CABINET rank.

Chancery One of the key discussions about late Anglo-Saxon government is concerned with whether the 10th- and 11th-century kings had an organized writing office, or chancery, to produce CHARTERS and WRITS. The case is stronger for 10th-century kings such as ATHELSTAN and EDGAR than it is for later rulers, but numerous signs of central direction in the writing of documents, increasing use of a royal SEAL and the development of the writ seem to indicate that the king's clerks frequently supervised the content of documents written in his name.

Chancery was in origin the royal secretariat under the CHANCELLOR, which took formal shape in the 12th century and was housed permanently at WESTMINSTER from the 13th century. The systematic making and keeping of copies of royal letters in the form of chancery rolls – charter rolls, patent rolls and close rolls – dates to the chancellorship of Hubert WALTER (1199–1205). This marked the creation of the central government archives (now the PUBLIC RECORD OFFICE). Chancery's legal work derived from the referral to the chancellor by king and council during the 14th century of an increasing tide of subjects' petitions asking for royal intervention on their behalf. In dealing with these petitions, the chancellor had the prestige to fashion and enforce remedies for petitioners who could show that they could not secure justice in civil matters in the established courts, and gradually his activities in this sphere took on the more formal character of judicial inquiries under oath. By the later 15th century, then, chancery figures as both an administrative body and a court exercising a jurisdiction in equity.

Chancery's jurisdiction continued to grow after 1500, sometimes in conflict with the common law courts but increasingly in co-operation with them, and in 1873 chancery and the other main central courts were amalgamated under the Judicature Act.

Channel Islands, group of islands in the English Channel, close to the coast of France, of which Jersey and Guernsey are the largest, followed by Alderney and Sark. They enjoy an anomalous status within the British Isles, being self-governing bailiwicks. Originally part of the duchy of NORMANDY, and attached to England since the NORMAN CONQUEST, the principal islands remained loyal to King JOHN after the French conquest of Normandy in 1204. Many ANGLO-NORMAN institutions and terms still survive there. The islands' rights were confirmed by HENRY III, EDWARD I and RICHARD II, and separate bailiffs were appointed from 1290. Following continued attacks by the French, e.g. 1338 and 1454, the islands' neutrality was agreed in 1483.

The islanders adopted CALVINISM as their form of religion; yet they remained essentially ROYALIST in their sympathies in the CIVIL WAR, until PARLIAMENT's forces invaded Jersey in 1651. The islands were again the object of French aggression in the War of AMERICAN INDEPENDENCE and the FRENCH REVOLUTIONARY WARS, with attempted invasions in 1779 and the battle of Jersey in 1781; from 1793, after the harbouring of French royalists, the islands were defended and garrisoned. Following Napoleon's defeat (*see* NAPOLEONIC WARS) they saw little action until 1940, when they surrendered to invading German forces in July. Recent opening of the island archives has revealed the extent of collaboration with, as well as resistance to, the occupying German forces, until Liberation in May 1945.

In the post-war years there were major procedural and governmental reforms. Traditionally the islands' lieutenant-governors had come from Britain, the bailiffs from the islands; in 1948 the main islands agreed to maintain the governors and their staffs themselves, and elected assemblies were established. In return, British citizenship was conferred upon the islanders by the 1948 British Nationality Act. The Channel Islands have subsequently become important holiday destinations, while developing the banking institutions which have become their most important economic mainstay.

Chantries, endowments to celebrate MASSes involving prayers for souls departed (Latin *cantare* = 'to sing', from the convention that all masses were sung). Usually prayers were specified for the founder and other benefactors, and their nominees. Of the chapels that were provided for this celebration, some were ambitious free-standing buildings. The movement to found chantries gained popularity in the 13th century and was still vigorous in northern England at the REFORMATION. Chantries were suppressed by legislation in 1545 and 1547; on the first occasion, this was avowedly to raise money, and on the second, because they were associated with the doctrine of PURGATORY. Much informal schooling perished with the chantries, a temporary setback to educational provision.

Chapbooks, small printed books, often 16 pages long, which, from at least the 16th century, were distributed by itinerant dealers or 'chapmen'. They included ballads, jest books, song books, radically abbreviated chivalric and historical romances, and books of prayers and religious admonition. Their numbers and spread are an indicator of the extent of READING and LITERACY. In the era of the French Revolution LOYALISTS such as Hannah More adapted the chapbook medium to warn the lower orders against discontentment and rebellion. Although chapbooks went out of favour in the 19th century, supplanted by PENNY DREADFULS and later cheap NEWSPAPERS, the stories they contained have endured in the consciousness. Some of the adventures in BUNYAN's *Pilgrim's Progress*, for example, are clearly drawn from chapbook antecedents.

Chapel of Ease, an additional church built within a large PARISH to relieve overcrowding or to serve a remote area.

Chapel Royal, the institution which provides for the monarch's worship at COURT; in other words, the term includes the personnel of the chapel, clergy, choir, organists, administrators etc., not just the fabric of the chapel buildings, in various palaces.

Charge of the Light Brigade, disastrous episode in the CRIMEAN WAR, on 25 Oct. 1854 during the Balaclava offensive. A British cavalry charge led by the Earl of Cardigan on the main Russian artillery position – in mistaken error for an isolated enemy outpost – resulted in ignominious defeat and severe casualties and loss of life. Lord Raglan blamed Lord Lucan for the confusion, but the tragedy was added to the roster of complaints against his command. The episode highlighted British military incompetence, and elicited the poet Tennyson's immortal line, 'Into the valley of death rode the six hundred'.

Charity Commissioners, established by the Charitable Trusts Act 1853 to supervise charitable administration in England and Wales. There were four of them: three were paid; and at least two, one of them the chief commissioner, were required to be barristers of at least 12 years' standing. In 1879, the powers previously exercised by the ENDOWED SCHOOLS Commissioners were permanently transferred to the Charity Commissioners, who were also appointed the central authority under the War Charities Act 1916. The Charity Commissioners continue to register and monitor charitable organizations, and to ensure the maintenance of their stated aims.

Charity Organization Society Founded in 1869 to co-ordinate the administration of charity according to given principles, the COS (as it is widely known) believed that the indiscriminate giving of relief was demoralizing to the recipients. It urged the eventual abolition of outdoor relief and the offering of indoor relief to members of the poor who appeared capable of eventually achieving 'self-dependence'. Careful individual casework with families would enable the COS to distinguish between the deserving and undeserving, to decide which families would receive material assistance on a temporary basis and to offer 'education' in household management and the value system common to the Victorian middle and upper classes. The casework approach, although already practised, was pioneered on a grand scale by the COS and was extremely influential in the administration of social policy in both Britain and the USA from then on. Octavia Hill (1838–1912) and the powerful first secretary of the COS, C. S. Loch (who served 1875–1913), were among the most important figures in the society, which numbered among its adherents GLADSTONE and the social reformer Samuel Barnett (1844–1913). While the COS did modify its approach in response to criticism from within as well as without, it continued to insist that relief should be a charitable matter and that the state's role should be confined to relieving the residuum of 'undeserving poor'.

Charity Schools Schools established by charitable benefactions predate the REFORMATION, often being connected with CHANTRIES, but from the late 17th century, such institutions increasingly commonly targeted the young children of the poor. Their chief object was religious, and most were linked with the CHURCH OF ENGLAND. Schools funded by public subscription first appeared in LONDON, and were encouraged by the SPCK. Those providing free clothing as well as tuition were frequently known as 'Blue Coat' or 'Grey Coat' schools. Many charity schools were converted into national schools in the 19th century, but some survived into the 20th.

Charles I (1600–49), King of England, Scotland and Ireland (1625–49). Heir apparent to JAMES VI AND I after his elder brother Prince HENRY's death in 1612; from 1617 his marriage negotiations for the Spanish Infanta Maria caused much ANTI-CATHOLIC national anxiety, particularly when he went in person to Madrid in 1623. English joy at the end of these negotiations was tempered when in the following year he was betrothed to the French princess HENRIETTA MARIA, likewise a Roman Catholic. He succeeded to the throne and married in 1625. His affection for his father's former favourite, George VILLIERS, 4th Duke of Buckingham caused much ill-will nationwide until Buckingham's assassination in 1628. Thereafter Charles turned for companionship to Henrietta Maria, and they became a model of marital devotion, although he got little credit for this from a political nation suspicious of Catholic subversion. Popular worries accumulated because of his consistent favour to the ARMINIAN clergy (*see* LAUD) whom his father had begun to patronize, and also as a result of his difficult relationships with successive English PARLIAMENTS over a combination of financial, religious and political issues (*see* PETITION OF RIGHT; TONNAGE

AND POUNDAGE); he ceased to call Parliaments after 1629, and showed every sign that he did not intend to meet one again.

Charles's personal rule 1629–40 (the Eleven Years' Tyranny, *see* THOROUGH) was fitfully energetic (*see* BOOKS OF ORDERS) and rode out opposition, though marred by a series of public relations disasters in persecuting opponents such as Henry Burton; he also alarmed many English gentry by permitting Thomas WENTWORTH, his lord deputy in Ireland, ruthlessly to recover lands for the crown and the Established Church, from Anglo-Irish and NEW ENGLISH landowners. Equally insensitive to public opinion in his other kingdom of Scotland, he showed no comprehension of Scottish national pride despite his ancestry: his first visit to Scotland for his coronation in 1633 did not improve the atmosphere, and in particular he provoked fury among the Scots because of the English-style religious ceremonial which he worshipped at court. After the fiasco of the BISHOPS' WARS 1639–40, Charles was forced to recall the English PARLIAMENT (*see* LONG PARLIAMENT; SHORT PARLIAMENT) and make sweeping political concessions, which in effect redressed all the grievances which had built up against him and his advisers over the previous years.

What is remarkable, after this apparent settlement of the kingdom's worries, was that within two years Charles managed to throw away any goodwill thus gained and trigger a CIVIL WAR in England. His determination to seize back power on his own terms and his consistent betrayal of attempts at compromise (*see* FIVE MEMBERS) destroyed the trust of many. Confrontation over who would control an army to suppress the Irish Rebellion in 1641 became civil war in 1642, when Charles retreated from Westminster and raised his standard at Nottingham. Natural loyalty to the monarch among gentry and aristocracy, and widespread fear of what the radicals in the Westminster Parliament were intending, now created a constituency of ROYALIST support, and he set up his capital and Parliament at OXFORD.

Facing defeat by May 1646, Charles surrendered to the Scots, abandoning his previous commitment to the system of EPISCOPAL government in the Church in the hope of winning their support. However, negotiations were abortive and the Scots handed him over to the English Parliament. The next few years were filled with futile attempts at constructing a lasting settlement. Renewed royalist risings in summer 1648 persuaded army leaders that he must be destroyed. He won much sympathy by his dignity at his trial and execution (Jan. 1649), and a martyr's cult quickly developed, encouraged by the ghost-written account of his meditations in his last months *EIKON BASILIKE*, and much exploited in CHARLES II's RESTORATION.

Charles has always provoked sharply contrasting assessments. He was hard-working, personally impressive and charming, with an informed interest in art, and in combination with his posthumous image as defender of the Church of England (in reality rather tarnished by his Scottish negotiations of the late 1640s), material has always been on hand for a sympathetic and even admiring interpretation of his career. In recent years some REVISIONIST historians have challenged the negative view of Charles in a number of different ways; most successfully they have pointed out that the Eleven Years' Tyranny was not such a monolithic regime as has sometimes been asserted, and that it accommodated several different viewpoints among leading politicians. Another line has seen Charles's religious policy as a quest for consensus directed by the king, with Archbishop Laud merely as an agent of policies deriving from the king himself. It has also been asserted that opposition to royal religious and financial policies in the 1630s was less widespread than previously thought, and that the collapse of the regime in 1640 can therefore be blamed mainly on the immediate disaster of defeat in Scotland. Much remains to be investigated in the evidence for these arguments. However, what is difficult to escape is the atmosphere of isolation and confrontation which existed in Charles's immediate court circle against the wider political nation before the Civil Wars. He found it difficult to convey his intentions to the wider political audience, or even to see that there was a need to do so. The most likely verdict on Charles is that whatever his private virtues and admirable aesthetic sense, in public life he was selfish, inept and devious. *See also* *BOOK OF SPORTS*; FIVE KNIGHTS' CASE; FOREST LAW; SHIP MONEY.

Charles II (1630–85), King of England (1660–85), Scotland and Ireland (1649–85). Son of CHARLES I and HENRIETTA MARIA, as a 12-year-old he was present at the battle of EDGEHILL, and in 1645 was placed in nominal command of the ROYALIST forces in the south-west. He fled to the Continent in 1646. When his father was executed three years later, he was proclaimed king in EDINBURGH and DUBLIN, and in 1650 he gained Scottish support by accepting the COVENANT. The following year, he invaded England and was seriously injured at WORCESTER, hiding in the 'royal oak' at Boscobel, Salop, while making his escape.

He spent some years in Paris, then travelled elsewhere on the Continent. In 1659, he opened secret negotiations with MONCK, and in his Declaration of BREDA (April 1660), he promised general amnesty, religious liberty and other conciliatory measures: in the event, the RESTORATION settlement was to be somewhat more conservative.

He returned to England in May 1660 and was proclaimed king, his accession being formally backdated to 1649. Two years later, he married the Portuguese princess Catherine of Braganza, a move seen as anti-Spanish and therefore pro-French. His court was notorious for laxity of morals. Charles himself had numerous mistresses, including: Louise de Kéroualle, Duchess of Portsmouth; Eleanor ('Nell') Gwynn; Barbara Villiers, Duchess of Cleveland and Countess of Castlemaine; and Lucy Walter, mother of James SCOTT, Duke of Monmouth.

A pragmatic man, concerned to re-establish the claim of the Stuart house to rule a troubled kingdom, Charles experimented with a variety of domestic political strategies. Clarendon's (*see* HYDE, EDWARD) administration, the CABAL, Danby's (*see* OSBORNE, THOMAS) administration, the various expedients associated with the POPISH PLOT and the EXCLUSION CRISIS, and, finally, the period of TORY REACTION – all represented a series of improvisations as the king and his ministers strove to find a stable basis for government at a time when consensus on religious matters, touching the life of every subject, was notably absent, and the parliamentary support indispensable for the pursuit of any kind of enterprising foreign policy was obtainable only at the price of allowing MPs a powerful voice in such divisive matters.

Although he may have felt the occasional urge to emulate the splendour and self-assertiveness of some of his continental contemporaries, notably Louis XIV – and some of his subjects certainly feared that he might be tempted to aggrandize the powers of the crown – such admiration as he felt for the French seems to have been tempered by concern for British interests. Despite promising, in the secret clauses of the treaty of DOVER (1670), to announce his conversion to Catholicism in return for a French subsidy, he never wholeheartedly committed himself to the support of France, but rather tried to exploit potential antagonism between France and Holland to British advantage. In his later years, however, as his difficulties with Parliament made him increasingly dependent on French financial aid, his freedom of action was effectively constrained.

Having no legitimate children, he expected to be succeeded by his brother James, Duke of York (*see* JAMES II), a declared Catholic, and when the latter's claims came under serious attack during the Exclusion Crisis, Charles was unwavering in his support. On his deathbed, he pronounced himself a Catholic.

'Charles III', *see* STUART, CHARLES EDWARD

Charles, Prince of Wales (Charles Philip Arthur George) (1948–), heir apparent. The eldest son of Queen ELIZABETH II and Prince Philip, Duke of Edinburgh, Charles was the first heir to the throne to have been educated at a school and obtained a university degree. His life as heir apparent, with his adoption of the roles of architectural critic, ecological enthusiast, scourge of inner city deprivation and supporter of youth development projects, has been played out under full media scrutiny. His investiture at Caernarfon Castle as Prince of Wales on 1 July 1969 was watched by a television audience of some 200 million worldwide. He played himself in a television programme on the home life of the royals on the eve of the investiture, and his wedding in 1981 to Lady Diana Spencer was dubbed 'fairytale' and watched by 750 million viewers in 74 countries.

Two sons were born, Prince William (1982) and Prince Henry (Harry) (1984), but the marriage collapsed amidst mutual televised confessions of adultery and the couple were divorced in 1996. DIANA, Princess of Wales, died on 31 August 1997, since when Charles has struggled, with some success, to establish his credentials as a plausible monarch for the 21st century – when the post eventually falls vacant.

Charterhouse, *see* CARTHUSIANS

Charters, Anglo-Saxon An extremely important source for Anglo-Saxon history because they record the transfer of ESTATES, they sometimes describe their boundaries and frequently supply a list of witnesses present when the charter was drawn up. Over 1,000 survive from the 10th century onwards, although some have been the subject of subsequent interpolation and recopying, and some are forgeries. The charter, modelled on the Italian private deed, was introduced into England by the Roman missionaries (*see* CONVERSION). In form, they always remained ecclesiastical documents, although it is possible to argue that some in the 10th century were products of a royal CHANCERY. In the 11th century, some of their functions were taken over by the sealed WRIT.

Chartism, a working-class movement in favour of political equality, accountability and social justice. Its demands – embodied in a Bill or 'charter', for parliamentary approval – comprised six points: manhood suffrage, equal electoral districts, voting by ballot, annual parliaments, abolition of property qualifications for MPs, and payment for MPs. Notwithstanding local variations in its strength and character, chartism mobilized a larger proportion of workers than any other movement before the end of World War I. Its progress, however, was retarded by resolute opponents, differing regional attitudes and interests, and the leadership divisions over 'physical' and 'moral' force; in addition, its success in mobilizing its supporters was diminished in times of economic prosperity.

In May 1838, the People's Charter was published and a national campaign formed around it. A petition, with 1,280,000 signatures, was presented to Parliament in June 1839 and rejected a month later, by 235 votes to 46. A period of confusion and division followed, accompanied by intermittent attempts at resistance, boycott, general strike and insurrection. With the formation of the National Charter Association in July 1840 began the patient work of creating an effective national organization, and in 1842, a second monster petition was presented to Parliament. Its rejection provoked a further round of strikes, riots and arrests.

In the years that followed, Chartists debated the most effective way of achieving their aims. Socialism, republicanism and varying forms of a democratic polity were scrutinized; practical experiments in land reform were tried; and there were advocates of 'Bible Chartism', 'Teetotal Chartism' and 'Knowledge Chartism'. In Feb. 1848, following the revolution in France, and inspired by the example of the 'YOUNG IRELAND' movement, a final petition was launched, said to contain 5,706,000 signatures, and it was decided that a mass demonstration should march from Kennington Common on 10 April to present it to Parliament. The military were placed on stand-by in case the demonstration turned into insurrection. There was no need: it rained, the petition was delivered by cab, and the crowds went home. The petition was rejected. Chartism had peaked.

Historians are currently debating the extent to which chartism represented a new form of largely working-class politics embodying an anti-capitalist critique. Some, concentrating on a continuity of language and oratory, see chartism as a continuation of the 18th-century attack on 'Old Corruption'. Others see in chartist mobilization, oratory and action an important stage in the development of new oppositional politics in the industrial capitalist economy.

CHRONOLOGY

1836 London Working Men's Association (LWMA) formed by William Lovett.

1837, 28 Feb. Petition to the House of Commons adopted at meeting of RADICALS called by the LWMA. Feargus O'Connor founds *The Northern Star*.

1838 'People's Charter' published on 8 May; mass meetings to present Charter and elect delegates to proposed national convention are held throughout spring and summer.

1839, Feb. General Convention of the Industrious Classes is assembled in London.

1839, March ANTI-CORN LAW LEAGUE is founded.

1839, April Maj. Gen. Sir Charles Napier is appointed General Officer Commanding in the unsettled industrial North.

1839, May Llanidloes riots. Convention moved to Birmingham. Manifesto issued recommending 'ulterior measures' to be

implemented in the event of petition's rejection.
1839, 14 June Petition presented to Parliament by Thomas Attwood and Fickler.
1839, 8–15 July Birmingham Bull Ring riots.
1839, 9 July Lovett arrested.
1839, 12 July Parliament declines to consider petition. Convention calls for general strike.
1839, 6 Aug. General strike called off and Convention dissolved.
1839, 4 Nov. Newport rising: 14 were killed in clashes with the military.
1839, Dec. Mass arrests of Chartists and trial of John Frost on charge of high treason.
1840, Jan. Abortive risings in North. Armed Chartists arrested in London.
1840, March Trials of Chartists for riot and conspiracy.
1840, July National Charter Association founded in Manchester.
1841, April Lovett founds National Association of the United Kingdom for Promoting the Political and Social Improvement of the People.
1841, Aug. General election. Feargus O'Connor released from prison.
1842, April Complete Suffrage Union conference at Birmingham; National Charter Association convention, London.
1842, May Second national petition rejected by Parliament.
1842, Aug. Strikes in coalfields and other industries coalesce into general strike for the Chartists; PLUG RIOTS bring North to standstill.
1842, Dec. Collapse of Complete Suffrage Union.
1843, Sept. Land plan accepted by Chartist Convention at Birmingham.
1846, June Repeal of CORN LAWS.
1847, May TEN HOURS ACT passed. O'Connorville, an estate of smallholders, opened as part of Chartist Land Plan.
1848, 10 April Chartist Convention, London; national petition presented and rejected, followed by National Assembly.
1848, Aug.–Dec. Chartist disturbances in the North and London's East End.
1849, Dec. Chartist Delegate Conference.
1850, Jan. National Reform League founded.
1850, March National Chartist League founded.
1850, Aug. Chartist Land Congress dissolved by Parliament.
1858, Feb. Last Chartist Convention.

Chaseabout Raid, Scotland, summer 1565, a rebellion against MARY QUEEN OF SCOTS led by James Stewart, Earl of Moray, after her attempt to improve the position of the Catholic Church. It gained its nickname from the indecisiveness of the action: both sides hurried round Scotland without ever meeting. With no sign of the English support promised him, Moray fled to England on 6 Oct. 1565, and was received by ELIZABETH I, despite her public disavowal of his treasonous revolt.

Chatham, 1st Earl of, *see* PITT 'THE ELDER', WILLIAM

Chatham Chest, *see* DRAKE, SIR FRANCIS

Chaucer, Geoffrey (*c.*1340–?1400), poet. Chaucer's work – some of the greatest ever produced in England, especially the immediately popular *Canterbury Tales* – helped to establish the English of the south-eastern lowlands as the main language of English literature in place of French and Latin. Born into a family of wealthy London wine merchants, from 1357 onwards he was in royal service in a variety of military, diplomatic and administrative capacities. Married to Philippa Roet, daughter of an English royal herald from Hainault in the Low Countries, he became a justice of the peace and MP (1386) for Kent. He was buried in Westminster Abbey, not as the first inhabitant of Poets' Corner – a much later creation – but as a royal servant who had leased a house in the abbey precincts.

Chaucer's significance lies in the permanent currency which he gave to the linguistic forms of his day, especially since his writings included some of the earliest works printed by CAXTON (lesser poems in the 1470s, *Canterbury Tales*, 1478). This ensured his continued popularity as a story-teller in the Tudor age, despite large shifts in pronunciation and usage, and he was also influential in the more conservative linguistic world of early modern Scots literature. Some of the clerical characters in the *Tales* became much-imitated stock literary figures of ANTI-CLERICALISM both before and during the 16th-century REFORMATION.

Chelsea Hospital Founded as a home for retired soldiers on the basis of planning begun under CHARLES II, though the first residents were not admitted until 1690, the original hospital housed only 472 pensioners; many others were and are maintained on outpensions.

Chemical Industry From relatively small origins the chemical industry has become one of the UK's largest in the 20th century. It is very varied, but essentially involves the application of chemical change to convert raw materials into a consumable form – alkali into soap, iron slag into fertilizers, coal tar into dyes, sulphur by-products into acid. By the early 20th century man-made fibres, especially artificial silk (rayon), represented a new departure for the chemical industry, to be followed after WORLD WAR II by, e.g., nylon. The location of the chemical industry has relied heavily on tradition – hence the Cheshire SALT deposits to the south of Runcorn, Widnes and Warrington became the focus of giant chemical concerns, while the main ICI concern at Billingham, Cleveland, stemmed from the early development there of fixing atmospheric nitrogen in acid and fertilizer production. Since the 1940s, the chemical industries have expanded in further directions, with oil-based products and pharmaceuticals; but growth, however impressive, has been slow relative to overseas competitors, partly because of Britain's slower change from coal-to gas- or oil-based technologies, and tardiness in plastics manufacture.

Chester (*Deva*). One of the three LEGIONARY FORTRESSES established by JULIUS FRONTINUS between AD 73–4 and 77–8, it was a town of major importance throughout the Roman occupation, down to its abandonment in 383. It remained important in the medieval period because of its proximity to the Welsh frontier and its convenient siting for trade with Ireland. Partly because of the latter, it became an area in which significant SCANDINAVIAN SETTLEMENT took place. In the reign of EDWARD THE ELDER, a *BURH* was constructed, which became a MINT, and it was in Chester, in 973, that EDGAR displayed his IMPERIAL pretensions in the company of several British kings. It was briefly the site of a CATHEDRAL (1075–95) until the bishop moved to Coventry, but a diocese was re-established in 1541 with the former St Werburgh's Abbey as a cathedral. The town declined somewhat in the later Middle Ages when the harbour began to silt up.

Chevauchée, contemporary term, now historians' jargon, for the most characteristic form of medieval warfare: the mounted raid into enemy territory with the object of ravaging and looting while, if possible, avoiding fighting. A successful chevauchée simultaneously enriched the troops and inflicted damage on the enemy's economic resources.

Chichele, Henry (?1362–1443), Archbishop of Canterbury (1414–43). A lawyer, diplomat and administrator, he was made bishop of St David's in 1408, then in 1414 was HENRY V's choice as Archbishop of Canterbury. He helped to finance the war against France and organize the fight against LOLLARDY. Founder of All Souls College, OXFORD.

Chichester (*Regnum*). A settlement was established soon after the ROMAN invasion; the 2nd–3rd century wall, still substantially surviving in rebuilt medieval form, and the two crossing main streets still define the city centre. Nearby was the important 1st–4th-century local ruler's palace of FISHBOURNE. The diocese, virtually coterminous with the county of Sussex (unusual in medieval England), was moved from Selsey *c.* 1080, and the CATHEDRAL was established for SECULAR CANONS on an older parish church site. The present structure is still dominated by the 13th-century rebuilding programme, its spire remarkably successfully restored after its telescopic collapse in 1861. The city hospital of St Mary (founded 1158) is a remarkable survival of the medieval hospital type designed like a huge church: it is still occupied as ALMSHOUSES.

Child Labour, employment of children, especially in industry. The concept of childhood in which children are educated and not expected to work is a relatively modern one, coming to importance in late Victorian Britain. Previously most children would have been expected from an early age to make some contribution to the family economy, and many children would have left home, in their teens or even before, to enter SERVICE or be APPRENTICED. Criticism of child labour arose from the experience of early industrialization when it may have intensified, with the exploitation of children, especially pauper apprentices in factories, the long hours worked by children and women in COTTON mills and other manufacturing concerns, and the employment of small children in mines or as chimney-sweeps (*see* CLIMBING BOYS). Attention was drawn to the issue by social reformers – including the Earl of Shaftesbury, Charles Kingsley and the 1842 Royal Commission on children's employment. Gradually children's workload and working hours were reduced by FACTORY LEGISLATION and by rising incomes among the working-class.

Chimney Money, *see* HEARTH TAX

Chimney Sweeps Act 1875, *see* CLIMBING BOYS

Chindits, long-range penetrative groups organized by Orde Wingate (1903–44) during WORLD WAR II to fight behind Japanese lines in BURMA with supply by air. Active between Feb. 1943 and March 1944, their name derived from the mythical Burmese animal – the *chinthe* – that served as their emblem, and from the River Chindwin beyond which they operated. Despite only limited successes, they became an important symbol of British attempts to go on the offensive after their earlier defeats at Japanese hands.

Chinoiserie, a fashion in design employing 'Chinese' motifs, which reached the height of its popularity in the 1740s and 1750s. Chinese export wares were a source of inspiration, but the new motifs were set within a pre-existing ROCOCO stylistic framework. It was chiefly employed in interior decoration and the design of garden buildings. The 1738 Chinese pavilion at Stowe, Bucks., was an early example of the latter; the 1761 pagoda at KEW is the most famous surviving example.

Chivalry The word derives from the medieval French *chevalerie* which itself had a number of different, but to some extent overlapping, meanings. It could mean the special skills of the armoured warrior on horseback, the knight, skills which could be displayed in the tournament as well as in war; or it could mean a group of aristocratic warriors – as in the phrase 'the chivalry of England'; or it could refer to the code of values held by, or ascribed to, such a group. French historians, following Georges Duby, tend to use the word in the second sense, whereas British historians generally prefer the third. The third is also the sense which most obviously eludes precise definition, but it is usually held to include prowess and courage (especially when shown in good causes such as protecting the weak), loyalty, generosity, courtesy (especially in dealing with ladies), and the compassionate treatment of defeated enemies, particularly those who themselves belonged to the chivalric class, i.e. the élite. Since admiration for this combination of qualities is first clearly visible in the vernacular literature of the 12th century, this is often regarded as the beginning of the 'age of chivalry'. From then on rulers such as RICHARD I, EDWARD III and EDWARD THE BLACK PRINCE, and nobles such as William MARSHAL and John Chandos (?–1370) came to be regarded, quite soon after their deaths, as having embodied chivalric ideals. Twelfth-century writers already tended to lament the contrast between the current realities of war and the imagined conduct of the chivalrous heroes of the past (such as the knights of King ARTHUR), so the notion of a 'decline of chivalry' – often said to be a distinctive feature of the later middle ages – seems to have been a permanent characteristic of the chivalric ethos.

Chivalry, Orders of, especially honourable forms of KNIGHTHOOD. The following are the principal British orders, with dates of foundation, founder and home chapel of the order:

CHRONOLOGY

***c.*1346–8** GARTER; EDWARD III; St George's Chapel, Windsor.

1687 Thistle: JAMES VII of Scotland; St Giles High Kirk, Edinburgh.

1725 Bath: GEORGE I; Westminster Abbey, London (previously, knights of the Bath were created at coronations and other state occasions).

1788 St Patrick: GEORGE III; St Patrick's Cathedral, Dublin (order now closed).

1818 St Michael and St George: GEORGE IV; St Paul's Cathedral, London.

1896 Royal Victorian Order: VICTORIA (for personal services to monarch); no designated chapel.

Cholera, highly infectious and frequently fatal intestinal disease. The most significant influence on the SANITARY REFORM MOVEMENT and the campaign for state action to safeguard the nation's health, cholera first attracted the attention of Europeans as a consequence of its ravages in INDIA in 1817. From there, it spread westwards and northwards, and the first of its lethal EPIDEMICS in England began in Oct. 1831. It came a second time towards the close of 1848 and killed 52,201 people in England and Wales within a year. The third visitation, in 1853–4, accounted for a further 24,516 deaths. In 1854, Dr John Snow showed by careful observation in Soho, London, that the disease was spread by contaminated water. The Sanitary Act, passed during the epidemic of 1865–6, represented a positive, if belated, response on the part of the legislature; this and further regulation of sanitation eventually made cholera an extremely rare illness in Britain.

Christian Socialism, Christian response to CHARTISM developed by liberal theologian F. D. Maurice, John Malcolm Ludlow, and Charles Kingsley. Their idea was to Christianize socialism and socialize Christianity. Maurice rejected individualism and selfishness and embraced the idea that Christians must work for social salvation, based on Christian fellowship.

Christian socialists wished to replace capitalism with co-operation (*see* CO-OPERATIVE MOVEMENT). In the 1850s, they set up eight workers' associations, issued tracts to explain the movement's goals and published a journal *The Christian Socialist*. Their efforts ran into financial difficulties in the 1860s, and Christian socialism thereafter lost its momentum and was not revived until the later years of the century.

Christmas, Christian festival celebrating Christ's birth, held on 25 Dec. and incorporating the pre-Christian midwinter Yule festival. Although Christmas, with its ritual exchange of gifts is now the principal annual HOLIDAY, it has not always had that role; Twelfth Night, 6 Jan., was earlier the more important feast. By the 16th century Christmas had grown considerably in importance as a day of feasting, so much so that in the INTERREGNUM it was made a public fast day in some years so as to wean the population from popish survivals. The modern Christmas is largely a Victorian creation, with the fir tree introduced from Germany by Prince ALBERT, the custom of sending Christmas cards starting in the 1850s, self-conscious revival of carols and folk-songs, and the literary confections of Charles Dickens, especially in *A Christmas Carol* (1843).

Church: England

ROMAN AND ANGLO-SAXON

Although there is no reliable evidence as to when Christianity arrived in the Roman provinces of Britannia, three British bishops attended a council of Western church leaders at Arles, France (314). Archaeology has revealed much evidence of Christian presence in Britannia, and suggests a religion which was associated mainly with the towns and the Romanized rural élite. This church was forced westwards by the Anglo-Saxon invasions, and became central to Celtic civilization; the CONVERSION OF THE ENGLISH was achieved from 597 by a renewed mission from Rome under St AUGUSTINE. Its success was spectacular, the Anglo-Saxon Church leading missions into central Europe in a conscious effort to spread the new faith to ethnic cousins. Rivalry with the Celtic Church was settled (particularly at the Synod of WHITBY, 664) in favour of the Anglo-Saxons – predictably, since they had the closer links with the Western church which was increasingly being centralized in Rome. A PARISH system was well-developed by the 10th century.

CONDITION IN 1066

Beginning with the *VITA AEDWARDI REGIS*, historical writers of the late 11th and early 12th centuries attributed the English defeat in 1066 to the sins of the people and to the corruption of the Church in England. In doing this, they were following an ecclesiastical pattern of ideas whereby earthly events were regarded as direct manifestations of divine favour or disapproval. Modern scholarship generally recognizes these statements for what they are and, instead, stresses the Church's good health and institutional strength, while also acknowledging that there was no longer the dynamism associated with the TENTH-CENTURY REFORM. STIGAND, Archbishop of Canterbury from 1052 to 1070, was a dubious, worldly figure, but other bishops were men of ability and notable piety. New ideas were arriving from the Continent via the Lotharingians and Normans appointed to BISHOPRICS by EDWARD THE CONFESSOR, and the condition of most monasteries remained good.

MEDIEVAL AND TUDOR

After the NORMAN CONQUEST, the English Church was fully integrated into the Roman mainstream, adopting CANON LAW and developing its own system of CHURCH COURTS, despite persistent conflicts between the ANGLO-NORMAN monarchy and the Pope over the appointment of senior clergy (*see* BECKET); the headquarters of many DIOCESES were moved to major urban centres, and CATHEDRALS and major monastic churches were built on a massive scale. In the late 14th century, England generated one of medieval Europe's major movements of religious dissidence, LOLLARDY, but generally the late medieval English Church was efficiently led, less institutionally corrupt than the Scottish Church, and less chaotic than the Church in Ireland. Nevertheless, the Church authorities were ill-prepared for the onslaught by HENRY VIII which led to England's break with Rome and the establishment of the ROYAL SUPREMACY (1533–6), and they put up little resistance. After MARY I's brief reconciliation of England to papal obedience (1554–8), ELIZABETH I restored the Church as it had been before EDWARD VI's death. This ELIZABETHAN SETTLEMENT has always caused controversy about the theological nature of the Church (*see also* ANGLICANISM).

RISE OF DISSENT

In the British CIVIL WARS the future shape of English religion was a major issue, in particular the influence of ARMINIANS on CHARLES I's religious policies, but the abolition of the PRAYER BOOK and of EPISCOPACY by the LONG PARLIAMENT was reversed with remarkable ease at CHARLES II'S RESTORATION, leaving the various DISSENTING bodies who would not accept the new settlement as a vulnerable minority, subject to intermittently savage persecution. Efforts in the 1690s and 1710s to reunite Dissenters with the established Church, or at least to provide a broad scheme of COMPREHENSION, were thwarted by the intransigence of many Anglican clergy and politicians, although a significant number of HIGH CHURCH clergy and laity were also forced out of the Church by the NON-JURING controversy. The failure of attempts to heal divisions resulted in a permanent split within English PROTESTANTISM between the established Church and Dissent/NONCONFORMITY. At first, Dissent appeared to be a declining force, but during the mid-18th century the EVANGELICAL Revival brought new vigour both to Church and Dissent. It also created a new schism, as John WESLEY'S METHODIST societies found it increasingly difficult and in the end impossible to remain within the structures of the establishment.

19TH CENTURY

In the 19th century the established church was faced with an identity crisis, as non-Anglicans (eventually even non-Christians) gained full civil rights, and it became apparent that much of the population was indifferent to religious practice (*see also* ANTI-CLERICALISM). The OXFORD, Evangelical and BROAD CHURCH MOVEMENTS, CHRISTIAN SOCIALISM and Liberal CATHOLICISM can all be seen as attempts to provide further definition for the Church, despite their frequent mutual quarrels. Positive institutional change included the creation of many new urban parishes, a network of philanthropic organizations, the revival of the CONVOCATIONS, and the development of clerical training in theological colleges. Dissenters and Methodists (increasingly both known as FREE CHURCHMEN) imitated or anticipated these moves, their self-confidence boosted by their strong showing in the 1851 religious attendance census; and until WORLD WAR I, English politics were affected by Anglican–Free Church tensions, particularly struggles for an end to preferential treatment for Anglican schools.

MODERN DEVELOPMENTS

The Church of England and the Free Churches experienced sharp declines in active membership until the late 1980s, although from the 1960s there was growth among those congregations and new church bodies affected by the charismatic movement originating in the United States. Many Anglicans are now convinced of the value of a major modification in the Church's established status; nearly all churches have become involved in ecumenical discussions and co-operation, although the only substantial institutional fruit of this so far has been the formation of the United Reformed

Church from CONGREGATIONALISTS and the English PRESBYTERIAN Church in 1972.

CHRONOLOGY

314 Council of Arles: bishops of LONDON, YORK and COLCHESTER or LINCOLN present.
429 First visit of GERMANUS to Britannia to combat heresy of Pelagius.
597 Mission of AUGUSTINE to Canterbury.
664 Synod of WHITBY adopts Roman date of Easter and other Roman customs.
1170 Thomas BECKET murdered; humiliation for HENRY II follows.
1407 LOLLARD BIBLE banned by church Council of Oxford.
1533–6 Royal supremacy established by the REFORMATION PARLIAMENT.
1549 CRANMER's first PRAYER BOOK.
1552 Cranmer's second Prayer Book.
1553 Protestant 42 Articles of Religion, defining doctrine.
1554 England reconciled to papal obedience.
1559 ELIZABETHAN SETTLEMENT.
1563 39 Articles of Religion issued, modifying 42 Articles.
1645 Parliament replaces Prayer Book with Directory of Worship.
1646 Parliament declares EPISCOPACY abolished.
1660 RESTORATION includes all old institutions of the Church.
1662 Revised Prayer Book made mandatory: *c.*2,000 clergy refuse and are ejected on St Bartholomew's Day.
1689 NON-JURORS leave. TOLERATION ACT benefits DISSENTERS.
1744 Conference of METHODIST preachers first meets.
1828 Protestant NONCONFORMISTS allowed to hold public office.
1829 CATHOLIC EMANCIPATION (RELIEF) ACT.
1833 John Keble's Assize Sermon triggers the OXFORD MOVEMENT.
1870 Religious tests for OXFORD and CAMBRIDGE abolished, ending Anglican monopoly.
1972 Creation of the United Reformed Church.
1980 Church of England's Alternative Service Book published.

Church: Ireland Christianity followed contacts with Roman Britannia, and was already present when in the 5th century PATRICK began his mission to Ireland. Although he and other early missionaries had sketched out a system of EPISCOPAL government for the Irish Church, it became dominated by abbots and abbesses (*see* MONASTICISM, EARLY IRISH), usually members of the leading noble and royal families, and its remarkable missionary work to Scotland and central Europe was carried out by monks and nuns (*see* COLUMBA). The ANGLO-NORMAN invasion brought the same centralizing trends as in England, with the relatively new diocese of DUBLIN assuming increasing importance in the Church because of the English government based there, and the new monastic ORDERS spread through all parts of the island.

All through the medieval period, Irish religion reflected the kaleidoscopic nature of Irish politics, with English government influence weak and a complex relationship between Gaelic and Old English culture (*see* NEW ENGLISH). From the 1470s, a religious revival particularly encouraged by Franciscan FRIARS was spreading out from the Gaelic parts of the island, but DIOCESAN and PARISH organization was much less well developed than in England. The response to religious change under the Tudor monarchs was therefore confused. Officially the REFORMATION followed the pattern set in England from 1533, but bishops and clergy were slow to clarify where their allegiance lay between Rome or the crown, both of which appointed bishops. Monasteries and friaries were dissolved where the Dublin administration had influence, but many communities survived beyond the 16th century. Under ELIZABETH I, the increased interventionism of the English government alienated both Gael and Old English, and heightened loyalty to Rome became part of the struggle to resist English interference. The established PROTESTANT Church of Ireland was associated with the New English, and failed to engage the loyalty of most of the population. The majority remained Roman Catholic, despite repression of Catholicism throughout the later 16th and 17th centuries. In the north-east, from the time of the PLANTATIONS onwards, PRESBYTERIANISM, DISSENT and (from the late 18th century) METHODISM became well established as a result of Protestant immigration.

In the 18th century, persecution of Roman Catholicism slackened, and the Catholic

Church continued to command the allegiance of the majority. During the 19th century, the official position of the Church of Ireland was steadily eroded and was ended in 1871, although its constituency among the prosperous and well educated has given it a continuing influence disproportionate to its size. After the Partition of Ireland (1921), the Roman Catholic Church gained a leading role in the IRISH FREE STATE and later Republic. In more recent times, despite persistently high mass attendance, it is clear that Church influence on popular social attitudes has sharply diminished.

CHRONOLOGY

***c.*563** COLUMBA founds community at IONA.

***c.*590** Columbanus goes to Gaul to begin mission.

1111 Council of Rathbreasail.

1142 First Irish CISTERCIAN house established (*see* MONASTICISM).

1162 On the death of Gréne (Gregorius), Lorcán O Tuathail becomes 2nd Archbishop of Dublin; co-operates with Anglo-Normans, introducing Roman customs.

1533–6 ROYAL SUPREMACY established; monastic DISSOLUTIONS begin.

1607 FLIGHT OF THE EARLS removes Roman Catholic lay leadership; PLANTATION of Ulster follows.

1641 Gaelic and Old English Catholics rebel against Protestant government.

1642 Confederation of KILKENNY formed.

1652 Roman Catholics' resistance to English invasion ends; followed by large-scale confiscation of their lands.

1660 James Butler, Earl of Ormonde restores Protestant episcopal establishment.

1690–1 JAMES II defeated at the BOYNE and AUGHRIM: end of Roman Catholic hopes for regaining power. Penal legislation follows, designed to deny them wealth or influence.

1740s After fading of JACOBITE dynastic threat, official repression relaxes.

1795 Maynooth College founded to train Catholic clergy.

1829 CATHOLIC EMANCIPATION (RELIEF) ACT.

1833 Government reduces number of Protestant bishoprics and archbishoprics.

1838 End of obligation on Roman Catholic and Protestant DISSENTERS to pay tithe to Church of Ireland.

1871 Disestablishment and partial disendowment of the Church of Ireland.

1922 Formation of IRISH FREE STATE; special position of Roman Catholic Church recognized.

1937 Republican constitution strengthens rights of Roman Catholic Church.

Church: Scotland The Briton NINIAN is credited with bringing Christianity to the PICTS of southern Scotland, possibly in the early 6th century. A different mission from Ireland was pioneered by COLUMBA in the Western Isles, and this in turn evangelized in England, causing frequent tension with the Anglo-Saxon church directed from Rome. The Synod of WHITBY (664) was one episode in the gradual reorientation of the northern churches towards Rome, which was also marked by the establishment of EPISCOPAL authority; during the 9th century a bishopric for Scotland was sited at Dunkeld (later at the royal centre of Abernethy) and in the early 10th century relocated at the cultic centre of ST ANDREWS. The introduction at least in outline of a full-scale DIOCESAN and PARISH system similar to that in the ANGEVIN dominions, together with much encouragement of the new Monastic ORDERS, was the work of DAVID I, inspired by his English-born mother St MARGARET. Senior Scots churchmen, anxious to free themselves of domination by the English archbishops, generally identified with the fight against England in the 13th–14th-century wars of SCOTTISH INDEPENDENCE; however, the eventual establishment in the 15th century of two archbishoprics for Scotland bought a promise of institutional reform in the Church which remained unfulfilled. The parish system in the Scottish Lowlands was distorted by the diversion of revenues to collegiate chantry foundations (*see* CHANTRIES) designed for the uphill struggle to save the souls of the Scottish aristocracy, and in general the late medieval Scottish Church's wealth was channelled aside for the nobility's benefit.

There were marginal traces of LOLLARDY in Scotland, but a different pattern of 16th-century REFORMATION emerged from that in England, Wales and Ireland, based on CALVINISM. The present PRESBYTERIAN Church has resulted from a series of acts of defiance against the crown, first against MARY QUEEN OF SCOTS in the 1560s, then against

CHARLES I after 1637, then against the defeated JAMES II AND VII in 1690. The Church fiercely guarded its independence against English interference thereafter. Its commitment to Calvinist orthodoxy resulted in a number of schisms on the issue of state intervention in church affairs, most of which have been healed by reunions in the 20th century (but *see* CAMERONIANS), and its uncompromising Protestantism has left little room for the growth of DISSENT OF NONCONFORMITY in the English manner. Roman Catholicism failed to maintain much presence in Scotland during the 16th-century Reformation, except in the Western Isles and far north. Nineteenth-century Irish immigration much increased its numbers, especially in the west.

CHRONOLOGY

***c.*563** COLUMBA founds community at IONA.

664 Synod of WHITBY adopts Roman date of Easter and other Roman customs.

908 Scottish bishopric transferred from Abernethy to ST ANDREWS.

***c.*1070** MARGARET marries MALCOLM III CANMORE: major English influence on church organization.

1192 Scotland recognized as independent province, though without an archbishopric.

1472 DIOCESE of St Andrews elevated to an archbishopric.

1492 Diocese of GLASGOW elevated to an archbishopric.

1528 First burning of a LUTHERAN sympathizer, Patrick Hamilton.

1559 Rising against Catholicism and French influence.

1560 Reformed Church set up; Anglo-Genevan liturgy and BIBLE.

1578–1610 Episcopal control of presbyteries ebbs and flows under royal sponsorship.

1618 Five Articles of PERTH.

1637 CHARLES I imposes ARMINIAN-influenced PRAYER BOOK.

1638 National COVENANT.

1643 Solemn League and COVENANT.

1646 Westminster Confession completed.

1661–3 EPISCOPACY restored: bitter struggles result with COVENANTERS.

1690 Bishops refuse to break their oath to JAMES II AND VII, and are dismissed (*see* EPISCOPAL CHURCH OF SCOTLAND); Presbyterianism restored.

1843 Free Church of Scotland formed in the DISRUPTION.

1929 Reunion of most of previous Presbyterian secessions.

1969 Church of Scotland ordains women as ministers.

Church: Wales The origins of Welsh Christianity are difficult to unravel from pious legend, which luxuriates in the 6th-century 'Age of the Saints'; this was undoubtedly a time when the Church was well developed around MONASTIC centres, often very large. Four monasteries (Bangor, Llandaff, St Asaph, ST DAVID'S) developed into the headquarters of DIOCESES.

In the 12th and early 13th centuries vain attempts were made to establish a Welsh archbishopric and to free the Welsh churches from the growing authority of the church at Canterbury. Despite the adoption of Roman organization, with PARISHES and new Monastic orders, clerical CELIBACY was never successfully imposed.

The Welsh bishoprics remained much poorer than most English dioceses, and they suffered still further damage during GLYN DWR's revolt. Wales was included in the changes of the English REFORMATION (*see* CHURCH: ENGLAND), but its clerical resources remained smaller. Vigorous private enterprise by some PROTESTANT clergy and laity led to the translation of the BIBLE and PRAYER BOOK into Welsh, the centrepieces of a devotional literature which prevented a cultural gap appearing between Protestant culture and the Welsh-speaking majority. Roman Catholicism went into swift decline, only partly reversed by 19th-century Irish immigration.

During the 18th century, institutional decay and rapid NONCONFORMIST growth undermined the position of the established Church, which was increasingly identified with rural Wales and with the hegemony of the English-speaking establishment. Despite some 19th-century ANGLICAN recovery, which itself fuelled inter-church hostilities, LLOYD GEORGE championed the Church's disestablishment and partial disendowment to please radical Welsh opinion; the resulting parliamentary settlement defused religious tension.

CHRONOLOGY

1092 First bishop under Norman influence consecrated, for Bangor.

1567 William Salesbury publishes Welsh PRAYER BOOK and New Testament.

1571 Hugh Price founds Jesus College,

OXFORD: important for future training of Welsh Protestant clergy.
1588 William Morgan publishes complete Welsh Bible.
1639 SEPARATIST church established at Llanfaches (Mons.).
1662 ANGLICAN settlement enforced.
1811 Calvinistic METHODISTS formally split from established Church.
1904 Last major REVIVAL movement chiefly affects NONCONFORMIST congregations.
1920 By Act of 1914, Welsh Anglican dioceses detached from Church of England, partially disendowed and disestablished to form the Church in Wales.

Church Ales, medieval Church fund-raising events, usually involving the sale of specially brewed beer/ale. Later, PURITANS disapproved and campaigned for their suppression. Archbishop LAUD incurred Puritan fury when he sought to encourage the ales' revival. *See also* ALE AND ALEHOUSES.

Church and King, Anglican political slogan, implicitly conjoining religious dissent with political disloyalty, popular in the 1710s, 1740s and 1791–2. Church and King clubs were founded in the late 1780s in response to the campaign for the repeal of the TEST and CORPORATION Acts. The Manchester Club was implicated in anti-UNITARIAN riots in 1792; the slogan was also used in the Birmingham PRIESTLEY RIOTS.

Church Army Founded in 1882 by Wilson Carlile (1847–1942), an ANGLICAN clergyman, it sought to capture for the CHURCH OF ENGLAND the moral energy and practical philanthropy displayed by the SALVATION ARMY. Missionary work among the urban poor was extended in WORLD WARS I and II to include welfare work among the troops and their dependants. The Church Army continues to operate.

Church Assembly, *see* CONVOCATIONS OF CANTERBURY AND YORK

Church Commissioners, *see* ECCLESIASTICAL COMMISSIONERS

Church Courts, the Church's legal system that operated CANON LAW, and which evolved a complex structure from the 12th century. The REFORMATION made virtually no difference to their administration, and their chief weapons remained spiritual ones – e.g. EXCOMMUNICATION. However, their activity was temporarily supplemented by diocesan ecclesiastical commissions and courts of HIGH COMMISSION, deriving powers from the crown. Historians have made too much of hostile comment about Church courts from PURITANS and practitioners of the COMMON LAW; recent research has shown a system that thrived until the CIVIL WARS. Restored in 1660, the courts never again commanded universal consent, and the final blow to their power was the removal, in 1857, of WILL probate to civil authority. They now exist solely for internal administration of the Church of England.

'Church in Danger', an early 18th-century TORY propaganda slogan, especially associated with the SACHEVERELL AFFAIR, and with campaigns against OCCASIONAL CONFORMITY and DISSENTING ACADEMIES. Tories associated the WHIGS with religious dissent and atheism, and saw them as a threat to the influence and liberties of the Church. The slogan was revived when DISSENTERS attempted to repeal the TEST and CORPORATION Acts.

Church Missionary Society, *see* MISSIONARY SOCIETIES

Church of England, *see* CHURCH: ENGLAND

Church Papists, *see* RECUSANCY

Church Rate, rate levied by the churchwardens and vestry of a PARISH to provide for the repair and upkeep of the parish church and graveyard. Offensive to NONCONFORMISTS, and increasingly difficult to enforce in urban parishes, it was abolished in 1868 and replaced by a voluntary rate. One unintended consequence was the reduction of the power of the laity in the parish.

Church-Scot, *see* TITHES

Churchill, John (1st duke of Marlborough) (1650–1722), soldier. Son of a Dorset royalist, Churchill became a page to the Duke of York, and ensign in the Foot Guards. In 1673–4 he fought with an English regiment in French service. In 1677 he married Sarah Jennings, an attendant to, and close friend of the duke's daughter, Princess Anne (the future Queen ANNE). He accompanied the duke into exile in Brussels in 1679, then to Scotland. After the duke's accession as JAMES II, Churchill came to question his religious policies. He commanded against Monmouth's (*see* SCOTT, JAMES) rebels at SEDGEMOOR in 1685, but corresponded with William of Orange (the future WILLIAM III), and in the GLORIOUS REVOLUTION took his forces over to William's side. He was made an earl in 1689 and given command of the campaign in the Netherlands and against JACOBITE forces in Ireland. He was dismissed on charges of Jacobite plotting in 1692, and remained out of favour till 1698, when he was made governor to the Duke of Gloucester, Queen Anne's son and heir.

In 1701 he became commander of British forces in the Netherlands; on the accession of Anne he was made captain-general and commander of all the allied forces, a position he held through most of the War of the SPANISH SUCCESSION, in which he distinguished himself by the diplomatic skill with which he held together the alliance against France as well as by his string of victories, notably at BLENHEIM (1704), RAMILLIES (1706), Oudenarde (1708) and MALPLAQUET (1709). His great distinction as a commander lay in his development of tactics – a series of feints preparing the way for a devastating assault – that enabled him to achieve decisive victories. He had been elevated to a dukedom in 1702; in 1706–7 Parliament further marked its appreciation of him by making the title heritable by his daughters.

A courtier by upbringing and inclination, Marlborough did not adapt well to the changing character of British political life. He depended on WHIG support to prosecute the war, and was insufficiently sensitive to ebbing public support for its human and financial cost. After the TORIES gained power in government in 1710, he was dismissed in 1711, and threatened with prosecution for corruption. His wife Sarah had been in more or less open breach with the queen since 1708; this quarrel helped weaken the Whigs' position. Her own dismissal in Jan. 1711 paved the way for Marlborough's at the year's end. He remained on the Continent during 1712–14, when he was reinstated as captain-general by GEORGE I. The palace of Blenheim, at Woodstock near Oxford, named after his 1704 victory was built for him by Sir John Vanbrugh (1664–1726) from money granted by Anne. After his death his still formidable widow managed the Marlborough political interest in the Whig – latterly opposition Whig – cause until her own death in 1744.

Churchill, Sir Winston (1874–1965), politician and Prime Minister (1940–5, 1951–5) and world statesman. Son of Lord Randolph Churchill (1849–95), the conservative politician and leader of the 'FOURTH PARTY', and the American heiress Jennie Jerome, and grandson of the 7th Duke of Marlborough, he was born at Blenheim Palace and educated at Harrow before seeing military service in the army and as a war correspondent in the Sudan in 1898 and in the BOER WAR.

Churchill entered Parliament as a CONSERVATIVE in 1900, but defected to the LIBERALS four years later over TARIFF REFORM. As home secretary (1910–11) under ASQUITH, he dealt firmly with the industrial unrest in south Wales that culminated in the Tonypandy riots. Appointed first lord of the Admiralty in 1911, he resigned from the government in 1915 after the failure of the DARDANELLES CAMPAIGN, an episode that appeared to confirm his reputation for recklessness.

In 1917 he returned from France, where he had been commanding a battalion, to office in the LLOYD GEORGE coalition, serving as minister of munitions (1917–19), secretary for air and war (1919–21) and colonial secretary (1921–2), but lost his seat in 1922. After two years during which he wrote a five-volume history of WORLD WAR I, he was re-elected to Parliament as a Conservative. As chancellor of the Exchequer (1924–9), he returned Britain to the GOLD STANDARD in 1925, and took a tough line during the GENERAL STRIKE.

With the fall of the BALDWIN government in 1929, he became increasingly isolated over his opposition to INDIAN INDEPENDENCE and enhanced his reputation as a political maverick, remaining out of office throughout the 1930s. In particular, his early warnings about the need for rearmament to combat the rise of Fascism were out of step with the APPEASEMENT policies of the NATIONAL GOVERNMENT, but as disillusion over the effectiveness of these grew, especially after MUNICH, his views were increasingly seen as vindicated. With the outbreak of WORLD WAR II in 1939, he returned to government, again as first lord of the Admiralty, and was the natural successor as prime minister, even though it was the NORWEGIAN CAMPAIGN, essentially a naval disaster, that precipitated CHAMBERLAIN'S fall in May 1940.

Churchill formed an all-party Cabinet that united public opinion behind the war effort. He galvanized the British people at a time of national disaster and threat of invasion, after DUNKIRK and during the Battle of BRITAIN, when the country 'stood alone' (apart from the Empire troops) against the Nazi threat. He forged a strong personal relationship with US President Roosevelt, obtaining vital LENDLEASE agreements, and was active in encouraging US commitment to the war against Italy and Germany, as well as against Japan. His military contribution has been questioned; his interference in strategic and operational matters was often amateurish, but he successfully survived periods of unpopularity to provide a stable coalition government until the end of the war. Leaving much domestic policy to ATTLEE, BEVIN and MORRISON, he concentrated on high-level diplomacy in a series of wartime conferences that shaped the post-war settlement.

As the war neared its end, his attempts to preserve the interests of the BRITISH EMPIRE were only partly successful as Britain became the junior partner to the US and the Soviet Union. Although he accepted plans for social reform (*see* BEVERIDGE REPORT), his reluctance to see them implemented immediately distanced the Conservatives from the emerging consensus. In the 1945 election, Churchill's wartime prestige was insufficient to overcome the memory of pre-war dole queues and the strong desire for change which ultimately brought a Labour government under Attlee to power.

Out of office again, Churchill, who had never led a political party before, continued to play the world stage. Always a vociferous anti-Bolshevist and increasingly alarmed at the Soviet domination of Eastern Europe, he underlined the rhetoric of the COLD WAR with his 'Iron Curtain' speech delivered at Fulton, Missouri, in 1946. Returned again as prime minister in 1951, he led a government which removed controls on the economy but also encouraged measures such as house-building. His last years in office were affected by illness and old age and, in 1955, at the age of 80, he finally gave way to EDEN. His four-volume project *A History of the English-Speaking Peoples*, a view of the Anglo-Saxon world which informed his idea of Empire, appeared 1956–8. He was finally persuaded not to stand for Parliament at the 1964 election, and died within months of leaving the Commons aged 90. He was accorded a state funeral, the first commoner to be so honoured since Arthur WELLESLEY, Duke of Wellington in 1852.

A man of enormous energy and abilities, Churchill had a rare gift of oratory and inspired phrase-making, qualities which were crucial in maintaining Britain's will to fight on alone in her – and his – finest hour. Whilst his pre-war political career has been described as 'a study in failure', to his wartime deputy and post-war successor Attlee, Churchill was 'the greatest Englishman of our time'.

Churchwarden, annually elected officer in a PARISH representing the church or parish's interests. Churchwardens became of particular importance from the 16th until the early 19th century with the increasing administrative role of the parish, often having responsibility for PARISH REGISTERS, charitable doles, and presentation of miscreants to CHURCH COURTS when those were active, and working alongside OVERSEERS OF THE POOR for the administration of the Old POOR LAW.

Cinema The technical process of PHOTOGRAPHY applied to moving images, which is then projected, was simultaneously developed in the later decades of the 19th century in the USA, France, Britain, and elsewhere. The compact and efficient *Cinématographe* patented by the Lumière brothers in Paris in 1895, and first seen in London in 1896, won the day.

Projected moving films, initially regarded as a fairground amusement, quickly began to find permanent homes in the 'penny gaffs', which were usually converted shops, and then in specially-constructed buildings. The Central Hall in Colne, Lancs., opened in 1907, is generally considered to have been Britain's first purpose-built cinema; London's earliest specially-constructed cinema opened in 1912, in the wake of the first controlling legislation of 1909. Cinemas rapidly proliferated across the nation. The 1920s and 1930s were the heyday of British cinema construction and design, resulting in many most elaborate buildings, especially in the interiors, and the characteristic Art Deco-derived style of the Odeon organization. With the rise of television from the 1950s, cinema-going went into sustained decline from its wartime and post-war heights; from 1955–65 the number of cinemas in Britain halved.

Film production rapidly established itself in Britain after its first commercial exploitation. Early British films were, however, of a generally lower quality than those imported from the USA, and the British film industry's long decline started almost before the industry had begun. This perennial problem was countered in 1927 by the introduction of a quota system, designed to protect the home product and resulting in many worthless films as well as the higher-quality productions associated with Michael Balcon, Alfred Hitchcock, and others whom the measure was designed to assist.

The first British talking picture was Hitchcock's *Blackmail* (1929), the same year as John Grierson's *Drifters*, the seminal work in the characteristically British documentary movement. Through the 1930s, and in the patriotic and propagandist film-making of the wartime years, an indigenous cinematic style was developed, notably in the Ealing comedies, the entertainment films produced by Alexander Korda or the idiosyncratic work of Michael Powell and Emeric Pressburger, in contrast to the prevailing output of Hollywood, against which post-war British attempts at protectionism were disastrous.

There was a flurry of British cinematic activity in the 1960s, coincident with the era of 'Swinging London' and the rise to prominence of a range of directors, including Lindsay Anderson and John Schlesinger, the phenomenal success of the series of James Bond films, and the injection of American money into fashionable Britain. By the end of the 1960s that bubble had largely burst, and most successful British directors sought work in the USA. Occasional attempts at reviving British cinema production have largely failed, unaided by the abolition of the Eady levy in 1980. British cinema has had both a confrontational and symbiotic relationship with television, which since the mid-1980s has been the principal saviour of the film industry including *Four Weddings and a Funeral* (1994), one of the highest earning British films of all time.

Cinque Ports, a confederation of towns on the south-east coast of England that, during the Middle Ages, owed an annual service of ships to the crown to provide both coastal defence and the cross-Channel passage vital to the ANGLO-NORMAN REALM. When the confederation first emerged in the 12th century, there were five ports (hence the name): Dover, Hastings, Hythe, Romney and Sandwich. Winchelsea and Rye were added later. The loss of Normandy in 1204 meant that the Channel became a front line of war, and during the 13th century the Cinque Ports played a major naval role. Thereafter they were increasingly absorbed into the general administration of navy and coast, and subsequently, the office of Warden of the Cinque Ports became purely honorific.

Circumspecte Agatis, writ issued in 1286, later regarded as a statute, which defined some of the contentious boundaries between English secular and ecclesiastical jurisdiction. Its name is derived from its opening words: 'Act circumspectly'.

Cirencester (*Corinium Dobunnorum*). Soon after the start of the ROMAN CONQUEST in AD 43, Cirencester was established as a fort and communications centre to support further advance westwards. Within 30 years, it had become the capital of the *CIVITAS* of the DOBUNNI, and as its range of splendid public buildings illustrates, it thereafter developed into one of the great towns of Roman Britain – to a considerable extent because of its location at the crossing of important roads (*see* FOSSE WAY) – and, in the early 4th century, became one of the four provincial capitals (*see* CONSTANTINE I). It declined in the later Roman period and was taken over by the ANGLO-SAXON invaders after the battle of DYRHAM in 577. The town's continued importance is, however, testified to by the huge Anglo-Saxon abbey church, which was sited beside the magnificent surviving parish church. Cirencester's medieval and early modern wealth was based on the WOOL trade.

Cistercians, monastic ORDER which developed an especially austere practice of the BENEDICTINE Rule. The first house was founded in France by Robert of Molesme in 1098 at Citeaux ('Cistercium' in Latin). The Order spread rapidly through Europe during the 12th century; part of its wide popularity arose from its initial practice of allotting the community's manual labour to lay brothers, who need not be literate like monks in most Orders, thus giving opportunities to many more to enter the monastic life. The Cistercians were established in England from 1128, in Wales from 1130, in Scotland from 1136–7, and in Ireland from 1142.

Cit, short for 'citizen', was used from the late 17th century through the 19th century as a term of mockery or contempt for a townsman, especially a tradesman or shopkeeper, as distinguished from a gentleman.

Citrine, Walter (1st Baron Citrine) (1887–1983), trade union leader. As general secretary of the TUC (1926–46), he played a crucial role in establishing TRADE UNION influence within the LABOUR PARTY. In Aug. 1931, he opposed cuts proposed by MACDONALD's Cabinet, precipitating the fall of the second Labour government. He was then responsible, with BEVIN, for rallying the bulk of the Labour Party to oppose the NATIONAL GOVERNMENT and securing MacDonald's expulsion. From 1931, he increasingly asserted control of the trade union movement over Labour Party policy via the TUC-dominated National Joint Council. Under the post-war Labour government, he presided over the NATIONALIZATION of the electricity industry, serving on the National Coal Board and becoming chairman of the Central Electricity Authority (1947–57).

City, *see* BOROUGH; CATHEDRAL

City of London, *see* LONDON, CITY OF

Civic Gospel, a Christian response to the problems of faith in the city. Inspired by the 'gas and water socialism' pioneered in mid-Victorian Britain by Joseph CHAMBERLAIN, it was taken up by middle-class NONCONFORMITY and associated with a pronounced EVANGELICAL morality. Increasingly, the concept described the approach of those ministers of various denominations who sought to propagate the ideal of Christian participation in civic life and politics and in the administration and government of the rapidly growing urban areas during the 19th century.

Civil Law, the usual term in English usage for Roman law – i.e. the law of the Roman Empire, which, during the RENAISSANCE, was widely adopted in European countries as the basis of legal reform. In England, however, COMMON LAW resisted adaptation. Civil law's main application remained confined to maritime cases, since they might involve more than one nation, so it was mostly practised in the Admiralty court. Civil lawyers also practised in the CHURCH COURTS after the study of CANON LAW was abolished at the REFORMATION.

By contrast, in medieval Scotland, lawyers were trained largely on the Continent. As elsewhere, there was a major reform during the 16th century (the 'reception'), which made Roman law the framework of the Scottish legal system. This was not disturbed at the UNION of the crowns in 1707, and remains distinct in practice and courts. *See also* CIVIL LITIGATION; COURT OF SESSION.

Civil List, sum of money allocated by PARLIAMENT to the monarch, for the maintenance of the royal household and (originally) for the payment of certain official salaries. It was first distinguished from other public revenues in 1698, when Parliament decided to limit permanently the monarch's discretionary financial powers by keeping other aspects of public expenditure under its own control. During the 19th century, the Civil List was relieved of the burden of official salaries, and, at the accession of VICTORIA, of the cost of various pensions previously paid by the crown. The sum allocated to the Civil List in the early 20th century was less than the £700,000 originally allocated by Parliament in 1698, but the payments on the List remain controversial.

Civil Litigation, disputes between party and party, rather than cases brought by the crown. Not to be confused with CIVIL LAW. *See also* COMMON PLEAS; COUNTY COURT.

Civil Registration Act 1836 This made the registration of births, marriages and deaths compulsory, and marked an important advance in the gathering of data on which social and economic policy might be based.

Civil Rights Association, broadly based group of Irish Nationalists, liberals, trade unionists and students which from 1967 led the campaign for the reform of the Protestant-dominated Northern Irish political system. Drawing on the American precedents of the early and mid-1960s, it held civil rights marches in the summer and autumn of

1968, leading to the violent reaction of the Royal Ulster Constabulary and PROTESTANT mobs. The break-up of a 'freedom march' from BELFAST to LONDONDERRY in January 1969 and subsequent rioting between Catholics and Protestants (with the resurgent IRA (*see* IRISH REPUBLICAN ARMY) entering the power vacuum) led Terence O'NEILL to propose a reform package. By spring 1969 a UNIONIST revolt forced O'Neill's resignation and the introduction of the British army in a peacekeeping role.

Civil Service The term was originally applied in the 18th century to those administrative officials of the EAST INDIA COMPANY who were not part of the army or navy. By the mid-19th century it was commonly being used to describe the public administrative officers within Britain itself, and the usage has now become common throughout the successor states of the former BRITISH EMPIRE, including the United States of America.

The British civil service is the group of men and women who are paid by the state to put into effect government policy and to apply the law as defined in PARLIAMENT. In Britain, the bureaucracy thus described has a lineal continuity with administrative structures dating back at least to the 12th century (*see* CENTRALIZATION), and hence the term is occasionally used by medieval and early modern historians of the British Isles. However, this is probably unwise, because of the nuances of the phrase which are commonly understood in modern Anglophone politics: it implies the existence of a corps of administrators who are conscious of their impartial duty to the public of a democratic society, a duty which is owed beyond the party concerns of any one elected government. None of these conditions applied in pre-19th-century society, and there was a basic structural difference between these pre-modern bureaucracies and the modern civil service. Pre-modern administrators commonly relied for their main income on fees charged to those for whom they performed services, rather than on a substantial salary from the government; often they also expected gifts, which might easily shade into bribes. The ideal of the modern civil service is that such external inducements to action are strictly prohibited. However, the formal expression of modern civil service impartiality in British governmental theory is actually inherited from the older world of élite politics: rather than appealing to a democratic ideal, the rationale of impartiality is that civil servants are servants of the CROWN, rather than of the elected party government. In practice there is considerable confusion in the moral and political responsibility owed by civil servants, thanks to this constitutional fiction. Besides this peculiar British historical consideration, both the usage 'civil service' and the overtones which make of the phrase a definable political concept are notably absent from non-English-speaking political cultures, even close neighbours of Britain like France or the Netherlands. Even in the United States, the change of an administration on the inauguration of a new presidency results in the displacement of a whole host of administrative officers and their replacement by a new set of nominees on a party basis.

It has been suggested that the concept of a non-political civil service originated with the PLACE Acts of the early 18th century. From the mid-19th century a number of key reforms served to advance the establishment of a modern civil service ethos in Britain. In 1853, Charles Trevelyan and Stafford Northcote, at GLADSTONE's request, reported on the state of the civil service. They criticized the inefficient system of patronage recruitment and recommended the introduction of competitive entry examinations, promotion on merit and the introduction of a unified civil service that would incorporate all departments and make a distinction between policy-making and administration. In 1855, the creation of the Civil Service Commission was intended to introduce meritocracy and end patronage appointment: in practice, nothing much changed. An ORDER IN COUNCIL of 1870 introduced an open competition examination that appealed greatly to those who had attended public schools, and which eventually transformed the civil service. Civil servants were now loyal to the state rather than to a 'patron'. Women were excluded from élite civil service positions until well after World War I, but were involved in clerical work throughout the later 19th century, and in some departments were employed as inspectors to deal with female issues.

For most of the 20th century the civil service still operated under the same framework and expectations as had been established in the 19th century. However, the scope of its activity expanded enormously: as the state took on more and more responsibilities so recruitment to the main departments of state reflected this. By 1979 there were approximately 750,000 civil servants, of whom some 570,000 were non-industrial officials. The remaining 25 per cent were working in the defence industries, such as ordnance factories and naval DOCKYARDS. Even as late as 1939 there had only been a little over 200,000 and in 1960 some 375,000 civil servants.

Until the 1960s the service was divided into classes horizontally (higher and lower grades in the same area of work) and vertically (various skills or professional areas). Recruitment was to a particular level or functional area and this then determined career prospects and promotion. This was clearly inefficient and inflexible and in 1968 the Fulton Committee on the Civil Service suggested a unified grading structure with more open access. This was thought to be particularly important for the peak of the service where some 800 posts (Under Secretary, Deputy Secretary and Principal Secretary) could be recruited from within or outside the service itself. These and the other administrative posts were filled by open competition and were the responsibility of the independent Civil Service Commissioners, set up in the 19th century to counter patronage and corruption. After 1968, however, the commissioners were absorbed into the civil service department which is headed by the prime minister. It is this latter change which gave rise to a great deal of concern in the 1980s when it was felt that the incumbent prime minister was able to make use of this position to appoint people sympathetic to a particular political view. This would have the profound effect of changing the historical perception of the service as politically neutral. Since the election of the LABOUR government under Tony BLAIR in 1997, this perception has been sharpened with the appointment of government-appointed 'special advisers' from outside the civil service. These numbered 70 in 2000: they are paid from public funds to advise the government across a range of political issues.

Civil Wars, British, 1639–60. The sequence of Civil Wars which spanned more than two decades is often reduced in scope and duration by the description the 'English Civil War'. This is a measure of how a concentration on English history has distorted the history of the British Isles, and has impoverished itself by doing so. A series of conflicts spanning the three kingdoms of the Stuart Crown and all four nations of the British Isles needs to be considered.

During the 1630s CHARLES I's personal rule caused much discontent through his favouring of the ARMINIANS and his levying of non-Parliamentary taxation, but his regime found little difficulty in keeping the initiative until its double defeat by the Scots in the BISHOPS' WARS (1639–40). Collapse of the government's authority enabled the English PARLIAMENT to extort drastic constitutional and religious concessions, but Charles continued to intrigue to regain control, e.g. in his attempted arrest of the FIVE MEMBERS.

The flashpoint in 1642 was over control of an army to defeat the IRISH REBELLION (1641). Many in Parliament did not trust the king, but many others, increasingly frightened by what they saw as the radicalism of the opposition to Charles, rallied to his support. Both sides issued orders to raise troops, but it was Charles's attempt at Nottingham to rally the provinces against the capital which precipitated open conflict. Parliament thereafter split between the group directing war against the king at WESTMINSTER and a Parliament at the ROYALIST capital of OXFORD (so it is no more than a convenient shorthand to talk of a war between Parliament and the King). The Westminster Parliament entered an uneasy alliance with the victorious Scots armies against the king.

In the first – English and Welsh – Civil War (1642–6), the Westminster Parliament's major advantage was the possession of LONDON, with its major financial resources, and this became decisive once Parliament prosecuted the war with fresh vigour after the SELF-DENYING ORDINANCE and the formation of the NEW MODEL ARMY under Sir Thomas FAIRFAX and Oliver CROMWELL in 1645. Charles's defeat exposed the divisions not only between the Scots and the English but also between the Westminster Parliament and its army. Discontents multiplied as

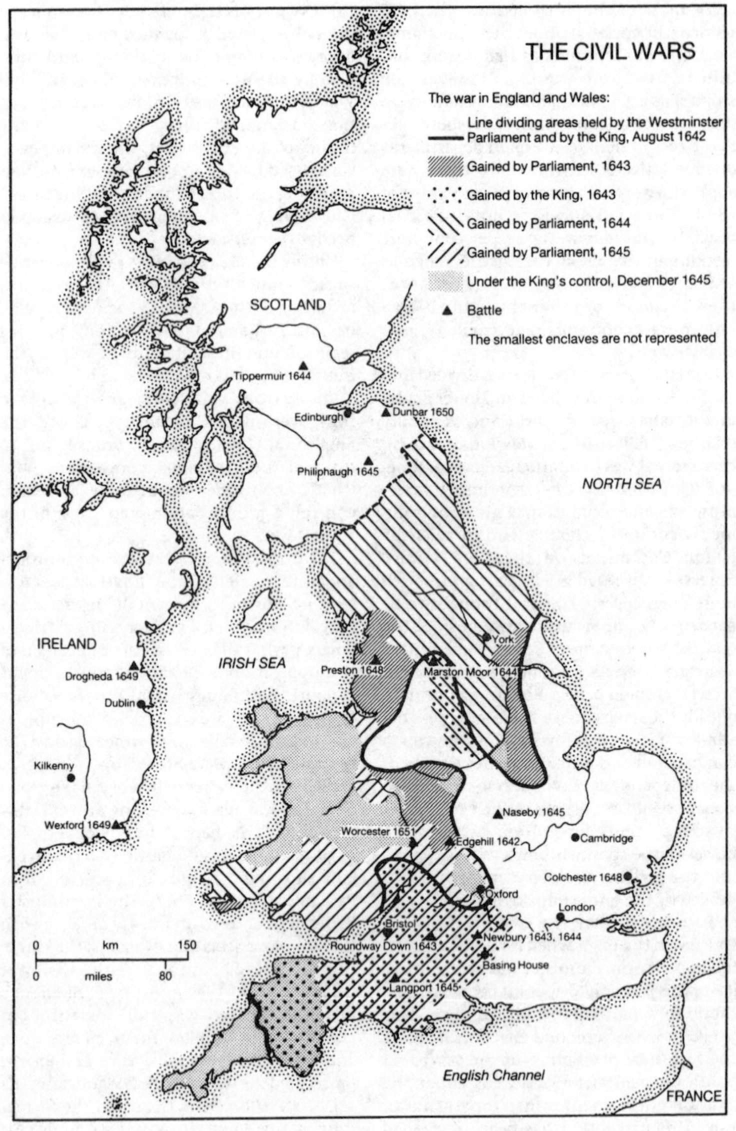
THE CIVIL WARS
The war in England and Wales:
Line dividing areas held by the Westminster Parliament and by the King, August 1642
Gained by Parliament, 1643
Gained by the King, 1643
Gained by Parliament, 1644
Gained by Parliament, 1645
Under the King's control, December 1645
Battle
The smallest enclaves are not represented
SCOTLAND
Tippermuir 1644
Edinburgh
Dunbar 1650
Philiphaugh 1645
NORTH SEA
IRELAND
Drogheda 1649
Dublin
IRISH SEA
Preston 1648
York
Marston Moor 1644
Kilkenny
Wexford 1649
Naseby 1645
Worcester 1651
Edgehill 1642
Cambridge
Colchester 1648
Oxford
London
Bristol
Roundway Down 1643
Newbury 1643, 1644
Basing House
Langport 1645
0 km 150
0 miles 80
English Channel
FRANCE

Charles I resisted all compromise proposals so requiring the maintenance of the army on a wartime footing and taxation at high levels. The upshot was the second English Civil War (spring–summer 1648), in which the New Model defeated English and Scots royalists aligned with discontented English provincials. Thereafter, the army's intervention in politics further escalated, climaxing in PRIDE'S PURGE and the trial and execution of Charles I in January 1649.

Fairfax having resigned his command over the king's trial, Cromwell succeeded to the command of the New Model and turned his attention to subduing Ireland. A brutally won English victory here (*see* DROGHEDA) was followed by an equally decisive campaign against the Scots armies now supporting Prince Charles (the future CHARLES II) as the inheritor of his father's throne. Over the next few years, English republican armies defeated guerrilla armies in Ireland and Scotland, and for the first time in British history, England completely dominated the British Isles (*see* INTERREGNUM).

Further royalist risings proved futile until MONCK, one of Parliament's own generals, stepped in to solve the constitutional deadlock after the death of Cromwell and set in motion the RESTORATION of Charles II. Charles reckoned his accession from the moment of his father's execution in 1649. *See also* COUNTY COMMITTEES; EASTERN ASSOCIATION.

Argument over the causes began even while conflict was going on, and remained central to party debates between WHIGS and TORIES into the 18th century. Victorian discussion became more detached: S. R. Gardiner and later G. M. Trevelyan saw the civil war as the culmination of a struggle for religious and political liberty by the PURITANS. Socialist historians, following R. H. Tawney, stressed long-term social and economic change; Lawrence Stone has placed a similar emphasis on a crisis in social structures (*see* ARISTOCRACY; GENTRY). Christopher Hill has taken an avowedly MARXIST exposition of the upheaval as a bourgeois revolution, but also as an ideological battle between conservative royalists and progressive Puritans.

By contrast, regional studies since the 1950s have suggested that Charles I's first opponents were conservatives defending England against what they saw as religious and constitutional innovations; this has created new interest in the religious issues.

Some American historians have argued against the Marxists that the wars were largely political conflicts within the governing class. G. R. Elton criticized long-term explanations, seeing origins in essentially short-term political events; similarly REVISIONIST historians have sought to minimize the extent of conflict between crown and Parliament under the early Stuarts.

CHRONOLOGY

1639 First BISHOPS' WAR: English defeated by Scots.

1640 Second Bishops' War: English defeated by Scots.

1641 Roman Catholic rebellion in Ireland (Confederation of KILKENNY).

1642 CHARLES I raises standard at Nottingham; war breaks out in England. Battle of EDGEHILL: indecisive.

1643 Scots renew war on Parliamentary side.

1644 Battle of MARSTON MOOR: royalist defeat.

1645 SELF-DENYING ORDINANCE and creation of NEW MODEL ARMY; Battles of Naseby and LANGPORT: royalist defeat.

1646 King surrenders to Scots, who hand him over to English Parliament.

1647 Peace talks with king stall; he is seized by English army.

1648 'Second Civil War' (*see* COLCHESTER): English royalist and Scots alliance defeated.

1649 King executed; CROMWELL recaptures most of Ireland; massacre of Drogheda.

1650 New alliance of CHARLES II and Scots defeated at battle of DUNBAR.

1651 Charles II and Scots defeated at WORCESTER.

1652 War in Scotland effectively over.

1653 War in Ireland effectively over. Guerrilla rising begins in Scotland.

1655 General MONCK suppresses Scottish rising; PENRUDDOCK'S RISING fails.

1659 Booth's Rising (unsuccessful) and other royalist disturbances. Monck marches on London.

1660 Charles II restored.

Civitas (plural *civitates*), the basic unit of local government throughout the Roman Empire, which was introduced into Britain from soon after the start of the ROMAN

CONQUEST in AD 43. Most of the *civitates* appear to have comprised the territory previously controlled by a British tribe, although a few were the result of Roman reorganization (*see* ATREBATES; BRIGANTES).

Each *civitas* was expected to be self-governing beneath the overall authority of the emperor's appointed officials, and had a specially built or redeveloped urban centre as its capital. These centres would, as a matter of course, have their own amphitheatres and public buildings, and were expected to replicate Roman civilization in the provinces.

While it is important to recognize that a lack of evidence can impede the identification of *civitates*, it is probable that there were about 15 in Britain by the time the Roman conquest was complete (*see* CAERWENT; CANTERBURY; CIRENCESTER; EXETER; SILCHESTER; VERULAMIUM; WINCHESTER; WROXETER; YORK). Together they did not, however, cover the entire province, since some of the more hostile regions – such as north-west England and north Wales – were not divided in this way.

The towns within the *civitates* often acted as centres of resistance during the English invasions of the 5th century. The *civitates* themselves may on occasion have determined later SHIRE boundaries, and their capitals often retained their importance as TOWNS.

Claim of Right, 1689, Scottish counterpart of the English DECLARATION OF RIGHTS, drawn up by the Scottish Convention Parliament following the GLORIOUS REVOLUTION. The offer of the crown to William of Orange (the future WILLIAM III) and MARY was made conditional on their acceptance of the Claim. It asserted that JAMES II AND VII had forfeited the throne by allowing Catholics to practise, teach and hold high office, by maintaining a STANDING ARMY, imposing magistrates on royal BURGHS, and imprisoning people without trial. It declared that no papist could become king or queen of Scotland or hold public office, and called for the abolition of the episcopal hierarchy, for more frequent parliaments, and for tighter limits on the use of judicial power and charges of treason.

Clapham Sect, Anglican EVANGELICAL group – also nicknamed 'the Saints' – centred around John Venn, rector (1793–1813) of Holy Trinity Church, Clapham, London. Its members, mostly influential laymen living in the area, engaged in philanthropic, missionary and other collective religious activities. They included William WILBERFORCE, the former governor of Sierra Leone, the 'freed slave settlement in West Africa', Zachary Macaulay, the banker and politician Henry Thornton and the lawyer James Stephen. Links between some of these families endured until the early 20th century, when they contributed several members to the BLOOMSBURY GROUP.

Clare, Richard de (2nd Earl of Pembroke) (*c*.1130–76), commonly known as 'Strongbow', soldier. He inherited his father's earldom of Pembroke in 1148, but, as STEPHEN's man, forfeited it when HENRY II came to the throne. In *c*.1166, still out of favour at court, he decided to risk accepting DERMOT MAC MURROUGH's offer of marriage to his daughter Aoife and succession to the kingdom of LEINSTER in return for military assistance. In 1170, Strongbow went to Ireland, occupied DUBLIN and Waterford and, in 1171, succeeded Mac Murrough. This precipitated Henry II's invasion of Ireland. Following it, Strongbow was recognized as earl and as Henry's representative in Ireland. His gamble had succeeded, and the English conquest of Ireland had begun.

Clarendon, 1st Earl of, *see* HYDE, EDWARD

Clarendon, Assize of, 1166. Regarded as an important step in the development of English criminal law, this ASSIZE required grand juries to present accused or suspected persons for trial before royal judges in county courts. *See also* JURY SYSTEM.

Clarendon Code, the collective name given to the four Acts passed by the RESTORATION Parliament which reinforced the position of the ESTABLISHED CHURCH and restricted the activity of DISSENTERS: the CORPORATION ACT 1661, the Act of UNIFORMITY 1662, the Conventicle Act 1664 and the Five Mile Act 1665. The name derives from that of Edward HYDE, 1st Earl of Clarendon, the chief minister, though he was not the prime instigator. The Acts were unevenly enforced: sporadic government pressure produced waves of local activity, but only the rare local enthusiast took every opportunity to harry his Dissenting neighbours.

Clarendon Commission Appointed in 1861 to examine the state of the great public schools under the chairmanship of the 4th Earl of Clarendon, it found little to criticize except outmoded methods of teaching Latin and Greek. It endorsed the centrality of classics, but recommended a broadening of the curriculum to encompass mathematics, modern languages and science. A response to the changing manpower requirements of an industrial economy, its recommendations, though advanced by contemporary standards, revealed the complacency and anti-industrial ethos of the Victorian governing classes.

Clarendon, Constitutions of, 1164, a written statement of HENRY II's view of his customary rights over the English Church. Summoning a council to Clarendon, Wilts. in Jan. 1164, the king issued the constitutions in an attempt to clarify and settle the issues at stake in his quarrel with Thomas BECKET. He required the BISHOPS to promise to observe these customs in good faith, but the effect was to escalate the dispute. Some of the Constitutions – including one perceived as undermining BENEFIT OF CLERGY – seemed to threaten the liberty of the Church and as such were condemned by Pope Alexander III.

Clarion The most successful of socialist weeklies, founded in 1891, it popularized socialism as the *Daily Mail* popularized conservatism. Robert Blatchford, its gifted editor, set out to entertain as well as instruct: readers were invited to join cycling and glee clubs and to propagate socialism through the Clarion Scouts and Clarion Vans. It was in its heyday during the 1890s; it finally folded in 1932.

Class and Class Consciousness The debate on the role of class and class consciousness (as conducted between MARXist and non-Marxist historians) is concerned with the origins and formation of a class society, the status and character of class conflict and the material and cultural factors in the growth of class consciousness.

For debate about class in the 18th and 19th centuries, the central study is E. P. Thompson's *The Making of the English Working Class* (1963). His thesis – that between 1780 and 1832 most English working people came to feel an identity of interest among themselves and against their rulers and employers – presented working-class consciousness as the ways in which the experience of industrial capitalism in its formative stages was embodied in traditions, value systems, ideas and institutional forms. Class, he argued, must be viewed as a relationship rather than a structure, and class formation as a dynamic process, with working people making their own history.

Critics thought otherwise. Thompson, it was claimed, had exaggerated the importance of marginal disaffected elements and neglected the mainstream of workers; had ignored critical divisions between artisans and labourers and the sectionalism of many occupational groups; had underplayed the brutal, drunken, xenophobic low-life element; and had adopted a simplistic two-class model that could not accommodate the intermediate strata and the cross-cutting pressures that made for stability and diminished class feeling.

The analysis presented in 1963 is still substantially valid in the view of its wide number of supporters. The controversy has revealed our profound ignorance of the formation and operation of social hierarchies and of the divisions both within and between classes. These deficiencies alone will ensure that the debate continues.

Class Structure, a broad concept denoting the different social strata in a society. The modern definitions and arguments regarding class principally derive from MARX. Many commentators draw a distinction between the pre-industrial social order of ranks and estates on the one hand, and the industrial formation of classes – working, middle, upper – marked by their possessions and wealth and by their relationship to the means of production. Early commentators, notably Weber and Herbert SPENCER, differed from Marx in their definition of class, especially the distinction between economic and social class (which Marx held largely to be the same thing), and those definitional problems remain an active subject of debate. Although Marx predicted that the increased exploitation of the working class would ultimately result in social revolution, the reality, at least in Britain and the West, has belied that prediction. Increased real WAGES, the regulation and institutionalization of social conflict in TRADE UNIONS and the like (*see* *also* LABOUR ARISTOCRACY), and the existence of cross-class social or religious divides, have all been features militating against social and political divisions based solely on class.

Classical Architecture, the family of architectural styles deriving from the buildings of ancient Greece and Rome. *See also* BAROQUE; NEO-CLASSICISM; PALLADIANISM; ROCOCO.

Classical Movement, an unofficial PURITAN attempt to set up a PRESBYTERIAN structure of synods (*classis*=synod) in the CHURCH: ENGLAND during the 1580s, to prepare for the replacement of EPISCOPACY, and to promote further church reform. The chief organizer, John Field, died in 1588, and three years later, when those remaining were discovered, arrested and intimidated by the STAR CHAMBER, the movement collapsed.

Claudius (10 BC–AD 54), Roman emperor (41–54). He launched the second successful Roman invasion of Britain (*see also* JULIUS CAESAR). His motives have been much discussed by scholars; his need to establish his personal prestige after the assassination of his predecessor Caligula, as well as the threat to Roman power in Gaul posed by the developing power of the CATUVELLAUNI, are likely to have been the predominant ones.

Claudius took part in the invasion himself, arriving when his army had reached the Thames and leading the triumphal entry into the Catuvellaunian capital of COLCHESTER. He appointed good generals – e.g. AULUS PLAUTIUS and OSTORIUS SCAPULA – and presumably contributed to the plans for the organization of the new Roman province.

Clause Four, *see* NATIONALIZATION

Clayton–Bulwer Treaty, 1850. An Anglo-American agreement, named after the principal negotiators, it defined the attitude of Britain and the United States towards Central America in connection with a possible transoceanic canal. The two powers agreed to a mutual 'hands off' policy in Central America and to abstain from seeking control over any such waterway. The treaty did something to improve relations between the two countries after the ANGLO-AMERICAN WAR.

Clean Air Act 1956 The first major piece of legislation to control air pollution provided for the control of smoke from factories and domestic fires in urban areas. The Act has had a dramatic effect on the appearance of LONDON and major industrial areas, substantially reducing smog in the capital and elsewhere.

Clearances, Highland The history of the Scottish Highlands and Islands is coloured by descriptions of the sufferings and brutality of mass clearances of people by landowners in the decades after 1800, principally so as to allow the introduction of large-scale sheep farming. Marked POPULATION decline occurred in many areas, with mass emigration, particularly to the United States and CANADA. Much of this MIGRATION has been shown by subsequent research to have been the result of overpopulation in a marginal economy, especially when the herring fisheries failed in the 1820s and the POTATO FAMINE came in the 1840s. Landowners used the vacant land to graze sheep and establish crofters. In some locations, violence did accompany the eviction of families for these ends, and in a few places there were sudden and mass clearances. The clearing of the Highlands was thus a combination of the population drifting away and their being forced to move, but its emotive power remains dominant.

Clearing Banks, *see* BANKS

Cleves, Anne of, *see* ANNE OF CLEVES

Client Kingdoms, Roman The establishment of client-kingdom relationships with neighbouring tribes was a feature of Roman frontier policy during the time that the empire came to dominate most of the known world, and it occurred in Britain from the earliest stages of the ROMAN CONQUEST. A relationship of this kind existed at some time with the BRIGANTES, the ICENI and the territory of the ATREBATES ruled by COGIDUBNUS.

The client kingdoms maintained a considerable amount of independence; their rulers were, for example, allowed to mint coin. None the less, the Romans always took the view that they could intervene in their internal affairs at any time, and sometimes did so with unhappy consequences (*see* BOUDICCA; CARTIMANDUA). Cogidubnus' career, on the other hand, is indicative of a successful client relationship during the first decades of the conquest. However, in the second half of the 1st century, Roman policy shifted inexorably towards direct rule.

Climbing Boys, chimney sweeps. One of the most scandalous uses of child labour during the early industrial period, the employment of children as chimney sweeps was also among the most intractable of social problems. Accounts such as Jonas Hanaway's *The Sentimental History of the Chimney Sweepers in London and Westminster* (1785), and Charles Kingsley's novel of the life of a climbing boy, *The Water Babies* (1863), failed to translate moral outrage into enforceable legislation until the passage of the Chimney Sweeps Act 1875 made the police the responsible licensing authority.

Clink, popular term for a prison, deriving from the name of a debtors' prison in Southwark, LONDON. The Clink itself was burned down in the GORDON RIOTS of 1780, though by then it was no longer in use as a prison. *See also* IMPRISONMENT FOR DEBT.

Cliometrics, term coined to describe the application of ECONOMETRICS in history. Named after the Muse of history, Clio, it is more commonly in use in the United States.

Clippers A much-misused word often appropriated for any fine-lined fast sailing ship, it originated in North America and was used for the fast PRIVATEER brigs and pilot schooners built in the Chesapeake. It then became applied to the larger ship-rigged vessels built for high speed in the low-bulk, high-value China TEA trade. British shipyards produced their own designs, successfully challenging the American record-breakers in the 1850s and 1860s, but in 1869 when the SUEZ CANAL was opened, the day of the true clipper was done and the emphasis shifted to larger vessels designed for carrying-power and low costs rather than outright speed.

Clipping, *see* COIN CLIPPING

Clito, William, *see* HENRY I

Clive, Robert (1st Baron Clive of Plassey) (1725–74), Indian adventurer. Having joined the EAST INDIA COMPANY in 1742, he spent three periods in INDIA, each time returning with a larger fortune and the opportunity to cut a more significant figure on the English social and political scene.

From 1746 to 1753, he took part in fighting against the French in India; on his return, he was elected MP. From 1756, he led a successful offensive against the French and the nawab of Bengal, whom he decisively defeated at PLASSEY; made governor of the Bengal Presidency, he consolidated the company's influence. Back in England, he was elected MP for Salop in 1761, and given an Irish barony. He returned to India in 1763 as governor and commander-in-chief, arriving after a crucial victory at Buxar. The Mughal emperor now granted the company responsibility for civil administration in Bengal, including the right to collect revenue.

When Clive came back to England for the final time in 1767, he used his by then fabulous wealth to build up a parliamentary interest, and in 1772 was made lord lieutenant of Salop. However, much of his later political career was spent justifying his position. Forced to defend his financial integrity to a parliamentary inquiry (1772–3) he committed suicide in Nov. 1774 even though the inquiry vindicated his conduct. Clearly a man of energy and courage, though often criticized for overwhelming ambition and ruthlessness, he was the most successful of the so-called NABOBS. His great collection of treasures from India survives, and is displayed at Powis Castle, Powys.

Cliveden Set, the allegedly pro-German group centred on Cliveden, the Berks. country home of Nancy and Waldorf ASTOR. Although accusations of a conspiracy were much exaggerated, the Astors did use Cliveden to entertain a PRO-APPEASEMENT group, including the foreign secretary Lord Halifax, Geoffrey Dawson, editor of *The Times*, and sympathetic MPs. Such influence as the group had was largely dissipated when Hitler conquered the whole of Czechoslovakia in the spring of 1939 and turned even the most avid appeasers against him, including the Astors.

Clodius Albinus (Decimus Clodius Albinus) (?–AD 197), Roman governor of Britain. He proclaimed himself emperor in 193, after the Emperors Commodus, Pertinax and Didius Julianus had all been murdered during the period 192–3. He took a large army from Britain to the Continent, but was defeated near Lyons by rival emperor SEPTIMIUS SEVERUS in 197.

Clontarf, Battle Of, near Dublin, 1014. In Irish and Norse legend, it was at this battle that BRIAN BORU, high-king of the Irish, defeated for ever the armies of the VIKINGS settled in Ireland. In fact, the battle was a major episode in the struggle for power between the kings of early 11th-century Ireland, with Irish and Vikings fighting on both sides. Brian Boru was victorious, but his death in the latter stages of the battle allowed MAEL SECHNAILL II, who had not taken part, to resume the role of high-king.

Closed Shop, *see* TRADE UNIONS

Cloth Industry Since clothing is a basic requirement in most societies, cloth manufacture is one of the first industries created by surplus purchasing power. In medieval and early modern Europe, England was one of the outstanding producers. Evidence of the industry goes back to earliest times, and during the 14th century it rapidly overtook raw wool exports as the most valuable national overseas trade (*see* STAPLE, COMPANY OF; WOOL SUBSIDY; WOOL TRADE).

From then until the 18th century, the technology of woollen cloth production changed little: raw wool was successively sorted (removing flaws and impurities), spun into yarn, dyed, woven, fulled (cleaned and milled), tentered (stretched) and finished (raised and cropped to smooth the surface). Most industrial innovation consisted of more ingenious variations in weaving techniques to produce different types of cloth. The so-called 'NEW DRAPERIES' (early worsted developments incorporating longer-stapled wool in warps) usually sought to combine strength with lighter weight and were important in expanding exports to southern Europe; some of these techniques were introduced by immigrant workers, notably from the Low Countries.

The industry lent itself to co-operative working by people with different skills. The main capital input was in the purchase of raw wool and in dyeing and finishing, so this was where large-scale clothiers and merchants concentrated their efforts. Much of the other work was done on a 'putting-out' system – farmed out to individuals usually working in their own homes frequently as a BY-EMPLOYMENT or, as in West Yorks., by small independent clothiers who bought raw wool and sold cloth at weekly cloth markets. From the 13th to the 18th centuries, the industry progressively moved out of towns to escape urban regulations and was concentrated in well-populated rural areas with plenty of cheap labour, especially in East Anglia, the West Country and West Riding, Yorks. This process was frequently accompanied by economic dislocation, especially in the 1530s to 1560s with the (temporary) collapse of trade in the 'OLD DRAPERIES'.

Historians have concentrated on the EXPORT trade, since there is more evidence available, but the industry was underpinned by domestic demand, particularly during the periods of population growth of the 12th and 13th centuries and 1500–1650. Later the prosperity of the trade (*see* WOOLLEN INDUSTRY) became one of the main stimuli of the INDUSTRIAL REVOLUTION. *See also* COCKAYNE SCHEME; COTTON INDUSTRY; MERCHANT ADVENTURERS.

Club, word increasingly used from the late 17th century to denote gatherings or associations of people, or the practice of pooling ('clubbing') money to finance social or other activities. By the early 18th century, clubs were being hailed – and satirized – as social phenomena distinctive of the age. Some clubs were no more than informal gatherings of friends at public houses; others shouldered formal responsibilities, such as the 'Jockey Club', which survives as a body regulating horse-racing. FRIENDLY SOCIETIES were commonly termed 'clubs'. Among the more notorious political clubs of the mid- and late-17th century were the ROTA (associated with James Harrington, the author of *The Commonwealth of Oceana* (1656)) and the GREEN RIBBON CLUB (associated with Anthony Ashley COOPER, 1st Earl of Shaftesbury). In the 18th century, as well as many local political clubs, there were clubs with many MPs among their members, such as the predominantly TORY 'COCOA TREE' and the WHIG 'Brooks's'. The early 19th century saw the development of the 'gentlemen's club' as a distinct building type, the Athenaeum (begun 1827) being a pioneering example.

Clubmen, local associations in the CIVIL WARS in south and west England, often without gentry leadership, which tried to keep both armies at bay. Different groups displayed differing biases, some ROYALIST and ANGLICAN, some PARLIAMENTARIAN. They had considerable nuisance value to both sides, but more to the undisciplined Royalist armies in the West.

Cluniacs, monastic ORDER strictly observing the BENEDICTINE Rule, with its mother house at Cluny in BURGUNDY. During the 10th century its observance was influential in other French monasteries, and in the 11th century Abbot Odilo developed a common organization which inspired many new foundations across Europe, loosely affiliated to Cluny. The particular characteristic of the Order was its attention to splendid liturgy, exemplified in its church at Cluny, the largest in 12th-century Europe. The first English Cluniac house was St Pancras, Lewes (Sussex), of 1077; the first in Scotland was Paisley Abbey, from 1163. There were never full-scale Cluniac foundations in Wales or Ireland.

Clydesiders, a militant TRADE UNION and socialist group led by shop stewards in the engineering industry and socialist MPs in and around GLASGOW during and after WORLD WAR I. They had representation on the Clyde Workers' Committee, formed initially to campaign against DILUTION, and later organized the series of strikes and demonstrations in 1918–19 known as Red Clydeside.

CND, *see* CAMPAIGN FOR NUCLEAR DISARMAMENT

Cnut (*c.*994–1035), King of the English (1016–35). The younger son of SVEIN FORKBEARD, King of Denmark, Cnut acquired the English kingdom by conquest in 1016. From 1019, he also controlled Denmark and later, briefly, the kingdom of Norway. The story of his reign is basically one of attempts to hold together a vast North Sea 'empire'. After some initial disturbances, England remained at peace, but Scandinavia was turbulent, and a great deal of Cnut's time was spent fighting there.

He became an ostentatious Christian, visiting Rome at least once and making extravagant benefactions to the Church. Despite this, his rule in England was fairly brutal: political rivals killed, Englishmen dispossessed of their lands, new Danish landholders appearing in almost every SHIRE, and exceptionally heavy taxation in the early years. He maintained two 'wives' – Queen EMMA and Ælfgifu of Northampton – the Scandinavian warlord always present beneath the veneer of the Christian, traditionally-minded king of the English. His 'empire' disintegrated after his death during the short reigns of his sons HAROLD HAREFOOT and HARTHACNUT.

The (possibly apocryphal) story telling how he demonstrated to his courtiers that he could not hold back the sea first appeared about a century after his death (*see* HENRY OF HUNTINGDON), its purpose being to show the humility of this former pagan and his awareness that the power of a king was limited.

In England, Cnut's achievement was the preservation of the strong monarchy created by the 10th-century kings, but he also symbolizes the long-standing Scandinavian interest in and influence on English affairs, which only came to an end after the NORMAN CONQUEST. Historians no longer use the Anglicized form of his name, Canute.

Coal Industry Coal was worked in Britain during the Roman period, but thereafter production seems to have lapsed until *c.*1200, when deposits began to be rapidly exploited in north-east England, the Pennines and the Forest of Dean, both for trade within England and for export: coal was used as a luxury domestic fuel, but also for iron-smelting, pottery-firing and limestone-burning, and a major seaborne trade to southern England developed from NEWCASTLE UPON TYNE. The development of the industry in size and geographical range was steady, until rapid growth occurred during the 16th century, when expanding production, thanks to the development of mechanical (animal-powered) pumping and better transport organization, made coal for domestic use comparatively cheap in most regions. National output may have increased fourfold between 1560 and 1690 and growth continued in the 18th century, aided by the use of steam-powered pumping engines.

Coal was the most important fuel of the INDUSTRIAL REVOLUTION. Stimulated by the sustained growth of POPULATION, improved transport, the application of STEAM POWER and the development of the metallurgical industries (*see* IRON AND STEEL), coal-mining expanded rapidly during the first four decades of the 19th century, through the action of entrepreneurs and landowners, and often on land forming part of great estates. The total output was about 16 million tons in 1816, 30 million in 1836 and 44 million in 1846.

As coal output increased, pits were sunk to greater depths, and problems relating to ventilation, haulage and winding became pressing, as did the greater exposure to explosive gases. By the 1840s, some of these problems had been resolved, and mechanical equipment to deal with them was installed throughout the mining industry over the next 40 years or so. However, the enormous expansion in output was achieved largely by muscle rather than machine power. Between 1850 and 1880, the number of miners rose from an estimated 200,000 to around 500,000, and by 1914, there were rather more than 1.2 million colliers working in some 3,000 mines – almost as many as the agricultural population and textile workforce combined. Coal-miners, often concentrated in mining villages in the South Wales, Som., Yorks., Notts., Cumbrian, Northumb., Scottish and other coalfields, developed a distinctive and often politically militant working-class culture of their own. The hazards of the mining process brought regulation to the industry, notably in the COAL MINES ACTS.

The economic importance of the coal-mining industry was enormous. The value of its output, equal to about 3 per cent of GNP in 1860, had risen to 7 per cent by 1913, and exports rose from 7 million to 73 million tons. Until the outbreak of World War I, Britain remained the world's leading coal exporter.

For all that, industrial performance gave cause for concern. Labour productivity began to decline from the 1880s, while that in the United States registered rapid and continuous advances. American coal owners were quicker than their British competitors in the application of labour-saving machinery; by the beginning of the 20th century, a quarter of US bituminous coal output was cut by machinery, compared to 1.5 per cent in Britain. The meaning of the comparison, however, remains unclear. Economic historians are divided as to whether management resistance to the mechanization of coal cutting was a rational response to unfavourable geological conditions or a sign of technological backwardness and entrepreneurial failure.

The coal industry was nationalized in 1947 (*see* NATIONALIZATION) and has undergone a lengthy period of contraction, largely as a result of international competition and the increased importance of OIL, GAS and ATOMIC ENERGY. The militant mining TRADE UNIONS succeeded in winning their struggle with the HEATH government, but were largely broken by the legislation of the THATCHER governments, the long and bitter miners' strike of 1984–5, and the subsequent mine-closure programme. The UK coal industry is now entirely in the private sector with 41 underground mines in production (including 19 major deep mines) employing around 10,500 workers and 59 open cast sites with a workforce of around 4,000.

CHRONOLOGY: INVENTION AND INNOVATION

1815 Safety lamp, invented by Sir Humphry Davy, enabled mining to be carried on in places previously too dangerous to work. Adopted very slowly and did not eliminate risk of explosion, particularly where pits did not have effective ventilation system.

1837 Exhaust fan developed by William Fourness of Leeds as safer alternative to practice of ventilating pits by means of burning furnace at bottom of upcast shaft; it is said to be capable of exhausting 420 cu. m. (4,500 cu. ft) of air per minute at a cost of 5–7.5 pence a day.

1840 Safer method of heating air by means of high-pressure jets of steam demonstrated at Seaton Delaval; subsequently applied in south Wales and elsewhere, but not widespread. Wire ropes, first used in Blackwall Tunnel, London, applied to pumping and winding in mines, replacing hempen ropes which were costly and short-lived. Raising of coal and men by means of cages running on guide rods or rails introduced and rapidly adopted, with safety devices to prevent cages falling.

1849 Centrifugal fan, invented by W. P. Struve, marked beginning of modern ventilation, whereby air can be forced down one shaft or drawn up another.

1849 Compressed air, first used for transmission of power in Govan mine, proved less dangerous than steam engines for haulage purposes, and spread rapidly.

Coal Mines Act 1872 gave protection to checkweighmen, who frequently acted as

TRADE UNION officials (*see* COAL MINES REGULATION ACT 1860) against arbitrary dismissal, though they could still be recruited only from among the men actually employed in the colliery concerned. Colliery managers were also required to carry state certificates of technical competence. Daily safety inspections were to be carried out, and miners received the statutory right to appoint (from their own ranks) inspectors who were entitled to oversee the safety arrangements undertaken by pit managers.

Coal Mines Act 1930 The working day of underground miners was limited to seven and a half hours. It had been reduced to seven in 1920, but increased to eight again after the failure of the GENERAL STRIKE in 1926.

Coal Mines Inspection Act 1850 Passed in the wake of a series of colliery disasters, it provided for the state inspection of the mines on the lines already introduced into the textile factories, and imposed minimum standards of lighting and ventilation.

Coal Mines Minimum Wages Act 1912 Passed in response to the first national coal strike (1912), it provided for conferences of owners and workers, with government representatives, to fix the minimum rate of wages in each district. An aggrieved miner could bring a civil action for recovery of the minimum wage to which he was entitled.

Coal Mines Regulation Act 1860 prohibited the employment of boys under the age of 12 – or 9–10 if they could produce a certificate of education – and granted the miners' right to appoint checkweighmen to check the weights of coal credited to them by colliery officials as a basis for calculating their piece-work earnings.

Coal Mines Regulation Act 1908 Hours of men working underground were regulated to eight hours – the first time they had been restricted by law.

Coalition, Wars of the First, 1792–7, and **Second**, 1798–1802, *see* FRENCH REVOLUTIONARY WARS

Cobbett, William (1763–1835), journalist and tribune of the poor. Born in Farnham, Surrey, the son of a small farmer, he served in the army, became a self-taught journalist, and shifted from extreme TORYism to extreme RADICALISM. In and out of debt, and sometimes in prison, he published transcripts of parliamentary debates and state trials, and from 1802 he was editor of *Cobbett's Political Register*, which spoke to as well as for workers, against privilege and corruption and the destruction of a familiar way of life. The large number of imitators testify to the paper's importance. Cobbett is most widely remembered for his *Rural Rides*, journals of his travels from 1821, which first appeared from 1830; they are distinguished by their appreciation of the countryside and their attacks on landlords, corruption and 'the Great Wen' (London).

Cobden-Chevalier Treaty, 1860, an Anglo-French trade arrangement by which France would admit British machinery, coal, textiles and iron on a reduced tariff and, in return, Britain would reduce duties on French wines, brandy and silks. Negotiated by Richard Cobden, the founder of the ANTI-CORN LAW LEAGUE, it represented a triumph for FREE TRADE.

Cockayne Scheme, a disastrous government attempt in 1614–16 to intervene in the CLOTH INDUSTRY. Alderman William Cockayne enlisted government aid to break the MERCHANT ADVENTURERS' monopoly in cloth export and to stimulate the English finishing industry by banning unfinished cloth exports. Corrupt and undercapitalized, his new company could not cope with the reorganization, and after a trade crisis, the Merchant Adventurers regained their privileges.

Cockerton Judgement, 1901. A catalyst to the passage of the EDUCATION ACT 1902, the successful case was brought by T. B. Cockerton, an auditor, who claimed that, according to the EDUCATION ACT 1870, provision of secondary education by the London School Board constituted an illegal use of the school rate.

Cockpit, originally an octagonal building to the north of present-day Downing St containing a cock-fighting pit, and forming part of WHITEHALL Palace. It gave its name to the entire set of buildings facing St James's Park, resided in by, among others, Oliver CROMWELL, MONCK, CLIFFORD, Danby (*see* OSBORNE, THOMAS) and the future Queen ANNE. The Cockpit itself was demolished *c.*1675 and replaced with offices occupied by the PRIVY COUNCIL from 1678.

Cocoa Tree, a COFFEE HOUSE which provided a meeting place for Edward Harley's Board (a Hanoverian TORY political club) from 1727, and thus became a focus for rank-and-file Tory MPs. By the 1740s and 1750s, the term was used as a synonym for parliamentary Toryism.

Codex Amiatinus This superb early 8th-century manuscript, produced at the twin abbeys of MONKWEARMOUTH and JARROW in the time of Ceolfrith (abbot, 688–716), is the earliest surviving complete text of the Latin Bible. It is now preserved in the Biblioteca Medicea-Laurenziana in Florence.

Coenobitic Life, *see* MONASTICISM

Coercive Acts 1774, *see* INTOLERABLE ACTS

Coffee Houses From the earliest known example, in Oxford in 1650, they proliferated in London in the late 17th century, and by the 1720s were also commonplace in provincial towns. In addition to chocolate and coffee (a relatively new commodity), they provided TOBACCO, as well as NEWSPAPERS and periodicals for customers to read. They might also serve alcohol: some were described as essentially ALEHOUSES masquerading under a more fashionable name. Together with taverns, they provided a setting for many forms of semi-public activity: they were often used as accommodation addresses, and served as meeting places for more and less formal groups. In London, Lloyd's Coffee House, a centre for shipping intelligence, provided the basis from which the INSURANCE brokers grew; White's Chocolate House became famous for gaming, and was later transformed into a private political club.

Coggeshall, Ralph of, *see* RALPH OF COGGESHALL

Coigny, Anglo-Irish term (also seen as 'coyne') derived from the Irish *coinnmheadh*, meaning the right of a chief to exact free billeting for soldiers and servants and sometimes for his horses and dogs.

Coin Clipping, term used to describe the widespread practice of making an illegal profit by shearing and then melting down slivers of silver or gold from the edges of COINS, common in the 16th–18th centuries, also thereby reducing their weight and so forcing good unclipped coins out of circulation. The introduction of milled edges on coins and the progressive reduction in the precious metal content curbed the practice, as did vigorous prosecution of organized criminal gangs in the 18th century.

Coins and Coinage Coinage is usually thought to demonstrate an ECONOMY in which the use of money is widespread, although in more primitive societies coins containing a high proportion of precious metals may have been minted on behalf of rulers who wished primarily to display their power. The study of coins found in hoards has made an extremely important contribution to knowledge of ancient and early medieval societies, where documentary material is in short supply.

PRE-ROMAN BRITISH

The British tribes of the late Iron Age began to mint their own coins during the 1st century BC. The majority of these were high-value gold or silver, suggesting that they were made for prestige and gift exchange rather than for a market economy. They imitate Gaulish patterns and are confined to southern and eastern Britain.

The location of finds is exceptionally useful for defining the areas of tribal predominance, showing, for example, the wide area controlled by the DOBUNNI or the power of the CATUVELLAUNI immediately before the ROMAN CONQUEST. The coins also illustrate the power of particular rulers (e.g. CUNOBELIN) and – because some of them used the title *Rex* on their coins – show how Roman ideas had penetrated Britain even before the conquest.

ROMAN

The coins that circulated in Britain during the Roman occupation were the official money of the empire – minted abroad and dispatched to pay the army's wages – and replaced the largely ceremonial coinages of the Iron Age tribes (*see above*). They were subject to constant debasement in the last centuries of the Roman Empire, which fuelled inflation and other economic ills. Because money was regularly reminted for successive emperors, it can be closely dated – a great aid to dating archaeological sites. The coinage apparently continued to be used for some time after the departure of the

Roman armies, only falling out of use after c.430.

ANGLO-SAXON

England appears to have depended on the circulation of continental coin until gold *THRYMSAS* began to be minted in the second quarter of the 7th century; silver coins known as *SCEATTAS* replaced them by the end of the century. The first major minting of the PENNY (*denarius*) occurred in the reign of OFFA of MERCIA, although the NORTHUMBRIAN kings continued to mint *STYCAS*. In the 9th and 10th centuries, the minting became progressively more of a royal monopoly and the number of active MINTS increased. After EDGAR's great reform of 973, only royal mints issued coin, which was of high silver quality and renewed at periodic intervals (*RENOVATIO MONETE*); the administrative processes involved must have been highly sophisticated. This established pattern lasted for almost a century after the NORMAN CONQUEST. The study of coins from this period has made an extremely important contribution to knowledge of government and the economy.

EARLY IRISH

Early medieval Ireland was a coinless society, and the early Irish LAW TRACTS supply plentiful information on the workings of a non-money economy. The first coins to be struck were silver pennies minted in the name of Sihtric Silkbeard, the VIKING king of DUBLIN, in c.995. They were direct copies of the English pennies of King ATHELSTAN, and continued to be produced in increasingly debased form until the middle of the 12th century.

MEDIEVAL

During STEPHEN's reign the crown's monopoly of minting coin broke down, as is testified by the survival of pennies struck in the names of various barons as well as on behalf of the Empress MATILDA. In 1158 HENRY II ordered the recoinage which reasserted royal control; this TEALBY coinage lasted until 1180 when it was replaced by the SHORT CROSS coinage. In 1247 HENRY III, helped by bullion provided by RICHARD OF CORNWALL, issued LONG CROSS pennies. From the later 12th century onwards the number of mints was gradually reduced; by the mid-13th century LONDON and CANTERBURY were responsible for virtually the entire currency. This same period saw a tremendous increase in the number of coins struck. Not until the 19th century was a greater weight of bullion turned into coin of the realm than had been the case in 13th-century England. That money was becoming useful in an ever greater variety of transactions is shown by the success of EDWARD I's decision to mint halfpennies and farthings as well as pennies in the recoinage of 1279. In 1279 GROATS did less well, but they proved popular when re-issued in 1351. Similarly a gold coinage had proved to be premature when tried by Henry III in 1257, but took off when EDWARD III issued his NOBLE coinage in the 1340s and 1350s. The reign of EDWARD IV saw the introduction of new gold coins: the ryal or rose noble (valued at 10 shillings, i.e. a half rather than a third of a pound), and the angel (which was valued at a third of a pound like the older noble, and became associated with touching for the KING'S EVIL).

EARLY MODERN TO THE PRESENT DAY

The late medieval English coinage had a high reputation in Europe for stability and reliability, but this national asset was squandered by the debasements of HENRY VIII's last years, and it was not until the reign of ELIZABETH I that the damage was finally undone. Elizabeth also initiated short-lived experiments with machine-milling of coins in an attempt to replace hammered (i.e. hand-struck) coins; in this she had been forestalled in Scotland by the government of MARY OF GUISE. However, there was much opposition from vested interests in the English mints, and the main operator, the French craftsman Eloye Mestrelle, was eventually hanged for forgery in 1578. During the 16th century various private mints maintained by bishops (e.g. at Canterbury, York and Durham) were closed and the minting of coin was thus once more monopolized by the monarchy. The CIVIL WARS of the mid-17th century saw many local coinages produced; separate official coinages for Ireland continued down to the 1801 Act of UNION, but the Scots mint was closed two years after the 1707 Act of UNION. Before 1707, Scottish denominations were generally worth one-twelfth of English, although the same general range of denominations had been struck.

A persistent problem with the English coinage was the lack of small change, and despite Elizabethan experiments with base metal coinage, a proliferation of unofficial tokens and semi-official issues under licence were all that was available until the reign of CHARLES II; he also finally introduced a permanent milled coinage. The hammered coinage was finally abolished as part of the complete 1696 RECOINAGE, an element in the financial innovations which also included the founding of the BANK OF ENGLAND. There were further acute problems with the supply of all coins under GEORGE III, exacerbated by the disruption of the NAPOLEONIC WARS, and once more there was a flood of local token issues. Intermittent efforts to remedy the situation culminated with the coming of peace in a general recoinage in 1816 based on the GOLD STANDARD; silver coins ceased to maintain more than a token silver content. This silver coinage was in turn ended in 1947, which together with the 1931 abandonment of the Gold Standard was an acknowledgement of Britain's financial decline. Efforts to reform the complicated system of pounds, shillings and pence which had been mooted since the mid-19th century were only put into effect in 1971 with the introduction of DECIMALIZATION. *See also* STERLING.

CHRONOLOGY

Late 8th century First known silver pennies minted by KENTISH kings.

973 King EDGAR's reform of English coinage establishes complete royal control over minting and a regular pattern of recoinage.

Mid-12th century DAVID I mints first Scots national coinage.

1279 EDWARD I produces new silver denominations including the groat (4 pence).

1344 First English national gold coinage – the florin (6 shillings); quickly superseded by the noble (half a MARK; 6 shillings and 8 pence).

1526 Minting of first CROWN: gold and worth 4 shillings and 6 pence (later 5 shillings).

1544 HENRY VIII begins serious debasement.

1553 Scots Testoon (SHILLING): the first mechanically manufactured (milled) British coin.

1560 Short-lived experiments with milled English coinage begin.

1562 ELIZABETH I completes efforts, begun under EDWARD VI and MARY I, to restore coinage.

1600 First (short-lived) coinage for English EAST INDIA trade, in dollar values.

1642–9 Several regional coinages during British CIVIL WARS.

1662 English milled coinage begins.

1663 Guinea first minted, from West African gold and worth 20 (later 21) shillings.

1672 First official copper coinage.

1695 Handmade (hammered) coinage demonetized.

1696 Major RECOINAGE undertaken.

1707 Scots currency united with English (previously, Scottish denominations generally worth one-twelfth of English).

1709 Scottish mint in Edinburgh closed down despite promises.

1722–5 WOOD'S HALFPENCE controversy.

1797 Great gold shortage: bank notes declared legal tender.

1816 GOLD STANDARD adopted; silver coinage given token silver content.

1931 Gold standard finally abandoned.

1947 Silver content of coinage ended.

1971 DECIMALIZATION implemented.

Coke, Sir Edward (1552–1634), lawyer. Coke began his career as legal adviser to the gentry of East Anglia, before breaking into office as solicitor-general in 1592, SPEAKER of the Commons in 1593 and attorney-general in 1594 – appointments that earned him the hatred of Francis BACON. Continuing to combine frequent Commons service with legal eminence, he began publishing law reports in 1600 and became chief justice of the COMMON PLEAS in 1606; his feud with Bacon and his independent attitude to JAMES I's government culminated in his dismissal in 1616.

Fiercely opposing James's pro-Spanish policies, he was sent temporarily to the Tower in 1622, but continued to personify legalistic opposition. Publication of his monumental *Institutes of the Laws of England* was only completed in 1644. This and his other writing decisively shaped the legal profession's view of its past and hence its priorities for the future – notably its sense of its own importance.

Colchester (*Camulodunum*), the chief town of the TRINOVANTES, which became the capital of the enlarged tribal confederation dominated by the CATUVELLAUNI. In AD 43, the emperor CLAUDIUS staged a ceremonial entry into the principal town of his main enemies to celebrate the success of the Roman invasion, and six years later, it became the first Roman *colonia* (i.e. settlement specially set aside for Roman citizens) in Britain. Sacked in 60–1 when the Trinovantes joined BOUDICCA's revolt, it was subsequently rebuilt and remained one of the major urban centres of Roman Britain, even though the provincial capital was moved to LONDON. It was severely damaged when besieged by PARLIAMENT's armies during the second CIVIL WAR (1648); its massive CASTLE keep (the largest in England), begun *c.*1080 and built on the substructure of a major 1st-century AD temple, was partially dismantled in 1683.

Cold War, name given to the period of heightened tension between the Soviet-dominated Communist bloc and the West from the mid-1940s to the late 1980s. The Cold War began in Europe with disagreements between the wartime allies – Britain, the United States and the Soviet Union – over the division and future of Germany and the nature of the regimes imposed on eastern Europe by the Soviet Union; CHURCHILL made a speech at Fulton, Missouri, in March 1946, describing an 'Iron Curtain' across Europe. Ideological differences between the Communist East and a capitalist West sharpened with the enunciation of the Truman doctrine and Western support for the non-Communist forces in the Greek Civil War, the provision of MARSHALL PLAN aid to shore up the democratic regimes in the West, the Soviet blockade of Berlin in 1948–9, and the Communist takeover in Czechoslovakia in May 1948. Those divisions were hardened into military alliance by the formation of NATO in 1949, of which Britain was a founder member, and of the Soviet-led Warsaw Pact, a balance of power increasingly expressed in the doctrine of nuclear deterrence. International politics became dominated by the ideological contest between the superpowers for influence, colouring regional tensions in hotspots such as the Middle East, southern Africa and Southeast Asia. Britain participated in the KOREAN WAR to resist Communist expansion, put down a Communist-led insurgency in Malaya (*see* MALAYAN 'EMERGENCY'), committed itself to maintain a large standing army on the Continent of Europe as part of its Nato obligations, and provided bases for American nuclear forces in the United Kingdom.

The Cold War reached its maximum intensity between the ending of wartime co-operation over occupied Germany in 1947 and the Cuban missile crisis of 1962. The subsequent period of relaxation and détente produced strategic nuclear arms limitation agreements SALT I and SALT II between the US and the USSR. This gave way to a new period of tension from the late 1970s, prompted by Soviet intervention in Afghanistan and increasing concern over the growth of Soviet nuclear and conventional forces under Brezhnev. US President Reagan instituted a large arms build-up and commissioned the Strategic Defence Initiative (Star Wars). However, the accession of Gorbachev as Soviet president in 1985 began a rapid thaw in East–West relations which culminated in the collapse of the Communist regimes in eastern Europe, leading Presidents Bush and Gorbachev in December 1989 to declare the Cold War 'at an end'.

Coldstream Guards, *see* GUARDS AND GARRISONS

College of Arms, *see* HERALDRY AND HERALDS

College of Justice, *see* COURT OF SESSION; JAMES V

Collegiate Churches, churches served by a corporation (college) of clergy who are not monks. They were common in Anglo-Saxon England as MINSTERS, and in the high Middle Ages as the most expensive form of CHANTRY foundation. Most were suppressed at the REFORMATION, but a few – e.g. WESTMINSTER ABBEY, St George's Chapel, Windsor, Southwell Minster – survived for miscellaneous reasons.

Collins, Michael (1890–1922), Irish nationalist leader and soldier. The son of a farmer from West Cork, he returned to Ireland after a period in London, to take part in the EASTER RISING of 1916. After his release from subsequent internment in December 1916, he became secretary to the reformed IRISH REPUBLICAN BROTHERHOOD. He was a member of the provisional Dáil Éireann and minister of finance in the provisional government, but also organized and led attacks on British forces from 1919, including the killing of 11 British intelligence officers in DUBLIN in November 1920. Collins proved both a ruthless and energetic guerrilla commander, and a skilful negotiator in the Dáil's delegation to the London Conference of October 1921. He was one of those who signed the ANGLO-IRISH TREATY of December 1921 which led to the setting up of the IRISH FREE STATE with Dominion status.

Collins became Ireland's first prime minister in January 1922, when DE VALERA and his followers denounced the treaty. During the IRISH CIVIL WAR which followed between pro- and anti-treaty forces, he became the Free State's commander-in-chief, but was killed in an ambush at Beal na Blath in County Cork in August 1922. Widely admired as a courageous and romantic leader of the Irish revolution, he was known universally as 'the Big Fellow'.

Colonial Laws Validity Act 1865 A landmark in the evolution of the British COMMONWEALTH, passed under Palmerston (*see* TEMPLE, HENRY), it clarified the constitutional principles on which imperial authority rested, and recognized the right of colonies to pass legislation limited only by the doctrine of repugnancy, which held that any colonial Law should not conflict with the provision of any Act of Parliament relating to that colony. It ceased to apply to laws made by DOMINION parliaments under the provisions of the Statute of WESTMINSTER, 1931.

Colquhoun, Patrick (1745–1820), magistrate and pamphleteer, Lord Provost of Glasgow (1782–3), he founded the CHAMBER OF COMMERCE (1783) and was its first chairman. In 1789, he moved to London and three years later was appointed one of the new metropolitan police magistrates through the patronage of Henry Dundas (1742–1811), the Scottish lawyer and politician. In numerous pamphlets, he attempted to estimate the extent of London's vice and crime, and suggested schemes for improving public institutions and policies, his works including *Treatise on the Police of the Metropolis* (1795), *A Treatise on Indigence* (1806), and *Treatise on the Wealth, Power and Resources of the British Empire* (1814), which historians frequently use as a basis for estimating the distribution of wealth in the early 19th-century social structure.

Columba (Columcille), St (*c*.521–97), Abbot of Iona (563–97). An Irish nobleman who, apparently after being driven out of Ireland, founded the abbey of IONA, the island community which then became the centre of a monastic confederation within the Scottish kingdom of DALRIADA. Columba has acquired a reputation as the evangelist of the PICTS, but this may not be historically accurate since no mention is made of such work in ADOMNÁN's biography, the source of much of our knowledge of Columba's career. His achievements at Iona were certainly the basis for the later CONVERSION of the Picts and also for St Aidan's missionary work in NORTHUMBRIA. In his last years, Columba founded abbeys in Ireland, which gave him great influence there.

Combat, *see* TRIAL BY BATTLE

Combination Acts 1799, 1800, 1824, 1825 A response to the increased economic uncertainty associated with the development of industrial capitalism, 'combinations' – i.e. proto-TRADE UNIONS – to improve wages and conditions were regarded by government, especially in wartime, as a dangerous form of subversion that ought to be suppressed. The 1799 Act consolidated legislation passed (from the 1720s) against workers' combinations in many particular trades into a general statute banning all such combinations. The 1800 Act, which superseded it, provided for arbitrators to settle disputes over work or wages, failing which either party might appeal to a MAGISTRATE. Workers none the less continued to undertake collective action, often linked, during the Napoleonic War period, to political underground movements. Although prosecutions were brought under the new acts, more were brought under pre-existing legislation.

The Acts of 1799 and 1800 were enforced irregularly and repealed in 1824 following the campaign organized by Francis PLACE and Joseph Hume. An upsurge of STRIKES and industrial violence prompted new restrictive legislation in 1825; attempts to enlarge the sphere of collective bargaining by strike action henceforth exposed trade unionists to prosecution for criminal conspiracy. The legal status of trade unionism remained ill defined and uncertain, with a series of legal judgments failing to clarify it, until the passage of the TRADE DISPUTES ACT 1906. *See also* TRADE UNIONS.

Commendation, Anglo-Saxon The act of *commendation*, whereby a lesser man submitted himself to a greater one or to a powerful church, is frequently mentioned in the documents of late Anglo-Saxon England. Interpretation of its obscurities is important to the discussion of whether FEUDALISM existed in England before 1066. The surviving texts often imply that commendation was a personal bond that could be transferred from one lord to another. However, the increasing emphasis on the role of LORDSHIP in the recruitment of Anglo-Saxon armies (*see FYRD*) suggests that this possibility was often more apparent than real.

Commercial Revolution, historians' term for the expansion in English – or more generally British – overseas trade *c.* 1650–1750. The foundations for this expansion were laid in the 16th and early 17th centuries with the diversification of British manufacturing production, and the establishment of colonies in North America and the West Indies and of trading bases in Asia and West Africa. The NAVIGATION ACTS (*see* MERCANTILISM) attempted to ensure that commercial profits arising from this expansion accrued to the English, and not to Dutch middlemen. The English profited from a growth in sales of new textiles to the Mediterranean, from the sale of extra-European products in the form of RE-EXPORTS, and the sale of goods to extra-European markets. Income generated by these forms of trade in turn helped to create a buoyant market for imports, especially of SUGAR, TOBACCO and East Indian cloth. Growth in trade resumed after KING WILLIAM'S WAR and the War of the SPANISH SUCCESSION, the export of manufactures to the American colonies representing the most dynamic element in this period. The SLAVE TRADE was also important. It has been estimated that by the fall of WALPOLE in 1742, the British merchant marine was carrying half the commerce of the known world.

Commission of the Peace, *see* JUSTICES OF THE PEACE

Committee of Both Kingdoms, set up in Feb. 1644 after the COVENANT as a mostly civilian executive to put more vigour into the efforts of the Scots and the English Parliament during the CIVIL WARS. It prosecuted the war to victory by 1646. With the alliance abandoned, it was replaced by the DERBY HOUSE COMMITTEE in Jan. 1648.

Committee of Safety, a joint committee comprising members from the Lords and the Commons, established in July 1642 to fight CHARLES I. Too large and divided over strategy to be effective, increasing military reverses led to its replacement by the COMMITTEE OF BOTH KINGDOMS. A further Committee of Safety was appointed in the confusion of 1659.

Committee of the Whole House, *see* COMMONS, HOUSE OF

Common Agricultural Policy (CAP), *see* EUROPEAN UNION

Common Burdens, the label favoured by modern scholars to describe the obligations owed by landholders in Anglo-Saxon England. The term *trinoda* (or *trimoda*) *necessitas* (literally 'the three necessities') is also used. The obligations were: to serve in the king's army (*see FYRD*), to repair *BURHS* (i.e. fortifications), and to repair bridges (*see* BRIDGE-WORK). The three duties were normally reserved by kings when estates were granted to their subjects. The origins of the 'common burdens' have been located in the 8th-century kingdom of MERCIA, from where they were subsequently imposed on the others. The inspiration may have been CAROLINGIAN.

Common Era (CE) Dating, now much used for dating, especially by historians of religion, since it removes the obvious Christ-centred reference of BC ('before Christ') and AD ('*Anno Domini*') dating. BC dates become BCE, AD dates CE; the reference point remains the same.

Common Fields, Common Land, *see* ENCLOSURES; OPEN FIELDS

Common Law, term used to describe the English legal system from the 13th century to the present day. The law was 'common' in the sense that it was regarded as being uniformly applied throughout the kingdom. It was also seen as 'routine' – i.e. a royal judicial system had developed to the point of claiming to be routinely available, through the mechanisms of WRITS, royal judges (*see* EYRE) and a network of courts (both SHIRE-COURTS and central courts at WESTMINSTER – *see*

COMMON PLEAS; KING'S BENCH), to all the king's *free* subjects – though until the demise of villeinage (*see* SERFDOM) in the 14th and 15th centuries, this was a significant restriction. Although pre-12th-century English law was more uniform than was believed by, e.g., the author, perhaps Ranulf Glanvill (Glanville), of the 12th-century work *Treatise on the Laws and Customs of England*, it was the rapid expansion of the machinery of justice in the latter part of the 12th century – some of it documented in the ASSIZES of HENRY II's reign – and then the emergence *c.* 1200 of a group of professional lawyers specializing in English law that gave the common law its distinctive character, self-consciously different from CANON and Roman law as well as from local custom. The beginning of RICHARD I's reign (1189) was later considered the beginning of legal memory.

Besides the criminal law, in which those accused of major offences (felonies) were for the most part prosecuted in the king's name, private individuals were quick to use the system to bring civil cases against each other. By the 14th century, the secular legal profession had developed its own training system in INNS OF COURT. 'Common law' was saved from traditionalist rigidity by inventing numerous LEGAL FICTIONS, and through the complementary role of equity in CHANCERY; it was therefore vigorous enough to resist the European-wide reception of Roman law during the 16th century (*see* CIVIL LAW), although WOLSEY is said to have contemplated such a step. Tudor and Stuart common lawyers – e.g. Edward COKE – determinedly asserted the superiority of common law over the royal PREROGATIVE COURTS, and Coke gave new stress to the importance of the MAGNA CARTA. This attitude decisively prevailed both after 1641 and after the RESTORATION of 1660. *See also* BRACTON; HALE.

Common Lodging Houses Act, *see* LABOURING CLASSES LODGING HOUSES ACT 1851

Common Market, *see* EUROPEAN UNION

Common Pleas, Court of, Common Law court, also known as *De Banco* ('of the [Justices'] Bench'), which evolved from HENRY II's systematization of centralized royal justice. Its record of proceedings on Plea Rolls began in the 1190s, by which time it generally met at WESTMINSTER – a practice confirmed by the MAGNA CARTA's stipulation that common pleas should be heard in some fixed place. A separate chief justice of common pleas was appointed from 1272. Its business came to concentrate on disputes between private individuals (CIVIL LITIGATION), and on the registering of land transactions, and it developed many LEGAL FICTIONS in order to extend its freedom of action in these matters. It was united with KING'S BENCH and the Court of Exchequer of Pleas in 1873. *See also* COMMON LAW.

Common Prayer, Book of, *see* PRAYER BOOKS

Common Wealth, the party founded by former Liberal MP Richard Acland in 1942 to campaign for 'progressive' policies and to contest by-elections during the electoral truce proclaimed by the major parties. Its three by-election successes between 1943 and 1945 were widely interpreted as expressing public support for improved welfare and full employment policies after the war. Membership of Common Wealth was proscribed by the LABOUR PARTY in 1943. In the 1945 election, the new party put up 23 candidates, but only one was successful, and this MP and Acland both subsequently joined the Labour Party.

Commonplace Books, a popular form of self-cultivation in the 16th and 17th centuries: personal notebooks containing quotations, transcriptions, original compositions and/or personal and financial jottings. A glorious lucky dip for the researcher when they survive.

Commons, House of The Commons has evolved from the secondary role which it enjoyed in the PARLIAMENTS of medieval England to its modern position as the main effective player in the parliamentary trinity of crown, LORDS and Commons, despite continuing to be known as 'the Lower House'. In the 13th century, representatives of the SHIRES and BOROUGHS were first summoned by the crown to Parliament to supplement the advice offered by spiritual and temporal magnates. During the later 13th century, representatives of the communities of the realm (the shires, the boroughs, and, on occasion, the lower clergy) were summoned by the crown to some of the assemblies that contemporaries styled parliaments. From the monarch's point of view, their principal purpose was to give consent to taxation on behalf of those who had sent them (since the great men of the realm professed to be no longer able to speak for those who were not their own tenants). From the local communities' perspective, the summons was more a burden than a privilege, though it allowed them to bring petitions concerning matters of local import to the king and his council's attention. In a sense, then, the element of bargaining between the king and the representative elements in Parliament was present almost from the outset, while the representatives' role in the grant of taxes gradually won for them recognition as an essential part of Parliament. The name 'Commons' was frequently used from the 14th century, when the appointment of a Commons clerk was first recorded. The general pattern of election of two knights from each shire and two burgesses from selected boroughs persisted until the 19th century, with some later survivals; from 1429 to 1832, the shire electorate was defined as those FREEHOLDERS with more than 40 shillings a year in land. Numbers in the Commons increased from 296 to 462 in the 16th century, in part through gentry pressure on the crown for additional seats – a pressure foreshadowed by the GENTRY's increasing appearance as members for boroughs (especially lesser boroughs) during the preceding century.

In 1549, the Commons acquired its first permanent meeting place: the derelict COLLEGIATE chapel of St Stephen in WESTMINSTER Palace. Its choir-stall seating arrangement has influenced Commons procedure ever since. Controversy remains about the significance of clashes between the Commons and the Stuart monarchy in the early 17th century; modern historians are not inclined to give these disputes the great significance in the development of English liberties which they were afforded by Victorian and early 20th-century constitutional historians. More emphasis has been placed on the continuing importance of the House of Lords, which contained the most wealthy and powerful people in England, but whose members often chose to fight their battles with the monarch by proxy, using agents and friends in the lower house. The mid-17th-century CIVIL WARS, however, sidelined the upper house: the Westminster Parliament's war effort against CHARLES I increasingly fell into the hands of the leaders in the Commons, especially after the SELF-DENYING ORDINANCE, and the Lords were abolished along with the monarchy in 1649. The various INTERREGNUM experiments with legislatures culminated in an all-Britain 549-member House of Commons in Jan. 1659, the largest assembly to that time, but the old FRANCHISE was restored in 1660, and the restored Lords regained much of their influence, particularly in the election of borough MPs (*see* POCKET BOROUGHS; ROTTEN BOROUGHS).

Repeated proposals for PARLIAMENTARY REFORM during the 18th century produced no result until 1832. Thereafter the franchise was steadily widened and, during the 20th century, the superior will of the Commons over the Lords asserted by legislation (the PARLIAMENT ACTS, 1911, 1949). The number of MPs today, each representing a geographical DIVISION (CONSTITUENCY), fluctuates around 650 due to the regular redrawing of boundaries. Whether the present status and powers of the Commons really deserve the description 'parliamentary democracy' is debatable; *see* PARLIAMENT.

Discussions continue about an alternative to the 'first past the post' electoral system, but proposals for a complicated form of proportional representation recommended by a committee set up under the former Labour chancellor, Roy Jenkins, which reported in 1998, were received with palpable lack of enthusiasm – a situation that seems likely to pertain whilst either of the two major parties commands a comfortable majority. *See also* BURGH; KNIGHTS OF THE SHIRE; LOBBY; SPEAKER.

COMMONS CHRONOLOGY

1264 SHIRE knights summoned to Parliament.

1265 Two knights from each shire and two burgesses from some BOROUGHS summoned.

1295 'Model' parliament summoned by EDWARD I with two shire knights, two citizens from each city and two burgesses from each borough.

1341 Commons gain their own chamber.

1376 First SPEAKER chosen.

1388 APPELLANTS use their dominance in

the MERCILESS PARLIAMENT to convict a group of RICHARD II's followers of treason.
1407 Commons granted priority over LORDS in granting of funds to the monarch.
1414 Accepted that when Commons draft a bill and send it for royal approval, the monarch can accept or reject but not amend it.
1529 First known committee.
1532 First known division (vote).
1604 Commons APOLOGY.
1606 Committee of the Whole House first used: enables Commons to replace speaker with elected chairman.
1641 First TRIENNIAL ACT, mandating a maximum of 3 years between parliaments.
1642 CHARLES I attempts to arrest the FIVE MEMBERS in the chamber of the Commons. He fails and flees London.
1648 RUMP PARLIAMENT formed after PRIDE'S PURGE of the LONG PARLIAMENT removes all of Charles I's remaining supporters from the chamber.
1653 Oliver CROMWELL ejects Rump Parliament (not recalled until 1659).
1660 CONVENTION PARLIAMENT (1660–1) elected which accepts Charles II's declaration from BREDA without conditions.
1679–81 CHARLES II dissolves Parliament three times when MPs vote to exclude his heir, the future JAMES II, from the succession during the EXCLUSION CRISIS.
1694 Revised Triennial Act mandating no more than 3 years for the duration of a parliament.
1707 Scottish MPs sit in Commons following the Act of UNION.
1716 SEPTENNIAL ACT extends the maximum duration of parliament to 7 years.
1769 Commons rejects RADICAL John WILKE's election for Middlesex three times, thus adding a British dimension to the American claim for 'no taxation without representation'.
1771 London printers reprimanded for publishing parliamentary debates. Lord Mayor and two aldermen imprisoned for breach of privileges of Commons. No subsequent serious attempts made to interfere with parliamentary reporting.
1800 Act of UNION returns some 100 Irish MPs to Commons.
1829 CATHOLIC EMANCIPATION (RELIEF) ACT allows Roman CATHOLICS to sit in Commons.
1832 First major reform of FRANCHISE (*see* REFORM ACT 1832).
1867 Second REFORM ACT.
1872 BALLOT ACT introduces secret ballot for elections.
1884 Third REFORM ACT.
1911 PARLIAMENT ACT; LORDS loses its power of veto over Commons.
1918 REPRESENTATION OF THE PEOPLE ACT and Qualification of Women Act.
1928 Equal Franchise Act.
1950 Last two-member constituencies removed.

Commonwealth, the British Commonwealth of Nations, a group of self-governing states and their dependencies which were formerly within the BRITISH EMPIRE, and which are united by the strong but elastic link of former ties to Britain. The queen is head of the Commonwealth, and also queen of those Commonwealth countries which have not chosen to become republics. The phrase 'Commonwealth' began to appear in the late 19th century and slowly gained currency, particularly in regard to the status of the DOMINIONS, but only came to be generally applied in the years after WORLD WAR II when Britain was beginning to dismantle its imperial structure. The shift was signalled by Empire Day being renamed Commonwealth Day in 1958. Regular meetings of Commonwealth prime ministers and heads of state, as well as the economic and trade relations which have survived (although considerably diminished since Britain's accession to the EUROPEAN UNION) have maintained the Commonwealth and its institutions.

Commonwealth Ideas in the 16th Century In the 1530s, Thomas CROMWELL encouraged discussion of legislation for religious, social, economic and political reform in the English realm or 'commonwealth'. Some was eventually embodied in his policies; some remained as discussion and was revived in the reformist atmosphere of EDWARD VI's administrations. Some historians have envisaged an Edwardian commonwealth 'party' patronized by PROTECTOR Somerset (*see* SEYMOUR, EDWARD), with Hugh Latimer as spokesman and John HALES as policy-maker. The group was never so coherent, although as an attitude 'commonwealth' rhetoric, which had been common in the Middle Ages, persisted in late Tudor politics.

Commonwealth Immigrants Act 1962 Passed by a CONSERVATIVE government, the Act controlled IMMIGRATION of COMMONWEALTH citizens into Britain for the first time. Immigration was restricted to those who had a work voucher from the ministry of labour, to their dependants, and to students. A major reversal of Britain's hitherto 'open door' to Commonwealth immigration, the Act was aimed directly at fears aroused by growing black and Asian immigration. The 1979 Act removed the automatic right of husbands or fiancés of women settled in the UK to join them, and further restrictions were introduced on the entry of parents, grandparents and children over 18. The 1988 Act further tightened controls, particularly on wives and children, while the 1993 Asylum and Immigration Appeals Act, a measure against supposed 'economic migrants', restricted those asylum seekers allowed 'exceptional leave to remain' in Britain.

Commonwealth of England, *see* INTERREGNUM

Communist Party of Great Britain (CPGB), founded in August 1920 by representatives of various small socialist groups, notably the British Socialist Party. Early attempts to affiliate with the LABOUR PARTY were rebuffed, and the Communists' close association with Moscow led to hostility from both Labour and the establishment, seen in the ARCOS RAID and in the Labour and TUC bans on them. The party enjoyed little electoral success between the wars and, by 1932, had only 6,000 members. However, it had a wider impact through 'front' organizations such as the NATIONAL UNEMPLOYED WORKERS' MOVEMENT, as well as intellectual influence with the development of 'united front' strategies against Fascism prior to 1939.

Membership rose to 43,000 at the height of Anglo-Soviet co-operation during WORLD WAR II, but the party's appeal remained limited by Labour hostility and the COLD WAR. Its pro-Soviet stance on the Hungarian rising of 1956 lost it members, and in the 1960s and 1970s, it faced competition from other left-wing groups. Splits led to a breakaway New Communist Party in 1977 and a further creation – the Communist Party of Britain – in 1987. In 1991, following the collapse of the Soviet Union, the remaining 6,300 members of the CPGB renamed themselves the 'Democratic Left', committed to a democratic structure and a pluralistic, radical stance. The *Morning Star* newspaper (formerly the *Daily Worker*) remains the party's main organ.

Companies Act 1844 Following the repeal of the BUBBLE ACT, this statute did away with the necessity for royal authorization for the formation of a JOINT STOCK company with transferable stock; all that was needed was registration in compliance with specified regulations. Further amendment of the law followed, especially the LIMITED LIABILITIES ACT 1855.

Compotus, the science of understanding the ecclesiastical calendar – of vital importance for the early Church in Britain when the basic chronology of time, the dates of Christian festivals and the calendar were uncertainly understood. BEDE's computations on the date of EASTER were a major contribution, as was the work of BYRHTFERTH of Ramsey.

Comprehension, the 17th-century redefining of ANGLICAN doctrines or practices, with the object of making adherence to the Established Church palatable to some who, on grounds of conscience, were reluctant to adhere to it. It was promised in the Worcester House Declaration of 1660, but hopes that the RESTORATION religious settlement might include an element of comprehension were dashed with the passage of the Act of UNIFORMITY 1662. Proposals for comprehension were mooted in 1667 and again in 1674, but the rumoured bills were never brought into parliament. A bill for comprehension (along with a separate bill for toleration for those DISSENTERS who could not be comprehended) was introduced into the Commons in Dec. 1680; it was sponsored by a coalition of Anglicans and PRESBYTERIANS, but got no further than a second reading before the Houses were dissolved. However, it was these bills, but little modified, that Daniel Finch, 2nd Earl of Nottingham (one of the leading advocates of the measures in 1680) brought into Parliament in March 1689. Yet contrary to expectations (and to many moderate Anglicans' hopes), comprehension failed over the issue of Dissenters' eligibility for office, and only the TOLERATION ACT was eventually passed. Proposals for comprehension were mooted again in the mid 1690s and mid 18th century, but 1689 was effectively its last gasp.

Comprehensive Schools, schools designed to provide the whole range of secondary education, for children of all abilities, within the same institution. This differed from the tripartite division of schools for children of different abilities set up under the EDUCATION ACT 1944, where the type of school attended was determined by results in the ELEVEN PLUS examination. Growing opposition to 'selection' at eleven and the second-class education offered to the majority of children in the non-academic secondary modern schools led to experiments with 'multilateral' or comprehensive schools in both London and some rural areas. After initial hostility, the LABOUR PARTY supported plans to make all secondary education comprehensive, and phase out GRAMMAR SCHOOLS in the name of social justice. In 1965 the newly elected Labour government instructed all local education authorities to prepare plans for the creation of comprehensive schools, either by amalgamation of existing sites or by new building. In consequence of the policies followed by both Labour and CONSERVATIVE governments after 1965, the majority of grammar schools were amalgamated into comprehensives or became independent by 1990. The policy has remained controversial because of arguments about its success in raising educational standards.

Compton Census, a survey of religious adherence carried out in 1676 on the initiative of Danby (*see* OSBORNE, THOMAS), who hoped to persuade CHARLES II that the DISSENTERS were not a significant force and could be crushed by rigorous enforcement of the penal laws. Henry Compton's (1632–1713) name is attached to it because the ailing Archbishop of Canterbury entrusted him to oversee it. Returns from the dioceses suggested that only one in 22 adults – under 5 per cent – did not adhere to the Established Church. This proportion should probably be regarded as a minimum: it seems likely that many clergy counted partial conformists as ANGLICANS. The Compton census returns, like those under the HEARTH TAX, are used by both local historians and HISTORICAL DEMOGRAPHERS as a basis for estimating the size of POPULATION in the late 17th century.

Compton, Spencer (Earl of Wilmington) (?1673–1743), Whig politician. Commanding trust, but of no great ability, Compton was elected Speaker of the Commons in 1715. He served as treasurer to the household of the Prince of Wales, whose intention on succeeding as GEORGE II was to make him first minister, but WALPOLE was so evidently more capable that the king dropped the plan. In 1728 Compton went to the Lords as Wilmington; in 1730, he became lord president of the Council. In 1742, when Walpole fell, the king turned to the elderly Wilmington to head a ministry also comprising the more significant John Carteret, and William Pulteney. On his death in 1743 PELHAM became first minister.

Compurgation, a system of defence in Anglo-Saxon customary law against an accusation which was dependent on the sanctity of the OATH. The accused was required to swear his or her innocence, and also had to produce a specified number of people, usually twelve ('oath-helpers') to swear that the sworn statement was true. It was much used at first by the COMMON LAW (where it was known as 'wager of law'), but also in CHURCH COURTS, as well as in local courts such as those of MANORS; after being generally superseded in common law practice by JURY trial, it was finally abolished in 1833. *See also* TRIAL BY BATTLE; TRIAL BY ORDEAL.

Comyn, John (Lord of Badenoch) (?–1306). As head of the senior branch – the Red Comyns – of the Comyns, the most powerful of the Scottish baronial families, he was generally known as 'the Red Comyn'. From 1298 until he submitted in 1304, he was one of the leaders of Scottish resistance to EDWARD I. As John BALLIOL's nephew and son of one of the competitors in the GREAT CAUSE, he stood close to the Scottish throne, and it was presumably this that lay behind his long-standing rivalry with Robert BRUCE, which culminated in his murder at Bruce's hands in the Greyfriars kirk of Dumfries on 10 Feb. 1306.

Concert of Europe, *see* VIENNA, CONGRESS OF

Conciliation Act 1896 The only positive outcome of the ROYAL COMMISSION ON LABOUR, it empowered the BOARD OF TRADE to appoint arbitrators if both sides in an industrial dispute agreed, and to inquire into the causes of the dispute. In effect, it gave statutory recognition to current practice.

Condition of England Question, an agenda-setting phrase from the discourse of the 1840s, summarizing the anxieties and problems posed by industrialism, urbanism and CLASS conflict.

Confessional State, a state in which full political rights, including rights to hold public office, are restricted to adherents of particular religious confessions. The term is arguably applicable to England throughout the era of the TEST AND CORPORATION ACTS (1661–1828), although exclusion was unevenly supported and variably enforced.

Congregationalists, Protestant separatists who see the voluntarily constituted local congregation as the chief expression of the Christian church, and therefore reject all church hierarchy. They were usually known as Brownists (after Robert Browne, *c.* 1550–1633) during the late 16th century and INDEPENDENTS during the 17th and 18th. An interest in association and co-operation grew with the involvement of many Congregationalists in the EVANGELICAL movement. In May 1831, the Congregational Union of England and Wales was formed, which two years later produced a *Declaration of Faith, Church Order and Discipline*. By 1838, 49 country and district associations had joined, but fears that this would lead to clerical domination over independent churches meant that the Union was deprived of financial support. At the time, the number of Congregationalists in England stood at 127,000 and in Wales at 43,000, representing a tripling of numbers since 1800. There were 435,000 members in England and Wales in 1900.

The *Congregational Year Book* was established in 1846. The Congregationalists led the NONCONFORMISTS in creating theological colleges on the basis of the older DISSENTING ACADEMIES: there were 16 by 1871. In 1886, Mansfield College, the first Nonconformist college in the ancient universities, was established at Oxford. A majority of Congregationalists united with the PRESBYTERIAN Church of England to form the United Reformed Church in 1972.

Congress System, system established in 1815 to maintain the peace in Europe after the NAPOLEONIC WARS by regular diplomatic conferences between Britain, Austria, Russia and Prussia. This quadruple alliance met at Aix-la-Chapelle (1818), Troppau (1820), Laibach (1821) and Verona (1822). However Britain, increasingly critical of the interference in the internal affairs of other nations, was not present at the final congress at St Petersburg in 1825.

Connacht, Irish kingdom. The early medieval kingdom of Connacht was dominated by two families – the Uí Briúin and the Uí Fiachrach – both of which came to prominence in the early 8th century. The kingdom's history was typified by dynastic conflict among several families (*see* KINGSHIP, EARLY IRISH). There were occasional periods of submission to dominant kings from either the UÍ NÉILL or from MUNSTER, but in the 12th century, the descendants of the Uí Briúin – the O Connors – were the most powerful kings in Ireland (*see* TURLOCH O CONNOR). English royal authority over Connacht (*anglice* Connaught) was established peacefully in 1585, thereby avoiding the policy of PLANTATION that so deeply affected the other provinces.

Consanguinity, the blood-relationship between two people. In CANON LAW, consanguinity renders a marriage null within certain degrees of relationship (for instance, sister and brother), although the computation of these degrees has varied over time. *See also* AFFINITY.

Conscientious Objectors, people who refuse military enlistment on religious or other grounds of 'conscience'. During WORLD WAR I, their position became a highly emotive issue in Britain, especially with the introduction of CONSCRIPTION in 1916. Those claiming exemption were screened by local tribunals, and some 16,000 were excused military service and given noncombatant duties or work in labour camps. Some who were not excused continued to refuse military discipline, leading to 41 being sentenced to death; after an outcry they were reprieved, but joined a total of 1,298 imprisoned for their views, of whom 70 died. Although public attitudes to conscientious objectors were almost invariably hostile, leading to their disenfranchisement by the REPRESENTATION OF THE PEOPLE ACT 1918, their cause was supported by influential campaigners such as the philosopher Bertrand Russell and the Labour politician Fenner Brockway, who also contributed to the growth of anti-war and pacifist feeling between the wars. One result was that the Conscription Acts from 1939 made more generous provision for conscientious objectors; nevertheless several were imprisoned for refusing to take on war-related work during WORLD WAR II. *See also* QUAKERS.

Conscription, compulsory enlistment of citizens, usually in the armed services. Exceptionally amongst the larger European states, Britain had no peacetime conscription before 1914 and fought the first year and a half of war by raising volunteers. After considerable controversy and the use of schemes which fell short of compulsion, such as the 'Derby Scheme' named after the Secretary of State for War (*see* STANLEY, EDWARD), the ASQUITH government was forced to introduce conscription under the Military Service Act of 1916 to meet the demands for men in the great attritional battles of the Western Front. The attempt to extend conscription to Ireland, however, aroused intense opposition, and when passed in 1918 proved largely ineffective. Conscription lapsed in 1919, but was introduced for the first time in peace in May 1939 to meet the anticipated demands for the coming war. Once war broke out, conscription of men became universal and was extended to unmarried women between the ages of 18 and 50 by 1943, either for war work or for service in the women's branch of the armed forces. The NATIONAL SERVICE Act of 1947 provided for the continuation of conscription, initially for one year, but raised to two in 1950. In 1957 the government announced the phasing out of conscription, which finally came to an end in 1963. *See also* CONSCIENTIOUS OBJECTORS.

Conservation, preservation of historic buildings, landscape, wildlife, environment, or natural resources, or their use in such a way as to prevent their unnecessary waste. The conservation movement has been an important force in British society, especially since the later 19th century in both architecture and landscape, its influence increasing from the 1960s onwards (*see* PLANNING).

The most obvious instances are in historic buildings, where the foundation of the SOCIETY FOR THE PROTECTION OF ANCIENT BUILDINGS in 1877 was followed by increased protection to ancient monuments. The Ancient Monuments Protection Act of 1882 provided for the public guardianship or acquisition of a scheduled (usually prehistoric or Roman) monument by the Commissioners of the Board of Public Works, to which the Ancient Monuments Protection Act 1900 added medieval buildings, while in 1913 the first powers of 'listing' monuments were introduced. Lobby and pressure groups have continually been formed.

The NATIONAL TRUST, its origins in landscape conservation, soon began to acquire historic buildings, which have since had an ever greater part in their conservation strategy. The Georgian Group, founded in 1937, was a reaction against destruction of Georgian buildings, particularly in London. Further impetus was given by wartime bombing: the Town and Country Planning Act 1944 provided for the listing of buildings of special architectural or historical interest. Campaigns by the Civic Society, founded in 1957 amidst concern at the destruction of the fabric of towns and the problems of town planning, resulted in the Civic Amenities Act of 1967, which embodied the concept of 'conservation areas' within towns and villages and provided for statutory consent for demolition within a conservation area. The founding of the Victorian Society in 1958 was a reaction to the wholesale destruction of Victorian architecture. Its first major successes were the saving of a large part of WHITEHALL, and securing the statutory listing of Victorian buildings. The Town and Country Planning Act 1968 reactivated the listing survey, adding new powers for local and national authorities, while European Architectural Heritage Year in 1975 brought issues of conservation to a wider audience, with a rush of books exposing the threat to the historic built environment. The provision within government for historic buildings, the remit of the Department of the Environment and its predecessor ministries of Public Works, was given in 1984 to English Heritage, Historic Scotland, and Cadw (for Wales).

The conservation of open spaces became a battleground of the later decades of the 19th century, with activists of the calibre of Octavia Hill (1838–1912), joint founder of the National Trust. The preservation of the English Lake District and of common land and woods around London are among the most obvious of the movement's early successes, leading to the formation of the NATIONAL PARKS at the end of WORLD WAR II. The seemingly unstoppable process of urban growth has refocused attention on the countryside, with the foundation of wildlife groups, again from the closing years of the 19th century. The power of the conservation movement has been augmented by the continuing rise from the late 1960s of the environmental or 'green' movement, often challenging ECONOMIC GROWTH and its past and future effects on landscape, built structures, air quality, use of non-renewable natural resources, etc. Conservation has moved within one hundred years from being a fringe activity to one of central social and political importance.

Conservative Party Pragmatic, eschewing general theoretical principles, preferring practical responses to particular situations, the Conservative Party, emerging from the TORY (a name still in common use to designate Conservative) grouping, was essentially a creature of the Victorian era. PEEL'S TAMWORTH MANIFESTO (1834) and DISRAELI'S concept of TORY DEMOCRACY supplied a set of principles and policies that brought mass support to the defence of privilege and tradition.

The extension of the FRANCHISE prompted the development of an extra-parliamentary party. The National Union of Conservative and Constitutional Associations, formed in 1867, opened a two-way channel of communication between the party and the electorate it served. Popular Toryism was also fostered by the PRIMROSE LEAGUE, as well as the identification of the Conservatives with IMPERIALISM and social reform.

The popular base of Toryism remains a matter of controversy among historians; its reality, though, is not in question. During the 128 years between the passing of the 1867 REFORM ACT and 1995, the Conservatives have held office for 71 years. Without substantial working-class support, the Conservative Party could not have maintained the dominant position it has held in British politics since 1867.

In the general election following the 1832 REFORM ACT, 175 Conservative MPS were elected. Peel's recognition of the implications of the Act, and his attempt to balance the interests of an industrial bourgeoisie with the agricultural interest of his 'country party', led to divisions in the parliamentary party over the repeal of the CORN LAWS in 1846, when Peel was forced out of office.

In the ensuing split many PEELITES joined the LIBERAL PARTY, whilst the Conservative Party grouped around DISRAELI'S commitment to maintaining traditional institutions, defending the BRITISH EMPIRE and introducing a limited programme of social reform consistent with a view of Tory paternalism. However, apart from three brief ministries (1852, 1858–9 and 1866–8), the Conservatives were out of office for a quarter of a century, finally profiting from Liberal dissension, particularly over GLADSTONE'S policy of HOME RULE for Ireland after 1886, and the party's growing electoral appeal in more prosperous city and suburban areas as well as successful campaigning in traditional working-class regions such as Lancs.

Salisbury (*see* CECIL, ROBERT GASCOYNE), who had resigned in protest over the 1867 REFORM ACT, became prime minister from 1886 – a post he twice combined with that of foreign secretary. Salisbury was a consummate diplomat – not only in foreign relations – and his instinctive empathy with the Conservative Party as it was at the end of the 19th century enabled him to control his unruly party. His commitment to moderate social reform and opposition to Irish HOME RULE enabled him to form the UNIONIST alliance, which dominated British politics between 1886 and 1906. However, under the leadership of BALFOUR (1902–11) the split in the Conservative Party finally did happen over an ideological issue – that of the ex-Liberal Joseph CHAMBERLAIN'S policy of TARIFF REFORM – and the Conservatives were again in opposition after the Liberal landslide in the 1906 election until the party was able to profit from the disagreements in the Liberal Party over their response to the outbreak of WORLD WAR I. The Conservative leader Bonar LAW then accepted the Liberal prime minister Herbert ASQUITH's invitation to join a coalition government in May 1915 in order to avoid a political crisis following the scandal over lack of shells for the Western Front and the failure of the DARDANELLES expedition.

In Dec. 1916, with Asquith under increasing pressure over the conduct of the war, Bonar Law declined the king's invitation to try to form a government, but instead backed the replacement of Asquith by LLOYD GEORGE. The Coalition won the post-war 'coupon election' in Dec. 1918 and continued until 1922, but the Conservatives became increasingly dominant. In Oct. 1922 a revolt by Tory MPs and peers at the CARLTON CLUB, led by Stanley BALDWIN, caused the fall of the Lloyd George government. In the resulting general election the Conservatives were returned to power with Bonar Law as prime minister. The following year Bonar Law resigned on health grounds and was replaced by Baldwin, the chancellor of the Exchequer, rather than by Lord Curzon, the foreign secretary. Baldwin, distrusted by Austen Chamberlain and other ex-Coalition Tories, tried to consolidate his position by calling a snap election at the end of 1923, ostensibly on the issue of higher tariffs. The result was a hung Parliament, with the Conservatives as the largest party. Baldwin lost a vote of confidence in Jan. 1924 and gave way to a minority LABOUR government, which survived until the general election in Nov. 1924 returned Baldwin to power with an overall majority.

The 1929 general election resulted in another hung parliament with, for the first time, the Conservatives having fewer seats than Labour, and led to a second minority Labour government. Baldwin and the Conservatives came to the rescue of MACDONALD in 1931 during the financial crisis, forming a NATIONAL GOVERNMENT under his continuing premiership when the majority of his own party deserted him. The Conservatives became the increasingly dominant force within the National Government and Baldwin became prime minister when MacDonald resigned because of ill health in 1935. After the general election at the end of 1935 the National Government in effect became a Conservative government, which lasted under Baldwin and then Neville CHAMBERLAIN until May 1940, when CHURCHILL formed a coalition government which included Labour and Liberal leaders in the Cabinet.

Under Baldwin in the 1920s the Conservatives restored their image as the natural party of government, which the Liberals had captured in the period between 1906 and the end of WORLD WAR I. They stood for free trade, a balanced budget and the GOLD STANDARD. During the depression of the 1930s, after the government had come off the Gold Standard, the party became more protectionist in trade policy.

The party's overwhelming defeat by Labour in the post-war 1945 general election led to a drastic modernization of its policies, centred on a new Conservative Research Department organized by R. A. BUTLER. The new conservatism stressed the need for positive state action in economics and welfare, aimed at releasing private energy, increasing industrial and commercial competition, and assistance for those in need. *The Industrial Charter* presented in 1947 a new formula for planning in a mixed economy. The party returned to power in 1951 and remained in office until 1964, winning general elections in 1955 and 1959. Under successive prime ministers, Winston Churchill, Anthony EDEN, Harold MACMILLAN and Alec DOUGLAS-HOME, the party, while denationalizing the steel industry (*see* IRON AND STEEL INDUSTRY), came to accept the broad sweep of the mixed economy and the WELFARE STATE (*see* BUTSKELLISM). It also came to accept the accelerating pace of DECOLONIZATION and, after the SUEZ CRISIS in 1956, the reality of Britain's reduced world role.

Labour were in power from 1964 to 1970, when Edward HEATH won a general election and became prime minister until 1974. This period saw sustained levels of public spending and, in 1973, British membership of the European Economic Community (*see* EUROPEAN UNION). The government's policies for reforming the TRADE UNIONS and its incomes policy brought it into conflict with the trade union movement in general and the National Union of Mineworkers in particular, causing the introduction of the THREE-DAY WEEK at the end of 1973 which was largely responsible for its defeat in the Feb. 1974 general election. After a second general election defeat in Oct. 1974, Margaret THATCHER challenged Heath and became Leader of the

Opposition in 1975. Under her leadership the party abandoned any consensus approach and developed radical new policies. These featured the rolling back of the functions of the state, the reduction in the levels of taxation on incomes and property, and the adoption of a monetarist and 'market'-oriented approach to economic management and industrial policy. Thatcher won the 1979 general election but faced substantial public hostility towards her policies, largely because of the high levels of inflation and unemployment they produced. The 1980s, however, proved to be a period of consolidation and expansion of 'Thatcherite' conservatism – the privatization of state-controlled industries, the sale of council houses, and a tax-cutting agenda for the well off – which came to end in a singular sense when Thatcher lost the leadership to John MAJOR in 1990 seen initially as a 'safe pair of hands', and a more flexible and conciliatory leader than the increasingly isolated Thatcher, who was regarded by many of her colleagues as an increasing electoral liability. Major, however, soon began to appear dull, rather than safe, unable to keep his party together over Europe and increasingly vacillating and economically inept. The divided party, tainted by accusations of sleaze both sexual and financial, and no longer seen as the only party with which the economic health of the nation would be assured, lost humiliatingly to Labour in the 1997 election (165 seats to Labour's 418) with not a single Conservative MP left in either Wales or Scotland. The replacement of Major by William HAGUE immediately after the election has done little to make the Conservative party seem a credible party of government.

Conspiracy and Protection of Property Act 1875 It established the principle that a trade union could not be prosecuted for an act which would be legal if performed by an individual. Since it was not illegal for an individual to cease work, it followed that a union could not be prosecuted for conspiracy if it organized a STRIKE. Peaceful picketing was also allowed. An example of DISRAELI-style social reform, this change in the labour laws reflected the growing importance and standing of TRADE UNIONS in industrial Britain.

Constable In origin the leading military officer of the king's court, the word was early appropriated for a variety of law enforcement officers, especially those appointed for PARISHES (petty constables) and HUNDREDS (high constables), who were initially chosen by the court leet (*see* COURT BARON) but, from the later 16th century, by the JUSTICES OF THE PEACE. The word survives for their successors, as the junior rank in the POLICE forces, and for the military governor of castles, e.g. Dover and the Tower of London.

Constantine I King of Scots (862–77). A son of KENNETH MAC ALPIN, he ruled during a period when northern Britain was attacked by powerful VIKING armies. He appears to have tried to maintain an alliance with some of the Viking war bands while the land of the PICTS and the kingdom of the STRATHCLYDE Britons were ravaged (*see* DUMBARTON ROCK). However, eventually he was himself defeated by a war band led by HALFDAN in 875, and was killed two years later.

Constantine I the Great (*c.*274–337), Roman emperor (306–37). Proclaimed at YORK on the death of his father CONSTANTIUS I during the latter's campaign that had taken him north of HADRIAN'S WALL, he is generally regarded as one of the greatest of the Roman emperors, making Christianity the empire's favoured religion and building the new capital at Constantinople. The notion that his mother was British is a myth invented in the Middle Ages.

Because of his many concerns elsewhere, he may not have revisited Britain after 314. The manner in which he was proclaimed emperor, while showing the power of the Roman army in Britain to influence the imperial succession, also contributed to the long-term disruption of the empire by causing civil war and demonstrating how a strong man could use local troops to support personal ambition. *See also* CARAUSIUS; CONSTANTINE III; MAGNUS MAXIMUS.

Constantine II (?–952), King of Scots (900–43). A recent commentator, Professor Alfred Smyth, has remarked that Constantine's reign was the time when 'the medieval kingdom of Scotland came of age'. It is clear from the fragmentary evidence that Constantine finally secured the kingdom against the VIKINGS and, having built on the domination gained by his predecessors over the PICTS and STRATHCLYDE Britons, consolidated the territory they had won (*see* DONALD II; KENNETH MAC ALPIN).

He first fought against the Vikings when RAGNALL was establishing his rule over the kingdom of YORK, but he later supported the Norsemen against the northwards advance of the kings of WESSEX (*see* CORBRIDGE; BRUNANBURH). The evidence suggests that he manipulated the rulers of Wessex and DUBLIN to his advantage, and his treaties with ATHELSTAN demonstrate that, by the 930s, he was securely established as the strongest ruler in northern Britain. In 906, he had sworn to uphold the rights of the Scottish Church, another sign of the expanding notions of the duties of KINGSHIP. He retired to the monastery at ST ANDREWS in 943, and died in 952.

Constantine III, Roman emperor (407–11). The last of the many Roman emperors to be proclaimed by the army in Britain (*see* CARAUSIUS; CONSTANTINE I THE GREAT; MAGNUS MAXIMUS). By removing most of the remains of the Roman army in Britain to fight on his behalf against his rivals, he effectively left the Britons to fend for themselves. *See also* HONORIUS; ROMAN CONQUEST.

Constantius I (Constantius Chlorus), Roman emperor (305–6). From 293, he was 'Caesar' (in this case the term signifies 'co-emperor') with special responsibility for the western provinces of the empire. He visited Britain on two occasions: in 296 to defeat the followers of CARAUSIUS, and in 305–6 to campaign north of HADRIAN'S WALL against the PICTS. He is also credited with the military reorganization of northern England after a period of weakness. In 306, he died at YORK, where his son was immediately proclaimed as Emperor CONSTANTINE I.

Constituency, word of comparatively recent invention to describe the area designated to elect a Member of PARLIAMENT. It was first used informally after the REFORM ACT 1832, and was then increasingly used as a formal term as the old distinction among MPs between BURGESSES and KNIGHTS OF THE SHIRE became obsolete.

Constitutions of Clarendon, *see* CLARENDON, CONSTITUTIONS OF

Contagious Diseases Acts 1864, 1866, 1869, legislation introduced in 18 garrison and port towns to combat the spread of VENEREAL DISEASE among enlisted men, by identifying and registering 'common prostitutes' (*see* PROSTITUTION). The women then had to undergo fortnightly internal examinations, and if found to be suffering from gonorrhoea or syphilis to be interned in hospital for up to nine months. The legislation embodied a 'double standard', since no attempt was made to curb the sexual activities of men, and often non-prostitutes were degraded. Proposals were made to extend the Acts to the north of England and perhaps make them general. The vigorous campaign against the Acts began in 1869, led at first by the largely male National Association, but soon joined and overtaken by Josephine Butler and the Ladies' National Association. The most successful of all the Victorian social purity movements, the long and often bitter campaign finally resulted in the Acts' repeal in 1886.

Continental System, a form of economic warfare initiated by Napoleon. The Berlin Decrees of 1806, designed to close continental ports to British commerce, were subsequently extended to Russian ports and made more stringent with the Milan Decrees of 1808. In retaliation, the British ORDERS IN COUNCIL of 1807 closed the ports of France and her allies and threatened the ships of neutrals who traded there with seizure. The transformation of the struggle between Britain and France into a war of mutual economic strangulation was more than either side could afford. It was abandoned in 1812, by which time it had led one party into the ANGLO-AMERICAN WAR and the other into the PENINSULAR WAR and Russian campaign.

Contraband, traffic in smuggled or illegal goods. Contraband trading has had at certain times an important impact upon Britain. The early and successful introduction of TOBACCO in the late 16th century occurred through contraband trading with the Spanish in the Orinoco region of South America. The heavy duties on TEA, WINES, and many other foreign goods in the 18th century sparked an enormous contraband trade – it has been estimated that three times more tea was smuggled than imported legally 1710–45 – while contraband helped undermine Napoleon's attempt to isolate Britain with the CONTINENTAL SYSTEM. The advent of FREE TRADE made contraband a generally less universal and lucrative activity after the 1840s.

Contraception, *see* BIRTH CONTROL

Conventicles, name given in the 16th and 17th centuries to independent gatherings of SEPARATISTS or DISSENTERS for worship.

Convention Parliament, 1660–1, the parliament convened in April 1660, with a lower house consisting of members elected following the dissolution of the RUMP PARLIAMENT in March, and an upper house speedily augmented by the admission of young lords who had come of age since it last met. It laid the groundwork for the RESTORATION settlement, sorting out the terms of an amnesty, a land settlement and fiscal arrangements adopting a more conciliatory stance than its successor, the CAVALIER PARLIAMENT.

Convention Parliament, 1689, the parliament elected to decide upon a constitutional settlement following the GLORIOUS REVOLUTION. In Dec. 1688 a group of about 60 lords met to agree on a formal address to William of Orange (the future WILLIAM III) asking him to take on the powers of government and call an election; a convention of about 300 former MPs, those elected to any of CHARLES II's parliaments, and the lord mayor, aldermen and common council of LONDON endorsed the address. Elections were held; the resulting Convention Parliament met on 22 Jan. 1689. It agreed, after some dispute, to state that JAMES II, by deserting, had abdicated, and left the throne vacant; it settled the royal succession on William and MARY II, and modified the powers of the crown by the DECLARATION OF RIGHTS.

Conversion of the English to Christianity This began in 597 with the arrival in the kingdom of KENT of the mission dispatched by Pope Gregory the Great and led by St AUGUSTINE. By the time of the synod of WHITBY in 664, the rulers of the main ANGLO-SAXON kingdoms had all been converted, although pagan worship continued in some places into the 8th century. The chief historical source for the conversion is BEDE's *Ecclesiastical History*, which inevitably takes a Christian and sometimes idiosyncratic view of events.

Conversion was accomplished through the uncoordinated (and sometimes hostile) efforts of the Roman missionaries who accompanied and succeeded Augustine, as well as through the work of Irish missionaries, many of whom came from the Scottish monastery of IONA. The Roman missionaries, like Augustine himself, brought clear ideas of organization, whereas the Irish, of whom Aidan is an especially good example, were ascetic monks who relied more on the impact of an austere life-style. However, conversion was far from a smooth process, the missions suffering numerous setbacks. Some kingdoms converted to Christianity and then returned to paganism: King REDWALD of EAST ANGLIA kept altars dedicated to both forms of religion in the same building (*see also* COIFI). The conversion of the last great pagan kingdom, King PENDA'S MERCIA, came about only after his military defeat at the battle of WINWAED river.

Although the persistent missionaries must take a lot of the credit for the eventual conversion of the English, it is obvious that the attitude of the most powerful kings – the *BRETWALDAS* – was often crucial. It is arguable whether political reasons – notably the fact that most of 7th-century Europe was already Christian – or religious ones can explain the conversion. What is clear is that it came about through numerous compromises with existing customs; the Teutonic origins of the current names of the days of the week are just one indication of this.

Convertible Husbandry, also known as up-and-down husbandry or ley farming: a system of cultivation in which land alternated every 7–12 years between tillage and grass leys. Widely adopted in the 18th century, in place of the permanent assignment of land to one or the other use, it improved soil fertility while extracting the greatest possible animal and cereal yield.

Convocations of Canterbury and York After the 12th- and 13th-century clashes between the English monarchy and the papacy resulted in substantial victory for the crown, kings summoned representatives of the lower clergy to PARLIAMENT. However, in the 14th century their attendance at Parliament became redundant since they also gathered in two synods for the provinces of Canterbury and York, known as 'Convocations'. The upper clergy, already represented in the House of LORDS, also formed the Upper Houses of both Convocations. Usually more compliant than Parliament, Convocations lost most of their independent initiative in the SUBMISSION OF THE CLERGY of 1532, but did not surrender their right to grant clerical taxation independently until 1664. They were dissolved in 1717 to quell Church controversy. As part of the CHURCH OF ENGLAND's 19th-century institutional revival, Canterbury met again in 1852 and York in 1861; a House of Laymen was introduced, albeit without effective powers, in 1885. In 1904 a Representative Council, drawn from both Convocations and the two Houses of Laymen, was initiated for discussing church policy, but a 1919 Enabling Act led to the calling in 1920 of a Church Assembly with legislative powers, subordinate to the control of Parliament. This body was replaced by the General Synod of the Church of England in 1969, although symbolic formal meetings of the Convocations continue.

Convoy System, the best way of protecting MARITIME TRADE by using warships to escort a group of merchantmen. Dating back to the Middle Ages, it was highly developed by the 18th century, with legal and INSURANCE backing. Mistakenly thought inappropriate for the 20th century, it was revived in 1917 to save Britain from defeat by submarine blockade. It proved the best way of sinking submarines as well as depriving them of easy targets.

Cook, James (1728–79), navigator and explorer. He joined the navy as a seaman and became an officer through his skill in navigation. He was responsible for the successful piloting of the fleet which took QUEBEC (1759) and taught himself surveying techniques. In this he was so successful that he was selected to command the *Endeavour* on her voyage on behalf of the ROYAL SOCIETY to make astronomical observations from Tahiti. He also successfully charted NEW ZEALAND, the eastern coast of AUSTRALIA and Hawaii. His second Pacific voyage successfully disproved the geographic concept of a 'Great Southern Continent' and charted some of Antarctica. His third voyage charted the north-western coast of North America, in the search for a NORTHWEST PASSAGE (*see* NOOTKA SOUND). His usually good touch with the local inhabitants finally deserted him and he was killed in a skirmish by Hawaiians.

Cooper, Anthony Ashley (1st Earl of Shaftesbury) (1621–83), politician. He fought for the crown in the early stages of the CIVIL WAR, but changed sides in 1643. A member of Oliver CROMWELL'S COUNCIL OF STATE, and of the BAREBONES PARLIAMENT from 1653, he sided with the opposition from 1654. Pardoned by CHARLES II, he was appointed chancellor of the Exchequer in 1661. He opposed Clarendon (*see* HYDE, EDWARD), and served in the CABAL ministry, becoming president of the Council of Trade and Plantations and, later, lord chancellor. Sympathetic to DISSENT but not to Catholicism, he supported both DECLARATIONS OF INDULGENCE, and was not informed of the secret clauses in the treaty of DOVER.

After the break-up of the Cabal, he opposed the king's Catholicizing and arbitrary tendencies, and was dismissed from the PRIVY COUNCIL and other offices. His *Letter from a Person of Quality to his Friend in the Country* (1675) provided an influential formulation of COUNTRY ideology. Exploiting the POPISH PLOT to attack Danby (*see* OSBORNE, THOMAS), he also sponsored extra-parliamentary opposition. Although appointed president of the Privy Council, he continued to oppose royal policies, supported EXCLUSION and, when Parliament was dissolved, organized petitions for its recall, among other WHIG activity. After the final failure of exclusion, he was charged with high treason but cleared by a sympathetic jury. After a period in hiding, he went to the Netherlands in 1682, where he died. John Dryden (1631–1700) satirized his ambitions in *Absalom and Achitophel*.

Co-operative Movement, an attempt to eliminate the antagonism between capital and labour by making the worker a capitalist. Its ethos and programmes were strongly influenced by Robert OWEN; its practical existence started in 1844 with the establishment in Rochdale of the Pioneer Society, founded by 28 men contributing £1 apiece, buying their own supplies and dividing profits according to the amount of their purchases. Co-operation as applied to the distribution and retailing of goods became, and remains, the dominant form; producers' co-operatives were invariably short-lived.

Copyhold Tenure, a form of MANORIAL land tenure which evolved out of SERFDOM in medieval England. Unfree manorial tenants could not transfer their interest in land without their lords' consent. The transaction was therefore done in the manorial court (COURT BARON), and the tenant given a copy of the entry on the court roll as proof of tenancy – hence 'copyhold'. On manors where it evolved, it became distinct from serfdom because it was regulated by the custom of the manor, so the lord could not exercise arbitrary jurisdiction over copyholders; during the 15th century, most serfs became copyholders and in some areas of the country it remained the dominant form of landholding into the 19th century.

COMMON LAW courts did not offer any remedies for disputes between manorial lord and unfree tenant, but in the 15th century, CHANCERY and equity provided increasingly complete legal protection for copyholders. This form of tenure was only abolished in 1926, when copyholders became regarded as FREEHOLDERS by law.

Coram Rege, *see* KING'S BENCH, COURT OF

Corbridge (*Corstopitum*). This Roman settlement lies just south of HADRIAN'S WALL and is now one of the most impressive Roman sites to visit. From the time of AGRICOLA, it was of strategic importance since it lay on Dere Street, the best road into the SCOTTISH LOWLANDS, and at a major crossing of the River Tyne. Archaeological excavation has shown that it played an important role during the campaigns that established the ANTONINE WALL and during the wars of SEPTIMIUS SEVERUS. The extensive civilian settlement outside the walled area has led to the suggestion that Corbridge may also have been a *CIVITAS*.

Corbridge, Battles of, Northumb., 910s. The VIKING war leader RAGNALL won two battles here against the NORTHUMBRIANS and the Scots before seizing the kingdom of YORK in 919.

Coritani, one of the tribes that dominated pre-Roman Britain, with lands approximating to the modern counties of Leics. and Lincs. It appears that, before the end of AULUS PLAUTIUS' governorship in AD 47, the Romans had absorbed their territory, which was converted into a *CIVITAS* with its capital at Leicester; a *colonia* (settlement specially for Roman citizens, who were very often retired army veterans) was established at LINCOLN.

Corn Law Act 1815 Protective duties on corn were first introduced in 1804. In the Act of 1815, brought forward by Liverpool's (*see* JENKINSON, ROBERT) administration, these duties were reintroduced to protect the landed interest following the collapse of the artificially high prices caused by the FRENCH REVOLUTIONARY and NAPOLEONIC WARS. The Act prohibited the importation of corn (i.e. cereal generally, not just maize) into Britain until the price of that on the domestic market had reached 80 shillings a quarter. The price of bread, kept higher than it might have been, made post-war adjustment more difficult than necessary. Advocates of FREE TRADE associated the Act with monopoly, PROTECTIONISM and aristocratic misrule; the labouring poor with class oppression. The most sustained and politically effective criticism came from the ANTI-CORN LAW LEAGUE, which mobilized the moral energies of the middle classes and presented the corn laws as the epitome of the inefficiency and immorality of the old regime. The Act was finally repealed under PEEL in 1846, in the aftermath of the Irish POTATO FAMINE.

Corn Laws, *see* CORN LAW ACT 1815

Corn Production Act 1917, a measure enacted during WORLD WAR I giving farmers a guaranteed price for cereals, in order to encourage domestic production during the German U-boat campaign against merchant shipping. (It also guaranteed minimum wages for farm labourers.) A reversal of Britain's pre-war FREE TRADE policies in agriculture, it was repealed in 1921, with considerable economic dislocation ensuing in some agricultural regions.

Cornish Rising, a rebellion in 1497 against the raising of taxes for Scottish wars, led by Bodmin lawyer Thomas Flamank and maverick nobleman James, Lord Audley. Thousands marched eastward, killing a tax commissioner at Taunton, but were defeated on 13 June 1497 at Blackheath outside London by Giles, Lord Daubeney.

Cornovii, one of the tribes that dominated pre-Roman Britain, with territory in the modern counties of Ches., Staffs., Salop, Clwyd and Powys. The Romans probably moved in at a relatively early date; the second governor, OSTORIUS SCAPULA, appears to have used WROXETER as a fortified base from which to launch campaigns into Wales *c.*AD 50. The territory became a *CIVITAS* containing the LEGIONARY FORTRESS of CHESTER, with its capital at Wroxeter.

Cornwall, Earl of, *see* GAVESTON, PIERS

Cornwallis, Charles (1st Marquess Cornwallis) (1738–1805), soldier and governor-general of India. He joined the army in 1756, and in 1760 became an MP, moving to the Lords on the death of his father, the 1st Earl Cornwallis, later the same year. He was a commander in the War of AMERICAN INDEPENDENCE, with successes at Camden, New Jersey, in 1780 and Guilford courthouse in North CAROLINA in March 1781, but in Oct. was forced to surrender at YORKTOWN, Virginia.

He was appointed governor-general of INDIA in 1786. In the wake of major controversy concerning the EAST INDIA COMPANY'S role in the country, he carried out administrative reforms, and in 1792, he defeated the sultan of Mysore in the Third MYSORE WAR. His successes helped to give retrospective credibility to PITT THE YOUNGER'S INDIA BILL. As lord lieutenant of Ireland, he organized the suppression of the 1798 IRISH REBELLION, and four years later, he helped negotiate the peace of AMIENS. He returned to India in 1804 to serve again as governor-general, but died the following year.

Coronation, ceremony involving the anointing and crowning of the king or queen at or near the start of a reign. The first king known to have been anointed was Ecgfrith, son of OFFA, King of MERCIA, in 786. The ceremony was probably an imitation of that of the CAROLINGIAN Pippin the Short in 751, which may itself have been derived from Celtic models. A new ritual was devised by the followers of the TENTH-CENTURY REFORM for the IMPERIAL coronation of EDGAR in 973, and this, with modifications, forms the basis of the modern ceremony.

Since 1066 English coronations have almost without exception taken place in WESTMINSTER ABBEY, and include the anointing with sacred oils and vesting with the crown of St EDWARD THE CONFESSOR, a ring, and the orb and sceptres signifying power. The monarch sits in the chair which holds the Stone of SCONE on which the Scottish kings had once been instituted, and receives the fealty of the lords and the acclamation of the people. The stage-managed ceremonial at the last coronation, in 1953, was in contrast to some of its predecessors – for example, the physical exclusion of Queen CAROLINE from GEORGE IV'S, or the confusion at Queen VICTORIA'S, recorded with amusement in her diary. The principal items in the regalia, which had been destroyed during the INTERREGNUM, were remade for the coronation of CHARLES II in 1661. The regalia, or Crown Jewels, are housed in the TOWER OF LONDON; the Scottish regalia, lost after the Act of UNION until rediscovered by Sir Walter Scott, are displayed in EDINBURGH castle.

Coronation Charter, 5 Aug. 1100, issued by HENRY I on the day of his coronation. Correctly anticipating that his rule would be challenged, he renounced oppressive practices and promised good government. This charter was rediscovered in JOHN'S reign and served as a model for MAGNA CARTA.

Coroner, one of the offices of English local government which emerged in the 12th century, as the monarchy experimented in devising institutions which would effectively represent the power of the centre in the localities. However, coroners were elected by the COUNTY COURT, so the king did not allow their power to develop, instead granting powers by commission to individuals who came to be known as JUSTICES OF THE PEACE. Coroners were soon restricted to determining by inquest the causes of death in cases where there were suspicious circumstances. Many FRANCHISES and BOROUGHS became entitled to choose their own coroner. When county councils were created (*see* LOCAL GOVERNMENT ACT 1888) they were given the power to appoint coroners.

Corporation Act 1661, one of the Acts that made up the CLARENDON CODE. It required all municipal officeholders, within 12 months of election, to: take the OATHS of allegiance, supremacy (*see* ROYAL SUPREMACY) and NON-RESISTANCE; renounce the Solemn League and COVENANT; and receive the sacrament after the forms of the Church of England (*see* OCCASIONAL CONFORMITY ACT). From 1727, its provisions were mitigated by the passage of INDEMNITY ACTS, which protected those not prosecuted within a set period, but despite several earlier attempts at repeal, the Corporation Act remained on the statute book until 1828.

Corporations of the Poor, bodies set up, on local initiatives, to take over from PARISHes responsibility for relieving the poor. Characteristically they incorporated numerous parishes, therefore potentially achieving economies of scale. The first was established in LONDON in 1647; it collapsed but was revived in 1698. Local acts sanctioned a wave of provincial corporations from 1696, especially in the south-west. Rural incorporations were pioneered in East Anglia from the 1750s. In the absence of an Irish poor law, Irish corporations, set up from the 1760s, relied on charitable donations.

Poor law reformers often urged that the whole country should be reorganized into such large units. This was ultimately accomplished for England with the formation of poor law 'unions' under the POOR LAW AMENDMENT ACT of 1834, and for Ireland with the introduction of a national poor law in 1847.

Corporations, Remodelling of, an attempt by CHARLES II and JAMES II to secure loyal and biddable corporations, by changing their governing personnel. The CORPORATION ACT of 1661 allowed commissioners to remove corporation officials and to fill vacancies until 1663. Initiated by ANGLICANS anxious to purge DISSENTERS and their sympathizers, the Act was amended in the LORDS more generally to strengthen the powers of central government over corporations. Subsequently, other corporations – including not only cities and BOROUGHS but also the INNS OF COURT, livery companies, the College of Physicians and the Virginia Company – were charged with having failed to observe details of their charters; *QUO WARRANTO* writs were issued, and charters revoked and reissued. During the TORY REACTION of the early 1680s, the City of LONDON and 56 other corporations were remodelled. As James II prepared for the election of 1688, government agents were sent out by the Board of Regulators to check the loyalty of corporations, and further *quo warranto* writs issued as necessary. A conciliatory act of 1690 attempted to resolve the legacy of controversy.

Corresponding Society Term applied in the 18th century to any society set up to correspond with other societies for a common end, but chiefly associated with RADICAL societies of working men established in the 1790s with the common object of obtaining PARLIAMENTARY REFORM. Provincial societies included the Manchester Constitutional Society, established in 1790; the Norwich Revolution Society, probably dating from late 1790; and the Sheffield Constitutional Society of late 1791. This last was dominated by working men, and acquired a national reputation for radical extremism. The LONDON CORRESPONDING SOCIETY, established in Jan. 1792, joined and sought to maintain a pre-existing network. Societies lost support as the increasing radicalism of the FRENCH REVOLUTION scared off members; the TWO ACTS of 1795 further hampered their operations. The London Corresponding Society was specifically banned by an act of 1799. Though it, and other societies, may have survived a little longer on a more informal basis, their heyday passed with the decade.

Corrupt Practices Acts 1883, 1888 A consequence of electoral reform, these measures were designed to check electoral abuses and make effective the rights created by the REFORM ACTS. They form the basis for current electoral procedures. The Act of 1883 fixed a limit for election expenses in proportion to the number of voters. The Act of 1888, which stopped political parties paying election helpers, created scope for women's political participation as volunteer canvassers, such as those mobilized by the PRIMROSE LEAGUE for the Conservatives and the Women's Liberal Federation for their opponents.

Cottar, *see* BORDAR

Cotton Industry The pre-industrial CLOTH INDUSTRY, consisting mainly of wool, was organized on the domestic system using hand-powered machinery (*see* BY-EMPLOYMENT). By 1850, this system was rapidly giving way to the FACTORY SYSTEM and to

STEAM POWER, and the primacy of wool was replaced by the primacy of cotton. Textiles were transformed; cotton became king. In 1830, it constituted 50 per cent by value of all British exports and, until the end of the 19th century, cotton textiles remained Britain's leading industry in terms of value added. Although historians now less readily accord to cotton the status of the prime mover of the INDUSTRIAL REVOLUTION, and point to the relatively few large factories there were before 1850 and the continuation of HANDLOOM WEAVING, cotton was always the most visible industrial-growth sector and dominated trade fluctuation before the RAILWAY era.

The imbalance between the efficiency of spinning and weaving determined the nature of mechanization in the cotton industry. The mechanization of spinning and its concentration in factories – arising from the invention of the water frame and the 'MULE' – was achieved during the 1780s and 1790s. This impelled the mechanization of weaving although it was not dominant until the 1820s. Improvement and innovation served to sustain Lancashire's international pre-eminence and MANCHESTER's wealth, aided by the infra-structural, mercantile and financial advantages which accrued from the increasing regional concentration of the sector. But the threat from overseas competitors grew from the mid-19th century.

Historians used to think that the subsequent collapse of cotton was due to the conservatism of British manufacturers. On the eve of WORLD WAR I, so it was argued, the cotton textile industry was highly developed, but technologically stagnant and structurally unsound, largely the result of the failure of new generations to innovate. Manufacturers, the indictment read, had neglected ring-spinning and the automatic loom which would have led to higher labour productivity. In some quarters, the British industrialist has now undergone a rehabilitation. American scholars now insist that the British preference for the self-acting 'mule' over the ring frame and the non-adoption of the automatic loom were economically rational responses to the pattern of costs and to the traditional markets of their industry which favoured yarns made by older methods. The effects of growing international competition, increasingly from Asia, were the main cause of British textile decline after 1914, and were felt acutely in the inter-war period.

Historians have debated the role of the state in ameliorating decline. Tariff preferences in the DOMINIONS and quota restrictions on colonial imports helped a little, and the Lancashire Cotton Corporation, established in 1929 with BANK OF ENGLAND assistance, helped to scrap much capacity, encourage the merger of small firms, and introduce technological innovations. In 1936 the government finally intervened directly with the Cotton Industry Reorganization Act, but some historians argue that the industry's inevitable decline should have been allowed to happen more quickly, with government action concentrated on the redeployment and retraining of labour. The development of synthetic fibres further affected cotton after World War II, and the industry quickly shrank to a small specialized sector using, by the 1980s and 1990s, computer-aided technology developed abroad.

CHRONOLOGY: INVENTION AND INNOVATION

1733 Invention of John Kay's flying shuttle, enabling shuttle to be passed automatically across loom to accelerate weaving process; begins to be adopted during 1750s.

1764 Invention of James Hargreaves' SPINNING JENNY (patented 1770), a hand machine that originally worked eight spindles but was subsequently modified to cope with 100.

1769 Invention of Richard Arkwright's water frame, a spinning machine driven by water power, marks the beginning of move from domestic production to factory system.

1775 Arkwright invents carding machine to comb out cotton fibres.

1779 Samuel Crompton's 'MULE' (so called because it was a cross between jenny and frame), capable of spinning fine-quality thread.

1786 Power loom, invented by Edmund Cartwright, completes mechanization of weaving but encounters popular resistance from HANDLOOM WEAVERS.

1822 Richard Roberts' improved power loom produces 3–4 times as much cloth per unit of time as hand loom and makes triumph of factory system inevitable; installed in ever-greater numbers 1820s and 1830s.

1825 Self-acting 'mule' invented by Richard Roberts with operating costs 15 per cent lower than those of traditional semi-manual 'mules'.
1828 Patenting of ring-spinning in US by J. Thorpe; widely used there, but does not cross Atlantic until 1860s and is not widely adopted for some time. Its advantages are that it makes spinning continuous, and it can be worked by women at high speed. Quality of resulting yarn does not suit English conditions.
1892 Automatic loom perfected in US. Most suitable for weaving plain fabrics and not so well adapted for those produced in Lancs.; barely penetrates English industry before 1914.

Council, King's, *see* KING'S COUNCIL

Council Houses, name given to local authority housing, usually for rent. Although some small estates were built before 1914, the first large-scale local authority schemes were begun under the HOUSING AND TOWN PLANNING ACT 1919 with government subsidy. During the interwar years, combined with a freeze on urban rents, a succession of HOUSING ACTS were passed under which over one million homes for rent were built by local councils, many of them in new 'council estates' on the fringes of the large conurbations.

Local authority housing received new impetus after WORLD WAR II in the drive to solve housing problems left over from the pre-war years and to meet post-war demands for better housing. Over 3 million council houses and flats were built between 1945 and 1985 with the aid of further Housing Acts offering government subsidies, raising the proportion of people living in council-owned accommodation to one in three by 1979.

The THATCHER government dramatically reversed this trend. The drastic reduction in the building of council houses, the 'right to buy' legislation introduced in 1980, and the subsequent legislation allowing private landlords to take over former local authority housing estates, has meant that the proportion of people renting from local authorities has fallen to less than one in five, while the number of owner-occupiers has risen to record levels.

Council in the Marches of Wales, appointed by EDWARD IV and HENRY VII to administer estates of the Prince of Wales, and by WOLSEY for Princess Mary (the future MARY I). Thomas CROMWELL made it a permanent part of Welsh administration, based at Ludlow. It was revived after the INTERREGNUM by CHARLES II in 1660, but was again dissolved in 1689, ending any unified focus for Welsh government.

Council in the West Parts, set up for western England in 1539 under Lord John Russell's presidency by Thomas CROMWELL, after the destruction of Henry Courtenay, 1st Marquess of Exeter's local power. It was dissolved in 1540.

Council Learned in the Law, a subcommittee of the KING'S COUNCIL set up by HENRY VII *c.*1498. It included most leading lawyers, and under Reynold Bray and later Edmund Dudley and Richard Empson, it played the chief part in Henry's government. So closely was it associated with Henry's cold efficiency that it became as swift a casualty of his death as Empson and Dudley. Its importance remained unrecognized until this century, when much of its archive was found lodged in the Duchy of Lancaster records.

Council of Europe, founded on 5 May 1949 to achieve greater unity of action between members of the EEC (*see* EUROPEAN UNION) through co-operation in economic, social, cultural and other spheres. Britain and the majority of other European countries were the original signatories, joined subsequently by West Germany, Greece, Turkey and Cyprus, and following the collapse of the Soviet bloc in 1989, former Czechoslovakia, Hungary and Poland became members. 'Special guest status' has been granted to Armenia, Azerbaijan, and Bosnia and Herzegovina. A council of ministers meets twice a year, and there is also a consultative assembly of appointed representatives, which meets at Strasbourg. The Council has drawn up more than 70 conventions and agreements – the most important of which has been the European Convention on Human Rights – which are adjudicated by the European Court of Human Rights in Strasbourg, but they only have force if the member states ratify them.

Council of Officers This initially informal

caucus of army officers emerged in 1647, after CHARLES I's defeat, to defend army interests and the political gains made in the war; INDEPENDENTS and BAPTISTS were prominent on it. It nominated the BAREBONES PARLIAMENT in 1653, and when threatened in 1659, it removed the hostile regime of Richard CROMWELL.

Council of State, an executive body that tried to cope with INTERREGNUM government. First set up by the RUMP PARLIAMENT in 1649, and often at loggerheads with the ARMY, it was remodelled after the ejection of the Rump in April 1653 by the COUNCIL OF OFFICERS. Having elected Oliver CROMWELL lord protector, it continued as his executive, and was twice reconstructed after Richard CROMWELL's fall.

Council of the North When RICHARD III was Duke of Gloucester with his base in Yorks., he appointed a council, and on his accession to the throne, he continued to use this as an agency of royal government in the North. HENRY VII appointed such a council in 1489 to advise the infant Prince ARTHUR as titular warden-general in the North. In 1537, after the PILGRIMAGE OF GRACE, Thomas CROMWELL remodelled it and extended its jurisdiction, giving it a headquarters at YORK. Membership was by royal appointment, and it acted for the North as the STAR CHAMBER and the Court of REQUESTS did in Westminster; it also played an important role in directing Church affairs. A forceful Elizabethan president was Henry Hastings, Earl of Huntingdon. The council's operation became increasingly controversial under the presidency in the 1630s of Thomas WENTWORTH, Viscount Stafford: it was abolished by the LONG PARLIAMENT in its first session.

Counter-Reformation, the movement in which the remnants of the Western Church loyal to Rome renewed their confidence and regained ground from PROTESTANTISM. The strategy for recovery, which rejected any compromise with the Protestants, was determined between 1545–7, 1551–2 and 1562–3 by sessions of the Council of Trent, whose Latin name has given rise to the adjective 'Tridentine'. Characterized by fierce papal loyalty, it encouraged exuberant, emotional piety and the renewal of REGULAR religious life; its chief agents were the JESUITS.

In Britain, the Counter-Reformation faced hostility from post-1558 governments and, after *c.*1580, from most ordinary people outside Ireland. In Ireland, it transformed traditional religion to forge a new alliance between the Roman Catholic Church and resistance to English rule (*see* CHURCH: IRELAND). Some historians have argued that, in England, the missionaries neglected the more promising highland zone, and that Catholic survival owed more to traditionalism and the witness of pre-Tridentine clergy. Although there is force in this, the vital contribution of the missionaries was probably in fostering unprecedented papal loyalty in the RECUSANT community.

Country Party Members of Parliament who stressed the need to give priority to the interests of the country as a whole, and who were wary of the proceedings of the court and courtiers, were sometimes described as spokesmen for 'the country' from the early 17th century. Later in the 17th century, it became increasingly common to speak of a country 'party', in the loose sense of a body of men holding common views. Men of the country party, for whom Anthony Ashley COOPER, 1st Earl of Shaftesbury, and his followers claimed to speak, were not all landowners sitting for country constituencies, but such men epitomized disinterest and therefore best embodied the group's self-image. They contrasted their views with what they saw as the narrow self-interest of the COURT PARTY. After the GLORIOUS REVOLUTION of 1688, the close association between the Whig JUNTO and the strengthening of the military and fiscal powers of the central government encouraged men of the 'country party' to identify with the TORIES; and in the early 18th century HARLEY and other dissident WHIGS helped to form a NEW TORY party, although there remained some country Whigs.

After the HANOVERIAN SUCCESSION some Tories, such as Henry ST JOHN, Viscount Bolingbroke, anxious to discard a discredited political title, insisted that the true divisions in politics lay between court and country, identifying themselves with the latter. In the 1734 and 1741 elections, numerous urban and rural constituencies were successfully contested by Tory/dissident Whig 'country' alliances. Supporters of 'the country' also called themselves PATRIOTS, from the Latin *patria* (country, fatherland). However, once GEORGE III's withdrawal of support from the WHIG OLIGARCHY had dissolved the formerly close identification between Toryism and opposition, the term 'country' lost its traditional reference point: terms such as Whig, independent, patriot, son of liberty, reformer and latterly JACOBIN were preferred. In the early 19th century, the Ultras sometimes referred to themselves as the 'country party', signifying by this that they were hostile to the reforming designs of ministers insufficiently sensitive, as they thought, to national, especially rural, interests.

County, territorial division of each country within the British Isles, mainly deriving from the Danish and Anglo-Saxon kingdoms (*see* SHIRES, ORIGINS OF). The county, under its SHERIFF and other officers appointed by the crown, was an important element in local administration throughout the succeeding centuries, in areas such as the ASSIZES (*see also* COUNTY COURT), road and bridge maintenance, POOR RELIEF and VAGRANCY. Under the County Councils Act 1889, new elected authorities were instituted for each county. Reorganization of counties took place in 1974, which created a number of new counties on the basis of centres of economic activity, such as Cleveland, and metropolitan counties around conurbations in the manner of the GREATER LONDON COUNCIL. The ancient counties of Scotland and Wales were also reorganized, into large regions in the Scottish case and new large counties (mainly bearing the names of the old Welsh kingdoms) in Wales.

County Committees in the English Civil War Committees proliferated, particularly on the PARLIAMENTARIAN side. At a local level, the most important were those in the counties, which mediated Westminster's demands and helped to organize the heaviest taxation in Britain before the 20th century. They evolved from the pre-war organization of the LORDS LIEUTENANT, supplanting the powers of the JUSTICES OF THE PEACE, and were exempted from control by the courts. In many counties, they displaced traditional notables and attracted much unpopularity.

County Community Local studies of medieval and early modern England have been dominated by the county unit, encouraged by the county arrangement of both local and central records. In addition, the notion of a development in local identities, centred on the GENTRY society of each county, has been important.

Gentry county communities – of which different studies have found traces from the 12th century onwards – expanded with the growth in the number of gentry families in the late 16th century. This county-based localism has been seen as crucial in tensions between centre and locality leading up to the CIVIL WARS. However, objectors have pointed out that units larger and smaller than the county commanded regionalist loyalties, and that highland counties reveal much less evidence of community feeling. Certainly major aristocratic estates spanning large areas formed one alternative focus for gentry loyalties, and below the social level of gentry, there were less strong motives for county feeling.

Nevertheless, the 16th- and 17th-century growth of county ANTIQUARIAN studies, and the behaviour of many local gentry societies during the civil wars, both argue for strong county feelings, which the post-RESTORATION concentration of power in the county benches of JUSTICES OF THE PEACE did nothing to weaken. *See also* COURT VERSUS COUNTRY.

County Councils, *see* LOCAL GOVERNMENT ACT 1888; LOCAL GOVERNMENT REORGANIZATION ACT 1972

County Court *or* **Shire Court,** an institution which predated the introduction of COMMON LAW. It was descended from the assemblies of free men in the SHIRES of Anglo-Saxon England; it was presided over first by the EALDORMAN, later by the SHERIFF, and from the late 12th century the CORONER was also present.

In the medieval period, the court lost virtually all its judicial functions to other institutions, such as the ASSIZES, central common law and equity courts (*see* CHANCERY) and the JUSTICES OF THE PEACE, retaining its place mainly as the setting for declarations of

OUTLAWRY and for elections of KNIGHTS OF THE SHIRE. However, during the 19th century, the moribund institution was revived in a new form, particularly by the County Court Act 1846, which instituted a nationwide system of county courts with paid MAGISTRATES to deal with minor civil cases; the courts' functions have continued to expand. They have often been called both the most ancient and the most modern of English courts, a pleasing conceit, but inaccurate because of the 18th-century break in institutional continuity. The ghost of the old shire or county court was laid with its formal abolition in 1977.

County Hideage, an administrative document, probably from the early 11th century, which supplies important information on the hideage assessment of 13 shires (*see* HIDE). It provides intermediate evidence between early texts such as the *BURGHAL HIDEAGE* and the later *DOMESDAY BOOK*.

County (Rural) Police Acts 1839, 1856 The 1839 Act enabled county magistrates to establish a police force funded out of the rates. The expense was generally regarded as prohibitive, and by 1853, action had been taken by only 22 counties, a response that underscores the importance of ratepayer priorities in the evolution of a nationwide police force.

The 1856 Act was prompted by this patchy development of provincial police forces. It required all counties and BOROUGHS without such a force to create one, with authority to organize it on the lines of the Metropolitan POLICE or any other force. Financial assistance was available to those forces that made annual returns on crime statistics and submitted to a newly appointed inspectorate of constabulary. The criminal thus came to confront an organized police presence in every country in England and Wales.

'Coupon' Election, 1918. General election named after the letter of approval or 'coupon' signed by LLOYD GEORGE, prime minister and leader of the Coalition LIBERALS, and Bonar LAW, leader of the CONSERVATIVES, sent to candidates who formed a coalition: 531 'coupons' were distributed, 150 to Coalition Liberals, to signify that they were not to be opposed by other pro-coalition candidates. The effective electoral pact between Coalition Liberals and Conservatives confirmed the division in the Liberal Party between Lloyd George's pro-coalition followers and ASQUITH's supporters or 'WEE FREE's. 468 'coupon' candidates were elected, 335 Conservatives and 133 Liberals, providing the basis for the post-war coalition government led by Lloyd George until 1922.

Court Baron, the court of a Manor. The JURY was drawn from the FREEHOLDERS (who were originally the judges), presided over by the lord's steward or BAILIFF, but otherwise from the 13th century the courts lost their jurisdiction over freeholders to COMMON PLEAS. Some MANORS also had leet jurisdiction and view of frankpledge (i.e. competence over minor criminal matters), which would be indicated in the title of the court. Courts baron retained an importance for COPYHOLDERS in registering their title up to the abolition of copyhold tenure in 1926. Other minor actions at law triable in courts baron were transferred to the COUNTY COURTS in the 19th century. Some are still held for purely ceremonial purposes, but all residual legal functions were abolished in 1977.

Court Leet, *see* MANOR

Court of Exchequer, Pleas, *see* EXCHEQUER

Court of Session, the supreme court of the Scottish legal system. It originated in the Session, a council which was set up in the 15th century to consider appeals made to the king; JAMES V reconstituted this as the College of Justice in 1532, modelling it on the *Parlement* of Paris, and the lawyers who practised there formed a College of Advocates. Because the Court derived from the royal PREROGATIVE (like the English STAR CHAMBER), it was able to build up its own procedure and criteria for deciding the law; most of the lawyers who worked in it were trained in Roman law in continental universities, and hence the legal system which they developed increasingly diverged from English COMMON LAW (*see* CIVIL LAW). Since 1707, appeals have been allowed from the Court of Session to the House of LORDS, but they are heard there on the principles of Scottish law.

Court Party, term in use from the late 17th through to the early 19th centuries for those holding posts at court or in the administration, or generally supportive of measures tending to strengthen the military or fiscal power, or political influence of the crown and its ministers. The knowledge that ministers enjoyed royal favour meant that they could generally count upon the parliamentary support of placemen and pensioners (*see* PLACE BILLS), though they could win parliamentary majorities only with additional support from other political groupings and from backbenchers.

The term was pejorative in connotation: members of the court party were suspected of putting the narrow interests of the court above those of the country as a whole, while those dubbed the COUNTRY PARTY claimed by contrast to give priority to the public good. *See also* COURT VERSUS COUNTRY; DUNNING'S MOTION.

Court, Royal, the main arena for politics before the modern atrophy of royal power. The English court achieved a sophisticated organization by the early 12th century, earlier than in most European states, but it later tended to borrow its style from other courts such as that of BURGUNDY in the 15th century, the French and Italian courts in the 16th and the French in the late 17th.

Historians have sometimes underestimated the court's importance because of its apparently pointless display, ceremony and entertainment. However, these were essential ways of controlling a largely male aristocratic institution that had originated in the king's armed retinue; a court where aggression was allowed to breed through unregulated boredom could have had serious consequences. Court offices close to the monarch, such as those of the Tudor PRIVY CHAMBER, could be vital weapons in seizing and maintaining power alongside control of the formal structures of government, often themselves fossilized institutions of the court (e.g. CHAMBER; CHANCERY; EXCHEQUER).

A court had other functions. It should provide honourable office for those who felt themselves naturally entitled to it, and courtly magnificence should impress and entertain the king's subjects. A court that became isolated and difficult to enter, as did CHARLES I's, did the monarch serious harm. *See also* COURT PARTY; COURT VERSUS COUNTRY.

Court Versus Country, part of the rhetoric of politics in the 17th and 18th centuries: metropolitan and central government attitudes versus the rugged honesty, localist loyalties and hostility to taxation in the SHIRES. The stereotype was always inaccurate: an urban sophisticate in local life might leap to the defence of his locality in central politics, and might also turn to 'country' attitudes if he felt excluded from rewards at court. Emphasis on localism has also minimized the local informed interest in national affairs that was obvious in many general elections.

The artificiality of the division was shown in the national crisis of 1642, when both 'parties' were torn apart between king and Parliament. None the less, the terms COURT PARTY and COUNTRY PARTY retained political significance. *See also* COUNTY COMMUNITY; PLACE BILLS.

Courtenay, William (*c*.1341–96), Archbishop of Canterbury (1381–96). As bishop of London (from 1375) and then archbishop of Canterbury, he led the opposition within the English church to WYCLIF and the LOLLARDS.

He was particularly influential in driving them out of Oxford, the university at which he had been a student and was to become chancellor.

Courts of Law, *see* ASSIZES; CHANCERY; CHURCH COURTS; COMMON PLEAS; CORONER; COUNTY COURT; COURT BARON; COURT OF SESSION; CUSTOMARY LAW; EXCHEQUER; EYRE; JUSTICES OF THE PEACE; KING'S BENCH; MANOR; REQUESTS; SHERIFF; STAR CHAMBER; WARDSHIP

Covenant (Scottish National Covenant, 1638, and Solemn League and Covenant, 1643) Exploiting the rhetorical use of the idea of covenant popular in the Reformation, covenants against Catholicism were a recurrent feature of the 16th-century Scottish REFORMATION. After CHARLES I's attempt to impose the 1637 PRAYER BOOK (*see also* BISHOPS' WARS), most Scots noblemen and a third of the clergy signed a national covenant in Feb. 1638 committing themselves under God to restore the purity of the KIRK. Attracting signatures nationwide, it flatly rejected EPISCOPACY in favour of PRESBYTERIANISM, and became the Scottish manifesto throughout the 1640s.

Its objectives were incorporated in the English PARLIAMENT's alliance with the Scots – the Solemn League and Covenant – in Sept. 1643, the doctrinaire presbyterianism of which was opposed by INDEPENDENTS as well as ROYALISTS. The Scots COVENANTERS saw Charles's execution as a violation of the Covenant, leading to open war with England. After the RESTORATION, it was a rallying point for opposition when in 1662 EPISCOPAL government and patrons' rights were restored in Scotland, and some 300 ministers were ejected. The PENTLAND RISING of 1666 expressed Covenanter grievances. Government policy swung between attempts to conciliate moderates and more swingeing repression. DECLARATIONS OF INDULGENCE of 1669 and 1672 allowed the appointment of ejected ministers; by contrast, CONVENTICLES were suppressed, sometimes by soldiers. Lauderdale (*see* MAITLAND, JOHN) favoured repression after 1673 and some Covenanters were transported. In 1678 the assassination of Archbishop Sharp prompted new action against conventicles, and in 1679, James SCOTT, Duke of Monmouth, defeated some 4,000 Covenanters at BOTHWELL BRIDGE. A third indulgence allowed house conventicles south of the Tay, except around major cities, but the TEST ACT of 1681 required all officeholders to swear they held the Protestant faith as expressed in the Scots confession of 1560; BURNET and others were deprived of their livings for refusing.

When the Covenanter Convention of Societies issued its *Apologetical Declaration and Admonitory Vindication of the True Presbyterians of the Church of Scotland* (1684), the government ruled that whoever failed to disown it and take the oath of abjuration would be summarily executed. The CAMERONIANS, a small sect of covenanting Presbyterians, were treated harshly, but Presbyterians as such were rarely executed. A further Declaration of Indulgence in 1687 removed all restrictions on Presbyterians except that on open-field preaching. Presbyterian ministers were released from prison, and many returned from exile. With the abolition of episcopacy in 1690, ejected ministers were allowed to return to their parishes. However, a sizeable number remained outside this settlement, considering it incomplete and therefore a betrayal of the Covenants. The memory of the Covenant was potent enough in ULSTER for the name to be used by the Unionists under Edward Carson in 1912.

Covenanters, name applied to those adhering to the various covenants in the Scottish REFORMATION, but in particular to those resisting the introduction of EPISCOPACY to Scotland during 1661–3, when some 300 ministers were ejected from their PARISHES. *See also* CAMERONIANS; COVENANT (SCOTTISH NATIONAL COVENANT, 1638, AND SOLEMN LEAGUE AND COVENANT, 1643).

Covent Garden, district in WESTMINSTER north of the Strand, which was the first self-conscious new urban development in pre-Civil War LONDON, with a square and church built to the designs of Inigo Jones for the 4th Russell Earl of Bedford. Covent Garden was famous for its fruit and vegetable market, set within the original square right through to the 1970s, and as a focus of social, literary and theatrical life. The first Covent Garden Theatre was built in 1732, and the district remains a prime focus of London THEATRE with the Royal Opera House, built in 1858, at its heart.

Coventry The city's success has been built upon a succession of industries, from medieval times onwards. The rise of commerce from the 13th century, in the CLOTH and especially the cap-making trades, transformed medieval Coventry into one of the five wealthiest and largest towns in England, reflected in the numbers of religious houses and merchants' dwellings, a few of which survive. After a period of decline in the 16th and 17th centuries, growth resumed in the 18th with watch- and ribbon-making, the latter coming to dominate 1820–50. From that grew a succession of ENGINEERING industries: sewing machines, bicycles, and finally motor cars, with Daimler's works being the first in 1896. Coventry's population grew tenfold from the mid-19th century to the 1970s. German bombing in Nov. 1940 devastated much of the central area; out of the ruins rose Sir Basil Spence's new CATHEDRAL (1951–62), one of the most potent images of post-war reconstruction, and the opportunity to put into practice the now-controversial comprehensive PLANNING scheme, first mooted in 1941.

Craftsman, The, one of the most successful 18th-century opposition periodicals. Started in 1726 and run for ten years by Nicholas Amhurst, it had an estimated circulation of 500–1,250 a week, and aimed to expose political 'graft' and corruption. Purportedly edited by 'Caleb d'Anvers', its contributors included Bolingbroke (*see* ST JOHN, HENRY) and William Pulteney. It subjected WALPOLE's policies, and particularly the Excise Bill (*see* EXCISE CRISIS), to sustained and well-informed attack.

Cranbourne, 1st Viscount, *see* CECIL, ROBERT

Cranmer, Thomas (1489–1556), Archbishop of Canterbury (1533–56). A member of a minor gentry family of Nottinghamshire, his worthy but unspectacular Cambridge academic career abruptly changed direction in 1529 when he joined the team working for HENRY VIII's first divorce. After service on foreign embassies, Henry engineered his appointment as archbishop of Canterbury in 1533, and he soon presided over the king's unilateral annulment. Already a convinced reformer, he married the niece of the German Lutheran theologian Osiander in 1532 while clerical marriage was still illegal in England. In 1536, he granted Henry a further annulment from ANNE BOLEYN, and worked closely with Thomas CROMWELL to further the English REFORMATION. He survived Henry's final unpredictable years to become a chief architect of the Edwardian religious changes, constructing the PRAYER BOOKS of 1549 and 1552, the ORDINAL of 1550, the THIRTY-NINE ARTICLES and the abortive *REFORMATIO LEGUM*.

Cranmer's relations with John DUDLEY, Duke of Northumberland, were strained, but he acquiesced in the unsuccessful attempt to put Lady JANE GREY on the throne. He was convicted of treason in 1553 and, the following year, of HERESY. Demoralized by his long imprisonment, he signed six recantations, but was still condemned to burn at the stake at Oxford. Realizing that no mercy would be shown him, he made a final bold statement of his PROTESTANT faith.

Perhaps too fair-minded and cautious to be a ready-made hero in Reformation disputes, Cranmer was an impressively learned if unoriginal scholar, and his genius for formal prose has left a lasting mark on ANGLICAN liturgy.

Crécy, Battle of, near Abbeville in France, 26 Aug. 1346. It was a victory for EDWARD III over Philip VI of France, and one of the main English successes in the HUNDRED YEARS WAR. After a destructive march through Normandy, Edward crossed the Somme, then offered battle. With his men-at-arms and archers standing on the defensive, he enjoyed a tactical advantage. The superiority in numbers of the French made them overconfident, and their disorganized attacks were beaten back with heavy losses. Edward immediately capitalized on this by besieging CALAIS, which fell in 1347.

Creed, brief and officially approved statement of the salient points of Christian doctrine. Those formulated in the early Church – most notably, the Apostles', Nicene and Athanasian creeds – are the most important. They were frequently used as tests of the orthodoxy of Christian belief, as standards to which Church members, office holders and clergy must assent, and as a convenient summary of belief for purposes of worship. Much religious conflict in Victorian Britain centred on the extent to which theological liberals doubted, rejected or reinterpreted certain items of various creeds. Controversies concerned the 'damnatory clauses' of the Athanasian Creed (i.e. those that consigned non-believers to hell) and whether credal references to the Resurrection and the virgin birth should be understood symbolically or as statements of historical fact.

Crime, any activity which is illegal according to law. As the law changes over time, so does the legal status of many activities, although murder, violence and theft tend to be classified as crime in most societies and periods of history. Crime has become an important focus of historical study in recent years, alongside the growing popularity of 'history from below' and SOCIAL HISTORY in general. Crime statistics are notoriously difficult to interpret because they have to be gathered from a variety of different sorts of courts, and reflect changes in the law and in the efficiency of policing and the legal process (often influenced by media-created or media-enhanced moral panics), as much as they reflect changes in the level of crimes themselves. Research however suggests that the late 16th and first half of the 17th centuries were turbulent and violent in crime terms, whereas the 18th century saw a relative decline in criminal prosecutions and in harsh punishments, especially hanging. Although the 18th century saw a multiplication of statutes defining an array of capital crimes (*see* CAPITAL PUNISHMENT), the death penalty was used sparingly and as a deterrent (TRANSPORTATION, especially to AUSTRALIA, grew to replace it for a time). The biggest change in the 18th century was the greater emphasis on the defence of property, and commercial transactions which occurred with industrialization, and an increasing criminalization of the poor associated with POPULATION growth, PROLETARIANIZATION MIGRATION and UNEMPLOYMENT. The poor were coming to be regarded as the dangerous classes, a trend which became even more apparent in the first half of the 19th century which saw a major acceleration in criminal prosecutions (relative to population growth). In this period of industrialization, rapid urbanization and social unrest, crime was often associated with political conflict and therefore increasingly feared by the propertied classes. Historians are only just beginning to consider why markedly fewer women were and are involved in criminal activity outside of PROSTITUTION, which became a major focus of prosecutions in the late 19th century. By the same token, youth crime appears to have been a marked and enduring feature over the centuries and needs explaining in terms other than the general factors affecting the needs or proclivities of the lowest social classes. In the 20th century white-collar crime and fraud have increased in importance, aided by modern methods of financial and other transactions, whilst petty crime and theft appear to be associated with unemployment and with the mentality of free market economics. *See also* PUNISHMENT; SOCIAL CRIME.

Crimean War, 1853–6. An episode in the EASTERN QUESTION, known to contemporaries as the 'Russian War', the war was precipitated by Russian occupation of Moldavia and Wallachia in 1853, in response to the Ottoman Turkish rejection of demands for a Russian protectorate over Orthodox Christians within their borders. The Turks, encouraged principally by French support, declared war on Russia, which won the naval battle of Sinope in the Black Sea in Nov. 1853. Wishing to see Russia's power curbed, Britain joined France in a declaration of war on 28 March 1854, with political support from Austria.

A British Army contingent under Lord Raglan, joined the French in landing in the Crimea, fighting at the Alma on 20 Sept. and laying partial siege to Sebastopol. Russian attempts to relieve the siege included the battles of Balaclava on 25 Oct., including the disastrous CHARGE OF THE LIGHT BRIGADE under the Earl of Cardigan, and Inkerman (a 'soldiers' battle') on 5 Nov. On 8 Sept. the British captured but failed to hold the Redan, and the French captured the Malakoff redoubt. The Russians abandoned Sebastopol the next day, but the Allies were unable to advance and occupy the docks, and the fighting continued over a second winter.

The campaign in the Baltic, conducted entirely by the navy, was less spectacular but more important to the war's progress. Britain built a floating siege train of over 350 bombardment vessels, to attack the Russian naval base at Kronstadt. The threat of this led the Russians to make peace and concessions by the Treaty of Paris of 30 March 1856, including accepting the neutrality of the Black Sea.

At the time the Crimea was a by-word for incompetence. Altogether 4,600 soldiers died in battle, 13,000 were wounded and 17,500 died of disease. The Aberdeen government (*see* GORDON, GEORGE) fell in 1855 as a result of its failure to prosecute the war properly. But although important ARMY reforms came from the war, many were already in place at its start. The appalling conditions for the soldiers were no worse than in many previous campaigns, the product of a British system which cut military spending to the bone in peacetime. In the second war winter it was the French, not the British, who suffered most. The difference was that this time London 'public opinion' knew of the soldiers' experience through, in particular, W.H. Russell of *The Times*, the first man to be called a 'war correspondent', the work of photographers like Roger Fenton, and the self-publicity of Florence NIGHTINGALE in promoting better hospital conditions.

The limited victory won by Britain and France ended Russian expansion south into the Balkans for a generation, and west into Scandinavia for good, forcing her to abandon her dominant position in central Europe. This compares favourably with more ambitious attempts to conquer Russia by Napoleon and Hitler.

CHRONOLOGY

1853, 31 May Tsar Nicholas I of Russia dispatches troops to occupy Moldavia and Wallachia in defence of Christian Ottoman population.
1853, 4 Oct. Turkey declares war on Russia.
1853, 30 Nov. Russia sinks Turkish ships anchored at Sinope Harbour.
1854, Feb. Anglo-French ultimatum sent to Russia, demanding evacuation of principalities.
1854, 28 March British and French declare war on Russia.
1854, June Allied troops ordered to Varna in support of Turks.
1854, 14 Sept. Allied invasion of Crimea following Russian withdrawal across Danube, intent on capturing Sebastopol and destroying Russian fleet.
1854, 20 Sept. 40,000-strong Russian force defeated at battle of the Alma; 2,000 British casualties.
1854, 17 Oct. Siege of Russian-held Sebastopol begins.
1854, 25 Oct. Russians repelled in costly battle at Balaclava, which includes suicidal CHARGE OF THE LIGHT BRIGADE.
1854, 5 Nov. Russians repelled again in even bloodier encounter at Inkerman.
1854/1855 British spend winter holed up in Crimea; over-extended and poorly supplied, they suffer badly. Public opinion outraged by daily reports from *The Times* war correspondent W. H. Russell.
1855, Jan. Aberdeen government brought down on the radical MP John Roebuck's motion to appoint a committee of inquiry.
1855, April Military and administrative reforms improve flow of supplies and restore fighting effectiveness.
1855, 11 Sept. Fall of Sebastopol.
1856, Feb. Hostilities cease.
1856, 30 March Peace concluded at Paris.
1871 Russians refortify Sebastopol.

Criminal Law Amendment Act 1871 Designed to prevent a repetition of events like the SHEFFIELD OUTRAGES, it made picketing illegal, and revived much of the terminology of the COMBINATION ACTS. 'Molestation', 'intimidation' and 'obstruction' became imprisonable offences and STRIKE action difficult.

Criminal Law Amendment Act 1885, *see* HOMOSEXUALITY AND BRITISH LAW; PROSTITUTION

Cripps, Sir Stafford (1889–1952), Labour politician. After a highly successful career at the Bar, becoming the youngest KC in 1927, Cripps was drawn into LABOUR PARTY politics in 1929. His uncle by marriage, Sidney WEBB, and his father were both Cabinet ministers in Ramsay MACDONALD's government, and in 1930 Cripps became SOLICITOR-GENERAL. He declined the invitation to continue in that post in the NATIONAL GOVERNMENT of 1931 and threw himself with zeal into militantly socialist politics. His willingness to work with communists led both to his expulsion from the Labour Party and to his election to the national executive at the 1937 party conference. Re-admitted to the party, he was expelled again in Jan. 1939 for advocating a cross-party Popular Front to oust Neville CHAMBERLAIN's government. Party and public opinion was divided about him; sent as ambassador to Moscow in 1940, Cripps was convinced of the need to persuade Stalin away from the Nazi–Soviet Pact of 1939. After Hitler attacked the Soviet Union in June 1941, Cripps' role in furthering the Anglo-Russian accord was significant. As a member of the war CABINET, he was sent to INDIA to gain Indian support for the war effort; he failed, and left the Cabinet to become minister of aircraft production until 1945.

Cripps became president of the Board of Trade in the 1945 ATTLEE government, and so prime mover of the difficult post-war economic reconstruction strategy and its accompanying AUSTERITY. Becoming chancellor of the Exchequer in 1947 after Hugh Dalton's resignation, Cripps had the difficult task of implementing wage and dividend freezes, but in Sept. 1949 was forced into a

DEVALUATION of the pound. Ill-health forced his resignation in Oct. 1950.

The mixture of wealthy grandee and ardent socialist, combined with the force of personality which allowed an unpalatable economic policy to be maintained for so long, made Cripps an important figure in Labour politics through the 1930s and 1940s. Yet his legacy gave opponents of subsequent Labour governments the ready charge that theirs was the devaluing party, and with his departure the general resentment in the country at his economic measures became only too apparent.

Cromwell, Oliver (1599–1658), statesman. The scion of a very minor gentry family in Huntingdon; a nervous breakdown seems to have led him to a PURITAN conversion in the early 1630s, and he became a client of Puritan aristocrats. Elected to the LONG PARLIAMENT in 1640, he rose to prominence in the EASTERN ASSOCIATION in 1642–4, becoming steadily more critical of the high command.

A leading engineer of the SELF-DENYING ORDINANCE of 1644, he backed FAIRFAX's command of the NEW MODEL ARMY, emerging after notable victories at MARSTON MOOR and NASEBY as the most powerful military commander, with INDEPENDENT sympathies manoeuvring against the PRESBYTERIAN group in Parliament. He became convinced that no deal could be made with CHARLES I and, after the Presbyterian opposition had been swept aside (*see* PRIDE'S PURGE), superintended Charles's trial and execution in 1649; however, he also successfully blocked the rise to power of the LEVELLERS.

In Aug. 1649 he faced the formidable challenge to Parliament offered by the Irish coalition led by James Butler, Earl of Ormond; landing at Ringsend (Dublin) and marching north to DROGHEDA, he treated the town ruthlessly after capturing it, and behaved equally savagely in his southern campaign at Wexford. Both these atrocities may later have been exaggerated, but they were real; Cromwell had no hesitation in regarding them as God's judgement on a bloodthirsty and barbarous enemy. By Dec. he held the whole of the east coast of Ireland, and by the time he left Ireland to face a new threat from Scotland in May 1650, the English forces held the advantage. He went on to defeat the Scots in 1650–1 (*see* DUNBAR; WORCESTER).

His wars against the DUTCH (1652–4), Tunisian piracy (1655) and the Spaniards (1655–8) were broadly successful; less happy were his efforts to find a lasting balance of army power against civilian longing for peace and proper representation in government. From late 1653 until his death, he was lord PROTECTOR, a title that gave him supreme legislative and executive power in association with Parliament and the COUNCIL OF STATE; he eventually refused urgings that he should assume the crown, since the army was hostile to the idea, but he lived in increasingly monarchical splendour. His settlement of the Church in England was a comprehensive and tolerant PROTESTANTISM, amid which ANGLICANISM maintained a clandestine life and Roman Catholics were less molested than for a century; he was also responsible for the readmission of JEWS into England in 1655. In 1660, his body, buried in Westminster Abbey, was dug up and ceremonially executed.

A great military commander and religious idealist, he lacked personal ambition, and had a strong streak of humility and self-doubt that was most apparent in his political leadership.

Cromwell, Richard (1626–1712), politician. Son of Oliver CROMWELL, he found himself lord PROTECTOR for want of an alternative on his father's death in 1658, having previously served conscientiously in second-rank offices. His regime at first appeared stable, but was undermined by financial chaos and confrontation between government and army. The army forced him to dissolve PARLIAMENT in April 1659, and he was overthrown in May. He later lived in retirement unmolested, first in Paris, then in London and Hampshire: an amiable, hard-working man thrust into power at the most difficult of times.

Cromwell, Thomas (16th [1st Cromwell] Earl of Essex) (*c.*1485–1540), royal servant. Son of a Surrey tradesman, Cromwell gained an all-round education through a colourful if obscure early career comprising continental travel and commerce, acquiring enough legal expertise to rise high in WOLSEY's service from the 1510s. Admirably loyal to Wolsey when he fell from power in 1529, he transferred to royal service with quiet efficiency after the cardinal's death the next year, and rapidly gained HENRY VIII's trust, becoming royal councillor in 1531, master of the jewels and of the wards (*see* WARDSHIP) in 1532 and king's secretary in 1534.

Opinions differ on how far he originated the idea of breaking with the papacy to solve Henry's matrimonial problems. Although it is likely that the concept was the king's, Cromwell certainly supervised the detailed working out of the scheme behind the Act in RESTRAINT OF APPEALS 1533 and subsequent legislation (*see* REFORMATION PARLIAMENT; ROYAL SUPREMACY). He was the first royal minister to be thoroughly at home in the House of COMMONS, and used parliamentary legislation to the full to pursue the royal will.

Appointments as vicar-general and then vice-gerent in spirituals in 1535 (*see* VICE-GERENCY) gave him use of the new royal powers in the Church. He was committed to drastic Church reform and had many long-standing links with reforming circles, working closely with Archbishop CRANMER. Reformist views did not, however, stop him securing the downfall of his former ally ANNE BOLEYN in 1536. From that year, he masterminded the DISSOLUTION of all monasteries and friaries, having gained experience of suppressions in Wolsey's service. He also undertook reforms of government that, although incomplete and often designed for his own political advantage, were of great long-term importance (*see* COUNCIL IN THE MARCHES OF WALES; COUNCIL OF THE NORTH; *TUDOR REVOLUTION IN GOVERNMENT*).

He survived the attempt of the PILGRIMAGE OF GRACE to destroy his power. Thereafter, his one fatal blunder came with the ANNE OF CLEVES marriage fiasco in 1540. After apparently weathering this storm, even gaining an earldom, he was suddenly arrested and executed through the plots of conservative clergy and noblemen. *See also* CATHERINE HOWARD.

Crowland Abbey, Lincs. In *c.*700, St GUTHLAC established a hermitage on an island in the Fens. The community disappeared during the VIKING invasions, but was refounded in *c.*971 during the TENTH-CENTURY REFORM. The body of Waltheof (?–1076), Earl of Northumbria, the last Anglo-Saxon earl to survive in office, was entombed at the abbey, and (it was said) miracles subsequently occurred there. Also sometimes spelt 'Croyland', the abbey was dissolved in 1539.

Crown Since Britain has an unwritten constitution under its monarchy, the descriptive uses of this vital term are vague and various. It is applied to the central government of the United Kingdom of Great Britain and Northern Ireland; the combination of traditional departments in the royal household, such as the Lord Chamberlain's Department; the combination of those offices of state in executive government which are formally based on exercise of the royal PREROGATIVE, such as secretaries of state; the power exercised by the courts of the COMMON LAW; the authority exercised by the monarch as supreme governor of the Church of England (*see* ROYAL SUPREMACY); and the combined action in decision-making of monarch and PARLIAMENT. *See also* FORTESCUE, JOHN; KINGSHIP.

Crown, a COIN introduced in England in 1526 in imitation of the French écu, as a gold coin worth 4 shillings and 6 pence, and which took its name from the large crowned shield which formed its reverse. From 1551 it was normally issued as a silver coin worth 5 shillings (a quarter of £1). Crowns ceased to be a part of commonly used currency in the early 20th century, but they are still minted for commemorative purposes.

Croydon Treasure Hoard, Surrey. Discovered in 1862, this hoard is remarkable for the diversity of 9th-century coins. Its mixture of Arabic, Frankish and English types suggests that it was deposited by a much-travelled member of the GREAT ARMY of the late 860s, and thereby indicates the range of VIKING activities.

Cruiser In the 18th century a 'cruiser' was any warship on detached service, not a particular type; it was not until the last quarter of the 19th century that it replaced 'frigate' and 'corvette' as a designation for the next type of warship down from the battleship – ships with more range or greater speed, but less protection and less powerful guns, than the contemporary capital ships. Whilst the battleship was intended to fight for control of the seas, the cruiser was intended to make use of that control, for trade protection, policing, and many other purposes. Generally there were two types of cruiser – larger ones for general-purpose world-wide use, and smaller ones for use as fleet scouts – though there was also the very large armoured cruiser which evolved into the battlecruiser, which could be larger and faster though weaker than the contemporary battleship, an expensive and mistaken development of the two decades before 1914. The British NAVY, with its world-wide commitments, required cruisers in larger numbers than any other.

Crusades, military expeditions authorized by the pope, launched against people identified as enemies of the Church, and in which those participants who had 'taken the Cross', i.e. had made a vow to join the expedition, were believed to obtain a spiritual reward, the INDULGENCE. The first crusade was preached by Pope Urban II in 1095. With ROBERT II Curthose as one of its leaders, it ended with the capture of Jerusalem from the Muslims in 1099, and the subsequent establishment of the kingdom of Jerusalem and other crusader states.

This success, against all odds, sparked off a remarkably enduring enthusiasm for crusading throughout Europe, including England and Scotland, though less so in Wales and hardly at all in Ireland. Twelfth-century crusades were directed either against pagans in the Baltic region or against Muslims in the Middle East or Spain – in 1147 an English crusading fleet contributed to the capture of Lisbon. The collapse of the kingdom of Jerusalem in 1187 led to the SALADIN TITHE and to the third crusade under RICHARD I's inspirational leadership. Although increasingly hard-pressed, the kingdom survived until the 1291 fall of Acre – in part thanks to the efforts of a continuing stream of crusaders such as the future EDWARD I.

Although in the 13th century both heretics (the Cathars) and the papacy's political enemies within Christendom were added to the list of crusaders' targets, crusading against non-Christians remained a generally acknowledged ideal. In the 14th century many English nobles such as Henry of Lancaster and HENRY IV went to Prussia to crusade against Lithuanians (until they inconveniently converted to Christianity). Even Protestant Englishmen cheered when a Catholic prince, Don John of Austria, defeated the Turks at the battle of Lepanto (1571). However, Philip II of Spain's habit of having his expeditions against England, including the 1588 ARMADA, declared crusades, helped to ensure, from the 17th century onwards, a widely held English perception of crusades as 'popish superstition'. The use of the word 'crusade' in the wider sense of the vigorous pursuit of a just cause goes back to the 18th century.

Crystal Palace, the enormous glass conservatory, over 1,800 feet (550 metres) long and at its broadest 450 feet (140 metres) wide, designed by Sir Joseph Paxton to house the GREAT EXHIBITION of 1851. After the exhibition was over, the innovatory iron-framed, glazed building was removed from Hyde Park and reassembled in Sydenham, south London, as the centrepiece of an amusement park with facilities for concerts, drama and exhibitions, as well as a menagerie. It was destroyed by fire on 30 Nov. 1936, although the area is still known as 'Crystal Palace'.

Cuerdale Treasure Hoard, Lancs., one of the largest coin hoards ever found in western Europe, probably buried in the early 10th century. Discovered in 1840, it contained more than 7,000 coins, over 5,000 of which came from VIKING-controlled areas of England, as well as numerous pieces of silver. It is a crucial source for understanding the Viking kingdom of YORK and its relations with DUBLIN and the rest of Ireland.

Culdees, Scottish and Irish monks or nuns (name probably derived from the Old Irish *céle dé*, 'companion'). There is evidence for their communities from the 8th century, although they may originally have been hermits. Gradually they relaxed their monastic rule, and there are examples of married Culdees before 12th-century reforms replaced most of their communities, generally with Augustinian CANONS. By the 14th century the remainder had become indistinguishable from colleges of secular CANONS. *See also* AUGUSTINIAN RULE.

Culen, King of Scots (966–71). A son of King

INDULF, he seized the kingdom from King DUB, possibly because he had been excluded from the sub-kingdom of STRATHCLYDE contrary to a succession pattern that had existed for much of the 9th century. Culen's usurpation began a feud which lasted for a century (*see* KINGSHIP). He was himself killed by a son of Donald, who had kept him out of Strathclyde.

Culloden, Battle of, north-east of Inverness, 16 April 1746. Prince Charles Edward STUART, the 'Young Pretender', landed in Scotland on 25 July 1745 and defeated the government forces at Prestonpans on 20 Sept. In Nov., his forces invaded England, capturing Carlisle and reaching Derby on 4 Dec. But faced with the vastly superior forces of General Wade and WILLIAM AUGUSTUS, Duke of Cumberland, the JACOBITE army retreated, and at Culloden Moor, they were defeated. Cumberland's ruthless pursuit of the defeated soldiers and his killing of wounded men earned him the nickname 'The Butcher'. Charles Edward escaped to France. Although Jacobite intrigues continued into the next decade, in retrospect this battle can be seen to have marked the effective defeat of the Jacobite cause.

Cumann na Ngaedheal, Irish organization founded in 1900. Originally intended to act as a loose co-ordinating body for movements involved in the struggle for Irish independence, in 1923 it was re-established to rally these forces in favour of the ANGLO-IRISH TREATY during the IRISH CIVIL WAR, and formed a government in Aug. of that year. It saw the IRISH FREE STATE through its first decade of independence and the re-admission of anti-treaty forces to Parliament. Losing power in 1932, the following year it formed – with elements of other groupings – the nucleus of a new party: FINE GAEL.

Cumberland, 3rd Duke of, *see* WILLIAM AUGUSTUS

Cunard Line, shipping company, founded as the British and North American Royal Mail Steam Packet Company, but better known by the name of its founder Samuel Cunard, who was awarded the first North Atlantic mail contract in 1839. The company commenced service on 4 July 1840, at first to Halifax and Boston, but from 1848 also to NEW YORK. The line earned a reputation for safety and reliability which helped to keep it in business in spite of strong competition (and early complaints about the food). Only the competition of the airlines finally brought an end to the regular passenger service, although Cunard even now retains the distinction of operating the last passenger liner on the Atlantic run: the *QE2*.

Cunningham, Andrew (1st Viscount Cunningham) (1883–1963), Admiral of the Fleet and Britain's most successful naval commander of WORLD WAR II. As commander-in-chief in the Mediterranean, he showed far-sighted appreciation of the use of carrier-borne aircraft in the successful assault on the Italian fleet in Taranto harbour in Nov. 1940. He then succeeded in worsting the Italians again in the night battle off Cape Matapan in March 1941, forcing their powerful fleet on to the defensive. In 1942–3 he was naval commander-in-chief under Eisenhower of Anglo-American naval forces expelling the Axis from North Africa. In Oct. 1943 he became first sea lord, and was CHURCHILL's chief naval adviser until the end of the war.

Cunobelin (*fl.* 1st century AD), King of the Catuvellauni. The historical basis of SHAKESPEARE's Cymbeline, he ruled the CATUVELLAUNI from *c.*AD 5 to 41, during which time he made them the dominant power in south-eastern England. The extent to which he did this can be seen in his COINAGE, which shows that he had taken over COLCHESTER, the chief town of the TRINOVANTES. There are signs that he developed his rule along Roman lines, but there is no evidence either of direct relations with the empire or that he in any way provoked CLAUDIUS' invasion in 43.

Cura Pastoralis ('Pastoral Care'), an immensely popular medieval text written by Pope Gregory the Great (590–604). It was one of those selected for translation and dissemination among his people by ALFRED THE GREAT. Alfred's purposes are transparent; the book gives advice on Christian pastoral responsibilities and lays a heavy stress on the importance of education. His preface contains his famous commentary on the decline of learning in England.

Curragh 'Mutiny', incident in 1914 when 57 officers of the 3rd Cavalry Brigade stationed at the Curragh Barracks, near DUBLIN, said they would resign their commissions rather than impose HOME RULE on Ireland against the wishes of the people of ULSTER. The War Office gave assurances that they would not be asked to do so, but the incident showed the sympathy of sections of the army for Ulster's resistance and cast doubt on whether Britain could effectively coerce Ulster.

Curthose, Robert, *see* ROBERT II

Custody of Infants Act 1839. This gave mothers of 'unblemished character' access to their children in the event of a separation or divorce, a right for which Caroline Norton (1808–77) campaigned after battles with her estranged MP husband over access to her own children (*see also* WOMEN, LEGAL STATUS OF).

Custom, a set of locally established practices and rights in law which arise and are justified by their repeated operation rather than recorded as rights in written form. Appeals to custom were often used from the 16th century during periods of economic change, and especially in the 17th and 18th centuries when communities felt the impact of changes in AGRICULTURE (including ENCLOSURE), mining (including shifts in mining rights), INDUSTRY and long-distance trade (including shifts in labour hierarchies and remunerations, in local food supplies, and attempts by both central and local governments to tax new sources of wealth). Custom was based in law upon oral culture and memory, and struggles over customary rights provide historians with interesting insights into the contested nature of the past and into the invention of traditions. Custom was also important as the legal foundation for the monarchy and the state.

Customary Law, *see* BLOOD FEUD; BREHON; COMMON LAW; COMPURGATION; FLYMENAFYRMTH; *GLANVILL*; HAMSOCN; HYWEL DDA, LAWS OF; LAW CODES, ANGLO-SAXON; LAW TRACTS, EARLY IRISH; MANOR; TANIST; TRIAL BY ORDEAL

Customs, duties on imports and EXPORTS, collected by or on behalf of the crown. *See also* CONTRABAND; EXCISE.

Custos Rotulorum, *see* JUSTICES OF THE PEACE

Cymmrodorion Society, formed in 1751 by a group of Welsh businessmen living in London, under the patronage of the prince of Wales, to promote Welsh culture and literature, study antiquities, customs and manners, language, natural philosophy and manufactures, and educate and relieve their distressed countrymen; Richard Morris, editor of the Welsh Bible, was an active member. It was dissolved in 1787, but some of its projects were carried on by the Cymreigyddion Society, established by the older society's assistant secretary in 1772; this group revived the EISTEDDFOD in 1789. The Cymmrodorion Society, refounded in 1820 with a more strictly literary emphasis, organized the modern EISTEDDFODAU from 1821. It too declined, but was refounded once more in 1873.

Cyprus Taken from the Ottoman Empire in 1878, as a potential British military and naval stronghold in the eastern Mediterranean, the island of Cyprus was formally transferred in the aftermath of WORLD WAR I. From the 1950s the majority Greek-speaking population began to demand *enosis*, union with mainland Greece. These demands were resisted by Britain, partly because of Cyprus' strategic role, partly because of the danger of outraging Turkey and pushing her into the arms of the Soviet Union. A terrorist campaign was conducted by EOKA, under the command of George Grivas, from 1955, with British military personnel and installations the principal targets. The British solution was to make any change conditional upon agreement from both Greece and Turkey, and to attempt to drive a wedge between the various interests on the island. Archbishop Makarios, the leader of both the Cypriot church and state, was offered the choice between partition of the island or complete independence. Makarios chose the latter, and in 1959 Cyprus became an independent republic, with the British retaining military bases there 'in perpetuity'. The revival of the idea for a 'Greater Greece' under the Colonels, the ruling military *junta* in Greece, prompted an attempted Greek invasion of Cyprus in 1974. Turkey intervened, and a *de facto* partition of the island has been in place since.

D

Dafydd ap Gruffudd (?–1283), youngest, ablest and most ambitious of the siblings of LLYWELYN AP GRUFFUDD, prince of Wales. His readiness to seek English aid against his brother was one of the latter's most intractable problems in the 1260s and 1270s. Although EDWARD I provided for Dafydd out of conquered territory in 1277, five years later English oppression pushed him into joining Llywelyn in a war of national liberation. After the prince's death in 1282, Dafydd became leader of the Welsh cause, but he was captured in June 1283, convicted of treason and hanged.

Dafydd ap Llywelyn (*c.* 1208–46), Prince of Gwynned. During his father LLYWELYN AP IORWERTH's lifetime, he was generally recognized as heir to GWYNEDD and to all his father's authority over native Wales. But after Llywelyn's death in 1240, HENRY III's government – posing as the guardian of Welsh tradition – set out to undermine the embryonic principality. By supporting all of Dafydd's rivals – other princes as well as his half-brother Gruffudd – it forced him to accept humiliating terms in 1241. However, by 1244 English high-handedness had provoked a Welsh rebellion, which Dafydd was leading when he died.

Dáil, the bicameral parliament of the IRISH FREE STATE and subsequently the Republic of Ireland, first established in DUBLIN in 1918 by the 73 Sinn Féin MPs elected to WESTMINSTER who refused to take their seats there. First sitting in the Mansion House, since 1924 (two years after the establishment of the Free State) the Dáil has sat in the former Leinster House, built 1745.

Dál Cais, a powerful family who originated within a sub-kingdom of MUNSTER on the southern Irish coast. In the 8th century, they conquered the eastern parts of Clare, and in the 10th, they supplanted the Eóganacht kings of Munster. This increase in their power was accomplished by King MATHGAMAIN and, after his murder in 976, by his brother BRIAN BORU. The family's period of domination within Munster came to an end in 1063 when it was supplanted by TURLOCH O BRIEN supported by DIARMIT MAC MÁEL NA MBÓ.

Dalriada, a kingdom created out of the migration of the SCOTS from Dalriada in north-east Ireland into modern Argyll around AD 500. Its establishment involved conflict with the PICTS, who were already settled in the area.

Knowledge of most of the kingdom's history is inevitably sparse because of the lack of sources. The connections with Ireland appear to have remained strong for a long time, being amended at the Convention of DRUMCEAT in 575, and not brought to an end until the battle of MAG RATH in 637. It was these connections that brought St COLUMBA to IONA in 563. There was a period of military expansion in the time of the king AIDAN MAC GABHRÁIN, but many setbacks in the reign of DOMNALL BRECC. What is known about the kingdom's organization comes from the 7th-century document *SENCHUS FER NALBAN*. Dalriada was united with the kingdom of the Picts in the time of KENNETH MAC ALPIN in the 9th century.

Dame Schools, common term for schools, particularly of the 18th century where a limited education was provided for the children of the poor (especially younger children before they became economically useful). They were run by an elderly woman who might teach reading, sewing and other useful arts. The growing realization among historians of the extent of READING and LITERACY suggests that these small informal schools had a greater social and economic impact than was previously believed.

Danby, 1st Earl of, *see* OSBORNE, THOMAS

Danegeld, the 12th-century name for the tax ('geld') created in the reign of ETHELRED II THE UNREADY to buy peace from the Danes. It was afterwards transformed into an all-purpose general tax and continued to be levied until 1162. *DOMESDAY BOOK* and other 11th- and 12th-century records reveal a well-established structure of local assessment based on HIDES and *CARUCATES*, as well as an equally well-established system of exemptions for subjects favoured by the king.

Danelaw, a term used in the 11th and 12th centuries to describe the area of the English kingdom where Danish legal customs prevailed. It referred above all to the east Midlands, East Anglia and Yorkshire, although the term is sometimes inclusive of all of eastern and northern England. In practice, the differences between Danish and English England were not that great, and not all the differences are to be explained by Danish settlement. *See also* CARUCATE; SOKEMAN; *WAPENTAKE*.

Dardanelles Campaign, Feb. 1915–Jan. 1916, an attempt by British, Dominion and French forces in WORLD WAR I to seize the Turkish Dardanelles strait (connecting the Sea of Marmara with the Aegean), with the aim of knocking Turkey out of the war and thereby relieving pressure on Russia. After an unsuccessful attempt to force the strait by an Anglo-French fleet in Feb. 1915, landings were made on the Gallipoli peninsula in April, which incurred heavy losses for no significant gains. Further landings in Aug. failed to break the stalemate, and after 250,000 casualties had been sustained, all forces were withdrawn between Dec. 1915 and Jan. 1916.

The débâcle led to FISHER's resignation as first sea lord, forced CHURCHILL from the Admiralty and contributed to the political crisis that compelled ASQUITH to form a coalition government in May 1915. The failure to open a successful 'second front' committed the Entente powers to the Western Front as the decisive theatre of conflict.

Darien Scheme, a plan for the foundation of a Scottish colony – New Caledonia – on the Central American isthmus of Darien (now Panama). The colony was to be managed by the Company of Scotland, founded in 1695 and trading with Africa and the Indies. The chief object was to annex a part of England's entrepôt trade, though it was also hoped that the colony might provide a market for Scottish goods.

The English WHIG opposition tried to make political capital of the threat to the English EAST INDIA and ROYAL AFRICAN companies. In the event, Spanish opposition, underfunding and mismanagement led to the scheme's failure. English sabotage was blamed, there were anti-English riots in EDINBURGH, and Anglo-Scottish relations were strained. However, the episode also served to convince many Scots that they could not hope to prosper unless they could gain access to England's protected trading sphere. This was to be a key feature of the UNION of 1707.

Darnley, Lord, *see* STEWART, HENRY

Darwin, Charles (1809–82), scientist. Born in Shrewsbury, the grandson of the botanist and radical Erasmus Darwin (1731–1802) and educated in Edinburgh and Cambridge, Darwin was the naturalist on the expedition of the *Beagle* to South America in 1831–6, discovering and describing many new species of plant and animal. In 1859 he published his great work *On the Origin of Species by Means of Natural Selection*, in which he posited the idea of evolution, a theory he had devised alongside Alfred Wallace. He argued for a natural rather than a divine origin of species, where in the struggle for existence creatures with advantageous mutations would survive, evolving into new species. Herbert Spencer coined the description 'survival of the fittest'. Darwin's theories caused enormous controversy, which increased when he published *The Descent of Man* (1871), in which he argued that man had also evolved from the higher primates. Modern ideas of evolution, often termed neo-Darwinism, were synthesized in the 1920s, with the application of Mendel's discoveries in genetics, originally published in 1865.

David, St (Dewi) (*fl.* 6th century). Little is known about the historical St David. Although the first life of him was written only in the late 11th or early 12th centuries, it is clear – from the combined evidence of church dedications in Wales and early sources in Ireland and Brittany – that, from at least the 7th century, David was the most popular Welsh saint. His fame accelerated in the 12th century during the failed attempt to elevate the church of ST DAVID'S into an archbishopric (*see* BARRI, GERALD DE), which was to provide the basis for his status as the patron saint of Wales.

David I (*c.*1082–1153), King of Scots (1124–53). Youngest son of MALCOLM III CANMORE and St MARGARET, he spent much of his early life at the Anglo-Norman court of HENRY I, where he was married to Maud, daughter of Earl Waltheof, and, in 1113, was granted the earldom of Huntingdon. After the deaths of all his older brothers, he came to the Scottish throne in 1124.

He welcomed Englishmen and Frenchmen to his court, adopting a style of kingship open to up-to-date European fashions – seen, for example, in his patronage of CISTERCIAN monasteries. He was the first Scottish king to issue his own coin, found chartered BURGHS (from BERWICK to Inverness) and establish new-style sheriffdoms. According to WILLIAM OF MALMESBURY, he promised tax rebates to those subjects who adopted a civilized life-style and, in consequence, was able to introduce a measure of refinement to a previously barbarous people. The 1130 rebellion of Angus of MORAY may reflect the hostility of traditionalists to so many newfangled and foreign ways.

The English succession dispute between his niece, the Empress MATILDA, and STEPHEN gave David the chance to press his wife's claim to the earldom of Northumberland. He led several invasions of England and, despite defeat at the battle of the STANDARD in 1138, was able to secure the recognition of his son Henry as earl of Northumberland in the treaty of Durham the following year. Since he also acquired control of Cumbria, this meant that, for once, a Scottish king was able to face the kings of England on almost equal terms. However, Henry died in 1152, and David's decision to designate his young grandson, the future MALCOLM IV, as his heir was to put much of his remarkable achievement at risk.

David II (1324–71), King of Scots (1329–71). As the only surviving legitimate son, he succeeded his father Robert BRUCE in 1329, by which time he was already married to EDWARD III's sister Joan. In 1331, he became the first Scottish king to be crowned and anointed (*see* SCONE), but three years later, he was sent to France for safe-keeping in face of the invasion by the DISINHERITED and Edward BALLIOL. He returned to Scotland in 1341, committed to the AULD ALLIANCE, and as a consequence invaded England in 1346.

He was captured at NEVILLE'S CROSS and, by the treaty of Berwick (1357), agreed to pay a ransom of 100,000 marks. During the negotiations, he considered making EDWARD III, with whom he shared a taste for chivalrous and amorous pursuits, his heir-presumptive – a reflection of the recurrent tension between David and his nephew Robert the Steward (later ROBERT II), which led to the abortive rising of 1363. About half of the ransom was, in fact, paid; raising the money meant developing direct and indirect taxation as well as a general overhaul of government and the extension of its authority in the highlands and islands. David still had no heir when he died unexpectedly while trying to divorce his second wife Margaret Logie in order to marry his latest mistress, Agnes Dunbar.

Davies, Clement (1884–1962), Liberal politician and party leader. A successful barrister, he was MP for Montgomeryshire (1929–62). In 1945, he accepted the party leadership after SINCLAIR's defeat in the general election. In 1951 he considered but declined CHURCHILL's offer of a Cabinet post, choosing to maintain the LIBERALS as an independent force. He saw the party through the nadir of its fortunes when reduced to only six MPs in the 1951 and 1955 elections, and witnessed the first signs of a Liberal revival when the leadership passed to GRIMOND in 1956.

D-Day, 6 June 1944, the Anglo-American cross-channel amphibious landings in occupied Normandy, France, at the start of Operation OVERLORD, the largest and most difficult amphibious operation ever mounted in warfare, and a crucial event of WORLD WAR II. Led by a major night drop by airborne forces on 5 June, 156,000 British, American and Canadian troops under MONTGOMERY, supported by 8,000 ships and craft and 13,000 aircraft, broke through the German defences of the Atlantic Wall, landing over beaches rather than at a major port. The

Allies compensated for lack of port provisions by heaving concrete cassions, 'Mulberries', across the channel and assembling them to provide artificial harbours. The Germans, anticipating that the invasion would come in the Pas de Calais where the Channel was at its narrowest, were caught unprepared with uncoordinated resistance to the Allied attack.

US losses were the heaviest at 6,603; overall Allied losses exceeded 10,000. D-Day was a military planning term to indicate the day that any battle starts. Only this one has become famous.

De Banco, *see* COMMON PLEAS

De Courcy, John (?–*c.*1219), a minor Som. landowner who in five years (1177–82) of audacious soldiering, CASTLE building and diplomacy – he married a daughter of the king of MAN – conquered the northern Irish kingdom of Uladh, carving out a virtually independent principality of ULSTER for himself. None of this was to the liking of King JOHN who, during 1201–5, employed Hugh de Lacey II (*see under* DE LACEY) to attack and overthrow him.

De Heretico Comburendo, *see* HERESY

De Lacey, Hugh (?–1186), English baron. He played a key role in the early stages of the English conquest of Ireland. HENRY II granted him the entire Irish kingdom of Meath in 1172, and subsequently appointed him governor of Ireland. However, de Lacey's marriage to Rory O'CONNOR's daughter gave rise to rumours that he was planning to make himself king of Ireland; Henry is said to have been relieved when he was killed by the Irish. His younger son, Hugh de Lacey II, was created the first earl of ULSTER in 1205.

De Montfort, Simon, *see* MONTFORT, SIMON DE

De Valera, Éamon (1882–1975), Irish politician and Prime Minister. Born in New York of Irish-Spanish parents, he was educated in Ireland and taught mathematics there. In 1913, he joined the Irish Volunteers and commanded a battalion in Dublin during the EASTER RISING of 1916. He was captured and condemned to death by the British, but his sentence was commuted and he was released in 1917. Elected a SINN FÉIN MP the same year, he remained leader of the movement until 1926.

Interned in Lincoln Gaol in 1918–19, he escaped to the US, where he raised funds for the ANGLO-IRISH WAR. In 1919, he was appointed president of Sinn Féin's provisional government, but then disputed the terms of the 1921 ANGLO-IRISH TREATY, lending his support to the anti-treaty forces in the IRISH CIVIL WAR. He split from the militant Sinn Féiners in 1926, founding his own party, FIANNA FÁIL, and re-entered the Dáil (parliament).

His victory in the election of 1932 began a 16-year period as Irish prime minister, during which he promoted Irish independence through a trade war with Britain and the framing of a new constitution, which established the republic of EIRE in 1937. He also maintained Irish neutrality during WORLD WAR II, causing much bitterness in Britain. He lost office in 1948, but later returned as prime minister (1951–4, 1957–9); he was president from 1959 until his retirement, aged 90, in 1973. An implacable nationalist, he remained a direct link with Ireland's struggle for independence.

DEA, *see* ECONOMIC AFFAIRS, DEPARTMENT OF

Dean (from Latin *Decanus*, which also gives the word 'deacon'), the clergyman presiding over the chapter (corporate body) in a COLLEGIATE CHURCH or CATHEDRAL (*but see also* PROVOST). The CHURCH OF ENGLAND has revived the medieval system of 'rural deans', senior parish clergy who perform minor supervisory duties within a grouping of parishes.

Dearth, *see* FAMINE

Death Penalty, *see* CAPITAL PUNISHMENT

Death Rate, the annual number of deaths calculated per 1,000 of the total POPULATION estimated to exist midway through a calendar year. This is technically known as the 'crude death rate'; 'standardized death rates', first devised for the UK on the basis of the 1901 population, take into account the age and sex structure, both of which have marked effects on crude rates.

Debasement, addition of base metals to the precious metal content of coins. The succession of debasements to the English COINAGE in the 16th century, notably in the 1540s, contributed to public distrust and helped fuel the price INFLATION of that era.

Debating Societies The first society established for the specific purpose of encouraging formal debate appears to have been the Robin Hood Society, founded in a tavern of that name in 1742. It spawned several imitators, and in the early 1780s entrepreneurs launched numerous such clubs as commercial ventures, including a Ladies' Debating Society. Radical CORRESPONDING SOCIETIES of the 1790s drew on the debating society tradition.

Debtors' Prisons, *see* IMPRISONMENT FOR DEBT

Deceangli, the pre-Roman British tribe that settled in northern GWYNEDD and northern Clwyd. The Romans launched campaigns against them as early as AD 48, but they and their neighbours were not fully subjugated until the governorship of JULIUS FRONTINUS in 73, 74–7. Unlike many tribal territories, the region was not made into a *CIVITAS*, the Roman presence remaining confined to forts.

Decimalization, conversion of the British currency in 1971, from a system where the £ was divided into 20 shillings (s) and 240 pennies (d) to one where it was divided into 100 new pence (p). *See also* COINAGE.

Decimation Tax, imposed in 1655 on wealthy former ROYALISTS to maintain new MILITIAS. It was very unpopular, and the rejection of a Bill for its extension in 1657 marked the end of the rule by the MAJOR-GENERALS and the disappearance of militias.

Declaration of Rights, document presented by the CONVENTION PARLIAMENT to William of Orange (the future WILLIAM III) and MARY II together with the offer of the crown on 13 February 1689. The Declaration stated that Parliaments must be held frequently; that elections must be free; that freedom of speech, and debates and proceedings in PARLIAMENT should not be questioned other than in Parliament; and that parliamentary consent was necessary to suspend statutes, levy taxation and maintain a peacetime STANDING ARMY. It condemned as illegal various acts of CHARLES II and JAMES II: the use of the royal DISPENSING POWER, the ECCLESIASTICAL COMMISSION, the prosecution of petitioners and the imposition of cruel and unusual punishments.

Declarations of Indulgence CHARLES II first attempted to introduce religious toleration through the exercise of his prerogative SUSPENDING AND DISPENSING POWERS in 1662, but quickly backed down in the face of opposition. Several attempts by, for example, George Villiers, 5th Duke of Buckingham, and Shaftesbury (*see* COOPER, ANTHONY ASHLEY) to secure toleration acts failed during the next decade. Charles tried again in 1672, a year when Parliament did not meet. The Declaration of 1672 suspended the penal laws against DISSENTERS and Catholic RECUSANTS. It allowed Protestant Dissenters to worship in licensed buildings; Catholics, in their homes. Some 1,500 Dissenting ministers took out licences. When Parliament was summoned in 1673 in the context of the Third DUTCH WAR, the Declaration was withdrawn as a *quid pro quo* for MPs' support of the war effort.

JAMES II's 1687 Declaration was an element in the radicalization of his religious policies. It differed from Charles's in promising to protect, not the Church of England as an institution, but its members' religious practices and possessions, and in allowing Catholics to worship in public. This renewed bid for the support of Protestant Dissenters had only a limited effect in sustaining their backing for the king's measures; and the king's command that the clergy of the state church read his Declaration from their pulpits spurred the petition of the Seven Bishops (*see* SEVEN BISHOPS CASE).

Declarations of Indulgence, Scottish Lauderdale's (*see* MAITLAND, JOHN) attempts to reconcile Scottish DISSENTERS had entailed the issuing of indulgences to ministers of religion who agreed to conform in behaviour, and to refrain from holding services outside their own PARISHES. The policy helped to divide moderates from extremists. In Feb. 1686, JAMES VII AND II announced that Catholics and QUAKERS engaging in private worship would thenceforth be protected from prosecution by his dispensing power (*see under* SUSPENDING). This was extended into a general toleration of worship in the summer of 1687. *See also* COVENANT.

Declaratory Act 1720, an Act of the British Parliament which attempted to resolve controversies about the constitutional relationship between Great Britain and Ireland that had flared up intermittently since the GLORIOUS REVOLUTION (1688). Matters came to a head in 1719 when the Irish House of Lords claimed, in relation to a property dispute (*ANNESLEY V. SHERLOCK*), to be the final court of appeal in Irish cases. The Act declared that the Irish House of Lords had no appellate jurisdiction, and that the kingdom of Ireland was subordinate to, and dependent upon, the imperial crown of Great Britain. The king and British PARLIAMENT therefore had full power and authority to make statutes binding on Ireland – although in practice Irish domestic legislation continued to issue from the Irish PARLIAMENT. The Act was repealed in 1782, when the Irish Parliament was given LEGISLATIVE INDEPENDENCE.

Declaratory Act 1766 An Act brought forward by the Rockingham (*see* WENTWORTH, CHARLES) ministry when they repealed the STAMP ACT. It affirmed the right of PARLIAMENT to enact laws relating to the American colonies; the principled case of American critics against the Stamp Act was therefore not conceded. PITT THE ELDER tried unsuccessfully to insert a clause distinguishing fiscal from other legislation, as requiring consent. The issue was to remain a bone of contention between his followers and the Rockinghamites, but in America the Act excited relatively little notice.

Decolonization This has been one of the major forces in 20th-century international politics. Since the BRITISH EMPIRE was the largest of the world's empires, decolonization by Britain has affected almost every part of the globe. The greatest extent of empire, in 1919, was quickly followed by the loosening of bonds with the white DOMINIONS. The Statute of Westminster of 1931 gave formal legislative autonomy to CANADA, NEWFOUNDLAND, SOUTH AFRICA, AUSTRALIA and NEW ZEALAND as part of the British COMMONWEALTH. The granting of self-government to the largest of the non-white colonies, INDIA, proved more protracted (*see* INDIAN INDEPENDENCE). Britain also loosened its formal control in the Middle East with the ANGLO-EGYPTIAN TREATY of 1936 (she retained control of the SUEZ CANAL) and by granting independence to Iraq in 1932. The independence of PALESTINE, however, was increasingly complicated by the antagonism between the indigenous Arab population and a growing tide of Jewish settlers (*see* BALFOUR DECLARATION).

On the eve of WORLD WAR II the defence of the Empire was still central to Britain's strategic and diplomatic position. But the rapid overrunning of the European colonies in the Far East by Japan and the economic cost of the war forced Britain to adjust to the dismantling of a large part of her pre-war Empire. India and PAKISTAN became independent in 1947, BURMA and CEYLON in 1948, while the creation of the state of Israel in 1948 ended the Palestine MANDATE. Although Britain fought protracted campaigns against the MAU MAU in KENYA and against Communist subversion in MALAYA during the 1950s, it was clear that Britain had no wish to emulate France in full-scale wars to resist decolonization. The SUEZ CRISIS of 1956 also faced Britain with the realities of her weak post-war position, increasing the pace of decolonization. The first of the African colonies, GOLD COAST, became independent as Ghana in 1957, followed by NIGERIA in 1960. MACMILLAN'S 'WIND OF CHANGE' SPEECH in 1960 foreshadowed the rapid granting of independence to almost all of Britain's remaining colonies over the next 20 years. Only in exceptional circumstances, such as the intransigence of the white settler regime in Southern RHODESIA, and those colonies and dependencies where the indigenous population wished to remain attached to Britain, as in GIBRALTAR and the FALKLAND ISLANDS, was the process delayed or held back.

CHRONOLOGY

1900 AUSTRALIA becomes a Dominion.

1907 NEW ZEALAND becomes a Dominion.

1910 Union of SOUTH AFRICA formed (inc. SWAZILAND) and becomes a Dominion.

1922 EGYPT becomes independent; IRISH FREE STATE becomes a Dominion.

1932 Iraq becomes independent.

1933 NEWFOUNDLAND reverts to colonial status.

1937 Irish Free State becomes a republic.

1947 INDIA and PAKISTAN become independent.

1948 CEYLON (now Sri Lanka) and PALESTINE become independent; Newfoundland federates with CANADA; BURMA (now Myanmar) becomes independent from India.

1957 The GOLD COAST (now Ghana) and MALAYA become independent.

1960 CYPRUS and NIGERIA become independent.
1961 Sierra Leone and TANGANYIKA (now Tanzania) become independent.
1962 JAMAICA, TRINIDAD & TOBAGO and UGANDA become independent.
1963 KENYA and Northern RHODESIA (now Zambia) become independent.
1964 MALTA and NYASALAND (now Malawi) becomes independent.
1965 The GAMBIA and SINGAPORE become independent; Southern RHODESIA declares UDI.
1966 BARBADOS, BASUTOLAND (now Lesotho), BECHUANALAND (now Botswana) and BRITISH GUIANA (now Guyana) become independent.
1967 ADEN (as South Yemen) becomes independent.
1968 MAURITIUS and SWAZILAND become independent.
1970 FIJI becomes independent.
1971 Bangladesh becomes independent from Pakistan.
1973 The BAHAMAS become independent.
1974 GRENADA becomes independent.
1976 SEYCHELLES becomes independent.
1978 DOMINICA and The SOLOMON ISLANDS become independent.
1979 ST LUCIA, ST VINCENT & GRENADINES and Southern RHODESIA (now Zimbabwe) become independent.
1981 ANTIGUA, BRITISH HONDURAS (now Belize) and VANUATU become independent.
1983 ST KITTS & NEVIS become independent.

Decorated, name given to architectural style of the period *c.* 1280–1350. It was characterized by the ogee arch, a double curve, and by flowing and inventive window tracery and lighter vaulting, especially in churches; EXETER cathedral is a prime, early example of the style. It was more lavish and inventive than any contemporary European style.

Defence of the Realm Act 1914 (DORA) Passed in August 1914 and subsequently extended, this WORLD WAR I measure gave the government emergency powers to requisition property, apply CENSORSHIP, and control labour. It marked a significant erosion of traditional liberties to meet the strains of modern warfare. In 1920 it was succeeded by the Emergency Powers Act, which rendered DORA obsolete by allowing the sovereign to declare an emergency by proclamation.

Defenders, an Irish popular protest movement first taking shape in the 1780s, with its roots in ULSTER when Catholics banded together to defend themselves against PROTESTANTS. Influenced by the ideals of the French Revolution, early Defenderism, unlike WHITEBOYism, took on an explicitly political dimension. Defender organization may have been influenced by FREEMASONRY: members were organized into lodges run by committees, and developed secret signs, symbols and rituals. The movement faded away with the disintegration of the UNITED IRISHMEN after the IRISH REBELLION of 1798.

Defoe, Daniel (*c.* 1660–1731), writer. Son of a London butcher, he was educated at a DISSENTING academy at Newington Green. He took part in Monmouth's (*see* SCOTT, JAMES) rebellion in 1685, but escaped after SEDGEMOOR. By that time established as a merchant, he went bankrupt in 1692, and took to pamphleteering. He was a very prolific writer – though he probably did not write all that has been attributed to him. His satirical *Shortest Way with Dissenters* (1702) led to his imprisonment for libel. HARLEY helped to secure his release in 1703, subsequently employing him to gather political intelligence; Defoe was his chief agent in Scotland during the UNION crisis.

From 1704 to 1713, Defoe edited the *Review of the Affairs of France*, in the TORY interest, sometimes going against his own beliefs in the process. When the WHIGS came to power in 1714, they demanded as the price for not prosecuting Defoe that he continue to write for the Tory press but 'soften' it to help the Whig cause. In this capacity, Defoe was employed on the Tory *News Letter* from 1715 and the JACOBITE *Mist's Journal* from 1717. He also started writing novels, publishing *The Life and Surprising Adventures of Robinson Crusoe* in 1719 – a lasting success, and one of the few 18th-century novels to appear also in CHAPBOOK form. Other well-known works include *Moll Flanders* (1722), *Journal of the Plague Year* (1723) and *Tour of the Whole Island of Great Britain* (1724–7).

Degsastan, Battle of, exact location unknown, 603. A victory for King Ethelfrith (?–616) of Northumbria over the Scots king

AIDAN MAC GABHRÁIN of DALRIADA. It saw the end, until the early 10th century, of the Scots' interest in expanding into the Lowlands, and laid the basis for the increase in the power of the kings of NORTHUMBRIA.

Deheubarth, *see* DYFED

Deiniol, St (*fl.* 6th century), one of the more important of the early Welsh saints, venerated in both north Wales and Ireland, of whom little is known. The centre of his cult was at Bangor and at BANGOR-ON-DEE.

Deira, Kingdom of, along with BERNICIA, one of the two main kingdoms established in the North by the ANGLES, possibly in the second half of the 5th century. Its southern and northern frontiers were (roughly) the Humber and the Tees. Ethelfrith of Bernicia (593–616) was the first to combine the two kingdoms into a single kingdom of the NORTHUMBRIANS, but there were further periods of separation during the 7th century.

Deism, belief in God (from Latin, '*deus*', God) but not in revealed religion. The term began to be used in Britain in the early 17th century. It was applied in connection with various individuals, from Lord Herbert of Chirbury to John WILKES, sometimes by others, sometimes by themselves, but was never given formal definition by any organized group. Deists commonly held that underpinning diverse systems of belief were certain common principles, which could be established by empirical study and the use of reason. They opposed priestly hierarchies as inimical to rational religion, and favoured religious toleration.

Delaware, one of the original Thirteen Colonies which broke with Britain in 1776 to form the USA. Named after the river, Delaware was originally a territorial appendage of Pennsylvania, founded in 1682. It had a half-way status, being mentioned in Pennsylvania's original grant but not in the charter, until it acquired its own legislature in 1704 and executive in 1710.

Demesne, the land within a medieval MANOR that the lord did not lease to tenants but reserved for his own use. In favourable market conditions – e.g. in the 13th century – the demesne could be run for profit; this is sometimes known as demesne farming. 'Royal demesne' refers to the lands of the medieval English CROWN.

Demetae, the pre-Roman British tribe that occupied DYFED. It is not clear at which stage during the campaigns of AD 50–80 they were finally subjugated to Roman power. The tribe's territory was subsequently formed into a *CIVITAS* with its capital at Carmarthen.

Demise In legal terminology from the 12th century onwards, 'to demise' is to lease. Not to be confused with 'to devise' – i.e. to bequeath by will (*see* WILLS).

Democratic Unionist Party (DUP), Northern Irish political party formed in 1971 and led by Ian PAISLEY. Representing the more militant and fundamentalist wing of LOYALIST opinion, it effectively broke the unity of the old ULSTER UNIONIST PARTY. Usually electing at least three MPs to PARLIAMENT, it has increasingly co-operated with the official Unionist Party in opposing the Anglo-Irish agreement of 1985 and preserving the status of PROTESTANTS in Northern Ireland.

Whilst Paisley opposed the Good Friday Agreement in 1998 (*see* ULSTER), the DUP supported the executive and won 20 seats at the election, whilst claiming that it did not recognize its Sinn Féin colleagues.

Demographic Transition, change from a situation in which FERTILITY and MORTALITY are both high to one where both are low, often associated with socio-economic change. The classical theory, first propounded in 1929, assumed that a fall in mortality caused by economic improvement would trigger a fall in fertility, and envisaged the changes seen in 19th-century Europe being emulated in developing countries. This has been extensively revised in recent years. Research in HISTORICAL DEMOGRAPHY has shown that levels of fertility and mortality in pre-19th century England (and to a lesser extent Scotland) were both low in comparison with other European nations and with modern developing societies, while Britain was comparatively late in undergoing its transition. Marked decline in both fertility and mortality did not come until the 1870s and 1880s, when Britain was already very economically advanced. Recent theories have stressed the importance of changes in fertility resulting from shifts in income levels with greater use of and more reliable contraceptive aids (*see* BIRTH CONTROL). Since the inter-war years, Britain has entered a post-transitional phase of low or negative POPULATION growth.

Deodand, from the Latin *Deo dandum* ('to be given to God'), the philanthropic medieval legal custom whereby anything – animate or inanimate (e.g. a horse or a mill-wheel) – that had caused the death of a person was forfeited to the court and sold for the benefit of the poor. Deodand was abolished in 1846.

Depression, Agricultural, 1873–1914. The threat to British farming posed by the repeal of the CORN LAWS became real in the 1880s, when the RAILWAY and the STEAMSHIP had opened up the American prairies to allow the importation of cheap grain into Britain. The development of refrigerated holds also made livestock farmers vulnerable, particularly to NEW ZEALAND lamb and Argentinian beef; by 1895, one-third of the meat consumed in Britain was imported.

Arable farmers, especially in Lincs. and East Anglia, abandoned HIGH FARMING and sought to reduce their costs by cutting labour and production. By 1914, domestic production accounted for just 20 per cent of the cereals required by the British market. Livestock farmers fared much better since demand for fresh meat remained buoyant. Dairy farmers, benefiting from the fall in cereal prices and the increased purchasing power of industrial workers, also found a ready market for their products. The development of market gardening close to large cities represented another profitable response to changed conditions, but there was no reversion to the 'golden age of British AGRICULTURE'.

Depression, Great, a contested concept applied to the years 1873–96, an age of falling prices, reduced profits, rising unemployment, decelerating growth and increasing foreign competition. Closer inspection indicates a need for revision. Industrial output grew during these years, though Britain's share of world markets began to decline. Although wages did not rise, the fall in prices meant that these were prosperous years for the average worker in employment, who also benefited from cheap food imports. The 'great depression' is now generally considered more an expression of contemporary concern about the growing challenge to Britain's industrial supremacy than an accurate summary of the nation's economic health.

Depression, The The 'slump' of the 1920s and 1930s was the most severe and protracted economic downturn experienced by the British ECONOMY since the mid-19th century. It caused mass unemployment on an unprecedented scale, widespread suffering and deprivation. It was responsible for the fall of the second LABOUR government of 1929–31 and for tarnishing the reputation of the NATIONAL GOVERNMENT that succeeded it. The Depression bequeathed a legacy of concern about the social and political consequences of mass unemployment, which had a decisive effect on the agenda of British politics for more than a generation after WORLD WAR II.

Economic depression arose from the dislocation of the world economy following WORLD WAR I and the reduction in markets for the staple industries of COAL, IRON AND STEEL, textiles and SHIPBUILDING, which had been the foundation of Britain's industrial and commercial prosperity before 1914. Following a brief post-war boom, these major industries were affected by a slump that resulted in unemployment rising to almost 2 million in the winter of 1921–2.

Although there was some recovery in the mid-1920s, unemployment was not to fall to under 1 million – i.e. one in ten of the working population – until 1940. During the grimmest phase, following the Wall Street crash of 1929, it rose to a peak of almost 3 million during the winter of 1932–3. The worst affected areas were the centres of traditional staple industries: Scotland, the North-east, Lancs. and south Wales, some of which suffered semi-permanent job loss reaching as high as 80 per cent of the workforce.

The governments of the inter-war years grappled ineffectively with the effects of the Depression. In the 1920s, hopes were pinned on a return to 'normalcy', such as the reversion to the GOLD STANDARD in 1925. Economic policies were dominated by a belief in balanced budgets and sound finance; alternative views, such as those of KEYNES, were still regarded as unorthodox. These policies produced the 1931 crisis of the Labour government, when its commitments to unemployment benefits could not be reconciled with the demands for a reduction in government spending. The CONSERVATIVE-dominated

National Governments after 1931 pursued a predictably orthodox path, reducing government expenditure (including cuts in state salaries and unemployment benefit), introducing the MEANS TEST, and giving only limited assistance to particularly depressed areas through the SPECIAL AREAS ACT.

The apparent failure of the existing political system stimulated extremist movements of the left and right. The COMMUNIST PARTY increased its membership and influence, though failing to achieve a political breakthrough because of TUC and Labour Party opposition. Attempts were also made to mobilize the unemployed through the Communist-led NATIONAL UNEMPLOYED WORKERS' MOVEMENT, which mounted a series of hunger marches. On the right, Oswald MOSLEY's British Union of FASCISTS also attempted unsuccessfully to capitalize on dissatisfaction with the status quo.

Despite their limitations, the National Governments stabilized Britain during the troubled 1930s, securing an overwhelming majority in the 1931 election and an even larger one four years later. Unemployment began to fall after 1935, and recovery was evident in the new consumer-based industries of the Midlands and South and in a house-building boom which was aided by a cheap money policy (low interest rates). Rearmament in the late 1930s added to the recovery of employment and output in shipbuilding and producer goods sectors. The continuing plight of the depressed areas, epitomized in the JARROW CRUSADE of 1936, damaged the government's reputation and left a legacy of bitterness and waste. By the outbreak of World War II, there was a growing consensus that planning and Keynesian economics could provide an alternative system of economic management. The demands of the war led increasingly to calls for 'full employment', a commitment confirmed by the BEVERIDGE REPORT and by the coalition government. Labour owed its victory in 1945 in no small part to the memory of the Depression, and this ensured that full employment remained a commitment of governments for much of the post-war era.

CHRONOLOGY

1922 Ending of post-war boom; unemployment reaches 2 million.

1925 Britain returns to GOLD STANDARD, leading to overvaluation of currency and restriction of exports.

1926 Crisis in COAL INDUSTRY, partly caused by loss of export markets, produces GENERAL STRIKE.

1929 Wall Street crash in US ends period of partial recovery and introduces most severe phase of Depression.

1930 LABOUR government fails to adopt MOSLEY's proposals for KEYNESian-style reflation of economy.

1931 MAY COMMITTEE calls for reduction in government expenditure to meet financial crisis (July). Labour government resigns following failure to agree package of cuts (24 Aug.). Formation of NATIONAL GOVERNMENT led by former Labour premier MACDONALD. Government removes Britain from gold standard (21 Sept.), undertakes emergency package of cuts and introduces MEANS TEST; wins overwhelming majority at general election (27 Oct.), reducing Labour Party to 52 seats.

1932 Mosley founds Britain Union of FASCISTS. NATIONAL UNEMPLOYED WORKERS' MOVEMENT mounts series of demonstrations and marches, leading to serious disorder in LONDON, BELFAST and Birkenhead.

1933 Unemployment reaches almost 3 million: one in four of working population.

1934 SPECIAL AREAS ACT offers help worth £2 million to most depressed areas.

1935 Government attempts to rationalize unemployment relief under UNEMPLOYMENT ASSISTANCE BOARD leads to widespread protests and standstill of new regulations.

1936 Unemployment falls below 2 million for the first time since 1930. JARROW CRUSADE to London highlights continuing problem of depressed areas. Keynes' *General Theory of Employment, Interest and Money* provides first full articulation of his economic theories.

1939 Rearmament, introduction of CONSCRIPTION (March) and outbreak of WORLD WAR II (Sept.) begin transformation of employment situation.

1940 Unemployment falls below 1 million for the first time since 1921.

1942 BEVERIDGE REPORT assumes conditions of 'full employment' in post-war Britain.

Derby, one of the five Danish *BURHS* of the Midlands, and a regional fulling and malting centre in the later Middle Ages, the town came to particular prominence with industrialization. John and Thomas Lombe's first silk mill was built there in 1717. Derby grew especially from 1867 when it became a major RAILWAY station, and with the establishment of the principal railway carriage works of the London and Midland Railway, while in 1907 Rolls-Royce opened their first motor-car works. It has been the SEE of an Anglican BISHOP since 1927. The town has been considerably affected by the decay of some of its industries since the 1960s, especially with the collapse and rescue of Rolls-Royce and the shrinking of the railway works. *See also* MOTOR INDUSTRY.

Derby, The, leading English horse race, that was run on the Epsom (Surrey) course on the last Wednesday in May or the first Wednesday in June (now it is run on a Saturday). Originated in 1780 by the 12th Earl of Derby, it carries a substantial stake and is competed for by the best three-year-olds. It also remains a principal event in the English social calendar.

Derby, 23rd Earl of *see* STANLEY, EDWARD

Derby House Committee, the parliamentary committee (named after its Westminster meeting place) that replaced the COMMITTEE OF BOTH KINGDOMS in Jan. 1648 as a *de facto* executive body. It was dominated by Denzil Holles's PRESBYTERIAN circle, which the army swept from power in PRIDE'S PURGE in Nov. 1648.

Dermot mac Murrough (Diarmait mac Murchada) (*c.*1107–71), King of Uí Chennselaig and Leinster. In 1152, he abducted Devorgilla, wife of Tiernan O Ruairc, together with her dowry, and so incurred the long and bitter enmity that notoriously contributed to the overwhelming defeat he suffered in 1166 when all his enemies took advantage of the fall of MUIRCHERTACH O MAC LOCHLAINN (Dermot's longstanding ally) to wreak their vengeance. Driven out of Ireland, he sought English help, even breaching Irish custom by offering Strongbow (*see* Richard de CLARE) the succession to LEINSTER together with the hand of his daughter Aoife. With the help of mercenaries recruited in South Wales, he recovered Uí Chennselaig in 1167. As more troops came, so his ambitions increased until, in 1170, Strongbow himself arrived with a force large enough for Dermot to contemplate overthrowing Rory O'CONNOR and making himself high-king. But these developments persuaded HENRY II that it was time to invade Ireland himself.

These events at the end of his reign (which had begun in 1132) transformed Dermot into the VORTIGERN of Irish history, responsible, in national tradition, for 'the beginning of the woes of Ireland'. Catholic defenders sometimes mitigate his 'guilt' by emphasizing his association with Church reformers, especially with LORCAN O TUATHAIL, but this was probably an aspect of a life-long struggle to control DUBLIN.

Derry, *see* LONDONDERRY

Desmond, 14th Earl of, *see* FITZGERALD, GERALD

Destroyer, the small fast torpedo boat evolved in the last quarter of the 19th century as a menace to the BATTLESHIP. In the 1890s the British produced a larger and faster version, the 'torpedo boat destroyer', which superseded the smaller type. During both world wars destroyers proved useful escorts against submarine and air attack, and it is for ships specializing in the latter role that the name is still used.

Dettingen, Battle of, June 1743, fought between French and British forces near Hanau, in the War of the AUSTRIAN SUCCESSION. When Prussia withdrew from the war in 1742, the French position in Bavaria became untenable and they retreated westwards with heavy losses. The British forces hoped to separate the French from the Bavarians, but found themselves trapped at Dettingen. The French left a secure position to attack what they thought to be a smaller force, and were badly beaten. GEORGE II led an infantry counter-attack, but on the advice of the army's commander, Lord Stair, did not pursue the victory. Stair resigned, the French withdrew to Alsace, and peace negotiations were opened. This was the last occasion on which a reigning British monarch fought in battle.

Devaluation, reduction in the official value of a country's currency against gold, the US dollar or some other standard. Under the regime of fixed exchange rates between major currencies, the defence of the pound STERLING at a given exchange rate regularly became a symbol of political competence for the government of the day, requiring the BANK OF ENGLAND to sell its gold and dollar reserves and the TREASURY to keep interest rates high in order to counter speculative selling in the foreign exchange markets.

Devaluations have generally been welcomed by industry since they make imports more expensive and exports cheaper in sterling terms. But they have done severe political damage to the government involved. Under the BRETTON WOODS system LABOUR governments were forced by the markets to devalue the pound from $4.03 to $2.80 in 1949 and from $2.80 to $2.40 in 1967.

After 1972 the pound was allowed more or less to find its own level in the foreign exchange markets, with its value moving at times wildly against other currencies. More recently, attempts have been made to stabilize exchange rates with the EC (*see* EUROPEAN UNION) though this is proving difficult because of different rates of growth and economic change between member nations. In May 1998 a meeting of EU heads of state agreed that 11 of the 15 EU member states would take part in the single European currency from 1 January 1999 when the euro became the legal currency and the European Central Bank took responsibility for formulating the monetary policy of the EU area. Britain was not one of those 11, and the government has not yet committed to a date when membership of the single currency will be in the economic interests of the UK. *See also* EUROPEAN MONETARY SYSTEM.

Devereux, Robert (19th [2nd Devereux] Earl of Essex) (1566–1601), soldier and courtier. At the age of nine he inherited the earldom (and heavy debts); later, he became ward to William CECIL, while his mother married Robert DUDLEY, Earl of Leicester. The latter brought Essex to court and, in 1586, took him on campaign to the Netherlands. Here, the death of his cousin Philip SIDNEY left Essex under the delusion that he should carry on Sidney's legacy of PURITAN chivalric virtue (he did marry Sidney's widow).

Essex's good looks and charm, which considerably outranked his talents, fascinated ELIZABETH I, particularly from 1587. Throughout the 1590s, he exploited her affection to act as a loose cannon in politics, seeking glory and power to the exclusion of all rivals, including such similar glamour boys as Walter RALEIGH as well as the very different Robert CECIL. His military endeavours were showy, expensive and progressively more unsuccessful: the siege of Rouen (1591), the sack of Cadiz (1596), the abortive Azores attack on the Spanish treasure fleet (1597) and, most disastrously, the expedition to Ireland as lord lieutenant (1599–1600). Essex squandered the best-equipped English army yet sent to Ireland, then rushed back to court in Sept. 1600 to explain his initiative in signing a truce with the rebel Tyrone (*see* O'NEILL, HUGH). An embarrassing confrontation with Elizabeth at NONSUCH Palace led to house arrest. Faced with financial ruin, convinced that his enemies were intent on destroying him, and surrounded by young aristocratic would-be heroes, Essex staged a pathetic attempt at a *coup d'état* in Feb. 1601. After a trial, he was executed; his fellow-conspirator Thomas Wriothesley, 5th Earl of Southampton, had his sentence commuted.

Devise, *see* WILLS

Devolution, term used to describe schemes for the establishment of local assemblies in the constituent nations of the United Kingdom. Northern Ireland had devolved rule via the STORMONT parliament from 1921 until its suspension in 1972. The word became current in the 1970s to describe the demand for Scotland and Wales to be given greater autonomy following successes in parliamentary elections for PLAID CYMRU and the SCOTTISH NATIONAL PARTY and a growing tide of support for greater independence. The Kilbrandon Report in 1973 recommended the setting up of elected assemblies in Wales and Scotland and formed the basis of referendums held on 2 March 1979. However, in Scotland 33 per cent of the electorate voted in favour of a Scottish assembly – short of the 40 per cent threshold required by the Referendum Act – and in Wales the pro-devolution vote was only 12 per cent. Although the devolution issue was temporarily laid to rest, it revived in the late 1980s under the impact of renewed nationalist successes.

As one of its first acts in government in 1997, the LABOUR party held a referendum on devolution to an elected assembly in

Scotland and Wales. 74.3 per cent of Scots who voted endorsed government proposals, as did 50.3 per cent for Wales. The parliament and executive (Scotland) and assembly (Wales) administer the budgets previously in the charge of the Secretary of State for Scotland (nearly £16 billion 1998–9) and for Wales (some £7 billion). In the first election to the devolved assemblies held in May 1999, Labour was the largest party in Scotland with 50 Members of the Scottish Parliament (MSPs) but without a majority; the SCOTTISH NATIONALIST PARTY (SNP) returned 35 MSPs; the Liberal Democrats 17; Conservatives 18; others 1, so the Labour First Minister, Donald Dewar, has been working in conjunction with the Liberal Democrats. In Wales, Labour failed to achieve an overall majority (28 seats; PLAID CYMRU 17; Conservatives 9; Liberal Democrats 6) and runs the Assembly as a minority administration. Both Wales and Scotland continue to return the same number of MPs to Westminster as previously, which raises interesting issues about the governance of England. NORTHERN IRELAND will have a devolved Assembly when cross-community agreements are finally in place. Limited central government powers over LONDON devolved to the elected Greater London Assembly (GLA) led by a mayor, after the elections of May 2000.

Devonshire, 8th Duke of, *see* CAVENDISH, SPENCER

Dewar, Donald (1937–), politician. Son of a dermatologist, educated at Glasgow University where he was President of the Union, Dewar worked as a solicitor before being elected Labour MP for Aberdeen South in 1964 aged 29. His first job was as Anthony Crosland's PPS (1967–9). He lost his Aberdeen seat in 1970 and was out of the Commons for eight years until he took Garscadden, Glasgow, for Labour at a by-election in 1978. Holding a brief for Scotland during Labour's years in opposition before becoming shadow spokesman for Social Security (1992–7), Dewar was appointed Secretary of State for Scotland following the labour victory in May 1997, and when the Scotland Act 1998 established a Scottish parliament, was elected an MSP in the May 1999 elections. With Labour's coalition partners the Liberal Democrats providing his deputy, Dewar was appointed First Minister of the Scottish Executive.

Diarmit Mac Máel na-mBó (?–1072). King of the Uí Néill Chennselaig and Leinster (1046–66). Diarmit Mac Máel na mBó was a member of the Uí Chennselaig, one of the dynasties of LEINSTER. In a career that began in the 1030s, he seized the kingdom of Leinster by force in 1046, took over the VIKING kingdom of DUBLIN in 1052 and then assisted decisively in the efforts of his protégé TURLOCH O BRIEN to become king of MUNSTER. He also gave succour and military assistance to the sons of the English king HAROLD II after 1066. Until his death in battle, he was undoubtedly the strongest king in Ireland.

Diceto, Ralph (*c.*1125–*c.*1200), historian. His name suggests that he came from Diss in Norfolk. As dean of St Paul's, London, he was well connected and well informed about English affairs. His erudite *Epitome of Chronicles* covers the period from the Creation to 1148, his *Images of History* from 1148 to 1200.

Dictum of Kenilworth, *see* KENILWORTH, DICTUM OF

Diego Garcia, *see* BRITISH INDIAN OCEAN TERRITORIES

Dieppe Raid, northern France, 19 Aug. 1942. 'Operation Jubilee' was a WORLD WAR II Anglo-Canadian amphibious raid to capture the port of Dieppe temporarily, organized by MOUNTBATTEN from a plan initially devised by MONTGOMERY. Designed to raise morale and test concepts of amphibious warfare, the attack by 6,000 troops was a disaster, over half the force (chiefly Canadians) being lost. It was concluded that the D-DAY landings must be made over beaches and would require artificial prefabricated harbours, rather than capturing one from the sea.

Dig for Victory, slogan adopted for British WORLD WAR II campaign to increase domestic food production by the cultivation of all spare land, including parks, sports grounds and allotments.

Diggers, a group that, from April 1649 and under Gerrard Winstanley's leadership, set up communal farming communities on former crown and common land, especially at St George's Hill, Surrey. By spring 1650, local opposition combined with army hostility destroyed them, though the movement had created about ten communities, some as far away as the Midlands. It was one of the most radical initiatives of social experimentation amid the new possibilities opened up by the INTERREGNUM. *See also* RANTERS.

Dillon, John (1851–1927), Irish nationalist leader. Born in Dublin, the son of a noted nationalist, he was a qualified surgeon but more interested in politics. He was thrice imprisoned for his support of the IRISH LAND LEAGUE, but became leader of the anti-PARNELL group after the divorce case in which Parnell was involved. Dillon was succeeded by John Redmond (1856–1918) in 1900, but returned, briefly, to lead the parliamentary party on Redmond's death in March 1918. His principal concern was to defend HOME RULE against PROTESTANT and nationalist extremism. However, by this time SINN FÉIN had become a significant political force, and he himself was defeated in East Mayo by the imprisoned DE VALERA in Dec. 1918.

Dilution, WORLD WAR I term for the use of unapprenticed labour, including women, to do the skilled work previously reserved to craftsmen in order to increase production, especially of munitions. By the 'Treasury Agreement' of 1915, the unions sanctioned the suspension of the normal 'trade practices' for the duration of the war in return for a tax on excess profits. The terms were enshrined in the July 1915 Munitions of War Act, subsequently amended in 1916. The operation of dilution continued to provoke unrest, however, especially on the Clyde in 1917, and disputes continued into 1918–19, the resultant STRIKES and agitation earning the region the epithet 'Red Clydeside'.

Diocese Originally a late-Roman administrative unit, the term was borrowed by the Church for the area governed by a bishop, usually taking its name from the city where his throne (*cathedra*) is situated. *See also* SEE.

Diplock Courts, non-jury courts introduced in Northern Ireland to deal with terrorist offences from 1972. Following the imposition of DIRECT RULE from Westminster in Northern Ireland in 1972, the British government appointed Lord Diplock to head an inquiry into the legal processes for dealing with political violence. Concern at the intimidation of witnesses and jurors led to the proposal for the establishment of non-jury courts. In the first instance, defendants on terrorist charges are tried before a judge sitting alone, while all appeals are heard before three judges.

Diplomatic Revolution, 1756, breakdown of the 'old alliance' between Britain and the Holy Roman Empire/Austria, which characterized all major wars since 1689, and of the alliance between France and Prussia, forged in the War of the AUSTRIAN SUCCESSION. That war had revealed a widening gap between British and Austrian interests. In 1755 this divergence became unmistakable when, in the context of the conflicts which were to escalate into the SEVEN YEARS WAR, the British asked for Austrian aid against the French, and Austria demurred unless offered guarantees against Prussia. In the circumstances, the easiest way for the British to defend vulnerable Hanover against possible Prussian manoeuvring seemed to be to seek alliance with Prussia itself. In Jan. 1756 Britain and Prussia signed the Convention of Westminster, by which Prussia guaranteed Hanoverian neutrality, and both powers pledged to resist any foreign power attacking Germany. In May, Britain declared war on France. France and Austria reciprocated with a defensive alliance; Frederick of Prussia's attack on Saxony in Aug. pushed these powers into a full offensive alliance in May 1757.

Direct Rule, description of the government of ULSTER from Westminster following the suspension of the provincial STORMONT government in March 1972. The ending of over 50 years of considerable autonomy for Northern Ireland was a response to the onset of the TROUBLES and the inability of Northern Ireland politicians to defuse the situation. Since 1972, attempts to restore a degree of devolved power have been unable to survive sectarian conflict.

Following the referendum in May 1998 as a result of the Good Friday Agreement (see ULSTER), a new Northern Ireland Assembly was constituted and in elections in June 1998, 108 members were elected from the existing 18 Westminster constituencies. The Assembly met for the first time in July 1998 and elected a First Minister (designate) on a cross-community basis, plus several committees including one to advise on the consequences of devolution. However, in January 2000, following the IRA's failure to decommission arms, direct rule was again imposed from Westminster.

Directory of Worship, *see* WESTMINSTER ASSEMBLY

Disinherited, the name given to two groups during the Middle Ages. The first were those followers of Simon de MONTFORT who were deprived of their estates in 1265. (For their continuing fight *see* KENILWORTH, DICTUM OF.)

The second comprised the Scottish landowners disinherited by Robert BRUCE after his victory at BANNOCKBURN in 1314. For the next few decades, as advocates of war against Scotland, they were to be an influential group at the English court (*see* DUPPLIN MOOR).

Dispensaries, institutions providing free medicines and medical treatment for the poor, founded in many towns in the late 18th and the 19th centuries. They were funded by donations and public subscription, subscribers having the right to nominate a number of poor patients for treatment.

Dispensing Powers, *see* SUSPENDING AND DISPENSING POWERS

Disraeli, Benjamin (1st Earl of Beaconsfield) (1804–81), Conservative politician and Prime Minister (1868, 1874–80), and novelist. The son of a writer, Isaac D'Israeli, he was brought up as a Christian but remained profoundly influenced by his Jewish origins. The first of several satirical novels on English political society, *Vivian Grey* (1826), caused a stir, but it was not until 1837, after several unsuccessful attempts, that he was elected to PARLIAMENT in the TORY interest. His political outlook, expressed in his *Vindication of the English Constitution* (1835), was an extension of the CONSERVATIVE ideology of Bolingbroke (*see* ST JOHN, HENRY) and BURKE. For Disraeli, too, the nation was an organism where well-being depended on the preservation of a balanced hierarchy between crown, church and aristocracy. Leadership, in his view, required a benign paternalism embodied in the Tory Party and embracing a concern for the conditions of the newly urbanized working class. Denied a seat in PEEL's Cabinet of 1841, the alienated Disraeli became the leader of the Romantic dissidents gathered in the YOUNG ENGLAND movement. *Coningsby* (1844), *Tancred* (1847) and *Sybil* (1845) – the CONDITION OF ENGLAND novel *par excellence* – were its political manifesto. Disraeli's emphasis on the regeneration of the natural leadership of the aristocracy supplied a unifying theme that gave the trilogy a coherence and continuing importance.

It was the CORN LAW crisis of 1845–6 that enabled Disraeli to drive Peel from office and assume with Derby the leadership of the PROTECTIONIST party. Thereafter, he divested himself of protectionism without loss of position. In 1852, he became chancellor of the Exchequer in Derby's government, was chancellor in his second administration of 1858–9 and again in 1866–7. His position as heir-apparent was secured largely on the strength of his own exertions and managerial skills.

Disraeli was briefly prime minister in 1868 before being rejected by the enlarged electorate that he himself had created with the REFORM ACT 1867. The years of his second administration (1874–80) were identified with a widespread programme of social reform – concerned with housing, safety at work and the regulation of food and drugs – the promotion of EMPIRE and the extension of British influence overseas. He purchased a controlling share for £4 million in the SUEZ CANAL from the Khedive of Egypt in anticipation of parliamentary approval, and in 1876 enabled Queen VICTORIA to assume the crown as Empress of INDIA. At the Congress of BERLIN in 1878, Disraeli's efforts did much to avoid further European conflict in settling the EASTERN QUESTION following the Russo-Turkish war, and he returned to England proclaiming that he had achieved 'peace with honour' (a phrase Neville CHAMBERLAIN would use again in 1938) and agreement for Britain to occupy Cyprus.

Between 1868 and 1880 Victorian politics were dominated by Disraeli and GLADSTONE who alternated as prime minister. Disraeli achieved his rise to power – from impecunious notoriety to leader of the nation – through a fierce ambition to climb 'to the top of the greasy pole' in a party thin on talent after the split of 1846. He owed his success to his superb skill as a parliamentarian and his appreciation of the practicalities of political management, while presenting a romantic view of England which appeared to give the landed classes a continuing role in a society of mass democracy. His strong IMPERIALIST rhetoric and forward – and often wayward – foreign policy contrasted with the relentless and convoluted moralizing of his LIBERAL rival and endeared him to the queen, who made him her personal and political ally. In 1880 Gladstone triumphantly proclaimed that 'the downfall of Beaconsfieldism is like the vanishing of some vast magnificent castle in an Italian romance' for Disraeli was, in his own words and the opinion of many of his party, 'never respectable'.

Historians continue to debate the substance of his achievements – and measure his long-term principles of Empire and his perception of British, or English, interests against his short-term expediencies, cynicism and opportunism. He may not be the 'founder of the modern Conservative Party' as was once claimed, since that accolade perhaps already belonged to Peel, but he bequeathed to the party a philosophical justification in the concept of 'one nation', which it has found useful to invoke in the 20th, as well as the 19th, century.

Disruption of the Church of Scotland The secession in 1843 of about 40 per cent of the membership and clergy of the Church of Scotland to form the FREE CHURCH was the greatest upheaval in the religious life of Victorian Scotland. It was the culmination of a protracted campaign within the Established Church between the MODERATE and EVANGELICAL parties, prompted by conflict over patronage as well as CALVINIST resentment at the role of the state and denial of a proper spiritual independence.

But it was more than that. Apart from the religious and ecclesiastical issues, the disruption possessed nationalist and social-class dimensions. The Anglicized landowning class that controlled patronage was unpopular with the Scottish middle class, while the English government's indifference to evangelical enthusiasms was equally vexing.

CHRONOLOGY

1773 Secession from Establishment and formation of Associate Presbytery in response to Patronage Act 1712.

1752 Further secession from Establishment also prompted by opposition to patronage in Church.

1820 United Secession Church formed, one of several fragments from previous disruptions of 18th century. (Others include Original Secession Church, Relief Church, and Reformed Presbyterian Church that originated from CAMERONIAN Sect of 1690.)

1833 Evangelical party led by Thomas CHALMERS wins control over General Assembly.

1834 The 'Nonintrusionists' object to 'intrusion' of ministers contrary to wishes of congregations; on motion of CHALMERS, Veto Act is passed by General Assembly, which compels presbyteries to reject nominees of lay patrons on objection of members of congregation even though no ground of objection is stated. Chapel Act passed by General Assembly admits to membership of church courts ministers of extension churches and CHAPELS OF EASE, who previously had no real status before law or Church.

1838 Legality of Veto Act challenged. In Auchterarder case, House of Lords, on appeal, confirms decision of COURT OF SESSION, which had ordered presbytery of Auchterarder to accept as minister a Mr Young, presented by Lord Kinnoul, in spite of protest from congregation. House of Lords declares Veto Act illegal.

1839–40 Strathbogie case: Mr Edwards, presentee to parish of Marnoch, obtains decision from Court of Session requiring presbytery of Strathbogie to accept him despite objections of congregation. General Assembly prohibits presbytery from obeying this order and, on their complying with it, supersedes them from their clerical duties. Right of presentation has become a question of authority of civil government over Church.

1842 General Assembly sends two addresses to crown, one protesting against 'encroachments of the Court of Session', other demanding abolition of lay patronage. Unfavourable answer sent by crown.

1843, 18 May Secession of 395 ministers, who then formed Free Church of Scotland.

Dissenters In religious terms, the general name for those Protestants who refused to accept the 1660–2 reimposition of EPISCOPACY and the PRAYER BOOK in the Church of England: such church bodies as the BAPTISTS, INDEPENDENTS, PRESBYTERIANS and QUAKERS. Commonly in use in the later 17th and 18th centuries, during the 19th century the label changed to NONCONFORMIST or FREE CHURCH. *See also* NEW DISSENT.

Dissenting Academies Called academies in imitation of CALVIN's Academy, established at Geneva 1552, they were university-level institutions for DISSENTERS. They trained students for the ministry and for professions, and in the 18th century also for business; science bulked larger in their curriculum than at the UNIVERSITIES. Latin as a medium of instruction gave way to English by 1750. Twenty-two were founded 1663–90 and 34 1691–1750: many had short lives.

Dissenting Deputies The Protestant Dissenting deputies were formed in 1732 as a permanent body to look after the interests of the three Dissenting denominations: every PRESBYTERIAN, INDEPENDENT and BAPTIST congregation within ten miles of London elected two members, who in turn elected a committee of 21. Links with the provinces were maintained by correspondence. The deputies lobbied PARLIAMENT on such matters as the repeal of the TEST and CORPORATION ACTS, continuing active in this role down to the early 20th century.

Dissolution of the Monasteries The confiscated revenues resulting from dissolutions of ALIEN PRIORIES in the early 15th century and those by WOLSEY in the 1520s were redirected to the Church or educational purposes. In the 1530s, HENRY VIII's advisers – chiefly Wolsey's former servant Thomas CROMWELL – organized a remarkably efficient dissolution of all English monasteries and nunneries, confiscating revenues for the crown and giving most RELIGIOUS adequate pensions. The Henrician government's motives for dissolution remain controversial. Probably there was a mixture of impulses, with conservative politicians interested in the financial gain to be made, and others determined to destroy an important aspect of traditional religion.

A 1536 Act of Parliament dissolved the smaller monasteries; the rest were induced to surrender individually to royal commissioners (1537–40), together with all friaries (1538). A 1539 Act 'for the dissolution of abbeys' merely recognized a *fait accompli*. All monastic cathedrals except COVENTRY were refounded as SECULAR colleges, and some new cathedrals were set up (*see* BISHOPRICS, ENGLISH); otherwise most property was sold to pay for government expenditure, and for a substantial burden of pension payments.

The lack of resistance is surprising, but the dissolution's piecemeal nature (probably reflecting a lack of overall government strategy) made it difficult to focus opposition. In southern England, the government benefited from widespread indifference to monastic life, even among religious conservatives; in the north, greater indignation led to the PILGRIMAGE OF GRACE in 1536–7, the defeat of which encouraged total dissolution. The destruction of art, architecture and manuscripts was immense. However, there was no formal statutory condemnation of monastic life, making it possible for ANGLICANS to found new nunneries and monasteries from the 1850s. Irish religious houses were dissolved from the 1530s as the English extended their control, although unlike those in England, many communities kept together. In Scotland, piecemeal and largely peaceful dissolution was achieved over 30 years from 1560. Dissolution everywhere was accompanied by a massive increase and quickening of the land market and by changes in land ownership and land use. Dissolution may also have contributed to an increase in poverty because of the disappearance of monastic alms (food and money distribution to the poor). These problems were in part responsible for the introduction of the Elizabethan POOR LAW. *See also* MONASTICISM.

Distraint of Knighthood, the practice, begun in HENRY III'S reign, whereby English kings, in an attempt to increase the numbers of knights who could be called upon to perform military and other duties in their service, required men of sufficient wealth to become knights or pay a fine. Used as a money-raising device by monarchs up to CHARLES I, in 1641 it was condemned as one of the king's abuses of power.

District and Parish Councils Act 1894 A complement to the LOCAL GOVERNMENT ACT of 1888, it established rural and urban district councils, provided for female representation, an enlarged suffrage, and the transfer of administrative duties previously discharged by PARISH vestries. *See also* BOROUGHS.

Divine Right of Kings Most monarchies in the ancient world claimed sacred status to some degree, and Roman emperors quickly assumed a claim to divinity during the 1st century AD. However, a specifically Christian dimension was given to monarchy in the early medieval period, when CAROLINGIAN kings initiated a religious CORONATION CEREMONY, which was imitated in England by MERCIAN kings in the late 8th century. The anointing of the king in the coronation signified a divine right to rule, and this remained part of the ideological armoury of medieval monarchy, emphasized particularly during the 11th- and 12th-century conflicts with the papacy.

Early modern European discussion about the nature and justification of the state became increasingly secular, particularly under the influence of Roman law (*see* CIVIL LAW). English COMMON LAW, however, resisted such changes, and the English REFORMATION's strong emphasis on a divinely given ROYAL SUPREMACY in the Church encouraged monarchs to continue seeing their role in religious terms, involving a God-given mandate to rule. An elaborate coronation ceremony was retained, the Tudor monarchs were frequently described in terms borrowed from Old Testament Israelite kingship, and English society as a whole saw its hierarchy as ordained by God. Hence, in the 17th century, there was nothing new about the Stuarts' employment of divine-right language to describe their rule, although no monarch before JAMES I had rushed into print on the subject. The novelty was the number of people with the classical education to see that there were other ways of describing governmental power.

Far from deciding the issue, the CIVIL WARS (particularly CHARLES I's 'martyrdom' and *EIKON BASILIKE*) polarized opinion, and divine-right theory became a favourite in ANGLICAN sermons and TORY ideology after the RESTORATION. The GLORIOUS REVOLUTION of 1688–9 proved a merely temporary embarrassment, even among those who rejected JACOBITISM, and it was only during the 18th century that the idea lost its credibility. Echoes could still be heard in early 19th-century Anglican circles.

Division, a term with two meanings in the usage of the British PARLIAMENT. First, since the 16th century it has been the description of votes taken in either house which cannot be determined simply by the Speaker's or the lord chancellor's estimate: those present leave their seats to divide into groups to pass through two different lobby chambers 'Aye' and 'No'. The names of members passing through the lobbies are recorded and published. Second, it is the official description for CONSTITUENCIES, the electoral districts which elect Members of Parliament. The term was first used in 1832 for the two-member divisional areas created within the old county seats (*see also* KNIGHTS OF THE SHIRE), and then since 1885 for the divisions of BOROUGH seats as well.

Divorce and British Law English law long followed CANON LAW in distinguishing between *a vinculo* divorce (dissolution of the marriage 'bond') and *a mensa et thoro* (legal separation from 'table and bed'). The first was seen as impossible: dissolution could only be achieved by annulment (which was informally and loosely called *divortium*) – i.e. a pronouncement that, for a variety of reasons, there had never been a marriage (HENRY VIII sought annulment in his marriage to CATHERINE OF ARAGON). The second could be granted by a CHURCH COURT. Despite many REFORMATION proposals for liberalization, including in the abortive *REFORMATIO LEGUM*, this remained the legal position in the Church of England, uniquely among Protestant Churches.

Alongside separations under decrees of the ecclesiastical courts, private separations became increasingly common from the mid-17th century, but these did not entitle the parties to remarry. Not until 1670 (in the case of Lord Roos) did Parliament, by private act, enable a party, separated under a church court decree, to remarry, and such acts were not at all numerous before the later 18th century. Even then, they were not easy to obtain, with the prerequisites being both a church court decree for separation and a successful civil action by the wronged party (almost always the husband) for 'criminal conversation' (adultery) against the spouse's lover. Not surprisingly, the process, costing hundreds of pounds, was sufficiently expensive as to be confined for the most part to the well-off, with successful petitioners for such legislation averaging less than four per annum between the 1780s and 1840s. Radical change only began when, in 1857, the English church courts lost marriage jurisdiction, and a Divorce Act set up secular court procedures. The divorce rate thereafter remained fairly static until successive liberalizations of the law in 1923, 1937, 1969 and 1971 (the act that allowed divorce on the grounds of the irredemable breakdown of the marriage, and the initiation of divorce by one partner even against the wishes of the other) after each of which the number of divorces increased substantially. Safeguards were put in place for the welfare of the children of a marriage, and the 1996 Divorce Act sought to establish a more equitable distribution of property and pension rights etc. Despite the long-term trend of a rising divorce rate, numbers appear to have levelled off since the mid 1990s with 13 per 1,000 married people divorcing – though the rate of marriage (rather than cohabitation) is also falling. Approximately 7 out of 10 divorces are now initiated by women, usually on the grounds of unreasonable behaviour.

Ireland broadly followed English practice up to 1922, but in the Irish Republic, divorce was made illegal.

In Scotland, as elsewhere, divorce was introduced during the Reformation. From 1573, it was granted in the Commissary Court for adultery (which was a criminal offence) or desertion, with remarriage permitted to the innocent party. Until the 20th century, however, the divorce rate remained tiny. *See also* MARRIAGE; WOMEN, LEGAL STATUS OF.

Dobunni, the British tribe that occupied the area of modern Glos. and Avon and parts of Som., Oxon., Herefords,, Worcs. and Warwicks. The pre-Roman urban centre of the kingdom lay at Bagendon, Glos. During the early 1st century AD, some of the kingdom appears to have come under the control of the CATUVELLAUNI, which may explain why the Dobunni seem to have come quickly to terms with AULUS PLAUTIUS after 43. CIRENCESTER, the chief town of the region, was soon being used by the Romans as a base for campaigns into Wales, and also became the capital of the *CIVITAS* of the Dobunni.

Dock Strike, 1889. One of the key moments in British labour history, the successful STRIKE of the London dockers in support of a pay increase from 5 to 6 pence (the 'dockers' tanner') an hour, modifications in work practices, and 8 pence an hour for overtime, had a profound effect on middle-class opinion. The unexpected capacity for organized and disciplined action displayed by hitherto unorganizable (and therefore dangerous) elements of the population gave promise of a peaceful outcome to the social unrest of the period. Members of the LABOUR ARISTOCRACY were also surprised by the upsurge in general unions of the unskilled that followed in the wake of the strike. Contemporaries attributed the growth of the NEW TRADE UNIONISM to the influence of a revived socialism; historians now give more attention to the TRADE CYCLE and relations within particular industries, rather than the role of ideology, in the formation of general unions. *See also* TRADE UNIONS.

Dockyards The Royal Dockyards were vital elements in the strength of the NAVY, and the largest and most complex economic and industrial units anywhere until well into the 19th century. They included building and repairing facilities, with dry (and later wet) docks, stores of timber and other materials. Permanent yards at Deptford and PORTSMOUTH were established by the reign of HENRY VIII. Chatham followed in the reign of ELIZABETH I, and Woolwich and Sheerness soon after. With France becoming the chief enemy another yard was begun at PLYMOUTH (later known as Devonport) in 1689. During the 18th century overseas yards were added: GIBRALTAR, JAMAICA, BERMUDA, ANTIGUA, Bombay, Halifax (NOVA SCOTIA) and Port Mahon (Minorca); in the early 19th century MALTA, Trincomalee and Simonstown; and later in the century HONG KONG. This network of overseas bases was a vital element in the world-wide dominance of the Royal Navy. During the NAPOLEONIC WARS a specialized shipbuilding yard was set up at Pembroke, and an Irish yard at Berehaven (Cobh). After 1900 with the growing threat of the German navy, a yard was created at Rosyth. In the latter half of the 20th century the number of dockyards has steadily shrunk, with Gibraltar the last of the overseas ones to go, and the home yards reduced to Rosyth (about to close), Portsmouth (on a limited basis) and Plymouth.

As was inevitable with such large employers of labour, the dockyards experienced some of the first STRIKES and other labour disputes. Up to the introduction of the IRONCLAD (*c.* 1860) the dockyards built nearly all the navy's peace-time tonnage, but in war concentrated on refit and repair. Thereafter the yards continued to build ships as a check on commercial building prices and practices.

Dole Originally a charitable apportionment of money, food or other gifts associated with monasteries and churches, and later with charities and the Old POOR LAW (*see* POOR RELIEF), it was applied in a pejorative sense to the 'out-of-work donation' issued at the close of WORLD WAR I. The benefit received under the Unemployment Insurance Act 1927 was also commonly referred to as the 'dole', which has since become a generic term for such payments.

Domesday Book, the record of a comprehensive and detailed survey of English landholdings undertaken on the orders of WILLIAM I THE CONQUEROR. According to the ANGLO-SAXON CHRONICLE, a few days after Christmas 1085 'the king had much thought and very deep discussion with his council about this country – how it was held and with what sort of people. Then he sent his men over all England into every shire and had them find out ... he had a record made of what or how much, in land or livestock, everybody had who was holding land in England, and how much money it was worth'. This record was initially kept in the royal TREASURY in Winchester and is today held in the PUBLIC RECORD OFFICE. For centuries it survived in two manuscript volumes: the first, known as Little Domesday, covers Essex, Norfolk and Suffolk; the second, Great Domesday, covers the rest of the English counties south of the River Tees, but in less detail. Great Domesday is thought to represent the final stage of a long and complex editorial process which was halted soon after William I's death and before it reached the three eastern counties.

It is the most remarkable statistical document in European history. It records detailed information on some 45,000 landholdings in about 14,000 named places, providing geld assessments (*see* DANEGELD) and valuations of the estates both for Jan. 1066 (when EDWARD THE CONFESSOR died) and 'now', i.e. 1086. In its surviving form it contains a few lacunae – LONDON and WINCHESTER, for example, are omitted – but there is nothing else on this scale before the 19th century. Although in making the survey William's government was able to utilize Anglo-Saxon administrative records, there was clearly no precedent for the scale and thoroughness of 1086, hence the shocked comment of the *Anglo-Saxon Chronicle*: 'so very strictly did he have the enquiry carried out that – it is shameful to say it, but it did not seem shameful to him to do it – not one ox, nor one cow nor one pig escaped notice in his survey'. In fact this was an exaggeration since the survey was intended to assist the king's fiscal exploitation of his new kingdom, and this meant that his agents were only really interested in the wealth at the disposal of the élite. Since the survey shows that by 1086 only a handful of the élite still bore Anglo-Saxon names, one of its effects was to set a seal on the dispossession of the old aristocracy as a result of the NORMAN CONQUEST. According to Richard Fitznigel in his *Dialogue of the Exchequer (Dialogus de Scaccario* written in the late 1170s), within its own sphere *Domesday Book* was as authoritative as the Last Judgment, hence the name by which it was then (in the 1170s) already known.

Domestic Service, employment of servants to perform tasks within the household. The institution of service (*see also* SERVANTS IN HUSBANDRY) was important in early modern, and probably medieval, society, when young people left home and worked in other households, frequently for a year at a time. Such a service was a qualifying category for a SETTLEMENT under the 18th-century settlement laws. During the 19th century, as these older forms of service declined, the employment of domestic help increased, and more servants worked for life rather than just during a phase in their lives. Service also became a predominantly female occupation. Although the employment of servants was an indicator of social status, households at most levels in 19th-century society might employ a servant, either living-in or working by day. The high-water mark for domestic servants was in 1881. Thereafter the numbers of servants went into sustained decline. By the inter-war period domestic technology removed many of the labour-intensive tasks servants had previously performed, and the employment of servants was increasingly restricted to the wealthiest members of society.

Dominica, Commonwealth of, former British colony in the WINDWARD ISLANDS and one of the poorest Caribbean islands. Its position between Martinique and

Guadeloupe made control fragile; fought over by the British, French and native Caribs, Britain's possession was settled in 1805. A generally neglected island of small estates, Dominica achieved independence in 1978.

Dominicans, *see* FRIARS

Dominions, self-governing former colonies within the BRITISH EMPIRE and subsequently the COMMONWEALTH. CANADA was the first to be given dominion status in 1867 under the BRITISH NORTH AMERICA ACT, with AUSTRALIA following in 1900, NEW ZEALAND in 1907 and SOUTH AFRICA in 1910.

Don Pacifico Incident, 1850. This arose out of a denial of compensation to a Gibraltar-born merchant whose property had been destroyed in 1847 in riots in Athens against the Greek government. David (known as Don) Pacifico, a British subject, then appealed to London. Palmerston (*see* TEMPLE, HENRY) ordered the fleet to Athens and threatened to bombard the city if the Don's claims were not satisfied. The Greeks succumbed. Richard Cobden, John BRIGHT and GLADSTONE protested at this example of 'GUNBOAT DIPLOMACY' but were routed in the Commons. Palmerston concluding his defence with the peroration: 'A British subject, in whatever land he may be, shall feel confident that the watchful eye and the strong arm of England will protect him against injustice and wrong.' The incident appealed to the unthinking patriotism and growing IMPERIALISM of Britons in the heyday of their industrial and naval supremacy.

Donal Ban, *see* DONALD III BAN

Donald I (?–862), King of Scots (858–62). The brother and successor of KENNETH MAC ALPIN, he continued the latter's conquest of the PICTS by imposing the laws of DALRIADA on them, a significant step towards unification. Little else is known about his reign, and later events suggest that Scottish hegemony over the Picts remained unstable (*see* CONSTANTINE I). It is possible that Donald was assassinated.

Donald II (?–900), King of Scots (889–900). A son of CONSTANTINE I, he took advantage of a lull in VIKING activity, and of the confusion that followed the siege of DUMBARTON ROCK, to install his family as kings over the STRATHCLYDE Britons. In 890, he banished the remnants of the latter's aristocracy, who then sought refuge in north Wales.

Donald II was the first Scot to be called 'King of Scotland' (by the *ANNALS OF ULSTER*). This territorial title acknowledged the hegemony that his predecessors had established over other northern British tribes such as the PICTS and the Strathclyde Britons, and, in this single stray reference, suggested the possibility of territorial unification in northern Britain.

Donald III Ban (*c*.1033–1100), King of Scots (1093–4, 1094–7). Son of DUNCAN I, he seized the throne of his brother MALCOLM III CANMORE in 1093 and promptly reversed Malcolm's policy of welcoming Englishmen to court. He was defeated and dethroned by his nephew DUNCAN II in May 1094, but before the year was out he had recovered power and procured Duncan's death. Three years later, another nephew, EDGAR, captured and blinded him. As champion of the native cause against growing Anglo-Norman immigration and influence, it is appropriate that Donald should be the last Scottish king whose bones were claimed by the Gaelic monastic community of IONA.

DORA, *see* DEFENCE OF THE REALM ACT

Dorchester-on-Thames, Bishopric of, the first bishopric of the kingdom of WESSEX, created for BIRINUS in *c*.635. After the site of the cathedral was moved to WINCHESTER in 660, Dorchester-on-Thames was only intermittently a bishopric. When the Leicester bishopric was destroyed by the Scandinavian invasions of the late 9th century, the Dorchester diocese stretched from the Humber to the Thames. The cathedral was relocated at LINCOLN after the NORMAN CONQUEST.

Dort, Synod of, synod of the Dutch Reformed Church called to Dort (Dordrecht) in 1618–19 to crush the ARMINIAN movement. English and Scots representatives were among the foreigners invited, and subscribed (some with misgivings) its ultra-CALVINIST Articles.

Doublecross system, highly successful counter-espionage policy adopted by British intelligence in WORLD WAR II. German agents sent to Britain were 'turned' into double agents sending misleading information back to Germany about Anglo-American intentions.

Douglas, James (4th Earl of Morton) (?1516–81), politician. After becoming earl (in right of his wife) in 1553, he subscribed the LORDS OF THE CONGREGATION's first BOND in 1557, but withdrew his support two years later. He was lord chancellor in 1562. Having reluctantly supported MARY QUEEN OF SCOTS's marriage to Darnley (*see* STEWART, HENRY), he was one of RIZZIO's murderers in 1566. Darnley hypocritically denounced him, but he returned from his flight to England when pardoned by Mary. He seized Edinburgh in revolt against Bothwell (*see* Hepburn, James), and was again lord chancellor in the regime proclaiming JAMES VI in 1567. Furious at the murder of the regent, James Stewart, Earl of Moray, he induced ELIZABETH I to recognize James in 1570.

As regent himself from 1572, he reformed justice, secured peace on the Borders and strengthened PROTESTANTISM, beginning to rebuild an EPISCOPAL system. Losing the regency when James VI was persuaded to assume government in 1578, he was rapidly reinstated by Parliament. However, with James's connivance, Matthew Stewart, Earl of Lennox, unjustly accused him of procuring Darnley's murder, and he was executed on the guillotine that he had reputedly introduced.

Douglas-Home, Alec (Baron Home of the Hirsel) (1903–95), Conservative politician and Prime Minister (1963–4). As Lord Dunglass, he was parliamentary private secretary to Neville CHAMBERLAIN (1937–40), whom he accompanied to MUNICH in 1938. After the war he was a junior minister at the Scottish Office (1951–5), and then secretary of state for Commonwealth relations (1955–60), and leader of the House of Lords (1959–60). He was foreign secretary under MACMILLAN (1960–3), securing the NASSAU AGREEMENT and the PARTIAL TEST BAN TREATY.

Invited unexpectedly by the Queen to become prime minister in succession to Macmillan in 1963, after the traditionally obscure consultation procedures, he renounced his peerages and returned to the House of Commons via a by-election. His aristocratic demeanour and career were in stark contrast to WILSON's modern and technocratic image; but despite this, and the fact that the CONSERVATIVES were beset by scandal and had been in office for 13 years, he only lost the 1964 election by four seats. He resigned as leader in 1965 and MPs chose HEATH as his successor, using for the first time a formal voting system put in place on his initiative. He was foreign secretary again (1970–4).

Dover, Treaty of, 1670, concluded between CHARLES II and Louis XIV in May, as the outcome of discussions pursued intermittently since 1661. Charles was anxious not to face another Franco-Dutch alliance against England, as in the Second DUTCH WAR, but did not share what was at this point Parliament's inclination to maintain the Protestant TRIPLE ALLIANCE against France to which England had formally committed itself in 1668. The treaty embodied an attempt to secure French favour through a series of promises. It committed England and France to declare war on Holland; if the attack succeeded, England was to receive Zeeland. In return for Ostend, prospective conquests in South America and £225,000 a year, England was also to assist Louis' claim to the Spanish succession. Ultra-secret clauses, known only to Arlington, Arundel and CLIFFORD among the ministers, stated that Charles II would re-establish Catholicism in return for £150,000 and the use of 6,000 French troops to cope with internal resistance. A 'simulated treaty', omitting these secret clauses, was signed in Dec., setting the scene for preparations for a war intended to begin in 1672.

Drake, Sir Francis (?1542–96), naval hero. From a Devon family that was already, at that early date, fiercely Protestant, Drake was apprenticed to a Thames captain and then, in 1563 and 1566, joined his distant cousin John HAWKINS' voyages to Africa. His first command coincided with violent Spanish reaction to Hawkins' smuggling trade with their American colonists. He was soon planning a voyage of revenge against Spain, and achieved spectacular success in seizing bullion in America and the Atlantic in 1572–3, and then in circumnavigating the globe (1577–81). By now he was being encouraged by ELIZABETH I, who regarded his activities as a useful way of distracting the Spaniards from following up their military successes in the NETHERLANDS. This was the first time that English ships had sailed the

Pacific, anticipating England's later interest in the East Indies; it included, in June 1579, a landfall in what is thought to be California, which Drake declared annexed to the English crown. The expedition brought him great wealth and Elizabeth, ignoring furious Spanish protests, ostentatiously knighted him on his own ship, the *Golden Hind* (subsequently preserved at Deptford as a tourist attraction).

On his return, he continued his feud with Spain, this time openly backed by the queen. There followed destructive raids on the Spanish Caribbean in 1584–5 (also including the rescue of the remaining English colonists in VIRGINIA), the wrecking of the Spanish fleet at Cadiz in 1587 – the so-called singeing of the king of Spain's beard – and then a major command against the ARMADA. He masterminded the fireship attack which broke the Spaniards' formation at Gravelines. Though not in supreme command such was the power of his name that both friend and foe spoke as if he was. After the Armada, his career declined, including a disastrous attack on Portugal in 1589. He died from sickness during an unsuccessful Caribbean venture in 1596. Nevertheless, his achievements had been astonishing, and he had played a unique part in the denting of Spanish overseas prestige.

Dreadnought Launched in 1906, *Dreadnought* was the first battleship to be completely armed with the very largest guns rather than a variety of sizes. Dreadnought then became the name of a new series of BATTLESHIPS built in the ensuing race to equip the British and German navies. The *Dreadnought*'s construction in only a year remains a record, but within a decade she was rendered obsolete by the development of larger and more powerful 'super dreadnoughts'.

Dream of the Rood, The, one of the greatest of the surviving poems written in Old English (*see* ANGLO-SAXON). As well as its religious content – it describes a vision of Christ's crucifixion – it draws on images of contemporary secular society; as the historian Patrick Wormald has remarked, 'All Creation is seen as Christ's warband.' Although the text survives in a 10th-century manuscript, its composition must have been much earlier since parts of it are transcribed in a RUNIC inscription on the RUTHWELL CROSS.

Drogheda, Massacre of, Co. Louth, 11 Sept. 1649, a massacre by Oliver CROMWELL's troops of all men found in arms after the capture of the town; perhaps 2,000 died. A similar massacre soon after at Wexford was made worse by the accidental drowning of many non-combatants. The scope and exceptional nature of the massacres have often been exaggerated, not least in Irish nationalist folk-memory, although they were horrible enough, and Cromwell showed unpleasant pious relish in reporting them to Parliament.

Droitwich, *see* SALT INDUSTRY

Droving Trade, trade in cattle and other animals where the beasts walked from upland areas to the larger centres of population, especially LONDON. For many areas of Scotland, Wales and northern England, as well as with cattle imported from Ireland, the trade was a mainstay of the agricultural economy, notably from the mid-17th century to the mid- or late 19th century. The economies of the Lake District or Dumfries and Galloway, for example, depended upon it. A network of drove roads, often away from centres of population and the tolls on TURNPIKE roads, criss-crossed the countryside.

Drug Abuse Many dangerous or addictive substances were freely available prior to the 20th century. Growing concern about the widespread use of opiates as sedatives, especially on young children, led to the Pharmacy Act of 1868 which permitted the sale of opium only through licensed pharmacists. By the inter-war years most of the more dangerous substances were also controlled, but drugs were considered a minor problem compared with drink until the rise of the rock and pop culture of the 1960s. The fashionable use of cannabis, amphetamines, hallucinogenic drugs such as LSD, and 'hard drugs' such as heroin and cocaine, became a widespread cause of concern. The Misuse of Drugs Act 1971 tightened the law against drug-taking and drug-trafficking, while considerable government effort was devoted to enforcement, the rehabilitation of drug-users, and publicity to dissuade young people from drug-taking. The advent of AIDS has led to increased awareness of the spread of infection through shared needles amongst those who inject drugs. Campaigns to legalize cannabis and also other non class A drugs in the 1990s have met with resistance from both CONSERVATIVE and LABOUR governments.

Druids, the priests of pre-Roman CELTIC religion. They were primarily concerned with the organization of a religion dominated by nature and the agricultural seasons, and with the performance of magical rites. Although identified by the Romans as a political threat in Gaul, the same may not have been true in Britain, where references are much scarcer. It is likely that St COLUMBA and others who worked to convert the PICTS would have had to combat druidical practices. The Irish *FILIDH* can, in some respects, be seen as their successors. 17th- and 18th-century ANTIQUARIES, inspired by the uncritical fantasies of John Aubrey, were prone to ascribe all mysterious prehistoric antiquities to the Druids, a syndrome which has left traces in popular historical memory. A small modern revival holds a ceremony at STONEHENGE every summer solstice.

Drumceat, Convention of, Co. Derry, 575, a meeting attended by AIDAN MAC GABHRÁIN, King of Scottish DALRIADA, St COLUMBA and Aed mac Ainmerech, high-king of Ireland, with the object of changing the terms on which the Dalriada kings had ruled their Irish territories since the Scottish kingdom was established *c.*500. The outcome was that the kings based in Scottish Dalriada no longer ruled their Irish lands directly, but instead acknowledged the overlordship of the Irish king, while still being permitted to receive tribute.

Drummond, William (1585–1649), writer. Having studied at Edinburgh, Bourges and Paris, he succeeded as laird of Hawthornden in 1610. He designed various measuring instruments and weapons, and wrote accomplished and innovative poetry (in southern English rather than Scots), a *History of Scotland* and tracts designed to seek peace in the CIVIL WARS. He protested against the COVENANTS and advocated negotiations with CHARLES I after his 1646 defeat. His death was reportedly hastened by the king's execution.

Dry-Stamp Royal Signatures, used on behalf of HENRY VIII in his last years of illness and of the young EDWARD VI: the stamp made an impression on a document which was then inked in by authorized royal servants. Possession of the dry stamp and authorization to use it were vital factors in the EVANGELICAL ascendancy of Henry's last months and in the power of Somerset (*see* SEYMOUR, EDWARD) and Northumberland (*see* DUDLEY, JOHN). ELIZABETH I kept hers secure and rarely allowed it to be used.

Dub (?–966), King of Scots (962–6). A son of MALCOLM I, he was challenged and overthrown by CULEN, a son of King INDULF – a usurpation that began a violent BLOOD FEUD lasting many years. The outbreak of this feud within the Scottish royal family occurred when the threat from the VIKING war bands had died away. In this time of apparently increased security, the Scottish rulers re-embarked on the kind of family warfare that was typical of many early societies (*see* KINGSHIP).

Dublin, capital city of the Irish Republic. With YORK and Rouen, Dublin was one of the three great VIKING towns of north-western Europe outside Scandinavia. Archaeological discoveries have shown that the town, first settled by Scandinavians in 841, became a great centre of trade, and for several decades after 995, its Norse rulers had COINS minted on their behalf. Its kings were frequently involved in attempts to maintain rule over an 'Irish Sea Empire' combining Dublin and the kingdom of York (*see* IVAR THE BONELESS; OLAF SIHTRICSSON; RAGNALL), and in events on the Scottish islands (*see* OLAF THE WHITE).

After the mid-10th century, Dublin became no more than one of the many participants in Irish dynastic politics (*see* KINGSHIP), and in the 11th, it was frequently controlled by its more powerful Irish neighbours. The city was finally captured by the English in 1171, and HENRY II encouraged settlement from BRISTOL by royal charter. From then on Dublin was the principal centre of 'old English' settlement and its castle was the seat of English royal administration, although frequently royal control was reduced to a small area of the PALE around the city; from the 14th century the Irish PARLIAMENT normally met there. Clerical rivalries in the 12th century led to the foundation of two CATHEDRAL churches, Christ Church and St Patrick's, both of which are still used by the CHURCH OF IRELAND (there is no Roman CATHOLIC full cathedral in Dublin).

Dublin's heyday was in the 18th century, the years of the PROTESTANT ASCENDANCY, when the city was considerably expanded with grand public buildings, gracious streets and squares, becoming the second city of the British Isles. Trinity College became one of the pre-eminent UNIVERSITIES of the English-speaking world. The UNION of 1801, removing the Irish Parliament, brought that era to a close. James Joyce's *Ulysses* (1922) evoked the city of 1904, on the eve of the upheavals which came in the wake of the EASTER RISING of 1916. The grand buildings of the British era were taken over by the emerging Irish state after 1919, the former Mansion House becoming the first home of the DÁIL, and the Four Courts the centre of justice. Since the 1970s, and accession to the EUROPEAN UNION, Dublin has undergone rapid economic and architectural change, with the arrival of many international financial institutions.

Dublin Society, a semi-official organization founded in 1731 to promote the useful arts, agriculture, trade and manufactures – in effect, Irish economic development. Its members included MPs, doctors, clerics and academics, and it was financed by public subscriptions, later assisted by parliamentary grants, which were disbursed in the form of 'premiums' (prizes) for useful inventions or improvements. It set up a botanic garden as a site for experiments, imported new implements and skilled men to demonstrate their use, and circulated accounts of new techniques. It conducted mineral and agricultural surveys and, in 1800, offered rewards for the publication of county natural histories on the model of those commissioned by the BOARD OF AGRICULTURE in Britain; 23 had been published by 1832.

Dudley, John (7th Baron and Viscount Lisle, 19th Earl of Warwick, 1st Duke of Northumberland) (*c.*1504–54), politician. Son of Edmund Dudley (?1462–1510), the effects of his father's ATTAINDER were lifted in 1512; he was probably brought up by his guardian Sir Edward Guildford. He received legal training but, in 1523, began a military career in France; by the 1530s, he was taking part in court life. Service in the 1540s in Scotland and France, including the capture of Boulogne in 1544, brought him his earldom of Warwick in 1546.

Although he acquiesced in Somerset's (*see* SEYMOUR, EDWARD) seizure of protectoral powers in 1547, he encouraged Lord Thomas SEYMOUR's fruitless intrigues, and defeated KETT'S REBELLION in Norfolk in Aug. 1549. In the aftermath of Somerset's overthrow in Oct., he adroitly outmanoeuvred conservative nobility to dominate the KING'S COUNCIL, a triumph sealed by his appointment as lord president of the Council in 1550 and by his dukedom of Northumberland the following year. After a fragile reconciliation, Somerset was arrested, and was executed in Jan. 1552.

Northumberland furthered PROTESTANT reforms and began to sort out chaotic government finances, while continuing to line his own and his supporters' pockets; however, all depended on EDWARD VI's survival. When the boy became fatally ill in the winter of 1552/3, the young king and Northumberland decided to divert the succession to JANE GREY (who was originally responsible for the idea is not certain), but now the duke's ruthless sureness of touch in politics faltered as his own health deteriorated. The Council were persuaded to agree to Jane's accession to the throne, she was married to Northumberland's own son Guildford, and on Edward's death, the plan seemed to have succeeded – until a wholly unanticipated nationwide revulsion in favour of MARY I intervened. Northumberland was sent with an army to confront her, but at Bury St Edmunds he lost his nerve and turned back to Cambridge, proclaiming Mary queen himself. At his execution on 22 Aug., he affirmed his Catholicism (to Jane's disgust); his family was once more attainted. Dudley remains a mysterious figure, despite his political prominence.

Dudley, Robert (14th Earl of Leicester) (1532/3–88), courtier and politician. The fifth son of John DUDLEY, Duke of Northumberland, he tried strenuously to hold Norfolk for JANE GREY in 1553, but was pardoned and lived obscurely until he was allowed to fight against France in 1557, which resulted in the reversal of his ATTAINDER.

Immediate favour and appointment as master of the horse came with ELIZABETH I's accession. With this exceptional treatment, it was difficult for scandal not to attach to the mysterious death of his wife Amy Robsart in

Sept. 1560 (the likelihood is that it was accidental). The queen's continuing affection was shown in the grant of Kenilworth Castle in 1563 and by his earldom in 1564. When she came to realize that marriage to him was politically impossible, she tried to persuade him to marry MARY QUEEN OF SCOTS. Through the 1560s, Leicester's relations with William CECIL were sometimes tense, but thereafter they worked on the PRIVY COUNCIL in general harmony, although Leicester was more inclined to urge an aggressive policy to support PROTESTANTISM abroad.

His place at court was repeatedly put in jeopardy by his flirtations – he was desperate for an heir – and most seriously by his eventual marriage to Lettice Knollys, widowed mother of Robert DEVEREUX, Earl of Essex, in 1578 (and probably earlier in secret); their son died in 1584. Partly to reassert his court position, he pushed for command of an expeditionary force to help the rebel Dutch (*see* NETHERLANDS, REVOLT OF THE). In 1585, Elizabeth reluctantly agreed, but was furious when he accepted the Dutch supreme governorship. By 1587, the expedition had become a fiasco, and he was recalled; he was only beginning to regain favour with energetic preparations to fight the ARMADA when he died in 1588. The queen mourned him deeply. A fascinating combination of flamboyant courtier and PURITAN patron, Leicester was the most powerful English nobleman of his age.

Duke, highest rank in the PEERAGE, from the Latin *dux*, leader. The title was first conferred by EDWARD III in 1337 on the PRINCE OF WALES, making him Duke of Cornwall. The rank was exclusive to Princes of the Blood Royal until RICHARD II extended its use. The honour was rarely conferred until after the reign of ELIZABETH I. The last non-royal duke to be created was Arthur WELLESLEY, Duke of Wellington (1814).

Dumbarton Rock, Siege of, 870. The four-month siege of the chief fortress of the kingdom of the STRATHCLYDE Britons, by a VIKING army led by OLAF THE WHITE, King of DUBLIN, and IVAR THE BONELESS, was a formidable military achievement. The serious defeat inflicted on the King of Strathclyde did much to bring that kingdom under the domination of the King of Scots. The Vikings may have been supported by the Scottish King, CONSTANTINE I, whose son, DONALD II, was able to establish Scottish pre-eminence over the Strathclyde Britons.

Dumnonia, post-Roman British kingdom. At its greatest extent, it consisted of the modern counties of Cornwall and Devon and the western parts of Som. and Dorset. It lost its independence in two stages: Devon was incorporated into the kingdom of WESSEX during INE's reign; and Cornwall during EGBERT's, after the battle of HINGSTON DOWN. Documentary evidence is thin, but archaeological evidence and monumental remains indicate a kingdom that had rich and diverse contacts with Wales, Ireland and BRITTANY. *See also* OGHAM.

Dumnonii, the peoples who inhabited the modern counties of Cornwall and Devon and parts of Som. in the pre-Roman period. It is thought unlikely that they formed a single tribe. They appear to have submitted in the early stages of the ROMAN CONQUEST, during the governorship of AULUS PLAUTIUS. EXETER was first established as a LEGIONARY FORTRESS and then, in *c.*75, was transformed into the capital of the *CIVITAS* of the Dumnonii.

Dunbar, Battle of, Lothian, 3 Sept. 1650, English PARLIAMENTARIAN victory by Oliver CROMWELL over the Royalist PRESBYTERIAN Scots. With the subsequent battle of WORCESTER (1651), it was the fatal blow to CHARLES II's hopes of regaining his throne with Scots help.

Duncan I (*c.*1010–1040), King of Scots (1034–40). Having succeeded his grandfather MALCOLM II, he was killed six years later by MACBETH, Earl of Moray. The manner of his death identifies him as a victim of the long-standing BLOOD FEUD fought over the Scottish kingdom, and more recently of his father's destruction of the descendants of Kenneth III, whose grand-daughter GRUOCH was Macbeth's wife. SHAKESPEARE's play greatly simplifies the complex social conditions that led to Duncan's death (*see* KINGSHIP).

Duncan II (*c.*1060–94), King of Scots (1094). Son of MALCOLM III CANMORE and his first wife Ingibiorg, he was sent in 1072 as a hostage to the court of WILLIAM I THE CONQUEROR, where he remained until after his father's death. With the help of an army supplied by WILLIAM II RUFUS, he defeated his uncle DONALD III BAN in May 1094. However, his foreign supporters were detested, and although he promised to introduce no more Englishmen or Normans into Scotland, this was not enough to save him: Donald engineered his murder on 12 Nov. 1094. Duncan II's brief reign graphically illustrates the dynastic and ethnic tensions in late 11th-century Scotland.

Dundee, 1st Viscount, *see* GRAHAM, JOHN

Dungannon Conventions, 1782, 1783, 1793. Delegates from Ulster volunteer corps gathered in Dungannon, ULSTER in Feb. 1782 to carry forward the campaign for IRISH LEGISLATIVE INDEPENDENCE. A small group including Henry Flood and Henry Grattan had prepared resolutions demanding legislative independence, the repeal of POYNINGS' LAW, and the independence of the Irish judiciary. They resolved to use every constitutional means to attain their objectives and to support at the ensuing general election only those who accepted their programme. The espousal of the reform programme by armed and mobilized corps intensified pressure on the Irish administration to make concessions. Many were, however, left unsatisfied when the reform programme was implemented later that year: the lord lieutenant's influence over the legislature was argued to nullify the spirit of the reform. It was argued that a further measure of PARLIAMENTARY REFORM was needed to make Parliament more effectively reflective of the electorate.

The issue was agitated in the 1783 election: in Sept. a provincial convention of nearly 400 volunteer delegates again assembled in Dungannon and approved a programme of annual elections, secret ballots, the abolition of some small BOROUGHS, and the opening up of the borough FRANCHISE. The issue of whether Catholics should be able to vote was remitted to a national convention to be held in Dublin, dubbed the ROTUNDA PARLIAMENT.

The FRENCH REVOLUTION having given a new boost to Irish radicalism, a third Dungannon convention was held in 1793 under the sponsorship of UNITED IRISHMEN and county notables. Delegates from five Ulster counties supported a moderate reform programme. The outbreak of the FRENCH REVOLUTIONARY WAR put an end to this phase of Ulster constitutional reformism.

Dunkirk, Evacuation of, remarkable rescue of British and Allied troops from Dunkirk and neighbouring beaches in late May and early June 1940. The German breakthrough in the Ardennes and drive to the English Channel trapped the BRITISH EXPEDITIONARY FORCE and elements of the French and Belgian armies. Desperate rearguard actions kept Dunkirk and its beaches open for evacuation, assisted by a halt in the German advance on the port, and allowed more than 330,000 troops, 233,000 of them British, to be taken off by an armada of ships, both large and small. The 'miracle' of Dunkirk allowed Britain to remain in WORLD WAR II by saving her only large body of trained troops at the cost of most of their equipment.

Dunkirk, Treaty of, March 1947, Anglo-French agreement to provide mutual assistance against German aggression. It was a reaffirmation of Anglo-French co-operation following the events of WORLD WAR II.

Dunning's Motion, 6 April 1780. 'The influence of the crown has increased, is increasing and ought to be diminished' – this parliamentary motion was brought by John Dunning, a follower of William PETTY, Earl of Shelburne, at a time when the troubles associated with the War of AMERICAN INDEPENDENCE were diminishing public confidence in the NORTH ministry, and the ASSOCIATION MOVEMENT's demands for PARLIAMENTARY REFORM were gaining a sympathetic hearing. The implication was that crown patronage was sustaining an incompetent and unpopular ministry.

The motion was carried 233 to 203; resolutions relating to the reform of the royal household and the CIVIL LIST also passed. However, on 24 April, a motion that Parliament should not be prorogued until measures had been taken to reduce crown influence failed to win support, demonstrating the limits of MPs' willingness to back the opposition against king and ministry. *See also* ECONOMICAL REFORM; PLACE BILLS.

Dunstan, St (*c*.909–88), Archbishop of Canterbury (959–88). Dunstan and the younger Ethelwold and OSWALD were leaders of the TENTH-CENTURY REFORM in Anglo-

Saxon England, the basic principles of which Dunstan began to develop following his appointment as abbot of GLASTONBURY in 940. Although his historical reputation rests on his achievements as an ecclesiastical reformer, he was also a profoundly political figure. He had family ties with the highest levels of the aristocracy, acted as chief adviser at the courts of kings EDMUND and EADRED, and was almost instantly appointed to the archbishopric of Canterbury after EDGAR'S accession. His regular attendance at court was fundamental to his partnership with Edgar, which permitted radical changes within the English Church.

Dupplin Moor, Battle of, 12 Aug. 1332, victory near Perth for the DISINHERITED, led by Edward BALLIOL, over a larger force of overconfident Scots fighting in support of DAVID II.

Durham The town's importance stems from the transfer there, in 995, of the relics of St CUTHBERT, whose reputation made the church in which he was buried by far the wealthiest and most prestigious in the region. The superb ROMANESQUE cathedral, started in 1093 and containing the tombs of BEDE and Cuthbert, and the massive CASTLE, begun in 1072 and much extended in the 12th century, are powerful reminders of the town's significance in the history of northern England. Locally, the bishops became not only the greatest spiritual authority, but also the most powerful secular lords. The so-called 'PALATINATE of Durham', within which the bishops exercised all administrative and jurisdictional authority until the 19th century, was well on the way to formation in the 12th century; of the medieval English Palatinates, only Durham remained in the hands of a subject of the crown. A 1536 Act transferred much judicial power to the crown, but the attempt at abolition by Northumberland (*see* DUDLEY, JOHN) in 1552 was overtaken by his fall, and apart from the INTERREGNUM, the jurisdiction remained in the bishop's hands until 1836. Continuous parliamentary representation dates only from after the RESTORATION.

Durham House Set, the nickname of the ARMINIAN group, including LAUD and Richard Montagu, which met at Richard Neile's London house while he was bishop of Durham between 1617 and 1628. The group spearheaded the later Arminian advance against the CALVINIST Church establishment.

Durotriges, the pre-Roman British tribe that inhabited the modern county of Dorset and parts of southern Som. and Wilts. They were subdued soon after AD 43 during the early campaigns of AULUS PLAUTIUS, although archaeological finds at several hillforts within their territory suggest fierce fighting. In *c.*75, the tribal territory became a *CIVITAS* with its capital at Dorchester, close to the Durotriges' magnificent hillfort at MAIDEN CASTLE.

Dutch Wars, the first of three conflicts (1652–4) between two PROTESTANT powers of northern Europe who by tradition and culture ought to have been natural allies (*see* NETHERLANDS, ENGLAND AND THE REVOLT OF THE). The problems arose over the development of both England and the newly independent United Provinces of the Netherlands as worldwide maritime powers, which from the beginning of the 17th century caused increasing friction, particularly in the East Indies (notoriously in the 1623 AMBOINA MASSACRE). However, open confrontation in European waters was postponed until the INTERREGNUM. Dutch merchants were annoyed by the seizure of Dutch ships and cargoes by both sides in the English CIVIL WARS, and Dutch opinion was outraged by the execution of CHARLES I (1649), leading to toleration of English ROYALIST refugees in the Netherlands. The official end to the long conflict between the Dutch and Spain at the end of the THIRTY YEARS WAR in 1648 also made the Dutch less inclined to conciliate the English, and immediately resulted in great expansion of Dutch maritime activity. The English Republican government was nervous in case William of Orange (the father of the future WILLIAM III of England), a relative by marriage of the Stuart dynasty, built on his family's traditionally prominent role in the United Provinces to gain a recognized constitutional status there, either as stadholder or captain-general. Negotiations in 1651 for a close alliance (even diplomatic and commercial union) between the Dutch and the English broke down and were followed by the RUMP PARLIAMENT passing the first NAVIGATION ACT (*see* MERCANTILISM). When war broke out in May 1652, it was provoked by long-standing Dutch anger at the English claim to right of search of all ships in English waters. There were engagements in the Channel and the North Sea, in which the Dutch suffered heavier losses. When making peace in the Treaty of Westminster (1654), the Dutch made concessions, including financial compensation for the Amboina incident and an agreement not to give official positions to William of Orange.

This war established the concept of fighting in line of battle at sea – with the concomitant that only the most powerful ships (the 'ships of the line') could stand in the line. This gave a definite advantage to the English who had more, bigger and more powerful ships than the Dutch, relied less on hired and converted merchant-men, and had more of the infrastructure of a regular NAVY. The process of supplanting the Dutch in international trade was begun in this and subsequent Dutch wars, which were (for England) entirely maritime. England was helped throughout by her geographical position, across the Dutch routes to the outer world, but never managed, despite her considerable advantages, to defeat her hard-fighting adversary completely.

Second Dutch War, 1665–7, like the first was the outcome of Anglo-Dutch trading rivalries, exacerbated by the NAVIGATION ACT's restriction of certain trades to English shipping. There were conflicts in West Africa between 1661 and 1663 and in America in 1664 when the British captured New Amsterdam and renamed it NEW YORK. The Duke of York (the future JAMES II) backed the more aggressive merchants; CHARLES II was more cautious, but as confrontations continued and Parliament voted extra funds, he declared war in March 1665. English naval victory at Lowestoft in June led the French to try to negotiate a peace, in order to leave themselves more room for manoeuvre on the European scene. This having failed, in Jan. 1666, in accordance with treaty obligations, the French entered the war in support of the Dutch, being joined in Feb. by Denmark. English diplomats, by contrast, failed to secure European allies. At the Four Days Battle in early June, the English, having split their fleet to cope with the threat from the French, were caught at a disadvantage by the Dutch and suffered heavy losses. The GREAT FIRE OF LONDON, fears of invasion, the burden imposed by heavy war taxation, exacerbated by the decline in trade, and the strengthening COUNTRY opposition in Parliament forced a near bankrupt king to begin peace negotiations in May 1667. The fleet was laid up at Chatham. In June the Dutch took advantage of this to sack Sheerness, sail up the Medway and capture or destroy several of the most important English warships. They then blockaded the Thames. The English were forced to make terms by this combination of humiliation and danger. Peace was concluded at BREDA in July 1667. Disappointment at the outcome of the war led to Clarendon's (*see* HYDE, EDWARD) dismissal, and the setting up of a parliamentary Accounts Commission to investigate war finance. Louis XIV of France, who had already invaded the Spanish Netherlands in May, was left free to pursue his ambitions. The build-up of the French navy effectively threatened the maritime power of both the English and the Dutch.

Third Dutch War, 1672–4. The treaty of DOVER (1670) had bound the English to join with the French in attacking the Dutch; as planned, war was begun in March 1672, though CHARLES II did not, as promised, announce his conversion to Catholicism, contenting himself with issuing a DECLARATION OF INDULGENCE. Naval victory proved elusive: the Anglo-French fleet received a setback at Solebay in May and then were prevented from gaining decisive victory in a series of brilliant defensive actions fought by the weaker Dutch fleet in their home waters in the summer of 1673. Despite the pre-war suspension of loan repayments, the STOP OF THE EXCHEQUER and French subsidies, the cost of war proved difficult for the English government to meet; in 1673, however, Parliament agreed to raise taxes in return for the rescinding of the Declaration and passage of the TEST ACT (1673) which, by prompting the resignations of the Duke of York (the future JAMES II) and others, demonstrated the truth of the charge that there had been Catholics in high places. Meanwhile, the Dutch had succeeded in strengthening their position. In Aug. 1672 a revolution in the United Netherlands brought William of Orange (the future WILLIAM III) to power as stadholder. In Aug.–Sept. 1673 Spain, Austria and Brandenburg, and, in Jan. 1674, Denmark joined in the war on France. Dutch propaganda encouraged the development among sections of the English Parliament and public of the belief that the war reflected a betrayal of PROTESTANT interests by high-placed Catholics. Following Parliament's refusal to grant further funds, the English government concluded a separate peace with the United Provinces by the Treaty of WESTMINSTER (1674).

Dyfed (Deheubarth). Although the south-western Welsh kingdom of Dyfed is first mentioned in the 6th century, it should certainly be regarded as a reorganization of the pre-Roman DEMETAE. Always one of the most prestigious of the early Welsh kingdoms (*see* KINGSHIP), its politics were recurrently disturbed by feuds within the ruling kindred and with other Welsh families, although it tended to be dominated by GWYNEDD in the 10th and 11th centuries (*see* GRUFFUDD AP LLYWELYN). The kingdom was virtually destroyed by the Normans in 1093, but revived after 1135, only to fall into disarray again in the early 13th century. Its name has been given to a modern county.

Dyrham, Battle of, 577. A victory in Som. gained by the English forces of CEAWLIN of WESSEX and Cuthwine (apparently his co-king) over an army of Britons, which was followed by the English capture of GLOUCESTER, CIRENCESTER and BATH. The battle signalled the resumption of the advance of the English peoples (basically ANGLES and SAXONS) after the long period of peace that followed the battle of Mount BADON.

E

Eadmer (*c.*1060–*c.*1130), hagiographer and theologian. In 1093, this CANTERBURY monk entered ANSELM's household and became the archbishop's companion and historian. In Eadmer's *History of Recent Events in England*, the main theme was Anselm's public career; in his strikingly original *Life of Anselm*, he reconstructed the saint's conversations in order to shed light on his character. In 1120 Eadmer was chosen Bishop of ST ANDREWS but resigned before being consecrated.

Eadred (?–955), King of the English (946–55). His election as king of YORK by its inhabitants, probably in 952, followed by the second expulsion of ERIC BLOODAXE in 954, brought to its completion the absorption of lands conquered by the Scandinavians by the 10th-century kings of WESSEX. He also advanced the careers of both DUNSTAN and Ethelwold, thereby greatly assisting the development of the TENTH-CENTURY REFORM. Despite his successes, he left money in his will to pay the VIKINGS not to attack in the future – an indication that he was prey to the anxieties typical of all 10th-century English kings.

Eadwig (*c.*940–59), King of the English (955–9). Eldest son of EDMUND, he was about 15 when he became king. There appears to have been a succession dispute with his younger brother EDGAR, presumably fomented by factions among the nobility, and after 957, Eadwig's authority was reduced to control over WESSEX as the result of the rebellion launched on Edgar's behalf. Eadwig's reputation was posthumously vilified (perhaps unfairly) by Edgar's supporters, who included DUNSTAN.

Ealdorman, an Anglo-Saxon term that translates literally as 'senior man' and therefore refers to the greatest magnates, often men of royal blood. Ealdormen with administrative responsibilities appear as early as the time of King INE. In 9th-century WESSEX, an ealdorman was normally responsible for a single SHIRE, but the office's status was greatly elevated in the time of ATHELSTAN, who seems to have created single ealdormen for NORTHUMBRIA, MERCIA and EAST ANGLIA. After CNUT's conquest of England in 1016, these same officials were more commonly referred to by the Anglo-Scandinavian word 'earl' (*see* EARLDOMS, ANGLO-SAXON).

Ealdred (?–1069), Archbishop of York (1060–9). He typifies the extravagant display of the late Anglo-Saxon state, as well as the co-operation between churchmen and secular authority. At one stage in the 1050s, he held three bishoprics, attended papal councils in Rome and, in 1054, led the diplomatic mission to Germany that negotiated the return to England of EDWARD THE EXILE. He was, in addition, a great church-builder and collector of valuable books. He appears to have quickly appreciated the decisiveness of the Norman victory in 1066, since he crowned WILLIAM I THE CONQUEROR in WESTMINSTER Abbey on Christmas Day 1066, and was well regarded by the Normans.

Earl, third in the rank of PEERAGE titles, between MARQUESS and VISCOUNT. In Old English the word meant a Danish under-king, but the title in the modern sense was first applied by the Normans as equivalent to the continental title of count, hereditary magnates with residual administrative and military duties in the shires: hence, e.g. earls of Oxford.

Earldoms, Anglo-Saxon The great 11th-century earldoms of WESSEX, MERCIA and NORTHUMBRIA were King CNUT's enlarged version of the territorial units controlled by EALDORMEN, which had been typical of 10th-century England. The earls held extensive powers within their borders, such as the right to receive one-third of royal revenues from the operation of local courts (the 'third penny') and from the BOROUGHS, and to preside over the SHIRE-COURTS.

The greatest of the earls – GODWINE of Wessex, LEOFRIC OF MERCIA and SIWARD of Northumbria – also exercised great influence over the kingdom's destiny. Conflict between them – as in 1051–2, when Godwine and his family were temporarily exiled by EDWARD THE CONFESSOR supported by Leofric and Siward – could shake England to its foundations. Smaller earldoms, some the size of a single SHIRE, were carved out for members of these earls' families in Edward's reign.

Whether the 11th-century earldoms constituted incipient 'territorial principalities', whose existence might eventually have dismembered the English monarchy and regionalized its power, is a controversial and unanswerable question – all earldoms consisting of more than one shire were abolished by WILLIAM I THE CONQUEROR.

Early English, architectural style of the period *c.*1120–1280, the first phase of GOTHIC architecture in England. It was characterized by pointed arches, height, and narrow, lancet windows, with much less solid masonry than in the previous ROMANESQUE style. SALISBURY cathedral, Wilts., is one of the finest examples of this period, built almost in one phase.

East Anglia, Kingdom of This covered the modern counties of Norfolk and Suffolk. Its origins date from the early 6th century, although the names of the earliest kings are unknown. In the time of King REDWALD (*c.*599–*c.*625), the kingdom was the most powerful in southern England, and Redwald was included in BEDE's list of what were later termed *BRETWALDAS*. It is possible that an early 6th-century king (perhaps Redwald himself) was buried at SUTTON HOO. Until the martyrdom of EDMUND and the Danish conquest of 869/70 (*see* VIKINGS), East Anglia was frequently under the domination of the kings of MERCIA. After 869/70, there was a short succession of Danish kings before East Anglia was absorbed into the single kingdom of the English during the reign of EDWARD THE ELDER.

East India Company The dominant force in the extension of indirect imperial control of INDIA, it was chartered by ELIZABETH I in 1600 to challenge the Dutch–Portuguese monopoly of the spice trade. From 1612, voyages were undertaken on a JOINT-STOCK basis. Sir Thomas Rowe, sent as emissary to the Mughal Emperor in 1615–19, gained some trading privileges for the Company, and it established trading posts or factories (*see* FACTORY SYSTEM) in the Bay of Bengal; but conflict with the Dutch led to the massacre of English merchants in Amboina in the Moluccas in 1623 (*see* AMBOINA MASSACRE). Thereafter, the Company concentrated on Indian trade; in 1640, it acquired the site of modern Madras, and built a base there. The Charter was renewed in 1647, constituting the Company as a joint-stock company. Major growth in the Company's activities after 1660 was accompanied by the issue of five further charters, giving it the rights to acquire territory, exercise jurisdiction, make alliances, declare war and conclude peace, command troops and coin money. It acquired the site of modern Bombay in 1667, and founded Calcutta in 1690.

A rival company was formed in 1698, but the two merged in 1702 as the United Company. Along with the BANK OF ENGLAND and the SOUTH SEA COMPANY, the East India Company was a major lender to government – adding a fiscal to a commercial reason for public interest in its affairs.

A problem for the Company was that British demand for Indian goods outstripped Indian demand for British goods, with the result that a surplus of purchases had to be financed by the export of bullion, widely perceived to be against the public interest. Spices and light cloths – calicoes and silks – were from an early date prominent among Indian exports. A triangular trade also developed whereby opium and other goods were exported from India to China, whence tea was exported for European markets. After protests from domestic producers, Indian printed calicoes were excluded from Britain in the early 18th century, but these and other Indian goods bulked large among RE-EXPORTS. A reverse trade in British woollens, from small beginnings, prospered in the later 18th century, which together with a trade in metal goods helped the balance of payments.

From the mid-18th century, the Company extended its territorial power in India as a result of wars among Indian powers and with other Europeans. Major territorial gains in Bengal arose in the SEVEN YEARS WAR, notably as a result of the battle of PLASSEY. Some individuals were able to make fortunes in the heady years after Plassey, earning notoriety on their return as nouveaux-riches 'NABOBS'. Hopes that the Company would be able to contribute substantially to public funds were disappointed when it ran into economic difficulties. (It was in order to assist in the difficulties of a company in whose affairs the public interest was seen to be involved that the Company was given permission to ship tea directly to America – sparking the BOSTON TEA PARTY.) Hopes that territorial revenues might be used to purchase Indian goods for sale in European markets likewise failed to be realized: the costs of administering territories, and above all the costs of war, were to eat up those revenues, and indeed necessitate government subsidies.

Growing parliamentary and public interest in the Company's governmental activities gave rise to a Regulating Act (1773) providing for a government-appointed governor-general, and to PITT THE YOUNGER's 1784 INDIA BILL, creating a BOARD OF CONTROL to oversee the Company. Wars with MYSORE and the Maratha Confederacy in the later 18th century produced further territorial gains; in the early 19th century, Sind and the Punjab were taken in the first AFGHAN WAR, as well as coastal BURMA.

During the 18th century the Company built up an army of its own, or rather three separate armies based on the Presidencies of Bombay, Madras, and Calcutta – the latter was the army that mutinied in 1857 (*see* INDIAN MUTINY). Many additions to the BRITISH EMPIRE, in and beyond India, were won by the sepoys (Indian soldiers) of the Company's army with their British officers. This local army, first owned by the Company and later – after the British crown had assumed full sovereignty over India in 1857 – part of the British Indian Army, was, in combination with the Royal NAVY, the foundation of British power in Asia. The Company also had its own small navy, the 'Bombay Marine', mostly for dealing with pirates on the Indian coast or the Persian Gulf. The huge fleets of east indiamen, the large merchant ships which traded between Britain and the East, were not owned by the Company, though they were licensed and controlled by it. The groups of shareholders who actually owned the ships were also shareholders in the Company.

The Charter Act of 1813 ended the Company's trading monopoly (as response to demands from would-be entrants to the trade), while the Charter of 1833 removed its China trade. It ceased to be a trading concern, and survived solely as an administrative body. More rigorous and systematic in its approach to administration than was the British government of the time, the Company was the original source of the term 'civil servant' (as opposed to a military servant), and pioneered the use of administrative training colleges. In 1858, the crown assumed full sovereignty over India in the aftermath of the 1857 Indian Mutiny. *See also* CIVIL SERVICE; CLIVE, ROBERT; HASTINGS, WARREN.

Easter, Christian festival celebrating Christ's resurrection from the dead. Easter is a moveable feast in spring, its date determined by the phases of the moon; its dating was a major source of difference between the Roman and some of the Irish missions to Britain in the 7th century (*see* CONVERSION). It was also a special interest of BEDE's, which may have resulted in historians overestimating the heat that the arguments generated. Controversy arose because of differing interpretations of earlier Church legislation and the computational complexities of Easter tables (*see COMPOTUS*). The superiority of the Roman calculations was accepted for NORTHUMBRIA at the synod of WHITBY (664) and was eventually accepted throughout the British Church.

Easter was an important time for the laity to take communion, and after the REFORMATION many PARISHes kept Easter books to record attendance. Many CALENDAR CUSTOMS are associated with Easter, commonly involving eggs and other fertility symbols, as well as fairs and local football matches.

Easter Rising, April 1916, armed insurrection in DUBLIN to assert Ireland's claim for independence, led by a faction of the IRISH REPUBLICAN BROTHERHOOD. Plans by Roger Casement to land German arms proved abortive, but on Easter Monday Patrick Pearse and James Connolly seized the General Post Office and other buildings in Dublin. Pearse proclaimed the Irish Republic and himself as president of its provisional government. After five days of heavy street fighting, British troops forced the rebels to surrender. Connolly, Pearse and 12 other leaders were summarily tried and executed. Though the rising was initially unpopular with much Irish opinion, the execution of its leaders increased sympathy for their cause. The rising marked the beginning of a major swing in Irish sentiment from the moderate HOME RULERS to the nationalist aspirations of SINN FÉIN, so that Pearse's doomed rising became a celebrated moment in Ireland's campaign for independence from Britain.

Easterlings, *see* HANSEATIC LEAGUE

Eastern Association The only success story (but a fairly moderate one) among PARLIAMENT's attempts to set up regional military organizations in 1642–3 during the CIVIL WARS, it linked the East Anglian counties with Herts. and Lincs. Under the command of Charles Montagu, Earl of Manchester, it held the region firm against the ROYALISTS. Its role effectively ended with the creation of the NEW MODEL ARMY in 1645.

Eastern Question A dominant concern of British foreign policy in the 19th century, and a key element in the making of the CRIMEAN WAR, it arose out of the need to preserve the Ottoman Empire – 'the sick man of Europe' – against Russian encroachment in defence of Britain's interests in INDIA. Turkish decline was evident in the 18th century. The Russians, who had established themselves on the Black Sea, obtained, in the treaty of Kuchuk Kainardji, concluded with the Turks in 1774, certain ill-defined and easily invocable rights of interference in favour of the Christian subjects of the sultan. The Crimean War resulted from Russian attempts to exercise these rights and the consequent opposition from Britain and France. British military and diplomatic support, coupled with a growing pressure for administrative reform within the Ottoman Empire, ultimately alienated the Turks to Germany's advantage in 1914.

Eastland Company, set up in 1579 to regulate the English Baltic trade, which was particularly important for mast timber and other naval stores. With the HANSEATIC LEAGUE's privileges removed and their share of English trade in steep decline, the company remained a vigorous cloth exporter into the 17th century. Its privileges were confirmed in the NAVIGATION ACTS but abrogated in 1673. After the early 18th century, it had a merely formal existence.

EC, *see* EUROPEAN UNION

Ecclesiastical Commission, a court set up by JAMES II in 1686 to enforce ecclesiastical discipline, after Bishop COMPTON had refused to remove a clergyman charged with seditious preaching. The commission suspended both the clergyman and Compton. Critics suggested that it recalled LAUD's Court of HIGH COMMISSION, abolished by Parliament in 1641. The Ecclesiastical Commission was itself dissolved in Oct. 1688, when William of Orange (*see* WILLIAM III) was about to appear on the scene and James was desperate to rally support.

Ecclesiastical Commissioners, an incorporated body which, from 1835 until 1948, was responsible for the administration of the estates and revenues of the Church of England. The Commissioners were principally concerned with the augmenting and endowment of BENEFICES. In 1948 the Ecclesiastical Commissioners and QUEEN ANNE'S BOUNTY united in a new body, the Church Commissioners for England.

Ecgfrith (?–685), King of Northumbria (670–85). A notably warlike king who briefly extended NORTHUMBRIAN power to its furthest limits. His ambitions in the south were thwarted by Ethelred of MERCIA in 679, but in the north he crushed the PICTS in *c.*672 and established a bishopric at Abercorn on the Firth of Forth in 681. Four years later, he set out to invade Ireland, but was defeated and killed at NECHTANESMERE in the kingdom of the Picts. His first wife was ÆLTHELFRYTH, founder of ELY abbey. Although Ecgfrith's reputation for piety has remained intact, he was involved in a spectacular quarrel with Bishop WILFRID, which seems to have been caused by the encouragement Wilfrid gave to Ælthelfryth to leave her husband.

Econometrics, the investigation of economic relationships using mathematical and statistical techniques based within economic theory. The application of econometrics to economic history has become increasingly marked in the past 30 years, and its techniques are being applied to a variety of debates: most notably the contribution of RAILWAYS to economic growth, the profitability of SLAVERY, entrepreneurial performance, and technological choices. Some of the most enthusiastic claims about the advantages of this approach in eliminating subjectivity and uncertainty from aspects of the ECONOMIC HISTORY of the past are now derided, but the technique remains useful in contributing to cyclic debates. The greatest body of work is being done in the USA, often under the title of the New Economic History or CLIOMETRICS.

Economic Affairs, Department of (DEA), part of a failed administrative reorganization by the newly elected WILSON government of 1964 which is often seen as a symbol of its overall performance. The new ministry was set up in 1965 under George Brown, intended to act as a counterweight to the TREASURY and take a more strategic view of the economy. It introduced a Prices and Incomes Board and in Sept. 1965 produced a 'National Plan', envisaging a 25 per cent growth in national output by 1970. Growing balance of payments problems almost immediately rendered the Plan unrealistic. Brown, its main advocate, transferred to the foreign office in 1966, and the new ministry was eventually wound up in Oct. 1969.

Economic Growth, an increase over time in real national income, or in real national income per head (national income being defined as either the *gross* or the *net* national product). The definitions may vary, but the core concept of expansion over a sustained period of time, usually measured in annual percentage terms, remains the same. In modern industrial countries the rate of economic growth has commonly been between 1 and 2 per cent per annum, although it has been higher in many post-1945 economies. The expansion of the British economy in the period from the mid-18th century has been largely seen as one of almost unbroken economic growth, with the exception of the depths of the Victorian TRADE CYCLES and the DEPRESSION of the inter-war years.

Economic History Interest in economic history developed strongly from the late 19th century both inside and outside academic circles. Early compilers of economic statistics such as J. E. Thorold Rogers and William Beveridge (*see* BEVERIDGE REPORT) provided the basis for an understanding of the broad movements of prices and wages and detailed studies of the economy. But interest in the economic and social life of the past was also a feature of the early LABOUR movement and was strongly represented in adult education through University Extension courses and the WORKERS' EDUCATIONAL ASSOCIATION, to which several of the pioneer economic historians, such as R. H. Tawney, devoted much of their time. By the inter-war years economic historians including Tawney, Barbara and John Hammond, G. D. H. Cole, Eileen Power, and J. H. Clapham had produced important studies of the medieval, early modern, and industrial periods. Issues were emerging concerning the nature of industrialization, the relationship of religion to the rise of capitalism and the standard of living during the INDUSTRIAL REVOLUTION. The Economic History Society and its journal *Economic History Review* provided an increasingly important focus for academic work in the area during the post-1945 period. From then economic history developed a harder, quantitative edge, the so-called 'New Economic History' reflecting ECONOMETRICS and the increasingly mathematical nature of economics. Other specialisms have also emerged, such as business history, transport history and financial history, although in recent years the subject has moved into closer alliance once more with social and cultural history.

Economical Reform The expenditure of public money on salaries for placemen, and on pensions for various nobility, gentry and others with some claim on the crown, was a target for criticism throughout the 18th century – the more so since it was suspected that the object was in effect to buy votes, and so 'increase the influence of the Crown' (i.e. of the king and his ministers). In 1780, when the War of AMERICAN INDEPENDENCE was inflating expenditure, and when the increasing likelihood that the American colonies would be permanently lost was causing many to doubt the soundness of the political system, 'economical reform' – a new catchphrase of the period – became one of the chief objects of oppositional campaigning. Yorks. freeholders, under the leadership of Christopher Wyvill, spearheaded a petitioning movement which was supported by a majority of English counties and a number of cities. The COMMONS approved DUNNING'S MOTION, condemning the increasing influence of the crown, but specific opposition proposals, including a wide-ranging scheme put forward by BURKE, were defeated. NORTH, however, agreed to set up commissioners for examining the PUBLIC ACCOUNTS. More radical steps were taken when the ROCKINGHAMITE WHIGS came to power in 1782. Burke's Establishment Bill (1782) abolished several offices, including the BOARD OF TRADE, and imposed economies on the royal household. Clerke's Bill, which excluded from the Commons all holders of government contracts, and Crewe's Bill, which deprived revenue officers of the vote, were passed in the same year. *See also* PLACE BILLS.

Economy, general term used to describe the interaction of the various areas of economic activity within a locality, region, nation or larger entity. The term, in a historical context, will usually encompass agricultural production, industrial production, the amount of non-productive employment an economic system can support, etc. The word originally meant 'management' and retains that sense in phrases such as 'domestic economy'; the study of economics was similarly traditionally called 'political economy', i.e. study of the management of the economic system.

Often a distinction is drawn between the formal economy, which includes all regulated and officially recorded economic activity, and the informal economy, which includes unregulated production, trade reciprocities and economic relationships. In modern economies part of this informal economy is sometimes referred to as the black market, which flourishes where people can gain from illegal trades and/or by evading taxation. In most economies, and especially in early and pre-industrial ones, a very large part of economic life takes place informally and is embedded in social and cultural practices, conventions and relationships.

ROMAN

The nature of Roman Britain's economy has to be largely deduced from archaeological evidence. It was undoubtedly organized in a way that was typically Roman, and therefore differed radically from what came before and after. TOWNS and associated VILLAS were deliberately and extensively constructed in the areas most securely under Roman control – namely, the south and east – and became centres of demand and supply. Development was somewhat slow in the early stages of the ROMAN CONQUEST; much important building work seems to date from the later years of the 1st century AD.

The sheer survival rate of coin indicates a money economy (*see* COINS AND COINAGE, Roman), although it should be noted that the finds of coin suggest a much greater supply in the 2nd century. State-controlled exploitation of mineral mining made Britain an exporter of gold, silver, copper, iron and tin. There was industrial development – for example, in the manufacture of pottery – and Britain became increasingly self-sufficient in many items. POPULATION may well have been as high as 3–4 million, which is considerably greater than during the early medieval period.

Although towns were undoubtedly declining during the 4th century, there are signs that the Roman economy continued beyond the departure of the Roman armies. Nevertheless, the collapse during the 5th and 6th centuries was certainly severe.

ANGLO-SAXON

There can be no doubt that the wealth of Anglo-Saxon England was one of the factors – and perhaps the major one – that attracted the VIKINGS' attacks and the NORMAN CONQUEST of 1066. That this wealth existed is now accepted by all modern commentators, but its sources remain mysterious, as also does the economy that created it.

It appears that, after the departure of the Romans, the use of money virtually disappeared; the importance of towns certainly declined dramatically. None the less, the sophisticated manufacture of brooches and the extensive international contacts indicated by SUTTON HOO and other archaeological finds suggest an economy that was far from rudimentary.

Native coins were again minted in the second quarter of the 7th century (*see* COINS AND COINAGE, Anglo-Saxon), and King OFFA of MERCIA negotiated a treaty on behalf of English merchants abroad. The England of the 10th and 11th centuries was rich in silver, perhaps because of a favourable balance of trade with the Low Countries and the Rhineland. The towns that developed from the Alfredian *BURHS* and as a result of the SCANDINAVIAN SETTLEMENTS often became notable centres of manufacture and local and international trade (*see* YORK). *DOMESDAY BOOK* and the DANEGELD both demonstrate the widespread use of money as a medium of exchange.

MEDIEVAL

Economic recovery beginning in the late Anglo-Saxon period meant that the landscape of dispersed population characteristic of the early post-Roman centuries – with very few towns and nearly everyone living in hamlets and isolated farmsteads – was transformed by the gradual emergence of a much more nucleated settlement pattern, a countryside of villages and market towns. The evidence of *DOMESDAY BOOK* indicates that some 150 towns and markets existed in England, enabling historians to estimate that by 1086 the proportion of the total English population living in towns was as high as in 1586 (though less than 10 per cent at both dates). Throughout the 12th and 13th centuries old towns continued to grow – recent studies suggest that by 1300 London contained about 100,000 inhabitants, several times more than previously thought. At least 140 new ones were founded. In village after village churches were newly built, or rebuilt in stone. By 1300 the English POPULATION reached a level not exceeded until *c.*1750. During the 12th and 13th centuries many thousands of English families, seeking new opportunities, migrated to the more fertile parts of Ireland as well as northern and western Britain where the pace of economic development had hitherto been noticeably slower than in England.

Shortage of silver meant probably that for a century or so after 1066 less coin was minted than in the late Anglo-Saxon period, but then the opening of new silver mines in Germany led to a massive increase in the output of the English mints. By 1250 over 100 million silver pennies were in circulation in England, five times as many as a century earlier, and with the minting of new coins of smaller denomination – farthings and halfpence in 1279 and 1280 – money could be used for a wider range of transactions. The volume of silver circulating as coin in later 13th-century England was not exceeded until the 19th century. Improved methods of harnessing allowed greater use of horses (instead of oxen) to pull carts as well as ploughs. Thus the inhabitants of the new market towns – the bakers, butchers, fishmongers, brewers, weavers, tailors, shoe-makers, building-workers and carpenters, smiths and metal workers – were able to provide a greater range of goods and services for the villagers of the surrounding countryside as well as for their fellow townspeople. As carts loaded with building stone, grain and cloth went to and fro on the roads linking villages and towns so, to cope with the increased volume of traffic, a road network emerged which was not significantly extended until the motorways of the 20th century. Hundreds of bridges were built, or rebuilt in stone, over the country's rivers. Similar developments all over Europe meant that England became part of a single trading area reaching from Russia and the Middle East to Spain and Ireland. Thus many of the new towns, e.g. Hull, LIVERPOOL, PORTSMOUTH, were ports, their quays built to accommodate the cog, a ship of new design, well-suited to carry bulk cargoes such as the bales of high-quality English WOOL much sought after by the emerging cloth industries of Europe's most urbanized regions, northern Italy and the Low Countries.

Other technological innovations such as the windmill and spinning wheel improved the capacity to process the raw material of a fundamentally agricultural economy. Whether primary production could have continued to keep pace with the rising population is a moot point. However the dramatic population fall caused by the BLACK DEATH and subsequent plagues led to the permanent abandonment of many villages and postponed that challenge for several centuries. In the early 15th century money supply was shaken by a Europe-wide bullion shortage. Despite such shocks, however, improvements in ship design as well as the development of clocks, firearms and the printing press indicate continuing technological development in the later Middle Ages.

EARLY MODERN

The Tudor period was marked by the development of greater political stability and national unity which provided a firm basis for the further development of the economy, although there were many severe problems. The 16th century witnessed POPULATION growth, urbanization (particularly the growth of LONDON), ENCLOSURE and price inflation. Price rises were caused partly by population growth and rising demand for food and raw materials, but were exacerbated by DEBASEMENT of the COINAGE and (from the 1590s) by a major inflow of gold bullion into Western Europe from the Americas. The crown's need for money in order to wage war necessitated a debasement in 1526–7 followed by the 'Great Debasement' of 1544–51 which possibly doubled the circulating medium. Population increase, high prices (especially for cereals) and changes in AGRICULTURE (especially enclosure for sheep-rearing to take advantages of increased international prices for wool before the 1520s) combined to aggravate problems of UNEMPLOYMENT and POVERTY. These peaked with periods of bad harvests creating severe crises with high MORTALITY rates. High food prices encouraged the extension of the cultivated acreage and gave smaller landowners, lesser GENTRY and yeomanry of the Tudor and early Stuart period the opportunity to increase their wealth and status. In this they were joined by new entrants to landowning: lawyers, burgesses and government office-holders. The crown and Church both lost lands, the former through sales to raise finance, the latter through both sales and confiscations. The DISSOLUTION OF THE MONASTERIES, as well as adding massively to the active land market, meant that monastic sources of charity for the poor dried up at the same time as the monasteries themselves were forced to shed their many thousands of employees, contributing to the problems of poverty and VAGRANCY. These developments resulted in the Act of Elizabeth 1601, which consolidated the establishment of the Old POOR LAW.

External and internal trade were stimulated in the 16th century by price rises and by growing populations and urban concentrations throughout much of Europe. From the 1460s England's export trade recovered from the doldrums of the earlier 15th century, marked very significantly by an increase in exports of cloth in addition to wool. The European market for English broad-cloths and particularly for kerseys was much extended, and this was joined from the late 16th century by an expansion of exports of 'NEW DRAPERIES' (early worsted mixes), in which the MERCHANT ADVENTURERS (a regulating, guild-like London company) was very prominent. From its joint headquarters in London and Antwerp it controlled entry to trade, won government support, chartered ships and kept out interlopers. In the 1560s war between France and Spain had a drastic impact upon the Antwerp money market, and there were Europe-wide harvest failures and grain crises. The English cloth trade decayed for a time and the Merchant Adventurers lost their Antwerp base.

Trade aspirations turned away from concentration on Europe and, in a climate of wars, of aggressive nationalistic commerce and of MERCANTILIST ideas, the state granted rights and support to a series of major trading companies to assist with the politico-economic battle for world commerce: the RUSSIA COMPANY (1553), Spanish Company (1577), EASTLAND COMPANY (1579), the LEVANT COMPANY (1581), the EAST INDIA COMPANY (1600), the Virginia Company (1606) and others of the early 17th century for trading to the Americas. The privileges so established for London merchants created great resentment and opposition in the provinces. Despite voyages of discovery and the work of the long-distance trading companies, until the 18th century English trade continued to be focused on Europe, consisting of about 86 per cent wool and cloth exports, and the bulk was carried in foreign vessels as the domestic mercantile marine remained small. Although English overseas trade benefited from neutrality during the THIRTY YEARS WAR, especially in developing RE-EXPORTS and in Spanish American commerce, only the foundations for later empire and world trading had been laid at this point.

The growing domestic trade of the 16th century was interrupted in the 17th by population crises, notably by visitations of Plague (the last of importance and the worst, the GREAT PLAGUE in London in 1665–6), influenza and smallpox. Poor climatic conditions aggravated the increased death rates though England was spared the severe decimations of population experienced in much of Europe during the 17th century. Slow rates of demographic increase, which continued to the mid-18th century, were also caused by high ages of MARRIAGE and lower marriage rates than those commonly found after the late 18th century. These were perhaps the reaction to poor economic prospects, though for those in waged work low food prices (before the late 18th century) created reasonable living standards. Buoyant domestic demand amongst some sectors of the population in the late 17th and early 18th centuries created a vital home market from an expanding range of manufactured goods and services, including clothing and household wares, a trend further encouraged by the growth of retailing and continuing urbanization. Much manufacturing during the early modern period and in the 18th century came to be carried out in households in the countryside, using family labour often working a 'dual economy' (INDUSTRY alongside agriculture). Soaking up unemployed and underemployed rural labour (including that of women and children) in PROTO-INDUSTRY often occurred at the expense of older-established urban industries in the old corporate towns, which used more expensive male artisan labour. Thus, for example, YORK declined in the 15th and 16th centuries whilst West Yorks. rural cloth-manufacturing expanded, and along with it the newer industrial towns of Halifax, LEEDS and Wakefield. Despite sluggish population growth and political instability, the 17th century also witnessed major expansion in COAL and lead mining, involving deeper pits, more capital investment and larger-scale concerns often employing several hundred persons.

The 17th century stands out because of the English CIVIL WAR, and there has been much debate about the connection between it and the later RESTORATION of a limited monarchy (the so-called English revolution) on the one hand, and economic changes, in particular the 'rise of the gentry' and the development of capitalism. MARX and Engels saw the revolution as a turning-point in establishing a political structure which represented the interests of the capitalist classes. R. H. Tawney and other historians argued that the civil war arose because the increasing economic power of commercial landowners was not reflected in their political power or status. Others have argued that only a narrow group of the lower gentry were experiencing economic improvement. Whatever the cause, the economic effects were substantial, arising from the sequestration and sale of ROYALIST lands, the disruption and destruction of parts of the country, of manufacture and of trade, and the longer-term representation in Parliament of the commercial landed élite who had much in common with the manufacturing bourgeoisie. The restoration of the monarchy, followed by shifts during the following decades in state policy to reform national finances, to secure private property rights, to extend agricultural improvement, trade and manufacture, ushered in a century or so of marked, though interrupted, economic progress which laid foundations for the INDUSTRIAL REVOLUTION of the later 18th century. *See also* BANK OF ENGLAND; BOARD OF TRADE; CLOTH INDUSTRY; COMMERCIAL REVOLUTION; DROVING TRADE; ENUMERATED GOODS; EXCISE; EXPORTS; FINANCIAL REVOLUTION; GRAIN RIOTS; INFLATION; IRON AND STEEL INDUSTRY; LEAD MINING; MIGRATION; MINERAL AND BATTERY WORKS AND MINES ROYAL; MONOPOLIES; NAVIGATION ACTS; PALAVICINO, HORATIO; PLANTATIONS; RE-EXPORTS; STOCK EXCHANGE; SUGAR; TOBACCO; TONNAGE AND POUNDAGE; URBAN RENAISSANCE; WOOLLEN INDUSTRY.

THE 18TH AND EARLY 19TH CENTURIES

Sluggish rates of population growth were transformed by the 1760s to a marked acceleration, influenced by lowering ages and higher rates of marriage, increased illegitimacy, and by general improvements in death rates (although urban death rates continued markedly to exceed those in rural areas). Under the impact of population pressure and accompanying urbanization (felt in the growth of London and in provincial industrial and port towns and cities) prices began a marked upward movement, especially for foodstuffs. The intersectoral TERMS OF TRADE moved in favour of agriculture, which encouraged heavy investment in the sector, particularly during the NAPOLEONIC WARS.

The output of foodstuffs only just kept pace with population increase, and it was the production of industrial manufactured goods which increased most rapidly (especially the output of textiles) under the impetus of buoyant domestic and overseas demand, and with the aid of numerous technical and organizational improvements of the industrial revolution.

Big shifts occurred in overseas trade in the 18th century. Imports and exports both increased more than fivefold, and re-exports expanded ninefold to account for a third of the total value of exports at their peak of influence in the third quarter of the century. External demand was important to industrialization, since around 30–35 per cent of English manufactures were exported at this time and levels of demand often changed at such a pace as to provoke major innovations. Cotton cloth overtook woollens as the major export in the late 18th century and iron exports grew in importance. Re-exports consisted mainly of colonial consumer goods such as SUGAR, TOBACCO, TEA, coffee, rum and spices. These were shipped to Europe, enabling England to continue to buy linen, timber, naval supplies and other products from the continent. The high level of trade in re-exports, together with growing domestic demand for colonial groceries and for raw cotton, sustained purchasing power in North America and the WEST INDIES for English manufactured goods and thus gave the Atlantic economy a key role during a century in which protectionism in Europe placed restrictions on the expansion of trade there. Growing trade with colonies of European settlement was very important in stimulating demand for manufactured goods that could be mass-produced: printed and plain textiles, blankets, nails, ropes, cordage, buckets, hand tools, copper and wrought-iron products, linens and sails, as well as fashion products such as silks, hats, pewter, buckles, buttons and toys. The SLAVE TRADE underpinned the growth of the Atlantic economy and of trade with North America and the West Indies.

State policy, protectionism, militarism and diplomacy lay behind English overseas expansion in the 18th century. Wars with the French and the Dutch secured an expanding place in trade and in shipping. By the late 18th century, and with the aid of the NAVIGATION ACTS, Britain monopolized much of the world's shipping and mercantile activity, spawning marine insurance, underwriting, banking and multilateral, international credit and bill networks. London replaced Amsterdam as the major international capital market. Overseas investment was stimulated, and by 1850 around £200 million of foreign securities was held by British subjects mainly in the United States and in the colonies.

After 1815 cotton and other exports to Europe declined in relative terms and Britain came increasingly to depend on more distant markets and upon IMPERIALISM both formal and informal. Britain succeeded in endorsing a dominant relationship with the underdeveloped world (AFRICA, Asia, the Near East, AUSTRALIA and Latin America), and control of INDIA made the subcontinent the vital linchpin of Far Eastern expansion after the 1830s, providing some compensation for the decline of the West Indies markets. At home, though there is little evidence that average real earnings were increasing before the 1840s, there appears to have been a big increase in domestic demand for a greater variety of manufactured goods from the third quarter of the 18th century – so much so that historians have used the term 'consumer revolution' and suggested that it was caused by the increased earnings of women and children in industry – and by a spirit of social emulation (tastes and demands being stimulated by the consumption patterns of the élites and middle classes). Other historians, notably Jan de Vries, have suggested that increased consumption during this period was caused largely by an 'industrious revolution' whereby more and more households (and especially their female members) became involved in wage labour outside the home and therefore turned to the market to buy those sorts of manufactured goods (candles, plates, butter, cheese, clothing, cloth) which they had formerly produced on a subsistence basis.

The quickening pace of industrial production in households, workshops and (in the case of some restricted sectors, notably textiles) FACTORIES was accompanied by innovation, of new technologies and methods of organizing production, such as subcontracting and sweating (*see* SWEATED TRADES). These developments involved new ways of employing labour, the increased employment of women and children in manufacturing, new labour discipline and a destruction of old labour hierarchies and established rhythms and routines of working which had often fitted around the agrarian calendar. Instead of taking time off to do harvest work, or for feast days, manufacturing workers now had to work regular, often long, hours throughout the seasons. The cultural and social dislocations of these changes, coupled with the hardships of urbanization and high indirect taxation, precipitated the widespread social protests of the early 19th century in movements such as the LUDDITES, the ANTI-POOR LAW movement, factory reform, Owenite socialism (*see* OWEN, ROBERT) and CHARTISM.

In the countryside the 18th and early 19th centuries saw continued agricultural change and enclosure. Agriculture absorbed only one-third of the labour force by 1800, compared with two-thirds a century earlier, although absolute numbers on the land did not fall until after the mid-19th century. Population growth, rural UNEMPLOYMENT and the loss of valuable income-earning supplements from CUSTOM, common rights and common lands added to the hardships experienced by ordinary people in the process of economic transformation and structural change. *See also:* BANK OF ENGLAND; BOARD OF CONTROL; BOARD OF TRADE; CANALS; CHAMBERS OF COMMERCE; COAL INDUSTRY; COTTON INDUSTRY; DROVING TRADE; EAST INDIA COMPANY; EXCISE; EXCISE CRISIS; EXPORTS; FINANCIAL REVOLUTION; GRAIN RIOTS; INFLATION; IRON AND STEEL INDUSTRY; LINKAGES; MIGRATION; MULE; NATIONAL INCOME; PLANTATIONS; RE-EXPORTS; SHIPBUILDING; SOUTH SEA BUBBLE COMPANY; STEAM POWER; STOCK EXCHANGE; TAKE-OFF; TRIANGULAR TRADE; URBAN RENAISSANCE; WOOLLEN INDUSTRY.

SINCE THE MID 19TH CENTURY

By the 1850s Britain had become the dominant industrial power in the world economy. While this initial dominance was based on textiles, a new wave of innovations in STEAM POWER, RAILWAYS and steel which promised to consolidate that position were under rapid development. The accumulation of capital accelerated with beneficial effects on labour productivity (output per head). Despite this acceleration, however, it was becoming clear that the UK's position was not unassailable: thus the United States and then Germany were seen to be catching Britain up – indeed the former passed Britain in terms of GDP per capita in the 1890s.

By the 1870s, however, complaints were already being expressed in the UK about lower rates of technical progress and an educational system that was élitist and antipathetic to business. There is also some evidence that the pound was becoming overvalued so that export performance began to suffer. The possibility of DEVALUATION as a way of retaining competitiveness was simply unthinkable as the pound was the key currency in the financing of international trade and devaluation was thought likely to damage the UK's financial and commercial interests. Britain's role as an imperial power, the international orientation of her financial institutions and the overvaluation of the pound resulted in a larger outflow of capital than had been seen before or since. From 1900–14 foreign investment was as large as domestic investment, so that by the outbreak of WORLD WAR I assets owned overseas were one and a half times larger than the GDP. As a result the flow of income from ownership of these assets comprised nearly 10 per cent of the GDP. This compared with only 2 per cent in the 1850s.

Britain came out of World War I with less physical damage and loss of manpower than her continental neighbours, but a return to the *status quo ante* was impossible. The 1920s were a period of stagnation and class conflict, while in the United States they were years of boom. The thrust of economic policy seemed to be driven by desire to return to the stability of the GOLD STANDARD. The folly of this nostalgic policy was the desire to return to the gold standard at the pre-war parity: given the way in which productivity and prices had evolved since before the war this implied an overvaluation of the currency. How much the pound was overvalued remained a contentious issue even in the 1980s, but the implication of sustaining any overvaluation was the need to bring down domestic wages and prices relative to the UK's major competitors. Hence the mid-1920s were riven with industrial relations conflicts as employers in the main export industries, particularly coal, attempted to bring down their labour costs.

Following the Wall Street crash of 1929, the American economy collapsed into the great depression, and this had serious consequences for the world economy including Britain. International trade contracted as country after country introduced 'beggar my neighbour' policies such as import quotas, tariff barriers and exchange controls. The 1930s were widely regarded as years of failure, but the impact of the DEPRESSION was not felt equally throughout Britain. It was particularly acute in the North of England, South Wales and Scotland: these were areas where older manufacturing activity was located – such as textiles, SHIPBUILDING, IRON AND STEEL making – and they were particularly susceptible to the collapse of overseas markets. The problems faced by these areas received political recognition as it was during the 1930s that embryonic forms of regional policy began to appear. It has been argued by some economic historians that, despite the depression, the record of the 1930s was not a complete and unmitigated failure, that there were a number of significant advances. Thus new emerging industries, predominantly orientated to the domestic market, enjoyed a sustained period of growth: for example, aeronautics, synthetic materials, electrical goods, fine chemicals and pharmaceuticals, were established and began to be available to middle-class households. House-building of course enjoyed the benefits of cheap money – very low interest rates – and the quality of the housing stock in suburbia increased markedly. For the most part, these new industries and the house-building boom were located in the Midlands and the south-east of England, so that these areas escaped the worst ravages of the depression.

WORLD WAR II had remarkable effects on the British economy and society. First, the rearmament programme made rapid inroads into unemployment; second, the rate of technical advance accelerated as public funds flowed into the development of RADAR, AIRCRAFT and TELECOMMUNICATIONS; third, the scope for government economic and social policy was demonstrated across a whole range of activities; fourth, the TRADE UNION movement was 'co-opted' as an important partner in the prosecution of the war; fifth, the recruitment of women into the labour force on a larger scale than ever before portended changes in the post-war world; and finally, the social solidarity engendered by the war produced some diminution of the class conflict which had been a feature of the 1920s and 1930s.

By the end of the war, however, the economy was in a parlous condition. Apart from war damage the capital stock was badly run down – little or no investment had taken place for over half a decade, particularly in the transport and fuel supply industries. In addition, balance of payments difficulties immediately became apparent: the US administration ended its commitment to LEND-LEASE immediately hostilities ceased, yet Britain was in no position to sell exports to replace the loss of dollar inflows. Inflation was a constant threat from pent-up consumer demand, the need to renew the capital of the economy and the commitment to public spending. As a result, for the next five to six years the ATTLEE government maintained most of the wartime controls, and the population was subject to continued rationing and general austerity: consumer spending was restrained to make room for exports and public expenditure. The latter was maintained at a particularly high level as the government set up the WELFARE STATE and undertook an extensive programme of nationalization. Recovery was of course helped by the use of Marshall Aid (*see* MARSHALL PLAN) in the late 1940s, but substantial devaluation could not be avoided in 1949. The final death blow to the government's anti-inflationary strategy was dealt by the outbreak of the KOREAN WAR. This had two sorts of impact: it drove up international commodity prices, and in addition the government embarked on a rearmament programme which put enormous demand pressures into the economy.

The coming to power of the CONSERVATIVES in the 1951 general election represented a political change but there was considerable cross-party agreement on economic management. Indeed, the era is often referred to as that of BUTSKELLISM because the differences between the main parties on the objectives of policy were so small that it was described by conflating the names of R. A. BUTLER, the Tory chancellor, and Hugh GAITSKELL, his immediate predecessor as LABOUR chancellor. The 1950s were years of prosperity and stability: unemployment averaged only 1–1.5 per cent; the annual rate of inflation rarely exceeded 2 per cent; at the same time economic growth was proceeding at nearly 3 per cent per annum. This was a performance unmatched in British history. It is hardly surprising that some degree of complacency affected the UK's political and business élites. The economy was clearly performing well; Japan and Germany were recovering their international position but not yet challenging too seriously; on the commercial/industrial front Britain was first to develop a civilian jet airliner and first to develop nuclear power for peaceful purposes. This complacency may have contributed to the decision to remain aloof from the Mistune conference which led to the Treaty of Rome and founding of the EEC (*see* EUROPEAN UNION).

By the 1960s there was the clear feeling that, while the UK's economic performance was better in terms of the level and stability of employment and output growth than at any time since the 19th century, this did not compare with what was occurring in Germany, France, Italy and some of the smaller European countries (not to mention Japan). The Conservative government began to espouse some of the ideas that had apparently worked well in the French context, and started to introduce new institutions and use the language of planning in the conduct of economic policy. In turn there was also a belated conversion to the idea of joining the EEC – an effort which met with a decided 'Non' from the French president de Gaulle. The return of a Labour government in 1964 was marked by a long but ultimately unsuccessful attempt to avoid devaluation of the pound. INCOMES POLICIES of various types were introduced but to no avail, and the pound was devalued from $2.80 to $2.40 in 1967.

As the 1960s wore on, the trade union movement was perceived as becoming more powerful and truculent, and attempts in 1969 to change their legal status and powers by the minister of labour, Barbara Castle, were defeated. The election of a Conservative government headed by Edward HEATH in 1970 was somewhat unexpected. It had a right-of-centre programme, including the introduction of a completely new, legally-based system of industrial relations (*see* INDUSTRIAL RELATIONS ACT 1971). However, the economic situation was deteriorating sharply: for the first time since the 1930s, unemployment rose to over one million in the winter of 1972 as a result of domestic deflation and a slowdown in the world economy. The government then performed a complete volte-face, reflating the economy by expanding the money supply very rapidly, and at the same time imposing an incomes policy which was, by the standards of previous attempts, fairly generous. The incomes policy placed the government on a course which led to confrontation with the miners' union and ultimately to defeat in the general election. This plus the U-turn on economic policy burned itself into the minds and hearts of the Tory party, particularly a then junior minister, Sir Keith Joseph, and his later protégée Margaret THATCHER.

The 1970s were by any post-war standards a disastrous decade. First, the breakdown of the BRETTON WOODS system of international payments in 1972/3 ushered in greater financial and monetary instability and showed how performance of different economies was diverging sharply. Second, the world economy was brought to a halt by the oil-price increases of 1973/4. Third, inflation accelerated sharply and the capacity of governments to manage their economic affairs with any authority was undermined by soaring and apparently uncontrollable budget deficits. The problem of stagflation resulted also in much sharper industrial relations conflict as trade unions struggled to maintain their members' incomes. Finally, the decade was brought to an end with a further crippling rise in oil prices in 1979 and a rash of strikes in the public sector. This helped to bring Mrs Thatcher into office determined to shift the locus of political debate radically to the right, a determination deeply influenced by the Heath government's volte-face on economic policy in 1972 and ultimate loss of power following the 1974 general election.

The number one target for the 1980s was tackling inflation with reduced subsidies to industry despite the cost of this in the manufacturing sector, and unprecedented high levels of unemployment – 3 million unemployed in 1982. But the middle years of the decade saw the arrival of the 'Lawson boom' (named after THATCHER's Chancellor of the Exchequer) when deregulation of financial controls and institutions and easy credit fuelled an unprecedented – and unsustainable – consumer boom. Consumer spending exceeded GNP (Gross National Product) and house prices doubled between 1985 and 1989, but the rate of savings fell to 4 per cent, the lowest for 10 years. The widening gap between domestic savings and investment resulted in a balance of payment deficit of £14 billion with interest rates soaring to 15 per cent in Sept. 1989. In October Lawson resigned. The boom, predictably, was followed by a deep recession in the early 1990s and control of inflation again became the government's priority, though unemployment which had remained high throughout the boom years stayed at around 2 million. By 1995 the 'green shoots' of economic recovery could be detected: this time tight monetary and fiscal control resulted in a slower rate of consumer demand and export growth, due in part to a strong pound, but also to the slowdown of the global economy. The fastest growth area is now the service sector with manufacturing contributing less than a quarter of GDP compared to over a third in 1950. *See also* AGRICULTURE; AUSTERITY; BANKS; BOARD OF CONTROL; BOARD OF TRADE; CANALS; CHAMBERS OF COMMERCE; CHEMICAL INDUSTRY; COAL INDUSTRY; CORN PRODUCTION ACT 1917; COTTON INDUSTRY; EAST INDIA COMPANY; ENGINEERING INDUSTRY; EXPORTS; FAIR TRADE LEAGUE; FINANCIAL CRISES; FREE TRADE; GENERAL CHAMBER OF MANUFACTURERS; GENERAL STRIKE; HUNGRY FORTIES; IMPERIAL PREFERENCE; IMPORT DUTIES ACT 1932; INFLATION; KEYNES, J. M.; *LAISSEZ-FAIRE*; *LOMBARD STREET*; MERCHANT SHIPPING ACTS; MIGRATION; MOND–TURNER TALKS; MOTOR INDUSTRY; NATIONAL ASSISTANCE ACT; NATIONALIZATION; STEAM HAMMER; STERLING AREA; STOCK EXCHANGE; STRIKES; TARIFF REFORM LEAGUE; THREE-DAY WEEK; TOBACCO; TRADE BOARDS ACT; WOOLLEN INDUSTRY.

Ecumenicism, the attempt to reunite the divided Christian Churches: the word derives from the Greek 'Oikoumene', the whole inhabited world. All initiatives in the 16th century to heal the Catholic/Protestant breach by negotiation failed, and PROTESTANTS remained divided between Lutheran, REFORMED ANGLICAN confessions, together with many more minority radical groupings. The first major modern initiative for Protestants was a missionary conference at Edinburgh (1910), which was the origin of prolonged discussions leading to the formation of the World Council of Churches (1948); eastern Orthodox Churches joined the Council. Prominent in this and in later warm overtures to Roman Catholicism was Geoffrey Fisher (1887–1972), Archbishop of Canterbury (1945–61). Several unions between Protestant churches have occurred in the United States and former BRITISH EMPIRE, but so far the only British structural unions have been among METHODIST churches (principally 1932) and the creation of the UNITED REFORMED CHURCH (1972). Repeated efforts to reunite the Church of England and Methodism have been blocked by minority opposition. A different and differently spelled derivative of the same Greek root-word, 'Oecumenical', is used as a description for the early general councils of the Church which are recognized as authoritative for doctrine by most mainstream Churches, including the Church of England.

Eden, Sir Anthony (1st Earl of Avon) (1897–1977), Conservative politician and Prime Minister (1955–7). Son of an eccentric Co. Durham baronet, awarded the Military Cross in WORLD WAR I, Eden studied Oriental languages at Oxford and developed a lifetime's interest in the Middle East. MP for Warwick and Leamington (1923–57), he became foreign secretary in 1935 at the young age of 38, when HOARE resigned over the HOARE–LAVAL PACT. While Eden increasingly came to oppose CHAMBERLAIN's policy of APPEASEMENT towards Germany, he made his resignation stand three years later on the issue of the government's recognition of Italy's conquest of Abyssinia. He returned as secretary for the dominions (1939–40), secretary for war (1940), and again as foreign secretary (1940–5) when, in tandem with CHURCHILL, he played a major role in Britain's wartime foreign policy.

He was again foreign secretary in 1951. When Churchill finally resigned in April 1955, Eden, so long the heir apparent, duly became prime minister and the following month won a general election with an increased majority. Dogged by poor health following an operation, and influenced by his experience of appeasement in the 1930s, Eden was tempted into taking a strong line against

Egypt's Nasser. By breaking off negotiations with the Egyptians and colluding with the French and Israelis in mounting an invasion of Suez in Oct. 1956, he aroused immense opposition at home and abroad. The resulting SUEZ CRISIS – and the subsequent withdrawal of British troops in what was seen as a humiliating climbdown – ruined his career, and he resigned on grounds of ill-health in 1957. Eden's distinguished pre-war career in foreign affairs and his prolonged role as Churchill's lieutenant had left him ill-prepared to deal with the rise of Arab nationalism and Britain's diminished world status after 1945; the Suez fiasco exposed Britain's inability to act independently as a great power.

Eden Treaty, 1786, commercial treaty with France, named after the British negotiator, William Eden. This was unfinished business from the peace negotiations that ended the War of AMERICAN INDEPENDENCE. French exports to Britain had been subject to prohibitive duties for most of the 18th century; the treaty provided for reciprocal duties on a 'most favoured nation' basis, which proved more advantageous to Britain.

Edgar (944–75), King of the English (959–75). After seizing NORTHUMBRIA and MERCIA from his brother EADWIG in 957, and then succeeding him as king of the English two years later, Edgar's reign was apparently largely peaceful and successful. The most famous event was his 'second coronation' at BATH in 973, followed by a meeting with the British kings at CHESTER, who subsequently rowed him on the River Dee to demonstrate their subjection. All the evidence suggests that these dramatic and unusual incidents allowed Edgar to consolidate his 10th-century predecessors' claims to imperial domination over Britain (*see* IMPERIAL IDEAS). He was also important for his support of the TENTH-CENTURY REFORM, his LAW CODES, and his fundamental reform of the COINAGE, which took place in 973.

Edgar's reign marks a high-point in the theory of Anglo-Saxon KINGSHIP, with its emphasis on the king's direct responsibility to God for the performance of his duties. Many of its governmental achievements endured, but the conflicts that began during the reign of Edgar's son, EDWARD THE MARTYR, demonstrate the fragility and personal nature of kingly power.

Edgar (*c*.1074–1107), King of Scots (1097–1107). The eldest son of MALCOLM III CANMORE and St MARGARET, he took refuge in England when his parents died in Nov. 1093. After the death of his half-brother DUNCAN II the following year, he became the Anglo-Norman candidate for the Scottish throne, which he won in 1097 with the aid of an army supplied by WILLIAM II RUFUS, overthrowing DONALD III BAN. In 1098, he recognized the King of Norway's lordship over the Western Isles. His reign was an unusually peaceful one, probably thanks to substantial Anglo-Norman support – in 1100, he gave his sister MATILDA in marriage to HENRY I. He died unmarried and was buried in Dunfermline priory.

Edgar the Ætheling (*c*.1052–*c*.1125), son of EDWARD THE EXILE. The word 'Ætheling' signifies a prince of royal blood, and was used regularly in the 10th and 11th centuries. In 1066 he was proclaimed king in London after HAROLD II's death, but was almost at once forced to submit to WILLIAM I THE CONQUEROR. Deeply involved in the abortive revolts of 1069–70, he then went into exile. Even after his reconciliation with William in 1074, his status as a potential English candidate for the throne meant he had an awkward time at court, and he travelled a good deal, taking part in the First CRUSADE. He generally supported ROBERT II Curthose and consequently was taken prisoner at the battle of Tinchebrai in 1106; after his release, he settled for a quiet life in the country.

Edgehill, Battle of, Warwicks., 23 Oct. 1642, the first major battle of the English CIVIL WAR, between the PARLIAMENTARIAN forces of the Earl of Essex (Robert Devereux) and the ROYALIST army. It was indecisive, although Essex withdrew in good order to London.

Edinburgh The name is probably an Anglo-Saxon version of the Gaelic *Din Eidyn*, 'the fort on the hill slope', with reference to the mile-long rock which now bears the castle and the old town. There is little evidence for Roman occupation of this strategic site, but perhaps in the 6th century it became a main stronghold for the VOTADINI, succumbing to a siege by Anglian invaders in 648. From royal buildings on the castle site there remains a small early 12th-century chapel dedicated to St Margaret, and there was clearly a substantial adjacent urban settlement by then. The abbey of Holyrood at the other end of the ridge to the castle was founded in 1128 (the monks were dispersed in 1559), and by the 15th-century, the monarchy had established a palace in its precinct, lavishly rebuilt by JAMES IV in 1501–5. This sealed the 15th-century establishment of Edinburgh as unchallenged capital of the Scottish kingdom, the home of the central law courts and the normal meeting-place for PARLIAMENTS. A UNIVERSITY was founded in 1582. The PARISH church of St Giles was briefly raised to cathedral status with the founding of a DIOCESE of Edinburgh by CHARLES I in 1633.

The city was confined on its rock, with a single main street ('the Royal Mile') as its spine, until the draining of a loch to the north and the laying-out of a New Town on open land beyond, from 1767. This magnificent planned development made a fitting setting for the social and cultural life associated with the SCOTTISH ENLIGHTENMENT.

Since its inauguration in 1947, Edinburgh has been renowned for its three-week international festival held in the late summer, the largest and most prestigious in the UK. This has also attracted an increasingly large and diverse 'Fringe' of often experimental music, theatre and comedy.

Edinburgh Review, The, leading quarterly periodical, published between 1802 and 1929, and established by Henry BROUGHAM, Sydney Smith and Francis Jeffrey with a strongly WHIG bias. Almost every major writer and critic of the 19th and early 20th centuries was published in the *Review*, and especially in its earlier years it was a major platform for reform and political economy.

Edinburgh, Treaty of, 1560, between England, Scotland and France. All foreign troops were evacuated from Scotland, giving the LORDS OF THE CONGREGATION the chance to establish a provisional government.

Edington, Battle of, Wilts., 878, ALFRED THE GREAT's decisive victory over the VIKINGS, after he left his refuge at ATHELNEY and rallied an army from the south-western SHIRES. He was subsequently able to conclude the favourable peace of WEDMORE.

Edington, William (?–1366), royal servant. He was an efficient and reforming royal minister (treasurer, 1344–56; chancellor, 1356–63) who did much to restore public confidence in EDWARD III's government. When appointed treasurer, he inherited a legacy of debt and financial chaos; his innovations in EXCHEQUER procedure and record-keeping allowed ministers to obtain a clear overview of the state of royal finances. By taking the increasingly lucrative WOOL SUBSIDY into direct government control, he tapped the resources that enabled Edward to mount some of the major campaigns of the HUNDRED YEARS WAR. As bishop of Winchester (1346–66), he began rebuilding the nave of the cathedral.

Edith (?–1075), Queen of the English, wife of EDWARD THE CONFESSOR, daughter of Earl GODWINE of WESSEX and sister of King HAROLD II. She was patron of the *VITA AEDWARDI REGIS*, in which the childlessness of her marriage to Edward was said to be due to the agreement reached by the pious couple to become celibate. She lived on under Norman rule.

Edmund (*c*.921–46), King of the English (939–46), the son of EDWARD THE ELDER and brother of King ATHELSTAN. Edmund's reign was notable for continuing (but not completing; *see* EADRED) the military successes against the Scandinavian rulers of northern England (*see* YORK; OLAF GUTHRICSSON). He also supported his nephew, the CAROLINGIAN King Louis IV, in his wars in France; continued the ANGLO-SAXON practice of issuing LAW CODES; and patronized the Church. When he was about 25, he was killed while trying to protect his steward from an attack by an outlaw.

Edmund Ironside (*c*.981–1016), King of the English (1016). A son of ETHELRED II THE UNREADY, he rebelled against his father in 1015, was reconciled and then succeeded him. He was briefly successful in resisting the Danish armies of King CNUT, with whom he made a short-lived partition of the English kingdom in 1016 after the battle of Ashingdon (*see* ALNEY, PEACE OF). His subsequent early death enabled Cnut to take the entire kingdom. Edmund was nicknamed 'Ironside' (probably by contemporaries) as a tribute to his courage.

Edmund, St (*c*.841–70), King of EAST ANGLIA (*c*.855–70). After defeat by a Danish army during the campaigns in which the

GREAT ARMY sought to conquer the English kingdoms, Edmund may have died in a ritual sacrifice to Scandinavian gods (the evidence is slender; *see* IVAR THE BONELESS). By the year 900, he was already regarded as a saint, and in *c.*1020, the monastery of BURY ST EDMUNDS was founded to house his tomb. Although very little is known about the historical Edmund, his cult developed in such a way that later ages regarded him as the epitome of a good king. His shrine at Bury was destroyed in 1538, although a group of bones formerly preserved at Toulouse and now at Arundel is claimed to be his.

Education The sources of educational reform for British children were as diverse as the forms of provision. Some were moved by religious and humanitarian motive and some by economic and industrial concerns. Issues of class control and class advancement were never far from the surface. The contested relationship between educational reform and social inequality, a recurrent motif in public discussion of the question, is certain to fuel debate well into the 21st century.

Britain took to system building in education long after the principal states of Western Europe, partly because the British schooling system was reasonably responsive to the requirements of an industrializing economy, but also because the improvements in national efficiency and national integration that might come from increased state intervention entailed religious and denominational conflict which successive governments shied away from.

Until 1870, England and Wales were without a national system of education; provision depended on voluntary effort organized principally by religious philanthropic and private bodies. The religious conflicts associated with the control of education limited the state's role to a modest supervisory one. The earliest formal state intervention occurred in the FACTORY ACT 1833, which insisted on the provision of half-time education for employees under 13 years. Employers often evaded this responsibility by employing children on a relay system. The education of working-class children was parcelled out among the RAGGED SCHOOLS Union, the SUNDAY SCHOOLS and, above all, the National Society for Promoting the Education of the Poor in the Principles of the Church of England, and its Nonconformist counterpart, the BRITISH AND FOREIGN BIBLE SOCIETY. The MONITORIAL SYSTEM, employed by both these bodies, made for efficiency and orderliness. Curricular innovation, never large, was stifled by the recommendations of the NEWCASTLE COMMISSION, the subsequent concentration on the '3 Rs' and the introduction of PAYMENT BY RESULTS.

The EDUCATION ACT 1870, which opened the way to free and compulsory elementary education, marked the transition to a more interventionist role by the state and a growing recognition of the significance of increased schooling in a modern and democratic industrial society. The EDUCATION ACT 1902, which made secondary education the responsibility of counties and county boroughs, laid the basis for a co-ordinated system of this level of education. The increased opportunities for secondary education were extended to all by the EDUCATION ACT 1944.

A further assault on social inequality and deprivation was made with an attempt to improve the quality of provision. This was initiated with the controversial COMPREHENSIVE experiment of the 1960s, which remains the main basis of the current system. *See also* BOARD SCHOOLS; CHANTRIES; ELEMENTARY EDUCATION ACTS; ELEMENTARY SCHOOLS; ENDOWED SCHOOLS ACT 1868; GRAMMAR SCHOOLS; PUBLIC SCHOOLS; SCHOOL-LEAVING AGE.

CHRONOLOGY

1870 EDUCATION ACT introduces secular rate-supported ELEMENTARY SCHOOLS administered by about 2,000 school BOARDS.

1880 Education Act introduces compulsory schooling.

1902 EDUCATION ACT extends opportunities for secondary education.

1906 EDUCATION (PROVISION OF MEALS) ACT provides for supply of cheap SCHOOL MEALS for children attending state elementary schools, the cost to be shared by local and central governments.

1907 EDUCATION (ADMINISTRATIVE PROVISIONS) ACT provides for medical inspection for elementary schools. A free-places quota is introduced.

1912 Board of Education makes grants to local education authorities (LEAs) to make possible the medical treatment of children.

1918 EDUCATION ACT makes compulsory attendance universal until age 14; day continuation classes introduced for children between SCHOOL-LEAVING AGE and 18.
1921 Free milk supplies to children in need (subsidized by the Milk Marketing Board from 1934, and from 1946 to 1971 is free to all).
1936 Education Act makes provision for school-leaving age to be raised to 15 in Sept. 1939; is deferred due to war.
1944 In EDUCATION ACT, president of Board of Education becomes minister of education; primary and secondary education are divided at ELEVEN PLUS; and secondary education is provided in GRAMMAR, technical and secondary modern schools. School-leaving age is raised to 15 (becomes operative in 1947).
1964 School-leaving age to be raised to 16 in 1970/1 (change eventually made in 1973).
1965 Department of Education asks all LEAs to submit plans for reorganizing secondary education on comprehensive lines, with view to ending both selection at 11 and tripartite system; policy then suspended.
1972 Department of Education accepts that, by 1982, it will provide nursery education for 90 per cent of four-year-olds and 50 per cent of three-year-olds.
1974 Comprehensive system revived by Government Circular 4/74.
1976 Direct grant system phased out (most went independent). Education Act requires LEAs to submit proposals for comprehensive schooling.
1980 Education Act establishes 'assisted places scheme' to provide financial support for some students in independent education; changes made to increase parental choice and participation.

Education Act 1870 The Act, primarily the work of the Liberal politician W.E. Forster (1819–86) was a landmark in the development of education, it marked the transition of state responsibility from a supervisory role to a more direct interventionist one. It initiated the school BOARD era, with local action to supplement voluntary provision. Elected school boards were empowered to levy a rate and given discretionary powers to enforce attendance (with exemptions) to the age of 13. By 1874, 5,000 new schools had been founded. *See also* SCHOOL-LEAVING AGE.

Education Act 1902 This abolished school attendance committees and school BOARDS, and transferred control of education to 140 new local education authorities (LEAs). For higher (i.e. secondary) education, the county and borough councils were made responsible in all cases. For elementary education, urban district councils with populations of over 20,000 and boroughs with populations of over 10,000 became the LEAs. In other cases, the county and borough councils became responsible for all forms of education. Each LEA was required to appoint an education committee approved by the Board of Education. The Act also provided for the support of voluntary schools from the local rates, in addition to government grants. The recognition of local responsibility in the provision of public secondary education stimulated the development of higher education. *See also* COCKERTON JUDGEMENT.

Education Act 1918, known as the 'Fisher' Act after the president of the Board of Education, H. A. L. Fisher (1865–1940). Part of the RECONSTRUCTION legislation after WORLD WAR I passed under LLOYD GEORGE, it raised the SCHOOL-LEAVING AGE to 14 and abolished any remaining fees for elementary education. Plans to provide part-time 'continuing education' for 14–18-year-olds were shelved because of government economies in 1921.

Education Act 1944 Known also as the Butler Act after R. A. BUTLER, minister of education in the wartime coalition government, the legislation set the structure for the post-war British education system. It raised the SCHOOL-LEAVING AGE to 15 and, in the state-maintained sector, provided for universal free secondary education in three different types of schools: GRAMMAR, secondary modern and technical. These were supposed to cater for the different academic levels and other aptitudes of children, with selection usually the result of an ELEVEN PLUS examination. The Act also formed the basis on which church schools formed part of the state-maintained sector, while retaining their religious affiliations. Its only statutory requirement over curricula was that each school day should start with an act of collective worship.

The Act was a major plank in the programme of progressive social legislation developed for the post-war reconstruction of Britain. Later, the educationally and socially divisive effects of the way in which the eleven plus examination streamed a minority of children at an early age into academically oriented grammar schools, while condemning the majority to under-resourced secondary modern and technical schools, came under heavy criticism from supporters of COMPREHENSIVE SCHOOLS.

Education (Administrative Provisions) Act 1907 This authorized local education authorities (LEAs) to attend to the health and well-being of scholars; to provide vacation schools and camps, play centres, school baths and gardens; and to award scholarships and bursaries. The Act laid the foundations of the School Medical Service.

Education (Choice of Employment) Act 1910 This empowered local educational authorities (LEAs) to make arrangements for vocational guidance and set up juvenile employment bureaux, the foundation on which the Youth Employment Service was later based.

Education (Provision of Meals) Act 1906 A response to the fears of national degeneration, as disclosed in the *Report of the Inter-Departmental Committee on Physical Deterioration* (1904), it empowered local education authorities to make arrangements for the provision of SCHOOL MEALS to deserving students. By 1914, 150,000 children were in receipt of such meals. The measure was permissive rather than compulsory, and the problem of malnutrition among the school population remained a serious one.

Edward I (1239–1307), King of England (1272–1307). As a young man during the turbulent years 1258–65, he found himself torn between his position as HENRY III's heir and his sympathy for some of the measures proposed by the king's opponents. He changed sides several times before ending up as his father's most energetic champion, only to be defeated by Simon de MONTFORT at LEWES in 1264 and taken hostage. The next year he escaped and organized the campaign that led to de Montfort's death at EVESHAM. While on CRUSADE (1270–2), he was wounded in an assassination attempt. On his way home, he heard of his father's death (Nov. 1272), but he stayed on the Continent until 1274, detained by the affairs of AQUITAINE – the last reigning king of England to visit the duchy.

His determination to improve the efficiency of royal justice led to the stream of statutes (1275–90) on which his reputation as the 'English Justinian' is based. No English king made greater efforts to rule the whole of Britain. In two campaigns – 1276–7 and 1282–3 – he defeated LLYWELYN AP GRUFFUDD and conquered the principality of Wales. He reorganized its government by the Statute of Wales (1284, *see* RHUDDLAN), and, in 1301, granted the principality to his eldest son: a precedent followed by every English monarch who could. In 1290, he expelled the Jews (*see* JEWS IN BRITAIN) – a measure that reflected his own religious convictions and was applauded by the anti-Semitic majority of his subjects. Two years later, he awarded the Scottish throne to John BALLIOL, but his subsequent attempts to dominate Scotland only provoked the wars of SCOTTISH INDEPENDENCE.

During the first 20 years of his reign, Edward seemed the master of events, but in 1294, after Philip IV of France pronounced the confiscation of Aquitaine, he found himself fighting on three fronts – against the French, the Scots and the Welsh rebels. From that year, he taxed his subjects ruthlessly, which, in 1297, sparked off a protest movement that, while he was abroad, forced concessions from his ministers. On his return, he continued to spend huge sums on war, invasions of Scotland and the construction of castles in Wales. He died, deeply in debt, at Burgh-by-Sands (Cumbria) in 1307, while leading his army on yet another campaign. By his two wives – ELEANOR OF CASTILE and MARGARET OF FRANCE – he probably had 17 children, and he was succeeded by Eleanor's last-born son EDWARD II.

The reign of Edward I left an enduring imprint on English government and society. The WOOL SUBSIDY, which he instituted in 1275, provided both useful revenue and the security on which the crown could borrow. To meet the rising costs of war in the 1290s, he turned increasingly to PARLIAMENT, summoning representatives of SHIRES and BOROUGHS in the expectation that they would give their consent to taxation. Even more profound legacies of Edward's rule were the expulsion of the Jews, the destruction of the last independent Welsh principality and an enduring hostility between English and Scots: in the 16th century, the words 'Hammer of the Scots' were inscribed on his tomb in Westminster Abbey.

Edward II (1284–1327), King of England (1307–27). Born at Caernarfon, the 14th and last child of EDWARD I and ELEANOR OF CASTILE, in 1301 he became the first heir to the throne to bear the title 'Prince of Wales'. A contemporary chronicler described him as 'fair of body and great of strength'; sadly he was also little of brain. Even before his accession in 1307, his political and financial indiscretions had caused anxiety; in the end, these same failings were to lead to his downfall and death.

The early years of Edward II's reign were bedevilled by quarrels with the barons, who were disturbed – as his father had been – by his (possibly homosexual) infatuation with Piers GAVESTON. In 1311, in an attempt to restrain his excessive generosity, they imposed the ORDINANCES on him; Edward's refusal to accept Gaveston's exile only exacerbated the situation. The upshot was civil war and, in 1312, Gaveston's murder. The Scottish victory at BANNOCKBURN two years later added to Edward's humiliations, forcing him to acquiesce in the *de facto* take-over of government by his cousin THOMAS OF LANCASTER – the man he held responsible for Gaveston's death.

During these years (1315–17), Edward showed himself capable of politic behaviour, gradually forming a group of allies among the aristocracy, and by 1318, he was in a position to reassert his own authority. However, in 1319, his inadequacy as a military leader was demonstrated again, at the siege of BERWICK, and in the following years, he showed he was still susceptible to the blandishments of an avaricious favourite – this time, Hugh Despenser. By 1321, a widespread anti-Despenser movement had led to renewed civil war.

The defeat of Thomas of Lancaster at BOROUGHBRIDGE in 1322 was followed by a series of executions and a reign of terror, Edward's revenge for Gaveston's death. After destroying their principal opponents, Edward and the Despensers set about enriching themselves with scant regard for law or justice. In 1324, the war of SAINT-SARDOS broke out, and ISABELLA OF FRANCE, whom Edward had married in 1308, was sent to Paris to discuss peace terms with her brother Charles IV. When she refused to return to England, it became clear that the Despensers' ascendancy had led to the complete alienation of the queen.

In Sept. 1326, Isabella and Roger MORTIMER invaded England. They had only a small force, but since virtually no one would obey Edward's orders, it was more than sufficient. Edward fled but was captured and taken to Kenilworth. In Jan. 1327, Parliament accepted a damning – and largely accurate – indictment of his rule, concluding that, since he was 'incorrigible without hope of amendment', he should be deposed. Edward then abdicated in favour of EDWARD III, and was imprisoned in Berkeley Castle, Glos.

However, while alive, he remained a potential threat to Mortimer and Isabella, and attempts to an rescue him sealed his fate: it was later announced that he had died at Berkeley on 21 Sept. Almost certainly he was murdered, perhaps in gruesome fashion, and stories of the tragic fate of this anointed king led to a short-lived cult focused on his tomb in Gloucester cathedral. Others – notably his son's foreign enemies – preferred to believe that he had escaped and was living incognito as a hermit.

Edward III (1312–77), King of England (1327–77). Proclaimed king in 1327 after the deposition of his father EDWARD II, he was still only 17 when, in 1330, he organized the coup that sent Roger MORTIMER, his mother's lover, to the scaffold, and took over the reins of power himself. Determined to erase the memory of recent humiliations in the wars of SCOTTISH INDEPENDENCE, he espoused the cause of Edward BALLIOL. This prompted Philip VI of France to assist the Scots by adopting a more aggressive policy towards AQUITAINE. Thus, from 1337, it was the war with France rather than with Scotland that chiefly engaged Edward's attention.

In 1340, primarily to please his Flemish allies (who were technically French subjects), he decided to assume the title 'king of France'. Despite the victory at SLUYS, the early part of the HUNDRED YEARS WAR achieved little and was phenomenally expensive, precipitating the crisis of 1340–1 when

LORDS and COMMONS united against a combination of misrule and heavy taxation. However, Edward persisted, and in 1346, with the victories of NEVILLE'S CROSS and CRÉCY, the fortunes of war swung in his favour. Celebratory tournaments and the foundation of the Order of the GARTER (1348–9) asserted Edward's claim to be at the pinnacle of European CHIVALRY – a claim that the god of war seemed to endorse when King John of France was captured at POITIERS (1356). Although peace negotiations revealed that Edward was prepared to drop his pretensions to the French throne, the territorial gains registered in the treaty of BRÉTIGNY gave him everything that his predecessors had been fighting for since 1259.

Between 1360 and 1371, his subjects enjoyed the longest respite from direct taxation for more than a century, yet revenues from the WOOL SUBSIDY and the profits of war, including two kings' ransoms, enabled Edward to embark on a major building programme (notably the palatial rebuilding of Windsor castle). He owed much of his success – and his popularity with patriotic Englishmen – to his own enthusiastic participation in the theatre of war, deeds of arms and courtly spectacles. Meanwhile, the Statute of LABOURERS, enacted in the aftermath of the BLACK DEATH, had shown that crown and ruling classes were just as united against the wage demands of their poorer compatriots as they were against the French.

Aged 55 when war was renewed in 1369, it is not surprising that the easy-going Edward wished to leave such matters to his son, EDWARD THE BLACK PRINCE. Unfortunately the latter's illness meant that he proved ineffective at a time when Charles V was leading a French recovery. Moreover, that year had seen the death of Queen PHILIPPA and her replacement in the king's bed by Alice PERRERS, a mistress with political ambitions. The dominance that she and a clique of courtiers eventually obtained over a senile king provoked an explosion of criticism in the GOOD PARLIAMENT of 1376. Edward died on 21 June 1377, and was succeeded by his grandson RICHARD II, the Black Prince having died the year before.

Despite the scandals that overshadowed Edward's last years, his long reign had provided a sense of stability, and it was his achievements that were remembered when he died – military triumphs and a period of domestic peace longer than any hitherto. These were all the more remarkable given the low ebb to which the events of 1327–30 had brought the English crown. For much of the 19th and 20th centuries, historians sceptical of the adulation of Edward's contemporaries tended to believe that these achievements were bought at the price of concessions alleged to have undermined the long-term future of the monarchy. In the 1990s, historians are less inclined to hold Edward responsible for events that occurred 20 years and more after his death.

Edward IV (1442–83), King of England (1461–83). Unexpectedly propelled to the throne at the age of 18 in the midst of one of the most tumultuous periods of the WARS OF THE ROSES, he seized every opportunity with courage and aplomb. When his father, RICHARD OF YORK, was killed at WAKEFIELD in Dec. 1460, Edward became the YORKIST heir to HENRY VI. The following Feb., Warwick's (*see* NEVILLE, RICHARD) defeat at ST ALBANS allowed the LANCASTRIANS to recover possession of King Henry, and so the Yorkists were forced into a hasty assertion of Edward's kingship – a momentous step facilitated by the young man's recent victory, in his first independent command, at Mortimer's Cross. No sooner had he been proclaimed king in March than he marched north and crushed the Lancastrians at the battle of TOWTON.

The crisis over, he relaxed and enjoyed the pleasures of being king – though his always remained the guiding hand behind major issues of policy (somewhat to the chagrin of Warwick who felt it should be his). Possessing the natural politician's gift of never forgetting a name or a face, Edward probably had too much faith in his ability to retain friends and charm enemies; at least this meant that he was rarely unforgiving.

The only major mistake he made, in political terms, was to marry 'beneath' him and for love. The fact that, for four months, he kept his May 1464 marriage to Elizabeth WOODVILLE a secret from even his closest advisers shows that he foresaw some of the consequences that would flow from marrying a widow with two children, five brothers and seven unmarried sisters. The marriage also contributed to the breakdown in trust between Edward and Warwick, which precipitated the second crisis of the reign: in July 1469, Warwick, conspiring with Edward's brother Clarence, took the king prisoner, only to be forced by public opinion to release him two months later.

In March 1470, Edward's prompt and ruthless response to the Lincolnshire Rising forced the two conspirators to escape to France, where they joined forces with MARGARET OF ANJOU. In Sept., it was Edward's turn to flee when taken by surprise by Warwick's hitherto loyal brother, John Neville, Marquess of Montagu. However, with naval support from Charles of Burgundy, the king was able to return to England in March 1471. Within two nerve-wracking months, he had recovered the throne, acting first deviously (to disarm the opposition), then diplomatically (to win over Clarence), and finally with such speed and determination that he was able to bring his enemies to battle separately, at BARNET and TEWKESBURY. Henry VI, whom Edward had captured in 1465 and allowed to live, was now murdered on his orders. Clarence, after continuing to intrigue against his brother, was finally to meet the same fate in 1478.

In 1475 Edward invaded France, but allowed himself to be bought off by the treaty of PICQUIGNY. Five years later, he resurrected English claims to lordship over Scotland, setting up the Duke of Albany as a puppet king against his brother JAMES III; in 1482, English troops captured BERWICK. Edward's death came suddenly on 9 April 1483, the result of an illness that some historians blame on his own excesses.

In the crises of his reign, Edward IV demonstrated courage, political intelligence and leadership of the highest order. However, his promiscuous life-style offended puritans both then and since, and this has sometimes led to unrealistic denunciations of him as a lazy and pleasure-loving monarch who failed to foresee that the consequences of over-indulgence would be his own early death and the tragic circumstances in which his brother, the future RICHARD III, would ascend the throne.

Edward V (1470–?83), King of England (1483). Son of EDWARD IV and Elizabeth WOODVILLE, he was at Ludlow, Salop, where his household as prince of Wales was based, when he succeeded to the throne on 9 April 1483. The council, dominated by his mother's relatives, fixed his coronation for 4 May, and he was on his way to London in the care of Anthony Woodville, Earl Rivers when, on 30 April, his uncle Richard of Gloucester (*see* RICHARD III) arrested Rivers and took the 13-year-old boy into custody. Richard then made himself PROTECTOR and postponed the coronation until 22 June.

Government business continued to be transacted in Edward V's name until 16 June when another postponement of the coronation (until Nov.) made it plain that the protector had something else in mind. From 22 June, Richard's adherents put forward the argument that all the children of Edward IV and Elizabeth Woodville were illegitimate – though hitherto their legitimacy had been taken for granted – and on 26 June, Edward was dethroned and Richard III proclaimed king. Despite at least one scheme to rescue them, Edward and his younger brother Richard, Duke of York, remained in the TOWER OF LONDON. During the autumn of 1483, while rumours of their deaths circulated, King Richard made no attempt to prove that the boys were alive, most probably because he had by then disposed of them.

In 1674, two skeletons discovered in the Tower were identified as being those of Edward and Richard – the 'princes in the Tower' – and were buried in WESTMINSTER ABBEY. Although a forensic examination carried out in 1933 claimed to confirm this finding, scientists since then have generally remained sceptical.

Edward VI (1537–53), King of England and Ireland (1547–53). HENRY VIII's longed-for son by JANE SEYMOUR (who died soon after his birth), he was king from 28 Jan. 1547. His tutors were men of reforming sympathies, particularly Roger Ascham, John Cheke, Richard Cox and Anthony Cooke, and his father left a council of regency weighted towards Protestant sympathizers, including his uncle Edward SEYMOUR who became lord PROTECTOR and Duke of Somerset. The latter's efforts to monopolize access to the young king were challenged unsuccessfully by Thomas Seymour and successfully by Northumberland (*see* DUDLEY, JOHN), control of the boy's person being crucial in the government crisis of Oct. 1549.

Edward never exercised independent initiative except in his last months, when he felt his previous good health give way to tuberculosis in the winter of 1552/3. Having absorbed his tutors' PROTESTANTISM, he was appalled at the prospect of his half-sister MARY becoming queen, and he and Northumberland moved to divert the succession from her and ELIZABETH to JANE GREY. Edward's death came quicker than expected, which may account for the inept failure to round up Mary and neutralize her bid for the throne. Edward's surviving papers give witness to a lively mind quick to learn; little contemporary comment suggests personal warmth.

Edward VII (1841–1910), King of Great Britain and Ireland (1901–10). The second child of Queen VICTORIA (who was inclined to blame the scandal associated with his wayward behaviour on his father ALBERT's untimely death), Edward was Prince of Wales from the age of one month to 60 years. Largely excluded from royal duties during his near lifetime as heir apparent to the throne, he devoted his attention to society, being cited in two divorce cases, but also encouraged his mother to return to public life after her long withdrawal following the death of Albert.

Coming to the throne on Victoria's death in 1901, Edward proved to be an effective and popular monarch. He was an excellent linguist who was interested in and well informed on foreign affairs. His pro-French sympathies accorded well with GREY's foreign policy. However, contrary to received opinion, the king was not the architect of the ANGLO-FRENCH *ENTENTE* (the *Entente Cordiale*) of 1904 nor the Anglo-Russian agreement of 1907. His was a role of enthusiastic supporter and European contacts man rather than of instigator. Although, as during the build-up to the PARLIAMENT ACT 1911, he revealed that he could occasionally be heir to his mother's tradition of political intervention, in general he played the role of a 20th-century constitutional monarch, who, though he enjoyed and understood the role of monarchical pomp and circumstance, also understood the limits of royal authority.

Edward VIII (1894–1972), King of the United Kingdom (1936). The eldest son of GEORGE V and called David by his family, he was created Prince of Wales in 1911, and achieved considerable popularity for his youth, charm and concern for the unemployed. His wish to marry Wallis Simpson, an American divorcee, precipitated the ABDICATION CRISIS and caused him to relinquish the crown in favour of his brother (who became GEORGE VI) after a reign of less than a year (Jan.–Dec. 1936) and to go into exile. Created the Duke of Windsor, he married Mrs Simpson in June 1937. He served as governor of the Bahamas (1940–5), but lived most of the rest of his life in France shunned for the most part by the rest of the royal family.

Edward the Black Prince (1330–76), Prince of Wales. The name Black Prince was given (for unknown reasons) to EDWARD III's eldest son in the 16th century. His semi-legendary fame is chiefly due to Jean Froissart's romanticized and unreliable story of the rise and fall of a chivalric hero. Having been entrusted by his father with nominal command of the van at CRÉCY so that (in Froissart's phrase) 'the boy might win his spurs', he went on to become one of the outstanding English leaders in the HUNDRED YEARS WAR. In 1355 he conducted a destructive and profitable CHEVAUCHÉE through Languedoc; the raid of 1356 culminated in the battle of POITIERS, where he plucked triumph out of near-disaster. Having married JOAN OF KENT (presumably for love) in 1361, he then intervened in Spain on behalf of Peter I of Castile, winning the battle of Najera in 1367, but also contracting the disease (possibly a form of dysentery) that was to dog the last ten years of his life. He expected the population of AQUITAINE, of which he had been made prince in 1362, to meet the costs of the Spanish campaign. However, his tax demands provided some of the more independent French lords, already hostile to a regime that took little account of regional tradition, with the perfect opportunity to challenge English lordship. In the war that followed, the Black Prince took the city of Limoges by assault (1370) and, according to Froissart, ordered the massacre of its inhabitants. The following year he returned to England where, although he enjoyed tremendous prestige, his illness kept him in the background.

Edward the Confessor, St (*c.*1005–66), King of the English (1042–66). The eldest son of ETHELRED II THE UNREADY and the latter's second wife EMMA, he was driven into exile in 1013 by the Danes, and remained abroad (often in Normandy: *see* RICHARD II, Duke of the Normans; ROBERT I) until recalled to England in 1041 by King HARTHACNUT. He succeeded peacefully to the throne, and with the exception of the years 1051–2, his reign was one of internal peace. Yet his lack of an heir, the rivalries among the aristocracy and the persistent threat of invasion from Scandinavia were permanent sources of tension.

In 1045, Edward married EDITH, daughter of GODWINE, Earl of WESSEX and the most powerful member of the aristocracy that Edward inherited. Six years later – and for slightly obscure reasons, probably connected with his determination to advance ROBERT OF JUMIÈGES to the archbishopric of Canterbury and his recent promise of the throne to Duke William of Normandy (the future WILLIAM I THE CONQUEROR) – he drove Godwine into exile, only for the earl to return with overwhelming military force in 1052. After Godwine's death the following year, his sons were promoted to earldoms and the family apparently dominated the kingdom until TOSTIG's exile in 1065. Edward's attitude towards the succession to the kingdom seems to have vacillated, perhaps as a diplomatic ploy. By 1066, claimants included several from Scandinavia as well as young EDGAR THE ÆTHELING, Duke William, and Godwine's son HAROLD, Earl of Wessex and the recipient of Edward's deathbed bequest (*see* SUCCESSION).

The *VITA AEDWARDI REGIS* (Life of King Edward), composed over the year 1066 on behalf of the monarch's widow, is the crucial source for Edward's religion and his supposed chastity. However, neither can be taken at face value, and political considerations were certainly behind his canonization in 1161. The extent of his culpability for the bloodbath of 1066 will always be debated by historians.

The title 'the Confessor' was given to Edward in the papal bull of 7 Feb. 1161 which confirmed his canonization. At that date it can be taken as meaning someone who had demonstrated his religion in the face of the world's temptations. It is possible that the title was given to distinguish Edward from his predecessor EDWARD THE MARTYR.

Edward the Elder (*c.*870–924), King of the English (899–924). After defeating his cousin ETHELWOLD's challenge to his succession, Edward spent most of the rest of his reign subduing the Danes south of the Humber. After the death of his sister ETHELFLÆD in 918, he added MERCIA to his kingdom by means that may not have been entirely peaceful or just; his conquests mark the start of the true UNIFICATION of England. He consolidated his acquisitions through the construction of *BURHS*, and issued LAW CODES and patronized the Church.

Edward the Martyr, St (*c.*963–78), King of the English (975–8). He was about 12 at the time of his accession, and the sparse evidence suggests that his reign was typified by conditions approximating to civil war. He was murdered on 18 March 978 by retainers serving his younger half-brother Ethelred (*see* ETHELRED II THE UNREADY), who then became king. By 1000 Edward was widely regarded as a saint and miracles were recorded at his tomb in SHAFTESBURY ABBEY. There can be little doubt that his posthumous reputation was enhanced by the disasters that befell England during Ethelred's reign.

Edwin (?–633), King of Northumbria (616–33). The son of a king of DEIRA, he was driven into exile by Ethelfrith, the first king of the united NORTHUMBRIA, and spent his youth at the court of REDWALD of EAST ANGLIA. In 616, he and Redwald defeated and killed Ethelfrith in battle, and Edwin succeeded to the Northumbrian throne. He had a Christian wife and also allowed the missionary PAULINUS to come into his kingdom; his own CONVERSION – accomplished by Paulinus and described by BEDE – seems to have taken a long time. He was a great warrior, who was included in Bede's list of what were later termed *BRETWALDAS* and was said by him to have been more powerful than any previous English king. He died in battle at Hatfield Chase near Doncaster, defeated by PENDA of MERCIA and the British king CADWALLA of GWYNEDD. *See also* KINGSHIP.

EEC, *see* EUROPEAN UNION

Egbert (?–839), King of Wessex (802–39). A great warrior king, who briefly dominated all the other kingdoms of England (*see* ELLENDEN). This achievement should not be seen as a true UNIFICATION, since its character was as personal and ephemeral as the supremacy of the Mercian kings ETHELBALD and OFFA. MERCIA and NORTHUMBRIA threw off WESSEX's control in 1830. Egbert's permanent achievement was the incorporation of south-west England and KENT into Wessex. He thereby created the kingdom that would eventually form the basis for the unification of England that began under ALFRED THE GREAT.

Eglinton Tournament, *see* TOURNAMENT

Egypt British involvement persisted through the 19th century and well into the 20th, until the débâcle of Suez (*see* SUEZ CRISIS). The Ottoman Empire, which had won Egypt in 1516, largely administered it through the Mamluks, the former rulers. A French expeditionary force under Napoleon Bonaparte took the country in 1798, but was forced to retreat in 1801 after defeat by British, Ottoman and Mamluk forces. A period of anarchy ensued (with Britain vainly attempting an invasion in 1807 on behalf of the deposed Mamluks), out of which the Ottoman leader Muhammad Ali emerged, defeating the Mamluks in 1811. In the ensuing years, Egypt was opened up to European gaze and influence: ARCHAEOLOGY began to flourish and collectors and travellers brought home artefacts, while the European-trained army under Ibrahim Pasha extended Egyptian rule through SUDAN and the Middle East. After Muhammad Ali had defeated the Ottomans in 1839, the European powers were moved to intervene, the 1840 Convention of London and 1841 Treaty of London restoring all but Egypt and Sudan to Ottoman rule.

During the years after 1854, westernizing policies were pursued vigorously, with the SUEZ CANAL their greatest memorial, but Egyptian indebtedness to European banks grew inexorably. Expansion into Africa after 1867 was a costly affair, and from 1875 Egypt's shares in the Canal were to be sold and its finances placed under international control. European representatives were added to the Egyptian cabinet from 1879, which was a spur to nationalist anger culminating in the 1882 Arabi Rebellion. In crushing the rebellion, the British established *de facto* rule of Egypt. Through Britain, Egypt continued its claim to Sudan, which was lost to the MAHDI in 1885 and regained in 1896–8. Egypt was formally given the status of a British protectorate in 1914; previously the fiction of Ottoman sovereignty had been maintained. Between 1883 and 1907, under Evelyn Baring, Lord Cromer, Egyptian public life was modelled along British colonial lines; but in the years of WORLD WAR I nationalist feeling was rekindled, and rebellion ensued in 1919. Although suppressed by the British, the rebellion's strength indicated the degree of disaffection; the Milner Mission of 1919–20, despatched to investigate conditions, recommended terminating the protectorate. Although the British government was unwilling for that, the fracturing of nationalist politics and the strong urging of the high commissioner, Sir Edmund Allenby (1861–1936), resulted in the termination of the protectorate in 1922, Egypt becoming an independent monarchy, but retaining a large British military presence.

The final vestiges of British rule were removed by the ANGLO-EGYPTIAN TREATY of 1936, although Britain reserved rights of intervention and control regarding the Suez Canal. British military pressure in WORLD WAR II ensured Egypt's non-belligerence and its support for the Allied war effort. Its poor military showing against the nascent state of Israel in PALESTINE in 1948, and its fractured domestic politics, resulted in the 1952 military coup, and the emergence of Gamal Abdel Nasser in 1954. His subsequent nationalization of the Suez Canal was the spark for Britain's final humiliation in Egypt.

Eikon Basilike (*The Royal Image*), supposedly written by CHARLES I as a pious meditation on his sufferings (in fact, it was probably mostly composed by his chaplain John Gauden). It was a bestseller on its publication soon after Charles's execution in Jan. 1649, and created his image as a martyr for the ANGLICAN cause. Arguably the most influential new book in 17th-century English politics.

Eire, name adopted by the IRISH FREE STATE under DE VALERA's 1937 constitution. As the Gaelic for 'Ireland', it retained nationalist aspirations for a united Ireland, and the constitution declared Eire 'a sovereign, independent, democratic state', though still theoretically a member of the Commonwealth. Under the Republic of Ireland Act of 1948, Ireland left the Commonwealth and the official name for southern Ireland became the Irish Republic.

Eisteddfodau, literally 'sittings' in Welsh. From the 12th century, congresses of bards were often held at the capitals of the Welsh princes – for instance, at Cardigan in 1176 – as much for regulation as for performances of music and poetry. The English monarchs continued to permit them and occasionally, until 1576, summoned them by royal mandate; thereafter, and until the late 17th century, private patrons sponsored them. The 18th century saw their near-extinction, but by the end of the century, local literary societies were encouraging a cultural revival (*see* CYMMRODORION SOCIETY). In 1819 came the first of a series of nationwide meetings, which have since become annual and a central feature of Welsh national consciousness. The 19th century added much archaizing ceremony to the Eisteddfod.

Ejectors, *see* TRIERS AND EJECTORS

El Alamein, Battle of, 23 Oct.–4 Nov. 1942. Launching an attrition battle in imitation of WORLD WAR I techniques, MONTGOMERY wore down Rommel's forces with mass firepower. Badly overstretched and short of fuel, Rommel was in no position to defend against the onslaught, and the TORCH landings in North Africa four days later forced a precipitate retreat. The Germans and Italians lost about 2,000 dead but more than 30,000 captured. British losses were about 13,500.

Eleanor Crosses, the most elaborate series of funeral monuments ever built for an English monarch. After the death of ELEANOR OF CASTILE in 1290 at Harby, Notts., EDWARD I ordered the construction of commemorative crosses at each stopping place of the cortège on its way to WESTMINSTER Abbey. There were 12 in all, the last at Charing Cross in London.

Eleanor of Aquitaine (1122–1204), Queen of England. A vast inheritance (the duchy of AQUITAINE), a formidable personality and a long life made her the most powerful woman of her age. However, there is little evidence that she championed women's rights or courtly love or even that (as has been sometimes stated) she was an unusually influential patron of troubadours.

In 1137, she was married to Louis VII of France. Her inheritance enormously increased her husband's wealth and standing, but when she bore him only two daughters, the marriage broke down and was annulled in 1152. Eleanor promptly married Henry of Anjou (later HENRY II), and in the next 15 years, they had eight children, including five boys: William, HENRY (later called 'the young king'), the future RICHARD I, Geoffrey and JOHN.

In 1173, she led young Henry, Richard, Geoffrey and the barons of Poitou into a war against her husband. The king's agents arrested her while she was making her way, disguised in male clothing, to the court of his principal enemy, her ex-husband. These events generated immense controversy then and subsequently. The reasons behind her rebellion are obscure, although she was probably fighting for the independence of Aquitaine rather than for the independence of women. None the less, what she did was extraordinary and she paid for it. While Henry forgave his rebel sons, his wife remained his prisoner until he died.

She was released on RICHARD I's accession in 1189. During his absences on CRUSADE and in prison (1192–4), she played an important part in curbing JOHN's acquisitive instincts. On Richard's death in 1199, she helped John – now her only surviving son – win over Anjou from ARTHUR OF BRITTANY. Three years later, Arthur revived his claim, and it was while besieging her at Mirebeau that he fell into his uncle's hands.

Towards the end of her life, she retired to the abbey of Fontevrault in the Loire valley, and in April 1204, she was buried there, near Richard and King Henry. Throughout her adult life, Eleanor remained the lawful ruler of Aquitaine, and her death marked another stage in the collapse of the ANGEVIN EMPIRE, for her subjects immediately transferred their allegiance to the king of France.

Eleanor of Castile (1242–90), Queen of England. Daughter of Ferdinand III of Castile, she married Prince Edward (later EDWARD I) in 1254, becoming her husband's constant companion and accompanying him on CRUSADE, as well as to Gascony and Wales. She probably bore 14 children – the last of them, the future EDWARD II, at Caernarfon. She was reputed to be a grasping woman; none the less, historians have sometimes argued that Edward became a harsher ruler after her death. In her memory, he erected the ELEANOR CROSSES.

Eleanor of Provence (1223–91), Queen of England. Daughter of Raymond Berenguer, Count of Provence, and Beatrice of Savoy, she married HENRY III in 1236; five of their children – including the future EDWARD I – survived infancy. Henry was devoted to Eleanor, and his generosity to her uncles – the Savoyards – provoked criticism. A lady of strong opinions – including anti-Semitic ones – she remained an influential figure during the reigns of both her husband and her son, until she became a nun at Amesbury in 1286.

Electricity Industry Electricity was first discovered in the 1830s but the electricity industry owes its origins to the invention of the carbon filament lamp in the 1870s. Electric street lighting made its first appearance in 1881, and in 1882 the BOARD OF TRADE was empowered to license local authorities (or private companies approved by the local authorities) to supply electricity. Until the end of the century it was confined to lighting, but with the development of electric motors it began to be used for both traction and industrial machinery. A national grid controlled by the Central Electricity Generating Board was completed by 1938.

The industry was nationalized in 1947 with a two-tier structure: the British Electricity Authority, responsible for organizing and pooling electricity-generating capacity, and retail distribution through 14 area boards. Electricity generation was based on coal-powered stations, but cheap OIL became available in the 1950s and natural GAS in the 1960s–70s. In the 1950s there was also great optimism about nuclear power (*see* ATOMIC ENERGY) as a cheap source of electricity. In the event, technological and environmental concerns have cast doubt on the case for the expansion of nuclear power.

The 1989 Electricity Act allowed for the transfer of the electricity supply industry to the private sector. There are now 12 privatized regional companies supplying electricity from the national grid to consumers via local networks. Eight are owned by overseas companies.

Elementary Education Acts 1876, 1888 These made education compulsory up to the age of 10. In 1893, the SCHOOL-LEAVING AGE was raised to 11 and, in 1899, to 12. In 1891, elementary education was made free.

Elementary Education (Blind and Deaf Children) Act 1893 This made special provision for disabled children unable to attend ordinary elementary schools; as a result, blindness and deafness were no longer an excuse for absence. The Act did not apply to those classed as 'idiots' and 'imbeciles' or to POOR LAW children. The Elementary Education (Defective and Epileptic Children) Act 1899 applied the same principles to those who were mentally disabled and those suffering from epilepsy. These acts laid the foundations for provision for children with 'special needs'.

Elementary Schools, term applied to both BOARD SCHOOLS and National Society schools (*see* MONITORIAL SYSTEM), which catered from the mid-19th century to the mid-20th for children through to the SCHOOL-LEAVING AGE. Secondary schools were originally fee-paying and intended for middle-class children, so educational institutions were largely segregated on class lines. The EDUCATION ACT 1902, which abolished school boards, brought all elementary schools under the control of 140 new local education authorities which could draw on local rates and grant aid to run elementary schools, and to build (or aid) secondary schools. The chance of a working-class child securing a secondary education improved with the Free Place Regulations of 1907; by 1912 one-third of pupils at maintained secondary schools were former public elementary pupils receiving free tuition. From 1926 it became official policy to phase out all-age elementary schools and replace them with primary and secondary schools divided at the age of 11. Local authorities, especially in depressed areas, were slow to respond: in 1938 over one-third of children over 11 were still in the old elementary schools, and many reorganizations were only token. The EDUCATION ACT 1944 was the final death-knell for the elementary school.

Eleven Plus, examination taken by children aged 11 to determine whether they should attend the GRAMMAR, technical or secondary modern schools set up under the EDUCATION ACT 1944. Almost all schoolchildren after 1945 sat the eleven plus examination, which was increasingly seen as a pass or fail examination for entry into grammar school. Growing concern in the 1950s about the efficacy and equity of the tests contributed to a campaign to remove them and adopt a system of COMPREHENSIVE SCHOOLS. After the LABOUR PARTY'S 1964 election victory, the eleven plus exam was largely phased out.

Eleven Years' Tyranny, *see* THOROUGH

Elgin Marbles, a large collection of sculptures, bought by the 7th Earl of Elgin in Greece, and brought to England in 1812. The work of Phidias, they had once formed part of the Parthenon in Athens. They were purchased by the BRITISH MUSEUM where, for the present, they can still be seen. Their repatriation, which has been requested by heritage-minded Greek governments, remains a contentious issue.

Elizabeth I (1533–1603), Queen of England and Ireland (1558–1603). Daughter of HENRY VIII and ANNE BOLEYN, she was declared illegitimate after her mother's execution in 1536, but was given a royal humanist education and from 1544 was once more included in the succession. Thomas Seymour tried to win her love in 1547–9 and the traumatic effect of these overtures from a man nearly three times her age may have a bearing on her later emotional difficulties over marriage. Her position during MARY I'S reign was sometimes dangerous, though nothing was ever proved to link her with PROTESTANT conspiracies against the queen; her friends quietly prepared the ground for a trouble-free accession on 17 Nov. 1558. Immediately she sanctioned restoration of a Protestant church settlement, carefully drawn to accommodate her own prejudices against CALVINISTS (*see* ELIZABETHAN SETTLEMENT). The prospect of marriage was a long-standing problem; although her preference for Robert DUDLEY quickly emerged as politically unacceptable, a queue of foreign suitors included PHILIP II of Spain (1559), the Austrian Archduke Charles (1564), Henry Duke of Anjou (1571) and FRANCIS OF VALOIS, Duke of Alençon (1572–81). Much negotiation was diplomatic play-acting, much reflected her ministers' nervousness (she nearly died of smallpox in 1562), and some, particularly the Alençon match, came near to persuading her.

Partly by their manipulation of these foreign marital possibilities, Elizabeth and her ministers preserved the regime in its fragile opening decade from any hostile Catholic intervention in English affairs, and they kept an increasingly uneasy peace with English Catholic sympathizers; however by 1568 domestic and foreign tensions began to accumulate, especially because of the flight to England of the Catholic heir to the throne, the much-married MARY QUEEN OF SCOTS, who became Elizabeth's prisoner. In 1569 ill-prepared Catholic conspiracies aimed at destroying the government were defeated with relative ease (*see* NORTHERN EARLS' RISING), but resulted in Elizabeth being declared excommunicate by Pope Pius V and in consequence deposed, in his bull *Regnans in Excelsis* (1570). Her subsequent relationship with the captive Mary was tense, and she agonized for years before agreeing to Mary's execution in 1587. Her caution in overseas military adventures was defeated by the international situation which saw her presiding over a world war and an attack on Gaelic Ireland by the late 1580s; yet these enterprises met with long-term success from the perspective of her kingdom's assertion of its place in the world. It was a result of the oceanwide seaborne operations in her reign, partly building on her father's investment in the NAVY, that England became a major force in maritime warfare and trade.

In her last years, death robbed Elizabeth of many politicians who had been her faithful if occasionally exasperated servants since the 1550s, in succession Dudley, Earl of Leicester, WALSINGHAM, Christopher Hatton and William CECIL. Her choice of men with first-class political talent and her dominance of court quarrels then faltered, particularly in combination with the inept selfishness of Robert DEVEREUX, Earl of Essex, until he brought ruin on himself in 1601. Her neurotic refusal to name an heir to the throne added to the atmosphere of insecurity in the 1590s and much alarmed the obvious candidate JAMES VI of Scotland, but capable senior politicians, particularly Robert CECIL, managed the transition on her death with exemplary efficiency.

Although documentation about her is abundant, Elizabeth has guarded much of her privacy from subsequent scrutiny. Highly self-conscious, she was a brilliant self-fashioner, exploiting her indispensability for the Protestant cause in England and genuine popular affection and loyalty, for instance in the official encouragement of spontaneous celebrations for her ACCESSION DAY and in the use of PROGRESSES throughout the country (*see also* PRODIGY HOUSES). Her personal sense of theatre encouraged the creation of her image as patriotic, Protestant and classical heroine, fostered by ceremony and painting; often her skills needed to be employed to mend fences broken by her own ill-tempered defence of her PREROGATIVE, especially in foreign and religious policy. Yet as a woman in a political world designed for men, she succeeded in remaining dominant in a situation full of potential dangers.

Elizabeth II (1926–), Queen of Great Britain and Northern Ireland and Head of the Commonwealth (1952–). She married Philip Mountbatten (created the Duke of Edinburgh) in Nov. 1947, and, as eldest daughter of GEORGE VI, succeeded to the throne on 6 Feb. 1952. She has four children: CHARLES, PRINCE OF WALES (1948–); Anne, the Princess Royal (1950–); Andrew, Duke of York (1960–); and Edward (1964–). Her CORONATION in June 1953 – the first to be televised – marked the beginning of a reign in which the monarchy has had to respond to increasingly intense and intrusive media coverage, partly accommodated by a greater openness about the workings of the royal household, and, increasingly, this has had the effect of contributing to growing speculation about the monarchy's future role. The queen has travelled extensively, paying particular attention to the affairs of the COMMONWEALTH.

Elizabethan Settlement The 1558–9 settlement of religion on ELIZABETH I's accession has always generated controversy, because it bears on the question whether the Church of England should be seen as PROTESTANT or CATHOLIC. In the early 1950s, Sir John Neale suggested that Elizabeth wanted only to create a semi-Catholic Church like that of HENRY VIII, but was pushed into a more Protestant programme by activists in the House of COMMONS. This theory gained remarkable sway in textbooks, but has no real basis.

Hesitations in the legislation, which Neale noticed, were caused by government politicking round Catholic bishops and peers until a LORDS majority could be constructed to pass the Settlement. Elizabeth did have some conservative personal religious preferences, but little was allowed to influence the Settlement; what emerged was a barely modified fossilization of the Protestant state of the Church at the death of EDWARD VI. This gave no ground to the CALVINISTS who wished to create a settlement more in the image of recent developments on the Continent: Elizabeth distrusted Calvinist ideas on the independence of the Church, and personally detested the Calvinist spokesman, John KNOX. *See also* CHURCH: ENGLAND.

Ellandune, Battle of, 825, a victory gained by King EGBERT of WESSEX over Beornwulf, king of MERCIA, probably at Wroughton, Wilts. It was followed by a Wessex take-over of KENT, Surrey, SUSSEX and ESSEX and, in 829, of Mercia itself, and marked the end of the period of Mercian supremacy, even though the new Mercian king, Wiglaf, threw off Wessex's overlordship in 830.

Elmet, British kingdom established in the 5th century after the departure of the Romans. It was located in the foothills of the Pennines around the modern city of Leeds. Although information about its history is very sparse, it appears to have put up a long resistance to the invading English, and to have been incorporated into NORTHUMBRIA only during the reign of EDWIN in the first half of the 7th century.

Ely Abbey, Cambs., first founded as a double monastery (i.e. for men and women) in 673 by Queen ÆLTHELFRYTH of NORTHUMBRIA. Destroyed in the second half of the 9th century during the Danish invasions, it was refounded in *c.*970 under the aegis of St Ethelwold with monks from ABINGDON, and thereafter grew rapidly in wealth and prestige. Its estates were plundered after the NORMAN CONQUEST because of its support for HEREWARD the Wake, but in 1109, it was made the seat of a bishopric. When the monastery was dissolved in 1539, the cathedral became a SECULAR foundation.

Emancipation, Catholic, *see* CATHOLIC EMANCIPATION

Emigration, *see* MIGRATION

Emma (?–1052), Queen of the English, daughter of Count Richard I of the Normans, wife (in turn) of ETHELRED II THE UNREADY and his supplanter, CNUT, and mother (by Ethelred) of EDWARD THE CONFESSOR and (by Cnut) of HARTHACNUT. A strong personality and a manipulative politician, the chief long-term result of her career was the creation of dynastic links between England and NORMANDY (where she placed the young Edward in exile), which contributed to the NORMAN CONQUEST (*see ENCOMIUM EMMAE REGINAE*).

Empire, British, *see* BRITISH EMPIRE

Employers and Workmen Act 1875 This reduced the legal inequality of TRADE UNIONS with respect to breach of contract. Previously, under the Master and Servants Act (a revealing terminology), workers who broke their contracts were exposed to criminal prosecution with the possibility of imprisonment. For employers, by contrast, the same action was classified as a civil offence punishable by a fine. This Act made breach of contract a civil offence for both worker and employer.

Employers' Liability Act 1880 A response to TRADE UNION pressure, it extended the liability of employers to include accidents caused by the negligence of managers, superintendents and foremen, or by the obeying of improper rules. Railway companies were also made liable when their employees were injured through the negligence of signalmen, drivers and pointsmen. An important step forward, the Act nevertheless left workers unprotected against accidents that were caused by their fellow workmen.

Enclosure Acts, *see* ENCLOSURES

Enclosures (also Inclosures), the conversion of landholding and agricultural practice from OPEN FIELD farming to SEVERALTY – i.e. compact holdings held by a single proprietor – and often involving the transfer to private ownership of land previously subject to communal rights. Some areas (Kent, parts of East Anglia, Devon and Som.) may never have been open field, and many lowland areas were enclosed from the 12th century onwards. However, enclosure for sheep-runs became widespread during the 15th- and 16th-century booms in the WOOLLEN INDUSTRY, mainly in the Midlands, and the practice, which did indeed lead to depopulation of some villages, became a scapegoat for resentment at imperfectly understood economic and social change. An easy target for governments wishing to be seen to be doing something, enclosures were attacked by legislation from 1489, and investigated by major commissions in 1517–19 and 1548–9; the effect was minimal.

Under pressure for food production, enclosure later became more diverse in aims and scale, ranging from piecemeal arable agreements to major single schemes and wetland reclamation (*see* FEN DRAINAGE); from the early 17th century, many such schemes were passed by parliamentary private Act, the first in 1604. Consistently, they raised the rentable value of the land involved, and to gain total control of farming practice, all resulted in a loss of rights in common land – i.e. manorial waste land in which all the tenants of the manor enjoyed certain defined rights of exploitation. Such commons were of great importance to the poor, and the chief focus of continuing discontent. There were recurrent enclosure RIOTS, which often comprised the orderly communal removal of fences, designed to generate legal arbitration. Much enclosure took place without the sanction of parliamentary acts, but a great deal of land still remained for the attentions of the 18th-century enclosure movement.

Lands remaining unenclosed as late as the 18th century were often largely in the hands of small owners who found it hard to reach agreement as to their interests, or were subject to common rights prized by commoners. PARLIAMENT was prepared to order enclosure so long as landowners owning a major proportion of the land in question were agreed. Most acts were concentrated in the years 1755–80 and 1790–1815; it has been estimated that within a century 2.4 million hectares (5.9 million acres) had been enclosed by 4,000 acts of parliament (*see also* GENERAL ENCLOSURE ACTS 1801, 1836, 1845). The Midlands, heartland of the open field system, was most heavily affected. In Scotland, several acts promoting enclosure and facilitating the abolition of RUNRIG passed between 1661 and 1695; local enclosure acts were not a feature of the Scottish enclosure movement. The results of the movement have been much debated.

The improvements in the production and output of food and livestock made possible by enclosure, and the positive contribution it may have made to the industrializing process, need to be set against the unquantifiable social costs that followed from the unplanned and arbitrary dispossession of cottagers and squatters. *See also* AGRICULTURE.

Enclosures of Commons Act 1876 An environmental protection measure, it prevented landowners from incorporating into their estates what remained of the old common lands. It was a triumph for the Commons Preservation Society who campaigned to retain substantial open spaces such as Hampstead Heath and Epping Forest for public enjoyment. In asserting a public interest beyond the claims of private landowners, the Act saved thousands of acres from being built on and marked a signal advance in the development of a public responsibility for the environment.

Endowed Schools Act 1868 A measure designed to modernize PUBLIC SCHOOLS through the more efficient use of their endowments, it was also an expression of GLADSTONIAN LIBERALISM and its concern for the renovation of the state and its institutions. Passed in response to the work of the CLARENDON COMMISSION and the TAUNTON COMMISSION, the Act extended its provisions to the education of the middle classes by appointing three commissioners to review and revise the trust deeds of all endowed schools and by enabling the use of obsolete charities for educational purposes. These commissioners' duties were taken over by the CHARITY COMMISSIONERS in 1874, with a brief to expand secondary education provision for girls.

Engagement, a treaty (Dec. 1647) between CHARLES I and the PRESBYTERIAN leadership in Scotland which bitterly divided the Scots. The Engager army under James, Duke of Hamilton invaded England but surrendered at Uttoxeter, Staffs. in Aug. 1648.

This Engagement should be distinguished from the ENGAGEMENT CONTROVERSY, and from the Solemn Engagement drafted by Henry IRETON and agreed by the English army in June 1647, which, in the face of hostility from Presbyterians in Parliament, asserted its unity and determination not to disband.

Engagement Controversy An 'engagement' was introduced by the RUMP PARLIAMENT in Jan. 1650, requiring all adult males to 'engage obedience' to the current government. It aroused anger and pamphleteering about the nature of loyalty, even among PRESBYTERIANS who had fought CHARLES I but who now felt compromised by his execution. Where the engagement was conscientiously enforced, there were often sweeping purges in local offices. It was repealed in 1653.

Engineering Industry The importance of engineering largely began in the mid-19th century, before which local metalworking and machine-making trades were dominant. Most machines, in textile industries and elsewhere, could be made in small works and foundries, and only the large STEAM and WATER POWER companies acquired any wider reputation. After the 1820s the importance of the RAILWAYS, and the ever-wider application of steam power, increased the need for skilled boiler-makers, machine-tool engineers, etc. Some areas, such as MANCHESTER, the West Midlands and GLASGOW, came to be important in machine-tool making, while elsewhere new types of machinery production emerged, e.g. small arms in BIRMINGHAM, bicycles and sewing machines in COVENTRY, agricultural machinery in LINCOLN, and armaments at NEWCASTLE. Some of these traditions were to be translated in the early 20th century into the emergence of the MOTOR INDUSTRY and then the production of electrical goods. Electrical engineering rose steadily to overtake mechanical engineering in importance in post-WORLD WAR II Britain, while many of the old machine-tool trades experienced gradual but eventually total eclipse in the face of growing international competition.

English Language, Development of Its history is normally divided into three periods: Old English (before *c*.1150); Middle English (*c*.1150–*c*.1500); and Modern English (*c*.1500 to the present). The transformation from one period to another is characterized principally by its ceasing to be an inflected language – i.e. by the gradual disappearance of the practice of adding endings to words or of combining words together to produce new meanings – features still normal in modern German. There have always been distinctive English regional dialects, and – to state an obvious but important truism – the English language is constantly changing.

Modern English is a direct descendant of the language spoken by the ANGLES and SAXONS who invaded and settled much of England in the 4th and 5th centuries (*see* ANGLO-SAXON SETTLEMENT). The language was surprisingly little influenced by that of the Celtic peoples already inhabiting the islands – i.e. the precursor of modern Welsh, Gaelic and Cornish. This can be explained in terms of Anglo-Saxon political domination rather than the extermination of the British population of England (*see* BRITISH SURVIVAL), a factor that also explains why English spread to Scotland and Ireland.

The English language has subsequently been most heavily influenced by the Scandinavian speech of the VIKINGS (*see* SCANDINAVIAN SETTLEMENT) and, after the NORMAN CONQUEST, by French (*see* ANGLO-NORMAN). The former, a Germanic language similar to Old English, was much more influential, arguably because the numerous common features made linguistic interchange easy. The effects of the latter are mostly confined to the areas of government and law.

In the time of the Tudors, people had a sense of their language's comparative youth and of its continuing development: Stephen Gardiner, Bishop of Winchester, remarked that it was only two centuries old, while TYNDALE had to update a LOLLARD text for southern readers, which he promised to print in its original form for northerners and Scotsmen to appreciate. Among dialects, the dominance of south-eastern usages – apparent since the adoption of English at court in the 14th century – became complete, aided by the London-based PRINTING industry, which encouraged gradual standardization. Direct French influence was declining with the loss of England's continental possessions, but HUMANIST scholarship was adding a host of new Latinate words (*see RENAISSANCE*).

Selection of permanent additions was now largely determined by a handful of major texts such as the PRAYER BOOKS and the translations leading up to the Authorized Version of the BIBLE, both fairly conservative in their usage. The main work on these texts, done in the 1530s and 1540s, was decisive in producing a language for the future, one that was hybrid and capriciously spelled but largely devoid of inflections. In the 1560s, the Scottish CHURCH adopted a BIBLE and liturgical texts in southern English, beginning the long decline in the Scots form of English.

English, Origins of the The idea that England was inhabited by a single people known as 'the English' is a literary and political creation of the Anglo-Saxon period (*see* UNIFICATION, ENGLISH). BEDE's treatment of the CONVERSION of what he called the English peoples to Christianity as a literary unity is the first clear expression of this. Those included by him under this one name comprised the many small groupings that made up the early kingdoms and the peoples referred to as ANGLES, SAXONS and JUTES, as well as other smaller tribes. The English were contrasted with the *Britones* (*see* BRITISH SURVIVAL) who inhabited the parts of western and northern Britain we now call Wales, Scotland and Ireland.

In the 8th century, MERCIAN kings such as ETHELBALD and OFFA, who exercised hegemony over other kings, began the practice of proclaiming themselves kings over a single English people, which was continued by ALFRED and his successors. Of course, Anglo-Saxon England (*Anglia*) was actually inhabited by a number of different peoples, of whom the Angles, Saxons, British andSCANDINAVIANS were the most prominent.

These distinct identities were fast disappearing by the time of the NORMAN CONQUEST, and in writs, charters and chronicles written in the 12th century, they were completely submerged in the general designation of *Angli* – the Latin word for 'English' used in such documents. Even at that early date, the English were said to have certain characteristics peculiar to themselves, one of which was untrustworthiness. They also showed the imperialistic trait of considering themselves superior to their Celtic British neighbours.

Engrossing This term has two separate usages historically: in legal terminology, 'to engross' is to make a formal final copy of a document, traditionally on parchment; in economic history, 'to engross' was to indulge in sharp commercial practice – buying up goods wholesale in order to sell them at an inflated price (to REGRATE them). *See also* GRAIN RIOTS.

Entail, the succession of specified persons by which property descends in FEE TAIL.

Enthusiasm In the 17th and 18th centuries, this term was applied to misdirected religious emotion, frenzied and extravagant speculation or claimed supernatural inspiration. Dr JOHNSON defined it as 'a vain confidence of divine favour or communication'. Those who valued tradition, ceremony or reason – supporters of the ANGLICAN establishment, and some DISSENTERS – commonly employed the term to condemn adherents of the various sects that proliferated in the mid-17th century, including QUAKERS, and later used it against the METHODISTS.

Entrepreneur, a leader and/or manager of business. The precise function of the entrepreneur varies with the nature and size of business operation and has changed very much with the evolution of firms (particularly since the 18th century) from small owner-operated and family-based private partnerships to a modern mix which includes large corporations and a divorce of ownership from management (*see* FAMILY FIRMS; JOINT STOCK). During the INDUSTRIAL REVOLUTION the entrepreneur was often works manager, financier, accountant, sales and personnel manager, architect and inventor all in one, whereas today many functions are the province of salaried specialist professionals. Britain's early lead in industrialization has often been attributed to the quality of entrepreneurship. Joseph Schumpeter argued that the dynamic, risk-taking entrepreneur was the prime mover in economic change, but that entrepreneurship inevitably suffered with the divorce of ownership from management because the high level of direct interest in the business was lost.

The declining competitiveness of British industry from the late 19th century has been attributed to declining entrepreneurship, particularly in sales and technology and associated with the preference for *rentier* and financial careers or the aristocratic lifestyle promoted by the PUBLIC SCHOOL culture surrounding second- and third-generation offspring of English industrialist families (*see* GENTLEMANLY CAPITALISM).

Although entrepreneurship is important in understanding the pace of ECONOMIC GROWTH and change it is likely that the uniquely favourable environment for British industry in the late 18th and early 19th centuries, followed by the catching up of rival economies from the late 19th century, are more important factors in explaining major shifts in the pace and nature of British economic growth.

Enumerated Goods, forms of colonial produce listed in the 17th-century NAVIGATION ACTS and later legislation. Enumerated goods could not be shipped directly to foreign markets, but had to be sent to England (later Britain) for RE-EXPORT. The commodities originally enumerated were SUGAR, TOBACCO, cotton wool, indigo, ginger, fustic and other dyeing woods. Subsequent acts both added to and subtracted from the list: coffee, raw silk, naval stores and pig and bar iron were added; rice was added in 1706 and then removed in 1730; sugar was removed in 1739. The object was to ensure that Britain had a cheap supply of goods which were not easily procurable, or regarded as especially important for national defence. This trade regulation also increased the demand for British shipping and the potential revenue from customs.

Eoka, *see* CYPRUS

Epidemics In recorded historic time, there is a pattern of east–west movement of epidemics, generally identified as the blood-borne bacterial diseases BUBONIC and pneumonic plague, which are spread through the bites of rat fleas affecting humans. The incidence of plague is associated with major population movements from a heartland in central Asia, but the periods of quiescence in plague are much less straightforward to explain. The outbreaks have triggered successive waves of death through western Asia and Europe, with the British Isles as one of the last areas to fall victim; such continent-wide epidemics are known as pandemics. A major pandemic in the 6th and 7th centuries is sometimes termed Justinian's Plague, since its first spectacular destructive effect in southern Europe occurred in 541–4, during the reign of the Byzantine emperor. It was not until much later that a major outbreak occurred in England (recorded by BEDE in 664), and it spread throughout the British Isles; however, thereafter the plague seems to have disappeared from Britain for nearly seven centuries, until the advent of the BLACK DEATH from the same central Asian source. After 1348–9 bubonic plague remained endemic in Britain; pneumonic plague, far more virulent, was fortunately much rarer. Although declining from *c.*1550, local outbreaks (mostly urban) continued (*see* GREAT PLAGUE); disappearance after 1667 remains mysterious. Growing realization of the effectiveness of quarantine may have contributed; the rats which transmitted plague may have suddenly developed greater immunity.

In the 1490s there was sudden Europe-wide panic about an epidemic of syphilis, a spirochete infection associated with sexual and intimate contact, which, in a pattern of development different to that of plague, seems to have spread rapidly from southern to northern Europe, including Britain, during the decade. Modern archaeology has revealed evidence of cases in early 15th-century Ireland; traditional theories about the emergence of syphilis as a result of Columbus's voyages to the NEW WORLD are therefore discounted today. Throughout the 16th century, syphilis was a major killer, but its virulence thereafter declined, even though it remains a serious endemic disease, now on a worldwide basis. It may have caused a revolution in 16th-century public manners, in which intimate bodily contact in courtesy became far more restricted, and it probably contributed to the century's noticeably heightened anxiety about sexual behaviour, including the widespread closure of previously legalized brothels (*see* STEWS). Nevertheless, far more serious killers in 16th-century England were the mid-century outbreaks of influenza.

After the sudden disappearance of bubonic plague, the late 17th and the 18th centuries saw recurrent regional epidemics of typhus, and a new virulence in smallpox. The epidemic disease associated with the very rapid urban growth of the early 19th century was CHOLERA, a water-borne bacterial infection which took advantage of the crowded and ill-planned cities created by the INDUSTRIAL REVOLUTION; the first major outbreak was in 1831–2. It was quickly noticed that its worst virulence was in poverty-stricken areas (although Prince ALBERT was one exalted victim in 1861), and the connection with water supply was eventually made; the disease's decline was largely a result of the provision of pure water supply rather than of any advance in medical technique.

A consistent feature of epidemics is the natural human desire to find a scapegoat for them; in the absence of detailed knowledge of medical pathology before the 19th century, moral explanations seemed more rational than medical ones, especially in the case of syphilis, with its sexual associations. Even in the supposedly better-informed 20th century, this same process of moral scapegoating has been applied in affluent western culture, Britain included, to AIDS. Since infectious disease characteristically affects a stable population as a result of outside contacts, there is a certain grim rationale for the outbreaks of racism or xenophobia which also feature in popular explanations of epidemic disease. Similarly, and especially in the case of cholera, class-based explanations at first predominated: the poor were regarded as a source of disease as a result of their moral behaviour, rather than simply as a result of the conditions in which they were forced to live as a result of their poverty. Overall, there is much to be said for the view that before the mass campaigns of preventive INOCULATION and VACCINATION sponsored since the late 1940s by the NATIONAL HEALTH SERVICE, medical science contributed remarkably little to the defeat of epidemic disease, in comparison with social and environmental changes and reforms which created a healthier population with greater resistance to serious infection.

CHRONOLOGY: THE INCIDENCE OF EPIDEMICS

541 'Justinian's Plague' begins in southern Europe: approximately quarter of the population dies.

664 First recorded major outbreak of plague in England.

1348 Arrival of BLACK DEATH, Melcombe, Dorset.

1361–2 Fresh plague outbreak: 'the plague of children', also apparently affecting males more than females.

1473 'The flux': apparently a dysenteric form of plague.

1490s Sudden widespread syphilis outbreaks, western Europe.

1551, 1555–9 Influenza (sweating sickness), the century's worst mortality: especially affects the elderly, including MARY I's elderly political and religious supporters.

1563, 1593, 1603, 1625 Further BUBONIC PLAGUE epidemics, in London, with provincial repercussions.
1650s Widespread plague and depopulation in Ireland, associated with constant troop movements in warfare.
1665–75 Last nationwide bubonic plague, beginning in London (*see* GREAT PLAGUE).
1831–2 First major CHOLERA outbreak.
1848–9, 1854, 1861 Further cholera outbreaks.
1918–19 Influenza epidemic.
1950s Isolated cases of deaths in England, now retrospectively diagnosed as AIDS (Acquired Immune Deficiency Syndrome).
1981 First recognized incidence of AIDS in Britain.

Epidii, a tribe that inhabited modern south-west Argyll, Kintyre and Islay during the time of the ROMAN CONQUEST and occupation of Britain. Little is known about their history; they were conquered during the 5th century by the SCOTS of DALRIADA.

Episcopacy, government by bishops. It was universal in the Church from the 2nd to the 16th century and thereafter controversial, especially during the English and Scottish REFORMATIONS. It is seen by Roman CATHOLICS and some ANGLICANS as essential to the perfection of the Church. *See also* BISHOPRICS; METHODISM; NAG'S HEAD CONSECRATION.

Episcopal Church of Scotland The REVOLUTION SETTLEMENT made the PRESBYTERIAN Church the Established Church in Scotland. Episcopalian ministers who took oaths of loyalty to the new regime were allowed to continue, and their position was protected by legislation in 1712. Many, however, chose to become non-juring JACOBITES (*see* NON-JURORS). After the failure of the 1745 Jacobite rebellion, which the church had supported, penal laws against episcopalians were reinforced, and many gentry supporters deserted the Church for PRESBYTERIANISM. On the death of Charles Edward STUART, the Young Pretender, in 1788, most episcopalians acknowledged GEORGE III. In 1792, episcopal priests who subscribed to the THIRTY-NINE ARTICLES were freed from disabilities.

The Church played an important part in the future shape of American religion when in 1784 the first ANGLICAN bishop in north America, Samuel Seabury, was consecrated for the Anglican church in the newly independent United States; because of the political situation he could not be consecrated by English bishops, so Scottish bishops performed the ceremony. During the 19th century the Scottish Episcopal Church reorganized itself and experienced modest growth. Since its reason for existence was its loyalty to High Church principles (*see* HIGH CHURCHMANSHIP), it proved very receptive to the ideas of the OXFORD MOVEMENT.

Equal Opportunities Commission, statutory body set up in 1975 to enforce the SEX DISCRIMINATION ACT 1975 and the EQUAL PAY ACT 1970. Its duties are to work towards eliminating sex discrimination and to promote equality of opportunity. The Commission assists in test cases before courts and tribunals, conducts investigations and issues notices requiring discrimination to stop, as well as advising ministers on amendments to legislation.

Equal Pay Act 1970, act introduced under a LABOUR government by Barbara Castle providing for equal remuneration for men and women for work of 'equal value'. The full implementation of the Act came into force in 1975. It was broadly successful in raising women's wages to the same level as men's where equality of value could be proved though there is evidence that a lack of parity remains in some areas 40 years on.

Equity, *see* CHANCERY; EXCHEQUER

Equivalent, the, the sum of £398,085.10 paid to Scotland at the UNION (1707), representing the capitalized value of that part of existing tax yields that was to be used to service the English national debt. A 'rising Equivalent' was to provide compensation for anticipated tax increases and further contributions to the English debt in the following seven years. These funds were intended to finance the Scottish national debt, to settle deferred pay and pensions, compensate losers from the failure of the COINAGE and DARIEN schemes, and to encourage the woollen industry and other economic activity. In the event, most of the funds went to meet the claims of higher officials and noblemen, and the scheme became a focus for popular discontent with the Union.

Erasmus, Desiderius (?1469–1536), Dutch leader of international HUMANIST scholarship (*see* RENAISSANCE) who made extended English visits on his perennial search for wealthy patrons and learned company to fill his loneliness. His 1499 visit to the English court and OXFORD was at the invitation of his pupil William Blount, Lord Mountjoy, and was important in turning his attention from Latin classical literature towards theology and the study of Greek (encouraged by John Colet). It also impelled him to begin *Adagia* (a collection of proverbs, and the first printed bestseller) as a money-spinner after Dover CUSTOMS officers confiscated all his English currency. His 1505 visit brought him patronage from Archbishop Warham, and most of his 1509–14 extended stay was spent at CAMBRIDGE; thereafter his huge correspondence included many English scholars and would-be humanists. His edition of the Greek text of the New Testament with his own translation into humanist Latin (1516 and later revisions) had a European-wide impact, providing a new view of the biblical text for many future PROTESTANT reformers.

There is a lazy tendency to term all Tudor humanism 'Erasmian'; nevertheless the influence of Desiderius Erasmus was very great, although his vision of a tolerant Christianity minimizing the power of the clergy was much retarded by the ideological struggles of the REFORMATION.

Erastianism, the belief that the state should control the Church – or, more technically, arguments of the Swiss theologian Thomas Erastus (1524–83) that the Church should have no independent initiative in moral discipline. Although Erastus' specific ideas had no influence in Britain, the word is often used loosely to describe the Church–State relationship created in England by the REFORMATION, and in particular by the ELIZABETHAN SETTLEMENT. Not to be confused with Erasmianism, the northern European humanism of ERASMUS.

Ergyng, *see* ARCHENFIELD

Eric Bloodaxe (?–954), the last VIKING king of YORK, whose blood-soaked career fully justifies his nickname. Briefly king of Norway – where he certainly killed his brother and committed the other acts of unbridled violence that led to his expulsion in 946 – he controlled York 947–8 and 952–4, but was expelled by the NORTHUMBRIANS at the end of both periods as the English armies of King EADRED were marching north. He was then betrayed and handed over to his enemies, who had him killed.

Escheator, royal official who from the 1230s onwards took over some of the duties previously performed by the SHERIFF, i.e. the administration of lands either belonging to wards in the king's custody (*see* WARDSHIP) or which had fallen into the king's hands as a result of forfeiture or because the tenant had died without an heir (this was known as an 'escheat'). From 1377–8, escheators were responsible for a county or group of counties to the EXCHEQUER of audit. The post was abolished in 1660.

Essex, 16th Earl of, *see* CROMWELL, THOMAS

Essex, 19th Earl of, *see* DEVEREUX, ROBERT

Essex, Kingdom of Although Essex was one of the earliest areas of English settlement, which took place in the 5th and 6th centuries, there is no clear evidence for a king of the East Saxons before the late 6th century. The kings of Essex were always among the lesser Anglo-Saxon rulers, sometimes having control of neighbouring counties, but also usually subject to greater powers such as MERCIA. The kingdom was incorporated into WESSEX in 825 after EGBERT's victory at the battle of ELLENDEN.

Essoin, medieval Norman-French legal term for an excuse for non-appearance to a summons. Professional essoiners existed until the 14th century, after which their functions were undertaken by ATTORNEYS.

Estate, all property and people over which control is held through LORDSHIP, including both OPEN FIELDS and DEMESNES.

Étaples, Treaty of, 1492, a treaty between France and England, ending a brief war following French annexation of Brittany. It renewed France's subsidy promised in the treaty of PICQUIGNY and ended French support for Perkin WARBECK.

Etcetera Oath In May 1640 CONVOCATION required all clergymen and graduates to swear that the Church hierarchy (listed but tailed with 'etc.') accorded with the word of God. Amid acute national tension, this –

combined with other actions of the Laudian-dominated Convocation (*see* LAUD) – seemed to prove conspiracy theories of an ARMINIAN plot to subvert the evangelical protestant nature of the Church of England.

Ethelbald (?–757), King of Mercia (716–57). The first Mercian king to exercise domination over all the English kingdoms south of the Humber (*see* MERCIA). Like most of the early monarchs, he emerged from among available royal kindred by violence and force of personality. Little is known of his reign. His treatment of the Church and his sexual mores were criticized by St BONIFACE, although there is also evidence of constructive government and of support for the Church. However, the fact that he was murdered by his own war band points to serious political divisions within his realm.

Ethelbert (*c*.552–*c*.616), King of Kent (*c*.560–*c*.616). The first English king to convert to Christianity and the first to issue a LAW CODE. In 597, he welcomed St AUGUSTINE's mission to KENT – interestingly, according to BEDE, he was only prepared to meet the Christians in the open air for fear of their magic. Third on Bede's list of what were later termed *BRETWALDAS*, he used his power to assist the spread of Christianity to ESSEX and EAST ANGLIA. His reign established that powerful connection in England between KINGSHIP and the Church, which was to remain a significant feature of the country's history for centuries. *See also* CONVERSION.

Ethelflæd (?–918), 'Lady of the Mercians'. The daughter of ALFRED THE GREAT, her political marriage to Ethelred, Ealdorman of MERCIA, cemented an alliance that was to be decisive for English resistance to the Danes. After her husband's death, she continued his policies of military campaigns and the construction of *BURHS*, in co-operation with her brother EDWARD THE ELDER.

Ethelred II the Unready (966–1016), King of the English (978–1016). He became king at the age of 12 after the murder of his half-brother, EDWARD THE MARTYR, and died when his realm had been almost completely conquered by the Danish king CNUT. The raids from Denmark began in 980 – at first on coastal districts for the extraction of plunder and tribute. In 991, Ethelred and his advisers decided to pay DANEGELD, a well-established tactic of his more successful predecessors, including ALFRED THE GREAT. In this case, however, it provided only a temporary respite, and from 1009, large armies under SVEIN FORKBEARD and Thorkell the Tall arrived bent on exacting massive wealth and, ultimately, conquest.

Historians debating the extent of Ethelred's personal responsibility for the disasters that befell his kingdom have highlighted the size of the invading armies, and have pointed out that the main documentary source for the reign – the *ANGLO-SAXON CHRONICLE*, which is sharply critical of the king – was largely compiled with the benefit of hindsight after his death. The Danes' fleets gave them mobility and the ability to make surprise attacks, and their bases in Ireland (*see* DUBLIN) and NORMANDY were strategically helpful. There were also many Scandinavian settlers (*see* SCANDINAVIAN SETTLEMENT) – particularly in northern England – whose loyalties are likely to have been divided.

Ethelred's responses to the Danish threat were praiseworthy in many ways: he built a large fleet; some of his campaigns were well conceived; by marrying the Norman princess EMMA in 1002, he sought to neutralize the duchy; and the collection of Danegeld must have involved a complex administrative effort. However, his leadership was not of the calibre needed to unify his people, his reign was littered with political murders, and there were periods when he disregarded the property rights of his subjects. It is also clear that nobles such as Eadric Streona were lining their pockets with the proceeds of Danegeld. As a result, corruption and disunity appear to have undermined attempts at effective resistance.

The nickname '*Unraed*' – 'no-counsel', i.e. taking no or bad advice – was a play on words that originated in the 12th century, and is in many ways apt.

Ethelwold (?–902). The son of Ethelred I of WESSEX, ALFRED THE GREAT's elder brother, Ethelwold contested the succession of Alfred's chosen heir, EDWARD THE ELDER, and died in battle in 902. His willingness to ally himself with the VIKINGS shows the depth of division within the Wessex family, which in turn emphasizes how this successful kin-group resembled all contemporary royal families.

Ethelwulf (?–858), King of WESSEX (839–58), a monarch notable for his personal magnificence and his firm resistance to the early VIKING attacks. Having five sons (the youngest being ALFRED THE GREAT), he tried various partition schemes to check disagreement over the succession. These involved the sons succeeding him in turn, and the younger ones acknowledging the supremacy of the eldest. Although there were quarrels, these plans did, in fact, work. However, the chance occurrence that most of the sons died young without heirs is probably the most convincing explanation for their success.

Ethiopian crisis, *see* APPEASEMENT; HOARE–LAVAL PACT

Eugenics, the science of improving the human race through selective breeding. The term, which literally means 'well born', was coined by Francis Galton (1822–91), Charles DARWIN's cousin, and derived from Darwinian ideas of evolution and selection. Positive eugenics encourages the reproduction of 'superior' humans; negative eugenics discourages those with 'undesirable' traits from reproducing, often by sterilization. Eugenics first became a popular social movement in Edwardian Britain, with widespread middle-class support (*see also* BIRTH CONTROL; FABIAN SOCIETY) stimulated by the belief that progress in the BOER WAR, and later WORLD WAR I, was slow because of the degeneracy of the British race. Negative eugenics was taken up enthusiastically in some parts of the USA and, notoriously, in Nazi Germany. Since WORLD WAR II the links with Nazism and revised views on race and social fitness have largely made eugenics a reviled or forgotten study.

Eurobond Market, market for internationally traded securities. The first Eurobond issue was initiated in 1963 by Warburg's, the London MERCHANT BANK, in collaboration with several foreign banks. This has since grown to be the world's largest source of international capital: sovereign governments, corporate entities and supranational organizations such as the World Bank are regular borrowers in the Eurobond market. While the majority of the issues in the early phase were in US dollars (US dollars lent outside the US), by the later 1960s Eurobonds denominated in Deutschmarks, francs, guilders and STERLING were being issued. Later still, bonds denominated in a mix of currencies emerged, e.g. the Ecu bond. The market is not regulated by any national authorities but is subject to self-regulation via the London-based International Securities Marketing Association. The bonds, which are usually in bearer form, are sold world-wide to clients in major financial centres but banks and securities houses in London are responsible for being lead managers for approximately 70 per cent of total issuance. The Eurocurrency and Eurobond markets have been extremely influential in bringing about the integration of world capital markets and in fostering a high degree of financial innovation. In addition, in the view of some authorities, these markets were responsible for re-establishing London as one of the world's three main financial centres.

European Community, *see* EUROPEAN UNION

European Economic Community, *see* EUROPEAN UNION

European Free Trade Association (EFTA), free trade area formed by the Stockholm Convention on 3 May 1960 between Britain, Denmark, Norway, Portugal, Austria, Sweden and Switzerland. Seen as a counterweight to the European Economic Community (EEC), formed in 1957, EFTA was simply a free trade area with few communal institutions. Britain left EFTA, with Denmark, when she joined the EEC in 1973.

European Monetary System (EMS), the framework of co-operation between central banks of the EUROPEAN UNION instituted in 1978, with transactions denominated in the European Currency Unit (ECU). Its central feature is the exchange-rate mechanism (ERM) under which members are required to intervene in foreign exchange markets to keep the value of their currency within a band around the average for all participating currencies. The ERM was thus intended as a staging post to the ultimate goal of a single currency for the whole Community. After considerable debate Britain joined the EMS in Oct. 1990, but was forced to leave it in Sept. 1992. From 1 Jan. 1999 the euro became the legal currency of those EU countries that had agreed to take part in a single currency: this did not include the UK.

European Union (EU), intergovernmental and supranational organization, formerly known (before 1993) as the European Community, previously the European Economic Community, and colloquially as the Common Market. The desire for international reconciliation after WORLD WAR II was the spur for the formation of what has become the European Union. The European Coal and Steel Community, founded by the 1951 Treaty of Paris and instituted in 1952, was its first expression – coal and steel resources were pooled between Belgium, France, Italy, Luxembourg, the Netherlands and West Germany. This common market was the framework for the more comprehensive European Economic Community (EEC), founded in 1958 by the same six countries under the terms of the 1957 Treaty of Rome. The two organizations, together with EURATOM, the European Atomic Energy Community, were united in 1967. Under the EEC, ever-wider policies of harmonization of indirect taxation, regulation, border policies, monetary policies, agriculture, fisheries and many other areas of life have been pursued. British attitudes towards European integration have been consistently ambivalent. Although there had been some official consideration of the merits of joining the original Community, the residual imperial role and the SPECIAL RELATIONSHIP with the USA kept the UK aloof. Attempts at joining the Community and making what seemed to be an increasingly rational move were rebuffed in 1963 and again in 1967, notably by the vetoes from France under President de Gaulle. Britain was finally admitted in 1972, after protracted negotiations and a keenly-fought campaign for and against membership – and the original six members of the community became nine on 1 Jan. 1973 with the accession of the UK, Denmark and Ireland. Greece joined in 1981, Portugal and Spain in 1986, the former East Germany on German reunification in 1990, and Austria, Finland and Sweden in 1995.

The ideal of political unification has animated many who adhere to the 'European ideal', while fear of such unification, of the loss of national sovereignty, and of rule by bureaucrats from Brussels, the principal headquarters of the European institutions, has sown mistrust and opposition. Britain has had a love-hate relationship with European integration since the 1950s. The formation in 1960 of the now largely defunct EUROPEAN FREE TRADE ASSOCIATION (EFTA), consisting of a wide range of European nations with less ambitious economic and political ideals, was one expression of that persistent mistrust; its members have with few exceptions joined the EU over the years, while EFTA and the EU have co-operated since 1991 in the agreement on the European Economic Area and a single European market.

Common policies have been inaugurated in many areas of economic, and increasingly of political, life. In the wake of the original common coal and steel markets, the Common Agricultural Policy (CAP) was inaugurated in 1962, as a boost to farm production and farmers' incomes. A strongly interventionist agricultural regime, it has been one of the principal targets for opposition to European integration. The CAP was reinvigorated by the 1969 summit meeting at The Hague, shortly after de Gaulle's resignation, when active steps were taken to expand the union, and the principle of economic and monetary union (EMU) was advanced. The initial steps towards currency harmonization, the 'snake' within which currencies were allowed to fluctuate against each other, were vitiated by the monetary instabilities of the mid-1970s; further steps were taken in 1979 with the establishment of the EUROPEAN MONETARY SYSTEM (EMS), having eventual currency union as its goal, and the Exchange Rate Mechanism (ERM), a system of semi-fixed exchange rates which has tended to benefit the more stable currencies but has been difficult, and sometimes dangerous, for the more vulnerable currencies – the peseta, lira, and the pound. The 1992 Maastricht Treaty, a comprehensive revision of the original Treaty of Rome agreed at a summit in Dec. 1991, both reinvigorated the movement towards greater integration and harmonization and galvanized opposition towards it. The importance of 'Euro-scepticism', especially within the CONSERVATIVE governments of Margaret

THATCHER, John MAJOR and William HAGUE with the debate over the single currency continuing to be a rallying point for arguments over sovereignty as much as economic policy, has been a source of division in British political life.

CHRONOLOGY

1951 Treaty of Paris between France, West Germany, Italy and the Benelux countries – 'The Six' – setting up 'common market' in coal and steel; Britain declines to join.
1957 Treaty of Rome between 'the Six' sets up European Economic Community (EEC).
1959 Formation of European Free Trade Association (EFTA) as counterweight to EEC.
1961 Britain, Ireland, Denmark and Norway apply for membership of EEC.
1963 De Gaulle vetoes British application.
1967 De Gaulle again opposes British membership.
1971 Negotiations opened on British entry to EEC.
1972 Britain signs treaty of accession to EEC with effect from 1 Jan. 1973.
1975 WILSON'S LABOUR government puts question of Britain's membership of EEC to nationwide referendum, which votes decisively in favour.
1979 European Monetary System (EMS) introduced. Britain holds first direct elections to European Parliament.
1981 Greece to become 10th member of the EEC.
1985 Spain and Portugal signatories to an access treaty to join EC from 1 Jan. 1986.
1986 Single European Act signed providing for the free movement of people, goods, services and capital within the EU came into effect in 1993. European flag adopted.
1988 Mrs Thatcher's 'Bruges' speech attacking plans to create a European 'superstate'.
1989 Austria applies to join EEC.
1990 First stage of European Monetary Union (EMU) starts on 1 July. In October Britain joins EMS.
1991 10 Dec. Maastricht Treaty: Summit of European leaders to agree terms of the Treaty of the European Union. John MAJOR leading a Conservative Party deeply divided over Europe obtains opt-out clauses on a single currency and the social chapter, the provisions of which seek to improve living standards, health and safety at work, employer/worker relations etc.
1992 Britain leaves EMS 'temporarily' in Sept.
1993 British parliament eventually passes Maastricht Bill despite a prolonged campaign for a referendum on the Treaty led from the House of Lords by Margaret (now Baroness) Thatcher.
1994 European Union comes into force.
1997 UK accepts social chapter and agrees to implement measures already adopted under it by other 14 member states.
1999 May Amsterdam Treaty signed in 1997 comes into force: the provisions include co-ordinated measures to cut unemployment, and new mechanisms to improve the effectiveness of the Common Foreign and Security Policy (CFSP) which, since 1993, has provided for EU member states to agree unanimously a common foreign and security policy and underpin it with a credible, fast response European military capability. Recent examples of joint action and a common policy have included punitive measure against Serbia over violence in KOSOVO, and the resumption of dialogue with Iran.

Evacuation Precautionary programme at the outbreak of WORLD WAR II in 1939 whereby urban children and, in some cases, their mothers were moved to areas where they would be safer from bombing. Many soon drifted back during the PHONEY WAR. A second wave followed the onset of the BLITZ, though only a minority of children were ever involved. The dispersal of some of the poorest slum dwellers, often to better-off homes, did much to increase awareness of poverty and to encourage support for the creation of a WELFARE STATE.

Evangelicalism From the Greek *evangelion* ('good news', or the Gospel: hence the whole message of the New Testament), 'evangelical' has acquired a number of religious nuances. In the 16th-century REFORMATION, it became associated with the message of Martin Luther, and many LUTHERAN Churches are officially titled Evangelical. Many English historians have adopted the word to describe English religious reformers in the reign of HENRY VIII, considering the description 'PROTESTANT' premature for the variety of half-formed opinions and outlooks at this early stage of the English REFORMATION; this usage remains controversial.

From the 18th century evangelicalism has been associated with Protestants preoccupied with sin and the need for redemption: they place particular emphasis on personal conversion and salvation by faith in Jesus Christ, whose death was a perfect atonement for human sin. This outlook is compatible with a variety of theological stances: some 18th-century evangelicals were CALVINISTIC (e.g. George Whitefield), others ARMINIAN (e.g. the WESLEYS). *See also* LOW CHURCH.

The religious energy inspired by these beliefs triggered an Evangelical Movement which affected both the Church of England and DISSENT, and created METHODISM. Some early leaders habitually preached to large numbers, often outdoors (especially Whitefield and later the Wesleys), provoking scenes of 'ENTHUSIASM' deplored by RATIONALISTS. In the later 18th century, members of the socially elevated CLAPHAM SECT adopted an evangelical stance, and the movement spread among both clerics and laity, particularly through the influence of Charles Simeon at CAMBRIDGE UNIVERSITY. In this phase, it was associated with support for social reform – e.g. the anti-slave trade campaign (*see* ANTI-SLAVERY; SLAVE TRADE) – and missionary endeavour at home and abroad. Its primary effect was in the early 19th century; Anthony Ashley Cooper, 7th Earl of Shaftesbury, was the only major evangelical figure of VICTORIA's reign. The movement later became excessively absorbed with biblical literalism and struggles with ANGLO-CATHOLICS, and within the Church of England it has only reasserted significant influence from the mid-20th century.

In Scottish Protestantism, with its distinctive preoccupation with CALVINISM, the word 'evangelical' had a particular association with 18th- to early 19th-century struggles within the Established PRESBYTERIAN Church; evangelicals were strong Calvinists distinguished by their distaste for interference in church affairs by the state, as opposed to 'moderates' who were happy with the status quo, and well disposed to the Enlightenment.

Evesham, Battle of, Worcs., 4 Aug. 1265, the decisive royalist victory in the BARONS' WAR. By fine generalship, Prince Edward (later EDWARD I) defeated the Montfortians before they could unite their forces. A dawn attack (2 Aug.) at Kenilworth took Simon de MONTFORT's son Simon by surprise; then a night march (3/4 Aug.) trapped de Montfort *père*. In an unusually savage battle, the outnumbered Montfortians were slaughtered and Earl Simon himself was killed and mutilated.

Evil May Day, 1517, London RIOTS inspired by xenophobia. Londoners' habitual distrust of resident foreign merchants was inflamed by a sermon preached on 14 April at St Mary Spital by one of its CANONS, Dr Bele. Two weeks later, a group of apprentices used traditional May Day celebrations to start riots in which thousands attacked foreigners and their property. No lives were lost, except in the subsequent executions, but these were the most serious public disorders in Tudor London.

Exchequer At first merely a useful auxiliary to the CHAMBER, the exchequer became the main financial department of the increasingly bureaucratic English government in the 12th and 13th centuries. It comprised an office of receipt, the Lower Exchequer, and an office of audit, the Upper Exchequer. Twice a year it called SHERIFFS and other officials to account following the procedure described in Richard Fitznigel's *Dialogue of the Exchequer*. Its name derives from the chequered table cloth which served as a counting board on which calculations were made in the sight of both sheriffs and exchequer officials.

Although both the earliest references to the Exchequer and its earliest extant record, a PIPE ROLL, date from HENRY I's reign, a central office of receipt and audit had probably existed much earlier – if under another name – at the royal treasury at WINCHESTER. From the 1170s onwards it was generally based at WESTMINSTER, though it moved to YORK during EDWARD II's and EDWARD III's campaigns against the Scots. In the early 14th century the Exchequer occasionally lost its control of government finance to one of the spending departments attached to the royal household – the Chamber or the WARDROBE – but the reforms of William EDINGTON who was treasurer (1344–56) and chancellor (1356–63) reasserted its traditional dominance of financial administration.

Ousted from a central financial role under the YORKISTS and early Tudors by the CHAMBER and PRIVY CHAMBER, the

Exchequer regained its position by amalgamations in 1554, although not all revenue departments were incorporated. Chamber procedures continued to function alongside medieval Exchequer routine (complete with TALLIES), and government finance remained bedevilled by extreme official conservatism, departmental infighting and downright corruption. In the late 16th century, the TREASURY (yet another informal interloper) began to develop as a separate department, and took over most revenue administration during the 17th century; the Exchequer was abolished in 1833 (though its name survives in the title of the CHANCELLOR OF THE EXCHEQUER). The Court of Exchequer was the oldest of the COMMON LAW courts. Its original function was to adjudicate issues related to the royal revenue, its case load was substantially enlarged in the 17th and 18th centuries, both in common law and in equity, by accepting fictitious pleas of suitors that they were debtors of the crown. The Court was absorbed into the Supreme Court of Judicature in 1873.

Excise, from the Dutch *excijs*: an inland duty on the wholesale or, less often, retail value of commodities, which became a common revenue device in early 17th-century Europe. CHARLES I considered introducing it in 1628; despite the fury this caused, the Long Parliament made it a cornerstone of its war effort against the king from July 1643. No subsequent government relinquished it; indeed, the abolition of royal FEUDAL rights in 1660 meant that the crown exchanged a revenue device burdening the privileged for one affecting everyone (*see* WARDSHIP).

Cut back after the RESTORATION, excises were again exploited to finance wars following the GLORIOUS REVOLUTION. Excise collection, previously farmed out, was taken under direct governmental control from 1683. Excisemen were sometimes portrayed as intrusive agents of governmental power, and, in 1733, opposition to the extension of the excise precipitated the EXCISE CRISIS. The excise service could, however, also be viewed as a model bureaucracy, and, in the later 18th century, other parts of the machinery of government were restructured partly on the basis of practices well established in the excise. During the 18th century the excise accounted for between a third and a half of government revenue and was more important than either CUSTOMS or direct taxation. Taxation fell disproportionately upon necessities such as salt, candles, beer, soap, leather and coal. In addition much of the excise revenue was immediately transferred as interest payments to holders of government stock, so the tax system was doubly regressive.

Excise Crisis, 1733, political storm-in-a-teacup precipitated by Robert WALPOLE's decision to allocate to the reputedly more efficient EXCISE service responsibility for collecting customs duties on goods imported into Britain but destined for RE-EXPORT. He hoped to use the profits to reduce taxes on land, and had expected the plan to be broadly welcomed, but it alarmed commercial interests, whose anxiety was whipped up by the opposition into an anti-government campaign of 'INSTRUCTIONS' to MPs. Worried by indications that the furore was undermining the king's confidence in him, Walpole abandoned the plan. The incident was frequently cited during the 18th century as an example of the hubbub that could result when 'public opinion' was temporarily alienated from government.

Exclusion Crisis, 1679–81. CHARLES II dissolved three PARLIAMENTS in rapid succession when each showed a disposition to bring forward legislation to exclude his heir – his Catholic brother, James, Duke of York (*see* JAMES II) – from the succession on religious grounds. James's Roman Catholicism had stirred up controversy previously: the TEST ACT 1673 had been in part aimed against him. The POPISH PLOT of 1678–9 helped to revitalize fears of 'popery' and to undermine confidence in royal government. After a general election (Feb. 1679), a Bill to exclude James was brought before the COMMONS in May 1679. Fear that Charles's illegitimate son Monmouth (*see* SCOTT, JAMES) would replace James led some to oppose it, but it passed by a substantial majority, upon which the king dissolved Parliament and the Bill was lost. Recalled after another general election (Aug./Sept. 1679), the Commons again passed the Bill, but the LORDS rejected it in Nov. 1680. In Jan. 1681, the Commons responded by voting that no supplies be granted until the Bill passed; opponents of the Bill were condemned as traitors in the pay of the French. Parliament was again dissolved, but when it reassembled in OXFORD in March 1681 (after a third general election in Feb.), it still insisted on the Bill.

Observers of all persuasions saw parallels with events of the reign of CHARLES I; Sir Robert Filmer's *Patriarcha* was just one of several early 17th-century tracts that were distributed. Among the many terms coined to describe supporters and opponents of exclusion, WHIG and TORY, respectively, proved enduring. In practice, there were serious divisions among as well as between those who lined up on each side: exclusionists, for example, were not agreed as to who should succeed Charles.

The king's refusal to allow any Parliament committed to exclusion to remain in existence frustrated exclusionist leaders; they contemplated rebellion, and faced discredit when the government implicated them in the RYE HOUSE PLOT. Charles summoned no further Parliaments before his death in 1685. Historians have termed the period following the crisis the TORY REACTION.

Excommunication, exclusion by the Church from the community of the faithful. Medieval 'greater excommunication' deprived an offender of all contact with fellow-Christians and, in England, resulted in a writ *de excommunicato capiendo* issued to the SHERIFF for the offender's arrest. This was only abolished in 1813; similar provisions in Scotland disappeared in 1690.

Exercises of Preaching, meetings designed to improve preaching in the post-REFORMATION Church; the clergy of a district would meet to preach and be assessed by leading local clergymen (moderators). ELIZABETH I, perhaps frightened by the lurid alternative name 'prophesyings' (in fact deriving from the *Prophezei*, a prosaic institution of the Zürich church), ordered their suppression as subversive, leading to a bruising confrontation with Archbishop GRINDAL in 1577. They were quietly revived, renamed 'exercises', without her noticing.

Exeter (*Isca Dumnoniorum*). The town of Exeter was chosen as the site for a LEGIONARY FORTRESS soon after the Roman invasion of Britain (*see* ROMAN CONQUEST). Although the legion was transferred to CAERLEON soon after AD 70, the town remained an important Roman centre, and was established, as archaeological investigations have shown, as the urban hub of the *CIVITAS* of the DUMNONII.

There was a decline in the 5th century, followed by a revival under the Anglo-Saxon kings; its port became an important focus of trade in the Middle Ages, and the town itself became a fortified *BURH* in the time of ATHELSTAN. The bishopric for western England was moved there by Bishop Leofric (?–72) shortly before the NORMAN CONQUEST. From the 15th century Exeter became one of the South-West's chief CLOTH markets; and although that importance diminished, as did the port trade, it evolved in the 18th and 19th centuries into a city of genteel retirement. The city was badly bombed in 1942, and considerable destructive redevelopment of the historic fabric occurred in the 1950s and 60s.

Exeter Book, The, a verse collection compiled in the late 10th or early 11th century, that survived in the library of Bishop Leofric of Exeter to become one of the principal sources of our knowledge of ANGLO-SAXON poetry. It contains, for example, two poems by Cynewulf as well as *THE WANDERER, THE SEAFARER, THE WIFE'S LAMENT*.

Exeter Hall, erected in the Strand, London, in 1831 as a centre for EVANGELICAL activity. It became the focal point of the many philanthropic and religious societies and served to reinforce the cohesion and commitment of the evangelical community. Its famous 'May Meeting', which brought believers together from many parts of the country for prayer and deliberation, rapidly became a key event in the Christian calendar. Exeter Hall also came to signify a certain outlook – high-minded, austere and devoted to Christian duty. The building was purchased by the YMCA in 1880 and demolished to make way for the Strand Palace Hotel in 1909.

Exports The economies of the British Isles, have always depended on overseas trade. England exported gold, silver, copper, IRON and TIN in Roman times. In the Anglo-Saxon period, its wealth may well have in part derived from trade, and in the 10th and 11th centuries, it appears to have had a formidable balance of trade with Flanders and the

Rhineland, which could have already been based on the export of wool. In medieval England the WOOL TRADE was pre-eminent. Between the 15th and 18th centuries, English exports underwent two periods of boom flanked by severe recessions. The first boom (1475–1550) saw a major expansion of the woollen CLOTH trade in newly prospering but long-established central European markets. Poverty caused by war and disease halted this, and revealed the vulnerability of a trade based on one product, one market area and complacent marketing strategy.

The next boom (1630–90) had two bases: first, patient exploration of alternative markets in the far north and in southern Europe, where the English and Dutch competed fiercely to win trade lost by declining industries in Spain and Italy; second, the growth of RE-EXPORTS of colonial goods – TOBACCO, SUGAR, cotton calico. Overall, exports may have accounted for as much as a quarter of national production, with imports feeding a similar proportion of consumption. Only the Netherlands could match this scale of trade. In the following two centuries the British ECONOMY was to be heavily dependent upon exports. The export of textiles and other manufactured goods, particularly to the American colonies, was, together with the import of cotton and sugar, a keystone of 18th-century expansion. In the 19th century the export of IRON, STEEL and RAILWAY rolling stock was added to the existing range of consumer-goods exports, with major markets gained in parts of the world experiencing political and/or economic domination by Britain. Britain's trading and economic superiority made it the centre of a vast re-export trade.

Decline in the relative economic position and competitiveness of the UK economy, the rise of protectionism abroad and an increasingly 'free trade' policy domestically for most of the time since the later 19th century has resulted in an ever worsening balance of payments problem. The value of imports has consistently and increasingly outstripped the value of exports – the gap being closed by the invisible earnings of shipping and insurance services and interest from various areas. In the 20th century invisibles have increasingly failed to cover the deficit exacerbated by increased imports of consumer goods from the Far East in particular and by the erosion of key elements of Britain's manufacturing and exporting infrastructure. Since 1983 Britain's exports of manufactured goods have not been sufficient to balance imports of manufactured goods.

External Relations Act 1936, Irish legislation, passed by DE VALERA, limiting the ability of the British crown to act on behalf of the IRISH FREE STATE in external affairs and allowing it to do so only with the approval of the Irish government. The Act was part of the process of stripping away the terms of the ANGLO-IRISH TREATY of 1921, and was followed by a new constitution in 1937 which further asserted Irish independence.

Eyre (Norman-French, from Latin *iter*, 'journey'), a circuit on which teams of royal judges rode to administer justice (*see* COMMON LAW). The system was created by HENRY II, who completed it by organizing the kingdom into six circuits in 1176. The justices in eyre generally held their sittings in the COUNTY COURT. At first irregular in their occurrence, but later settling down to a seven-year pattern of recurrence, eyres were more wide-ranging than merely legal hearings, taking in any matter which the crown wanted examining, and reputedly they inspired widespread terror. The crown eventually recognized that eyres were not only unpopular but inefficient because of their infrequency, and they were allowed to lapse during the 14th century, giving way to the six-monthly ASSIZE circuit system evolved in the late 13th century. They were never abolished; as late as the 16th century they were occasionally held for special inquiries, and chief justices in eyre for the royal forests north and south of the River Trent only ceased to be appointed in 1817.

F

Fabian Society Founded in 1884, its first members included Beatrice and Sidney WEBB and Bernard Shaw. The Fabians took their name from the Roman general Quintus Fabius (?–203 BC) who favoured a strategy of cautious advance rather than a pitched battle in the campaign against Hannibal. The peaceful and democratic revolution that its members favoured was thus to be inaugurated by educating public opinion and securing the gradual adoption of their socialist policies through the infiltration of local government. The success of their programmes and policies has been much exaggerated, not least by themselves. Nevertheless, they were a great influence on the LABOUR PARTY, supplying its leaders with statistics, background information and ideas vital for the formulation of policy, and the society remains an important source of policy initiatives within the party.

Faction As a form of political conflict, faction is a useful concept, if elusive to definition. It does have a number of recognizable characteristics. First, it is primarily about power, whereas (party) conflict at least aspires to be about ideology, religious or secular. Second, it takes place in a small, face-to-face political setting with few natural divisions of class or wealth. Third, it is personal, centring on individuals or families.

Medieval and early Tudor politics provided these conditions, operating in a small military and aristocratic world where the importance of personal honour easily caused conflicts when gentlemen asserted their dignity, and where the route to the top demanded clientage links with a patron. The best patron to have was the monarch, but few reached that level without lesser patrons on the way; so clientages bred factions. The religious passions of the REFORMATION introduced a new ideological element that offered faction an escape route towards party self-righteousness, but in England towards the end of ELIZABETH I's reign, full-blooded faction re-emerged, mainly thanks to Robert DEVEREUX, Earl of Essex's inability to act the Puritan nobleman convincingly. Much early Stuart politics was faction dressed up with political slogans, but the CIVIL WARS added new issues around which to polarize. The years of 18th-century WHIG OLIGARCHY renewed factional conflict, but thereafter, British politics have rarely offered the preconditions for factions in their pure form.

Factory Legislation, the most widely diffused form of intervention into social organization during the 19th century. Beginning with a hesitant and imperfect measure of control intended for the benefit of POOR LAW APPRENTICES for whom the state was already responsible, government was driven by humanitarian pressures, mobilized by the EVANGELICAL movement and by popular agitation, to expand its coverage to take first children, then young persons, then women, under its protection, and to extend the operation of the acts to one industry after another. The regulation of hours, from being lax and indefinite, became more stringent and specific, and the provisions for health and safety, which began as little more than an injunction for cleanliness, developed into precise codes of special means of prevention of the dangers and insanitary conditions incidental to certain industrial employments. Inspection and monitoring, the key to effective intervention, followed a comparable course, evolving into a body of professional experts able to police the acts and create opinion in favour of their further extension.

According to Sidney WEBB, the developments chronicled below were a typical example of English practical empiricism. Reviewing developments over the course of the 19th century, he wrote: 'We began with no abstract theory of social justice or the rights of man. We seem always to have been incapable even of taking a general view of the subject we were legislating upon. Each successive statute aimed at remedying a single ascertained evil.'

FACTORY ACT 1819
The first of a series of measures to regulate the working conditions created by the INDUSTRIAL REVOLUTION and the FACTORY SYSTEM, it provided for the exclusion of children under nine years from working in cotton mills; those over nine were limited to a 12-hour day. The Act's significance lies less in the detail than in the acknowledgement of an enforceable obligation in the workplace.

FACTORY ACT 1833
The first breakthrough for the TEN HOURS MOVEMENT, it prohibited the employment of children under nine in textile mills, and limited the working of children between nine and 13 to a maximum of nine hours a day and 48 hours a week. Those between 13 and 18 were to work a maximum of 12 hours a day and 69 hours a week. Night work was forbidden for those under 18. The Act also insisted on educational provision for children up to the age of 13 and, most important, provided for the appointment of four full-time, paid inspectors to enforce the terms of the Act. It represented a significant departure in terms of the political and administrative processes of factory legislation.

FACTORY ACT 1844
A further response to the TEN HOURS MOVEMENT, it limited the employment of children between the ages of 9 and 13 to a maximum of 6½ hours a day, permitted women and young persons between 13 and 18 to work up to 12 hours a day, prohibited the cleaning of moving machinery and provided for the compulsory fencing off of textile machinery. The latter clause reflected the progressive influence of the new factory inspectorate. The Act encouraged the movement for factory reform without satisfying its claims.

FACTORY ACT 1850
This embodied the controversial compromise formula that divided the TEN HOURS MOVEMENT from its erstwhile leader, Anthony Ashley Cooper, 3rd Earl of Shaftesbury, who had agreed to extend the working day for women and young persons to up to 10.5 hours provided they worked only between 6 a.m. and 6 p.m. (6 a.m. to 2 p.m. on Sundays) to surmount the problems posed by the 'relay system'.

FACTORY ACT 1864
An addition to the ever-growing body of factory legislation designed to improve health and safety at work, it prohibited the employment of children under the age of eight in 'workshops' – i.e. firms employing fewer than 50 workers. *See also* FACTORY SYSTEM.

FACTORIES AND WORKSHOPS ACTS 1878, 1891
The 1878 Act codified the existing factory legislation that had grown in extent and complexity since the FACTORY ACT 1833. In the 1860s alone, the lace industry and bleaching, dyeing and domestic fustian workers had become subject to the Factory Acts. The laws controlling hours and conditions of work were thus made clearer and more consistent. The 1891 Act gave the home secretary powers to issue special regulations for the large number of trades that might be scheduled as 'dangerous'.

Factory System 'Factory' was the term used from the late 16th century to denote an overseas base for mercantile agents or 'factors'; by the early 17th century, it was also employed as a synonym for 'manufactory', a place of production. The word 'mill', meaning a factory employing some form of machinery, dates from the same period. In the early 19th century, factories and mills were already seen as standard emblems or symbols of the new 'industrial society' that contemporaries perceived to be taking shape.

The factory system – i.e. the centralization of production in one establishment, application of large-scale units of operation, labour-saving machinery and a disciplined labour force – spread slowly from the COTTON and IRON industries to replace the decentralized domestic system of manufacture (*see* BY-EMPLOYMENT; PROTO-INDUSTRIALIZATION). It was a painful and protracted process that began in the 18th century and was not completed even in those industries where the factory came to dominate until the end of the 19th (*see* INDUSTRIAL REVOLUTION).

The gains and losses of the factory system have been much debated. Some historians see it as the crucible of working-class consciousness and cohesion; others are appalled by the social costs of its unplanned and arbitrary nature, and the alienation of labour; others again emphasize the long-term improvement both in the production of goods and the standard of living that its advent made possible. *See also* FACTORY LEGISLATION.

Fagel's Letter A letter written by Mijn Heer Fagel, pensionary – i.e. head of the 'states' or ruling body – of Holland, in consultation with William of Orange (the future WILLIAM III), was distributed in England in large numbers in early 1688, in a bid to strengthen William's position. The letter was addressed to James Stewart, a Scots Presbyterian lawyer who had lived in Holland, but returned to Britain following JAMES II'S DECLARATION OF INDULGENCE. The king was angling to secure the support of DISSENTERS such as Stewart for a policy of toleration that also extended to Catholics. Fagel condemned James's policies, inasmuch as they opened the way for Catholics to acquire political power, but at the same time identified William and Mary (the future MARY II) with the view that no Christian should be persecuted for his conscience. The king responded by ordering the return of all English soldiers serving with the Dutch army.

Fair Trade League A symptom of relative economic decline, it was formed in 1881 by a group of northern businessmen who pressed for the imposition of tariffs on imports to match those charged by other countries on British exports, in order to prevent 'unfair' competition. The challenge to FREE TRADE moved from the periphery to the centre of politics at the turn of the century when Joseph CHAMBERLAIN tried to convert the CONSERVATIVE PARTY to PROTECTIONISM.

Fairfax, Sir Thomas (3rd Baron Fairfax of Cameron) (1612–71), a professional soldier who, though knighted by CHARLES I in 1641, became PARLIAMENTARY general of horse the following year. Fairfax proved an outstanding commander, outshining his father Ferdinando, who also fought for Parliament. He shared in the MARSTON MOOR victory (1644) and, as lord general of the NEW MODEL ARMY, commanded at NASEBY and LANGPORT (1645). He recaptured COLCHESTER from the ROYALISTS in 1648 but, increasingly unhappy at army militancy, took no part in Charles's trial. Although he relished suppressing the LEVELLERS, he resigned his command rather than invade Scotland in 1650. He was returned as a member for the parliaments of 1654–5 and 1656–8, but boycotted both, and though he played a part in the recall of CHARLES II retired to Yorkshire, shunning active involvement in politics.

Falaise, Treaty of, 1174, imposed by HENRY II on WILLIAM I THE LION of Scotland, whom he held prisoner in Falaise castle in NORMANDY. According to its terms, William had to do homage to Henry for Scotland, and the Scottish nobles had to swear allegiance to Henry and hand over sons as hostages. In addition, English garrisons were installed in the castles of EDINBURGH, BERWICK and Roxburgh. Edinburgh was restored in 1185 – as Henry's wedding present to his vassal – but it was not until after Henry's death, when RICHARD I was raising money to finance his CRUSADE and agreed to the Quit Claim of Canterbury, that William was able to recover Scottish independence in return for 10,000 MARKS.

Falkirk, Battle of, 22 July 1298, a major setback for the Scots in the wars of SCOTTISH INDEPENDENCE. Their army – led by William WALLACE, and largely composed of spearmen drawn up in defensive formations known as schiltrons – was easily defeated by EDWARD I, thanks to the overwhelming superiority of the English in both archers and cavalry.

Falkland Islands, British dependency in the south Atlantic, off the coast of Argentina, which was the scene in 1982 of Britain's last colonial war. First discovered in the 16th century, the islands were claimed for Britain in 1690 and named after the then treasurer of the NAVY, Viscount Falkland. A British settlement was founded there in 1766, two years after a French attempt at settlement on the islands (which the French named after St Malo, from which derives their Spanish name, Las Malvinas). Argentine attempts at settling the islands in the early 19th century were thwarted when they were formally made a British colony in 1843. Sheep-farming became the islands' economic mainstay, while they also acquired importance in world TELECOMMUNICATIONS as a relay station, and gave Britain a territorial foothold in southern waters and, later, claims upon Antarctica.

Continued claims by Argentina upon the Falklands and their dependent islands were rejected by the British government. Early in 1982 Argentina occupied the island of South Georgia, and then on 2 April invaded and swiftly captured the Falklands. The British 'task force' retook them, after vicious combat by air, land and sea, on 28 June when Argentina surrendered. The Falklands war was a signal event in British politics – the CONSERVATIVE government under Margaret THATCHER was swept back into office on a jingoistic tide in 1983 – and also in Argentine politics, proving to be the nail in the coffin of the ruling military *junta*.

Family Allowances Act 1945 This introduced payments, originally of 5s (25p) a week, for all children except the eldest. Family Allowances had long been advocated as a means of relieving poverty in large families and were regarded as a significant part of the creation of the WELFARE STATE in the BEVERIDGE REPORT. Granted as a universal benefit without a MEANS TEST, payments were paid direct to the mother to help to ensure that they were spent on the children for whom they were intended. They are now called Child Benefit.

Family Firms In the absence of efficient capital markets family resources may provide the vehicle through which business enterprises emerge and grow. This happened in Britain in the 18th century (when the law in any case prohibited JOINT-STOCK enterprises in most sectors). In Britain and some other West European countries (France in particular) small family-based firms continued to be the most prominent feature of the business structure in most sectors until the late 19th century, despite the extension of limited liability and INCORPORATION. Some historians have attributed much of Britain's lack of international competitiveness from the late 19th century to the conservatism of these entrenched structures, especially in contrast to the dynamic American model of the large corporation. Others, however, have pointed to the flexibility, innovativeness and diversification of family firms and their adaptation to the fragmentation of markets and the different economic environment of Britain compared with the United States. Family firms in the 20th century are predominantly small but some large concerns remain in private hands – Littlewoods, the stores and pools empire, for example. Today the ownership of most corporate giants and multinationals is in the hands of a mass of shareholders and financial institutions.

Family, History of the Since the 1960s historians have turned their attention increasingly to family relationships, and in so doing have constructed their own soap opera. The history of the family derives from work in HISTORICAL DEMOGRAPHY and investigations into social structure and the household, from a deeper interest in SOCIAL HISTORY, and from the application of insights from social anthropology and sociology (*see* KINSHIP, ANGLO-SAXON; MARRIAGE). Historians have been interested in both the character of familial arrangements – discovering small, nuclear families to have been the norm in England and to some extent in Scotland and Ireland, as far back as records allow – and in the relationships between family members. The conflict between those who have seen the history of these relationships as becoming ever more loving and companionable over time, and those who see personal family affection to have been present at every period in the past, received its most public airing with Lawrence Stone's book *The Family, Sex and Marriage in England 1500–1800* (1977) and the counterblast led by Alan Macfarlane.

These controversies have mainly been the concern of early modern historians. Historians of the 19th and 20th centuries have been more interested in the position of the family as an economic and work unit, often in the context of INDUSTRIALIZATION, and the changing status of women (*see* INDUSTRIAL REVOLUTION; WOMEN, LEGAL STATUS OF).

Family of Love, the only ANABAPTIST offshoot to make a lasting impression in England. Founded by the Dutch mystic Hendrik Niclaes ('H.N.' to his followers), it arrived under EDWARD VI and persisted until the CIVIL WARS. Members believed themselves pure and united with God, and entitled to lead a life of complete deception amid the outside world, so they frequently denied any connection with their sect, and fitted without trouble into the ordinary life of the official Church. It is clear that ELIZABETH I knowingly tolerated them among her personal servants, though PURITANS hated them and encouraged persecution of them.

Family Planning Association, a pressure group that campaigns for contraceptive knowledge to be made more freely available, and runs BIRTH CONTROL clinics to advise on contraception. The name was adopted in 1939 by the former National Birth Control Association, formed eight years earlier from an amalgamation of five separate family planning groups.

Family Reconstitution, a technique used in HISTORICAL DEMOGRAPHY, first developed in France in the 1950s and 1960s, involving the linking of data on baptisms, marriages and burials from parish REGISTERS to provide a basis for multi-generational family histories. The technique makes it possible to associate 'vital events' with the circumstances of particular individuals, and contributes to an understanding of the behaviour patterns and social mechanisms driving demographic trends. In England, its use has been popularized by the Cambridge Group for the History of Population and Social Structure. On the basis of data derived in this way, the Cambridge Group has argued, for example, that throughout the 17th and 18th centuries, English women frequently delayed marriage until their late 20s, and that such small changes in ages at marriage were crucial to changes in FERTILITY and hence to POPULATION changes.

Famine, lack of food leading to widespread mortality. The earliest records to supply usable statistical evidence have been employed by some historians to argue that famine was a MALTHUSian reality in early medieval England. This may not be entirely convincing, but there is no doubt that after the 12th- and 13th-century POPULATION boom, lack of food weakened resistance to disease in the early 14th, leading to abrupt population decline. After that, the reduced population did not place similar strains on AGRICULTURE until the 1590s, when parish REGISTERS reveal a nationwide crisis in 1597–9 and more frequent regional disasters in remote areas with bad transport: most of the North was hit in 1623. More common was food shortage (dearth), detectable in evidence of increased infant MORTALITY and lowered FERTILITY in poor women. Episodes of dearth were common in the 18th century, aggravated by war, grain exports and hoarding middle-men. Agricultural change in the 17th and 18th centuries meant that England and the Netherlands became the first European countries to avoid famine permanently, though only by a small margin before the 19th century. After a final disaster in the 1690s, Scotland followed suit, but 19th-century Ireland still had to endure the POTATO FAMINE.

Farming, High, *see* HIGH FARMING

Fascists, British Union of, a political organization founded by Sir Oswald MOSLEY in Oct. 1932, on his return from a visit to Mussolini's Italy. Its avowal of anti-Semitism led to violence at meetings and demonstrations, particularly in the East End of London. Its activities were checked in 1936 by the PUBLIC ORDER ACT and the BUF was banned under wartime regulations in May 1940.

Fawcett, Dame Millicent Garrett (1847–1929), women's suffrage leader. The younger sister of Elizabeth Garrett Anderson and friend of Emily Davies, she married Henry Fawcett in 1867. His blindness led her to work as his political secretary and gave her access to the world of politics. She published *Political Economy for Beginners* in 1870 and was active in campaigning for university education for girls, and married women's property rights, but it was the cause of WOMEN'S SUFFRAGE that was her lifetime crusade. She became president of the NATIONAL UNION OF WOMEN'S SUFFRAGE SOCIETIES in 1897, as well as speaking out against HOME RULE in Ireland and being sent on a delegation to investigate concentration camps in South Africa during the BOER WAR. With the rise of the PANKHURSTS' militant suffrage movement, the WOMEN'S SOCIAL AND POLITICAL UNION, Fawcett continued to recruit women who sought the vote through constitutional means and to strengthen party political alliances to this end. A conservative and patriot, she linked enfranchisement with social purity and hoped that when women had the vote domestic values would become the standard in public life. On the outbreak of WORLD WAR I she, like Mrs Pankhurst, urged her fellow suffragists to prosecute the war with vigour, but in 1916 she again petitioned for women's suffrage, which was passed by both Houses of Parliament in 1918.

Fawkes, Guido (Guy), *see* GUNPOWDER PLOT

Feathers' Tavern Petition, 1772, petition to Parliament from a group of liberal ANGLICANS, influenced by the principles of BLACKBURNE's *Confessional*, for the relief of the Anglican clergy, civil lawyers and physicians from the requirement to subscribe to the THIRTY-NINE ARTICLES. Parliament voted to reject it, and also rejected a second petition presented in 1774. Remarks made in debate encouraged certain DISSENTING ministers to apply for relief from the requirement that they subscribe to 37 of the articles in 1772 and 1773; these petitions were also rejected. Also associated was an attempt to remove subscription requirements for students at OXFORD and CAMBRIDGE.

Federal Theology, *see* COVENANT THEOLOGY

Federated and **Unfederated Malay States** The various small states and kingdoms in the Malay peninsula, which Britain had governed since the 1824 Treaty of London and the formation of the STRAITS SETTLEMENTS, were progressively combined into new British colonial protectorates. The Treaty of Pangkor 1874, which had established a system of British residential administration, had sparked off revolts in Penang, Selangor, Negri Sembilan and Pahang, which were incorporated into the Federated Malay States in 1876. Subsequently, in 1909, Kedah, Perlis, Kelantan and Terengganu accepted British control, joined by Johore in 1914, to form the Unfederated Malay States. They were all incorporated into the new MALAYA after the Japanese occupation 1941–5.

Fee Simple, a legal term used from the 13th century onwards to describe an estate ('fee') that the holder was free to dispose of as he chose.

Fee Tail, a legal term used from the 13th century onwards to describe an estate ('fee') granted to a number of persons in succession; thus no one possessor was free to deal with it as he chose. Therefore, his fee was, in law French, '*taille*' – that is, cut back, restricted. *See also* ENTAIL; STRICT SETTLEMENT.

Feidlimid mac Crimthainn (?–847), King of Munster (820–47). One of the most powerful kings of MUNSTER before the time of BRIAN BORU, Feidlimid mac Crimthainn was able to impose his superiority over neighbouring kingdoms such as LEINSTER, and even claimed domination over the UÍ NÉILL. He was also a monk and interfered directly in ecclesiastical as well as secular politics. His readiness to burn monasteries founded by rival families made him notorious (*see* KINGSHIP).

Felony, in COMMON LAW, a heinous act of wrongdoing (such as murder), for which the offender should forfeit life and lands. Felony was distinct from a trespass or misdemeanour, lesser offences which merited imprisonment, corporal punishment or a pecuniary fine, and in some cases, compensation to the injured party. The practical distinction between felonies and misdemeanours was abolished in 1967. *See also* CAPITAL PUNISHMENT.

Fen Drainage, reclamation of land in the wetlands of East Anglia, Lincs. and Som. The process has certainly been going on since Roman times, although the gains in that and later ages were usually lost. In the 15th century, Bishop MORTON and Lady Margaret BEAUFORT began the modern sequence of artificial rivers to divert water and expose land. From 1626, the crown and wealthy individuals such as Francis RUSSELL, Earl of Bedford, sponsored major schemes, employing the Dutchman, Cornelius Vermuyden. All drainage upset the delicate balance of richly varied resources that had sustained a large population on the margins of the fens, and CHARLES I's enterprises faced especially violent opposition, which continued under the INTERREGNUM. Such resistance postponed drainage in many areas until the 19th century when the draining of the fens was largely completed. The use of steam-driven pumping engines, as opposed to windmills, permitted a firmer control over the waters. Serious flooding has none the less continued into the 20th century, most catastrophically in 1947.

Fenians, a secret Irish nationalist organization formed about 1858 by James Stephens (1824–1901) with the avowed object of establishing a republic of Ireland; its name was taken from the *feinne*, legendary Irish warriors. The movement spread to the US, and assumed serious proportions. In 1867, there was an abortive invasion of Canada and plans for a rising in Ireland, a policeman was shot during the rescue from a prison van of two Fenian prisoners in Manchester, and 20 people were killed when part of Clerkenwell prison in London was blown up in an attempt to rescue a Fenian inmate.

The dual significance of the movement was that it pressured GLADSTONE to address the IRISH QUESTION, and also established a transatlantic connection that would continue to provide material and moral support for Irish patriotism.

Feoffees for Impropriations The revenues of BENEFICES '*ap*propriated' to support monasteries were sold off at the DISSOLUTION as pieces of property to become '*im*propriations' to lay people (*see also* RECTOR). Many thought this a scandalous diversion of Church revenues, and a consortium of PURITANS constituted themselves as 'feoffees' (trustees) to buy impropriations to endow preaching. LAUD saw their efforts as subversive, particularly as they concentrated on BOROUGHS that elected MPs – their chosen preachers might have influenced parliamentary elections in these communities. He therefore had their corporation dissolved in 1633, causing much Puritan anger.

Fertility, childbearing performance. Although fertility is often assumed to have been relatively high in pre-modern times until the onset of the DEMOGRAPHIC TRANSITION, recent investigations have suggested, particularly for England, that fertility from the early modern period if not earlier was comparatively low; that it varied with changes in the age at MARRIAGE; and that fertility was in the long term of greater importance than MORTALITY in determining the pace of POPULATION growth and decline since the 16th century. Demographers make the distinction between controlled fertility, i.e. the use of BIRTH CONTROL of some form within marriage to restrict the number of children born, and natural fertility, where such control is absent. Biological fertility, the theoretical maximum number of children a woman could bear, has never been attained and hardly even approached by recorded populations. *See also* CENSUS; ILLEGITIMACY.

Festival of Britain, 1951, celebration of Britain's scientific, industrial and artistic achievements held on the South Bank of the Thames in London, marking the centenary of the GREAT EXHIBITION of 1851. Although most of the buildings were temporary, the Festival Hall was a permanent legacy. The Festival was an important symbol of post-war optimism as Britain emerged from AUSTERITY.

Feud, *see* BLOOD FEUD

Feudal, an adjective derived ultimately from the Latin noun *feudum* (or *feodum*), a term that became common in 12th-century England. Although it had different meanings at different times and in different contexts, *feudum* is generally taken to refer to property held from a landlord by a tenant in return for rent in the form of service – military or administrative service in the case of a high-status tenant. It is usually translated as 'fief', or sometimes 'fee', as in KNIGHT'S FEE.

The idea that laws and customs relating to land tenure could be grouped together and termed 'feudal law' goes back to the 17th century, to the Scottish legal scholar Sir Thomas Craig and to Sir Henry Spelman. However, since Spelman's day the word 'feudal' has been used so widely and loosely as to have become little more than a synonym for 'medieval'. *See also* FEUDALISM.

Feudal Levy, *see* KNIGHT SERVICE

Feudal Quota, *see* KNIGHT SERVICE

Feudalism, an abstract term, coined in the 19th century and analogous to the earlier French term *féodalité*. It, like 'feudal system', is commonly used to highlight those features that are held to be characteristic of the state of society in western Europe during the Middle Ages. Exactly what those features were is, and has long been, a matter of debate, but most discussions have emphasized one or other (or both) of two distinct elements: the weakness of central government; and the performance of service, not in return for money – regarded as being in short supply in less developed economies – but in return for

FIEFS (land grants). Not surprisingly, it is the second aspect that has tended to dominate MARXist discussions of the subject along with the stress upon coercion rather than the 'free-labour' contract as the basis of the employment relationship. But it also led conservative historians to develop the concept of BASTARD FEUDALISM.

In the 18th century, Montesquieu developed the theory that royal authority in France collapsed in the late 9th century when fiefs became heritable. One effect of his brilliant hypothesis was to launch the notion that feudalism started in France. This in turn led to the belief that it was introduced into England as a result of the NORMAN CONQUEST, then brought to Wales, Scotland and Ireland by French and English invaders and settlers during the course of the next two centuries. However, since it is clear that, throughout the British Isles, rulers before 1066 expected political, administrative and military service from the landed élites in their kingdoms, those historians who believe that WILLIAM I THE CONQUEROR 'feudalized' England have had to define feudalism precisely in terms of those elements which they believe William introduced – in particular, the CASTLE and the feudal quota (*see* KNIGHT SERVICE).

One problem with feudalism is that the 'facts' on which it is said to be based – e.g. Montesquieu's view that fiefs became heritable in the late 9th century, or the view that William introduced the quota – are themselves highly debatable. Another problem is that so many different – and often contradictory – definitions of feudalism have been offered (or, much worse, assumed) at one time or another. In these circumstances, it is not surprising that many historians would now like to abolish the word.

So far, however, the concept of feudalism has proved more resilient than the feudal regime abolished by the French National Assembly in 1789. French historians, more at ease with abstractions than their Anglo-Saxon colleagues, continue to use the term freely, though in France feudalism tends to be discussed in terms of the breakdown of public power with (ever since Georges Duby wrote of a 'feudal revolution *c.*1000') a new orthodoxy placing the transition roughly a century later than it was in Montesquieu's chronology.

Fianna Fáil ('soldiers of destiny'), one of two main Irish political parties (rival to FINE GAEL). Founded by DE VALERA in 1926, it has been the dominant party of government since 1932, and is the constitutional base of those opposed to any vestiges of British rule and of supporters of the eventual unification of Ireland. The constitution drawn up by the Fianna Fáil government in 1937 confirmed the Catholic character of the Irish state.

The party's unity was severely strained during the ULSTER crisis (from 1968), when it was alleged that members of the government were supporting the IRA. In 1985, despite tensions with the British government, Fianna Fáil's most prominent recent leader, Charles Haughey, supported the Anglo-Irish agreement as a basis for dealing with the Ulster question.

Fief, an estate – a realm or an acre – held in return for homage and service to an overlord. *See also* FEE SIMPLE; FEE TAIL; FEUDALISM.

Field of the Cloth of Gold, French/Calais border, June 1520, meeting between HENRY VIII and Francis I of France. The focus of its staggeringly expensive splendour was a series of tournaments, designed – in vain – to end the prolonged hostility between England and France. The next year WOLSEY concluded a treaty with Charles V against France.

Fifteenths and Tenths, parliamentary tax on movable property: one-fifteenth for lay people, one-tenth for clergy. From 1334, it was imposed on communities at a fixed rate; by the 16th century, it was becoming increasingly unrealistic, and was supplemented by the SUBSIDY.

Fifth Monarchists, a MILLENARIAN grouping with an urban and army constituency, which emerged during the CIVIL WARS. Inspired particularly by CHARLES I's execution, they expected the imminent rule of Christ with his saints (the 'fifth monarchy' foretold in Daniel 2). Their initial support of Oliver CROMWELL ended in disillusion, and VENNER'S RISING (1661) was their last fling.

Fihtwite, in Anglo-Saxon LAW CODES, the fine imposed for brawling or fights between individuals or groups. The payment was made to the king if someone were killed, and was in addition to compensation paid to the lord (*manbot*) and to the kin (*WERGELD*).

Fiji, South Pacific island nation and former British colony. After occasional sightings and visits by explorers, Fiji was opened up by the French and Americans in the 1830s. Escaped convicts from AUSTRALIA had been the first white men to settle there; during the American Civil War, enterprising Australians established COTTON production. Thereafter Fiji descended into increasing lawlessness until in 1874 Britain acceded to requests to annex it as a colony. SUGAR production had been established, and Indian INDENTURED workers were imported in large numbers between 1879 and 1916 to cut the cane. The Indian-Fijian political, ethnic and social divide has been, and continues to be, a major element and frequent difficulty in the nation's life. From 1904 various forms of representative and self-government were given, always divided along ethnic lines. Fiji became independent from Britain in 1970.

Filidh, revered poets and scholars of early Irish society. Their origins were pre-Christian; it is possible to see them as DRUIDS converted to a Christian purpose. They existed to memorize and maintain the traditions of the people in an essentially oral culture, and to remind kings and their followers of their genealogies and of the exploits of their predecessors (*see* KINGSHIP).

Financial Crises In Britain in 1825–6, 1847, 1857, 1866, 1878, 1890, 1914, 1920, 1931, and 1973, financial institutions failed and businesses collapsed, accompanied by considerable personal and economic distress. The essence of these crises was uncontrolled expansion and speculation followed by loss of confidence, a lack of liquidity and retrenchment. Harvest failure prompted the collapse of 1847, while fluctuations in the trade cycle accounted for that of 1878. These particular crises were, however, largely home-grown; subsequent ones were imported by over-exposed banks that had made unwise overseas loans, such as those of BARING in Argentina in 1890. Uncertainty about the role of the BANK OF ENGLAND (as a private profit-making institution) in controlling crises, and difficulties in controlling private notes and the money supply, meant that the Bank only started to act effectively in the later 19th century. The Bank did contain domestic crises through the manipulation of interest rates and money supply, but was less able to safeguard the nation from disasters such as the beginning of the DEPRESSION in 1931, which began overseas, destroyed the GOLD STANDARD and swept away the second LABOUR government. Since the end of WORLD WAR II, government intervention, the development of institutions such as the International Monetary Fund, and the co-operation of central banks, have improved the control of financial markets and made for greater stability. However, the dismantling of investment regulation and exchange controls, the EURODOLLAR MARKET and the attraction of private speculation currently form a growing destabilizing force.

Financial Revolution, the term used by historians to denote the fiscal innovations introduced to finance KING WILLIAM'S WAR in the 1690s, and thereafter retained as the basis of public finance. The core feature of the financial revolution was the systematization of government borrowing, largely (though by no means exclusively) through institutional intermediaries such as the BANK OF ENGLAND and the EAST INDIA and SOUTH SEA companies. PARLIAMENT secured the confidence of creditors by 'funding' (underwriting) much of the debt, 'appropriating' (assigning) the proceeds of certain taxes to meet the interest payments.

Fine Gael ('Tribe of Gaels'), one of the two main Irish political parties, rival to FIANNA FÁIL. It was formed in 1933 from the ANGLO-IRISH TREATY supporters of CUMANN NA NGAEDHEAL after their defeat in the 1932 election, with elements of the Farmers' Party and Eoin O'Duffy's right-wing National Guard. Under its leader, Garret Fitzgerald, it held office in the 1980s.

Fire, Great, *see* GREAT FIRE OF LONDON

First Fruits and Tenths, papal taxation of the clergy, including their first year's income in a benefice; generally known in the medieval period as 'annates'. First claimed by Pope Clement V (1305–14), it was appropriated by HENRY VIII, who set up a court to administer it in 1540; this was amalgamated with the EXCHEQUER in 1554. The revenues were transferred to QUEEN ANNE'S BOUNTY in 1704.

First Lord of the Treasury, since the 18th century the formal title for the leading member of the government, known informally as the PRIME MINISTER. During the later 17th century lords commissioners were frequently appointed to run the TREASURY rather than a single lord high treasurer; the first lord presided at its deliberations in the absence of the monarch, which became frequent in the reign of ANNE and more or less permanent from 1714. Robert WALPOLE first saw the potential of the office in ensuring the control of government patronage, on which his continued power depended. However, since prime ministers were in practice the effective head of government, they in turn began to attend Treasury Board meetings as first lord only rarely, and in the first lord's absence the normal president became the chancellor of the EXCHEQUER.

First World War, *see* WORLD WAR I

Fiscal Feudalism, *see* WARDSHIP

Fishbourne, Sussex, the most extensive and magnificent Roman VILLA to be excavated in Britain. Arguably more appropriately styled a palace, the site is particularly interesting because it may have belonged to the British client-ruler COGIDUBNUS. Excavations, which began in the 1960s, have shown that it was built around AD 80, replacing an earlier stone villa.

Fisher Act, *see* EDUCATION ACT 1918

Fisher, John (1469–1535), Bishop of Rochester. A CAMBRIDGE humanist scholar of international reputation, he became confessor to Lady Margaret BEAUFORT, persuading her to benefit Cambridge with a divinity chair (to which he was appointed in 1503) and the foundation of colleges. He was made bishop in 1504 and did not seek a wealthier diocese; unusually for a SECULAR priest, he became a renowned preacher. He brought ERASMUS to Cambridge in 1511, and they remained lifelong friends.

In the 1520s, Fisher wrote important defences of Catholic theology, and pleased HENRY VIII by defending the king's *Assertio Septem Sacramentorum* following attacks by Martin LUTHER. However, from *c.*1526, he threw his considerable moral influence against Henry's search for a marriage annulment, and bitterly opposed the break with Rome. Arrested with MORE in 1534 (provocatively, the pope gave Fisher a Cardinal's hat), their execution the following year for refusing the ROYAL SUPREMACY horrified European monarchs and scholars.

Fisher, John (Jackie) (1st Baron Fisher of Kilverstone) (1841–1920), Admiral and naval administrator. A man of great energy and enthusiasm for new naval technologies, he made his mark in the adaptation of electricity to naval purposes, particularly in mining. Appointed commander of the Mediterranean fleet (1899–1902), he was then made first sea lord (1904–10) and he reorganized many aspects of the NAVY and introduced the DREADNOUGHT. His reforms of the conditions for the men were wholly beneficial, his interventions in ship design controversial, especially his erroneous advocacy of battle-cruisers, whilst he split the officer corps and failed to introduce a naval staff. CHURCHILL called him back from retirement at the beginning of WORLD WAR I, his immense energy fuelling an enormous building programme, but he brought down his patron by resigning over clashes over the DARDANELLES CAMPAIGN.

Fitzgerald, Lord Edward (1763–98), Irish revolutionary. Younger son of the Duke of Leinster and a cousin of Charles James FOX, Fitzgerald received a Whiggish and reformist upbringing on his family's Irish estate (his mother's educational views were influenced by Rousseau), joined the British army, but was cashiered in 1792 for having attended a revolutionary banquet in Paris where he was hailed as Citizen Fitzgerald. Elected to the Irish Commons, he was almost expelled in 1793 for derogatory remarks about the lord lieutenant. In 1796 he joined the UNITED IRISHMEN, rose speedily in its hierarchy, and became its military commander. In March 1798, in an attempt to forestall a rising, the Irish administration ordered the arrest of members of the Leinster Directory of the United Irishmen. Fitzgerald escaped, but in May was mortally wounded evading arrest and died in prison, securing for himself a place in the canon of Irish patriot martyrs.

Fitzgerald, Gerald (8th Earl of Kildare) (*c.*1456–1513), Irish leader. Known as 'the Great Earl', from the time of his succession to the title in 1477, he was effectively ruler of Ireland (officially lord deputy from 1480). Pardoned for supporting Lambert SIMNEL's imposture in 1487, in 1494 he was attainted (*see* ATTAINDER) on suspicion of supporting Perkin WARBECK in his plotting against Henry VII, and was imprisoned in the Tower of London. Nevertheless HENRY VII recognized his usefulness in sustaining fragile English power in Ireland, and as lord deputy again from 1496, Kildare remained loyal against Warbeck and reigned supreme. A skirmish with a rival led to his death from wounds.

Fitzgerald, Gerald Fitzjames (14th Earl of Desmond) (*c.*1533–83), Irish leader. One of the most powerful men in Ireland and a constant problem for ELIZABETH I, he was imprisoned in London from 1567 to 1573 for feuding with his stepson, James Butler, Earl of Ormond. Thereafter he intrigued with Catholic overseas powers until openly rebelling in MUNSTER in 1579. The rebellion was gradually beaten back, and he was in hiding, his family's power destroyed, when he was treacherously murdered by his own followers.

Fitzroy, Augustus Henry (3rd Duke of Grafton) (1735–1811), Whig politician and Prime Minister (1767–70). Elected MP in 1756, he moved to the Lords on succeeding his grandfather the following year. One of several well-born young men who came to the political fore in the 1760s, he was made northern secretary of state in Rockingham's (*see* WENTWORTH, CHARLES) 1765–6 ministry, and first lord of the Treasury in Chatham's (*see* PITT THE ELDER) ministry of 1766. When Chatham fell ill, Grafton became head of the administration, but his ministry lacked cohesion and incurred unpopularity over the WILKES affair, and he resigned in 1770. He served as lord Privy Seal under NORTH (1771–5), resigning over American policy. He was again lord Privy Seal under Rockingham in 1782–3, then retired from political life. A rake as a young man, he subsequently reformed and wrote several religious tracts.

Five Boroughs, the, a term used in the 10th and 11th centuries to refer to the former Scandinavian fortified towns of Nottingham, DERBY, Stamford, Leicester and LINCOLN. The earliest reference to them as a confederation occurs in the 940s, and their distinctive identity was such that ETHELRED II THE UNREADY directed a separate law code to the region (*see* SCANDINAVIAN SETTLEMENT).

Five Knights' Case, 1627, a *cause célèbre* in which five knights (John Corbet, Thomas Darnell, Walter Earle, Edmund Hampden, Walter Heveningham) refused to pay a FORCED LOAN demanded by CHARLES I, and were imprisoned. They appealed for a writ of *HABEAS CORPUS* to KING'S BENCH, which returned them to prison, but avoided making a final decision in their case. They were released in 1628.

Five Members, Attempted Arrest of, the hamfisted effort by CHARLES I on 4 Jan. 1642 to round up (forcibly and personally) Lord Mandeville and five MPs – HAMPDEN, the leading INDEPENDENT, Arthur Haselrig, (?–1661), Denzil Holles (1599–1680), PYM and William Strode (?1599–1645) – on treason charges. The intended victims had been tipped off and were absent; Charles faced an embarrassing scene in the COMMONS chamber. The episode turned many moderates against him, and the king soon left London.

Flanders, County of This emerged as a separate principality in the late 9th century, and its proximity meant that it was consistently important in England's medieval history (*see also* BURGUNDY AND ENGLAND). There were always strong economic links, which became especially important in the later Middle Ages when the Flemish CLOTH INDUSTRY relied extensively on English WOOL. In the 11th century, Flanders played an important political role, harbouring the exiled Earl GODWINE of WESSEX from 1051 to 1052, and contributing many men to the invading force of WILLIAM I THE CONQUEROR in 1066.

Fleet Marriages Until the passage of HARDWICKE'S MARRIAGE ACT 1753, irregular marriages performed by clerymen were binding in both ecclesiastical and COMMON LAW – even if canons had been ignored, e.g. regarding proper public notice. The Fleet Prison, one of the great London debtors' prisons (*see* IMPRISONMENT FOR DEBT), was well known as a place where such marriages might be obtained. It has been estimated that, between 1694 and 1754, 2–300,000 Fleet marriages were performed. Their attractions were that they offered some legal security, allowed people to marry without attracting the notice of parents, masters, poor law officials or other authorities, and were cheaper than ordinary church marriages.

Fleet Prison, *see* IMPRISONMENT FOR DEBT

Flight of the Earls, the flight to the Continent of the Ulster lords Hugh O'Donnell, chief of Tyrconnell, and Hugh O'NEILL, Earl of Tyrone, in 1607, fearing arrest by the English government. This removal of Gaelic Ireland's remaining leadership is often seen as a turning-point in Gaelic fortunes. Systematic colonization of ULSTER began soon after. *See also* PLANTATIONS.

Flodden, Battle of, Northumb., 9 Sept. 1513, between England and Scotland after JAMES IV had abandoned his alliance with HENRY VIII and invaded England. A crushing English victory, resulting in the deaths of James IV and many Scottish aristocrats, the battle has retained a special, almost mythical, place in both English and Scots folk-memory.

Flymenafyrmth, in Anglo-Saxon law, the offence of harbouring an outlaw or a fugitive from justice. The penalties were set out in several 10th- and 11th-century LAW CODES, and the right to receive fines was occasionally granted to great landowners.

Folkland, an obscure but important Anglo-Saxon term that has provoked much discussion among historians. In the 19th century, it was believed to mean 'common land', but today a plausible definition is thought to be 'land subject to all customary legal burdens, which could not be alienated [i.e. could not have its ownership transferred] by its owner outside his or her kindred'.

Foot, Michael (1913–), Labour politician and party leader. The son of the radical Liberal MP, Isaac Foot, and a distinguished journalist and man of letters, he was a follower of Nye BEVAN whose biography he wrote, a member of the TRIBUNE GROUP and a supporter of the CAMPAIGN FOR NUCLEAR DISARMAMENT. Foot was first elected in 1945 as LABOUR MP for Plymouth, but he lost this seat in 1955 and was out of Parliament until he took over Bevan's constituency of Ebbw Vale on his death in 1960; he became a dissident voice on the left and focus of the 'Tribunites' for a decade. It was 1970 before he entered the Shadow Cabinet as a somewhat unlikely spokesman for fuel and power. In 1976 Foot challenged CALLAGHAN for the party leadership when WILSON unexpectedly resigned, but subsequently gave his support to Callaghan's premiership, acting as mediator with the increasingly vocal left of the party. He was secretary of state for employment (1974–6) and leader of the House of COMMONS (1976–9). He won the leadership contest against HEALEY in 1980, but resigned in 1983 when Labour lost a second consecutive general election.

Forced Loans Royal demands for loans from the wealthy were common – though never popular – under the Tudors. The loan of 1626–7 to finance war abroad was levied to remedy PARLIAMENT's intransigence on taxation in 1625 and the failure of a BENEVOLENCE in 1626; it affected more people than in the past, and involved much personal pressure from local commissions. CHARLES I refused to allow its legality to be tested in the courts by five knights, and widespread opposition was reflected in the parliamentary elections of 1628. A further loan was levied by the king in 1640 and by Parliament in 1643. *See also* FIVE KNIGHTS' CASE.

Fordun, John of, *see* JOHN OF FORDUN

Forest Charter, 1217, a charter issued by the government of HENRY III's minority as part of its campaign to win support for the war against Louis IX of France and a revealing indication of the unpopularity of FOREST LAW. The charter was essentially an extension and clarification of the forest clauses that, in 1215, had been included in MAGNA CARTA. Impediments were imposed on extortion by forest officials, and arrangements were made for forest boundaries to be checked.

Forest Law, a body of English law, originally intended to protect the king's hunting, and probably introduced into England by WILLIAM I THE CONQUEROR. The law protected both 'vert' and 'venison' – i.e. the vegetation that nourished and harboured deer and wild boar, as well as the hunted beasts themselves. Thus it hampered agricultural expansion and prohibited poaching. Moreover, it applied not only to actual forest but everywhere that royal authority determined should be designated 'forest'. Since fines could be imposed at arbitrarily high levels, 12th-century English kings both vastly extended the area so designated – e.g. the whole of Essex – and set up a special forest administration to enforce this lucrative institution.

As the most unpopular aspect of royal power, forest law came under attack in MAGNA CARTA, and in 1217 a separate FOREST CHARTER was issued. However, throughout the 13th and early 14th centuries, forest law remained an issue over which king and baronial critics clashed. Eventually, in 1327, the crown accepted that the boundaries of a forest should be those recognized by the local juries that had investigated the matter during EDWARD I's reign. In addition, as taxation income increased so the crown could afford to treat offices in the forest administration as items in a patronage system rather than as important sources of royal revenue. Forest law was no longer a thorn in the side of the rich and influential; on the other hand, a statute of 1390, which in effect forbade the poor from hunting anywhere, marked the beginning of the law that protected the 'gentleman's game'.

Forest law was revived in the 1630s as one of CHARLES I's efforts to raise non-parliamentary revenue. Royal forest boundaries were extended and landowners punished for encroachments on them, although many of the forests had long been mere legal memories. Charles sincerely believed that he would gain goodwill by imposing large fines and then remitting most of them; the revenue gained by this public relations disaster was minimal. Forest law was abolished with other royal rights in 1660.

Foresteall, an Anglo-Saxon legal term that appears to have referred to the offence of obstructing the investigation of crime and/or the operation of God's and the king's law. The normal monetary penalty – five pounds – was, for the time, a very large one. The term remained in use in relation to marketing into the 18th century (*see* GRAIN RIOTS).

Formigny, Battle of, 15 April 1450, a French victory near Caen over an English expeditionary force sent across the Channel in a vain attempt to halt Charles VII's reconquest of Normandy in the closing stages of the HUNDRED YEARS WAR.

Formularies, documents that define articles of belief, or regulations concerning worship – e.g. the Westminster Confession (*see* WESTMINSTER ASSEMBLY) or the THIRTY-NINE ARTICLES; also books of formulae, or books of form letters.

Fortescue, John (?1394–1479), lawyer and political writer. A lawyer of Lincoln's Inn, he was eight times an MP between 1421 and 1437 and chief justice of KING'S BENCH from 1442, but as a prominent LANCASTRIAN he was dismissed and attainted (*see* ATTAINDER, ACT OF) by EDWARD IV in 1461. He followed the Lancastrian royal family into exile in Scotland and Flanders as their titular chancellor, and returned with MARGARET OF ANJOU in the READEPTION (1471). Captured at the battle of TEWKESBURY (1471), he agreed to recognize Edward as king in 1473 and lived in retirement on his estates until his death.

His works included several defences of the title of the House of Lancaster to the throne, and (in 1473, to seal his change of allegiance) one defending Edward's title; but of more permanent influence were two treatises about the nature of English government, written during his exile in the 1460s. *On the Governance of the Kingdom of England* remained in manuscript until 1714. *De Laudibus Legum Angliae* ('Praises of the Laws of England', first printed 1537) compared English and French law, and expressed the idea that judges were loyal to the COMMON LAW and an impersonal entity called the CROWN (the king in parliament), as much as to the physical person of a particular monarch. Fortescue claimed that England, unlike exclusively 'regal' France, was a mixed monarchy (*regnum politicum et regale*), where the 'politic' element was based on the consent of the monarch's subjects. He took a very high view of the legislative powers of PARLIAMENT, which he expressed both in his legal judgments and in his writings, reflecting ideas for a refoundation of trust in the monarchy which had been expressed in Parliament during the 1450s. Fortescue is not generally considered an original thinker, which makes his expression of such ideas all the more interesting as evidence for the commonplaces of legal thought in 15th-century England.

Forts, *see* HILL FORTS; LEGIONARY FORTRESSES; RING FORTS; SAXON SHORE

Forty-Two Articles, *see* THIRTY-NINE ARTICLES

Foss or Fosse Way, one of the major roads built in Britain by the Romans, eventually stretching from Topsham in Devon, via BATH,

CIRENCESTER and Leicester, to LINCOLN. The fact that most of it was constructed by AD 47 has led to the suggestion that it was, at that stage, a frontier marking the limits of the Roman advance. However, the existence of many forts to the west of it implies that, along much of its length, it was, in fact, a vital strategic route to support the Roman advance westwards (*see* ROMAN CONQUEST).

Foundling Hospital Established after a lengthy campaign by the merchant Thomas Coram, the hospital, with buildings in Lambs Conduit Fields in London, received a royal charter in 1739. It took in illegitimate infants, sent them to foster mothers in the country, and then brought them back to London to be taught useful skills and found APPRENTICESHIPS. It was financed chiefly by charitable contributions, and in the 18th century was an important focus for cultural display: for instance, HANDEL (who left the hospital the rights to the *Messiah*) gave fund-raising concerts in its chapel. The site was sold in 1926, but a charitable foundation for children survives.

Four Days Battle, *see* DUTCH WAR, SECOND

Fourth Party, the nickname given to a parliamentary ginger group, led by the young Lord Randolph Churchill (1849–95), who were critical of Sir Stafford Northcote's flaccid leadership in the Commons and took every occasion to harry the second GLADSTONE ministry. The CONSERVATIVE leadership was shaken by the amount of support which its critics enjoyed within the party, and moved to limit the damage by admitting Churchill into the leadership in 1884. With his death the Fourth Party died.

Fox, Charles James (1749–1806), politician. Younger son of Henry Fox (reputedly an excessively indulgent parent), Charles became MP for Midhurst in 1768 (while technically still too young to stand) and initially supported Grafton's (*see* FITZROY, AUGUSTUS) ministry, taking part in attacks on WILKES. A dandy and heavy gambler, Fox was thought self-willed and ambitious; nevertheless, he was made a lord of the Admiralty by NORTH. He resigned and was reappointed in 1772, but two years later was dismissed for his bumptious disrespect for North's authority in the COMMONS.

He then changed his political colours, associating with BURKE and the ROCKINGHAMITE WHIGS, and opposed North's American policy. When the ASSOCIATION MOVEMENT put PARLIAMENTARY REFORM on the agenda, Fox indicated support. In 1781, he was elected MP for Westminster and, when Rockingham (*see* WENTWORTH, CHARLES) came to power the following year, was made secretary of state. Because of personal and political differences with Shelburne (*see* PETTY, WILLIAM), he resigned immediately after Rockingham's death and teamed up with his old enemy North – an unprincipled alliance, in the opinion of some observers.

Together they came to power in April 1783, under the nominal leadership of Portland (*see* BENTINCK, WILLIAM CAVENDISH). GEORGE III had no wish to see either Fox or North as his ministers, and did his utmost to make life difficult for them. When Fox introduced an INDIA BILL, the king used it as an excuse to force him from power, convincing Fox that it was the king and the king's friends who posed the chief threat to the Constitution. Fox favoured the FRENCH REVOLUTION, which led to a public split with Burke and, in 1794, to division within the WHIG ranks, when Portland and many others joined PITT THE YOUNGER's government.

Fox effectively withdrew from public life between 1797 and 1802, but regained interest when Pitt's resignation opened up the prospect of significant change. In 1804, he helped to force out ADDINGTON, and, despite the king's opposition, he was made foreign secretary in GRENVILLE'S 1806 MINISTRY OF ALL THE TALENTS. He died in Sept. of the same year.

Fox's lack of respect for conventional morality – his marriage to his mistress, Elizabeth Armistead, in 1795 (not announced until 1802) did little to mollify moral rigorists – and his tolerance for RADICAL politics, which he thought less threatening to the Constitution than the wiles of the establishment, caused many to mistrust him. But he was beloved by a small circle of Whig aristocrats, and earned the qualified respect of more radical figures. His persistent defence of civil liberties in the face of counter-revolutionary panic, his support for CATHOLIC EMANCIPATION and his opposition to the SLAVE TRADE played an important part in defining the character of early 19th-century

Whiggery. His admirers founded 'Fox Clubs' to perpetuate his memory.

Foxe, John (1516–87), writer. A former OXFORD don, he fled to the Continent under MARY I and developed John Bale's scheme of collecting the history of anti-papal martyrs, producing first (1554) a Latin work and then (1563) the English *Acts and Monuments*, complete with grisly pictures (all the more effective for being rare in English PROTESTANT literature). Quickly nicknamed 'Foxe's Book of Martyrs', it was a huge publishing success, running to enlarged editions, and is still invaluable for the information it has preserved, despite its obvious bias. It had a profound impact on the English Protestant outlook. Foxe was unusual in the 16th century for believing that burning people was a bad idea.

Framework Knitting, knitting with the aid of a hand-powered knitting-machine. The 'stocking frame' was first invented by William Lee in 1598; at first used in London, by the late 17th century it had moved out to Notts., Derbys. and Leics. where stocking knitting became an important BY-EMPLOYMENT. Although the numbers of workers in the industry continued to expand in the early 19th century, long hours, low wages and allegedly falling standards of craftsmanship – in a word, SWEATING – inspired discontent and protest. STEAM POWER was introduced in the 1850s and 1860s, and in the 1880s decisively superseded outwork.

Franchise or Franchize, a term which has several distinct historical usages, all derived from its primary meaning of 'privilege'. The manumission or freeing of a SERF was known as 'enfranchisement'; another specialized use of enfranchisement was in reference to grants in new royal charters for BOROUGHS which gave them the right to send representatives ('burgesses of PARLIAMENT') to the House of COMMONS. The term franchise was commonly used in medieval law to refer to a subject's right to exercise jurisdiction; the term 'liberty' was synonymous. Possession of a franchise by custom or by grant (*see* CHARTER) conferred on the holder a degree of immunity, not always clearly specified, from the regular sphere of operations of the Crown's law officers; the greatest franchises were known as PALATINATES. In 13th-century England, the *QUO WARRANTO* inquiries marked one of the ways in which franchise holders came under increasing government supervision. In 1536 most privileges of franchises which had remained outside crown control were abolished by Act of Parliament, an important stage in the Tudor programme of CENTRALIZATION.

From the general medieval usage of the word, there developed in the 18th century a specialized meaning referring to the privilege of voting, and hence to the qualifications for voting. This has now become the usual modern political reference of the term; so one speaks of the widening of the franchise in the REFORM ACTS of 1832 etc. (cf. the similarly specialized modern development of the word CONSTITUENCY). *See also* entries under REPRESENTATION OF THE PEOPLE ACT.

A commercial use of the word has become very common in the late 20th century: 'to franchise' is to grant a right to market certain goods, usually employing a well-known name or brand label, in a restricted region or timespan. The practice has even spread to the granting of higher degrees in some institutions of learning.

Francis of Valois (Duke of Alençon) (1554–84), youngest surviving son of Henry II of France. Duke of Alençon until 1574, he succeeded his brother Henry as Duke of Anjou (do not confuse them; Henry became King Henry III of France, 1574–89). Both Henry and Francis were put forward by their mother Catherine de' Medici as suitors for ELIZABETH I, but Francis was the more serious contender, 1572 and 1579–81. On the second occasion his diplomatic importance was considerable as he was playing a leading role in the NETHERLANDS Revolt against Spain. Elizabeth was genuinely fond of him, calling him her 'Frog', and may have seen him as a last chance to marry; she showed real grief when it became obvious that his Roman Catholicism would be widely unpopular, making marriage impossible.

Franciscans, *see* FRIARS

Frankfurt, Troubles at, complicated disputes that raged between 1554 and 1558 in the English PROTESTANT community of MARIAN EXILES at Frankfurt. The disputes centred on how much the PRAYER BOOK should be further modified and whether the congregation, rather than clerical organization, should control religious policy. When the conflicts were described in a pamphlet of 1574 (probably by the PURITAN clergyman William Whittingham), they were already seen as prefiguring the puritan disputes of the Elizabethan Church.

Franklin, a member of the highest rank in village society in later medieval England.

Frankpledge, *see* COURT BARON; MANOR

Frederick (1707–51), Prince of Wales. Father of GEORGE III, he was often at odds with his own father GEORGE II. In 1737, he was banned from court after he had removed his wife Augusta, daughter of the Duke of Saxe-Coburg, from Hampton Court Palace to prevent his second child being born there; he then set up a rival court at LEICESTER HOUSE, which became a centre of opposition to WALPOLE. The latter's fall in 1742 brought no more than a partial reconciliation between father and son. However, Frederick died unexpectedly after being hit by a tennis ball.

Free Church, a church denying the doctrines, polity or discipline of the Established Church. The term, used widely in the 19th century, also embraces denominations described as DISSENTING and NONCONFORMIST churches. The term was first used in England in the late 1860s, being derived from the Free Church of Scotland formed by the DISRUPTION of 1843.

Free Trade, a 19th-century reaction against the 18th-century mercantile system (*see* MERCANTILISM). Adam SMITH, its principal theorist, argued that the removal of trade restrictions between nations would encourage the exploitation of natural advantages, resulting in an efficient international division of labour and the promotion of world peace. The liberation of trade policy, begun by PITT THE YOUNGER and William Huskisson, president of the Board of Trade (1823–7), came to fulfilment in the 1840s. The budgets of 1842 and 1845 replaced or eliminated duties on large numbers of raw materials and manufactured goods; the CORN LAWS were repealed in 1844; most remaining duties were swept away in the budgets of 1853 and 1860. Britain became the 'workshop of the world', taking full advantage of her early lead in industrial innovation. 'Free Trade' went hand in hand with political and economic domination, enabling Britain to buy its raw materials in the cheapest markets and sell its manufactures in the most costly. Its limitations became apparent in the later 19th century with increased competition, and the growth of PROTECTIONISM among non-imperial trading partners.

After an attempt to restore free trade in the 1920s, the collapse of the world economy in the 1930s produced a wholesale retreat into protections with tariffs, quotas and exchange rate restrictions multiplying rapidly. This was self-defeating and simply exacerbated the DEPRESSION. In 1944 BRETTON WOODS produced the institutional framework within which post-war international economic policy was to develop. The IMF, World Bank and specifically GATT came into being with the objective of restoring a liberal trading order. Successive rounds of multi-lateral tariff reductions over the next 30–40 years helped world trade to grow at well over 7 per cent per annum, fuelling the post-war boom. Instead of tariffs and quotas, however, there have grown up less visible barriers such as voluntary export restraints, higher safety or environmental standards, bureaucratic procedures and legal restrictions.

Freehold, the normal form of landholding in modern England, descended from the more humble FEUDAL tenures grouped together as 'tenures in socage'. The feudal services due on socage land usually consisted of labour services or small money payments, most of which had become worthless by the late medieval period. Increasing amounts of land were therefore considered freehold (i.e. held free of feudal obligations); a mark of the changing character of landholding was that from 1429, possession of freehold land worth 40 shillings a year was considered a minimum qualification for being a person of substance, someone who was therefore suitable to vote for the election of KNIGHTS OF THE SHIRE to the House of COMMONS. In 1660 the distinction between KNIGHT SERVICE and socage tenure was removed. From 1926 virtually all other forms of feudal tenure were abolished, together with any remaining feudal INCIDENTS or peculiar customs of INHERITANCE (e.g. BOROUGH, ENGLISH; GAVELKIND) in freehold lands held in socage; thenceforward, in feudal terms, all

English lands were nominally considered as tenancies-in-chief (*see* TENANT-IN-CHIEF) by socage held of the crown. In practice, this means that English land law now recognizes only freeholds and LEASEHOLDS. *See also* COPYHOLD.

Freemasonry Much written about the ancient beginnings of freemasonry may be disregarded. The most plausible account of early freemasonry, which subsequently became a worldwide movement, locates it in late 16th- and early 17th-century Scotland, growing out of the normal secrecy of skilled-trade associations. In a country where buildings were being erected on a large scale, and where the intelligentsia were interested in the mystical nature of mathematics and proportion, some trade lodges began to take on non-professional members, encouraged by William Shaw, master mason to JAMES VI. There was no hostility from the Scottish Church, although during the Enlightenment many lodges became linked with DEISM. Freemasonry had spread to England by the late 17th century, and members of the ROYAL SOCIETY included many early masons. A constitution promulgated in 1723 was endorsed by all official lodges. Spreading abroad, freemasonry was condemned by Pope Clement XII in 1738.

The special allure of freemasonry lay in its alleged contact with a universal and ancient wisdom embodied in mathematical and architectural skills; celebration of God as a great architect whose handwork was the natural world fitted with the fashion for natural religion. It flourishes today as a global organization, the secret and exclusive nature of which still engenders outsiders' suspicions.

French, John (1st Earl French) (1852–1925), soldier. A distinguished cavalry commander in the BOER WAR, he rose steadily to become chief of the imperial general staff in 1912, but was forced to resign in 1914 when the government disavowed a letter he had written to Irish officers at the CURRAGH, assuring them that they would never be called upon to force ULSTER to accept HOME RULE. Commander-in-chief of the BRITISH EXPEDITIONARY FORCE, he led it during the opening phases of WORLD WAR I. Following the retreat from MONS and in the first battle of the MARNE, French led a series of offensives which involved further heavy casualties. His relations with the French were poor, and in Dec. 1915 he was replaced as commander-in-chief on the Western Front by HAIG. He spent the rest of the war as commander-in-chief of Home Forces and from 1918–21 served as lord lieutenant of Ireland, where he proved ill-equipped to deal with Irish nationalism.

French Revolution, 1789–99, a process of reform and restructuring, undertaken in the conviction that the old regime was simply incapable of governing France, and in particular of resolving the fiscal crisis. It took dramatic form in 1789 when Louis XVI summoned the Estates General (last convoked in 1614). Reconstituting themselves as a national assembly, the deputies worked to create a constitutional monarchy, and initiated a programme of radical reform, including the abolition of feudal rights (1789), nationalization of the Church, and development of a written constitution (1791). Fearing that other European powers would act to suppress the revolution, the French declared war on Austria in April 1792; then in Aug.-Sept. a popular insurrection in Paris destabilized the regime. The king was imprisoned, and a 'Convention' elected which declared France a republic; in Jan. 1793 the king was guillotined.

The widening of the FRENCH REVOLUTIONARY WAR in the autumn of 1792 and spring of 1793 destablized this regime; in June the more moderate 'Girondin' deputies were arrested, and effective power passed into the hands of the Parisian 'Committee of Public Safety', dominated by Robespierre. A period of 'Terror' followed, associated both with aggressive prosecution of war abroad with military, judicial and terroristic action against enemies of the revolution at home. Christianity was superseded by deism in the form of the 'Cult of the Supreme Being'. The 'Thermidorean reaction' came in 1794 when the Convention withdrew support from Robespierre, who had threatened to extend purges through their ranks. In 1795, under a new constitution, executive power passed into the hands of the 'Directory', who maintained political stability by quashing elections which swung too far to right or left. Campaigns in Italy and EGYPT helped to bring Napoleon Bonaparte to prominence among republican generals; on '18 Brumaire'

(9 Nov.) 1799, a coup brought him to power as FirstConsul. Though Napoleon preserved certain revolutionary institutions and ideas, his regime was autocratic, and many of his values conservative. He agreed a concordat with the papacy in 1801 and proclaimed himself emperor in 1804; most emigré nobles returned to France.

In Britain, the early reformist phase of the revolution was widely welcomed, though the special enthusiasm shown for it by RATIONAL DISSENTERS and the more radical WHIGS alarmed those most firmly wedded to the Established Church, aristocracy and traditional parliamentary government, notably BURKE. radicalization of the revolution in 1792, by contrast, provoked panic; a royal proclamation against seditious activity focused hostility on British JACOBINS and popular CORRESPONDING SOCIETIES. In Feb. 1793 Britain joined other powers in making war on the French republic. Charles James FOX and others maintained that the 'Terror' was in large part a response to foreign aggression, but in 1794 Portland (*see* BENTINCK, WILLIAM CAVENDISH) led a Whig secession into alliance with PITT THE YOUNGER. After the overthrow of Robespierre, British responses became more diverse and complex. Burke and other conservative Whigs favoured a war to restore the monarchy; Pitt aimed primarily to curb French aggression; William WILBERFORCE among others argued the time had come to make peace. Though the repression of popular political activity was continued by the passage of the TWO ACTS, people began to count the economic costs of war. Bad harvests (especially in 1795 and 1800–1), and other social problems at home, helped to spur broadly-based interest in social reform, reflected in the founding of the SOCIETY FOR BETTERING THE CONDITIONS AND INCREASING THE COMFORTS OF THE POOR. The problem of containing disaffection in Ireland – which took armed form in the IRISH REBELLION of 1798 – divided ministers: William Wentworth-Fitzwilliam, resigned on the issue in 1795, and Pitt himself did likewise in 1801. Meanwhile the increasingly imperialistic expansionism of revolutionary France, and development of french government into a form of militaristic autocracy, rallied a broader spectrum of British public opinion behind the war effort. The threat of French invasion in 1798 prompted mass enlistment in the volunteers. The MINISTRY OF ALL THE TALENTS (1806–7) briefly saw Whigs and Pitties on the one hand jointly prosecuting war, and on the other enacting one of the more radical reforms of the period: the abolition of the SLAVE TRADE (*see* ANTI-SLAVERY).

French Revolutionary Wars, 1793–1802. Austria and Prussia formed a protective alliance, and considered invasion of France to uphold the monarchy. GEORGE III and PITT THE YOUNGER were initially determined to hold aloof, but in Sept. 1792, having defeated the Prussians at Valmy, the newly established French Republic set out on an expansionist course. Announcing an intention of extending to their 'natural frontiers', the Rhine and the Alps, the French conquered the Austrian Netherlands and annexed Savoy.

In Jan. 1793 Louis XVI was executed: the National Convention then declared war on Britain, commissioning several members of the Convention, including Thomas PAINE, to draft an appeal to the British people. Holland, Spain, Portugal and several Italian states, interlinked by a complex web of treaty obligations, also came into the 'War of the First Coalition'. Britain's concern with the Low Countries was a constant; she had just (1790) intervened in both Holland and the Austrian Netherlands against internal revolt.

Links forged between French revolutionaries and domestic RADICALS, e.g. members of the LONDON CORRESPONDING SOCIETY, were also a source of concern. Radicalization in Britain aided Pitt inasmuch as it produced serious tensions within the WHIG opposition.

Initial British reactions were to send armies to the Low Countries and to seize French West Indian SUGAR islands (which had been the main contributors to French economic growth). It soon became clear that the Revolution had all but wrecked the French navy, with dire results on its performance against an increasingly predominant Royal Navy. However, the French began to show an equal predominance in land warfare. Total mobilization and reorganization of their army led to the conquest of the Low Countries and the proclamation of the Batavian Republic, the British army being driven out, thereby ending for many years successful British military involvement on the continent. From then on Britain's main involvement would be naval, colonial, and in providing subsidies to allies. French royalists had handed over the naval base of Toulon to the British Mediterranean fleet in 1793 but it could not be held, whilst support of royalist risings in Brittany and the Vendée merely resulted in disaster to the insurgents. Initially successful, the WEST INDIES campaign soon bogged down, with huge losses of troops to fever. In 1794 the battle fought so far out into the Atlantic that it is known by its date – 'the Glorious First of June' – confirmed the fighting efficiency of the British fleet, though the French achieved their object of getting an urgently needed grain convoy through. An Anglo-American treaty of commerce, the JAY TREATY, headed off the threat of a Franco-American alliance. The government clamped down on French sympathizers at home: in May 1794, responding to radical calls for the summoning of a British Convention, Pitt suspended *HABEAS CORPUS* and arrested leading radicals; Horne Tooke, Thomas Hardy and others were charged with treason. In July, the government was strengthened by the accession of the Portland (*see* BENTINCK, WILLIAM CAVENDISH) Whigs, who supported these repressive policies, and their further extension by the TWO ACTS of 1795. In 1795, the British secured the trade route to INDIA by seizing Capetown from the Dutch, as well as bases in CEYLON, and West Indian islands. Some prospect of peace opened up, provoking debate in Britain about war aims.

In 1795 Prussia, several other German states and Spain made peace with France. Britain explored the possibility of making peace that year and the next, but it became clear that France would demand not only her 'natural frontiers' but also the return of all colonial conquests. From that point, the war turned against Britain. In Oct. 1796 Spain entered on the French side; the British fleet was forced to withdraw from the Mediterranean. Attempts were made to land troops to foster rebellion in Ireland, and to prepare a landing in Britain itself. The danger of this was greatly increased by the Spithead and NORE MUTINIES putting most of the fleet in home waters out of action. However Admiral Duncan's victory over the Dutch fleet at Camperdown in Oct. 1797 showed that the crews who had mutinied would still fight, and for the time being brought the danger of invasion to an end. Meanwhile, in Feb, 1797 Jervis had beaten the Spanish fleet at St Vincent though financial crisis forced the abandonment of the GOLD STANDARD.

When royalist resurgence at the elections of 1797 seemed to threaten the French government, peace seemed temporarily attractive – but the Directory re-established its power with the *coup d'état* of Fructidor, and talks collapsed. French forces under Napoleon captured Lombardy and advanced into Carinthia. In Oct. the Austrians made peace with France by the Treaty of Campo Formio. The 'First Coalition' collapsed. Renewed threat of French invasion prompted the mobilization in Britain of a multitude of VOLUNTEERS. Napoleon, however, persuaded the Directory that Britain could best be hit indirectly. Bases should be established in the Near East to support an attack on India and allies sought among south Indian powers, notably Tipu of Mysore (who in the event was defeated in the second MYSORE WAR). Abandoning those in Ireland – and thereby helping to doom the IRISH REBELLION of 1798 – Napoleon seized MALTA and landed in EGYPT. However, in Aug. 1798 his hopes were dashed when NELSON destroyed the French fleet in the Battle of the NILE, stranding French forces in Egypt. British naval mastery in the Mediterranean was established, Malta was besieged and would fall into British hands.

This victory made possible a second anti-French coalition, comprising Britain, Austria, Russia, Portugal, Naples and the Ottoman Empire. An Anglo-Russian expedition to North Holland won the surrender of the Dutch fleet, but achieved nothing on land. Though there were coalition victories elsewhere, a British expedition to Holland failed and problems of co-ordination emerged. Napoleon abandoned his army and returned to France; in Nov. 1799 he seized power as 'First Consul'. He assumed control of the army in northern Italy, 1801, after defeating the Austrians at Marengo, persuaded them to confirm the conditions of the previous peace of Campo Formio with a new peace of Luneville. Russia made peace, and joined with Sweden, Denmark and Prussia to form a new League of ARMED NEUTRALITY in 1800, challenging British control of the seas.

However, a rapid and successful maritime strike at COPENHAGEN, combined with the assassination of Tsar Paul, the chief architect of the League, dispelled this threat. In 1801 Pitt resigned because he could not persuade the king of the need for CATHOLIC EMANCIPATION to complement the ACT OF UNION with Ireland. Under the much weaker ADDINGTON, Britain failed to drive a hard bargain at the Peace of AMIENS. Though Pitt supported Addington, GRENVILLE and other Pittites repudiated him.

The French Revolutionary War highlighted British strengths and weaknesses. British efforts to contain a dynamic continental enemy proved totally inadequate; her strengths were maritime and imperial. The threat of domestic subversion, whether in JACOBITE or other form, had been an element in most of Britain's 18th-century wars. If Pitt's government had a special advantage it lay in the breadth of support it enjoyed among the parliamentary and ruling classes: this was the only 18th-century war in which disputes about the conduct of the war did not topple at least one administration. The possibility that lower-class discontents might transmute a French-style revolution in Britain was, in an era of rising prices and occasional disastrous harvests, the stuff of nightmares for the propertied, but the widespread participation in the Volunteer movement of 1798–9 suggests that, whatever their discontents, English working men were by and large prepared to rally against a republic whose credentials as the champion of liberty, equality and fraternity were in any case debatable. The war stimulated Anglo-Irish parliamentary union, but government otherwise underwent no major structural change. Its administrative capacities were strikingly displayed: income tax was introduced in 1799; unprecedentedly high proportions of the male population were mobilized for military or naval service; concern about food supplies prompted a series of nationwide crop surveys; and 1801 saw the first English CENSUS.

Friars (Latin *fratres*, i.e. 'brothers'), a variety of religious communal life which evolved to meet the new challenges facing the Western Church from religious dissent and the evolution of new urban centres during the 12th century. The two dominant early figures were a Spanish AUGUSTINIAN canon, Dominic (1170–1221), who obtained sanction for his Order of Preachers (Dominicans, or 'Black Friars') from Pope Honorius III in 1216, and the Italian Francis of Assisi (1181/2–1226), who secured approval for his Friars Minor (Franciscans, or 'Grey Friars') from Pope Innocent III in 1209–10.

Although the founders were very different personalities, the mainstream of their movements quickly developed in very similar ways (and were therefore great rivals); unlike many monastic ORDERS, they both emphasized close contact with the laity, preaching and hearing confessions and siting their convents accessibly in towns. They also developed a special ministry to UNIVERSITIES, and many friars became major figures in medieval scholarship. The Dominicans first arrived in England in 1221 and the Franciscans in 1224. Other orders of Friars evolved, including the Augustinian ('Austin') Friars, the Carmelites ('White Friars'), Trinitarians ('Red Friars') and Crossed (or Crutched) Friars.

Friendly Isles, *see* TONGA

Friendly Societies Prior to the introduction of national insurance in 1911, friendly societies, operating on a contributory basis, provided workmen with protection against unemployment and sickness, and with pensions and death gratuities. Originating in the 17th century, often as trade CLUBS, with parliamentary approval from 1793 and a sound legal status they increasingly flourished. Estimated membership rose from 0.7 million in 1801 to 4 million in 1874 and upwards of 6.5 million in 1913. Their size, success and importance frequently made the skilled workers for whom they catered suspicious of state intervention in welfare provision.

Friends, Society of, *see* QUAKERS

Frigate, a ship-type name which varies in meaning according to date, context and user. In the mid- to late 17th century it meant a type of ship copied from Dunkirk PRIVATEERS, low lying and fine-lined, and could include line-of-battle ships. In the early 18th century it could mean any warship of 50 guns to 20 guns used for cruising purposes, or even the smaller sloops. The merchant frigate was a ship (usually fine-lined) with two decks. Just before 1750, copying the French, the NAVY adopted a new type which was a vessel, originally of 28 or 32 guns, with two continuous decks but no guns on the lower one. This proved to be the ideal type for cruising duties, was built in large numbers, and grew in size and power till by 1815 the largest carried 50 to 60 guns. The type was adapted for steam, but around 1880 the name was replaced by CRUISER. Inappropriately revived in the middle of WORLD WAR II to describe a new type of anti-submarine escort, the name 'frigate' is now used to describe most surface warships.

Fulford Gate, Battle of, Yorks., 20 Sept. 1066. A hard-fought engagement in which HARALD HARDRAADA of Norway and Earl TOSTIG defeated the northern English Earls Edwin of Mercia and MORCAR. However, the battle weakened the Norwegian army so much that, five days later, it succumbed to the forces of HAROLD II of England at STAMFORDBRIDGE. As a result of their losses in these two battles, the northern English were unable to assist Harold at the battle of HASTINGS.

Fursa, St (?–*c*.650), an Irish monk who undertook missionary work in EAST ANGLIA during the 630s. An ascetic in the Irish monastic tradition (*see* MONASTICISM), and representative of its highly individualistic evangelism, he travelled to East Anglia in the aftermath of its king's CONVERSION through the influence of EDWIN of NORTHUMBRIA. St Fursa subsequently founded a monastery near Paris.

Fyrd, the Anglo-Saxon term for a king's army. The 19th-century notion of the original equality of all members of Anglo-Saxon society has largely been abandoned, but the associated idea of a universal obligation to do military service has not been entirely jettisoned. Nevertheless, the emphasis is now increasingly on the central role of lordship and land tenure as the organizational basis of Old English armies. The history of the COMMON BURDENS indicates that there was, from an early date, an association between military service and the status derived from the tenure of land, which is further illuminated by more plentiful 11th-century evidence. This later material also suggests a territorial basis for service, and identifies specialized warriors such as HOUSECARLS, BUTSECARLS, LITHSMEN and simple mercenaries.

The Anglo-Saxon army appears to have been an infantry force, although references to the use of horses, as well as archaeological discoveries of what looks to be cavalry equipment, should not be neglected. The *fyrd*'s composition and tactics remain controversial among historians and are inextricably entangled with discussions of FEUDALISM.

Fyrdwite, the penalty incurred by anyone who failed to respond to a summons to join a royal Anglo-Saxon army (*see* FYRD). The fine appears as early as the laws of King INE, and its frequent mention thereafter indicates an efficient system of military organization.

G

Gaelic, the Celtic languages spoken in what are now Ireland and Scotland. Together with the Manx language of the Isle of MAN (extinct as a living tongue in the 19th century), Irish and Scots Gaelic are members of the Goidelic or 'Q-Celtic' or Brythonic grouping of languages, as opposed to the 'P-Celtic' grouping of Welsh, Cornish and Breton: note, for instance, the contrast between the words for 'son' – 'mac' in Gaelic, 'ap' in Welsh. In both Ireland and Scotland, from the medieval period Gaelic faced competition from English (known in Scotland as 'Scots'); most of lowland Scotland was culturally English, while the extreme north-east and Orkney and Shetland were culturally Scandinavian. The first book to be printed in Gaelic was *Foirm na n-Urrnuidheadh*, a free translation of John KNOX's *Book of Common Order* by Superintendent John Carswell (*c.*1520–72), published at Edinburgh, 1567; this was still in a literary form of the language common to Ireland and Scotland ('classical common Gaelic'), but by then the unity of the Goidelic language-family was breaking up.

Despite the inroads made on Irish Gaelic by English colonial policies in Ireland during the 17th and 18th centuries, the language remained dominant in the rural west during the 19th century, but it received a further blow from the POTATO FAMINE. On the establishment of the FREE STATE it was made the first official language, with English as a second official language. Despite (or because of) this, Irish suffered considerable further decline, although since the 1970s there has been a revival of popular interest, and the areas where it is spoken (the Gaeltacht) have been given special economic assistance.

In Scotland the Gaelic-speaking areas of the west and north have been steadily contracting since the 18th century. Recent efforts at revival are producing some results. *See also* CELTIC REVIVAL; CELTS.

Gaimar, Geoffrey, 12th-century author of the ANGLO-NORMAN *L'Estoire des engles* (*c.*1140) – the earliest extant historical work written in French. Conceived as a continuation of GEOFFREY OF MONMOUTH's *History of the Kings of Britain*, it covers the period from the ANGLO-SAXON SETTLEMENTS to the reign of WILLIAM II RUFUS in a romantic and courtly manner intended to appeal to the Anglo-Norman aristocracy.

Gaitskell, Hugh (1906–63), Labour politician and party leader. He joined the LABOUR PARTY during the GENERAL STRIKE while still at Oxford, was Hugh Dalton's (President of the Board of Trade 1942–5) private secretary during WORLD WAR II and became MP for Leeds in 1945. In 1947 he was made a junior minister and was appointed chancellor of the Exchequer in 1950. A rising star on the right wing of the party, he came into conflict with the left over the need to finance increased defence expenditure because of the KOREAN WAR, and the introduction of some NATIONAL HEALTH SERVICE charges. In opposition over the following decade, Gaitskell and BEVAN were the main protagonists on the opposing wings of the party. When ATTLEE resigned as party leader after losing the 1955 general election, Gaitskell defeated both Bevan and MORRISON for the succession.

Tested almost at once by the SUEZ CRISIS, he showed skill in opposing the government's policy as a matter of principle without seeming unpatriotic. After Labour's third consecutive election defeat in 1959, he initiated a basic review of Labour's policies and machinery, seeking unsuccessfully to persuade the party to drop Clause Four of its constitution (*see* NATIONALIZATION), which committed Labour to the common ownership of the means of production and distribution. He bitterly contested the vote for UNILATERALISM at the 1960 party conference, and by diligent work with trade union leaders behind the scenes he secured its reversal the following year. Between then and his death as a result of a mystery virus, his prestige and control of the party were at their height; he was considered by many to be the outstanding representative of the social democratic tradition within the Labour Party.

Galanas, the Welsh equivalent of WERGELD, the payment to be made by the kindred in compensation for a serious crime committed by one of its members. The BLOOD FEUD played a central role in early Welsh society, as did mechanisms of compensation, which are elaborately described in the earliest law texts (*see* HYWEL DDA).

Gallipoli, *see* DARDANELLES CAMPAIGN

Galloway, the region in the extreme southwest of Scotland that emerged as a distinct and highly Gaelicized political entity in the early 12th century under Fergus, son-in-law to HENRY I. The gradual extension of the authority of Scottish kings provoked local rebellions in 1160 and 1174. In 1234, ALEXANDER II ousted the illegitimate son of the last Galwegian prince – Alan, son of Roland – and partitioned Galloway between Alan's daughters, treating it not as a principality but as a great estate. But Galwegians continued to live by their customary law, including the BLOOD FEUD, which had led the English, from the 12th century onwards, to regard them as 'savages'.

Galloway Levellers Although localized and short-lived, the 'levellers' revolt' in Dumfries and Galloway in the summer of 1724 was the most substantial agrarian protest in Britain in the 18th century (Ireland furnished more examples; *see* WHITEBOYS). When small tenant farmers were evicted by lairds wishing to breed more cattle for English markets, the Levellers issued a manifesto demanding justice for the poor, and pulled down ENCLOSURES and killed and mutilated cattle. At Kirkcudbright, they responded to the reading of the RIOT ACT by reading the Solemn League and COVENANT of 1643. Trouble continued until the autumn, despite the arrival of troops. The government and army tried to avoid a provocative response, and only two protesters were TRANSPORTED. *See also* LEVELLERS.

Gallowglass, a Scottish mercenary employed in Ireland to fight as a heavily armed foot soldier, from the 13th to the 17th centuries. The term derives from the Irish *galloglaigh*, 'foreign soldiers'.

Gambia, the, a tiny, and artificially created, west African republic and former British colony, its territory extending along the lower reaches of the river of the same name. The borders were drawn up by Britain and France in 1889. The territory's origins lie in the wider Senegal which surrounds it (except for its short coast); the Gambia River was an important trading post from the mid-16th century, and especially from the mid-17th century. James Island in the river became a major base of the ROYAL AFRICAN COMPANY from 1661. The abolition of the SLAVE TRADE in 1808 provoked Britain to control the merchants and the territory directly. Gradually the British sphere of influence spread; when Britain and France confronted each other in the region during the first SCRAMBLE FOR AFRICA, Gambia and Sierra Leone were separated and their boundaries settled in 1888–9. Nationalist sympathies were slow to develop, although native political parties were emerging by 1959. Self-government came quickly thereafter, in the 'WIND OF CHANGE' in 1963, with independence in 1965.

Game Laws, an intricate set of laws passed between 1671 and 1831 to restrict the hunting of game – especially pheasant, partridge and hares – to landed proprietors. The qualification remained steady at £100 p.a. in freehold land, or £150 leasehold, the sons and heirs of esquires being exempted. The laws, frequently modified to discourage particular forms of poaching, were much resented because they were seen as restricting access to the fruits of nature, and because those entitled to could pursue game over others' land. Poaching was neither a FELONY nor a CAPITAL CRIME, but the most severe legislation – the Night Poaching Law of 1817 – made offenders liable to TRANSPORTATION.

Gaol Delivery, *see* ASSIZES

Gaols Act 1823 Introduced by Home Secretary PEEL, the measure represented a move towards a penal policy based on rehabilitation and reform rather than punishment and deterrence and, as such, reflects the work of John Howard (1726–90), who is commemorated in the name of the Howard League for Penal Reform, and Elizabeth Fry (1780–1845) the philanthropist and prison reformer. The Act provided for regular visits by prison chaplains, the payment of gaolers, the abolition of fees, the institution of a reforming regime, the appointment of female staff for women prisoners, and a prohibition on the use of irons without prior knowledge of the magistrates. Impressive on paper, it was useless in practice because of the non-provision of an inspectorate. Such provision had to await the Prison Act 1853.

Garden City Movement This applied the ideas of Ebenezer Howard (1850–1928) to the built environment, with the intention of combining the energy and dynamism of town life with the beauty and delight of the countryside. BOURNVILLE was an important precursor. Garden cities were to be self-supporting towns of 30,000 people, owned by the residents and equipped with a central park containing public buildings; factories, workshops, and warehouses were to be located on the periphery and separated from other towns by a green belt of farmland and forests. The first garden city, Letchworth in Herts., was started in 1903, and was followed by a second at Welwyn in 1920. They became models for the NEW TOWNS built after World War II.

Gardiner, Stephen (*c.*1497–1555), Bishop of Winchester (1531–55). A Suffolk cloth-maker's son whose kinship with Richard Eden, clerk of HENRY VIII's council, encouraged his legal career and the beginning of a lifelong association with CAMBRIDGE. As WOLSEY's secretary (1525), he was drawn into the royal divorce negotiations, which he energetically promoted without sharing his colleagues' religious reformism; his book *De Vera Obedientia*, ably supporting the ROYAL SUPREMACY (1535), would later prove to be an embarrassment. Bishop of Winchester from 1531, he missed the archbishopric, which went to CRANMER, and Henry never fully trusted him or allowed him and his allies to destroy Cranmer. As a rallying figure for conservatism, he spent most of EDWARD VI's reign in prison, but MARY I made him lord chancellor. He reluctantly accepted Mary's Spanish marriage, and initially promoted the campaign of burning HERETICS. His reputation as 'wily Winchester' has exaggerated his conspiratorial skills and ignored his frequently self-destructive temper. He consistently used his attention to detail and brilliant command of sarcastic English in his role of arch-defender of conservative religion.

Garter, Order of the, an order of CHIVALRY founded by EDWARD III in 1348–9 as a select group comprising 26 companions and the sovereign. The first group had contributed to the 1346 CRÉCY campaign, the outcome of which was felt to vindicate Edward's claim to the French throne. The colours of the order – gold on blue – seem to be an allusion to the royal arms of France; certainly the words *Honi soit qui mal y pense* ('Shame on him who thinks evil of it') had originally been Edward's motto for the 1346 campaign (not, as later tales have it, the words with which he retrieved the garter of a lady of somewhat dubious reputation).

By associating the order with his well-endowed refoundation of the royal chapel of St George's (itself later rebuilt by EDWARD IV) in Windsor castle, with 26 impoverished veteran knights representing the companions at daily services, Edward gave his order the financial security that has helped it to survive to the present day, both as an élite club and as a symbol of the continuity of the English monarchy – though not of its claim to France.

Gas Industry The use of coal gas for lighting was pioneered in the late 18th century by William Murdock at Boulton and Watt's Soho factory and was introduced into Manchester cotton mills by the early 19th century. By mid-century gas lighting had become widespread in streets, factories, shops, inns, stations, etc., and private gas companies were common in urban centres. The first municipal PUBLIC UTILITY gas company was opened in MANCHESTER in 1820, more towns and cities following with public provision especially in the later 19th century. The gas industry consumed around a million tons of COAL annually by the late 1840s, and the tar and ammonia by-products were increasingly absorbed by the developing

CHEMICAL INDUSTRY. In the late 19th century gas remained predominantly a fuel for lighting and cooking but its industrial potential continued to grow. During WORLD WAR I its role as an industrial fuel was considerably expanded and the by-products from the extraction of gas from coal – coke, tar and benzole – became substantial additional sources of revenue. Between 1920 and 1939 the number of gas consumers rose by 50 per cent but gas sales only increased by 25 per cent as ELECTRICITY made inroads into the household demand for energy.

Gas reasserted its importance during WORLD WAR II when, unlike coal and OIL, it was never subject to rationing. NATIONALIZATION followed in 1948. By the 1950s the industry was perceived as in decline compared to electricity and nuclear power (*see* ATOMIC ENERGY). Then natural gas was discovered in the North Sea, and the development of more efficient gas appliances allied to aggressive advertising gave the industry new impetus. The noxious leftover fuel from the 19th century came to be seen as a modern, clean, controllable product able to deliver heat more rapidly than competitor fuels.

The Gas Act (1986) paved the way for the privatization of the gas industry but it had a limited effect on competition as British Gas maintained a monopoly on domestic supply, but the 1995 Act allowed competition in all areas and by May 1998 over 2 million customers had changed suppliers. The new regulator of the Industry (appointed in 1998) had his brief extended to include the ELECTRICITY supply in Jan. 1999 in recognition of the convergence between the two power supply industries.

Gascony, the French region lying between the Pyrenees and the River Garonne. In the 11th century, Gascony was acquired by the dukes of AQUITAINE, and came into PLANTAGENET hands in 1152 when ELEANOR OF AQUITAINE married HENRY II. As a result of the military defeats suffered in the early 13th century, the later duchy of Aquitaine actually consisted of little but Gascony.

Although the English spent remarkably little money and time on retaining Gascony – EDWARD I was the last reigning king to visit it – Gascon appreciation of the value of the English market for the Bordeaux WINE TRADE, and their feeling that the Paris government represented a greater threat to their traditional independence than did the English, meant that the duchy remained attached to the English crown. In the later stages of the HUNDRED YEARS WAR, there were few major campaigns in Gascony; it was the débâcle at FORMIGNY in Normandy in 1450 that enabled the triumphant French king Charles VII to conquer it with some ease in 1450–1. A belated expeditionary force under TALBOT was temporarily able to exploit Gascon resentment of French rule, but the 1453 battle of CASTILLON marked the end of English Gascony.

Gascoyne-Cecil, Robert, *see* CECIL, ROBERT GASCOYNE

Gasworkers' Strike, 1889, an illustration of the tendency for TRADE UNION membership to expand in sudden dramatic bursts. The formation of a general union of gasworkers in 1888 and its unexpectedly successful demand for an eight-hour day without a strike or a reduction in wages reflects the importance of the trade cycle and tightening labour market on the genesis of the NEW UNIONISM.

GATT, *see* GENERAL AGREEMENT ON TARIFFS AND TRADE

Gauge Act 1846 This imposed a standard (and still current) gauge for RAILWAYS (i.e. width between rails) of 4 feet 8.5 inches (1.44m), and thus introduced a measure of public control over the privately developed railway network in order to promote the through traffic of goods and passengers. BRUNEL's Great Western Railway, which had opted for an exceptionally broad gauge, was forced to make rapid adjustments.

Gaunt, John of, *see* JOHN OF GAUNT

Gavelkind, the custom of dividing a tenant's estate equally between his surviving sons. In the 12th and 13th centuries, the term was used to describe Kentish practice; subsequently it was extended to refer to similar customs in Wales and Ireland.

Gaveston, Piers (?–1312) (3rd Earl of Cornwall), royal favourite. Son of a Gascon noble in EDWARD I's service, his close, possibly homosexual, relationship with EDWARD II ended in personal and political disaster. The extent of Edward's infatuation became clear when, in 1307, he asked his father to make Gaveston Count of Ponthieu, which resulted in the first of Gaveston's short-lived banishments.

Immediately after Edward II's accession in July, Gaveston was recalled, created Earl of Cornwall and given a dominant place at court. This so disconcerted the other earls that, in 1308, they combined to compel Edward to send Gaveston to Ireland. His return to court a year later led, in 1310, to the earls forcing Edward to appoint the ORDAINERS. To many contemporaries, including the king, the most important ORDINANCE issued by these men was the clause expelling Gaveston yet again, but by Christmas 1311, he was back with Edward. The earls took up arms, besieged Gaveston at Scarborough and captured him. Then a group of them, headed by THOMAS OF LANCASTER, used the dubious authority of the Ordinances to sentence him to death for treason. Edward II never forgave those whom he held responsible for his friend's execution, and he took his revenge after his victory at BOROUGHBRIDGE.

Geddes 'Axe', economies in government spending recommended by a committee appointed by Prime Minister LLOYD GEORGE in Aug. 1921 under businessman Sir Eric Geddes (1875–1937). The appointment of the committee reflected the new climate of economy which curtailed the plans for RECONSTRUCTION after WORLD WAR I. By the time it reported in 1922, many of the programmes in HOUSING and EDUCATION had already been cut back by the coalition government, marking the apparent betrayal of earlier promises.

Genealogy, family history, the construction of pedigrees to illuminate ancestry, and study of the historical features surrounding those pedigrees. It is an ancient pursuit, important for the transmission of property and status, and for the distinction and legitimacy it might confer upon an individual. In particular periods, such as the late Elizabethan or early Victorian, it has been of immense social and artistic importance. Genealogy, and its broader outgrowth FAMILY HISTORY, have now become one of the largest pastime pursuits in Britain and the USA; it is of particular, and religious, importance for members of the Mormon church. There are obvious links, especially in the study of PARISH and CIVIL REGISTERS and the CENSUS, with the study of HISTORICAL DEMOGRAPHY. *See also* HERALDRY.

General Agreement on Tariffs and Trade (GATT) The BRETTON WOODS Conference in 1944 proposed three institutions: one to deal with international liquidity and the exchange rate regime – the International Monetary Fund; the second to deal with reconstruction and development – the World Bank; the third to supervise world trade – the World Trade Organization. The US Congress refused to ratify the third proposal as it would have implied some loss of sovereignty in trade matters. In 1948, therefore, a much weaker organization, the General Agreement on Tariffs and Trade, was set up. AGRICULTURE was kept out of the GATT framework at American insistence, and services only became part of its remit in the 1980s.

GATT was the main forum used to negotiate reductions in barriers to trade, such as quotas and tariffs, on a multilateral basis – the Kennedy round, the Tokyo round, and so on. In the recessionary 1970s, however, new sorts of non-tariff barriers to trade began to emerge, e.g. regulations on technical or safety standards, import licensing, subsidies, and discriminatory public procurement procedures. Thus GATT was forced to widen its horizons and try to formulate general rules to deal with these new problems to achieve fair trade.

The eighth (Uruguay) GATT round (1968–94) led to the formation of the World Trade Organization (WTO) and a new set of agreements to cover not only tariffs but also trade in subsidies, services and intellectual property. A WTO Ministerial Conference convened in Seattle (US) at the end of 1999 had to be abandoned amidst protests that the WTO was an interest group of the G8 (the world's industrialized nations) whose actions over such issues as third world debt, environmental and trade policies were deemed detrimental to the rights and interests of the developing world.

General Chamber of Manufacturers, a lobbying group established in 1785, with MANCHESTER and BIRMINGHAM men prominent, to co-ordinate the representation of manufacturing interests while a commercial treaty with Ireland was being considered in Parliament. The Staffs. pottery manufacturer Josiah Wedgwood (1730–95) was first chairman of its executive committee. Two years later, the group split when discussions of a proposed commercial treaty with the French exposed conflicts of interest. *See also* CHAMBERS OF COMMERCE.

Historians have seen the formation of the chamber as an important stage in the development of a distinct manufacturing (as opposed to general commercial) self-consciousness. Although not novel, it was a striking organizational initiative, and its members were influential in such campaigns for social reform as that against slavery (*see* ANTI-SLAVERY).

General Enclosure Acts 1801, 1836, 1845 An aspect of the ENCLOSURE movement, these enactments aimed to simplify and expedite the administration of enclosures. The Act of 1801 provided a model for the drafting of appropriate legislation; that of 1836 enabled farmers to enclose land without direct reference to Parliament; and the Act of 1845 created a cadre of specialist peripatetic commissioners to supervise a speedier procedure. The parliamentary commissioners responsible for the surveying and allocation of the enclosed fields and strips – accused by social historians J. L. and L. B. Hammond of partiality and malpractice – have been rehabilitated by more recent research.

General Strike, May 1926, nine-day stoppage called by the TRADES UNION CONGRESS in support of the COAL miners. It began following a TUC pledge in 1925 to back the miners in their dispute with the coal owners, if necessary by calling a General Strike. Following the lockout of the miners on 30 April and a breakdown of negotiations with the BALDWIN government over continuation of a subsidy to the mining industry, the TUC called a General Strike on 4 May. The first workers called out were in transport, construction, printing, and IRON AND STEEL, with an almost 100 per cent response.

The government, however, was well prepared. Declaring the strike unconstitutional, it utilized plans for the emergency movement of supplies and mobilized middle-class volunteers to maintain skeleton services. An emergency newspaper, the *British Gazette,* was produced by the government and radio used to maintain a semblance of government control. The police and troops remained loyal throughout, making over 5,000 arrests. Although further workers were called out on strike after a week, the TUC increasingly felt itself to be losing control of the situation and on 12 May abjectly surrendered without obtaining any worthwhile concessions for the miners. The miners, under their leader A. J. Cook, refused to compromise and remained out on strike until forced to return to work in Nov.

A humiliating and historic defeat for the labour movement as a whole, the strike was followed by the passage of the TRADE DISPUTES ACT (1927) to prevent similar sympathetic action in the future. For the TUC it contributed to a rapid fall in membership and an increasing willingness to develop closer ties with the LABOUR PARTY and pursue parliamentary rather than industrial action.

General Surveyors, Court of, *see* CHAMBER, ROYAL, AND FINANCE

General Synod, *see* CONVOCATIONS OF CANTERBURY AND YORK

General Warrants, warrants issued for the arrest of unspecified persons, provided for under the LICENSING ACT 1662 for use against the authors, publishers and distributors of seditious publications, and retained after the lapse of the Act in 1695. They became a focus of controversy in 1763–5 when they were issued against those responsible for publishing No. 45 of WILKES' weekly paper *NORTH BRITON*, which attacked the king's speech to PARLIAMENT. In 1765, Lord Chief Justice Camden ruled them unconstitutional.

Geneva Convention Signed by the principal European powers in 1864, it defined the 'rules of war' for the protection of servicemen and guaranteed the neutrality of ambulances, hospitals, sanitary officers, chaplains and others engaged in aiding the sick and wounded. All persons employed in such work are required to wear a Geneva cross – i.e. a red cross on a white ground – as an indication of their special status. The adoption of the Convention was, in essence, the beginning of the International Red Cross.

Gentlemanly Capitalism, a term which has been used to describe the peculiar nature of the English economy and society since the late 19th century. Several historians have emphasized the theory that the British INDUSTRIAL REVOLUTION was incomplete because INDUSTRY and the industrial bourgeoisie never really came to dominate the older aristocratic society and culture based on wealth derived from empire, financial activities and the land. Provincial industrial cities obviously felt the impact of new industrial wealth and of the politics of industrial ENTREPRENEURS who came to dominate LOCAL GOVERNMENT and civic culture. However, the major focus of personal wealth remained in the hands of the landed and financial élite, largely in the south of England and in the City of LONDON. Cain and Hopkins have argued that the development of British overseas trade and empire has always been dominated by the imperatives and needs of finance rather than industrial capital and macro-economic policy, since the late 19th century is often seen to have favoured rentier and financial rather than industrial interests (see ECONOMY). Most influentially, Martin Wiener, amongst others, has suggested that the dominance of aristocratic culture and privilege since the late 19th century, seen in PUBLIC SCHOOLS, Oxbridge and in an anti-industrial mentality, has endorsed the gentlemanly form of British capitalism and ensured the long-term failure of the industrial spirit.

Gentry, a general term from the 16th to the 19th centuries for the families of gentlemen. In the Middle Ages, knights and other gentlemen were sometimes reckoned minor nobility; in early modern England, a 'gentleman' was defined chiefly by his ability to convince others that he was one. The main criteria were that he should live a leisured lifestyle and be entitled to his own family HERALDRY; that he should own a respectable amount of land was also preferred. The gentry ranged greatly in income, from wealthy knights and esquires to minor or parish gentry. An aristocrat or nobleman – i.e. a member of the PEERAGE – was a gentleman with a title giving him the right to sit in the House of LORDS.

Once, no undergraduate was safe from discussing whether the gentry of the 16th and 17th centuries had risen or fallen at the expense of the ARISTOCRACY, despite the somewhat artificial distinction between these two categories. This 'gentry controversy', begun by R. H. Tawney and stimulated by H. R. Trevor-Roper and Lawrence Stone, was worthwhile for encouraging detailed research, which was unsurprising in its inconclusive outcome.

It is certain that there were more gentlemen (thanks to expanding national prosperity) and fewer peers (thanks to deaths and few creations) in 1600 than in 1500; this gave the gentry temporarily more say in local government and defence. Both groups benefited from the REFORMATION share-out of Church lands (*see* DISSOLUTION), the gentry proportionally more. Recent research has, however, redressed previous neglect of the peerage both in late Tudor politics and in the outbreak of the British CIVIL WARS. After the RESTORATION, gentry power in the counties was checked by aristocratic LORDS LIEUTENANT, and in Parliament by the electoral influence of the peerage. The TORY party presented itself as the party of the rural gentry *par excellence*, but failed to dislodge the WHIG OLIGARCHY. The years 1760 to 1815 were something of a golden age for the gentry: GEORGE III rehabilitated former Tories; PITT THE YOUNGER raised many to the peerage; and agricultural income boomed.

The gentry were classically landowners, but many spent some of the year in towns; historians have coined the term PSEUDO-GENTRY to describe the increasingly numerous group who lived entirely in towns and might derive their income from non-landed sources, but who lived in the leisured and 'polite' style of the gentry. Gregory KING estimated in 1690 the annual income of baronets, knights, esquires and gentlemen respectively to be £880, £650, £400 and £240; it has been suggested that corresponding figures for 1790 would be £2,000, £1,000, £400 and £400.

In what survives of landed society in post-INDUSTRIAL REVOLUTION Britain, the remnant of aristocratic wealth is in a healthier state than that of the gentry.

Geoffrey of Monmouth (?–1155), author of the Latin prose 'History of the Kings of Britain' (which included the *Prophecies of Merlin*) and the Latin verse *Life of Merlin*.

These works were chiefly responsible for taking two figures from CELTIC legend – King

ARTHUR and MERLIN – and launching them on to the wider stage of European culture, where they have remained ever since.

Geoffrey referred to himself as 'of Monmouth', but despite this, many modern scholars have argued, probably mistakenly, that his sympathies, and perhaps his descent, were Breton rather than Welsh. Between *c.*1130 and *c.*1150, he was based at OXFORD, probably as a CANON of the collegiate church of St George; in 1152, he was consecrated bishop of St Asaph. His *History*, which he claimed to have based on 'a very ancient book in the British tongue', was completed by 1139 and primarily dedicated to ROBERT OF GLOUCESTER. Covering the reigns of 99 British kings from the mythical foundation of Britain by Brutus, great-grandson of Aeneas of Troy, until AD 689, it became an instant 'bestseller', its readers sharply divided between those (such as WILLIAM OF NEWBURGH) who dismissed it as a tissue of lies, and those who saw it as genuine history.

If, as most scholars now accept, there was no 'ancient book', then the *History* was an astonishingly original historical fantasy. Geoffrey's purposes in writing fiction masquerading as history have been much debated. Probably he was, at one level, mocking the recent work of English historians such as WILLIAM OF MALMESBURY and HENRY OF HUNTINGDON. But at another and deeper level, he was providing his people – the 12th-century descendants of the Britons – with a splendid and civilized past.

George I (1660–1727), King of Great Britain and Ireland (1714–27), and Elector of Hanover. Son of Ernest Augustus, Duke of Brunswick-Lüneburg and the first Elector of Hanover, he fought in the imperial army in wars against the Dutch, the Turks, in the Nine Years War and in the War of the SPANISH SUCCESSION. He married Sophia Dorothea, daughter of the duke of Celle, but divorced her and kept her closely confined for adultery in 1694. He succeeded as elector in 1698. When the Act of SETTLEMENT 1701 placed him in line for the British throne – after his mother Sophia, granddaughter of JAMES VI AND I – he established contacts with WHIG leaders, who were to remain his chief allies thereafter.

Following Queen ANNE's death in 1714 (some seven weeks after the Electress Sophia), he came speedily to England, and appointed a predominantly Whig ministry, within which STANHOPE and Sunderland (*see* SPENCER, CHARLES) gained ascendancy. The following year, George's claim to the throne was challenged by a JACOBITE rebellion, but the rebels were defeated, and the episode served further to strengthen the Whigs' position – historians have termed the reigns of the first two Georges the era of WHIG OLIGARCHY.

George was on bad terms with his son, the future GEORGE II, whom he refused to make regent during his periodic absences in Hanover. Expelled from court in 1717, the prince set up his own household at LEICESTER HOUSE, which became a focus for opposition to the ministry (a pattern that would be repeated when George II's son FREDERICK came of age). WALPOLE and TOWNSHEND – Whigs but, at this time, opponents of government – were prominent members of this circle. In 1720, the king and his son were reconciled; Walpole and Townshend moved closer to the centre of power, and were to dominate the remainder of the reign.

George was as much concerned with Hanoverian as with British affairs, spending the summer in Hanover whenever possible, but his hold on British politics should not be underestimated. His uncertain command of English was not a crippling constraint; French served for most political business. He attended formal CABINET meetings, and though Walpole and Townshend's cohesion and strong power base in the COMMONS reduced the king's room for manoeuvre, that development can be argued to have been largely independent of any characteristics of the king's. Judged cold and dull by some English observers, George was a cultured man and a shrewd and pragmatic ruler, who followed his father in building up the power of Hanover and then, as king and elector, won himself a pivotal position in the complex diplomacy of the period. He responded with restraint to anti-Hanoverian sentiment in Britain, and supported religious toleration. He died on the way to Hanover, where he was buried.

George II (1683–1760), King of Great Britain and Ireland (1727–60), and Elector of Hanover. The only son of GEORGE I – who had imprisoned his mother for life in 1694 on a charge of adultery – he was admitted to the British line of succession by the Act of SETTLEMENT 1701. He married Caroline of Ansbach in 1705, and fought as a cavalry commander in the War of the SPANISH SUCCESSION. In 1714, he accompanied his father to England, where he was made Prince of Wales.

He was often on bad terms with his father, and in 1717 was banished from court when this quarrel came to a head over the christening of his second son. He established a rival court at LEICESTER HOUSE, among whose principal members were WALPOLE and TOWNSHEND. In 1720, father and son were formally reconciled.

George succeeded to the throne on the unexpected death of his father in June 1727 and, after initially asking Spencer Compton, Earl of Wilmington (?1673–1743) to form a ministry, reappointed Walpole and Townshend. His difficulties with his father were replicated in those he experienced with his own son: in 1737, a serious quarrel prompted FREDERICK to establish a rival court at Leicester House. Queen Caroline died in the same year.

The War of the AUSTRIAN SUCCESSION posed a series of problems for the king, who was especially concerned about the position of Hanover; widespread suspicion that the war was being waged more in Hanoverian than in British interests was a source of trouble for successive ministries. George played an active part in the war, commanding the allied army in the Low Countries, and leading them to victory at DETTINGEN in 1742 – the last occasion on which a reigning British monarch commanded in battle – attracting critical comment by wearing Hanoverian colours for the occasion. War constrained his political freedom: in 1742, he was forced to accept Walpole's resignation; in 1744, to dismiss John Carteret, Earl Granville; and in 1746, to accept PITT THE ELDER as paymaster of the forces. To forestall this last demand, he entreated Granville and William Pulteney, Earl of Bath, to form a ministry, but they failed to attract sufficient support. PELHAM and subsequently his brother Newcastle (*see* PELHAM-HOLLES) remained to the fore for the rest of the reign, although from 1754 Pitt became a contender for power in his own right.

The SEVEN YEARS WAR was less problematic for the king than the Austrian conflict. New imperial acquisitions were acclaimed in Britain, and although complaints of Hanoverian bias were once again heard, Pitt headed them off with flamboyant patriotic gestures.

Opinionated and assertive, George was a force to be reckoned with throughout his reign. Recognizing that his ministers needed parliamentary support, and that this limited his own freedom of action, he still resented being a 'king in toils'. He oversaw a broadening in the political basis of the regime. He flirted with the TORIES before succeeding to the throne, and in 1744 they were admitted to minor positions in Pelham's BROAD-BOTTOM MINISTRY; Pitt also cultivated their support. However, George by and large accepted that leading ministers should come from among OLD CORPS WHIGS – a convention that his grandson and successor GEORGE III thought was a mistake.

George III (1738–1820), King of Great Britain and Ireland (1760–1820), and Elector of Hanover. Grandson of GEORGE II, he was the first of the Hanoverian kings to be born and bred in Britain. Because of this, his leading ministers could not plausibly argue (as his grandfather's sometimes had) that they knew the constitution better than the king. Pious, chaste and conscientious, George was firmly convinced of his own rectitude. When he came to the throne in 1760, he hoped to inaugurate a new era in politics, above all by ending the exclusion of the TORIES from royal favour, court and other office. The gestures he made to this end did win him the loyalty of many former Tories and certain independents, but a section of the OLD CORPS WHIGS took offence. This group, who were to spend most of the king's reign out of office, did much to blacken his reputation. They accused him of unconstitutionally plotting to enhance the power of the crown; he, in turn, believed them to be motivated by self-serving ambition.

The first five decades of the reign were troubled by the growth of extra-parliamentary RADICALISM, the extraordinarily destructive GORDON RIOTS of 1780, and war with the North American colonies – which resulted in AMERICAN INDEPENDENCE – as well as troubled relations with IRELAND and INDIA, and a prolonged and taxing war with France. In the early 1780s, the king more than once contemplated abdication.

As George saw it, successive crises revealed that not merely the more obviously (from his point of view) 'unreliable' public figures of the day, but also those apparently more worthy of trust could not in the end be trusted to stand firm. Thus, in the Gordon riots, metropolitan magistrates proved unwilling to stand up to the rioters and George himself had to order in troops. In the concluding stages of the American War, even NORTH, his trusted minister for 12 years, became convinced, contrary to the king's own judgment, that it was necessary to accede to American demands – and resorted to resignation to force the king's hand, delivering him into the hands of that very group (ROCKINGHAMITE, subsequently FOXITE WHIGS) that the king found it so difficult to respect or trust. In 1801, PITT THE YOUNGER, who in 1783 had rescued him from the hands of that group, resigned because the king would not agree to his wish for a further measure of CATHOLIC EMANCIPATION.

Throughout his reign, George showed himself willing to go behind the backs of his leading ministers if necessary in search of figures he felt he could trust – a propensity which encouraged the perception that he showed an unconstitutional predilection for favourites. His former tutor, Bute (*see* STUART, JOHN), did indeed have the position of a favourite early in his reign; though the king ceased to consult him from 1765, the opposition continued to suspect that he was a power behind the curtain. In the later stages of North's ministry, George made a confidant of secretary at war Charles Jenkinson, who consequently became, and remained, a focus for similar suspicions.

George married Princess Charlotte of Mecklenburg Strelitz (his field of choice was of course restricted to Protestant princesses) in 1761. A devoted husband and father to their 15 children, George attempted to restrict his children's personal lives, and above all their marital choices, in ways many of them found oppressive. Like his grandfather and great grandfather before him, he had a stormy relationship with his eldest son (later GEORGE IV), whose taste for high living and loose company his father blamed in large part on the debauching influence of Fox and his cronies.

He also suffered recurrent outbreaks of 'madness' (now retrospectively diagnosed as a symptom of the kidney disorder porphyria), giving rise to REGENCY CRISES in 1765 and 1788. In 1811 he became permanently incapable, and his son was made regent. Yet, curiously, in the later decades of his reign, when he had entered his final descent into insanity, the king's personal popularity within Britain, which had never been inconsiderable, blossomed – in part as a result of LOYALIST rallying in response to the FRENCH REVOLUTIONARY and NAPOLEONIC WARS.

George IV (1762–1830), King of Great Britain and Ireland, and King of Hanover (1820–30). Eldest son of GEORGE III, he became Prince Regent in 1811 because of his father's incapacity, and succeeded him in 1820. Like most of the Hanoverians, his relationship with his father was oppositional and antagonistic, which had a considerable effect on his morals. Clever, indolent, a dandy when young and in later life obese – he was known in some circles as 'Prince of Whales' – George 'married' Mrs Fitzherbert, a Catholic, in 1785 and the invalid union continued until 1811 although the king legally married CAROLINE of Brunswick in 1795 and they had a daughter, Charlotte (1796–1817). The scandal surrounding his attempt to divorce Caroline and have her excluded from his coronation further damaged a monarchy already held in low esteem and some ridicule. However, for all his excesses, George IV was a man of culture, a patron of the arts and admirer of fine architecture – he is particularly associated with the seaside resort of BRIGHTON where he built an elaborate dome- and minaret-encrusted pavilion for Mrs Fitzherbert.

George V (1865–1936), King of the United Kingdom and Emperor of India (1910–36). Second son of EDWARD VII and Queen Alexandra, he served in the NAVY from 1877–92, marrying Princess Mary of Teck (1867–1953) in 1893. He became heir following the death of his elder brother Clarence in 1901, and acceded to the throne in 1910, holding a memorable coronation durbar in INDIA the following year. Initially showing little zest for kingship, he nevertheless proved a dutiful and conscientious monarch, attempting to assist in the reconciliation of the HOME RULE crisis at a conference at Buckingham Palace in 1914 and providing leadership during WORLD WAR I. In 1917 he changed the royal family's name from Saxe-Coburg to Windsor. He played a role in politics through his choice of BALDWIN as prime minister in 1923, and in persuading MACDONALD to form a NATIONAL GOVERNMENT in 1931. He began the tradition of Christmas broadcasts to the country and Empire in 1932, and his Silver Jubilee in 1935 was genuinely popular. He was succeeded by his eldest son, EDWARD VIII.

George VI (1895–1952), King of the United Kingdom (1936–52) and Emperor of India (1936–47). The second son of GEORGE V and Queen Mary, as Prince Albert he served in the Royal NAVY (1909–17), being present at the battle of JUTLAND, and then for a year in the ROYAL AIR FORCE. Created Duke of York in 1920, he married Lady Elizabeth Bowes-Lyon (1900–) in 1923. Long in the shadow of his more outgoing elder brother David, who became EDWARD VIII, he came to the throne as a result of the ABDICATION CRISIS of 1936. Overcoming both shyness and a stammer, he did much to restore the credibility of the monarchy, especially during WORLD WAR II by maintaining residence in Buckingham Palace during the BLITZ and visiting bombed areas with the queen. He was succeeded by his daughter ELIZABETH II.

Georgia, youngest and southernmost of the 13 colonies that formed the USA. Founded in 1723 by James Oglethorpe, the philanthropist and Tory MP (1696–1785), and named after GEORGE I, it was originally intended to be free of SLAVERY, but the rice PLANTATION ECONOMY quickly demanded the system's introduction.

Geraldines, the name given to the early 16th-century Irish following and sphere of influence of the FITZGERALD Earls of Kildare. It is also used by historians of the FitzGerald family in Ireland from the 12th century onwards.

Gerald of Wales, *see* BARRI, GERALD DE

Germanus (?–*c*.437), Bishop of Auxerre. The record of Germanus' two visits to Britain in the early 5th century is one of the few documentary sources for conditions in Britain after the end of Roman rule. Since the purpose of his journeys was to combat the heresy of PELAGIUS, it can be presumed that Britain was still largely Christian. The story of Germanus' part in a military victory over the PICTS and SAXONS demonstrates a British community still successfully resisting its invaders (*see* ANGLO-SAXON SETTLEMENT). *See also* BRITISH SURVIVAL; AMBROSIUS AURELIANUS; BADON, MOUNT.

Gervase of Canterbury (*c*.1145–*c*.1210), chronicler. A monk of Christ Church, CANTERBURY, his devotion to his abbey led him to its archives and then to the writing of a number of historical works in which the affairs and especially the litigation of Christ Church were central themes. Of inestimable value to architectural historians is his detailed description of the rebuilding of Canterbury cathedral after the fire of 1174.

Gesith, a term used to describe a nobleman (literally 'companion') in early Anglo-Saxon society. By the 10th century, it had been superseded by *THEGN*, which has implications of service.

Ghana, *see* GOLD COAST

Ghent, Treaty of, *see* ANGLO-AMERICAN WAR

GIs, popular name for the American troops who came to Britain after the US had entered WORLD WAR II, to prepare for the Allied invasion of occupied Europe (*see* D-DAY). The word means 'Government Issue', and by May 1944 1.5 million GIs were 'over paid, over sexed and over here', in the phrase of the time.

Gibbon, Edward (1737–94), historian. He conceived the idea for his massive *History of the Decline and Fall of the Roman Empire* while touring Italy in 1763–4. The first volume appeared in 1778 and was well received, although his pessimistic assessment of the effects of Christianity attracted criticism, which he answered in *A Vindication* (1779). Gibbon became an MP in 1774, served as a commissioner of trade and plantations to 1782, and consistently supported NORTH's ministry on the War of AMERICAN INDEPENDENCE. The final volumes of the *Decline and Fall* were completed in Lausanne in 1788. Although based on very extensive reading, it is remarkable chiefly as a literary and semi-philosophical exploration of cultural and political change.

Gibraltar Britain's smallest colony, situated at the southernmost point of the Iberian peninsula and the entrance to the Mediterranean. It has long been, and remains, a source of contention with Spain (see GIBRALTAR BLOCKADE). The rock was taken by the British under Sir George Rooke in 1704, and Britain took full possession in 1707, confirmed by the treaty of UTRECHT, 1713. The object of continuing attack and siege, notably in 1779–81, Gibraltar thereafter remained firmly in British hands. 'As safe as the Rock of Gibraltar,' the saying went. Gibraltar's enduring strategic importance was proved in both WORLD WARS I and II and in the FALKLANDS War. The Gibraltarians' special status was confirmed by being made full British subjects in the 1981 nationality legislation.

Gibraltar Blockade Persistent Spanish claims to the important British naval base of Gibraltar became pressing under General Franco, the Spanish dictator from 1939. A referendum in 1967 produced an overwhelming majority in favour of maintaining British rule, and was accompanied by greater moves towards self-government in 1964 and in 1969. The latter led Franco to impose a blockade of Gibraltar by closing the land frontier with southern Spain in June 1969. The declining strategic importance of Gibraltar, Spain's desire for support for its entry into the European Economic Community (*see* EUROPEAN UNION) and the death of Franco brought about new talks in 1977. Agreement was reached in April 1980 to ease restrictions, and in Jan. 1982 Spain agreed to lift the siege of the colony in return for talks on Gibraltar's future. Although negotiations were interrupted by the FALKLANDS War, the border was reopened on 15 Dec. 1982 and the final restrictions lifted in Feb. 1985.

Gibson, Edmund (1669–1748), cleric and religious writer. Educated at Oxford, ordained and elected a fellow in 1694, he edited several historical works, including the *ANGLO-SAXON CHRONICLE* (1692) and CAMDEN's *Britannia* (1695), and published several pamphlets in the controversy over the rights of CONVOCATION (1701–2). His best-known work, *Codex Iuris Ecclesiae Anglicanae* ('Book of the Law of the Church of England'), appeared in 1712 and was long the standard authority on ecclesiastical law. He became Bishop of Lincoln in 1716 and of London in 1720. As WALPOLE's chief adviser on ecclesiastical matters, he was called 'Walpole's Pope'; they split in 1736 when Gibson opposed the Quaker Relief Bill (designed to protect QUAKERS who refused to pay TITHES for conscientious reasons from legal harassment), and he was passed over when the archbishopric of Canterbury fell vacant the following year. Offered the post in 1747, he declined on grounds of ill health.

Giests A word of uncertain derivation (perhaps from 'joists' in the sense of supports or stages), it is a list of places and hosts on the itinerary for royal PROGRESSES in late medieval and early modern England. The list was published before the start of each annual progress, and was eagerly (or apprehensively) awaited by GENTRY and nobility to find out where the monarch would be, what that indicated in terms of political favour, and what opportunities for lobbying or influence the locations might offer.

Gilbertines, the only monastic order indigenous to England. Gilbert of Sempringham's (?1087–1139) first foundation was originally for nuns only, but by the 1150s, the distinctive Gilbertine mix of nuns and regular canons served by lay sisters and brothers had developed. Men and women lived in separate enclosures but shared a church – with a wall running east–west down the middle to ensure that neither saw the other (at mass, communion was passed via a turntable). Despite scandal and rebellion in the 1160s, the order survived until the DISSOLUTION but never expanded much beyond the borders of Lincs.

Gilbert's Act 1782, permissive legislation empowering groups of PARISHES to unite and establish a common WORKHOUSE, in which children and the aged poor (but not the able-bodied) might be confined. Because these workhouses could not be used to deter the able-bodied poor from claiming POOR RELIEF, it has been described as a humanitarian measure, but at the time, its policy of even limited confinement was controversial.

It was the only successful bill among a number to amend the poor laws promoted by Thomas Gilbert, MP for LICHFIELD and vigorous developer of the agricultural and industrial estates of Earl Gower. Its effects were very limited: by 1830 only 927 parishes had adopted it, forming 67 unions.

Gildas, author of the tract called the *De Excidio Britanniae* (The Ruin of Britain), which is an important, if exceedingly obscure, record of the period of the English invasions of the 5th and 6th centuries. Probably written in the middle of the 6th century, it tells of the peace after the battle of Mount BADON, censures the ineffectuality and quarrelsomeness of several named British kings, and predicts that disaster will follow. Interestingly, it contains no mention of King ARTHUR.

Gilds, *see* GUILDS

Gilts/Gilt-Edged Market Gilts are bonds issued by British governments as one way of covering their borrowing needs. Most of these bonds pay the buyer a fixed interest and are redeemed at a fixed maturity date. The terms gilts or gilt-edged simply refer to the fact that these have the highest degree of security against possible default. Governments have rarely had sufficient sources of revenue to cover all their spending – this has been particularly true of periods when wars have had to be prosecuted. Thus they are faced with the need to borrow considerable sums of money. This has become more acute in the 20th century as the role of government has expanded. The gilt-edged market emerged in the 18th and 19th centuries and has become an integral part of government finance. The BANK OF ENGLAND sells new issues of government bonds on behalf of the government while the London STOCK EXCHANGE provides a secondary market in which existing bonds can be bought and sold. The gilt-edged market is particularly important for institutional investors such as PENSION FUNDS and INSURANCE companies since they require safe and profitable outlets for the vast flow of savings.

Gin Acts 1729, 1736, 1743, 1751 Introduced to Britain from the Netherlands in the 1690s, gin was cheap and proved popular. The belief that gin-drinking encouraged idleness and vice prompted, first, an increase in duty in 1729, and then, in 1736, the introduction of harsh penalties for the infringement of regulatory laws. The 1736 Act was both unpopular and ineffective; in 1743, the new PATRIOT ministry reduced duties and penalties, claiming that moderate measures would be easier to enforce. In 1751, renewed calls for action, in the context of concern about crime, prompted a further rise in duties that effectively curbed consumption.

Giraldus Cambrensis, *see* BARRI, GERALD DE

Girl Guides, *see* SCOUTING MOVEMENT

Gladstone, W(illiam) E(wart) (1809–98), Liberal politician and Prime Minister (1868–74, 1880–5, 1886, 1892–4). The personification of Victorian LIBERALISM, he entered Parliament in 1832 as Conservative MP for Newark. He began his political career as an arch reactionary opposed to FACTORY LEGISLATION, the abolition of SLAVERY and virtually anything that smacked of reform. His drift from the HIGH TORYISM of his youth began in the 1840s and found final confirmation when, in 1859, he quit the CONSERVATIVE PARTY to join Palmerston's (*see* TEMPLE, HENRY) government. The shift in outlook reflected the combined effects of a new conception of religious freedom, the influence of Sir Robert PEEL and the principle of nationality.

The first of these liberalizing influences stemmed from a conviction that Church-state relations were a hindrance to faith and that freedom and equality for all creeds and sects were essential requirements of true belief. The personality and performance of Peel – whom Gladstone served as president of the Board of Trade (1843–4) and colonial secretary (1845) – were no less important. Peel's mastery of government and administration and his devotion to duty and economic liberalism made a deep imprint on the style and substance of Gladstone's politics.

The third influence, that of nationality, derived from Gladstone's interest in the language and culture of Italy, from which emerged a growing sympathy for the cause of Italian unity and liberty. It was an aspect to which he would later return during the BULGARIAN AGITATION of 1876, and would develop more fully in the campaign for Irish HOME RULE. Indeed, it was the nationalist sympathies aroused by Italian unification that enabled him, as a leading Peelite, to leave the political wilderness and accept office under Palmerston. From that point onwards began his years as a constructive statesman.

Gladstone's most notable achievements lay in the field of finance. As chancellor of the Exchequer (1859–66), he set out to complete Peel's FREE TRADE programme, reduce public expenditure and cut taxes with the aim of promoting freedom, prosperity and social peace. This, though, was no narrowly based middle-class or privileged conception of progress. GLADSTONIAN LIBERALISM was founded on the cultivation of a skilled working class, whose vital interests as citizens and producers he supported, and on the strength of NONCONFORMITY. For Gladstone, the moral basis of politics was as important as the material. His personal religiousness and defence of civil equality – particularly the abolition of CHURCH RATES and the opening up of OXFORD and CAMBRIDGE – won over the Nonconformists and helped transform the LIBERAL PARTY into a force that was larger than the sum of its parts. It was the successes of his first great ministry (1868–74) – above all, the reforms of the ARMY, CIVIL SERVICE, LOCAL GOVERNMENT and law courts – that gave substance to his claims of having 'liberated' the people from unjust restraints on freedom and personal advancement.

In foreign affairs, there was a complementary commitment to the notion of the 'law of nations', an overriding imperative working for world peace and mutual understanding. This perspective informed his criticism of Palmerstonian foreign policy and his approach to the settlement of the *ALABAMA* CLAIMS. But in an age of resurgent IMPERIALISM, his pacific outlook made him vulnerable to jingoistic critics and their demands for a more aggressive foreign policy. Despite a reputation for convoluted and confusing policy declarations, in a successful attempt to win the Conservative-held seat of Midlothian Gladstone emerged from the semi-retirement into which he had retreated after DISRAELI's Conservative government came to power in 1874 to spearhead an attack on Disraeli's foreign policy in a series of mass meetings in 1879–80. His oratorical power on the 'stump' around Scotland demonstrated the potential of a national leader making direct appeal to a mass electorate.

His subsequent ministries – 1880–5, 1886, 1892–4 – were not as productive as the first. The Liberal Party, distracted by the IRISH QUESTION, was less responsive to the changing ambitions and interests of the working classes, who gave priority to the improvement of social and economic conditions over constitutional or religious questions. In foreign and colonial affairs, too, contemporaries thought that the application of Gladstonian high principle led to a denial of the benefits to which the nation felt entitled.

Gladstonian Liberalism As propounded by William GLADSTONE in the 1860s and 1870s, it had three defining features: peace, retrenchment and reform. The first was designed to promote trade and industry and reduce taxation; the second, to keep public expenditure to a minimum on the assumption that economic and social progress was best secured by allowing people freedom to spend their money as they pleased; and the third, to reform the institutions and laws that prevented people from acting freely. The centre of Gladstonian liberalism, then, was individualism. It emphasized the reason and moral dignity of the individual and opposed political, economic and social restraints on individual liberty. *See* LIBERAL PARTY.

Glanvill, a pioneering treatise (of uncertain authorship) on COMMON LAW entitled *De legibus et consuetudinibus regni Angliae*, written *c.*1187, and like the *DIALOGUS DE SCACCARIO*, celebrating the administrative achievements of HENRY II. It listed the royal WRITS then in use, and popularized the view that the customs of the king's court constituted the law and custom of the realm, taking precedence over local customary law; a version of it also circulated and had influence in 13th-century Scotland. *See also BRACTON*.

Glasgow The evidence of prehistoric and Roman settlement is to be expected, given Glasgow's position as one of the lowest convenient crossing-points on the River Clyde; however, the present community is first associated with the late 6th-century/early 7th-century gift of land to St Kentigern (or Mungo) by Rhydderch Hael,

King of STRATHCLYDE, for a monastery, now the site of the medieval cathedral, one of the largest and best preserved in Scotland. A continuous episcopal succession is known from the 12th century, and a royal charter granted in the 1170s bears witness to a growing commercial community; a UNIVERSITY was established in 1451.

The city, famed for its architectural beauty during the 17th century, expanded very rapidly from the mid-18th century, taking a major role in transatlantic trade, and during the 19th century it became a major centre for textile manufacture, mining and heavy industry, establishing a pre-eminence in SHIPBUILDING; the wealth thus created was responsible for some of the finest urban architecture of the period (coexisting with some of Britain's worst slums) – the most popular today being the distinctive art nouveau work of Charles Rennie Mackintosh (1868–1928) including the Glasgow School of Art (1897–1907). The collapse of Glasgow's overseas trade and manufacturing base in the 1970s and 1980s was to some extent compensated for by its vigorous cultural revival.

Glastonbury Abbey The origins of religious life at Glastonbury go back at least to the 5th century. In the 7th century, the site was patronized by the kings of WESSEX, and in the 940s it was placed firmly under the BENEDICTINE Rule following the appointment of DUNSTAN as abbot. *DOMESDAY BOOK* shows that, by the 11th century, it had become the wealthiest monastery in England. Its great antiquity meant that it had numerous connections with the CELTIC Church as well as some alleged relics of St PATRICK. The tomb of King ARTHUR was supposedly found there in 1191. The abbey was dissolved in 1539 and its last abbot executed by HENRY VIII, on trumped-up charges of treason and theft from his own abbey; he was hanged from the chapel on Glastonbury Tor. The Tor and the town's Arthurian associations have made modern Glastonbury a centre of occultism and mysticism.

GLC, *see* GREATER LONDON COUNCIL

Glencoe Massacre, near Ballachulish, Lochaber, 13 Feb. 1692. WILLIAM III's strategy for pacifying the Scottish Highlands in the face of opposition from Dundee (*see* GRAHAM, JOHN) and others required clan chieftains to take the OATH of allegiance. Macdonald of Glencoe took it after the deadline, and the Campbells, rivals for influence, used this as an excuse to launch a surprise attack on an unprepared community. They killed 38 Macdonald clan members, and of those who escaped, some subsequently died of their wounds. The attack was condemned in the Scots Parliament and led to the fall of William's secretary of state, John Dalrymple. Implicit in this critical response was the application to Highland warfare of standards of conduct current elsewhere in Europe.

Glendower, Owen, *see* GLYN DWR, OWAIN

Glorious Revolution, 1688–9, the sequence of events which led to JAMES II's replacement on the throne by WILLIAM III and MARY II. Building on the foundations of the TORY REACTION to the EXCLUSION CRISIS of 1679–81, James was able to pursue policies of strengthening royal power and improving the lot of Catholics without serious hindrance until early 1688. In that year a series of massive purges of commissions of the peace and BOROUGHS undertaken by the Board of REGULATORS, which were intended to prepare the way for the election of a biddable parliament, alienated TORY supporters. In April–June the SEVEN BISHOPS resisted the command that a new DECLARATION OF INDULGENCE be read out in churches, and were tried and acquitted. In June, a son (the future 'James III' – *see* James Edward STUART) was born to James and his Catholic second wife, and, following soundings from the Prince of Orange (the future William III) among opposition leaders, the IMMORTAL SEVEN invited him to invade.

William's eagerness to act at this time was affected by wider European considerations: in the new Elector of Brandenburg he had an ally against Louis XIV, while in Sept., large numbers of French troops were sent into Germany. William published a 'Declaration' proclaiming that it was proper to use force against tyrannical monarchs, and his own intention of restoring England's laws and liberties (*see* DECLARATION OF RIGHTS). James then panicked, withdrew the writs for the new election, abolished the Commission for Ecclesiastical Causes, and attempted to put into reverse the remodelling undertaken by the Board of Regulators. Initially delayed by storms, William was lucky enough to avoid interception by the English fleet and landed at Torbay on 5 Nov. with some 20,000 troops. He was supported by Devonshire Tories under Sir Edward Seymour; there were other small risings in Yorks. (led by Danby [*see* OSBORNE, THOMAS]), Cheshire and Notts. James prepared to fight him at Salisbury but, unnerved by defections in the army, retreated to London; he opened talks with William and reissued election writs, but then attempted to flee to France. Halted and returned to London, he opened discussions with the bishops, but, under pressure from William, fled again.

Power had meanwhile passed into the hands of an assembly of peers in the Guildhall under Rochester (*see* HYDE, LAURENCE) and Halifax (*see* SAVILE, GEORGE), and, *de facto*, to City authorities, who had invited William in. The peers, and an Assembly of Commoners summoned by William (consisting of MPs from CHARLES II's parliaments and London aldermen and common councilmen) asked him to take charge of the government. Elections in Jan. 1689 produced a CONVENTION PARLIAMENT, which began to work out the terms of the REVOLUTION SETTLEMENT. William and Mary were offered the crown jointly in Feb., but faced armed opposition in Scotland and Ireland, and from Louis XIV. William declared war on France (KING WILLIAM'S WAR) in May. Scots rebels under John GRAHAM, Earl of Dundee, were defeated in Aug.; and fighting in Ireland, where James had convoked a JACOBITE PARLIAMENT, continued until the battle of the BOYNE in July 1690, after which James returned to France.

Though representatives of a broad spectrum of views helped to shape the course of the Revolution (with varying degrees of enthusiasm and regret), later, it acquired partisan connotations. In the early 18th century, WHIGS enthusiastically endorsed it; some TORIES (such as SACHEVERELL) expressed doubts. Late 18th-century RADICALS promoted the view that it had not been radical enough. Mid-20th-century historians contrasted the conservatism of the 'Glorious Revolution' with the greater radicalism of the mid-17th century. Recently, though stressing that crucial decisions were made by a few key actors, historians have explored evidence for support at all social levels; have emphasized the (political) radicalism of some revolutionary ideologists, notably LOCKE; and have argued that the Revolution and subsequent reshaping of English government – necessitated by European war, but coloured by reforming aspirations – did in truth mark a watershed in British political and cultural development, as well as transforming Britain's international standing.

Gloucester (*Glevum Colonia*). One of the more important towns of Roman Britain, it was briefly a LEGIONARY FORTRESS in *c.*AD 65 and was made a *colonia* (a settlement for retired Roman soldiers) between 96 and 98. Excavation has revealed all the customary features of a Roman town, although it may have been somewhat overshadowed by neighbouring CIRENCESTER. Its Anglo-Saxon history is rather obscure. It was visited on occasion by the later Old English kings and, as a result, became the centre where the Norman kings traditionally spent Christmas. They also contributed generously to the development of the abbey of St Peter's. The town's location on the River Severn gave it some importance as a port. St Peter's became the CATHEDRAL of a bishopric in 1541. CHARLES I failed to capture Gloucester in a siege in Aug./Sept. 1643, thus preventing the ROYALISTS consolidating their position in the Severn Valley.

Gloucester, Humphrey of, *see* HUMPHREY OF GLOUCESTER

Gloucester, Robert of, *see* ROBERT OF GLOUCESTER

Glyn Dwr, Owain (Owen Glendower) (*c.*1355–*c.*1416), leader of the last major Welsh revolt against English rule. He was descended from the princes of POWYS and Deheubarth (*see* DYFED), and after the murder of Owain Lawgoch, legitimist Welsh hopes centred on him. During the 1380s, he served the English crown, but in subsequent years, his own disappointed ambitions meant that he came to share the anger of his fellow-countrymen against the arrogant and oppressive nature of English rule.

In Sept. 1400, rebels proclaimed him Prince of Wales and, in the next few years, he won an increasing measure of support from all sections of Welsh society. From 1403 onwards, his revolt found friends outside

Wales: the Percys (*see* PERCY REBELLION) whose rebellion in England culminated in Glyn Dwr's claims for an enlarged Wales in the Tripartite Indenture of 1405; the French, who sent military aid in 1403 and 1405; and the Avignon papacy, which prepared to liberate the Welsh Church from English control. In the event, the capture of Harlech and Aberystwyth in 1404 and the holding of Welsh parliaments in 1404 and 1405 were to mark the summit of Glyn Dwr's achievements.

Once HENRY IV had survived the financial and political difficulties of his early years, the much greater English resources were bound to tell. In 1408, the Percy rebellion was crushed at BRAMHAM MOOR; English cannon enforced the recapture of both Harlech and Aberystwyth. From then on, the Welsh cause was hopeless. But Glyn Dwr never submitted. His extraordinary ability to inspire loyalty from his close associates meant that he was still at large when he died – at a place and on a date unknown to mere historians. In the words of the Welsh annalist: 'Very many say he died; the prophets insist he did not.' He had joined that select band of heroes – such as King ARTHUR – whose time had been, but was also to be.

Glywysing, Welsh kingdom that first appeared during the 7th century and retained some sort of hegemony over the peoples of south-east Wales until the 10th century. The evidence for early Welsh KINGSHIP is sparse, but it appears as if fragmentation into smaller units (*see* GWENT; MORGANNWG) began *c.*950. Even during Glywysing's heyday, several kings from within the reigning kindred often shared the kingship, even if one was given preeminence.

Godden v. Hales, 1686, case devised to test the legality of the king's DISPENSING POWER (*see under* SUSPENDING), the outcome of which was to uphold it. A previous judgment in 1674 had found that the king might dispense from the laws if no individual's interest was adversely affected. Hales was a Catholic officer, who was challenged under the TEST ACT. JAMES II removed six judges who seemed disinclined to deliver a favourable verdict; 11 of the 12 who finally heard the case found in Hales' favour.

Goderich, Viscount, *see* ROBINSON, FREDERICK

Godiva, Lady (?–*c.*1080), the wife of Earl LEOFRIC OF MERCIA, now famous for her legendary ride, naked, through the streets of COVENTRY in an attempt to persuade her stubborn husband to reduce the taxation on the people of the town. Little is known about the historical Godiva (Godgifu), except that she and her husband were generous patrons of several churches. The story of the ride originated in the 13th century.

Gododdin, British kingdom that lay around the Firth of Forth. It was created by the tribe known as the VOTADINI, who lived to the north of HADRIAN'S WALL in the eastern SCOTTISH LOWLANDS. The expansion of BERNICIA confined Gododdin to an increasingly smaller area, despite the kingdom's possible involvement in the famous, but possibly legendary, raid as far south as Catterick, which must date to *c.*600, and which is described in the poem *GODODDIN*. The kingdom was eventually subjugated in the 7th century by OSWALD of NORTHUMBRIA.

Gododdin, an Old Welsh poem supposedly written in the late 6th century by Aneurin, court poet of RHEGED. The text survives only in a 13th-century manuscript, and its tradition, and therefore also its historical value, are somewhat uncertain. It describes a crushing defeat inflicted on the warriors of the kingdom of GODODDIN by Ethelfrith of NORTHUMBRIA, and shares with the poem *Maldon* the theme of heroic devotion to the chieftain in a lost cause.

Whether this campaign happened when it is said to have happened in the poem is a matter of scholarly controversy. However, like other early poems (*see BEOWULF*), *Gododdin* is invaluable for its depiction of the ethos of a warrior society. *See also* MERLIN.

Godolphin, Sidney (1st Earl of Godolphin) (1645–1712), politician. A courtier of CHARLES II, MP from 1668 and a lord of the Treasury from 1679, he remained in favour during and after the EXCLUSION CRISIS despite having urged concessions to the WHIGS. In 1684, he became secretary of state, then succeeded Rochester (*see* HYDE, LAURENCE) as lord high treasurer.

He was removed from office on the accession of JAMES II, but entrusted to hold secret negotiations with Louis XIV; in 1687 he again became a lord of the Treasury. He was among the last ministers to remain loyal to James, and was sent to negotiate with William of Orange (the future WILLIAM III) in Dec. 1688. He voted for William to be regent rather than king, but agreed to head the Treasury (1690–6) though continuing to correspond with James and JACOBITE agents; when this was exposed, he resigned.

He returned to the Treasury in 1700–1, and under ANNE served as lord treasurer (1702–10), grappling effectively with the demanding task of financing the War of the SPANISH SUCCESSION, and working closely with Marlborough (*see* CHURCHILL, JOHN). He became increasingly dependent on the support of the Whigs, and in 1710 he favoured the IMPEACHMENT of SACHEVERELL, after which the queen asked him to resign.

Charles II said of Godolphin that he was never 'in the way or out of the way'. His reliability as an administrator was the key to his success.

Godwine, Earl of Wessex (1018–53), the most powerful man in England (after the king) during the reigns of CNUT, HAROLD HAREFOOT, HARTHACNUT and EDWARD THE CONFESSOR. The father of HAROLD II, he was an adroit survivor of the dynastic and political crises that shook the Anglo-Saxon state in the 11th century.

An Englishman of relatively obscure origins, in 1018 he was created Earl of WESSEX by Cnut and married into the Danish royal family. In the time of Harold Harefoot, he organized the capture of Edward the Confessor's brother ALFRED and was therefore an accomplice to the blundered gouging out of his eyes, which was probably the cause of his death. However, he so ingratiated himself with Edward that the latter married his daughter EDITH in 1045. A complex quarrel broke out between Godwine and Edward in 1051, which resulted in the earl's exile until the autumn of the following year, when he secured his reinstatement with the backing of an overwhelming military force.

Godwine must have been an able man, who may well have come close to dominating his king in the 1040s. He was notably irreligious, and typified the Anglo-Scandinavian character of the Old English aristocracy of his time.

Gold Coast, former British colony, now Commonwealth nation of Ghana. British official involvement with the west coast of Africa began with the establishment of the ROYAL AFRICAN COMPANY in 1676, and trading settlements on the Gold Coast, Sierra Leone, and the GAMBIA. Gold and slaves (*see* SLAVE TRADE) were the most important commodities in the early Gold Coast, through trade with the highly militarized Asante and Dahomey tribal states. Both Christian missionaries and guns came to west Africa from the 1820s; until 1874 British power was limited to the coastal forts, while inland slaving continued despite abolition of the British trade. Britain bought the Danish forts on the Gold Coast in 1850, and was given the Dutch forts in 1872. The SCRAMBLE for territorial power culminated in the annexation of the Asante territory in 1896 and of the Northern Territories in 1901, to forestall French expansion. Thereafter a cash crop economy grew, with gold mining supplemented by rubber and then especially cocoa. After World War II the tide of nationalism, which had had its origins in the 1910s, was sweeping through the colony, led by Nkrumah. Independence came in 1957, the precursor of rapid DECOLONIZATION in west Africa.

Gold Standard, the currency system operating from 1816 to the outbreak of war in 1914 under which the value of the pound sterling was fixed against other currencies on the basis of its value in gold, with banks being obliged to exchange notes for gold coin on demand. Winston CHURCHILL as chancellor of the Exchequer in the CONSERVATIVE government under BALDWIN returned the pound to the gold standard for all external transactions in his April 1925 budget, hailing the move as proof that Britain's post-war economic recovery allowed a return to 'normal' conditions. The pound at once rose to its pre-war level of $4.86, an overvaluation which contributed heavily to the depth of the slump during the rest of the decade. The political and financial strains involved in continued adherence to the gold standard brought down the MACDONALD LABOUR government in Aug. 1931. Bowing to continuing speculation against the pound, the new NATIONAL GOVERNMENT finally came off the gold standard in Sept. and allowed the pound to devalue to about $3.40.

Goldsmith, Oliver (1730–74), writer. Son of an Anglo-Irish curate, he was rejected for ordination, and instead became a physician. He wrote many biographies, translations and other literary hackwork, edited *The Bee* and *The Lady's Magazine*, and joined Dr JOHNSON's literary club. Although he had to struggle to remain solvent, Goldsmith was a relatively successful example of the professional littérateur in a period that saw the emergence of that species. His best-known works include: *The Citizen of the World* (1762), a series of satirical letters supposedly by a Chinese visitor to London; *The Vicar of Wakefield* (1766); the poem *The Deserted Village* (1770); and the play *She Stoops to Conquer* (1774).

Goltho, Lincs, a site crucial to discussions of the origins of the CASTLE in England. Excavations here have shown that, in the late 11th century, a motte-and-bailey was built within a fortified residence constructed in *c.*850. This appears to confirm what had been suggested from other evidence – namely, that an Anglo-Saxon *THEGN*'s residence was a fortified dwelling, and that the architectural changes after 1066 were ones of style rather than function.

Good Parliament, 1376. As it met in an atmosphere of general public hostility to the allegedly corrupt clique of courtiers dominating the old and sick EDWARD III, this Parliament – for the period, a remarkably well-documented one – witnessed crucial developments in the powers of the COMMONS. Apparently managed by the first SPEAKER of the Commons, Sir Peter de la Mare (*fl.*1370), not only did the members refuse the request for a tax grant – itself enough to win the Parliament its epithet – but for the first time in the history of representative institutions, the procedure of IMPEACHMENT was used to secure the dismissal of ministers.

Gordon, Charles (1833–85), soldier. Having served with distinction in the CRIMEAN WAR, he had considerable success in China, as explorer and then as commander of the force that ultimately suppressed in 1864 the mystical and agrarian unrest of the Taiping Rebellion, which was destabilizing both the Chinese rulers and European influence. Subsequently known as 'Chinese Gordon', he entered the service of the Khedive in EGYPT, administering the SUDAN (1874–80) and helping stamp out the SLAVE TRADE there. Sent back to Sudan in 1884 to rescue garrisons isolated by the MAHDI's revolt, he was cut off in Khartoum, where he died after a 10-month siege. His death unleashed public indignation in Britain against GLADSTONE that a relief force had not been dispatched, and he became a hero of EMPIRE. His heroic status was reduced by his inclusion in Lytton Strachey's scathing series of portraits of *Eminent Victorians*.

Gordon, George (4th Earl of Huntly) (1513–62), politician. With a formidable power base in northern Scotland, he was regent in 1536 and high chancellor in 1546–9 and 1561–2. He supported Cardinal Beaton against the pro-English James Hamilton, Earl of Arran. After defeating the English at Halidon Hill in 1542, he suffered defeat at PINKIE in 1547; he christened this defeat 'the rough wooing', a *bon mot* later applied to the whole series of English campaigns of 1544–5. Although Catholic, he was loth to choose between the factions under MARY QUEEN OF SCOTS, and rebelled against her when she deprived him of the earldom of Moray in 1562. James Stewart, the new Earl of Moray, defeated him in battle, and he died – probably of a heart attack (he was extremely overweight) – the same day.

Gordon, George (4th Earl of Aberdeen) (1784–1860), Conservative politician and Prime Minister (1852–5). As special ambassador, he negotiated the treaty of Toplitz that created the great power alliance against Napoleon, and served as foreign secretary under Wellington (*see* WELLESLEY, ARTHUR) (1828–30) and PEEL (1841–6). His ministry saw the conclusion of the OPIUM WARS, the creation of the *entente cordiale* with France and a significant improvement in Anglo-American relations. His reputation never recovered from his mismanagement of the CRIMEAN WAR.

Gordon Riots, 1780, prolonged and destructive ANTI-CATHOLIC riots that broke out on 2 June, following Parliament's unsympathetic response to a petition for the repeal of a 'Relief Act' of 1778. The latter had in turn repealed certain harsh anti-Catholic laws of the late 17th century. Riots in Glasgow and Edinburgh had apparently dissuaded Parliament from extending the Act to Scotland; the London-based PROTESTANT ASSOCIATION collected signatures to a request for repeal, and demonstrators, led by the association's president, Lord George Gordon (1751–93), marched on Parliament to present it. Catholic chapels were attacked the same day; clashes between crowds and authorities then produced a spiral of violence.

London was in turmoil for ten days. The houses of Catholics and supposed sympathizers were attacked, as well as prisons and other public buildings, and many were destroyed; 12,000 troops, summoned by the king, fired on unruly crowds. By these and other means, some 700 died. About 450 were arrested and 160 indicted, leading to 25 executions. Gordon was tried for high TREASON, but was acquitted; the lord mayor of London was fined £1,000 for criminal negligence. Anti-Catholics made the traditional equation between Catholicism, superstition and tyranny; supporters of relief argued that anti-popery was itself superstitious and tyrannical.

Gosforth Cross, Cumbria, one of the greatest remaining examples of VIKING art in Britain. The sculpture on it contains both Christian and pagan Scandinavian motifs, a vivid commentary on the pluralistic culture of 10th-century northern England (*see* SCANDINAVIAN SETTLEMENT).

Gothic, general name given to the architectural styles of the 12th to 15th centuries which employed pointed arches, derived supposedly from the Goths of Germanic Europe. The name is also applied to its revival in the 19th century, often known as 'Victorian Gothic'. PUGIN and RUSKIN were the great publicists for the 19th-century revival, which was seen as particularly and appropriately Christian. The so-called 'battle of the styles' from the 1830s to the 1850s, between the Goths and the Classicists, was essentially won by the Gothic camp, although the classical vein remained a rich one in 19th-century architecture. *See also* PARLIAMENT; WHITEHALL.

Gothick, a self-conscious, often prettified and romanticized, 18th-century revival of medieval styles. Its origins are particularly associated with Horace Walpole and his house at Strawberry Hill, Twickenham, and a significant number of country houses were ornamented in Gothick styles or had mock medieval ruins built in their landscape gardens. The 19th-century GOTHIC revival had greater scholarly rigour, expressed in the architect Augustus Pugin's (1812–52) work and the writings of John Ruskin (1819–1900), whose work *The Stones of Venice* (1851–3) contains the famous essay 'The Nature of Gothic'.

Gough, Richard (1635–1723), ANTIQUARIAN and local historian. Gough's memorial is his history of his native Shropshire PARISH of Myddle, north of SHREWSBURY, composed *c.*1700. It is a remarkable LOCAL HISTORY which is organized on the basis of family histories and engaging anecdotes concerning the occupiers of the pews in the parish church, and hence the properties to which those pews were allocated. Gough's history has been edited and published a number of times since 1834.

Government of India Act 1935, *see* INDIAN INDEPENDENCE; SIMON COMMISSION

Grafton, Richard, *see* STOW, JOHN

Graham, James (5th Earl and 1st Marquess of Montrose) (1612–50), soldier. He initially fought for the COVENANTERS, but was alienated by his suspicion of the Argyll CAMPBELLS. In 1641, he was imprisoned for communicating with CHARLES I, and in 1643, he joined the king at Oxford. From autumn 1644, he led a ROYALIST campaign in the Highlands, using Highland and Irish forces with spectacular success against the Covenanters, but in the Lowlands his troops began to desert and he was defeated by superior forces at PHILIPHAUGH in Sept. 1645. After foreign service, he fought for CHARLES II in northern Scotland in 1650. Betrayed after defeat in battle, he was executed in Edinburgh. His poetic skill helps to make a convincing picture of a romantic hero.

Graham, John (1st Viscount Dundee) ('Bonnie Dundee', Graham of Claverhouse) (*c.* 1649–89), soldier and rebel. A relative of James GRAHAM, Marquess of Montrose, whom he admired, he was educated at Aberdeen, then spent some years in military service abroad under William of Orange (the future WILLIAM III) among others. From 1677 he was employed in Scotland under the Duke of York (the future JAMES II), repressing COVENANTERS, which he did with notorious rigour. In 1688, he took Scottish forces to join James II at Salisbury, and was made a viscount; after James's flight, he was allowed to return to Scotland. He attended the Scots CONVENTION PARLIAMENT, but withdrew, claiming there was a plot to kill him. When he refused an order to return, he was proclaimed a traitor. He assumed the leadership of Highland clans loyal to James and led them to victory at KILLIECRANKIE in July 1689, despite dying in action.

Grain Riots, crowd action designed to stop the movement of grain out of a region, to force the vending of stockpiles, or to reduce prices, usually in years of poor harvests and consequent high prices. There are documented instances from the 16th century, but the late 18th century seems to have been the heyday of the grain riot. Wageworkers dependent on the market for food were the main activists, and women appear to have been centrally involved, partly because these riots often occurred in the market place. Local authorities and central government responded with varying combinations of repression and (no doubt often pragmatically calculated) sympathy: laws forbidding 'forestalling and regrating' (hoarding in anticipation of a rise in price, selling outside the market place) might be reiterated, 'just' prices advocated, and EXPORTS abroad restricted. In the later 18th century, interfering with the market was increasingly frowned upon by the authorities, and charitable support of the purchasing power of the poor via POOR RELIEF advocated. After the early 19th century, grain riots became more unusual and localized. Wage rates, work conditions and unemployment replaced price rises as the major focus of discontent. *See also* RIOTS.

Grammar Schools, schools usually of relatively ancient foundation, notably in the 16th century, which gave boys a basic grounding in the classics. Frequently these schools were established in towns, with many or all places intended for non-fee-paying scholars. In some cases the schools had become PUBLIC SCHOOLS by the 19th century, but in many cases they survived to be gradually absorbed into the state system. These were among the secondary schools which gave middle-class boys, and sometimes girls, an education in the later 19th century, as opposed to ELEMENTARY SCHOOLS. In many areas of England and Wales in the 1920s and 1930s, the local education authorities (established in 1907) instituted grammar schools, sometimes as new foundations, sometimes based upon older, often charitable, institutions. Under the EDUCATION ACT 1944, which established the binary divide for children at ELEVEN PLUS, the name grammar school was usually given to the school for the academic higher-achievers. The number of such schools declined in the post-1960s shift towards COMPREHENSIVE EDUCATION. *See also* EDUCATION.

Grammar Schools Act 1840, a sequel to the MUNICIPAL CORPORATIONS ACT 1835, which had provided for improved local trustees. It freed grammar schools from the narrowness imposed by the LEEDS GRAMMAR SCHOOL CASE and allowed for the introduction of new subjects into a curriculum that had remained unchanged since the 17th century.

Grand Assize, 1179. One of the ASSIZES OF HENRY II's reign, it marked a stage in the development of trial by JURY, since it gave a defendant involved in a dispute over property the right to choose to have the case decided by a jury rather than by TRIAL BY BATTLE.

Grand Jury, *see* JURY

Grand Remonstrance, Nov. 1641. A sweeping indictment of CHARLES I's rule including accusations of popish conspiracy, by which PYM tried to regain opposition momentum as the COMMONS' appetite for confrontation faltered. Passed by a narrow margin after stormy debates, its rejection by Charles in Dec. hastened full-scale conflict.

Grand Tour, a tour of continental Europe, often focused especially upon Italy, which became fashionable from the early 17th century. It was characteristically undertaken by young men of aristocratic or gentry background, in the company of a tutor (humorously dubbed a 'bearleader'), supposedly for educational purposes, but often involving gambling and carousing in the company of other young Britons as well as sitting to fashionable portrait painters. The fashion was associated with interest in Italian art and architecture, though critics worried about the effects of exposure to Catholicism and supposedly lax continental manners. After the SEVEN YEARS WAR numbers of travellers expanded, and diversified socially. The FRENCH REVOLUTIONARY and NAPOLEONIC WARS interrupted travel and brought an end to the classic grand tour.

Grattan's Parliament, name applied to the Irish parliament of 1782–1800: the heyday of Irish LEGISLATIVE INDEPENDENCE. The Parliament abolished itself in Aug. 1800, by voting in the Act of UNION.

Great Army, The, name given to the VIKING army that landed in England towards the end of 865 under the leadership of brothers HALFDAN and Ingwaer (*see* IVAR THE BONELESS). It completed the conquests of the kingdoms of NORTHUMBRIA, EAST ANGLIA and MERCIA – in 867, 870 and 874, respectively – before being subdued by ALFRED THE GREAT in 878. There is little doubt that this was a large force intent on conquest. It was reinforced in 871, but became weakened when sections decided to settle on conquered land in 874 and 877 (*see* SCANDINAVIAN SETTLEMENT).

Great Britain, steamship. Largest ship of her day and the first large screw steamer as well as the first really large IRON steamer, she displaced 3,270 tons. Designed by BRUNEL and built at Bristol, she was launched in 1843. She was used as an Atlantic LINER, but soon ran aground and demonstrated the strength of her construction by being pulled off 11 months later. Eventually converted to sail, she was abandoned in the FALKLAND ISLANDS. The hulk was recovered in 1970 and is now a heritage attraction in Bristol docks, restored to her original appearance.

Great Cause, The, the dispute over the succession to the crown of Scotland, which followed the death of MARGARET, MAID OF NORWAY in 1290. Thirteen more or less serious contenders – known as the 'Competitors' – recognized EDWARD I's overlordship and agreed to abide by his arbitration. In 1292, he settled the issue by awarding the throne to John BALLIOL.

Great Contract, 1610, an abortive attempt by Robert CECIL at a parliamentary deal to bring permanent security to the crisis-ridden royal finances. He sought a lump sum to clear debt as well as a permanent revenue settlement, in return for abolition of the Court of Wards and Liveries (*see* WARDSHIP). PARLIAMENT raised an accumulation of grievances about central government, and JAMES I, primed by Cecil's opponents, was lukewarm. Parliament was prorogued in Feb. 1611 with nothing achieved.

Great Council, medieval assembly distinct from PARLIAMENT called to advise the king, and which included the PEERAGE and anyone else whom the king chose. Great Councils continued to be summoned under the LANCASTRIANS; HENRY VII revived their use, perhaps after observing similar institutions in his Continental exile. After this, they were occasionally called by HENRY VIII, but thereafter were only fleetingly revived by CHARLES I in the 1640 crisis. Not to be confused with the KING'S COUNCIL.

Great Depression, *see* DEPRESSION, GREAT

Great Eastern, steamship. Launched in 1858 and intended by BRUNEL to carry passengers and mail to INDIA around the Cape of Good Hope without needing to refuel, her enormous size (18,914 tons and accommodation for 4,000 passengers, unequalled for nearly half a century) was conditioned by the need to carry enough coal for this. Her size entailed new constructional techniques and the first steering engine. Too advanced and never a success, except when laying a transatlantic cable, she was scrapped in 1888. Her attempt to combine paddle and screw propulsion was also a failure.

Great Exhibition, 1851. The brainchild of Prince ALBERT, it was held in London's Hyde Park in a specially constructed CRYSTAL PALACE between May and Oct. 1851. The 13,000 exhibits were seen by 6.2 million people who came to celebrate Britain's industrial ascendancy and a renewed confidence in the possibilities of peaceful social progress. The income generated by the exhibition was applied to the advancement of cultural, educational and scientific learning, institutionalized in London at the new museums in South Kensington, the Albert Hall, the Royal College of Music and Imperial College of Science and Technology.

Great Famine, *see* POTATO FAMINE

Great Fire of London, 2–6 Sept. 1666. More than two-thirds of the City was destroyed by a fire that raged for five days. St Paul's cathedral, 89 parish churches, the Guildhall, 44 halls of livery companies, the Royal Exchange, the Customs House and 13,200 houses went up in flames, but few people died. The second DUTCH WAR was then being fought, and many attributed the fire to papists and foreigners – a charge which, at the time of the EXCLUSION CRISIS, was inscribed on the Monument, built in 1671–5 near the fire's origin in Pudding Lane. The architect Sir Christopher Wren, the diarist Sir John Evelyn (1620–1706), and others devised grandiose schemes for rebuilding LONDON on a new plan, but the old street pattern was reinstated. However, Parliament passed Acts laying down regulations for uniform building types to make future fires less likely. A coal duty was levied to help pay for public rebuilding and improvements, including street widening and the relocation of markets, under the direction of royal commissioners.

Great Matter, *see* HENRY VIII

Great Plague, 1665. The last major EPIDEMIC of plague in England – blamed by contemporaries on merchandise imported from the Levant via Holland. In London, 70,000 deaths were reported – perhaps 15 per cent of its population. Official regulations for controlling the epidemic followed a model established in 1625, including the isolation of infected houses. The worst-affected provincial centres included Norwich, Southampton, Portsmouth, Newcastle and Sunderland. Its impact on historical consciousness owes much to the vivid descriptions of its effect on London in the diary of Samuel PEPYS. *See also* BLACK DEATH; EPIDEMICS.

Great Seal, still the main and original seal of authentication used by English monarchs. The first example is from the reign of EDWARD THE CONFESSOR. It retains its original circular shape and is double-sided; it was, from early times, put in the care of the CHANCELLOR. As the chancellor's officials in CHANCERY became permanently based at Westminster, a formal procedure evolved for authenticating crown grants, which needed to be originated by a written warrant under the PRIVY SEAL. The Scottish Great Seal, which had a similar evolution to that of England, was in the hands of the Scottish chancellor or a keeper until the death of the last chancellor in 1730; after that, its keeper continued to rank as a senior officer of state until 1885, when custody was vested in the secretary for Scotland (from 1926 the secretary of state).

Great Sessions, Welsh COMMON LAW courts similar to the English quarter sessions, set up in 1543 in the creation of counties ('shiring'), systematizing earlier arrangements. Held in each county twice yearly, they were abolished in 1830.

Great Western, steamship. The first steamer designed as a transatlantic LINER, she was just beaten across by the much smaller *Sirius* as the first vessel to steam all the way in 1838, but was the ship that proved it could be done, with fuel in hand, as a practical economic proposition. She was the largest steamer of her day and, like all her contemporaries, a wooden-built paddler. BRUNEL conceived her transatlantic service as the continuation of his Great Western Railway from London to Bristol.

Greater London Council (GLC), elected authority set up in 1965 to replace the former LONDON COUNTY COUNCIL (LCC) and covering a wider area of Greater London. The GLC led by Ken Livingstone, became a centre of left-wing activism and of opposition to the early THATCHER government. In 1985 the government abolished the GLC, vesting its powers in the constituent boroughs and thus ending 100 years of unified municipal government in London.

Green Ribbon Club, founded by politicians of the sort who would shortly be called WHIGS, at the King's Head Tavern in London's Chancery Lane in 1675. The 150 or so members included both MPs and Londoners, many of them DISSENTERS. They wore green ribbons as tokens of membership, probably choosing green because it had been the LEVELLERS' colour. The club provided a meeting place for

WHIG activists during the POPISH PLOT and the EXCLUSION CRISIS, and played a part in producing and disseminating Whig propaganda, as well as organizing 'pope burnings': the ceremonial burning, in a bonfire, of an effigy of the pope. The club was seen by critics as a focus for conspiracy, and at the time of the RYE HOUSE PLOT, there were demands that the PRIVY COUNCIL investigate its activities. It disintegrated with the 1st Earl of Shaftesbury's (*see* COOPER, ANTHONY ASHLEY) decline and exile, and had ceased to exist by 1688.

Greenwich Hospital, founded in 1695 as a home for retired and disabled seamen in what had been the royal palace of Greenwich in London. Designed by a committee including Sir Christopher Wren, Nicholas Hawksmoor (1661–1736) and Sir John Vanbrugh (1664–1726), its magnificent buildings have more recently been occupied by the Royal Naval College.

Gregorian Calendar, a calendar reform by Pope Gregory XIII dating from 15 Oct. 1582, which replaced the Old Style or Julian calendar introduced by JULIUS CAESAR in 45 BC. England resisted introducing the Gregorian (or New Style) calendar until 1752, out of PROTESTANT prejudice; as a result, for 170 years English dates were at first 10, then 11 days behind the Continent's. When the Gregorian calendar was introduced, there were riots about the lost 11 days. It is important, in historical narratives, to check carefully which system of dates is being used.

Grenada Settled by France from 1650, the Caribbean island was ceded to Britain under the Treaty of PARIS, 1763. Regaining control in 1779, the French returned it to Britain in 1783 under the Treaty of VERSAILLES. Spice cultivation then became a mainstay of the economy. Grenada joined the WINDWARD ISLANDS FEDERATION in 1833, and the Federation of the WEST INDIES in 1958. It gained independence in 1974. The advent of a left-wing government prompted an invasion by the USA in 1984: British complicity in this remains a subject of debate.

Grenadier Guards, *see* ARMY; GUARDS AND GARRISONS

Grenville, George (1712–70), politician and Prime Minister (1763–5). Educated at Eton and Oxford, Grenville was called to the bar in 1735, and elected MP in 1741. He was made a lord of the Admiralty in 1744 and then treasurer of the NAVY under Newcastle (*see* PELHAM-HOLLES). Closely associated with PITT THE ELDER, who was his brother-in-law, he was dismissed in 1755 for criticizing the ministry's foreign policy, but returned to office in Pitt's two administrations. Upon Pitt's resignation in 1761, he remained in the ministry and became first lord of the Admiralty. A conscientious man, with a taste for the technical work of administration, he was made FIRST LORD OF THE TREASURY on Bute's (*see* STUART, JOHN) resignation in 1763, and turned his attention to the rebuilding of resources drained by the SEVEN YEARS WAR, and to the rationalization of imperial administration. He devised the 1765 STAMP ACT, which started the train of events which led to the War of AMERICAN INDEPENDENCE. GEORGE III found him tedious and didactic, and continued to consult Bute; in 1765 he replaced him with Rockingham (*see* WENTWORTH, CHARLES). Reunited with Pitt (now Chatham), he played a part in the opposition to Grafton (*see* FITZROY, AUGUSTUS). He successfully put forward an Election Act in 1770, which reformed the procedure the COMMONS used to determine contested elections.

Grenville, William (1st Baron Grenville) (1759–1834), politician and Prime Minister (1806–7). The younger son of George GRENVILLE, he entered the Commons in 1782 and was foreign secretary for ten years during PITT THE YOUNGER's first ministry. Coming under the influence of FOX, he refused office in Pitt's second ministry but, after Pitt's death, returned to lead the 'MINISTRY OF ALL THE TALENTS', which abolished SLAVERY. Grenville, though, was unable to control the coalition after Fox's death in Sept. 1806 and resigned in 1807 over the Catholic question. He never held office again.

Gresham's Law Named after Sir Thomas Gresham (1519–79), a wealthy London merchant who became England's leading operator in the international money market and CLOTH trade, doing much to reduce royal debt abroad under both EDWARD VI and MARY I. This was the notion that 'bad money drives out good', which might be observed in times of INFLATION or clipping of the coinage (*see* COIN CLIPPING; COINS AND COINAGE). It suggests that in using money as a medium of exchange people will prefer to pass on the clipped, depreciated forms and hold onto the non-depreciated money.

Grey, Charles (2nd Earl Grey) (1764–1845), Whig politician and Prime Minister (1830–4). A conservative WHIG, Grey was nevertheless a long-time campaigner for PARLIAMENTARY REFORM. He was a founder member of the Society of the Friends of the People in April 1792, a group committed to 'more equal representation of the people in parliament', and introduced an unsuccessful FRANCHISE bill in 1797. Grey was also a strong opponent of PITT THE YOUNGER's foreign and domestic policies during the 1790s (as a friend of FOX he was closely involved in the move to impeach Warren Hastings (1732–1818), governor-general of British INDIA 1773–84. First lord of the Admiralty in 1806, Grey succeeded Fox as foreign secretary but resigned in protest at GEORGE III's demand for a pledge not to introduce CATHOLIC EMANCIPATION. In opposition from 1807 (having succeeded to the earldom in that year), Grey was invited to form a ministry in 1830 and the following year made another attempt at parliamentary reform. The bill was defeated: Grey called an election on the issue of reform and when returned introduced a new bill which passed through the COMMONS but was defeated by the LORDS. Grey resigned but, having secured a commitment from WILLIAM IV that he would create a sufficient number of peers sympathetic to reform to secure the passage of the bill through the Lords, returned to office a few days later in May 1832. Although Grey intended that the REFORM ACT would settle the question of parliamentary reform, the 1832 Act proved only the beginning of the nearly century-long process of enfranchising the adult British population (*see also* REFORM ACTS 1867, 1884). Grey himself resigned in 1834 over CABINET disagreements over his Irish policies, and retired from political life.

Grey, Sir Edward (1st Viscount Grey of Falloden) (1862–1933), Liberal politician. Appointed foreign secretary in 1905 he held the post for 11 years, the longest tenure of that office in British history. Grey made the defence of France against German aggression the central feature of British foreign policy through a number of pledges and 'military' conversations, but diminished their deterrent force by not transforming them into public alliances. This, and his support for France during the first (1905–6) and second (1911) Moroccan Crises, led to criticism from his own LIBERAL backbench and fuelled charges of 'secret diplomacy' against him. Seeing no alternative to fulfilling Britain's 'obligations of honour' towards France, he took Britain into WORLD WAR I, uttering his prescient prophecy: 'The lamps are going out all over Europe; we shall not see them lit again in our lifetime.' His reflections on the causes of the war led him to active membership of the LEAGUE OF NATIONS Union after 1918.

Grey, Lady Jane, *see* JANE GREY

Grey, Lord Leonard (1st Viscount Grane) (*c*.1490–1541), courtier. He became marshal of the English forces in Ireland in 1535 and, the following year, lord deputy. Although he achieved much in pacifying the country and defeated a joint Scottish/Irish force at Bellahoe in 1539, his conciliatory attitude to religious conservatism and to his GERALDINE in-laws aroused royal suspicion. On returning to England in 1540, he was arrested, then executed. ST LEGER, his successor as lord deputy, continued his reconciliation policy.

Griffith, Arthur (1871–1922), Irish journalist, political leader and first President of the IRISH FREE STATE. Born in Dublin, he worked in South Africa (1896–8), before returning to Ireland to found a nationalist weekly *The United Irishman*. Advocating Irish separation from Britain, he formed and became president of SINN FÉIN in 1905. He joined the Irish Volunteers in 1913 and, although he took no part in the EASTER RISING, was temporarily imprisoned as a leading supporter of Irish nationalism. Elected vice-president under DE VALERA in the provisional government set up in 1918, he instituted during the president's absence in the US a 'shadow' administration to that of the British government. Imprisoned again (1920–1) during the ANGLO-IRISH WAR, he was released following the truce of Aug. 1921 and led, with COLLINS, the Irish delegation which negotiated the ANGLO-IRISH TREATY in Dec. He defended the treaty before the Dáil and secured its ratification, becoming president on de Valera's resignation in Jan. 1922, and going on to win a majority for the pro-treaty forces in the June general election (*see* CUMANN NA NGAEDHEAL). He died suddenly on 12 Aug. 1922, just as fighting between pro- and anti-Treaty forces was breaking out.

Grimond, Jo(seph) (Baron Grimond of Firth in the County of Orkney) (1913–93), Liberal politician and party leader. Married to ASQUITH's granddaughter, Grimond trained as a barrister before becoming LIBERAL MP for Orkney and Shetland from 1950 to 1983. In 1956, at the nadir of his party's fortunes, he took over the leadership from Clement DAVIES and gave the party fresh vision and drive, making particularly good use of the new medium of television. In 1958 the Liberals achieved their first by-election success since 1928 at Torrington; Orpington followed in 1962, and in the decade leading up to 1966 the number of Liberal MPs doubled from six to 12. Grimond's political beliefs were in individual liberty, decentralization – he supported Home Rule for Scotland and Wales – and participatory democracy made possible by electoral reform. If the precise implementation of these beliefs was not clear – after the Orpington by-election he rallied his party to 'march towards the sound of gunfire' – his aim was to create an effective radical non-socialist party of the left, an electable alternative to the CONSERVATIVE PARTY. This had only been partially achieved by the time he resigned in 1967, with the Liberals still a minority force in Parliament.

Grindal, Edmund (?1519–83), Archbishop of Canterbury (1575–83). His Cambridge career, interrupted by MARIAN EXILE, made him an obvious high-flyer in the Elizabethan Church, and he became bishop of London (1559), archbishop of York (1570), then of Canterbury (1575). Here a distinguished ministry foundered when ELIZABETH I ordered him to suppress the EXERCISES OF PREACHING. His defiance led to his suspension and house arrest in 1577, and he had not recovered favour at his death. He is often seen as a lost hope of official rapprochement with PURITAN activists.

Grithbryce, an Anglo-Saxon legal term for the crime of breach of the peace or breach of special protection that the king might choose to confer on an individual. The offence was normally punished by a fine.

Groat, a silver coin worth 4 pence (4d). Although a few were issued by EDWARD I, it first came into general circulation in 1351 when minted by EDWARD III in imitation of Italian and Flemish issues; it remained in general circulation until the 16th century. Its name – derived from the Flemish *groot* ('big') – reflects the fact that it was a larger coin than the silver PENNY. *See also* COINS AND COINAGE.

Grosmont, *see* HENRY OF LANCASTER

Grosseteste, Robert (*c.*1170–1253), Bishop of Lincoln. Despite his name, he was no 'fathead' but a dominating figure of 13th-century English intellectual and religious life. Very little is known about his first 50 years, only that, as an author of scientific treatises, he composed works – particularly on light and optics – of such quality that one 20th-century scholar chose to title his book *Robert Grosseteste and the Origins of Experimental Science*.

In later years, Grosseteste turned more to philosophy and theology – for which he learned Greek – and after ten years lecturing at OXFORD, he was consecrated bishop of Lincoln in 1235. Within a year, he had quarrelled with his cathedral canons and deposed 11 heads of religious houses. 'A heartless tyrant,' observed Matthew PARIS. However, Grosseteste's intense concern for pastoral care led him to welcome the FRIARS; it also meant that no one – pope, king or ordinary parishioner – was immune from his starkly expressed views (often delivered in person) on how they could do better. By the time he came to write the bishop's epitaph, Paris had found much to praise.

Groundnuts Scheme, notorious development scheme by the ATTLEE government in 1948–9 to grow groundnuts (peanuts) in TANGANYIKA (now Tanzania). The scheme proved an almost total failure, incurring heavy losses, because of poor planning and unsuitable agricultural techniques. Often cited as an example of the limitations of PLANNING in the period after World War II.

Grub Street, a street near Moorfields, London, now under the site of the Barbican Centre, which, in the 17th and 18th centuries, was a squalid area. In the 1620s, the name was first applied to poor hack writers, many of whom lived there.

In the 18th century, Dr JOHNSON wrote that it was 'much inhabited by writers of small histories, dictionaries and temporary poems'; POPE satirized them in his *Dunciad*. Grub Street was renamed Milton Street in 1830, but the term lived on to be revived by George Gissing in his 1891 novel of literary poverty and failure *New Grub Street*.

Gruffudd ap Cynan (*c.* 1055–1137), Prince of Gwynedd. The only Welsh ruler to be the subject of a surviving near-contemporary biography – the anonymous *Historia Gruffudd vab Kenan* – he made his first bid for power in 1075. However, it took three turbulent decades – one of them spent in a Norman prison – before he finally established himself on the throne of GWYNEDD, for much of the time as client of HENRY I. Although he was constantly at war with rival princes, his biographer gives him credit for an economic revival. He was succeeded by his son OWAIN OF GWYNEDD.

Gruffudd ap Llywelyn, King of Gwynedd (1039–63). The first and last king of Wales, his career was one of relentless military campaigning against other Welsh kings and the English. He emerged from DYFED in 1039 when he seized GWYNEDD by killing its king; in 1055, he overcame Dyfed, and dominated south Wales from about the same date. His wars also enabled him to take territory from the English, and he temporarily stopped VIKING attacks on Wales from Ireland. His achievements eventually provoked a two-pronged assault by sea and land led by Earls HAROLD and TOSTIG in 1063. After his defeat, he was killed by his own men, most probably as a result of a Welsh dynastic feud; kings from local dynasties then re-emerged in the various Welsh kingdoms. *See also* KINGSHIP; MORGANNWG; POWYS; BLEDDYN AP CYNFYN.

Gruffudd, Rhys ap, *see* RHYS AP GRUFFUDD

Gruoch, Queen of Scots (1040–57). The historical 'Lady Macbeth': wife of MACBETH, Earl of Moray (and later king of Scots), and a descendant of earlier Scottish kings. Nothing is known of her actions or personality except that she was a woman of legitimate royal stock, and therefore a suitable wife for a universally accepted king. Her reputation as a ruthlessly ambitious woman who pushed her husband into a succession of murders is SHAKESPEARE's invention. The violence of the time is explicable in terms of the long-standing feud to control the Scottish kingdom (*see* KINGSHIP).

Guards and Garrisons 'Our [the King's] Guards and Garrisons' was the official title of the British ARMY from 1661 until the Declaration of Right of 1689. CHARLES II's army consisted originally of regiments of foot guards and horse guards taken from both ROYALIST and PARLIAMENTARY forces in a gesture of reconciliation. The Duke of Albermarle's Horse became the Life Guards, and the Earl of Oxford's Horse the Royal Regiment of Horse Guards ('the Blues'). Charles's own expanded guard regiment became 1st Foot Guards (renamed the Grenadier Guards in 1815), with MONCK's regiment, previously quartered at Coldstream, as 2nd Foot Guards (the Coldstream Guards). The 3rd Foot Guards (the Scots Guards) was added in 1678, together with the Earl of Dumbarton's or Royal Regiment of Foot (the Royal Scots), which claimed even earlier creation as the oldest regiment in the army. The first 'garrison' was the Tangier Horse (1st Dragoons) and the Tangier or Queen's Regiment. When Tangier, which formed part of Queen Catherine of Braganza's dowry to Charles, was abandoned in 1684, both became part of the British army.

Guelph, *see* HANOVERIAN SUCCESSION

Guildford, 2nd Earl of, *see* NORTH, FREDERICK

Guilds (or 'gilds'), voluntary organizations, bound by oath and membership levy, with common purposes. They existed in Anglo-Saxon times, and expanded greatly in number in later centuries, becoming, in G. H. Martin's phrase, 'as unselfconscious and ubiquitous as the committee is today'. At one time, an artificial distinction was made between trade and devotional guilds. However, a single one could evolve in a variety of directions – e.g. as trade regulator (craft and merchant guilds), local government agency, social club, loan club, special interest devotional group – but many of them were associated with their local PARISH church. They were the only area of medieval devotion controlled by the laity. The 1545 CHANTRIES Act gave HENRY VIII the right to dissolve guilds, but most were only dissolved after a second Chantries Act of 1547, whose passage was fiercely contested. Some urban guilds, particularly in the City of LONDON and incorporated towns, survived to regulate trade, control APPRENTICESHIP or for administrative purposes. With the principal exception of London, their influence had largely disappeared by the late 18th century.

Gumley, Council of, Leics., 749. Presided over by ETHELBALD of MERCIA, this released the churches of the kingdom from all dues except the COMMON BURDENS. It is important evidence of the Mercian kings' imposition of extensive military service on their subjects, as well as of their efforts to conciliate the Church.

Gunboat Diplomacy, the use or threat of naval force to obtain concessions. The history of the 19th-century NAVY includes many examples, ranging from the bombardment of Algiers (1816) to that of ZANZIBAR (1893), from the use of the fleet to frighten European powers into concessions (*see* DON PACIFICO INCIDENT), to a gunboat punishing the killers of a missionary on a Pacific island. The intervention of British fleets in the Baltic during the 1710s or of carrier-borne forces in Tanzania or the Persian Gulf in the 1960s are equally examples of this use of seapower.

Gunpowder Plot, 5 Nov. 1605. A few desperate Roman CATHOLIC gentry led by Robert Catesby decided to destroy the persecutors of their community by blowing up JAMES I, the Lords and the Commons at Parliament's formal opening. Ambrose Rookwood, Everard Digby and Francis Tresham were designated to lead a rebellion, and their agent was Guido (or Guy) Fawkes. The plans were betrayed by Tresham and other Catholics reluctant to see friends killed; the government may have allowed the plot to go forward in order to round up the conspirators. Further persecution followed, and the anniversary merged with earlier PROTESTANT Nov. celebrations to become a permanent commemoration (*see* GUY FAWKES NIGHT).

Guthlac, St (*c.*675–714), hermit. The surviving near-contemporary life of Guthlac, written by the otherwise unknown monk Felix, is an important source for early Anglo-Saxon lay and ecclesiastical society, describing as it does his military career and his eventual retirement to become a hermit at CROWLAND in the Fenland. It shows, for example, how Guthlac as a young warrior pillaged the countryside and had little to do with the royal court, and also the way in which a hermit acted as a counsellor to many people, including kings.

Guthrum (?–890), a VIKING chieftain who, in 875, led the spectacular attack that penetrated into WESSEX as far as EXETER and almost defeated ALFRED THE GREAT (*see* GREAT ARMY). After his defeat at EDINGTON, Guthrum accepted terms and converted to Christianity. In 880, he set himself up as king of EAST ANGLIA, made a treaty with Alfred to define a common frontier, and appears to have ruled constructively.

Guy Fawkes Night, annual commemoration on 5 Nov. of the foiling of the GUNPOWDER PLOT in 1605, when fireworks are let off, bonfires lit, and effigies of the conspirator Guy Fawkes burned. The commemoration has often been the occasion for ANTI-CATHOLIC sentiment; in previous generations, effigies of the pope or other public hate-figures were burned, a tradition which survives in a few places. The bonfire festivities have often been the occasion for public lawlessness, both in the late 19th century and in very recent years.

Guyana, *see* BRITISH GUIANA

Gwent A kingdom of Gwent is known to have existed in the 6th century, and there are also references to several kings in the 11th century. It is likely that the region was absorbed into GLYWYSING for much of the early medieval period. However, the practice of giving the title of 'king' to more than one member of kingly families assisted its subsequent re-emergence alongside MORGANNWG (*see* KINGSHIP).

Gwynedd, a kingdom first mentioned by GILDAS and which clearly originated during the 5th century following the Roman withdrawal. Its earliest kings (*see* MAELGWYN) were often referred to as 'kings of the Britons', thereby establishing its pre-eminence among the British/Welsh kingdoms, which endured until the principality's conquest by EDWARD I in 1282.

Gwynedd's expansion within Wales began in the 9th century when RHODRI MAWR overcame BUELLT, CEREDIGION and POWYS and established the pattern whereby members of his kindred often ruled in both DYFED and Gwynedd. Despite their achievements, the 9th- and 10th-century kings frequently had difficulty fighting off VIKING attacks from Ireland. The internal politics of the kingdom were turbulent, and it was as a result of a BLOOD FEUD that GRUFFUDD AP LLYWELYN emerged as king. His domination over Wales ended with his murder in 1063.

Perhaps as a result of Gruffudd's conquests, his kingdom was remorselessly attacked by the Normans. None the less, a revitalized principality of Gwynedd emerged in the early 12th century in the time of GRUFFUDD AP CYNAN. *See also* KINGSHIP.

H

Habeas Corpus ('you have the body'), WRIT in COMMON LAW ordering the addressee to deliver a person in his custody to a court for a specified purpose – most famously, to restore someone to liberty. CHARLES I tried to bypass the writ in 1627, triggering protests that led to the PETITION OF RIGHT; further tussles resulted in the passage of the Habeas Corpus Act 1679, defining its use. Subsequently, Parliament has temporarily suspended the act in times of emergency, as in 1715, 1794 and 1817. *See also* SOMERSET CASE.

Haddington, Treaty of, Lothian, 1548. Agreement between Scotland and France: in return for marriage between the French Dauphin Francis and MARY QUEEN OF SCOTS, the French would provide military support for Scotland. This was the beginning of 11 years of close association between the two countries.

Hadrian (76–138), Roman Emperor (117–38). The decision to build what has come to be known as HADRIAN'S WALL was undoubtedly taken during his visit to Britain in 122. His reign marks an important stage in the evolution both of the Roman Empire and of Roman Britain, since it was from this time that the empire effectively ceased to expand. Coming after AGRICOLA'S campaigns in Scotland, Hadrian's policies demonstrate a more cautious approach to controlling the British province.

Hadrian (?–709/10), Abbot of Canterbury. A native of North Africa, Hadrian joined Archbishop THEODORE OF TARSUS at CANTERBURY. He is reputed to have been a great teacher – his pupils included St ALDHELM – and he and Theodore together made Canterbury into an important intellectual centre.

Hadrian IV, *see* ADRIAN IV

Hadrian's Wall, Cumbria, Northumb., Tyne & Wear. Begun in the time of the Emperor HADRIAN, this was one of the most elaborate building projects ever undertaken by the Romans, and is now a magnificent reminder of their capabilities. It stretches some 74 miles – from Wallsend, Tyne & Wear, to Bowness-on-Solway, Cumbria – with a ditch behind it along its entire length. Forts were built on it at intervals of one Roman mile (slightly less than a modern mile), which were supported by large barracks at such places as CORBRIDGE and Housesteads. The construction of the wall was a complex process, and it is now agreed that there were several changes of plan.

Its purpose was probably to indicate the dividing-line between the Roman Empire and the barbarian world, to act as a kind of frontier control rather than a fortification. It was occasionally overrun by tribes from the north, but was always restored. Briefly abandoned when an attempt was made to place the frontier further north at the ANTONINE WALL, after 160 it remained the northern limit of Roman Britain until the Roman armies finally departed in the early 5th century. *See also* CONSTANTIUS; MAGNUS MAXIMUS; SEPTIMIUS SEVERUS.

Hague, William (1961–), politician. A pupil at a Yorks. comprehensive school when he made a speech to the 1977 Conservative Party conference when he was 16 calling for the party to 'roll back the frontiers of the state' to the accolade of the then leader Margaret THATCHER who hailed him as 'possibly' comparable to Pitt the Younger. Hague was president of the Oxford Union, then a management consultant before entering the Commons as MP for Richmond

(Yorks.) in 1989. Secretary of State for Wales (1995–7), he was elected party leader in 1997 following John MAJOR's resignation after the disastrous general election in which a deeply divided and compromised party was reduced to 165 seats, its smallest number since 1906, with no members in Northern Ireland, Scotland, or Wales. A consummate parliamentary speaker who regularly bests Tony BLAIR at Prime Minister's Question Time, nevertheless Hague's forceful style and right-of-centre policies made little progress in restoring his party's electoral credibility, or giving direction to its divided stance over Europe.

Haig, Douglas (1st Earl Haig) (1861–1928), soldier. Son of a Scottish distiller, and educated at Oxford and Sandhurst, he was commissioned into the 7th Hussars in 1885, serving in the SUDAN under KITCHENER (1898) and the Second BOER WAR (1899–1902). From 1906–9 he was a key figure in the reforms by Richard Haldane, the secretary of state for war. On the outbreak of WORLD WAR I he commanded part of the BRITISH EXPEDITIONARY FORCE under FRENCH, fighting at MONS, the MARNE and First YPRES. In Dec. 1915 he succeeded French as commander-in-chief on the Western Front and was promoted field marshal in Dec. 1916. Strongly supported by William Robertson, Chief of Imperial General Staff (1915–18), and by political leaders as well as GEORGE V, he shared a mutual loathing with LLOYD GEORGE who felt politically unable to dismiss him. Immensely controversial for his planning and conduct of costly battles such as the SOMME, ARRAS and Third Ypres (Passchendaele), he achieved victory in 1918 at AMIENS and in the 'Hundred Days' battles. He devoted his later years to work for ex-servicemen, instituting the 'Haig fund' with its 'Poppy Day' appeal. His unattractive personality and reputation as a profligate with men's lives has coloured debate on his achievements and disguised his considerable ability as a general.

Hainault, Philippa of, *see* PHILIPPA OF HAINAULT

Hale, Matthew (1609–76), lawyer. During the CIVIL WARS, he acted as defence counsel for several ROYALISTS, but he was prepared to serve the Commonwealth; from 1652 he presided over the RUMP PARLIAMENT's major commission on law reform, and in 1654 he became chief justice of COMMON PLEAS. He was prominent in the CONVENTION PARLIAMENT, and chief justice of KING'S BENCH from 1671; his broad sympathies led him to friendships with SELDEN, Richard Baxter (1615–91) and leading LATITUDINARIAN clergy. He is chiefly important for his extensive writings on COMMON LAW, although he also wrote on theological and scientific matters; his legal histories (principally *The History of the Common Law* and *The History of the Pleas of the Crown*) were only published after his death, but his opinions are still cited by lawyers.

Halfdan (?–877), VIKING chieftain. He was among the leaders of the GREAT ARMY of 865, which by the late 870s had destroyed all the English kingdoms except the WESSEX of ALFRED THE GREAT. In 875, Halfdan appears to have abandoned the attempt to conquer Wessex, and the following year is said to have 'shared out the land of the NORTHUMBRIANS' among his followers. He was killed in a sea battle fought at STRANGFORD LOUGH.

Halifax, 1st Marquess of, *see* SAVILE, GEORGE

Hall, Edward (1496/7–1547), historian. Cambridge-educated lawyer and veteran MP with reformist religious sympathies, his major historical work – *The Union of the Two Noble and Illustre Families of Lancaster and York* (1548, enlarged by Richard Grafton, 1550) – was much used by SHAKESPEARE in his history plays, and is still of major value for eyewitness (if ultra-loyal) accounts of central politics under HENRY VIII.

Hamilton, John (1511–71), Archbishop of St Andrews. Illegitimate son of the 1st Hamilton Earl of Arran, his predictably rapid Church career included the abbacy of Paisley from 1525, the bishopric of Dunkeld and – the ultimate prize – the archbishopric of St Andrews in 1547 (effective tenure from 1549). He showed far greater talent and commitment to Catholicism than his half-brother, the 2nd Hamilton Earl of Arran. His efforts at Church reform included the sponsoring of a Scots CATECHISM; during the 1560s, he resisted the REFORMATION and faithfully supported MARY QUEEN OF SCOTS (even though she connived in his imprisonment, 1563–6), baptizing her son, the future JAMES VI. After

Mary's flight, he was hanged for complicity in the murder (1570) of the regent, James Stewart, Earl of Moray; his knowledge of Darnley's (*see* STEWART, HENRY) murder is more doubtful, though he had encouraged Mary's marriage to Bothwell (*see* HEPBURN, JAMES) in 1567.

Hamilton By-Election, 1967 *see* SCOTTISH NATIONAL PARTY

Hampden, John (1594–1643), politician. He was a member of an old Bucks. family with an extensive cousinage combining PURITANISM with an increasing suspicion of CHARLES I's political intentions. Repeatedly elected to Parliament from 1621, he sprang to prominence in 1627 for refusing to pay the FORCED LOAN. In 1635 his refusal to pay SHIP MONEY gave rise to a major test case, only narrowly won by the Crown in 1637. A natural COMMONS hero in 1640, he collaborated closely with John PYM in pressing for strong curbs on Charles's power, and was one of the FIVE MEMBERS who escaped the royal arrest attempt in 1642. On the outbreak of war, he was an active commander, urging vigorous attack against the ROYALIST armies. His death from wounds after a skirmish at Chalgrove Field, Oxon., was a severe blow to the preservation of consensus on the PARLIAMENTARIAN side.

Hampton Court, royal palace situated beside the river Thames upstream from London. It was originally built 1515–25 for Cardinal WOLSEY, in brick with early Renaissance detailing, and was subsequently given by him to HENRY VIII, who considerably extended the buildings. Half of the Tudor palace was rebuilt by Sir Christopher Wren for WILLIAM III and MARY II, in imitation of Louis XIV's Versailles. Hampton Court was the venue for the conference of 1604 (*see below*) which led to the translation of the King James BIBLE. Ceasing to be a royal residence in the mid-18th century, it was the first royal palace to be opened to the public in an early act of VICTORIA's reign.

Hampton Court Conference, 1604, convened by JAMES I, in response to PURITAN petitions, to consider Church reform. The bishops, led by Archbishop BANCROFT and given unexpectedly forceful backing from James, were not conciliatory to the Puritan representatives. The only substantial result was a decision to undertake a new BIBLE translation (the Authorized Version).

Hamsocn, an Anglo-Saxon legal term that first appears in LAW CODES dating from the mid-10th century. It signifies forcible entry or assault inside a house. Punishment at first was forfeiture of lands, but this appears to have evolved into a money payment.

Handloom Weavers, weavers in the COTTON and WOOLLEN INDUSTRIES, who used hand-powered looms. These were to be largely superseded during the INDUSTRIAL REVOLUTION by looms at first powered by WATER and then by STEAM POWER. Such weavers were usually men, though women were more commonly employed as weavers in the 19th than the 18th century, perhaps because of the decline in spinning as a domestic industry. The greatly increased output resulting from the developments in spinning technology led first to a vast increase in the numbers of weavers needed to cope and then to comparable advances in weaving technology. Even after a relatively severe industrial crisis in 1826, there were nearly 250,000 cotton handloom weavers; but by 1850 their numbers had fallen to only 40,000, by which time there were 250,000 power looms compared with only 2,400 in 1813. The handloom weavers, thrown out of work by these changes, have been seen either as the necessary victims of progress or as symbols of the waste of human potential and the heartlessness of industrialization. Displaced handloom weavers were prominent in many early 19th-century protest movements, notably CHARTISM. Revisionism in this, as in other topics of early industrial change, suggests a less stark picture. There seems to have been a gradual shift in weaving, given the slow pace of adoption of new technologies, with handloom weavers moving into specialized weaving and the manufacture of particular fine cloths; their demise was, in fact, a very drawn-out affair, especially in areas of Lowland Scotland.

Hannington, Walter (1896–1966), TRADE UNION official and political activist. Born in London and trained as a toolmaker, this self-taught Marxist became active in the SHOP STEWARDS' MOVEMENT during WORLD WAR I. He joined the Amalgamated Engineering Union (AEU) and was a founder member of the COMMUNIST PARTY OF GREAT BRITAIN in 1920. In 1921, he set up the NATIONAL UNEMPLOYED WORKERS' MOVEMENT (NUWM) and led a series of demonstrations throughout the early 1920s, being imprisoned for his activities in 1922, 1925–6 and 1932. He organized national 'hunger marches' in 1932, 1934 and 1936 to campaign for improved treatment of the unemployed, and led the opposition to the MEANS TEST of 1931 and the UNEMPLOYMENT ASSISTANCE BOARD legislation of 1935. Although he failed in his larger purpose of politicizing the unemployed on behalf of the Communist Party, he did achieve widespread publicity for their plight. After the NUWM suspended activities in 1939, Hannington returned to trade union work as a national organizer for the AEU from 1942 to 1951, only retiring in 1961. He wrote *Unemployed Struggles, 1919–1936* (1936), *Ten Lean Years* (1940) and an unfinished autobiography, *Never on Our Knees* (1967).

Hanover, Treaty of, 3 Sept. 1725, an agreement between Britain, France and Prussia designed to counterbalance the treaty of Vienna between Spain and Austria, which had shattered the QUADRUPLE ALLIANCE. Britain's interests were threatened by the Vienna treaty's commitment to restore the Stuart dynasty, and compel the return of GIBRALTAR and Minorca. The Hanover treaty provided for mutual aid if any of the signatories were attacked. A key object – perhaps overemphasized by ministers in the hope of gaining mercantile approval – was to force Charles VI of Austria to withdraw the Ostend Company from trade with the East Indies, in violation of the BARRIER TREATY.

Hanoverian Succession The Electors of Hanover gained title to the British throne by the Act of SETTLEMENT 1701, as being the Protestants closest to the line of succession. When ANNE died childless in 1714, George Ludwig of Hanover succeeded as GEORGE I, setting aside the stronger hereditary claim of the Catholic STUARTS. All British monarchs were also Electors – after 1815 Kings – of Hanover until the accession of VICTORIA in 1837. The Hanoverians were sometimes referred to as Guelphs, because they descended from the Guelph family which had contested the imperial crown with the Hohenstaufen emperors in the 12th century, and sometimes as the House of Brunswick, because they also held the title of Duke of Brunswick-Wolfenbüttel.

Hanseatic League (also known as the Hansa), a league of north German and Baltic towns, established *c.*1350 to control the activities of German merchants operating from the privileged overseas trading posts known as *Kontore*.

The presence of German businessmen in England is documented from the 11th century onwards; by 1157, Cologne merchants possessed a guild hall in London (*see also* STEELYARD). The expansion of Anglo-Baltic trade in the 13th century brought in merchants from Hamburg, Lübeck and the Baltic ports – collectively known as Easterlings – to join their Rhinelander colleagues. In 1281, the English government recognized the existence of a self-governing community of Germans in London: the Hanse of Almain. Other *Kontore* emerged at Hull, Boston and (King's) Lynn. In 1303, the Hansards were granted extensive trade exemptions throughout the realm; the preservation of this privileged position then became one of the main functions of the League.

Naturally, English merchants tried to undermine the League, especially those who wished to break into the Baltic trade. As disputes led to reprisals, relations with the Hansa tended to be one of the main commercial preoccupations of the English government in the 14th and 15th centuries. In 1468, EDWARD IV attempted to break the power of the Hansa but, after a six-year war at sea, accepted defeat in the treaty of Utrecht (1474). In the 17th century, changing patterns of trade and the rise of Sweden led to the League's demise.

Hansom Cab The patent safety (Hansom) cab was a particularly popular Victorian form of transport which plied the streets for hire. Patented by the inventor and architect of Birmingham town hall, Joseph Hansom (1803–82) it was a two-wheeled horse-drawn vehicle accommodating two passengers with the driver seated behind.

Harald Hardraada ('The Ruthless') (1015–66), King of Norway (1045–66). A great Scandinavian warrior who set himself up as king of Norway in 1047 after a life of exile and freelance violence. Claiming the kingdom of the English on the basis of a promise supposedly made by King HARTHACNUT to his predecessor King Magnus (*see* SUCCESSION), he invaded in 1066. He was defeated by HAROLD II and killed at the battle of STAMFORD-BRIDGE.

Hardie, Keir (1856–1915), Labour leader. An illegitimate child who was compelled to work from the age of eight and was employed in mining from the age of 10, Hardie was victimized for his attempts to organize the Scottish coalfields. He studied at night school, gave up mining, became a journalist, contested the Mid-Lanark parliamentary seat (1888), and was returned for West Ham South (1892–5) and for Merthyr (1900–15). Founder-editor of the influential *Labour Leader* (1889) and creator of the INDEPENDENT LABOUR PARTY (1893), he was instrumental in the formation of the LABOUR REPRESENTATION COMMITTEE in 1900 and became chairman and leader of the Parliamentary LABOUR PARTY in 1906. TRADE UNIONIST, EVANGELICAL, pacifist, internationalist, vigorous supporter of the cause of women's suffrage, and Christian and TEMPERANCE reformer, though he never himself held public office, he identified the Labour Party with a pragmatic form of socialism that, in due course, made it the principal alternative to the CONSERVATIVE PARTY.

Hardwicke's Marriage Act 1753, legislation designed by the WHIG lord chancellor, Philip Yorke, 1st Earl of Hardwicke (1690–1764), to curb the practice of clandestine MARRIAGES, most notoriously those conducted in the Fleet prison, and so protect particularly the inheritance of landed estates. The Act specified that the only valid marriages, with very few exceptions operating, in England (Scotland continued to operate the older system in which a promise made a valid marriage) were conducted in the Church of England by banns or licence, before witnesses, while those under the age of 21 had to obtain parental consent.

Harley, Robert (1st Earl of Oxford and Mortimer) (1661–1724), politician. Son of a PRESBYTERIAN gentleman, he was educated at DISSENTING schools. In 1688, he helped hold WORCESTER for William of Orange (shortly to be WILLIAM III) and the following year, elected MP, he emerged as leader of the 'COUNTRY' Whigs. He helped secure the TRIENNIAL ACT 1694, and worked with country Tories on the Committees of PUBLIC ACCOUNTS.

After his election as SPEAKER in 1701, he associated with GODOLPHIN and John CHURCHILL (the future Duke of Marlborough). When HIGH TORIES were ejected in favour of Tory moderates in 1704, Harley was made secretary of state. He disliked Godolphin's promotion of JUNTO Whigs. When one of Harley's clerks was revealed to be a French spy and he resigned, Bolingbroke (*see* ST JOHN, HENRY) and other moderate Tories followed him into opposition. In 1710, he returned as chancellor of the Exchequer and effective head of the ministry, and established the SOUTH SEA COMPANY to complement the BANK OF ENGLAND as a holder of the NATIONAL DEBT (*see* FINANCIAL REVOLUTION). Surviving an assassination attempt, he became lord treasurer in 1711.

His attempts to secure peace with France ran into trouble in the LORDS; they were quelled by Queen ANNE, who dismissed Marlborough and created new peers. Outmanoeuvred by Bolingbroke, Harley was dismissed shortly before the queen's death. He had corresponded with JAMES II in exile, and was suspected of supporting a JACOBITE restoration. Impeached in 1715 (*see* IMPEACHMENT) for his part in obtaining the peace of Utrecht, he was imprisoned for two years but finally acquitted. He and his son Edward, the 2nd Earl, amassed a large collection of books and manuscripts, now in the British Library.

Harold Godwinson, *see* HAROLD II

Harold I Harefoot, King of the English (1037–40). The son of King CNUT and Ælfgifu of Northampton, he was initially regent for his half-brother HARTHACNUT. Then, in 1037, he seized the throne with the aid of his mother and a party of nobles. Little is known about his reign, although he apparently had a colourless or weak character.

Harold II (Harold Godwinson) (?1020–66), King of the English (1066). The last Anglo-Saxon king of the English was the second son of GODWINE, Earl of Wessex. In 1044, he was given the earldom of EAST ANGLIA, and when, nine years later, he succeeded to his father's earldom, he was undoubtedly the most powerful man in England after King EDWARD THE CONFESSOR.

His route to the throne is unclear, since nothing is known of his personal motives. He appears to have been involved in the schemes to bring EDWARD THE EXILE back to England, and in 1064 or 1065, he went (or was sent by King Edward) to NORMANDY, where he was made to swear an oath in support of the claim to England of Duke William, the future WILLIAM I THE CONQUEROR (*see* SUCCESSION). The dying King Edward then chose Harold as his heir, and he was crowned on 6 Jan. 1066, the day after the Confessor's death.

Government continued to function effectively during Harold's brief reign, but – inevitably – his chief preoccupations were to unite the nobility and to counter invasion. A judicious marriage gained him an alliance with EDWIN, Earl of MERCIA, and the latter's brother MORCAR, Earl of NORTHUMBRIA. On 25 Sept., Harold defeated the army of HARALD HARDRAADA, king of Norway, and his own brother TOSTIG at STAMFORDBRIDGE, but on 14 Oct. he was himself defeated by Duke William of Normandy at the battle of HASTINGS.

Harold's generalship is open to criticism. He rushed south in an attempt to take William by surprise, leaving some of his army behind, and was himself taken unawares and forced to fight a long defensive battle with tired troops. However, his personal conduct on the battlefield was courageous. The manner of his death towards the end of the day – although not a matter of any great historical importance – remains controversial. Was he killed by an arrow through the eye? Interpretations of the crucial scene in the BAYEUX TAPESTRY will always differ.

Harrying of the North, winter 1069/70, WILLIAM I THE CONQUEROR's systematic devastation of the northern counties in reaction to three NORTHUMBRIAN revolts within two years. The bulk of the population either died or became refugees. *DOMESDAY BOOK* shows that, 16 years later, in 1086, northern land values were still only a fraction of what they had been in 1066.

Harthacnut (?1019–42), King of the Danes (1028–42) and of the English (1040–2). The only legitimate son of King CNUT, he was prevented from acquiring England after his father's death by the military threat to Denmark from Magnus of Norway. When Harthacnut became king of Denmark in 1035, the throne of England was taken by HAROLD I HAREFOOT, whose death in 1040 made Harthacnut's projected invasion unnecessary. Harthacnut's reign was notable only for a number of brutal acts and for the invitation to return to England made to EDWARD THE CONFESSOR, which eventually restored the kingdom to a descendant of the WESSEX dynasty.

Harvey, William (1578–1657), physician. After gaining his Cambridge BA in 1597, he studied medicine at Europe's foremost medical faculty at Padua, where he became interested in the problem of blood circulation. He acquired a Cambridge MD in 1602, then practised in London. Seven years later, he became physician to St Bartholomew's and, in 1615, began anatomical lectures, during which, and for the first time in medical history, he outlined the true circulation of the blood, illustrated by dissections. He quickly gained a European-wide reputation, which earned him honour under the Commonwealth despite his CIVIL WAR position in ROYALIST Oxford. He also made important investigations in embryology, and was physician extraordinary to JAMES I and physician-in-ordinary to CHARLES I.

Hastings, Battle of, 14 Oct. 1066, a victory for Duke William of Normandy (*see* WILLIAM I THE CONQUEROR) over HAROLD II. Harold's army fought on foot, defending a strong position – which William subsequently insisted should be the site of the abbey he called BATTLE in Sussex – against the attacks of Norman cavalry and infantry. After a long struggle, lasting (intermittently) for most of the day, Harold was killed and the Normans victorious.

From this one battle, historians used to infer that the English always fought on foot and that Anglo-Saxon England was an archaic society, doomed when challenged by the more advanced Normans – both dubious propositions. *See also* BAYEUX TAPESTRY.

Hawkesbury, 2nd Baron, *see* JENKINSON, ROBERT

Hawkins, Sir John (1532–95), trader and naval commander. Son of a Plymouth merchant, he began the English involvement with the African SLAVE TRADE on a voyage in 1562–3 to West Africa and then to the Spanish Caribbean settlements, where he sold the people he had acquired by a combination of capture and purchase. Foreigners were forbidden to trade with Spanish colonies, and the Spanish authorities caught up with Hawkins on his third voyage at San Juan d'Ulloa, where he was attacked. From 1577 he was a naval administrator, and seems to have been responsible for introducing a new type of warship and for other reforms. Second-in-command against the ARMADA, in 1595 he was joint commander with his younger cousin DRAKE of an unsuccessful attack on the WEST INDIES during which both died.

Heads of the Proposals, the terms offered in 1647 by ARMY leaders to CHARLES I independently of Parliamentary negotiations. They were more generous than PARLIAMENT'S in restoring powers to him, in return for toleration of INDEPENDENT congregations and sweeping PARLIAMENTARY REFORM. Despite modern controversy over their authorship, it is likely that the initiative came from army officers led by IRETON, with some support in the COMMONS and from Parliamentary peers such as William Fiennes, Viscount Saye and Sele.

Healey, Denis (Baron Healey) (1917–), Labour politician. He served as defence secretary in the first WILSON government (1964–70) and as chancellor of the Exchequer in the second Wilson and CALLAGHAN governments (1974–79). His defence reviews at first tried to preserve the majority of Britain's military commitments round the world, but ended with extensive retrenchment. At the TREASURY he was faced with high and rising inflation and UNEMPLOYMENT. His involvement in trying to devise an effective incomes policy to cope with this situation brought him from 1975 onwards into bruising conflict with the TRADE UNIONS and the left of the party. The collapse of sterling in 1976 forced him to apply to the International Monetary Fund for a $3.9 billion loan and to accept spending cuts and other conditions to get it. In opposition, he was shadow foreign secretary (1980–7).

From being a member of the COMMUNIST PARTY in his youth, Healey became a political and intellectual heavyweight of the Labour right. He stood three times for the party leadership, coming closest to winning in 1980, when the parliamentary party rather surprisingly preferred FOOT.

Health and Morals of Apprentices Act 1802 This prohibited workhouse APPRENTICES in textile mills from working more than 11 hours a day, banned night work and required improved accommodation and provision of elementary education. The Act included provision for local supervision, but failed to create an independent inspectorate to make it effective. It was in spirit more akin to the Elizabethan poor laws (*see* POOR RELIEF) than to the Victorian FACTORY ACTS.

Hearth Tax From 1662, hearth tax, or 'Chimney money', was levied at 2 shillings per hearth, paid twice yearly, except by those exempted on grounds of poverty. The tax was repealed at the GLORIOUS REVOLUTION as an oppression on the poor as well as an infringement of liberty, inasmuch as it allowed the searching of taxpayers' homes. Hearth tax records, with their local listings of inhabitants and taxpayers, have been much used by historians to study social structure and population size (including debatable household multipliers).

Heath, Sir Edward (1916–), Conservative politician and Prime Minister (1970–4). He became CONSERVATIVE MP for Bexley in 1950. In successive Conservative governments, he was chief whip (1955–9), minister of labour (1959–60), lord Privy Seal (1960–3) and secretary of state for industry and trade (1963–4). He became Conservative leader in 1965, the first to be chosen by a ballot of MPs, and the first grammar school boy to hold the post. He became prime minister following the party's unexpected victory in 1970.

A strong supporter of the EEC (*see* EUROPEAN UNION), in Jan. 1973 he signed the treaty of accession that gained Britain membership. His attempts to reform industrial relations produced two confrontations with the TUC and the miners, leading to the THREE-DAY WEEK in the winter of 1973–4. Combined with the collapse of the economic boom fostered by his chancellor, Anthony Barber, this led to a narrow defeat by LABOUR in a snap election called in Feb. 1974 on the issue 'Who governs Britain?' when the miners refused to call off an all-out strike. He also lost the Oct. 1974 election by a wider margin. The following year, Heath was ousted from the party leadership by Margaret THATCHER. His government left few lasting legacies, and under Thatcher there began a sharp redefinition of Conservatism.

From the back benches Heath has remained a sonorous critic of his party's right-wing, anti-European shift, both under THATCHER and then HAGUE, but he remains an isolated figure with little political impact.

Hebrides, Scandinavian Lordship Over VIKING raids on the Western Isles (Outer Hebrides) began in the late 8th century and continued until the middle of the 9th. The raiders slaughtered many monks and eventually forced the abandonment of the great abbey of IONA. Alongside the raids, colonization took place; PLACE NAME evidence has suggested that the culture of much of the region became predominantly Norse.

Danish and Norwegian rulers competed for control over the islands, with the latter achieving predominance in the middle of the 9th century. Following the defeat of the kindred of KETIL FLATNOSE in *c.*870, settlers in the Hebrides colonized Iceland and, subsequently, Greenland. In 1079 the Hebrides were included with the Isle of Man in the Kingdom of MAN AND THE ISLES, which in theory remained under the rule of the kings of Norway until the treaty of PERTH in 1266.

Hengist (?–?488), King (?) of Kent. Later traditions (of which the earliest is recorded by BEDE) identify Hengist as the first king of KENT. The story is that, in the mid-5th century, he and his brother Horsa were invited into Kent to serve as mercenaries by the Romano-British ruler VORTIGERN, whom Hengist subsequently overthrew. His historical existence is unverifiable, but archaeological evidence does at least show English settlement in Kent at a time when Hengist might have been leading English warriors into the region.

Henrietta Maria (1609–69), Queen of England. Youngest daughter of Henry IV of France, she married CHARLES I in 1625. Their initially cool relations turned to devoted love after the murder of George VILLIERS 4th Duke of Buckingham in 1628. She never liked LAUD or Strafford (*see* WENTWORTH, CHARLES), forming a curious alliance in the 1630s with PURITAN courtiers to obstruct a diplomatic rapprochement with Spain; however, her Catholicism fuelled public fears about Catholic influence on Charles. Her schemes and her fund-raising from Catholics were both a help and a hindrance to Charles's war effort; although often politically inept, she did her best to persuade him to be flexible in negotiations after his defeat. Having moved to France in 1644, she was left poverty-stricken after Charles's execution, and angered exiled ANGLICAN courtiers by her efforts to convert her children to Rome. She returned to England from 1660–5, but then went back to France.

Henry I (1068–1135), King of England (1100–35). WILLIAM I THE CONQUEROR's third surviving son was well educated, hence his subsequent nickname 'Beauclerk' ('the learned'). In 1087, his father left him a huge sum of money, but his prospects remained uncertain until 2 Aug. 1100, the day on which, whether by chance or by design, WILLIAM II RUFUS was killed. Henry, who was near by, rode to WINCHESTER where he took possession of the TREASURY, and then to WESTMINSTER where, on 5 Aug., he had himself crowned and issued his CORONATION CHARTER.

In Nov. 1100, by marrying MATILDA II, descendant of Anglo-Saxon kings and sister of EDGAR of Scotland, Henry strengthened his claim and the security of the North. But his elder brother ROBERT II, Duke of Normandy, disputed Henry's right to the throne and enjoyed the support of such powerful magnates as ROBERT OF BELLEME. The war of succession lasted until 1106, when Henry won the battle of Tinchebrai, captured his brother and conquered Normandy, thus re-establishing the ANGLO-NORMAN REALM. Robert spent the last 28 years of his life as Henry's prisoner. His son, William Clito, born four years before his father's incarceration, grew up to be a thorn in his uncle's flesh, since the king of France and the count of Anjou, alarmed by Henry's power, recognized Clito's claim. While England was at peace throughout the remainder of Henry's long reign, in Normandy he constantly had to fight hard.

The king's need for money to fund the defence of the duchy led to administrative developments in England and the rise of

ROGER OF SALISBURY. Henry has been credited with the centralization of royal power – the earliest extant references to the EXCHEQUER date from his reign – and the employment of 'new men' of relatively humble origins in government service. But although Henry, like all kings, employed some 'new men', he depended much more on the greater, and better rewarded, services that magnates could give him.

Early in his reign, royal authority had faced an unprecedented challenge. ANSELM, an Archbishop of Canterbury ultimately loyal to a militant and reforming papacy, brought the prohibition of lay investiture to England, thereby threatening the customary power of the king to control ecclesiastical appointments – a serious matter at a time when prelates were great landowners and men of political weight. Eventually, in a series of agreements made between 1105 and 1107, Henry was able to retain the reality of control while renouncing the traditional ritual of investiture. By giving this up, he was acknowledging the fundamentally secular nature of kingship.

Diplomatic, realistic and secular-minded, Henry's ecclesiastical policy was entirely characteristic of the man. Morally dubious though many of his actions were thought to be, he was always able to justify them as necessary for the well-being of the state. Even the sex drive that resulted in 20 acknowledged bastards – more than any other English king so far – was justified in political terms: he used his illegitimate children as diplomatic pawns to construct marriage alliances.

Yet for all his fertility of brain and body, Henry had only one legitimate son: William, drowned in the WHITE SHIP disaster in 1120. From then on, the problem of the succession dominated the reign. Queen Matilda had died in 1118, and less than three months after William's death, Henry took a second wife, ADELA OF LOUVAIN. But the male heir desperately hoped for was never born. In 1127, Henry made his barons swear to recognize his only legitimate daughter, the Empress MATILDA, as heir, and the following year, he married her to Geoffrey of Anjou (*see* PLANTAGENET). But the king was reluctant to part with any of the power he had exercised for so long.

The chronicler HENRY OF HUNTINGDON portrayed him as a man made permanently miserable by anxiety: 'Each of his triumphs only made him worry lest he lose what he had gained.' At the time of his death on 1 Dec. 1135 – supposedly from a 'surfeit of lampreys' – he was quarrelling violently with Geoffrey and Matilda. This quarrel reopened old divisions within the Anglo-Norman baronage and allowed STEPHEN to snatch the crown from the hands of Henry's designated heirs. During the civil wars that followed, the English would look back on Henry's stern rule as an age of peace under a 'Lion of Justice'. *See also* ROBERT OF GLOUCESTER.

Henry II (1133–89), King of England (1154–89). The eldest son of Geoffrey PLANTAGENET, Count of Anjou, and of Empress MATILDA, by the time he was 14 Henry was already taking an active part in the campaign to wrest control of his mother's inheritance, the ANGLO-NORMAN REALM, from STEPHEN. In 1151, his father died and Henry took over the rule of Anjou and Normandy; the following year, he married ELEANOR OF AQUITAINE, and began to rule her duchy in her name. Astonishingly swiftly, the 19-year-old had become the richest prince in France – more powerful than Louis VII, Eleanor's ex-husband.

In Dec. 1153, Stephen reluctantly acknowledged Henry as his heir, and the next year, the young man became Henry II of England, ruler and, in large part, creator of the ANGEVIN EMPIRE. As contemporaries observed, in the extent of his dominions he was a greater king than any of his predecessors.

During the first 20 years of his reign, Henry was a belligerent ruler, chiefly interested in territorial expansion at the expense of his neighbours – taking Northumbria from MALCOLM IV, and launching attacks on the Welsh and the Bretons. In 1171, he invaded Ireland and was recognized as lord by nearly all the Irish kings. Although the acquisition of the Quercy region of south-west France had been regarded as a disappointing outcome of his massive 1159 invasion of Toulouse, in 1173 the Count of Toulouse was persuaded to do homage. During this period, with the exception of his appointment of BECKET as Archbishop of Canterbury, Henry suffered few serious setbacks. But the rebellion of his wife and sons HENRY THE YOUNG

KING, Geoffrey and Richard (the future RICHARD I) in 1173–4 marked a major turning-point. From then on, he was mainly on the defensive, concentrating on holding what he had won and giving a higher priority to internal affairs.

To the end, Henry remained a man of boundless energy, always hunting or riding from one part of his dominions to another. The sheer size of his empire inevitably stimulated the growth of localized administrations that could deal with routine matters of justice and finance in his absence. The result was – especially in England, a country where a bureaucratic tradition was already strong – the rapid development of the institutions of government, notably the creation of the COMMON LAW administered by a more centralized judicial system. Since the 18th century, the 'making of the common law' has been regarded as the most significant aspect of Henry's reign, and in consequence, he has been seen as a king with a genius for law and government. This, however, is not how his contemporaries viewed him.

By the end of his reign, he was seen as an unpopular ruler who appointed corrupt judges, oppressed the Church and failed to manage his family (there were further rebellions of his sons in 1183 and 1188–9). Despite urgent pleas from his hard-pressed cousins, the rulers of the kingdom of Jerusalem, he did not go on CRUSADE. To most people, it seemed that his only contribution to the Third Crusade was to lay a massive tax – the SALADIN TITHE (1189) – on his subjects. The accession of RICHARD I was greeted with relief.

Henry III (1207–72), King of England (1216–72). Eldest son of JOHN and ISABELLA OF ANGOULÈME, he succeeded in Oct. 1216, a nine-year-old king whose realm was torn apart by the civil war provoked by his father's misrule. However, while he was still a minor, the government headed in turn by William Marshal, Peter des Roches and Hubert de BURGH coped very well with the immense military, financial and political problems facing the crown. Only in Poitou, overrun by LOUIS VIII in 1224, did Henry suffer a permanent loss of rights.

He declared himself to be of age in 1227, but not until after his marriage to ELEANOR OF PROVENCE in 1236 did he take personal control of government. The delay was entirely characteristic of a king who occasionally made ambitious policy pronouncements, on both foreign and domestic affairs, but lacked the drive and determination to see them through. After the humiliating failure of the Taillebourg campaign (1242), he made little effort to recover the Plantagenet continental dominions lost in John's reign; indeed, in the 1259 treaty of PARIS, he renounced them. As a good family man, he promoted the interests of his foreign relatives – first the Savoyards, then the LUSIGNANS – but in ways that alienated an aristocracy that was increasingly conscious of its Englishness.

From 1244 onwards, those who doubted his capacity to rule were advocating reforms that were, in effect, reversions to the practice of his minority – government by ministers accountable to GREAT COUNCILS (assemblies of lay and ecclesiastical magnates) rather than to the king. In 1258, his financial predicament – the result of his misguided SICILIAN ADVENTURE – and his failure to keep court FACTION within bounds made it impossible for him to avoid one such reform scheme: the PROVISIONS OF OXFORD. Naturally he tried to escape these constraints as soon as he could, and the outcome was years of tense political manoeuvring, culminating in the BARONS' WAR. After being defeated and captured at LEWES in 1264, he was effectively dethroned by Simon de MONTFORT. However, the following year, he was restored thanks to the victory won at EVESHAM by his eldest son, the future EDWARD I.

By now, Henry was head of the family in name only and could safely leave politics to others while he concentrated on rebuilding WESTMINSTER Abbey. At the end of a very long reign, he was at least still king of England. Naïve, pious and well-meaning, he loved quiet as well as peace, and generally let events take their course. His claim that he had given his subjects peace would have been justified had it not been for the drift into civil war in the 1260s.

Henry IV (1366–1413), King of England (1399–1413). Born at Bolingbroke, Lincs. – hence the name by which he is commonly known – as JOHN OF GAUNT's son he was heir apparent to the richest estate in England, and his prospects improved still further when, in

1380, he married Mary de Bohun (died 1394), co-heiress of the earldom of Hereford. In 1387, he was one of the APPELLANTS and the victor at Radcot Bridge. However, there is some evidence that, at this date, he may have argued against the deposing of RICHARD II.

During the early 1390s, Bolingbroke's chivalric reputation was enhanced by CRUSADES with the Teutonic knights and a pilgrimage to Jerusalem. However, in the tense political climate created by Richard, charges and counter-charges of treason led to his exile in 1398 and, in his absence, the seizure of the duchy of Lancaster. In 1399, with just a few hundred men, he returned to England, seeking the restoration of his inheritance and posing as a champion of the rule of law against a tyrannous king. It was soon clear that the throne was there for the taking, and with decisive support from the PERCYS, Henry took it, asserting in justification a non-existent hereditary right. Richard was deposed and imprisoned in Sept. 1399, and the following Feb., after a failed rescue attempt, Henry had him murdered.

The new king's previous denunciations of Richard's extravagance made him very vulnerable on the same score: the PARLIAMENTS of 1401–6 complained angrily of the costs of the royal household, of excessive annuities and of taxes misspent. On several occasions, he had to accede to the COMMONS' demands – thus the Victorian interpretation of him as a constitutional monarch. Cash shortages crippled his response to GLYN DWR's revolt and meant that he treated the Percys, especially Thomas, less well than they expected. His swift reaction to the news of the PERCY REBELLION took him to victory at SHREWSBURY in 1403, though it was not until 1408 that his baronial enemies finally gave up.

Their defeat eased his money problems and, consequently, his relations with parliament, but by this time he had a new enemy: ill-health, brought on (according to later chroniclers) by his execution of Richard Scrope, Archbishop of York, who had joined the Percy Rebellion in opposition to the king's taxation of the clergy and in fear of clerical disendowment in 1405. After this date, the king who had come to the throne with a reputation for physical strength was hardly ever capable of leading his troops in person. He died at the age of 46 after a number of severe and temporarily incapacitating (if unidentifiable) illnesses, which forced him at least once, in 1411, to ward off an attempt to make him abdicate in favour of his eldest son (the future HENRY V).

In his last two years, he hardly left London except to go to BECKET's shrine at Canterbury, where he opted to be buried, and where his second wife, JOAN OF NAVARRE, was to join him on her death.

Henry V (1387–1422), King of England (1413–22). Created Prince of Wales in 1399, a month after HENRY IV's accession, he was soon employed in suppressing GLYN DWR's revolt. (Tales of Prince Hal's misspent youth were first recorded after his death, when he was regarded as a figure from the heroic past.) By 1406, he was actively involved in court politics, and relations with his father were tense; in 1411, he was probably in favour of the unsuccessful move to force the monarch to abdicate.

In 1413, soon after Henry IV's early death and his own accession, the new king faced two challenges – Sir John Oldcastle's, LOLLARD rising (1414) and the Southampton Plot – and overcame both. As a sincere champion of religious orthodoxy, he felt he deserved divine support, and it was in this mood that he decided to vindicate his right – if necessary via trial by battle – to the crown of France. In 1415, he captured Harfleur, then marched through Normandy to AGINCOURT, winning enormous acclaim at home.

For five years, enthusiastic parliaments voted Henry all the money he needed, and never again did a French army dare to stand in his way. The Englishness of his government was emphasized by his policy of having official documents written in English. He built up a NAVY, clearing the Channel of enemy shipping and using his vessels for trading to meet part of the cost. He led a second army to France in 1417 and methodically and ruthlessly conquered Normandy. By the treaty of TROYES, Charles VI recognized him as his heir, and in June 1420, he married the French king's daughter CATHERINE OF VALOIS. The next day, he marched off to continue the conquest of his kingdom, only to die of dysentery a few weeks before his father-in-law.

In his short reign, Henry V impressed

foreign enemies as well as loyal subjects. A pious, self-disciplined and obsessively efficient ruler, who ensured that the English position in France remained tenable and profitable for at least 20 years after his death, he conformed so effectively to the model of the ideal king that, as SHAKESPEARE's *Henry V* makes plain, for centuries posterity regarded him as England's perfect monarch – as, indeed, some historians still do. Yet doubts remain. Some have wondered whether his ambitions did not finally exceed those of his subjects – at the end of his reign, ADAM OF USK wrote of 'the smothered curses of the taxpayers' – or whether his brilliant exploitation of opportunities did not lead him into conquests that, in the longer term, would have proved impossible to maintain.

Henry VI (1421–71), King of England (1422–61, 1470–1). He became king in Sept. 1422 at the age of nine months, following the early death of his father HENRY V. In Oct., after the death of his maternal grandfather, Charles VI of France, and in accordance with the treaty of TROYES, he was proclaimed king of France. The governments of his minority in both kingdoms were remarkably effective; problems multiplied after he was declared of age in 1437.

His love of peace may have been genuine, but it went hand in hand with inertia – in his entire reign, he visited his continental kingdom only once, when he was taken there as a boy in 1430–2. When he married MARGARET OF ANJOU in 1445, he promised to surrender Maine to her uncle, Charles VII (who, as French dauphin, had declared himself king of France within two weeks of Henry being proclaimed), a promise that had to be kept secret from his advisers and was not fulfilled until 1448. The humiliating military defeats (1449–53) in the closing stages of the HUNDRED YEARS WAR shocked his subjects, precipitating CADE'S REBELLION at home and culminating in the final loss of Normandy and AQUITAINE. In Aug. 1453, a few days after the news of CASTILLON, he suffered a total breakdown. Although he recovered what passed for his right mind in 1455, he played an increasingly passive role thereafter.

Loyalty to his person still counted for something – as was apparent when he relieved RICHARD OF YORK of the second protectorship in 1455 and at the confrontation with the YORKISTS at Ludlow in 1459 – but he became little more than a symbolic parcel of monarchical authority passed from hand to hand as the fortunes of the WARS OF THE ROSES swayed from side to side at ST ALBANS, NORTHAMPTON and St Albans again. After EDWARD IV's crushing victory at TOWTON in March 1461, Margaret took Henry to Scotland.

His occasional appearances in Northumbria failed to revive the LANCASTRIAN cause, and when deprived of Scottish aid by Edward's truce with the Scots in 1463, after the last Lancastrian strongholds in Northumbria had been captured, he became a king in hiding. Discovered by the Yorkists in 1465, he was imprisoned in the Tower. There he might have lived out his days had he not been restored to the throne in Oct. 1470 (after Edward's flight to Holland), and then deposed again in April 1471 after Edward's return. The killing of his only child, Prince Edward, at the battle of TEWKESBURY sealed Henry's fate. He was now the last obvious representative of the Lancastrian dynasty, and Edward judged that he could no longer allow him to live: Henry VI was murdered on 21 April 1471.

After 1485, it became politically convenient to present Henry as a pious king, pure and blameless, an innocent unjustly dethroned by the Yorkists, and even to press for his canonization. Undoubtedly his life had been tragic, but for his subjects, his reign had been calamitous. He had stood helplessly by as England slid into the Wars of the Roses, and as well as losing the throne of England twice, he witnessed from afar the loss of all his dominions in France except CALAIS.

Henry VII (1457–1509), King of England (1485–1509), Lord of Ireland. Son of Edmund Tudor, Earl of Richmond, he was brought up in Wales until he fled to Brittany in 1471. His highly shaky royal claim through his mother Margaret BEAUFORT only gained real significance after EDWARD V's murder and Henry STAFFORD, Duke of Buckingham's unsuccessful rebellion (*see* BUCKINGHAM'S REBELLION) in 1483. Moving to France to avoid betrayal, Henry was joined by a few remaining LANCASTRIANS. He landed at the Welsh port of Milford Haven in 1485, defeating and killing RICHARD III at BOSWORTH and taking the throne.

In 1486, he honoured the public pledge he had made in Brittany to marry Elizabeth of York, EDWARD IV's daughter, though not his pledge to rule jointly with her. He faced repeated dynastic rebellions notably from Lambert SIMNEL and Perkin WARBECK, together with some serious popular unrest, especially in Yorks. (1489) and Cornwall (1497), and he only secured his rule in Ireland in 1494; however, he made busy efforts to restore central authority. He won goodwill in the potentially hostile North because his opponents allied themselves with the Scots, the traditional enemies of northern Englishmen.

After initial hesitation, he used Yorkist CHAMBER methods of revenue control, and exploited his FEUDAL financial rights to the full. Having little acquaintance among English aristocrats, he manipulated the legal system to intimidate them and curb private lawlessness; he shared government sparingly with a close circle of acquaintances, mostly efficient bureaucrats. His treaty of ÉTAPLES in 1492 brought profitable peace with France, and although he was troubled by the successive pretenders backed by Margaret of Burgundy, the *INTERCURSUS MAGNUS* of 1496 stabilized trade with the Low Countries. The one fruit of much convoluted marital diplomacy surrounding his sons ARTHUR and Henry (the future HENRY VIII) was the alliance with Aragon and Castile that brought CATHERINE OF ARAGON to England in 1501.

Henry VII is often seen as cold and calculating; however, his relationship with his family was close and affectionate, particularly with his wife and his remarkable mother. His intimate circle was small, but he had good reason to distrust most prominent politicians. He balanced his private style of government with a recognition of the need to impress his subjects by the magnificence of his court (*see also* PRIVY CHAMBER).

At his death, there were murderous COURT tensions, which destroyed Richard Empson and Edmund Dudley, but the king left his surviving son Henry a peaceful and united realm, ending 15th-century instability and securing the future of his Tudor dynasty.

Henry VIII (1491–1547), King of England (1509–47), Lord then King of Ireland. There is a reliable tradition that, as the second son, Henry was intended by his father HENRY VII for a senior position in the Church before he became heir to the throne on the death of his elder brother ARTHUR in 1502. At his accession, his ebullience, sporting prowess and genuine, if fitful, interest in RENAISSANCE humanist learning were a welcome contrast with his introvert father, and he soon completed long-drawn-out negotiations for marriage with Arthur's widow CATHERINE OF ARAGON. Bored by detailed administration, he found the ideal bureaucrat-minister in Thomas WOLSEY, who by 1511 was supplanting the council of cautious aristocrats and bishops who had initially dominated government. Henry rapidly turned to a traditional source of English royal glory in the first (1512–13) of several expensive wars with France; ironically, he fought this war as a crusade on behalf of the pope, with whom the French king was then at war. Throughout the reign, his ministers were forced to devise new sources of revenue to finance war, including a cynical and damaging debasement of the COINAGE in the 1540s.

Henry used Wolsey's talents in complex and often contradictory diplomacy designed to secure an equal place with the much more powerful Holy Roman Emperor and the French king Francis I. The confusing and wasteful character of his foreign policy was symbolized in 1520 when he staged an immensely lavish meeting to establish close friendship with Francis at the FIELD OF THE CLOTH OF GOLD, only a few weeks before making a secret agreement with the emperor not to ally with France. However, his marital troubles further complicated matters. His marriage to Catherine of Aragon was ruined by his obsession with securing a male heir, since apart from a series of miscarriages, she had only produced one surviving daughter, Mary (the future MARY I) in 1516.

From early 1527, his love for ANNE BOLEYN made matters worse, but his quest to have his marriage declared invalid (soon tactfully known as the king's 'Great Matter') was made harder by his insistence that it was a theological issue, in which the pope must acknowledge that the papacy had made a fundamental mistake when it had originally granted a papal dispensation for the marriage to take place; he ignored any easier approach. In 1529 the resulting inevitable deadlock made Henry jettison Wolsey. He also forgot his earlier extravagant papal loyalty, which in 1521 had won him the title 'Defender of the Faith' for writing (or taking the credit for) the anti-Lutheran *Assertio Septem Sacramentorum* ('Defence of the Seven Sacraments'); instead, he built on his equally long-standing conviction of his own God-given place at the head of the English Church. Out of this, a committee of clerical academics created a theory of ROYAL SUPREMACY, and the means to put it into effect was created by Thomas CROMWELL in the Parliaments of the 1530s. Henry used this new royal power to sanction the DISSOLUTION of all monasteries, nunneries and friaries by 1540, and also to allow the publication of an official translation of the BIBLE in English in 1538.

Henry's marital misfortunes continued when he was persuaded of Anne Boleyn's adultery (1536); after her execution, a new wife, JANE SEYMOUR, provided him with his son EDWARD, but died of illness as a result (1537). Genuinely heartbroken, Henry nevertheless entered fresh matrimonial adventures: the ANNE OF CLEVES fiasco (1540) was followed by the undoubted adultery and consequent execution (1542) of CATHERINE HOWARD; and only with CATHERINE PARR (1543) did Henry find a contented partnership for his last years. Meanwhile he kept a careful and cruel balance between religious reformists and conservatives at COURT, using their murderous struggles to sanction the destruction of MORE and FISHER (1535), the Courtenays (1538), Cromwell (1540), and the HOWARDS (1546/7) – besides numerous figures across the spectrum of belief who died for not conforming to his religious blueprint. A further consequence of the break with Rome was that he decided that he must replace his title 'Lord of Ireland', since it was widely believed that it was derived from the supposed 12th-century papal grant by ADRIAN IV (*see LAUDABILITER*). He was therefore declared King of Ireland by the Irish Parliament in 1541 and by the English Parliament in 1542.

As his REFORMATION progressed, Henry's own religion grew complicated, puzzling both contemporaries and modern observers. He lost any strong sense of PURGATORY, a central medieval belief, and besides a strong dose of aristocratic ANTI-CLERICALISM, he remained proud of his part in sponsoring an English Bible and curbing the cult of images and destruction of shrines. He put his son's education in the hands of CAMBRIDGE reformists. Nevertheless he never accepted the Reformers' PROTESTANT emphasis on justification by faith alone; despite some late hesitations, he maintained the provisions of the savagely Catholic SIX ARTICLES (1539). His most enduring conviction was that next to God, he knew best.

Henry's place in folk-memory has been assured by his eccentric marital history, and by the enduringly vivid visual images of himself and his court provided by the drawings and paintings of Hans Holbein the Younger (*c.*1497–1534). However, his reign was genuinely of great significance in British history, not merely for the religious break with Rome. It marked an important stage in the CENTRALIZING assertion of WESTMINSTER government within England, and of England in the Celtic lands of the British Isles. Within England itself, patterns of medieval government through JUSTICES OF THE PEACE and ASSIZES which had only fully operated in the south-eastern and Midlands heartland were now made effective also in the north and west. From 1536 Wales was also assimilated to English administrative institutions (*see* UNION OF WALES AND ENGLAND), and relations between Anglophone and Gaelic culture in Ireland were permanently altered as the English government determined on more aggressive policies. Henry also reasserted claims over the Scottish kingdom which were ironically to be fulfilled in reverse in 1603 when JAMES VI AND I, a Scots descendant of his sister Margaret, the wife of JAMES IV, assumed the English crown. He took a keen personal interest in the NAVY, investing much money in new ships.

Much debate has raged over how far Henry can be given credit for developments in the reign; the ultimate reaction against seeing him as an all-powerful, all-controlling tyrant came in the 1950s with the work of Sir Geoffrey Elton (*see TUDOR REVOLUTION IN GOVERNMENT*), who saw the vital changes as resulting from the conscious strategy of Thomas Cromwell. Recent research tends to restore credit to Henry, even if he was shrewd enough to delegate hard detailed work (and frequently also the blame for unpopular policies) to ministers of great talent.

Henry of Blois (?–1171), prince bishop of the English Church. Son of Count Stephen of Blois, he was brought up as a monk in the abbey of Cluny. Then, in 1126, his uncle HENRY I gave him the abbey of GLASTONBURY and, three years later, the bishopric of Winchester. Since he contrived to hold both for over 40 years, he was the richest prelate in England and, in 1135, helped his brother STEPHEN obtain the throne.

Although he failed either to become archbishop of Canterbury or to convert Winchester into a metropolitan see, he played an extraordinarily prominent political and even military role throughout Stephen's reign. This was particularly true during the years 1139–43, when the struggle between the king and the Empress MATILDA was at its most intense, and when he used his authority as papal legate to hold councils in highly publicized, if largely unsuccessful, attempts to settle the affairs of the kingdom. At HENRY II's accession in 1154, he withdrew to Cluny, but returned four years later to play the part of elder statesman. Since he was also a builder of CASTLES and palaces (notably Wolvesey at Winchester), as well as a connoisseur who brought back pagan statues from Rome because he appreciated them as works of art, he inevitably encountered the wrath of the austere St Bernard of Clairvaux, in whose eyes he was the 'old wizard' and the 'whore of Winchester'.

Henry of Huntingdon (?–*c.*1160), historian. Archdeacon of Huntingdon, he was the author of the Latin *History of the English* covering the period from Caesar's invasion of Britain to his own day, initially up to 1129, then in subsequent editions to 1154. A very organized thinker, his systematic analysis of Anglo-Saxon history was to prove influential – for example, he introduced the notion of the HEPTARCHY. He is also responsible for the story of King CNUT trying to hold back the waves – to illustrate a sensible king's scorn for the flattery of courtiers.

Henry the Young King (1155–83), son of HENRY II and ELEANOR OF AQUITAINE. For reasons that are still unclear, in 1170 he was crowned by the Archbishop of York (*see* BECKET, THOMAS); thus he was referred to as both 'Henry III' and 'the Young King'. He initiated the great rebellion of 1173–4 against Henry II, and he was again in revolt against his father when he died in 1183. This turbulent history may explain why he remains the only heir to the English throne to be crowned during his father's lifetime. Contemporary chroniclers describe him as a charming but feckless playboy; he was doubtless frustrated by the fact that he was heir to dominions (Anjou, NORMANDY and England) over which his father had no intention of relinquishing control.

Hepburn, James (Baron Hailes, 4th Earl of Bothwell) (*c.*1535–78). In 1556 he succeeded to the power in the Scottish Borders wielded by his father Patrick, an opponent of the REFORMATION and an unsuccessful suitor of MARY OF GUISE. Although a PROTESTANT, he opposed the LORDS OF THE CONGREGATION, endearing him to MARY QUEEN OF SCOTS. At her entreaty of help against the Earl of Moray's rebellion, he returned from exile in 1565, and as she increasingly turned her affections towards him, he determined to supplant Darnley (*see* STEWART, HENRY) as royal consort. After the latter's murder in 1567, a farcical trial acquitted Bothwell of any involvement; he then seized the queen, probably raping her at Dunbar, and secured a hasty annulment from John HAMILTON, Archbishop of St Andrews, of his first marriage. He and Mary were rapidly married at Holyrood Palace, Edinburgh.

Immediately national anger combined against them, resulting in their defeat at Carberry Hill (15 June). By the end of the year, he was a fugitive, stripped of his honours. He sailed to Norway, where old creditors and relatives of a wronged former mistress seized him and took him to prison in Denmark. Never released, he died in chains, stark mad. The occasional modern efforts at rehabilitating him are doomed to failure.

Heptarchy, The, the term frequently used to refer to the seven major English kingdoms in existence at the end of the 7th century: WESSEX, KENT, SUSSEX, ESSEX, EAST ANGLIA, MERCIA and NORTHUMBRIA. These comparatively large territories are thought probably to have evolved from competitive struggles among much smaller units. In any case, the term Heptarchy makes the political situation appear more clear-cut than in reality it was, and is applied to a stage of political development which was reached more than two centuries after the original settlement by the English. *See also* HENRY OF HUNTINGDON.

Heraldry and Heralds Heraldry is the science of identifying families in a symbolic pictorial language. It developed in the 12th century out of the earlier practice whereby (as a means of identification on the battlefield) fighting men put individual symbols on their shields; the shield was to remain the conventional frame for designs as the symbolism evolved and became fixed. Coats of arms were soon hereditarily annexed to particular families, and a fixed descriptive language for the symbols evolved – in Britain, a debased Norman–French.

Heralds began as announcers and organizers of tournaments, and thus had a professional interest in shields and the coats that they displayed. Originally also employed on diplomatic missions, during the 16th century they were largely supplanted by a new diplomatic service but, at the same time, gained formal jurisdiction over the granting and definition of coats of arms.

In England, the College of Arms, presided over by the GARTER King of Arms, was given formal existence in 1484 and acquired its present central London site in 1555. By that stage, families' GENEALOGIES and their right to bear arms were being investigated by heralds in regular VISITATIONS, which continued into the late 17th century. In Scotland, a similar system of regulation evolved under the Lord Lyon King of Arms; both systems still function.

Nowadays a pleasant diversion, heraldry was once of vital political significance and has many continuing uses for the historian, notably as a way of dating or provenancing objects that incorporate coats of arms.

Heresy, obstinate persistence in error against official Church doctrine. When the Church became established in the 4th-century Roman Empire, it adopted the pagan punishment of burning alive for religious error, but very few heretics suffered this fate before the 11th century. In England, CANON LAW and COMMON LAW were intertwined by the Act *DE HERETICO COMBURENDO* of 1401, by which secular authority carried out the burning. HENRY VIII replaced this by new legislation, which was abolished by EDWARD VI, but it was restored by MARY I. ELIZABETH I's further abolition of it did not prevent her burning certain ANABAPTISTS (Edward VI had also burned two), as did JAMES I in 1612, for the last time. *See also* BLASPHEMY; FOXE, JOHN.

Heretable Jurisdictions Act 1747, Act abolishing legal jurisdictions which passed by inheritance in some parts of Scotland. Heretable (or heritable) jurisdictions were scattered through the Highlands and Lowlands, varying in size and in the extent of the rights associated with them: lords of regalities had very considerable civil and criminal powers. JAMES VII AND II had contemplated their abolition; their removal after the defeat of the 1745 JACOBITE rising represented part of a larger programme for the modernization of Scotland.

Hereward (*fl. c.*1070), rebel soldier. The most celebrated leader of English resistance to the NORMAN CONQUEST, in 1070 he plundered PETERBOROUGH ABBEY to finance the revolt in the Fenlands; a year later, when other leaders surrendered to WILLIAM I THE CONQUEROR, he and his followers escaped from the Isle of Ely. After that, nothing certain is known of his career, only that, by fighting on, he became, by the mid-12th century, a legendary figure, called (for unknown reasons) 'Hereward the Wake' from the 13th century onwards.

Heriot, a death duty paid from a man's estate to his lord. After the NORMAN CONQUEST, this Old English word was no longer appropriate for high-status transactions, and so, where members of the French-speaking élite were concerned, it was replaced by a new term: RELIEF. However, it presumably continued to be used at village level because it re-emerged in 13th-century surveys, normally for a payment made to a lord of the manor when a tenant in VILLEINAGE died.

Hermeticism, RENAISSANCE philosophy inspired by NEO-PLATONIC mystical writings (mainly 3rd century AD) attributed to the imaginary Hermes Trismegistus ('thrice mighty'), a Neo-Platonic name for the ancient Egyptian god Tut. Hermetic treatises presented a picture of the universe as containing patterns of magical forces upon which humans might call, after appropriate investigation. They much excited intellectuals throughout early modern Europe, encouraging scientific, astrological, alchemical and magical research; hence they were a major stimulus to experimental science, although until recent years scientists had forgotten this mystical parentage. Hermeticists with a major influence in England were John Dee (1527–1608), an outstanding CAMBRIDGE scientist, geographer, astronomer and mathematician, with a reputation as a magician, and Giordano Bruno (1548–1600), an Italian philosopher, friend of Philip SIDNEY and Robert DUDLEY, Earl of Leicester, who was burned at the stake in Rome.

Hertford, Synod of, 672, the first council of the entire English Church, held under the presidency of Archbishop THEODORE OF TARSUS. Although not all English bishops attended, the synod was a landmark because of its general legislation on, for instance, the role of bishops, the requirement for annual Church councils, marriage, and the size of DIOCESES, and because of the way in which bishops, whose dioceses often coincided with a kingdom, were drawn into a consideration of wider concerns.

Hide, the most widely used unit of assessment in the English kingdom for tribute, taxation and military service until the 12th century (*see also CARUCATE*). It was not strictly a measure of area. Instead, it seems originally to have signified the amount of land sufficient to support a family, but it had already become a unit of assessment by the time of BEDE. It may have had a relationship with economic resources, although numerous examples of 'beneficial hidation' show that it could be manipulated in favour of chosen individuals or institutions. *See also BURGHAL HIDEAGE; COUNTY HIDEAGE; TRIBAL HIDEAGE.*

Higden, Ranulf (?–*c.*1364), historian. A BENEDICTINE of St Werburgh's, Chester, and author of treatises on preaching, he is now best known for his Latin history of the world, the *Polychronicon*, which was translated into English by John Trevisa (*c.*1342–1402) and remained the most popular account of world history available in England until Walter RALEIGH's in the early 17th century.

High Churchmanship, vague but useful term, first used in the 17th century, referring to the recovery of CATHOLIC insights by one group in the post-REFORMATION Church of England. High Churchmen emphasize continuity with the pre-reformation Church, the power of the sacraments and the value and authority of the EPISCOPAL ministry; they often delight in liturgical splendour and artistic creativity. High Churchmanship was first prominent in the early 17th-century ARMINIAN movement led by LAUD, and was a strong force after the RESTORATION and through the reign of Queen ANNE, when High Churchmen led the defence of the Church of England's privileges and opposed concessions to DISSENTERS (*see also* HIGH TORY). The term fell from favour in the more pacific religious climate of the mid-18th century, but came back into use in the 1790s. In the 19th century, the High Church party, always influential in North American ANGLICANISM, experienced an English revival in the OXFORD MOVEMENT (*see also* ANGLO-CATHOLICISM; RITUALISM; TRACTARIANISM); their activities aroused fierce opposition from EVANGELICALS or Low Churchmen (*see* LOW CHURCHMANSHIP).

High Commission, Courts of The 1559 Act of Supremacy (*see* ROYAL SUPREMACY) recognized the CROWN'S PREROGATIVE to set up commissions for ecclesiastical affairs. Under ELIZABETH I, besides temporary commissions in most dioceses, commissions for the provinces of Canterbury and York quickly turned into two permanent courts of High Commission. Many practitioners of COMMON LAW resented their activities, and their association with LAUD's policies led to their abolition in 1641. A similar institution, the ECCLESIASTICAL COMMISSION, was set up by JAMES II but collapsed with his regime.

High Farming, term first introduced by James Caird in 1848 in response to the repeal of the CORN LAWS. He argued that high, or scientific, farming – farming that was more business-like and progressive – could overcome the threat of foreign competition and was the best alternative to PROTECTIONISM. The term is also used by medieval historians to refer to the methods employed in 13th-century England by a lord running a DEMESNE for profit.

High Tory, a subgroup of TORIES in the early 18th century, distinguished above all by their fierce commitment to the Church of England. The three main High Tory connections were led by Rochester (*see* HYDE, LAURENCE), Daniel Finch, Earl of Nottingham and Sir Edward Seymour; spokesmen in the COMMONS included William Bromley, Sir Thomas Hanmer and Sir Arthur Annesley. They went into opposition in 1704, attempted to tack a bill against OCCASIONAL CONFORMITY on to the Land Tax Bill in 1704–5, and opposed the UNION with Scotland (1707) because of the guarantees it offered to the PRESBYTERIAN Church. Rochester died in 1711, and Nottingham went over to the WHIGS; Annesley, by this time Earl of Anglesey, remained as their leader in the LORDS, Bromley in the Commons.

Highland Clearances, *see* CLEARANCES, HIGHLAND

Highway Act 1835, a general enactment that developed the system of maintenance for the highways of each PARISH, and empowered the parish to levy a rate for that purpose. The Act required the appointment of parish or district surveyors. Experience proved that the parish was too small an administrative unit; as a result, the PUBLIC HEALTH ACT 1848 made the new local Boards of Health surveyors of highways.

Hillforts, fortified upland settlements of the Iron Age, first appearing *c.*400 BC, with massive, commonly multiple ramparts and complicated entrances. They are evidence of growing wars and tension, following what was probably a relatively peaceful pastoral age, possibly because of increasing pressure of POPULATION. The forts probably served as administrative centres as well as strongholds in time of trouble. The spirited defence of hillforts like MAIDEN CASTLE at the time of the ROMAN CONQUEST, when the CELTIC tribes were defeated, shows how strong the defences could be.

Hingston Down, Battle of, 838, a victory in Cornwall for EGBERT of Wessex over an alliance of Cornishmen and VIKINGS. The battle consolidated Egbert's control over Cornwall and completed the region's subjugation to the kings of WESSEX – and, after them, to the kings of England.

Hispaniola (Little Spain), the Caribbean island, now comprising Haiti and the Dominican Republic, which was unsuccessfully attacked by English forces in 1655. Captain William Kidd, the pirate, claimed to have buried his treasure there at the end of the 17th century.

Historical Demography, the study of POPULATION in the past, especially the application of the methods of demography to historical records. A historical dimension has always been integral to the work of statisticians and political economists interested in population (*see*, e.g., KING; MALTHUS). The modern rise of historical demography dates largely from the 1950s, with the rise of the subject in France and then the UK and USA. Research in the UK has been particularly associated with CAMBRIDGE UNIVERSITY, where it has been linked with the history of the FAMILY. *See also* AGGREGATIVE ANALYSIS; CENSUS; DEMOGRAPHIC TRANSITION; FAMILY RECONSTITUTION; FERTILITY; MORTALITY.

Historical Materialism, a notion fundamental to the writings of Karl MARX; aspects of this have therefore been assimilated into a great deal of ECONOMIC and SOCIAL HISTORY by Marxists in particular. The central idea is that social, cultural and political life is broadly determined by the nature of economic production and distribution, and that the dynamic behind historical change is the tension and conflict between the forces of production (utilization of the resources and technologies of the ECONOMY) and the relations of production (employment and other social and political relations) which follow from this. There is a danger of oversimplifying the notion and ignoring more sophisticated uses and insights gained from it. Critics have done this, arguing that use of the idea of historical materialism has distorted historical interpretations and is reducible to a crude economic determinism. There has, however, always been a range of historical approaches which stress the importance of material production and reproduction and of change in the ownership and distribution of resources in understanding broader social, cultural and political phenomena. In British history this has shown itself in interpretations of the social and political impact of industrialization, for example, and it has been formative in much of the traditional periodization of social and economic history. Today post-structural and post-modern approaches have dismissed the idea of historical materialism, preferring to see the autonomy of culture and language and to question any broader analysis of history which may be seen to serve or even relate to any long-term political purpose or structure.

History Workshop, organization dedicated to 'history from below' and the encouragement of ordinary men and women to write and record their own history. History Workshops were held at the TRADE UNION-funded adult education college, Ruskin College, Oxford from 1967. Led by Raphael Samuel, the group was associated from its early days with the Oral History Society and the Society for the Study of Labour History. It has produced a series of studies of working-class life and other collective works considering popular culture, gender and, more recently, nationalism. The journal *History Workshop* (from 1976) is one of the major forces in broadening historical studies although much of the content is more academic than was initially intended. For much of its existence the journal described itself as one of 'socialist' and 'feminist' historians but this has been recently dropped from the manifesto in the light of the contemporary post-structuralism debate. The organization has been very influential in Britain and outside, particularly in central Europe and Scandinavia, where it has inspired many to follow the same approach.

Hlothere, King of Kent (673–85). He is notable because of his continuation of the tradition of law-giving established in KENT by ETHELBERT. In 684, Hlothere was defeated by his brother Eadric and, after a family feud typical of these early centuries, was forced to share the kingdom.

Hoare–Laval Pact, Dec. 1935, secret agreement devised by Samuel Hoare, the British foreign secretary, and Pierre Laval, the French prime minister, to resolve the Abyssinian crisis following the Italian invasion in Oct. 1935. It was proposed that Italy would receive two-thirds of Abyssinia, enlarging the existing Italian colonies in East Africa and giving further scope for Italian settlement and economic development. In return, Abyssinia was to receive a narrow strip of territory and access to the sea. When news of the pact reached the press on 10 Dec. it was widely denounced as APPEASEMENT of Italian aggression, forcing both Hoare and Laval to resign.

Hobbes, Thomas (1588–1679), philosopher. Oxford-educated and long-term tutor, secretary and friend to the Cavendish family, the Earls of Devonshire, he was one of the Great Tew Circle, discusants who met at the Oxon. home of Lucius Carey. Having already travelled widely on the Continent, from 1641 he sat out the CIVIL WARS in Paris, at one stage tutoring CHARLES II, but returned to England in 1652 to make peace with the regime. At the RESTORATION, Charles gave him a pension and protection from churchmen infuriated by his writings, which included an autobiography. A mild man horrified by the violence around him, his works on law, society and philosophy – particularly his *Leviathan* (1651) – have profoundly influenced political thought, through both their bleak view of human nature and their radical scepticism about the claims of organized religion and traditional legitimacy. *See also* LOCKE, JOHN.

Holidays The word originally meant 'holy-days', the principal feasts of the medieval Church on which the faithful were not supposed to work (*see* CALENDAR CUSTOMS). It has come to mean, especially since the 19th century, time off work and spent away from home, associated with the rise in popularity of the seaside and pleasure resorts. The development of Wakes' Weeks and similar mill and factory shut-downs in industrial towns provided the opportunity to go away, and the RAILWAY system gave many the transport to do so. The rise of Blackpool and other resorts at the end of the 19th century derived from these developments, as well as the institution in 1861 of bank holidays, statutory non-religious days off work in the best time of year to travel. Reductions in working hours and improved pay encouraged the rise of the holiday away; in the 1920s, 1.5 million workers were entitled to paid holiday, a figure which had doubled by 1938, and which octupled in 1939 with the Pay Act. The idea of a paid period to go away, once seen as a luxury for the few, came to be viewed as a right for the many.

Holinshed, Raphael (?–*c.*1580), historian. A London printer, in 1577 he completed a collaborative project – the *Chronicles of England, Scotland and Ireland* – which was entirely dependent on others' research, for example William Harrison's *DESCRIPTION OF ENGLAND* (1577), but a great publishing success. This and later enlarged editions attracted government CENSORSHIP. SHAKESPEARE's history plays are indebted to Holinshed.

Holy Orders, *see* ORDER

Homage, the medieval ceremony by which a tenant acknowledged that he held his land as a FIEF (*see* FEUDAL) from a lord and that he owed obligations to that lord – i.e. that he had become the lord's man (the word is related to the French *homme*). In its classic form, the ceremony involved the tenant, who might be kneeling, putting his joined hands between his lord's. Conventionally it is regarded as FEUDALISM's most characteristic ritual and survives in the CORONATION ceremony.

Home Front, term first coined in WORLD WAR I. It implies that some wars are fought not just by the armed services but by civilian production and the 'nation in arms'. The home front is associated with widespread CONSCRIPTION, RATIONING and government intervention to create a command economy producing munitions rather than consumer goods. In some views it also legitimizes attacks on the enemy civilian population by naval BLOCKADE or bombing. The effort made by France during the FRENCH REVOLUTIONARY and NAPOLEONIC WARS is seen as the first modern case of a home front.

Home Guard, popular name for the Local Defence Volunteers, the volunteer force formed in May 1940 to protect Britain from invasion. Following a stirring speech by CHURCHILL in July, the force's name was officially changed to the 'Home Guard'. It was made up of almost one million men, exempt from military service because of their age or occupation, who responded to a radio appeal for volunteers. Although poorly equipped, the Home Guard symbolized Britain's determination to resist invasion in the summer of 1940. The force, which reached a maximum of 1.6 million in 1942, was never called into action, though sections of it manned anti-aircraft batteries during the BLITZ. It was officially disbanded on 31 Dec. 1944.

Home of the Hirsel, Baron, *see* DOUGLAS-HOME, ALEC

Home Rule, the movement of the 19th and early 20th centuries in favour of the repeal of the Act of UNION with Ireland and of the establishment of a parliament in DUBLIN responsible for internal affairs. It found expression in the Home Government Association founded in 1870 by Isaac BUTT, which won over 50 seats in the general election of 1874. PARNELL's more aggressive leadership concentrated attention on the IRISH QUESTION and helped to convert GLADSTONE to Home Rule in 1885. His conversion split the LIBERAL PARTY and led to the secession of the LIBERAL UNIONISTS. A Home Rule Bill, carried against a background of rising violence, was placed on the statute book shortly before the outbreak of WORLD WAR I in 1914, on the understanding that its implementation would be delayed until after the war. Whatever opportunities may have existed for a peaceful resolution of the Irish Question had by then disappeared, and the Home Rule question was overtaken by the events of the EASTER RISING and the coercion and fighting that followed. *See also* IRISH QUESTION.

Homilies, Book of, a book of sermons issued by the English government. First proposed under HENRY VIII, its publication was delayed until 1547, then it was enlarged in 1563 and 1571. Most Elizabethan clergy had no licence to preach sermons so, in theory, could only preach from the *Book of Homilies*.

Homosexuality and British Law British law has always concerned itself only with acts, not with the abstract notion of homosexuality, which is a comparatively recent concept. CANON LAW penalized homosexual acts, although up to the 12th century, the Church was not consistent in regarding them as a serious sin. English law took its cue on male homosexuality from the Church until recent years, although it has never taken any notice of female homosexuality.

CHRONOLOGY

1534 First parliamentary legislation against all forms of buggery, homosexual or heterosexual: death penalty.

1861 Offences against the Person Act replaces death penalty with imprisonment.

1885 Amendment to CRIMINAL LAW AMENDMENT ACT by Henry Labouchère criminalizes all acts, even those carried out in private.

1895 Trial of Oscar Wilde stimulates public discussion.

1898 Vagrancy Act criminalizes homosexual importuning.

1921 Attempt to legislate penalties against lesbianism fails.
1957 WOLFENDEN REPORT recommends decriminalization.
1967 Sexual Offences Act: homosexual acts decriminalized between civilian consenting adults over 21 in private in England and Wales.
Between **1981 and 1993** homosexual acts were decriminalized in Scotland, Northern Ireland and finally in the Republic of Ireland.
1994 The age of consent for homosexuals was reduced to 18 and legislation is underway to bring it in line with the age of consent for heterosexuals which is 16.
2000 The ban on homosexual men and lesbian women serving in the armed forces was lifted.

Hong Kong, British crown colony on the south coast of China, some 90 miles south of Canton. The territory comprises a total land area of 410 square miles and consists of the island of Hong Kong, the Kowloon peninsula and the adjoining New Territories. As a result of the OPIUM WARS with China, Hong Kong Island was ceded to Britain in perpetuity under the terms of the Treaty of Nanking (1842) and Kowloon was also ceded in perpetuity by the Convention of Peking (1860). The New Territories were leased for a period of 99 years dating from 1 July 1898. Neither the treaties nor the lease have been recognized by the People's Republic of China.

Hong Kong has been a vital strategic base in the Far East; in Dec. 1941, after valiant resistance, it surrendered to the invading Japanese. After WORLD WAR II over a million Chinese refugees fled to Hong Kong and it became an increasingly prosperous centre for the manufacturing production of domestic and electrical goods, international commerce and banking. However the fact that the British government agreed in 1984 to hand back all of Hong Kong (not just the New Territories as they were mandated to do) in 1997 to China – albeit with guarantees about civil and economic freedoms – led to an initial flight of business and capital and continuing anxiety. The 1984 Sino-British Joint Declaration which designated Hong Kong as a Special Administrative Region (SAR) set out guarantees about Hong Kong's way of life until at least 2047. As a thriving capitalist economy with autonomy in all but defence and foreign affairs, it is this prosperity that still seems Hong Kong's greatest safeguard against any interference in its laws and social customs from the Chinese mainland.

Honorius, Roman Emperor (395–423). He is famous as the emperor who, in 410, instructed the people of Britain 'to look to their own safety' – a declaration that marked the effective end of Roman rule in Britain. At the time, however, the order was probably intended to be a temporary measure enabling Honorius to cope better with the usurper CONSTANTINE III as well as the invaders who were attacking Gaul and Italy. In practice, Rome never again possessed the resources to restore its authority in Britain (*see* ROMAN CONQUEST).

Hood, Robin, outlaw. If he ever existed, he probably waylaid travellers going through Barnsdale, Yorks. on the Great North Road (rather than Sherwood Forest in Notts.). Many attempts have been made to identify him – and his great rival, the Sheriff of Nottingham – but none has so far succeeded in pinning him down.

The now familiar dating that places him in RICHARD I's reign was first made by the Scottish historian John Major in 1521, but it is at least as likely that his was a name to conjure with as early as the 13th century since the surname 'Robinhood' has been found in documents dating from that period. The earliest surviving ballads date from the 15th century, but LANGLAND, writing in the late 1300s, already refers to tales about him.

A yeoman in the earliest ballads, by the 16th century he has acquired noble status and an association with Maid Marian. In other ways, the legends came to reflect the hopes and fears of later ages: after the REFORMATION, he became more hostile to rich prelates; and for the 18th-century RADICAL, Joseph Ritson, editor of the first systematic collection of Robin Hood tales and ballads, he was the egalitarian hero who robbed the rich to give to the poor. The notion that he led Anglo-Saxon resistance to Norman oppression goes back no further than Walter Scott's *Ivanhoe*.

Hooker, Richard (*c.*1554–1600), writer. Exeter-born Oxford academic who, on his marriage in 1584, resigned his fellowship for a series of Church appointments – notably, from 1585, the mastership (chaplaincy) of the

Temple Church, London, where he found himself drawn into clashes with his PURITAN colleague Walter Travers. His great work *On the Laws of Ecclesiastical Polity* was published in sections between 1594 and 1662. Although its majestic language has earned him a reputation as 'judicious', it was an all-out attack on PRESBYTERIAN doctrine and a passionate defence of the ELIZABETHAN SETTLEMENT on philosophical grounds. Hooker played a great part in the formation of ANGLICAN theology.

Hooper, John (*c.* 1495–1555), Bishop of Gloucester. A former CISTERCIAN monk, he fled England in 1540 because of his reformist religious views; experience of Zürich (1547–9) made him more radical still. Edward SEYMOUR, Duke of Somerset, made him his chaplain on his return. In 1550–1, he caused a stir by refusing to accept the bishopric of Gloucester if he had to swear a CATHOLIC form of ROYAL SUPREMACY oath and wear certain traditional vestments at his consecration. His climbdown on the latter point was an important indication of the limits on radical change in EDWARD VI's Church. Proving a model PROTESTANT bishop, he was an obvious target for MARY I; his death at the stake for HERESY was unusually agonizing.

Hornby v. Close, 1866. The safety of TRADE UNIONS under the FRIENDLY SOCIETIES Act of 1855, which enabled properly constituted trade societies to prosecute defaulting or dishonest officials, was by this judgment shown to be illusory. The Court of Queen's Bench held that trade unions, though they had ceased to be illegal in 1825, were still established for objects that *were* illegal, because they were in restraint of trade; as a consequence, trade unions were outside the scope of the Act of 1855.

Horsa, *see* HENGIST

Hotspur, *see* PERCY, HENRY

House of Commons, *see* COMMONS, HOUSE OF

House of Correction Corrective prison, to which poor men and women might be sent to be whipped and set to work, and for which London's BRIDEWELL provided a model. Sixteenth-century statutes, culminating in an act of 1610, directed counties to establish such institutions. Misdemeanours such as idle and disorderly conduct, PROSTITUTION, offences against the POOR LAWS, misconduct at work and petty thefts might be punished by short terms in these houses; from the early 18th century, they were also used for the pre-trial detention of petty criminals. From the late 18th century gaols, originally essentially holding institutions, increasingly took on functions previously associated with houses of correction. In 1866, the two institutions were merged into the new category of 'local prison'.

House of Industry, a term that came into favour in the late 18th century, usually denoting a non-residential WORKHOUSE (by then, the latter term had acquired the connotation of residence), often specializing in the training and employment of children. The special advantages of non-residential institutions were that they were cheaper to run, and did not remove children from families.

House of Lords, *see* LORDS, HOUSE OF

Housecarls, an Anglo-Saxon term once believed to describe an axe-wielding troop of élite warriors, created by King CNUT in the early 11th century, who were subject to an elaborate code of behaviour. But modern authorities, rejecting the relevance of late 12th-century Scandinavian sources such as the *Lex Castrensis*, suggest that housecarls were typical members of medieval royal and noble military households.

Housing Act 1923, also known as the 'Chamberlain' Act, as it was passed when Neville CHAMBERLAIN was minister of health. It provided a prototype for subsequent inter-war Housing Acts by attaching a limited subsidy of £20 a year for a fixed period of 20 years for all new houses commissioned by private builders before Oct. 1925. It therefore avoided the open-ended financial commitment which had forced suspension of the 'Addison' Acts (*see* HOUSING AND TOWN PLANNING ACT 1919). Although the Act was initially seen as an emergency programme of limited duration, the time period for commissioning houses was extended until 1929 by the LABOUR government of MACDONALD. 438,000 houses were built under the Act, mainly by private builders.

Housing Act 1924, the most successful of the inter-war Housing Acts. Known as the

'Wheatley' Act after the LABOUR minister of health, John Wheatley, it was aimed primarily at stimulating rented local authority housing. It was to run for 15 years and gave a government subsidy of £9 for 40 years to local authority or private building for rent. The incoming CONSERVATIVE government of 1924 reduced the subsidy to £7 10s in 1926 and it was ended altogether by the NATIONAL GOVERNMENT in 1932. By then, however, over 520,000 houses had been built, mainly by local authorities, the largest number under any inter-war Housing Act.

Housing Act 1930 Known as the 'Greenwood' Act, after the LABOUR minister of health, Arthur Greenwood, the Act laid the basis for large-scale SLUM CLEARANCE. It introduced a subsidy specifically for slum clearance and related to the number of people displaced and rehoused. By paying a subsidy of £2 5s od for 40 years for each person, it encouraged the rehousing of large, poor families and allowed extra subsidies where rehousing costs would be high. Local authorities were allowed to adopt any scheme of rebates or renting they chose, up to a limit of contribution from the rates of £3 15s od per house or flat. All local authorities were also required to draw up plans for clearance of all slums within a five-year period. Owing to the financial crisis of 1931, the Act was not fully implemented until 1933. Under its provisions, 250,000 slum houses were demolished by 1939 and the residents rehoused. By that time, however, it was estimated that there were still over 200,000 slum dwellings remaining.

Housing Act 1946 Passed by the ATTLEE government, the Act granted local authorities a government subsidy of £16 10s od per house built for 60 years, provided this was matched by a local authority subsidy of £5 10s od. Additional grants were available for building on high-cost land, in rural areas, and for the construction of flats. The Act saw 900,000 houses built by 1951, though this fell below the target figure of 240,000 houses a year, a shortfall which contributed to LABOUR's defeat at the polls in 1951.

Housing Act 1952 The Act was passed by the CONSERVATIVE government in order to redeem its election pledge in 1951 to build 300,000 houses per year, following the failure of ATTLEE's government to reach its targets. Housing minister MACMILLAN raised the subsidy for houses built to £26 14s od per house and encouraged private builders to contribute to the programme. The government achieved its target in 1953 with 319,000 houses built, and 348,000 in 1954. By 1957 nearly 1.5 million houses and flats had been constructed.

Housing and Town Planning Act 1919, known as the 'Addison' Act after the minister of health, Christopher Addison, in the postwar coalition government. In part a fulfilment of LLOYD GEORGE's wartime pledge of 'Homes for Heroes', the Act required local authorities to survey housing needs in their areas and make plans for providing the houses indicated. All costs beyond the yield of a penny rate were to be borne by the TREASURY. Rents were to be fixed independently of costs and in line with existing controlled rents for working-class housing. A further Act, the Housing (Additional Powers) Act, offered a subsidy of £150–£160 to any builder to build houses for sale or rent. Although the quality of housing constructed was high, the large costs attached proved insupportable for the Treasury; the operation of the Acts had to be suspended in 1921 because of government economies, and the system of open-ended subsidy was deemed a failure. Only 214,000 houses of the estimated 500,000 required were built before the scheme was wound up, though the provision of government subsidy for house-building marked a major innovation in housing policy and was soon followed by fresh legislation in the HOUSING ACT 1923.

Housing Legislation Grossly substandard housing and accommodation shortages in the 19th century – problems requiring private and public action – resulted from the unplanned growth of industrialization and urbanization earlier in the century. The migration of the surplus rural population to the towns, poverty, the want of scientific and medical knowledge, and the predominant *LAISSEZ-FAIRE* outlook of the time made for a lethal combination that defied all remedial efforts, despite the exposure of scandalous living conditions in such publications as the REPORT ON THE SANITARY CONDITION OF THE LABOURING POPULATION (1842), the work of the SANITARY REFORM MOVEMENT, and the voluntary initiatives of BUILDING

SOCIETIES and philanthropists such as Octavia Hill and George Peabody whose experiments with flatted accommodation (known as model dwellings) were the best known of several similar attempts to show that cheap sanitary accommodation could be built in central London at rents that the working classes could afford. The visual impact of model dwellings was much greater than the numerical effect of such provision which barely touched the fringe of the subject. More important, in the long term, was the framing of housing management principles which became widely diffused through the public sector. State policy was concerned with the closure and clearance of slum properties, and recoiled from any direct engagement with problems of supply and management.

There was no simple unilinear progression from philanthropy through to regulation and state intervention. The first significant departure from the minimalist policy embodied in existing legislation followed the imposition of rent controls in response to popular agitation during WORLD WAR I. Political pressures thereafter prevented any withdrawal from the provision of state-subsidized local authority housing until the 1980s. Then Margaret THATCHER's determination to roll back the frontiers of the WELFARE STATE managed to dislocate the consensus and revolutionized housing policy. COUNCIL HOUSING was sold off, responsibility for finance and construction transferred from local authorities to private housing associations, and restrictions on private, rented accommodation were relaxed to encourage more housing to let in the private sector. For all that, the housing problem remains as intractable as ever.

CHRONOLOGY

1838 SMALL TENEMENTS RECOVERY ACT introduces summary form of eviction.

1840 Select Committee on Health of Towns exposes the extent of slum dwellings in urban areas.

1851 Permissive legislation to enable local authorities to build or purchase houses for working classes concludes in LABOURING CLASSES LODGING HOUSES ACT.

1868 Artisans' and Labourers' Buildings Act empowers local authorities to compel owners to demolish or repair unsanitary houses.

1875 Artisans' and Labourers' Buildings Improvement Act provides for compulsory purchase of areas 'unfit for human habitation'.

1885 Royal Commission on the Housing of the Working Classes appointed, following the publication of *Bitter Cry of Outcast London*.

1890 Housing of the Working Classes Act codifies and consolidates housing legislation, embodying in one act the triple concerns of housing requirements: control of individual houses, treatment of insanitary areas, provision of new accommodation; powers of compulsory purchase were also granted. However, before 1914, little municipal housing was built.

1909 Housing and Town Planning Act amends law relating to housing of working classes, and provides for town-planning schemes.

1915 Increase of Rent and Mortgage Interest (Restrictions) Acts mean that rents of working-class houses controlled, and tenants protected from eviction.

1919–24 In Housing Act 1919 and HOUSING ACTS 1923 and 1924, subsidies provided to encourage building of new houses for working classes.

1930 HOUSING ACT extends subsidies and powers for slum clearance.

1933 Housing (Financial Provisions) Act increases subsidies for SLUM CLEARANCE.

1939 Rent and Mortgage Interest (Restriction) Act extends rent restriction and security of tenure to decontrolled and new houses.

1946 HOUSING ACT.

1947 Furnished Houses (Rent Control) Act establishes rent tribunals to fix the prices of furnished lettings.

1949 Landlord and Tenant Rent Control Act authorizes rent tribunals to determine 'reasonable' rents on application of tenants, who could also apply for recovery of premiums on unfurnished houses and flats.

1952 HOUSING ACT.

1954 Housing Repairs and Rents Act authorizes landlords to increase rents where sufficient repairs to property had been carried out; rent could also be raised to cover increase in maintenance and other costs since 1939.

1957 RENT ACT decontrols large numbers of properties and permits substantial increases in controlled rents.

1958 Housing (Financial Provision) Act provides grants for improvements to private houses.
1959 House Purchase and Housing Act extends grants for improvements.
1961 Housing Act compels landlords of rentals to keep property in repair and proper working order.
1964 Protection from Eviction Act prevents landlords of residential premises from recovering possession without county court order.

Housing Act creates Housing Corporation to assist housing associations in provision of accommodation.
1965 RENT ACT provides for registration of rents, and security of tenure subject to certain conditions; right to possession against tenant not enforceable without court order.
1966 Building Control Act results in improved regulation and control of building and construction work.
1967 Housing Subsidies Act provides financial assistance towards provision, acquisition or improvement of dwellings.

Leasehold Reform Act allows tenants of houses held on long leases at low rents to acquire freehold or extended lease.
1969 Housing Act makes further provision for grants by local authorities towards cost of improvements and conversions; also raises legal standard of fitness for human habitation.
1971 Housing Act increases financial assistance for housing subsidies in development or intermediate areas.
1972 Housing Finance Act provides national rent rebate scheme for council tenants and rent loans for private tenants of unfurnished accommodation; also bases rent of public sector and private unfurnished accommodation on 'fair rent' principle.
1974 Rent Act extends indefinite security of tenure and access to rent tribunals to furnished tenants; residential furnished tenancies of absentee landlords brought into full protection of Rent Acts.

Housing Act enlarges functions of Housing Corporation, provides for registration and giving of assistance to housing associations, and introduces new powers for declaration of Housing Action Areas.
1975 Housing Rents and Subsidies Act repeals provision of Housing Finance Act 1972 related to fixing of public sector rents; new subsidies for local authorities and new town corporations introduced and certain housing associations made eligible for grants.
1976 Rent (Agriculture) Act grants security of tenure for agricultural workers housed by employers, and imposes duties on housing authorities in respect to agricultural workers.
1977 Housing (Homeless Persons) Act requires local authorities to house those homeless persons in 'priority need' – i.e. those with young children or those who are in some other way vulnerable – unless homelessness is shown to be intentional. The Act gave rise to the widespread use of bed and breakfast accommodation to cope with homeless people for whom councils had no other housing available.
1978 Home Purchase Assistance and Housing Corporation Guarantee Act creates 'Homeloan' scheme to provide reduction in cost of house purchase for first-time buyers.
1980 Housing Act introduces flexible subsidy system, repeals 'no-profit rule', and gives local authority tenants of three years' standing right to buy their houses at discounts ranging from 33 to 50 per cent; extended in 1984.

Housing Act transfers remaining rent-controlled dwellings to regulation; 'shorthold' tenure introduced, with security of tenure for limited period.

Howard, Catherine, *see* CATHERINE HOWARD

Howard, Charles (2nd Baron Howard of Effingham, 10th [3rd Howard] Earl of Nottingham) (*c*.1536–1624), Admiral and politician. Lord chamberlain from 1585, in the same year – after various naval and military commands – he became lord high admiral, and directed operations against the 1588 ARMADA. His inharmonious joint command with Essex (*see* DEVEREUX, ROBERT) of the raid on Cadiz (1596) provoked a long feud, fuelled by Howard's creation as earl in 1597, which led to Essex insisting on upstaging him with a grant of the earl marshalcy. Howard supervised the suppression of Essex's 1601 rebellion, and led the Anglo-Spanish peace negotiations of 1604–5, a turning-point in English diplomacy, after a quarter-century of alliance with the

Netherlands. He bitterly resented the growing influence of his cousin, Henry HOWARD, Earl of Northampton, on JAMES I. In 1619 he was removed as lord high admiral, leaving behind a spectacular administrative mess for his successor George VILLIERS, 4th Duke of Buckingham.

Howard, Henry (9th [1st Howard] Earl of Northampton) (1540–1614), politician. The execution of his elder brother – Thomas, the 4th HOWARD Duke of Norfolk – in 1572 left him poverty-stricken, and his lifelong, semi-secret attachment to Catholicism led to repeated investigations and imprisonments. He began to revive the family fortunes in the 1590s, allying himself with Essex (*see* DEVEREUX, ROBERT) against Robert and William CECIL, but full reward awaited the accession of his fellow-intellectual and homosexual JAMES I, who made him Earl in 1604. After Robert Cecil's death, he consolidated his position, backing a policy of reconciliation with Spain and wrecking the ADDLED PARLIAMENT. A fascinating if unlikeable man, he was one of the cleverest and most devious politicians of his day; his numerous writings on politics, philosophy, liturgy and religion await full investigation.

Howard, Thomas (14th Earl of Surrey, 8th [3rd Howard] Duke of Norfolk) (1473–1554), royal servant and soldier. Son of the 2nd Howard duke, he was created Earl in 1514 when his father was restored to the ducal title, for their parts in the FLODDEN victory; he succeeded as duke in 1524. His long life was spent in royal service: lieutenant in Ireland (1520–2), lord high treasurer (from 1522), general against the Scots (1542) (*see* SOLWAY MOSS), and in France (1545). At court, he represented traditionalist aristocratic Catholicism with no liking for clergy or RENAISSANCE HUMANIST reform. His relations with WOLSEY and Thomas CROMWELL were characterized by jealousy coloured by bluff friendship until the time seemed ripe to attack them. His investments in successive nieces – ANNE BOLEYN and CATHERINE HOWARD – as royal wives did not pay off, but he adroitly abandoned them. However, his skills in political escapology were not equalled in his son, Henry Howard, Earl of Surrey, and a bewildered Norfolk found himself in the Tower in Dec. 1546; only HENRY VIII's death saved him from execution. Released and restored to his honours on MARY I's accession, his geriatric last military command against WYATT'S REBELLION in 1554 was a humiliating failure. His second marriage, to the spirited daughter of Edward Stafford, Duke of Buckingham, had ended in a spectacularly messy separation in 1533.

Howard, Thomas (15th Earl of Surrey, 9th [4th Howard] Duke of Norfolk) (1538–72), nobleman. Son of the executed Henry Howard, Earl of Surrey, he dutifully acted his role as England's senior peer with a military command in Scotland (1559–60), but in the crisis of the late 1560s caused by MARY QUEEN OF SCOTS' flight to England, he became a leading candidate for her hand. However, by then grief at the death of successive wives had left him unable to cope with the strain of high politics; he was arrested in 1569 after he fled to his East Anglian estates. Evidence of continuing involvement with the plots around Mary led to his execution in 1572 (*see* RIDOLFI PLOT). Though central to Catholic hopes and a patron of religious conservatives, he died proclaiming his PROTESTANTISM, still valuing the friendship of his old tutor John FOXE.

Howard, Thomas (1st Baron Howard de Walden, 11th [1st Howard] Earl of Suffolk) (1561–1626), seafarer. Second son of the executed 4th HOWARD Duke of Norfolk, his rehabilitation began in the 1580s and was encouraged by his energetic naval service both against the 1588 ARMADA and later, although his 1591 Azores expedition against Spain was marred by Sir Richard Grenville's death. JAMES I gave him his earldom; with his uncle, Henry HOWARD, Earl of Northampton, he formed a pro-Spanish and Catholic-tinged FACTION in government, increasingly influential after Robert CECIL's death in 1612. After triumph in wrecking the ADDLED PARLIAMENT, he became lord high treasurer in 1614. The enmity of George VILLIERS, Duke of Buckingham, led to his dismissal for embezzlement in 1618; he was imprisoned and heavily fined and his career was ruined. His profiteering in government had, however, enabled him to build a monstrously large mansion at Audley End, Essex.

Howden, Roger of, *see* ROGER OF HOWDEN

Hudson's Bay Company, major trading company which opened up the northern and interior regions of CANADA. Prince RUPERT was one of the prime movers to try to wrest the lucrative beaver fur trade from the French. He promoted the syndicate, led by Radisson and Groseilliers, to explore Hudson's Bay, and CHARLES II gave the new company its charter on 2 May 1670. The territory it was given encompasses some 40 per cent of modern Canada, from the Arctic to the Great Lakes. Its first governor (1674–83) was Charles Bayley, a tempestuous QUAKER who was specially released from the Tower of London to take up office. Bayley established trading posts at the mouths of rivers. Highly organized, even ritualized, trading ceremonies were instituted, with muskets, hatchets and needles exchanged for fur, while some tribes, notably the Cree, assumed the role of middlemen and so gained in importance.

The territory controlled by the Company was subsumed into the newly-emerging provinces of 18th- and 19th-century Canada. The first permanent white colony on the central prairies, established on Company land in 1812, was the attempt to settle Scottish Highlanders evicted in the CLEARANCES on the Red River in what would become MANITOBA. The scheme was ill-fated, and settlement was only properly established when the Hudson's Bay Company amalgamated with its younger and jealous rival, the North-West Company, whose Indian traders had massacred the new colonists. In 1869, the Company sold its lands to the new DOMINION of Canada to the east, and the centre and west of the continent were thereby opened up.

Huguenots, nickname of French PROTESTANTS, of uncertain derivation. Persecution by the CATHOLIC French monarchy, particularly in the 1550s and 1560s, brought refugee communities to England. When, in 1685, Louis XIV revoked the Edict of Nantes, which had guaranteed their position, half a million more Huguenots fled, many of them to Britain, carrying tales of French Catholic oppression and cruelty. By 1700, there were about 30 Huguenot churches in LONDON (*see* STRANGER CHURCHES); other communities settled in BRISTOL, PLYMOUTH, Dartmouth, EXETER, EDINBURGH, DUBLIN, Wexford, Cork and elsewhere. Many of the exiles were skilled craftsmen, and they have been credited with the introduction of a variety of new techniques particularly in the weaving of textiles and most notably the production of silk. *See also* MIGRATION.

Hulk, a type of medieval trading ship. By *c.* 1700 the word had come to mean an old ship, dismasted and turned into a harbour depot ship, a hospital, an accommodation ship or a floating crane ('sheer hulk'). The NAVY made much use of hulks instead of shore installations up to the early 20th century. They were also used for prisoners of war (especially 1793–1815) and for convicts, including those awaiting TRANSPORTATION to AUSTRALIA.

Humanism, the mode of thought which pays particular attention to the dignity of humanity and to the importance of human experience. The term is used in two senses: first, the Christian humanism of the 14th- to 16th-century RENAISSANCE; and second the non-theistic humanism of the 19th and 20th centuries.

Humble Petition and Advice, constitutional plan of 1657 produced by a moderate parliamentary majority, seeking to make Oliver CROMWELL into a constitutional monarch. After ARMY opposition to KINGSHIP, a revised version re-established a two-chamber PARLIAMENT but continued the Protectorate (*see* INTERREGNUM). The army remained unenthusiastic.

Hume, David (1711–76), philosopher. A native of Edinburgh, who spent some time at the university in his early teens, Hume passed his career on the fringes of the legal and governmental world, finally as under-secretary of state (1767–8). His philosophical works – including the *Treatise of Human Nature* (1739–40) and the *Enquiry concerning Human Understanding* (1748), which followed LOCKE's example in linking a study of the human mind and emotions with an assessment of the nature and limits of human knowledge – were better regarded on the Continent than in Britain. His political and economic essays, and his *History of England* (1754–62) enjoyed greater success. A sceptical critic of simple moral and political postures, he also attracted notice for his atheism: James Boswell noted with fascination his serene acceptance of death. Hume is today regarded as one of the most powerful thinkers of the SCOTTISH ENLIGHTENMENT.

Humphrey of Gloucester (1390–1447), youngest son of HENRY IV. He was created Duke of Gloucester in 1414. He fought at AGINCOURT, and was prominent in HENRY V's conquest of Normandy. A man of wide intellectual interests – founder of Duke Humphrey's Library at Oxford and a notable patron of scholars – he was also an erratic politician who never quite held the power to which he aspired.

He was PROTECTOR of England only during Bedford's (*see* JOHN OF LANCASTER) absences and regent only when HENRY VI was in France (1430–2). His marriage to Jacqueline of Hainault in 1422 and his subsequent pursuit of her inheritance threatened to undermine the vital Anglo-Burgundian alliance (*see* BURGUNDY AND ENGLAND). In 1428, his marriage was annulled and he married his mistress, Eleanor Cobham; later, when Humphrey was heir presumptive, she was accused of plotting the king's death by sorcery.

After 1435, as Henry V's sole surviving brother, Humphrey saw himself as the executor of the policy of conquest and was bitterly opposed to all peace-making; this resulted in renewed quarrels with Cardinal Henry BEAUFORT and then with the dominant Suffolk (William de la Pole) faction. In 1447, the Earl of Suffolk planned to put him on trial on charges of treason, but five days after his arrest at Bury St Edmunds, Humphrey died, probably of a stroke. He became a political martyr, the 'Good Duke' to whose memory all those who opposed either the court or peace with France would appeal.

Hundred, from the late Anglo-Saxon period, a local territorial unit that was a subdivision of the SHIRE. In theory – but often not in practice – it comprised 100 HIDES.

All the freemen domiciled within a hundred would meet monthly as a 'hundred-court', which was responsible for solving local disputes, overseeing the peace and punishing crime (*see also* TITHING). Although first mentioned only in the 10th century – in the Hundred Ordinance of EDGAR's reign (or a little earlier) – it is assumed that such a local institution had existed for a long time previously. Its responsibilities were greatly increased by the legislation of later Anglo-Saxon kings, and it became the bedrock of English LOCAL GOVERNMENT for many years afterwards. For instance, the evidence supplied on oath by juries from each hundred-court was crucial to the collection of the material written down in *DOMESDAY BOOK* and the HUNDRED ROLLS. They also gave testimony on crime and property to the king's itinerant justices.

Hundred Days, the period from March to June 1815 during which Napoleon escaped from exile on Elba and was finally overthrown at WATERLOO.

Hundred Rolls, the name given to the records of two inquiries carried out by EDWARD I's government. The first, in 1274–5, investigated the loss of royal rights and the misdeeds of officials. The second, in 1279, was a village-by-village survey of landholding in England, which was more comprehensive than the *DOMESDAY BOOK* survey, though less used by historians largely because the returns survive for only five counties. *See also* HUNDRED.

Hundred Years War, a term invented in the late 19th century and conventionally applied to the Anglo-French wars between 1337 and 1453. Tension over the status of AQUITAINE had already led to the wars of 1294–1303 and 1324–6, but the renewal of this conflict in 1337 took on a new twist in Jan. 1340 when, under pressure from his Flemish allies, EDWARD III formally assumed the title 'King of France'. Although France was larger and richer than England, its kings Philip VI and John II could never match Edward politically or militarily, and they suffered humiliating defeats at SLUYS, CRÉCY and POITIERS (where John II was captured). This enabled Edward to negotiate the profitable treaty of BRÉTIGNY in 1360.

However, in Charles V, the French found a king who could skilfully exploit his resources, and following the renewal of war in 1369, they generally had the upper hand. In 1396, RICHARD II agreed to a 28-year truce. Charles VI's mental illness led to savage rivalry between the Burgundian and Armagnac factions, and the ruthless HENRY V found irresistible the opportunities that then presented themselves. The triumph at AGINCOURT, the conquest of Normandy (*see* VERNEUIL), the Burgundian alliance and the treaty of TROYES left his baby heir, HENRY VI, widely recognized as king of France, and the English in control of Paris and much of northern France as well as Aquitaine.

However, Charles VII did not yield, and after 1429 – in part thanks to Joan of Arc – the fortunes of war swung back in France's favour, as became clear at the Congress of ARRAS in 1435. The English held on stubbornly for years, but then, between 1450 (the battle of FORMIGNY) and 1453 (the battle of CASTILLON), they were swept out of both Normandy and Aquitaine. Although this is traditionally regarded as the end of the conflict, the intermittent sequence of wars continued until the fall of CALAIS in 1558; indeed, English rulers bore the title 'King of France' until 1802.

Hunger Marches, *see* JARROW CRUSADE

Hungry Forties, phrase that is at once an evocation and summary of the deep depression, widespread unemployment and popular discontent that characterized the 1840s, the decade that witnessed FAMINE and mass MIGRATION from Ireland as well as the CHARTIST challenge on the mainland.

Huntingdon, Henry of, *see* HENRY OF HUNTINGDON

Husbandry Convertible, *see* CONVERTIBLE HUSBANDRY

Hwicce, Kingdom of the, an Anglo-Saxon kingdom in the Severn valley, roughly coterminous with the modern dioceses of Worcester and Gloucester. It is generally assumed that it was formed on the basis of a distinct Anglo-Saxon settlement by King PENDA of Mercia in the early 7th century. The kingdom, which had its own bishopric at Worcester, is mentioned as paying tribute in the *TRIBAL HIDEAGE*, and was eventually incorporated into MERCIA in the time of OFFA.

Hyde, Edward (1st Earl of Clarendon) (1609–74), politician and historian. The son of a Wilts. gentleman, he was educated at Oxford and called to the bar. He became a member of the Great Tew Circle gatherings at the Oxon. home of Lucius Carey (or Cary), 2nd Viscount Falkland (*c.* 1610–43), at which thinkers and writers sympathetic to Christian humanism met to discuss issues of the day as rationally and openly as possible. Hyde was elected MP in 1640 and was associated with the opposition. In the LONG PARLIAMENT he supported the impeachment of Strafford (*see* WENTWORTH, CHARLES), though he tried to prevent his execution. In 1641 he voted against the GRAND REMONSTRANCE, and became an adviser to CHARLES I. He drafted several declarations for him, and was expelled from Parliament. He was made chancellor of the Exchequer in 1643, and as councillor to the Prince of Wales (later CHARLES II) from 1644 was a (usually unheeded) voice against CAVALIER extremism. In 1646 he accompanied the Prince of Wales to Jersey, and there began writing a *History of the Great Rebellion* – one of the most important contemporary accounts of the CIVIL WARS and INTERREGNUM. During the next few years he lived in several parts of the Continent, latterly with the exiled king, standing in defence of ANGLICANISM against Roman Catholic courtiers.

In 1660 he was closely involved in drawing up the Declaration of BREDA. In the same year his daughter Anne married James, Duke of York (the future JAMES II) – a marriage that was to produce the princesses (and future queens) MARY and ANNE. Accompanying Charles II on his return to London, he was created Earl of Clarendon in 1661 and dominated the administration for the next few years. He favoured the restoration of moderate EPISCOPACY, and opposed the king's policy of indulgence, though the repressive CLARENDON CODE was not wholly of his devising. Cautious and conservative in government, Clarendon failed to see the need to conciliate and manage PARLIAMENT, and he soon became vulnerable to his courtier enemies. In 1663 there was an abortive attempt to impeach him, while the unsuccessful Second DUTCH WAR of 1665–7 generated further criticism. His dismissal was engineered by Sir Henry Bennet, 1st Earl of Arlington, and Sir William Coventry in 1667. Fearing IMPEACHMENT, he went into exile in France, where he completed his *History*.

Hyde, Laurence (4th [1st Hyde] Earl of Rochester) (1641–1711), politician. Second son of Edward HYDE, 1st Earl of Clarendon, he returned to England at the RESTORATION and became an MP. His sister's marriage to the Duke of York (later JAMES II) made him uncle to James's children, putative heirs to the throne; both his nieces, MARY and ANNE, were in fact to become queen. Rochester became a lord commissioner for the Treasury on Danby's (*see* OSBORNE, THOMAS) resignation in 1679, and first lord after Shaftesbury's (*see* COOPER, ANTHONY ASHLEY) dismissal. He resisted calls for the recall of Parliament after the EXCLUSION CRISIS. Riding high in royal favour, he was made an earl in 1681, and under James II was made lord high treasurer. He took instruction in Catholicism, but refused to convert, was edged out by the more compliant Sunderland (*see* SPENCER, HENRY) and dismissed in 1687. After the invasion of William of Orange (the future WILLIAM III), he proposed the calling of Parliament, where he argued for a regency in order to preserve the notion that James was the rightful king. Later he became close to Mary and was leader of the HIGH CHURCH party. He was made lord lieutenant of Ireland in 1700 but never took up his post. During the first year of his niece Queen Anne's reign, he, Daniel Finch (1st Earl of Nottingham), and Edward Seymour represented the HIGH TORIES in an administration headed by GODOLPHIN and the Duke of Marlborough (*see* CHURCHILL, JOHN), but his insistence on the pursuit of HIGH CHURCH measures led to his resignation in 1703. During these years, he oversaw the publication of his father's history of the civil wars which was published in 1702–4.

Hywel Dda ('The Good') (?–950), King of DYFED. A grandson of RHODRI MAWR, he became king before the year 918. The English kings generally accorded him pre-eminence among the Welsh rulers, and after 942, he used his dynastic links to impose his rule on GWYNEDD.

There are three reasons why he occupies a special place in the history of early Welsh KINGSHIP: his reputation as the instigator of the written collection of the customary laws of the Welsh (*see* HYWEL DDA, LAWS OF); his pilgrimage to Rome in 928 or 929; and his status as the only pre-Norman Welsh ruler from whose reign a coin survives (a single penny minted at CHESTER). He seems to have been a powerful ruler inspired by the example of his 10th-century English contemporaries (*see* ATHELSTAN), but his involvement in Welsh dynastic politics in no way differed from that of his predecessors or successors.

Hywel Dda, Laws of All collections of early medieval Welsh law survive in 13th-century manuscripts. Many of these manuscripts attribute the collection of this material to the 10th-century King HYWEL DDA, but it is impossible to believe that he did more than start the process. Disentangling the early material within the law texts is a complex task, but it is at least clear that some of it must date from long before the surviving manuscripts. A strong candidate for organizing the compilation of the laws is RHYS AP GRUFFUDD.

I

Iceni, the pre-Roman British tribe established in modern Norfolk and northern Suffolk. Before the ROMAN CONQUEST, they showed little sign of having been influenced by either Rome or their southern tribal neighbours. The Iceni were given CLIENT KINGDOM status during the early stages of the conquest and retained this until the death of their king Prasutagus in AD 60. Roman intervention then provoked the savage revolt of his widow, Queen BOUDICCA, and the Iceni thereafter came under the direct rule of Rome. The territory formed a *CIVITAS* with its capital at Caistor-by-Norwich.

Iconoclasm, the destruction of religious imagery and art (hatred of such imagery being 'iconophobia'). Inherited from Judaism, the impulse to exclude art from religion has, in Christianity, constantly been at war with the ideas of the beauty of holiness and of worshipping God with the aid of art. Medieval LOLLARD iconophobia occasionally broke out in iconoclasm, but it was not until the English REFORMATION that image-smashing became prominent, backed by the authorities under EDWARD VI and ELIZABETH I (despite her personal attempts to discourage it).

Love of religious art grew once more under the early Stuarts, particularly among ARMINIANS, but the violent reaction to Arminianism in the CIVIL WARS of the 1640s produced further iconoclastic outbreaks with official encouragement. Thereafter, iconoclasm ceased to be of significance, although Low Churchmen remained suspicious of religious art (*see* LOW CHURCHMANSHIP).

Illegitimacy, birth outside marriage. Illegitimacy, or bastardy, has always been a recognizable feature of British social systems. It has rarely carried enormous stigma, particularly given the fluid unofficial definition of MARRIAGE among lower-status communities, its loose official definition until HARDWICKE'S MARRIAGE ACT of 1753 in England and Wales, and the separate nature of marriage law in Scotland. Where illegitimacy figures can be recovered from parish REGISTERS and later sources, they show substantial variations over both time and place, with historically very high levels at the end of the 16th century, very low levels at the end of the 17th, and rising rates in the 18th and early 19th centuries as well as in recent decades. These shifts reflect changing attitudes to extra- or pre-marital sex. There has been some consistently high local concentration of illegitimacy over several centuries, for example in north-east Scotland, indicating the importance of long term and often localized cultural factors.

Illustrated London News, the first of the weekly pictorial papers to be published in England. It was founded in 1842 by Herbert Ingram, an American printer and newsagent, who had noted the enormous popular interest generated by a few crude illustrations in one of the ordinary weeklies. *ILN's* staff artists travelled the globe to supply sketches of battles, explorations and courtroom dramas. The paper's woodcuts, drawings and latterly photographs have made it the most important single pictorial source for the social history of modern Britain.

Immigration, *see* MIGRATION

'Immortal Seven', 1688, the signatories of the 30 June invitation to William of Orange (the future WILLIAM III) to invade England. They were Danby (*see* OSBORNE, THOMAS), Shrewsbury (*see* TALBOT, CHARLES), Devonshire, Lord Lumley, Edward Russell, Henry Sidney and Bishop Compton of London.

Impeachment, criminal trials initiated in the House of COMMONS, with the House of LORDS acting as judges: this form of procedure is a survival of the normal procedure in a MANORIAL or seigneurial court leet, with the Commons representing the presenting jury, the Lords the suitors of the Court and the lord CHANCELLOR the office of the manorial lord. It evolved during the 14th century (*see* GOOD PARLIAMENT), fell into disuse after the mid-15th century, and was revived, at the initiative of Sir Edward COKE, in the Parliament of 1621. Frequently started or threatened as a way of trying to oust unpopular royal ministers (including Roger Boyle, 1st Earl of Orrery; Lionel Cranfield, 1st Earl of Middlesex; Warren Hastings, governor general of British India; and Robert Heath, Chief Justice of the KING'S BENCH (1642–5)); *see also* HYDE, EDWARD; LAUD, WILLIAM; WENTWORTH, THOMAS, it was used with diminishing frequency after GEORGE I's reign, with its last employment in Britain coming in 1806 (though a similar procedure is still very much a part of the US constitution).

Imperial Institute One of many initiatives designed to give the BRITISH EMPIRE purpose and cohesion, it was founded in 1887 as a memorial to Queen VICTORIA's Jubilee and formally opened in 1893. Its object was to bring together into one permanent exhibition the products of the British colonies and dependencies, and generally to collect statistics and useful information respecting local conditions. It came under the control of the BOARD OF TRADE in 1902.

Imperial Preference, a concept associated with Joseph CHAMBERLAIN which summarized his plans for the development of the resources of the BRITISH EMPIRE behind a defensive tariff. A central feature of the campaign for tariff reform, imperial preference represented the most controversial attempt to halt Britain's relative economic decline before the debate on Britain's entry into the EEC (*see* EUROPEAN UNION). It was adopted by the NATIONAL GOVERNMENT in 1931, during the international depression, was extended to the DOMINIONS by the Ottawa Agreement of 1932 (*see* OTTAWA CONFERENCE), and applied to the Crown Colonies in 1933. Preferential arrangements for goods traded within the COMMONWEALTH survived until Britain's entry into the Common Market in 1973, after which they were gradually phased out to conform to EEC regulations. Some special agreements have survived to support particularly vulnerable groups of Commonwealth producers. *See also* TARIFF REFORM LEAGUE.

Imperial Theory of Kingship English kings in the 10th and 11th centuries adopted the practice of making occasional use of imperial titles. These reflect their predominance over British (i.e. Cymru or Welsh) rulers who, from time to time, attended their courts. King EDGAR received a quasi-imperial coronation in 973, and Byzantine titles such as *basileus* were used up until the time of WILLIAM I THE CONQUEROR. The conquest, and attempted conquest, of Wales, Ireland and Scotland in the 12th and 13th centuries ensured that the English monarchy retained this imperial character, sometimes bolstered by allusions to King ARTHUR's rule over the whole of the British Isles.

In medieval political thought, an empire was a jurisdiction that had no earthly overlord under God. Naturally most kings took for granted that they were emperors within their own kingdoms. During the RENAISSANCE, political theorists were encouraged to look afresh at the powers of ancient Roman emperors as relevant to modern kingdoms. The claim that England was an empire of itself was an important part of HENRY VIII's break with the pope, but there remained an unresolved tension between the ancient Roman precedents of absolute power concentrated in the monarch and the role played by PARLIAMENT in English government.

Imperial rhetoric faded from royal claims during the 17th century, but an informal use of the term 'BRITISH EMPIRE' arose as a result of renewed colonial conquests in the 18th and 19th centuries. In 1876, DISRAELI revived the imperial title of INDIA and annexed it to the British crown; this title was extinguished by the India Independence Act 1947. *See also* DIVINE RIGHT; IMPERIALISM.

Imperialism, extension of the power of the state through the acquisition of other territories to create an empire, the subjugation of the people in those territories (often through war), and their economic exploitation. The term itself emerged in the 1890s, taken up by Joseph CHAMBERLAIN and his followers as part of the move to develop and extend the

BRITISH EMPIRE rather than concentrate on home development. The word was swiftly taken into other languages, in the contest between the European powers for territorial gains in the SCRAMBLE FOR AFRICA and other confrontations. All apologists for empire claimed they were extending the bounds of civilization for the common good. Within a short space of time the term was being subjected to critical scrutiny, first in J.A. Hobson's *Imperialism* (1902), which was developed in Lenin's *Imperialism as the Highest Stage of Capitalism* (1915). Lenin argued that the tendency of capitalism towards MONOPOLY, to safeguard profits, drove capitalists to search for new profits abroad through imperial expansion; rival empires would inevitably fight and this was the final stage of capitalism before revolution supervened.

However, he failed to recognize non-economic elements in imperial expansion, such as race or national power. Certainly, territorial empires have tended to founder in the course of the 20th century, but not necessarily through war and revolution. The newer manifestations of imperialism have tended to be the cultural imperialism of the multinational economic combines, especially of the USA, summed up in the term 'Coca-Colanization'. *See also* INFORMAL EMPIRE.

Imperium, *see* BRETWALDA

Imphal-Kohima, Battle of, *see* KOHIMA-IMPHAL, BATTLE OF

Import Duties Act 1932 The Act broke with Britain's tradition of free trade by placing import duties on most foreign goods. Passed by the NATIONAL GOVERNMENT at the trough of the DEPRESSION, it provided significant relief for hard-pressed domestic industries. The OTTAWA CONFERENCE led to preferential treatment of goods from the COMMONWEALTH.

Imprisonment for Debt From 1352, courts would, under certain circumstances, order the imprisonment of debtors until they had satisfied creditors who had sued for the recovery of debts. In the 16th century the high courts, competing with one another for business, developed new 'expeditious' forms of action, facilitating imprisonment. From the 16th until the mid-19th centuries, imprisoned debtors constituted a large proportion of the total prison population. Concentrated especially in the high court prisons, Fleet and King's Bench, the CLINK (until the early 18th century) and the MARSHALSEA, they could also be found in town and county gaols. Since their imprisonment could be argued to serve private rather than public interests, their plight attracted widespread concern. 'Acts of grace', providing for their release under certain conditions, were issued by the crown in the early 17th century, and by Parliament from the mid-17th century. In the early 18th century the bankruptcy laws were liberalized, to facilitate non-punitive settlements, and procedures were established whereby debtors whose cases had gone to court could seek release at any time. Because they were held on civil and not criminal charges, debtors were allowed substantial autonomy, and (if they could pay) relatively comfortable living conditions, including sometimes the privilege of making day trips out, or settling in the immediate neighbourhood of prisons (termed 'living within the rules'). Creditors complained that such conditions were insufficiently deterrent; in the mid- and later 19th century, stricter regulations were imposed. However, pre-trial imprisonment was progressively restricted from 1729, and abolished in 1838. Creditors' powers were further abridged in 1869. It remains possible for courts to order the imprisonment of persons not making payments – such as fines or alimony – ordered by the courts.

Impropriations, *see* FEOFFEES FOR IMPROPRIATIONS

Improvement, standard approving term for change from the late 17th century, when its use was extended from a primarily agricultural to a broader economic and social context, for example in the title of Andrew Yarranton's *England's Improvement by Foreign Trade* (1677). The contrasting term of disapproval was 'innovation'. Local acts to provide urban public services – paving, lighting, cleansing, policing and the like – common from the mid-18th to the later 19th centuries, were termed 'improvement acts', and the bodies set up to administer these services 'improvement commissions'. Their role was taken over by local authorities at the end of the 19th century.

Improvement Commissions, *see* IMPROVEMENT

In Place of Strife, title of a White Paper prepared by Barbara Castle, Secretary of State for Employment and Productivity, for the WILSON government in 1969 to regulate the power of the TRADE UNIONS, with the ultimate sanction of legal proceedings if infringed. The legal provisions raised bitter controversy within the Labour movement, and with many MPs threatening to vote against the Bill, the government was forced to drop the legal sanctions, relying instead on voluntary agreement by the unions to abide by the spirit of the proposals. Seen as a humiliating climbdown by the Wilson government in the face of union pressure, it fuelled the determination of the HEATH government to attempt its own INDUSTRIAL RELATIONS ACT in 1971.

Inchtuthil, site near Dunkeld, Tayside, chosen for the new LEGIONARY FORTRESS that was set up in *c.*AD 83 to consolidate AGRICOLA's conquests in Scotland. It was intended to be the centre of a ring of fortifications around the Highlands, which have been traced by archaeological excavation. However, it was abandoned and systematically dismantled soon after 86 when the Romans decided to base their troops in the SCOTTISH LOWLANDS.

Incidents of Feudalism, *see* ESCHEATOR

Inclosures, *see* ENCLOSURES

Income Tax, 'progressive' tax on earned and unearned income. Introduced by PITT THE YOUNGER in 1798 as a war emergency measure, it was abolished in 1816 but restored by PEEL in 1842 (at a rate of 7 pence in the pound on incomes over £150) to smooth the transition towards a FREE TRADE economy. GLADSTONE, though equally keen to abolish what he regarded as a temporary tax, was forced to raise it to 1 shilling 2 pence in the pound on the outbreak of the CRIMEAN WAR. It was only towards the close of the 19th century that taxation came to be thought of as an essential instrument of social betterment and economic management. In the 20th century, this has been one of the principal purposes of income tax, especially under LABOUR governments who have seen the tax system as a means of helping balance inequalities of wealth, though in the 1997 election Tony BLAIR was convinced that any threat of an increase in the rate of income tax would weaken LABOUR's chances of electoral victory and has been anxious to portray Labour as a party of low taxation in government.

Incomes Policies Deployed periodically by a succession of UK governments from 1948 until 1978, they were an attempt to deal with the persistent problem of INFLATION by obtaining a collective agreement between TRADE UNIONS, employers and the government that wage settlements would be kept within a certain limit or 'norm'. Policies varied according to whether they were voluntary or backed by legal compulsion. The defeats of the HEATH government in 1974 and the CALLAGHAN government in 1979 were attributed to the too inflexible imposition of incomes policies. They were eschewed by the CONSERVATIVE government of Margaret THATCHER as being incompatible with a free market economy. *See also* STOP-GO.

Incumbent, *see* PARISH

Incunabula (or incunables), term for the earliest books, those printed before 1501. The word derives from the Latin for 'swaddling clothes'.

Indemnity Acts, any acts indemnifying people from punishment. The term is applied especially to a series of acts passed from 1727, protecting DISSENTERS who had failed to take the sacrament before taking public office, as required by the CORPORATION ACT of 1661. The acts enabled them to escape without incurring penal consequences.

Indenture, a form of written contract between two parties – so called because the document was cut in pieces along an indented line and each party kept a matching portion. 'Indentures of retainer' record the terms on which a man was engaged to serve his lord, normally specifying his wages and, if it was a long-service contract, his retaining fee. The earliest surviving indentures of retainer date from the 13th century, but references in narrative sources suggest that retainers received fees and wages much earlier. The most common form of indenture in later centuries was for APPRENTICESHIP.

Indentured Servants Young men and women escaped 17th-century British economic misery by contracting under INDENTURE to work in one of the NEW WORLD colonies for a term of years, in return for the costs of emigration and maintenance and an eventual cash payment. Although their labour was crucial, particularly to developing plantations, they were replaced during the 18th century (and even earlier on West Indian islands) by large-scale importation of African SLAVES. Indentured labour was also important in providing work forces for many 19th-century imperial ventures, e.g. Chinese in AUSTRALIA and Indians in Southern and East AFRICA.

Independent Labour Party, parliamentary political party which was the precursor of the post-1900 LABOUR PARTY, and existed alongside it until soon after WORLD WAR II. Founded by Keir HARDIE in 1893 to have working-class members returned to PARLIAMENT who were unconnected with the LIBERAL PARTY, the party was one of the affiliated organizations in the LABOUR REPRESENTATION COMMITTEE of 1900. It had not previously had direct links with TRADE UNION organizations and continued to tread a separate path; ILP MPs were not bound to take the Labour whip, although they almost always followed the broad party line. Although the party won three seats in the 1945 general election, any remaining influence was lost with the death of its leader, James Maxton, in 1946.

Independent Television (ITV), commercial television network financed by advertising, founded in 1956 as a counterweight to the licence-funded BBC. ITV has usually followed a more populist path in programme-making. Regional television companies are given fixed-term franchises, all of which are reviewed together, to broadcast programmes.

Independents, a term first used in the 1640s, which is confusing because it was employed in two different senses – religious and political – to describe groups that overlapped but were not identical.

In church government, the Independents normally rejected separatism but advocated decentralized authority, and their brethren in Massachusetts Bay did implement such a church order; for this reason, in both England and NEW ENGLAND, their 19th-century descendants were styled CONGREGATIONALISTS. Similarly, it was on grounds of church government that the Independents opposed even a modified Presbyterian restructuring of the Church of England in the WESTMINSTER ASSEMBLY. During Oliver CROMWELL's ascendancy, with clergyman John Owen much in his confidence, several hundred Independent ministers served in parish posts. Their position was spelled out in detail in the Savoy Declaration of 1658.

In politics, the Independents were, among those fighting CHARLES I, the least enthusiastic about an alliance with the Presbyterian Scots, and less convinced than 'political Presbyterians' of the need to negotiate a deal with the king. This group included Oliver Cromwell, and was stronger in the army than in PARLIAMENT.

After the failure of COMPREHENSION in 1689, Presbyterians and Independents attempted a rapprochement known as 'the Happy Union' (1691), but it soon collapsed amid theological wrangles. None the less, the two groups did collaborate in lobbying for removal of the remaining civil disabilities upon Protestant Dissenters (*see* DISSENTING DEPUTIES).

In the 18th century the term 'Independent' was principally used to refer to backbench MPs who did not owe their seats to patrons, and prided themselves on judging 'measures not men'.

India The 'jewel in the crown' of 19th-century British IMPERIALISM, its protection was crucial to Britain's foreign policy in the Far East, with the movement of Indian opium to China providing an important linchpin for many decades. The administration and army in India shaped the employment and outlook of the British middle classes.

English interest in Indian trade developed from 1600, when the EAST INDIA COMPANY was founded. The initial intention was to tap into the production and trading networks of a developed society, and acquire exotic goods, especially spices, for European markets. The trade was controversial because English goods were not in great demand in India, and purchases had to be financed by exports of bullion. The development of a trade in Indian printed calicoes caused further controversy *c.*1720: domestic producers argued that English manufact-urers were disadvantaged by the trade and protective legislation was introduced in the course of the 18th century; however, Indian demand for British WOOLLENS and metalware especially expanded. Also important was the blossoming of a triangular trade, whereby Indian goods – including opium – were exported to China, and Chinese goods – including TEA – to Britain and elsewhere. Trade within the Indian ocean was not a Company monopoly, and numerous British and other European 'free merchants' developed that sector or activity. The British relationship with India changed in the 18th century as the Mughal Empire slowly disintegrated and was superseded by a heterogeneous mass of successor states, and as the increasing propensity of European powers to pursue European rivalries by engaging in heavy armed conflict with competitors in extra-European settings spurred the Company to shift the focus of its activities initially in a military, latterly in a governmental direction. During the SEVEN YEARS WAR, British troops in the service of the Company defeated both French and Indian forces. As a result, Company power extended outwards from its three trading bases, Bombay, Madras and Calcutta – significantly in the case of Madras, but most dramatically in Calcutta where the British effectively reduced the Nawab of Bengal to a puppet, and were granted certain jurisdictional rights over the whole province by the Mughal emperor. Subsequently a kind of 'domino effect' became evident, that was to provide the basis for much of the ensuing extension of British power in India: some Indian rulers who sought British protection lost their autonomy; others who defied them were regarded as disloyal and/or aggressors, and crushed.

The expansion of British power caused problems of discipline within the Company. Great fortunes (the PITT family's, for example) had sometimes previously been made in Indian trade. Opportunities expanded after PLASSEY. The wealth and misdeeds of former company officers enriched by Indian gains – so-called NABOBS – became a byword in Britain, and ambitious young men rushed to enlist in the Company's service. Successive Company administrators, CLIVE and Warren Hastings (1732–1818), tried to curb the corrosive effects of private interest by limiting or forbidding the taking of presents or bribes, and the participation in trade by Company officers with administrative rather than trading responsibilities. (In practice, the chance to make a killing seems to have waned from the 1770s. From that time, it has been argued, British traders in India could by sustained application amass enough wealth to sustain a genteel lifestyle, but rarely more.) Concern that the process of extracting wealth from India did not get out of hand, and that a portion of such gains be directed to public coffers, prompted various parliamentary interventions from the later 1760s, notably the Regulating Act of 1773, which established the post of governor-general, supreme over the governors of the other trading regions, and the INDIA BILL of 1784, which subjected the Company's governmental activities to the supervision of a BOARD OF CONTROL. Expectations as to standards of propriety developed in Britain, however, rose more quickly than men on the spot were able, or perhaps even wanted to achieve, resulting in fierce criticism of both Clive's and Hastings' activities, pursued, in Hastings' case to the point of IMPEACHMENT.

The later 18th century saw the growth of scholarly interest in Indian civilization among Company officials and others, including Hastings himself, and Sir William Jones (1746–94), first judge of the British Supreme Court in Calcutta. In part a manifestation of sympathetic interest such scholarship was also intended to provide the basis for more effective British rule. The War of AMERICAN INDEPENDENCE and FRENCH REVOLUTIONARY and NAPOLEONIC WARS saw British troops again in combat with French forces and their Indian allies, and further extensions of British power, though westward expansion met formidable opposition from the dynamic Marathas. CORNWALLIS, when he took over as governor general in 1786, inherited a Company already largely reconfigured by his predecessors into a military and administrative body; his period of office consolidated it in that mould. Cornwallis, who had recovered in esteem after the débâcle of YORK TOWN, firmly placed his stamp upon India, over which he had been given a personal authority almost unique in its history. He reasserted the power of the state and the Company, and cleansed its administration, dividing it into the commercial and political branches, which was the beginning of the CIVIL SERVICE, while Europeanizing the service by dismissing all Indian high officials. He also tackled the revenue and land tenure system, introducing reform which persisted until 1947 and beyond, and brought in an English-style legal and penal code. Cornwallis's rule until 1793 effectively made the British the replacement of the Mughal emperors, both in overall control and in the manner of working through client dependent states.

Cornwallis had not pursued an aggressive military policy; his successor, Lord Wellesley, did, especially because of French involvement in India, notably through the southern Indian ruler Tipu Sultan. Victory over Tipu Sultan at Seringapatam in 1799 ended the MYSORE wars and gave Britain the beginnings of dominance in the south, as well as opening the way to further territorial ambitions and gains: annexing Madras and the Carnatic, half of the northern state of Oudh, establishing garrisons in Hyderabad, and the first victories against the warrior Marathas. After Wellesley's recall in 1805, India was freer of British military activity, although it was the springboard for the seizure of Mauritius and Java (*see* SINGAPORE), while banditry flourished in many central regions.

Trade with India was one of the consistent underpinnings of British rule. The new Company charter of 1813 was a recognition of the need for freer trade. Exports of COTTON goods to India flourished, especially at the cheaper end of the market, at the end of the Napoleonic Wars, while the promotion of a domestic cotton industry and the first stages of tea-growing brought economic change in many regions. The arrival of the Marquess of Hastings in 1813 meanwhile saw the revival of military action: a frontier war with the Gurkhas in Nepal in 1815–16, the defeat of the Pindari bandits in central India by 1818, and the associated eclipse of the Marathas. Many Indian states concluded treaties with the British, becoming their client. Thus by 1818 British control was extended over very considerable portions of India; successive administrators saw it as their task not only to extend that control further, but to bring new prosperity, and moral and religious change, to India.

The Evangelical and Utilitarian impulses, the former given shape in the toleration of Christian missionary activity from 1813 and the latter embodied in James Mill's 1817 *History of India*, were given full rein during Lord William Cavendish-Bentinck's governor-generalship from 1828–35. The moralistic crusade against *suttee*, the burning of widows on their husbands' funeral pyres, and *thuggee*, the central Indian practice of robbery and ritual murder in the name of the goddess Kali, were the most visible aspects. Longer-lasting in its impact was the far greater Anglicization of Indian education and institutions, with the establishment of schools and colleges, the imposition of English as the official language of India (replacing the Persian of the Mughal Empire), and legal codification and reform under Thomas Babington Macaulay (1800–59).

Territorial expansion had continued with the conquest of parts of BURMA after the war of 1823–6 (with the annexation of Lower Burma in 1852 and of Upper Burma in 1886), while the threat posed by Russia prompted the first of the AFGHAN WARS of 1838–42. Failure at Kabul was compensated by the annexation of Sind in 1843, and then, following the two Sikh Wars of 1845 and 1848–9, the annexation of the Punjab. The Punjab was to become a model of British administration and control, and prospered; however, the new governor-general, James Ramsay, Marquess of Dalhousie, who ruled from 1848–56, continued a vigorous westernizing policy. This was to extend British rule but cause considerable animosity and resentment which flared up in the INDIAN MUTINY of 1857–8, a year after his recall.

The Mutiny was a shock, and a turning-point in British involvement in India, for after it the East India Company was disbanded under the Government of India Act of 1858. Responsibility was transferred to a new department of government, with a secretary of state, a legislative council, and a viceroy in place of the governor-general. With a new form of administration, albeit one firmly based upon the Company's antecedents, came a new consciousness and the full flowering of the British Raj, which had extended its control over virtually the entire sub-continent. The restraint in managing India in the aftermath of the Mutiny, under 'Clemency' Canning, Dalhousie's successor from 1856 and first viceroy, 1858, was accompanied by a realization that westernizing policies could be taken too far, although more Indians themselves came to adopt the ways and aspirations of their British rulers. Reforms in the army, in financial administration, and changed, more positive attitudes towards native Indians, remained the basis for British rule until independence came in 1947. After the flood of westernizing changes of the previous half-century, the revision of the penal code in 1861 was the last piece of social legislation to be enacted until 1929 and the Age of Consent Act; however, the railway system, which had begun construction in 1853, continued to be built at considerable speed, reaching completion by 1900.

A succession of viceroys ruled India during its heyday in the second half of the 19th century overseeing, sometimes with indolence, occasionally with energy, the economic and industrial development of India: railways and irrigation schemes, cotton and jute plantations, coal fields and ironworks. In his stories and poetry Rudyard Kipling (1865–1936) was to become the quintessential voice of British India, which received its crowning, literally, in DISRAELI's creation of Queen VICTORIA as Empress of India in 1876. Soon after, war was again prosecuted, with the second AFGHAN WAR of 1878–80, an expression of British alarm at Russian expansionism, and the annexation of Upper Burma in 1886. Meanwhile, Lord Ripon, GLADSTONE's nominee as viceroy between 1880 and 1884, had instigated liberal-style reforms, notably a measure of local self-government and expanded educational opportunities for Indians; when he proposed that Indian judges be allowed to try Europeans, he was enveloped in a racial storm.

Within this period of relative quiet the seeds of the INDIAN INDEPENDENCE movement were sown, and the story of British involvement in 20th-century India is told under that head. There was a British expectation of eventual self-government, Britain's role being expressed by Lord Curzon, viceroy between 1899 and 1905, as that of trustees of India's past and tutor to her future. India had come to underpin the British imperial system; its eventual 'loss' prefaced the final and rapid dissolution of Empire (*see* DECOLONIZATION).

India Bills 1783–4, Bills reconstructing the relationship between the EAST INDIA COMPANY and the British government, in the light of growing unease about the Company's competence to govern its Indian territories. Two Bills, largely drafted by BURKE, were brought in by the short-lived FOX–NORTH administration. The first proposed to replace the Company's directors with a board of commissioners; the first commissioners, named in the Bill, were all friends of the ministry. GEORGE III made it known to the LORDS that he would consider anyone voting for the Bill an enemy; it was then defeated and the ministry dismissed.

The charge – although almost certainly ill-founded – that the Bill had been designed to augment ministerial patronage played a part in ensuring that the 1784 election was a triumph for the king and his new chief minister, PITT THE YOUNGER. The latter's own India Bill, which passed in 1784, left the Company intact, but subjected it to the supervision of a BOARD OF CONTROL.

Indian Independence In the course of the first half of the 20th century, having been the finest adornment of the BRITISH EMPIRE, India became the first part of the Empire to achieve separate nationhood and independence. Even in the later 19th century many in Britain and the colonial service had come to foresee independence as the logical outcome of British rule, but it was not given without considerable struggle.

Indian political activism pre-dated the INDIAN MUTINY, with the murmurings about Indian government by Bengal landlords in 1853, but received its first concrete expression, again in Bengal, in the Indian Association of 1876, which was highly critical of the imperial policies pursued by the viceroy Lord Lytton. Lord Ripon's projected judicial reforms under the Ilbert Bill of 1884, which provided for Indian judges to be able to try Europeans and was met with a storm of indignation, proved the crucible for a native political movement with its strength located in the emerging professional and business groups.

The Indian National Congress first met in Bombay in Dec. 1885, and had spread across India by 1900. The Indian Councils Act 1892 was a small measure of reform, widening the scope of locally-elected provincial councils, which served to excite further political interest, while the imposition in Britain of an EXCISE duty on imported Indian textiles was seen as naked protectionism of the home COTTON industry. The rule of Curzon as viceroy between 1899 and 1905 was the high point of British imperialism in India; his administrative reforms, less confrontational frontier policies but controversial attempts to move into Tibet in 1904, promotion of higher education, and the partition of Bengal to form new provinces, were all conducted with good intent but quickly aroused opposition from within India as well as Britain.

With growing extremism and the advent of terrorism among Congress supporters, the need for reform became pressing. The Morley–Minto reforms of 1909, in the Indian Councils Act, enlarged provincial executive councils and gave membership to Indians, including separate Muslim representation. The Muslim League had been founded in 1906, to counter fast-growing Hindu political influence. With the accession of GEORGE V, and his magnificent Durbar in 1911 when the capital was transferred to Delhi from Calcutta, the Bengal partition was reversed and the pace of change accelerated. In WORLD WAR I, initial Indian support for the Allied effort rapidly waned; Home Rule Leagues were established in 1916 by Annie Besant and Bal Gangadhar Tilak, and Tilak concluded the Lucknow Pact with Muslims which gave their support to Congress in return for separate Muslim constituencies. The MONTAGU–CHELMSFORD REFORMS, produced in the final months of war, were part of the radical British initiative on India envisaging DOMINION self-rule.

The resulting Government of India Act 1919 provided for a majority of Indians to sit on the Central Legislative Council and in provincial councils; however, there would continue to be nominees on the councils, and in the provinces control over revenue matters and law and order were reserved to non-Indian officials. This form of devolution by stages was inadequate for many Indians who wanted rapid change, not least as reward for Indian involvement and sacrifice in the Great War. Terrorism reappeared, but indignation found its leader and philosophy in the non-violent person of Mohandas, later styled 'Mahatma', Gandhi (1869–1948), a lawyer who had recently returned from SOUTH AFRICA, and its cause in the AMRITSAR MASSACRE of 1919, when 379 unarmed civilians were killed in the Punjab, shot by Gurkhas commanded by General Dyer, and the harsh measures that succeeded it. Gandhi swung towards a policy of non-co-operation with the British, and advocated passive resistance; although the campaigns were short-lived, not least because Gandhi himself was imprisoned in 1922, they had forged a new political will and a keen sense of unity within India.

Although liberal reforms were enacted, including the abolition of British duty on Indian cotton and much wider Indian recruitment to the civil service, India was angered by the imposition of a salt tax which later occasioned Gandhi's most eloquent protest. Gandhi remained at the centre of Indian politics, slowly transforming ideas of caste and race among the Indian political classes. The SIMON COMMISSION, appointed in 1927, was greeted with shock since it had an all-British composition, and prompted a call from Congress for complete independence and dominion status.

Radical sentiment, led by Jawaharlal Nehru (1889–1964) and Subash Chandra Bose, was opposed to the British offer of a round-table conference, and Gandhi led the anti-salt tax protest which occasioned riots and protest across India; over 100,000 were imprisoned including Gandhi. Although a round-table conference was convened in London in 1930, after the non-Congress Indian politicians had agreed to attend it, the results were inconclusive and civil disobedience recommenced in 1931–4, including Gandhi's fast to near-death in gaol. The Government of India Act 1935, which was the concrete result of the 1930–2 round-table conferences, introduced a federal structure including the native princely states and fully responsible provincial government; its passage had been delayed by the die-hard resistance of Winston CHURCHILL and others.

Faced with radical anger, notably from Nehru and Bose, Gandhi defused their opposition to his policies, first by choosing Nehru as his successor – Nehru became president of Congress in 1936 – and then by manoeuvring to prevent Bose's re-election as president in 1938 and forcing his resignation from Congress. Although the 1935 constitution was a prelude to independence, it had failed to give proper recognition to Muslims and was seen as devised in favour of Hindu interests, while the continued prominent role of princely rulers was seen as reactionary. The previously divided Muslim parties were united under Muhammad Ali Jinnah (1876–1948), who began to campaign vigorously against the Congress party in the aftermath of the 1936 elections which swept Congress to power in most provinces.

The new constitution had barely begun to take shape when India was plunged into WORLD WAR II. Indian troops fought in the Allied effort, while the politically-exiled Bose led the pro-Japanese Indian National Army. Political deadlock in the country was broken by the mission led by Sir Stafford CRIPPS in 1942 which offered India full dominion status, including the right of secession from the COMMONWEALTH. Following Gandhi's lead, Congress politicians rejected the offer; the ensuing 'Quit India' period of civil disobedience ensured a return to the deadlock, while Congress had lost the opportunity to dominate a new India and to smother the ambitions of the Muslim League to partition India and form a new state, PAKISTAN.

The return of the 1945 LABOUR government in Britain and the swift end of the war against Japan propelled India rapidly towards independence. Congress remained opposed to partition, and India slid towards civil war on the question of the formation of Pakistan. Attempts by a Cabinet mission in 1946, again including Cripps, to reconcile the parties to a united India failed, and were followed by serious rioting in Aug. when the Muslim League declared a Direct Action Day. The viceroy, Archibald Wavell, drew both sides into an interim government, but failed to establish a Constituent Assembly for a united India. Nehru and Congress went over Gandhi's head and approved partition, and independence for the new nations came at midnight on 14/15 Aug. 1947, overseen by the last viceroy, Lord MOUNTBATTEN, who had only been installed on 24 March.

The two new states of India and Pakistan (the latter divided into West and East, subsequently Bangladesh) came into being amidst large-scale violence, rioting and massacres, and the mass exodus of refugees from areas where they constituted a religious minority – some 5.5 million in each direction. Partition cost upwards of 250,000 lives, among them Gandhi himself who was assassinated by a Hindu fanatic on 30 Jan. 1948 after fasting for Hindu–Muslim unity. In the new constitution which was implemented from 1950, India became a federal republic within the Commonwealth. Links with Britain have been maintained in language and institutions, as well as the volume of IMMIGRATION to the United Kingdom from the Indian subcontinent.

Indian Mutiny, 1857–8, a series of military mutinies and civil revolts, which arose out of the Indians' resentment of the governor-general, Lord Dalhousie's (1848–56) extensive institutional reforms, fear of forcible conversion to Christianity, and their suspicion that cartridges issued to sepoys – Indian soldiers under British discipline – were greased with cow-fat (and therefore repugnant to Hindus) or pig-fat (offensive to Muslims).

The outbreak, which began on 10 May 1857 at Meerut, was followed by the seizure of Delhi by three mutinous regiments and the proclamation of the elderly Mogul Emperor, Bahadur Shah II (1775–1862), as their leader. As the rebellion spread, British forces and their families, cut off at Cawnpore, were taken prisoner and murdered. Order was gradually restored but not before there had been a good deal of blood-letting on both sides. In Sept., Delhi was retaken, followed by Cawnpore and the Lucknow residency; central India was recovered in spring 1858, and in July came an official declaration of peace.

The following month, legislation was passed transferring Indian administration from the EAST INDIA COMPANY to the crown. A secretary of state for India was created, with a council of persons well versed in Indian affairs to assist him. Further measures of pacification included promises of religious toleration, equal justice and an amnesty to all except murderers.

Indulf (?–962), King of Scots (954–62). The son of CONSTANTINE II, he had ruled the sub-kingdom of STRATHCLYDE before his elevation to the kingdom of the Scots. His reign is notable for the expansion of the Scottish kings' power into Lothian, and specifically for the acquisition of EDINBURGH. The collapse of the Scandinavian kingdom of YORK provided the opportunity for this advance.

Indulgence, a Church grant that remits penances due either in this life or in

PURGATORY, in penitence for sin. Indulgences became common from the end of the 11th century, at first to encourage participation in the CRUSADES. Later, scandal arose from their unregulated sale, and they are famous as the cause of LUTHER's breach with the 16th-century papacy. In 1567, indulgences were forbidden to be sold; they are still granted, but only with careful explanation about their purpose. The earliest datable surviving piece of English PRINTING is an indulgence of 1476. *See also* DECLARATIONS OF INDULGENCE.

Industrial Districts, seen by many economists, notably the neo-classical economist Alfred Marshall (1824–1924) and Philip Sargant Florence, as important in the growth of sectors of INDUSTRY since the later 18th century. It has been argued that the dynamism of small-scale businesses in particular was aided by the EXTERNAL ECONOMIES which derived from the clustering of appropriate infrastructures, trading and credit and subcontracting networks, and by conglomerations of skill, knowledge and information which characterized areas such as the West Midlands, parts of south Lancs., the West Riding and South Yorks., and Teesside. *See also* FAMILY FIRMS; INDUSTRIAL REVOLUTION.

Industrial Relations Act 1971, a doomed attempt to solve the TRADE UNION 'problem'. Passed by the HEATH government, it placed industrial relations within a framework of law under a new National Industrial Relations Court. It also provided for compulsory union recognition, legally binding contracts between employers and employees, strike ballots, 'cooling off' periods, and the registration of trade unions. The TRADES UNION CONGRESS bitterly opposed the Act, seeing it as an infringement of 'free collective bargaining', and most unions refused to register. The Act was repealed by the WILSON government when it came to power in 1974.

Industrial Revolution, historians' term, classically applied to the period *c.*1750–1850. Contemporaries began to describe their society as 'industrial' from the early 19th century; the term 'industrial revolution' was coined by a French envoy to Berlin, Louis Guillaume, in 1799. It was used by the French communist Auguste Blanqui in 1837, and by Friedrich Engels in his *Condition of the Working Classes in England* (1845). It entered general usage with the publication of the historian Arnold Toynbee's notes and lectures in the 1880s. Features of the period which have been held to justify the label include an expansion in the size and relative significance of the industrial workforce; expansion in industrial output and productivity, and the introduction of new technologies, especially the mechanization, first of spinning, then of weaving; in association with this, expansion and change in the use of energy sources, water- or windmills, STEAM POWER and the use of COAL in an extended range of industrial processes; changes in the social relations of production associated with the accumulation of capital and growth of wage-labour, and in the physical organization of production, associated with the rise of the FACTORY SYSTEM. The period saw notable changes in the regional distribution of industrial activity: industry developed most rapidly in the GLASGOW region, the industrial north and Midlands of England, and in south Wales; some older industrial regions, e.g. East Anglia and the West Country, declined in relative significance.

Heroic accounts of the industrial revolution stress the role of inventors and ENTREPRENEURS such as Richard Arkwright (1732–92) whose invention of a water-powered spinning frame for producing strong cotton thread was the basis of the expansion of the COTTON industry in the north of England; Matthew Boulton (1728–1809) who, in conjunction with James Watt, developed a steam engine which powered early factory production; Henry Cort (1740–1800), an ironmaster whose PUDDLING AND ROLLING process revolutionized iron production; Samuel Crompton (1753–1827), inventor of the 'MULE' to produce finer, strong spun-cotton thread; James Hargreaves (?–1778), who devised the SPINNING JENNY which enabled several yarns to be produced at once; John Kay (1704–post 1764), who patented his inventions for a twisting machine and 'flying shuttle' which made it possible for a single weaver to produce broader cloths – this was widely adopted and helped speed the expansion of the cotton and WOOLLEN industries; James Watt (1736–1819), celebrated as a pioneer of industrialization for the steam engine he invented and manufactured with Matthew

Boulton; and Josiah Wedgwood (1730–95), whose innovative approach to pottery production and design at his factories near Stoke on Trent and Chelsea (London) served a rapidly expanding market, but historians now stress the role of market opportunities, political stability and the myriad of piecemeal technical and organizational improvements which lay behind industrial expansion. The term is sometimes used more generally to encompass a host of economic and social changes taking place in Britain over the same period, including the so-called AGRICULTURAL REVOLUTION, transport developments, especially the development of TURNPIKES, CANALS and, later, RAILWAYS, urbanization and unprecedented rates of POPULATION growth. The limitations of the evidence make it impossible definitively to establish the scale, pace and precise character of change in the industrial economy: debate continues as to how significant productivity gains were, and whether they were confined to particular sectors (notably cotton textiles: *see* COTTON INDUSTRY), or spread across a broad front. The adoption of steam power has been shown to have been a slow process; the factory remained an atypical work-place even in the late 19th century; and a skilled artisanate continued to exist. Marked increases in the use of fossil fuels and in the scale of capital accumulation, and a shift in favour of producer rather than consumer goods were features of the railway era rather than of the 'early industrial revolution'.

Historians have also stressed the extent of industrialization before 1750. By 1700, England was already importing mainly raw materials, and (RE-EXPORTS apart) exporting mainly manufactured goods. It has been suggested that in 1700 the proportion of the workforce engaged in AGRICULTURE (perhaps 60 per cent) was already notably low by European standards; the proportion engaged in INDUSTRY (perhaps 20 per cent), notably high. Conversely, at no point has the British ECONOMY achieved rates of productivity growth comparable with those achieved by industrializing nations of the late 19th century, such as Germany and the USA. As 'industrial revolutions' go, Britain's may have been early, but it was also slow and protracted.

Industrial Revolution, Second, a term sometimes used by historians to describe the growth of new light industries from the 1880s to 1914, notably CHEMICALS, machine tools, bicycles and cars (*see* MOTOR INDUSTRY).

Industrial Schools Act 1866 Under this Act, destitute orphans, children with parents in prison and vagrants between the ages of eight and 13 could be committed to a certified school to be lodged, clothed, fed and taught a useful trade. The preventive approach to juvenile delinquency was an advance on the thinking embodied in the Young Offenders Act 1854.

Industry, manufacture of products from raw materials, or, more generally, an area of economic activity other than AGRICULTURE. The word industry was rarely used before the later 18th century, 'trades' being preferred to describe manufacturing and other industrial activities, perhaps reflecting the low levels of fixed capital (plant and equipment) as opposed to circulating capital (credit and trade finance) engaged. From the earliest times some forms of manufacture have existed – metal goods, textiles, pottery, etc. The long-term trend has been for industrial production to assume an ever-greater share of economic activity, with the coming of the INDUSTRIAL REVOLUTION in the 18th and 19th centuries transforming the basis of economic activity, and widening the range of production. In the 20th century, however, the importance of the industrial sector has diminished. *See also* CHEMICAL INDUSTRY; CLOTH INDUSTRY; COAL INDUSTRY; COTTON INDUSTRY; INDUSTRIAL DISTRICTS; IRON AND STEEL INDUSTRY; MOTOR INDUSTRY; PROTO-INDUSTRIALIZATION; SHIPBUILDING; WOOLLEN INDUSTRY.

Ine, King of Wessex (688–726). He extended the domination of the WESSEX kings over southern England as far as the still-independent south-western kingdom of DUMNONIA – a process apparently begun a century earlier by his predecessor, CEAWLIN. Ine, a vigorous supporter of the Christian Church, was also the first king of Wessex to issue a LAW CODE. This shows both a rudimentary structure of local administration and that payments to the Church, such as 'church-scot', were regarded as compulsory (*see* TITHES).

Infangenetheof, one of the powers most frequently granted to the lords of estates in late Anglo-Saxon England. It involved the right to try and hang thieves caught red-handed within an estate, and gave lords extensive responsibilities for the maintenance of local law and order.

Infant Mortality, deaths of live-born children who have not reached their first birthday. The infant mortality rate should be the death rate per 1,000 children under the age of one, but for technical reasons is often calculated by taking as base the number of children born in the particular calendar year. The infant mortality rate is often considered one of the best indicators of the health and material well-being of a POPULATION. Its decline has been the greatest single contribution to MORTALITY decline since the 18th century.

Infield–Outfield System, an agricultural system characteristic of Scotland and parts of northern and western England, as of other parts of Europe, where good arable land was in short supply and the accent was on livestock rearing. In this system, arable land was divided into two unequal parts: a small 'infield' close to the village or homestead, which was cropped and manured constantly; and a larger 'outfield', composed of waste, a part of which was ploughed up and cropped each season. The system developed over time, and it has been suggested that it may not have reached its classic form until the 15th or 16th century. It died out in England largely before the 18th century, and in Scotland in the course of that century. *See also* AGRICULTURE; ENCLOSURE; RUNRIG.

Inflation, a significant and persistent increase in prices, and therefore a decline in the purchasing power of the £ STERLING or other unit of money. In pre-industrial economies, the degree of inflation has been seen largely as an outcome of POPULATION pressure within an inelastic economy and/or the effect of an increasing quantity of money within the economic system. The 16th and early 17th centuries saw inflation across Europe, in the context of both increasing population and the injection of American silver through the Spanish transatlantic trade; it was given greater impetus in England by the series of DEBASEMENTS of the COINAGE and the economic dislocation resulting from dearth and FAMINE. Inflationary pressures were to reassert themselves in 18th-century Britain with the population rise, but industrial and trade expansion in the 19th century brought stable or falling prices.

In the 20th century, deflationary pressures were at their strongest in the DEPRESSION of the inter-war years, and inflation remained at low levels until the 1960s when prices began to rise again. Management of the ECONOMY, often under KEYNESian policies, resulted in the fine-tuning of the STOP-GO era of the 1960s and a sequence of PRICES AND INCOMES policies and restraints that had only a temporary effect in slowing inflation. Growing international trade in the 20th century meant that inflation became partly an international problem, but one from which the UK suffered particularly acutely, with annual rates surpassing 20 per cent in the mid-1970s, influenced by the OIL CRISIS.

Inflation has some beneficial effects, in encouraging new and ingenious responses to the economic situation, but has most commonly had a negative effect, sapping initiative, reducing living standards unless productivity increases are achieved, lowering real fixed incomes and so having adverse effects on the distribution of wealth.

Informal Empire, historians' term for a type of IMPERIALISM in which the imperial power does not rule the colonized territory directly, but leaves it formally independent while securing *de facto* control through economic penetration and exploitation. Such was characteristic of Britain in the late 18th century and of the United States in the mid-20th.

Informers The human instinct to tell tales was given formal encouragement during the 15th–17th centuries. A great variety of statutes of that period provided for rewards or a share of profits for private informers who exposed infringements of the law or initiated prosecutions (in the absence of an extensive, paid civil service to do the job), and some made a lucrative career out of informing (*see* WALSINGHAM, FRANCIS). Growing outrage at the practice led to repeated and, in the end, successful curbs on informers during the 17th century, although COMMON LAW still provides for legal actions brought to court by 'informations' (written accusations).

Ingimund (*fl. c.*910), a VIKING warrior based in DUBLIN who led the SCANDINAVIAN colonization of the Wirral in the early 10th century. The colony was prevented from expanding by a ring of encircling *BURHS* constructed on the orders of Ealdorman Ethelred and his wife Ethelflæd.

Ingwaer, *see* IVAR THE BONELESS

Inheritance, transfer of wealth between generations, usually at death. The term also applies to other forms of transfer on death, e.g. PEERAGE titles. Inheritance has been, and remains, the single most important factor in the distribution of wealth in Britain. With some exceptions (*see* BOROUGH-ENGLISH; GAVELKIND) the main system of inheritance in England, and often in other parts of the British Isles, has been PRIMOGENITURE, the bulk of an estate being inherited by the eldest son. This has tended to keep properties intact, rather than being split by partible forms of inheritance. Communal ideas of property, prominent in clan-based systems (*see* BREHON), cannot be discerned within English or Anglocentric systems. *See also* STRICT SETTLEMENT; WILLS.

Injunctions In Church administration, these were sets of instructions for action usually in connection with a VISITATION, issued especially by monarchs or bishops. During the REFORMATION, they often announced major religious changes, such as those of HENRY VIII and Thomas CROMWELL in 1536 and 1538.

In secular law, an injunction is an order issued by a court, originally in the equity system by CHANCERY. It is familiar from its modern employment by the courts to secure an immediate result, for instance in restraining publication of books, articles or information.

Inkerman, Battle of, *see* CRIMEAN WAR

INLA, *see* IRISH NATIONAL LIBERATION ARMY

Inns of Court, training institutions and professional societies for BARRISTERS, concentrated around the City of LONDON. They began taking corporate existence in the 14th century and were vital in building up practice of the COMMON LAW into a secular legal profession unique in medieval Europe. Main inns – the Middle and Inner Temples, Lincoln's Inn, Gray's Inn – still flourish, though lesser inns with a variety of training functions besides those for barristers were suppressed in the 19th century (*see* SERJEANTS AT LAW). Ordinary membership of the inns is now confined to barristers, but in 16th- and 17th-century England, a gentleman's education often included a stint at an inn which was not intended to lead to professional qualifications.

Inoculation, a technique for immunizing people against disease. It was first used for smallpox (when it was called 'variolation'): pustulous matter from a smallpox sufferer was inserted into a small scratch in the skin of someone who had not had the disease. The death rate was lower than when the smallpox was otherwise contracted, but deaths did occur and those inoculated became infectious and could spread the disease. Developed in the Middle East, the technique was promoted by the ROYAL SOCIETY in the 1720s, and it became popular from the 1750s. VACCINATION, a less dangerous alternative originally using matter from sufferers from the related cowpox, was established by Edward Jenner in 1798.

Inquest, *see* CORONER

Inquisitions In England, inquiries held by FEUDAL lords on specified matters – for instance, into the lands held by a deceased feudal tenant (inquisition *post mortem*), or as to whether a new grant would infringe existing rights (inquisition *ad quod damnum*). No inquisition into HERESY similar to the papal or Spanish inquisitions was ever active in the British Isles; action against medieval heretics was taken by individual bishops or archbishops.

Inspeximus (Latin for 'We have examined'), a document confirming existing privileges previously granted by CHARTER, after an investigation has been made by the descendant or successor of the original grantor.

Institute of Economic Affairs (IEA), a private body set up in 1957 as a forum for economists and political scientists to express what were then unorthodox views. The IEA had an avowedly right-of-centre philosophy and published pamphlets and papers critical of socialism and the WELFARE STATE, and in favour of free market economics; in this respect it could be termed the first of the so-called 'think tanks'. It was regarded as extremist and flying in the face of history in the 1960s when it advocated such schemes as privatization of public-sector industries and the NATIONAL HEALTH SERVICE, as well as vouchers for education. However, by the 1970s it began to influence political thought in the CONSERVATIVE PARTY, and was to see many of its views become the political/economic orthodoxy of the 1980s.

Institutes of Polity, the great work of political thought written by Archbishop WULFSTAN of York in the early 11th century. It set out to analyse the rights and duties of all grades of society, so that sin could be avoided and stability ensured, and is important for our knowledge of the religious and social ideas of late Anglo-Saxon England.

Instructions Directions by constituents to their MPs, usually endorsed at public meetings. During the EXCLUSION CRISIS of 1679–81, the WHIGS circulated instructions which might be presented to parliamentary candidates. Eighteenth-century RADICALS favoured them as devices to make MPs accountable, but they had no legal status, and their propriety was often questioned: it was argued that MPs were representatives, not delegates, and that, to function properly, they must preserve their independence.

Instrument of Government, 1653. The constitutional settlement created by the soldier John Lambert (1619–83) and the COUNCIL OF OFFICERS instituting Oliver CROMWELL'S Protectorate (*see* INTERREGNUM). It never received final shape from the PARLIAMENT that it had set up and, after much confusion, was replaced by the HUMBLE PETITION AND ADVICE of 1657.

Insurance The need to insure goods and property was first keenly felt in shipping, and the 17th-century insurance of shipping found institutional expression in the establishment of Lloyd's COFFEE HOUSE in London. Marine insurance came to be dominated by the business at Lloyd's, growing to be the world's most important insurance market. General insurance (fire and accident insurance) is normally taken out on an annual basis and the premiums companies receive are invested. There is great uncertainty with regard to paying out against the risks they insure – hurricanes, earthquakes and other natural disasters are not very predictable. It was only when life insurance became feasible in the 19th century that substantial growth in the assets of the insurance companies began to take place. The actuarial risks involved in life insurance are predictable; thus the long-term flow of contractual savings implied in the payment of regular premiums gave the organizations concerned the ability to invest in longer term assets which themselves could yield better returns. By the 1960s and 70s insurance companies had grown to become some of the largest financial institutions in the modern ECONOMY: by 1981 they owned 21 per cent of the value of quoted equities in the UK stock market – excluding other assets such as property, MORTGAGES, bonds, overseas government securities. By the early 1980s the value of their portfolios was some £106 billion, and by the late 1990s London was estimated to handle around 20 per cent of the general insurance business placed on the international market.

Intercursus Magnus ('Great Commercial Exchange'), 1496. Treaty between HENRY VII and Maximilian I, Holy Roman Emperor, which confirmed long-standing trade arrangements with the Low Countries and ended Habsburg help to the YORKIST rebels.

Internment in Northern Ireland Internment without trial was introduced in Northern Ireland in 1971 following attacks by the Provisional IRISH REPUBLICAN ARMY upon British soldiers and a worsening security situation. Both Catholic and Protestant suspects were rounded up, provoking particularly serious rioting in Republican areas. Widely condemned as having exacerbated an already difficult situation, from 1975 internment was phased out in favour of a policy of 'criminalization', whereby terrorist suspects were tried by special DIPLOCK COURTS and only those found guilty imprisoned.

Internment of Aliens Anti-German feeling at the outbreak of WORLD WAR I led to the rounding up of hundreds of aliens in Aug. 1914 in special camps, including the Olympia exhibition hall in London. The 1914 Aliens Act required aliens to register with the police and led to widespread internment of German aliens of military age. During WORLD WAR II residents in Britain of German and Italian extraction, many of them refugees from Hitler, were interned in 1940 as enemy aliens on the Isle of MAN, though most were soon released.

Interregnum, 1649–60. Literally the 'period between reigns', it consisted successively of Commonwealth, Protectorate and Commonwealth. The Commonwealth of 1649–54 was a republic, although it took some months after the execution of CHARLES I to work out its constitutional structure; it was ruled by a single-chamber PARLIAMENT and a COUNCIL OF STATE. The Protectorate of 1654–9 derived its name from the title of 'Lord PROTECTOR' granted to Oliver CROMWELL; in 1657, a second chamber of nominated 'PEERS' (mostly new creations by Cromwell) was added to Parliament. The fall of Richard CROMWELL in May 1659 led to the re-establishment of the Commonwealth and, after much confusion, to the RESTORATION of the Stuart monarchy the following year.

The regimes of the Interregnum enjoyed many military successes (*see* DUTCH WARS; NAVY), and the very loose structure of a state Church set up by Cromwell afforded toleration to most PROTESTANTS in England. However, all successive regimes represented a conquest of the British Isles by the English state, and even within England they faced the serious problem of winning firm, long-term allegiance: how to devise a constitutional settlement commanding assent not only from the general population – most of whom were shocked at the execution of Charles I – but also from the army (*see* NEW MODEL ARMY). The latter had won the conflicts of the 1640s, and was now determined to safeguard its achievements; it remained essential for suppressing disaffection in the newly conquered kingdoms of Ireland and Scotland, even though (and, again, even in England) it became increasingly unpopular (*see* MAJOR-GENERALS).

In the end, the effort involved in trying to please both people and army proved fruitless, and the restoration of CHARLES II provided an escape route from stalemate. *See also* CIVIL WARS, BRITISH.

CHRONOLOGY

1648–53 RUMP PARLIAMENT administers effectively, but fails to agree any long-term plans.

1649 CHARLES I executed after PRIDE'S PURGE; 'Commonwealth of England' declared.

1653 Oliver CROMWELL and army dismiss Rump. BAREBONES PARLIAMENT collapses and INSTRUMENT OF GOVERNMENT created. Cromwell created LORD PROTECTOR under Instrument.

1654 First Protectorate Parliament seeks to modify Instrument: dismissed.

1655–6 Local rule by MAJOR-GENERALS.

1656–8 Second Protectorate Parliament.

1657 Cromwell rejects Parliament's offer of crown, but accepts modified HUMBLE PETITION AND ADVICE. Major-Generals mandate extends.

1658 Parliament ends in uproar (Feb.). Political situation unresolved at Cromwell's death (Sept.). His son Richard succeeds as Protector.

1659, Jan. Parliament convened: COMMONS elected on modified pre-1640 franchise, with Scottish and Irish representatives.

1659, April Army dissolves Parliament and recalls Rump Parliament; Richard CROMWELL resigns.

1659, Oct. Army dissolves Rump. Chaos threatens.

1660, Jan. MONCK marches south, welcomed by restored Rump.

1660, Feb.–March Negotiations between CHARLES II and Monck.

1660, May CONVENTION PARLIAMENT votes to restore monarchy.

Intolerable Acts 1774, five Acts passed by the British Parliament, comprising four Coercive Acts, designed to end resistance in the colony of MASSACHUSETTS, and the QUEBEC ACT. The BOSTON TEA PARTY – the destruction of a shipment of tea subject to duties that some Americans denounced as unconstitutional – provided the immediate stimulus for the Coercive Acts. American colonists argued that these Acts revealed the British government's tyrannical inclinations. They represented one of the key causes of the discontent that led to the War of AMERICAN INDEPENDENCE

Inventories, post-mortem lists of the moveable property of a deceased person, particularly in the period, before 1838, of ecclesiastical control of WILLS and testaments. These documents, which survive in large numbers for the 17th and early 18th centuries, have been much studied by economic and social historians, particularly by those interested in the balance of agricultural and industrial activities during PROTO-INDUSTRIALIZATION, and by those researching the dissemination of new consumer goods in the early modern period.

Invergordon Mutiny, mutiny at Invergordon on the Cromarty Firth in Sept. 1931, involving 15 ships of the Atlantic Fleet, in protest against lower pay rates which were part of the NATIONAL GOVERNMENT's cuts in government expenditure following the MAY COMMITTEE report. The crews of several capital ships held meetings and refused to obey orders, though there was little violence. The mutiny was defused by Admiralty promises to revise the proposals, but it contributed to the run on sterling in the foreign exchange markets which forced the government to come off the GOLD STANDARD on 20 Sept.

Iona Monastery Founded by St COLUMBA in the 6th century on the Scottish island of Iona off the Ross of Mull, the monastery was, in many ways, the religious capital of northern and western Britain for several hundred years after its foundation. Monasteries connected with Iona existed throughout western Scotland and Ireland, and the community established from there on LINDISFARNE by St Aidan played a dominant role in the CONVERSION to Christianity of pagan English NORTHUMBRIA. Under such abbots as Adomnan (*c*.625–704) and Egbert (639–729), Iona remained extraordinarily influential, as well as a great centre of learning; the *BOOK OF KELLS* may have been produced there. The community was destroyed by VIKING attacks in the early 9th century, and although restored, it never regained its earlier pre-eminence. Much of what can now be seen on Iona is a restoration of the later medieval buildings, but there are still substantial remains from the abbey's heroic period. *See also* MONASTICISM.

IRA, *see* IRISH REPUBLICAN ARMY

Iraqi Mandate Britain received the LEAGUE OF NATIONS mandate for the area known as Mesopotamia, once part of the Turkish Empire, following WORLD WAR I. In 1921 the monarchy of Iraq was established and full independence was granted in 1932. *See also* MANDATE.

Ireland, English Conquest of The traditional Irish notion of 1169 as 'the year of destiny' encapsulates the fundamental point that the events of 1166 to 1171 transformed Irish history. In the words of an English historian of the time, WILLIAM OF NEWBURGH, they marked the end of freedom for a people who had previously been free since time immemorial, unconquered even by the Romans. Inevitably these events have been at the centre of intense political and historical controversy ever since, all the more so since HENRY II, the king of England who invaded Ireland in overwhelming force in 1171, justified his actions partly on the grounds that the Irish were a backward and immoral people and that he had been authorized by the pope to reform them (*see LAUDABILITER*). In fact Ireland already had its own reformers, particularly in ecclesiastical affairs where men such as MALACHY and Lorcan O Tuathail were consciously influenced by continental fashions. None the less there was considerable resistance to change and to many outsiders, Gerald de BARRI for example, Irish culture and society still seemed primitive. In political terms 12th-century Ireland was still a land in which many more or less independent kings engaged in a relentless struggle for power. At stake were both regional supremacies and then, for the most successful regional kings, such as TURLOCH O CONNOR and Muirchertach O mac Lochlainn (*fl. c*.1160), that dream of KINGSHIP over all Ireland (increasingly associated with rule over DUBLIN) that historians have labelled the 'high kingship'. When one such regional king, DERMOT MAC MURROUGH, went to Henry II's court for military help against his Irish enemies (in particular RORY O'CONNOR), he set in train the sequence of events which ended with what William of Newburgh in the 1190s was already calling 'the conquest of the Irish by the English'.

In the late 12th and 13th centuries English settlers crossed the Irish Sea in their thousands and English courtiers became great landowners in Ireland, some of them remaining absentee landlords. Irish kings continued to lose power and prestige. But although Irish political fragmentation meant that there was no single Irish ruler with the resources to defeat the English, it also meant that Ireland could only be conquered piecemeal. In the south-east where English settlement was thickest, the Irish were driven back into uplands and bogs, the poorest parts of the country, but elsewhere, the north-west for example, the O'Donnells and O'Neills were much more successful in retaining traditional – BREHON – law, and this meant keeping the English out. Indeed, in the 14th and 15th centuries, as the supply of English colonists dried up, the Irish were able to recover lost ground, gradually confining English power to the PALE. Thus for centuries Ireland remained a land of war, and on both sides attitudes hardened.

CHRONOLOGY

1166 DERMOT MAC MURROUGH asks HENRY II for military assistance.
1169 Invasion of GERALDINES. Capture of Wexford and restoration of Dermot.
1170 Arrival of Strongbow (*see* CLARE, RICHARD DE) and his marriage to Dermot's daughter. Capture of Dublin.
1171 Death of Dermot and invasion of Henry II. Most Irish kings submit.
1172 Henry II grants kingdom of Meath of Hugh DE LACEY.
1175 Treaty of WINDSOR between Henry II and RORY O'CONNOR.
1177 Henry II grants the lordship of Ireland to his son JOHN. John DE COURCY begins conquest of Ulster.
1180s Gerald de BARRI writes the *Topography of Ireland* and *The Conquest of Ireland*.
1210 King JOHN visits Ireland.
1258 Alliance between Aedh O'Connor and Brian O'Neill attempts to halt continuing expansion of English power.
1260 Brian O'Neill killed in Battle of Down.
1315 Arrival of Edward BRUCE and his proclamation as king of Ireland.
1318 Defeat and death of Edward Bruce in Battle of Faughart.
1361–6 Lionel of Clarence, younger son of Edward III, as king's lieutenant in Ireland.
1366 Statutes of KILKENNY.
1394–5 RICHARD II's first visit to Ireland. Submission of ART MAC MURROUGH.
1399 Richard II's second visit.
1449–50 RICHARD OF YORK as king's lieutenant in Ireland.
1460 Statute of Drogheda proclaims separate status of Ireland.

Ireland and England in the 16th and 17th centuries HENRY VII, insecure enough in England, was faced with negotiating his position in Ireland around the power of the two great late medieval ANGLO-NORMAN families, the Butler Earls of Ormond (based at Kilkenny) and the FITZGERALD Earls of Kildare and of Desmond (*see also* GERALDINES). Of these, the Geraldines were the more formidable because of their power in the Dublin PALE. Gerald FITZGERALD, 8th Earl of Kildare, had been an enthusiastic YORKIST, while the Butlers were LANCASTRIAN in sympathy. Kildare was nevertheless reappointed lord deputy in 1485. His official favour survived supporting Lambert SIMNEL in 1487, but not the Earl of Desmond's support for Perkin WARBECK (1492); this led to James Butler being given the novel title of governor. Kildare's further self-assertiveness led to his imprisonment in England and the arrival in Ireland of Sir Edward Poynings (*see* POYNINGS' LAW), but it was difficult to resist the power of the Geraldines for long, and by 1496 Kildare's power had been restored.

It might still have been possible for the lordship permanently to have become a semi-detached dominion of the English crown; however, Kildare's death (1513) led to further instability, an incentive for the Tudor dynasty to consider greater involvement to prevent repetition of its earlier embarrassments. The failure of the Kildare rebellion (1534) was a turning-point, since it resulted in the destruction of Fitzgerald power. It was followed by a drive by English administrators to reform government of the Pale, encouraged by Thomas CROMWELL; English REFORMATION legislation was obediently echoed by the Irish PARLIAMENT. Successive lord deputies Lord Leonard Grey and Sir Anthony St Leger also tried to pursue policies of winning over the Gaelic leaders and integrating them into an English-led system of government alongside the Anglo-Norman aristocracy; this culminated in the proclamation of a kingdom of Ireland in 1541 (*see* HENRY VIII; *LAUDABILITER*), and the granting of PEERAGE titles to Gaelic chiefs. However, success was hampered by the lukewarm English commitment to the conciliation policy, by the clash of English and Gaelic legal inheritance systems (*see* BREHON; SHANE; TANIST), and by increasing Irish resentment at the imposition of new religious policies in parallel with the English Reformation.

Nevertheless it was the Catholic regime of PHILIP II and MARY I which began implementation of a new policy, PLANTATION, which would remain the leading strategy of the English government in Ireland for a century, with dire consequences for the future. Under ELIZABETH I, successive Gaelic noblemen lost faith in the DUBLIN and WESTMINSTER governments, and led rebellions against English encroachment in Ireland. It became increasingly obvious that useful sources of support would be the papacy and Spain, and this helped to commit the disaffected Gaelic leadership to Roman Catholicism. The alignment culminated in 1595 when Hugh O'NEILL and his allies offered the Irish crown to PHILIP II of Spain. The defeat of O'Neill and the FLIGHT OF THE EARLS led to intensifying of the assault on Gaelic society and pursuit of the plantation policy: notable here was the English encouragement of Scots PROTESTANT settlement in the former Gaelic heartland of Ulster.

Resentment culminated in the IRISH REBELLION of 1641; this involved atrocities which lost nothing in the telling, and seemed to confirm the worst prejudices of English Protestants about Irish Catholics. Devastating civil wars followed, involving at least three combatant forces: Confederates (*see* KILKENNY, CONFEDERATION OF), ROYALISTS and PARLIAMENTARIANS. Between 1649 and 1650 the Parliamentarian forces won a ruthless victory (*see* CROMWELL, OLIVER; DROGHEDA), completing the ruin caused by the earlier campaigns and by serious EPIDEMICS; Catholic landowners were systematically dispossessed.

The RESTORATION of CHARLES II ended the legislative union of England and Ireland created by Cromwell and restored the pre-1641 institutions of the Irish kingdom. The land settlement, under the Irish Act of SETTLEMENT of 1662, confirmed a part but not the whole of the post-1641 grants to Protestants: Protestant holdings had increased from some 40 per cent in 1641 to over 90 per cent of the total by 1659, but were then cut back to some 80 per cent.

The new regime was dominated by James Butler, Earl of Ormond, and those noblemen who were Protestant, until JAMES II began returning power to Catholics and appointed Richard Talbot, Earl of Tyrconnel, lord deputy. Despite his initial hesitations about opposing WILLIAM III, Tyrconnel rallied to James when assured of French help; it took more than two years for William's armies to subdue the JACOBITES. This was the final disaster for the Catholic political élite: especially since promises made in the Treaty of LIMERICK were not honoured. The flow of Irish Catholic gentry and others – so-called WILD GEESE – into the service of continental Catholic monarchs, which had begun during the war, continued for decades. Such penal laws as had been passed when the attempt was made to extend the Reformation to Ireland had not been much enforced, but in the Irish parliaments of William and ANNE, a formidable new set of penal laws were enacted, exposing Catholic clergy to regulation and punishment, and depriving the laity of civil rights, including the right to bear arms, to marry Protestants, to have their children educated in Catholic schools, to pass on the bulk of their estates to their oldest sons, to hold land on long leases, and to vote. Though these too were unevenly enforced, they did constrain Catholic opportunities, and expose Catholics to harassment, especially in the first half of the 18th century.

CHRONOLOGY

1480 Gerald FITZGERALD, 8th Earl of Kildare, made lord deputy.

1487 Lambert SIMNEL wins support from Kildare and is crowned Edward VI in Dublin.

1491–2 Perkin WARBECK wins support from Kildare and the Earl of Desmond.

1494–6 Kildare imprisoned by HENRY VII; POYNINGS' LAW enacted 1494 to control Irish PARLIAMENT.

1504 Battle of KNOCKDOE restores Kildare's ascendancy.

1513 Death of 8th Earl of Kildare.

1534 Rebellion led by Thomas Fitzgerald, 10th Earl of Kildare; defeated by Lord Leonard Grey 1535.

1535 Monastic DISSOLUTIONS begin with Grane nunnery.

1536 ROYAL SUPREMACY established by Irish Parliament; as lord deputy, Lord Grey begins policy of conciliating Irish magnates.

1540 Lord deputy St Leger carries on previous conciliation policy.

1541 Con Bacagh O'NEILL ravages PALE; HENRY VIII proclaims himself King (instead of Lord) of Ireland; Gaelic leaders given PEERAGE titles.

1542 First brief and inconclusive visit of JESUITS to Ireland.

1552 First English PROTESTANT bishops appointed.

1555 St Leger finally removed as lord deputy; end of conciliation policies.

1557 First PLANTATIONS sponsored by PHILIP II and MARY I and organized by lord deputy Thomas Radcliffe, Earl of Sussex, in Leix and Offaly.
1566 Rebellion led by Shane O'NEILL.
1569 Rebellion in MUNSTER led by James Fitzmaurice Fitzgerald; ends 1573.
1579 Rebellion in Munster led by Gerald Fitzgerald, 14th Earl of Desmond; papal force under James Fitzmaurice Fitzgerald lands at Dingle: defeated by English.
1586 Plantation of Munster begins.
1595 Hugh O'NEILL, 3rd Earl of Tyrone, seizes English fort on the Blackwater river; offer of Irish crown to PHILIP II of Spain.
1598 Battle of YELLOW FORD; Tyrone defeats English army.
1599 Robert DEVEREUX, Earl of Essex, sent as lord lieutenant.
1600 After signing truce with Tyrone without consulting government in Westminster, Essex recalled and replaced by Charles Blount, Lord Mountjoy.
1601 Battle of KINSALE: besieged Spanish force defeated.
1603 Tyrone surrenders to Mountjoy at Mellifont.
1607 FLIGHT OF THE EARLS removes Catholic and Gaelic lay leadership.
1609 Plantation of ULSTER begins, encouraged by lord deputy Chichester.
1610 Plantation of LEINSTER and Leitrim begins.
1632 Sir Thomas WENTWORTH made lord deputy; introduces policies of THOROUGH.
1641 Gaelic and Old English Catholics rebel against Protestant government and NEW ENGLISH (*see* IRISH REBELLION 1641).
1642 Confederation of KILKENNY formed; early victories against ROYALISTS and PARLIAMENTARIANS, especially by Eoghan Ruadh O'Neill.
1643 Cessation. King's Lord Lieutenant James Butler, Duke of ORMOND, makes a truce with the Confederation of KILKENNY, which is regularly renewed over the following years.
1649 Jan. Grand coalition under James Butler, Earl of Ormond, including some confederate forces, formed to fight English Parliamentarians; defeated by Oliver CROMWELL from Aug. 1649.
1649 11 Sept. Massacre at DROGHEDA, followed (11 Oct.) by massacre at Wexford.
1652 Resistance to English invasion ends.
1654 Large-scale confiscation of lands of Catholics: forcible removal of owners to west coast; English settlement, especially by Parliamentarian ex-soldiers.
1660 Ormond made lord lieutenant; restores royal government and Protestant episcopal establishment.
1662, 1663 Acts of SETTLEMENT and Explanation confirm the greater part of the Cromwellian land settlement.
1663, 1667 CATTLE ACTS – early examples of acts restrictive of Irish trade – are passed.
1687 JAMES II makes Richard Talbot, Earl of Tyrconnel, lord deputy to replace Protestant Henry Hyde, 2nd Earl of Clarendon.
1688 Nov. Invasion of England by William of Orange (the future WILLIAM III) provokes Irish crisis; by Feb. 1689 Tyrconnel has declared for James II.
1689 12 March James II lands at Kinsale from France.
1689 April–July Unsuccessful siege of Protestant-held Derry/Londonderry by James II.
1690 1 July James defeated at the BOYNE.
1691 12 July Battle of AUGHRIM; defeat for James's last significant army.
1691 Oct. Treaty of Limerick ends war. It allows Irish soldiers to go to France, offers Catholics, as a minimum, the religious rights they had under CHARLES II and secures their possession of lands to which they had established a claim.
1691 Dec. Act of English Parliament disables Catholics from sitting in Irish Parliament.

Ireland and England in the 18th century This period is often termed the era of the PROTESTANT ASCENDANCY. Protestant gentry and townsmen monopolized power in PARLIAMENT, the counties and the boroughs until 1793. The nomination of lords lieutenant passed effectively into the hands of the ruling party in the British parliament; until 1767, they customarily resided in England. Although in this context the Irish politicians who administered government (lords justices) and managed parliament (UNDERTAKERS) enjoyed a measure of power and independence, the subordination of Irish parliaments – under the terms of POYNINGS' LAW, and by the convention (affirmed in the DECLARATORY ACT 1720) that the British parliament had the right to legislate for Ireland – provided a recurrent focus for controversy.

William Molyneux challenged these arrangements at the end of the 17th century, and Dean SWIFT, in the context of the WOOD'S HALFPENCE affair, in the 1720s. In many such disputes, constitutional and economic discontents intertwined. Though economic historians have questioned whether British PROTECTIONIST policies significantly stunted Ireland's ECONOMIC GROWTH in this period, the long series of acts regulating commerce between Ireland and Britain, from the CATTLE ACTS on, were motivated more by concern for British than Irish interests. Constitutionalist opposition to British claims blew up once more, in the context of a battle for control of 'surplus revenue', in the IRISH CRISIS OF 1753–6, and carried through from thence, under the leadership first of Henry Flood (1732–91) and later of Henry Grattan (1746–1820) into the campaign for Irish LEGISLATIVE INDEPENDENCE. From 1716 until 1768, Irish parliaments were dissolved and general elections held only upon the death of a monarch. The passage of an Octennial Act in 1768 – requiring that elections to parliament (which conventionally met biennally) be held at least once in every eight years – contributed to the burgeoning of a politicized public opinion.

The War of AMERICAN INDEPENDENCE inspired Irish self-assertion; meanwhile, the dislocation of the economy under the impact of war encouraged a push for enhanced powers of self-determination on economic as well as on constitutional grounds. The accession to power of the reformist Rockingham (*see* WENTWORTH, CHARLES) ministry in 1782 saw most of the Irish patriots' claims granted: Poynings' Law and the Declaratory Act were repealed; any residual claim the British parliament might have to legislate for Ireland was abjured by the RENUNCIATION ACT of the following year. British politicians, having made such concessions to make Ireland governable, worried about the sustainability of so loosely articulated a British/Irish relationship.

PITT THE YOUNGER's 1785 attempt to exact certain guarantees from the Irish parliament foundered both on Irish opposition and on the British manufacturing community's opposition to the COMMERCIAL PROPOSITIONS he intended as a quid pro quo. The REGENCY CRISIS of 1788 underlined the constitutional problem when British and Irish legislatures differed in the terms in which they provided for a regent. The era of GRATTAN'S PARLIAMENT (1782–1801) in one sense saw the apotheosis of Irish Protestant ambitions. However, executive power remained in the hands of British-appointed lords lieutenant, and their ability to construct parliamentary majorities through a variety of forms of influence led radicals to begin to press for PARLIAMENTARY REFORM as the necessary complement to earlier achievements: a VOLUNTEER convention, the ROTUNDA PARLIAMENT, meeting in Dublin in 1783, drafted a reform bill; in the following year, a more radical urban reform movement began to take shape – but at the price of alienating many gentry. A yet more difficult challenge was presented by a notable rise in Irish Catholic assertiveness. What remained of an Irish Catholic landowning élite was increasingly afforced by the development of a Catholic middle class of merchants and professionals. Exploiting the willingness of successive British cabinets and lords lieutenant to offer them concessions in return for promises of loyal support, and the growth of tolerationist sentiment among some (especially Whig and radical) Irish Protestants, Irish Catholics, spearheaded from 1759 by an increasingly ambitious CATHOLIC COMMITTEE, sought modification of the penal laws; and from 1774–93 they secured the repeal of the greater part of them, gaining the vote in 1793. William Wentworth-Fitzwilliam, made lord lieutenant in 1795, would have gone further, admitting Catholics as MPs. Though Pitt himself was prepared to see Catholic MPs – he was to resign in 1801 when GEORGE III blocked his proposals for emancipation – Fitzwilliam was tactless and precipitate, and Pitt dismissed him.

In Ireland, as in Britain, the FRENCH REVOLUTION politicized popular discontent. Peasant or smallholders' grievances had for some decades found expression in WHITEBOYS, DEFENDERS and other such activist protest movements like the anti-TITHE riots in Munster. In the mid 1790s, largely urban-based UNITED IRISHMEN cooperated with rural leaders to plan a rising against British rule. United Irishmen in France, including Wolfe TONE, lobbied for French military backing. After an unsuccessful invasion attempt in 1796, a co-ordinated rising and military landing were planned for 1798 (*see*

IRISH REBELLION). Despite the defeat of the Rebellion an embattled Protestant ascendancy was little inclined to resist British proposals for a Union in 1800–1. From the point of view of the British government, the incorporation of the Irish into a new imperial parliament removed the threat, a source of special worry since 1782, that Ireland might adopt economic or defence policies adverse to British interests.

CHRONOLOGY

1696–1709 Main series of penal laws passed. Catholics are disarmed and forbidden from owning any horse worth more than £5, from running schools, or from having their children educated abroad. In 1697, modifying the treaty of LIMERICK, Catholics exercising ecclesiastical jurisdiction or belonging to religious orders are made liable to TRANSPORTATION; several hundred are transported. Catholics are forbidden to intermarry with Protestants (Protestants who defied the ban were to be treated as Catholics). In 1704 ordinary clergy entering the kingdom are made liable to transportation; priests within the country required to register. Property must be evenly divided among all children; no Catholic might buy freehold land or purchase a lease for more than 31 years. Sworn declarations – affirming that post-revolutionary monarchs were 'rightful' sovereigns and denying transubstantiation – to be taken by any Catholic wishing to vote. Requirement that national and civil office-holders take the sacrament in the Church of Ireland restricts civil rights of DISSENTERS. In 1709 previous penal legislation is tightened up. Registered priests to abjure transubstantiation (made inoperable by mass refusal).

1696 William Molyneux's *Case of Ireland's being bound by Acts of Parliament in England Stated*, asserting the Irish parliament's sole right to legislate for Ireland, is published and condemned.

1719 *ANNESLEY V. SHERLOCK*: Irish House of Lords claims to be the final court of appeal in Irish cases.

1720 DECLARATORY ACT by the British parliament confirms its right to legislate for Ireland.

1722–5 WOOD'S HALFPENCE crisis: Irish interests said to be subordinated to English profiteering.

1748–9 Charles Lucas first comes to public notice as Dublin agitator, laying blame for Irish misfortunes on British misgovernment.

1753–6 Crisis (*see* IRISH CRISIS) in relations between British government and the Irish parliamentary élite, focusing on the disposal of 'surplus revenue'.

1759 CATHOLIC COMMITTEE first meets in Dublin, aiming to relieve legal restrictions on Catholics' religious and civil activities.

1760 Death of GEORGE II and accession of GEORGE III brings first Irish general election since 1727.

1761 First outbreaks of WHITEBOY protest among smallholders in Tipperary.

1763 *Freeman's Journal* founded by Lucas and others as organ of reformist opinion.

1767 Lord lieutenant, Lord Townshend, takes up residence in Ireland, ending the convention whereby the lord lieutenant only attended biennial parliamentary sessions.

1768 Octennial Act provides for general elections at least every eight years.

1770 Townshend persuades various patriots, including Henry Flood, to accept government offices.

1774 Relief bill, providing a simple declaration by which Catholics could attest their loyalty, marks the first significant step towards CATHOLIC EMANCIPATION.

1776 The outbreak of the War of AMERICAN INDEPENDENCE disrupts the Irish economy; Irish VOLUNTEER corps formed to maintain law and order during the absence abroad of troops.

1778–82 Campaign for removal of British restrictions on Irish trade, and for LEGISLATIVE INDEPENDENCE: Grattan and latterly Flood prominent among parliamentary leaders. Support expressed by Irish Volunteers at a convention held at DUNGANNON in 1780.

1778, 1782 Catholic relief bills remove prohibition on Catholics holding land on long leases and purchasing freeholds. Catholics are allowed to run schools under certain restrictions and members of the ecclesiastical hierarchy and of religious orders are allowed to enter the country. Priests no longer have to register.

1780 Sacramental test – which barred Dissenters from public life – is abolished.

1782 Repeal of POYNINGS' LAW and the DECLARATORY ACT.

1783 RENUNCIATION ACT renounces any residual claim of British Parliament to legislate for Ireland.
1783 Sept. Volunteer convention meets at Dungannon to press for parliamentary reform.
1783 Nov. ROTUNDA PARLIAMENT drafts a reform bill, later defeated in Parliament.
1785 PITT THE YOUNGER's attempt to barter commercial concessions (the COMMERCIAL PROPOSITIONS) for an Irish guarantee of conformity to British wishes in matters of imperial finance and trade is rebuffed in both islands.
1788 REGENCY CRISIS: English and Irish Parliaments differ in the terms on which they approve a regency.
1791 UNITED IRISHMEN formed.
1792 Modest Catholic relief bill – allowing Catholics to become barristers and marry Protestants – spurs Catholic committee to further efforts: Wolfe TONE is hired as an organizer and a convention of delegates meets in Dec.
1793 Dungannon Convention supports a moderate measure of parliamentary reform. Relief measure gives Catholics right to bear arms, removes most restrictions on Catholic political participation: admitting them to the magistracy and juries and giving them the right to vote (the British law banning Catholics from sitting in Parliament remains in force).
1794 United Irish agent W. F. Jackson is arrested on his return from a mission to procure French aid for Irish insurrection. United Irishmen are officially suppressed.
1795 Wentworth-Fitzwilliam, the new lord lieutenant, tries to advance towards total Catholic emancipation – and is dismissed by Pitt. Activities of Catholic DEFENDERS prompt formation of first lodges of ORANGE ORDER. Wolfe Tone leaves for America.
1796 Insurrection Act makes it a capital offence to administer an oath and increases powers of authorities. Yeomanry formed. Tone goes to France soliciting support for a rising. In Dec. there is an abortive invasion attempt under Hoche.
1798 British try to forestall the IRISH REBELLION by arresting the leaders. In March Lord Edward FITZGERALD is captured and mortally wounded. In May scattered risings are put down by the British army; largest clash at VINEGAR HILL in June. Belated arrival of French expeditionary force in Aug.
1799 Act of UNION recommended in speech from throne.
1800 Aug. Act of Union passed uniting British and Irish Parliaments from Jan. 1801. Pitt resigns in Feb. when GEORGE III will not allow complementary measure of Catholic emancipation.

For Ireland from union to free state *see* IRISH QUESTION (IRELAND: UNION TO FREE STATE).

Ireland, 1st Duke of, *see* DE VERE, ROBERT

Ireland, New English in, the name given to 16th- and 17th-century English settlers in Ireland, mostly PROTESTANTS (*see* PLANTATIONS IN IRELAND), in contrast to the 'Old English', whose families had often been in Ireland for centuries and few of whom accepted the REFORMATION. The difference is important in 17th-century Irish conflicts: the Old English tended to side with the CATHOLIC Gaelic population in bitter resentment against the New English. Historians often call the Old English 'Anglo-Irish', a term used more loosely in the 19th and 20th centuries to describe Irish people of English descent.

Ireland, Northern, *see* ULSTER

Ireland, Plantations in, *see* PLANTATIONS IN IRELAND

Irish Catholic Committee, *see* CATHOLIC COMMITTEE, IRISH

Irish Church Act 1869 An aspect of GLADSTONE's programme for the pacification of Ireland, it provided for the removal of a PROTESTANT establishment that was offensive to the generality of Irish Catholics. The Church of Ireland was disestablished on 1 Jan. 1871, the courts spiritual were abolished, and provision made for the organization of a non-established EPISCOPAL church. Curates and incumbents received compensation. *See also* CHURCH: IRELAND.

Irish Civil War, 1922–3. The divisions within Irish nationalism caused by the ANGLO-IRISH TREATY of 1921, narrowly accepted by the Irish DÁIL in Jan. 1922, broke out into open warfare during that summer. The Republican or 'anti-treaty' faction, including DE VALERA, refused to accept the partition of Ireland and the continuing link with Britain symbolized by the declaration of faithfulness to the crown. Republicans began to carry out raids on ULSTER and ambushes of government forces in the IRISH FREE STATE. Following victory by the pro-treaty faction in the June 1922 general election, a group of Republicans seized the Law Courts Building in DUBLIN and held it for two days before destroying it (together with virtually all Ireland's historic official archives) and being forced to surrender. In early Aug. an IRISH REPUBLICAN ARMY assault on Dublin was beaten back, but later that month the nationalist leader Michael COLLINS was ambushed and killed in Co. Cork. By May 1923 the Free State had hunted down and imprisoned virtually all the anti-treaty forces, carrying out many executions for treason, and the rebels called for a ceasefire. De Valera and other political prisoners were released in July 1924.

This bitter 'Free State War' polarized Irish politics for decades. The victorious pro-treaty forces set up a new governing party, and re-established CUMANN NA NGAEDHEAL, while the remaining SINN FÉIN members refused to accept the outcome or to take their seats in the Dáil. In 1926 De Valera, who had been a non-combatant supporter of the anti-treaty side, formed a new party, FIANNA FÁIL, as an anti-British republican party with the aim of altering the treaty by peaceful means.

Irish Combination Acts Similar in content to English COMBINATION ACTS, these had a distinct history. The most sweeping such act to be passed by the Irish parliament before the UNION was an Act of 1780, reflecting in part concern at the increasingly prominent role the Dublin guilds were playing in political agitation in the era of the campaign for LEGISLATIVE INDEPENDENCE. All such acts applying to Ireland, as well as to England and Scotland were repealed in 1824.

Irish Crisis of 1753–6, crisis of governance in Ireland, involving a series of stand-offs between lords lieutenant (or the lords justices who ruled the island in their absence) and leading Irish parliamentarians, mobilized in a form of patriot opposition. Dissatisfaction with Ireland's subordination to English government, as embodied most notably in POYNINGS' LAW, had surfaced on several previous occasions, having been stirred by the 1689 JACOBITE PARLIAMENT, at the turn of the century by the scholar and writer William Molyneux author of *The Case of Ireland's being bound by Acts of Parliament in England Stated* (1696), an attempt to establish Ireland's independence, and others, and in 1722–5 during the crisis over WOOD'S HALFPENCE. Troubles at mid-century focused especially on controversies over who had the right to dispose of a revenue surplus – the king (since the surplus arose on the hereditary revenue), or the Irish parliament, argued by some to possess a constitutional right to determine the disposition of moneys raised by Irish taxation. The emergence of an opposition press from the 1740s, and the activities of the demagogue Charles Lucas (1713–71), sometimes called 'the Irish WILKES', helped to create a context in which some parliamentarians were emboldened to adopt a defiant stance. In 1753, a clash between the British PRIVY COUNCIL and Irish Parliament led the lord lieutenant, Dorset, to prorogue Parliament. Archbishop Stone, the dominant figure among the lords justices, dismissed major office-holders. A general election was contemplated but the administration was not confident that it would strengthen its position. The crisis was resolved by a new lord lieutenant, William CAVENDISH, Marquess of Hartington (who succeeded as 4th Duke of Devonshire in 1755), whose family owned great Irish estates and whose kin networks encompassed Irish political families on all sides of the dispute. Erstwhile critics of government were made lords justices or promoted or restored to other political offices. The fragility of Devonshire's settlement was however revealed when his successor, John Russell, 7th Duke of Bedford faced similar constitutionalist complaints. Building up through the 1760s and 1770s, the patriot campaign was to culminate in the winning of Irish LEGISLATIVE INDEPENDENCE in 1782.

Irish Famine, *see* POTATO FAMINE

Irish Free State, independent state formed in Ireland (less the six counties in ULSTER) in 1922, with DOMINION status and an oath of allegiance to the crown. The refusal of many to accept the oath led to the IRISH CIVIL WAR, in which the Republicans were virtually stamped out and leaders like Michael COLLINS, who had signed the treaty with the

British, were killed. In 1932, when DE VALERA came to power, the process of dismantling the Free State was begun, with the oath of allegiance abolished in 1933 and a new constitution in 1937 changing the name of the Irish Free State to EIRE. In 1949 Eire became the Irish Republic.

Irish Land Act 1870 A central feature of GLADSTONE's attempt to pacify Ireland, it gave tenants protection against arbitrary eviction, established a right to compensation for improvements, and provided loans to tenants who wanted to buy their holdings. It ended the absolute right of the landowner to his land but did not protect tenants against exorbitant rents or achieve its goal of ensuring peace between landlords and tenants.

Irish Land League, an association formed in 1879 by Michael Davitt with PARNELL as president in reaction to the worsening plight of tenant farmers in Ireland. Set up as a moral force, it aimed to compel a reduction in the rents of land and, where proprietors refused to comply, to withhold the payment of rent. It was seen in the government's eyes as a physical force as well, and the League was an important step on the road to Irish independence. Its principal weapon was the BOYCOTT, which was ultimately successful since the passage of the 1881 Irish Land Act guaranteed the 'Three Fs' – fair rent, free sale, fixity of tenure – for which it had been fighting. Although the land war continued into 1882, it died out as the Act took force, but the identification of the national movement with the land problem was a significant development of the IRISH QUESTION, and made the League an important influence on the growth of HOME RULE agitation. The League itself provided the framework for Parnell's new political movement, the NATIONAL LEAGUE.

Irish Land Purchase Act 1903 (the Wyndham Act). A generous scheme that aimed to strike at the root of the Irish land agitation, it made £100 million available for land purchase by tenants. However, although this was not too little, it was too late; nationalism was too deeply embedded to reconcile the Irish Catholic peasant to English rule.

Irish National Federation (INF) Anti-PARNELLite organization formed in March 1891, led by John Dillon and others, it was stronger than the NATIONAL LEAGUE, from which it had broken. Throughout the 1890s the wrangling between the various nationalist groups fostered disillusionment. As a response to the rise of the United Irish League founded in 1898, the INF and the National League reunited in 1900 under John Redmond in the United Irish League.

Irish National Liberation Army (INLA), breakaway nationalist paramilitary organization within Northern Ireland, which first announced its existence with the car-bomb murder of Airey Neave MP at Westminster in March 1979. *See also* IRISH REPUBLICAN ARMY.

Irish Question (Ireland: Union to Free State) One of the longest-running and most intractable issues in British politics, the critical concerns of the Irish question have revolved around land, religion and the political conflicts arising from these.

The arrested economic development of Ireland – above all, the lack of a much-needed agrarian revolution – left a growing population dangerously dependent on a diminishing means of subsistence. In the 1840s, famine followed the failure of the staple crop, the potato, on which the population largely depended, and mass emigration followed. Three-quarters of Ireland's population were Catholic, whereas the majority of landowners were absentee Protestants.

Increasing resistance from the Catholic peasantry was met with coercion and conciliation, sometimes singly and sometimes in combination, but always to no avail. With Irish MPs now at Westminster, the political arena moved from Dublin to London. Irish nationalism grew inexorably and, by the 1870s, HOME RULE was the most consistently important demand in British politics, with increasingly vociferous and militant groups being formed in Ireland for its prosecution (*see* FENIANS; IRISH LAND LEAGUE; IRISH NATIONAL FEDERATION; NATIONAL LEAGUE; PARNELL, CHARLES). The outbreak of WORLD WAR I postponed this demand, but also offered Irish nationalists the opportunity for action – possibly with the support of Germany. The EASTER RISING of 1916 was suppressed by British forces, but it ushered in a period of conflict – the ANGLO-IRISH WAR (*see* BLACK AND TANS) – which was not resolved until the ANGLO-IRISH TREATY 1921.

The treaty finally recognized the whole of Ireland (with the exception of the six counties of Ulster) as the independent IRISH FREE STATE, with DOMINION status within the BRITISH EMPIRE.

CHRONOLOGY

1801 Irish Parliament abolished by Act of UNION in expectation that Catholics will receive equal rights with Protestants. PITT THE YOUNGER's intentions frustrated by GEORGE III's refusal to countenance CATHOLIC EMANCIPATION.

1823 O'CONNELL forms Catholic Association to unite religion and nationalism in peaceful campaign for equal rights.

1825 Catholic Association declared illegal.

1828 O'Connell's victory at Co. Clare election compels Wellington (*see* WELLESLEY, ARTHUR) and other defenders of PROTESTANT ASCENDANCY to concede Catholic Emancipation as alternative to civil war.

1829 CATHOLIC EMANCIPATION ACT grants civil equality to Irish Catholics; O'Connell takes seat in Commons.

1835 Lichfield House Compact, anti-CONSERVATIVE alliance supported by O'Connell in hope of securing WHIG support for repeal of Union and reform.

1843 O'Connell's climbdown over prohibited Clontarf meeting widens breach with nationalist militants, offended by his brinkmanship and outraged by his concession of federalist solution instead of full repeal of Union.

1845 Failure of potato crop followed by POTATO FAMINE and emigration; CORN LAWS repealed too late to save lives. POPULATION falls from 8.1 million in 1841 to little more than 6.5 million in 1851; increasing bitterness informs Anglo-Irish relations thereafter.

1847 YOUNG IRELAND organization formed to promote national regeneration along Mazzinian lines of a Young Italy movement.

1848 Poorly organized rising in Tipperary led by Young Ireland, suppressed with violence.

1867 FENIAN insurrection. Campaign of bombings, gaol-breaks and murders; formation of Special (Irish) Branch follows.

1868–71 GLADSTONE makes pacification of Ireland a priority, disestablishes Irish Church and tackles land problem, but evictions continue.

1877 PARNELL becomes leader of Irish Home Rule Party and pursues policy of obstruction in House of Commons to underscore urgency of HOME RULE.

1879 IRISH LAND LEAGUE formed to resist eviction; Parnell, elected president, orders supporters to have nothing to do with those taking over farms after evictions; Captain BOYCOTT the first victim.

1881 W. E. Forster, chief secretary for Ireland, introduces Coercion Act to allow arrests without trial, and Land Act providing fair rents, fixity of tenure and free sale; Parnell imprisoned in Kilmainham Gaol.

1882 Under Kilmainham treaty, Parnell agrees to call off violence in return for improved government assistance for tenants in arrears; Forster resigns in disgust. Successor, Lord Frederick Cavendish, and his under-secretary both assassinated shortly afterwards in PHOENIX PARK. New Coercion Act passed and violence continues.

1885–6 Parnell holds balance of power after general election in Nov. 1885; Gladstone declares for Home Rule in Dec.; Salisbury's (*see* CECIL, ROBERT GASCOYNE) minority government turned out in Jan.; Home Rule Bill introduced in April, defeated in June; Gladstone resigns.

1886 Ulster Protestants – mobilized by Lord Randolph Churchill (under slogan 'Ulster will fight and Ulster will be right') – threaten civil war to prevent Home Rule.

1890 Parnell cited as co-respondent in O'Shea divorce case; alliance with Liberals abandoned and Home Rule party split.

1892 Gladstone tables second Home Rule Bill. Commons rejects it and he resigns, having split his party without pacifying Irish.

1893–1905 Ireland under Salisbury administrations pursues a policy of firm government coupled with a number of Land Purchase Acts (*see* IRISH LAND PURCHASE ACT 1903) which aim to assist creation of body of contented Irish proprietors. Support for Home Rule not diminished.

1907 SINN FÉIN founded by Arthur Griffith.

1910–12 LIBERAL government, dependent on Irish nationalist support in Commons, concedes PARLIAMENT ACT 1911 to prevent Lords' veto on passage of Home Rule Bill 1912, which, though defeated in Lords, will become law in 1914.

1912–13 Ulster Protestants organized into volunteer army, with Tory Party support;

pledge to defend Union with guns from Germany. Formation of Irish Volunteers, nationalist defence force, increases likelihood of civil war.

1914 CURRAGH MUTINY by British army officers (March); resignations of war minister, chief of the imperial general staff and other officers follow. Since reliability of army in Ulster doubtful in event of civil war, when Home Rule Bill becomes law in Sept., it is agreed to suspend it until after WORLD WAR I.

1916 EASTER RISING: militant nationalists, seizing opportunity created by World War I, carry out insurrection. It is bloodily suppressed, creating martyrs and nucleus of expanding Sinn Féin independence party; by end of war, this completely eclipses John Redmond's Home Rule movement.

1919–20 Britain attempts to coerce Ireland by armed police, regular soldiers, irregular auxiliaries and notorious BLACK AND TANS. Proposed division of Ireland, embodied in Government of Ireland Act 1920, unacceptable to Sinn Féin; fighting continues.

1921 Treaty is agreed providing for formation of IRISH FREE STATE excluding six counties of the north.

Irish Rebellion, 1641–52. Sparked by discontent over increasing English and Scottish colonization (*see* PLANTATIONS), the uprising had the backing of both Gaelic and OLD ENGLISH. In turn, the news of the uprising, accompanied by greatly exaggerated tales of the massacre of Protestants, reached London on 1 Nov. 1641, greatly heightening tensions between CHARLES I and those of his English subjects already fearful of 'Popish' conspiracies. The rebellion provided an essential element in the formulation of the GRAND REMONSTRANCE, and the question of who should control the army to be raised to suppress the uprising constituted one of the key factors in the subsequent breach between Charles I and the Houses. In the event, the uprising was only suppressed after Charles I's execution (and after the Catholic rebels had allied with a segment of Irish Protestant royalists). The suppression was followed by a short-lived legislative union of the two kingdoms and by a more lasting and massive dispossession of Irish Catholic landowners.

Irish Rebellion, 1798. In the aftermath of the FRENCH REVOLUTION, socio-economic and sectarian discontent (of the sort that had previously found expression in WHITEBOY, DEFENDER and other movements) fused with a campaign for radical constitutional change promoted by the UNITED IRISHMEN to produce widespread politicized unrest among both Catholics and Protestants. Legislation was introduced, as also in England, to strengthen the government's hand, notably an Insurrection Act of 1796, in which year a yeomanry force was also formed. Lobbying of the French revolutionary government for support by UNITED IRISH agent Wolfe TONE produced an abortive invasion attempt in Dec. of that year. In 1797 the government ordered the disarming of ULSTER (unlike Catholics, Protestants had traditionally been allowed to bear arms, and many remained as a legacy of the VOLUNTEER movement). Government attention then turned to LEINSTER, in the east, where an attempt to arrest leaders early in 1798 led to the mortal wounding of the radical son of a leading WHIG family, Lord Edward FITZGERALD. May–June saw a series of uncoordinated risings, most widespread in the south-east, where a final stand was made at VINEGAR HILL on 21 June. Risings in ULSTER subsided after a major battle at Ballynahinch. French expeditionary forces were belatedly sent in the later summer and autumn and were speedily repelled. The revolutionary and separatist movement then went underground. In all, some 30–50,000 men were involved in risings in 18 counties; total deaths – mainly of rebels – may have numbered 20,000. The rebellion played a formative part in the development of an Irish radical/revolutionary tradition, and was frequently harked back to by later generations. People convicted of involvement in the rising or of other seditious activity, and sentenced to TRANSPORTATION to AUSTRALIA, cherished memories of the rising, and fought their own 'battle of Vinegar Hill' against government forces outside Sydney in 1804.

Irish Republic, *see* EIRE

Irish Republican Army (IRA), Irish nationalist paramilitary organization, split since 1970 into two rival groups, 'Official' and 'Provisional', both dedicated to the unification of Ireland into an autonomous republican state. A direct descendant of a number of anti-British, often revolutionary, organizations, from the FENIAN movement of 1858 (reconstituted as the Irish Revolutionary Brotherhood in 1873) onwards, the IRA emerged in 1919 out of the defeat of the 1916 EASTER RISING and the struggle against the British in the aftermath of WORLD WAR I. In rejecting the ANGLO-IRISH TREATY partitioning Ireland, it also came to fight the bitter and bloody civil war with the newly formed IRISH FREE STATE.

Thereafter, the IRA became a secret underground organization, generally marginal to Irish politics but mounting sporadic bombing campaigns in ULSTER and on the mainland until the mid-1950s and the border campaign of violence between 1956 and 1962. The standing of the IRA was revived with renewed violence and struggle in 1969, with the failure of the CIVIL RIGHTS movement and the hard-line response of ULSTER UNIONISM. Armed with weapons smuggled in from the Irish Republic, and in part funded by American sympathizers, the IRA stepped into the power vacuum and rallied the nationalist cause.

In 1970 the Belfast-based leadership split from the Dublin-based Army High Command to form the Provisional IRA, which quickly came to dominate the armed struggle in Northern Ireland, their campaign of bombings, assassinations and attacks on troops – who had first been dispatched to the province in 1969 – competing in violence with the actions of Protestant, LOYALIST paramilitary groups which had sprung up in response. The political party associated with the IRA, Provisional SINN FÉIN, has acted as the constitutional wing of the organization, putting up candidates in parliamentary and local elections.

Following the Downing Street Declaration issued by the British and Irish governments in December 1993 which reiterated the constitutional possibilities open to all for peace in Northern Ireland, the IRA declared a cease fire in August 1994 suspending military operations: it ended with a bomb explosion at London's Canary Wharf in Feb. 1996.

All-party peace talks recommended in 1997, culminated in the Good Friday Agreement in April 1998, authorizing a referendum on the settlement of Northern Ireland and elections to a new Northern Ireland assembly.

Irish Revolutionary Brotherhood (IRB) A direct descendant of the anti-British, often revolutionary organizations loosely known as the FENIAN movement of 1858, the Irish Revolutionary Brotherhood was reconstituted in 1873. In its new constitution it declared that the Irish people should decide the fit hour for inaugurating war against England; but the means for achieving that often proved confused in the fractured state of late 19th-century Irish politics. Some members joined the Home Rule League and obstructed proceedings in the COMMONS at Westminster; the rise of the IRISH LAND LEAGUE and, following it, the NATIONAL LEAGUE prompted some in the IRB to form new political alliances within the more extremist nationalist groups. Although support for the IRB was falling in the 1890s, it had a brief resurgence in 1898 amid the centenary celebrations for the IRISH REBELLION, and a more lasting revival under the leadership of younger men after 1904. The IRB and its paramilitary sister group, the Irish Volunteer Force, were the main movers in the abortive EASTER RISING in 1916. Out of their defeat and the split in the IRB during the IRISH CIVIL WAR (leading to its dissolution in 1924) the IRA (*see* IRISH REPUBLICAN ARMY) was founded.

Irish Treaty Ports, four naval bases in the Irish Free State over which Britain retained control as part of the ANGLO-IRISH TREATY of 1921. As part of an Anglo-Irish Agreement signed by Neville CHAMBERLAIN and DE VALERA in 1938 they reverted to Irish control as a gesture of British goodwill. Irish refusal to allow Britain the use of the ports at the outbreak of WORLD WAR II caused great bitterness in Anglo-Irish relations. De Valera insisted on strict Irish neutrality, even to the point of refusing to consider a negotiated unification of all Ireland after the war in return for use of the bases.

Irish Volunteers, *see* IRISH QUESTION

Irish War of Independence, *see* ANGLO-IRISH WAR

Iron and Steel Industry Iron was mined and worked in Britain during the Roman occupation, and there is some evidence of this continuing in the Anglo-Saxon period. From the 11th century the Forest of Dean (Glos.) was the main centre, but other areas gradually began production, notably in a resumption of earlier activity in the Weald (Sussex and Kent), which rapidly developed its armaments industry in the 1540s, encouraged by HENRY VIII. The first reference to a blast-furnace in England comes from the Weald (1496), and by the late 16th century, blast-furnaces were to be found in the northern areas of the industry. By 1700 many industrial villages had particular specializations, in locks, knives, chains or the like. By later standards, however, output was small up to the mid-18th century.

The iron industry was then to play a leading role in the industrialization of Britain between 1790 and 1850 (*see* INDUSTRIAL REVOLUTION). During the 18th century, it was able not only to supply other industries but also to contribute to the EXPORT market. The transformation was due to a series of technical improvements associated with the work of Abraham Darby, Benjamin Huntsman and Henry Cort, and to the efforts of a remarkable series of ironmasters such as John Wilkinson, Robert Crawshay and Samuel Walker.

The substitution of COAL for charcoal as the energy source and the application of STEAM to the manufacturing process served to liberate the foundry from the forests, freed the industry from dependence on inadequate supplies of WATER POWER and concentrated production on the coalfields. The important iron-producing districts were South Wales, Staffs., Salop and Scotland. The scale of operations varied. The leading firms were integrated, having their own coal and iron mines and being able to undertake refining and rolling as well as smelting operations.

In the half-century that followed VICTORIA's accession in 1837, the iron and steel industry went from strength to strength. After 1815, the demand for armaments gave way to orders for boilers, machine parts, water pipes, RAILWAY lines, rolling-stock, bridges and ships. The extraordinary expansion of steel production was in no small part due to the respective inventions of Henry Bessemer (*see* BESSEMER PROCESS) and Sidney Gilchrist Thomas. The latter's BASIC PROCESS, designed to cope with phosphoric ores, led to the growth of new steel-making centres located on the ironstone of the Cleveland Hills and the subsequent development of Middlesbrough.

For most of the 19th century, Britain was world leader in both production and consumption, but by WORLD WAR I, German and American competition had outstripped the British in terms of output and per capita consumption. Britain's share of world production and world exports fell sharply: in 1880, iron and steel had ranked second to COTTON textiles among its industries, but by 1907, they had fallen to eighth place. Contemporaries were critical, and wondered what had gone wrong. Relative economic decline, historians suggest, was simply the penalty of previous success; entrepreneurial behaviour in iron and steel after the 1880s appears to be poor only because it had formerly been so good and had enjoyed a lack of effective competition in export markets.

The 20th century has witnessed further contraction in the iron and steel industry, with continued success only coming in those products where high-grade materials are important: stainless and special steels, for example. The decline of the industry intensified difficulties in ASSISTED AREAS, while NATIONALIZATION made British Steel a political football.

CHRONOLOGY: INVENTION AND INNOVATION

1740 Benjamin Huntsman of Handsworth near Sheffield devises process of producing crucible or cast steel.

1760 Carron Ironworks opens to carry on coke smelting.

1769 James Watt's first engine set up at Carron Ironworks.

1783–4 Puddling and rolling perfected by Henry Cort, enabling pit coal to be used in production of bar iron of high quality.

1800–30 Boulton and Watt engines employed in iron industry.

1806 Charcoal iron accounts for 7,800 tons out of total output of 258,206 tons.

1829 James Neilson's hot blast, patented and tried out at Clyde Ironworks in Scotland, produces massive fuel efficiencies in productive process.

1856 Patenting of BESSEMER converter, which removes impurities from pig iron.

1856–7 William Siemens develops 'open-hearth' steel production to obtain greater range of hardness and mildness, and metal that is more uniform and reliable throughout than Bessemer steel.

1879 Basic Process, perfected by Sidney Gilchrist Thomas, allows phosphoric iron ores to be used.
1900 Commercial introduction of Talbot tilting furnace, designed to deal with problem of slag accumulation that is particularly acute in open-hearth process.

Irvingites, *see* CATHOLIC APOSTOLIC CHURCH

Isabella of Angoulême (c. 1188-1246), Queen of England. Daughter and heiress of Audemar, Count of Angoulême, she married King JOHN in Aug. 1200, despite already being betrothed to Hugh of Lusignan. The following year, angered at John making light of his protests, Hugh rebelled and appealed to Philip II Augustus of France for justice, an action that was to lead directly to the collapse of the ANGEVIN EMPIRE.

Isabella bore John five children. In 1218, two years after his death, she returned to Angoulême and married Hugh of Lusignan (the son of her former fiancé). Their nine children are known collectively in English history as 'the LUSIGNANS'. In 1242, she encouraged HENRY III, her eldest son from her first marriage, to undertake the disastrous Taillebourg campaign. The following year, she retired to Fontevrault Abbey, where she was eventually buried.

Isabella of France (1293-1358), Queen of England. Daughter of Philip IV of France and reputed to be one of the most beautiful women of her time, she was married to EDWARD II in 1308. Convention required the queen to play the role of mediator, so her husband's alleged preference for GAVESTON must have made her introduction to the English political scene a remarkably difficult one. However, once Gaveston was dead, she managed to bear the king four children (between 1312 and 1321). In fact, she lived up to the expectations placed in her so well that she clearly enjoyed widespread sympathy when, in 1325, she chose to disobey her husband and strike out on an extraordinary path of her own.

Having been sent to France – with her son, the future EDWARD III – to negotiate with her brother, Charles IV, the ending of the war of SAINT-SARDOS, she refused to return. In Paris, she became Roger Mortimer's mistress, and together they planned and executed an invasion of England, landing in Sept. 1326. Virtually no one was prepared to fight for King Edward and his favourites, Hugh Despenser (*c.*1287–1326) and his father, within a matter of weeks, Mortimer and Isabella were in control. In Jan. 1327, Edward III was proclaimed king – as a 14-year-old, he still did what his mother told him – and for the next three years, she and her lover ruled England.

However, they were soon faced with gathering resentment of their ostentatious lifestyle and policies; Edward II's murder, the humiliating treaty of NORTHAMPTON and the execution for treason of the king's uncle, Edmund, Earl of Kent, were all laid at their door. On 18 Oct. 1330, the young king forced his way into his mother's chamber in Nottingham Castle and arrested Mortimer. Isabella was forced to forfeit her estates, but the substantial allowance of £3,000 a year she received enabled her to live very comfortably indeed, until, towards the end of her life, she took the habit of the Poor Clares. She has not enjoyed a favourable press since 1327, and is still widely known by the nickname given to her by Thomas Gray: the 'She-Wolf of France'.

ITV, *see* INDEPENDENT TELEVISION

Ivar the Boneless, King of Dublin. One of the great VIKING warriors of the sagas, a literary creation of the 12th and 13th centuries, he was a superhuman figure invented in an age that mythologized its Viking past. He may have been based on Ingwaer (?–873), who, with his brother HALFDAN, led the GREAT ARMY. Ingwaer pursued a spectacular career of violence and plunder in Ireland (*see* DUBLIN), England and Scotland (*see* DUMBARTON ROCK) between 857 and 873. One of his possible exploits was the murder of EDMUND, King of EAST ANGLIA.

J

Jacobins, name applied to political RADICALS from the 1790s and derived from the Jacobin Club (1790–4), the best known and most influential of the political clubs which appeared in France during the FRENCH REVOLUTION. British radicals were commonly sympathetic to some of the French revolutionaries. British conservatives played up the connection, attempting to tar British radicals with the taint of disloyalty and extremism. The reference was built into the title of one of the more influential anti-radical organs of the period: the *Anti-Jacobin Review and Magazine* (1798–1821) – succeeding the short-lived *Anti-Jacobin* (1797–8).

Jacobite Parliament, 1689. Summoned by JAMES II after the GLORIOUS REVOLUTION, this was the only Irish PARLIAMENT to be opened by the king in person until 1921. The fact that the English parliament no longer recognized James as king required this parliament to challenge the English parliament's claims, but James would not allow the repeal of POYNINGS' LAW which required that not only the Irish but also the English PRIVY COUNCIL must previously assent to any bill brought into the Irish parliament. After long wrangling, it was agreed that a Court of Claims should be established, where landowners who had lost lands in 1641 might sue for their recovery; those who had bought them might be compensated with land confiscated from adherents of WILLIAM III. Predominantly Catholic in membership, though with four CHURCH OF IRELAND bishops attending, the parliament also passed an Act for Liberty of Conscience. All its acts were annulled by order of the parliament of 1695, the first called by William III.

Jacobites, those who remained loyal to the Stuart dynasty in exile after the GLORIOUS REVOLUTION of 1688–9 (from *Jacobus*, Latin for James). It is difficult to establish the extent of Jacobitism. Information gathered by an ever-hopeful Jacobite court probably overestimated its strength, while more direct evidence probably underestimates it: it seems probable that prudent Jacobites would have suppressed evidence of potentially treasonable activity. Until the HANOVERIAN SUCCESSION was securely established, many politicians hedged their bets. Sentimental Jacobitism, expressed in the drinking of toasts and wearing of WHITE ROSES, and an enduring belief that the Stuarts had the strongest claim to the throne, not necessarily coupled with any desire to unseat the current occupant, may have been quite widespread down to the mid-18th century. In practice the restoration of the Stuarts could probably only have followed foreign-backed invasion. The timing of several such attempts – 1708, 1715, 1719, 1745 – was significantly influenced by international events. James Edward STUART (the Old Pretender) in 1715 and Charles Edward STUART (the Young Pretender) in 1745 attracted substantial support in Scotland, and some support from English Catholics and from some northern TORIES, but little from any other quarter. Both risings were militarily defeated: the '15 at SHERIFFMUIR, the '45 at CULLODEN. The defeat of the '45, and modification of the exclusiveness of WHIG OLIGARCHY from the 1740s, all but extinguished Jacobite hopes. The cause finally collapsed with the death of Charles Edward in 1788, though the claim was notionally continued by his brother Henry, a cardinal from 1747.

Jamaica, Caribbean island and former British colony. The island was seized from Spain in Oliver CROMWELL's war of 1655. It rapidly became a SUGAR-based economy, attracting a large number of planters and utilizing slave workers (*see* SLAVERY). The island was also a base for pirates and buccaneers; the destruction of the original main town, Port Royal, in 1690 by an earthquake was seen as a Sodom and Gomorrah-like judgement. The new capital, Kingston, was then built on the southern side of the island. Bauxite-mining for aluminium production became a very important trade in the 20th century, but it and many of the older industries have experienced substantial decline. Jamaica provided the majority of Caribbean immigrants (*see* MIGRATION) to Britain in the 1950s and 1960s, while its music industry has been of critical importance as a source of innovation since the 1960s. The influential black religion of Rastafarianism, with its hope of returning to an Ethiopian 'homeland' and veneration for Emperor Haile Selassie, is also a particularly Jamaican phenomenon.

Jamaica Insurrection A rising in this British colony in Oct. 1865 – by exploited Caribbean workers against planters and magistrates – led to the proclamation of martial law, and the inflicting of savage punishments: 439 black people were executed, 600 (women included) flogged and 1,000 homes burned. William Gordon, a champion of the plantation workers, was brought by unlawful means before an illegal tribunal, tried and executed. Governor Eyre, appointed in 1861, was exonerated of any charge of wrong-doing in suppressing the rebellion. The incident displayed Victorian racism at its worst.

James I (1394–1437), King of Scots (1406–37). In 1406, shortly after falling into English hands while being sent to France for safety, he succeeded his father ROBERT III. The 12-year-old king remained a captive until 1424. In James's view, this was because the Duke of Albany, Scotland's governor and his uncle and heir-presumptive, did nothing to secure his release, and it was only after agreeing to pay a 50,000-mark ransom that he was freed. He used the enforced leisure to compose the greater part of a long, allegorical and romantic poem, the *Kingis Quair*, which includes a description of how he fell in love with Joan Beaufort, whom he married in Feb. 1424.

On his return to Scotland, James initiated a flood of statutes. Very little escaped his paternalist and interventionist concern for law and order and the well-being of his subjects – e.g. he forbade the playing of football. He also imposed taxes, ostensibly to raise the money for his ransom. He had other ways of filling his treasury: in 1425, he executed the leading members of the house of Albany and confiscated their estates, and by meting out similar treatment to other nobles, including Highland chiefs, he was able to treble the royal estates.

Inevitably, there were some who saw him as a tyrant. In 1437, a group of conspirators broke into his chamber at Perth and murdered him.

James I, King of England, *see* JAMES VI AND I

James II (1430–60), King of Scots (1437–60). Although king in name ever since the murder of his father JAMES I in 1437, it was his 1449 marriage to Mary of Guelders, niece of Duke Philip of BURGUNDY, that marked his assumption of power. By the marriage treaty, he was bound to pay her the immense dower of £5,000 a year.

His first moves were directed against the Livingstons, one of the families that had dominated Scottish politics during his minority. Then, between 1450 and 1455, he launched a series of attacks on the Black Douglases, including the murder of Earl William Douglas in Feb. 1452 at Stirling Castle – a flagrant breach of his sworn word, since the earl had been under safe-conduct. The ensuing confiscations and revocations of earlier grants meant that the crown emerged much richer. In 1458, a compliant Parliament announced that 'all rebels and breakers of his justice are removed'.

An aggressive and warlike king, fascinated by the latest weaponry (i.e. guns), in his legislation James proclaimed his concern for justice, order, economic stability and royal authority. In 1460, intending to use the disarray south of the border to put an end to the English occupation of Teviotdale, he was besieging Roxburgh when one of his siege guns blew up and killed him.

James II, King of England, *see* JAMES VII AND II

James III (1452–88), King of Scots (1460–88). Proclaimed king in 1460 after the death of his father JAMES II, six years later – during one of the factional struggles that characterized his minority – he suffered the indignity of being kidnapped. On taking over power in 1469, he had his abductors, the Boyds, punished as traitors. In the same year, he married Margaret of Denmark – whom, after her death in 1486, he tried to have canonized.

In 1479, he confiscated the estates of his brothers, the Duke of Albany and the Earl of Mar. The latter died in suspicious circumstances, and Albany fled to England. James attempted to make peace with England, betrothing his sister to Anthony Woodville, Earl Rivers, but when she was found to be already pregnant, negotiations collapsed, war broke out, and in 1482 the English, accompanied by Albany, invaded Scotland. James mustered an army at Lauder only to be seized by a group of conspirators led by the Earl of Angus. He was held prisoner in EDINBURGH Castle until the following year, when, by exploiting divisions between his various opponents, he was able to secure his restoration. However, his attempts to use the judicial process to punish his enemies only led to a renewal of opposition, this time led by his own heir, the future JAMES IV.

James III was killed at or after the battle of Sauchieburn on 11 June 1488. The historian Hector Boece (?1465–1536) described him as the king who subdued the Highlands and brought peace to the whole of Scotland, but the prevailing image created by historians of the 16th and later centuries is of a king corrupted by low-born counsellors. Although many of the details of that image appear to be based on little more than legend, successive Parliaments in the 1470s and 1480s did criticize his greed and laziness, and Lauder and Sauchieburn bear witness to the degree of hostility felt by significant numbers of his more powerful subjects.

James IV (1473–1513), King of Scots (1488–1513). Son of JAMES III, he did penance on his coronation in 1488 for his part in his father's death, which caused him long-term guilt. He was energetic in crushing internal opposition and defending his frontiers; he extended effective royal control to the Western Isles, and developed EDINBURGH's role as royal capital and seat of the law courts. Intelligent and popular, he was a great builder and actively encouraged education, literature and the arts, becoming patron of the new university college at ABERDEEN in 1505, and licensing Scotland's first PRINTING press.

He supported Perkin WARBECK in 1495–7, but his multi-faceted diplomacy also included marriage to HENRY VII's daughter Margaret in 1503. Relations with HENRY VIII deteriorated. Signing an alliance with France against England in 1512 – part of a grand strategy for satisfying his lifelong obsession with a crusade against the Turks – James invaded Northumb. in 1513, but was defeated and killed at FLODDEN, his lavish spending on the ARMY and NAVY having been completely misused.

James V (1512–42), King of Scots (1513–42). His long minority from his father JAMES IV's death in 1513 was dominated by struggles between his mother Margaret (daughter of HENRY VII) and noblemen ruling or seeking to rule in his name – principally John STEWART, Duke of Albany (1515–24) and Margaret's estranged second husband, Archibald Douglas, Earl of Angus (1525–8). Their conflicts were a confusing mixture of selfishness and genuine disagreement about whether England or France should be Scotland's ally. Despite Margaret proclaiming James fit to rule in 1524, only in 1528 did he manage to assert himself, and begin rebuilding the fragmented power of the crown.

In 1532, he established a central CIVIL LAW court, the College of Justice (*see* COURT OF SESSION). This was endowed out of Church revenues as part of a profitable financial agreement with Church authorities, but James's continued desperate search for money embittered his relations with many noblemen. Irritated by his uncle HENRY VIII's condescending advice, he refused to follow the English king into a break with Rome, and allowed the persecution of some HERETICS while sponsoring minor Church reforms. He married successively two French princesses: Madeleine (1537–8) and MARY OF GUISE.

After James snubbed Henry by not turning up at a meeting at York in 1541, Anglo-Scots relations descended once more into war, leading to the Scots defeat at SOLWAY MOSS in 1542. James died in a state of nervous breakdown after hearing of this disaster, leaving the new-born infant MARY QUEEN OF SCOTS as his only legitimate heir. His illegitimate offspring – particularly the future regent James Stewart, Earl of Moray – continued to complicate Scots politics.

James VI and I (1566–1625), King of Scots (1567–1625) and King of England and Ireland (1603–25). After the deposition of his mother MARY QUEEN OF SCOTS in 1567, when he was just a year old, James was a royal victim of Scots political instability through a long minority under regencies. He began claiming real power only in 1581, when he helped the first of many male favourites, the personable, French Esmé Stuart, overthrow James DOUGLAS, Earl of Morton; thereafter the king had to endure seizure by Protestant noblemen in the RUTHVEN RAID (1582) before regaining his freedom of action.

His adult reign in Scotland was marked by increasing surefootedness in countering powerful aristocrats – e.g. the GOWRIE CONSPIRACY – and power-seeking PRESBYTERIAN clergy, and even after going south, he continued to exert effective absentee control over Church and state in Scotland (*see* LORDS OF THE ARTICLES; PERTH, FIVE ARTICLES OF). His grief at the execution of his mother in 1587 was softened by the absence of any personal memories of her, by his marriage in 1589 to Anne of Denmark, and by the prospect of succession to the English throne in right of his great-grandmother Margaret, daughter of HENRY VII.

After much anxious intrigue with anyone who might prove useful to him, he succeeded ELIZABETH I without fuss in 1603. Finding the Established English Church much to his liking, he disappointed PURITAN high hopes at the HAMPTON COURT CONFERENCE (1604), and – particularly after the GUNPOWDER PLOT (1605) – showed much less favour for Roman CATHOLICS than they had anticipated. His delight at his new kingdom's comparative wealth was soon soured by the failure of its antiquated revenue system to provide enough money for normal government, let alone for his family's personal extravagance; successive ministers, notably Robert CECIL and Lionel Cranfield, found no solutions. James also failed to interest either kingdom in his pet project of full political union. His relations with the English PARLIAMENT sometimes produced angry stalemate (*see* ADDLED PARLIAMENT), although the long-term significance of such conflicts has probably been exaggerated. Some of his homosexual favourites brought severe political troubles through their incompetence and greed, notably Robert Carr, Earl of Somerset, and George VILLIERS, 4th Duke of Buckingham.

Bored by the minutiae of government business, James was rightly proud of his peacemaking achievements, curbing the feuds of aristocratic Scots, ending the Anglo-Scots border war and the Irish and Spanish wars, and drawing away from the aggressive Elizabethan alliance with the Dutch United Provinces (*see* NETHERLANDS). His rather unconventional abilities, his wit and his genuine talent as scholar and writer are generally held in high regard among modern historians.

James VII and II (1633–1701), King of England, Ireland and Scotland (1685–8). The second son of CHARLES I and brother of CHARLES II, James was created Duke of York in 1643. He was captured at the surrender of Oxford in 1646, but escaped to Holland in 1648 and served in the French and Spanish armies. He married Anne Hyde in 1660; their daughters MARY and ANNE were brought up as Protestants. He was a successful lord high admiral during the Second and Third DUTCH WARS.

James's conversion to Catholicism in the 1660s was widely known from about 1668, and the passage of the TEST ACT in 1673 compelled him to resign office. In the same year, his first wife having died, he married Mary Beatrice, the Catholic daughter of the Duchess of Modena, prompting parliamentary attempts to prevent consummation of the marriage, exclude him from the throne, or compel future children to be brought up as Protestants. The POPISH PLOT of 1678 was supposedly designed to place James on the throne; an exclusion bill was brought in, precipitating the EXCLUSION CRISIS. James went briefly into exile, but returned as lord high commissioner for Scotland from 1680–2, where he reversed Lauderdale's (*see* MAITLAND, JOHN) policy of concessions to dissent. In 1684 he was reappointed lord high admiral, and although his succession to the throne in 1685 was challenged by risings led by Monmouth (*see* SCOTT, JAMES) and Archibald CAMPBELL, 9th Earl of Argyll, both were defeated. The Parliament summoned at his accession, displaying a loyalty deriving from the TORY REACTION, voted a generous financial settlement, whose value was further enhanced by buoyant economic conditions.

Devoutly committed to reviving Catholicism in Britain, and displaying no sense of the limits of his subjects' tolerance, James promoted Catholics to governmental and military posts, using his DISPENSING POWER (*see under* SUSPENDING) to nullify the Test Act, and obliging the universities to admit Catholics. A DECLARATION OF INDULGENCE of 1687 gave relief to both Catholics and DISSENTERS. James began sounding out local élites to see whether they would countenance the repeal of the Test Act, and set up a Board of REGULATORS to oversee the remodelling of CORPORATIONS in anticipation of a parliamentary election. When SEVEN BISHOPS refused to read out a second Declaration of Indulgence of 1688, they were tried for seditious libel.

Matters came to a head when, in June 1688, the birth of a male heir (James Edward STUART) was announced. Conspirators invited James's daughter Mary's husband, William of Orange (the future WILLIAM III), to intervene to ensure the parliament that met was a 'free parliament'. In Sept. 1688 James belatedly made concessions, abolishing the Commission for Ecclesiastical Causes, which he had used to impose royal policy on the church, and reinstating corporate charters. When William invaded in Nov., James fled London but was captured in Kent and returned. In Dec., William encouraged him to leave for France, opening the way for William to assume power and for the set of constitutional changes known together as the GLORIOUS REVOLUTION. James established a court in exile at St Germain near Paris with the help of Louis XIV. In 1690 he landed in Ireland with French military assistance, and summoned the JACOBITE PARLIAMENT, but was defeated at the Battle of the BOYNE in July and returned to France. By the Treaty of RYSWICK of 1697, the French recognized William III as rightful king. James's later years were clouded by morose religiosity.

'James VIII and III', *see* STUART, JAMES EDWARD

Jameson Raid, crucial event in the prelude to the BOER WAR. On 29 Dec. 1895 Dr Storr Jameson, administrator for the British South Africa Company, led a force of 470 men from BECHUANALAND into Transvaal, intending to cross to Johannesburg and join the non-Boer population in overthrowing Kruger's government. The conspiracy failed, and Jameson was soon apprehended. RHODES was forced to resign because of his connivance at the escapade, while the Boers, having received the congratulatory KRUGER TELEGRAM, came to expect German support in any future war with the British. Joseph CHAMBERLAIN, the colonial secretary, was officially exonerated, but evidence suggests he knew and approved of the intended revolt. Jameson himself later became premier of CAPE COLONY 1904–8.

Jane Grey (1537–54), Queen of England (1553). Victim of her descent as great-niece of HENRY VIII through her mother, the Marchioness of Dorset and Duchess of Suffolk, Lady Jane Grey used learning and PROTESTANT piety as a refuge from a bleak, over-regulated childhood. However, in 1553 she became a passive conspirator against MARY I's succession, when she was married to Guildford Dudley, son of John DUDLEY, Duke of Northumberland, as part of a scheme – concocted by Northumberland and the fatally ill EDWARD VI – to defy the provisions of HENRY VIII's will and divert the succession to the Grey line. Jane's recognition as queen on Edward's death on 6 July at first seemed unstoppable, backed as it was by all the leading politicians, but a wide spectrum of English opinion was outraged at the exclusion of the Tudor daughters. Following provincial uprisings, the regime collapsed within a fortnight; Mary acceded to the throne on 3 Aug. and 19 days later Northumberland was executed. Mary initially spared Jane, but following WYATT'S REBELLION, she was executed on 12 Feb. 1554.

Jane Seymour (*c.* 1509–37), Queen of England. Sister of Edward SEYMOUR, Duke of Somerset, and Thomas Seymour, she entered CATHERINE OF ARAGON's service in 1529, later serving ANNE BOLEYN. As the latter's marriage ran into trouble, Anne's conservative enemies brought Jane to HENRY VIII's attention; Henry rose to the carefully tutored bait and married Jane only two days after Anne's execution. Despite her brothers' later PROTESTANTISM, Jane's religion was conventionally conservative; she argued against the DISSOLUTION, and even tried to get MARY restored to the succession. She bore Henry's longed-for male heir, the future EDWARD VI, on 12 Oct. 1537, but died soon after, to Henry's intense grief.

Jarrow Crusade, the most famous of the hunger marches of the 1930s when 200 men from the unemployment blackspot of Jarrow on the Tyne marched to London in Nov. 1936 to seek aid for their town. Led by the local MP, Ellen Wilkinson, the march was officially non-political to distinguish it from other marches organized by the COMMUNIST-backed NATIONAL UNEMPLOYED WORKERS' MOVEMENT. The march, which has come to symbolize the plight of the unemployed between the wars, received much sympathetic publicity and a petition was presented to Parliament, though little practical help was forthcoming. *See also* DEPRESSION.

Jarrow Monastery BEDE spent his entire life at this monastery in Co. Durham (now Tyne & Wear), founded in 681 or 682. With its twin monastery of MONKWEARMOUTH (founded in 674), it constituted one of the most important religious centres of early Anglo-Saxon England. Its benefactors made it rich, and the interests of its founder, Benedict Biscop, ensured that it kept in close touch with Mediterranean culture and possessed an excellent library. Although the community was destroyed by the VIKINGS, some of the original buildings survive. Later merely a cell of DURHAM Cathedral, it was dissolved in 1536. Recent excavations have greatly illuminated our knowledge of the place. *See also CODEX AMIATINUS.*

Jay Treaty, 1794, treaty of commerce between Britain and the United States, named after its American negotiator, John Jay, and the first treaty between the two countries since the British had recognized American independence by the Peace of PARIS in 1783. The British were anxious to dissuade the Americans from supporting France in the FRENCH REVOLUTIONARY WARS: President Washington was in any case set on a policy of neutrality. The British finally agreed to fulfil part of the Peace of Paris by withdrawing forces from the American north-west. They also granted limited trading rights with the WEST INDIES. The United States agreed to meet an outstanding grievance by setting up a commission to consider claims by British creditors left unsatisfied at the end of the War of AMERICAN INDEPENDENCE; they also accepted much of the British position regarding the rights of belligerent powers at sea. The two powers agreed to reciprocal most-favoured-nation agreements, to FREE TRADE across the American–Canadian frontier and free navigation on American rivers. American vessels were given free access to British possessions in Europe and the East Indies.

Jellicoe, John (1st Earl Jellicoe) (1859–1935), Admiral. A gunnery expert, naval administrator and protégé of FISHER, he was given command of the Grand Fleet on the outbreak of WORLD WAR I. He trained the fleet well. On 31 May 1916, despite a lack of information from his subordinates (especially BEATTY), he contrived to put his ships exactly where needed at JUTLAND. Conscious of being 'the man who could have lost the war in an afternoon' (CHURCHILL) he was cautious in closing the German fleet and was much criticized immediately after the battle. Nowadays it is generally considered that he did well but was let down by others' failings, both in the fleet and the ADMIRALTY. He then became first lord of the Admiralty in Nov. 1916, serving a year till his obstinate failure to consider the introduction of CONVOY against submarine attack (shared with most senior naval officers, an aberration which nearly resulted in defeat) caused LLOYD GEORGE to dismiss him. He served as governor-general of NEW ZEALAND (1920–4).

Jenkins, Roy (Baron Jenkins of Hillhead) (1920–), politician. The son of a Welsh miner and LABOUR MP, he was educated at Oxford and became an MP himself in 1948. As home secretary under WILSON (1965–7), he oversaw the liberalization of ABORTION and family planning law. In 1967, he took over as chancellor of the Exchequer on CALLAGHAN's resignation and, through deflation in 1968–9, achieved a trade and revenue surplus. However, his neutral budget of April 1970 is often seen as contributing to Labour's defeat in June. Returning as home secretary in 1974, he was responsible for the passing of the PREVENTION OF TERRORISM ACT. After Callaghan became Labour leader in 1976, Jenkins left Parliament to become the first British president (1977–81) of the Commission of the EEC (*see* EUROPEAN UNION).

In Nov. 1979 he launched a campaign for a new centre party and, in March 1981, returned from Brussels to co-found the Social

Democratic Party (SDP), with the 'gang of four' Labour MPs, himself, David OWEN, William Rodgers and Shirley Williams. The SDP forged electoral alliances with the LIBERAL PARTY in 1983 and 1987, leading to a formal union in 1987. In 1998 Jenkins chaired the independent Committee on Voting Systems. Its complicated proposals for proportional representation have yet to be taken up.

Jenkins' Ear, War of, 1739–48, war with Spain, declared after the Convention of PARDO failed to resolve Anglo-Spanish differences. Captain Jenkins' loss of an ear to Spanish *guarda-costas* was one of a series of notorious incidents about which British merchants had given evidence to Parliament. There had also been disagreements over the borders of CAROLINA and GEORGIA. Admiral Vernon's spectacular success in capturing Porto Bello in 1739 'with six ships only', and the capture of Chagres in 1740, was followed by an unsuccessful attack on Cartagena in 1740 and a mismanaged landing on Cuba in 1741. A squadron under Commodore George Anson sent from Britain in Sept. 1740 to raid Spanish colonies returned in 1744 having circumnavigated the world. From late 1740, Britain was involved in the wider European War of the AUSTRIAN SUCCESSION; in 1744 the two conflicts formally converged when the French signed a compact with the Spanish and declared war on Britain. Receiving less support from the French than they had hoped, the Spanish entered into peace negotiations in 1747. The Treaty of AIX-LA-CHAPELLE in 1748 provided for the extension of the ASIENTO, but this was surrendered after further negotiations in 1750.

Jenkinson, Robert (2nd Baron Hawkesbury, 2nd Earl of Liverpool) (1770–1828), politician and Prime Minister (1812–27). A TORY MP in the COMMONS from 1790, he was called to the LORDS as Lord Hawkesbury (1803), and became 2nd Earl of Liverpool (1808). As foreign secretary (1801–3) he was responsible for the Treaty of Amiens with Napoleon in 1802; he was home secretary (1804–6, 1807–9) and secretary for war and the colonies (1809–12) during the PENINSULAR WAR. Liverpool succeeded PERCEVAL as prime minister in 1812. One of PITT THE YOUNGER's 'men of business', he was an able administrator who managed to consolidate the disparate interests and abilities of his party to rally against the Napoleonic threat.

From 1815 his government was faced with a severe post-war fiscal crisis, the call for PARLIAMENTARY REFORM and for CATHOLIC EMANCIPATION. Liverpool and his government – 'a government of departments', claimed the Prince Regent (the future GEORGE IV) – were ill equipped to co-ordinate a political strategy in the face of severe social unrest and demands for reform; they responded with a series of repressive measures, including the draconian SIX ACTS (1819). In 1822, after the suicide of Castlereagh (*see* STEWART, ROBERT), Liverpool moved to liberalize his administration by appointing CANNING as foreign secretary and bringing in PEEL to replace Sidmouth (*see* ADDINGTON) as home secretary, and appointing William Huskisson at the Board of Trade and ROBINSON as chancellor of the Exchequer in 1823. This period of 'liberal Toryism' introduced a series of domestic reforms to reduce the preposterous number of crimes that carried the death penalty (*see* CAPITAL PUNISHMENT), rationalize the system of criminal justice, and advance the policies of moderate FREE TRADE and tariff reform. Liverpool resigned in 1827 after a stroke, his reputation still tainted for many of his contemporaries and subsequent historians by the years of political and social repression between 1815 and 1822.

Jesuits, members of the Society of Jesus, the highly disciplined and intensively trained religious order founded by Ignatius Loyola in 1534 and given a papal charter in 1540. Their crucial role in the European COUNTER-REFORMATION was marginal in Britain. They arrived too late to give any help in MARY I's attempt at CATHOLIC restoration, and their later missionary heroism – e.g. in the work of Edmund CAMPION – achieved little in the face of repression from Elizabethan and Stuart governments, which identified them as the most dangerous group among the Catholic clergy. They established a separate administrative province for England in 1623.

Paradoxically, when the Jesuits were suppressed by the papacy in 1773, one of their refuges was PROTESTANT Britain: in 1794, they established a school at Stonyhurst, Lancs., which gained a significant place in English Catholic society. Formally restored to the Roman Catholic Church in 1814 by Pius VII, today they maintain their pastoral and educational work in England.

Jews in Britain There were undoubtedly Jews in the towns of the Roman provinces of Britannia, but the next definite evidence of Jewish communities, again normally in commercial centres, occurs after the NORMAN CONQUEST of 1066. As elsewhere, these Jews were associated with money-lending and commerce, and were subject to periodic attacks of murderous bigotry. The massacre of 150 men, women and children at YORK in 1190 was the worst in a series of incidents encouraged by the Christian invention of ritual child-murder legends – the so-called 'blood libel' – which resulted in cults of spuriously 'martyred' children such as St William of Norwich (*c.* 1132–44) and little St Hugh of Lincoln (*c.* 1246–55). In 1231, Simon de MONTFORT expelled the Jews from Leicester, and in 1290, EDWARD I expelled the entire Jewish community from England, the first European monarch to do so. For the next three centuries, there is little trace of a Jewish presence, although during the 16th century, there were clandestine Sephardic (i.e. Spanish/Portuguese) communities in English ports. Jews were also active in some of the early 17th-century North American colonies.

The upheavals of the CIVIL WARS and INTERREGNUM saw mounting excitement about MILLENARIAN ideas. Although one of the signs of the 'last days' would supposedly be the conversion of the Jews, an obstacle to this was that there were apparently none in England; this encouraged a movement to readmit them. In 1656, following a mission to England by Rabbi Manasseh ben Israel of Amsterdam, Oliver CROMWELL tacitly rescinded the ancient expulsion order, and a test case at law the following year confirmed Jewish property rights.

The Jewish community in England became, once again, commercial and urban in character. In 1757–8, London saw the establishment of the Chief Rabbinate and, in 1760, a representative body: the Board of Deputies of British Jews. However, in 1753, government legislation to facilitate the naturalization of Jewish immigrants was dropped after shows of popular opposition, and in 1847, following his election as MP for the City of London, Lionel Rothschild was not allowed to take his seat in Parliament. A major row ensued but in 1858–60, after further confrontations, Jews were granted full parliamentary rights.

The character of the community was transformed, and its numbers much increased, when large-scale tsarist pogroms (massacres), which began in 1882, were followed by waves of initially destitute Russian/Polish immigrants into Britain. An anti-Semitic reaction persisted into the 1930s, exemplified by the activities of the short-lived British Union of FASCISTS led by Oswald MOSLEY.

From the end of the 19th century, the movement for a Jewish homeland – ZIONISM – was the cause of bitter debate among British Jews. The BALFOUR DECLARATION of 1917 was a commitment by the British government to the creation of this homeland in PALESTINE, its signing having been influenced by government contact with Zionist sympathizers such as Chaim Weizmann. However, it was followed by cautious government responses when the British MANDATE was established in Palestine. Similar caution marked official British reaction to the persecution of the Jews by the Nazis in the 1930s; although much private effort to help the refugees was undertaken, this was frequently in the face of obstruction and feet-dragging by the government.

The modern British Jewish community contains a spectrum of identities, from religious orthodoxy through religious liberalism to secularism. It comprises a total of about half a million individuals. *See also* JUDAISM, REFORM.

Jingoism, a form of imperialistic chauvinism. 'Jingoists' became a nickname for those who supported DISRAELI's policy of sending a British fleet into Turkish waters to check the advance of the Russians in 1878. The term itself came from the music-hall song: 'We don't want to fight,/But by Jingo if we do,/We've got the ships, we've got the men,/We've got the money too.'

Joan of Navarre (*c.*1373–1437), Queen of England. Daughter of the King of Navarre, she was the widowed Duchess of Brittany when she married HENRY IV in 1403. Widowed again ten years later, in 1419 she was accused of (unsuccessfully) contriving the death of her stepson, HENRY V, by sorcery and necromancy. Although never tried, she was held in custody for three years until Henry, on his deathbed, ordered that she be released and that her dower – worth 10,000 marks a year – be restored.

Jocelin of Brakelond (*fl.c.*1200), historian, author of a history of the abbey of Bury St Edmunds from 1180–1202. As an unrivalled account of life in the cloister and a fine biographical portrait of a great BENEDICTINE abbot (Samson, whose chaplain Jocelin was from 1182–7), it inspired Thomas Carlyle's *Past and Present* (1843).

John (1167–1216), King of England (1199–1216). Youngest son of HENRY II and ELEANOR OF AQUITAINE, he grew up fearing that everyone was against him and determined to outmanoeuvre them. His father gave him the lordship of Ireland, but when John went there in 1185, he alienated both English colonists and Irish kings. Henry's subsequent attempts to provide for John – already nicknamed 'Lackland' – at the expense of the future RICHARD I provoked the latter to rebel; in 1189, when he calculated that his dying father would lose, John joined the revolt. From 1191–4, he first intrigued and then, in alliance with Philip II Augustus of France, rebelled against his absent crusader-king brother. However, two months after his return, in May 1194, Richard forgave him, and five years later designated John his heir.

Despite doubts about his trustworthiness and competence, in 1199 he succeeded to the whole of the ANGEVIN EMPIRE remarkably smoothly; only in Anjou itself did he have to overcome some armed opposition. But his marriage to ISABELLA OF ANGOULÊME and his maladroit handling of the LUSIGNAN family provoked a rebellion in Poitou. The general belief that he murdered his nephew, Arthur of Brittany, his rival to the succession, in April 1203 meant that, when Philip Augustus invaded Normandy and Anjou in 1203–4, very few thought John was worth fighting for – especially since John himself retired to the safety of England. From then on, he was known as 'Softsword'.

The loss of Anjou, Normandy and much of Poitou meant that, from 1204, John spent more of his time in the British Isles, even taking the opportunity to visit the north of England and Ireland. For ten years, he prepared his counter-attack against Philip, building up a war chest and using it to buy political and diplomatic support. The French king's response was to plan an invasion of England. In May 1213, John – who had quarrelled with the papacy over the appointment of Stephen LANGTON – made England a papal fief in order to obtain Pope Innocent III's injunction against Philip; but in the end, it took an English naval victory at DAMME to halt the French invasion. In 1214, John's grand strategy collapsed when his dearly bought allies were defeated at the battle of BOUVINES; inevitably, baronial rebellion followed. John was forced to seal MAGNA CARTA, but had no intention of implementing its terms. His reign ended with England torn by civil war and many of his former subjects giving their allegiance to Louis of France.

Earlier this century, the misconceived perception of John as an essentially English king, combined with the systematic study of the voluminous records of English government, led to John, after centuries of denigration, being regarded in a more positive light – as a hard-working king who stayed 'at home' and presided over important administrative developments. But what historians came to see as administrative progress, contemporaries saw as oppressive government that could have been justified only by military and political success. In these spheres, John's record was remarkably poor.

John of Fordun (*fl.*1380s), historian, and author of the earliest (*c.*1385) surviving full-scale history of Scotland: *Chronica gentis Scotorum*. Since Fordun's purpose was the patriotic one of providing an ancient pedigree for an independent Scotland, his chronicle is naturally fairly scrappy on the relatively well-documented 13th and 14th centuries and much more detailed on the earlier centuries, about which so little was known that myth-making could run riot.

John of Gaunt (1340–99), Duke of Lancaster, King of Castile and Léon, Duke of Aquitaine. As his titles suggest, although most familiar as the patriotic elder statesman who spoke for England in SHAKESPEARE's *Richard II*, John of Gaunt's own concerns were both dynastic and international. A younger son of EDWARD III, born in Ghent (hence 'Gaunt'), his ancestry, wealth and ability made him a key figure in the European politics of the HUNDRED YEARS WAR. In 1359, he married Blanche, daughter of Henry of Lancaster, and, three years later, inherited the entire Lancaster estate – becoming the greatest landowner in England – and was created duke. His second wife, Constance of Castile, whom he married in 1371, brought him his royal title and a deep involvement in the affairs of south-western Europe, which was reinforced by his role first as lieutenant (1370–1, 1373–4, 1388–9), then as duke of AQUITAINE from 1390.

Although a seasoned and competent soldier, prepared to fight for his rights (as in Spain, 1386–7), these interests made him quicker than most to see the advantages of a negotiated settlement with France. Since he was also deeply suspect in ecclesiastical eyes as an open adulterer and patron of WYCLIF, it is not surprising that, in the 1370s – when the ill health of his father and older brother left him the most prominent member of the royal family – he should become the victim of rumours that he was plotting to kill the bishop of London or usurp the throne. However, although conventionally ANTI-CLERICAL, he was a devout Catholic as well as loyal to his young nephew, RICHARD II. Yet these tales bore fruit in the violent hostility shown to him during the PEASANTS' REVOLT, notably the destruction of his London palace, The Savoy, and then in the increasingly tense relations between him and the adolescent king.

In 1386, after more than ten years of defending royal authority in England, he sailed to pursue his claim to Castile and Léon. He conquered Galicia, but it soon became evident that, even in alliance with Portugal, his resources were inadequate. In 1387–8 he negotiated a settlement – the treaty of Bayonne – renouncing his claim to the Spanish thrones in return for £100,000 and an annual pension. His return to England in 1389, with his wealth greatly enhanced, marked the restoration of political stability after the APPELLANTS crisis of 1387–8.

In 1396 – to general astonishment – he married his long-term mistress, Catherine Swynford, and then secured the legitimization of their children, the BEAUFORTS. In 1397–8, as his health became increasingly poor, he acquiesced in Richard's revenge on the Appellants, including his brother THOMAS OF WOODSTOCK and even his own heir Bolingbroke (the future HENRY IV), unable to do more than arrange for his son's period of exile to be reduced from ten years to six. John of Gaunt's death in 1399 ushered in the last crisis of Richard's reign.

John of Lancaster (1st Duke of Bedford) (1389–1435), a younger brother of HENRY V. He was created duke in 1414 and served as regent of England while Henry V was in France. During the minority of HENRY VI (1422–9) he acted as PROTECTOR of the realm of England. However, he was chiefly responsible for pressing on with the conquest of France. He won the battle of VERNEUIL in 1424, and was generally successful in maintaining the strategically vital alliance with the Duke of Burgundy (whose sister he married in 1422). *See also* BURGUNDY AND ENGLAND.

John of Salisbury (*c*.1120–80), scholar and cleric. His letters and books reflect both the range of his scholarship and the vicissitudes of a remarkable ecclesiastical career. Born at SALISBURY, he drew on his student days (1136–46) in the Paris of Abelard to defend, in his *Metalogicon*, the value of logic as an intellectual discipline. As political secretary to Archbishop Theobald (1147–61), he used his friendship with ADRIAN IV to promote Canterbury's interests at the papal curia, and then, in his *Policraticus*, his insider knowledge to discuss both contemporary history and the theory of relations between Church and state. He acted as an adviser to BECKET during his quarrel with HENRY II and, after the former's murder, was active as a hagiographer promoting the cult of the martyred archbishop. In 1176, he was elected bishop of Chartres.

Johnson, Dr Samuel (1709–84), essayist and critic. Son of a LICHFIELD bookseller, he briefly kept a school there, but left for LONDON with David Garrick (1717–79), the actor-manager, one of his pupils, in 1737. He wrote parliamentary reports for the *GENTLEMAN'S MAGAZINE*, and in 1747 was commissioned by a consortium of booksellers to compile a new dictionary illustrated by quotations, which established his reputation when it appeared in 1755. Debt impelled him to recurrent spurts of productivity: his novel *Rasselas* (1759) was written in seven days. He also wrote essays collected as *The Rambler* (1750) and *The Idler* (1758), produced a new edition of SHAKESPEARE (1765) and *Lives of the English Poets* (1777). In his own day, Johnson was both respected as a scholar and renowned as an eccentric personality. The Scots lawyer, James Boswell, who first met him in 1763, immortalized his character and conversation in his *Life* (1791).

Joint Stock, a way of spreading the ownership of a corporate entity and at the same time making it possible to expand the capital base. Ownership is split into a large number of units – equities or shares – which are sold to generate more funds. While joint-stock companies were formed in growing numbers for the conduct of trading and industrial ventures beginning in the later 16th century (*see* EAST INDIA COMPANY; RUSSIA COMPANY; STOCK EXCHANGE), their proliferation was curbed by the BUBBLE ACT 1720 as a means of restricting stock market speculation; after the repeal of the 1720 Act in 1825 and especially after the passage of the LIMITED LIABILITIES ACT 1855, joint-stock corporations became increasingly common. The resulting wider distribution of ownership means that control of the organization is more likely to become the domain of professional managers and hence divorced from the owners, and in this way the objectives of the firm may change. The divorce of ownership from control is one of the key features of modern capitalism, a fact highlighted by Joseph Schumpeter.

Josselin, Ralph (1616–83), diarist. Obscure Essex PURITAN clergyman, vicar of Earl's Colne for most of his adult life, who has achieved posthumous fame by keeping a lively and detailed diary. Last edited by A. Macfarlane, it has been much used as a source for 17th-century cultural, economic and social history.

Joust (occasionally the archaic spelling 'just' may still be found), a form of armed contest between mounted knights which first appears in the early 12th century. Knights rode against each other, trying to use the weight of their horse's charge combined with the newly developed technique of the couched lance to unhorse their opponents. Originally jousting occurred during the preliminaries of either battle or TOURNAMENT, but from EDWARD I's reign until the 17th century more or less regulated jousts between pairs of knights became particularly popular events at those courts – above all in England, but also in Scotland – where CHIVALRY was cultivated. They provided better opportunities for the display of individual prowess than did the crowded *mêlée* of the *tournoi* (tourney). Jousts *à plaisance* were tests of horsemanship and dexterity using blunted lances: jousts *à outrance* were fought not necessarily to death but at least to defeat or injury.

JPs, *see* JUSTICES OF THE PEACE

Julian Calendar, *see* GREGORIAN CALENDAR

Julius Caesar, Gaius (c.102–44 BC), Roman statesman and general. His expeditions to Britain in 55 and 54 BC are well-known historical events, even though their actual results were small. The invasions took place during his conquest of Gaul and were probably intended both to stop the Britons assisting his Gaulish enemies and to enhance his personal prestige.

The first expedition appears to have been no more than a reconnaissance; the Romans left fairly rapidly after landing at Deal in Kent and meeting stiff resistance. Caesar returned the following year at the head of a large army comprising five legions (around 27,000 men). Despite defeating the British under their leader CASSIVELLAUNUS and marching beyond the River Thames, Caesar soon made treaties with his opponents and returned to Gaul where his military position was still precarious.

Evidence of subsequent economic contact between southern Britain and Roman Gaul suggests that Caesar's expeditions brought Britain into closer touch with Roman power. His campaigns also provided lessons that assisted the later successful conquest begun by Emperor CLAUDIUS (*see* ROMAN CONQUEST).

Julius Frontinus, Sextus (*fl.* AD 70s), Roman governor. In office from 73 (or 74) to 77 (or 78), he continued the policy of aggressive campaigning that had been resumed by bis predecessor PETILLIUS CERIALIS. His major successes were against the SILURES, and he appears to have largely completed the subjugation of the tribes in Wales. He may also have been the founder of YORK. His governorship seems to be associated with major public building at, for example, VERULAMIUM (St Albans) and CIRENCESTER.

Junta, The, a term (taken from the Spanish *junta* meaning council or committee) coined by Sidney and Beatrice WEBB to describe the unofficial Cabinet that guided the mid-Victorian labour movement, made up principally of the leaders of the NEW MODEL UNIONS. They represented the outlook and interests of the skilled artisans for whom they claimed a status comparable with that of professional men.

Junto, from the Spanish *junta*, a council or committee, applied by contemporaries to a group of aristocratic WHIG politicians who exercised great influence in a series of ministries at the turn of the 17th and 18th centuries.

Jure Divino, 'by divine law', or DIVINE RIGHT. The term describes systems of government in Church and state that claim to derive their authority from God – e.g. (in intransigent moods) EPISCOPACY or PRESBYTERIANISM, as well as monarchy.

Jury, a panel of persons called to answer specified questions. The early function of juries was to give evidence or make statements, rather than to decide on guilt or innocence in criminal cases, and this primary function persisted in the procedure of the EXCHEQUER and other revenue departments of the crown up to their reform in the early 19th century. From an early date, the scriptural number 12 seems to have been common. There is evidence for such juries in criminal cases in the DANELAW, and the Assize of CLARENDON (1166) provided for them in cases before the justices in EYRE; their function was to name ('present') crimes and suspected criminals in their area. These juries were called 'Grand Juries', and customarily came to be 23 in number; they were called at the ASSIZES until their abolition for most cases in 1933.

After the abolition of TRIAL BY ORDEAL by the Church in 1215, the English crown had quickly to devise an alternative mode of determining guilt or innocence. The solution, worked out in most particulars by 1222, was to employ petty juries of 12 men of the locality (presumed to have access to information about the crime and the accused) to decide the guilt or innocence of the accused. Such information might well come from trial jurors who, as members of a presentment or grand jury (by this juncture in use for over half a century), had previously returned the presentment. However, during the 14th and 15th centuries, as the two juries became distinct in membership and as the requirement for residence in the locality where the offence occurred was relaxed, so whatever 'self-informing' capacity the trial jury may originally have possessed was almost wholly eroded, though the legal presumption of 'self-informing' lingered into the later 17th century. Local knowledge was also the underlying logic of the even earlier employment, under the PETTY ASSIZES, of the trial jury in civil cases (i.e. between party and party). Use of the civil trial jury was made optional in 1854, with trial by the judge as the alternative, and the latter has become the norm since 1933. The COMMON LAW requirement for unanimity in verdicts (established by a leading case of 1367) was replaced by the option of majority voting in 1967. In 1998 the Labour home secretary, Jack Straw, proposed to limit the right of defendants to choose to be tried in front of a jury in certain categories of criminal case. The power of decision will lie with MAGISTRATES.

Just, *see* JOUST

Justices of Assize, *see* ASSIZES

Justices of the Peace (JPs) From the 14th to the 19th centuries, these were the most important officers in LOCAL GOVERNMENT, a lasting success out of various 12th-century experiments in royal administration – and all the more attractive to the crown for being unpaid. They were named for each county by commission during royal pleasure (the commission of the peace) and, from 1363, were ordered to hold sessions four times a year: the quarter sessions. Their records were held by a senior JP – the *custos rotulorum* – assisted by the clerk of the peace, and from the 15th century, those with most experience, particularly lawyers, were named as being of the *quorum* (i.e. those who had to be present to make a sessions meeting valid). Their duties were much increased by various 16th-century parliamentary statutes, particularly in connection with POOR RELIEF, and again in the 18th and early 19th centuries, and the scope of their powers was only reduced with the setting up of county councils. Nevertheless they remain an essential part of the English structure of justice, disposing of minor charges, committing more serious ones to trial, and granting licences for the sale of intoxicating liquor.

They provide – together with the JURY system – a witness to the principle that law is too important to leave to the professionals.

Justiciar, sometimes 'chief justiciar'. From HENRY II's reign to HENRY III's, this was the title borne by the minister with overall responsibility for the government of England, particularly for judicial and financial business during the king's absences abroad. Following the collapse of the ANGEVIN EMPIRE in the early 13th century, the monarch rarely left England, and as a result, the post of justiciar remained unfilled from 1234–58. Revived briefly by the baronial reformers as a check on royal power, it was finally abolished in 1265.

Jutes, one of the three peoples (*see also* ANGLES; SAXONS) identified by BEDE as having taken part in the 5th-century invasion and settlement of Britain. His statement that the Jutes came from Jutland and settled mostly in Kent, the Isle of Wight and Hants. has been confirmed by archaeological evidence.

Jutland, Battle of, 31 May 1916. The only time the main British and German fleets clashed in WORLD WAR I, it started with a clash of the battlecruiser forces where the Germans caused serious losses to the British (*see* BEATTY). The British Grand Fleet under JELLICOE then caught the German High Seas Fleet at a disadvantage, between it and its base, and gave much more than it got. However the Germans on their second attempt to do so disengaged, and during the night managed to escape behind their enemies. Failure of subordinates to report and mistakes in the communication of vital signals intelligence from the ADMIRALTY deprived the British of a probably decisive confrontation the next morning. The British lost more ships and men, the Germans had more ships damaged, and were aware that they were lucky to escape. They did sortie into the North Sea again, but with increased caution. An American journalist summed it up: the German fleet had assaulted its jailor but was still behind bars.

Juxon, William (1582–1663), Archbishop of Canterbury (1660–3). Oxford-educated, and a friend of William LAUD, he was made bishop of London in 1633. His appointment in 1636 as the first clergyman for more than a century to be lord treasurer was a mark of the ARMINIAN triumph, although his personal kindness and tolerance prevented him attracting the hatred stirred by fellow-Arminians. As he attended CHARLES I at his execution (1649), his RESTORATION appointment as archbishop after years of retirement was a predictable reward for a venerable symbol of the royal martyrdom.

K

Keeper of the Great Seal, *see* CHANCELLOR

Kellogg–Briand Pact, 1928, popular name for the pact signed by Britain in Paris on 27 Aug. 1928, derived from the names of the French foreign minister, Aristide Briand, and the US secretary of state, Frank B. Kellogg. Briand proposed in April 1927 that France and America should sign a pact renouncing war and expressing an intention of seeking settlement of disputes by peaceful means. To widen support, a nine-power conference was called in Paris (attended by Britain, Belgium, Czechoslovakia, France, Germany, Italy, Japan, Poland and the United States). Eventually 65 states were to sign the pact; however, the agreement provided no machinery to restrain aggression should it occur and it was soon rendered ineffective by the international tensions of the 1930s.

Kells, Book of, *see* BOOK OF KELLS

Kemp, John (?1380–1454), lawyer and royal servant, Archbishop of Canterbury (1452–4). Initially HENRY V's keeper of the Privy Seal and chancellor in Normandy, he became one of the longest-serving and most influential members of HENRY VI's council, as well as serving two terms as chancellor of England. Few English prelates have held such a string of bishoprics: Rochester (1419–21), Chichester (1421), London (1421–5), York (1425–52) and then Canterbury. Naturally he also acquired a cardinal's hat, in 1439.

Kempe, Margery (*c.*1373–*c.*1440), mystic. Her autobiography, the earliest surviving in the English language, is a remarkably intimate and revealing work, which she dictated in the late 1430s. By birth and marriage, she belonged to the prosperous business community of Lynn in Norfolk, but in about 1410, after many personal crises, she committed herself to celibacy and religion, including pilgrimages to Jerusalem and Compostela. Although consciously orthodox, both her intense – and often exasperatingly tearful – devotion and outspoken criticism of contemporary churchmen made her vulnerable to accusations of LOLLARDY.

Kenilworth, Dictum of, Oct. 1266. Statement of the terms on which DISINHERITED supporters of Simon de MONTFORT – who were holding Kenilworth Castle, Warwicks., and the Isle of Ely, Cambs., against HENRY III's government – agreed to end their resistance if allowed to buy back their confiscated estates. However, it took a further modification of these terms in 1267 before peace was fully restored.

Kenneth mac Alpin, King of the Scots and Picts (840–58). His origins are obscure; all that is clear is that, by *c.*847, he had managed to impose himself by violence on the kingdoms of both the PICTS and the SCOTS at a time when they were threatened by VIKING assaults from the north, west and south. It is probable that he received indirect assistance from the Vikings, since they appear to have inflicted a great military defeat on the Picts in 839. There had been previous temporary unions of the two kingdoms, but Kenneth's conquest of the Picts was converted by his successors into a lasting one (*see* KINGSHIP).

Kenneth II, King of Scots (971–95). Son of MALCOLM I, he took over the Scottish KINGSHIP from the collateral line of kings INDULF and CULEN. His raid on Stainmore on the border of Cumbria and Yorks. shows how far south his power extended. He also attended the famous meeting with King EDGAR at CHESTER in 973. Otherwise his reign is notable for the way in which he sought to settle kingship on his son (the future MALCOLM II) to the detriment of the descendants of kings Indulf and DUB. This exacerbated tensions within the ruling kindred and began a feud that lasted for almost a century.

Kennington Common A well-known London meeting place on the south side of the Thames, it was a fairground in the 16th century, the scene of religious meetings held by both WESLEY and George Whitefield, and, until the early 19th century, the principal location of the Surrey county gallows. The venue for the great CHARTIST demonstration of April 1848, it subsequently became the home of Surrey County Cricket Club.

Kent, Kingdom of Legends abound concerning the creation of the kingdom of Kent in the mid-5th century, notably the story of HENGIST and Horsa. The name 'Kent' is pre-Roman, and in all probability the invaders – the ANGLES, SAXONS and JUTES – took over an existing region. They initially ruled it as two kingdoms, which were finally amalgamated in the time of King ETHELBERT. In his day, Kent was the most powerful of the English kingdoms, but its decline thereafter meant that it was often a sub-kingdom of MERCIA in the 7th and 8th centuries, before its eventual absorption into WESSEX during the reign of EGBERT.

Kenya, Commonwealth state and former British colony and protectorate. The spheres of growing economic interest in east Africa between British and German traders were settled by treaty in 1886, and the area which has subsequently become Kenya was acquired by the British East Africa Company the following year in a lease from the sultan of ZANZIBAR. The company's rule was superseded by that of the crown in 1893, with executive and legislative councils first established in 1906. In 1920 British East Africa was renamed Kenya, and in the ensuing decades railways penetrated further into the interior and Kenya became an important centre of white farming settlement. The so-called Happy Valley provided a notorious refuge for the ne'er-do-wells of British high society. The activities of the MAU MAU in 1952–6 caused serious disturbances to public peace and order, and the British tried to clamp down on the growing tide of nationalist fervour, gaoling leaders like Jomo Kenyatta (*c*.1894–1978). Eventually Kenya was given its independence in 1963, becoming a republic in 1964. Kenyatta became its first president.

Kern, Anglo-Irish term referring, in the Middle Ages, to native Irish soldiers; derived from the Irish word *ceatharnaigh*.

Ketil Flatnose (*fl.* 850s), ruler of the Western Isles. The best-known of the early Scandinavian rulers of the Western Isles (Outer Hebrides), he either conquered the islands on behalf of the king of Norway, or did so independently and was then forced to submit to him. After Ketil's death, his family's influence quickly collapsed, and his daughter, Aud the Deep-Minded, and her brothers became central figures in the early Scandinavian settlement of Iceland. *See also* HEBRIDES; VIKINGS.

Kett's Rebellion, 1549. Part of widespread disturbances in south-east England, East Anglia and the Thames valley, the main motivation for Kett's rebellion was – unlike the near-simultaneous WESTERN REBELLION – not religious but anger against local misgovernment and a mistaken belief that Edward Seymour, Duke of Somerset's (?1500–52) (*see* SEYMOUR, EDWARD) regime was going to sponsor reforms. In the second week of July, trouble erupted very suddenly, suggesting widespread co-ordination; the protesters seized prominent gentry and set up camps (producing the nickname 'the camping time'). Most camps dispersed after negotiation, except the one at NORWICH led by Robert Kett, a substantial farmer of Wymondham. Here, government forces blundered into military confrontations; on 28 Aug., an army led by John DUDLEY, Earl of Warwick (later Duke of Northumberland), massacred the protesters at Dussindale on Mousehold Heath. Robert Kett and his brother William were among those subsequently executed.

Kew Gardens, London. The Royal Botanic Gardens here were begun during the reign of GEORGE II, when Queen Caroline leased the nearby Kew Palace (the Dutch House), and were further developed by FREDERICK, Prince of Wales, his widow Princess Augusta, and John STUART, Earl of Bute, who added garden buildings in classical and Chinese styles. The gardens were relandscaped by William

Chambers in the 1760s, when the botanic collection was reorganized on a more scientific basis. Since 1840 the gardens have been open to the public, and now perform an important role in education and in the conservation of endangered plant life.

Keynes, J(ohn) M(aynard) (1st Baron Keynes) (1883–1946), economist. Keynes' father was a Cambridge lecturer in logic and political economy who was a founder member of the rigorous Cambridge 'school' of economics, while his mother was the first woman mayor of the city. At CAMBRIDGE UNIVERSITY Keynes read mathematics and was influenced by the ideas of the philosopher G. E. Moore; he was a member of the exclusive 'APOSTLES' around whom the BLOOMSBURY GROUP formed. In 1906 he entered the India Office, returning to Cambridge in 1908 to continue his research on probability and to work with the economist Alfred Marshall.

He worked at the Treasury during WORLD WAR I, and was its chief representative at the PARIS PEACE CONFERENCE, but resigned in protest at the harshness of the planned German REPARATIONS, which he criticized in his book *The Economic Consequences of the Peace* (1919). In the 1920s, he developed radical proposals for dealing with mass UNEMPLOYMENT by deficit financing and state intervention, which influenced LLOYD GEORGE's election campaign of 1929 and MOSLEY's proposals to the second LABOUR government in 1930.

Keynes' main theoretical work is contained in *The General Theory of Employment, Interest and Money* (1936), which inspired the 'Keynesian revolution' in economic thinking during and after WORLD WAR II. He rejected the belief of classical economists that the economy is self-regulating and will absorb unemployment if wages and interest rates are allowed to fall, stressing the benefits of government expenditure and economic management to maintain maximum output and produce full employment; he also saw a link between economic prosperity and cultural progress. During WORLD WAR II, he returned as an adviser to the Treasury, and co-operated with William Beveridge (*see* BEVERIDGE REPORT) over proposals for the funding of the WELFARE STATE. In 1944, he was the chief British delegate at the BRETTON WOODS conference and in the discussions leading to the creation of the International Monetary Fund and the World Bank.

A theoretical economist who was able to put his ideas into practice, Keynes himself became wealthy through financial speculation. He was also a patron of the arts, founding the Arts Theatre in Cambridge and becoming the first chairman of the ARTS COUNCIL. His immense influence – his ideas on economic management became the economic orthodoxy from the 1940s to the mid-1970s – waned thereafter with the apparent inability of 'Keynesianism' to cope with the simultaneous onset of economic stagnation and price inflation, and with the rise of monetarism.

Khaki Election, the popular name for the general election called in 1900 since this was the colour of the British ARMY's new combat uniform. It was hoped that the election would mobilize popular support generated by the BOER WAR. The CONSERVATIVES won with an overall majority of 134 seats.

Kildare, 8th Earl of, *see* FITZGERALD, GERALD

Kilhamite Methodists, *see* METHODIST NEW CONNEXION

Kilkenny, Confederation of, a government set up in 1642 by the Gaelic and Old English CATHOLIC alliance after the 1641 IRISH REBELLION against English rule. From the beginning it was troubled by basic policy divisions – on attitudes to the Stuart crown and the return of property to the Catholic church and to Catholic Irish families. It negotiated truces with ROYALIST representatives in 1643 and 1645, but in England, the presence of Irish Catholic troops in ROYALIST armies did much propaganda harm to CHARLES I. The Confederation attracted increasing Royalist support after the king's English defeat in 1646, and kept control of most of Ireland until it was smashed in Oliver CROMWELL's 1649 invasion.

Kilkenny, Statutes of, 1366, legislation enacted in a Parliament held at Kilkenny and presided over by LIONEL DUKE OF CLARENCE, which attempted to deal with the problems perceived by the English in Ireland as threatening to undermine their community (*see*

PARLIAMENT, IRELAND). The statutes range very widely, including matters such as the conduct of officials and the evils of hurling. However, their most significant aspect has always been seen in the preamble's assertion that 'many English [now] comport themselves according to the customs, fashion and language of the Irish enemies, and have entered into numerous marriages and alliances between themselves and the aforementioned Irish enemies'. The statutes' prohibition of all these practices throws a revealing light on the situation of the English colony in later medieval Ireland.

Killiecrankie, Battle of, 27 July 1689, between JACOBITE Highland clans, under John GRAHAM, Earl of Dundee, who had been laying siege to Blair Castle in Atholl, and WILLIAM III's troops. Though the Jacobites won, Dundee's death effectively doomed their cause, and government troops triumphed at Dunkeld in Aug., effectively securing the GLORIOUS REVOLUTION in Scotland. Fears that the rebel remnant might receive support from Ireland continued to cause concern until the Treaty of LIMERICK in 1691.

King, Gregory (1648–1712), political arithmetician. Son of a Lichfield mathematician and land surveyor, he was employed variously as clerk, genealogist, mathematics and writing teacher, and cartographer's engraver, and finally at the heraldic offices of the Rouge Dragon Pursuivant and Lancaster Herald. One of the first practitioners of the new science of POLITICAL ARITHMETIC (i.e. economic statistics), he used tax and other information to analyse POPULATION and the economy; his *Natural and Political Observations and Conclusions upon the State and Condition of England* (1696), with estimates of population size and income distribution, and detailed consideration of LONDON, was first printed in full by the statistician George Chalmers in 1801, and continues to be a basis for historians' understanding of elements of early modern demography and social structure.

'King and Country' Debate, 9 Feb. 1933, debate in the OXFORD UNIVERSITY Union debating society, when the resolution 'That this House will in no circumstances fight for its King and Country' was passed by 275 votes to 153. It is often cited, with only limited justification, as a symbol of the pacifist and anti-war feeling of the 1930s, and seen as indicating support for the policy of APPEASEMENT.

King William's War, 1689–97. WILLIAM III's chief aim in coming to England and precipitating the GLORIOUS REVOLUTION had been to secure English aid against the French. Once the French had aligned themselves with JAMES II's attempt to recapture his throne, war became inevitable; it has been suggested that it might plausibly be termed 'the war of the British succession'. James landed in IRELAND with French troops in March 1689; Dundee (*see* GRAHAM, JOHN) raised JACOBITE forces in Scotland. In May, William declared war on France. The French Navy had been built up to a strength more than equal to the English and Dutch fleets combined, and a French naval victory at Bantry Bay underlined the need for a mustering of anti-French forces: in May/June, a Grand Alliance of England, the United Provinces, the Holy Roman Empire, Spain, Savoy and many German states was formed. After a Pyrrhic victory at KILLIECRANKIE in July, Scots Jacobite resistance was quickly crushed. Following the 1690 parliamentary session William left for Ireland, and defeated Irish Jacobite forces at the Battle of the BOYNE. Catholic resistance continued into the following year but ended with the surrender of Limerick in Oct. 1691, and was sealed by the Treaty of LIMERICK.

In June 1690 the French succeeded in beating the combined Anglo-Dutch fleet at Beachy Head. The Allies, however, managed to keep a 'fleet in being' which warded off the danger of French invasion, that year and the next, despite widespread fear. In May 1692 the Allied fleet won its revenge, dispersing the French fleet at Barfleur and then burning numbers of ships that had taken refuge at La Hogue and Cherbourg. After this the financial effort of keeping up a battle fleet became too much for the French, and they went over, very successfully, to commerce raiding. Both British and Dutch navies took a long time to come to terms with the French privateers.

Meanwhile the English military effort focused on campaigns in the Netherlands. After an attack by a French fleet on an Anglo-Dutch convoy had caused great losses to the

LEVANT COMPANY in 1693, an English fleet was sent out to operate in the Mediterranean from 1694–6, but it was recalled to combat a new invasion threat – averted when Sir John Fenwick's conspiracy, planned to coincide with a French landing, was unmasked. The Grand Alliance began to crumble in 1696: Savoy, exposed by the withdrawal of the English fleet, made peace in Aug.; in the autumn the emperor conceded defeat in Italy and began to withdraw his troops. In May 1697 a peace conference assembled; the Treaty of RYSWICK was signed in Sept.

The war was unprecedentedly expensive. Difficulties in agreeing what form of financial settlement should be made in the post-Revolutionary era, coupled with the need to finance expensive war, gave rise to prolonged debate, and prompted the formation of a PUBLIC ACCOUNTS Commission. In the event, the war was funded partly by borrowing, underpinned by land taxes, customs, duties and excises. The establishment of the BANK OF ENGLAND in 1694 facilitated borrowing; the RECOINAGE of 1696 attempted to restore faith in a currency depleted to meet the demand for bullion. Unease about the costs of a war whose management was seen to lie largely in the hands of a WHIG JUNTO stimulated the growth of a COUNTRY opposition, and increased the popularity of the TORIES. The ending of the war produced controversy as to whether the STANDING ARMY should be disbanded. The decision to retain a force in being, though heavily reduced, reflected general acceptance by the parliamentary class that the demands of the post-Revolutionary era necessitated a permanently enlarged and strengthened apparatus of government – even though debate continued as to how best to secure efficiency and effective parliamentary oversight of the executive in the new era.

Kingmaker, the, *see* NEVILLE, RICHARD

King's Bench, Court of, COMMON LAW court, also known as *Coram Rege* ('in front of the king'), which evolved from HENRY II's systematization of centralized royal justice. Originally it was the court of the king sitting in person, and it followed him on his journeys. It settled down at WESTMINSTER in the early 14th century, although it continued to be sent out on occasions to individual counties. Because of the intimate royal connection, it retained its dominance in criminal cases, but secured its share of lucrative civil litigation by devising LEGAL FICTIONS. In particular, an aggrieved party could claim that his grievance related to a violent offence committed in Middlesex (over which the court had jurisdiction), and so he could be heard in the court by a 'Bill of Middlesex'. King's Bench was united with Common Pleas and the Court of Exchequer of Pleas (*see* EXCHEQUER) in 1873.

King's Bench Prison, *see* IMPRISONMENT FOR DEBT

King's Book, 1543, statement of the English Church's official religious doctrine – *A Necessary Doctrine and Erudition for Any Christian Man* – revising the *BISHOPS' BOOK* (1537). Substantially reflecting HENRY VIII's own religious views, most of its changes were in a conservative CATHOLIC direction.

King's Confession, *see* NEGATIVE CONFESSION

King's Council All monarchs need advice, and their leading subjects are only too anxious to give it. Advisers have persistently sought to take on a formal role, particularly in crises, and historians have sometimes mistaken these attempts for formal continuity. Strong medieval kings tended to call not only on noblemen who regarded themselves as natural councillors, but also on advisers of their own choice. Councils only took more institutional form in royal minorities such as that of RICHARD II or under weak monarchs such as HENRY VI. The YORKIST monarchs bolstered their shaky position by gathering a permanent Council, and HENRY VII followed suit. Therefore, under the Yorkists and Tudors, institutional continuity becomes apparent.

However, the Council remained too large to be a single executive institution. Councillors performed tasks assigned them by the king – for instance Henry VII's COUNCIL LEARNED IN THE LAW or, from the time of WOLSEY, the sittings in the STAR CHAMBER. From 1536, the PRIVY COUNCIL played a new executive role. (The King's Council should not be confused with the GREAT COUNCIL.)

King's Counsel, *see* BARRISTER

King's Evil, Touching for the Scrofula, a glandular disease, became known as the 'king's evil' after the growth of a belief in 11th-century England and France that it could be healed by the royal touch. English monarchs from HENRY III down to ANNE practised ceremonial touching as a potent part of the royal mystique. The Scots monarchy never had such healing pretensions, and JAMES VI AND I disliked the practice, but his Stuart successors took it up with enthusiasm to demonstrate their DIVINE RIGHT to rule, particularly in the years when they had lost the throne. The Hanoverians never tried it.

Kingship, Origins of in Britain and Ireland

ANGLO-SAXON

The origins of Anglo-Saxon kingship are obscure. The earliest settlers appear to have comprised a multiplicity of war bands whose leaders became kings. Many of these early kingdoms are scarcely known to us; by the 7th century, they were being absorbed into the seven kingdoms of the HEPTARCHY. Those aspiring to kingship frequently relied on an ability to defeat and slaughter rivals, although there also appears to have been an acceptance that kings could come only from certain noble families. There is no doubt that the institution of kingship was reinforced by Christianity, since biblical texts legitimized it and gave it responsibilities. For this reason, although SUCCESSION feuds remained common, powerful kings increasingly stressed their roles as law-givers and protectors of the Church. By the 9th century, England was dominated by the three kingdoms of WESSEX, MERCIA and NORTHUMBRIA. Their successor, the single kingdom of the English, developed great powers and elaborate rituals, such as the CORONATION ceremony, but remained territorially and dynastically somewhat unstable (*see* UNIFICATION).

EARLY IRISH

Until the 12th century, Ireland was a land of multiple kingdoms, with as many as 100 before the 9th century, although in practice there were gradations within kingship and some rulers were much more powerful than others. From the 5th century, northern Ireland was dominated by the confederation of the UÍ NÉILL (*see also* DALRIADA; ULAID), and the south by the kings of MUNSTER. The other major kingdoms were LEINSTER and CONNACHT. By the 8th century, lesser kingdoms were being downgraded, and within three centuries, the concept of the 'high-king' or 'king of all Ireland' had appeared. Certain rulers aspired to this – e.g: BRIAN BORU, MÁEL SECHNAILL II, DIARMIT MAC MÁEL NA MBÓ and TURLOCH O BRIEN – but their status was temporary and personal.

The institutional basis of Irish kingship was flimsy: kings were basically war leaders, although by the 11th century they were starting to take on responsibilities for law-making and protecting the Church. Their persons were originally considered sacred, and pagan inauguration rituals endured long into the Christian era. They were also polygamous, thereby creating an extensive royal kindred. Certain groups within kindreds tended to monopolize kingship, but Irish society was fiercely competitive and the warfare that was engendered was apparently unending (*see* BLOOD FEUD).

EARLY SCOTTISH

The single kingdom of the SCOTS was formed during the 9th and 10th centuries as the kings of DALRIADA from the time of KENNETH MAC ALPIN imposed their authority over the traditionally independent territories of the PICTS to the north and east and those of the STRATHCLYDE Britons to the south. The Scottish kings were remarkably successful in expanding their lands, and by the 11th century, the frontier, which had run along the Forth–Clyde line, had been pushed south to the Solway and the Tweed. Although, in the meantime, Scandinavian settlers had taken control of ARGYLL, the Western Isles (Outer HEBRIDES) and the far north (*see* ORKNEY), the Scots' rulers seem to have manipulated VIKING armies from YORK, DUBLIN and Scandinavia with some skill.

The Scottish royal family appears to have developed a particularly subtle means of organizing the succession, which involved passing the kingship back and forth between the two main branches of the family with the line that was not ruling the Scots being installed in the sub-kingdom of Strathclyde from the late 9th century onwards. This practice did, however, break down in the 970s (*see* CULEN; INDULF) as attempts were made to establish a more lineal pattern of succession. The result was a feud that, until the time of

MACBETH and MALCOLM III CANMORE, claimed many lives.

EARLY WELSH

Like England and Scotland until the 10th century, early medieval Wales was a land of many kingdoms. Unlike them, however, Wales experienced no unification under a single ruler and the multiplicity survived until the Norman invasions of the 11th and 12th centuries. The earliest and most important kingdoms were DYFED, GLYWYSING, POWYS and (usually the most powerful) GWYNEDD (*see* RHODRI MAWR; GRUFFUDD AP LLYWELYN) – all of which first appeared in the 5th and 6th centuries. Smaller kingdoms were recorded at various times in BRYCHEINIOG, CEREDIGION, Ergyng (ARCHENFIELD), GWENT and MORGANNWG.

Kingly power was generally exercised with one eye on England, Welsh rulers usually acknowledging their subordination to their more powerful neighbours who might intervene if they believed it necessary. Even a king such as HYWEL DDA visited the English court, and Gruffudd ap Llywelyn's power was destroyed from England. Welsh kings were primarily war leaders and gift-givers; there is little sign in the earliest law texts (*see GALANAS*) of any responsibility to keep the peace. Their incessant dynastic feuds were fuelled by a complex kindred structure and the practice of conferring kingly titles on several members of a particular family. There was no organized COINAGE until the time of Hywel Dda; kings drew their resources from a system of 'food-renders', but details of its practical operation are extremely unclear (*see* CANTREF).

Kinnock, Neil (1942–), politician. A Welshman educated at Cardiff University, Kinnock was elected MP for Bedwelty (subsequently Islwyn) 1970–95. Leader of the party in succession to Michael FOOT (1983) following Labour's crushing defeat in the General Election, Kinnock, determined, impulsive and emotional and initially regarded as on the left, instigated a radical programme of restructuring and modernization of the Labour Party, launching attacks on the extremist Militant Tendency, and ditching the party's commitment to unilateral nuclear disarmament. Despite expectations of victory, Labour lost the 1992 election after which Kinnock resigned to be replaced by John SMITH. In 1994 he accepted the post of European Commissioner.

Kinsale, Battle of, 1601, defeat of a joint Irish/Spanish army in Co. Cork by English forces under Charles Blount, Lord Mountjoy. A decisive end to Irish hopes of reversing the Tudor conquest of Ireland.

Kinship, Anglo-Saxon The family was one of the most powerful social and political units in post-Roman societies. A man's kindred guaranteed his status in society and, in the event of his violent death, would normally be expected to exact revenge (*see* BLOOD FEUD). The kindred was also the unit that determined the distribution of family property, which, unless a WILL had been made, would not normally be alienated outside the kindred.

What 'family' meant at this time is an unexplored minefield; the definition may well have varied according to circumstances. In terms of language, specific terms developed in Old English (as in its successor, modern English) only for close relatives; therefore, it appears that it was usually only close kindred who really mattered. It is at least clear that, throughout the Anglo-Saxon period, the untrammelled power of the family had to struggle against the rival power of kings and the Church, who sought, among other things, to mitigate (with some success) the effects of the blood feud and the practice of passing churches to relatives.

These seemingly remote developments of the early centuries AD – the most obvious of which are the role of the nuclear family and the expectation that close relatives would obtain a share in family property – established patterns that still dominate English and western European society. *See also* FAMILY, HISTORY OF THE.

Kirk, Scots word for 'church', often used to describe the PROTESTANT Church of Scotland, established after 1560, particularly in its PRESBYTERIAN form (*see* CHURCH: SCOTLAND).

Kit Kat Club, a WHIG club set up in London in 1703, providing an opportunity for Whigs to cement socially their political loyalties. Until about 1720, it met in the house of the confectioner Christopher Kat in Shire Lane near Temple Bar, at the junction of Fleet Street and the Strand. Its 48 members included such outstanding literary and political figures as the essayist, Joseph Addison (1627–1719), Steele, Marlborough (*see* CHURCHILL, JOHN), SOMERS, Charles Montagu, 3rd Earl of Halifax, and WALPOLE. Some of the three-quarter-length portraits of members commissioned to hang in the club room – the so-called Kit Kat portraits – survive in the National Portrait Gallery.

Kitchener Armies, newly raised armies of volunteers called for by Lord Kitchener, the war minister, in the early months of WORLD WAR I: the recruiting poster bore his finger-pointing image above a legend 'Your country needs YOU'. In the absence of CONSCRIPTION and with only a small body of trained troops, Kitchener's far-sighted anticipation of a long war led him to seek authorization to raise an extra 500,000 men in Aug. 1914. On 7 Aug. he called for a first 100,000 volunteers to form the basis of a 'new army'. Patriotic enthusiasm produced a huge surge of recruits: over one million had volunteered by the end of 1914, many of them in 'Pals' battalions of men from the same neighbourhood, workplace, or organization. The new armies required extensive training and many only saw service for the first time in the disastrous SOMME offensive of 1916.

Kloster-Zeven, Convention of, 8 Sept. 1757. In the second year of the SEVEN YEARS WAR, French forces defeated the German army of WILLIAM AUGUSTUS, Duke of Cumberland, at Hastenbeck in July 1757, cutting off their retreat to the Elbe. The convention allowed the Hanoverians to disperse and the Hessian and Prussian troops to return home. It was violently attacked in both Prussia and England; its terms were repudiated by the ministry of Newcastle (*see* PELHAM-HOLLES) and PITT THE ELDER, and Cumberland was removed as captain-general.

Knatchbull's Act 1723, *see* WORKHOUSES

Knight Service (*servitium debitum*), military service performed by well-armed and mounted soldiers and owed to a lord – e.g. the lord king – in return for land held from that lord. It is generally accepted that troops raised under this obligation (commonly called 'feudal levies') comprised a significant part of the English king's military forces in the 12th and early 13th centuries.

According to the returns to the 1166 inquiry that established how many soldiers each tenant-in-chief owed (commonly known as the FEUDAL or knightly quota), HENRY II could call upon 6,000 men to serve, usually without pay, for 40 days each year. As this limitation indicates, knight service could never have been the sole – or even the most important – part of the politico-military system. It was probably always most useful as a means of extracting money in the form of SCUTAGE, but as quotas were revised downwards in the 13th century, it lost even this. The last summons of the feudal levy occurred in 1385.

Much more controversial is the question of the introduction of knight service. In 1895, J. H. Round argued that the system was brought to England by WILLIAM I THE CONQUEROR. Although Round's thesis has since been modified to allow for a continuing process of negotiation of quotas during the reigns of WILLIAM II RUFUS and HENRY I, it is still central to those who believe that the NORMAN CONQUEST saw the advent of FEUDALISM in England.

Knight's Fee, a landholding from which the service of one knight is due – i.e. the basic unit of the KNIGHT SERVICE system. *See also* FEUDAL.

Knights of the Shire, the pair of representatives from each SHIRE or county elected to the House of COMMONS until 1832. They were generally senior gentry of the COUNTY COMMUNITY, usually indeed knights, and were considered superior in status to the BOROUGH representatives, the 'Burgesses of PARLIAMENT'. They were elected in the COUNTY COURT with the SHERIFF presiding, and election was by acclamation, i.e. the two candidates with the loudest shouts from the crowd won (although from the 17th century, head-counts were customary, resulting in POLL-BOOKS). The term has survived as a jocular usage for traditionalist CONSERVATIVE MPs from rural CONSTITUENCIES.

Knockdoe, Battle of, 1504. Gerald FITZGERALD, 8th Earl of Kildare, defeated MacWilliam of Clanricarde, a rival for power in western Ireland, in Galway. A milestone in Kildare's winning of supremacy, in Irish affairs under HENRY VII's loose overlordship, it was said to be the first occasion when guns were used in battle in Ireland.

Knox, John (*c*.1513–72), religious leader. Church lawyer turned tutor, he became a PROTESTANT under George Wishart's influence. In 1547, he became preacher to the Protestant garrison in St Andrew's castle, and although he had not been involved in their murder of Cardinal Beaton (1546), he was nevertheless made a galley slave when the French besieged and captured the castle. He was released in 1549 and went to England, where he actively promoted the government's Protestant changes. Fleeing from MARY I to Geneva and Frankfurt, he championed thoroughgoing CALVINIST reform among the English exiles. His *First Blast of the Trumpet against the Monstrous Regiment of Women* (1558) – an attack on the two Catholic rulers, Mary of England and, in Scotland, MARY OF GUISE – denied that women could hold power. This theory, unfortunately and accidentally, also applied to the Protestant ELIZABETH I, and she scuppered any hopes Knox might have had of resuming his English career. Instead he returned to Scotland, following an invitation from some of the LORDS OF THE CONGREGATION in 1557. From 1559, he was the clerical leader of the Protestant, anti-French revolution, leading the construction of a Calvinist Church settlement and, from 1561, bitterly opposing the government of MARY QUEEN OF SCOTS, who obligingly behaved badly enough to be deposed (1567).

Following the murder in 1570 of James Stewart, Earl of Moray, Knox's influence lessened, but after his death he remained a potent symbol of the Scottish REFORMATION. He had been a crucial player in this, although he was more flexible and Anglophile than either his detractors or his PRESBYTERIAN near-idolators have later recognized.

Kohima–Imphal, Battle of, 8 March–4 July 1944, the decisive battle of the Burma Campaign of WORLD WAR II. The Fourteenth Army under SLIM inflicted a major defeat on the Japanese. Slim kept his forces supplied from the air through months of intense jungle fighting, assisted by the operations of the CHINDITS under Orde Wingate deep in the Japanese rear. By 27 April when the monsoon broke the Japanese had failed to take either town and were forced to retreat.

Korean War, 1950–53, the first major war of the nuclear age, and the only war fought under the colours of the United Nations. After WORLD WAR II, Korea was divided at 38 degrees latitude (the 38th Parallel), and puppet regimes established in the north and south by the Soviet Union and United States respectively. On 25 June 1950 Communist North Korea invaded South Korea. In the absence of the Soviet Union, the UNITED NATIONS (UN) Security Council passed several resolutions authorizing military intervention. The resulting war lasted two more years, an armistice being signed on 27 July 1953. By this time 20 other countries including Britain had sent troops or medical units to the UN command. Counted as a victory for containment, the war gave the UN a credibility lacked by its predecessor, the LEAGUE OF NATIONS. In Britain the burden of supporting even a relatively small contingent led the ATTLEE government to switch spending from the WELFARE STATE to rearmament.

Kosovo Following the break up of the Paris Peace Conference called in March 1999 in an attempt to solve the situation in Kosovo (Federal Republic of Yugoslavia) with repression and violence by the Serbs against the overwhelmingly Albanian population, a NATO force including British military aircraft and personnel began an intensive bombing campaign of Kosovo. On 3 June 1999, the Yugoslav government under President Slobodan Milosevic accepted the peace terms proposed by EU and Russian envoys. These included the deployment of an international security presence to ensure the withdrawal of Serbian security forces and the return of displaced people and refugees to their homes in what was intended to become a substantially autonomous province. On 12 June the UN, NATO and other forces including around 10,000 British troops began the difficult and very long-term task of restoring peace to the province.

Kruger Telegram, sent by Kaiser Wilhelm II on hearing the news of the JAMESON RAID. In the telegram the Kaiser congratulated SOUTH AFRICA's President Kruger, and sent his best wishes for the preservation of Transvaal independence. The telegram exposed Britain's isolation in the international community and fuelled growing ANGLO-GERMAN RIVALRY.

L

Labour Aristocracy, a contested concept that defines a distinct upper stratum within the working class that is alleged to have exerted a major influence on the militancy of the labour movement and the relationship between classes in mid-Victorian Britain. The historians E. J. Hobsbawm and Royden Harrison have argued for the concept, while its most notable critic has been Henry Pelling. The labour aristocracy is generally distinguished in terms of higher income, regularity of employment and living standards. It size is uncertain. It might have been co-extensive with the 10–15 per cent of workers who were organized by the craft unions, or possibly with the 40 per cent of workers who may have been members of FRIENDLY SOCIETIES. Whatever their number, labour aristocrats are invariably assumed to have been adult males. Six criteria are commonly cited to identify them: the level and regularity of a worker's earnings; his prospects for social security; his conditions at work and the degree of job control; his relations with the social strata above and below him; his general living conditions; and his and his children's prospects for advancement.

However, questions have arisen about the extent of social and economic differences within the working class. The privileged position of certain skilled workers in the division of labour, demonstrated in studies of particular industries, has not provided a basis for safe generalization, while another approach directs attention away from economic and industrial structures to show how values and life-styles distinguished labour aristocrats from the unskilled masses. Measures of social distance include HOUSING, MARRIAGE and membership of voluntary associations. Earlier formulations which presented the labour aristocracy as the prime source of mid-Victorian stability, have now been discarded. Likewise, the Marxist–Leninist location of the origins of British reformism in the existence of a labour aristocracy is now best considered a part of the history of ideas.

Labour Exchange Act 1909 Intended to reduce UNEMPLOYMENT and increase mobility, it created a national system of labour exchanges. Although they could not create additional jobs, they reduced the average period of unemployment by improving the organization of the labour market.

Labour Party The party had its origins in the development of TRADE UNIONS and socialist societies in the late 19th century. In 1900 the INDEPENDENT LABOUR PARTY (ILP), the Marxist-based SOCIAL DEMOCRATIC FEDERATION (SDF), the FABIAN SOCIETY and trade union organizations formed the LABOUR REPRESENTATION COMMITTEE (LRC). The fundamental aim of the LRC was to get working people's interests directly represented in parliament and to seek a redress for unfavourable judgements such as the TAFF VALE case which threatened the trade union movement. An electoral pact with the Liberals in 1903 paved the way for Labour candidates to be elected in 1906, and in the same year the Labour Party was formed from the 29 LRC members elected to the House of COMMONS. In 1918 the party's constitution was drafted, laying down the objectives and principles of the party as a parliamentary socialist party, committed to NATIONALIZATION and egalitarianism.

The growth in trade union membership, and the involvement of Labour politicians in the wartime government at a time of increasing state control, saw the party positioned to take advantage of the wartime decline of the LIBERAL PARTY. Labour gained

57 seats in 1918, increasing these to 142 in 1922 in the face of Liberal disarray. In 1924 Ramsay MACDONALD became Labour's first prime minister, presiding over a minority Labour government which was dependent on Liberal support and which lasted for only 10 months. A cautious administration with a limited legislative effect, its real achievement was to establish the Labour Party as the natural opposition to the CONSERVATIVE PARTY.

During the 1920s the influence of trade unions in the party's organization increased, most Labour MPs being trade union-sponsored. A second minority Labour government held power from 1929–31 under MacDonald. However, in the world financial DEPRESSION of 1931, the trade unions and the majority of the party refused to co-operate with proposed reductions in unemployment benefit and public expenditure. Instead of resigning, MacDonald formed a NATIONAL GOVERNMENT with Conservative and Liberal support which secured a huge majority over Labour – the party was reduced to 52 seats – in the Oct. 1931 general election.

Labour was out of office for the remainder of the decade, under the leadership of Arthur Henderson (1863–1935), George Lansbury (1859–1940) and Clement ATTLEE. The party recovered ground in the 1935 election and by 1937 its principal policy statement advocated nationalization of most major industries and financial institutions; it also proposed a radical overhaul of the existing social services.

During WORLD WAR II, the party joined the all-party coalition formed by CHURCHILL in May 1940 and advocated the implementation of the wartime reformist reports and white papers – such as the BEVERIDGE REPORT – which were eventually incorporated in the party's 1945 manifesto, *Let's Face the Future*. The pre-war failures of the Conservatives' economic and employment policies helped build momentum for Labour in the 1945 general election when it won 394 seats, an overall majority of 146. Its first majority government under Attlee's premiership passed an extensive nationalization programme, including COAL, steel, ELECTRICITY, GAS, aviation, the RAILWAYS and the BANK OF ENGLAND, and created the post-war WELFARE STATE including a NATIONAL HEALTH SERVICE. The party was faced with serious economic difficulties and shortages of food and raw materials which it met with increasing AUSTERITY measures as a result of the wish not to divert resources away from its export drive. The general election in 1950 was won by only a narrow majority, but Labour was defeated in 1951 whilst obtaining its highest vote ever – 13.9 million.

During the following 13 years in opposition, Labour was beset by internal disputes, particularly when Hugh GAITSKELL replaced Attlee as leader, with his main concern being to make the party electable by espousing a pragmatic, reformist policy. This was at odds with the left wing of the party who were opposed to Gaitskell's proposal to scrap Clause Four of the party constitution, which committed Labour to the common ownership of industry.

In 1963, following the sudden death of Gaitskell, Harold WILSON became leader, and succeeded in identifying Labour as the party of modernization in a world of technological change. Labour won the general elections of 1964 and 1966. During the party's period in office, dogged by severe economic problems, the Wilson government pursued an orthodox economic policy including an eleventh-hour DEVALUATION in 1967 and retrenchment in defence and social spending, while in 1969 it was forced to abandon its proposed industrial relations legislation in the face of opposition from the trade unions and the left wing of the party (*see IN PLACE OF STRIFE*). In domestic affairs, the Labour government was reformist: CAPITAL PUNISHMENT was abolished – but the House of LORDS was not; in EDUCATION the number of COMPREHENSIVE SCHOOLS grew apace, and the OPEN UNIVERSITY was established; the laws relating to RACE RELATIONS were stiffened whilst those concerned with DIVORCE, ABORTION and HOMOSEXUALITY were relaxed.

Contrary to expectations, Labour lost the 1970 election but was returned to power in Feb. 1974 in a minority government, and in Oct. the same year Wilson again went to the country for a mandate to govern. A negotiated 'social contract' with the trade unions and the creation of a national enterprise board were key planks in the government's strategy to hold down inflation and encourage economic growth, as were strategies to regulate prices and harness the benefits of NORTH SEA OIL for the nation. Britain's first-ever referendum was held in 1975 on the renegotiated terms of Britain's membership of the EEC (*see* EUROPEAN UNION). With the cabinet divided on the issue, the government recommended a 'yes' vote which the nation endorsed with a ratio of 2:1.

Wilson unexpectedly resigned in March 1976, to be replaced by CALLAGHAN. By-election losses meant that by Jan. 1977 Labour had a majority of only one, and survived the next two years with the support, first of the Liberals (*see* LIB-LAB PACT), and then the SCOTTISH NATIONAL PARTY (SNP), who were anxious not to compromise the introduction of a DEVOLUTION Bill for Scotland and Wales. But in a referendum held in March 1979 the Welsh people voted firmly against devolution, whilst in Scotland the proposal failed to reach the 40 per cent 'yes' vote required. The government was already beset by industrial disputes among public sector workers in what became known as the 'WINTER OF DISCONTENT', and on 28 March it was defeated in a vote of confidence in the Commons, and defeated in the country in the election on 3 May 1979. The Conservatives under Margaret THATCHER came to power and the Labour party went into what often seemed like permanent opposition for 18 years.

Following the Labour defeat in the 1979 election, James Callaghan resigned (Nov. 1980) and the left-winger Michael FOOT became party leader. Constitutional changes won by the left precipitated the defection of four prominent right-wing Labour MPs to form the SOCIAL DEMOCRATIC PARTY. Foot led Labour to heavy defeat in the 1983 election. Foot (and his deputy Denis Healey) resigned to be replaced by the 'dream ticket' of Neil KINNOCK with Roy Hattersley as his deputy. Kinnock's consistent aim was to move the party to the centre to make it electable: hence the Party's commitment to UNILATERAL DISARMAMENT was abandoned; its anti-European stance reversed, and Kinnock waged a campaign against the hard left Militant Tendency and attempted to reduce the influence of the TRADE UNIONS on party policy. In 1992, despite great Labour optimism, the electorate rejected the red rose of modern Labour as it had the red flag of Old Labour, and the Conservatives under John MAJOR won that election too. Kinnock resigned to be replaced by John SMITH, another centrist politician. Smith died of a heart attack in May 1994.

The new leader, Tony BLAIR, in his single-minded commitment to end Labour's wilderness years embarked on a thorough-going modernization of the new styled 'New Labour', including dropping clause four, and making overtures to business. His strategy succeeded triumphantly with a landslide victory in the 1997 election, wining 418 seats; the highest number ever for the party. Determined to break the pattern of one-term Labour governments, Blair has been assiduous in keeping his party 'on message' in government and whilst, after an ecstatic 'honeymoon period' for the government there have been minor rebellions, sackings and resignations, the government has marched apparently unitedly behind Blair's somewhat presidential-style of leadership in its first term, despite some disquiet on the back benches and in the country at his welfare reforms and continuing focus on the concerns of 'middle England'.

Labour Representation Committee (LRC) A forerunner of the modern LABOUR PARTY, it was formed following a conference of socialists and TRADE UNIONISTS held at the Memorial Hall, Farringdon St, London on 27 Feb. 1900. Ramsay MACDONALD was nominated secretary with a brief to establish a Labour group in Parliament to promote the direct interests of labour. The LRC would be financed by groups paying an affiliation fee of 10s (50p) per 1,000 members. In the general election of 1900, two of its candidates won seats. An electoral pact with the LIBERALS, concluded in 1903, was critical to its subsequent growth. In the general election of 1906, LRC candidates won 29 seats out of 50 contested, and the Committee was renamed the Labour Party with Keir HARDIE as chairman.

Labourers, Statute of, 1351, a government attempt to control the labour market in the interests of employers – principally by fixing wages at pre-plague rates – at a time of labour shortage in the aftermath of the BLACK DEATH. Initially issued as a royal ordinance in 1349, it was converted into a parliamentary statute in 1351. In the long run, it was unenforceable, but for three decades, JUSTICES OF THE PEACE in some areas worked hard to enforce it, their efforts adding to the tensions that exploded in the PEASANTS' REVOLT.

Labouring Classes' Lodging Houses Act 1851 Sometimes referred to as the Common Lodging Houses Act, it gave local authorities powers of supervision and inspection in respect of common lodging houses; urban authorities with populations of at least 25,000 were empowered to provide new accommodation and to borrow for this purpose. Little advantage was taken of these provisions, principally on grounds of cost.

Lacey, Hugh de, *see* DE LACEY, HUGH

Lady Chatterley's Lover, novel by D. H. Lawrence, written in 1928, but unpublished in Britain in unexpurgated form for over 30 years for fear of prosecution under the obscenity laws. It became the subject of a celebrated case at the Old Bailey in 1960, when Penguin Books were prosecuted under the Obscene Publications Act 1959 for planning to publish it in full in Britain for the first time. The jury found for Penguin and the first edition of 200,000 sold out on the day of publication. The trial was widely seen as exposing the gulf between popular and official attitudes towards the publication of sexually explicit material, and the verdict reflected the emerging permissive ethos of the 1960s.

Laibach, Congress of, 1821–2. At this follow-up to the Congress of VIENNA, Austria, Prussia and Russia tried unsuccessfully to win Castlereagh (*see* STEWART, ROBERT), who though conservative in his politics was liberal in his foreign policy, round to their brand of interventionism in defence of monarchical power (*see* HOLY ALLIANCE). The unsatisfactory results of the Congress were symptomatic of the growing strains between the liberal British and their more conservative allies.

Laissez-Faire By the 1860s, this term – borrowed from 18th-century French advocates of FREE TRADE – had entered common usage in Britain and had become a shorthand for a non-interventionist approach to government, as well as the antonym of collectivism. Political economists supplied the intellectual case for a minimal role for government, albeit with numerous exceptions, but the dominant position of *laissez-faire* in 19th-century political discourse owed much to the fact that it coincided with the instincts and interests of politicians and the financial and business élites. The experience of industrialization and free trade, and an entrenched localism and opposition to direct national taxation, gave it a resonance it might otherwise never have possessed. This also explains its variable application: government withdrew from the sphere of foreign trade but increasingly intervened in the workplace, the schoolroom and in public health.

The trend has led some historians to argue in favour of a 'revolution in government' inspired by a BENTHAMite RADICALISM in which, so it is claimed, reside the origins of the WELFARE STATE. The substitution of one form of government ideology for another in the 19th century, however, has been challenged by historians who prefer a pragmatic and less Whitehall-centred approach, maintaining that the debate on *laissez-faire* and state intervention underestimates the evolutionary character of governmental growth at both local and national levels in the mid-19th century. *See also* BRIGHT; MANCHESTER SCHOOL; RICARDO.

Lamb, William (2nd Viscount Melbourne) (1779–1848), Whig politician and Prime Minister (1834, 1835–41). A WHIG MP, and follower of Charles James FOX from 1806–12, he returned to the Commons in 1816 and was appointed secretary of state for Ireland in CANNING's liberal TORY administration, a post he held briefly under Wellington (*see* WELLESLEY, ARTHUR) in 1828. Home secretary in GREY's Whig ministry, Melbourne (who had succeeded to the title in 1829) was an unexpectedly assiduous minister, ruthless in his control of RADICAL dissent and agricultural unrest. After considerable hesitation he succeeded Grey as prime minister in 1834; however, his government was weak, and when WILLIAM IV objected to the inclusion of the radical Whig, Lord John RUSSELL, as chancellor, Melbourne was happy to offer his resignation, which was seized on by the king in Dec. He was prime minister again from 1835, when he proved unsympathetic to CHARTIST demands and growing pressure to repeal the CORN LAWS in the face of a deepening economic depression.

Melbourne is generally remembered as prime minister when VICTORIA came to the throne in 1837; he warmed to his role as mentor and paternal adviser on matters of state and politics to the 'girl queen'. His own private life was turbulent: his wife, Lady Caroline Lamb had a public infatuation for the poet Byron, and they had a judicial separation in 1825; and in 1836, whilst prime minister, he was cited in the divorce case George NORTON brought against his wife Caroline, though their friendship was shown to be platonic. Melbourne resigned after the Whigs were defeated by one vote on a motion of no confidence in June 1841, and he suffered a severe stroke the following year.

Lambarde, William (1536–1601), historian. Kentish gentleman and government archivist who wrote *Eirenarcha* ('Rule of Peace', 1581), a classic handbook for the increasingly busy JUSTICES OF THE PEACE, and also researched and published diligently on history. His deservedly popular *Perambulation of Kent* (1570) was the first substantial British work on LOCAL HISTORY.

Lambton, John (1st Earl of Durham) (1792–1840), Whig politician. One of the four people who drew up the REFORM BILL of 1832, he served as lord Privy Seal in the administration of Earl GREY (his father-in-law), but is best known for his dictatorial rule as governor-general of CANADA (1837–8) and his report recommending self-governing status for that Dominion in regard to internal affairs.

Lancaster, Duchy of, *see* PALATINATE

Lancaster, Thomas, *see* THOMAS OF LANCASTER

Lancaster House Agreement, Dec. 1979, agreement which ended the war in Rhodesia (*see* RHODESIA, SOUTHERN) between the Ian Smith regime and guerrilla groups. Talks at Lancaster House, London, under the chairmanship of the British foreign secretary, Lord Carrington, agreed a ceasefire and free elections on the basis of one person, one vote. The agreement effectively marked the end of opposition to black majority rule in Rhodesia and was a major diplomatic success for the early THATCHER administration, bringing an end to an increasingly costly war and paving the way for the Feb. 1980 elections in which Robert Mugabe came to power as the first prime minister of an independent Zimbabwe.

Lancastrian, term used to describe the monarchs HENRY IV, HENRY V and HENRY VI and their families, Henry IV before his usurpation being duke of Lancaster in succession to his father JOHN OF GAUNT. It is also used to describe their supporters in the WARS OF THE ROSES.

Land Banks Several banks whose capital took the form of landed property were established in the 1690s. Such schemes were attractive to landed men suspicious of the MONEYED INTEREST, and were promoted particularly by TORIES. The most promising was the National Land Bank of England, formed in 1696 from the merger of two other schemes. Subscribers mortgaged land to the bank, which made loans of up to three-quarters of the value and charged lower interest than the BANK OF ENGLAND. Parliament agreed to borrow money from the National Land Bank, but a run on the Bank of England frightened investors and insufficient funds were raised. This failure helped to discredit such schemes.

Land League, *see* IRISH LAND LEAGUE

Landau, a type of horse-drawn carriage, popular in Victorian Britain. Named after the German city in which it was first made, its distinguishing feature was that the covered top was in two parts that could be let down or raised as required.

Lanfranc (*c.*1010–89), Archbishop of Canterbury (1070–89). A native of Italy, he left home *c.* 1030 to pursue his studies in France. He entered the poor and recently founded Norman monastery of Bec in 1042, becoming prior about three years later; as a biblical scholar of international repute – notably in his defence of orthodoxy against the eucharistic heresy of Berengar of Tours – his teaching did much to make Bec famous and wealthy. By 1063, when William of Normandy (*see* WILLIAM I THE CONQUEROR) appointed him abbot of his foundation of St Stephen's, Caen, Lanfranc was evidently the duke's man, and was probably responsible for presenting to the papacy the case for William's claim to England.

Made archbishop by William in 1070, he had the task of managing, reforming and reorganizing the English Church, and rebuilt CANTERBURY Cathedral on the model of St Stephen's. During the king's absences, he also took on wider responsibilities for the government of England. In return, William supported Canterbury's hotly disputed claim to primacy over York, the Conqueror seeing this as a means of bolstering his precarious authority over the North.

Lang, Cosmo Gordon (1864–1945), Archbishop of Canterbury (1928–42). Although brought up as a PRESBYTERIAN, he was ordained into the CHURCH OF ENGLAND in 1890. After a brief period as curate of Leeds parish church, he became vicar of St Mary's, university church of OXFORD (1894–6), and of Portsea (1896–1901). He became suffragan bishop of Stepney (1901), then archbishop of York (1908–28). As archbishop of Canterbury he played an important role in the ABDICATION CRISIS in Dec. 1936. He retired in 1942.

Langland, William (*fl.* *c.*1380), poet. Author of *Piers Plowman*, the visionary poem written in three different versions in the last three or four decades of the 14th century. Of Langland's life nothing is known apart from what can be inferred from the poem: that he came from the West Midlands and lived on Cornhill in the City of London. His poetic ability to re-create people and places in vivid and concrete detail while shifting to and fro between religious allegory and ironic social criticism makes him an extraordinary witness to the world in which he lived.

Langport, Battle of, July 1645, crushing defeat in Som. by the NEW MODEL ARMY of Lord Goring's ROYALIST western army during the CIVIL WARS.

Langside, Battle of, May 1568, final defeat near Glasgow for MARY QUEEN OF SCOTS by the forces of the regent, James Stewart, Earl of Moray, after which she fled to England.

Langton, Stephen (*c.*1156–1228), Archbishop of Canterbury (1207–15, 1218–28). Educated at Paris, he stayed on to teach theology. He revised the order of the books of the Bible and their arrangement into chapters. Created cardinal by Innocent III in 1206, in the following year the pope consecrated him archbishop of Canterbury against King JOHN's will. John's refusal to admit Langton into England led to a quarrel between king and pope that lasted until John submitted in 1213.

Once in England, Langton's concern for lawful government made him an important mediator between the king and his baronial opponents, and he played a key role in negotiating MAGNA CARTA. Once this had been sealed, he remained fully committed to its principles – a stance that brought him into conflict with a pope now wholeheartedly on the side of a submissive king. Langton was suspended in Sept. 1215 and went to Rome. He returned to England in 1218, but it was only after he had paid another visit to the curia (1220–1), to secure the recall of an uncomfortably influential papal legate, that he was free to play an active role in English affairs. Until 1226, his moderating presence and co-operation with Hubert de BURGH did much to keep the peace during the minority of HENRY III.

Lansdowne, 1st Marquess of, *see* PETTY, WILLIAM

Largs, Battle of, 2 Oct. 1263, fought on the beach at Largs on the Firth of Clyde between Norwegians under King Haakon and Scottish levies on behalf of ALEXANDER III. In the face of rising Scottish pressure, Haakon had judged that a show of strength was necessary if the Western Isles were to continue to owe allegiance to Norway. In view of the numbers engaged, this drawn 'battle' was little more than a skirmish, but its consequences for Scottish history were immense: the treaty of PERTH and the ending of the Norse presence in Scotland.

Last Determinations Act 1729, an Act intended to prevent bribery and corruption in parliamentary elections. Among its provisions was the stipulation that, in cases where there was disagreement as to who was entitled to vote, if the matter had previously come before the COMMONS, that body's last determination was to be binding.

Lastingham Along with JARROW, LINDISFARNE and WHITBY, the monastery at Lastingham, Yorks., was one of the major monastic foundations of the 7th-century CONVERSION period. It was established by St Cedd on the Irish model, and was subsequently ruled by his brother St Chad. In the 1080s the monks moved permanently to YORK.

Latitudinarians Influenced by the Cambridge PLATONISTS of the mid-17th century, the so-called 'men of latitude' – a label implying (not necessarily favourably) a degree of doctrinal flexibility and ecclesiastical broadmindedness – comprised some of the leading figures of the later 17th- and early 18th-century ANGLICAN establishment. Two of their number, John TILLOTSON and Thomas Tenison, were to be elevated to the archbishopric of Canterbury after the non-juring schism. Others included Joseph Glanville, Edward Stillingfleet, Bishop of Worcester, and Simon Patrick, Bishop of Ely. They condemned both religious ENTHUSIASM and the learned wrangling that had characterized much religious writing in the earlier part of the century, and instead preferred to emphasize the simple moral fundamentals which, as they saw it, underlay Christianity. Their support for toleration played a part in attracting to them charges of doctrinal laxity, specifically Socinianism (*see* UNITARIANISM). *See also* NON-JURORS.

Laud, William (1573–1645), Archbishop of Canterbury (1633–45). An OXFORD don with a lifelong detestation of the CALVINISM dominant in the CHURCH OF ENGLAND of his youth, he rose through patronage, principally from Richard Neile and George VILLIERS, 4th Duke of Buckingham, to lead the ARMINIAN party under CHARLES I; his preferment culminated in the archbishopric in 1633. He was determined to impose conformity on the Church, using the STAR CHAMBER and HIGH COMMISSION to impose often savage penalties on opponents, for example Henry Burton (1578–1648) and the polemicist lawyer William Prynne (?1602–69) both of whom had their ears slashed off. He harassed reluctant older bishops into disciplinary campaigns, and he encouraged the compilation of the 1637 Scottish PRAYER BOOK, which sparked the BISHOPS' WARS. An obvious target for popular revenge when Charles's regime collapsed, he was imprisoned in 1641, IMPEACHED and executed. Laud remains a controversial figure; some REVISIONIST historians do not see him as the driving force behind the official religious programme of the 1630s, merely as a willing agent of the king. This may be to take too seriously Laud's own public affirmation of his secondary role in the radical change of atmosphere among the Church hierarchy. Personally kindly and austere, but a lonely bachelor, he was never prepared to recognize that there might be other ways than his of viewing the Church of England, or that those who disagreed with him were anything else than enemies – usually to be dismissed with the abusive label 'PURITAN'. He never appreciated the importance of conciliation or even of favourably publicizing his vision of a CATHOLIC Church free from Roman Catholic error.

Laudabiliter, the name of the controversial papal bull allegedly granting Ireland to HENRY II in 1155 or 1156 so that he could reform its 'rough and ignorant people'. The authenticity of this document has long been disputed. However, there is no doubt that, at that time, Pope ADRIAN IV granted Henry II possession of Ireland, or that the text of *Laudabiliter* – whether it is a 12th-century forgery or not – reflected a view of the Irish that was then widespread.

Lauderdale, 2nd Earl and 1st Duke of, *see* MAITLAND, JOHN

Law, Andrew Bonar, (1858–1923), Conservative politician and Prime Minister (1922–3). Born in CANADA of an ULSTER Presbyterian father and Scottish mother, he was brought to Scotland after his mother's death and at 16 started work in her family's ironwork business. He entered Parliament in 1900 when his strong pro-BRITISH EMPIRE stand during the BOER WAR won Glasgow Blackfriars from the LIBERALS. In the sparse ranks of able CONSERVATIVE MPs after the 1906 Liberal landslide, Law's support for TARIFF REFORM earned him a reputation as a tough debater. When BALFOUR resigned in 1911, he succeeded to the leadership after the deadlock in the war of succession between Austen CHAMBERLAIN and Walter Long. As LLOYD GEORGE perceptively remarked, 'the fools have stumbled on the right man by accident'. As Conservative leader in opposition Law's task was to unite the party – which meant supporting Ulster's resistance to HOME RULE.

On the outbreak of WORLD WAR I the IRISH QUESTION was subsumed to that of winning the war with Germany, and Law agreed to suspend the usual parliamentary opposition for the duration. When a Liberal/Conservative coalition was formed under ASQUITH in May 1915, as Conservative leader he could have expected a senior post, such as chancellor of the Exchequer or minister of munitions. In fact Asquith decided to offer him neither, but rather the second-rank post of colonial secretary, which was a personal slight to Law and meant that his party received only one major CABINET post out of the six on offer (Balfour at the Admiralty). That this was a deliberate slight is undoubted, but the reason is less clear: it was partly to do with Asquith's low estimation of Law's abilities, partly to do with the taint that a firm with which he was involved had been trading in iron ore for armaments with Germany in Aug. 1914, partly because Asquith's own position in the wartime Cabinet would be strengthened if its Conservative members had no clear leader, and partly because Law's own party was less than totally enthusiastic about its leader. It was not until the fall of Asquith in Dec. 1916 that he moved to the political centre stage when he was appointed chancellor of the Exchequer by the new prime minister, Lloyd George, and effectively his second-in-command. In this role he was an able manager of the wartime coalition, sustaining it into the peace until he resigned because of ill-health in March 1921 – and was replaced by Austen Chamberlain who was not able to restrain the growing tide of Conservative anti-coalitionists. At the CARLTON CLUB meeting on 19 Oct. 1922 Law, fearful that if he did not act the Conservative party would be irrevocably split, reluctantly put himself at the head of the Conservative revolt against the coalition, pledging a quiet political life for the country, and this ensured a second term in office. Law resigned because of ill-health in March 1923 and was dead 7 months later. He was buried in Westminster Abbey, the grave of the 'unknown prime minister' close to that of the Unknown Warrior.

Law Codes, Anglo-Saxon Law codes were drawn up in the names of several early kings of KENT from ETHELBERT onwards, and in the name of INE, King of WESSEX. ALFRED THE GREAT devised an extensive one, and his 10th- and 11th-century successors produced a considerable body of legislation. The last surviving code is CNUT's.

The codes are an important source for our knowledge of Anglo-Saxon society, and are also a tribute to the power of the kings. There is controversy, particularly in relation to the early codes, as to whether they were the result of genuine legislation or simply symbolic demonstrations of power and statements of existing custom. The 10th-century codes are very concerned with public order; it is from them, for example, that we learn a great deal about the HUNDRED, the TITHING and the BLOOD FEUD.

Law Reports, *see* YEAR BOOKS

Law Tracts, Early Irish The extensive records of early Irish law, which survive in manuscripts dating from the 8th century onwards, are among the most important sources for understanding so-called 'Dark Age' societies. As with all other early law texts (*see* LAW CODES, ANGLO-SAXON; HYWEL DDA, LAWS OF), it is now thought that these were descriptive records rather than legislation. They reveal an extensive system of social gradations stretching down through society from the kings, and also describe the workings of a largely coinless economy (*see* COINAGE). Irish society was also typified by a special class of learned lawyers, whose task was to commit the law to memory (*see* BREHON).

Laxton Notts. parish, and last surviving example of communal OPEN FIELD farming where farmers still work strips of land allocated in an annual ballot. The farming system there is jealously preserved for its historical rarity and value.

Lay Readers, a class of ministrants reintroduced into the CHURCH OF ENGLAND in 1866 in an attempt to increase the involvement of the laity in worship (there had been previous short-lived experiments in the 1560s during a shortage of clergy). Their duties are to read certain portions of the service and otherwise assist in church work; they are not ordained or entitled to be addressed as 'Reverend'.

LCC, *see* LONDON COUNTY COUNCIL

Lead Mining Lead has long been valued as a high-quality roofing material, for a variety of military uses, and (as is now realized, disastrously for human health) as a flexible metal for piping to convey water. Extensive archaeological work has shown several mines in operation soon after the Roman conquest; in the Mendips (Som.) a town grew up near the modern Charterhouse, entirely devoted to servicing the extensive local industry, and all the later areas of major exploitation were already being worked. Activity continued in the Anglo-Saxon period. Later medieval evidence witnesses a revival of mining particularly in the Pennines and the Mendips; the industry in central Wales was less profitable, but was sustained because of the possibility of silver extraction from the lead seams. There was a general intensification of activity during the 16th century, when the introduction of furnace smelting from the Continent represented major cost savings on fuel for the industry; lead became a major English export. This particularly affected Derbys., which was probably the area most economically dependent on the industry. Britain remained, with Spain, one of the world's main producers of lead up to the early 19th century.

League of Augsburg, War of, *see* AUGSBURG, LEAGUE OF

League of Nations, international organization set up following WORLD WAR I, inspired by US President Wilson, who included it among his Fourteen Points. The League was established at the PARIS PEACE CONFERENCE, which handicapped it from the outset by associating it with the harsh settlement to the war, and it was further weakened when the US Congress failed to ratify American membership of their president's brainchild. Based in Geneva, the League was intended to prevent the antagonistic armed alliances which had led Europe to war in 1914, but with only Britain and France as great powers amongst its 53 members, it lacked the means to impose its will. It did not in any case have powers to authorize military action, but relied instead upon non-military measures such as SANCTIONS. The League enjoyed minor successes in the 1920s, arbitrating in disputes and organizing plebiscites in areas such as Silesia and the Saar, but proved powerless to deal with the increasing turbulence of the 1930s. Both Japan and Italy committed aggression while still members, in Manchuria (1931) and Abyssinia (1935) respectively, and the League's imposition of sanctions against Italy was undermined by the British and French policy of APPEASEMENT. In any case, aggressors preferred to leave the League rather than accept censure. Germany became a member in the 1920s but left when Hitler came to power, and the organization was increasingly ignored as WORLD WAR II approached, with members resorting to rearmament and old-style alliances to protect themselves. The League was formally dissolved with the formation of the UNITED NATIONS in 1945.

Leasehold, a property right whereby the lessor grants the lessee rights in property for a fixed term. It was originally often employed as security on a loan of money, and had no existence in FEUDAL law, although COMMON LAW came to devise means to give leaseholders some protection. *See also* BURGAGE; FREEHOLD; TACKSMAN.

Leeds Yorkshire's largest city, Leeds' rise to prominence is principally the result of its key role in the 18th- and 19th-century WOOLLEN INDUSTRY. The town's commercial traditions extend back to the 15th century and the CLOTH INDUSTRY, and by the early 18th it had acquired a considerable reputation in wool manufacture and wholesaling. The earliest woollens factory was begun in 1792, and the solid architecture of mills, warehouses and offices continued to expand in Leeds throughout the 19th century. The town hall (1853–8) is one of the proudest of all Victorian civic buildings. The eclipse of the woollen industry, as with MANCHESTER'S cotton industry, has seen both large-scale demolition of warehouses and subsequently their CONSERVATION and re-use, while Leeds has continued to grow strongly as a regional, trading and financial centre.

Leeds, 1st Duke of, *see* OSBORNE, SIR THOMAS

Leeds Grammar School Case, 1805, a celebrated legal case in which the Tory lord chancellor, Lord Eldon, judged that grammar schools could not use their endowments to teach non-classical subjects. Until the GRAMMAR SCHOOLS ACT 1840, schools of this type had to teach the same curriculum that had been established by their statutes in the reign of ELIZABETH I.

Leet, *see* MANOR

Leeward Islands Federation, colonial administration of British possessions in the eastern Caribbean, which lasted from 1872 to the 1950s when most began to run their own affairs and gradually attain independence. *See* ANGUILLA; ANTIGUA; BRITISH VIRGIN ISLANDS; ST KITTS AND NEVIS.

Left Book Club Established in 1935 by the publisher Victor Gollancz, the political scientist Harold Laski, and the writer and theoretician John Strachey, to disseminate political writings of the left – largely communist – in cheap editions, by 1937 it had 500,000 members.

Legal Fictions As the COMMON LAW developed, fictions rapidly became a pronounced feature of property law. Most fictions were devised either to extend the jurisdiction of a particular tribunal, to expedite the course of suits, or to facilitate the transfer of entailed land. While the adoption and proliferation of fictions greatly enhanced the flexibility of the law, their repetition as common form added additional mystery, if not absurdity, to legal process, and one of the achievements of 19th-century legal reform was to end fictions in procedure.

Legate, a representative of the pope. In pre-Reformation England, the archbishop of Canterbury was automatically *legatus natus* ('legate born'). A 'legate *a latere*' ('on the side') was a special envoy with papal powers bypassing normal arrangements (*see* WOLSEY, THOMAS).

Legionary Fortresses The legion, the basic unit of organization of the Roman army, theoretically consisted of just over 5,000 men. Four were sent to Britain during the early stages of the ROMAN CONQUEST (*see* CLAUDIUS), and it is clear that they were flexibly deployed during the first decades, with legionary fortresses known to have existed at various stages at EXETER, GLOUCESTER, USK, COLCHESTER, LINCOLN, WROXETER, YORK and CHESTER. After *c.* AD 87, the number of legions was reduced to what became the normal level of three. It was also from about this time that the three great legionary fortresses of CAERLEON, Chester and York were transformed into permanent bases. *See also* VEXILLATION FORTRESSES.

Legislative Independence, Irish A goal of Irish PATRIOT agitation in the early 1780s, it was largely accomplished with the repeal by GRATTAN'S PARLIAMENT in 1782 of the DECLARATORY ACT of 1720, affirming the right of the British PARLIAMENT to legislate for Ireland and of POYNINGS' LAW which required the previous assent of both Irish and English PRIVY COUNCILS to bills brought into the Irish parliament. The RENUNCIATION ACT of 1783, renouncing any residual legislative right the British parliament might be thought to retain, completed the package. The executive remained dependent on the British crown, and the lord lieutenant retained substantial influence in Parliament, based in part on patronage powers leading some to argue that only when measures of economic and PARLIAMENTARY REFORM had been obtained would independence be complete.

Leicester, 6th Earl of, *see* MONTFORT, SIMON DE

Leicester, 14th Earl of, *see* DUDLEY ROBERT

Leicester House, London household maintained by two Princes of Wales: the future GEORGE II (1717–20), and FREDERICK (1737–51). Situated in what is now Leicester Square, it functioned as a centre for opposition politicians.

Leinster Like other early Irish kingdoms it was divided among several kingly families (*see* KINGSHIP). It is notable for its successful resistance to the larger Irish kingdoms – MUNSTER and the UÍ NÉILL – throughout much of its history until the time of BRIAN BORU in the late 10th century. From the 7th century, the kingship was usually monopolized by the Uí Dúnlainge family, but in the 11th century, they were overthrown by the rival line of DIARMIT MAC MÁEL NA MBÓ, who went on to become the dominant king in Ireland. Leinster's influence then became localized until the 1170s, when it was taken over by Richard de CLARE, Earl of Pembroke ('Strongbow').

Lend-Lease, the system used during WORLD WAR II by US President Roosevelt to provide first Britain and then the Soviet Union and other Allied countries with vital supplies, with the question of payment or return of equivalent equipment left until after the war. By early 1941, Britain was in urgent need of both munitions and raw materials but had exhausted cash reserves and credit. Under the Lend-Lease Act passed by the US Congress in

March 1941, the Allies were provided with whatever American industry could produce to support their war effort. Lend-Lease was decisive in providing Britain with the means to fight on alone during 1941, while allowing the US to support the anti-Nazi cause without formally breaking American neutrality. The arrangement continued after Germany declared war on the US in Dec. 1941, and by the end of the war lend-lease shipments to Britain amounted to some $30 billion. It was terminated by President Truman on 2 Sept. 1945.

Leofric (*c.* 1023–57), Earl of MERCIA. A member of a prominent English family, he was created one of the most powerful men in the kingdom by King CNUT. Thereafter he was at the forefront of English politics, favouring HAROLD HAREFOOT in 1037 and at times counter-balancing Godwine under EDWARD THE CONFESSOR. He was a generous benefactor of the Church. *See also* EARLDOMS, ANGLO-SAXON; GODIVA.

Lesotho, *see* BASUTOLAND

Letchworth, Herts., the first GARDEN CITY, embodying the vision of Ebenezer Howard, founded in 1903. The architects employed an ARTS AND CRAFTS architectural idiom which mingled urban and rustic features, in both blocks of pretty cottages and grander buildings like the Spirella corset factory and the THEOSOPHICAL College. It also boasted the first roundabout in Britain on its roads. Letchworth bears many of the marks of its foundation today – it is still without public houses – and is the ageing prototype for suburban and new urban housing across the nation.

Letters of Marque, *see* PRIVATEERING

Letters Patent, literally 'open letters' (and pronounced with a short 'a'): royal commands and grants in letter form with seal appended. Like the more private 'letters close', from the chancellorship of Hubert WALTER they were recorded in a series of rolls; the patent rolls continue for royal grants to the present day. Since 1853, 'patents of invention' have been dealt with separately by the Patent Office.

Levant Company English trade with the eastern Mediterranean (the Levant) blossomed in the 1580s, and in 1592 two companies of London merchants trading with Turkey and Venice amalgamated to form the Levant Company (chartered in 1605). Members of the company dealt mainly with Constantinople, Aleppo and Smyrna, exporting cloth, tin and lead and importing cotton yarn, silk, spices, drugs, wine and currants. In the late 17th century, after it attacked the EAST INDIA COMPANY's export of bullion, the latter company was required to export English goods, but this rebounded, since the two companies then competed for markets in Persia. In 1744, the Levant Company's monopoly was modified by a grant to the RUSSIA COMPANY of the right to import Persian silk. Ten years later, Parliament facilitated entrance to the Levant Company by removing the requirement that its members be merchants and freemen of the City of London, and by reducing admission fees. The company surrendered its charter in 1825.

Levellers, originally an abusive nickname for the loose grouping of reformists whose assorted ideas were publicized from 1645 principally by John LILBURNE, Richard Overton and William Walwyn, particularly in the pamphlets of 1647: *The Case of the Army Truly Stated* and *The Agreement of the People*. Advocating extensive reforms in society and government and a parliamentary FRANCHISE open to all males except servants, they drew their support from the PARLIAMENTARIAN armies and humble and middle-ranking people in London and southern England. The ARMY leadership increasingly confronted them, particularly in the PUTNEY DEBATES of late Oct./early Nov. 1647, and they were repressed after army mutinies in 1649, although these disturbances were mostly only very distantly connected with them. Subsequently the movement disintegrated. *See also* GALLOWAY LEVELLERS.

Lewes, Battle of, 14 May 1264, Simon de MONTFORT's victory in Sussex in the BARONS' WAR against HENRY III and (the future) EDWARD I. While the left wing of de Montfort's army was chased from the battlefield by Edward, his right and centre defeated the main body of royalists. When Edward returned to Lewes, he found his father surrounded and Richard of Cornwall (1209–72), the younger brother of Henry III, captured. In the negotiations that followed, de Montfort gained possession of the king, the heir to the throne and the government of the kingdom.

Lexington, Battle of, *see* AMERICAN INDEPENDENCE, WAR OF

Ley Farming, *see* CONVERTIBLE HUSBANDRY

Libel Act 1792, also known as 'FOX's Libel Act' after its promoter. This declared the right of a JURY to find a general verdict on the whole matter of an alleged libel, and not, as before, only to pronounce on whether or not a supposed libel had been published by the accused. Juries had recurrently claimed the right to determine whether something was in substance libellous from at least the time of BUSHELL'S CASE, but judges had resisted the claim.

Liber Landavensis ('Book of Llandaff'), an extensive collection of copies of CHARTERS made at Llandaff in S. Glam. in the late 11th and early 12th centuries. The collection was compiled to impress the Normans with the antiquity of the bishopric of Llandaff. Scholars have debated the authenticity of the charters, which purport to cover the period from the 6th century onwards, but used with care, they are a crucial source for early Welsh history.

Liberal Democratic Party, *see* LIBERAL PARTY

Liberal National Party (National Liberal Party after 1948), LIBERAL group formed in 1931 by 23 Liberal MPs who split from the official party to join the NATIONAL GOVERNMENT. The group won 35 of the 41 seats they contested in the 1931 general election, although in 1932 the followers of Herbert Samuel, the Samuelites, left the National Government in protest at its PROTECTIONIST policies. Other Liberal Nationals, the SIMONITES, remained, securing 33 seats in 1935. In 1940 Ernest Brown succeeded Sir John Simon as leader and in 1945 only 13 of the Liberal Nationals were elected. In 1947 an agreement between the CONSERVATIVES and Liberal Nationals proposed that the constituency parties combine, and in 1948 the Liberal Nationals adopted the name the National Liberal Party. In 1966 the last MPs abandoned the National Liberal label.

Liberal Party Emerging in the late 1850s through the fusion of WHIGS, PEELITES and assorted Radicals, it combined a commitment to liberty, representative institutions, social progress and non-interventionism abroad with the fervour of militant NONCONFORMITY and the harsh precepts of LAISSEZ-FAIRE economics. J. S. MILL was its most articulate theorist and GLADSTONE its most effective exponent and practitioner.

Between the passing of the REFORM ACT 1867 and the outbreak of WORLD WAR I, the Liberal Party held power on five occasions: 1868–74, 1880–5, briefly in 1886, 1892–5 and 1906–16. Between 1867 and 1894 it was dominated by Gladstone, who championed moderate reform, FREE TRADE and a restrained foreign policy (*see* GLADSTONIAN LIBERALISM). However, the party was split by Gladstone's commitment to HOME RULE for Ireland (*see* LIBERAL UNIONISTS) and was out of office until a landslide victory in 1906. *De facto* the party of the working class, the Liberal Party under CAMPBELL-BANNERMAN and ASQUITH, after 1908, introduced a programme of far-reaching social and TRADE UNION reforms, extending concepts of state intervention. During this period, however, Liberal strength, strongest in Scotland and Wales, diminished markedly in England and it became more of a class-based party. The nature of the party's performance, doctrine and identity are, however, imperfectly understood, and the discrepancy between its pre-war achievements and post-war demise has been the cause of much historical controversy.

The outbreak of war in 1914 temporarily eased the pre-war crises faced by the Liberal government, but the demands of modern industrialized warfare were to prove almost fatally disruptive. Asquith's leadership came increasingly into question and he was forced to form a coalition government in May 1915 with CONSERVATIVE and LABOUR support, and put his dynamic colleague, LLOYD GEORGE, in charge of a newly-created ministry of munitions. By late 1916 Asquith's lacklustre performance led to him being deposed as premier by Lloyd George with Conservative backing, dividing the Liberal Party in the process. Although Asquith remained supportive of the government, his followers formed a rival faction to that led by Lloyd George. Lloyd George's decision to fight the general election of 1918 under the Coalition banner led to outright rivalry in which Asquith's followers were reduced to a mere 22 seats. While the Coalition Liberals returned 133, they only did so through the absence of Conservative opposition.

Meanwhile, the LABOUR PARTY had revamped its constitution, organization and programme, fighting as a national party for the first time and beginning to feel the beneficial effects of the REPRESENTATION OF THE PEOPLE ACT of 1918, which had virtually trebled the electorate. When Lloyd George was forced to resign over the CHANAK CRISIS in 1922, the divided Liberals faced the full impact of both Labour and Conservative opposition, falling to a combined total of 116 seats, and behind Labour. Although the party's factions reunited under Asquith in 1923 to fight another election, they again finished in third place and saw Labour form its first government. A further election in 1924 saw the party reduced to a mere 40 seats. Although there was a flurry of policy initiatives after Lloyd George assumed undisputed control of the party in 1926, and a bold election manifesto attempting a cure for mass unemployment in 1929, the party could only obtain 59 seats and was losing ground on almost every front. The crises of the early 1930s saw the party split further, a section of LIBERAL NATIONALS under Sir John Simon eventually becoming virtually indistinguishable from the Conservatives. A small independent element led by Herbert Samuel with few policies other than free trade and internationalism obtained a mere 20 seats in 1935. Decline continued after 1945, when only 12 seats were won, and took the party to the brink of extinction during the early 1950s.

A Liberal revival began under the new leadership of GRIMOND from 1956, marked by by-election victories at Torrington in 1958 and Orpington in 1962, where the Party benefited from capitalizing on a 'protest' vote. The Liberal share of the vote at general elections increased, although the party was unable to win sufficient seats to threaten the position of Labour and the Conservatives. During the 1960s, the party also attracted an influx of activist 'Young Liberals' which assisted it to a stronger base in local councils. The party also expanded its range of issues, emphasizing electoral reform, regionalism, freedom of information, and 'community politics'. In the first general election of 1974, the party won sufficient seats to negotiate a possible coalition with HEATH, but this failed to materialize. Temporarily set back by the THORPE affair and by his resignation as leader, David STEEL took the party into the LIB-LAB PACT with GALLAGHAN in 1976 to re-establish some credibility. Little advanced by the 1979 election, the party saw a chance to break the mould of British politics with the formation of the Social Democratic Party in 1981, with which it was to form a sometimes troubled alliance, until the two parties merged in 1988 to become the Liberal Democrat Party. David OWEN, leader of the SDP since 1983 and joint leader of the Liberal/SDP Alliance, resigned as leader of the SDP over the merger to lead the 'continuing SDP' until its demise in June 1990. In 1992 the Liberal Democrats under Paddy ASHDOWN won 18.3 per cent of the vote in the election, but with 20 MPs failed to hold the balance of power. The Labour landslide in the 1997 election denied the Liberal Democrats any such hope, though they achieved 46 seats and continuing dialogue with the government, though this did not please many of their grass-root supporters who insisted that the party should remain a third force in British politics rather than eliding with Labour's 'third way'. In 1999 Ashdown's long-announced departure took place and he was replaced by Charles Kennedy.

Liberal Unionists This parliamentary group was created as a result of the split in the LIBERAL PARTY over Irish HOME RULE in 1886, and became, in effect, the progressive wing of late-Victorian Conservatism. Liberal Unionists were opposed to Home Rule. Initially, the secessionists were divided into two, led, respectively, by Joseph CHAMBERLAIN and the Marquess of Hartington (*see* CAVENDISH, WILLIAM); in 1889, the groups merged to form the National Liberal Union. The failure of GLADSTONE's second Home Rule Bill divided the Liberal Party further and brought them closer to the CONSERVATIVE PARTY. In the 1895 general election, 70 Liberal Unionists were elected; Chamberlain and Hartington (now Duke of Devonshire) joined Salisbury's (*see* CECIL, ROBERT GASCOYNE) cabinet. The Liberal Unionists, with their interest in WORKMEN'S COMPENSATION, LOCAL GOVERNMENT, HOUSING and

PUBLIC HEALTH, had become the standard-bearers of Tory social reform.

Liberalism, Gladstonian, *see* GLADSTONIAN LIBERALISM

Liberalism, Theological, a wide-ranging term used in the 19th century, which includes the exponents of the higher criticism of the Bible and the upholders of an enlightened moral view of doctrine. Within the Church of England, it was used by its opponents as a term of criticism rather than as a description. *See also* CATHOLICISM, LIBERAL; CHURCH: ENGLAND; *ESSAYS AND REVIEWS*.

Liberty, *see* FRANCHISE

Lib-Lab Pact, agreement formed between the LIBERAL PARTY in Parliament under David STEEL and the CALLAGHAN government in March 1977 in order to keep the latter in office in the face of a vote of no confidence. The agreement allowed the LABOUR PARTY to survive the vote of no confidence on 23 March and the pact was renewed in autumn 1977. Although the continuation of the agreement was approved by the Liberal Assembly early in 1978, Steel formally ended the pact in June judging it to have become a liability in the run-up to the next general election.

Lib-Labs, a group of working-class MPs prominent in the generation before WORLD WAR I, who represented the labour interest but were elected with the support of the LIBERAL PARTY. The first were Thomas BURT and Alexander MACDONALD, who were subsequently joined by Henry Broadhurst, who held junior office under GLADSTONE; by 1885, there were 12 Lib-Labs in Parliament. Principally they were TRADE UNION members whose commitment to the radical wing of the Liberal Party was broadly representative of the political outlook of the skilled working class. They found the case for independent labour representation increasingly difficult to deny as Liberalism failed to protect essential trade union interests or keep abreast of increasing demands for a better standard of living. By the close of World War I the group no longer existed.

Libraries, repositories of books and manuscripts with access provided for readers and scholars. During the Middle Ages, ecclesiastical institutions housed the most important libraries, but with the advent of PRINTING the acquisition of a library became increasingly possible for private individuals. By the 18th century every gentleman was expected to have one, while from the 19th century onwards public access to books had vastly increased through the establishment of public and lending libraries.

From the 17th century, public access to libraries was increased through the opening of institutions such as Chetham's Library, MANCHESTER, and the establishing of circulating libraries where members of the public could borrow books on payment of a fee. The first such was Ramsay's, founded in EDINBURGH in 1726, and circulating libraries flourished in the later 18th and 19th centuries, supporting the growth of a READING – mainly novel-reading – public. The libraries operated by W. H. SMITH, Boots, Mudie's, and others in the 19th century had enormous influence on public taste; but all these circulating libraries have died out in the 20th century.

Their place has been taken, and surpassed, by public libraries, normally providing access and borrowing without payment of a fee. Apart from local benefactions, the first public libraries were established in various towns in 1847–50; the Public Libraries Act of 1850 empowered local authorities to levy a halfpenny rate to fund libraries and museums. Progress was relatively slow, although around 400 libraries had been opened by 1900. Added impetus was given before WORLD WAR I by the considerable philanthropy of the Dunfermline-born American steel magnate Andrew Carnegie, and then in 1919 by the Public Libraries Act which removed the rate limitations and gave counties the power to establish library services. Since the 1920s library services have expanded considerably, both through central government provision and the post-war growth of the county libraries; although periods of recession, notably the early 1930s, and the spending restrictions of the post-1979 period, have seen retrenchment.

Under the Copyright Act 1911 the BRITISH MUSEUM (since 1973 the British Library), the Bodleian Library, OXFORD, CAMBRIDGE UNIVERSITY Library, the National Libraries of Scotland and Wales, and Trinity College Dublin, are entitled to a free copy of every book published in the United Kingdom. Of these copyright and national libraries the oldest is the Bodleian, founded in 1602.

Licensing Acts (16th–17th centuries). The requirement that books be licensed by the PRIVY COUNCIL or other royal officers was introduced in 1538 and periodically revised. From 1586, no printing press could be set up except in LONDON, OXFORD and CAMBRIDGE, and, in 1588, 12 people were appointed to license books for printing.

The licensing system collapsed at the outbreak of the CIVIL WAR but was revived in 1643. In 1662, a new Licensing Act forbade the printing of any book against the doctrine or discipline of the Anglican Church or tending to the scandal of Church or government. It also required that all books and pamphlets be licensed, and allowed the king's messengers to search for unlicensed publications. This law lapsed in 1679; publishers were then prosecuted under other laws. In 1685 the system was revived, but ten years later, it lapsed for the final time, having proved inadequate to prevent the publication of seditious material. However, authors and publishers remained liable to prosecution for seditious libel or TREASON. *See also* CENSORSHIP OF THE PRESS.

Licensing Act 1872 This gave powers to magistrates to grant licences and check for adulteration of alcoholic drinks, and fixed closing hours of public houses at 11.00 p.m. for the country and midnight for London. It displeased both the temperance supporters (who thought it too lenient) and the licensed victuallers (who thought it excessive).

Licensing Act 1904 This raised a levy on the whole licensing trade to provide compensation for publicans who had lost their licences. The treatment of publicans as a vested interest helped further to rally NONCONFORMIST opinion, which had already been antagonized by the EDUCATION ACT 1902, against the CONSERVATIVE government.

Lichfield, Staffs. Briefly an archbishopric from 787–802/3, its elevation to metropolitan status was brought about by OFFA of MERCIA to counteract the influence of the archbishop of CANTERBURY, whose see lay within the rival kingdom of KENT. The one consecrated archbishop of Lichfield, Hygeberht, resigned before the papacy agreed to his see's demotion to become again a BISHOPRIC, which it has remained almost continuously to the present day. During the CIVIL WARS, the cathedral was the only one in England to suffer ruinous structural damage, being three times involved in sieges (twice in 1643 and in 1646); it was reconstructed from 1661–9. Dr JOHNSON is Lichfield's most famous son.

Life Cycle, the sequence of stages through which individuals or families pass in the course of life: from birth to death, or from marriage to dissolution of a union by death or divorce. The concept has been widely used in HISTORICAL DEMOGRAPHY and SOCIAL HISTORY to focus study of, e.g., the institution of DOMESTIC SERVICE at adolescent and young adult ages, entry to MARRIAGE, retirement, and ageing.

Life Expectancy, the average number of years a person would expect to live. Life expectancy is frequently expressed as from birth although it can be calculated from any age. Research in HISTORICAL DEMOGRAPHY has shown that in much of the early modern period, life expectancies at birth have been in the range 35–45 years and they have remained at these levels for low-income city and town dwellers into the 19th century, while those in the present day are in excess of 70. These figures reflect the heavy incidence of infant and child MORTALITY in the past, and are *not*, as is often erroneously supposed, the standard (or even upper) age at which adults are expected to die. Life expectancies have almost always been lower for men than for women.

Life Peerages Act 1958 A partial reform of the House of LORDS which allowed the creation of non-hereditary life peers, including women. The possibility of the government recommending the creation of hereditary PEERAGES remained, but was not exercised again until 1983 when Margaret THATCHER recommended William Whitelaw and ex-Speaker George Thomas for viscountcies. Neither had heirs, but in the following year Harold MACMILLAN (who did) accepted an earldom.

Life Table, numerical description of the MORTALITY of a population, giving the probability of dying or surviving at each age. The application of a particular life table produces the figure of LIFE EXPECTANCY among its statistics. Model life tables, based upon empirical observation, are frequently used in HISTORICAL DEMOGRAPHY for estimating mortality.

'Lilliburlero', a popular 17th-century political song written by Thomas, Lord Wharton (1648–1715) and portraying Catholics as determined on the massacre of Protestants. It is said to have greatly influenced popular opinion in 1688: the chorus – 'lilliburlero bullenala' – was thought to have been a password used by Irish Catholics when murdering Protestants in 1641. The tune is now the call sign of the BBC World Service.

Limerick, Treaty of, 3 Oct. 1691. This was signed in Ireland between JACOBITE and Williamite forces at the conclusion of the second siege of Limerick in the aftermath of the GLORIOUS REVOLUTION. The military treaty allowed Irish soldiers to go to France, and 11,000 did so. The civil treaty promised an amnesty to all who took an OATH of allegiance, and offered Catholics at least the religious rights they had had under CHARLES II, as well as secure possession of lands to which they had established a claim. The wholly Protestant Irish PARLIAMENT complained that these provisions were too generous; they were not confirmed by statute until 1697, and then only in substantially modified form.

Limited Liabilities Act 1855 This allowed companies registered under the COMPANIES ACT 1844 to limit the liability of individual investors to the value of their shares. Such limited liability, which ended the risk of investors in failing companies being exposed in law to the seizure of their other properties to pay the company's debts, is said to have done much to encourage investment in trade and industry, though good evidence for this assertion is lacking. Further legislation consolidating this and related statutes was passed in 1857 and 1862. *See also* INCORPORATION; JOINT STOCK; STOCK EXCHANGE.

Lincoln Situated at the junction of FOSSE WAY and Ermine Street, this was one of the major cities of Roman Britain, emerging in the late 3rd century as the capital of one of Britain's four newly created provinces. The town's fortunes declined sharply between the 5th and 9th centuries, recovering in the 10th as a result of the economic impact of the VIKINGS. The Normans built the CASTLE and the CATHEDRAL that still dominate the town. Lincoln was very prosperous in the medieval period because of the WOOL TRADE, but declined to the status of a provincial town in the 16th century.

Lincoln, Battles of The first took place on 2 Feb. 1141, and was a key moment in the war between STEPHEN and the Empress MATILDA. Stephen, who was laying siege to Lincoln Castle, was defeated and captured by a relieving army led by the earls ROBERT OF GLOUCESTER and Ranulf of Chester.

The second battle (20 May 1217) was the turning-point in the war between LOUIS VIII of France and the supporters of HENRY III. While besieging the castle, Louis was caught off-guard and defeated by a force led by William Marshal, Falkes de Breauté and Peter des Roches.

Lincolnshire Rebellion, *see* PILGRIMAGE OF GRACE

Lindisfarne The monastery on the island of Lindisfarne, Northumb. was, from the time of St Aidan, the centre for Irish MISSIONARY activity in northern England during the period of the CONVERSION to Christianity. It remained a great religious centre for two centuries until its destruction by VIKINGS in 793, including among its inmates St Cedd, St Chad and, most importantly of all, St Cuthbert, and producing that superb illuminated manuscript, the *Lindisfarne Gospels*, which can now be seen in the BRITISH MUSEUM. Later it became merely a cell to DURHAM Cathedral and was dissolved in 1537; the ruins remain extensive and dramatic.

Lindsey, Kingdom of The origins of this obscure early Anglo-Saxon kingdom lie in the 4th or 5th centuries, and its last recorded ruler lived in the late 8th century. Its independence between the two powerful kingdoms of MERCIA and NORTHUMBRIA was never secure, and documents such as the *TRIBAL HIDEAGE* show that its status must frequently have been that of a tribute-paying dependency.

Liner, a merchant ship, either passenger or cargo, which plies on regular routes to a fixed timetable. The first liners were the early 19th-century North Atlantic sailing packets. By 1840 steamships were carrying passengers and mail on the North Atlantic. Air transport killed off the passenger liner (except for cruises) by the 1970s but most larger cargo ships are now either containerized liners or bulk carriers.

Lisle Letters The surviving correspondence of the courtier, Arthur Plantagenet, 6th Viscount Lisle (*c.*1480–1542), the illegitimate son of EDWARD IV, with his household and his masterful second wife. The letters have been edited by Muriel St. Clair Byrne (1981).

Literacy Living in a society with a very high literacy rate, we tend to take its importance for granted. However, in earlier societies, literacy may not have seemed worth acquiring even by the powerful; for much of the medieval period, the clergy (the word-association of 'cleric' and 'clerk' is not accidental) provided the necessary specialist labour like any other variety of craftsman. Moreover, our educational system teaches READING and writing together, but they are different skills that can be acquired separately and which may have different uses. It is useful to distinguish between 'active' literates (writers as well as readers) and 'passive' literates (readers but not writers).

Problems remain in the history of literacy despite great recent advances in research – for example, by Michael Clanchy on the great, though unquantifiable, increases in literacy in the 12th and 13th centuries. The easiest data to gather are the proportion of people able to write their signature ('signature literacy'), but this overestimates writing skills and reveals little about who can read, usually a much higher proportion. Nevertheless, signature data form the basis of information on England from the early 16th century. This indicates substantial increases in literacy during that century at all social levels except among labourers and vagrants, where near-total illiteracy rates prevailed into the 19th century. Overall male literacy rose slowly from about 30 per cent in 1550, with the north catching up with the south during the 17th century; women consistently lagged far behind in ability to write, although probably not in reading. Literacy rates were fairly similar in Lowland Scotland, although during the 19th century, Scotland surged ahead of England in basic literacy. After 1600, illiteracy was virtually unknown among the English, Scots and Irish merchant class, gentry and aristocracy. At all stages, there were major regional variations.

Explanations for these early modern developments are varied and often oblique. Literacy was associated with power. Lay jealousy of clerical power (*see* ANTI-CLERICALISM) and the emphasis in PROTESTANTISM on personal understanding of the Bible were important factors, prompting CATHOLICS to acquire literacy in self-defence. In Scotland, there may have been a determination to outdo the more powerful English neighbour. The increase in trade and commercial AGRICULTURE made a mastery of written figures and agreements desirable. Early modern government produced much more documentation, which it was as well to understand – but was this growth a stimulus to or an effect of literacy? Discussion continues.

The rise or fall of literacy during the period 1780–1870 also remains controversial. It is agreed that literacy rose in the first two-thirds of the 18th century, but not what happened then. The historian Lawrence Stone argued, on the basis of marriage licences and parish registers, that literacy in England and Wales rose from around 56 per cent in 1775 to around 65 per cent in 1800, and to 66 per cent in 1840 in response to industrialization and the new demand for a literate workforce. Others dispute these figures, arguing that the POPULATION growth of the period swamped the available schools, that working-class children employed in factories had neither the time nor the energy for education, and that after the collapse of HANDLOOM WEAVING, families were more than ever dependent on child earnings. SUNDAY SCHOOLS seem to have maintained the status quo rather than improving literacy levels, especially as they ceased teaching writing in the 1790s. R. S. Schofield has demonstrated a marked decline in literacy levels in industrial areas between 1760 and 1820. In all probability, there were wide regional variations, with decline in industrial districts balanced by stability or a rise in rural areas.

Through the course of the 19th and into the 20th century almost universal literacy was achieved, more especially after compulsory schooling was introduced in 1870.

Literary and Philosophical Societies, societies founded from the late 18th century – in, for example, MANCHESTER (1781), NEWCASTLE (1793) and BIRMINGHAM (1800) – for the discussion of literature and natural philosophy, in imitation of French and other continental societies. Professional men and industrialists, some of them DISSENTERS, were prominent among their members.

Lithsmen, one of the categories of English warrior mentioned in 11th-century sources. Their function is uncertain, although some historians have perceived similarities with the HOUSECARLS. 'Sailors who received pay' is a possible definition. *See also* FYRD.

Liverpool, the town developed on the neck of land between the wide River Mersey and the tidal creek known as the Pool of Liverpool. A CASTLE was built in 1235, and a small but important settlement grew up, although Liverpool only became a PARISH in its own right in 1699; by this time it was growing in economic importance, especially due to shipping sailing to and from the WEST INDIES and North America. Spectacular growth occurred in the 18th century, when the population may have rocketed from 6,000 to 80,000; Liverpool traded in SUGAR, TOBACCO, and COTTON and was prominent in the trade in SLAVES shipped from Africa to the Americas. Nearly 5,000 ships a year were visiting in the late 18th century, from which time considerable areas of formerly genteel housing survive. The pace of growth continued in the 19th century, with Liverpool becoming the premier Atlantic trading port and the point of arrival for many Irish MIGRANTS, especially in the wake of the POTATO FAMINE. The city had over 250,000 inhabitants in 1841, and nearly 700,000 by 1900. The most eloquent survival of that age is the series of docks, notably the Albert Dock with its massive architecture, which was built by Jesse Hartley from 1824–60. Liverpool vied with all the other great provincial cities in the magnificence of its public buildings, pre-eminently St George's Hall (1839–56). The Anglican cathedral, designed by Giles Gilbert Scott in 1909, was only completed in the 1970s; a Roman Catholic cathedral later emerged, designed in 1959 by Sir Frederick Gibberd with a great lantern roof which, like the Anglican cathedral's tower, is a dominant accent in the city skyline. By the post-war years, Liverpool's heyday had long passed, and the docks and associated industries progressively shrank, as did the population. Having no large manufacturing base independent of trade and the port, Liverpool in the later 20th century has become almost a byword for urban deprivation. However, with its idiosyncratic 'scouse' wit it has also been an important and distinctive post-war cultural force, especially with the Beatles and the 'Mersey Sound' in the 1960s, and a succession of actors, poets, novelists and playwrights.

Liverpool, 2nd Earl of, *see* JENKINSON, ROBERT

Livery, from the French *livrée*, 'delivered'. The word can refer to the act of providing food, drink or clothing to servants or retainers, or to the provisions or clothing so dispensed. Hence it has come to mean the distinctive, uniform clothing bestowed by a lord on his retainer as a badge of allegiance. As an outward sign of aristocratic power and sometimes linked with MAINTENANCE, livery was a controversial issue in English politics from the 14th to the 16th centuries.

Livingstone, David (1813–73), explorer and missionary. Born in Lanarks., where he initially worked in a COTTON mill, Livingstone saved to study for a medical degree which he took in 1840. Thereafter his entire career was spent in AFRICA, first in BECHUANALAND where he was sent by the London Missionary Society. He combined missionary zeal, medicine and exploration: between 1849 and 1856 he discovered the Victoria Falls and Lake Ngami, and explored the Zambezi; between 1858 and 1864 he explored the Zambezi's eastern tributaries and discovered Lake Nyasa; and in 1865 he set out in search of the sources of the Nile. Nothing was heard of him until 1871, when he was found by H. M. STANLEY, the Welsh-born American journalist who had mounted an expedition to locate the veteran explorer. They met on Lake Tanganyika in Oct., Stanley – according to tradition – greeting him with the words, 'Dr Livingstone, I presume?' Livingstone's explorations continued for a further two years until his death at Ilala (Northern RHODESIA) in May 1873. He inspired not only hearts and opinions at home in Britain, but continued to be remembered and revered in Africa by succeeding generations.

Llancarfan, S. Glam. One of the major monastic sites of early medieval Wales, its most renowned abbot was the 6th-century St CADOG, who made Llancarfan the centre of a monastic confederation. Some early CHARTERS that have fortuitously survived give insights into the economic resources of a very early religious community. It does not seem to have survived later than *c.* 1100.

Llanilltud Fawr (Llantwit Major), S. Glam., the site of one of the most important monasteries of early medieval Wales. Its most distinguished abbot was St Illtud who lived in the 6th century, and its inmates at one stage or another included St Samson, Bishop of Dol (*fl.* 6th century) and, possibly, St DAVID. It does not seem to have survived later than *c.* 1100.

Lloyd George, David (1st Earl Lloyd George) (1863–1945), Liberal politician and Prime Minister (1916–22). Raised in a Welsh chapel household with an early intention of 'getting on', he became a solicitor before being elected as Liberal MP for Caernarvon Boroughs in 1890. He served as president of the Board of Trade (1905–8) before becoming chancellor of the Exchequer (1908–15), when he proved to be a radical social reformer, introducing the OLD AGE PENSIONS ACT 1908, National Insurance and the PEOPLE'S BUDGET, the latter precipitating a clash with the LORDS which culminated in the Lords being curbed by the PARLIAMENT ACT 1911.

As minister of munitions (1915–16), secretary for war (1916) and prime minister (1916–22) after ASQUITH was deposed, he proved an efficient and dynamic administrator and wartime leader. Even before the end of the war, he began a reconstruction campaign to appease working-class discontent and fulfil his radical aspirations. The HOUSING AND TOWN PLANNING ACT was passed in 1919, education reform introduced and social insurance extended. However, these programmes were cut short by a round of economies in 1921: the GEDDES AXE. Although he pursued a vindictive policy towards Germany in the run-up to the 1918 election, at the PARIS PEACE CONFERENCE he tried to moderate French demands. He also brought the immediate Irish conflict to a conclusion by the ANGLO-IRISH TREATY of 1921, which set up the IRISH FREE STATE.

Lloyd George's decision to oust Asquith from the premiership in 1916, and then to continue the wartime coalition with the CONSERVATIVES after the COUPON ELECTION of 1918, had done devastating harm to a LIBERAL PARTY already in disarray over attitudes to the war, and had permanently damaged his own reputation. The Conservatives who made up the majority of the coalition grew restive under his leadership, and in 1922 he was forced to resign over the CHANAK CRISIS. Although he made a temporary truce with Asquith to fight the 1923 election, he retained his own organization and funds, and in 1926, he assumed the leadership of a Liberal Party that had been reduced to a mere 40 seats in the 1924 election.

He showed considerable interest in policies designed to solve the problem of mass UNEMPLOYMENT, producing the *Orange Book* in 1929, offering a programme of public works and government spending that drew on the ideas of J. M. KEYNES. He was still a contender for office in 1931, but lost his chance through illness when crisis hit the second LABOUR government; he also gave up the Liberal leadership in that year. He continued to promote ideas for economic regeneration, and expressed admiration for what Hitler was doing in Germany. He was again considered for office in 1940, in the war cabinet, but felt he was too old to carry the responsibilities inherent in such a post. He was created an earl in 1945.

Llywelyn ap Gruffudd (*c.* 1228–82), Prince of Wales. In 1255, he obtained mastery of GWYNEDD by defeating his brothers in battle, and at once set about reversing the setbacks that the Welsh had suffered at English hands since the death of his grandfather LLYWELYN AP IORWERTH. Taking advantage of the political disarray in England, and in alliance with Simon de MONTFORT, he won a remarkable string of victories. By restoring lands to their rightful dynasties, often retaining only 'fame and honour' for himself, he persuaded all the rulers of Wales to accept the jurisdiction of his court, in this way creating a principality more extensive than his grandfather's. In 1267, the English acceptance of his achievement in the treaty of MONTGOMERY meant that he had become the first – and last – native Prince of Wales to be recognized by the English crown.

Subsequently Llywelyn showed less sensitivity towards the claims of local dynasties, and in 1274, his brother DAFYDD AP GRUFFUDD plotted his murder. Two years later, EDWARD I, angered by his independence, condemned him as a rebel. He was then overwhelmed by English military power and forced to accept the peace of Aberconwy (1278). However, English high-handedness and the menace contained in the CASTLES that Edward now began to build fuelled Llywelyn's insecurity and also exacerbated Welsh resentment, and in 1282, a war of national liberation exploded. In Dec., while Edward's fleet and armies advanced against Gwynedd, Llywelyn was killed near Builth. The following year, his principality was annexed to the English crown.

Llywelyn ap Iorwerth (?–1240), Prince of North Wales. Known as 'the Great' within a few decades of his death, he achieved a greater and more lasting dominance within Wales than any previous ruler – though he stopped short of calling himself 'prince of Wales' and he always acknowledged the overlordship of the English crown. Between 1194 and 1201 he won control of GWYNEDD at the expense of his dynastic rivals, and in 1205 he married Joan, illegitimate daughter of King JOHN, whose recognition enabled Llewelyn to annex southern POWYS and CEREDIGION in 1208. But three years later, John seemed set on the conquest of Wales, and it was by surviving this great crisis in 1211–12 that Llywelyn established his reputation as the leader of all the Welsh.

During 1215–17, he exploited the MAGNA CARTA movement to extend his authority as far south as Swansea. An alliance with Ranulf, Earl of Chester – whose heir married one of Llywelyn's daughters – then enabled the Welsh prince to retain his dominance for more than 20 years. Although he could not guarantee the undisputed succession of his only legitimate son DAFYDD AP LLYWELYN to the principality of north Wales together with his overlordship over the rest of the country, he had at least established the pre-eminence of Gwynedd, which lasted until brought down by EDWARD I.

Lobby, derived from a late medieval term for a passage or corridor, the perfect place to linger and wait to ask a favour from a powerful person. From this derive various usages of the term in modern parliamentary politics. 'To lobby' is to approach a Member of Parliament to further a group interest. A lobby is also the institutional arrangement to organize such pressure, long recognized and organized on a commercial basis in the United States, and now also well established in Britain. Additionally in Britain, 'the lobby' is the term used for the group of newspaper political correspondents who are given supposedly privileged access to government opinions.

Local Government The concept of local government is inseparable from that of a political entity with a central administration; the centre creates institutions which are intended to gather revenues and carry out its policies throughout its territories. One must therefore distinguish local government from the seigneurial institutions, such as the MANOR, whose jurisdiction derives from the immediate FEUDAL lord rather than from the ultimate feudal superior (*see* COURT BARON). Neither can one usefully talk of 'local government' in relation to the fragmented political structures of Wales and Ireland before they were invaded and partly colonized by the kingdom of England. However, in England, the precocious CENTRALIZATION of the kingdom, already perceptible in the late ANGLO-SAXON period, created officers and institutions of local government which derived directly from royal power. Some of these like the EALDORMAN, HUNDRED and WAPENTAKE, have not survived, but others have lineal connections with modern administration (*see* COUNTY; COUNTY COURT; SHERIFF; SHIRE; WRIT).

The Norman and Angevin monarchy developed this county-based organization still further, particularly through HENRY II's expansion of the competence and effectiveness of COMMON LAW, but also for purposes of revenue collection. Central government also delegated its powers in certain areas to feudal lords in liberties or FRANCHIZES, and used local officials to regulate its relationships to its own tenants, principally the ESCHEATOR and later the feodary (*see* WARDSHIP). Urban communities were given royal CHARTERS specifying their privileges and often details of their system of government; lords also granted similar charters (*see* ALDERMAN; BOROUGH; WARD).

A similar pattern developed in the kingdom of Scotland, although there the feudal institutions remained stronger in relation to a weak central government right up to the 17th century (*see* BURGH).

A problem in the centre's attitude to local political institutions has always been to create institutions of local government which are effective, yet whose independent power does not come to represent local interests against central policy. A further constant struggle for the medieval royal government which came to settle at WESTMINSTER was to find ways of bridging the gap between the judgments of central courts and the administration of royal justice locally. From the 12th century, the institutions first of the EYRE and more lastingly of the ASSIZES and the CORONER were evolved to fulfil this need, but the most successful and flexible institution of local government came to be the system of JUSTICES OF THE PEACE meeting in Quarter Sessions, the dominant setting for both justice and administration between the 15th and the 19th centuries (for Wales, *see also* GREAT SESSIONS). Equally long-lasting was the institution during the later 16th century of permanent LORDS LIEUTENANT, prompted by the need to co-ordinate national and local defence (*see also* MILITIA); the administration of POOR RELIEF was also much expanded from *c.*1600, organized on the basis of the much older ecclesiastical system of the PARISH.

From the time of WOLSEY up to its abolition by the LONG PARLIAMENT in 1641, the Court of STAR CHAMBER (the KING'S COUNCIL sitting as a court at Westminster) acted as a major monitor on the behaviour of local institutions. The Tudor monarchs also established the royal COUNCIL IN THE MARCHES OF WALES and the COUNCIL OF THE NORTH to act as regional governments on Westminster's behalf; an experimental COUNCIL IN THE WEST PARTS (1538–40) proved unnecessary. The troubles of the mid-17th-century CIVIL WARS destroyed the authority of the regional royal councils, and led to various nationwide experiments and expedients such as the COUNTY COMMITTEES and the MAJOR-GENERALS, none of which proved lasting.

During the 19th century, the growing ascendancy of the ideal of mass political representation led to the reform of local government, reducing the functions of Justices of the Peace to purely judicial matters, and gradually restricting the functions of the lords lieutenant to ceremonial matters; in their place a structure of popularly elected county, borough, district and even parish councils was instituted (*see* LOCAL GOVERNMENT ACT 1888; DISTRICT AND PARISH COUNCILS ACT 1894). This has been subject to frequent adjustment in its functions and geographical organization (*see* e.g. LOCAL GOVERNMENT REORGANIZATION ACT 1972), and elected bodies with specialist functions, for instance in monitoring the POLICE, controlling education and health authorities, were also created. In more recent years, representative local government has seen its powers eroded by a return to non-elected administrative bodies appointed by central government (quangos), a controversial development. *See also* COMPURGATION; CONSTABLE; CONSTITUENCY; COUNTY COMMUNITY; COURT VERSUS COUNTRY; DIVISION; *FLYMENAFYRMTH; HAMSOCN; INSPEXIMUS*; MARCHER LORDSHIPS; MAYOR; PALATINATE; PALE; PETTY SESSIONS; PROVOST; *QUO WARRANTO*; REGISTERS, PARISH; SANCTUARY; THOROUGH; TURNPIKES.

Local Government Act 1888 A response to population movement, the growth of democracy and the increasing role of the state, it created county councils, elected by rate-payers, to replace county MAGISTRATES nominated by LORDS LIEUTENANT. The 66 county councils were to be elected by household suffrage for three years, with ALDERMEN elected by the councillors. The corporations of BOROUGHS with populations of more than 50,000 were to act as borough councils independent of their counties. LONDON became a separate county (*see* LONDON COUNTY COUNCIL) with special provision for the City, which was to retain its own rights and be governed by its corporation, and for the METROPOLITAN POLICE, who were to remain directly responsible to the home office. The new county councils became responsible for the management of roads, bridges, drains and general county business. Control of the county POLICE outside London, however, was vested in a joint committee of magistrates and councillors. The Act was extended to Scotland in 1889.

Local Government Act 1929 Passed by Neville CHAMBERLAIN as minister of health, it gave county and borough councils control over public assistance to the poor and the chronically sick and over POOR LAW hospitals. It abolished the Boards of Guardians which had administered POOR RELIEF since 1834.

Local Government Board Act 1871 This transferred the functions and duties of the Poor Law Board of 1854 to a newly created department of state – the Local Government Board – under the auspices of a Cabinet minister (this was amalgamated into the ministry of health in 1919).

Local Government Reorganization Act 1972 The Act set up a new system and boundaries for local government in England and Wales to operate from 1974, and in Scotland from 1975. Six metropolitan county councils, covering the larger conurbations, were created on the existing model of the GREATER LONDON COUNCIL, together with 39 county councils to act as strategic authorities administering major functions such as transport, EDUCATION and social services. A second tier of district councils was to provide local services such as HOUSING, refuse collection, and leisure amenities. A third tier of 7,000 parish councils was to deal with local issues. The Act imposed a new administrative map of Britain, often cutting across historical boundaries. The metropolitan counties, such as Merseyside and West Midlands, were carved out of former counties; smaller counties, such as Rutland, were swept away; and new counties such as Avon and Humberside were created. In Scotland and Wales, the effect was particularly far-reaching, grouping several existing counties into much larger administrative units. The changes caused much local ill-feeling and complaints of excessive bureaucracy and increasing cost. In 1985 the GLC and the metropolitan counties were abolished and their functions devolved to the lower tier. A further review of local government in 1994 has led to fresh proposals to alter the provisions of the 1972 Act and re-establish former counties such as Rutland.

Local History, the study of the history of a particular village, town or locality. It has an important place in the writing of history today, as it had in previous generations (*see* e.g. GOUGH). Often derived from ANTIQUARIAN or personal interest, and frequently the preserve of amateurs (as is also the case with genealogy), local history has also become ever more important in the academic sphere. The so-called 'Leicester school', led by W. G. Hoskins, who wrote the classic *The Making of the English Landscape* (1954), took a new approach to the in-depth local study as the basis for comparative work. The most important work using local history has been done in Europe, and especially in France through the *Annales* school, named after the academic journal founded by Marc Bloch. Italian historians coined the term 'microhistory' for these studies which 'attempt to see the world in a grain of sand'.

Locarno Treaty, Oct. 1925, a mutual security pact signed in Switzerland by Britain, France, Italy, Belgium and Germany. The prime movers were the French and British foreign ministers, Briand and Austen Chamberlain, both of whom were concerned to ease European tensions. The treaty, and a linked series of agreements signed at the same time confirming the inviolability of Germany's borders with France and Belgium and the demilitarized status of the Rhineland, were intended as a symbolic reconciliation between Germany and its recent European enemies. Notably, however, no statement was made about guarantees for Germany's eastern border following the Treaty of Versailles (*see* PARIS PEACE CONFERENCE). Germany, France and Belgium entered into a mutual non-aggression pact and France offered Poland and Czechoslovakia protection in the event of German attack. The agreements were hailed as a major achievement in European co-operation, and remained the basis of European security policy until Hitler's remilitarization of the Rhineland in 1936.

Locke, John (1632–1704), philosopher. Son of an ATTORNEY who had fought on the PARLIAMENTARIAN side in the CIVIL WARS, Locke both studied and taught at OXFORD UNIVERSITY. In 1667, he became attached to the household of Anthony Ashley COOPER, 1st Earl of Shaftesbury, henceforth his political patron. Holding minor office when Shaftesbury was in power, Locke went to France when the earl was out of favour (1676–9), and to Holland when the exposure of the RYE HOUSE PLOT shattered his circle. The GLORIOUS REVOLUTION allowed him to come back to England in 1689, and from 1696 he once more played a part in public life, serving as one of the most active members of the newly founded BOARD OF TRADE.

His writings, published only after 1689 although much was written earlier, include three *Letters* advocating religious toleration (1689, 1690, 1692); *Two Treatises of Government* (1690), a classic exposition both of the right to resist misgovernment and limit its activities, and of the right to hold private property; and *An Essay on Human Understanding* (1690), a book which was to be hailed as seminal by thinkers of the Enlightenment for its advocacy of the primacy of individual human experience in the perception of truth. *Some Thoughts Concerning Education* (1693) and *The Reasonableness of Christianity* (1695) followed; the latter became a key text for LATITUDINARIANS and DEISTS (although Locke himself disapproved of the description 'Deist'). What made Locke's *Two Treatises* appear subversive to his more conservative readers, then and later, was his justification of the subject's right to resistance should the ruler (or governing authority) violate the trust invested in him. And Locke seems to have been well aware of the work's radical thrust; not only did he publish it anonymously, but he also consistently denied authorship, though frequently taxed with it, until his death. His political ideas were to have a considerable influence on the American colonists in their breach with Britain.

Lock-outs, *see* STRIKES

Locomotives Act 1865 A measure designed to regulate the speed of traction engines, it provided that mechanically driven vehicles were not to run at more than 4 mph and were to be preceded by a man carrying a red flag. The flag was abandoned in 1878, but the low speed restriction remained until the Locomotives on Highways Act of 1896, when the limit was raised to 14 mph (*see* MOTOR INDUSTRY).

Lollards, a medieval name for the followers of John WYCLIF – the word being a term of abuse for a religious zealot of suspect views. The Lollards shared with most of their pious but orthodox contemporaries a critical view of the clergy; where they differed was in espousing Wyclif's denial of transubstantiation in the MASS, and in arguing that a programme of clerical disendowment was the best way to return the Church to apostolic poverty and purity. Their belief that Holy Scripture was divinely inspired and ought to be accessible to everyone resulted in the Lollard BIBLE, an English translation made in the 1390s.

In its early stages, Lollardy enjoyed some support from within the political establishment – the Lollard knights – but in 1401, HENRY IV's statute *DE HERETICO COMBURENDO* introduced death by burning as a punishment for HERESY, and in 1407 the Lollard Bible was banned. The link between Lollardy and treason was confirmed by the rising led by Sir John Oldcastle in 1414. After this, Lollardy won no support from politically important groups, so the authorities generally took a fairly relaxed view of it. It survived as an underground movement with its own priests, schoolmasters and literature. Early 16th-century evidence (mostly derived from sporadic official persecution) suggests that, although Lollardy was not producing new literature, it commanded entrenched support in certain communities of southern England, which were able to keep in contact with each other. South-west Scotland produced one mysteriously isolated outbreak of Lollardy in the Kyle in the 1490s. Lollards quickly co-operated with those influenced by the continental Reformation and their traditional theological concerns – especially hatred of images and shrines (*see* ICONOCLASM), attacks on the Mass and an interest in the role of moral law in the Christian life – are significantly reflected in later English REFORMATION theology.

Lombard Street, a book by Walter BAGEHOT, published in 1873, which spelled out for the first time the principles of central banking and the BANK OF ENGLAND's functions and responsibilities.

London London's history is inextricably bound up with the histories of England and the United Kingdom. Since its foundation *c.*AD 50 after the ROMAN CONQUEST, and particularly from Anglo-Saxon times, London was the largest and politically most important town in Britain, and from the 13th century it has almost without exception been the seat of government and royal power, a principal port, manufacturing and trading centre.

The Roman town of *Londinium*, at the lowest crossing point on the River Thames, was established as the capital of the province of Britain after BOUDICCA's rebellion. The Roman wall, enclosing a square mile from Blackfriars in the west to the Tower in the east, established the boundary of London until the 16th century, a boundary which is still that of the City of London (*see* LONDON, CITY OF). ARCHAEOLOGY has revealed an exceptionally large forum, numerous wharves, a bridge, and evidence of considerable wealth.

During the Anglo-Saxon period, London retained its position as the most important town in the British Isles. St Paul's cathedral was established in 604. By the early 8th century, after decline in the 5th and 6th, BEDE could describe it as a market frequented by many who came there by land and sea. In the later 10th century its economic and political importance was such that it probably minted a quarter of the kingdom's COIN. The city's basic governmental organization of folkmoot and husting court probably originated in the 10th century. The absence of an entry for London in *DOMESDAY BOOK* makes an estimate of its early medieval population very hazardous, but a reasonable guess would be around 25,000.

WESTMINSTER, upstream, developed as a royal centre from the 10th century, especially under EDWARD THE CONFESSOR, and WILLIAM I THE CONQUEROR was crowned there. Also after the NORMAN CONQUEST, the TOWER OF LONDON was built as the dominating feature of the city. The transfer of the EXCHEQUER from WINCHESTER in the 12th century, and the development there of permanent courts of justice in the 13th, consolidated its political importance (*see* CHANCERY; COMMON PLEAS; KING'S BENCH). Medieval London was characterized by the number and wealth of the ecclesiastical foundations within its walls and the density of its population (estimated at 100,000 before the BLACK DEATH). London's wealth became so great that it could bail out the crown at times of difficulty, and leading citizens, such as the real Dick Whittington (?–1423), were among the wealthiest men in the kingdom. The city became a focus of both overseas trade (*see* STEELYARD) and inland traffic.

The evidence suggests that London, like many towns, was suffering in the early 16th century, but witnessed massive growth thereafter, its population doubling and redoubling in a generation (rising from 50,000 in 1550 to 600,000 by 1700). For the first time the population began to break out beyond the line of the walls, and after the 1620s most of the significant expansion took place in the suburbs, especially west towards Westminster (*see* COVENT GARDEN) or immediately downstream where port and industrial activity met. *See also* BILLS OF MORTALITY.

The density of housing and poor water supplies made London prey to the periodic and catastrophic outbreaks of BUBONIC PLAGUE and other infectious diseases, with the last visitation in 1665 (*see* GREAT PLAGUE), followed in 1666 by the GREAT FIRE. The fire gave the impetus both to the rebuilding of the ancient city and to further expansion outside, and by the late 17th century a series of squares, new streets and public buildings had arisen in Westminster. London's growth was undiminished, although by the 18th century other towns, especially ports and manufacturing centres, were growing at a faster rate. London was still the great political and social centre as well as a trade centre, and it became the pre-eminent financial centre; the Acts of UNION with Scotland and then Ireland further fuelled its growth as their capitals were eclipsed. By 1800 London's population had reached one million.

As London increased in size and the brick-built terraces snaked ever further out, so the number of houses within the City at the core fell. The 19th-century developments were marked by major changes in transportation, with the opening of the docks in the east and the coming of the RAILWAYS, both overground (from 1836) and underground (from 1863). These, and the programmes of SLUM CLEARANCE at the centre, pushed the limits of the built-up area out further still; yet the East End, where William Booth and others sought out poverty and vice, was in itself as large as many a European city. Meanwhile London was acquiring the grand buildings befitting its status as the great commercial and imperial capital.

London lost its title as the world's largest city in the 1920s, and from the 1930s the total population began to fall from its peak of 9 million as people moved out further still. The need to provide coherent government for London had resulted in the formation of the METROPOLITAN BOARD OF WORKS in 1867, with fuller powers given to the LONDON COUNTY COUNCIL in 1889, and the extension of the area designated as Greater London with the formation of the GREATER LONDON COUNCIL in 1965 (abolished in 1985); on each occasion the City retained its separate privileges and jurisdiction. In the BLITZ London, and especially the docks and East End, were badly devastated. The plan by Sir Patrick Abercrombie (1879–1957) envisaged a London for a new age; however, only parts of the plan and of its successors ever came to fruition. Indeed, almost every proposal for root-and-branch renewal in London from 1666 onwards has resulted in piecemeal change instead. In modern times some of the capital's traditional features, notably its port traffic and industry, have diminished or disappeared; but it remains the focus of population, government, the law, the arts, commerce and wealth which it has been for almost two millennia. The LABOUR government issued proposals in 1997 for establishing a Greater London Authority made up of an elected mayor and separate elected assembly: the first elections were held in May 2000 and Ken Livingstone, leader of the former GLC and standing as an Independent, was elected.

London, City of, self-governing corporate entity within the original confines of London, the 'Square Mile' principally defined by the ancient line of the Roman walls. The lord mayor, elected annually, has been since the 13th century one of the highest-ranking commoners in England, reflecting the financial and strategic value of the capital. Until the 17th century the history of the metropolis has mainly been that of the ancient City, but since then continued expansion has reduced its population (to almost zero) and geographical share. It was and remains the pre-eminent financial centre, housing most of the important BANKS, the exchanges in stocks and shares and in many commodities, and a wealth of other financial services. The City as it is known today is largely a creation of the late 19th century, with the expansion of the BRITISH EMPIRE and overseas finance, together with a more highly capitalized industrial structure at home, while its modern success against other international financial centres has been partly due to the wealth of its expertise and the creation of new markets in e.g. futures and Eurobonds. The separate privileges of the City have been confirmed in all modern legislation dealing with the expansion and reorganization of London. *See also* EUROBOND MARKET; EURODOLLAR MARKET; INSURANCE COMPANIES; GENTLEMANLY CAPITALISM; PENSION FUNDS.

London Companies, *see* PLANTATIONS IN IRELAND.

London Corresponding Society (LCS) The Society was founded in Jan. 1792 by the RADICAL Thomas Hardy, to maintain a correspondence with other reformers, especially with other CORRESPONDING SOCIETIES in the provinces, with the aim of achieving fair, equal and impartial representation of the people in Parliament. Its organizers and members were mainly artisans and working men. The LCS opposed the FRENCH REVOLUTIONARY WARS, and early in 1794 discussed with the SOCIETY FOR CONSTITUTIONAL INFORMATION the possibility of calling a National Convention in London. The society was infiltrated by government spies, and in May 1794 some of its leaders were arrested. Hardy, John Horne Tooke and John Thelwall were tried for treason, but acquitted; charges against other leaders were dropped. Maintaining its anti-war stance, the LCS organized large open-air meetings in 1795, helping to prompt the repressive TWO ACTS. In Feb. 1798 John Binns, a leading member, was arrested along with UNITED IRISHMEN leaving for France with a message for the French government; arrests of other members followed. The LCS was declared an illegal organization in 1799, along with other radical organizations, and retained little influence during its short informal existence thereafter.

London County Council (LCC), governing body for a newly-formed County of LONDON, created in 1889 by the 1888 LOCAL GOVERNMENT ACT, and superseded by the GREATER LONDON COUNCIL in 1965. The LCC was the first metropolitan-wide form of general LOCAL GOVERNMENT; it had been preceded by the METROPOLITAN BOARD OF WORKS. In 1888 the counties of Middlesex, Kent and Surrey gave away the areas which had become greater London to form the new administrative county, with new boroughs formed from the old mixture of vestries and districts. Elections were held in Jan. 1889, and the new council met under the chairmanship of Archibald PRIMROSE, Earl of Rosebery. The LCC took a leading role in school reform, provision of infrastructure, building control and town planning; its magnificent County Hall headquarters stood across the Thames from the Houses of PARLIAMENT. Continued anomalies, particularly the relationship between London and Middlesex, and the ever-greater spread of the built-up area, produced pressure for reform. The Royal Commission which reported in 1960 proposed a new Greater London, with fewer boroughs and an enlarged area; the proposals were mainly incorporated into the London Government Act 1963. When the new Greater London Council (GLC) was elected in April 1964 its make-up, with 64 LABOUR members and 36 CONSERVATIVE, reflected the balance of metropolitan politics for much of the 20th century.

London Government Act 1899 This created 16 independent boroughs within the area of the LONDON COUNTY COUNCIL and continued the privileges of the City of LONDON. Passed by a CONSERVATIVE administration, it was motivated less by a preference for decentralized self-government than by an intention to check the allegedly extravagant policies pursued by a PROGRESSIVE-dominated LCC.

London Missionary Society, *see* MISSIONARY SOCIETIES

London Naval Treaty, 1930. Signed in London as a follow-up to the WASHINGTON NAVAL AGREEMENT, it agreed that the building of large warships should be suspended for six years and that Britain, the United States and Japan would reduce their numbers of capital ships to 15, 15, and nine respectively. A further conference in 1936 agreed limits on the size of warships' guns and of aircraft-carriers. Japan, France and Italy refused to co-operate, rendering the agreement ineffective.

London, Treaty of, 1604, the treaty that ended two decades of war between Spain and England.

London, Treaty of, Aug. 1641, the treaty that ended the BISHOPS' WARS.

London, Treaty of, 26 April 1915. A secret treaty that brought Italy into WORLD WAR I on the side of Britain, France and Russia. It offered Italy territorial gains at the expense of the Austro-Hungarian Empire, implying substantial revision of the Empire's borders. The terms of the treaty were to cause difficulties for the peacemakers after 1918 because the promises made to Italy came into conflict with US President Wilson's Fourteen Points and with the proposal to create a Yugoslav state from territory assigned by this treaty to Italy.

Londonderry (Derry), second city of Northern Ireland. The city has had a long history of siege and destruction, from the VIKINGS in 783 to the great siege of 1689 by JAMES II. The eradication of the old city in 1600 by Sir Henry Docwra's English forces started Derry's history afresh. In 1613 the City of LONDON became responsible for the city in the PLANTATION of ULSTER – hence the name Londonderry. A new planned town was built, which withstood both CIVIL WAR sieges and the 105-day siege by the recently-deposed James II. Again the destroyed town was rebuilt, but it stagnated under London's control until the 1780s, when commercial expansion, especially of the port, began. Growth was fastest from 1863, with warehouses, textile works, and docks for passenger and commercial shipping. Even more than BELFAST, Londonderry fell into economic decline in the 20th century, until the world awoke to the disadvantages suffered by the CATHOLICS – in a majority, though this was disguised by electoral gerrymandering. The disturbances of the TROUBLES had their most visibly violent expression in the 'Battle of the Bogside' in 1969 and on BLOODY SUNDAY.

Londonderry, 2nd Marquess of, *see* STEWART, ROBERT

Long Cross Coinage, name given to COINAGE struck between 1247 and HENRY VII's reign. As a precaution against CLIPPING, the cross shown on the reverse was extended to the edge of the coins. *See also* SHORT CROSS COINAGE.

Long Parliament, 1640–60. Its life was uniquely and bizarrely prolonged from the national crisis of 1640 by the CIVIL WARS and INTERREGNUM. ROYALIST MPs and peers reassembled at OXFORD from 22 Dec. 1643, while from 1645 the Westminster PARLIA-

MENT, by now winning a full-scale war against its king, held RECRUITER elections. The Commons of the Long Parliament was purged on 6 Dec. 1648 by a regiment of the NEW MODEL ARMY commanded by Colonel Thomas Pride (*see* PRIDE'S PURGE); this purged body – nicknamed the RUMP – became the governing authority of England (the Commonwealth, so called) after the death of CHARLES I and the abolition of the monarchy and the House of LORDS. But the army, despairing of its slowness to implement reform, ousted the Rump on 20 April 1653. Six years later, after Oliver CROMWELL's death and the collapse of the Protectorate, the army recalled the Rump on 7 May 1659, and the Rumpers were rejoined by all other surviving members of the Commons on 21 Feb. 1660. It was this body, then, which voted on 16 March 1660 to dissolve the Long Parliament in order to make way finally for new elections – a decisive advance down the road to the restoration of the House of Lords and the monarchy.

Lord Chancellor, evolution of the title CHANCELLOR, first used for Thomas WOLSEY in 1515.

Lord Keeper of the Great Seal, *see* CHANCELLOR

Lord Protector, *see* PROTECTOR, LORD

Lords Appellant, *see* APPELLANTS

Lords, House of The upper house of PARLIAMENT, the Lords have their precursors in the great men of the kingdom who customarily counselled the monarch in pre- and post-NORMAN CONQUEST England. In their initial form, PARLIAMENTS were simply gatherings of the king's principal advisers and officials, with the great landholders in attendance. Only gradually did representatives of the communities of the realm come to be associated with these gatherings, and only gradually did Parliament assume its familiar bicameral (two-chamber) form. Moreover, although the COMMONS assumed a leading role in the grant of taxation as early as the 14th century, and thereby became the more important of the two houses after 1688 when the crown became almost wholly dependent on parliamentary supply, up to the 19th century the Lords contained the most powerful men of the realm considered as individuals, and members of the upper House continued to predominate in numbers in the CABINET (*see* PEERAGE). Indeed, it is a measure of the Lord's continuing importance that Robert HARLEY and Queen ANNE were prepared to resort to the unprecedented expedient of creating 12 new peers at one fell swoop in order to prevent the upper House from voting down the peace preliminaries with France in 1711–12.

Despite the continuing prestige and influence of the upper House, it did undergo two alterations, one temporary and one of longer duration, in the course of the 17th century. Firstly, largely by reason of a failure of moderate PARLIAMENTARIAN peers to continue attending the Lords in late 1648, the House was abolished, not to be restored until 1660; even so, a realization of the utility of a second House as a balance between the Commons and the executive prompted the experiment in the latter years of the Protectorate (*see* INTERREGNUM) of a non-hereditary upper chamber. Secondly, CATHOLIC peers, despite their hereditary claims to writs of summons to the Lords, were barred from sitting, under the terms of the 1678 TEST ACT, for a century and a half.

While the CATHOLIC EMANCIPATION ACT of 1829 brought with it the return of the excluded peers to the Lords, during the course of the 19th century the gradual shift in balance between landed and industrial wealth undermined the position of the upper House, a process aided by the general disappearance in the western world of political systems based on hereditary privilege; its 20th-century history has been a story of progressive curbs on its powers.

In 1999, the Labour government introduced the House of Lords Bill which removed the right of 750 so called hereditary peers to sit in the Lords; 92 existing hereditary peers (chosen by a vote amongst themselves) were allowed to sit temporarily in the upper House until a full reform programme is implemented. A Royal Commission set up in Feb. 1999, to determine the role, function and composition of a reformed second chamber, reported in 2000. Concern has been expressed that the reformed House would mean the replacement of hereditary peers with the placemen of whichever party is in power. *See also* PARLIAMENT ACT 1911; TACKING.

CHRONOLOGY

1387 Baronies first created by royal LETTERS PATENT: beginnings of fixed hereditary lay PEERAGE.

1516 Judgment that Parliament can meet without the lords spiritual (i.e. bishops and abbots) if necessary.

1539 King's officers of state given precedence over all other peers except royal dukes.

1540 By now, DISSOLUTION of the monasteries has removed abbots, and the prior of St John of Jerusalem, from Lords; the latter and the abbot of WESTMINSTER briefly restored under MARY I.

1544 First recorded use of term 'House of Lords'.

1653-7 Interregnum experiments with single-chamber assemblies.

1660 Old parliamentary arrangements restored.

1668 *SKINNER V. EAST INDIA COMPANY* results in limit on judicial role.

1703 *ASHBY V. WHITE* case.

1707 UNION of English and Scottish Parliaments: 16 Scottish peers, elected by their fellows, added to the House.

1801 UNION with Irish Parliament: 4 Irish bishops added (removed 1869) and 28 representative lay peers (phased out from 1921).

1832 First major reform of Commons franchise; further franchise reforms in 1868 and 1884 draw attention to anomaly of Lords' position.

1911 PARLIAMENT ACT restricts Lords' powers.

1949 Further Parliament Act reduces Lords' delaying power.

1958 LIFE PEERAGES ACT.

1999 House of Lords Bill removes the right of hereditary peers to sit and vote in the second chamber.

Lords Lieutenant First appointed for groups of counties during the troubled reign of EDWARD VI to supervise local military arrangements, they became a permanent part of LOCAL GOVERNMENT during the reign of ELIZABETH I; ideally they were great aristocrats trusted by the crown and respected in their localities. After the RESTORATION, their presiding local role over the JUSTICES OF THE PEACE was confirmed by the convention of choosing them also as *custos rotulorum*; this dominance, which had expanded far beyond their original military competence, lasted unmodified into the 19th century and the creation of COUNTY COUNCILS. Lords lieutenant are still appointed to the post-1974 counties, but their duties as representatives of the monarch are now virtually all ceremonial.

Lords of the Articles, committee of the Scottish PARLIAMENT set up to prepare legislation in detail. First referred to in 1426, it included bishops, nobility and SHIRE and BURGH representatives, chosen by a complex procedure that gave the monarch the possibility of manipulating parliamentary business, and which was particularly exploited by JAMES VI, who added officers of state. Loss of royal control after 1639 was a mark of the acute crisis facing CHARLES I. Lords of the Articles were abolished in 1689 as part of the GLORIOUS REVOLUTION, thus greatly enhancing the autonomy of the Scottish Parliament.

Lords of the Congregation In Dec. 1557, Scottish PROTESTANT noblemen opposing the French-dominated regency of MARY OF GUISE signed a BOND to join together in the 'Congregation of Christ Jesus in Scotland'. A number of them then invited John KNOX to return from Geneva.

An augmented group made a fresh bond and formed an army in May 1559; in Feb. 1560, they concluded the treaty of BERWICK with England, which brought English troops and the defeat of the French forces supporting the Guise regime. The Lords of the Congregation were dominant in the 1560 Parliament that enacted REFORMATION legislation.

Lordship, rights granted over an area of land, often a MANOR, including the services of resident SERFS and VILLEINS, subject to their COMMON LAW rights. It also often included special dispensations giving, for example, the right to hold fairs. Lordships have nothing to do with the modern PEERAGE.

Louis VIII (1187–1226), King of France (1223–6), offered the English throne. In late 1215, after the Peace of Runnymede (otherwise known as MAGNA CARTA) had broken down, the rebel barons offered JOHN's throne to Louis, son and (then) heir of Philip Augustus, king of France. The following May, he arrived in England and soon won many supporters, but when John died in Oct., Louis faced the harder task of depriving a child – the nine-year-old HENRY III – of his natural inheritance. In 1217, after Louis' forces were defeated at the battles of LINCOLN and Sandwich, he agreed, in the treaty of Kingston of Sept. 1217, to abandon his claim. As king of France, he continued the process of dismembering the ANGEVIN EMPIRE by his 1224 conquest of Poitou.

Lovett, William (1800–77), Chartist leader. One of the founders of the London Working Men's Association (1836), Lovett was also the chief drafter of *The People's Charter* (1838), but as a moderate 'moral force' CHARTIST who believed that it was necessary to make an alliance between 'the virtuous exceptions' among the middle classes and the 'reflecting part' of his own (working) class. He was appalled by the tactics of his more militant colleagues – Feargus O'Connor in particular – though he was himself imprisoned for a year in 1839 for publishing a pamphlet complaining about POLICE methods.

Low Churchmanship, a style of British Protestantism, particularly within ANGLICANISM, which emphasizes the heritage of the REFORMATION and the central place of the Bible as the Word of God. It is inclined to value the clergy's role as preachers rather than as dispensers of the sacraments, and has generally thought little of the use of art and ceremony in worship. It was asserted in the 19th-century EVANGELICAL revival and has remained in tension with ANGLO-CATHOLICISM. *See also* BROAD CHURCH; HIGH CHURCHMANSHIP.

Loyalists

(i) Term for the residents of the 13 North American colonies who did not agree with the move to independence in 1776. Some fought alongside the British in the War of AMERICAN INDEPENDENCE, while many returned to Britain or moved to CANADA. They were also known as 'Empire Loyalists'.

(ii) Name applied both by contemporaries and by historians to those who most energetically identified themselves with the cause of King and Constitution during the 1790s. The radicalization of the FRENCH REVOLUTION in 1792 prompted GEORGE III to issue a proclamation against seditious writings in May. This evoked supportive addresses; the RADICAL writer Thomas PAINE was burnt in effigy in many towns and villages. In Nov., John Reeves attempted to mobilize loyalist forces to form an 'Association for the Defence of Liberty and Property against Republicans and Levellers'. Fear of French invasion prompted some to form VOLUNTEER forces, but the Volunteer movement only gathered force when invasion came to seem a real possibility, from 1798. It is impossible meaningfully to estimate what proportion of the population were loyalists: many, perhaps most, people were prepared to rally against invasion and to protest loyalty in general terms but by no means all of those wished to stigmatize their neighbours as disloyal, or to restrict their freedom of expression or action.

(iii) General term for those within ULSTER who support the UNION with Great Britain. The term ultimately refers back to the PROTESTANT settlement established after WILLIAM III's victory over JAMES II at the BOYNE (1690). Loyalism is expressed in parades and membership of the ORANGE ORDER or, in extreme cases, paramilitary groups, in contradistinction to Nationalism, which supports the notion of a united Ireland and severance of the Union (*see* UNIONISTS).

Lucius Brutus, *see* GEOFFREY OF MONMOUTH

Luddites, an early 19th-century anti-industrial protest movement with revolutionary undertones, directed at plant and machinery by distressed HANDLOOM WEAVERS, FRAMEWORK KNITTERS and others of the North and Midlands whose handicrafts and status were declining in the face of industrial innovation. Organized machine-breaking occurred in Nottingham in 1811 and was associated with a youth called Ned Ludd, who quickly acquired mythical status as 'King Ludd', rumoured to have his headquarters in Sherwood Forest. Despite government repression, machine-breaking spread to Yorks. and Lancs. Factories and mills were attacked and blood spilt: 17 Luddites were executed at York in 1813, and class bitterness was intense. The York executions, however, broke the movement. Historians present the Luddites either as backward-looking, semi-criminal and misguided or as progressive revolutionaries upholding communitarian values against those of the new industrial capitalism. But the evidence is thin enough to make either view seem plausible. Luddism should be seen as a peak in a longer tradition of machine-breaking and industrial sabotage which preceded and continued after Luddism itself.

Lulach, King of Scots (1057–8). The son of Queen GRUOCH and King MACBETH, he was briefly proclaimed king after the latter's death in battle against MALCOLM III CANMORE. He was himself killed by Malcolm's forces at Essie in Aberdeens.

Lumphanan, Battle of, 1057, the battle in Grampian at which MALCOLM III CANMORE finally defeated and killed MACBETH. It virtually ended the feud (*see* BLOOD FEUD) between the two families that had begun in 1040, and secured Malcolm's rule over all Scotland. *See also* LULACH.

Lunacy Act 1890 A consolidating measure that compelled 'local lunacy authorities' (i.e. county and borough councils) to provide asylum accommodation for all persons in their areas are who were of unsound mind and unable to provide for their full maintenance and care either themselves or through their legally liable relatives. Those who, in consequence, became chargeable to public funds through this Act became known as 'pauper lunatics'.

Lunar Society, a small informal club, formed about 1775, which met in Birmingham regularly (when the moon was full) for dinner and discussion. The original members comprised the engineer and inventor, Matthew Boulton (1728–1809), the doctor and botanist Erasmus Darwin (1731–1802), the scientist and discoverer of oxygen Joseph Priestley (1733–1804), the inventor of the steam engine, James Watt (1736–1819), the pottery manufacturer Josiah Wedgwood (1730–95), Thomas Day, Richard Lovell Edgworth, Samuel Galton and six others. Historians have represented it as illustrative of the social milieu in which a new culture conducive to the INDUSTRIAL REVOLUTION was forged; recently, however, it has been stressed that similar societies met in country and cathedral towns, and were attended by gentry and clergy. Interest in science was by no means confined to DISSENTERS and industrialists.

Lusignans As the leading aristocratic family in Poitou in the 12th century, they played an important role in the politics of the ANGEVIN EMPIRE; their revolt in 1201 following JOHN'S marriage to Hugh of Lusignan's fiancée ISABELLA OF ANGOULÊME precipitated the empire's collapse. Isabella's subsequent marriage to Hugh's son (also known as Hugh of Lusignan) provided her son by John, HENRY III, with a clutch of Poitevin half-brothers: William, Aymer, Guy and Geoffrey, often referred to collectively as the Lusignans. They arrived in England in 1247 and were soon basking in Henry's favour. English magnates resented them, and ordinary people suffered from the extortions of their officials, but Henry's protection seemed to place them above the law. Their unpopularity made hostility to foreigners a major factor in English politics in the 1250s and 1260s. They were driven into exile or returned to England according to the ebb and flow of events during the BARONS' WAR.

***Lusitania*, Sinking of the,** 7 May 1915, the sinking of a liner by a German submarine off the south coast of Ireland during WORLD WAR I, drowning 1,198 passengers, including 128 Americans. The sinking followed a German declaration of a submarine war zone around the British Isles in Feb. 1915. It provoked extensive anti-German riots in Britain, and produced a major outcry in the still neutral United States which, compounded by two more American deaths when a submarine sank the British passenger ship *Arabic* in Aug., forced the Germans to cease their unrestricted submarine campaign on 1 Sept. 1915.

Lutheranism Without Martin Luther (1483–1546) there might have been no REFORMATION in 16th-century western Europe. His university career (principally at Wittenberg) forced him into increasing doubts about late medieval ideas on salvation, which came to a head in 1517 in his anger at a campaign promoting INDULGENCES. Matters escalated out of his control and he found himself leading a full-scale revolt against Roman authority, and at the head of a new Lutheran Church complete with doctrinal statements set out in the Augsburg Confession (1530; revised text, the *Variata*, 1540, preferred in some churches). Many princes of the Holy Roman Empire sponsored Lutheran reforms in their dominions, and in 1531 formed a defensive league of Schmalkalden against potential attacks from the Emperor CHARLES V. In England, Luther's ideas stirred up much interest and provoked official repression in the 1520s. HENRY VIII personally detested him after their literary clash (1521), and principled Lutheran opposition to Henry's quest for annulment of his first marriage made matters worse. Thereafter the king only encouraged dialogue with Lutherans when diplomatic necessity demanded. Subsequently English PROTESTANT theology diverged from Lutheranism, developing more personal contacts and sympathy for the Strasbourg reform of Martin Bucer (1491–1551), and with Swiss REFORMED CHURCHES.

Lux Mundi ('Light of the World'), a series of articles on the incarnation published in 1889 by a group of ANGLICAN scholars under the editorship of Charles Gore. Attention focused on Gore's acceptance of the new critical views of the Old Testament which had caused much dismay and heart-searching among the Tractarians (*see* OXFORD MOVEMENT) and the older school of High Churchmen (*see* HIGH CHURCHMANSHIP). The series dealt with ethics, politics and doctrine, and represented the clearest statement of liberal CATHOLICISM within the Church of England.

Lyons v. Wilkins**,** 1896, one of a series of decisions given against the TRADE UNIONS, which culminated in the TAFF VALE DECISION. Mr Lyons secured an injunction against the Amalgamated Trade Society of Fancy Leather Workers to prevent the picketing of his establishment. The union, believing its actions were protected under the CONSPIRACY AND PROTECTION OF PROPERTY ACT 1875, appealed to the High Court, who held that the injunction should stand. The right to picket, so central to collective bargaining, was again in doubt.

M

Mabinogion, The, the name popularly given to the earliest surviving Welsh vernacular prose tales: 'The Four Branches of the Mabinogi', and the separate tale, 'Culhwch and Olwen'. Very complex in theme, the stories are also rich in adventure, magic and wonders and make exciting reading. The date of their composition has been much discussed: a date in the 11th or 12th centuries is likely, although the earliest surviving manuscript copies are from the 14th century.

Mac Finguine, Cathal, *see* CATHAL MAC FINGUINE

Mac Máel na mBó, Diarmit, *see* DIARMIT MAC MÁEL NA MBÓ

Mac Murrough, Art, *see* ART MAC MURROUGH

Mac Murrough, Dermot, *see* DERMOT MAC MURROUGH

Mac Néill, Muirchertach, *see* MUIRCHERTACH MAC NÉILL

Macbeth, King of Scots (1040–57). The *mormaer* ('great steward', or earl) of Moray, he killed DUNCAN I in 1040 when the latter attacked him – the continuation of a feud that had begun in the 970s (*see* KINGSHIP). Macbeth then ruled the whole of Scotland until 1054, when he was defeated by SIWARD, Earl of NORTHUMBRIA, who had invaded to install MALCOLM III CANMORE, Duncan's son. Macbeth was finally killed at the battle of LUMPHANAN three years later. In view of his evil reputation – a creation of 14th- and 15th-century chroniclers immortalized by SHAKESPEARE – it is important to emphasize that Macbeth was regarded by all his contemporaries as a legitimate Scottish king. *See also* GRUOCH; LULACH.

MacDonald, Alexander (1821–81), trade unionist. Having worked in the coalmines from the age of eight, he paid his way through Glasgow University and acquired a small fortune through commercial speculation. A capable organizer and lobbyist, he promoted mining unions and mining legislation and was one of the two working men elected to Parliament in 1875. *See also* LIB-LABS.

MacDonald, Ramsay (1866–1937), Labour politician and Prime Minister (1924, 1929–31, 1931–5). The illegitimate son of a Scottish farmgirl, he was secretary of the LABOUR REPRESENTATION COMMITTEE (1900–5) and then of the LABOUR PARTY (1906–12). He became an MP in 1906 and leader of the parliamentary party in 1911. He resigned the post in 1914 because of his pacifist opposition to WORLD WAR I and lost his seat in the 1918 COUPON ELECTION, but he returned to head the party from 1922, seeking to make it a 'responsible' party of government. He led Labour's first short-lived (minority) government in 1924, as well as serving as foreign secretary, then headed the minority second Labour government (1929–31).

MacDonald's determination to maintain the GOLD STANDARD amid the economic crisis of 1931 led to a split in the Cabinet over the question of reducing unemployment benefits. His decision in Aug. 1931 not to resign with his colleagues but to accept the leadership of a NATIONAL GOVERNMENT with CONSERVATIVE and LIBERAL support, and to campaign against Labour in the subsequent general election, led to his being branded a traitor and to his expulsion from the party. He remained prime minister until 1935, after which – under BALDWIN – he became lord president of the Council until his death.

MacDonald was a tragic figure, whose readiness to accept the conventional parameters of politics and economics estranged him from the party he had served so loyally from its earliest days and which he had brought to power.

Macmillan, Harold (1st Earl of Stockton) (1894–1986), Conservative politician and Prime Minister (1957–63). Grandson of a Scottish crofter who founded the family publishing house, Macmillan was strongly influenced to achieve by his American mother. He attended Eton and Balliol College, Oxford before serving in WORLD WAR I, when he was wounded on three occasions.

As MP for Stockton-on-Tees (1924–9, 1931–45) his first-hand experience of the DEPRESSION set the pattern for his lifelong Tory paternalism, and the progressive interventionist views expressed in his book *The Middle Way* (1938) influenced the post-war government's economic policy. An opponent of APPEASEMENT in the 1930s, he played a key role as CHURCHILL's political representative in North Africa (1942–5). On the re-election of a CONSERVATIVE government in 1951, he made a domestic reputation as minister of housing (1951–4), when he surpassed election pledges to build 300,000 houses a year, and he subsequently served as minister of defence (1954–5), foreign secretary (1955) and chancellor of the Exchequer (1955–7). He became prime minister on EDEN's resignation in 1957.

Macmillan's premiership was marked domestically by rising living standards and wider consumer choice, which allowed him to claim in 1957 that 'most of our people have never had it so good' and helped him to victory in the 1959 election. In foreign affairs, he signed the PARTIAL TEST BAN TREATY, as well as, in 1962, the NASSAU AGREEMENT that gave Britain access to the American POLARIS nuclear deterrent; his 'WIND OF CHANGE' speech in Cape Town in 1960 heralded a speeding-up of DECOLONIZATION. His last years as premier witnessed de Gaulle's first veto of Britain's application to join the EEC (*see* EUROPEAN UNION) and growing balance of payments problems. Although a skilled politician and publicist – famously dubbed 'Supermac' – he was rattled by by-election defeats and undertook a drastic purge of his Cabinet ('the night of the long knives') in July 1962. By the time he retired due to ill health in Oct. 1963, he had been criticized for his 'grousemoor' image and embarrassed by the PROFUMO AFFAIR.

Dominating and flamboyant, Macmillan may have given his name to a prosperous era of Conservative government, but his premiership is often interpreted as one in which fundamental decisions on Britain's world role and economic performance were left unresolved.

MacWilliam, the name given to those descendants of William, son of DUNCAN II, who unsuccessfully claimed the Scottish throne at various times during the late 12th and 13th centuries. Donald MacWilliam challenged WILLIAM I THE LION until his head was brought to the king in 1187. Donald's son Guthred claimed the throne in 1211–12, but was captured and beheaded; Guthred's brother Donald took up the challenge in 1215, but he too lost his head. In 1230, the rebellion of another (unknown) MacWilliam ended with the smashing of his baby daughter's head against Forfar market cross.

Maeatae, the name given to the tribes living immediately north of the ANTONINE WALL from the late 2nd century AD onwards. It seems that, at this time, all the Highland tribes merged into the two groupings of Maeatae and CALEDONII. The lands of the Maeatae are likely to have been around Stirling and in Fife. They were involved in the invasions across HADRIAN'S WALL that prompted the campaigns of the Emperor SEPTIMIUS SEVERUS in the early 3rd century. The name 'Maeatae' appears to have been later replaced by that of 'PICTS'.

Máel Sechnaill I (?–862), King of Tara. Máel Sechnaill became king of the southern UÍ NÉILL in 846. His career included important victories over the VIKINGS, and his military success gave him domination over all the Irish kingdoms (*see* KINGSHIP). The first northern Irish king to have his superiority acknowledged by MUNSTER, he is therefore also the first who could be said to have been, in some sense, king of all Ireland. His successors sustained this domination for a further two generations. *See also* TARA.

Máel Sechnaill II (?–1022), King of Tara. In 980, he became king over both the northern and southern UÍ NÉILL. His reign was dominated by the struggle with BRIAN BORU of

MUNSTER for control over all the Irish kingdoms. A formidable warrior who defeated the VIKINGS of DUBLIN on three occasions, Máel Sechnaill was obliged to acknowledge Brian's superiority in 1002. However, after the latter's death at the battle of CLONTARF in 1014, Máel Sechnaill resumed his earlier role as the dominant Irish king. *See also* KINGSHIP; TARA.

Maelgwyn (?–549), King of Gwynedd. Described by GILDAS as the mightiest of the kings of the Britons, little is known about his actual career, except that he may once have been a monk and that he killed many of his relatives in the pursuit of power. His somewhat lurid prestige provides an early indication of the importance that the kingdom of GWYNEDD was to have in Welsh and British history.

Mafeking, Relief of, a crucial event in the second stage of the BOER WAR, when early Boer successes were being reversed. The British garrisons in Mafeking, as well as those in Ladysmith and Kimberley, had been besieged by Boer forces in late 1899. British counter-offensives under Lord ROBERTS lifted the sieges, with Mafeking relieved after 217 days on 12–16 May 1900. There was immense public celebration in Britain, and the Relief was taken as a symbol of a new imperial unity forged in war. Robert Baden-Powell's valour in the siege made him the hero of Mafeking and he caught the popular imagination.

Mag Rath, Battle of, 637, a battle fought in Co. Down between the Irish royal dynasty of UÍ NÉILL and DOMNALL BRECC, king of Scottish DALRIADA, which ended in a decisive victory for the Uí Néill. This effectively ended the control that the Scottish kings had exercised over their Irish lands since Dalriada had been established in *c.*500, and also annulled the terms of the convention of DRUMCEAT.

Magdalen College, Expulsion of Fellows from When the President of Magdalen College, OXFORD, died in March 1687, the fellows and JAMES II fell out over his replacement. James then imposed a candidate of his own, the Bishop of Oxford, Samuel Parker. The fellows refused him. The ECCLESIASTICAL COMMISSION heard the case, and deprived most of them of their fellowships, and associated spiritual and temporal emoluments. This was represented as an assault on property. Some of the fellows appointed to fill the resultant vacancies were CATHOLICS. When Parker died in 1688, James replaced him with a Catholic, Bonaventure Gifford. However in Oct., trying to rally support so as to be able to cope with the threatened descent of William of Orange (the future WILLIAM III), James restored the fellows to their places.

Magic Lantern, an apparatus for throwing pictures or images painted on a glass screen on to a screen or wall, invented by the German-born Athanasius Kircher in the 17th century, and consisting of a lantern with reflector and a set of lenses that enlarged the object to be shown. The forerunner of the modern CINEMA, the magic lantern show was a major popular entertainment in the 19th century.

Magistrate, a general term in Roman and CIVIL LAW for someone with judicial or governmental functions. In England, with its COMMON LAW traditions, the term has only comparatively recently acquired a formal legal usage for minor or subordinate judicial officers: stipendiary magistrates were appointed in London under the Metropolitan Police Courts Act 1839, elsewhere under the Stipendiary Magistrates Act 1863, and in BOROUGHS by the Municipal Corporations Act 1882. The unpaid JUSTICES OF THE PEACE are also now commonly known as magistrates. In Ireland and colonial territories of the BRITISH EMPIRE, the term was introduced at much the same time.

Magna Carta, the charter sealed by King JOHN at Runnymede in June 1215. By the mid-13th century, it was generally regarded as the fundamental statement of English liberties; hence the Latin term *Magna Carta* was understood to mean 'Great Charter' – although, when first used, it meant no more than 'big charter' to distinguish it from the much shorter FOREST CHARTER issued in 1217.

The Runnymede charter was a product of rebellion. John was a discredited and distrusted king, but would-be rebels could not look for leadership – as was customary – from a discontented member of the royal family: in 1215, John was the only adult male Plantagenet alive. In this predicament, John's baronial opponents took the revolutionary step of devising a new kind of focus for revolt – a programme of reform, which they drew up in a charter. After the rebels captured LONDON, John decided to seal this charter of liberties, but only to buy time; thus the peace achieved by the Runnymede charter lasted for only a few months. When war broke out again, the rebels reverted to traditional practice, calling in an anti-king, the future LOUIS VIII of France.

After John's death in 1216, the supporters of his son, HENRY III, reissued a modified charter; they did so again in 1217 (together with the Forest Charter), and produced yet another one in 1225. These reissues ensured that the charter was imprinted on the consciousness of the nation, and it was the 1225 text that entered the statute book as the first and most fundamental of English laws. Indeed, three of its 63 chapters still stand, including the promise that freemen will be judged by their peers and that 'to no one will we sell, to no one will we deny or delay right or justice'.

Whenever opponents of the crown in the 13th and early 14th centuries put forward reform programmes of their own – e.g. the 1258 PROVISIONS OF OXFORD and the ORDINANCES of 1311 – they believed they were following in the footsteps of the men who made Magna Carta. Those who devised the PETITION OF RIGHT in 1628 and the GRAND REMONSTRANCE of 1641 thought in similar terms. Exaggerated respect for the charter eventually led to the early 20th-century fashion for debunking it. Many scholars came to believe that 17th-century constitutional lawyers – COKE and others – had created an anachronistic myth, and that the charter, seen in its own context, had in fact been nothing more than a 'FEUDAL' document reflecting narrow baronial interests.

Certainly some of its chapters inevitably reflected the grievances and ambitions of rebel barons – in particular, their claim that they had been wrongfully dispossessed of lands, castles and privileges. But it was a long and detailed document, intended to win support at a time of crisis; its shape and contents were not just the result of criticism of the way John had been treating the barons, but were a thoroughgoing commentary on the whole system of royal government. Thus it was explicitly granted 'to all freemen of the realm and their heirs for ever', and it dealt with an immensely wide range of issues, containing something for virtually everyone; although originally conceived by rebels, it could, as in 1216 and 1217, be taken over and exploited by royalists. In this combination of wide appeal and adaptability lay – right from the outset – the making of the Magna Carta myth.

Magnus Intercursus, *see* INTERCURSUS MAGNUS

Magnus Maximus, Roman Emperor (383–8), was yet another Roman general based in Britain who declared himself emperor (*see also* CARAUSIUS; CLODIUS ALBINUS; CONSTANTINE I; CONSTANTINE III), gaining control of Gaul and Spain before his defeat by the Eastern emperor Theodosius I. The extent to which he contributed to the eventual collapse of Roman power in Britain by removing troops is unclear. He is known to have defeated the PICTS in 382 and HADRIAN'S WALL was still securely held at that time. However, the evidence for a Roman withdrawal from Wales during his rule is much stronger.

Magnus of Orkney, St (*c.*1080–*c.*1116). Viking ruler. For some years, he and his cousin Haakon were co-rulers of the virtually autonomous earldom of ORKNEY. According to a later biography, his policy of taking cold baths whenever he was tempted meant that his wife remained a virgin throughout their ten-year marriage. This apart, both his life and the manner of his death – killed by his cousin in a struggle for power – seem to have been those of a typical VIKING ruler. Yet a martyr's cult began to develop, which was institutionalized when his nephew Rognvald, Earl of Orkney, founded the cathedral of St Magnus at Kirkwall.

Magonsaetan, Kingdom of the, an exceptionally obscure, early kingdom whose area covered the modern counties of Herefords. and southern Salop. It must have been formed from English settlements made, in all probability, during the later 6th century, and was created a kingdom by PENDA, King of MERCIA, for one of his sons, who took the Welsh name Merewalh. It received a bishopric when the diocese of Hereford was created in 680, but was subsequently absorbed into Mercia.

Mahdi, an influential Arab leader with

powers akin to those of a Messiah. The term was applied from the 1880s to insurrectionary leaders in the SUDAN who claimed to be the expected Mahdi. Claimants to the title caused the Victorians a great deal of difficulty, especially Mohammed Ahmed (1840–85) who, in 1882, raised a revolt against Egyptian rule in the Sudan, defeated the Egyptian army, and besieged and captured Khartoum in 1885, killing General GORDON and his garrison. After the Mahdi's death, his successor ruled Sudan until he was defeated by KITCHENER at the battle of OMDURMAN in 1898.

Maid of Norway, *see* MARGARET OF NORWAY

Maiden Castle, massive Iron Age HILL FORT near Dorchester, Dorset, which was stormed by the ROMANS in a great battle in AD 44. The fort was the subject of a much-publicized ARCHAEOLOGICAL excavation led by Sir Mortimer Wheeler in 1934–8, and is the subject of further current excavations.

Main Plot, 1603. This was the scheme of Henry Brooke, 11th Baron Cobham, to replace JAMES I with his cousin Arabella Stewart (1575–1625), the daughter of Darnley's (*see* STEWART, HENRY) younger brother. The plot was quickly betrayed to the government; RALEIGH was among those convicted, but the leaders escaped execution. The government tendentiously linked it with a contemporary Roman Catholic scheme to kidnap James and extort a promise of toleration from him (the Bye Plot); the leaders of that plot were executed. Official manipulation of both conspiracies remains obscure but likely.

Maine Northernmost of the founding states of the USA in 1776, Maine, like NEW HAMPSHIRE, was subjected to repeated French attack, especially in the years around 1700. It was theoretically separate from MASSACHUSETTS, but was in reality a district of the larger and older colony until nationhood.

Maintenance, *see* LIVERY

Maitland, John (2nd Earl and 1st Duke of Lauderdale) (1616–82), royal servant. Having been appointed Scottish secretary of state at the RESTORATION, Lauderdale, who was close to CHARLES II, was the chief architect of British government policy in Scotland for two decades. Although he had himself been a PRESBYTERIAN, he helped to reimpose EPISCOPACY, and readily resorted to armed force to suppress religious and political opposition. The battle of BOTHWELL BRIDGE (1679), though a success within that framework, was judged to have exposed the bankruptcy of his approach in that such a conflict had taken place at all, and resulted in his fall.

Major, John (1943–), politician and prime minister. Son of a former circus trapeze artist, Major left school at 15, and did a variety of jobs (insurance clerk, labourer) before being elected CONSERVATIVE MP for Huntingdonshire in 1979. A steady parliamentary rise saw him as the youngest member of the Cabinet as Chief Secretary to the Treasury (1987), Foreign Secretary (1989–90) and Chancellor of the Exchequer (1990) after Nigel Lawson's resignation, taking Britain into the ERM (European Exchange Mechanism) in Oct. Regarded as a safe pair of hands after the boom and bust policies of the 1980s (*see* ECONOMY) the same perception propelled Major to Downing Street in Nov. 1990 when Margaret THATCHER conceded defeat in the leadership election. Very soon, however, what had appeared to be a steady and conciliatory premiership, seemed dull, offering weak leadership and paucity of vision. Though he saw off a leadership challenge from John Redwood (1995) when the Conservative party, mired in allegations of sleaze, incompetence and at war with itself over Europe, lost the 1997 General Election so resoundingly that it was left with no representation in Scotland or Wales and only 165 seats in England, Major resigned to be replaced by William HAGUE. In March 2000 he announced his intention not to stand for PARLIAMENT at the next election.

Major-Generals, ten leading army officers (later 11) commissioned in Aug. 1655 to supervise groups of counties and collect the DECIMATION TAX after PENRUDDOCK'S RISING. Their activities were sometimes heavy-handed, sometimes ineffective; given inadequate support from Westminster, they were bitterly resented locally. PARLIAMENT saw to their abolition in early 1657.

Malachy, St (Máel Maedoc Uá Morgair) (1094–1148), Archbishop of Armagh.

Formerly a priest from ARMAGH, as bishop of Down from 1128, archbishop of Armagh from 1132 and papal legate from 1139, he pressed for changes intended to bring the Irish Church more into line with the norms of the Latin Church on the Continent, in particular the establishment of a DIOCESAN structure and the introduction of the CISTERCIAN and AUGUSTINIAN rules. In the face of fierce opposition from traditionalists, especially in Armagh, he looked to Rome for support, but he died at Clairvaux while on one of his journeys to the papal curia.

The *Life of Malachy*, written in 1149 by his friend Bernard of Clairvaux, depicted him as the model of a reforming bishop, and as such, he was canonized in 1190. Ironically St Bernard's vivid description of the difficulties encountered by Malachy helped to establish the new image of the Irish as barbarous. *See also* CHURCH: IRELAND.

Malawi, *see* NYASALAND

Malay States, *see* FEDERATED AND UNFEDERATED MALAY STATES

Malaya, former federation of British colonies in South-East Asia, specializing in rubber and tin production. It was a combination of the various Federated and Unfederated states in the Malay peninsula, e.g. Kuala Lumpur, STRAITS SETTLEMENTS, Melaka, Penang, and was established after the resumption of British rule following the defeat of Japan in 1945. Local antagonism towards British rule, hostility between the Malay, Indian and Chinese populations, and the steady rise of Communist influence, fostered armed rebellion. The MALAYAN 'EMERGENCY' lasted from 1948 to 1960; eventually Britain, which had poured troops into the region, gave Malaya its independence in 1957. SINGAPORE, originally part of the new nation, was expelled in 1965, in the midst of the armed struggle against Indonesia. *See also* FEDERATED AND UNFEDERATED MALAY STATES.

Malayan 'Emergency', a major British success in defeating Communist forces during the 1950s. The Federation of MALAYA was proclaimed on 1 Feb. 1948, but insurgent communist guerrilla activity began, and in June a state of emergency was declared. In Jan. 1952, after the murder of the British high commissioner, Sir Henry Gurney, the preceding Oct., General Sir Gerald Templer was appointed high commissioner and director of military operations, and a new anti-guerrilla offensive was launched. On 8 Feb. 1954 the British authorities announced that the Communist party's high command in Malaya had withdrawn to Sumatra. The emergency was officially ended on 31 July 1960.

Malaysia, *see* MALAYA; STRAITS SETTLEMENTS; SINGAPORE; FEDERATED AND UNFEDERATED MALAY STATES

Malcolm I, King of Scots (943–54). He consolidated the achievements of his predecessor, CONSTANTINE II, and in 945 was recognized as controlling STRATHCLYDE and Cumbria by the English king EDMUND. He none the less had to surmount a difficult crisis when ERIC BLOODAXE temporarily obtained control of ORKNEY and the kingdom of YORK; his reaction was to renew Constantine's alliance with the kings of DUBLIN. Malcolm was killed by the men of Moray in 954, a sign of the instability of the nascent kingdom of the Scots.

Malcolm II (*c.* 954–1034), King of Scots (1005–34). A son of KENNETH II, he acquired the throne by killing Kenneth III (reigned 997–1005), the representative of a rival line. Malcolm's reign is notable for the way in which he tried to exploit the distracted English kingdom during the reign of ETHELRED II THE UNREADY to expand his power into BERNICIA. In particular, he gained a notable victory at the battle of CARHAM in 1018, but was eventually forced to submit when King CNUT and his army marched north in 1027. Malcolm's violent acquisition of the KINGSHIP and his determination to secure the succession for his grandson, the future DUNCAN I, meant that the feuds that had typified Scottish history since the 970s continued.

Malcolm III Canmore (*c.* 1031–93), King of Scots (1058–93). He succeeded to the throne after killing his predecessor MACBETH and the latter's stepson LULACH – events that brought to an end the long-standing feud for the Scottish kingdom. Malcolm's first marriage was to the daughter of Earl THORFINN THE MIGHTY of ORKNEY. His second – to Margaret, sister of the English pretender EDGAR THE ÆTHELING – involved him in the politics of the NORMAN CONQUEST.

He launched several invasions of northern England, without acquiring more than booty and slaves. WILLIAM I THE CONQUEROR's invasion of Scotland in 1072 forced him to accept the peace of Abernethy and become William's vassal; a similar settlement was made with WILLIAM II RUFUS in 1093.

Malcolm IV (1141–65), King of Scots (1153–65). Son of Henry, Earl of Northumberland, he was only 11 years old when his father died in 1152. Even so, his grandfather DAVID I persuaded the Scottish magnates to recognize him as the heir to the throne, and the next year the boy became king. In 1157, he agreed to surrender Cumbria and Northumb. to HENRY II, realizing, as WILLIAM OF NEWBURGH put it, 'that the king of England had the better of the argument by reason of his much greater power'. As compensation, Malcolm received Huntingdon. His youth and what many Scots regarded as his subservience towards the king of England meant that his was a turbulent reign. But he had successfully overcome internal opposition – notably in GALLOWAY and from SOMERLED of ARGYLL – when he died in 1165, still unmarried and with a reputation for chastity (hence his nickname 'the Maiden').

Maldon, Battle of, 991, Historically the occasion of the defeat and death of Ealdorman BYRHTNOTH of ESSEX at the hands of a VIKING army that included Olaf Tryggvason, later king of Norway. The battle, fought in Essex, is also the subject of a famous poem celebrating the heroism of Byrhtnoth and his followers, who preferred death to retreat. The poem's date and composition remain controversial, although it is generally accepted that it is almost contemporary with the battle. Its importance rests on the fact that, despite the poet's embellishments, it provides the only account of an Anglo-Saxon army in battle. Its emphasis on LORDSHIP and the military household echoes the world of the HOUSECARLS and the chivalric military household, groupings that are sometimes wrongly thought to be typical of later historical periods (*see* FYRD).

Malmesbury Abbey, Wilts. Founded by an Irish monk in the 7th century, the BENEDICTINE Rule was introduced in *c.*965 after DUNSTAN removed a community of clerks. Malmesbury at certain periods had a great reputation as a centre of learning, associated especially with St Aldhelm (*c.* 640–709) who had studied under both Roman and Greek scholars and, in the 12th century, WILLIAM OF MALMESBURY. It was dissolved in 1539; part of the magnificent 12th-century church remains in use.

Malmesbury, William of, *see* WILLIAM OF MALMESBURY

Malory, Sir Thomas (*c.*1416?–*c.*1471?), writer. Author of one of the greatest, and in terms of its impact on subsequent Arthurian literature, most influential romances ever written in English: the *Morte d'Arthur*, completed by 1470. Of the several known mid-15th-century Thomas Malorys, the writer is generally identified with a knight of Newbold Revel, Warwicks. who, in the 1450s, spent some years in prison facing (probably politically motivated) charges that included rape and theft, and who, released without trial, went on to play a minor role in the WARS OF THE ROSES. However, if, as some literary scholars suggest, the author helped CAXTON revise the version printed in 1485, he must have been a different Malory. *See also* ARTHUR, KING.

Malplaquet, Battle of, 11 Sept. 1709, the bloodiest battle in the War of the SPANISH SUCCESSION and indeed the entire 18th century. Marlborough's (*see* CHURCHILL, JOHN) army of 100,000 British, Dutch, German and Austrian soldiers intended to besiege Mons but were met by a French force of 90,000. After two days the allied forces attacked the fortified French position; in seven hours' fighting they lost 24,000 killed or wounded, the French 12,000. The French withdrew and Mons surrendered, but the heavy losses prevented further exploitation of the victory. Marlborough's last major battle was followed by two years of inconclusive manoeuvring and minor sieges.

Malta Acquired from the French (who had themselves only held the island for a few days having seized it from the religious-military order of the Knights of St John) by NELSON in 1799, the island of Malta came, in the same way as GIBRALTAR, to symbolize British naval dominance in the Mediterranean. During the early days of British rule, control was in the hands of semi-independent proconsuls, such as 'King' Tom Maitland, a Scotsman who ran both Malta and the Ionian Islands like a personal fiefdom. With the firm establishment of colonial rule from London in 1836, Malta became one of the BRITISH EMPIRE's most important naval fortresses, grafting a new architecture and social structure onto a proud and ancient history. In WORLD WAR II it was subject to both heavy aerial bombardment and naval BLOCKADE by the Axis powers between 1940 and 1943, for bravely withstanding which GEORGE VI awarded the island the George Cross. Malta's stand had pinned down German and Italian forces, thereby signally contributing to Allied victory. The sentimental and strategic links between post-war Malta and Britain were broken by the tide of national self-determination that swept through almost all Britain's colonial outposts, and in 1964 the island was granted independence and the British naval bases were withdrawn.

Malthus, Thomas Robert (1766–1834), economist and demographer. In his *Essay on the Principle of Population* (1798) Malthus advanced the notion that POPULATION had an inbuilt propensity to rise, and to outstrip any possible increase in food supply. The necessary conclusion was that population growth would be checked, either by the 'preventive' check of prudence or the 'positive' check of FAMINE or calamity, which would reduce numbers to a proper level again. In later years he extended the analysis, and came to view the preventive check as being more possible than he had initially imagined. Malthus' name is erroneously linked for posterity with the idea that the positive check is inevitable. His ideas were important influences on the thought of DARWIN, Alfred Wallace, John Stuart MILL and Herbert Spencer. His belief that indiscriminate charity would encourage population growth was influential in harsher 19th-century attitudes to the poor and exemplified in the New POOR LAW of 1834. Although he saw BIRTH CONTROL as wicked, the Malthusian (later Neo-Malthusian) League formed in 1861 openly advocated population control through contraception.

Malthus is hailed as the founding father of modern demography; but he was also an important economist, engaging in lengthy dispute with RICARDO about rent and other topics. His economic views were re-evaluated in the 20th century by KEYNES.

Maltote, a term, meaning 'bad toll', originally applied to any particularly unpopular toll on trade and, as such, prohibited in MAGNA CARTA. In 1294, EDWARD I raised the customs duty on a sack of wool from 6 shillings 8 pence (6s 8d) to £2, and from then on, the term normally referred to the high duty on wool exports used by Edward I and EDWARD III to pay for their wars with France, which was imposed without the consent of Parliament. Although *maltotes* were condemned by statute in 1340 and 1362, various Parliaments granted kings the WOOL SUBSIDY they wanted.

Man, Isle of Situated in the Irish Sea – in the midst of the VIKING settlements of the kingdoms of YORK and DUBLIN and elsewhere in the HEBRIDES, Ireland and northern Britain – the Isle of Man was, from the first attacks in the 8th century, seen by the Norsemen as a convenient base for raiding, and was subsequently a place where heavy SCANDINAVIAN SETTLEMENT took place. Archaeological excavation has revealed dramatic remains including a ship burial. The Isle long remained a part of the Scandinavian world. Its king fought on the losing side at the battle of STAMFORDBRIDGE in 1066. In *c.*1079, Godfred Grovan, probably one of the Norse of Dublin, founded the kingdom of Man and the Isles, which included the Hebrides. In theory, the kings of Man owed allegiance to those of Norway, but in practice they were largely independent since only occasionally, as in 1098, did a king of Norway come to the islands and reassert his authority.

After the late 12th-century English conquest of the coast of ULSTER, the kings of Man lost some freedom of action, and even more after the annexation of GALLOWAY by the Scottish kings in the early 13th century. In 1264, after the battle of LARGS, King Magnus Olafsson acknowledged the reality of Scottish power in the Western Isles and submitted to ALEXANDER III. In 1290, EDWARD I took control of the Isle of Man, and except briefly (1313–15), it has remained a possession of the English crown ever since. Its institutions – including its parliament, the Tynwald – still show traces of Scandinavian influence. To the Scandinavians, these were the southern isles' – '*Sudreys*' – and to this day there is still a 'Bishop of Sodor and Man'.

Manbot, *see* FIHTWITE

Manchester Third largest city in England, Manchester's growth was the epitome of the INDUSTRIAL REVOLUTION. An important regional textile-weaving town from the later Middle Ages, its principal expansion came with the COTTON INDUSTRY in the late 18th and early 19th centuries. It was important as a weaving town, but even more so as a trading and warehouse location serving the wider south Lancs. cotton manufacturing region, and as the focus of transport networks – the CANAL system of Lancs., the early RAILWAYS, the Ship Canal to the sea (1894), and latterly motorways. Perhaps more than any other city it is the embodiment of the Victorian architectural ideal, with public buildings such as the GOTHIC Town Hall and the more CLASSICAL Free Trade Hall, as well as many warehouses, and commercial and bank buildings, in an eclectic medley of styles. With the decline in the cotton industry Manchester's economy (and commercial architecture) suffered, but it has revived considerably since the 1960s. It was the centre of 19th-century economic liberalism, leading the campaigns for FREE TRADE and the abolition of the CORN LAWS, and gave its name to the *LAISSEZ-FAIRE* economics of the MANCHESTER SCHOOL.

Manchester School, the name given to the political grouping led by the northern MPs Richard Cobden and John BRIGHT who advocated the principles of FREE TRADE. Their name was coined (derisively) by Benjamin DISRAELI, to denote their *LAISSEZ-FAIRE* principles and sectional self-interest in favour of northern manufacturing. It has subsequently become attached to the LIBERAL followers of Cobden and Bright, and to *laissez-faire* economists.

Mandate, power of territorial administration given by the LEAGUE OF NATIONS in 1919 in the aftermath of WORLD WAR I, especially in areas formerly within the Ottoman Empire. The United Kingdom was given mandates over, e.g., IRAQ and PALESTINE. Taken together with the existing empire the mandated territories increased the BRITISH EMPIRE to its greatest ever extent.

Mandeville's Travels, the title of an immensely popular 14th-century book, allegedly the story of Sir John Mandeville's journeys in the Middle and Far East. Whether the *Travels* were really composed by an English knight from St Albans named Mandeville, or whether this was a pseudonym adopted by the real author, possibly a Frenchman, continues to be debated among literary scholars. Either way, the author took the familiar genre of a narrative of a pilgrimage to the Holy Land and transformed it into a work of fantasy, skilfully using scientific commonplaces – e.g. the circumnavigability of the world – to place his imaginative descriptions of marvels within an apparently realistic framework. The book proved to be a resounding success, soon translated from the original French into English, Latin and many other languages.

Manitoba Central province of CANADA, it was opened up with the establishment of grain agriculture on the prairies in the 1880s, although fur trading had been established with the HUDSON'S BAY and North West Companies from the 17th century. The Red River colony, near modern Winnipeg, the province's capital, was established in 1812 under Lord Selkirk by Scottish and Irish settlers, many of whom had been the victims of Highland CLEARANCES, but the settlers were massacred in 1816 by Indians and traders of the North West Company. Later generations of Scottish EMIGRATION provided a very strong Caledonian presence, while the failure of the Red River rebellions of 1869 and 1885 by Métis, people of mixed white and Indian descent, paved the way for Manitoba's full integration into the Canadian federation.

Manningham Mills Strike, 1891. A landmark in the development of independent labour representation, this five-month stoppage in Bradford was provoked by the imposition of wage cuts in the depressed Yorks. WOOLLEN trade. The defeat of the workers and the bitterness engendered exposed the deficiencies of local LIB-LABS and led to the formation of the Bradford Labour Union to press for a workers' political party. It was no accident that the INDEPENDENT LABOUR PARTY's inaugural conference was held at Bradford two years later.

Manor The word 'manor' derives from the Latin *manerium* and the French *manoir*. Both terms were introduced into England after the NORMAN CONQUEST and signify an ESTATE organized around a lord's chief residence. This included individual peasant holdings, with, at their centre, the lord's reserved estate (the DEMESNE), on which the peasantry worked on the lord's behalf.

Debates about the origins of this form of social organization used to be influenced by a belief that English society once consisted of equals beneath a king, and that servitude and gradations in status emerged only gradually. Modern commentators generally emphasize the presence of LORDSHIP from the very beginnings of Anglo-Saxon society, pointing to evidence in the most ancient of the Anglo-Saxon LAW CODES of estates where lords exercised extensive powers over their peasantry.

DOMESDAY BOOK supplies a mass of valuable evidence, showing that manors differed greatly in form, with many having outlying estates, and in the services owed by the peasants. The greater uniformity implied by institutions such as manorial courts (in which lords exercised jurisdiction over their tenants) and SERFDOM was encouraged, first by the Norman conquest, and afterwards by the development of an English COMMON LAW in the 12th and 13th centuries.

Some manorial courts exercised FRANCHISE jurisdiction beyond their purely FEUDAL functions, including the trial of minor criminal offences; such jurisdiction was conducted in sessions called 'courts leet' or 'views of frankpledge' (*see* COURT BARON). Despite constant pressure from the crown to reduce such rights, some franchisal rights survived in operation as late as the 19th century. Manorial courts were still important for conveyancing where COPYHOLD tenure survived up to 1926; the continuing functions of manors now are purely part of the British heritage industry.

Manumission, *see* SERFDOM; SLAVERY

Maps, Mapping, *see* ORDNANCE SURVEY; ROY'S MILITARY SURVEY

March, 1st Earl of, *see* MORTIMER, ROGER

Marcher Lordships These comprised a great variety of jurisdictions in the Marches of Wales (the English/Welsh border) and south Wales, which were established by Norman attacks on the Welsh. The expansion by leading TENANTS-IN-CHIEF of the crown in the 11th century was initially rapid, but was halted by Welsh uprisings in 1094–8; a stable agreement between Marcher barons and native Welsh rulers was not achieved until the late 12th century. The Marcher lords' spirit of baronial independence proved almost as troublesome to the English kings as the activities of the Welsh princes, especially during the 15th century, and they lost their powers in the Acts of Welsh Union with England of 1536–43 (*see* UNION OF WALES AND ENGLAND).

Marconi Scandal The Marconi Company's successful tender in 1912 for a government scheme for an 'Imperial wireless chain' led to enduring scandal and political trouble. Since TELECOMMUNICATIONS were then in their infancy, such a major undertaking prompted a huge rise in Marconi share prices. The company's rivals cried foul, and rumours circulated that ministers in ASQUITH's government had corruptly influenced the outcome in order to profit from share deals. The ministers named in the French press as the profiteers, the postmaster-general, Herbert Samuel, and the attorney-general, Sir Rufus Isaacs, successfully sued for libel. Controversy continued, and although Samuel was exonerated by the subsequent parliamentary inquiry, other ministers, including LLOYD GEORGE, were found to have acted improperly. The scandal rumbled on into mid-1913; a select committee, and subsequently the COMMONS, divided on party lines and corruption charges were rejected. The scandal undermined public confidence in the government, the whiff of corruption remained in the air, and the vindictiveness of the CONSERVATIVE opposition had been exposed to full view.

Margaret, Maid of Norway (1283–90), Queen of Scots (1286–90), only child of King Eric of Norway and Margaret, daughter of ALEXANDER III of Scotland. The deaths of her mother (probably in giving birth to her) and her uncles led to her being recognized, in 1284, as heir presumptive to the Scottish throne. When Alexander died two years later, she became, in her absence, queen of Scotland and was then betrothed to Edward, the eldest son of EDWARD I. But she saw neither husband nor kingdom, dying at the age of seven at Kirkwall in Orkney in Sept. 1290. Her death precipitated the GREAT CAUSE and thus the most serious crisis in the history of Anglo-Scottish relations.

Margaret of Anjou (1430–82), Queen of England. Daughter of René of Anjou, she was married to HENRY VI in 1445. She soon found herself in an extraordinarily difficult situation, partly because her husband was utterly feeble, partly because as a Frenchwoman she was awkwardly placed when the HUNDRED YEARS WAR ended in 1449–53, with what, to Englishmen, seemed shocking abruptness. Since Henry, partly to please her, had surrendered Maine to her uncle, Charles VII of France, in 1448, she was inevitably blamed for a policy of appeasement widely perceived as leading to catastrophe.

More than most queens, she needed friends, but finding them in the Suffolk–Somerset faction – the de la Pole and Beaufort families – also meant that she made enemies of RICHARD OF YORK and the NEVILLES. Thus instead of performing the traditional queenly role of peacemaker, she bears some responsibility for the outbreak of the WARS OF THE ROSES. Henry's deteriorating health and the birth of their only child, EDWARD, Prince of Wales, in Oct. 1453 gave her further reasons to fear the possible consequences of York's ambition. After Somerset was killed at ST ALBANS in 1455, she became the real leader of the court party, building up a power base away from London and provoking the renewal of fighting in 1459. at NORTHAMPTON in 1460, Henry was captured and Margaret fled, first to Harlech, then to Scotland. However, the disinheritance of her son in the Parliament of Oct. 1460 created a fund of sympathy for her, and after York's death at WAKEFIELD, she joined her English supporters, most of them northerners, and moved south. The YORKIST portrayal of this as a war of the North against the South meant that, despite her victory (and the rescue of her husband) at the second battle of ST ALBANS in Feb. 1461, London refused to open its gates.

She returned to the North and then, following EDWARD IV's victory at TOWTON in March, to Scotland again, taking her husband and son with her. For two years, she struggled to organize a recovery, sailing to France and back, surviving shipwreck, surrendering BERWICK in return for the promise of Scottish support. But after the failure of the siege of Norham in 1463, she returned to France, taking Edward with her and leaving Henry behind; she never saw him again. In 1470, her old enemy Richard NEVILLE, Earl of Warwick, in revolt against King Edward, visited her and was reconciled. But the inevitable distrust between them meant that she remained in France until 14 April 1471, by which time, although Warwick, the 'King-maker', had restored Henry to the throne, he himself had been defeated and killed at BARNET – just hours before Margaret landed at Weymouth. On 4 May, her own army was defeated at TEWKESBURY and her son killed. She remained Edward IV's prisoner until released in 1476 and allowed to return to Anjou.

Margaret of France (*c.*1282–1318), Queen of England. Half-sister of Philip IV of France, she was married to EDWARD I (about 40 years her senior) in 1299. She bore him three children, but her chief role was the traditional queenly one of peacemaker – between the kings of France and England, and between her husband and her stepson, the future EDWARD II.

Margaret, St (*c.*1046–93), Queen of Scots. Although the 'royal saint' of Scotland, she was of English descent. Brought to Scotland when her brother EDGAR THE ÆTHELING fled from WILLIAM I THE CONQUEROR, her marriage (*c.*1070) to MALCOLM III CANMORE marked an important stage in the anglicization of the Scottish court. She and her husband had eight children, none of whom were given traditional Scottish names; three of their sons became kings of Scotland (*see* EDGAR; ALEXANDER I; DAVID I). According to the 'official' biography written by her chaplain, Turgot of ST ANDREWS, she was an exceptionally devout and charitable queen who did much to persuade her husband to bring the practices of the Scottish Church into line with the mainstream of Latin Christendom. She died on 16 Nov. 1093, immediately after hearing of the deaths of her husband and eldest son at Norman hands. Her most enduring memorial was the priory (later abbey) she founded at Dunfermline, where she and her descendants were buried. She was formally canonized in 1250.

Marian Exiles, Protestants who escaped abroad under MARY I, primarily religious exiles concentrated in Germany and Switzerland, with others in France and Italy. Many took leading places in Church and state under ELIZABETH I, and they produced much literature (*see* FOXE, JOHN; GRINDAL, EDMUND; KNOX, JOHN). Christina Garrett's theory that their flight was a carefully planned stratagem has never gained much favour.

Maritime Trade and the Merchant Navy Maritime trade has been of importance to the islands of Britain since well before the ROMAN CONQUEST. It is no accident that the chief town of Roman Britain was LONDON, the major port. The economic position of Britain, its Empire and its world leadership in the economic take-off into industrialization in the 18th and 19th centuries owes much to success in the combined and interlinked fields of maritime trade and naval strength.

In the later medieval period the British Isles were part of the trading area dominated by the German trading confederation of the Hanse. Much of the English WOOL trade was initially carried in foreign ships, including the Italian galleys which were the first LINERS running a scheduled service. One of the main trades in which English ships took a major part was the wine trade with GASCONY, and ships from both BRISTOL and Hull developed a trade to Iceland. However the chief English trade was with the Low Countries. In the early Tudor period there were signs of increasing adventurousness with voyages to NEWFOUNDLAND and the start of a trade with the Eastern Mediterranean. Trade with Russia via the White Sea began in MARY's reign, and the beginnings of the SLAVE TRADE between West AFRICA and the WEST INDIES and then the first contacts with the East Indies in ELIZABETH I's – though PRIVATEERING against Spain was probably the more successful maritime activity at this time. English merchantmen were mostly powerfully armed and well crewed; good fighting ships in dangerous trades, but poor carriers in the bulk trades in which the more economical and better cargo ships of the Dutch were winning ascendancy, putting the English very much into second place during the first half of the 17th century. The DUTCH WARS were fought over trade and resulted in the English acquiring large numbers of the Dutch cargo ships by capture, and then copying the designs, particularly for the colliers used in the growing coastal COAL trade between the Tyne and London. English naval strength was used to support trade – particularly in the Mediterranean, and later in the West Indies. The NAVIGATION ACTS gave legal protection to the growing English merchant fleet trading with the expanding colonies in North America and the West Indies. Increasing British naval and mercantile ascendancy went hand in hand during the 18th century as the Dutch fell behind and the threat of French competition was met and mastered. By the end of the NAPOLEONIC WAR, not only was the British merchant fleet by far the largest in the world, but Britain had a lead both in industrial exports and a dominance in the world outside Europe which made her the greatest trading nation in the world, in both her own products, in re-exports – particularly of tropical produce – and in the carrying trade between other countries. During the remaining years of the 19th century, developments in SHIPBUILDING and marine engineering reinforced this dominance. British ships and firms were generally more up-to-date and efficient than others. Towards the end of the century some half of the world's mercantile tonnage was British. The development of the RAILWAYS in Britain reduced the relative importance of the coastal trade, but railways and machinery swelled the exports from Britain carried by ship. With such an ascendancy there was little need for protective legislation or monopolistic trading companies and the theories of FREE TRADE swept away these relics of the past. The British merchant navy remained the largest in the world into the second half of the 20th century, but by the 1970s changing patterns of trade and investment, a comparative lack of government support and increasing use of 'flags of convenience' had caused a steep decline in the numbers and tonnage of British-owned ships – a decline which still continues.

Up to the middle of the 18th century shipowning had not been a profession as such, and the ownership of individual vessels tended to be split between numbers of merchants, small investors and, often, ships' captains. There then came an increasing tendency for the growth of specialized shipowners, and by the middle of the 19th century the concept of 'lines' of ships, such as the P&O, Holt's or CUNARD, was becoming familiar. It was also at this time that the training and qualification of ships' officers came under state supervision and certification, as did the seaworthiness of merchant ships (mainly due to Samuel Plimsoll's agitation – the draft marks on the sides of ships known as the 'Plimsoll line' are his memorial), and other areas like signal flags and navigation lights. In these areas, as in maritime insurance, Britain, as the leading maritime nation, took a leading part.

Mark ('merk' in Scotland). Originally a unit of weight – two-thirds of a pound, either in gold or silver – by the 11th century it had become a unit of account, worth 13 shillings and 4 pence (13s 4d), i.e. two-thirds of a pound sterling. In England reckoning in marks finally died out in the 18th century.

Markievicz, Countess (*née* Constance Gore-Booth) (1868–1927), Irish revolutionary. Born in London but educated in Ireland, she married a Polish count while studying art in Paris. She was involved in the DUBLIN cultural milieu of the Abbey Theatre before joining SINN FÉIN in 1908 and, the following year, founding Na Fianna, a paramilitary organization for boys. She was condemned to death for her part in the EASTER RISING, though the sentence was commuted. Freed by an amnesty in 1917, she was elected a Sinn Féin MP in 1918 – the first woman to be elected to the British Parliament – but refused to take her seat in accordance with the party's boycott of Westminster. The following year she became minister of labour in the provisional Sinn Féin government and was twice imprisoned during the ANGLO-IRISH WAR; because of her opposition to the ANGLO-IRISH TREATY, she was also imprisoned by pro-treaty forces. Joining FIANNA FÁIL in 1926, she was elected to the DÁIL just before her death.

Marlborough, 1st Duke of, *see* CHURCHILL, JOHN

Marne, Battles of the, northern France, 6–11 Sept. 1914, and 15 July–2 Aug. 1918, key battles of WORLD WAR I. The first battle, or 'miracle of the Marne', fought mainly by the French but with the BRITISH EXPEDITIONARY FORCE playing an important role, ended the threat of a rapid German victory.

The second battle was the first Allied counter-attack, marking the failure of the German offensive of spring 1918. The French were supported by TANKS, and by American troops in significant numbers for the first time.

Marprelate Scandal In 1588–9, PURITAN pamphlets by 'Martin Marprelate' (never caught; probably Job Throckmorton, a talented Warwicks. gentleman) appeared, which satirically attacked leading churchmen. Older Puritans were shocked, and investigations by a furious government incidentally provided much material for anti-Puritan repression (*see* CLASSICAL MOVEMENT).

Marquess *or* Marquis, second highest PEERAGE title, between DUKE and EARL. It was first bestowed in the English peerage in the late 14th century, in the Scottish a century later.

Marriage From the 9th century, the Church increasingly claimed marriage as one of its sacraments; however, despite some efforts at a complete clerical takeover, the marriage service remained the work of the couple, with the priest merely a witness. Significantly, the vows said by the couple in the marriage service were the only part of medieval liturgy not in Latin, and their English form can be found already in 15th-century texts. In his PRAYER BOOK, Thomas CRANMER, England's first married archbishop, added a new justification of marriage to that of procreation: the couple might enjoy one another's company. From the 1580s, the English CHURCH managed to end the social acceptance of sexual relations between betrothal and marriage. In spite of attempts at post-REFORMATION reform, and at forcing marriages to take place in church, a valid marriage remained the simple exchange of vows. This led to many complications, and to the notoriety of clandestine and FLEET MARRIAGES. HARDWICKE'S MARRIAGE ACT of 1753 significantly tightened the conditions for English marriage, making the ceremony in an Anglican church, by banns or by licence, the only valid form. In 1836, marriage before a registrar or with non-ANGLICAN rites was legalized. The marriage registers themselves, with ages of spouses given and their signature or mark, have been a vital source of information in many fields of enquiry. Scots marriage law and that of the Irish Republic remain distinct.

Historians have taken a variety of views on marriage in the past, some stressing the lovelessness of many unions and arrangements to find partners, others remarking on the close companionship evident from an early date. Certainly, the late ages at marriage evident from FAMILY RECONSTITUTION suggest a high degree of choice of partner. Marriage has always been a fluid institution for some, not infrequently ending in DIVORCE or, more commonly in the past, separation. The number of consensual unions without marriage has probably always been considerable – although rarely visible – especially where social or religious controls have been weak. Probably at no time in the past has the number and duration of such unions exceeded that seen since the 1960s. *See also* DIVORCE AND BRITISH LAW.

Marriage, Age at, statistic frequently used by demographers, and commonly calculated before the advent of CIVIL REGISTRATION from FAMILY RECONSTITUTION studies. Changes in age at marriage were an important regulator of FERTILITY and of POPULATION growth before the DEMOGRAPHIC TRANSITION of the later 19th century.

Married Women's Act 1882, *see* WOMEN, LEGAL STATUS OF

Married Women's Property Acts 1870, 1882, 1884, *see* WOMEN, LEGAL STATUS OF

Marshal, William (*c.*1147–1219), soldier and courtier. The younger son of a royal official, he attracted attention as both a TOURNAMENT champion and a courtier in the service of HENRY THE YOUNG KING, and entered the household of HENRY II in 1186. His prudent military advice and his loyalty, even when the old king's fortunes were rapidly declining, won the admiration of RICHARD I, and in 1189, he was rewarded with the hand of the heiress to the vast estates of Richard de CLARE (Strongbow) in Ireland, Wales and the ANGLO-NORMAN REALM.

He put his political skills to the test when – despite the loss of Normandy in 1204 – he retained his estates there by doing homage to Philip II Augustus of France. Yet somehow he survived JOHN's reign with his influence intact and his reputation barely tarnished. As an experienced soldier and a shrewd operator, Marshal was a natural choice for regent during the civil war that marred the start of HENRY III's reign. Defeating the future Louis VIII of France in the battles of LINCOLN and Sandwich in 1217 meant that a remarkably long and successful career ended in a blaze of glory.

His significance became even greater with the discovery in the late 19th century of the near-contemporary *Histoire de Guillaume le Maréchal*. This long poem – the earliest vernacular biography of a non-royal layman in British history – extols him as 'the best knight in the world' and offers a unique window into the courtly and chivalrous milieu of the 12th- and 13th-century aristocracy.

Marshall Plan, American plan for the economic reconstruction of Europe following WORLD WAR II, announced by US secretary of state General George C. Marshall in June 1947. The plan was implemented by the European Recovery Programme (1948), under which 16 nations in western Europe received $13 billion (Britain received about $2,693 million) in grants and loans between 1948 and 1952. Together with the Truman Doctrine, the plan was at least partly designed to diminish the growth of Communist influence in western European politics. The western powers organized a conference in Paris in July 1947 to discuss the allocation of aid, and in April 1948 set up the Organization for European Economic Co-operation (*see* ORGANIZATION FOR ECONOMIC CO-OPERATION AND DEVELOPMENT), to administer the programme with the United States Economic Co-operation Administration. With the assistance of Marshall aid, all the participating nations had, by 1951, raised their production capacities beyond pre-war levels. In contrast to the DEPRESSION which followed WORLD WAR I, the Plan added a crucial margin of investment resources which enabled European economic reconstruction to proceed without greater austerity, thereby assisting the re-establishment of political stability.

Marshalsea Prison, formerly a house of detention in Southwark, standing near St George's Church. Originally a prison for royal servants, from 1842–9 it was a debtor's prison; it is depicted in Charles Dickens' *Little Dorrit*. *See also* IMPRISONMENT FOR DEBT.

Marston Moor, Battle of, July 1644, crushing defeat of Prince RUPERT'S ROYALIST army, losing CHARLES I the North. Fought in Yorks., it was the biggest battle of the CIVIL WARS.

Marx, Karl (1818–83), political and social theorist. Settling in London in the aftermath of the revolutions of 1848 which shook Europe, Marx, in association with Friedrich Engels, is credited with the formulation of the whole body of political thought usually dubbed Marxism. There are as many varieties of Marx's thought as commentators upon him, and just as many misinterpretations of the character of his ideas, but Marx's contribution to political economy has proved one of the most influential of all time.

Born in Prussia, Marx became editor of the Cologne newspaper *Rheinische Zeitung* in 1842, until the newspaper was suppressed for his extreme radicalism. In Paris, Marx met Engels, and there they began their collaboration in political writing. He returned to Cologne in 1848 where, with Engels, he briefly edited the *Neue Rheinische Zeitung* until both were expelled for their revolutionary views and settled in England where Engels was working in Manchester as an agent for his German family's cotton manufacturing firm, meaning he was able, on many occasions, to help the Marx family financially. The first fruits of their collaboration there were the *Communist Manifesto* (1848) and a series of other publications exposing the exploited social condition of workers, especially in MANCHESTER, the epitome of the INDUSTRIAL REVOLUTION.

Marx's principal contribution to political philosophy and economy is the form of communism described in *Das Kapital*, of which the first volume appeared in 1867 and the last was published posthumously by Engels in 1894. It contained Marx's criticism of capitalism, which was that capitalists appropriate the benefits of industry leaving the labouring classes in increasing misery. 'From everyone according to his abilities, to each according to his needs' was Marx's solution.

Marx's preoccupation with the analysis of the economic structure in relation to other parts of the social structure, with the formation of social classes and the theory of ideology, represented a coherent attempt to act both as an explanation of history and as a guide to political and social action. This idea that the mode of economic production and distribution of any society is an important determinant of that society's social, political and actual structure (*see* HISTORICAL MATERIALISM) has had a profound influence on the writing of economic and social history. Although he was actively involved in labour politics in the mid-Victorian period, his influence in his adopted land was limited by the absence of English-language translations of his chief writings and by the peculiarities of the economic and political structures of British capitalism. Marx is buried in Highgate Cemetery, London.

Mary I (1516–58), Queen of England (1553–8). Victim of her father HENRY VIII's estrangement from her mother CATHERINE OF ARAGON, she was bastardized on the ANNE BOLEYN marriage in 1533 and, after spirited resistance, was intimidated into a humiliating acknowledgment of her status in 1536. Her position thereafter improved, but during her half-brother EDWARD VI's reign (1547–53), she faced fresh troubles through her stubborn refusal to abandon the traditional CATHOLIC liturgy. The government tried to bypass her by placing JANE GREY on the throne in 1553, but with the aid of Catholic advisers, Mary drew on provincial outrage to stage a brilliantly effective *coup d'état*.

She moved swiftly to restore not only traditional worship but also (to the surprise of most of her subjects) obedience to the pope, although legal problems delayed this until Nov. 1554. She also brushed aside all objections to her marriage to PHILIP II of Spain, including the challenge of WYATT'S REBELLION. Equally unbending was her commitment to burning PROTESTANTS for HERESY, despite the propaganda asset that this became to her opponents. The loss of CALAIS in 1558, in an initially promising war with France, was a bitter blow, and illness in the summer proved not to be a sign of her longed-for child but fatal stomach cancer. Mary's reign and swiftly curtailed programme of Catholic restoration still provoke widely differing assessments, but her blighted personal history can only attract sympathy.

Mary II (1662–94), Queen of England, Ireland and Scotland (1689–94). The eldest child of James, Duke of York, later JAMES II, and his first wife Anne Hyde. Her education, under Henry Compton, bishop of London, was strictly PROTESTANT. The death of her only surviving brother in 1671 left her heir presumptive. In 1677 CHARLES II arranged her marriage to William of Orange (the future WILLIAM III) and she went to the Netherlands.

Following William's invasion, she returned to England early in 1689, and influenced the form of the REVOLUTION SETTLEMENT by refusing to contemplate serving as sole monarch. William and Mary were crowned joint sovereigns in April 1689. Personally pious, Mary encouraged schemes for the REFORMATION OF MANNERS. She died of smallpox in Dec. 1694.

Mary of Guise (1515–60), Queen of Scotland. A French princess spared a proposed marriage to HENRY VIII, she married JAMES V in 1538. As the symbol of French alliance, her political influence fluctuated in inverse proportion to that of the Anglophile party in Scotland. After PINKIE (1547), she took power beside James Hamilton, 3rd Earl of Arran, and in 1554 replaced him as regent to her 12-year-old daughter Mary (*see* MARY QUEEN OF SCOTS). Reluctant at first to persecute PROTESTANTS, she was pressured into aggression by the French and by increasing Protestant militancy, facing full-scale confrontation in 1559. She was driven out of EDINBURGH and replaced as regent by Arran (now Duke of Châtelherault); although fixed on continuing the fight, she was struck down by fatal illness. An able and resourceful woman, determined to protect her daughter's interests, Mary was unfairly demonized by later Scots Protestant writers.

Mary Queen of Scots (1542–87), Queen of Scotland (1542–67). Queen from six days old, after her father JAMES V's premature death, Mary was sent to France in 1548 while her mother, MARY OF GUISE, ruled Scotland. Briefly queen of France (1559–60) until her husband Francis II's early death, in 1561 she reluctantly returned to Scotland, where the Protestant LORDS OF THE CONGREGATION had filled a political vacuum. Her advisers helped her, a CATHOLIC monarch, preside uneasily over the steady PROTESTANT takeover.

Seeking freedom of action, she married her cousin Henry STEWART, Earl of Darnley, in 1566, but apart from producing the future JAMES VI, the marriage was a catastrophe, resulting first in Darnley leading the murder of her Italian favourite, David Rizzio (?1533–66) and then, in 1567, in Darnley's murder by a consortium including her next husband, James HEPBURN, Earl of Bothwell. By now the long-suffering Scots had had enough; Mary's supporters were defeated at Carberry Hill, and she was deposed in 1567. After escaping from prison, she was defeated again at LANGSIDE (1568) and fled to England, provoking an immediate political crisis and presenting a long-term problem.

A trial in 1568–9 decided that she was implicated in Darnley's murder (mainly on the strength of the 'casket letters', now lost and much debated), and she remained imprisoned, provoking plans for her remarriage and a series of Catholic plots. It took two decades and great political pressure for ELIZABETH I to overcome her qualms at ordering the execution of an anointed sovereign; it took place at Fotheringhay Castle, Northants. Recipient of an astonishing amount of romantic historical attention, Mary impresses by her ability to waste all the considerable assets that came her way.

Maryland, former British North American colony, and one of the original 13 states of the USA after the War of AMERICAN INDEPENDENCE. Maryland was founded in 1632 by Sir George Calvert (after whose title the principal city, Baltimore, was named) originally as a CATHOLIC enclave although it was never an exclusively Catholic settlement. It was second only to VIRGINIA in the cultivation of TOBACCO and in the speed with which its settlement expanded in its early years.

Masques, innovative dramatic form of the early Stuart court, a distinctive English contribution to a European-wide flowering of RENAISSANCE court spectacle. From 1605, the partnership of the dramatist Ben Jonson (1572–1637) and the architect and artist Inigo Jones (1573–1652) transformed traditional court pageantry into a virtuoso theatrical and intellectual display. Masques combined drama, music, dance and art, presenting monarchy's divine majesty through tableaux shaped by NEO-PLATONIC ideas and usually featuring symbolic or abstract characters.

Accessible only to an educated audience, during the 1630s court masques increasingly enunciated the absolutist ideology that so worried CHARLES I's politically aware subjects. However, perhaps the greatest example of the genre – *Comus* (1634) – was written by the uncourtly poet and writer John MILTON (1608–74), not for the royal court but for performance at the court maintained at Ludlow Castle, Salop, by the lord president of the COUNCIL IN THE MARCHES, John Egerton, Earl of Bridgwater. Masques ceased when war dispersed the king's court in 1642.

Mass, the name used from the 4th century in the Western Church, and still in the Roman Catholic Church and ANGLO-CATHOLIC congregations, for the eucharist or holy communion; taken from the puzzling last words of the Latin rite – *'Ite missa est'* ('Go, it is sent'). Like all the services of the early Church, it was chanted or sung, but the western Church from the 7th/8th century began multiplying the number of masses celebrated daily, to utilize the power of the prayer contained in them, particularly in MONASTIC communities. This meant that singing every mass became impossible, and two types of celebration therefore developed. One was the 'low mass', a said service often only involving one priest and, as a nominal congregation, one server; the other type, the 'high mass', remained an elaborately sung service, the focus for community and PARISH life, and around this has developed the main tradition of western church music (for example that of the composer William Byrd, 1543–1623). The late medieval theology of the mass as a repetition of Christ's sacrifice made on the Cross outraged the LOLLARDS and the 16th-century Reformers, and it was a main focus of their attack on the medieval Western Church.

Mass Observation, a project begun in 1937 when the ABDICATION CRISIS revealed the startling gap between the 'establishment' view and the opinion of the 'people'. The group was started by Humphry Jennings, Charles Madge and Tom Harrisson and its object was an 'anthropological study' of the British way of life – gathering information on subjects as diverse as 'sex in Blackpool' to 'anti-Semitism in the east end of London'. The most famous early mass-observation study was on the industrial life of 'Worktown' (Bolton, for which Humphry Spender took the photographs). A national panel of volunteers was set up to keep a detailed record of their daily lives, and these, which carried on throughout WORLD WAR II, still provide historians with an unmatchable source of information about life in Britain in the 1930s and 1940s.

Massachusetts, former British colony in North America and one of the original 13 states of the USA. The colony, like most in NEW ENGLAND, had its origins largely in religious affairs, as a haven for religious SEPARATISTS and PURITANS, beginning with the MAYFLOWER PILGRIMS landing at Plymouth in 1620 and the establishment of a colony in 1629. The Massachusetts Bay Company was, like the other colonial companies, a JOINT-STOCK venture to promote settlement and exploitation, but it was the least well funded of them all. The largest of the early migrations to the new colony was that led by John Winthrop in 1630. Church polity there was CONGREGATIONALIST and political power was to be in the hands of an oligarchy of religious divines; while the town meetings they instituted remained the basis of local and colonial government. Connecticut and Rhode Island were both offshoots from the parent colony. Boston became one of the most important of all the colonial trading cities, with its place in the shipping of the TRIANGULAR TRADE and one of the largest ports. The BOSTON TEA PARTY was one of the emotive events in the build-up to the War of AMERICAN INDEPENDENCE.

Match Girls Strike, 1888. A harbinger of the NEW UNIONISM, the strike was the unexpected outcome of the social reformer Annie Besant's exposure of the dangerous environment and abysmal wages paid at Bryant & May's match-making factory in East London. The wage increase won by the striking match girls in July 1888 encouraged unskilled and unorganized workers and showed that corporate solidarity was by no means exclusive to the craft unions (*see* NEW MODEL UNIONS).

Mathgamain (?–976), King of the DÁL CAIS (964–76). He overthrew the Eóganacht kings of MUNSTER and established his family's domination in southern Ireland. Seizing power in 964, he spent the subsequent years fighting neighbouring kings, dynastic rivals and the VIKINGS. Apparently secure by 974, he was defeated and murdered two years later in one of the recurrent feuds typical of early medieval Irish politics (*see* KINGSHIP). He was succeeded by his brother BRIAN BORU.

Matilda II (?–1118), Queen of England. Daughter of MALCOLM III CANMORE of Scotland and St MARGARET, she was married to HENRY I in 1100. Besides bearing two children, she was an important patron of music and literature (both Latin and ANGLO-NORMAN) and often presided over the council governing England while her husband was away in Normandy.

Matilda, Empress (1102–67). Daughter of HENRY I and MATILDA II, she became known as the 'Empress' because of her marriage, in Jan. 1114, to the Holy Roman Emperor, Henry V. (However, since she never received an imperial crown from the hands of a pope, formally her correct title remained 'Queen of the Romans'.) She returned from Germany in 1125 after her husband's death, and two years later, the ANGLO-NORMAN barons swore to accept her as their ruler if Henry I had no son. In 1128, she was married to Geoffrey PLANTAGENET, Count of Anjou, some ten years her junior. At first relations with her husband were troubled, but between 1133 and 1136, she bore him three sons.

Despite their oaths to Matilda, in 1135 most Anglo-Norman magnates acquiesced in the succession to the ANGLO-NORMAN REALM of STEPHEN, grandson of WILLIAM I THE CONQUEROR: for as long as military leadership remained one of the principal obligations of a ruler, thrones were usually reserved for men. But Matilda fought for her rights, initially in NORMANDY, then (from 1139) in England, leaving Geoffrey to complete the conquest of Normandy. When Stephen was captured at the battle of LINCOLN in 1141, she ought to have triumphed; for a while, many of Stephen's supporters, including his brother HENRY OF BLOIS, were prepared to acknowledge her as 'Lady of England and Normandy'. However, in this, the crisis of her life, she lacked judgment and alienated potential supporters, notably (by her financial demands) the citizens of LONDON. In consequence, her half-brother ROBERT OF GLOUCESTER, the mainstay of her party, was captured and had to be exchanged for Stephen. Matilda herself had a narrow escape when trapped in Oxford Castle in Dec. 1142.

Her authority in England remained restricted to the West Country. In 1148, realizing that she would never be accepted as queen and that the future of the Angevin cause lay with her son, the future HENRY II, she returned to Normandy. She was widowed again in 1151. The last 15 years of her life were both peaceful and reputedly influential. Henry II was widely believed to respect his mother's advice, and in his absence, she often presided over the government of the duchy.

Matilda of Boulogne (?–1152), Queen of England. Married to STEPHEN in 1125, the strategic location of her own inheritance – estates around LONDON in addition to the County of Boulogne – facilitated her husband's seizure of the throne in 1135. She played a very prominent role throughout the ensuing civil war, being much admired for her courage, sense of honour and diplomatic skill – an attractive contrast to the Empress MATILDA. Indeed, Stephen owed his throne to his wife's loyalty and leadership during the critical months of 1141, when he was imprisoned following his capture at the battle of LINCOLN. She bore him five children, and his cause did not long survive her death in 1152.

Matilda of Flanders (?–1083), Queen of England. Daughter of Baldwin V, Count of Flanders, she was married to Duke William of NORMANDY (the future WILLIAM I THE CONQUEROR) in 1050 or 1051. She was anointed queen in May 1068, but generally stayed in Normandy, often presiding over the council that governed the duchy during William's absences. She is sometimes said to have been only 4 ft 2 in (1.27 m) tall, but since she successfully bore at least nine children, this is almost certainly wrong.

Matrimonial Causes Act 1857, *see* WOMEN, LEGAL STATUS OF

Mau Mau Uprising, campaign of terrorism by a secret society of mainly Kikuyu tribesmen, with the aim of driving white settlers out of KENYA. Violence began in 1952 and continued for the next four years, mainly taking the form of attacks on the property of white settlers and on Africans who did not support Mau Mau; attacks on Africans far outnumbered those on whites. The emergency was ended in Jan. 1960, but Mau Mau cells continued to exist even after Kenyan independence in 1963.

Maundy Money, a distinctively English royal survival of ceremonies performed on Maundy Thursday in Holy Week, in commemoration of Jesus Christ's actions at the Last Supper, when he instituted the eucharist and washed his disciples' feet, at which the secular and spiritual leaders of medieval Europe washed the feet of the poor and gave them gifts. WILLIAM III decided to abandon foot-washing, but his successor monarchs have continued to give money to a group of the poor and elderly; the money has been specially minted since the reign of CHARLES II, and continues to be struck in silver with distinctive designs. The number of recipients chosen and the amount of money given corresponds to the years of the sovereign's age.

Mauritius British rule over this Indian Ocean island territory was established in 1810, along with the islands of the Seychelles, when they were captured from France, who had used them as bases for attacking British shipping. Under British control recognized in the Treaty of PARIS 1814, Mauritius became a SUGAR economy. A legislative council was put in place in 1947, with self-government in 1964 and independence in 1968. The Seychelles were a dependency of Mauritius between 1814 and 1903, when they became a crown colony. The coconut was an important crop, especially after SLAVERY was abolished in 1834. The Seychelles achieved independence in 1976.

May Committee, committee on the economy whose report, published in July 1931, precipitated the fall of MACDONALD's LABOUR government. Set up under the chairmanship of Sir George May, ex-secretary of Prudential Assurance, to estimate the budget deficit and ways of meeting it, the committee's report intensified the financial and political crisis facing the Labour government. The CABINET's failure to agree on cuts to the level required led to its break-up in Aug. 1931 and to the formation of the NATIONAL GOVERNMENT, led by MacDonald.

May Day, 1 May, traditionally one of the most popular HOLIDAYS, and associated in the past with a great variety of CALENDAR CUSTOMS – Morris dancing, the choosing and crowning of a May Queen, and local fairs. May Day is the most important workers' holiday in continental Europe, and in the 20th century its celebration came to be particularly associated with communist and socialist nations; a campaign for an official May Day holiday in Britain finally succeeded in 1977. *See also* EVIL MAY DAY.

Mayflower Pilgrims, or Pilgrim Fathers, SEPARATISTS who sought refuge from English persecution first in the Netherlands and then in the NEW WORLD. They sailed from Southampton in Aug. 1620, putting in for repairs at Plymouth, which provided the name for their landfall in NEW ENGLAND (on the coast of what became MASSACHUSETTS – although they had intended to land in VIRGINIA). Although far from being the first English settlers in the New World, they are often popularly regarded as such.

Maynooth, principal Irish Roman Catholic seminary and theological college, situated in Co. Kildare; founded in 1795. Its rebuilding caused a stormy passage in the fortunes of the TORIES under PEEL. When Peel proposed a grant of £30,000 towards the cost in April 1845 (15 years after the furore over CATHOLIC EMANCIPATION), the issue divided his party. Many WHIGS supported the move, but nearly half Peel's party voted against. The issue caused a vigorous mobilization of PROTESTANT opinion, and prefigured the split in the Conservative party over the repeal of the CORN LAWS.

Mayor, the presiding officer of a BOROUGH. Most English boroughs were originally ruled by one or more BAILIFFS, but the more independent-minded boroughs copied the revolutionary practice of towns in 12th-century France by choosing an elected leader, a 'greater man' (Latin *maior*). This became the aim of every town, despite general hostility from medieval kings and lords, but many boroughs did not succeed in acquiring mayors until the 19th century.

Means Test, introduced as an emergency measure by the NATIONAL GOVERNMENT in autumn 1931 for those in receipt of unemployment insurance beyond the statutory period of six months under the National Insurance Acts. Claimants had to undergo a 'household means test' carried out by the local Public Assistance Committees, the successors to the Poor Law Guardians (*see* POOR RELIEF). Any form of income, including contributions from sons, daughters or charities, could be taken into account, as well as savings, furniture and other effects.

By Jan. 1932, an estimated one million people had come within the scope of the 'tests', and within a year, 180,000 had been denied unemployment insurance.

The Means Test remained in operation for the rest of the decade, although its regulations were somewhat relaxed. It left a legacy of bitterness and has become a generic term for any restriction on benefits because of income.

Mechanics' Institutes, self-improving working men's adult education institutions of the 19th century. The institutes emerged in Scotland in the 1810s, in London in 1823, and soon appeared in the English provinces. The publication of BROUGHAM's *Observations upon the Education of the People* (1825) was influential in the movement's spread; TORIES criticized the growth of the 'reading rabble', while COBBETT scorned 'Scotch feelosophy'. Many institutes were sponsored and influenced by local industrialists and the middle classes, and, to that extent, may have been an element in social control as well as in working-class self-improvement. *See also* WORKERS' EDUCATIONAL ASSOCIATION.

Medina del Campo, Treaty of, 1489. A treaty made in Spain between HENRY VII and Aragon and Castile, it prevented YORKISTS taking refuge in Spain, and provided for the marriage between Prince ARTHUR and CATHERINE OF ARAGON. It began an 80-year English alignment with Spain. *See also* BURGUNDY AND ENGLAND.

Medway, Battle on the, AD 43. This two-day engagement on the River Medway in Kent, fought between the Roman armies commanded by AULUS PLAUTIUS and the Britons commanded by CARATACUS and his brother Togodomnus, was the decisive event in the early stages of the Roman advance into Britain. It was a fierce struggle, after which the Romans were free to advance to the Thames and beyond (*see* ROMAN CONQUEST).

Melbourne, 2nd Viscount, *see* LAMB, WILLIAM

Melville, Andrew (1545–1622), clerical politician. Studies at St Andrews, Paris and Poitiers culminated at Geneva (1569–74), which confirmed his enthusiasm for CALVINIST reform. On his return to Scotland in 1574, he did much for university reform and development, and was the prime mover for a pure PRESBYTERIAN system in the Church, provoking repeated clashes with JAMES VI AND I which led, in 1607, to imprisonment and, four years later, to French exile.

Mercantilism, a term describing a complex collection of economic theories particularly dominant in English state policy in the 17th century, although based on the commonplaces of government since the 15th century. Propounded most forcefully by the economist Thomas Mun (1571–1641), these theories stressed the importance of a positive balance of external trade for a state's well-being, and viewed world trade as a relatively fixed cake from which one country could benefit only at the expense of another. Official regulation of trade, of the import and export of bullion and COIN, and of agricultural and industrial production, together with the structuring of customs or other duties for economic ends, were considered vital, as was a system of regulation, protection and, where necessary, military intervention. The theory lay behind the NAVIGATION ACTS of 1651, 1660, 1662 and 1663, which protected the trade between England and her developing American colonies from external participation. With the aid of an increasingly effective NAVY, the Acts were vigorously enforced through the 18th century and only repealed in 1849. *See also* FREE TRADE.

Adam SMITH – who opposed such practices, believing that they served the interests of merchants at the expense of the community at large – first dubbed them the 'mercantile system'. Many historians have argued that the term 'system' is misleading: early economic writers developed no coherent body of 'mercantilist' doctrine, and 'mercantilist' policies were *ad hoc* and pragmatic, representing attempts to solve particular problems. However, the term continues in use as convenient shorthand.

Merchant Adventurers of London, an organization gradually consolidated by London merchants during the 15th century (with major royal charters in 1486 and 1505) become England's main overseas trading body possessing a series of overseas headquarters (STAPLES), notably in Antwerp (1446–93, 1496–1564) and Hamburg (1567–79, 1611 onwards). They concentrated on the CLOTH trade to the Netherlands and Germany, in which their dominance was confirmed by the failure of the COCKAYNE SCHEME (1614–16); monopoly companies in other arenas of trade were modelled on them. Changing trade patterns and balances of international power brought them steady decline during the 17th century, loss of monopoly in 1689 and formal disbanding in 1809.

Merchant Banks An important feature of the operation of LONDON's capital and securities markets, many were established in the 18th and 19th centuries – Baring Brothers, Hoare's, N. M. Rothschild – while others, like S. G. Warburg, came into being after World War II. They have some features in common with commercial or high street BANKS, such as accepting and discounting bills of exchange, or dealing in foreign exchange. However, they also differ in key respects: they are specialist organizations deeply involved in all aspects of corporate and government finance. Baring Brothers, for example, arranged the issue of bonds for a number of foreign governments in the early 19th century, and they also accepted and discounted commercial bills on behalf of corporate industrial clients. The following are the main activities of merchant banks, but not all are involved in every activity mentioned: as brokers, they arrange the sale of stocks and shares for companies which are raising new capital and in this context some have advised the UK and foreign governments in handling privatization issues; some merchant banks are also market makers in the secondary market – buying and selling securities which were issued some time in the past; in addition, they are frequently involved in mergers and takeovers – largely in an advisory capacity; finally they may have a function as managers of investment funds on behalf of individual or institutional clients – such as PENSION FUNDS and INSURANCE companies. Most of these activities are fee-earning and are therefore not risky; however, market-making is more risky as it requires the use of the banks' own capital. *See also* BANK OF ENGLAND; BARING CRISIS; GOLD STANDARD.

Merchant Shipping Acts 1850, 1876, 1877 Legislation was introduced in the late 19th century to regulate the carriage of goods at sea and improve safety standards. The Merchant Shipping Act of 1850 empowered the BOARD OF TRADE to train ships' officers and to insist that they be qualified to work on board a ship. It also introduced a code of standards to prevent exploitation by employers. Following the campaign of Samuel Plimsoll on behalf of seamen, the 1876 Merchant Shipping Act provided for the marking of a line on a ship's sides which would disappear below the water line if the ship was overloaded. A principal defect, the absence of a definition as to the location of the load-line on the ship's hull, was corrected in 1890. A further Act of 1877 imposed a limit on the weight of cargo which vessels were permitted to carry and created rules governing the engagement of seamen and their accommodation on board ship.

Mercia, Anglo-Saxon kingdom. One of the seven kingdoms of the HEPTARCHY, from the time of PENDA (626–55) it emerged alongside NORTHUMBRIA and WESSEX as one of the three most powerful kingdoms of pre-UNIFICATION England. There can be no doubt that, during the 8th and early 9th centuries, it was the strongest of these, and, despite a frustrating lack of evidence, a scholarly consensus has emerged that identifies the 'Mercian hegemony' as a brilliant political achievement.

The kingdom's origins were based on settlements in the north Midlands. Penda's kin-group, known as the Iclingas, were initially one of a number of families who fought for political control. His military achievements ensured their dominance, and in the time of ETHELBALD, OFFA and CENWULF, they dominated the other English kingdoms and the Welsh princes. If the *TRIBAL HIDEAGE* is, as many scholars believe, a Mercian tribute-list, we have an indication of how their extensive power was sustained.

The Mercian achievements include: the development of a new system of military obligation (*see* COMMON BURDENS); the production of the first COINAGE of silver pennies (*see* PENNY, ANGLO-SAXON); vast public works, of which OFFA'S DYKE is the most remarkable; a 'foreign policy' that enabled Offa to treat on equal terms with Charlemagne; and an ecclesiastical policy that briefly made LICHFIELD an archbishopric.

Mercia's supremacy was brought to an end by the victory gained by EGBERT of Wessex at the battle of ELLENDEN in 825. The kingdom itself was extinguished by the conquests of the Scandinavian GREAT ARMY in the late 860s and 870s, and after ALFRED THE GREAT's peace of WEDMORE, it was ruled by the ealdorman Ethelred. In the 11th century, CNUT created a large Mercian EARLDOM for LEOFRIC, which lasted until shortly after the NORMAN CONQUEST.

Merciless Parliament, the name given to the Parliament of Feb. 1388. After their victory at RADCOT BRIDGE, the APPELLANTS used their domination of Parliament to convict a group of RICHARD II's friends of treason. Nicholas Brembre and Chief Justice Tresilian were executed; others were exiled.

Merk, *see* MARK

Merlin (Myrddin), Arthurian figure. He first appeared as the wizard at the court of King ARTHUR in the 12th-century writings of GEOFFREY OF MONMOUTH, although, in an interpolated text of the supposedly 6th-century poem *GODODDIN* and in Welsh bardic tradition, there are references to a Myrddin who was an adviser to kings. Like Arthur, Merlin may be based on someone who actually lived in the 6th century, but the historical basis of Geoffrey's Merlin is flimsy and the modern Merlin of CAMELOT is pure legend.

Methodism The term 'Methodist' seems to have been used first in the 17th century as a jocular label for those leading a highly-structured devotional life, and in this sense it was applied to the 'Holy Club' established in the 1720s by a group of Oxford undergraduates, principal among them Charles Wesley; his elder brother John joined it and came to dominate it. By extension the name was applied to a variety of forms of 18th-century EVANGELICALISM, but as disagreements arose between the ARMINIAN Wesleys and the CALVINIST George Whitefield it came to be used exclusively for those who were directly influenced by John WESLEY. Wesley's movement, or 'Connexion', was characterized by tight organization of his followers into societies of members, grouped into circuits, with itinerant full-time preachers (meeting in an annual Conference from 1744) under his direct control.

After Wesley's death (1791) the absence of his powerful personality and the ambiguity of his future intentions led to increasing quarrels among his followers, particularly about the role of his Conference of preachers. Conference took on the government of 'Wesleyan' Methodism, and a series of schisms created new bodies, usually calling themselves Connexions, in imitation of the Wesleyan Connexion, and in conscious opposition to it. Matters were made worse by the personal dominance among the Wesleyans of the Rev. Jabez Bunting (1779–1858), a TORY autocrat who aroused much antagonism, but who nevertheless had a genius for organization at a time when Wesleyanism was administratively in chaos. Latent behind the many esoteric quarrels about church government were social tensions between the middle-class clerical leadership of Wesleyanism and the socially more humble elements, often lay people, who wished to embrace the dramatic missionary methods of Revivalism. Early 19th-century Methodism was therefore characterized both by extreme quarrelsomeness and continuing missionary vigour and expansion.

From the mid-19th century, tensions decreased among the Methodist Connexions, and the social distinctions between their leaderships lessened. The Wesleyans (increasingly alarmed at the growth of the OXFORD MOVEMENT in the Church of England) reluctantly accepted the reality of their permanent separation from ANGLICANISM, and took on the character of a FREE CHURCH, like the other Connexions; this included a general shift in political sympathies from their characteristic Toryism to the LIBERAL PARTY. A series of reunions took place, hastened by financial difficulties among the smaller Connexions, culminating in the major reunion of 1932. Repeated attempts from the 1960s to the 1980s to heal the original split with the Church of England came near to success, but foundered on a consistent opposition of a minority of Anglican clergy, mostly ANGLO-CATHOLICS.

CHRONOLOGY

1784 John Wesley's first ordinations. He

declares by deed that 100 members of Conference (to be replaced when necessary) will be his legal successor.
1795 'Plan of Pacification' seeks to end disputes about whether Methodist societies should celebrate holy communion separately from parish churches; societies can decide for themselves.
1797 METHODIST NEW CONNEXION secedes.
1807 First Revivalist meeting held at Mow Cop, Staffs., by Hugh Bourne; Conference furious.
1810 Conference expels William O'Bryan from Methodist membership for freelance preaching.
1812 Bourne and William Clowes, expelled by Conference, form Society of Primitive Methodists.
1815 O'Bryan forms Bible Christian Society, based mainly in Devon and Cornwall.
1827 Protestant Methodists secede in protest at Conference backing the installation of an organ in Brunswick Chapel, Leeds, against local opposition.
1835 Proposals to found a theological college arouse fears of clericalism: secession of Wesleyan Methodist Association results.
1842 First Wesleyan theological college opens, Didsbury, Manchester.
1846–8 Vitriolic anonymous attacks on Wesleyan leaders, the *Fly Sheets*, associated with earlier attacks by James Everett.
1849 Wesleyan Conference expels Everett and his associates. Everett forms Church of the Wesleyan Reformers. Serious temporary losses to Wesleyan membership.
1857 Wesleyan Reformers unite with Protestant Methodists as United Methodist Free Churches.
1907 Methodist New Connexion, Bible Christians and United Methodist Free Churches join as the United Methodist Church.
1932 Wesleyan Methodist, Primitive Methodist and United Methodist Churches unite as the Methodist Church of Great Britain.
1950–60s Official Anglican-Methodist conversations about reunion taking place.
1969 Anglican CONVOCATIONS fail to reach required majority for reunion scheme.
1974 First women ordained ministers.
1982 Anglican General Synod fails to reach required majority for Covenanting scheme for reunion.

Methodist New Connexion, also known as 'Kilhamite Methodists', named after Alexander Kilham, who in 1791 attacked the METHODIST Conference for allowing too small a role to the laity. A Plan of Pacification (1795) allowed the laity power at the level of the meeting only, and not in the decision-making at Conference. Kilham himself, expelled from the Conference, in 1797 formed a 'New Connexion' with more democratic organization and without ties to the Established Church. Kilham's New Connexion Chapel in Sheffield was well attended. He was accused of JACOBINism, and his followers were sometimes called 'Tom PAINE Methodists', but he denied any political motive. In 1907, the Connexion joined with Bible Christians and the United Methodist Free Churches to form the United Methodist Church.

Methuen Treaties, May, Dec. 1703. The first treaty brought Portugal into the Grand Alliance confronting France, Spain and Bavaria in the War of the SPANISH SUCCESSION. The effect was to commit England to an expansion of the war to the Spanish peninsula. The second allowed English cloth free access to markets in Portugal; in return, Portuguese wines were to bear significantly lower duties than French. This treaty helped Britain maintain a balance of trade during the war; British economic ascendancy in Portugal was maintained into the 19th century.

Metropolitan Board of Works, governing body for London between 1855 and the creation of the LONDON COUNTY COUNCIL in 1889. A myriad of over 300 local bodies – parish vestries, district boards, commissioners of sewers – together with the City of LONDON and SHIRE officials for Middlesex, Kent and Surrey, had been unable to run an ever-growing London effectively. The new Board, elected by the City, vestries and district boards, was the first entity to govern built-up London as a whole. Its main remit was ROADS and sewers, and the completion of 81 miles of main sewers, together with the construction of bridges and the Thames-side Embankment, were its principal achievements.

Metropolitan Police Act 1829 The Act replaced the medieval and Elizabethan law-enforcement system with a professional uniformed and preventative POLICE force for the metropolis (excluding the City of London) under the authority of two commissioners and the home secretary. The creation of the metropolitan police force – known as 'Peelers' or 'Bobbies' after the then home secretary – enhanced PEEL's reputation as an enlightened reformer. Its effects upon criminal activity remain conjectural.

Metropolitan Water Board Constituted by special Act in 1902, it consisted of 60 members and was responsible for the water supply of the metropolis. £42 million was paid in compensation to the water companies absorbed.

MI5, the British security system started by Vernon Kells in 1905, who headed it until his official retirement in 1924 – but in reality probably until 1940. Formed as Division 5 of the British Directorate of Military Intelligence, since 1916 it has been responsible for counter-espionage within and outside Britain, including the surveillance of groups deemed to be subversive, such as Communists and Fascists before 1939, and subsequently members of what are considered to be extremist organizations of the right or left. Although a significant arm of the state – the head of MI5 reports to the home secretary – MI5 has, until very recently, been cloaked in secrecy. Unable to make arrests, the organization works closely with Scotland Yard's Special Branch, which is empowered to do so.

MI6 Originally formed as Division 6 of the British Directorate of Military Intelligence, responsible for espionage outside Britain as a complement to MI5, it is in part a descendant of Francis WALSINGHAM's intelligence service in the 16th century. It has been in operation since 1911 when it was set up by Capt. Mansfield Cumming. Cumming used his initial 'C' to identify himself to his agents and heads of MI6 have called themselves 'C' ever since. MI6 was considered to have been successful during WORLD WAR I, but two of its operatives were kidnapped by the Germans at the start of WORLD WAR II and major responsibility for covert operations in Nazi-occupied Europe was not given to MI6 in 1940 but rather to a newly established SPECIAL OPERATIONS EXECUTIVE (SOE). During the COLD WAR MI6 was particularly concerned with the USSR and one of its successes was its information-gathering exercise with Colonel Oleg Penkovsky. He was executed by the Soviet authorities in 1963, the same year that Kim Philby defected to the Soviet Union claiming that during all the years he had worked for MI6 he had been spying for Russia. A reorganization of the service followed.

Middlesex Election, 1768–9, *cause célèbre* which helped to stimulate agitation for PARLIAMENTARY REFORM. John WILKES was elected for Middlesex in the general election of 1768, but in Feb. 1769 he was expelled for libel. Despite a parliamentary decision that his conduct made it impossible for him to take his seat (a decision which, given the precedent of *ASHBY V. WHITE*, could not be challenged in a court of law) the Middlesex electors three times re-elected him. On the third occasion, PARLIAMENT seated his opponent, Henry Lawes Luttrell, although Luttrell had received only 296 votes to Wilkes' 1,143. Critics of parliament claimed that its actions showed contempt for the manifest wishes of the electorate and therefore demonstrated the need for it to be made more accountable.

Midwives Act 1934 sought to improve the quality of care for pregnant women, following an outcry over the continued high rate of MORTALITY through childbirth. The Act provided for trained midwives to attend at births, and led to a fall in maternal mortality by the late 1930s.

Migration All the countries of the British Isles have traditionally been net losers of POPULATION through emigration since records began, and all – particularly England – have always been characterized by high levels of internal migration. Studies looking at periods from the 16th century onwards have shown both the rarity of a person spending the whole of his or her life in one community, and the frequency of movement, especially in youth (*see* APPRENTICESHIP; SERVANTS). Before the 18th century towns could usually only maintain their population, let alone grow as rapidly as they did, by sustained inward migration, while the rapid growth of industrial centres in the 19th century or the depopulation of some rural areas have largely been the effect of migration. *See also* SETTLEMENT ACTS.

From the late 16th century, the PLANTATIONS IN IRELAND and the NEW WORLD colonies resulted in emigration from Britain. The Scots plantation of ULSTER and the trade in INDENTURED SERVANTS of the 17th century are notable examples of this, while refugees from the Low Countries and, after 1685, HUGUENOT Protestants from France formed the principal incoming groups, frequently bringing important industrial and commercial skills with them. The flow overseas increased in the 18th and 19th centuries with the opening of new colonies, especially the USA, CANADA, AUSTRALIA and NEW ZEALAND. The effects of the POTATO FAMINE and poverty in Ireland caused the largest of all these migrations, many people coming to the British mainland, more going to other continents. The principal immigrant groups of the later 19th century were Russian and East European Jews.

Emigration to the traditional destinations has continued through the 20th century, while the most noticeable feature of immigration has been the arrival since the 1950s of substantial numbers from the Caribbean, the Indian sub-continent, and other parts of the COMMONWEALTH. Curbs on immigration have been imposed since the 1960s (*see* COMMONWEALTH IMMIGRANTS ACT), which have been portrayed by their critics as particularly harsh towards immigrants from the 'new' Commonwealth.

Militia Its origin (from *miles*, a soldier) was Anglo-Saxon (*see* ARMY; WARFARE, LAND). The 1181 Assize of Arms laid down regulations requiring all freemen to serve in defence of their locality, and the 1285 Statute of Winchester defined responsibilities under the SHERIFF. This system was changed by MARY I in 1558, placing the militia under the new post of LORD LIEUTENANT of the county. At the start of CHARLES II's reign three Militia Acts (1661–3) established the legality of the militia under the ultimate authority of the king. Thereafter service in the militia (together with its cavalry equivalent, the yeomanry) evolved to become essentially voluntary, except in times of threatened invasion when a ballot might be needed, as with the deeply unpopular 1757 Militia Act. Militarily broadly ineffective throughout its existence, and never required to repel an invasion, the militia's importance was in local politics and as a regional 'constitutional force' to balance the STANDING ARMY. The 1852 Militia Act finally placed the militia under the secretary for war. It was supplemented by a variety of 'fencibles' during the NAPOLEONIC WARS and by the Rifle Volunteers after the 1859 invasion scare, and in 1881 militia regiments were each attached to regular regiments of their own county. The militia ceased to exist under the 1907 Territorial and Reserve Forces Act, being absorbed into the Territorial Force (*see* TERRITORIAL ARMY).

Mill, John Stuart (1806–73), philosopher and social reformer. A leader and prophet of BENTHAMite UTILITARIANISM, very much in the mould of his father, the philosopher James Mill (1773–1836), he modified his views following a mental breakdown and developed a broader and more humanized version of utilitarianism which acknowledged differences in the quality as well as the quantity of happiness and incorporated idealistic and cultural values. The most influential of his books, *On Liberty* (1859), *Considerations on Representative Government* (1861) and *Utilitarianism* (1863), were concerned to defend individual freedom against both governmental control and popular pressure in a democracy. His belief in the extension of the FRANCHISE, a system of proportional representation, his support for local representative bodies, and workers' involvement in decision-making in industry, had less to do with an abstract notion of 'rights' than with trying to find under what conditions representative democracy was possible. He was convinced of the educative role of political participation which better trained people to become citizens rather than subjects, and thus better able to avoid the 'tyranny of the majority', which Mill saw as the danger of mass democracy. He credited his wife, Harriet Taylor, with co-authorship of all his works other than his early philosophical *The System of Logic* (1843), and *The Subjection of Women* (1869), a more controversial work, remains a founding text of feminism. Mill had practical experience of politics: he was a CIVIL SERVANT in the India office for most of his life, and was RADICAL MP for Westminster (1865–8).

Millenarianism (from the Latin *mille*, 'thousand'), the belief (inspired by various biblical references) that – in the near future, before time ceases – a chosen people will rule the earth for 1,000 years of blessedness.

Naturally attractive for the disorientated and those without much other worldly hope, millenarian movements have recurred throughout Jewish, Christian and Islamic history, and they were widespread in mainstream British PROTESTANTISM during the upheavals of the REFORMATION in the 16th and 17th centuries. The disturbance caused by the FRENCH REVOLUTION brought a similar outburst (for example, the prophetess, Joanna Southcott, 1750–1814). After a sad little Kentish revolt in 1838 led by 'Sir William Courtenay', a deranged conman, millenarianism ceased to have political significance, although the idea still excites fringe religious groups.

Milton, John (1608–74), poet and writer. Son of a minor composer, he was already writing accomplished poetry while at Cambridge. During the CIVIL WARS, he wrote with increasing radicalism on politics and (not least as a result of personal circumstances) advocated the free availability of DIVORCE; he also published pamphlets defending free speech and attacking the growing cult of CHARLES I. From 1649 to 1660, he was Latin secretary to the COUNCIL OF STATE, despite increasing blindness. Briefly imprisoned at the RESTORATION, he used his years of political disgrace to write some of his greatest poetry, including the final version of *Paradise Lost* (finished 1663), *Paradise Regained* and *Samson Agonistes* (both 1671).

Milton Keynes, new city in Bucks., founded in 1967, and the largest product of the NEW TOWN movement. It was based upon an ancient village already bearing the name, and was not called, as is sometimes thought, after two giants of English literature and economics.

Mineral and Battery Works and **Mines Royal,** two companies given a royal charter in 1565 and 1568 to manufacture brass sheet and wire and copper respectively. Their official backing arose from the government's concern to foster the armaments industry and to cut down on imports. They were the first English companies set up for the manufacture of a product, rather than for trading goods.

Mines Act 1842 Passed in the wake of the Royal Commission on Children's Employment in Mines and Manufacturies, the Act prohibited the employment underground of boys below the age of ten and of women and girls. The absence of limitations on the hours of labour and of provision for proper inspection have long been noted; the gendered nature of the legislation and its effects on women workers have recently begun to receive attention.

Mines Royal, *see* MINERAL AND BATTERY WORKS

Ministers of the Crown Act 1937, *see* CABINET; PRIME MINISTER

Ministry of All the Talents, 1806–7. The death of PITT THE YOUNGER in 1806 left no single political leader or grouping in the ascendant. GEORGE III offered the Treasury to Lord Grenville, accepting the admission to office of Grenville's ally, Charles James FOX. Some posts were given to the Carlton House set attached to the Prince of Wales (later GEORGE IV), others to followers of Sidmouth (*see* ADDINGTON, HENRY). The NAPOLEONIC WAR was inevitably the ministry's main concern. The conflicting views of its members hampered initiative on other fronts: Fox had agreed not to press for PARLIAMENTARY REFORM; Sidmouth opposed CATHOLIC EMANCIPATION. The major legislative success was the abolition of SLAVERY in 1807 (*see* ANTI-SLAVERY). Weakened by the death of Fox in Sept. 1806, the ministers fell out with the king over their desire to respond to Irish pressure with a further extension of Catholic emancipation, and he dismissed them.

Ministry of Munitions, new ministry created in May 1915 after the formation of a coalition government led by ASQUITH. The ministry was headed by LLOYD GEORGE and intended to overcome the shortages of munitions which had led to criticism of Asquith's LIBERAL government during the spring in the SHELLS SCANDAL. Lloyd George brought energy and drive to the task, securing DILUTION agreements with the TRADE UNIONS and greatly accelerating arms production. He was succeeded by Edward Montagu in July 1916, then by Christopher Addison and CHURCHILL in succession. The ministry was renamed the ministry of supply in 1919 and eventually abolished in 1921. A key administrative innovation, it gave Britain a much more committed war effort at a vital stage in WORLD WAR I.

Minor Orders, *see* ORDER

Minsters Churches known as minsters were the earliest form of pastoral organization in the ANGLO-SAXON Church after the CONVERSION. Served by groups of priests or monks – the distinction is sometimes impossible to make in the early centuries (*see* MONASTICISM) – they supplied places of religious ministry that were often responsible for large geographical areas. The development of local churches and a system of PARISH churches in the 10th century began the decline of the minster's role, which was largely complete by the 12th century. Their former importance is shown by such place names as Wimborne Minster (Dorset) and Leominster (Herefords.); by the way in which the term is still sometimes attached to CATHEDRAL churches such as York minster and Lincoln minster; and by the existence of especially large rural churches with Anglo-Saxon features, such as King's Sutton, near Banbury, Oxon.

Mint, *see* COINS AND COINAGE

Mints, Anglo-Saxon The relatively small number of mints producing COIN in the 7th and 8th centuries had grown to around 60 by the year 1000, after the kings of the previous century decided to establish one in every major *BURH*. The mints were integrated into a structure whereby the dies for each recoinage (*see RENOVATIO MONETÉ*) were designed centrally. Some mints were served by several moneyers (individuals who made the coins) who paid heavily for the privilege of minting. The organization involved is generally seen as testimony to the administrative effectiveness of the late Anglo-Saxon state.

Missionaries, Anglo-Saxon At certain periods, missionary activity on the Continent was a very important aspect of the work of the Anglo-Saxon Church. This is particularly true of the 8th century, when St BONIFACE and several others were exceptionally active in Germany, and the late 10th and early 11th centuries, when English churchmen played a major part in the conversion of Scandinavia. It is certainly true to say that the spread of Christianity accomplished by these individuals had a major impact on western European history; their role in extending CAROLINGIAN rule eastwards was, for example, very important in bringing together the lands which later formed Germany.

Missionary Societies When European great powers began acquiring colonial empires outside Europe at the end of the 15th century, the official Church was not slow to begin mission work among the peoples encountered. This was undertaken largely by religious orders, particularly the FRIARS and, later, the JESUITS. England was late on the colonial scene after the Catholic empires of Spain and Portugal, and at first English Protestants did not make much effort to undertake missions, for instance on the frontiers of their colonies in North America. They could not directly imitate Catholic methods, since they had no monks or friars to undertake the work, and when a systematic effort was made to begin missions at the end of the 17th century, it took the characteristic contemporary form of voluntary lay societies (*see also* REFORMATION OF MANNERS MOVEMENT). The first societies involved were dominated by HIGH CHURCH ANGLICANS: the SOCIETY FOR THE PROMOTION OF CHRISTIAN KNOWLEDGE, which worked with Danish and German missionaries in southern INDIA from 1710, and the SOCIETY FOR THE PROPAGATION OF THE GOSPEL, which sent missionaries to North America, and once, in 1742, to West Africa. Missionary zeal flourished in the 1790s, in the context of the rise of NEW DISSENT, and the MILLENARIAN climate associated with the French Revolution. The Particular BAPTIST Missionary Society was founded in 1792, the London Missionary Society (at first interdenominational, later CONGREGATIONALIST) in 1795, the (METHODIST) Wesleyan Missionary Society in 1813; the BRITISH AND FOREIGN BIBLE SOCIETY, founded in 1804, still maintains its work of bible translation and distribution on a strictly interdenominational basis (*see also* BIBLE SOCIETIES). Though many of the established Churches were wary of missionary enthusiasm, the (CHURCH OF SCOTLAND) Scottish Missionary Society was set up in 1796, and the (Anglican) Church Missionary Society in 1799, under EVANGEL-

ICAL influence. From the 1840s, the dramatic journeys in Africa of David LIVINGSTONE, a self-educated Scots missionary at first working for the LMS, aroused great enthusiasm in England; and consequently in 1857, ANGLO-CATHOLICS overcame previous hesitations and founded the Universities Mission to Central Africa (united with the SPG to form the United Society for the Propagation of the Gospel, 1965). An extraordinary initiative was the single-handed founding of the interdenominational China Inland Mission by James Hudson Taylor (1865); this quickly outstripped all other missionary organizations working there. During the early 20th century, missionary societies were pioneers in Christian ECUMENICISM. Consistently, such missionary work has had little impact on the other great world faiths, such as Islam, Buddhism and Hinduism, particularly among their élites, but many indigenous churches flourish in Africa and North and South America as a result of missionary work; some now even undertake missions to Britain.

Mistery, a skilled craft, often regulated in medieval towns by a GUILD. Such guilds often contributed a play to a town cycle of religious drama apparently usually performed on Corpus Christi day: hence such cycles are known as 'mistery plays' (a more accurate reflection of their nature than the potentially misleading 'mystery plays').

Mob, a contraction of the Latin *mobile vulgus* the 'fickle multitude'. The term caught on from the 1690s, sometimes being used to describe riotous crowds, but also simply to mean 'the common people', and was less pejorative in tone than the earlier dominant and near-equivalent 'rabble'. The term 'mobility' was also occasionally used by analogy with 'nobility'. Historical research in the 1960s and 1970s by E. P. Thompson, George Rudé, Eric Hobsbawm and others looked at the order and thought behind crowd actions in the late 18th century and suggested that the use of the term mob was misleading.

Moderates, Scots PRESBYTERIANS claiming to favour moderation in KIRK politics – as opposed to the more dogmatically orthodox 'Popular' or EVANGELICAL party. The term refers especially to the group who emerged under the leadership of William Robertson from 1750. Initially comprising ministers and lay elders dismayed by the refusal of recalcitrant congregations to accept whatever ministers patrons appointed, the Moderates became associated with efforts to reconcile Presbyterianism, with 'politeness' and the Enlightenment.

Modernism, Religious, a term used in Roman Catholic circles at the close of the 19th century to denote the thinking of those who sought to assimilate traditional teaching to the new disciplines of science and historical and literary criticism. Modernism was the Catholic analogue of Protestant LIBERALISM. *See also* CATHOLIC LIBERALISM.

Mods, name given to stylistic youth group of the 1960s, characterized by short hair-cuts, suits, and motorscooters. The Mods achieved some notoriety for clashes with motorcycle gangs of ROCKERS at holiday resorts in southern England during the decade.

Modus Tenendi Parliamentum ('The Manner of Holding PARLIAMENT'), an early 14th-century lawyers' manual describing parliamentary procedure. Its great emphasis on the importance of KNIGHTS OF THE SHIRE – asserting that, on questions of taxation, they 'have a greater voice than the greatest earl in England' – once caused some scholars to deny its authenticity.

Monasteries, Dissolution of the, *see* DISSOLUTION OF THE MONASTERIES

Monasticism, the specialized religious discipline which seeks to refine and deepen experience of God by renouncing certain aspects of ordinary human life. Characteristically, monks, nuns and FRIARS take vows of poverty, chastity and obedience. Monasticism originated in late 3rd-century Egypt, and by the 4th century it had developed two main forms: the life of an individual in a completely solitary existence (as a hermit), and life in a community according to agreed customs and rules (coenobitic life). There were already monastic communities in southern Europe by the 4th century, and in Britain certainly by the 5th (*see also* CULDEES).

EARLY ENGLISH

The monasteries founded after the CONVERSION OF THE ENGLISH TO CHRISTIANITY were notable for their diversity. The Rule of St Benedict, although well known in England in the 7th century, did not become the normal form of monastic organization until the 10th (*see* BENEDICTINE MONASTICISM; TENTH-CENTURY REFORM). Monasteries such as WHITBY and LINDISFARNE were strongly influenced by Irish practice (*see below*), whereas JARROW and MONKWEARMOUTH drew their inspiration from Mediterranean models. It was often difficult to distinguish between communities living under a Rule and those performing pastoral work (*see* MINSTERS). Some communities were very large, whereas others were small family concerns whose corruption was condemned by BEDE. The great majority of them were all destroyed or abandoned as a result of the VIKING attacks.

EARLY IRISH

It differed from the Mediterranean Benedictine variety by its emphasis on a monk's solitary, rather than communal, life. The great period of monastic growth in Ireland took place in the second half of the 6th century, when large monastic confederations (*paruchia*) developed under the Rule of such inspirational abbots as St COLUMBA. These *paruchia* became very important in Irish ecclesiastical and political life, supplanting the bishoprics as centres of religious authority.

Many monasteries were also centres of learning (*see BOOK OF KELLS*), and their influence was deeply felt in the conversion of the English to Christianity and of the PICTS (*see* ALDHELM; IONA; LINDISFARNE; WHITBY). The weakness of Irish monasticism stemmed from monasteries being, in certain respects, extensions of kindred groupings; they were therefore often plundered in feuds between rival families (*see* KINGSHIP).

Monck, George (1st Duke of Albemarle) (1608–70), soldier and royal servant. A professional soldier, Monck (or Monk) fought for the king until captured in 1644 (*see* CIVIL WARS). Then, from 1647, he accepted PARLIAMENTARY commands, proving unbeatable in Ireland, Scotland and, transferred to naval command, the 1652–4 DUTCH WARS, winning CROMWELL's great trust.

In the mounting confusion of 1659, Monck's exasperated intervention with his northern garrison troops proved decisive: marching south in Nov. without making his purposes clear, he attracted a bewildering variety of future hopes. He ordered the unpurged LONG PARLIAMENT's reinstatement; spurning offers of supreme power, he opened negotiations with CHARLES II and secured his RESTORATION. Predictably loaded with honours, Monck retained military influence, playing an active role afloat in the later Dutch Wars, but kept out of politics and did not let his PRESBYTERIAN sympathies interfere with the ANGLICAN turnaround in the Church.

Mond–Turner Talks, discussions on industrial co-operation held in 1928 between the TRADES UNION CONGRESS (TUC) and leading industrialists, taking their name from the TUC chairman, Ben Turner, and the chairman of Imperial Chemical Industries, Sir Alfred Mond, whose initiative they were. Following the defeat of the GENERAL STRIKE and the passing of the TRADE DISPUTES AND TRADE UNIONS ACT 1927, influential union leaders such as BEVIN and CITRINE sought a more consensual approach and persuaded the TUC to take part. Though there was little direct outcome, the talks pointed the way to less militant and more collaborative industrial relations in the following decades.

Moneyed Interest, term employed from the early 18th century, especially by TORY propagandists such as SWIFT, to denote those (notably stockholders in the WHIG-dominated BANK OF ENGLAND and EAST INDIA COMPANY) whose investments in government funds supposedly gave them reasons to favour the continuance of the War of the SPANISH SUCCESSION, consequent government borrowing, and by implication the high taxes necessary to service the public debt. It is questionable whether investors ever formed quite so coherent an interest group. By the 1740s, if not earlier, many small investors had invested in government stock, or had an interest in it via insurance, pension funds or the like. The RADICAL critic of 'old corruption', John Wade, in his 1833 *Black Book*, explicitly recognized this: though critical of the 'funding system', he urged the importance of keeping faith with small investors.

Monitorial System, teaching system developed in the early 19th century by Andrew Bell and Joseph Lancaster, and applied by the National Society for Promoting the Education of the Poor in the Principles of the Church of England and the BRITISH AND

FOREIGN BIBLE SOCIETY. It relied upon grouping pupils by ability and the diffusion of knowledge downwards from the top group who, having benefited from instruction by a teacher, would divide to teach the students in the lower classes. The system, praised for its low-cost efficiency, was also thought to encourage the discipline and orderliness required of an industrial workforce, and was subsequently applied to public sector elementary schooling. *See also* EDUCATION; PUPIL-TEACHER SYSTEM.

Monk, George, *see* MONCK, GEORGE

Monkwearmouth This monastery in Northumb. (now Tyne & Wear) was founded by Benedict Biscop in 674 along with the neighbouring contemporary foundation JARROW. Together they constituted one of the most important religious centres of early ANGLO-SAXON England. Both houses were constructed in a style that owed something to Mediterranean architecture – part of the west front of the original Monkwearmouth church survives – and were furnished by their founder with fine libraries; their most famous early inmate was BEDE. The community at Monkwearmouth, dispersed during the VIKING attacks, was re-established in the 11th century. *See also CODEX AMIATINUS.*

Monmouth, 1st Duke of, *see* SCOTT, JAMES

Monmouth, Geoffrey of, *see* GEOFFREY OF MONMOUTH

Monmouth's Rebellion, *see* SCOTT, JAMES

Monopolies, licences by LETTERS PATENT granting exclusive rights in trade or manufacture to individuals or companies. In the 16th and early 17th centuries, the crown abused the system as a cheap way to reward courtiers at other people's expense. Despite ELIZABETH I's soothing replies to furious criticism in the 1597 and 1601 PARLIAMENTS, JAMES I and CHARLES I continued to misuse monopoly grants. Abolition by the LONG PARLIAMENT followed although the big trading companies (LEVANT and EAST INDIA) continued to exercise monopolies after this. In the late 19th and 20th centuries, monopolies have emerged in several sections of industry and in public utilities provision as a result of merger movements. This has resulted in the government establishing the Monopolies and Mergers Commission (MMC) which is charged with investigating industries with monopolistic structures. The minister of trade and industry may refer cases for investigation where a single firm controls 25 per cent or more of the supply of a particular good. Some monopolies occur because of the technology of production and economies of scale: in this case the dominance of an industry by a single firm may not be contrary to the public interest. Others may be the result of deliberate suppression of competitors by predatory practices and these may be more clearly against the public interest.

Mons, Battle of, Belgium, 23 Aug. 1914, the first clash between the BRITISH EXPEDITIONARY FORCE and the Germans at the start of WORLD WAR I, and the first British battle against a European enemy since the CRIMEAN WAR. Although greatly outnumbered and forced to retreat, the high fighting qualities of the BEF under Sir John FRENCH imposed the first check on the Germans and helped pave the way for the Battle of the MARNE a month later.

Mons Graupius, Battle of, AD 84. The Roman governor AGRICOLA gained a spectacular victory over an army of Highland tribesmen (*see* CALEDONII), which, according to TACITUS, may have numbered 30,000 men. The battle had no significant long-term results because 20,000 of the Highlanders escaped and the Romans soon abandoned any attempt to control the Highlands (*see* INCHTUTHIL). The site of the battlefield has never been convincingly identified.

Montagu–Chelmsford Reforms, reforms of Indian government based on the report of the secretary of state for India, Edwin Montagu (1879–1924), and Lord Chelmsford (1868–1933), viceroy of India (1916–21), and embodied in the India Act of 1919. The reforms led to the establishment of a bicameral parliament for all INDIA, enjoying partially responsible powers of government. The legislature, however, could not remove the executive and could not prevent the viceroy from governing by emergency decree. Similarly, in the provinces the permanent British officials retained control over major areas of activity or 'reserved subjects', and only some aspects were controlled by elected bodies. This system of partial self-government was criticized in the SIMON COMMISSION's report of 1930 and amended by the India Act of 1935.

Monte Cassino, Battle of, central Italy, Oct. 1943–May 1944. The 5th-century monastery of Monte Cassino, built high in the mountains south of Rome, was the key position of the 'Gustav Line' held by the Germans under Field Marshal Albert Kesselring during the Italian campaign of WORLD WAR II. A scene of very bitter fighting, it was attacked repeatedly by the Allied armies under ALEXANDER, including American, British, INDIAN, NEW ZEALAND and French troops. The monastery itself, a priceless historical monument, was destroyed by bombing on 15 Feb. 1944. On 18 May it was finally captured by Polish troops and the Gustav Line broken, enabling the allies to advance toward Rome, which was liberated on 4 June.

Montfort, Simon de (6th Earl of Leicester) (*c.*1208–65), statesman and soldier. One of the most controversial of politicians: so hated by his opponents that they killed him and dismembered his body; so passionately admired by his supporters that his grave in Evesham Abbey attracted pilgrims and reports of miracles.

Younger son of the Simon de Montfort who led the Albigensian crusade, he came to England from France in 1230. The following year, his claim to the earldom of Leicester was allowed, and he immediately expelled the JEWS from that city. In 1238, he married HENRY III's sister Eleanor. While on CRUSADE (1240–1), in Poitou (1242) and as seneschal of GASCONY (1248–52), he acquired a reputation as a soldier; he also developed a number of financial grievances against the king and a growing contempt for Henry's ability.

De Montfort became one of the moving spirits of the political revolution of 1258, helped to frame the PROVISIONS OF OXFORD and, more than any of his peers, was determined to abide by the terms of those Provisions. In 1261, when others acquiesced in the king's resumption of power, he withdrew to France. Two years later, and with dissatisfaction with Henry once more widespread, de Montfort's uncompromising record made him the natural leader of the reform movement. Since, when at bay, his instinct was to fight rather than negotiate, this led directly to the rejection of the mise of AMIENS and the outbreak of civil war. His aggressive generalship won the battle of LEWES in May 1264, and with both king and heir to the throne in his custody, he became *de facto* ruler.

He adopted policies designed to appeal to the GENTRY and, in an attempt to legitimize his regime, summoned both KNIGHTS and BURGESSES to a PARLIAMENT in Jan. 1265 – hence the 19th-century view of him as the founder of the House of COMMONS. But his use of government patronage to enrich his family made him vulnerable – both then and since – to the charge that he was ultimately self-seeking. This, together with his unyielding confidence in his own rectitude, exasperated his peers.

The future EDWARD I's escape from custody signalled the end of de Montfort's grip on power, yet he kept the loyalty of his followers right to the bitter end at EVESHAM in Aug. 1265. However mixed his motives may have been, he was widely regarded as a champion of liberty and political reform by, among others, the outstanding English churchmen of the day.

Montgomery, Bernard (Monty) (1st Viscount Montgomery of El Alamein) (1887–1976), Field Marshal. Son of a bishop, commissioned into the Royal Warwickshire Regiment in 1908, he was severely wounded at YPRES in Oct. 1914 at the start of WORLD WAR I, and had risen to command a battalion at the war's end. Between the wars he attended various military colleges, establishing a reputation as an obsessive and opinionated but highly professional soldier. In WORLD WAR II he commanded the 3rd Division of the BRITISH EXPEDITIONARY FORCE with distinction under BROOKE during the retreat and evacuation from DUNKIRK in 1940. Marked for high command by both Brooke and CHURCHILL, when ALEXANDER replaced Auchinleck in the Middle East in summer 1942, the chance death of another general in an air crash gave him command of the Eighth Army. His victories at Alam Halfa and EL ALAMEIN, although costly, did much to restore Britain's prestige. At the end of the war in North Africa in July 1943 he commanded Eighth Army in Sicily and Italy, and in Dec. 1943 was appointed to command the Allied land forces for the D-DAY invasion under Eisenhower.

A charismatic figure, Montgomery's fighting methods – emphasizing morale and a massive superiority over the enemy in firepower – were appropriate to conscript forces in mass industrialized war, but proved controversial in Normandy for their slowness. Promoted to field marshal in Sept. 1944, he confounded his critics with the speed of his advance across France, but overreached himself at ARNHEM, his only major defeat. Vain and egotistical, his behaviour inspired either fierce loyalty or equally fierce disdain in those who knew him. Although he led his armies to victory in 1945, he was remembered as much for his rivalries and arguments with other commanders, notably the Americans, as for his battles.

In 1946 Montgomery succeeded Brooke as chief of the imperial general staff. He also served (1951–8) as deputy supreme commander of NATO in Europe.

Montrose, 5th Earl and 1st Marquess of, *see* GRAHAM, JAMES

Montserrat, British dependent territory in the eastern Caribbean. The island was settled by Roman Catholics from nearby ST KITTS and religious refugees from VIRGINIA and IRELAND in the 1640s. The then-prosperous SUGAR economy was disrupted by slave rebellions in 1768 and by French invasions which ceased with the Treaty of VERSAILLES in 1783 when the island became a British possession. It has been a British Dependent Territory with internal self government since 1960.

Moral Economy, a term originally employed by early 19th-century critics of the nascent science of political economy, which was adopted and popularized by the historian E. P. Thompson, initially in an article of 1971. He employed the term to denote a vision of how economic relations should work, involving 'a consistent traditional view of social norms and obligations, of the proper economic functions of the several parties within the community'; and he applied it especially to ideas and practices associated with the regulation of trade in grain (*see* PRICE-FIXING).

'ENGROSSING', 'forestalling' and 'regrating' were offences at COMMON LAW, yet many farmers and merchants preferred the profits available through the bulk-sale of foodstuffs (perhaps to distant and even foreign parts) to those available from sale to local consumers in public markets. This often left local people with too little grain at too high a price. At times of dearth in the 16th–18th centuries, the PRIVY COUNCIL or local MAGISTRATES sometimes encouraged prosecutions, to protect consumer interests; when they did not, consumers sometimes took the law into their own hands, attacking the grain warehouses of traders and middlemen and sometimes selling the grain to local consumers at what was regarded as a 'just price'. In Thompson's view, in so doing they were defending a traditional 'moral economy', although proponents of unfettered trade did not see themselves as immoral. However, from the mid-18th century it was increasingly argued that interference with the market did more harm than good. *See also* GRAIN RIOTS.

Moravianism, Protestant sect which emerged from the Hussite wars in 15th-century Bohemia. Formally titled *Unitas Fratrum*, they broke with the papacy at their first synod in 1467. They sought to recapture the spirit and practice of the apostolic church, practising puritanical discipline and emphasizing good works. In the 18th century Count Nicholas Ludwig von Zinzendorf organized a Moravian settlement at Herrnhut. They began missionary activities in 1731, establishing a settlement near Leeds. In 1737, the archbishop of Canterbury declared the validity of Moravian ORDERS. They influenced John WESLEY and many aspects of METHODIST practice, including lay preaching, the band system, hymn singing and love nights.

Moray, region in Scotland north of the River Dee that was long ruled by kings – e.g. MACBETH – then by men whom the Scottish kings preferred to call *mormaers* ('great stewards'). Despite this downgrading, they remained a threat to the Scottish kings until DAVID I killed Angus of Moray in 1130 and mutilated Wimund. In 1312, Sir Thomas Randolph, one of Robert BRUCE's most prominent supporters, was created earl of Moray. Apart from a few interludes, the earldom remained in the hands of his heirs – the Randolphs, Dunbars and Stewarts – until the 18th century.

Morcar (?–*c*.1090), Earl of Northumbria. The son of Earl ÆLFGAR of MERCIA, he was installed as Earl of NORTHUMBRIA after the expulsion of

Earl TOSTIG in 1065. Defeated at the battle of FULFORD GATE by the invading forces of HARALD HARDRAADA and Tostig, Morcar supported HAROLD II, but afterwards came to terms with WILLIAM I THE CONQUEROR. He subsequently rebelled, was captured and remained a prisoner for the rest of his life.

More, Sir Thomas (1477/8–1535), politician and writer. After studying at Oxford, he followed his father's distinguished legal career, although he spent four years testing his vocation to monastic life. His fascination with humanism (*see* RENAISSANCE) produced much poetry and the enigmatic fantasy/travelogue *Utopia* (1516), winning him a European-wide audience and friendship with ERASMUS, John FISHER and HENRY VIII. However, from the 1520s, his horror at LUTHER's effect on the Western Church turned his literary talents to savage polemic, especially against TYNDALE.

Although he opposed Henry's obsession with the annulment of his marriage to CATHERINE OF ARAGON, the king insisted on his becoming lord CHANCELLOR on WOLSEY's fall in 1529. As Henry's other advisers encouraged the break with Rome, More's position grew increasingly unhappy, and outraged by the SUBMISSION OF THE CLERGY, he resigned the chancellorship in May 1532. Henry's adulation then turned to hatred.

Although More, in apolitical retirement, tried to concentrate on attacking religious reformers, his prestige made him an obvious opposition symbol, and he was arrested on treason charges for his cautious interest in Elizabeth BARTON's prophecies. His formidable discretion and legal acumen were no defence against Henry's fury at his rejection of ROYAL SUPREMACY. His last religious writings in the Tower have a serenity from which the earlier rage has faded; his execution shocked educated Europe.

Morganatic Marriage, marriage to a monarch or other person of high status which does not confer royal or aristocratic status on the spouse of inferior rank. The word derives from Old High German *morgangeba*, a morning-gift, i.e. the simple privilege of having been born, which is all the children of such a marriage can expect to inherit. Such a marriage was one of the options open to EDWARD VIII and Wallis Simpson in the ABDICATION CRISIS.

Morgannwg This Welsh kingdom came into existence in the mid-10th century within the older and larger kingdom of GLYWYSING. Its first king, Morgan Hen ('Morgan the Old'), gave his name to both the kingdom and the later county of Glamorgan. The 10th and 11th centuries were typified by dynastic instability, and Morgannwg was conquered by the Normans from the 1090s. The title 'king' was still occasionally used in the 12th century.

Morris, Sir Parker, *see* PARKER MORRIS STANDARDS

Morrison, Herbert (Baron Morrison) (1888–1965), Labour politician. A journalist, he became secretary of the London LABOUR PARTY in 1915 and Mayor of Hackney in 1919 before being elected to the LONDON COUNTY COUNCIL (LCC) (1922–45), and then to the House of Commons (1923–4, 1929–31, 1935–59). He joined MACDONALD's Labour government as minister of transport in 1929, and created the London Passenger Transport Board. London was always his political power base, and he oversaw the widespread development of the capital's housing, health, education and transport services. Appointed minister of supply in 1940 in the wartime coalition, he then became home secretary and minister of home security (1940–5) with responsibility for AIR-RAID PRECAUTIONS and emergency services (he created the National Fire Brigade to co-ordinate services during the BLITZ).

Morrison was primarily responsible for the manifesto commitments, including the blueprints for nationalized industries and for welfare programmes, that assisted Labour to victory in 1945. Deputy prime minister 1945–51, he served as lord president of the Council (1945–7) and, as leader of the Commons (1947–51), managed the passage of Labour's extensive legislative reforms, including the NATIONALIZATION programme. Briefly foreign secretary in 1951, he was an unsuccessful rival to GAITSKELL for the leadership of the party in 1955 as he had been to ATTLEE in 1935. He took a life peerage in 1959, became president of the British Board of Film Censors and led the fight against the abolition of the LCC.

Mortalism, a theological theory championed by Richard Overton (*fl.*1642–63).

According to this theory, the soul dies with the body's death, to be re-created only at a final clash of good and evil. Believed by many radical INTERREGNUM intellectuals – e.g. the poet John MILTON and Gerrard Winstanley (*see* DIGGERS) – it challenged the pretensions of institutional Churches that their structures and membership reflected the reality of the afterlife.

Mortality, the process in which deaths occur in a population. The interaction of mortality, FERTILITY and MIGRATION produce the prevailing POPULATION size. In addition to the crude DEATH RATE, which expresses deaths per 1,000 population in a given period, there are more sophisticated age-specific measures, such as INFANT MORTALITY, the likelihood of dying at certain ages (frequently expressed in a LIFE TABLE), and measures of LIFE EXPECTANCY. A distinction is made between *exogenous* mortality – death due to outside causes such as the action of infectious disease, or through FAMINE and poor nutrition; and *endogenous* mortality – death from, e.g., cardiovascular disease or cancers. The two overlap and are closely related but the former were more likely to occur in past populations, and the latter are more common in modern, developed societies. The theory of DEMOGRAPHIC TRANSITION presupposed that mortality was high in the past, falling to low modern levels; but research in HISTORICAL DEMOGRAPHY has suggested how comparatively low mortality was in the English, and other western, populations in the past, and how fertility rather than mortality has been the leading factor in bringing about population growth or decline.

Mortgage, a secured loan extended to landholders since at least the 13th century. The loan is related to a particular property or piece of land, which constitutes collateral for the loan. In the event that the individual fails to fulfil the conditions of the mortgage the property can be repossessed and sold by the institution which provided the mortgage. In the 20th century, and particularly since World War II with the spread of home ownership, mortgages have come to be associated largely with the household sector (*see* BUILDING SOCIETIES). However they were an important feature of agricultural and industrial finance in the 18th century and have remained important in company finance in the last two centuries.

Mortimer, Roger (1st Earl of March) (1287–1330), virtual king of England. As a great landowner in Ireland as well as heir to the Mortimer of Wigmore estates in the Welsh Marches, he was appointed lieutenant of Ireland by EDWARD II, and was responsible for its defence against Edward BRUCE's invasion (1316–18). However, by 1321 EDWARD II's new favourite, Hugh Despenser, was proving so dangerous and acquisitive a neighbour in the Marches that Mortimer joined a coalition of MARCHER LORDS against him; their revolt was swiftly suppressed. Mortimer was condemned to life imprisonment but, in 1324, escaped from the Tower and fled to the French court.

The next year he became Queen ISABELLA's lover and political adviser, and together they planned and carried out the deposition (and probably also the murder) of her husband, Edward II. Mortimer now became king in all but name and exploited his position greedily, taking the bulk of Despenser's estates in south Wales and then, in 1328, giving himself the unprecedented title of Earl of March. Inevitably he had enemies, notably within the royal family; military failure against the Scots in the Stanhope Park campaign, leading to the unpopular treaty of NORTHAMPTON in 1328, tarnished his reputation further. His execution of the Earl of Kent on a charge of treason in 1330 showed all too clearly that his regime was no better than Despenser's had been. In Oct. 1330, the 17-year-old EDWARD III entered Nottingham Castle by a secret passage and had Mortimer arrested in his mother's chamber; he was executed the following month. He was survived by his wife Joan, by whom he had 11 children.

Mortmain, literally 'dead hand', a term applied to land granted to a church in perpetuity. The 1279 Statute of Mortmain, clarifying a matter already dealt with in the PROVISIONS OF WESTMINSTER (1259), forbade such grants except with royal licence to protect crown revenues. The 1736 Act aimed to protect family interests by inhibiting death bed requests to charities.

Morton, 4th Earl of, *see* DOUGLAS, JAMES

Morton, John (*c.*1420–1500), royal servant and Archbishop of Canterbury (1486–1500).

An Oxford-trained CANON LAWYER, it was only in 1471 that he reconciled his LANCASTRIAN loyalties with EDWARD IV's regime; government and diplomatic service followed. RICHARD III arrested him as a dangerous opponent; having encouraged the abortive BUCKINGHAM'S REBELLION in 1483, he fled to FLANDERS and began intriguing for Henry Tudor (*see* HENRY VII), who on his victory summoned him home and made him archbishop of Canterbury in 1486.

He became lord chancellor in 1487 and cardinal in 1493, and was prominent in Henry's ruthless financial exactions, giving his name to the 'Morton's fork' principle for tax assessment – ostentation is proof of wealth, but a poverty-stricken appearance is proof of hidden savings. Building and FEN DRAINAGE also occupied his formidable energies.

Mosley, Sir Oswald (1896–1980), Fascist leader and politician. Son of a Staffs. landed family, he served in the ROYAL FLYING CORPS during WORLD WAR I; he was invalided out of the war in 1916 after a plane crash and in 1918 was elected CONSERVATIVE MP for Harrow, the youngest MP in the Commons. Impatient with what he saw as outworn parties and mediocre men, he left the Conservatives and was re-elected to his Harrow constituency as an INDEPENDENT (1922–4). His restless search for new answers and decisive action led him to cross the floor of the House, and in 1926 he was elected LABOUR MP for Smethwick. Appointed chancellor of the Duchy of Lancaster in the second Labour government in 1929, he resigned when his radical proposals for dealing with mass UNEMPLOYMENT (based on his reading of KEYNES) were rejected.

In 1931, he founded the NEW PARTY, but its failure in that year's election led him to form the British Union of FASCISTS in 1932, borrowing many of the attributes of continental fascism.

A brilliant orator, he based his appeal on vigorous anti-Communism and a programme of economic revival founded on protectionism. Violence at mass rallies cost him support and an increasing anti-Semitic tone alienated him from respectable opinion. Provocative marches through Jewish districts in London led to the PUBLIC ORDER ACT 1936, which banned the wearing of political uniforms and gave the home secretary the power to ban marches. In 1936, after the death of his first wife, Mosley married Diana Mitford in Goebbels' house in Berlin. Mosley launched a peace campaign (1938–9), not because he was a pacifist, but because of his belief in a 'Jewish conspiracy' that wanted war, and was interned under wartime regulations in 1940. Released three years later, he re-emerged in post-war politics to found the Union Movement in 1947, advocating British integration in Europe and opposing the immigration of people of colour.

Motor Cars Act 1903 It extended the speed permitted under the LOCOMOTIVES ACT of 1865 from 14 to 20 miles an hour, imposed penalties for reckless and dangerous driving and made the councils of counties and county boroughs responsible for the licensing of all motor cars. Licensing returns for the following year, which revealed only 8,465 cars in the United Kingdom, show the infant condition of the British MOTOR INDUSTRY.

Motor Industry The manufacture of motor vehicles in the UK began in 1893 with the establishment of the Daimler Motor syndicate operating under a German licence. Fairly rapidly rival manufacturers emerged, the first being Frederick Lanchester and Herbert Austin in BIRMINGHAM in 1895. By 1900 there were some 80 British motor manufacturers, mainly based in the West Midlands. This expansion had been facilitated by the passage of the Locomotives on Highways Act (1896) which had removed the 4mph speed limit and therefore opened up demand. The MOTOR CARS ACT of 1903 further liberalized road traffic and the number of manufacturers increased yet again. All models were hand-built and there was a bewildering variety of them. The industry was clearly ripe for standardization and a major change occurred in 1911 with the opening of Ford's Model T factory in MANCHESTER, which soon dominated the market. By the early 1920s many small producers were being forced out and the process of amalgamation via mergers and takeovers became a continuing feature of the industry. Periodic technical change improved efficiency: in 1927 pressed-steel bodies were introduced by William Morris, later Lord Nuffield, who had previously introduced welding techniques. His car sales rose from 3,000 in 1921 to 55,000 in 1925, and Morris and his rival Austin became dominant producers in the home market. Vauxhall meanwhile joined the American group General Motors. In 1931 Ford opened their huge plant at Dagenham, Essex, and mass-production began to revolutionize the economics of the industry.

After World War II the motor industry recovered only slowly, constrained by rationing of steel and by heavy taxation which held back demand. In the absence of competition from Germany and Japan, however, the industry was able to enjoy a period of international success exporting largely to the COMMONWEALTH. Domestic sales increased sharply in the 1950s stimulated by full employment, rising incomes and cheaper credit facilities. At the same time, major programmes of ROAD building and improvement began: by the mid 1950s the motorway system, based on the example of the German *autobahn*, was being planned and constructed. There were also advances in technical design and innovation – for example, improved gearboxes, steering and transmission systems were making driving easier and increasing the average vehicle speed. The Mini appeared in 1959 to universal acclaim. The expansion of the industry was taking place via the construction of new factories on green-field sites, sometimes with government prompting, for example Ford at Halewood and Vauxhall at Ellesmere Port. At the same time, the industry was facing the stirrings of TRADE UNION militancy which was to affect it for the next 20 years. This was not helped by a series of defensive mergers: for example BMC, the British Motor Corporation – itself the outcome of the amalgamation of Austin and Morris – was merged with Leyland Motors to form British Leyland (BL). The new entity was a mix of old plants producing too many different models with poor quality control, old-fashioned working practices and chaotic wage structures. As a result American, European and Japanese producers were penetrating the British market at an accelerating pace. Sales of new cars had passed the million mark in 1954 and were over two million by the late 1960s, but imports were taking a growing proportion of this total.

The 1970s were very difficult years for the motor industry world-wide as the OIL CRISES (1974, 1979) and the end to the post-war boom squeezed consumer incomes and drove manufacturers toward producing smaller, more fuel-efficient models. British manufacturing fared particularly badly and BL had to be rescued by being taken into public ownership. By the 1980s the domestic industry was dominated by a handful of mainly foreign owned companies – Ford, Vauxhall (both American) and Peugeot-Talbot (French), with BL a diminishing force. These accounted for 99 per cent of domestic car production and 97 per cent of commercial vehicles. British manufacturers were still an important presence at the luxury and specialist ends of the range, such as Jaguar, Morgan, Lotus and Rolls Royce, but even here pressures were being felt from BMW, Mercedes and the rapidly advancing Japanese. Working practices pioneered in Japan, allied to robotic technologies, produced revolutionary changes in the industry on a global scale and production facilities became more mobile than ever before. The UK became the largest recipient of the inflow of such foreign capital in Europe. The motor industry was a symbol of manufacturing skill and capacity for nearly a century and was a sector where British innovative design and engineering had made significant contributions. However, management failures, a lack of early integration, and an over-varied product line made UK manufacturers increasingly vulnerable to foreign competition and control. The 1980s saw something of a revival of production in the UK, albeit led by foreign producers. This, however, began to erode by 2000 when BMW withdrew from Longbridge, Birmingham, and other cutbacks were threatened.

Mount Badon, Battle of, *see* BADON, MOUNT, BATTLE OF

Mountbatten, Louis (1st Earl Mountbatten of Burma) (1900–79), Admiral and Viceroy of India. Son of Prince Louis of Battenberg (1854–1921) and uncle to Prince Philip (husband of ELIZABETH II), he served in battle-cruisers in WORLD WAR I. During WORLD WAR II, his ship, HMS *Kelly*, was sunk off Crete in 1941 while he was commanding the 5th Destroyer Flotilla. As chief of combined operations (1941–3), he planned raids on St Nazaire and DIEPPE. Supreme Allied commander in south-east Asia from Oct. 1943, he took the surrender of the Japanese forces in SINGAPORE in 1945. Appointed the last viceroy of INDIA in March 1947, he advised a speedy transfer of power and presided over partition and the independence of India and PAKISTAN (*see* INDIAN INDEPENDENCE); he remained as the first governor-general of India (Aug. 1947–June 1948). He later resumed his naval career, becoming first sea lord (1955–9), then chief of the defence staff (1959–65). Widely admired for his overall conduct of wartime operations in BURMA, and for his recognition of the need for a rapid transition to independence in the Indian subcontinent, he was assassinated by the IRA (*see* IRISH REPUBLICAN ARMY) in Ireland in 1979.

Muggletonians, an INTERREGNUM sect founded by the UNITARIANS John Reeve and his cousin Lodowick Muggleton, who claimed to have had the final revelation from God and to have been granted the power to decide who should be damned and who saved. Despite their estimable prohibition on seeking converts, Muggletonians survived as a quiet living link with the CIVIL WARS until their last member died in 1979.

Muirchertach Mac Néill (?–943), King of the Uí Néill. Muirchertach Mac Néill was one of the Irish kings who contributed most to containing the VIKING conquests in Ireland. Defeated by them in 921, he subsequently achieved victories on sea and land, attacked DUBLIN in 938 and even launched sea-borne raids against the Norse-held Scottish islands. He also built up considerable power over other Irish kingdoms (*see* KINGSHIP). His successes, and those of contemporary Irish kings, parallel the victories gained against the Vikings in England and Scotland by ATHELSTAN and CONSTANTINE II.

Mule, spinning machinery developed by Samuel Crompton in the 1780s, so called because it was a 'hybrid' combining elements of James Hargreaves' SPINNING JENNY – to which it added a roller draft to control the thread – and Arkwright's frame. One of its advantages over the jenny was that it could produce yarn suitable for relatively fine muslin cloths. Small models could be used in cottages or small factories. From the 1790s, some mules were water-, some STEAM-POWERED. Its rapid adoption helped speed spinning in the COTTON INDUSTRY and so in turn brought innovation in weaving.

Multilateralism, term often used to denote complex networks of international trade and the attendant financial settlements. Most commonly however the term refers to nuclear disarmament policy requiring the Soviet Union to begin reducing its NUCLEAR WEAPONS at the same time and at the same pace as the West. It was opposed by supporters of UNILATERALISM, who sought one-sided arms reductions from the West as a guarantee of good faith and the only means to begin genuine disarmament. The issue proved a major source of division within the LABOUR PARTY during the 1950s and 1960s (*see also* UNILATERALISM).

Mundbryce, an Anglo-Saxon legal term used in the 10th and 11th centuries to signify a breach of special protection (*mund*), often the king's. The king's *mund* is mentioned in LAW CODES, and a breach of it could include an attack on a man in holy orders or on one of the kingdom's ships.

Munich Agreement, 30 Sept. 1938, agreement signed between the British and French prime ministers, Neville CHAMBERLAIN and Daladier, and Hitler and Mussolini. Its main effect was to hand over German-speaking Sudetenland, the mountainous region of north and north-west Czechoslovakia, to Germany to avert Hitler's threatened military intervention in support of the Sudeten Nazis' demands for virtual autonomy. The Czechs were neither present nor consulted.

Chamberlain, who had feared a general European war over Czechoslovakia, for which Britain and France were ill-prepared, returned home to a hero's welcome, calling his agreement with Hitler a guarantee of 'peace for our time'. German troops led by Hitler crossed into the Sudetenland on 5 Oct. Munich immediately became, and has remained, a hotly debated episode. By some it is regarded as the culmination of APPEASEMENT and a shameful and ultimately pointless betrayal of the Czechs, as in March 1939 Hitler broke his agreement and occupied the rest of Czechoslovakia. By others it is seen as having bought time in which to prepare public opinion and the armed forces for war.

Municipal Corporations Act 1835 The Act abolished the municipal councils, which had previously been limited corporations that were not popularly elected, enjoyed trading privileges and were secretive and often corrupt. In their place came a uniform system of local self-government consisting of a town council, elected by the ratepayers in each WARD, and including a MAYOR, ALDERMAN and councillors. The new bodies were to administer accounts which were duly audited and published. The Act was in essence a necessary sequel to the REFORM ACT 1832. In 1882 a further Municipal Corporations Act consolidated the reforms of the 1835 Act, by bringing 74 of the 100 unreformed BOROUGHS that were outside the provisions of that Act within a uniform system of borough government. *See also* LOCAL GOVERNMENT.

Munitions, Ministry of, *see* MINISTRY OF MUNITIONS

Munster Like all the Irish kingdoms (*see* KINGSHIP), its origins are obscure and lie in post-Iron Age developments. The dominant family within early Munster was the Eóganacht, who were divided into two main branches. The province seems to have been even more fragmented than most, and its early medieval kings were always rather weak. The Eóganacht suffered a serious setback at the battle of BELACH MUGNA in 908 and, later in the 10th century, were replaced by the DÁL CAIS, the leading family of one of Munster's sub-kingdoms. During the reign of one of their number, BRIAN BORU, Munster dominated all Ireland, and came near to doing so again in the reigns of Turloch O Brien and MUIRCHERTACH O BRIEN.

Munster was the object of PLANTATION from the 1580s, following long years of rebellion between 1569 and 1583. In the later 18th century it was the initial centre of the attacks on people and property perpetrated by the WHITEBOYS.

Murdrum, a punitive fine introduced into English law after the NORMAN CONQUEST. It was assumed that every slain man was a Frenchman unless his Englishness was proved; if it were not and the slayer not found, then the HUNDRED was required to pay this fine.

Museums, repositories for the display and study of artefacts from the past. Museums as we know them developed from the collecting activities of interested amateurs of the 16th and 17th centuries with their 'cabinets of curiosities'. By the 18th century a national museum was the hallmark of every civilized state (*see* BRITISH MUSEUM), and in Britain, museum culture – partly fuelled by the explosion of interest in ARCHAEOLOGY – probably reached its apogee in the civic temples to the past established in almost every British town. Museums, with an ever-greater emphasis on 'accessibility' and avoidance of what is often seen as the overdidactic dryness of past examples, have experienced a significant revival in recent decades with the advent of the 'heritage industry'.

Music Hall Originating in the 1830s and 1840s, it became the dominant form of commercialized popular culture in urban areas. Early music halls, offering song, dance, MELODRAMA and comedy acts, were simply adjuncts to public houses. Purpose-built, grander halls followed, though they were still dependent upon sales of drink. By the 1890s music halls outnumbered THEATRES and music-hall artists such as Marie Lloyd became household names. Deluxe or variety theatres were introduced in the 1880s in a bid for respectability, but rising costs led to their decline and loss of independence. In 1896 the first silent moving film was shown in London (*see* CINEMA) and thereafter music hall lived on borrowed time.

Muslim League, *see* INDIAN INDEPENDENCE

Musselburgh Declaration, 1650, the reply by Oliver CROMWELL's army in Scotland to Scots PRESBYTERIAN criticism, before Cromwell's DUNBAR victory. It justified CHARLES I's execution, saying that Jesus Christ was the only king.

Mutiny Act, legislation first enacted in 1689, initially for six months but thereafter usually renewed annually, which was the basis of military discipline. The Act confirmed the articles of war, which set out discipline for the ARMY and NAVY. Its provisions were extended to the MILITIA when on active service from 1757.

Myanmar, *see* BURMA

Myddle, *see* GOUGH, RICHARD

Myrddin, *see* MERLIN

Mysore Wars, 1791–2, 1799. Mysore was a southern Indian principality hostile to

British power. Its late 18th-century ruler, Tipu Sultan, achieved notoriety in Britain as a result of press coverage of Indian affairs. In 1791–2 CORNWALLIS, the British governor-general, won the first Mysore War, acquiring new territories in consequence. In 1798 French strategy in the FRENCH REVOLUTIONARY WARS prompted intrigue with Tipu. In 1799 the British struck pre-emptively and Tipu died defending has fortress capital, Seringapatam. Mysore was partitioned between Britain and other Indian powers. Other south Indian territories were annexed on various related pretexts from 1799–1801; Britain was thus established as a major territorial power in southern INDIA.

Mystery, *see* MISTERY

N

Nabob, the 18th-century rendition of the Indian word for ruler, now commonly 'nawab', which was also applied to Englishmen who made their fortunes in EAST INDIA COMPANY service. The dramatic expansion of British influence in Bengal in the 1760s produced an upsurge of anxiety in Britain about returning nabobs and the uses to which they might put their wealth. These fears were exacerbated by the fact that some, like Robert CLIVE, did use their money to bribe electorates to return them to Parliament.

Nanking, Treaty of (1842), *see* OPIUM WARS

Nantwich, *see* SALT INDUSTRY

Napier, Sir William (1785–1860), soldier and military historian. His multi-volumed *History of the PENINSULAR WAR* (1828–40) – a defence of the reputation of Sir John Moore and the Duke of Wellington (*see* WELLESLEY, ARTHUR) – is an evocative work which combined narrative skill with a keen eye for personal detail. It remains highly readable and a valuable source of information.

Napoleonic Wars, 1803–15, a continuation and extension of the FRENCH REVOLUTIONARY WARS dominated by Napoleon Bonaparte since 1796. After a short-lived peaceful interlude following the collapse of the second coalition and the Peace of AMIENS, anxieties and suspicions were aroused by Bonaparte's annexation of Piedmont and Elba, his occupation of Switzerland and refusal to evacuate Holland. Fearing his designs on the Mediterranean, the British refused to honour treaty commitments and withdraw troops from MALTA, a valuable base in the event of the renewal of French ambitions in EGYPT. On 18 May 1803 hostilities were resumed.

The initial phase of the wars had been directed at containment of republican principles through the overthrow of the Republic and restoration of the monarchy. The phase of the conflict that followed the end of the Peace of Amiens was seen in more personal terms: Bonaparte had for the British become the personification of tyranny and deceit – the 'Little Boney' who figured in grotesque parodies in thousands of cartoons. First blood went to the British: on 23 July 1803 Robert Emmet's rising in Dublin was easily suppressed, while the defeat of the Marathas at Assaye and Argaun prevented successful French interference in INDIA. PITT THE YOUNGER, who had resigned the premiership in 1801, returned to office in May 1804 almost at the same time as Bonaparte proclaimed himself emperor of the French. Pitt set about the creation of the Third Coalition while the ruler of France set about the invasion of England.

For this purpose a force of 150,000 men, the so-called 'Army of England', was assembled at Boulogne where a fleet of transports was collected 'to force the wet ditch of the Channel'. The British government increased their fleet and army and enrolled a force of 300,000 VOLUNTEERS. Confident of victory, the emperor proceeded to strike medals to celebrate the conquest of England. Success depended upon the defeat of the Royal NAVY; the plan was to unite the French and Spanish fleets and convoy the transports to England after NELSON had been enticed to Egypt or the WEST INDIES. The French admiral Villeneuve escaped the blockade at Toulon and sailed to the West Indies. Evading Nelson's pursuit he returned at once to Europe to an indecisive encounter with Sir Robert Calder off Cape Finisterre on 22 July 1805. He then put into Cadiz to refit instead of uniting with the Brest fleet as Napoleon had planned. The chance for mastery of the Channel was lost. Nelson had returned; his victory over the combined Spanish and French fleets at TRAFALGAR on 21 Oct. ended the possibility of a French invasion and left Napoleon's grand strategy devoid of effective sea-power thereafter.

Even before the victory at sea had been secured, the likelihood of a successful invasion seemed increasingly remote. In April Russia and Britain concluded a treaty to drive the French from Switzerland and Holland; shortly afterwards Austria joined the coalition as a result of the annexation of Genoa by the French and the coronation of Napoleon as king of Italy. Sweden, too, joined the allied cause. Napoleon decided to strike at the Austrians before the arrival of the Russian armies in central Europe. The Army of England was removed from Boulogne to Ulm where, on 20 Oct., it defeated a 30,000-strong force under the Austrian general Mack; Vienna capitulated. Hopes aroused by the subsequent victory at Trafalgar were speedily dashed by the crushing defeat inflicted by Napoleon on the Austrians and Russians at Austerlitz on 2 Dec. Austria, knocked out of the war, had to submit to the treaty of Presburg by which Venetia was ceded to the French kingdom of Italy, and the states of the Lower Rhine were formed into the Confederation of the Rhine, dependent on France. Napoleon also recognized the electors of Bavaria and Württemberg as kings, independent of Austria, and exacted a war contribution of 40 million francs.

Pitt died on 23 Jan. 1806 with, it seemed, little to show for all his efforts. The Third Coalition had gone the way of its predecessors; Napoleonic power was still in the ascendant. The Prussians, who had hesitated to join the allied cause, found that French domination of Germany was a fact rather than a possibility. Having created the Confederation of the Rhine, a puppet state under French control, Napoleon turned his attention to North Germany, proclaiming himself 'Protector' of the Hanseatic towns. Hanover, dangled before Frederick William III in order to secure Prussian neutrality during the Austrian campaign, was subsequently offered in peace negotiations with England. The exasperated Prussians, who went to war in the autumn, were humiliated at Jena on 14 Oct.; 13 days later Napoleon entered Berlin in triumph. The following year he crushed the Russians at Eylau in Feb. and Friedland in June; Europe lay at his feet. In July he met with Tsar Alexander I at Tilsit to carve up their respective spheres of influence in eastern and western Europe.

Britain alone remained defiant. On 2 Sept. 1807 the Danish fleet was bombarded at COPENHAGEN by the Royal Navy in order to prevent it from being used by Russia or France. The army, though, could offer no comparable success as the disastrous WALCHEREN EXPEDITION of 1809 was to show. Both sides turned increasingly to a new kind of economic war to break the deadlock. Napoleon's CONTINENTAL SYSTEM and the British BLOCKADE of France and her satellites damaged each power as much as they damaged the other; by 1812, when the policy was finally abandoned, it had involved Britain in the ANGLO-AMERICAN WAR and France in the PENINSULAR WAR. It was the desire to make the Continental System more effective that led Napoleon to intervene in Spain, depose the Spanish monarch and replace him with his own brother Joseph. In so doing, he provoked a national resistance and a consequent diversion of resources that finally brought about his downfall.

The Russian campaign, like the Peninsular War, also sprang from the Continental System. By 1812 relations between the two former allies had so deteriorated that Napoleon determined upon a decisive blow. An army of 650,000 men was marshalled and crossed the Niemen between 23 and 25 June 1812 en route for Moscow. On 7 Sept. it fought a bloody and indecisive battle at Borodino where each side lost about 40,000 men; on the 14th the French entered Moscow which they proceeded to burn. Still the Russians refused to surrender. Exhaustion, winter and ferocious Russian resistance nullified strategic retreat; half a million men were lost in the long trail homewards.

The emperor of the French no longer seemed invincible. Defeat in Russia and in Spain encouraged the Prussians and Austrians to throw off French domination. The battle of Leipzig, which lasted for three days in Oct. 1813 and cost 110,000 casualties, left Napoleon incapable of resisting the allied invasion of France and he was defeated at Arcis-sur-Aube. The allies entered Paris on 31 March 1814.

Napoleon, though banished to Elba, escaped his captors and landed in Cannes on 1 March 1815. The hatred of allied domination of France and the promise of even greater triumphs brought him support from the veterans of the Grand Army. In less than three months he had raised a force of 280,000 front-line troops, with a reserve of 150,000. The allies determined to invade France from the south-west, through Alsace and Lorraine, and through the Low Countries. Napoleon decided to attack their extreme right in Belgium and crush its constituent parts – Wellington's (*see* WELLESLEY, ARTHUR) army near Brussels and Blücher's near Liège – before they could combine into a more formidable force. On 16 June 1815 at Ligny he defeated the Prussians, who retired in good order to Wavre. On the same day Wellington resisted Ney's attacks at Quatre Bras, withdrew successfully and prepared British reinforcements for the final onslaught. On 18 June he stood on the defensive at WATERLOO, and by nightfall he was vanquished, in flight from the combined British and Prussian attack.

The 23 years of war against the French Revolution and Napoleon had been colossally expensive. The loss of life among British servicemen was proportionately higher between 1794 and 1815 than between 1914 and 1918. The financial cost too was unprecedented. More than £1,500 million was raised in loans and taxes to pay for the war, much of it disbursed as subsidies to allied powers. In the short term the Wars may have CROWDED OUT civilian investment and slowed the INDUSTRIAL REVOLUTION, but in the longer term Britain gained enormously from the extension of trade at the expense of France.

Naseby, Battle of, *see* CIVIL WARS

Nassau Agreement, Bahamas, Dec. 1962, agreement reached between US president Kennedy and prime minister Harold MACMILLAN under which the US agreed to sell Britain its submarine-launched POLARIS missile on favourable terms. The agreement called into question the whole nature of the 'independent' British nuclear deterrent. The French president de Gaulle, who resented the agreement, used its evidence of Britain's continuing 'special relationship' with the US to reject Britain's application for EEC (*see* EUROPEAN UNION) membership, arguing that she was not yet ready to act as a European country.

Natal, small coastal trading settlement expanded by the Boers after the Great Trek in 1837, who fought with the native Zulus. Occupied by Britain in 1842 and abandoned by the Boers, it was the setting for the ZULU WARS.

National Assistance Act 1948 The Act provided, as of right, for cash payments for those in real need. Intended to act as a 'safety-net' as part of the WELFARE STATE, it finally removed the last elements of POOR RELIEF. The system was increasingly superseded by the introduction of new benefits, notably supplementary benefit, family income supplement, housing benefit, and cash grants for emergencies, many of which were revised and renamed under the Social Security Act 1986 and subsequent legislation.

National Charter Association, *see* CHARTISM .

National Council for Civil Liberties (NCCL), private organization founded in 1934 by a group of liberal and left-wing activists to observe and report on POLICE behaviour towards hunger marchers and anti-Fascist demonstrators. It attracted a distinguished group of sponsors, including ATTLEE, and established itself after 1945 as a significant pressure group concerned with encroachments of state or police powers upon the rights of the citizen. (It was renamed Liberty in 1990.)

National Democratic and Labour Party, a party formed in 1915 to organize support from within the LABOUR movement for WORLD WAR I and the LLOYD GEORGE coalition. Support was drawn from various union groups, notably the Liverpool dockers, textile workers and miners. The party later included Labour ministers who refused to resign from the coalition government in 1918, led by George Barnes (1859–1940). It put up 28 candidates in 1918, 15 of whom were elected. Prior to the 1922 election the group joined the LIBERAL NATIONAL PARTY, but only one MP was elected and the party ceased to exist in 1923. It was essentially a LIB-LAB faction of the more anti-socialist MPs who had wholeheartedly supported the war against Germany.

National Front, political party formed in 1966 from the merger of a number of racialist, neo-Fascist, and right-wing groups. The NF's aims were an end to immigration, especially of black immigrants from new COMMONWEALTH countries, repatriation of immigrants, withdrawal from the EEC (*see* EUROPEAN UNION), and a continued Union with ULSTER. The party contested parliamentary and municipal elections during the 1970s, although no candidates were elected. It earned notoriety for its marches and demonstrations which frequently led to clashes with anti-Fascist demonstrators or clashes between their opponents and the POLICE. The party split in 1982, when a breakaway British National Party was formed.

National Gallery, a pre-eminent national collection of paintings, founded in 1824. Formed from the collection purchased from the Lloyds' magnate, John Julius Angerstein, it was housed in a permanent building in London's Trafalgar Square, designed by William Wilkins, in 1838. Attendances were enormous and some, including the novelist Anthony Trollope, argued that admission charges should be imposed to permit true art-lovers to enjoy the collection in peace. As with most of the great collections in London (*see* BRITISH MUSEUM) however, the principle of free admission has been maintained except for a brief period during the HEATH government.

National Government, name adopted by administrations from Aug. 1931 to May 1940. The first National Government was formed by Ramsay MACDONALD on 24 Aug. 1931, following the collapse of the second Labour government. Most of the LABOUR PARTY went into opposition; the LIBERALS and CONSERVATIVES generally supported it. Originally a temporary arrangement to balance the budget, it took Britain off the GOLD STANDARD and decided in Oct. to fight a general election against Labour, winning the biggest victory in British electoral history, with 554 seats (470 Conservative) against Labour's 46. After the election the CABINET became increasingly Conservative-dominated, shedding the Samuelite Liberals and Philip Snowden over the issue of protection in 1932. During 1931–5 the National Government grappled with the DEPRESSION, imposing the MEANS TEST and cuts in expenditure, as well as facing questions over rearmament and the government of INDIA. In June 1935 BALDWIN, who as lord president of the Council had become the dominant figure in the Cabinet, replaced MacDonald as prime minister and secured an election victory over a still weak opposition later in the year.

Increasingly Conservative in all but name, the government was faced with crises over Abyssinia (*see* HOARE–LAVAL PACT) and the ABDICATION. In 1937 Neville CHAMBERLAIN succeeded Baldwin and pursued a policy of APPEASEMENT. Mounting criticism, especially over the MUNICH AGREEMENT, and the failure to solve the problem of mass UNEMPLOYMENT, was temporarily stilled with the declaration of war in Sept. 1939, but the lacklustre handling in spring 1940 of the NORWEGIAN CAMPAIGN brought about a crisis. Following bitter criticism in a debate on 7–8 May 1940, Chamberlain resigned, leading to the formation of an all-party coalition government led by CHURCHILL.

The National Government has suffered serious criticism for both its economic and its foreign policies. More positive views have stressed the stability it gave Britain in a troubled decade, the substantial recovery of parts of the ECONOMY by the late 1930s, and the difficulties of dealing with the dictators when public opinion was anti-war.

National Grid, a system of unified national electricity supply by high-tension transmission cables carried on pylons. Begun in 1926 under the newly created monopoly of the Central Electricity Board, it brought cheap electricity to almost every part of the British Isles. By 1939 two-thirds of homes were connected to the electricity supply.

National Health Service Act 1946 Passed by the LABOUR government under ATTLEE, it set up a free medical service for all. The National Health Service came into effect in July 1948. The Act was a fulfilment of objectives set out by the BEVERIDGE REPORT and the wartime coalition government, though its final shape was the result of protracted negotiations between the minister of health, BEVAN, and the medical profession. The Act provided a free general practitioner service and medical treatment, free hospital care, and free dental and optical services. Existing hospitals, whether voluntary or local authority-controlled, were to become part of the new National Health Service. Significant concessions were given to GPs by not making them state employees, and hospital consultants were allowed to keep private practice and fee-paying patients.

The financial demands of rearmament during the KOREAN WAR forced the first compromise with the principle of a completely free service, when charges for dentures and spectacles were introduced by GAITSKELL, the Labour chancellor, in 1951. This caused the resignations from the government of Bevan, by then minister of labour, WILSON, president of the Board of Trade, and John Freeman, a junior war office minister. In 1952 the CONSERVATIVES introduced the first charges for medical prescriptions which have increased and grown more comprehensive ever since. *See also* WELFARE STATE.

National Income, the income generated by the economic activity of the residents of a country. The term corresponds either to Gross National Product, or to Net National Product, the value of economic activity after deduction for the depreciation of capital. Incomes are included in the calculation where they derive directly from the production of goods or services, and taking account of the net flows of income from abroad. A succession of historians since the 1950s has developed increasingly sophisticated estimates of national income for the British economy, going back into the 18th century. It is partly on the basis of that work that revision of the impact and timing of the INDUSTRIAL REVOLUTION has been based.

National Insurance Act 1946, the Act which created the structure of the post-war WELFARE STATE envisaged in the BEVERIDGE REPORT and in the government White Paper on national insurance in 1944. The Act provided for compulsory contributions for unemployment, sickness, maternity and widows' benefits and old age pensions from employers and employees, with the Exchequer funding the balance. The Act aimed at a comprehensive system of social security which, allied with the NATIONAL ASSISTANCE ACT, the NATIONAL HEALTH SERVICE ACT, and the FAMILY ALLOWANCES ACT, provided a network of security 'from the cradle to the grave' as of right. Although additional benefits have been attached to its basic structure, and other benefits, notably state pensions, have been whittled away, it has remained the foundation of the welfare state.

National League, Irish nationalist political movement, inaugurated on 17 Oct. 1882 by Charles PARNELL. Replacing the short-lived IRISH LAND LEAGUE, the National League stood for national and local self-government, land reform, extension of the FRANCHISE, and economic encouragement; it backed the nationalist parliamentary party. Within three years the League had well over 1,000 branches; its affairs were skilfully controlled by Parnell, especially after 1884 when he had secured the backing of the Roman CATHOLIC hierarchy. Following the Nov. 1885 general election the Parnellites were successfully returned to the House of COMMONS with 85 seats in Ireland. Success continued until the party split in 1890–1 over Parnell's liaison with Mrs Kitty O'Shea; the rump continued under John Redmond while the majority of anti-Parnellites established the IRISH NATIONAL FEDERATION. The National League was finally replaced by the United Irish League in 1900 as the constituency organization for nationalists in Ireland when it rejoined forces with the INF.

National Liberal Party, *see* LIBERAL NATIONAL PARTY

National Parks and Access to the Countryside Act 1949, the Act which set aside areas of natural beauty and recreational value for special treatment as National Parks. A National Parks Commission was set up to designate the areas concerned: the first was the Peak District National Park (1951), followed by the Lake District, Snowdonia, and Dartmoor (all 1951), the Pembrokeshire Coast and North York Moors (both 1952), the Yorkshire Dales and Exmoor (1954), Northumberland (1956) and the Brecon Beacons (1957). The ten National Parks cover 9 per cent of the area of England and Wales. *See also* CONSERVATION.

National Service A shorthand for military CONSCRIPTION, the term was applied to compulsory service in WORLD WAR II; thereafter the National Service Act of 1947 provided for the continuation of compulsory military service in peacetime for all males over 18. The period of service was initially 12 months, increased to 18 months in Dec. 1948 and to two years in Sept. 1950 because of the KOREAN WAR. In 1957 the government announced a reduction in national service intake and no men were called after 1960. The economic, military and moral value of National Service was, and remains, deeply contested.

National Society for Promoting the Education of the Poor in the Principles of the Church of England, *see* MONITORIAL SYSTEM

National Trust, leading CONSERVATION body, founded in 1895 by the philanthropist, Octavia Hill (1838–1912) and others to preserve 'places of historic interest and natural beauty'. Originally formed to preserve threatened areas of landscape, especially in south-east England and the Lake District, the National Trust has since become the owner and guardian of many historic houses as well as of landscape, and is now the largest private conservation organization in England, Wales and Northern Ireland. The National Trust for Scotland was founded in 1926.

National Unemployed Workers' Movement (NUWM). It was originally formed as the National Unemployed Workers' Committee Movement in 1921 under the auspices of the COMMUNIST PARTY OF GREAT BRITAIN, its purpose being to organize and politicize the unemployed. Under its leader Walter HANNINGTON it organized HUNGER MARCHES and demonstrations during the early 1920s and during the worst years of the DEPRESSION from 1929–35. The movement had a peak membership of about 20,000 in 1932, but as many as 400,000 unemployed may have passed through its ranks. Apart from campaigns against the MEANS TEST and the UNEMPLOYMENT ASSISTANCE BOARD regulations of 1934–5, much of the NUWM's activity was directed to casework on behalf of the unemployed. Its influence was limited by opposition from the LABOUR PARTY and the TRADES UNION CONGRESS because of its communist leadership, its treatment by the government as a subversive organization and the failure of the unemployed to join in anticipated numbers. In 1939 the organization was wound up, having failed in its larger purpose of revolutionizing the unemployed, though it had attracted some publicity for their plight.

National Union of Women's Suffrage Societies (NUWSS) Formed in 1897 on the initiative of Millicent FAWCETT, it brought together the miscellaneous 'constitutional suffragist' groups that had been formed in the aftermath of the Reform Bill agitation of 1867 (*see* REFORM ACT 1867). By 1913 the NUWSS had a journal *The Common Cause* and 400 societies covering the country, with a membership of 500,000 and an annual income of £45,000. Its argument that women were rational beings capable of using the vote intelligently made little impact in Parliament, where nearly 30 private members' bills in favour of WOMEN'S SUFFRAGE were voted down between 1870 and 1914. Women impatient of change began to turn from peaceful petitions, processions and public meetings to the more militant methods of the WOMEN'S SOCIAL AND POLITICAL UNION. *See also* SUFFRAGETTES.

Nationalization, policy of taking major industries into state control. The LABOUR PARTY's Clause IV was generally seen to espouse nationalization, that is taking into state control public utilities – those basic services essential to the functioning of an entire ECONOMY. Government control of vital industries in both world wars and the establishment of public corporations such as the BBC and the Central Electricity Board between the wars provided examples of state ownership of major economic enterprises.

The Labour government of 1945 embarked on a sweeping programme of nationalization, including the BANK OF ENGLAND (1946), the COAL INDUSTRY (1946), civil aviation (1946), ELECTRICITY (1947), RAILWAYS, CANALS, docks, road haulage, GAS (1948) and IRON AND STEEL (1949), a policy continued by the WILSON government, which turned the Post Office (*see* POSTAL SERVICES) into a public corporation in 1969. The CONSERVATIVE governments after 1951 accepted nationalization of key sectors of the economy as part of a 'mixed economy', but denationalized others. Criticism from the free-market wing of the Conservatives led to some minor hiving-off of state-owned assets under HEATH but the collapse of Rolls-Royce led to a U-turn in government policy with the company being taken into state ownership. The Wilson-CALLAGHAN government pursued further nationalization, but under the THATCHER governments, nationalized industries were regarded as inherently inefficient, leading to a wholesale process of privatization. The Labour Party voted to replace Clause IV in 1995.

NATO (North Atlantic Treaty Organization). Created by the North Atlantic treaty signed in Washington on 4 April 1949, NATO was formed in response to the development of the COLD WAR and fears about the power of the Soviet Union in Europe, and especially the threat to Berlin and West Germany. The treaty states subscribed to the principle that an attack on one was an attack on all. They were obliged to take such action as was deemed necessary to assist in resisting aggression. Its original signatories were the United States, Canada, Britain, Belgium, Luxembourg, the Netherlands, France, Italy, Norway, Denmark, Iceland and Portugal. These were later joined by Greece and Turkey (1952), West Germany (1955), Spain (1982), and the Czech Republic, Hungary and Poland (1999) bringing the total to 19 member nations. Its key political and military importance was that it coupled the United States to the defence of western Europe, including the commitment of the American nuclear umbrella. Faced from 1955 by the Eastern bloc's rival organization, the Warsaw Pact, NATO member states maintained a permanent military presence in continental Europe under an American supreme allied commander, and nearly all the combat and support aircraft of the ROYAL AIR FORCE, some equipped with nuclear weapons, were also assigned to NATO. The Royal NAVY's submarine ballistic missiles were also targeted by NATO.

In spite of some easing of tensions with the Soviet Union during the 'détente' era of the late 1960s and 1970s, fears of Soviet nuclear and conventional superiority led to the deployment in the 1980s of US nuclear Cruise missiles and new tactical NUCLEAR WEAPONS in Europe. However, a decisive reduction of tension under Soviet premier Gorbachev and US president Reagan from 1985 altered the whole character of NATO, and in 1989–90 the coming to power of non-Communist governments in much of eastern Europe saw the effective dissolution of the Warsaw Pact. The London summit meeting of NATO leaders in July 1990 declared the Cold War at an end and began planning for NATO force cutbacks.

The evolution of a post-war world role for NATO has included the establishment of the Euro-Atlantic Partnership Council, a framework for co-operation between NATO and its partners (including former members of the Warsaw Pact). NATO forces (in co-operation with forces from non-NATO countries) implemented the military aspects of the Bosnian Peace Agreement (signed Dec. 1995) through IFOR, its multi-national implementation force, and in March 1999 following the collapse of negotiations over a settlement of the KOSOVO situation, the UK committed Royal Navy vessels and RAF (ROYAL AIR FORCE) support and strike aircraft as part of a NATO attack on Serbian targets. British forces are also part of the KFOR peace-keeping force remaining in Kosovo.

Naturalization Acts, Acts passed from the 14th century to naturalize named aliens, or to facilitate the naturalization of classes of aliens. A practical advantage of naturalization was that it freed aliens from restrictions which otherwise inhibited their ability to trade or purchase land. Moves to facilitate the naturalization of non-ANGLICAN foreigners were a source of recurrent controversy in the 18th century: a WHIG General Naturalization Act of 1709 was repealed in 1712 after the arrival of large numbers of PALATINES had caused concern; while in 1753–4, the so-called JEW BILL provoked a storm of controversy. An 1844 Act reduced the need for special legislation by allowing the crown to grant certificates of naturalization to aliens who had been resident in Britain for five years.

Naval Stores, the materials used for building and rigging wooden sailing ships. Principally these were timber for hulls, masts and spars; sailcloth; cordage; and tar for preserving these materials. The Baltic was the chief source, which helps to explain its strategic importance in the age of sail.

Naval Warfare, *see* WARFARE, NAVAL

Navigation Acts, legislation reflecting MERCANTILIST ideas, restricting the terms on which English (later British) and foreign shipping could trade with England and its colonies. The first Navigation Act of 1651, aimed against the Dutch carrying trade, provided that only English ships, or ships of the country originally producing the goods being carried, could import goods into England. The second Act (1660) restricted the types of colonial produce that could be exported, and specified that they could be carried only in English ships. In 1663, the colonies were forbidden to import goods in foreign ships. Subsequent Acts varied the 'enumerated' articles subject to particular restrictions (*see* ENUMERATED GOODS). The Navigation Acts were seen as central to the 18th-century colonial system, and as a hindrance by many colonists in North America.

After the American colonies left the BRITISH EMPIRE following the War of AMERICAN INDEPENDENCE, the system of restrictions was reviewed, but an Act of 1786 upheld the basic principles of the old system. The Navigation Acts were repealed in 1826. *See also* UNION (ENGLAND AND SCOTLAND), ACT OF, 1707.

Navvy, a shorthand for 'navigator', used to describe the large numbers of workers employed in the excavation and construction of earthworks such as CANALS, RAILWAYS and drains, and by extension other manual workers. At the peak of the RAILWAY MANIA an estimated 250,000 navvies were so engaged, with many of them coming from Ireland. They had to be peripatetic and tough – some were capable of moving 20 tonnes of earth in a day. Exploited by employers and feared by contemporaries, they led a rough, rumbustious and dangerous existence in shanty towns close to the tracks.

Navy The earliest evidence for a royal navy are documentary references to ships built for ALFRED THE GREAT to fight the VIKINGS. An impressive organization similar to the *FYRD* provided later Anglo-Saxon kings with a large fleet. Thereafter there are references to naval expeditions mounted on behalf of many kings, suggesting the continuous existence of a royal navy. Material from the 11th century also shows the existence of numerous SHIPSOKES, which were the basis of a system of naval military obligation, while HAROLD II is known to have stationed ships in the Channel in 1066.

After the NORMAN CONQUEST this no longer existed, and fleets, when needed, were mostly collected by the conversion of merchant ships, though most monarchs had a few 'king's ships'. It was not until the time of HENRY VII and HENRY VIII that anything approaching a permanent organized navy appeared, coinciding with developments in ships and their armament (*see* WARFARE, NAVAL) which made converted merchantmen less suitable for naval use. The simple organization of having a lord admiral and a keeper of the king's ships expanded under Henry VIII to include what would become the navy board, the committee which organized both the navy and its DOCKYARDS. Some men spent much of their lives as captains of the ships of this navy – the very beginnings of a corps of professional naval officers. However, though the most impressive naval force in north-west Europe, this was still a small number of 20 or so ships. Most of the ships which fought the Spanish ARMADA were still requisitioned merchantmen. After a period of neglect under JAMES I, CHARLES I built up the SHIP MONEY fleet which, ironically, turned against him and was a major factor in PARLIAMENTARY success in the first CIVIL WAR.

Equally ironically, the real foundation of the organization and the success of what would be eventually known world-wide as the Royal Navy was under the Republican and CROMWELLian regimes of the INTERREGNUM. The fleet was expanded to cope with war with the Dutch (*see* DUTCH WAR, SECOND) and then Spain. The ADMIRALTY board came into its own as the overall directing body. The navy was coming to be a career for a permanent cadre of officers, and men like the boatswains, carpenters and gunners. The English fleet was the most powerful and effective in Europe. It was less successful under CHARLES II, but the work of setting up a permanent organization was continued, particularly by PEPYS. Some of the worst economic problems of providing for this very expensive state organization were solved in the reign of WILLIAM III, and the financial underpinnings were vital to its continuing growth and success. A challenge from the navy of Louis XIV was beaten off, and well before the end of the War of the SPANISH SUCCESSION the British fleet was what it has remained, the largest naval force in Western Europe.

What is perhaps the real marker of the beginning of this predominance is it remaining the same size for the period of peace that followed. It grew during the next two wars with France, and by the end of the SEVEN YEARS WAR, reformed under Admiral George Anson (1697–1762), had achieved a total predominance which not even the years of adversity during the War of AMERICA INDEPENDENCE could really shake. During this war it had expanded almost twofold, and it did so again during the FRENCH REVOLUTIONARY and NAPOLEONIC WARS. By 1815 it was no longer, as it had been in 1792, first amongst equals, but was simply by far the largest and most powerful navy in the world. It remained this until the US Navy rivalled it in numbers of BATTLESHIPS during the 1920s and then left it far behind during WORLD WAR II.

The sailing navy never managed to solve the problem of recruitment to the lower deck – relying throughout on the PRESS GANG to make up numbers. It was not until the middle of the 19th century that a permanent career was offered to seamen – at almost the same time as a uniform was introduced. The navy board had already been abolished in 1832 to fit in with liberal ideas of efficiency, leaving the Admiralty to be overwhelmed by administrative detail in a period of accelerating technical change. Inventors eager to push their projects fostered a legend of Admiralty conservatism that has stuck. However it is no more than a legend: the navy has a generally good record of adopting technical developments just as soon as they became practicable – the steering wheel about 1700, coppering and the carronade later in the 18th century, the ironclad and steel in the Victorian period, the aircraft-carrier in the 20th century.

During most of the 19th century Britain's industrial strength enabled her to cope very easily with naval challenges from France and Russia. Meanwhile the navy gave Britain an immense influence around the world, where its actions against SLAVE TRADERS, pirates and opponents of westernization, and also in charting, gave teeth and reality to the concept of the era of the 'Pax Britannica'. RAILWAYS were giving continental powers new advantages. By the time of the Naval Defence Act of 1889, however, Britain's relative industrial and economic position, the foundation of her seapower, was worsening. The serious challenge from Germany caused a whole series of reforms, strategical, administrative and social, associated with FISHER in the first decade of the 20th century. The process of reorganization, reform and retrenchment has continued ever since, with readjustment to Britain's changing place in the world (and the loss of overseas bases), to changing social attitudes (the navy was obtaining half of its officers from the 'lower deck' in the 1960s), and to the pace of technical change which has replaced battleships with nuclear submarines and aircraft-carriers. With the decay of the Russian fleet, the Royal Navy is now again the third largest navy in the world, a junior partner to the US Navy and a major part of NATO's fleet; though how much longer any of these statements will remain true is open to question.

Since 1994 changes in the management structure, reduction in personnel strength, base closures and rationalization were instituted. The naval bases at Rosyth and Portland closed in 1995, the naval dockyards at Rosyth and Devonport have both been sold to commercial operators and the number of naval personnel (including Royal Marines) has dropped from 59.4 thousand in 1993 to an estimated 47.5 thousand in 1997.

The navy was always a more popular service amongst the British public than the ARMY, less of a threat and promising much more. Arguably the first real national armed service, with a longer continuous history than any other, the navy ('that most commercially-minded service' according to Eric Hobsbawm) has also played a very major part in the ECONOMIC GROWTH of the country – by supporting British overseas trade and empire, by reducing those of others, and also by exercising an influence on the growth of British industry as a major customer.

Nechtan, King of the Picts (706–24). By accepting the Roman calculation of the dating of EASTER and imposing it on his people, he played a significant part in the Romanizing of the British Church. His reign is otherwise notable for the generally peaceful relations with NORTHUMBRIA and for the internecine struggles among the PICTS during its last years. Nechtan retired to a monastery in 724, but emerged intermittently thereafter to fight rivals.

Nechtanesmere, Battle of, 685. An important battle at Dunnichen Moss in Tayside, at which BRUDE MAC BILI, king of the PICTS, defeated and killed ECGFRITH, king of

NORTHUMBRIA. The battle put an end to Northumbrian aspirations to dominate Britain north of the Forth and marks an important turning-point in the development of the political geography of 'Dark Age' Britain. It also prevented Archbishop THEODORE from establishing an English-style bishopric at Abercorn on the south of the Forth estuary.

Negative Confession, 1581. Drawn up to pre-empt Esmé Stuart's Roman CATHOLIC political revival in Scotland, its unpromising name derives from its denial of all religion and doctrine not in accord with the 1560 CALVINIST church settlement. Also known as the 'King's Confession' – because it was signed, reluctantly, by JAMES VI – it is an important source of the 1638 COVENANT.

Nelson, Horatio (1st Viscount Nelson) (1758–1805), sailor and naval commander. Son of a Norfolk clergyman, he joined the NAVY aged 12 in 1770. After service in the Arctic and the WEST INDIES, his first command took him to fight in the War of AMERICAN INDEPENDENCE. With war again imminent in 1793, he sailed with Admiral Hood to the Mediterranean, where he lost his right eye in fighting off Corsica, and was then involved in the victory against the combined French and Spanish forces at Cape St Vincent in 1797. He lost his right arm in an unsuccessful attack on Santa Cruz in Tenerife that same year, but he was again fighting against the French Revolutionary forces in the Mediterranean in 1798. It was at this time that he met Emma Hamilton, whose husband was British ambassador in Naples; their love affair lasted until Nelson's death. He returned to England and a hero's welcome for his devastating defeat of the French in the battle of the NILE (1798). Promoted to rear-admiral in 1801, he disregarded a vacillating superior to win the battle of COPENHAGEN. The tactic of breaking the line instead of fighting in line, first used by Rodney in the battle of the SAINTS (1782), was used by Nelson to devastating effect at the battle of TRAFALGAR in 1805. He was killed during the battle when his flagship, the *Victory*, came under heavy musket fire, but his destruction of the French fleet established Britain as the world's foremost naval power and Nelson in a frontline position in the pantheon of British heroes. *See also* FRENCH REVOLUTIONARY and NAPOLEONIC WARS; WARFARE, NAVAL.

Nelson Monument ('Nelson's Column'), Trafalgar Square, London, erected by voluntary subscription to commemorate NELSON's victory at Trafalgar. Sir Edwin Landseer was responsible for the bronze lions that were added to the base in 1867, 25 years after William Railton's 145-foot-high column was erected. Its appropriation by the masses and transformation into a platform of populist politics was neither foreseen nor intended.

Nennius (*fl.* early 9th century), Welsh scholar. One of the few surviving histories of 'Dark Age' Britain – the *Historia Britonum* ('History of the Britons') – has been attributed to him. However, it is now doubted that he was the actual author; rather, his name was probably appended to some of the surviving manuscripts of what was a complex editorial compilation. The *Historia* contains much material – a great deal of it the stuff of legends – on characters such as AMBROSIUS AURELIANUS, VORTIGERN and ARTHUR.

Neo-Classical Economics, the school of thought which emerged in the latter part of the 19th century. Its prime exponent in Britain was Alfred Marshall (1842–1924) who, as professor of economics at CAMBRIDGE, was very influential in affecting the thinking of the next generation of economists, including J. M. KEYNES. Unlike the classical school, which emphasized the factors which caused long-run growth and change in the capitalist ECONOMY, the neo-classical school shifted the focus of attention to the way given resources are allocated to meet the wants of the population. In neo-classical economics the market was portrayed as the mechanism which carried out this allocation, and at the same time harmoniously reconciled the interests of consumers and producers, of employees and employers. In this respect neo-classical economists devoted much effort to developing a theory of individual choice, built around the concepts of profit maximization by the firm and utility maximization by the individual consumer. Thus the individual decision-taker, rather than social categories such as class, became the unit of analysis. In this respect the neo-classical school was counterposed to MARXism, which emphasized the conflictual features of capitalist society. Mathematical modes of analysis also became more common-place as the chief exponents of the school sought greater rigour. The level of abstraction was signified by the fact that, whereas the classical school referred to the subject as political economy, the neo-classical school used the term economics.

Neo-Classicism, fashionable architectural style in the late 18th century. Classical aesthetics were reappraised following the publication of a number of archaeologically based studies of ancient architecture, notably Robert Wood's *Ruins of Palmyra* (1753), James Stuart and Nicholas Revett's *Antiquities of Athens* (1762) and Robert Adam's *Ruins of the Palace of the Emperor Diocletian* (1764). Adam's Kedleston Hall, Derbys. (1760–70) exemplified the new style, as did churches by Simon, Earl Harcourt and Stuart at Nuneham Courtney, Oxon. (1764) and by Revett at Ayot St Lawrence, Herts. (1778). Discoveries of relatively well-preserved buildings at Pompeii and Herculaneum influenced Adam's interiors. Other variants included Robert Mylne and Henry Holland's more austere, French-influenced neo-classicism, and a mannered version, largely abandoning classical ornament, associated with George Dance the Younger and John Soane. The style is to be distinguished from the earlier PALLADIANISM.

Neo-Harringtonianism, modern historians' term for a set of ideas – derived from or resembling those of the political writer James Harrington (1611–77) – espoused by some 'COUNTRY' critics of the political and social order established after the GLORIOUS REVOLUTION. Neo-Harringtonians idealized what they conceived to be Britain's ancient constitution, and emphasized the importance of civic virtue and a civic MILITIA. They feared corruption, STANDING ARMIES and the proliferation of placemen and pensioners. Some who held these views probably took them from the same sources as Harrington – from classical republican writers, or from Machiavelli and other Italian 'civic humanists'.

Neo-Palladianism, *see* PALLADIANISM

Neo-Platonism, the religious and mystical adaptation of the philosophy of Plato (427–347 BC), inspired by the writings of Plotinus (AD ?205–70) and his biographer Porphyry (?230–?305). Plotinus described God as being experienced in a threefold way. Most purely, God was the One or the Good, who could only be approached through the world of ideas (*nous* or 'thought'); in a yet lower form, God was the World Soul, a mediator between the world of ideas and that of tangible matter.

Despite official Christian distrust, Christian writers were very influenced by neo-platonism, especially Augustine of Hippo (354–430) and various mystics. The RENAISSANCE created a new passion for neo-platonism, and its literature had a wide if sometimes diffused influence on writers and scientists – e.g. Giordano Bruno (1548–1600), John Dee (1527–1608), Edward Herbert (1583–1648) and Philip Sidney (1534–86). Many of the works of continental neo-Platonists familiar to English Latin-speaking scholars in the 16th century, were only first published in English translation in the mid-17th century; more books on ALCHEMY were published between 1650 and 1680 than before or since, sustaining its influence on scientific enquiry. *See also* HERMETICISM.

Netherlands, Revolt of the The Netherlands, or Low Countries (roughly, the modern kingdoms of Belgium and the Netherlands), were England's chief trading partner during the late medieval and Tudor period. Their struggle against Spain for independence therefore vitally affected England and helped to end its Burgundian alliance (*see* BURGUNDY AND ENGLAND).

England's increasing involvement in the crisis was prompted by fears that one of the consequences of a Spanish victory would be an alteration in the equation of power in the North Sea. The alliance of England and the independent Dutch later faltered when the two countries became overseas commercial rivals (*see* DUTCH WARS).

CHRONOLOGY

1567 Duke of Alva's successful repression brings first large Spanish army to Low Countries; English alarm.

1572 New taxation plans cause renewed rebellion; probably to add to Spanish problems, ELIZABETH I expels Dutch PRIVATEERS ('sea beggars'); they seize Brill.

1581 United Provinces (federation of seven northern provinces of the Netherlands) formally depose Philip and declare independence.

1584 Dutch leader William the Silent assassinated; Spanish triumph.

1585 Collapse of French government, previously a check on Spain, persuades a reluctant Elizabeth that intervention is necessary: treaty of NONSUCH and Leicester's (*see* DUDLEY, ROBERT) none-too-successful expeditionary force.
1587–8 Instead of following up successes, Spanish army waits to liaise with ARMADA for (abortive) invasion of England.
1590s Dutch gain initiative; English backing, though useful, is secondary.
1609 Twelve Years' Truce between Spain and United Provinces recognizes military stalemate. Low Countries partitioned: south remains Spanish.

Neville, Anne, *see* ANNE NEVILLE

Neville, Richard (16th [1st Neville] Earl of Warwick)(1428–71), nobleman, known since the 16th century as 'The Kingmaker'. Son of Richard Neville, Earl of Salisbury, he became the richest of the English earls as a result of his marriage to the Warwick heiress, Anne Beauchamp. Traditional Neville enmity with the PERCYS induced Warwick and his father to support RICHARD OF YORK in the factional rivalry at HENRY VI'S court. In 1455, Warwick distinguished himself at ST ALBANS, and was appointed captain of CALAIS, in which office he made himself a popular hero (particularly in Kent and the rest of the south-east) by plundering neutral shipping and then defying the LANCASTRIAN government that reprimanded him. In consequence, he and other YORKISTS were indicted in 1459, and he fled with them from Ludlow when their appeal to arms failed. The following year, after raising troops at Calais and in Kent, he captured Henry at NORTHAMPTON, but then lost possession of him when MARGARET OF ANJOU defeated him at the second battle of St Albans in Feb. 1461.

Following EDWARD IV'S decisive victory at TOWTON, Warwick was given command of the siege operations against Lancastrian strongholds in Northumbria (1462–4). However, he increasingly felt denied the influence he thought was his due, and began to plot with the equally dissatisfied George Plantagenet, 3rd Duke of Clarence, younger brother of Edward IV, to whom he married his daughter Isabel in 1469. Then Warwick rebelled, killing those of his political enemies – WOODVILLES and Herberts – who fell into his hands, and capturing Edward. However, after holding the king in confinement for several weeks in the summer of 1469, he was forced to release him. He rebelled again in 1470, this time intending to put Clarence on the throne, but instead he was compelled to flee to France, where he came to terms with Margaret of Anjou.

In Sept. 1470, he invaded England, and when his brother, John Neville, Marquess of Montagu, decided to support him, it was Edward's turn to flee. Warwick now swore allegiance to Henry VI, but in 1471, his cautious strategy allowed Edward to recover possession of both London and the Lancastrian king. When Warwick belatedly risked battle at BARNET, he was defeated and killed.

Although Warwick was admired by many – 'the most courageous and manliest knight living,' wrote a London chronicler – his unscrupulous ambition and ruthless treatment of his enemies significantly exacerbated the brutality of the WARS OF THE ROSES.

Neville's Cross, Battle of, 17 Oct. 1346. While EDWARD III was engaged at the siege of CALAIS, DAVID II of Scotland invaded England in support of his French ally. He was intercepted near DURHAM by an army raised by the archbishop of York. Unable to stand on the defensive against the fire of English archers, the Scots attacked and were defeated, David being wounded and captured. His 11-year captivity and the need to raise taxes to pay for his ransom meant that this battle had major consequences in the development of Scottish government.

Nevis, *see* ST KITTS AND NEVIS

New Allies, *see* BROAD-BOTTOM MINISTRY

New Brunswick, eastern coastal province of CANADA, first explored and settled by the French in the 16th century. The French were ousted in 1703, although a prominent French community remains in Acadia. New Brunswick became a major destination of the 40,000 or more LOYALISTS from the former Thirteen Colonies in and after the War of AMERICAN INDEPENDENCE.

New Churches, Commission for The Commission, established by an Act of 1711 to superintend the construction of 50 new ANGLICAN churches in and around LONDON and WESTMINSTER – to be financed by a tax on coal – was a response both to metropolitan growth and to the threat of DISSENT. Only 12 were built. These included Gibbs' St Martin-in-the-Fields (1722–6) and St Mary-le-Strand (1714–17), and Nicholas Hawksmoor's Christ Church, Spitalfields (1714–29).

New Dissent, a late 18th-century Evangelical revival within the ranks of the old DISSENTING denominations, especially among INDEPENDENTS or CONGREGATIONALISTS and Particular BAPTISTS; General Baptists spawned a breakaway New Connexion in 1770. It was associated with an emphasis on conversion, repentance and faith, with the development of a more active, populist style (following METHODIST precedents) and with a rapid growth in membership. The term is also loosely applied to the Methodist connexions and their offshoots, in contrast to the older Dissenting bodies. Growth was sustained until about 1840, but slackened thereafter as the movement became institutionalized and ossified, and the Church of England was revitalized by EVANGELICALISM and the OXFORD MOVEMENT; absolute decline set in early in the 20th century.

New Draperies, term used to describe the lighter, finished, fulled and dyed WOOLLEN cloths which became more important in the English CLOTH INDUSTRY from the mid-16th century onwards. They replaced the OLD DRAPERIES; many of the styles and techniques were introduced by Flemish Protestant REFUGEES.

New England, name frequently given to the north-eastern states of the USA and former British colonies in North America, of which MASSACHUSETTS was and is the most important. JAMES II's intention to make them a formal grouping failed to come to fruition.

New English, *see* IRELAND, NEW ENGLISH IN

New Hampshire, one of the original Thirteen Colonies which broke with Britain in 1776 to form the USA. Originally a territory of the MASSACHUSETTS Bay Company, its status was anomalous until its separate identity was confirmed in 1692, following the short-lived experiment of a united NEW ENGLAND colony.

New Hebrides, *see* VANUATU

New Jersey, *see* NEW YORK

New Lanark, a cotton-spinning complex in Scotland acquired by Robert OWEN in 1799 and transformed by him into a model industrial community and showpiece of enlightened paternalism. Owen's 18th-century confidence in the perfectibility of man, allied to his belief in environment as a character-forming agent, prompted him to introduce improved housing, childcare, educational and leisure facilities at New Lanark, to restrict child labour and to abolish corporal punishment in schools and factories. The utopian community failed by 1828, but the buildings have been restored in recent years.

New Liberalism, a restatement of political principles and social philosophy in the early 20th century, which acknowledged the need for greater government involvement in social affairs so that the LIBERAL PARTY might be better placed to meet the challenges posed by the exposure of poverty and national inefficiency and the growth of socialism. The Liberal social welfare reforms of 1906–14, associated with LLOYD GEORGE and Winston CHURCHILL, were in part a reflection of the New Liberalism. *See also* LABOUR EXCHANGE ACT 1909; OLD AGE PENSIONS ACT 1908; TOYNBEE HALL.

New Model Army Following Parliamentarian reverses in autumn 1644 during the CIVIL WARS, the SELF-DENYING ORDINANCE removed army commanders, and the forces were restructured to form the 'New Model'. Officers were retained on the basis of competence, and after a shaky start, the new force's victories ended the first Civil War. Its high morale and discipline owed more to regular pay and tolerable relations between officers and men than to the radical religion that undoubtedly became common in its ranks. The majority in PARLIAMENT soon felt fear rather than gratitude towards it; its continued existence was one of the main political problems for regimes in the INTERREGNUM. Although most of its regiments were disbanded at the RESTORATION, the remainder formed the basis for the STANDING ARMY of CHARLES II and JAMES II.

New Model Unions, a term employed by Sidney and Beatrice WEBB to define the characteristic form of mid-Victorian craft unions. These unions of the LABOUR ARISTOCRACY were national in scope, centralized in management and socially exclusive, with high subscription rates to support an extensive range of payments for sickness, unemployment, pensions, funerals and emigration. Led by practical and capable men, who formed the so-called JUNTA, they were careful in the use of STRIKE action but tenacious in the defence of their craft privileges and social position. Though the Webbs placed emphasis on the novelty of this approach, modern historians have stressed continuity rather than discontinuity, highlighting the persistence of an artisanal culture based on several centuries of small-scale craft manufacture and associated guilds, alongside a mass of ephemerally organized workers just as prone to direct action in the third quarter of the 19th century as they had been before.

New Party Founded by Sir Oswald MOSLEY in 1931, following his resignation from the LABOUR government the previous year when his 'Memorandum' on unemployment was rejected, the party's objective was to put into effect his radical proposals to solve unemployment, published in the *Mosley Manifesto*. Seventeen Labour MPs signed the *Manifesto*, six of whom joined Mosley's party. The New Party put up 24 candidates in the 1931 general election but all were defeated, only Mosley saving his deposit. The total failure to attract support led Mosley the following year to abandon the constitutional path and found the British Union of FASCISTS, effectively dissolving the New Party.

New South Wales, first of the states of AUSTRALIA. COOK explored the coast in 1770, discovering BOTANY BAY, which became the setting for the 1788 penal colony. After initial privations farms were soon established, and by the 1820s settlement and exploration ranged wide. In 1850 it had the leading colonial economy, through WOOL, soon boosted by the GOLD RUSH and COAL-mining. In 1901 New South Wales joined five other colonies in the Commonwealth of Australia; it is and was the largest and most productive Australian economy.

New Statesman, independent weekly founded in 1913 by Sidney and Beatrice WEBB as a vehicle for the idea of the FABIAN SOCIETY. It merged in 1931 with the LIBERAL-oriented *Nation* and enjoyed a substantial growth in circulation and influence during the next 30 years under the editorship of Kingsley Martin. Later editors of note included John Freeman, Paul Johnson and Richard Crossman. A usual supporter of the LABOUR PARTY and a forum for debate about its policies and future, it merged with *New Society* in 1988 to become *New Statesman and Society*.

New Style, *see* GREGORIAN CALENDAR

New Towns, a term used specifically to describe the towns set up under the provisions of the New Towns Act of 1946 to provide new focuses of urban development and relieve urban congestion. The Act set up New Town Development Corporations with sweeping powers to create new communities: eight new towns were designated in the London 'overspill' ring by 1948 and more than 20 elsewhere in the country by 1970, including Peterlee, Co. Durham (1948), Cumbernauld, Strathclyde (1956), Skelmersdale, Lancs. (1962) and MILTON KEYNES, Bucks. (1967). Although affected by their share of economic and social problems, the new towns have been widely regarded as one of the most successful and imaginative schemes of British social policy since the war. The initiatives resulting from the 1946 Act are to be distinguished from those of the earlier GARDEN CITY MOVEMENT.

New Unionism, historians' term to describe the labour upsurge and the formation of an allegedly new kind of general labour union around the time of the DOCK STRIKE of 1889. Whereas the older trade societies were exclusive unions of craftsmen with high subscription charges and non-industrial functions (*see* NEW MODEL UNIONS), the new TRADE UNIONS were meant to embrace all workers regardless of skill or training, with low dues and without the provision of sickness, unemployment and other FRIENDLY SOCIETY benefits to impede the pursuit of a fighting policy. The new unionism was considered by G. D. H. Cole, writing in the late 1940s, and other historians to have been socialist in intention. However, the new unions are now considered to have been driven less by ideology and more by the requirements of survival in varying industrial contexts.

New Universities, a term used for UNIVERSITIES mainly created following the Robbins Report of 1963, which recommended a major increase in the provision of higher education. It proposed a target of 60 universities and 0.5 million students in higher education by 1980, and recommended that six new universities should be created immediately, existing universities should be expanded, and other higher education institutions should be given university status. Amongst the new universities to be given their charters in the 1960s were Sussex, York, Lancaster, Warwick, Stirling, Essex and East Anglia. By 1972 there were 45 universities compared with 17 in 1945, and the number of university students had doubled within a decade. The Robbins target, however, remained unattained in 1980, though much of the shortfall was taken up by students taking degree courses at the 30 POLYTECHNICS set up since 1967. In turn, the term 'new universities' came to be applied to the polytechnics when the binary line between the two types of institution was abolished in 1992.

New World English fishing fleets began visiting NEWFOUNDLAND as early as the 1480s. Under ELIZABETH I, English seamen performed spectacular feats of exploration and made various claims of territorial annexation in America, in an effort to outflank their Spanish rivals; however, all foundations of permanent colonies proved abortive until the early 17th century.

Thereafter, there was steady progress in acquiring territories in the Caribbean and mainland North America. Much settlement in the latter had a religious motive, with colonists seeking to escape the constraints of the English Established Church. As a result, there was an uneasy relationship between many colonial administrations and the royal government at home.

The colonies were split in their allegiances during the CIVIL WARS in Britain, but CHARLES I derived little useful help from those who supported his cause. The collapse of JAMES II's regime (1688–9) proved a blow to the efforts of Westminster to encroach on self-rule in North America. Through the 18th century, until the War of AMERICAN INDEPENDENCE, the relationship between the centre and the colonies remained problematic.

CHRONOLOGY

1480s English fishing fleets begin visiting Newfoundland.
1562 John HAWKINS first to seek English share of West African SLAVE TRADE to Spanish Caribbean colonies.
1583 Humphrey Gilbert formally claims Newfoundland.
1585–6 Expeditions sponsored by RALEIGH fail to establish permanent colony of VIRGINIA on Roanoke Island (now part of North Carolina).
1607 Jamestown established: first settlement of Virginia.
1609 BERMUDA settled.
1620 New England Council chartered for settlement further north than Virginia; achieves nothing (dissolved 1635), but agrees to SEPARATIST refugees founding Plymouth colony (*see* MAYFLOWER PILGRIMS).
1627 BARBADOS settled.
1628 PURITAN settlement in MASSACHUSETTS: John Winthrop first governor. Strict CONGREGATIONAL church establishment. NEVIS settled.
1632 MONTSERRAT and ANTIGUA settled; MARYLAND settled under George Calvert.
1635 Connecticut founded.
1636 Rhode Island founded by Roger Williams to escape New England intolerance.
1643 New England colonists back PARLIAMENT against CHARLES I.
1655 Conquest of JAMAICA from Spain.
1663 North and South CAROLINA established.
1664 English seize New Amsterdam from Dutch: renamed NEW YORK.
1665 New Jersey established.
1666 BAHAMAS and Virgin Islands settled.
1678 TURKS AND CAICOS ISLANDS settled.
1682 Pennsylvania established by William Penn.
1698–9 Attempted Scots settlement in DARIEN (Panama) fails; English not displeased.
1723 Foundation of GEORGIA.
1761 Conquest of DOMINICA from France.
1762 Capitulation of ST VINCENT and GRENADA by French.
1763 First cession of TOBAGO from France.
1767 Capitulation of TRINIDAD by Spanish.
1803 Reconquest of Tobago from French.
1832 Major slave rebellion in Jamaica.
1865 Brutal suppression of JAMAICA INSURRECTION.

New Year's Gifts Customarily given in medieval and early modern England on 1 Jan., rather than the GREGORIAN Old Style beginning of the New Year, 25 March, these became an important part of Tudor court ceremonial, ranging from simple tokens given by menial servants, to highly elaborate pieces of plate made specially for the occasion. Often they served as an indicator of political fortunes. Refusal of a gift by the monarch was a sure sign of political eclipse, and the relative value of a king's or queen's gifts, even the precise number of ounces of precious metal used, was an accurate comparative guide to the current pecking order at court.

New York, state of the USA and one of the Thirteen Colonies which broke from Britain in 1776 in the War of AMERICAN INDEPENDENCE. Originally a Dutch possession, New Netherland, the territory was acquired by England in 1665 in the Second DUTCH WAR. CHARLES II presented it to his brother, the Duke of York (later JAMES II), hence the name given to the colony. A slice of territory was presented to Sir George Carteret of Jersey and Lord Berkeley, and took the name New Jersey. The acquisition of these territories completed the line of British colonies along the north-eastern seaboard. New York city (formerly New Amsterdam), on the navigable Hudson River, rose to increasing prominence as a port and centre of population in the colonial era.

New Zealand Sighted by Captain James COOK in 1769, the islands remained unexploited by European trade and settlement until the 1830s. With the formation of the New Zealand Company (1839) under Edward Gibbon Wakefield, systematic colonization began. Formal annexation followed the Treaty of Waitangi (1840). Representative institutions were created in 1852 and ministerial responsibility was granted four years later. New Zealand's early years were troubled by the Maori Wars, but by the third quarter of the 19th century, the Maoris had been Christianized and granted access to public office. The economy was greatly boosted by the series of GOLD RUSHES initiated by the discovery of gold in 1861. Close ties were maintained with Great Britain through continued MIGRATION and military assistance in the BOER WAR and in both WORLD WARS. New Zealand acquired DOMINION status in 1907 and became a member of the COMMONWEALTH in 1947.

Newburgh, William of, *see* WILLIAM OF NEWBURGH

Newcastle, 1st Duke of, *see* CAVENDISH, WILLIAM

Newcastle, 4th Duke of, *see* PELHAM-HOLLES, THOMAS

Newcastle Commission, 1858–61. Chaired by Henry Pelham Clinton, 5th Duke of Newcastle (1811–64), and prompted by concern at the rising level of public expenditure and the growth of bureaucratic control, the Commission examined the measures required for the extension of sound and cheap elementary EDUCATION to all classes. Its report, published in 1861, recommended that public money for education be continued, with the proviso that such support should be dependent upon a system of PAYMENT BY RESULTS. Both proposals were accepted. *See also* EDUCATION.

Newcastle Upon Tyne, Tyne & Wear (formerly Northumb.), coal, shipbuilding and port city on the north bank of the River Tyne. A former Roman fort, Newcastle – a royal CASTLE intended to subdue the Scots and the northern barons – was given a charter in the 12th century. Despite constant warring with the Scots, a town flourished within the castle walls in the Middle Ages. It received county status in 1400, by which time the COAL INDUSTRY had already grown considerably. At first coal was taken from open workings on the town moor and in nearby settlements, but by the 15th century shallow pits were being dug. The coal trade provided domestic heating fuel which was increasingly being taken by coastal shipping to London, hence 'sea coal'. The town's wealth and size increased steadily with the trade; the writer Celia Fiennes, on her travels around England *c.* 1687–1701, remarked that it was the city most like LONDON for up-to-date buildings in 1698. Rapid growth occurred through the 18th century, as coal was used for industrial applications, and the city acquired its present NEO-CLASSICAL appearance.

The coming of the RAILWAY in 1849 caused the building of Robert Stephenson's High Level Bridge over the Tyne and the almost total destruction of the 12th- and 14th-century castle to build the station. A city of some 90,000 people had swollen to 250,000 by the 1911 census, with William Armstrong's works at Elswick for armaments, cranes and SHIPBUILDING a key element in the city's later 19th-century growth. Growth has been markedly slower in the course of the 20th century, especially within Newcastle itself, although all the Tyneside communities have ultimately grown into each other. The eclipse of coal and shipbuilding have hit both the city and its region hard; it was one of the most intense focuses of economic DEPRESSION in the inter-war years (*see* JARROW CRUSADE), and had ASSISTED AREA status from the 1920s onwards. Newcastle remains an important regional centre with a highly developed sense of identity.

Newfoundland, Canadian province and the first British possession in North America. Discovered by Sebastian Cabot in 1495, Newfoundland became the centre of the cod-fishing industry with a brisk business in dried fish, especially to Catholic Europe. Initially conducted by small individual traders, Basque and French as well as English, on the foundation of the Newfoundland Company in 1605 the trade was restricted to its members. Newfoundland was also the springboard for the foundation of the HUDSON'S BAY COMPANY, with its interests in fur trading and opening up the Canadian interior, which was chartered in 1670. A representative assembly for Newfoundland was set up in 1832, and self-government along the lines of the rest of CANADA followed in 1855. Grave financial problems bedevilled Newfoundland, which after 1933 reverted to being a crown colony with the UK responsible for its finances. In a 1948 referendum the population voted narrowly in favour of federation with Canada, of which Newfoundland became a province in 1949.

Newgate, the prison of the City of London and the county of Middlesex, also sometimes used to hold state prisoners. Originally housed above a City gate, it was removed to a new building in 1770. It was closed in 1880, and finally demolished in 1902 to make way for the Central Criminal Court of the Old Bailey. Public executions, previously staged at TYBURN (Marble Arch), took place outside the prison from 1783 to 1868. The *Newgate Calendar* was an occasional and popular publication of biographies of notorious criminals, first published in 1773.

Newman, John Henry (1801–90), churchman and Cardinal. From a pious EVANGELICAL background, he went to OXFORD UNIVERSITY and was elected a fellow of Oriel College in 1822, becoming vicar of St Mary's, the university church, in 1828. Here he became celebrated as a compelling preacher, with as much influence among undergraduates as SIMEON had on a previous generation at CAMBRIDGE. By then his theology had moved away from his childhood evangelicalism, and he was one of the circle of Oxford clerics who emerged as leaders of the OXFORD MOVEMENT after the enthusiastic reaction to John Keble's Assize Sermon in 1833. He became one of the principal editors of the propaganda series *Tracts for the Times* and the journal *The British Critic*, but was astonished and shocked at the public reaction (particularly from the bishop of Oxford) to his Tract 90 (1841), an ingenious if perverse attempt to argue that the 39 Articles of doctrine of the CHURCH OF ENGLAND were compatible with CATHOLIC theology. This furore accentuated his growing doubts about the claims to Catholic continuity of his Church. After a period of agonized reflection in charge of his DAUGHTER CHURCH and religious community at Littlemore, he renounced ANGLICANISM in 1842, being received into the Roman Catholic Church in 1845 – a move which profoundly shocked many of his fellow TRACTARIANS. After a period in Rome, he returned to England and founded the religious communities known as oratories at BIRMINGHAM (1847) and LONDON (1850); he was principal founder and first rector of a new Catholic university in DUBLIN (1854). He was made a cardinal in 1877, but was always regarded with suspicion as dangerously liberal by many Roman Catholics, especially his fellow-convert and cardinal Henry Manning. Among his voluminous writings, which include his sermons and some well-known hymns, outstanding is his account of his conversion to Rome, *Apologia pro Vita Sua* (1864), a riposte to Charles Kingsley.

Newspapers The regular circulation of news in print has its origins in the 17th century, especially in the ferment of the CIVIL WAR and the liberalization following the abolition of STAR CHAMBER in 1641. News-sheets, and then regular newsbooks such as *Mercurius Britannicus* from 1644, carried information, opinion and propaganda. The regular issue of newspapers after the RESTORATION, notably the eventual official journal of record, the *London Gazette* (originally the *Oxford Gazette*) from 1665, was controlled until the lapse of the LICENSING ACT in 1679. Before its control was reimposed in 1685 there was a flood of new titles. With the Act's final abolition in 1695, newspapers were given a new legal status; and although they were restricted by the stamp, paper, advertisement and other duties, until the final abolition of duty in 1855, newspapers with their news, gossip, advertisements and useful knowledge grew in number, range and status. There were 12 London newspapers in 1712, and 52 a century later; Sunday newspapers began in 1779. The growth in the English provincial press was even more marked, from 24 titles in 1723 to over 100 by 1805.

Massive growth occurred in the course of the 19th century, as fiscal restrictions were reduced in the 1830s and then abolished. Widening communications encouraged the thirst for news, and major events such as the CRIMEAN WAR revealed (and fostered) a public appetite for information. The professionalization of reporting and publication accompanied the constant growth in titles and circulation. *The Times*, which grew to pre-eminence in the years 1800–60, was gradually eclipsed by other national titles, each seeking to serve a particular set of interests. The premier newspaper in Scotland, *The Scotsman*, began production in 1817. The CHARTIST newspaper, Feargus O'Connor's *Northern Star*, was one of the pioneering organs of popular journalism, while the *News of the World*, founded 1843, is the great survivor of the then new phenomenon of popular Sunday papers. The 1840s saw the establishment of a new type of professional and general periodical press, including the *Lancet*, *Punch*, and the *Economist*, to stand alongside the existing quarterlies such as the *EDINBURGH REVIEW* and *QUARTERLY REVIEW*. The first cheap daily newspaper, the *Daily Telegraph*, founded in 1855, ushered in a new age, which distributors W. H. SMITH fully exploited with the expanding RAILWAY network.

The golden age of British newspapers is generally held to have been the period 1860–1900, with mass-production, technical advances in printing, new styles of journalism, and the prominence of a new breed of proprietors owning a portfolio of titles. The establishment of news agencies from 1863, notably the Press Association in 1868, provided new conduits for information-gathering, while news styles were transformed by the pioneering 'yellow journalism' of W. T. Stead and the *Pall Mall Gazette* from the 1880s. The *Yorkshire Post*, largest of the provincial newspapers, began daily publication in 1866, over a century after its foundation; Scotland's currently most popular newspaper, the *Daily Record*, was founded in 1895. The first mass circulation popular newspaper, the *Daily Mail* was founded in 1896 by Alfred Harmsworth (Viscount Northcliffe, 1865–1922) and by 1918 the 'busy man's journal' was selling over a million copies. Newspapers, often reflecting the stance of their owners, took an increasingly partisan political position at the turn of the century. This was most apparent in the years of WORLD WAR I, when the so-called press barons, the Harmsworth and Berry brothers, had become so dominant. The Harmsworth press was almost hysterically anti-German, and certainly also used its might in opposition to ASQUITH.

Fleet Street, the LONDON thoroughfare where newspaper production and ownership was concentrated, became the synonym for the industry. Increasing markets and decreasing numbers of newspaper owners in the inter-war years made the face of British newspapers recognizably that which they are today. The Harmsworths – Lords Northcliffe and Rothermere – and the Berrys – Lords Camrose (1879–1954) and Kemsley (1883–1968) – were joined by Max Aitken, Lord Beaverbrook in dominating the industry; there was also a recognizable journalistic left-wing trend to offset their influence. The profoundest change post-war was the rise of what has become known as tabloid journalism, with smaller page-size newspapers alongside the heavier-weight broadsheets; the prominence of Cecil Harmsworth King (1901–87), nephew of both Northcliffe and Rothermere, with the *Daily Mirror* at the centre of his International Publishing Corporation, was symptomatic of the newer style. The only provincial success against the overwhelming metropolitan bias was the transfer of the left-leaning *Manchester Guardian* to London in 1963. The legacy of the growing success in the 1960s of the heavier-weight Sunday newspapers, with their colour supplements and glossy advertising, persists.

Consolidation in the 1970s saw the first assault on the power of the Fleet Street TRADE UNIONS (eventually to result in the demise of the street itself as a centre of newspaper publishing and production), and the emergence of new journalistic styles, more aggressive – and, many said, down market – than ever before. The success of the Australian proprietor Rupert Murdoch (1931–), and particularly the *Sun*, is symptomatic of that shift. Newspapers continue to be bought and read in large numbers, despite the inroads which radio and TELEVISION have made.

CURRENT NATIONAL NEWSPAPERS WITH FOUNDING DATES

Daily Express	1900
Daily Mail	1896
Daily Mirror	1903
Daily Star	1978
Daily Telegraph	1855
Evening Standard	1827
Evening News (ceased 1980)	1881
Financial Times	1888
Independent	1986
Independent on Sunday	1990
[Manchester] Guardian	1821
Mail on Sunday	1982
News of the World	1843
The Observer	1791
The People	1881
The Sun	1964
Sunday Express/Express on Sunday	1918
Sunday Pictorial/Sunday Mirror	1915
Sunday Business	1998
Sunday Telegraph	1961
Sunday Times	1822
The Times	1785

Newton, Sir Isaac (1642–1727), mathematician and natural philosopher. Having left school to work on the family farm, he was sent back on the advice of an uncle, and then went to Cambridge, graduating in 1665. His three laws of motion, including the universal law of gravitation, overturned Aristotelian mechanics, and his method of fluxions formed the basis of differential and integral calculus. He published *Philosophiae Naturalis Principia Mathematica* in 1687, and *Optics*, which proposed a combination of wave and corpuscular theories of light, in 1704. He was interested in ALCHEMY and astrology, and was guarded about his religious beliefs, gaining a dispensation to hold a CAMBRIDGE professorship without being in holy orders. He twice served as MP for the university, became master of the Royal Mint in 1699, and president of the ROYAL SOCIETY in 1703. Celebrated in his own lifetime as a seminal thinker, he was revered by the philosophers of the Enlightenment.

Next Five Years Group, pro-interventionist pressure group formed in 1932 by ex-LABOUR PARTY politician Clifford Allen, who became a supporter of MACDONALD'S NATIONAL LABOUR PARTY. The NFYG sought to draw together 'progressive' opinion from all parties to work out an agreed programme of social, economic and international policy. In 1935 it published a programme *The Next Five Years* and produced blueprints for future policy. Amongst its influential adherents were Harold MACMILLAN, Seebohm Rowntree, and Eleanor Rathbone, and it became an important focus for 'middle opinion', arguing for government intervention in the economic and social sphere within a democratic framework. The group broke up in 1939 on the outbreak of WORLD WAR II.

Nigeria, Commonwealth nation and former British colony. Like the GOLD COAST and SIERRA LEONE, Nigeria's origins lay in the trading forts established by Britain with the foundation of the ROYAL AFRICAN COMPANY in 1673. By the early and mid-19th century, missionaries and guns had come to West Africa, while the SLAVE TRADE continued inland. European incursions into the interior and the Niger river basin were hampered by disease and high mortality. In 1851 Britain intervened in the war among the native peoples for Lagos, annexing it as a colony in 1861, and gradually extending control in the coastal and inland river regions through the 1870s. The borders of Nigeria were established under Salisbury (*see* CECIL, ROBERT GASCOYNE) by treaties with the French and Germans in 1890 and by taking control in 1900 over the area of northern Nigeria previously run by the Royal Niger Company. The colony was complete in 1902, but in two halves, northern and southern, until united in 1914 when under the governorship of Frederick Lugard (1858–1945). Like its neighbours, Nigeria then became primarily dependent on cash crops.

The process of West African DECOLONIZATION began in Nigeria, with the new federal constitution of 1954. Full independence came in 1960, delayed by the local interests which were to come bloodily to the fore in the crippling civil war between Nigeria and the breakaway Biafra between 1967 and 1970.

Nightingale, Florence (1820–1910), founder of modern nursing. Florence Nightingale was brought up to have the typical limited expectations of an early Victorian upper-class young woman.

Her wealthy father relented when she was 24 and allowed her to enter nursing, at a time when hospitals were regarded as little better than brothels. Later, she used her £500 allowance to establish an Institution for Sick Gentlewomen in London, and the next year in response to stories in *The Times* about the wretched conditions of British soldiers wounded in the CRIMEAN WAR, was put in charge of a team of nurses sent by the prime minister, Aberdeen (*see* GORDON, GEORGE), to Scutari. Despite hostility from the military leaders, Nightingale's political contacts, missionary zeal and ruthless efficiency enabled her drastically to improve cleanliness and sanitation in the hospital. In a few months the death rate had dropped from 42 per cent to 2.2 per cent and she also instituted educational reforms and improved pay for the soldiers.

In 1856 she was invalided home from the Crimea. She spent the rest of her long life in ill-health, but lobbying tirelessly – for improved medical and sanitary standards in health care, and improved welfare conditions in INDIA (which she never visited) – and promoting the status of nursing. In 1860, with £45,000 raised by public subscription in gratitude for Nightingale's work in the Crimea, she set up a school of nursing at St Thomas's Hospital, London, where she planned every detail of the nurses' training. Within 20 years trained nurses were working in most large British voluntary hospitals and WORKHOUSES, as well as abroad. In 1907 she became the first woman to be awarded the Order of Merit.

She was a heroine in her lifetime, although her theories of medical non-intervention and her reforming abilities have subsequently been questioned.

Nile, Battle of the, 1–2 Aug. 1798. After landing Napoleon's army to conquer EGYPT and drive eastward from there, the French fleet moored in a defensive position in Aboukir Bay. NELSON's intercepting fleet tracked them down there and, confident in their superior training although nominally weaker, Nelson launched the fleet straight into battle. Attacking at sunset, they overwhelmed the French during the course of the night, the French flagship catching fire and blowing up, and after the following day's mopping up, only two French ships of the line and two FRIGATES escaped. It was the most complete victory in the age of sail, and its effect was to isolate Napoleon and his army in Egypt, creating the conditions in which the coalition against France could be organized. It also made Nelson into a hero both at home and abroad.

Nine Years War, *see* KING WILLIAM'S WAR

Nineteen Propositions, 1642, proposals put to CHARLES I by the opposition in PARLIAMENT, with the aim of drastically limiting his power. Charles rejected them in a dignified answer framed by his more moderate advisers.

1922 Committee, backbench organization of CONSERVATIVE MPs. It derives its name from a meeting at the CARLTON CLUB, London in 1922 when Conservative MPs decided to withdraw support from the LLOYD GEORGE coalition, precipitating its breakup. Prior to this, there was no effective backbench organization of Conservative members in the House of COMMONS. The 1922 Committee has remained the major focus for the articulation of backbench and grass-roots opinion within the Conservative party and its chairman is an influential figure; it is also now responsible for organizing elections for the party leadership.

Nisi Prius, *see* ASSIZES

Noble, an English gold COIN minted from 1344 until the early 17th century. Until 1464, it was valued at 6 shillings 8 pence (6s 8d) – half a MARK – and thereafter (as a rose-noble or ryal) at 10 shillings (10s).

Nominated Parliament, *see* BAREBONES PARLIAMENT

Nonconformity, a general term describing English and Welsh PROTESTANT Christians who do not belong to the CHURCH OF ENGLAND. Early in the 19th century it comprised two groupings – Old Dissent (BAPTISTS, INDEPENDENTS (later known as CONGREGATIONALISTS) and QUAKERS), and NEW DISSENT (METHODISTS). The SALVATION ARMY and the Plymouth BRETHREN emerged later in the century. By 1900 it was more normal to stress the independent and positive characteristics of the denominations rather than their relationship to the Established Church, and the term 'FREE CHURCH' replaced 'Nonconformist'. In 1828 the TEST AND CORPORATION ACTS were repealed, heralding the end of Nonconformist exclusion from politics and society. However, the final removal of social inequality was achieved only in the 1880s with the abolition of burial restrictions. Politically Nonconformity was closely linked with the LIBERALS, and Nonconformists campaigned for disestablishment. The religious census of 1851 showed Nonconformist church attendance close to that of Anglicans and revealed it as stronger than ANGLICANISM in major manufacturing areas. By the end of the century active Free Churchmen outnumbered active Anglicans.

Non-Jurors, High Church clerics who refused to take the OATH of allegiance to WILLIAM III and MARY II in 1689 and were deprived of their livings. They included William SANCROFT, archbishop of Canterbury, and six bishops, five of whom had been among the SEVEN BISHOPS who had been tried and acquitted in 1688. About 400 clergy refused to sign the Abjuration Act of 1702, acknowledging William and ANNE as lawful and rightful monarchs. Non-jurors forged close links with the EPISCOPAL CHURCH OF SCOTLAND, and with French Gallicans. They maintained their own episcopal hierarchy, but the movement collapsed on the death of the last bishop, the Manchester watchmaker Charles Booth, in 1805. *See also* HIGH CHURCHMANSHIP.

Non-Resistance, the doctrine – associated especially with late 17th- and early 18th-century TORYism – that subjects should never resist the commands of their king, or take up arms against him, even to protect their lives, liberty and property. In 1661, PARLIAMENT imposed an OATH of non-resistance on all clergymen and officeholders. Non-resistance did not necessarily preclude refusal to comply with orders should those orders be positively contrary to the will of God. The ideology was compatible with a variety of political stances: Thomas Sherlock in a sermon of 1704 turned it against the JACOBITES, arguing that the subject is bound to obey whatever the prince lawfully commands, however that authority may have been acquired. *See also* DIVINE RIGHT.

Non-Subscribers, *see* SALTER'S HALL CONTROVERSY

Nonsuch Palace, Surrey. This was HENRY VIII's most fanciful construction project: demolishing a village church and manor at Cuddington to build a palace in 1538 which was intended to rival the palace of the King of France, Francis I's Chambord. Unfinished at Henry's death, it was itself demolished for the private profit of one of CHARLES II's mistresses.

Nonsuch Treaty, 1585. Signed at NONSUCH PALACE, by it ELIZABETH I finally agreed to help the NETHERLANDS' rebels against Spain by sending permanent garrisons and an expeditionary force under Robert DUDLEY, Earl of Leicester.

Nootka Sound, an inlet on the west coast of Vancouver Island discovered by James COOK in 1778. The hope that a NORTHWEST PASSAGE from Europe to Asia might exit in that region, and Cook's suggestion that it would make a good fur-trading base, aroused interest in Britain, France, America and Russia. The Spanish, however, maintained their right to rule the Pacific coast, and in 1789 they arrested British traders and declared the American coast as far as Alaska a Spanish possession.

A prolonged diplomatic crisis ensued. When the United States unexpectedly failed to support Spain, agreement was reached, in July 1790. Spain was not to possess sovereignty, and would compensate the traders, but neither Spain nor Britain renounced the right to set up an exclusive base in the Sound.

Nore Mutiny, 1797, third in a series of

mutinies over naval conditions and discipline, which disrupted parts of the fleet during the FRENCH REVOLUTIONARY WARS. The first broke out in the Channel Fleet at Spithead in April 1797; the ADMIRALTY responded with a number of concessions, and pardoned the leaders. A mutiny at PLYMOUTH was settled with some violence in mid-May. Meanwhile, a more serious mutiny had broken out in the North Sea Fleet at the Nore near Sheerness in the Thames estuary: mutineers demanded that the terms agreed with the Channel Fleet should be extended to them, and that arrears of wages had to be paid before they would set sail.

The government was intransigent and stopped supplies; the mutineers responded by blockading London and threatening to sail to France. French and English JACOBIN involvement was suspected at the time; historians continue to dispute its extent and nature. The mutiny disintegrated in the second week of June; the mutineers' elected president, Richard Parker, was tried and executed, as were at least 36 others.

Norfolk, 8th and 9th Dukes of, *see* HOWARD, THOMAS

Norman Architecture, term sometimes used to describe ROMANESQUE architecture (i.e. referring back, however tenuously, to the style of Ancient Rome) as it developed in Britain in the later 11th and 12th centuries. Norman architecture is characterized by the solidity of its masonry and round-headed arches, seen in both churches and CASTLES, and one of the most distinctive Norman introductions. However, the boundaries between ANGLO-SAXON and Norman styles are not as clear-cut as many assume.

Norman Conquest, 1066, the conquest of England by Duke William of Normandy (*see* WILLIAM I THE CONQUEROR). This did far more than just provide English history with its most famous date. It meant the imposition of a new royal family, a new ruling class, a new culture and a new language; within a few years of 1066, the English had become an oppressed majority in their own country.

This had not been William's intention. After his victory at HASTINGS and his coronation on Christmas Day 1066, he expected that most English landowners would settle down to enjoy their customary privileges under the new regime. William would build royal CASTLES in key towns and punish HAROLD II's close associates, but otherwise would leave things much as they had been. However, a series of English revolts over the next few years posed formidable problems for the relatively small Norman army of occupation, and William was driven to take extreme measures such as the HARRYING OF THE NORTH.

By 1075, he had decided that he would be safe only if control over the land of England was in French hands, and embarked on a policy of wholesale transfer. By 1086, only two TENANTS-IN-CHIEF were English; the rest were foreign-born – Normans, Bretons, Flemings. The new ruling class brought with them a new language (ANGLO-NORMAN), as well as new names such as Richard, Robert and William.

The Norman Conquest has become a controversial subject. So massive were the changes it wrought that many historians have believed that virtually every aspect of society must have been transformed by it. Against this, others have emphasized the capacity of ANGLO-SAXON institutions to survive cataclysmic political and cultural changes. Thus there are many hotly – some would say too heatedly – debated subjects. In central government, for example, there is the question of whether there was a CHANCERY before 1066, and in religion, whether the pre-1066 Church was in a decadent state.

Above all there are two related questions. Did William introduce a new system of military obligation – the so-called 'KNIGHT SERVICE' or feudal levy system? And if he did, does this mean that he brought FEUDALISM to a previously non-feudal society? For a long time, the orthodox answer to both these questions was 'Yes'. Since the 1960s, however, a number of historians have questioned both orthodoxies and some have doubted the usefulness of the 'feudal' terminology. But however fiercely historians may disagree on these matters, they would almost certainly all agree that the Norman Conquest constitutes the greatest crisis so far in English history. *See also* SUCCESSION, ENGLISH, IN 1066.

Normandy, Duchy of This was created in north-west France during the 10th century, following the agreement with the VIKING chieftain Rollo known as the treaty of Saint-Clair-Sur-Epte. The political orientation of this Viking colony across the Channel was a matter of serious concern to the English, especially when its rulers provided harbours of refuge for the armies of SVEIN FORKBEARD and CNUT. It is also clear that Scandinavians moved to and fro across the Channel with considerable freedom.

By the year 1000, the settlers in Normandy were to a considerable degree integrated into their Frankish environment. The Normandy of the 11th century is no longer regarded as an advanced FEUDAL state; its institutions and customs differed little from those of its neighbours. A period of internal turmoil between 1025 and 1050 was followed by the development of closer ties of lordship and vassalage between the duke and the aristocracy and a remarkably close alliance between Duke William (the future WILLIAM I THE CONQUEROR) and the greatest landed families. This meant that Normandy, although a well-organized principality, lacked the structured SHIRE-COURTS and HUNDRED-courts typical of England. The Church, which only recovered in the 11th century from the devastations of the 10th, played an expanding role in Norman society and attracted great teachers such as the Italian LANFRANC.

Normandy Landings, *see* D-DAY; OVERLORD, OPERATION; WORLD WAR II

North, Frederick (8th Baron North, 4th (2nd North) Earl of Guilford) (1732–92), Whig politician and Prime Minister (1770–82). Son of a courtier, and known as 'Lord North' by courtesy before his succession to the title late in life, he was elected MP for Banbury in 1754 and supported Newcastle (*see* PELHAM-HOLLES, THOMAS). He took a leading part in parliamentary proceedings against WILKES, declined to serve under Rockingham (*see* WENTWORTH, CHARLES), but became paymaster of the forces under Chatham (*see* PITT THE ELDER), and chancellor of the Exchequer and leader in the Commons in 1767. He became first lord of the Treasury upon Grafton's (*see* FITZROY, AUGUSTUS) resignation in 1770.

An affable and adept parliamentarian, with a sound grasp of the business of his office, North attempted in the early 1770s to steer a middle course in relations with the rebellious American colonists, combining conciliation and firmness. However, even without pressure from hardliners in his Cabinet, he would probably not have been able to stem the drift to war. Anxious to preserve him in office, as the only competent minister prepared to pursue a line of policy palatable to him, GEORGE III none the less made North's life difficult by his rigidity and his habit of talking to other ministers behind North's back. After several times threatening to resign, North finally did so in March 1782, clearing the way for the recognition of AMERICAN INDEPENDENCE.

Now at odds with the king, North joined with FOX, and the two forced their way back to power in 1783, serving as secretaries of state under the nominal leadership of Portland (*see* BENTINCK, WILLIAM CAVENDISH); the king used the issue of Fox's INDIA BILL to force them back out. North opposed PITT THE YOUNGER, supporting the IMPEACHMENT of Warren Hastings, but declining health and increasing blindness led to his gradual withdrawal from Parliament. In 1790, he succeeded to his father's title, thus gaining a seat in the Lords. The fact that he had presided over the loss of most of Britain's American colonies inevitably tarnished his record at the time and since; contemporaries, however, respected his parliamentary skills, and historians have questioned whether any other minister would have handled the crisis to better effect.

North Atlantic Treaty Organization, *see* NATO

North Britain, term used to describe Scotland after the UNION of 1707, symbolizing the absorption of Scotland into a unified British state. Though it continued in occasional use into the early 20th century, from the late 18th century new stress was laid on Scottish identity as compatible with a broader British identity – most dramatically in 1822, when GEORGE IV visited Edinburgh dressed in Stuart tartan – and the neologism declined in favour.

North Briton, a weekly essay paper started in 1762 by John WILKES. Its name alluded to its opposition to the government paper *The Briton*, as well as to the Scottish ('North British') chief minister, John STUART, Earl of Bute. Wilkes was prosecuted for seditious libel for issue NUMBER 45 for allegations in relation to the king's speech.

North Sea Oil Before the 1970s Britain was

almost wholly dependent for its oil supplies on imports (*see* OIL INDUSTRY). The first oil discoveries were made in the North Sea in 1969 and the first oil was brought ashore in 1975. The exploitation of the reserves required new and challenging techniques of oil drilling and collection from platforms in all weathers. The discovery of indigenous supplies had a major beneficial effect on the balance of trade and upon government revenues, and the economy of ABERDEEN and north-east Scotland was transformed. By the mid-1980s Britain was the world's seventh-largest oil producer and was also an oil exporter. Output declined gradually from the mid-1980s peak, but Britain remains a significant oil producer into the 21st century. There is much controversy about the extent to which the economy has benefited from North Sea Oil, given the costs of exploitation and the terms under which rights were leased to private companies by the THATCHER government.

Northampton, Assize of, 1176, a reissue and elaboration of the Assize of CLARENDON. Its division of England into six judicial circuits came to be regarded as a crucial step in the making of the COMMON LAW. *See also* ASSIZES.

Northampton, 9th Earl of, *see* HOWARD, HENRY

Northampton, Treaty of, 1328, treaty made by MORTIMER and ISABELLA OF FRANCE when they found themselves short of funds after the expensive and embarrassing failure of their Stanhope Park campaign against the Scots. In the treaty, they recognized Robert BRUCE's kingship and renounced all claims in and over Scotland. In return, Bruce agreed to pay £20,000, most of which found its way into the private coffers of Mortimer and Isabella. In the opinion of both the young EDWARD III and the English public, the treaty was a shameful sellout.

Northern Earls' Rising, 1569–70, one result of the crisis caused by MARY QUEEN OF SCOTS' flight to England in 1568. The CATHOLIC earls of Northumberland and Westmorland (Charles Neville) turned vague schemes of rebellion and freeing Mary into hasty action after the arrest of Thomas HOWARD, 9th Duke of Norfolk, in Oct. 1569; in Nov., Northumberland seized Durham cathedral to celebrate MASS. However, the earls found that religious conservatism and feudal prestige were not enough to unite the north, and their march to face Thomas Radcliffe, earl of Sussex, at York petered out. After ragged skirmishes and one battle – at Naworth, Cumbria, on 20 Feb. 1570 – the leaders fled to Scotland. Government repression was harsh; the potential power of English Catholicism was broken and PROTESTANTISM more firmly established.

Northern Ireland, *see* ULSTER

Northern Territory Early attempts to colonize this region of AUSTRALIA were frustrated until the establishment of Darwin (named after Charles) in 1869. GOLD and mineral finds after 1874 boosted the colony, which from 1911–78 was administered by the Commonwealth government. Japanese bombing in 1942–4 – and hence the prospect of its being the gateway into the continent – changed attitudes to its importance. Cattle and mining are and were the mainstay.

Northumberland, 1st Duke of, *see* DUDLEY, JOHN

Northumbria One of the Anglo-Saxon kingdoms of the HEPTARCHY, it was also, with MERCIA and WESSEX, one of the three major English kingdoms in the period before the VIKING invasions and the 10th-century UNIFICATION of England. Created in the early 7th century by Ethelfrith from the two earlier kingdoms of BERNICIA and DEIRA (as well as from smaller units such as ELMET), at its height it stretched from the Humber to the Firth of Forth, and sometimes exercised hegemony over the STRATHCLYDE Britons, the PICTS and English kings to the south. Its greatest days were in the time of the 7th-century *BRETWALDAS* – EDWIN, OSWALD and OSWY – but claims to wider authority faded with the rise of Mercia under ETHELBALD and OFFA and the defeat by the Picts at NECHTANESMERE in 685.

The kingdom had great cultural importance, with its northerly situation making it a meeting-place of Romanizing Christianity and the Irish and British Christianity associated with IONA and LINDISFARNE. The achievements of such luminaries as BEDE and ALCUIN had a significance that was not only British but European (*see* NORTHUMBRIAN RENAISSANCE). Given the paucity of the surviving sources, the kingdom's organization is inevitably obscure. Excavations at the former palace of YEAVERING point to the existence of several major royal centres, as well as an accompanying organization that may owe a great deal to British, rather than English, origins.

The politics of 8th-century Northumbria were exceptionally violent, even by the bloody standards of the time, as several families fought to hold on to the KINGSHIP. The kingdom came to an end when it was conquered by the Scandinavian GREAT ARMY in the late 860s and 870s. The region was thereafter fought over by Scandinavians, English and Scots until the kings of Wessex overcame the Viking kings of YORK. Thereafter the region was ruled on behalf of English kings by earls (*see* MORCAR; SIWARD; TOSTIG) until shortly after the NORMAN CONQUEST.

Northumbrian Renaissance, the great flowering of early Christian culture in northern England in the 7th and 8th centuries. It was based on such monasteries as JARROW, MONKWEARMOUTH, LINDISFARNE and WHITBY, the growth of libraries such as that collected by the monk Benedict Biscop (?628–89) for Jarrow and Monkwearmouth, and the important cathedral school that developed in YORK under Archbishop Egbert (732–66). The greatest figure of the Renaissance was undoubtedly BEDE, but its achievements were also due to the efforts of many others – e.g. Caedmon, Cuthbert, Egbert of Iona, WILFRID – and to the creators of such superb manuscripts as the *CODEX AMIATINUS* and the *Lindisfarne Gospels*. In turn, the Renaissance influenced the development of the Christian Church within the CAROLINGIAN Empire, through the careers of Anglo-Saxon MISSIONARIES including St Willibrord, and ALCUIN who was called to Charlemagne's court to act as a cultural and educational adviser. The achievements of these years owe much to Northumbria's proximity to other areas of cultural activity (*see* IONA; MONASTICISM, EARLY IRISH) and to the support of some Northumbrian kings – e.g. ALDFRITH. The period effectively came to an end with the destruction of the Northumbrian kingdom by the Viking GREAT ARMY after 865.

Northwest Passage, from the Atlantic to the Pacific through the Arctic seas. For centuries, discovering such a route was a dream of navigators and the object of numerous expeditions that were costly in lives and money. From 1715–1818 the British Parliament offered a substantial cash payment for such a discovery. Sir John Franklin's expedition of 1845, though probably successful, resulted in the death of its leader and all his associates. Sir Robert McClure (1807–73) achieved the passage in 1850–4 by land and sea, but since it was impassable for most of the year the discovery was of little practical value. In 1906, the Norwegian explorer, Roald Amundsen, completed an arduous three-year journey by sea in a converted herring boat, and it was not until 1944 that Sgt Henry A. Larson of the Royal Canadian Mounted Police made the journey in a single season on the schooner *St Roch*.

Northwest Territories, jurisdiction within northern CANADA between Alaska and Hudson Bay, with a principally Inuit (Eskimo) population and covering a third of the national territory (much within the Arctic Circle and inhospitable Canadian Shield), but itself the residue of the former extensive domain of the HUDSON'S BAY and North West Companies. Martin Frobisher and other seekers for the NORTHWEST PASSAGE entered in the 16th century, while company fur traders began to penetrate the region in the late 18th century, and the Yukon was the scene of the last of the great 19th-century GOLD RUSHES. ALBERTA and SASKATCHEWAN became provinces in 1905. Until 1951 the rest of the Territories were governed directly from Ottawa, but progressively since then elections and directly-accountable assemblies have been instituted.

Norwegian Campaign, April–June 1940, major British defeat in the opening stages of WORLD WAR II. German forces invaded Norway on 8–9 April 1940, and Oslo, the Norwegian capital, fell on 10 April. Britain had already prepared plans for a pre-emptive invasion of northern Norway to interrupt German access to supplies of Swedish iron ore being exported via Narvik. Hastily prepared Anglo-French forces were landed at Namsos, Åndalsnes and Narvik on 14–19 April but the first two had to be evacuated on 1–2 May. The forces at Narvik held on until 8–9 June.

Already, however, the forced withdrawal of troops and loss of Norway had provoked a bitter debate in the House of Commons, leading to the resignation of Neville CHAMBERLAIN'S NATIONAL GOVERNMENT and the formation of a coalition government under CHURCHILL. On the naval side the honours were slightly more even. The Germans lost much of their DESTROYER force in the two battles of Narvik, and Allied submarines did well against the invading forces. Although victorious, the German Navy was so crippled by losses that it was virtually out of action for most of the rest of 1940.

Norwich, principal city of East Anglia. One of the most important and populous English towns until the 18th century, Norwich usually vied with YORK and BRISTOL for second place in the urban hierarchy after LONDON. The city received its first charter in 1158, at about the same time that the square stone keep of its Norman CASTLE was built, while the CATHEDRAL was begun in 1091 after the translation of the SEE from Thetford. In the later 14th century the city's population was some 5,000, in 1700 some 30,000. Its medieval commercial prosperity, built upon the city's key position in the CLOTH INDUSTRY both in production and trading, is attested to by the many surviving parish churches in addition to the size and splendour of the cathedral. The trade was boosted by the influx of MIGRANTS from the Low Countries in the 1330s and again in the 1560s, bringing new skills and cloth varieties. Norwich's pre-eminent place was slowly whittled away by competition from elsewhere and the relative decline of the East Anglian textile trades, although its growing specialization in black crape-weaving in the 18th and 19th centuries helped maintain its importance, because of the size of the mourning 'industry'. It remained an important social resort for East Anglia, with assembly rooms and THEATRES. The grain market in the 19th century to some extent compensated for the demise of the cloth trade, and Norwich has since grown into a city of nearly 250,000, because of its regional status.

Notitia Dignitatum, a Roman administrative document of the early 5th century. It lists civil and military officials and military installations and commands throughout the eastern and western empires. Scholarly commentators disagree about its value, because it does not appear to be an official government document and because of the late date of the manuscripts.

It divides Roman Britain into five areas, and lists numerous forts, of which those on HADRIAN'S WALL and the SAXON SHORE are of particular interest. It also illustrates a complex bureaucracy and chain of command, and shows units of troops from Britain deployed elsewhere in the empire, a sign of overstretched resources and the British province's increasing vulnerability (*see* ROMAN CONQUEST).

Nottingham, 10th Earl of, *see* HOWARD, CHARLES

Novantae, a British people who inhabited what is now Dumfries and Galloway, about whom little is known. They must have fallen under Roman rule as a result of AGRICOLA'S campaign in AD 81, but would have regained their independence when the Romans finally retreated to HADRIAN'S WALL. The tribe appears to have been incorporated into the later British kingdom of RHEGED.

Nova Scotia, south-eastern province of CANADA, founded as New Scotland and the scene until the mid-18th century of constant skirmishing between British and French settlers and troops. The territory was ceded to Britain by the Treaty of UTRECHT in 1713. The Scottish BARONETCIES had been originally instituted for the settlement of Nova Scotia, while German and Swiss PROTESTANT settlement was encouraged in the 18th century, and Halifax was established in 1749 on the French enclave of Cape Breton. The final extinction of French hopes came with the defeat of the city of Louisbourg in 1758 and the deportation of the French Acadians in 1755. The population was augmented by the arrival of LOYALISTS in 1783 after the War of AMERICAN INDEPENDENCE.

Nuclear Energy, *see* ATOMIC ENERGY

Nuclear Weapons, weapons which use the energy released from the nuclei of atoms to create the largest man-made explosions ever produced, as well as large amounts of lethal radiation. The term 'atom bomb' was applied to the earliest nuclear weapons (developed under the secret American-sponsored

Manhattan Project during WORLD WAR II), which worked through nuclear fission – the splitting of atoms of uranium or plutonium – sparking off an uncontrolled chain reaction. The first atomic weapon was tested in New Mexico in July 1945 and used against the Japanese cities of Hiroshima and Nagasaki on 6–9 Aug. 1945, causing horrific casualties and forcing Japan to surrender.

Anglo-American nuclear co-operation broke down in 1946 when America placed restrictions on the sharing of nuclear secrets. As a result, the ATTLEE government pursued a programme to develop an independent nuclear capacity, exploding its first atom bomb in AUSTRALIA in 1952. By then the Soviet Union also possessed nuclear weapons and America had already exploded her first hydrogen bomb, a much more powerful device based on nuclear fusion – the forcing together of the nuclei of hydrogen isotopes. Britain exploded its first 'H-bomb' in 1957.

Britain's nuclear weapons were initially designed to be dropped by aircraft, leading to the development of the V BOMBER FORCE. The growing vulnerability of aircraft to anti-aircraft missiles led to the project for the Blue Streak ballistic missile. When this was cancelled, Britain obtained access at the NASSAU AGREEMENT in 1962 to the American system of POLARIS submarine-launched nuclear missiles, which remained the basis of the more powerful Trident system ordered in 1986. Britain also deployed aircraft equipped with nuclear bombs and short-range tactical nuclear weapons as part of the NATO forces defending western Europe.

Nuclear weapons have been a source of intense political controversy, between UNILATERALISTS (including the influential CAMPAIGN FOR NUCLEAR DISARMAMENT) and MULTILATERALISTS, but the possession of an at least nominally independent nuclear deterrent has remained a principle of British defence policy.

Number 45, political symbol associated with John WILKES, after government attempts to suppress issue no. 45 of his essay paper, the *NORTH BRITON*, aroused a storm of controversy. His supporters rang the changes on the number in social activities – e.g. holding dinners for 45 people – and it was displayed on commemorative items such as medals and badges, and chalked on walls and clothing.

Nun of Kent, *see* BARTON, ELIZABETH

Nyasaland, former British central African territory, known as Malawi since independence. A British protectorate was established in 1891, under the administration of the larger-than-life consul-general Harry Johnston. Originally called British Central Africa, the territory was renamed Nyasaland in 1907 and given a colonial governor. Local political associations grew up from an early date, and the Chilemwe rising of 1915 was a shock to the British and a signal for the need for reform. Nyasaland was placed as the weak partner in the short-lived Federation with Northern and Southern RHODESIA in 1953. Five years later the exiled Hastings Banda returned to take over the nationalist movement. A state of emergency was declared in 1959 given the level of trouble; independence was secured in 1964. Banda was given the position of life president in 1966 when the new Malawi became a republic and a single-party state.

O

Oak Apple Day, annual celebration on 29 May of CHARLES II'S RESTORATION and of his escape after the battle of WORCESTER in Sept. 1651, when he hid from his pursuers in an oak tree at Boscobel House, Salop. This CALENDAR CUSTOM was widely observed in the later 17th and 18th centuries as a reminder of the nation's delivery from the INTERREGNUM and the Restoration of the monarchy, although its association with the STUARTS made it less appealing after the JACOBITE rebellions.

Oath Helpers, *see* COMPURGATION

Oaths Oaths pledging loyalty to a lord (sometimes a king) were an essential part of the web of relationships in all early British societies, and were taken also by rulers, as a guarantee of the duties which were expected of them. The Coronation Oath of the British monarch is a survivor from this world. More generally, oaths pledging both allegiance to the monarch and due performance of responsibilities were customarily taken by the whole range of office-holders in medieval and early modern kingdoms; in addition, oaths affirming political and religious loyalties remained a favoured tool of government down to the early 19th century, especially in the wake of the religious and political divisions caused by the REFORMATION. The first attempt to use a nationwide oath was part of the 1534 Act of Succession, to secure loyalty to the issue of HENRY VIII and ANNE BOLEYN; this was hastily replaced in 1536 by similar provisions for the issue of JANE SEYMOUR. The Acts of Supremacy of 1534 and 1559 also provided for oaths to be administered to office-holders and certain others, including those taking degrees at universities. The governments of ELIZABETH I and the Stuarts (notably JAMES I in 1606) attempted to test the loyalty of Roman CATHOLICS by imposing oaths of allegiance, causing Catholics many difficulties and disagreements as to what they could in conscience accept. Similar quarrels affected the population at large during the CIVIL WARS as successive regimes attempted to ensure national loyalty, if only in qualified form (*see* ENGAGEMENT CONTROVERSY). The TEST ACT (1673) reaffirmed the older provisions for all office-holders to take the Acts of Allegiance and Supremacy. The BILL OF RIGHTS (1689) abrogated the Elizabethan oath of supremacy and Jacobean Act of Allegiance and substituted new oaths of allegiance and abjuration. Oaths were widely administered after the assassination attempt on WILLIAM III in 1696, and the ATTERBURY PLOT of 1722, and in the panic associated with the radicalization of the French Revolution in 1792. The TOLERATION ACT of 1689 required DISSENTING ministers to take oaths of allegiance and abjuration; the Catholic Relief Act 1778 and Dissenting Relief Act 1779 both imposed oaths on those wishing to have the benefit of the legislation. The taking of oaths not authorized by law was forbidden by the COMBINATION ACT of 1799. *See also* NON-JURORS.

Occasional Conformity Act 1711 Legislation designed to prevent DISSENTERS from evading the restrictive provisions of the TEST ACT by 'occasionally' taking communion in the CHURCH OF ENGLAND. First introduced in 1702 by Bolingbroke (*see* ST JOHN, HENRY) and others, it provided for a fine of £40 and dismissal of anyone who attended a CONVENTICLE or Dissenting meeting house after taking the ANGLICAN sacrament and test for office. It was three times defeated in the LORDS, but finally passed when Daniel Finch, Earl of

Nottingham, proposed to WHIG leaders that, in exchange for Whig support, TORIES discontented with their own leaders would join in opposing the peace of UTRECHT. At the same time the TOLERATION ACT was confirmed, and Dissenting ministers and schoolmasters licensed under it were specifically empowered to act in that capacity anywhere in the kingdom. The Act was repealed in 1719, together with the Schism Act.

O'Connell, Daniel (1775–1847), Irish nationalist, called the 'Liberator'. Landowner, barrister and founder of the Catholic Association (1823), and strategist of the campaign for CATHOLIC EMANCIPATION, he mobilized a degraded peasantry, disciplined its enthusiasm and organized it into a powerful instrument of public opinion. The failure of the IRISH REBELLION of 1798 convinced him that change could only be secured through legal and constitutional means. The Catholic Association – arguably the first political mass movement – showed that the threat of violence, held in abeyance – brinkmanship, as we should now call it – was sufficient to secure civil liberties. His success not only reflected superb organizational and political skills, it also derived from the primacy of Catholicism in his conception of Irish nationalism.

O'Connor, Rory, *see* RORY O'CONNOR

O'Connor, Turloch, *see* TURLOCH O'CONNOR

October Club, an extreme TORY organization, formed in 1710. It took its name from the password required for admission to its meetings in the Bell Tavern, Westminster: 'October', from October ale, symbol of country living. At the height of its influence, in 1711, about one-third of Tory MPs were associated with it, mainly back-benchers. Members proposed numerous COUNTRY measures in the 1710–11 and 1711–12 PARLIAMENTS. Robert HARLEY managed to curb its power in 1712, partly by the judicious use of patronage to wean away supporters.

Oda, Archbishop of Canterbury (941–58). Oda is important for having advanced the careers of later and more famous TENTH-CENTURY REFORMERs – his nephew St Oswald and St DUNSTAN – and for having begun, with royal support, to hold councils of the entire English Church. Oda's career also demonstrates the integration of Scandinavians into English society, since he was the son of a pagan who had come to England in the Danish GREAT ARMY, and he also organized the reintroduction of a bishopric amid the SCANDINAVIAN SETTLEMENTS of East Anglia.

Odo of Bayeux (*c.* 1030–97), Earl of Kent. In 1049, the young Odo was appointed bishop of Bayeux by his half-brother WILLIAM I THE CONQUEROR, and for more than 30 years, he was one of William's most powerful aides in both NORMANDY and England. The BAYEUX TAPESTRY represents him as a principal architect of the 1066 campaign; when William returned to Normandy, Odo was one of those left behind to complete the conquest. In consequence, by the 1070s he was Earl of Kent and by far the richest landowner in England. In 1083, for reasons that are not clear, William had him arrested. Released in 1087, he led the 1088 rebellion against WILLIAM II RUFUS on behalf of ROBERT II CURTHOSE but was defeated and banished. He accompanied Robert on crusade and died at Palermo.

OECD, *see* ORGANIZATION FOR ECONOMIC CO-OPERATION AND DEVELOPMENT

OEEC, *see under* ORGANIZATION FOR ECONOMIC CO-OPERATION AND DEVELOPMENT

Offa, King of MERCIA (757–96). The greatest of the line of 6th- and 7th-century kings of MERCIA (*see* ETHELBALD; PENDA; WULFHERE; CENWULF), he briefly established himself as 'King of the English' and was treated as an equal by Charlemagne. Following the Frankish ruler's example, he organized the first CORONATION involving anointing with holy oil, for his short-lived son Ecgfrith. OFFA'S DYKE and the minting of the first silver pennies (*see* COINAGE; PENNY, ANGLO-SAXON) are among achievements that are still visible to us – the former, in particular, testifying to a king able to deploy enormous resources.

His power was ultimately based on violence and was resisted. Some of his pet schemes, such as the archbishopric of LICHFIELD, were intended to undermine other kingdoms. His reign witnessed the suppression of minor kingdoms such as SUSSEX and LINDSEY, but his rule over England must be seen as much more of a Mercian hegemony than a genuine unification. Like previous Mercian 'empires', Offa's fell apart after his death.

Offa's Dyke, Prestatyn, Clwyd, to Chepstow, Gwent, the monumental earthwork by which OFFA of MERCIA defined the boundary between his own kingdom and the Welsh tribes to the west. About 80 miles of it survive, but it is now thought certain that, except where rivers supplied an adequate boundary, it formed a continuous earthwork 120 miles long up to its northern end in Clwyd, where WAT'S DYKE provided an alternative. The original structure consisted of a ditch about 1.8 m (6 ft) deep and a rampart around 7.6 m (25 ft) high from the bottom of the ditch.

We can only speculate on the purpose of the dyke; the current view sees it as both a defensive and an offensive frontier intended to stop Welsh raiding and to provide a base from which the English could attack. Other earthworks of this type are known elsewhere in Europe, but Offa's dyke is the largest of them all, testimony to the massive power of the king who had it made.

Offences Against the Person Act 1861, *see* BLOODY CODE

Ogham, an Irish Gaelic term used to describe an Irish script, now known mainly from monumental inscriptions, which was used between the 4th and 7th centuries. It resembles RUNES and was based on the Roman alphabet. The fact that ogham inscriptions occur in Ireland, Scottish DALRIADA, Wales and Cornwall (*see* DUMNONIA) shows the wide range of contacts that existed among the CELTIC peoples of western Britain during that period.

Ogle, 1st Earl, *see* CAVENDISH, WILLIAM

Oil Crisis, sharp rise in oil prices caused by the Arab embargo on oil shipments to the West in response to the 1973 Arab-Israeli war. OPEC, the Organization of Petroleum Exporting Countries, reduced production and quadrupled prices before the embargo was lifted in Jan. 1974 and were doubled again in 1979. The price rise stimulated worldwide INFLATION, but also saw the adoption of energy conservation measures in the West, the search for alternative energy, including nuclear power, and the rapid development of new, non-Arab reserves of Alaskan and NORTH SEA OIL.

Oil Industry One of the 20th century's most spectacular growth industries, oil has come to dominate the world's fuel supply, supplanting COAL which had principally powered the industrial revolutions of the 19th century. At the beginning of the 20th century, oil production was mainly centred in the USA and Russia, producing kerosene for lighting. Even then the tendency of the industry to be concentrated in a very few hands was evident, with the dominance of the Rockefellers' Standard Oil Company in the USA, the formation of the Royal Dutch Company in 1890 and the Shell Transport and Trading Company in 1897 to exploit the East Indies (merging in 1907 to form Royal Dutch Shell), and the foundation in 1901 of the Anglo-Persian Oil Company, subsequently NATIONALIZED and becoming British Petroleum (BP) from 1951.

World oil production increased tenfold to 200 million tons between 1900 and 1930, with the opening of fields in the Middle East and South America as well as the exploitation of Texas and other North American oilfields and continued trade with the East Indies. Fuel oil became the dominant product, especially with the growth of the MOTOR INDUSTRY and the shift from steam to oil within shipping, while technological improvements considerably enhanced both fuel-oil refining and exploration techniques. Britain's oil industry, although less advanced than the USA's, followed it both in aggressive exploration policies and in vertical integration of the oil enterprises, participating in every stage from the well to the consumer. The British oil industry has throughout its history had a closer relationship with government than any other power industry, especially because of the imperial and foreign policy implications of its operations. Lord Curzon in 1920 had remarked that the Allies in WORLD WAR I had 'floated to victory on a wave of oil', while MANDATES given to Britain in the Middle East considerably enhanced British involvement in exploration and production there.

Crude oil throughput in Britain has grown from 5 million tons in 1923 to 13 million tons in 1939, 58 million tons in 1959, and 139 million tons in 1979. Britain joined in the international shift after 1948 from oil refinement in the oilfields to refining in the importing countries, as a result of political instability (exemplified by the nationalization of the Anglo-Iranian refinery at Abadan in 1951; *see* ABADAN CRISIS), and to employ the greater skill available in industrialized importing nations. The political and economic muscle of exporting nations was made evident in the SUEZ CRISIS and the closure of the Suez Canal in 1956–7, the effects of the Egyptian-Israeli conflicts, and the OIL CRISIS of 1973. The polluting aspect of oil transportation had been made shockingly evident in the *Torrey Canyon* tanker disaster off Land's End in 1962.

In Britain, the continuing rise in oil prices from 1973 was further stimulus to home production of oil and GAS from the offshore continental shelf, with considerable economic implications both for the national balance of payments and for the success of towns like ABERDEEN. Exploration from the late 1960s had established the quantities of gas and oil available; between 1973 and 1983 the UK produced 35–40 billion cubic metres of gas per annum, the second-largest quantity in the world. NORTH SEA OIL production began in 1975, with BP and Shell the principal home-based explorers and exploiters, and by 1983 UK annual oil production was 100 million tons, making Britain the fifth-largest producer in the world.

Olaf Guthricsson (?–941/2), King of Dublin and of York. The son of Guthric, king of York (exiled 927), Olaf became king of DUBLIN in 933 and, after asserting his authority there, played a prominent part in the coalition defeated at the battle of BRUNANBURH. After King ATHELSTAN's death in 939, Olaf returned to England and, by 940, had achieved control over YORK and over MERCIA as far south as Watling Street. His career illustrates the continuing interest in northern England of DUBLIN's Norse rulers. His conquests disintegrated after his death, and English domination in the North was temporarily restored by King EDMUND.

Olaf Sihtricsson (?–981), King of Dublin and of York. The son of Sihtric, king of York, he was, like his cousin, OLAF GUTHRICSSON, a VIKING warlord with interests in Ireland. He briefly asserted his domination over YORK in the 940s, but was driven out in 952 and subsequently replaced by ERIC BLOODAXE; he remained king of DUBLIN until his death.

Olaf the White (*fl.*850s and 860s), King of Dublin. One of the great chieftains of the heroic VIKING age associated with the conquests of the GREAT ARMY, he was active not only in Ireland but also in the far north of Britain. He was associated with KETIL FLATNOSE and ROGNVALD OF MOER in the conquest of the HEBRIDES and ORKNEY, and was with Ingwaer, king of DUBLIN (probably the historical IVAR THE BONELESS) at the siege of DUMBARTON ROCK.

Old Age Pensions Act 1908 The Act was passed at the culmination of a debate that had lasted nearly a generation, over the form of pension provision. Pensions financed by a weekly contribution during working life, similar to those introduced in Germany in the 1880s, had been championed by Joseph CHAMBERLAIN; they were approved by the LABOUR movement which supported Charles BOOTH's proposal for universal pensions for all over 65. The LIBERAL government plumped for a higher pensionable age on grounds of economy, in spite of the evidence that working people were unable to support themselves by their mid-60s, and the legislation provided non-contributory pensions of 5s a week each for old people over 70, or 7s 6d for married couples. Although coverage was partial – only people with an income of less than £21 per year were entitled to benefit and pensions were withheld from lunatics and criminals – it represented a new and important use of the power of taxation for the redistribution of income, and as such constitutes a move away from the hold of the POOR LAW and a landmark in the development of the WELFARE STATE.

Old Corps Whigs, the largest parliamentary bloc of the mid-18th century: it consisted of a group of some 250 MPs who transferred their allegiance from WALPOLE to PELHAM, and thence to Newcastle (*see* PELHAM-HOLLES, THOMAS). When GEORGE III's accession in 1760 was followed by the fall of the coalition between PITT THE ELDER and Newcastle, the old corps disintegrated, some orienting themselves towards the court, others rallying to Pitt or Rockingham (*see* WENTWORTH, CHARLES).

Old Dissent, *see* NEW DISSENT

Old Draperies, term used to describe the late medieval, often unfinished and usually undyed cloth which was the traditional product of many regions specializing in the CLOTH INDUSTRY. These cloths were usually intended for EXPORT; the changes in fashion and the closing of many markets in the 16th century crippled production in a succession of areas from the 1530s onwards. Those which suffered early, like some parts of Suffolk, lost their previous industrial importance and wealth, whereas other regions in the west of England and elsewhere were able to take advantage of the economic benefits from production of the NEW DRAPERIES.

Old English, *see* ANGLO-SAXON

Old English in Ireland, *see* IRELAND, NEW ENGLISH IN

Old Poor Law, *see* POOR LAW, OLD

Old Pretender, *see* STUART, JAMES EDWARD

Old Style, *see* GREGORIAN CALENDAR

Olympia Meeting, rally at Olympia in June 1934 by MOSLEY's British Union of FASCISTS which proved a turning-point in its fortunes. The brutal treatment of anti-Fascist hecklers by BUF stewards aroused widespread condemnation, leading to a withdrawal of support by, among others, Lord Rothermere's *Daily Mail*.

Ombudsman, a term (taken from the Swedish) for an investigative officer dealing with complaints about maladministration. Britain appointed its first ombudsman in 1965 with the title of Parliamentary Commissioner for Administration. He can act only at the request of an MP and has no powers of enforcement, although his reports are usually acted upon. Specific ombudsmen for particular commercial sectors have also been created.

Omdurman, Battle of, military engagement on 2 Sept. 1898, across the Nile from Khartoum, in which superior Anglo-Egyptian weaponry overwhelmed the Dervish forces and confirmed the British reconquest of the SUDAN. The British forces, led by Kitchener, had embarked upon the campaign in 1895, and at Omdurman avenged GORDON's defeat and death a decade previously. The battle has frequently been dubbed the high-water mark of British imperialism.

Omnibus (Latin: 'for all'), a public four-wheeled vehicle for conveying passengers along certain routes at specified fares. French in origin, omnibuses were first introduced to London in 1820 by George Shillibeer (1797–1866), running between Paddington and the Bank of England, and carrying 22 passengers on two decks. The London General Omnibus Company was established in 1856 with a fleet of horse-drawn vehicles which by 1901 ran 16 million route miles and carried 101 million passengers per year for an average cost of a penny a mile. By that time omnibus services had spread to most provincial cities. Horse-drawn vehicles had by the close of World War I been superseded by motorized ones, to which the appellation – or more commonly its diminutive, 'bus' – was transferred.

O'Neill, Con Bacach (1st Earl of Tyrone) (*c*.1484–1559), Irish chieftain. Descended from ancient chiefs of Tyrone, O'Neill exemplifies the constant tensions between aggression and compromise in early Tudor Anglo-Irish relations. He spent much of the 1520s and 1530s fighting the English and their allies with occasional reconciliations. Staging a final devastation of the PALE in 1541, he only submitted after deputy Anthony St Leger had three times invaded Tyrone. In 1542, he went to England, renounced his chieftainship and was created earl, becoming PRIVY COUNCILLOR of Ireland in 1543; there seemed a good chance of the GAELIC north being reconciled with the DUBLIN government. However, in his grant of the earldom, he had passed over his legitimate son Shane O'NEILL in favour of his illegitimate son Matthew, and Shane began a bitter feud. Con was seen as a collaborator with English power; his prestige tarnished, he died as a refugee from Shane within the PALE, with English influence in ULSTER destroyed.

O'Neill, Hugh (3rd Earl of Tyrone) (1550–1616), Gaelic leader. On his return to Ireland in 1568, English hopes that his upbringing in England would make him useful in taming GAELIC ULSTER at first seemed justified; in the 1580s, he was granted wide powers in Ulster by royal commission and was recognized as earl. However, friction with the government increasingly outweighed his longstanding feuds with relatives. A clash with the English in 1594 was patched up, but O'Neill now saw his best chance in an alliance with England's enemies, Spain and the Pope.

In 1595, he seized a fort on the River Blackwater in Armagh, was proclaimed traitor and then succeeded to the ancient northern Irish royal title of 'The O'Neill' (*see* UÍ NÉILL). A steadily more successful Catholic crusade culminated in victory at the YELLOW FORD in 1598. After a personal truce with Essex (*see* DEVEREUX, ROBERT) the following year, he faced the more formidable Charles Blount, Baron Mountjoy; when Spanish intervention at KINSALE failed, O'Neill's power disintegrated, and in 1603, he submitted at Mellifont. Despite outward reconciliation, his distrust of English intentions led to the FLIGHT OF THE EARLS in 1607, and he died in Rome.

O'Neill, Shane (?1530–67), Gaelic leader. Eldest legitimate son and likely TANIST of Con Bacach O'NEILL, 1st Earl of Tyrone, his bitter resentment at being passed over in the earldom for his bastard brother Matthew proved fatal to English plans to anglicize northern Ireland's paramount family. Family warfare culminated in Matthew's murder in 1558. A shaky reconciliation with ELIZABETH I petered out in attacks on the O'Donnells and their Scots kinsmen, the MacDonnells, as well as in intrigues with Spain and the partisans of MARY QUEEN OF SCOTS. O'Neill's destructive rising in 1566 was beaten back from the Dublin PALE; when he overtrustingly took refuge with the MacDonnells, they murdered him, with English approval.

O'Neill, Terence (Baron O'Neill of the Maine) (1914–90), Unionist politician and Prime Minister of Northern Ireland (1963–9). A Unionist MP from 1946, as premier he sought to bridge the divide between the communities of Northern Ireland, visiting Catholic institutions and inviting the Irish prime minister to Stormont. His initiatives stirred up PROTESTANT opposition led by Ian PAISLEY and also stimulated the CATHOLIC civil rights movement. His 1968 offer to the Catholics of a package of local government reforms could not prevent growing polarization and violence. Having failed to strengthen his position after the election of Feb. 1969, which saw the break-up of the old ULSTER UNIONIST PARTY, he resigned in April in favour of Major James Chichester-Clark.

Ontario, province of CANADA midway between the Atlantic provinces and QUEBEC and the western provinces, and the most populous and prosperous part of Canada. Under French rule the vast area which is now Ontario, stretching from the Great Lakes up to the Canadian shield, was unsettled except for a few forts and missions. Fort York, which was to become the city of Toronto, Ontario's capital, was founded in 1793 after the capture of Canada from France. Settlement began with the arrival of the Empire LOYALISTS; the area west of the Ontario river was subsequently formed into the Province of Upper Canada by the Constitutional Act of 1791. Settlement continued to grow, and the population had reached 400,000 by 1841 when the Act of Union was passed. Upper Canada became the administrative district of Canada West; in 1867, at confederation, it became Ontario.

Open Fields, term used to describe the pre-ENCLOSURE agricultural landscape found in many parts of Britain, especially England, where large fields held in common (*see* COMMON FIELDS) were divided into strips, individual proprietors holding a number of strips in each of two, three or four fields. The open field system was extinguished progressively by enclosure from the 12th century onward, with the pace quickening in the 17th century; however, some areas (Kent, parts of East Anglia, Devon and Somerset, and upland northern regions) may never have had open fields. *See also* LAXTON.

Open University, non-residential degree-awarding UNIVERSITY opened in 1971, which uses distance-learning techniques – such as radio and television broadcasts and correspondence – to teach mature students studying from home. The pioneering scheme was legislated for by the WILSON government and its techniques have been borrowed extensively elsewhere in the world.

Opium Wars, 1839–42, 1856–60. The opium trade was one of the more lucrative in which British merchants were involved in 19th-century China from the 1810s. The high commissioner at Canton, Lin Tse-hsu, was an implacable opponent of the addictive effect of opium on his countrymen and the level of British exploitation. Acting on behalf of the Chinese emperor, he ordered the confiscation of all opium stored in Cantonese warehouses. The British government held that the Chinese could not authorize the seizure of British private property, and had no jurisdiction over British subjects (the Chinese were demanding that two British sailors who had killed a local villager be handed over for trial). The Chinese refused to make reparations, fired on British warships, and forbade trade with Britain. An unequal war ensued, in which Canton was bombarded and HONG KONG seized by the British. The treaty of Nanking (1842) ended the war, with the Chinese paying reparations, ceding Hong Kong, and opening five 'treaty ports' to British trade – Canton, Amoy, Fouchow, Nangpo, and Shanghai. The Opium War was a prime example of Palmerston's (*see* TEMPLE, HENRY) bullying foreign policy. When trouble recurred in the 1850s, once more largely prompted by Britain, the British were again victorious and free-trade access to China was opened up under the 1858 Treaty of Tientsin.

Oral History Born out of the belief that what people have to say is an essential part of history, oral history has extended the existing documentary evidence of the past and investigated those less literate sections of society which have either been ignored by historians through lack of 'evidence' or interest. The HISTORY WORKSHOP movement has, since the 1960s, done much to advance work in oral history, as have the Oral History Society and the National Sound Archives, and in British history this has largely centred on working-class oral testimony of rural and urban life in the 19th and 20th centuries – and notably in wartime too. The criticisms of oral testimony as a source cite the fact that people may be partisan and/or partial in their recollections of the past. In response, oral historians point out that the current practice of working with small groups enables oral testimony to be treated as any other historical source and checked against other data, and in any case how the past is remembered is a way of understanding the ideology and motivation of a period, which is as valuable as discovering empirical information about it. Many LOCAL HISTORY and community history groups are involved in oral history projects which successfully extend not only the field and methodology of historical enquiry, but also the range of people who can undertake it.

Orange Order The first 'Orange Lodge', comprising Irish PROTESTANT supporters of the principles of 1688 – 'Orange' referring to William of Orange (the future WILLIAM III) – was formed in 1795, during the FRENCH REVOLUTIONARY WARS, in response to the activities of the Catholic DEFENDER movement. Other lodges followed, and by 1797, members numbered about 200,000. The Orange Order was dissolved by the ASSOCIATION Act 1825, but the movement soon revived and, by 1836, had around 125,000 members in Ireland and 145,000 in England. The order was suspected of wishing to place its grand master, Ernest Augustus, Duke of Cumberland, rather than his niece VICTORIA on the throne and, after a parliamentary inquiry, was again dissolved. Revived in 1845, the Order was prominent in opposing Irish HOME RULE. In the 20th century, it has been conspicuous in Northern Ireland as a badge of Protestantism and strong adherence to the Union, and for its annual, sometimes provocative marches to mark William III's victory on the BOYNE. *See also* LOYALISTS.

Ordainers, the name given to the eight earls, six barons and seven bishops appointed in March 1310 to draw up the ORDINANCES for the reform of the English royal household and realm. Chief among the Ordainers were THOMAS OF LANCASTER and Archbishop WINCHELSEY of Canterbury. They continued to meet and issue more ordinances after their legal authority lapsed at Michaelmas 1311. By 1312, they were locked in armed struggle against EDWARD II and GAVESTON.

Ordeal, *see* TRIAL BY ORDEAL

Order A monastic order is an association living under a distinctive monastic rule. Holy orders are the higher grades of ministry in the Christian Church, i.e. bishop, priest, deacon, and from 1207 to 1972 in the Roman CATHOLIC Church, sub-deacon, an office now abolished. One can also refer to such people as being 'in orders'. Minor orders are the lesser grades of ministry: porters, lectors, exorcists and acolytes in the western church, and also lectors and cantors in eastern Orthodox Churches. *See also* MONASTICISM.

Orderic Vitalis (1075–*c*.1142), author of the *Ecclesiastical History*. Although Orderic, the child of an English mother and a Norman father, spent all but the first ten years of his life in the Norman monastery of St Evroul, his history, written between 1115 and 1141, ranges much more widely than its title suggests, offering a remarkably vivid portrait of Anglo-Norman society.

Orders, Books of, *see* BOOKS OF ORDERS

Orders in Council, issued by the sovereign as a result of the deliberations of the PRIVY COUNCIL and much favoured by government in war emergencies and other situations requiring more rapid measures than are provided for by normal parliamentary procedure.

Orders of Chivalry, *see* CHIVALRY, ORDERS OF

Ordinal, in ANGLICAN churches, the order of service by which bishops, priests and deacons are ordained. It was first issued in 1550, separately from the PRAYER BOOK.

Ordnance Survey, official British map-making organization. It was founded in 1791 for military purposes, as its name suggests, and to provide information for the defence of the realm. William Roy, the surveyor of the Scottish mainland (*see* ROY'S MILITARY SURVEY), had long campaigned for such a body. The first one-inch (representing one mile) maps (scale 1:63,360) were published in 1801, as the trigonometrical survey of Great Britain was established. The Ordnance Survey Act of 1841 formally established the agency. The Survey's military origins are still evident in the blankness of maps at military or sensitive installations, but they are now used as much for leisure enjoyment of the countryside as for official purposes.

Ordovices, a pre-Roman British tribe that settled in the southern parts of GWYNEDD. They proved to be especially obdurate opponents of the ROMAN CONQUEST, assisting CARATACUS in AD 51 (*see* CAER CARADOG) and apparently attacking the Romans on other occasions. SUETONIUS PAULINUS was campaigning against them in 60–1 when BOUDICCA's revolt broke out. They were finally overcome in 79 by AGRICOLA, whose campaign is said by his biographer TACITUS to have resulted in the near-extermination of the tribe.

Oregon Treaty, 1846. The treaty settled the western boundary between CANADA and the United States and relieved tensions brought about by American expansionism and British concern to secure the fur trade in the region between the Columbus river and the 49th parallel. Under the treaty, the USA obtained the territory now comprising the states of Oregon, Washington and Idaho; Britain acquired Vancouver Island.

Orford, 2nd Earl of, *see* WALPOLE, ROBERT

Organization for Economic Co-operation and Development (OECD) Its predecessor, the Organization for European Economic Co-operation (OEEC), was formed in April 1948 to co-ordinate MARSHALL PLAN aid and reconstruction in the European states after WORLD WAR II. It involved most western European countries, including Britain and the three western occupied zones of Germany, with the United States and CANADA as associate members. When Marshall Plan aid ceased in 1952, the OEEC was replaced by the OECD, and the US and Canada became full members. The OECD retained the objective of promoting economic growth in Europe but added a commitment to assist the economic expansion of developing countries. During its earlier phase the OEEC played a key role, through its executive committee based in Paris and its technical committees, in rebuilding the post-war European economy and infrastructure. The organization continued to grow and by the 1970s included nearly all the developed economies. It is a forum for the investigation of economic problems within member states and provides a venue for occasional ministerial meetings.

Orkney, St Magnus of, *see* MAGNUS OF ORKNEY

Orkney, Scandinavian Earldom of The Scandinavian conquest of Orkney is generally attributed to the family of ROGNVALD OF MOER in the mid-9th century, perhaps in co-operation with the king of Norway. Later earls such as SIGURD THE MIGHTY, SIGURD THE STOUT and THORFINN THE MIGHTY established control over considerable parts of northern Scotland, sometimes exercising lordship over the Western Isles (Outer HEBRIDES) and the Isle of MAN. The great power of the earls may well explain the distribution of OUNCELANDS and pennylands throughout the Scandinavian areas of Scotland.

The earls generally recognized the overlordship of the kings of Norway, a status that was symbolically demonstrated by the famous visit of King Magnus Barelegs in 1098. The islands remained a possession of the kings of Norway until 1472 when they were formally annexed to the Scottish crown under the terms of the dowry arranged when JAMES III married a Danish princess.

Orpington By-Election, *see* LIBERAL PARTY

Osborne, Sir Thomas (1st Earl of Danby, Marquess of Carmarthen, 1st Duke of Leeds) (1631–1712), statesman. Son of a Yorkshire ROYALIST, he was elected MP for York in 1665, and opposed Clarendon (*see* HYDE, EDWARD). He demonstrated his ability as treasurer of the NAVY from 1668; as lord treasurer from 1673, he improved the yield of hereditary crown revenues.

In 1675, he became the leading figure in a strongly ANGLICAN ministry, but his ascendancy was always qualified: the Earl of Shaftesbury hinted that his religious intolerance was popish in tendency, and in the POPISH PLOT investigations Danby was revealed to have conducted secret negotiations with France. The king dissolved Parliament to prevent his IMPEACHMENT and provided him with a pardon, but Parliament ruled the latter illegal, and he was imprisoned.

Released in 1685, he criticized JAMES II's Catholicizing policies and, in 1687, made contact with William of Orange (the future WILLIAM III), whose marriage to James's daughter Mary (later MARY II) he had organized. He was one of the 'IMMORTAL SEVEN' signatories to the invitation to William, and secured the north for him at the time of the GLORIOUS REVOLUTION. Made lord president of the Council, he was chief minister from 1690, but his appetite for wealth and honours attracted criticism. Though he was created a duke in 1694, his influence with William declined after he supported the TRIENNIAL Bill in that year; in 1695, he was impeached for accepting a bribe, but not convicted. Thereafter he had little influence.

Osborne Judgment, 1909, arose from the action of W. V. Osborne, a LIBERAL trade unionist, who objected to his TRADE UNION subscription being contributed to the funds of the LABOUR PARTY. The decision of the judges in the House of Lords that a trade union had no legal right to use its funds for political purposes threatened to undermine the political activities of the trade unions and the Labour Party, until the passing of the TRADE UNION ACT of 1913 nullified the judgment.

Osraige, medieval Irish kingdom. Originally part of MUNSTER, its rulers established its independence in the early 7th century, and it thereafter developed as a powerful small kingdom located between the stronger Munster and LEINSTER. It was occasionally subjugated by conquering kings such as BRIAN BORU, but was able to sustain its independence into the 12th century (*see* KINGSHIP).

Ostorius Scapula (?–AD 52), Roman governor. He succeeded AULUS PLAUTIUS as the second governor of Britain in 47, remaining in that position until his death. He pushed Roman power westwards into Wales, and his achievements included the defeat and capture of CARATACUS. British revolts, which prefigured the great rebellion of BOUDICCA in 61, began during his rule, and the Roman hold on southern Britain, although secure, continued to be threatened by disturbances among the natives.

Oswald, St, King of Northumbria (634–42). A son of Ethelfrith of Northumbria, he spent years in exile among the Irish and the PICTS during EDWIN's reign, before returning to establish himself not only in NORTHUMBRIA, but as *BRETWALDA* and lord over the Irish and the PICTS. The long-term significance of his reign stems from his invitation to St Aidan and monks from IONA to carry out the CONVERSION of Northumbria to Christianity. A great warrior, he was eventually killed in battle against his greatest English rival, PENDA of MERCIA.

Oswaldslow, an area within which, from

the 10th century onwards, the medieval bishops of WORCESTER exercised numerous privileges – including the right to summon the royal army – as a result of royal grants secured by St Oswald, Bishop of Worcester (961–92) and Archbishop of York (972–92), one of the major figures of the TENTH-CENTURY REFORM. The considerable quantity of documentary evidence that survives about the structure of the Oswaldslow is important for the understanding of ANGLO-SAXON leases and of the organization of military obligation (*see FYRD*).

Oswy, King of Northumbria (642–70). A younger brother of OSWALD, he maintained the supremacy of the NORTHUMBRIAN kings over the English and the Britons. He fought many wars during his reign, including a great victory at Winwaed over PENDA of MERCIA in 655. He used the time during which he exercised power over southern England to spread Christianity to Mercia, an important stage in the CONVERSION of the entire English people. Oswy was the king who called and presided over the crucially important synod of WHITBY.

Ottawa Conference, July–Aug. 1932, imperial economic conference held in Canada, at which Britain accepted a limited policy of IMPERIAL PREFERENCE. This allowed goods to be traded within the BRITISH EMPIRE on favourable terms, avoiding some of the restrictions imposed by the IMPORT DUTIES ACT 1932. Elements of the policies remained in force until Britain joined the EEC (*see* EUROPEAN UNION).

Otterburn, Battle of, 5 Aug. 1388. A Scottish raiding army led by the Earls of Douglas, March and Moray was confronted by the English in Redesdale, Northumb. Remarkable for being fought throughout a moonlit night, the battle ended in victory for the Scots – though Douglas was killed – and the English commander Hotspur (*see* PERCY, HENRY) was captured. The account in the English ballad *Chevy Chase* bears little relationship to the events of the real battle.

Ounceland, a medieval territorial unit that existed throughout the regions of Scotland settled by Scandinavians in the early Middle Ages, and which was frequently divided into 'pennylands'. Its purpose was to assist the levying of taxation and tribute and to act as the basis of a naval force. Its origins are uncertain. There are parallels with similar arrangements in Norway, and it is possible that the system was expanded outwards from the earldom of ORKNEY during the time of the most powerful earls in the late 10th and early 11th centuries.

Outlawry, the legal expulsion of an individual from society. In COMMON LAW, a criminal offender was summoned at four consecutive COUNTY COURTS, and if he did not respond, at a fifth court a declaration was made that his goods were forfeit to the CROWN and his lands for a year to the crown and then to his FEUDAL lord; only the king could reverse the proclamation, and the outlaw could be killed on sight. His only reasonably secure defence was flight to a recognized SANCTUARY. In practice, from the 13th century, lesser 'civil' forms of outlawry developed to cope with cases of debt or of minor recalcitrance in the face of court orders, often including possibilities for easy reversal on a technicality. *See also* CAPITAL PUNISHMENT; *FLYMENAFYRMTH*.

OVERLORD, OPERATION, 6 June–25 Aug 1944, codename for the Battle of Normandy, which began on D-DAY. After successful landings, Anglo-American forces under MONTGOMERY were pinned down a few miles inland by German troops. The Allies gave priority to securing a port for supplies, capturing Cherbourg at the start of July, and to wearing down the Germans with carefully planned land and air attacks. Montgomery's methods were slow but saved Allied lives as the intensity of the fighting rivalled that of the larger battles of WORLD WAR I. In late July the Allies broke through the weakened German defences and made rapid progress inland, liberating Paris at the end of Aug. and Brussels on 3 Sept. Only failure at ARNHEM and the worsening supply situation prevented the Allies invading Germany that year (*see also* SECOND FRONT).

Overseer of the Poor, annually elected PARISH official under the Old POOR LAW who administered poor relief and the collection of parish poor rates. The duties of the overseers were gradually extended both by statute, e.g. the SETTLEMENT Laws, and by practice, with increasing sophistication of relief or the institution of new methods like SPEENHAMLAND.

In some larger towns, the overseer became a paid official in the later 18th century, but generally he was unpaid as were most parish offices.

'Overspill' Towns, *see* NEW TOWNS

Overton, Richard, *see* MORTALISM

Owain of Gwynedd (?–1170), Prince of Gwynedd. He succeeded his father GRUFFUDD AP CYNAN as ruler of GWYNEDD in 1137 and took advantage of the troubles of STEPHEN's reign to make territorial gains, especially between the rivers Conwy and Dee. Although he was forced to submit to HENRY II in 1157 and 1163, his extraordinary success in leading united Welsh opposition to the English invasion of 1165 enabled him to reassert his independence and won for him a reputation as 'Owain the Great, King of Wales'.

Owen, David (Baron Owen) (1938–), Labour politician and leader of the Social Democratic Party. A doctor who was elected as LABOUR MP for Plymouth Sutton (1966–74) and for Plymouth Devonport (1974–81), he served in the government as health minister (1974–6) and foreign secretary (1977–9) at the age of only 38 – an achievement matched in the 20th century only by EDEN. His disillusion with the leftward drift and anti-European stance of the party under FOOT led, in 1981, to his co-founding the Social Democratic Party (SDP) with Roy JENKINS, Bill Rodgers and Shirley Williams, the 'Gang of Four'. As leader of the SDP from 1983, he worked in alliance with the LIBERALS until 1988 when part of the SDP merged with them against his will. He continued to represent Plymouth as an SDP MP until his withdrawal from parliament in 1992 with a peerage from John MAJOR. From 1992–5 Owen worked as an EU (*see* EUROPEAN UNION) peace negotiator trying to find a solution to the Bosnian crisis.

Owen, Robert (1771–1858), pioneer of the co-operative movement. A Welsh-born draper's assistant, he became a master spinner, and in 1800 he and others took over the NEW LANARK Mills in Scotland, originally founded by his father-in-law and Arkwright. In 1813 he published *A New View of Society* in which he propounded the view that character was formed by environment, and claimed that the churches should recognize the evils of capitalism rather than castigate individuals as sinful. He improved working conditions, housing, sanitation and the education of children in the model community and village he established at Lanark, and his CO-OPERATIVE ideas were put into practice in such experimental communities as New Harmony, Indiana, USA (1825), Orbiston, near Glasgow (1826), Ralakine, Co. Cork (1831) and Queenswood, Hants. (1839). None survived, nor did his Grand Consolidated National Trades Union founded in 1833, but his example influenced both the passage of the Factory Act 1819 (*see* FACTORY LEGISLATION) and various co-operative movements and communities subsequently, and gives him a place as one of the founders of English socialism.

Owen map Bili (*fl.* mid-7th century), King of Strathclyde. A king of the STRATHCLYDE Britons, Owen map Bili achieved domination over the Scots of DALRIADA during the fluctuating power struggles between his kingdom and the SCOTS and PICTS. He achieved this by defeating the Scottish king Domnall Brecc in battle. A further reflection of his power may well lie in the fact that his brother BRUDE MAC BILI subsequently became king of the Picts.

Oxford and Asquith, 1st Earl of, *see* ASQUITH, HERBERT HENRY

Oxford and Mortimer, 1st Earl of, *see* HARLEY, ROBERT

Oxford and Oxford University Oxford's position as one of the focal towns in southern England's road network, and its proximity to royal palaces, probably helped it emerge as a significant centre for scholars. A crisis provoked by murderous quarrels between town and scholars in 1209 was ended by a papal settlement in 1214 – effectively, the first charter for the university – and soon after, the first chancellor is mentioned. As at CAMBRIDGE, colleges began to be founded in the late 13th century. The work of John WYCLIF and LOLLARD scholars resulted in a fierce reassertion of official orthodoxy in the 15th century, yet the university became a centre of RENAISSANCE humanist learning. It was generally less rapidly receptive to the REFORMATION than Cambridge, perhaps because of the greater number of colleges with monastic and episcopal connections. Until the 1850s the university, a loose fedesration of residential colleges, remained primarily a training ground in the classics for Anglican clergymen. In 1854 the University of Oxford Act reformed the university by reducing the power of college heads, opening fellowships and studentships to free competition, allowing NONCONFORMISTS to take the BA and freeing fellows from the obligation to become priests. The UNIVERSITY TEST ACTS (1871) removed the religious tests. In 1877 the revitalization of the university was carried further with the foundation of faculties of arts, science, law and theology; the building of laboratories; and the abolition of life fellowships, the granting of permission to fellows to marry, and the standardizing of fellowship stipends. From 1878 halls for female students were founded but women were not admitted to full university membership until 1920.

During the 17th-century CIVIL WARS, Oxford was the ROYALIST capital from 1642–5, but was only lightly damaged in the sieges leading up to its surrender. During the 20th century, it has also emerged as a major centre for the MOTOR INDUSTRY and for tourism.

CHRONOLOGY: FOUNDATIONS OF COLLEGES AND HALLS TO 1990

1264 Merton.
1280 University.
1282 Balliol.
***c.*1278** St Edmund Hall.
1326 Oriel.
1340 Queen's.
1379 New.
1427 Lincoln.
1438 All Souls.
1458 Magdalen.
1509 Brasenose.
1517 Corpus Christi.
1525 Christ Church (as Cardinal College); refounded 1529, with cathedral from 1546.
1554 Trinity (Durham, *c.*1286).
1555 St John's (St Bernard's, 1437).
1566 Exeter (Stapledon Hall, 1314; Exeter Hall, 1404).
1571 Jesus.
1610 Wadham.
1624 Pembroke.
1714 Worcester (Gloucester, *c.*1283).
1740 Hertford (Hart Hall, pre-1282); refounded 1874.
1868 Keble.
1878 Lady Margaret Hall.
1879 Somerville.
1886 St Hugh's; Mansfield.
1889 Manchester (moved from Manchester).
1893 St Hilda's.
1896 Campion Hall.
1897 St Benets.
1910 Greyfriars.
1921 Blackfriars.
1929 St Peter's.
1937 Nuffield.
1940 Regent's Park (moved from Stepney).
1950 St Antony's
1952 St Anne's.
1962 Linacre St Catherine's.
1965 St Cross.
1966 Wolfson.
1979 Green.
1984 Templeton.
1990 Kellogg.

Oxford By-Election, Oct. 1938, sometimes known as the 'APPEASEMENT' by-election since it was held only a month after the MUNICH AGREEMENT. The pro-CHAMBERLAIN, CONSERVATIVE candidate, Quintin Hogg (later Lord Hailsham), was challenged by an Independent Progressive A. D. Lindsay, master of Balliol College, who had the support of CHURCHILL, EDEN and MACMILLAN. The Conservatives narrowly managed to hold the seat. A fortnight later, at Bridgwater, Som., an Independent Progressive did gain a seat from the Conservatives. The two results attracted considerable publicity and provided evidence of a growing hostility to the Chamberlain government's policy of appeasement.

Oxford Movement, a religious movement based first in the early 19th-century University of OXFORD, representing a revival of the CATHOLIC outlook of the High Church Party in the Church of England (*see* HIGH CHURCHMANSHIP) after a century of relative eclipse. The Movement has been seen by many historians as originating in a TORY reaction by churchmen at the curbing of ANGLICAN dominance in the British state by the reforming WHIG governments of the 1830s. Indeed its first major incident, the 'Assize Sermon', was a protest by John Keble at the government's suppression of certain bishoprics of the established CHURCH in IRELAND. The widespread interest in this unlikely cause proved that Keble had struck a vein of unease among clergy, including EVANGELICALS, and when a group of clergy led by Keble, NEWMAN and Edward Pusey began publishing the *Tracts for the Times against Popery and Dissent*, they found themselves national celebrities. The Tracts were aimed to defend the Established Church and its doctrines with a Catholic emphasis. However, the publication of Tract 90 (1841) resulted in the abrupt withdrawal of remaining Evangelical sympathy with Tractarian aims, and the majority of the bishops showed themselves hostile – a sad blow to a Movement which laid especial stress on the authority conferred on bishops by their APOSTOLIC SUCCESSION. The subsequent conversion to Roman Catholicism of key figures, including Newman, seriously harmed the movement's progress.

The growth of the Ritualist wing (*see* RITUALISM) fuelled continuing controversy in the Church, but also helped to give the movement a wider constituency to a previously rather academic and clerical movement. Against persistent hostility from Evangelicals, the Church hierarchy and even Queen VICTORIA, the Oxford Movement made steady progress in the Church, influencing many old and new PARISHES (*see also* REVIVALS), and contributed much to the steady professionalization of the clergy. It also revived monastic life in the Church of England, which was legally possible since no official statement during the DISSOLUTION had ever condemned MONASTICISM; consistently there have been more nunneries than male monasteries, a reversal of the medieval situation. Increasingly by 1900 those affected by the Oxford Movement were labelling themselves 'Anglo-Catholics', and many were moving from the Movement's original association with political conservatism, some flirting with socialism and even advocating disestablishment of the Church. By the 1950s, Anglo-Catholics were dominant in the Church, providing a large proportion of the bishops and clergy. However, in the 1960s, the grouping split in its reaction to the radical theology which was then beginning to convulse western Christianity. Anglo-Catholics were further divided about their reaction to the long arguments about the ordination of women, and the final Anglican decision to ordain women (implemented in 1994) is a new challenge to the Movement's identity.

CHRONOLOGY

1833, 14 July Keble preaches Assize Sermon in St Mary's Oxford on 'National Apostasy'.

1833, 9 Sept. First *Tract for the Times* published.

1836 Melbourne (*see* LAMB, WILLIAM) nominates Dr Renn Dickson Hampden, a BROAD CHURCHman, as Regius professor of divinity; outraged High Churchmen fail to prevent appointment.

1841 NEWMAN publishes *Tract 90*, an attempt to prove that the THIRTY-NINE ARTICLES are compatible with Catholic theology; he is horrified by the hostility which this arouses.

1841 Pusey receives monastic vows of Marian Rebecca Hughes, possibly the first in ANGLICANISM since the REFORMATION.

1845 Newman received into Church of Rome.

1846 *The Guardian* (not to be confused with the *Manchester Guardian*, now called *The Guardian*) founded to express High Church opinion.

1849 Convent of Holy Trinity (with Hughes as Superior) founded in Oxford.

1850 High Churchmen furious when the PRIVY COUNCIL upholds the right of Rev. C. C. Gorham to accept appointment to a parish in the diocese of Exeter, despite his CALVINIST views on theology of baptism.

1851 Archdeacon Henry Manning joins Church of Rome; later made a cardinal.

1863 *Church Times* founded, with aggressive High Church stance.

1865 Community of St John the Evangelist (the 'Cowley Fathers') founded at Oxford.

Oxford Parliament, March 1681, the third of the three Parliaments of the EXCLUSION CRISIS of 1679–81, convened in OXFORD by

CHARLES II because he feared riots in LONDON. Since it seemed disposed, like its predecessors, to support the Exclusion of James, Duke of York (the future JAMES II) from the succession, Charles dissolved it within a week.

Oxford, Provisions of, *see* PROVISIONS OF OXFORD

Oxford Union Debate, *see* 'KING AND COUNTRY' DEBATE

Oyer and Terminer, *see* ASSIZES

P

Paganism, Anglo-Saxon The regions that subsequently formed the kingdom of England were dominated by pagan tribes between the 5th and 7th centuries. Because Christian writers such as BEDE did not describe it, information about Anglo-Saxon paganism is limited. Burials (of which SUTTON HOO is the most renowned), over 50 PLACE NAMES such as Wednesbury or Thurstable, and some of the names of the days of the week that we still use show that pagan religion – with its panoply of gods, headed by Woden and Thor – was deeply entrenched in early society, satisfying obvious practical needs. The reluctance of kings such as PENDA of MERCIA and REDWALD of EAST ANGLIA to abandon it shows that it could represent a genuine alternative to Christianity (*see* CONVERSION).

Paine, Tom (1737–1809), writer and republican. Son of a Norfolk QUAKER farmer and corsetmaker, he too worked as a corsetmaker before becoming an EXCISEMAN – a position from which he was dismissed for writing a pamphlet arguing the case for higher pay. On the advice of Benjamin Franklin, whom he met in London, he went to Philadelphia in 1774 and became co-editor of the *Pennsylvannia Magazine*. The following year, he published *Common Sense*, a statement of the American case for independence. This made him famous, and he was appointed secretary to the Congressional Committee for Foreign Affairs in 1777, resigning two years later.

As clerk to the General Assembly of Pennsylvania, he went to Paris in 1781 to negotiate a loan. He returned there in 1787, then went to London to promote his invention of an iron bridge. While in England, he published the first part of *The Rights of Man* (1791) in response to BURKE's *Reflections on the Revolution in France*; it sold in enormous numbers. The second part appeared in 1792, as tension within Britain heightened. Paine, who had gone to Paris, was tried in his absence for seditious libel and throughout the country, loyalists organized 'Paine burnings', at which he was burnt in effigy.

He was elected a member of the French National Convention, but his opposition to the execution of Louis XVI led to his imprisonment in 1793, during which time he wrote *The Age of Reason*. Released after the fall of Robespierre in 1794, he remained in France, and helped Bonaparte plan the invasion of England. In 1802, he returned to America, and died in New York in June 1809.

A fierce critic of all unnecessary mystery in Church and state, and an ardent republican, Paine stood somewhat outside the constitutionalist mainstream of 18th- and 19th-century British RADICALISM, but was widely read and cited.

Paisley, the Revd Ian (1926–), Unionist politician. Head since 1951 of the fundamentalist Free Presbyterian Church in Northern Ireland, he attracted populist support for the ultra-LOYALIST Ulster Defence Committee from 1960 and founded the breakaway DEMOCRATIC UNIONIST PARTY in 1971. MP for North Antrim from 1970, he helped organize the UNITED ULSTER UNIONIST COUNCIL, which won 11 out of 12 Ulster seats in PARLIAMENT in 1974. He supported the ULSTER WORKERS' COUNCIL strike of May 1974, which brought down the power-sharing executive set up by the SUNNINGDALE AGREEMENT. A bitter opponent of the Anglo-Irish Agreement of 1985, he formed an electoral pact with the ULSTER UNIONIST PARTY to oppose it, which to some extent healed the rift in Unionist politics that had existed since 1971. An MEP since 1979, Paisley was the dominant voice of Loyalism until the late 1990s. As a bitter opponent of the Anglo-Irish Agreement (1985), he formed an electoral pact with the Ulster Unionist Party (UUP) to oppose it, and led dissident UUP members in vociferous opposition to the Good Friday Agreement (April 1998); though the Democratic Unionist Party accepted seats on the Assembly Executive in Nov. 1999.

Pakistan, officially the Islamic Republic of Pakistan. The area was previously part of INDIA during the British colonial administration. It was founded amidst considerable violence and bloodshed in 1947, at the partition of India on independence, as a separate state for the Muslim minority, and originally in two parts, East and West, in the north-eastern and north-western parts of the Indian sub-continent. Pakistan's politics have been notoriously unstable. War between the two parts led to eastern Pakistan gaining independence as the state of Bangladesh in 1971. *See also* INDIAN INDEPENDENCE.

Palatinate A palatinate (or regality) is a region whose lord enjoys semi-royal jurisdiction although still a subject and TENANT-IN-CHIEF of the CROWN – an arrangement that was designed mainly to strengthen defence against invasion.

Of the Norman palatinates – CHESTER, DURHAM, KENT and Shropshire – the last two were quickly suppressed. The earldom of Chester, held from 1254 by the king's eldest son, has been in crown hands ever since, and Lancaster (erected a ducal palatinate in 1351) since 1399; only Durham remained a private jurisdiction, until 1836. Courts and administration aping medieval WESTMINSTER government functioned in Chester, Lancaster and Durham until a 19th-century tidying-up, although remnants remain.

In Ireland, among various generally less powerful palatinates, the County Palatine of Tipperary (erected in 1328) reverted to the crown from the Butler earls of Ormond in 1715. Early NEW WORLD proprietary colonies followed the palatinate model.

Palatines, German refugees, mostly PROTESTANT, from the Rhenish Palatinate, 12,000–13,000 of whom arrived in London in 1709, fleeing from an unsympathetic religious regime and an exceptionally severe winter, and moved by the hope of emigrating to NEW ENGLAND. The government accommodated them in dockyards and warehouses; Queen ANNE sanctioned a charitable appeal for their support. TORIES blamed the influx on the General NATURALIZATION Act of 1709, intended, they claimed, to undermine the Church of England; they repealed the Act in 1712. Some Palatines were settled in England and Ireland, but most were sent to the colonies.

Palavicino, Horatio (*c.*1540–1600), financier. A Genoese merchant, his Netherlands business deals led him, on Sir Thomas GRESHAM's death in 1579, to take over as chief English financial and diplomatic agent abroad. As an international financier, he was in a unique position to gather information. Loss of ELIZABETH I's favour brought retirement in the 1590s, when he used his staggering wealth to set himself up as an English country gentleman, as well as helping Robert CECIL in his struggles with Essex (*see* DEVEREUX, ROBERT).

Pale, the, the territory around DUBLIN, where English law and royal administration were respected – i.e. where the CROWN's writ ran. The area fluctuated in extent from the 12th century, and in the mid-14th century comprised Dublin, Louth, Meath, Trim, Kilkenny and Kildare. However, by 1500, the Pale had diminished to only 50 miles north of Dublin and 30 miles inland. Later, the Tudors reasserted the English presence. The word gave rise to the phrase 'beyond the Pale', which is still in general use.

This was also the term given to the small English territory around CALAIS.

Palestine, area traditionally regarded as the Holy Land, which had become an area of Arab and nomadic settlement in the centuries after the diaspora of the Jews in AD 70, and was long under the rule of the Ottoman (or Turkish) Empire. Palestine became the focus of the growing Zionist wish to recreate a Jewish homeland from the late 19th century, and BALFOUR made his Declaration supporting the idea of a Jewish homeland in 1917. On the fall of the Ottoman Empire following its defeat in WORLD WAR I and the capture of Palestine by Sir Edmund Allenby in 1918, the LEAGUE OF NATIONS gave Britain a MANDATE over Palestine, which it exercised – in the face of growing violence from extreme Zionists – from 1920 until 1948 (when the UNITED NATIONS took over, before the foundation of Israel the following year). The subsequent tensions between Arabs and Jews in what was Palestine have been continuously important among world events, especially since the mid-1960s.

Palladianism, 18th century architectural style in conscious imitation and revival of that of the late RENAISSANCE Italian architect Andrea Palladio (1508–80), based upon antique Roman architecture. Inigo Jones (1573–1652) had first introduced Palladio's classical style to England, and Palladio's influence was rediscovered two generations after Jones's death. Palladianism was the pre-eminent style of the 18th century, with its classical rationality, antique precedents and mathematical proportions. It was a rejection of the fluidity and panache of the English BAROQUE, associated with Sir Christopher Wren (1632–1723), Nicholas Hawksmoor (1661–1736), and Sir John Vanbrugh (1664–1726); it also had a political dimension since the ardent Palladians were usually WHIGS, while the rump of the TORIES after the 1720s held onto the older Baroque style. This reintroduction of Palladio's architecture is particularly associated with the publicity engineered by Colen Campbell, who began the volumes of the *Vitruvius Britannicus* in 1715, and with the architect peer, Richard Boyle, Earl of Burlington (1695–1753), who built Chiswick House (modelled on Palladio's Villa Rotunda outside Vicenza) and Burlington House (since considerably altered and now the ROYAL ACADEMY) in the 1720s. The style, much used (and abused) since the 18th century, is also known as Neo-Palladianism.

Palmerston, 3rd Viscount, *see* TEMPLE, HENRY

Pandemics, *see* EPIDEMICS

Pankhursts: Dame Christabel (1880–1958), **Emmeline** (née Goulden) (1858–1928), **Sylvia** (1882–1960), Suffragettes. The daughter of well-off reformist Manchester parents, Emmeline worked with her husband, Dr Richard Pankhurst, a progressive barrister, for WOMEN'S SUFFRAGE and property rights in Manchester and London, and, following the omission of women's suffrage from the REFORM ACT 1884 joined the INDEPENDENT LABOUR PARTY in 1893. Opposition in the ILP to the cause of women's suffrage rather than universal manhood suffrage, drove Pankhurst and her daughter Christabel to found the WOMEN'S POLITICAL AND SOCIAL UNION (WPSU) in Manchester in 1903. In 1905 Christabel was arrested with Annie Kenney (1879–1953, the only working-class woman to attain a key position in the WPSU) and imprisoned for protesting the right of women to vote at a LIBERAL election meeting in Manchester. The WPSU became a national movement with a policy of militant action to secure votes for women. Christabel joined her mother (who had been widowed in 1898) in London in 1907 where she acted as an orator and organizer for the WPSU and later as editor of its newspaper *The Suffragette*, through which she personally sought to direct the organization's activities from Paris, where she fled to avoid arrest in 1912. Sylvia, an artist, who studied at the Royal College of Art, and lifelong socialist was also much involved in the WPSU and designed many of the movement's banners, publications and other campaigning artefacts, whilst Emmeline's eloquent, charismatic and often dramatic leadership and her bravery in enduring many prison sentences and forcible feedings under the notorious 'CAT AND MOUSE ACT' proved a considerable embarrassment to the Liberal government. The work of the Pankhursts and others succeeded in drawing the demand for votes for women to the attention of the British public. However, the escalation of militancy and the increasingly autocratic leadership of Christabel and Emmeline Pankhurst, led to defections from the ranks of the WPSU, including that of Sylvia, who believing the interests of working-class women also needed to be served, worked to build a democratic mass movement to campaign for the vote for all women, which became the East London Federation.

On the outbreak of war in 1914 Sylvia founded the pacifist, socialist journal *Worker's Dreadnought*, was a member of the Women's International League for Peace and Freedom, continued to campaign for women's suffrage and worked tirelessly in the East End of London establishing clinics and NURSERY EDUCATION, finding work for the unemployed and organizing servicemen's wives to fight for better pensions. The WPSU suspended the demand for women's suffrage on the outbreak of war and Emmeline Pankhurst became an enthusiastic propagandist for CONSCRIPTION, touring the US and Russia lecturing on the war effort and social purity, activities shared by Christabel. Mother and daughter both tried unsuccessfully to be elected to PARLIAMENT after the war, but all three Pankhursts were able to witness the REPRESENTATION OF THE PEOPLE ACT (1918) which gave the vote to women over 30.

Panopticon, model prison promoted by Jeremy BENTHAM in the late 18th century, in the context of widespread interest in PRISON REFORM. It was designed to maximize opportunities for prison staff to observe prisoners: cells were organized in circular tiers around a central observation platform. Health was to be preserved by central heating and running water. Bentham was convinced that the governor of such a prison could make a profit from prisoners' labour, and in 1794 contracted with the government to build and administer one, but the scheme was later abandoned, Bentham being compensated with £23,000.

Papal Aggression, *see* BISHOPRICS, ENGLISH

Pardo, Convention of the, Jan. 1739, preliminary to a general settlement of Spanish–British tensions, arising from Spanish police actions primarily aimed against British smugglers based in JAMAICA. Twelve British ships disappeared in the Caribbean in 1737. The opposition whipped up public feeling with accounts of Spanish cruelty, most notoriously in the case of Captain Jenkins whose ear had allegedly been cut off in 1731. Spain was to pay £95,000 for damages received by British merchants; in return, the SOUTH SEA COMPANY was to pay £68,000 owed to the Spanish crown for the privilege of its annual shipment to the Caribbean, but the Company refused to pay unless compensated for damages first. Negotiations collapsed, and Spain suspended the ASIENTO. In the summer of 1739, British warships were sent to intercept Spanish galleons; war – the War of JENKINS' EAR – was declared in Oct.

Paris, Matthew (*c.*1200–*c.*1259), writer. A monk of ST ALBANS, he was a prolific author of historical and hagiographical works, often strikingly illustrated with his own line drawings. His latin *Chronica Majora*, from the Creation to 1259 – an extension of ROGER OF WENDOVER's chronicle and the most comprehensive history written in England up to that time – was so long that he produced several shorter versions as well. His informants included the most powerful figures in the realm, including HENRY III, but his opinions remained very much his own: xenophobic, often critical, always vividly expressed.

Paris, Treaty of, May 1259, concluded between HENRY III and Louis IX of France, by which the English king was recognized as duke of Aquitaine and did homage to the king of France for the duchy, but relinquished all claims to Normandy, Anjou, Maine, Touraine and Poitou. These renunciations set the seal on the fall of the ANGEVIN EMPIRE.

Paris, Treaty of, Feb 1763, agreement between Britain, France and Spain terminating the SEVEN YEARS WAR; Austria and Prussia signed the separate Treaty of Hubertusburg. Britain gained QUEBEC, Cape Breton Island, DOMINICA, TOBAGO, GRENADA, ST VINCENT AND THE GRENADINES, Minorca and Senegal from France. She annexed CLIVE's conquests in INDIA, where France was to keep only trading posts occupied in 1749 and was to station no troops. Spain surrendered Florida to Britain in return for the restoration of Havana and Manila; she also received Louisiana from the French. The peace was attacked in Britain for failing to take sufficient advantage of overwhelming success: fishing rights off the coast of NEWFOUNDLAND, Guadeloupe, Martinique, Gorée, Belle-Île and some Indian possessions were restored to France. In the eyes of other continental powers Britain's power had none the less alarmingly increased; in the next few decades, it was to be difficult to procure allies.

Paris Peace Conference, 1919–20, the five-month-long peace conference that concluded WORLD WAR I, producing the treaty of Versailles with Germany. Dominated by the leaders of the victorious powers – British and French prime ministers LLOYD GEORGE and Clemenceau and US president Wilson – it denied Germany any influence on the settlement, giving rise to later claims that it had produced a 'dictated peace'. It became a source of contention in international relations throughout the inter-war years.

Despite Wilson's desire to see adherence to the Fourteen Points on which Germany had concluded the Armistice, French demands for harsh treatment set the tone of the proceedings. Lloyd George was also pledged 'to make Germany pay', but since Britain's interests lay in a swift return to normal economic activity, he sought to mitigate the harshest aspects of French demands.

Britain's major gains were the ending of the naval threat by the surrender of the German fleet, the territorial and military restrictions placed on Germany, the setting up of the LEAGUE OF NATIONS, and the placing of former German colonies under League MANDATES, many of them effectively under British control. British influence was not sufficient, however, to prevent a REPARATIONS burden, which was to inflict severe damage on the German economy, creating conditions favourable to the later rise of Nazism, and precipitate the DEPRESSION. The territorial settlement, left Germany largely intact and in a position to recover later. Other agreements signed at Paris included the treaties of St Germain (with Austria), Neuilly (with Bulgaria), Trianon (with Hungary) and Sèvres (with Turkey).

Parish, the unit of pastoral care in the Roman CATHOLIC and ANGLICAN Churches and the CHURCH OF SCOTLAND: ideally a single community and church served by a parish priest (or 'incumbent'), or in Scotland, by a parish minister. In ANGLO-SAXON England, the general proliferation of parish churches can be dated to the 10th century; before then, the clergy's pastoral role had been mostly carried out by groups of priests based at MINSTERS. Many local churches founded by noblemen are recorded from the 7th century onwards, as are payments for the clergy's upkeep, such as church-scot (*see* TITHES). However, it was usually local landowners who were the founders of parish churches throughout the Anglo-Saxon period, an important consideration in the development of legal concepts such as ADVOWSON, the right of appointment of the parish clergyman. Another consequence of this development is the frequency with which modern parish boundaries follow Anglo-Saxon estate boundaries.

The system was virtually complete by the 13th century (with *c*.9,000 English and Welsh parishes), changing remarkably little thereafter up to the 19th century. It worked best in lowland England; Scottish and Irish parish systems long remained ineffective. From the 16th century, English churchwardens and other parish officers took on many secular responsibilities, especially for POOR RELIEF. Nearly all these functions disappeared in the 19th- and early 20th-century reforms. Elected parish councils were set up by the DISTRICT AND PARISH COUNCILS ACT 1894. They aroused great hopes of grass-roots democracy and social change at the time, but, in general, their lack of financial resources has limited their importance. However, in rural areas the parish is still often a social unit of real vitality. *See also* REGISTERS, PARISH.

Parish Registers, *see* REGISTERS, PARISH

Parisi, one of the tribes of pre-Roman Britain, whose territory lay on the north bank of the River Humber. Little specifically is known about their history, but it is reasonable to assume that they came under direct Roman control soon after AD 70, at the same time as their much more powerful neighbours, the BRIGANTES. The *CIVITAS* of the Parisi was subsequently created around Brough-on-Humber, Yorks. *See also* ROMAN CONQUEST

Parker, Matthew (1504–75), Archbishop of Canterbury (1559–75). A distinguished CAMBRIDGE don and chaplain to ANNE BOLEYN, the Church preferments he gained for his evangelical sympathies under EDWARD VI were all lost under MARY I. Emerging from rural obscurity in 1558, he found to his horror that ELIZABETH I had decided that her mother's old chaplain would make an ideal archbishop of Canterbury. He did his gentle and conscientious best in the difficult opening years of the ELIZABETHAN SETTLEMENT; with little support, he performed a balancing act between the PURITANS and the Queen's demands for discipline (*see* VESTIARIAN CONTROVERSIES), and led an uninspired official BIBLE translation. Happiest in scholarship, he sponsored other historians, pioneering especially Anglo-Saxon studies, and preserved many precious medieval manuscripts.

Parker Morris Standards, official standards for HOUSING and house-building in the public sector, recommended by the planner Sir Parker Morris (1891–1972), town clerk of Westminster from 1929–56. The recommendations Morris made in his 1961 report *Homes for Today and Tomorrow* were made mandatory in 1967. The minimum areas for dwellings and their amenity standards, which were themselves the development of earlier official reports from 1918 and 1944, were more generous than many private builders offered; they were of key importance in providing quality in the housing expansion, whether in high-rise blocks or low-rise accommodation, of the 1960s and 1970s.

Parker Society, established in 1840 by leading Anglican EVANGELICALS such as Anthony Ashley Cooper, 7th Earl of Shaftesbury, to publish the works of scholars of the English PROTESTANT reformers of the 16th century. Named from Archbishop Matthew PARKER, it upheld the credibility of the Protestant REFORMATION as a spiritual movement against its detractors both in the OXFORD MOVEMENT and in Rome. The 53 volumes so produced are now a staple source of British historians of the early modern period.

Parliament, from French *parlement* ('discussion').

ENGLAND AND WALES

Most medieval kingdoms developed consultative/representative assemblies. England's was distinguished chiefly by its developing bicameral (two-chamber) form, with the upper house, the LORDS, consisting of the great landholders (lay and ecclesiastical), the lower house, the COMMONS, consisting of representatives of the communities of the realm (SHIRES and BOROUGHS) furnished with powers of ATTORNEY to give consent on behalf of those who sent them. In the mid and later 13th century, when contemporaries spoke of parliaments, they referred mainly to assemblies of the great men of the kingdom meeting at the king's summons and carrying out a wide range of advisory, administrative and judicial functions. Representatives were summoned only infrequently, with lay representatives sometimes being joined by representatives of the lower clergy.

In the centuries between EDWARD I'S death in 1307 and the GLORIOUS REVOLUTION of 1688, Parliament underwent a series of transformations. The Commons, now consisting solely of the representatives of shires and boroughs and meeting separately from the 1330s onwards, became a regular part of Parliament, valued chiefly for their consent to taxation by the crown but also active as presenters of 'common' petitions on matters of concern to the kingdom as a whole. By the early 15th century they had become a necessary part of the legislative process as reflected in the almost standard appearance in statutes of the phrase 'by advice and assert of the lords spiritual and temporal at the instance [or at the request] of the Commons'. The Lords, meanwhile, were transformed into a chamber of hereditary lay peers and spiritual dignitaries (archbishops, bishops and the heads of 27 of the more important religious houses). Given the composition of Parliament and its enhanced status in the later Middle Ages, it is not surprising that on occasion it became the place where political conflicts were determined, as, for example, in 1340–1, 1388, or the late 1450s, with the Lords, as the great men of the kingdom, playing very much the principal role. Again, it was claimed by the backers of HENRY IV that the deposition of RICHARD II in 1399 took place in Parliament, though in fact he was deposed by an *ad hoc* gathering of PRELATES, lords and commons who had originally been assembled to meet as a parliament. Indeed, not until the CIVIL WARS of the mid-17th century would Parliament play so important a role in high politics as it did in these years.

Parliamentary assemblies also became less frequent in the later 15th and into the 16th centuries. In part this was a consequence of the end of the HUNDRED YEARS WAR which, along with the expansion of the royal domain, eased the need for parliamentary supplementation of the crown's own revenues. None the less, Parliament had become too entrenched and too important to fade away, though a number of its continental counterparts were to do so. In particular, its legislative role was crucial in HENRY VIII's breach with Rome and in the subsequent twists and turns of royal ecclesiastical policy spanning the quarter-century between the 1533 Act in RESTRAINT OF APPEALS to the 1559 Acts of Supremacy (*see* ROYAL SUPREMACY) and Uniformity (*see* ELIZABETHAN SETTLEMENT). Thus, while parliament was convened on average only once every three years between 1485 and the breach with Rome in 1529, between 1529 and 1559 it met on average nearly once a year. At the same time, the DISSOLUTION of the religious houses in the later 1530s meant the removal from the Lords of the abbots and priors, thus leaving the lay peers in a decisive majority over the remaining spiritual peers.

Under ELIZABETH I and the early Stuarts, parliamentary sessions again became more infrequent, with royal parliamentary relations showing increasing signs of strain in the war decades of the 1590s and the 1620s. That strain escalated into direct confrontation between a majority in both Houses and CHARLES I when, after the king had declined to summon a Parliament for eleven years, he was compelled by defeat in the BISHOPS' WARS with Scotland to do so in 1640. And it was the second of the Parliaments he summoned in 1640, the so-called LONG PARLIAMENT, that waged and won the first CIVIL WAR against the king, just as it was the purged remnant of the Commons of that Parliament (the RUMP) which, at the bidding of the NEW MODEL ARMY, authorized the trial and execution of Charles I in 1649.

However, the institution of a parliamentary government from 1649–53 proved to be a blind alley both politically and institutionally (while experiments with redistribution of constituencies under the PROTECTORATE also were abandoned at the RESTORATION of 1660). Rather, Parliament's constitutional future lay in acting in conjunction with the monarchy – as JAMES II himself acknowledged in his frantic efforts of 1687–8 to organize the return of a compliant House of Commons. In turn, the GLORIOUS REVOLUTION of 1688–9, followed by a quarter-century of unprecedentedly costly warfare, established, beyond real controversy, the convention of annual sessions (even though not mandated by the TRIENNIAL ACT of 1694 or any other statute), the legal supremacy of parliamentary statute (as against royal powers of unilateral action), and the wisdom of co-operation between the monarch and the two houses – co-operation managed by royal ministers chosen by the monarch in large part because they were politically acceptable to a majority of MPs and peers.

From this perspective, Parliament's constitutional standing in the mid-18th century had never been higher, and it was parliamentary supremacy that, in no small part, was at stake in the escalating quarrels of the 1760s with the American colonies. Thus Parliament, in response to American arguments that they were not represented at WESTMINSTER and hence should not be bound by parliamentary statute, passed in 1766 an act affirming its legislative authority. Yet Parliament's assertion of authority rested on the House of Commons' claim to represent (in some sense) all whom it taxed and all for whom it legislated, and that claim was challenged not only by the American colonists but increasingly also by political dissenters at home. The agitation for electoral reform, first articulated in the early decades of GEORGE III's reign, did not achieve any kind of fruition until the 1832 REFORM ACT, followed in subsequent generations by further measures extending the FRANCHISE. And as the redistribution of parliamentary seats and broadening of the franchise renewed the Commons' claim to be the true representative of the people (*see* REFORM ACT 1867), so it enabled the Commons in the early 20th century to begin the process of restricting the legislative powers of the Lords on the grounds that the peers, who represented only themselves, should no longer be permitted to frustrate the will of the electorate. However, the Lords survived, if with curtailed powers, and the anomaly of a hereditary upper house was not much eased by the innovation of life peers.

In Jan. 1999, however, the LABOUR government introduced a Bill which, when enacted, will remove the rights of some 750 people to sit and vote in parliament solely on the basis that they inherited their seats (*see* LORDS, HOUSE OF).

In the meantime, the fact that 'parliamentary democracy' since the expansion of the electorate has taken the form of the dominance of the House of Commons by the PRIME MINISTER and the CABINET (that is, the leadership of the majority party in the Commons) now raises questions in some quarters about the effectiveness of Parliament, either in holding the executive to effective account or even in carefully reviewing projected legislation.

For chronologies of important dates, *see* COMMONS, HOUSE OF; LORDS, HOUSE OF. *See also* ADMONITIONS TO PARLIAMENT; ADDLED PARLIAMENT; *ASHBY V. WHITE*; BAREBONES PARLIAMENT; CONSTITUENCY; CONVENTION PARLIAMENT; GOOD PARLIAMENT; LONG PARLIAMENT; MAN, ISLE OF; MERCILESS PARLIAMENT; PARLIAMENT ACT 1911; PARLIAMENTARY REFORM; REFORMATION PARLIAMENT; RUMP PARLIAMENT; SHORT PARLIAMENT.

IRELAND

An Irish Parliament was created by the English authorities in the early 14th century, on the English model, and it thus included representatives of the lower clergy (later excluded from English parliaments and represented only in CONVOCATIONS). Medieval parliamentary membership was generally drawn only from the PALE and some OLD ENGLISH communities and noblemen (*see* KILKENNY, STATUTES OF). Later, England did its best to control the institution in central interests, not always with success. *See also* IRELAND, ENGLISH CONQUEST OF; IRELAND AND ENGLAND IN THE 16TH AND 17TH CENTURIES; IRELAND AND ENGLAND IN THE 18TH CENTURY; IRISH QUESTION.

CHRONOLOGY

1366 Statutes of KILKENNY enacted.

1494–5 Drogheda Parliament passes POYNINGS' LAW; thereafter Parliament virtually a registry for English government legislation.

1541 HENRY VIII recognized as king of Ireland: Gaelic chieftains granted PEERAGES and thus a place in Parliament.

1612–13 NEW ENGLISH and Old English clash, resulting in ANTI-CATHOLIC legislation and Catholics losing parliamentary majority.

1640 Opposition to Thomas WENTWORTH, Lord Strafford, culminates in New and Old English co-operating in parliamentary denunciations of royal government.

1642 Representative assembly of Catholics – Confederation of KILKENNY – repudiates the title 'parliament'.

1649 Kilkenny Assembly dissolved by treaty with James Butler, Earl of Ormond.

1654 Token number of Irish representatives in Westminster Parliament.

1661 Irish Parliament restored on old FRANCHISE; very few Catholics.

1689 JACOBITE PARLIAMENT called by JAMES II declares that English Parliament cannot legislate for Ireland; dissolved when James is defeated.

1782 Virtual repeal of Poynings' Law and other restrictive legislation in GRATTAN'S PARLIAMENT; *see* LEGISLATIVE INDEPENDENCE.

1783 ROTUNDA PARLIAMENT called.

1801 UNION of Irish and British Parliaments at Westminster.

1919 DÁIL Éireann, organized by SINN FÉIN, meets in Dublin; proclaims a Republic.

SCOTLAND

The Scots Parliament never achieved the exclusive position of its English counterpart. In the 16th century, other informal *ad hoc* assemblies – congregations and conventions – and, from the 1560s, the General Assembly of the KIRK (organized on CALVINIST principles) provided an alternative political focus. Parliament was not divided into Lords and Commons; astute monarchs could manage business by controlling the LORDS OF THE ARTICLES.

CHRONOLOGY: PARLIAMENT IN SCOTLAND TO 1707

1290s First references to KING'S COUNCIL as 'Parliamentum': soon defined as a court that declares the law.

1312 First evidence of presence (alongside nobles and PRELATES) of BURGH representatives: at first, for financial business only.

1420s Burgesses summoned for all business.

1428 Act stipulates that SHIRE commissioners (representatives) be summoned; not implemented.

1445 First creation of lords by the king (JAMES II): growing differentiation between lower and upper baronage, with upper barons attending Parliament.

1587 Franchise Act constitutes shire commissioners; determines parliamentary FRANCHISE until 1832.

1654 Token number of Scots representatives in Westminster Parliament.

1661 Parliament summoned to EDINBURGH on old franchise.

1689 Convention of Estates (in which supporters of the future WILLIAM III have slight majority) meets at Edinburgh; offers crown to William and MARY II. LORDS OF THE ARTICLES established.

1707 Scots Parliament votes for UNION with English Parliament.

Parliament Act 1911 A landmark in defining the constitutional relationship between the LORDS and the COMMONS, the Act arose from conflict between obstructive CONSERVATIVE peers and the reforming LIBERAL government of ASQUITH, and in particular from the Lords' attempts to block the passage of LLOYD GEORGE'S PEOPLE'S BUDGET. By its provisions, the veto power of the Lords over legislation initiated in the Commons was reduced to a power of delaying legislation to one month in the case of money bills (which were defined as such by the Commons) and for two years for other public bills (reduced to one year by the 1949 Parliament Act). At the same time the maximum length of time between general elections was reduced from seven years to five.

Parliament of Devils, *see* ATTAINDER, ACT OF

Parliamentarians, frequently used term for those fighting CHARLES I in the 1642–6 CIVIL WAR (although it should be noted that a substantial number of MPs and LORDS sat in the king's Parliament at OXFORD throughout this period). Also known as 'ROUNDHEADS'.

Parliamentary Privilege is designed to preserve the authority and independence of members of both Houses of PARLIAMENT, and relies both on ancient custom and statutory grant. Privileges include freedom from arrest (a privilege which has been successively narrowed and carefully defined) and freedom of speech within the precincts of the Palace of WESTMINSTER; freedom of speech was specifically granted in the BILL OF RIGHTS 1689. *See also* *ASHBY V. WHITE*; WILKES, JOHN.

Parliamentary Reform, campaign for the reform of the House of COMMONS, especially between the 1760s and the REFORM ACT of 1832. Attempts had been made in the INTERREGNUM to produce a pattern of parliamentary representation which more fairly reflected clusterings of population, but the status quo was restored at the RESTORATION. The COUNTRY party attacked undue royal influence in PARLIAMENT from the late 17th century; the late 17th and early 18th centuries saw attempts to restrict numbers of placemen and pensioners (*see* PLACE BILLS). TORIES and independents occasionally argued that seats should be redistributed, and the FRANCHISE extended.

More sustained pressure for reform arose in the course of the campaign in 1769–70 for the reinstatement of John WILKES as MP for Middlesex, and was carried forwards by the ASSOCIATION MOVEMENT. Excessive crown influence in Parliament, the inequitable distribution of seats and narrowness of the franchise were the main foci of concern. More and less radical changes were proposed, moderates characteristically favouring an increase in the number of county seats, RADICALS favouring manhood suffrage. Charles Lennox, Duke of Richmond, proposed manhood suffrage to the House of LORDS in 1780. A high point in the early movement was reached when PITT THE YOUNGER, as prime minister, moved that a committee consider parliamentary reform in 1783, although the proposal was soundly defeated. A similar campaign in IRELAND reached its peak with the calling of a national convention, the ROTUNDA PARLIAMENT, in the same year and the promotion of a reform bill in the Irish Parliament, which was defeated by a smaller, though still decisive margin. The SOCIETY FOR CONSTITUTIONAL INFORMATION initiated research into defects of the English representative system, bearing fruit in Thomas Oldfield's *History of the Boroughs* (initially published in 1792). During the FRENCH REVOLUTION, parliamentary reform was a staple demand of both middle- and working-class reform clubs, and retained élite supporters among FOXITE WHIGS, and the SOCIETY OF THE FRIENDS OF THE PEOPLE. Radicalization in France encouraged conservative alarmism, but a substantial minority of MPs none the less continued to favour reform: Charles GREY'S 1797 motion, for example, received 91 votes in favour, 256 against.

Calls for parliamentary reform, which had been muted during the NAPOLEONIC WARS, revived in the 1820s, with the Whigs under Grey's leadership pledging a definite commitment to reform. The 1832 Reform Act began the process of dismantling the old parliamentary system by abolishing some POCKET and ROTTEN BOROUGHS and extending the franchise. The REFORM ACTS

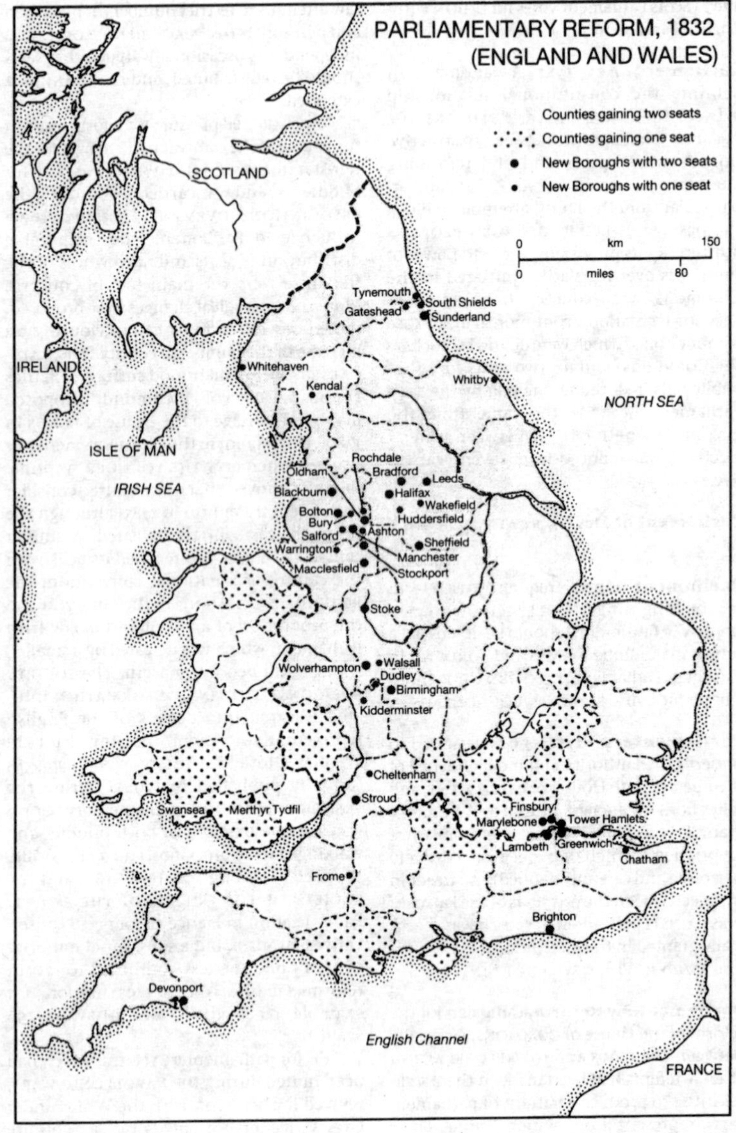
PARLIAMENTARY REFORM, 1832
(ENGLAND AND WALES)
Counties gaining two seats
Counties gaining one seat
New Boroughs with two seats
New Boroughs with one seat
0 km 150
0 miles 80
SCOTLAND
IRELAND
ISLE OF MAN
IRISH SEA
NORTH SEA
English Channel
FRANCE
Tynemouth
Gateshead
South Shields
Sunderland
Whitehaven
Kendal
Whitby
Rochdale
Oldham
Bradford
Leeds
Blackburn
Halifax
Wakefield
Bolton
Huddersfield
Bury
Ashton
Salford
Sheffield
Warrington
Manchester
Macclesfield
Stockport
Stoke
Walsall
Wolverhampton
Dudley
Birmingham
Kidderminster
Cheltenham
Stroud
Swansea
Merthyr Tydfil
Finsbury
Marylebone
Tower Hamlets
Lambeth
Greenwich
Chatham
Frome
Brighton
Devonport

1867 and 1884 gave the vote to a gradually wider section of the population and, during the 20th century, the REPRESENTATION OF THE PEOPLE ACTS took the process still further, culminating in full adult suffrage for all over 18 being granted in 1969.

In addition to the widening of the franchise, the BALLOT ACT 1872 introduced the secret ballot; the PARLIAMENT ACT 1911 curtailed the power of the LORDS and life peerages were introduced in 1958. Property qualifications for MPs were abolished in 1858 and, from 1912, MPs were paid a salary.

Parnell, Charles Stewart (1846–91), Irish nationalist politician. A PROTESTANT landowner, who came from an old and distinguished Anglo-Irish family, Parnell was seemingly an unusual exponent of HOME RULE. His mother was American, and he had come to hate the English and all their works. Entering Parliament in 1875, Parnell embarked upon a policy of obstruction rather than co-operation to advance the cause, especially obstruction of the working of parliamentary business, which succeeded in bringing the IRISH QUESTION to the forefront of British parliamentary politics. In 1879 he became president of the IRISH LAND LEAGUE, demanding considerable rent reductions and resisting evictions using BOYCOTTS in the face of continuing agricultural depression. The following year Parnell succeeded to the leadership of the Home Rule party, and obtained funds from sympathetic Americans to keep the cause going. He continually walked a political tightrope between advocating violence and following constitutional methods for change; he received libel damages from *The Times* for the suggestion that he had connived at the PHOENIX PARK MURDERS. The height of his power was reached in 1885 after the passing of the third REFORM ACT the preceding year, while after 1885 GLADSTONE had been converted to Home Rule and came into office in 1886 pledging to deliver it.

Parnell's fall came swiftly in 1890 when he was named in the DIVORCE case of Kitty O'Shea, with whom he had had a long-standing liaison. Most of his followers deserted him after Gladstone and the LIBERALS made it clear he should resign, and Parnell died in 1891, having clung on with a rump of his followers, his party divided, and the resolution of the Irish question barely advanced.

Parr, Catherine, *see* CATHERINE PARR

Partial Test Ban Treaty Signed in Aug. 1963 between Britain, the United States and the Soviet Union, the treaty banned nuclear tests in the atmosphere, underwater and in space. It followed growing public concern about the effects of radiation from the testing of NUCLEAR WEAPONS and was given urgency by the breakdown of a voluntary moratorium which had operated since 1958, as well as by the desire of the superpowers to cool their rivalries following the Cuban missile crisis of the previous year. It was seen as an important achievement for MACMILLAN, who acted as a useful intermediary between the US and the USSR.

Passive Obedience, political doctrine, especially associated with late 17th- and early 18th-century TORYism, and with the doctrine of NON-RESISTANCE. Subjects might not lawfully resist the king, but the doctrine held that if he issued a command contrary to the law of God they might not actively resist, but should refuse to act, and passively submit to consequent punishment, in the hope that divine judgment would ultimately reward them. NON-JURORS who refused to take OATHS of loyalty to WILLIAM III and MARY II after the GLORIOUS REVOLUTION on the grounds that they were not rightful monarchs, and who lost their places in consequence, could therefore regard themselves as acting in conformity with this doctrine.

Passfield, 1st Baron and Baroness, *see* WEBB, BEATRICE AND SIDNEY

Paston Letters, a collection of letters mostly written by or to members of the Paston family, Norfolk farmers who, in the 15th century, rose to become wealthy country GENTRY. As the earliest surviving collection of private papers in English history, the *Paston Letters* are immensely important, revealing for the first time how gentry and business people, women as well as men, felt about each other and the world in which they lived.

Pastor, title for a minister, usually of the FREE CHURCH or Pentecostal traditions, derived from the Latin word for 'shepherd'. It was first habitually used in Calvin's church in Geneva.

Patent, *see* LETTERS PATENT

Patrick, St (5th century), British missionary bishop and patron saint of IRELAND. Although some contemporary documents survive from his lifetime, his career in Ireland is surrounded by uncertainty and embellished with many legends. The precise dates of his mission are unknown, nor is it clear where he was based, though ARMAGH later came to be regarded as his principal church. It is now generally accepted that there were Christian communities in Ireland before Patrick's arrival, and that his work was undertaken as an agent of the Christian churches of post-Roman Britain.

Patriot, a person motivated by love of country (in Latin, 'patria'). In the 18th century, the name was used to commend people who engaged in a variety of attempts to improve public welfare, but was especially commonly associated with political activists, in or out of PARLIAMENT, who identified themselves in this way. From the era of WALPOLE to that of WILKES, the name was most commonly claimed by opponents of government. From the 1790s its usage was increasingly contested. At some point in the 19th century, the name came to be associated more with conservative politics.

Paulinus (?–644), Bishop of York. An Italian, in 601 he joined St AUGUSTINE's mission in KENT. In 619, he went to the court of the pagan EDWIN, king of NORTHUMBRIA, in the entourage of the latter's Christian bride, a Kentish princess. Paulinus eventually converted Edwin and many other Northumbrians, becoming the first bishop of YORK.

Paul's Cross, open-air pulpit beside St Paul's Cathedral during the Middle Ages. As London's most celebrated preaching-place, it was under close government control from the 1530s, and the choice of preachers there was a useful barometer of religious change. It was destroyed in 1643, paradoxically by sermon-loving PURITANS.

Pauper Lunatics, *see* LUNACY ACT 1890

Payment by Results, the principle, recommended by the NEWCASTLE COMMISSION, and embodied in the Revised Code of 1862, whereby schools could claim annually 4s for each pupil with a satisfactory attendance record, with an additional 8s if the pupil passed examinations in reading, writing and arithmetic. Schools were penalized by deductions from their grant in the event of failure. Payment by results, which lasted until 1897, though meant to raise standards and provide schools with an incentive to greater efficiency, was an intellectually deadening exercise, and its effect on standards remains debatable.

Payment of Members Act 1911 A measure designed to increase working-class representation in PARLIAMENT, it provided Members of Parliament for the first time with an annual salary (of £400). The Act did something to undo the effects of the OSBORNE JUDGMENT upon the development of the LABOUR PARTY.

Peace Ballot, five-question survey of 11 million people by the League of Nations Union in 1934–5. The results (June 1935) showed massive support for the LEAGUE OF NATIONS, disarmament, and the prohibition of private arms sales; and strong support for the abolition of military and naval aircraft and 'economic and non-military measures' against aggressor nations: 6.8 million voted for the use of force against aggressors, but 2.4 million voted against. The ballot was hailed as a high point of support for the League of Nations and anti-war policies, and was seen as contributing to the pro-APPEASEMENT policies of the BALDWIN government.

Peace of Utrecht, *see* UTRECHT, PEACE OF

Peace Pledge Union, pacifist and anti-war organization formed by Canon 'Dick' Sheppard of St Martin-in-the-Fields, London, in Oct. 1934. It appealed to men of military age to pledge themselves to renounce war, and expanded to an estimated 100,000 members by 1936. An important influence on APPEASEMENT and in support of the LEAGUE OF NATIONS, it declined with the rise of more militant anti-Fascist feeling and the evident failure of pro-peace movements to check the aggression of the dictators.

Peasants' Revolt, June 1381, the most significant popular rebellion in English history. The revolt had been unleashed by an unusual combination of circumstances. By the later 1370s, the demographic impact of the BLACK DEATH had been decisively reinforced by subsequent outbreaks of plague. Wage-earners and VILLEINS naturally resented the government's attempts to enforce the Statute of LABOURERS, legislation explicitly designed to prevent them taking advantage of the post-pandemic labour shortage. Military setbacks in the war against France added to the government's unpopularity and laid it open to charges of inefficiency and corruption. The last straw came with the imposition of the unjust POLL TAX of 1380 and the stringent measures taken, particularly in the south-east, to enforce its collection during the early summer of 1381. Yet, however unpopular his government, the king, RICHARD II (a boy of 13), was not held personally responsible for its failings. All this set the stage both for the widespread support that the revolt won in its early stages and for the way in which Richard brought about its collapse.

Rebel armies from Essex and Kent seized London, executed several government ministers and advisers, and seemed to have the young king at their mercy. But many rebels went home when he agreed to their demand that SERFDOM should be abolished. Those who remained in the capital, still trusting the king, allowed themselves to be dispersed when one of their leaders, Wat TYLER, was killed during a conference with the king's party at Smithfield (15 June). Richard then revoked his concessions, and the remaining rebel leaders were rounded up and punished; many were hanged, like John Ball (?–1381), the priest who had preached a sermon on the text 'When Adam delved and Eve span/who was then the gentleman?' to the rebels encamped at Blackheath. Risings elsewhere, notably in East Anglia, though provoked by local grievances, were inspired by news of the Kent–Essex march on London, and did not long survive its collapse.

Although the revolt failed, it made future governments more cautious about taxation and about interfering with the forces of supply and demand. For the poor, the continuing labour shortage meant that the 15th century was to be relatively prosperous.

Peculiar, a church or area of ecclesiastical jurisdiction which is exempt from control by the local bishop and answers only to a higher authority (e.g. an archbishop, a pope or the CROWN).

Peel Report, 1936, report of the royal commission sent to PALESTINE to investigate the Arab violence of 1935. It recommended that Palestine be divided into three parts: an Arab state; a Jewish state; and certain areas of strategic or religious importance that would remain under a British MANDATE. A source of the idea of partition as a solution to the Palestine problem, its recommendations were effectively rejected by a White Paper of 1939, leaving the problem still unresolved.

Peel, Sir Robert (1788–1850), Conservative politician and Prime Minister (1834–5, 1841–6). Son of a northern cotton magnate, and thus always conscious of being something of an outsider in the landowning parliament of the first third of the 19th century, he entered parliament as a Tory in 1809. His early career combined administrative efficiency with political reaction. As chief secretary for Ireland (1812–18) 'Orange Peel' was fiercely ANTI-CATHOLIC in policy and outlook. As home secretary (1822–7, 1828–30), he modified the criminal law and created the Metropolitan POLICE force, the 'Peelers' or 'Bobbies'. But he was no dogmatist. He was persuaded to change his views and broke his party over CATHOLIC EMANCIPATION in 1829, as he was again to do over the PARLIAMENTARY REFORM Movement, Ireland and PROTECTION in 1846. In fact, he did not find party leadership easy: the TAMWORTH MANIFESTO of 1834, often seen as a key document in the transition from old-style TORYISM to modern CONSERVATISM, was more an attempt to dispense with party opinion than to rally it. The repeal of the CORN LAWS in 1846 represented, albeit in extreme form, his abortive search for a non-party government. The FREE TRADE budgets and commercial measures of his two terms as prime minister laid the basis for subsequent economic progress. By 1846 he had repealed 605 duties and largely reduced a further 1,035 others.

When Peel failed to carry his cabinet with him – DISRAELI spearheaded a rebellion – over the repeal of the Corn Laws, which the Irish POTATO FAMINE had convinced Peel was necessary, he resigned and became a mainstay of the WHIG government. Four years later, on 29 June 1850, Peel was thrown from his horse when riding and died from his injuries three days later.

Peelites, CONSERVATIVES who remained committed to Peel's FREE TRADE policy after the party had been split by the repeal of the CORN LAWS in 1846. After Peel's death in 1850 they lost their coherence as a parliamentary force. Some returned to the fold; others, most notably GLADSTONE, joined the LIBERAL PARTY.

Peep O'Day Boys, *see* WHITEBOYS

Peerage The peerage was formalized in the 15th century out of the earlier baronage. *Peers temporal* are those who have the hereditary right to expect a personal summons by the monarch to attend Parliament; *peers spiritual* are those clergy (bishops and, until the DISSOLUTION, abbots) who enjoy a similar right by prescription – i.e. written precedent. There were separate peerages for Scotland and Ireland, who at the UNION sent representatives to Westminster (*see* LORDS, HOUSE OF; PARLIAMENT; PEERAGE BILL 1719).

Compared with most European aristocracies, British peers had few formal privileges – no separate taxation, for example. A peer's right to be tried by other peers was abolished in 1948. The LIFE PEERAGES ACT 1958 complemented the hereditary element in the Lords, and the 1963 Peerage Act made it possible for individuals to disclaim a hereditary peerage.

Peerage Bill 1719 Introduced by STANHOPE and Charles Spencer, Earl of Sunderland, First Lord at the Treasury, the Bill was an attempt to secure WHIG power in the LORDS. It provided for the replacement of the 16 elected Scots representative peers by 25 hereditary Scots peers to be nominated by the king (a large voting block who would normally vote as the king wished); six new English peers were to be created, but then no further additions were to be made except to replace extinct peerages. GEORGE I was prepared to accept the limitation of his ROYAL PREROGATIVE because this measure would also bind the hands of the future GEORGE II. The principal justification adduced for the measure was the abuse of the royal prerogative for political purposes (above all, in 1711–12). However, the Bill went down to defeat in the Commons after a memorable speech from WALPOLE, attacking both the motives of the sponsors and deploring the effect on aspiring GENTRY of sharply reducing any prospect of their descendants ever being elevated to the PEERAGE. Yet, since the Hanoverians up to the 1780s proved very conservative in the creation of new English peers, it may be said that something of the purpose of the abortive measure was achieved over the next half century.

Pelham, Henry (1696–1754), Whig politician and Prime Minister (1743–54). Younger brother of Thomas PELHAM-HOLLES, Duke of Newcastle, he entered Parliament in 1717. He was connected to both Charles, Viscount Townshend (1675–1738) and WALPOLE by marriage, and consistently supported them. Appointed to various second-rank offices in the 1720s and 1730s, he took over the leadership of the OLD CORPS WHIGS after Walpole's fall, and gained office as first lord of the TREASURY in 1743. After a showdown with the king in 1745, the Pelham brothers held power largely on their own terms; when Henry Pelham died suddenly, he was succeeded by his brother.

One of the longest-serving prime ministers of the 18th century, Pelham is now less renowned than Walpole, NORTH or PITT THE YOUNGER, perhaps partly because his emollient political style engendered less opposition. GLADSTONE admired his financial skill, and praised him as one of the few competent 18th-century statesmen.

Pelham-Holles, Thomas (4th [1st Pelham-Holles] Duke of Newcastle) (1693–1768), Whig politician and Prime Minister (1754–6, 1757–62). Upon inheriting his parents' estates in 1711–12, he became one of the largest English landowners. A supporter of the HANOVERIAN SUCCESSION, he was made a duke in 1715 and, three years later, married Marlborough's (*see* CHURCHILL, JOHN) granddaughter. He was made secretary of state in 1724, and went on to hold high office for longer than any other 18th-century politician. A keen manipulator of patronage, he played a crucial part in maintaining support for several ministries, but his garrulousness and emotional and demonstrative temperament excited derision. Normally content to play second fiddle to WALPOLE, he none the less developed strong independent views about foreign policy, which played a part in Walpole's downfall.

After the death of his brother Henry PELHAM in 1754, he succeeded him as first lord of the Treasury, but was unable to dominate politics and resigned in 1756. PITT THE ELDER, however, proved to need Newcastle's carefully cultivated network of connections, and they joined in a ministerial coalition the following year. Cornered into resigning by GEORGE III in 1762, Newcastle bewailed such ingratitude from a family whose fortunes he had so long espoused. He associated with opposition Whiggery thereafter, and enjoyed a final spell in office as lord Privy Seal in the first Rockingham (*see* WENTWORTH, CHARLES) ministry of 1765.

Pembroke, 2nd Earl of, *see* CLARE, RICHARD DE

Penal Laws, restrictions on the civil and political rights of those not members of the Established Church. *See also* CATHOLIC EMANCIPATION; CLARENDON CODE; CONFESSIONAL STATE; DECLARATIONS OF INDULGENCE; INDEMNITY ACTS; IRELAND; TEST ACTS; TOLERATION ACT.

Penal Servitude Acts 1853, 1857 A response to the ending of TRANSPORTATION, it sought to preserve prison capacity by reducing the maximum sentences for many offences and allowing prisoners with a record of good conduct to obtain a 'ticket-of-leave' and be released on probation. Courts claimed that it sacrificed punishment to expediency.

Penda, King of Mercia (?626–55). The first of the formidable line of MERCIAN kings, he remained an unregenerate heathen at a time when many English kingdoms were beginning to convert to Christianity (*see* CONVERSION; PAGANISM). His numerous wars expanded Mercian territory, including the conquest of the much smaller kingdom of the HWICCE. In the northern part of what came to be called England, he disputed supremacy with the kings of NORTHUMBRIA, and after killing EDWIN and OSWALD, he was eventually himself killed by King OSWY, probably at or after the battle of the Winwaed.

Peninsular War, 1808–14. Fought in the Iberian peninsula, it was Britain's main military contribution to the war against Napoleon (*see* NAPOLEONIC WARS). When the Spanish rose in revolt at the attempt by Napoleon to establish his brother, Joseph Bonaparte, on the Spanish throne, Britain seized the opportunity to establish a foothold on the continent. An early victory by Sir Arthur WELLESLEY at Vimiero (Portugal, 21 Aug. 1808) was squandered by the Convention of Cintra (30 Aug.) which allowed the French to withdraw. Sir John Moore then invaded Spain, found no support and was chased to Corunna, where a defensive victory caused his death but enabled his army to be evacuated by sea (16 Jan. 1809). Wellesley took over the army, in Portugal again, and won victories at Talavera (28 July 1809) and Busaco (27 Sept. 1810), then withdrew behind the lines (fortifications) of Torres Vedras he had caused to be built to protect Lisbon, and watched the attacking French starve and retreat. After another victory in 1811 (Fuentes de Onoro), his army stormed the Spanish border fortresses expensively but successfully early in 1812. Advancing into Spain he won at Salamanca, and then routed the French completely at Vitoria (21 June 1813) and in Nov. 1813 (by now the Earl of Wellington) he invaded France over the Pyrenees. His success owed much to the diversion of much of the French army in the Peninsula by Spanish armies, guerillas, and attacks from the sea by the ubiquitous Royal NAVY, which also ensured his supplies. His own army included excellent British-officered Portuguese units. The 'Spanish ulcer' drained French strength and helped in Napoleon's downfall.

Pennsylvania, former British colony in North America and founding state of the USA, founded by William Penn (1644–1718). In 1681 CHARLES II repaid a debt owed to Penn's admiral father by granting William a large province on the west bank of the DELAWARE river. Penn, a QUAKER, drew up a frame of government for the new colony, which he named Pennsylvania. Financial mismanagement forced him to mortgage his rights as proprietor of the colony.

Penny, Anglo-Saxon (*denarius*). The silver penny was the basis of early medieval English COINAGE. Although *SCEATTAS* and *STYCAS* are likely to have performed the function of pennies, the appearance of the *denarius* in the late 8th century was a major development. The earliest were minted by kings of EAST ANGLIA and KENT, but the great change is associated with the pennies of OFFA of MERCIA, the forms of which showed a CAROLINGIAN influence. For the rest of the Anglo-Saxon period and beyond, silver pennies were minted in numerous styles. Accurately interpreted, they form a fundamental source for understanding England's early ECONOMY and society.

Penny Dreadfuls, serialized NEWGATE biographies of murderers and other criminals, popular in the early 19th century. Edward Lloyd, the publisher, kept a stable of writers churning out such 'bloods', often replete with graphic and gory illustration. 'Improving' opinion thought they had an adverse effect on youthful morals. 'Pulp' fiction is their 20th-century descendant.

Penny Post, *see* POSTAL SERVICES

Pennylands, *see* OUNCELAND

Penruddock's Rising, the only substantial fruit of the ROYALIST conspiracy of 1655, yet the Wilts. gentleman John Penruddock and his minuscule force found little backing when they seized the SALISBURY assize judges. However, it was the main reason for Oliver CROMWELL instituting the MAJOR-GENERALS.

Pension Funds Many pension schemes, such as the state scheme introduced by LLOYD GEORGE at the beginning of the 20th century, are termed 'Pay As You Go' pension schemes and these do not accumulate assets: as the benefits are paid for from current contributions, in effect they are a form of transfer payment. However, the alternative is the funded scheme in which current contributions are paid into a fund; the fund builds up over time and acquires income-yielding assets from which future benefits will be paid. Many employers in the UK have set up occupational pensions arrangements for their employees; these take the form of funded schemes, and since the passage of the Occupational Pensions Act 1978 there has been a very substantial growth in such schemes. This partly reflects the very favourable tax treatment which governments have extended to pension funds, whereby all contributions are tax deductible and the funds' income and/or capital gains are not subject to tax. By the early 1980s pension funds were the largest holders of financial and other assets in the UK economy, with a total value of £108 billion; by the end of 1998 the total net assets of UK pension funds were estimated to be around £743 billion, and as major investors in the securities market hold around 22 per cent of the securities listed on the London Stock Exchange.

Pensioners, a royal bodyguard divided between gentlemen and yeoman pensioners, established in 1539. As so often with HENRY VIII, this was an imitation of a French institution.

Pentland Rising, 1666. Nearly 1,000 COVENANTERS, rebelling against the RESTORATION regime's support for episcopacy in Scotland, marched on EDINBURGH, until they were defeated by government forces at Rullion Green in the Pentland Hills. The rising provoked a rethinking of Scottish policy, and the rise to dominance of Lauderdale (*see* MAITLAND, JOHN) who embarked on a policy of concessions to DISSENTING groups.

Pentonville, model prison opened in London in 1844. A closely monitored daily routine of work, with short breaks for meals, writing letters (censored), silent exercise, worship and reading of an improving nature, exemplified the new view of the 1830s that humanitarian methods had failed and that what was needed was a tougher and uniformly enforced system of prison discipline which would reform the prisoner but be a proper deterrent and punishment. At Pentonville the prisoners were stripped of their identity, wearing masks when together and using a number not a name. Fifty-four new prisons had been built on the same lines by 1850.

People's Budget, 1909. The budget was devised by LLOYD GEORGE as a weapon of social change, to provoke the House of LORDS and to revive a flagging LIBERAL PARTY. He proposed to increase taxes on alcohol and TOBACCO and to introduce a motor-car licence. INCOME TAX was to be raised and a new super-tax imposed on the rich. Most controversial was the proposed duty of 20 per cent on the UNEARNED INCREMENT of land value, payable on the transference of property. It was rejected in the Upper House and a constitutional crisis ensued. Two general elections, and a threat by the king to create sufficient peers to carry the budget, were required before the Lords finally gave way. Conflict between the peers and the COMMONS prompted the PARLIAMENT ACT of 1911.

People's Charter, *see* CHARTISM

Pepys, Samuel (1633–1703), diarist and naval administrator. Secretary to the Admiralty from 1672–9, he was dismissed because of his close attachment to the Duke of York (the future JAMES II) and attendant accusations of popery. He was reappointed from 1684 and served until the GLORIOUS REVOLUTION, presiding over a phase of naval expansion, and has since been celebrated as a naval reformer. He also served for a term as president of the ROYAL SOCIETY. He is best known for the diary in which he candidly chronicled his daily life, which he left with the rest of his library to Magdalene College CAMBRIDGE: the surviving volumes in cipher date between 1660 and 1669, and were first deciphered and published in 1825. His marvellously vivid descriptions of his experiences in the GREAT PLAGUE and the GREAT FIRE OF LONDON have shaped our impressions of these events, but he has also endeared himself to his readers, and provided the archetype for diary-writers, by his rueful accounts of his varying fortunes in marital and extra-marital relations.

Perceval, Spencer (1762–1812), Tory politician and Prime Minister (1809–12). A barrister and TORY MP, Perceval served as solicitor-general in 1801 and attorney-general in 1802. He was chancellor of the Exchequer 1807–9, and succeeded Portland (*see* BENTINCK, WILLIAM CAVENDISH) as prime minister in 1809. Faced with economic depression and LUDDITE agitation at home, and the threat of Napoleon abroad, his administration was both divided and repressive. The only British prime minister ever to be assassinated, Perceval was shot in the lobby of the House of Commons on 11 May 1812 by a bankrupt who blamed the government for his troubles.

Percy Rebellion, 1403–8. Led by Henry Percy, 4th Earl of Northumberland (1341–1408), his son Henry (1364–1403), nicknamed 'Hotspur' by the Scots for his daring and prowess in battle, and his brother Thomas Percy, Earl of Worcester, the revolt very nearly dethroned HENRY IV in 1403. The plan was to join forces with the Welsh rebel GLYN DWR and make Edmund Mortimer, Earl of March (the young nephew of Hotspur's wife), king in place of the man they considered a usurper, who – or so they alleged – had deceived them in 1399 by swearing that he had come to England seeking not the throne but only his lawful inheritance.

In the years following 1399, the Percys had been at the pinnacle of their power and prestige, and they had, in fact, done more than anyone else to make Henry king. Yet despite their good fortune, Henry's reluctance to pay them the huge sums he owed them – most dramatically his refusal to let them keep the ransoms for the prisoners they had taken at HOMILDON HILL – fuelled their belief that they had deserved more. Nevertheless, their revolt came as a shock – which is why it nearly succeeded.

In the event, Hotspur published the rebel manifesto on 10 July, revealing his hand too early. Henry reacted swiftly and, at SHREWSBURY (21 July), before Northumberland or Glyn Dwr could intervene, the outcome was decided by Hotspur's death in battle, followed by Thomas Percy's execution. Although Northumberland formally submitted the following month, the catastrophe that had overwhelmed the family at Shrewsbury made genuine reconciliation impossible. Northumberland's discontent continued, spluttering into open rebellion again in 1405 – though he failed to support his ally Richard Scrope, Archbishop of York – and in 1408, ending only when he was himself killed in a desperate last throw at Bramham Moor.

Perpendicular, architectural style of the late 14th to 16th centuries which was typified, as its name implies, by the adoption of a more rectilinear, less flowing form. Perpendicular buildings, notably churches but also secular houses, often have enormous expanses of windows, with walls a buttressed frame of slender, vertically subdivided supports for the display of expensive glass. The royal chapels of King's College CAMBRIDGE and Henry VII's Chapel in WESTMINSTER ABBEY are among the finest examples of the style.

Perrers, Alice (?–1400), royal mistress. As EDWARD III's mistress, she procured promotion for her husband William de Windsor as governor of Ireland. Her dominating presence at court after Queen PHILIPPA's death in 1369 led to her being blamed for the setbacks and financial scandals that dogged the last years of a king who was growing senile. The GOOD PARLIAMENT of 1376 sentenced her to banishment and forfeiture of her estates, a sentence that, by 1379, had been reversed, reconfirmed and finally – at her husband's request – reversed again.

Perth, Five Articles of, 1618, articles imposed by JAMES VI in an only partially successful effort to make the Scots KIRK more like the Church of England. They included the obligation to observe Christmas and Easter.

Perth, Treaty of, 2 July 1266. A treaty between King Magnus 'the Lawmender' of Norway and ALEXANDER III of Scotland, whereby the former sold to the latter the rights of the Norwegian kings over MAN and the Western Isles (but reserving their rights over ORKNEY and Shetland). This epoch-making treaty, effectively marking the end of the VIKING period in Scottish history, had been forced on the Norwegian government by the outcome of the battle of LARGS.

Peruzzi, *see* BARDI AND PERUZZI

Peterborough Abbey, Cambs. Founded in the 7th century (when Peterborough was known as 'Medeshamstede'), it was at that time the centre of an extensive monastic federation that extended throughout MERCIA. Destroyed during the Danish invasions, it was refounded in 966 by St Ethelwold with monks from ABINGDON. It was dissolved in 1539 and refounded as a CATHEDRAL in 1541.

Peterborough Chronicle, the name given to the last sections of the ANGLO-SAXON CHRONICLE covering the years 1070–1154: the final phase of the Anglo-Saxon tradition of vernacular history. Apart from some interpolations in the earlier entries, only the section from 1122 onwards was actually composed at Peterborough. It ends with a famous description of STEPHEN's reign – 19 years 'when Christ and his saints slept' – and with a warm welcome for the accession of HENRY II: two attitudes that have shaped much subsequent English historical writing.

Peterloo Massacre, 1819. On 16 Aug. 1819, a crowd of 50–60,000 gathered at St Peter's Fields, MANCHESTER, to hear Orator Hunt speak on PARLIAMENTARY REFORM. The crowds were orderly. The magistrates, however, panicked, relying upon an incompetent yeomanry to arrest Hunt and disperse the assembly. Nine men and two women were killed and about 400 wounded. Within days, the term 'Peterloo' (a play on 'Waterloo') came to signify the horror, disgust and fury of the RADICAL commons for their so-called social superiors.

Peter's Pence, a regular annual payment in the Middle Ages from the English kingdom to the papacy. It may well have originated in ALFRED THE GREAT's reign, although there are instances of earlier, irregular payments.

Petillius Cerialis (Quintus Petillius Cerialis) (*fl.* AD 70s), Roman governor. His governorship of Britain – from 71 to 73 (or 74) – is notable for the resumption of conquest after the period of consolidation that followed BOUDICCA's revolt in 61. The Roman armies in Britain were brought back up to their former strength of four legions, and Cerialis launched campaigns that are thought to have conquered the BRIGANTES and let his forces go as far north as Carlisle. *See also* ROMAN CONQUEST.

Petition of Right, 1628. Officially, a legal document making a formal appeal to the monarch, this was a device resurrected from legal history by Sir Edward COKE to resolve the head-on clash between the COMMONS and CHARLES I: once accepted, such a petition could be recorded in the law courts, and would enshrine the subject's rights against royal PREROGATIVE. After it was approved by the LORDS, Charles grudgingly accepted it. He subsequently published a doctored version and then ignored its provisions.

Petty Assizes, sometimes known as the 'possessory assizes'. These ASSIZES, dating from HENRY II's reign, concerned disputes about recent possession of property (known as seisin), particularly inheritance disputes (the 'assize of *mort d'ancestor*') and cases where unlawful seizure was alleged (*novel disseisin*). They set up procedures whereby such disputes were heard before royal judges in the COUNTY COURTS, and verdicts were given by juries who – being 12 men of local standing – were expected to be well informed about the facts (*see* JURY). Litigants found the new procedures attractive, and in one form or another, they remained a part of the COMMON LAW until Victorian times.

Petty Sessions, literally 'little sessions'. Although not formally recognized until 1828, these became important from the 16th century in many areas as supplementary sittings of the JUSTICES OF THE PEACE to deal with greatly increased business.

Petty, William (3rd Earl of Shelburne, 1st Marquess of Lansdowne) (1737–1805), politician and Prime Minister (1782–3). Born in Dublin, educated at Oxford, he fought in the SEVEN YEARS WAR and became aide-de-camp to GEORGE II. He entered the LORDS on his father's death in 1761 and was employed as a mediator between Henry FOX and Bute (*see* STUART, JOHN). Fox judged him to have behaved duplicitously, an imputation he was repeatedly to attract. Much impressed by PITT THE ELDER, Shelburne resigned his post as president of the Board of Trade in 1763 to support him. In 1766, he became southern secretary of state under Pitt (now Chatham). Following Chatham in adopting a relatively conciliatory approach to American colonists, he differed from other colleagues in the ascendancy after Chatham's retreat to BATH with a nervous illness, and resigned in 1768. In opposition throughout the 1770s, his views were influenced in a RADICAL direction by his association with DISSENTERS such Joseph Priestley and Richard Price. His relations with the ROCKINGHAMITE WHIGS were uneasy. He was made secretary of state in the Rockingham (*see* WENTWORTH, CHARLES) administration of 1782. Favoured by the king, but distrusted by Charles James FOX, he replaced Rockingham on the latter's death that summer, but lost core Rockinghamite support. He was left with the difficult task of steering through PARLIAMENT preliminaries of the peace that was to end the War of AMERICAN INDEPENDENCE – a task made more difficult by his espousal of FREE TRADE notions, making him unusually ready to dismantle empire. The ministry was brought down in Feb. 1783 by an alliance between Fox and NORTH. Shelburne supported PITT THE YOUNGER in the 1780s, but in the 1790s preferred Fox.

Philip II (1527–98), King of England (1554–8) and King of Spain (1556–98), son of Emperor CHARLES V, who launched Philip on his dispiriting second marriage as king consort to MARY I of England. Philip, a conscientious and courteous man, did his best on two English visits in 1554–5 and 1557, but he was not impressed by English politicians' concern to restrict his rights. He had much else to distract him, especially when in 1555–6 Charles retired and partitioned the Habsburg inheritance between his brother Ferdinand and Philip; Philip received Spain and its NEW WORLD and Italian dominions, and the Netherlands. England followed him into war with France in 1557, losing CALAIS. On Mary's death, which deprived Philip of all rights in England, he rather tepidly offered marriage to ELIZABETH I, but his third and fourth wives were French and Austrian; by the 1580s his relations with England deteriorated into war. *See also* ARMADAS, SPANISH; NETHERLANDS, REVOLT OF THE; PLANTATIONS IN IRELAND.

Philiphaugh, Battle of, 13 Sept. 1645, a defeat in the Borders of Scots ROYALISTS under Montrose (*see* GRAHAM, JAMES) by COVENANTER armies (*see* CIVIL WARS).

Philippa of Hainault (?1314–69), Queen of England. Daughter of William, Count of Holland and Hainault, she was betrothed to the heir to the English throne (the future EDWARD III) in 1326 when his mother ISABELLA OF FRANCE wanted the Count's naval resources to carry out the invasion of England that she and MORTIMER were planning. The marriage took place in 1328. In 1347, Philippa successfully interceded for the lives of the six burghers of CALAIS whom Edward had wanted to execute when the town surrendered. Generally she seems to have been content with motherhood – she bore 12 children – and collecting fine clothes.

Phoenix Park Murders On 6 May 1882, in Phoenix Park, Dublin, Lord Frederick Cavendish, the Irish chief secretary and GLADSTONE's brother-in-law, and T. H. Burke, his under-secretary, were attacked and murdered. The two men were knifed to death at the hands of the 'Invincibles', a terrorist gang of Irish Nationalists (the members of which were later arrested and five of them hanged). British public opinion was outraged; fresh coercive legislation followed (*see* PREVENTION OF CRIMES ACT 1882). *See also* IRISH QUESTION.

'Phoney War', name given to the relatively inactive phase of WORLD WAR II between the fall of Poland in Sept. 1939 and the German invasion of Norway in April 1940. It is often seen as lulling the Western Allies into a false sense of security, which was rapidly shattered by the fall of Norway, Denmark, the Low Countries and France by the end of June 1940.

Photography The origins of photography stretch back to the *camera obscura*, used by artists from the RENAISSANCE onwards; the first photographs, fixed images using a pewter plate, were taken by the Frenchman Joseph-Nicéphore Niépce before 1827, and by his compatriot Louis Daguerre who had produced photographs by 1837. These took only 25 minutes exposure time to produce an image, compared to eight hours by Niépce's process. These images – known as daguerreotypes – were single positives; the first practical step forward – reproducibility – had already come with William Fox Talbot's invention of the negative in 1835. The next 70 years saw an explosion in photographic image-making and a series of technical improvements. Celluloid, the medium for the negative of the future, was introduced in 1888, by which time cameras were being mass-produced. At the century's end George Eastman's Kodak camera and the box Brownie camera brought photography within the grasp of any amateur. The 20th century has seen these developments continue, with the introduction of colour film (first invented in 1869 but not of major importance until the development of Kodachrome from 1935), the single lens reflex camera in 1903, 35mm cameras in 1924, and the instant Polaroid camera in 1947. Meanwhile, developments in swift exposures had promoted the development of the CINEMA at the very end of the 19th century.

The principal area of interest in photography in the 19th century was in portraiture – for the first time people could see themselves portrayed as others saw them at relatively modest cost. There were 51 photographers recorded in the 1851 census, 50 times as many 10 years later, and over 17,000 professional photographers by 1901. Fashions in photography – for stereoscopic pictures, small portrait *cartes de visite*, and later for unobtrusive 'detective' cameras or the first picture postcards – succeeded each other, as exposure times also shortened; art photographers like Julia Margaret Cameron (1815–79) rubbed shoulders with the enthusiastic amateur. By the close of the 19th century, half-tone printing techniques encouraged the rise of photo-journalism and illustrated NEWSPAPERS. Photographs are now regarded by historians as documents in their own right and as an independent art form.

Phrenology, study based on the scientific theory that the mental powers of the individual consist of separate faculties, each of which has its origin and location in a definite region or surface of the brain, the size or development of which is commensurate with the development of the particular faculty. The theory, originating in Germany and developed in France, was popularized in Britain through the writings of George Combe (1788–1858). There was a later 19th-century craze for bump-reading, the art of assessing character from the contour of the cranium. Phrenology, popular with serious scholars and the general public, was particularly influential in the fields of criminal and educational reform, but its respectability waned rapidly in the 20th century.

Picquigny, Treaty of, 1475, treaty made in northern France between EDWARD IV and Louis XI of France. In return for a pension worth £10,000 a year, Edward halted the invasion of France that he had launched in alliance with Burgundy. Inevitably his decision not to follow in the footsteps of HENRY V and prosecute his claim to the throne of France disappointed both Edward's allies and his more militant subjects.

Picts The term 'Picts' – first mentioned by a Roman author in AD 297 – signifies 'painted people' and was generally used in Roman times to describe the people living north of the ANTONINE WALL who habitually raided southwards. Scholarly discussion of the Picts' identity has, over the years, become immensely complicated. For example, on the basis of archaeological and PLACE NAME evidence, it has been suggested that they were a pre-CELTIC people. A more convincing approach regards them simply as a grouping together of the Celtic peoples who earlier had been identified by a number of different tribal names (*see* CALEDONII; TAEXALI; VENICOMES).

The lack of documentary evidence makes it difficult to know much about their history or their kings. There were clearly numerous conflicts with the SCOTS (who inhabited the rival kingdom of DALRIADA) and with the kingdom of STRATHCLYDE; the Pictish king BRUDE MAC BILI prevented NORTHUMBRIAN expansion north of the Firth of Forth (*see* NECHTANESMERE). The ebbs and flows of military fortune produced a number of temporary unions between the Picts and the Scots, the last of which, in the time of KENNETH MAC ALPIN, created a single realm that also dominated Strathclyde, and began the evolution through which these distinct peoples were formed into the kingdom of Scotland. *See also* KINGSHIP.

Picturesque, an aesthetic concept which became fashionable from the 1750s: landscape was prized inasmuch as it displayed characteristics familiar from the paintings of such artists as Salvator Rosa and Claude Lorraine. The fashion was associated with a growing interest in wild and remote scenes, to be found for example in the Lake District or Scotland. The concept's most famous exponent was William Gilpin, who published a series of accounts of his sketching tours from 1782. His efforts were parodied in William Combe and Thomas Rowlandson's *Dr Syntax in Search of the Picturesque* (1809–11).

Pilgrimage, devotion to the cult of holy places and SAINTS, often involving travel over long distances to get to a venerated site. Shrines (initially of martyrs) have existed in Christianity probably from the 2nd century, but there is little evidence for extensive travel to holy places until the official development of interest in the sacred sites of the Holy Land by the imperial entourage of CONSTANTINE I THE GREAT and his mother Helena in the early 4th century. A British example is the cult of St ALBAN at VERULAMIUM, which may date from the 4th century, and after the CONVERSION OF THE ENGLISH there was much interest among Anglo-Saxon royal and aristocratic families in pilgrimages to the tombs of Peter and Paul in Rome. From the 8th century, pilgrimage became a European-wide phenomenon, much encouraged by the Church's permission to substitute a pilgrimage for other forms of penance. This meant that relics of saints became valuable possessions for a church, monastery or royal dynasty, regarded as wielding considerable spiritual, political and even military power, and there were cases of theft by rival or aspiring pilgrimage centres.

Pilgrimages and shrines were an obvious target for PROTESTANT reforming hatred in the 16th century. Thomas CROMWELL encouraged propaganda against them and in 1538 ordered the destruction of the leading shrines, particularly Thomas BECKET'S; HENRY VIII continued the process after Cromwell's fall with orders of 1541. MARY I'S regime in this respect did little to revive the past: an interesting comment on the selective priorities of her CATHOLIC regime. Later, despite Protestant government disapproval, Irish Roman Catholics obstinately maintained pilgrimages, and on a lesser scale sacred sites maintained a clandestine role in the popular religion of Wales and western Scotland. Since the 19th century shrines have been restored on old sites throughout the British Isles, and pilgrimages are maintained by both ANGLICANS and Roman Catholics – even, at IONA, by the CHURCH OF SCOTLAND. Similar pilgrimages to ancient non-Christian sites (especially at STONEHENGE and AVEBURY) have been initiated by the modern revival of the DRUIDS and by various branches of New Age and pagan spirituality.

Pilgrimage of Grace, 1536–7, northern rising against HENRY VIII'S government. Various social and economic grievances (*see* USE) were united by resentment and apprehension at religious change, especially the DISSOLUTION of the monasteries; dissatisfied courtiers may also have played a part. Conservative religious rhetoric was prominent in the rebellion, as seen in the title 'pilgrims' that the rebels quickly assumed.

Trouble in Lincs. in Oct. 1536 was quickly imitated further north, with Robert Aske (?–1537), a Yorks. gentleman and London lawyer, as the main leader. Outright battle was prevented by royal pardons and promises of concessions, but fresh outbreaks in the winter of 1537 were excuse enough for the king to abandon these and wreak savage retribution. It was the most serious 16th-century English challenge to central government.

Pinkie, Battle of, 10 Sept. 1547, a Scots defeat near Musselburgh, Lothian by Somerset's (*see* SEYMOUR, EDWARD) army, in the course of his attempt to secure the marriage of MARY QUEEN OF SCOTS to EDWARD VI; it was nicknamed by George GORDON, Earl of Huntly, the 'rough wooing'. English garrisons were then planted in the Lowlands to subdue the Scots, to very little effect.

Pipe Roll, the principal annual record of the medieval EXCHEQUER on which the accounts of SHERIFFS and other local officials were recorded. The name probably derives from the fact that the record was made on parchment which was rolled up for storage and, in consequence, tended to look like a pipe. The Pipe Roll Society, founded in 1884, continues to publish and study the financial records of the medieval English crown.

Piracy, *see* PRIVATEERING

Pitcairn, remote British Pacific island colony, previously uninhabited, which became the refuge of the mutineers from HMS *Bounty*, led by Fletcher Christian, in 1789. Most of the handful of remaining islanders are descended from the original settlers. The island is now effectively ruled from NEW ZEALAND.

Pitt 'the Elder', William (1st Earl of Chatham) (1708–78), Whig politician and Prime Minister (1766–8). Grandson of an EAST INDIA COMPANY merchant, 'Diamond' Pitt, and son of an MP, he entered PARLIAMENT in 1735, and was associated with WALPOLE's 'boy patriot' opponents, also known as 'Cobham's Cubs' (after their leader Richard Temple, Viscount Cobham). In the 1740s, he attacked Hanoverian influence on British war policy, earning the king's dislike, but in 1746, the PELHAM brothers nevertheless forced his admission to office. As paymaster-general of the forces until 1755, he reinforced the reputation for disinterested patriotism that he was later to exploit.

Upon resigning office, he attacked and toppled Newcastle (*see* PELHAM-HOLLES, THOMAS), but failed to sustain support for his own ministry and, from 1757, governed in coalition. As southern secretary of state, he was effectively in command of the exceptionally successful SEVEN YEARS WAR, and was hailed as a 'PATRIOT minister'. Resigning when his desire to extend the war to Spain was thwarted in 1761, he spent most of the remainder of his career in opposition. GEORGE III, increasingly desperate for a reliable first minister, made him Earl of Chatham and first lord of the Treasury in 1766, but ill health, perhaps taking the form of a nervous breakdown, kept the new earl out of London and led him to resign in 1768. However he soon returned to politics and first took part in attempts to form a united opposition over the WILKES affair, then forcefully criticized the NORTH government's American policies.

At once cold and flamboyant, Pitt was a prima donna in politics. He was admired by some TORIES and extra-parliamentary groups for his 'patriot' stance, and influenced the political conduct of a younger generation of WHIGS, who, partly as a consequence, were also to spend much time in opposition.

Pitt 'the Younger', William (1759–1806), Tory politician and Prime Minister (1783–1801, 1804–6). Younger son of PITT THE ELDER, he was educated at Cambridge and then called to the Bar. From 1781, when he was elected MP for Appleby, he rapidly began to meet the high expectations his name aroused. He served as chancellor of the Exchequer under Shelburne (*see* PETTY, WILLIAM), refused GEORGE III's invitation to form a government on Shelburne's resignation, but later indicated his willingness to serve, thus opening the way for the king to engineer the overthrow of the FOX–NORTH coalition – and gaining Fox's undying enmity.

Pitt was 24 when he formed his minority government in Dec. 1783; the surprise general election of 1784 consolidated his position. Having earlier shown an interest in PARLIAMENTARY REFORM, he brought forward a plan in 1785, but failed to gain support. However, he advanced the ECONOMICAL REFORM schemes mooted earlier in the decade by appointing commissions to consider the scope for economies in government. In addition, the need to pay off debts incurred during the War of AMERICAN INDEPENDENCE led him to introduce several new taxes, which proved controversial. His failure to support Bills to repeal the TEST and CORPORATION

ACTS (1788–91) further alienated some of his original supporters.

During the FRENCH REVOLUTIONARY WARS, he was criticized for the repression of RADICALISM, his policies being (overdramatically) equated by some with the French reign of terror. He was also censured for his failure to seize the chance to make peace in 1795. However, he commanded very broad support among the propertied classes, and his ministry was strengthened in 1794 by the accession of the Portland (*see* BENTINCK, WILLIAM CAVENDISH) WHIGS. He resigned in Feb. 1801 when the king refused to allow him to bring in a measure of CATHOLIC EMANCIPATION, in Pitt's mind a necessary complement to the Irish Act of UNION. His successor ADDINGTON being unable to maintain Parliament's confidence in the face of the renewed outbreak of war, Pitt returned to office in 1804, but his health worsened and he died in Jan. 1806.

A bachelor, Pitt was reputedly temperamentally cold, though he displayed playfulness and warmth with old friends such as WILBERFORCE. Once circumstances had given him the chance to attain power, he dedicated himself to the task of maintaining effective government. While his critics denounced the pernicious 'Pitt system', his admirers, who were to include Liverpool (*see* JENKINSON, ROBERT) and PEEL, strove to emulate him. In retrospect, he was seen as a founding father of 19th-century TORYISM or Conservatism, though that casting entails some distortion: in particular members of early 19th-century Pitt Clubs, who made opposition to Catholic emancipation one of their badges of identity, strangely honoured a man who had staunchly supported that cause.

Place, Francis (1771–1854), trade unionist and social reformer. Known as 'the radical tailor of Charing Cross', he was a working-class autodidact who favoured the extension of the FRANCHISE by the progressive means advocated by the philosophical RADICALS in whose circles he moved. His lobbying and research made possible the repeal of the COMBINATION ACTS and played a significant part in the Reform Bill agitation (1830–2; *see* REFORM ACT 1832). He drafted the petition that later became the People's Charter (1838) (*see* CHARTISM) but abhorred violence. He was a steady, industrious artisan, who thought that self-improvement was as important as the extension of the franchise.

Place Bills, bills designed to moderate the power of the crown and executive to influence the House of COMMONS by restricting the number and type of holders of government offices, places or pensions who could sit as MPs since they were seen as being unduly susceptible to royal or ministerial influence. A variety of specific exclusions of placemen were attached to various revenue bills from 1694 onwards; much more sweeping was the bar on placemen sitting in the Commons incorporated in the 1701 Act of SETTLEMENT and intended to come into force at the accession of the first Hanoverian. Had this provision remained law it would have blocked the evolution of parliamentary government. It was, however, amended by the Regency Act of 1706, and this revision remained the basic rule until ECONOMICAL REFORM. Essentially, it provided that all holders of 'new' offices (those created since 1688) were ineligible to sit in the Commons, while holders of 'old' offices (unless specifically barred) would remain eligible provided that, if they accepted such office during the life of a parliament they would have to resign their seat and seek re-election from their constituency.

The effect of places and pensions on MPs' behaviour is not easily gauged. They might be rewards for loyalty, rather than the reason for it; those whose pensions or places were guaranteed for life could oppose governments with impunity. Reformers probably overstated their significance. Their reduced availability, combined with the growing power of party sentiment, did none the less weaken ministers' power in the Commons in the early 19th century, and much increased the likelihood of ministries falling on adverse swings of parliamentary opinion. *See also* COURT VERSUS COUNTRY.

Place Names as Historical Evidence The study of place names has made an important contribution to the understanding of the English and, more particularly, the SCANDINAVIAN SETTLEMENTS of the Anglo-Saxon period. Such research is, none the less, highly technical and fraught with difficulty since no one knows why the names of places change. The most profitable work of recent years has concentrated on the relationship of place names and the landscape. This has shown, for example, that places with purely Scandinavian names often tend to be on poor agricultural land, whereas Anglo-Scandinavian hybrids are frequently located on good soil. This suggests an initial take-over by a dominant people who were not necessarily that numerous, followed by colonization, rather than a single, large influx of people.

Placemen and Pensioners, *see* PLACE BILLS

Plague, *see* BLACK DEATH; BUBONIC PLAGUE; EPIDEMICS; GREAT PLAGUE

Plaid Cymru (Welsh Nationalist Party). The flag-bearer of Welsh nationalism during the 20th century, it was founded in 1925 by John Saunders Lewis with the aim of obtaining independence for Wales. It ran candidates in elections and by-elections without success until 1966, when its president captured Carmarthen at a by-election. By 1974 it had three MPs and was instrumental in forcing a DEVOLUTION Bill on a reluctant LABOUR government in 1979, against a background of rising support. However, the lack of public support for devolution in the Welsh referendum in early 1979 was a major setback, although the party retained two or three seats in Parliament throughout the 1980s and by 1992 returned four members to Westminster. In elections to the National Assembly for Wales in May 1999, established after a referendum had endorsed government proposals for devolution, Plaid Cymru won 17 seats compared to Labour's 28.

Plan of Campaign Instituted in Ireland on 21 Oct. 1886, it was provoked by the rejection of the HOME RULE Bill and severe agricultural depression. Tenants were instructed by the IRISH LAND LEAGUE to offer the landlord what they considered to be fair rent. Should the offer be refused, the rent was to be used to meet the expense of the Land War. *See also* IRISH QUESTION.

Planning, Town and Country Official planning of building and development grew out of the 19th-century PUBLIC HEALTH and SANITARY REFORM movements. New estates and towns like BOURNVILLE, PORT SUNLIGHT and then Hampstead Garden Suburb provided object lessons in what better housing might achieve. The first specific 'planning' Act was the Housing, Town Planning, etc. Act of 1909, which provided powers for local authorities to prepare schemes to control new HOUSING developments. Planning legislation gained momentum in the inter-war years, making local planning schemes mandatory and restricting the ribbon development which threatened to spoil both towns and countryside. Town and country planning became increasingly intertwined with economic PLANNING, especially in policies for the recovery of depressed areas (*see* ASSISTED AREAS). It was in this era that professionals like Sir Patrick Abercrombie (1879–1957) emerged and the ground was laid for the 1940 Barlow Report, outlining ways to control the location of industry and to permit expansion while improving the environment and amenities. Wartime destruction gave many planners the opportunity to develop new schemes, and urban renewal gathered pace (*see*, e.g., BIRMINGHAM; COVENTRY; PORTSMOUTH).

The note of optimism, building for a new age, has subsequently gone off key. Many urban planning schemes have failed to produce the benefits that were dreamed of, and the wholesale destruction in the 1950s and 1960s in many towns has produced a considerable backlash, notably from the CONSERVATION movement. Increasingly since the 1970s the presumption has been against rather than for wholesale renewal. Nevertheless, planning and the acceptance of regulation by the state for the general good has come to be an integral part of British society, and the effects are seen in roadsides and town fringes, which are tidier than in many continental countries and the USA.

Plantagenet, the name conventionally given to the English royal family descending from HENRY II. In the 12th century it was just a nickname given to Henry II's father, Geoffrey le Bel, Count of Anjou, while as a dynastic term, it seems to have been coined in the 15th century by supporters of RICHARD OF YORK. Its meaning is unknown, although in the later 19th century it was suggested that the name came from the sprig of broom *(Planta genista)* that Geoffrey might have been in the habit of wearing in his cap. This explanation has been widely accepted.

Plantation Economies, the widespread adoption of cash crops, notably TOBACCO, SUGAR, rice, and cotton, particularly in North America and the WEST INDIES, and later other tropical colonies, from the early 17th century.

Plantations in Ireland Plantations are attempts to colonize territory with a new settler population: 'ethnic cleansing'. Medieval IRELAND was divided ethnically between a Gaelic population and people of English descent who had settled piecemeal over centuries ('Anglo-Irish' and 'Anglo-Normans'). English determination to subdue Ireland by taming Gaelic culture and independence long veered between two strategies: co-operating with the Anglo-Norman aristocracy (e.g. the GERALDINES) while also finding some understanding with Gaelic chieftains; or imposing centralizing English-style royal government outwards from DUBLIN throughout the island. However, from the 1520s, schemes were mooted to dispossess and disperse the inconvenient native Gaelic population and introduce new settlers from outside the island to live alongside the existing ethnic English. This became a major feature of English intervention in the 16th and 17th centuries, as it had been in the 12th and 13th centuries.

The first efforts – sponsored, ironically, by the Catholic PHILIP II and MARY I – may have been encouraged by the example of Spanish NEW WORLD colonies; the settlers were either brought from England or had to be Englishmen who had been born in Ireland, and the existing Gaelic landowners were left with only one-third of their former lands. The pattern remained the same through the reign of ELIZABETH I; now settlers were mainly PROTESTANT and were known as New English, to distinguish them from the pre-Plantation Irish of English descent (now called 'Old English', and mostly Roman CATHOLIC in sympathy). The various Elizabethan efforts at plantation met with fierce resistance and were the main causes of the successive rebellions which culminated in the near-destruction of all plantations in Hugh O'NEILL's campaigns of 1595–8. O'Neill's defeat convinced JAMES I's government that it was essential to destroy the northern heartland of Gaelic culture and O'Neill's home territory in ULSTER: the way was made easier by the FLIGHT OF THE EARLS. From 1609, native inhabitants would be completely cleared from the land and replaced by reliably Protestant English and Scots settlers, with lands also reserved for the Protestant CHURCH OF IRELAND and Trinity College Dublin. The City of LONDON was given a county centring on the city of Derry (renamed LONDONDERRY). New plantations were also established elsewhere in the island, and in the years of THOROUGH Thomas WENTWORTH caused much New English and Old English resentment by radically extending crown control of them. The 1641 IRISH REBELLION was intended to destroy all plantations, but after the PARLIAMENTARIAN victory (*see* Oliver CROMWELL), by the end of the 1650s they had affected the whole island except for the counties of CONNACHT, Galway and Clare in the west – the poorest land in the island (for subsequent redistributions of land on religio-political grounds *see* SETTLEMENT, ACT OF (IRISH), 1662). In practice, plans usually fell short of their theoretical ruthless tidiness; nevertheless, the Gaelic landowning class was progressively ruined and virtually extinguished, and the legacy of bitterness, with populations keenly aware of their different cultural and ethnic loyalties, remains one of the root causes of Ireland's continuing troubles.

CHRONOLOGY

1557 Leix and Offaly renamed King's and Queen's County after PHILIP II and MARY I; settlement plans begin slowly there.

1571–2 Abortive Ards (Ulster) project, by Sir Thomas Smith.

1572–3 Abortive ULSTER plantation by Walter Devereux, Earl of Essex.

1586–7 Beginnings of MUNSTER plantation.

1598 English defeats by Hugh O'NEILL cause mass flights from Munster settlements.

1607 FLIGHT OF THE EARLS.

1609–13 Ulster plantation by English and Scots settlers; London livery companies prominent in organization. Derry renamed LONDONDERRY.

1610–20 Plantations in LEINSTER and Leitrim.

1635 Royal seizure of Londonderry causes fury in London and among settlers (*see* THOROUGH).

1641 Savage reprisals against settler population during Catholic rising; mutual atrocities result.

1654–9 Large-scale confiscations of Catholic lands throughout Ireland; former owners forcibly moved to CONNACHT, Galway and Clare. Much settlement, especially by ex-PARLIAMENTARIAN soldiers.

Plassey, Battle of, 23 June 1757, fought in West Bengal, INDIA, between Indian and EAST INDIA COMPANY troops under the command of Robert CLIVE, after the nawab (effectively the independent ruler) of Bengal had captured and sacked the Company's Calcutta settlement. British victory against huge numerical odds gave Britain immense military prestige and enabled Clive to replace the nawab with a successor dependent on Company backing, and this opened the way to a vast expansion in the Company's power and wealth. As a result, the British became incontestably the most powerful Europeans in India.

Platonists Also known as CAMBRIDGE platonists, this was a group of RESTORATION clerics, many of them fellows of Cambridge colleges – notably Ralph Cudworth, Henry More, John Smith, Benjamin Whichcote, John Wilkins and John Worthington – who reacted against doctrinaire CALVINISM and extolled the wisdom of the ancients, especially Plato and Plotinus. They championed the claims of reason and science, but took reason to include conscience and mystical insight. They influenced the LATITUDINARIANS, some of whom had been their pupils. *See also* NEO-PLATONISM.

Plegmund (?–923), Archbishop of Canterbury (890–923). Appointed to the archbishopric by ALFRED THE GREAT, he seems to have played an important role in the reigns of both Alfred and EDWARD THE ELDER. He advised Alfred on his translation of Gregory the Great's *CURA PASTORALIS*, created new DIOCESES and appears to have been deeply involved in early efforts to convert the DANELAW to Christianity.

Plough Monday, ancient holiday on the first Monday after Twelfth Night (6 Jan.), marking the resumption of work after the festivities and especially associated with the new agricultural season and particular CALENDAR CUSTOMS. Traditionally a plough was hauled along and the farmworkers demanded gifts.

Plug Riots, 1842. A phase of the HUNGRY FORTIES, the riots were provoked by UNEMPLOYMENT and wage reductions, and occurred principally in the north of England. They were so called because the rioters attacked mills and drew the plugs from the boilers to stop the machinery. In some areas, notably Yorks., the riots were clearly associated with the physical force side of the CHARTIST movement. In others the Chartists' attempt to identify it with the demand for the Charter merely exposed the gap between political and industrial unrest.

Plymouth, naval and port city in Devon, situated between the estuaries of the Rivers Tamar and Plym and on the natural harbour known as Plymouth Sound. A number of small settlements were incorporated in 1439, and became the nucleus of Plymouth, which expanded considerably in the 16th century. The town was important in the defeat of the Spanish ARMADA in 1588, and, in the 17th century, as the starting point for Atlantic voyages, notably of the MAYFLOWER PILGRIMS. From the reign of CHARLES II, Plymouth grew as a naval centre, especially after the foundation of the Devonport DOCKYARD in 1692. The town's strategic and commercial importance was reflected in dockyard fortifications and in the NEO-CLASSICAL grandeur of its early 19th-century houses and public architecture, much of which was erased by bombing in WORLD WAR II when 70,000 houses were damaged or destroyed. Post-war reconstruction was undertaken according to Watson and Abercrombie's radical plan, with ring roads and pedestrian shopping precincts. Plymouth's reliance upon the Royal NAVY has led to relative decline in recent years with the reduction in naval strength and expenditure.

Plymouth Brethren, *see* BRETHREN

Pocket Boroughs, a term used to describe those BOROUGHS with parliamentary representation in which seats were at the disposal of a patron or group of patrons in general election after general election (hence, 'in the pocket of'). The patron's 'interest' might range from unchallengeable power to nominate (to one or both seats in a given borough) or might be some lesser degree of influence. Such 'interest' might be based on the ownership of BURGAGE tenures in burgage boroughs (as in Old Sarum's burgage borough populated only on election day), on the packing of local councils in boroughs in which only the council had the FRANCHISE, or on the assiduous cultivation of boroughs with broader franchises in the vicinity of a patron's estates. Pocket boroughs, then, must be distinguished from wholly venal boroughs (*see* ROTTEN BOROUGHS). Approximately 120 English borough seats were subject to the nomination or continuing influence of private patrons in the early 18th century, at least 225 by 1761, and well over 300 by the 1806–7 election. In addition, 30 or so English borough seats were subject to crown influence in the early and mid-18th century, but thereafter the crown's electoral interest sharply declined. *See also* PARLIAMENTARY REFORM.

Poitiers, Battle of, 19 Sept. 1356, victory in western France for EDWARD THE BLACK PRINCE over King John of France. The numerical superiority of the French led them to attack the English who were drawn up in a strong defensive formation. The capture of John made this the most decisive of all the English victories in the HUNDRED YEARS WAR, and gave EDWARD III his strongest card in negotiating the treaty of BRÉTIGNY.

Polaris Submarine-launched ballistic missile system and part of the 'triad' of American strategic forces, it was also the basis, under the NASSAU AGREEMENT, of the British independent nuclear deterrent from 1962 until the introduction of the Trident system in the 1990s. Polaris has been at the centre of the debate about Britain's maintenance of NUCLEAR WEAPONS since the 1960s.

Police Police functions in Anglo-Saxon and ANGLO-NORMAN England were associated with individual communities. Within these communities CONSTABLES were elected to keep the peace at the assemblies known as 'views of frankpledge' (*see* MANOR); there were high constables for the HUNDREDS, generally chosen from the 16th century by JUSTICES OF THE PEACE.

The word 'police', from the Greek *politeia*, meant the management and good order of a city or territory; it was used occasionally in England during the 18th century, and concern about crime at the beginning of the 19th century saw the creation of parliamentary committees to investigate the 'police' of the metropolis. PEEL'S METROPOLITAN POLICE ACT 1829 signalled a break with the discretionary and parochial methods of law enforcement that hitherto had been the norm. In their place came a new system that was bureaucratic, hierarchically organized, and cast the new 'police constables' as impersonal agents of the law whose principle task was stated to be 'the prevention of crime'. They were to achieve this by the regular patrolling of individual beats. As a result of English fears of a continental police system involving spies and soldiers, the men were given uniforms more civilian than military, with a blue swallow-tailed coat and top hat, while their basic armament was limited to a wooden truncheon.

Local attempts at reorganizing police in the BOROUGHS were given a centralized focus by the MUNICIPAL CORPORATIONS ACT 1835 which required corporate boroughs to establish watch committees to supervise their policing. Legislation of 1839 and 1840 authorized any counties so inclined to create their own constabulary under the direction of a police committee of MAGISTRATES. Some 31 counties set up such forces for all or part of their jurisdiction before the County and Borough Police Act 1856 made police forces mandatory for both boroughs and counties, and subjected them to central inspection with EXCHEQUER grants available to those certified as efficient. By 1860 there were more than 200 separate borough and county forces in England and Wales. Similar developments were seen in Scotland; however the periodic troubles of Ireland led to the development of a more highly centralized, paramilitary organization, the Royal Irish Constabulary, commonly perceived as the model for British imperial police forces.

In England, Scotland and Wales the most common organizational model for the provincial forces was the Metropolitan Police, though this force was always independent of local government, being directly responsible, through its commissioners, to the home office. Attempts to bring it under the supervision of the new LONDON COUNTY COUNCIL were defeated, though under the LOCAL GOVERNMENT ACT 1888 the accountability of county police was shifted from police committees of magistrates to standing joint committees of magistrates and elected councillors. Fear of spies and political policing kept plain clothes and detective policing to a minimum in the early 19th century. A detective force was established at Scotland Yard in 1842, but it remained relatively small and, following the conviction of several senior officers in the Turf Fraud scandal of 1877, it was reorganized into the Criminal Investigation Department (CID) in 1878. From the beginning there was provision for a pension for policemen, though its discretionary nature led to much discontent. The Police Act 1890 guaranteed a pension after 25 years service, and this was followed by assistance with rents and a weekly rest day.

Although policemen were commonly deployed to 'keep the peace' during strikes in the Victorian and Edwardian periods, a union emerged among the police themselves shortly before 1914. The pressures of WORLD WAR I encouraged union membership and contributed to the police strikes of 1918 and 1919; these in turn brought about the POLICE ACT 1919. The war also led to the creation of the first women police, primarily as a force to protect and supervise the morals of young women in the vicinity of army camps or munitions factories. Women police were often unpopular with both senior officers and the rank and file. When financial stringency led to reductions in police numbers in the 1920s, women were commonly among the first to be dismissed.

Developments in motor transport during the interwar years put new burdens on the police and began to bring confrontations with members of the middle classes in a manner hitherto unknown. Over the same period the spread of suburbia and changes in leisure patterns began to make the traditional pattern of police beats redundant. On the eve of WORLD WAR II there were still some 200 separate police forces, and though the war provided the opportunity for the government to abolish some of these, the most significant amalgamations followed the POLICE ACT 1964. This legislation also led to the end of the borough watch committees and county standing joint committees.

From the late 1960s the fewer, much larger police forces usually had jurisdictions covering several counties and urban districts; they were accountable, in a very limited way, to committees of councillors and magistrates drawn from across their counties and districts. At the same time the policeman patrolling the beat to prevent crime was increasingly replaced by mechanized patrols and specialist units. Serious urban riots and industrial disorder during the 1980s made the question of police accountability a major political issue, while a steady rise in the statistics of crime prompted calls for a return to police on the beat to prevent crime, rather than just to respond to it in cars.

The official inquiry following the murder of the black teenager Stephen Lawrence in April 1993, reported in Feb. 1999 that there was institutionalized racism in the Metropolitan Police Force, and recommended a number of measures to raise awareness of racism, make police forces more accountable to their communities, extend the RACE RELATIONS ACT to apply to the police (as to other public servants), and establish a new Police Authority for London from July 2000, the majority of whose members will be elected. An initiative to set targets for the recruitment of more members of ethnic minority groups into police forces throughout the country was also signalled.

Police Act 1919 Passed following STRIKES by the Metropolitan POLICE (London) and the police in Liverpool for union recognition and better pay and conditions, the Act prohibited TRADE UNIONS in the police force but created the Police Federation to represent their interests. The home secretary was given powers to make pay and conditions uniform throughout the country. It was a crucial measure in taking the police force out of 'normal' industrial relations.

Police Act 1964 The Act provided for a major amalgamation of police forces, following on from an Act of 1946 which had removed 45 of the smaller constabularies. The Act reduced the number of police forces from 117 to 49 and encouraged the setting up of joint crime and traffic squads. It laid down that public complaints about police behaviour had to be investigated by an officer from another force.

Political and Economic Planning (PEP), pressure group launched in 1931 which attracted support from a range of businesses, politicians, and experts concerned with the need for a more thoroughgoing 'planned' approach to Britain's economic and social problems. It produced regular reports and a magazine *Planning*, which acted as a forum for views on the rationalization and reorganization of industry and the social services. PEP is often seen as a vehicle for 'middle opinion' in the 1930s which converged on the need for greater state involvement and improved welfare, and as a precursor of wartime and post-war measures. It merged in 1978 with the Centre for Studies in Social Policy to become the Policy Studies Institute. *See also* PLANNING.

Political Arithmetic, a term coined by Sir William Petty in the late 17th century to describe the application of arithmetical and mathematical analysis to the resources of the state. Early analyses were frustrated by the difficulties of obtaining reliable data as to POPULATION, trade or national wealth. Early practitioners included Gregory KING and Charles Davenant. Davenant was inspector-general of imports and exports, the first government office specifically devoted to compiling the statistics necessary for political arithmetic, set up in 1696.

Poll-Books Until 1832, elections of KNIGHTS OF THE SHIRE to the House of COMMONS were conventionally by acclamation (i.e. the two candidates with the loudest shouts from the crowd of electors won). However, such was the size of crowds and confusion on election day that during the later 16th century candidates frequently demanded a head-count (poll) of those voting. As elections became more commonly contested and party issues emerged in the later 17th century, the results of these polls were published as poll-books, although many also remain in manuscript form. They are an invaluable source for local and political history.

Poll Tax, a tax levied per head ('poll') of population. The financial costs of the HUNDRED YEARS WAR led the Parliament of 1377 to grant a tax of one groat (4 pence) on every lay person over the age of 14. Contemporary chroniclers regarded this as unprecedented; thus historians often refer to it as the first poll tax in English history. In fact, one intended to assist the kingdom of Jerusalem had been levied in 1222.

In 1379, another poll tax was granted, this time graduated according to wealth (as in 1222). It was the poll tax of 1380 – the third in four years and levied at the flat rate of 12 pence a head – that precipitated the PEASANTS' REVOLT. When the expected yield did not materialize, the government ordered commissioners to investigate evasion. Late in May 1381, defiance of the commission sitting at Brentwood by the residents of the Essex villages of Fobbing and Corringham rapidly escalated into armed rebellion, which was suppressed. Poll taxes were revived in the late 17th century as one among many revenue-raising devices, but these were usually levied only on more substantial earners, and it was to be nearly another 300 years before the next universal poll tax.

On 1 April 1989, the THATCHER government introduced a community charge (which became universally known as a poll tax) to replace the household rates in Scotland and on 1 April 1990 in England and Wales too. The rate was levied on individuals and took little account of the ability to pay and it was met with widespread protest including a major riot in Trafalgar Square on 31 March 1990 in which over 130 were injured, including 57 police, and 341 arrests were made. A year after the riot the government abandoned the poll tax and replaced it with a council tax, but the affair is widely believed to have been a contributory factor in Thatcher's downfall.

Polytechnics, institutions of higher education, mainly founded in the 1960s and originally intended to provide a more practical and technical education than the UNIVERSITIES, which they increasingly came to resemble; the distinction between polytechnics and universities was formally abolished in 1992.

Ponsonby Family, the most prominent of the small group of influential 18th-century Irish families, known as the UNDERTAKERS, who through their occupation of the main offices of state virtually controlled the government of Ireland, especially at mid-century.

Poor Law, New, term frequently used to describe the system of POOR RELIEF after the passage of the POOR LAW AMENDMENT ACT 1834, with its emphasis on harsher discipline and the WORKHOUSE, under the supervision of local boards from unions of PARISHES and a central national agency. Opposition to the introduction of the New Poor Law was intense in some areas, and persisted in northern industrial regions, while the stigma of the workhouse was hard to eradicate. The system was dismantled in the early 20th century with the introduction of old age pensions (*see* ANTI-POOR LAW RIOTS; OLD AGE PENSIONS ACT 1908; POOR LAW COMMISSION).

Poor Law, Old, term frequently used to describe the system of POOR RELIEF between 1552 and 1834. An Act in 1552 was refined by other Acts in 1597 and 1601 whereby JUSTICES OF THE PEACE were given overall responsibility for monitoring the system of relief locally, while within individual parishes OVERSEERS OF THE POOR were appointed annually to provide relief. The system was primarily based upon relieving the poor in their own homes, and a complicated set of rules governing SETTLEMENT, and hence entitlement to relief in a particular PARISH, evolved; the Old Poor Law began to crumble in the face of growing poverty, especially in southern rural counties, and the rise of UTILITARIAN political philosophies. *See also* POOR LAW AMENDMENT ACT; POOR RELIEF.

Poor Law Amendment Act 1834 Often hailed as one of the most important pieces of social legislation ever enacted, the measure was designed to discipline an 'irresponsible' and fast-growing POPULATION and to moderate the headlong rise in the cost of POOR RELIEF under the Old POOR LAW. The Act severely restricted access to outdoor relief, and made help available largely through the WORKHOUSE, entry to which was conditional upon passing a test to deter all but genuine cases of need. PARISHES were to be organized into Poor Law Unions under elected boards of guardians, to be supervised by the POOR LAW COMMISSION in London. The principal architect of the scheme was Edwin Chadwick (1800–90) who had largely been responsible for the report into the workings of the old laws in the same year; his UTILITARIAN sympathies were enshrined in statute, and Chadwick designed the workhouses to be, in his words, 'uninviting places of wholesome restraint'. *See also* ANTI-POOR LAW RIOTS; POOR LAW, NEW.

Poor Law Commission, a body consisting of three appointed commissioners set up to put the POOR LAW AMENDMENT ACT of 1834 into effect. Under its supervision a number of assistant commissioners were despatched around the country to group PARISHES into poor law unions, assist the formation of boards of guardians and, where appropriate, to advise on the construction of new WORKHOUSES. The Poor Law Commissioners also prepared diet sheets and the rules and regulations for the management of the union workhouses. The boards of guardians were required to keep minutes of their meetings and furnish annual returns on inmates and expenditure. By 1839 the nation's 15,000 parishes had been grouped into 600 poor law unions and 350 new workhouses had been built. The centralization of administration under the New POOR LAW was, however, controversial, and the 'three Bashaws of Somerset House', as the Poor Law Commissioners became known, were deeply unpopular. In 1847, following the ANDOVER SCANDAL, the Commission was wound up and replaced by a Poor Law Board which in 1871 united with the Public Health Board to form the LOCAL GOVERNMENT BOARD. *See also* ANTI-POOR LAW RIOTS.

Poor Relief Population growth in an undeveloped and slow-growing economy creates underemployment, UNEMPLOYMENT and VAGRANCY, prompting official worries about social unrest, as well as attempts to find remedies. The duty of care for the poor and travellers was supposedly a prime one for the many monastic institutions of medieval society, although it is still a matter of supposition how well that duty was carried out. Concern about the social consequences of poverty grew in the 14th century, resulting in the 1388 Statute of Cambridge. It contained two long-standing principles of the later Poor Law – a distinction between beggars considered 'sturdy' (capable of work) and those who were 'impotent' (unemployable through age or disability), and an attempt to settle the poor in a fixed place. The stagnation of POPULATION in the 15th century may have eased the general problem of poverty, but population growth in the 16th century and DISSOLUTION OF THE MONASTERIES made it ever more pressing. Piecemeal attempts were made at alleviating misery, combined with specific attacks on vagrancy. A growing tide of MIGRATION within England, from village to town, crowded area to marginal woodland, complicated the problem. Regular exhortations to charity were replaced by specific measures, with towns setting up workshops or investigating the extent of poverty, and growing systematization of the collection of PARISH funds for relief of the poor. The acute hardship of the 1590s, with social unrest, dearth and FAMINE, prompted the codification of the law in 1597, with its confirmation in 1601, generally known as the Old POOR LAW. The system in Scotland, until 1845, remained considerably less organized, based almost wholly on voluntary giving centred on the KIRK.

The Old Poor Law remained the basis of poor relief until the POOR LAW AMENDMENT ACT 1834, by which time both the scale of need and the sophistication of relief had far surpassed anything envisaged in the Elizabethan age. In practice, although not necessarily in statute, the system – at least where it was well administered – became caring both to those who, through age or sickness, were indigent, and to those who were overburdened with children or found work difficult to get, with relief administered on the basis of settlement. Relief was given as a supplement to wages – sometimes in relation to the price of bread or the size of families – and local poor houses took in the aged or sick and provided some work in local industries. After 1834, poor relief was supposed to be restricted to WORKHOUSE residents. Poor law reformers, notably Edwin Chadwick, promoted the view that relief was too generous, encouraging idleness and larger families, and sapping initiative. In practice, outdoor relief continued after 1834 because the workhouse system could not cope with the size of the problem – especially in the industrial areas during trade depressions. Crusades against outdoor relief occurred again during the 1870s, and such relief to the aged and widows with children was restricted. POVERTY remained widespread and poor law assistance continued to be significant well into the 20th century, despite the Liberal welfare reforms of 1906–14 and later extension of the incipient WELFARE STATE. *See also* APPRENTICES; GILBERT'S ACT; HOUSE OF INDUSTRY; POOR LAW, NEW; SPEENHAMLAND.

CHRONOLOGY

1388 Statute of Cambridge (*see above*).

1536 Beggars' Act: first attempt to regulate the raising of money for relief. Says 'sturdy' beggars should be put to work.

1547 Act introduces slavery for vagrancy; hugely unpopular and soon repealed. Provision for weekly exhortations to charity in churches.

1552 Systematization of PARISH poor relief collection.

1563 Greater powers to coerce those refusing to contribute.

1576 Legislation to encourage financing of work for poor. Large towns set up workshops.

1598, 1601 Social unrest, including OXFORDSHIRE RISING, prompts codification of law: JUSTICES OF THE PEACE gain major responsibilities and parish becomes unit for organization; parish overseers of the poor to be appointed, levying a poor rate (a local tax assessed on property) and, from it, administering relief.

1662 Act of SETTLEMENT to remedy previous inept attempts at defining settlement: parish responsible for poor who have lived there for 40 days. But without settlement gained from a £10 holding, a completed apprenticeship, hire for a year, or from paternal descent, this responsibility often extended only to removal.

1697 Overseers allowed to give ticket (token or certificate) to poor to find work outside parish; paupers must wear distinctive badges.

1723 WORKHOUSE Act allows overseers to make relief conditional on entry to a workhouse.

1782 GILBERT'S ACT passed. Meant as a humanitarian measure, it was the only piece of legislation successfully passed to amend the poor laws by Thomas Gilbert. Its effects were very limited.

1795 JUSTICES OF THE PEACE meeting at SPEENHAMLAND, Berks., agree rates should subsidize wages inadequate to cover high food prices.

1834 POOR LAW AMENDMENT ACT ushers in new POOR LAW. Poor relief continues for another century but is much more tightly and harshly administered, with the emphasis placed upon relief within the workhouse and largely for the aged, sick and orphaned.

Popish Plot, 1678–9, a conspiracy invented by Titus Oates and others. Oates swore on oath before the magistrate, Sir Edmund Berry Godfrey, that he knew details of a plot for CATHOLICS (with French assistance) to massacre PROTESTANTS, kill the king and install a Catholic ministry. Godfrey was later found murdered, and Oates' story gained widespread currency. Opponents of the Catholic Duke of York (the future JAMES II) fanned fears, and the Commons resolved that there was 'a damnable and hellish plot'. Many Catholics were tried and convicted, the most prominent being Lord Stafford, executed in Dec. 1680. Thomas OSBORNE, Earl of Danby fell, Parliament was dissolved, and the actions of the new Parliament precipitated the EXCLUSION CRISIS. A late execution, in June 1681, was that of the Irish Catholic primate Oliver Plunkett (subsequently canonized), who was tried in London on a charge of involvement in a complementary Irish plot.

Population, the total number of inhabitants within a territory. Any estimates of the numbers in the various countries before the 16th century are at best tenuous and often wild guesses, based upon extrapolation from a few locations and subject to radical revision. In the 16th century, at least in England, we enter the age of parish REGISTERS, from which source practitioners in HISTORICAL DEMOGRAPHY have produced ever more sophisticated estimates of total population, while similar work in the other countries of the British Isles has also begun to produce better estimates.

Present orthodoxy suggests a population figure of 3–4 million for England in Roman times, and perhaps 2 million for the 11th century. The latter figure is probably too low: the evidence of *DOMESDAY BOOK* has often been studied, but that source on closer inspection turns out to be a minefield of inconsistencies and *lacunae*. The physical evidence, of growing and shrinking settlements, together with economic evidence of hardship suggests rapid population rise until the early 14th century (by 1300, it may have been as high as 6 million), which was knocked back by a combination of FAMINE and restraint even in advance of the devastating MORTALITY of the BLACK DEATH. That same type of evidence then suggests little or no population growth until well into the 15th century, with the 16th century witnessing rapid and sustained increase.

With the introduction of parish registers from 1538, more accurate estimates become possible for England (and to some extent Wales), the most recent and sophisticated work being that of Wrigley and Schofield and their critics (*see* AGGREGATIVE ANALYSIS). Figures for Scotland and Ireland are necessarily very speculative, at least until the better record-keeping of the 18th century. The introduction of the CENSUS, first taken in 1801, provides a much firmer statistical basis for knowing the size and composition of the population. *See also* BIRTH CONTROL; DEATH RATE; EUGENICS; FAMILY RECONSTITUTION; FERTILITY; MALTHUS; MARRIAGE; MIGRATION; REGISTRAR-GENERAL.

Population (in thousands) of the British Isles: 1401–1991

Figures for England and Wales exclude Isle of Man, Channel Islands. Figures for Ireland exclude the Irish Republic after 1911.

	England & Wales	*Scotland*	*Ireland*
1401	2,100		
1481	2,000		
1500		500?	800?
1521	2,300		
1541	2,773		
1551	3,011		
1561	2,984		
1571	3,270		
1581	3,597		
1591	3,899		
1601	4,109	800?	1,000?
1611	4,416		
1621	4,692		
1631	4,892		
1641	5,091		2,100?
1651	5,228		
1661	5,140		
1671	4,982		1,700?
1681	4,930		
1691	4,930	1,230	2,000?
1701	5,057	1,000?	
1711	5,230		1,900?
1721	5,350		
1731	5,263		
1741	5,576		
1751	5,772		2,400?
1755		1,265	
1761	6,146		

	England & Wales	Scotland	Ireland
1771	6,447		3,584
1781	7,042		4,048
1791	7,739		4,753
1801	8,893	1,608	
1811	10,165	1,806	
1821	12,000	2,092	6,802
1831	13,897	2,364	7,767
1841	15,914	2,620	8,196
1851	17,928	2,889	6,514
1861	20,066	3,062	5,788
1871	22,712	3,360	5,398
1881	25,974	3,736	5,146
1891	29,003	4,026	4,680
1901	35,528	4,472	4,459
1911	36,070	4,761	4,390
1921	37,887	4,882	1,258
1931	39,952	4,843	1,243
1951	43,758	5,096	1,371
1961	46,105	5,179	1,425
1971	48,750	5,229	1,536
1981	49,154	5,130	1,491
1991	48,968	4,957	1,583

The next census will be 2001: the population of the UK in mid-1998 was estimated to be 59.2 million.

Port Sunlight, Ches. village built by Lever Brothers beside their Merseyside soap works as model cottage HOUSING. Begun in 1889, and ultimately having 1,000 houses, Port Sunlight (unlike its contemporary BOURNVILLE) was intended as a development to house only the Lever workers, and the company exercised benevolent patronage there. These and similar model developments were precursors of the GARDEN CITY, NEW TOWN and town PLANNING movements of the 20th century.

Porteous Riots, 1736. After rioting followed the execution of a smuggler, Williams, in Edinburgh, the English commander of the troops present, Captain Porteous, ordered them to shoot – without prior authorization from MAGISTRATES – and several rioters were killed. Porteous was tried and sentenced to death; when the execution was postponed, a lynch mob broke into the gaol and hanged him. The incident provided a focus for clashes between WALPOLE and his opponents, and Scottish resentment encouraged Walpole's political manager there, John CAMPBELL, Duke of Argyll, to turn against him and return opposition candidates at the 1741 election.

Portland, 3rd Duke of, *see* BENTINCK, WILLIAM CAVENDISH

Portsmouth, Hants., port and naval city. Founded at the mouth of the natural harbour in the late 12th century, it was granted a charter in 1194. During the Middle Ages it was far less important commercially than nearby SOUTHAMPTON, but was always important as a naval base. From 1418 to the mid-17th century successive monarchs strengthened the defences and improved the naval facilities; under CHARLES II Portsmouth became Britain's principal naval base, which it has essentially remained. The NAVY and an attendant garrison have framed Portsmouth's growth. From the 18th century new towns – Portsea, Landport and Southsea – grew outside the ancient walls, Southsea developing as a Victorian seaside resort. Extensive bomb damage in WORLD WAR II obliterated much of the city's ancient heart as well as causing major destruction in the naval base. Reconstruction has been less successful architecturally, and perhaps socially, than in some other towns. The declining importance of naval defence and the removal of the garrison have had an important effect on Portsmouth, which since the 1960s has become the home of newer, technologically based industries.

Possessory Assizes, *see* PETTY ASSIZES

Post Office, *see* POSTAL SERVICES

Postal Services The Post Office was founded in 1635, and gradually through the 17th and 18th centuries its tentacles spread, as the volume of mail rose with economic change, increased LITERACY, and the easier transport in the high-speed mail coaches on improved ROADS, particularly after 1784. The advent of organized postal services was also of strategic advantage – in 1655, for example, secretary of state John Thurloe had had an agent reading all ROYALISTS' letters, so was ready for PENRUDDOCK'S RISING when it came. The principal barrier to greater use of the postal service was its cost, since rates were calculated on number of pages sent and distance travelled, the cost usually being collected from the recipient on delivery rather than from the sender of the letter. Deliveries were only frequent in London.

The modern postal service emerged in 1840, when under Rowland Hill's urging

Parliament introduced the penny post, a uniform charge on letters of ½ oz in weight. This service was supplemented by book post (1849), reduced rate for cards and newspapers (1870), parcel post (1883), and a uniform imperial rate (1898). Telegraph companies were nationalized in 1870, and they too came under the aegis of the General Post Office, along with other financial transactions like savings (instituted in 1861 but first mooted in 1807) and postal orders.

The General Post Office had been among the early sponsors of Marconi's radio experiments, and became the main provider of TELECOMMUNICATIONS, adding the telephone to its services in 1890. This became a state monopoly when it acquired the trunk and provincial systems (with the exception of Hull) in 1892 and 1911, until the mid-1980s and privatization.

The General Post Office ceased to be a department of government under the postmaster-general in 1969, and its successor, the Post Office, was subsequently split in 1981, with responsibility for the telephone service being given to British Telecommunications, which was privatized in 1984.

Pot Wallopers, heads of households with their own fireplaces, who had the right to vote in certain BOROUGH elections. Prior to the REFORM ACT of 1832 their right to vote was conditional on their having 'boffed their own pot' in the borough in the six months preceding the election. The qualification was abolished by the 1832 Act.

Potato Famine Between 1845 and 1850, Ireland endured one of the worst FAMINES to strike the Western world in modern times: about one million people died, and another million emigrated. Ireland's POPULATION explosion over the preceding century, when it grew threefold, had been fuelled by the greater ability to subsist on potatoes. The arrival of the American potato blight in 1845 brought widespread suffering throughout Europe. Continually blighted crops, combined with atrocious winter weather, caused mass MORTALITY. Movement of starving people in search of food encouraged the rapid spread of disease, including dysentery and typhus. The repeal in 1846 of the protectionist CORN LAWS, a belated move to assist the distressed, had greater political repercussions in Britain than it had practical effect in Ireland. Remote areas of Scotland too were badly affected, although without the desperate plight of the Irish.

There was a 20 per cent fall in Ireland's population between 1841 and 1851. Every area except for DUBLIN and BELFAST lost population; ULSTER was less deeply ravaged than other parts. There was massive emigration to Britain. The poor in the central counties had perished in their hundreds of thousands, of hunger and disease. Ireland's population continued to shrink until 1926, through EMIGRATION and low MARRIAGE rates. The Famine was the most terrifying and public of events, and still lives on in the popular consciousness as an example of the hardships Ireland has suffered, and the indifference of mainland Britain to that suffering.

Potsdam Conference, last of the 'Big Three' wartime conferences between Britain, the United States and the USSR, held in a suburb of Berlin from 17 July–2 Aug. 1945 after the end of WORLD WAR II in Europe. America was represented by President Truman, and Britain's new prime minister ATTLEE took over from CHURCHILL after 27 July. The major issue was the future of Germany: it was agreed to give Poland a westward extension of its pre-war borders to the line of the Oder–Neisse rivers; REPARATIONS were also agreed. The summit marked the hardening of the divisions between Britain and the US on one side and the USSR on the other, which was to develop into the COLD WAR.

Poundage, *see* TONNAGE AND POUNDAGE

Poverty Usually measured with respect to some idea of the minimum subsistence required to maintain physical well-being, poverty has, however, since World War II come to be increasingly regarded as a relative phenomenon which changes with the movement of living standards and material expectations. Major crises of subsistence creating widespread disease and death through lack of food died out in Britain during the early modern period but chronic poverty remained. It had traditionally been seen as the occasion for acts of private charity in which the Church and monastic institutions were the central pivots. However, rising POPULATION and prices in the 16th century and the growing problem of VAGRANCY, coupled with the DISSOLUTION OF THE MONASTERIES and a decline in church almsgiving, combined to produce the Elizabethan legislation which created the Old POOR LAW, a system of parish-based relief of the poor. After the introduction of the New POOR LAW of 1834, per caput Poor Relief expenditure declined, although this was due less to the discriminatory policies of relief than to a general increase in employment and wages which characterized the later 19th century. Investigations of poverty at the end of the 19th and in the early 20th centuries, notably by Charles BOOTH and Seebohm Rowntree, showed its persistence amongst significant groups in the population. Rowntree identified an important LIFE CYCLE in poverty whereby a married couple might fare reasonably well until the arrival of children; loss of the wife's earnings and greater costs of a large family then combined to produce major hardship which was relieved only when older children became income earners or left home. He also distinguished between primary poverty, where income was less than that required to maintain physical efficiency, and secondary poverty, caused by unwise expenditure of income on alcohol or gambling or by inefficient housekeeping. Poverty has remained widespread in the 20th century, exacerbated by persistent, often increasing, inequalities in income, UNEMPLOYMENT, rising DIVORCE rates, and a persistence of the 19th-century view that generous state hand-outs might sap the energies needed for job seeking and self-betterment.

Power Loom, *see* COTTON INDUSTRY

Powys, early Welsh kingdom. Despite some difficulties in the early evidence, it is generally accepted that Powys had probably come into existence by the 6th century. Its rulers were involved in frequent conflicts with the kings of MERCIA. In 855, it was conquered by RHODRI MAWR and was treated as a part of GWYNEDD until the late 11th century, when it re-emerged as a principality.

Poynings' Law, part of HENRY VII's effort to revive English administration and challenge FITZGERALD power in Ireland. In 1494/5, the English troubleshooter, Sir Edward Poynings, forced the Irish PARLIAMENT to enact legislation to the effect that parliamentary sessions and proposed legislation in Ireland must be previously approved in England. Ironically, it was later used by Irish politicians to obstruct and delay English administration in DUBLIN. By the 18th century, the Irish Parliament habitually initiated legislation in the form of 'heads of Bills', but British governments also continued to find a use for Poynings' law, since this made it possible for proposed bills to be amended or blocked by either the Irish or the British PRIVY COUNCILS. Hated by Irish patriots, the law came under sustained attack when economic troubles associated with the War of AMERICAN INDEPENDENCE fuelled resentment of British rule. In 1780, demands for enhanced powers of self-government included one for the repeal of the law; two years later, it was denounced by the VOLUNTEER convention at DUNGANNON. The second Rockingham (*see* WENTWORTH, CHARLES) ministry, formed in 1782 and anxious to display statesmanship by quieting Irish troubles, allowed the Irish Parliament to pass Yelverton's Act in July, amending the law so drastically as to rob it of force. At the same time, the British Parliament repealed the DECLARATORY ACT. These measures inaugurated the era of GRATTAN'S PARLIAMENT.

Praemunire, Statutes of, 1353, 1365, 1393, enactments that aimed to prevent judgments given in the English king's courts being referred to courts outside the realm. Although not explicitly mentioned until the statute of 1365, appeals to the papacy were clearly meant. As a means of reinforcing the second statute of PROVISORS, the statute of 1393 (sometimes known as the Great Statute of Praemunire) imposed further constraints on communications between England and the papal court. The name 'Praemunire' (meaning 'summon') derives from the opening Latin word of the WRIT ordering a SHERIFF to summon offenders. These 14th-century statutes were, in turn, revived by HENRY VIII against Cardinal WOLSEY in 1529, and they were also used as ammunition in the king's jurisdictional battle with the papacy.

Prayer Book Rebellion, *see* WESTERN REBELLION

Prayer Books The 'prayer book' is the common name for the *Book of Common Prayer*, which was, in its various versions, the only legal liturgy used in the Church of England during the periods 1549–54 and 1559–1645 and then from 1662 to the 20th century. It has shaped all later ANGLICAN liturgical books, which also tend to be called 'prayer books'. *See also* CHURCH: ENGLAND.

CHRONOLOGY

1548 *Order of Communion* prepared by CRANMER: first in English.

1549 Cranmer compiles complete English *Book of Common Prayer*; much compromise with traditional rites, particularly Sarum rite; PROTESTANTS criticize.

1550 First ORDINAL in English.

1552 Second *Book of Common Prayer*: much more Reformed in character.

1553 Prayer book banned in MARY I's restoration of traditional CATHOLICISM.

1559 ELIZABETHAN SETTLEMENT resurrects **1552** prayer book, only slightly modified in Catholic direction.

1637 Prayer book prepared for Scotland by HIGH CHURCH Scots bishops working with LAUD; sparks off BISHOPS' WARS.

1645 Parliament replaces prayer book with CALVINIST *Directory of Public Worship*; much clandestine use of old book.

1662 New *Book of Common Prayer* produced by triumphant ANGLICANS; after this, no suggestions for modification succeed for more than 300 years.

1927–8 EVANGELICAL agitation leads to House of COMMONS twice rejecting new prayer book.

1965 Beginning of various new liturgies for CHURCH OF ENGLAND.

1980 Alternative Service Book published.

Prebendaries' Plot, 1543, amorphous agitation by conservative GENTRY and clergy, including CANTERBURY Cathedral PREBENDARIES, designed to destroy Archbishop CRANMER. HENRY VIII chose to back Cranmer; the plot disintegrated.

Prebendary, alternative term for a CANON. The *prebendary* (the office-holder) should not be confused with the *prebend* (the endowment that supports him).

Precedence, Statute of, 1539 This made new arrangements for seating during state business and meetings of PARLIAMENT. Great officers of state were given precedence over all other peers except royal dukes. Trivial at first sight, the statute actually reflected vital political struggles: it much enhanced Thomas CROMWELL's formal position, but great office-holders who were his enemies also gained. In the long term, it symbolized the importance of service to the crown against mere aristocratic birth – a chief Tudor goal achieved after the weakness of the crown in the 15th century.

Prefabs, temporary 'prefabricated' houses built as an emergency measure to cope with homelessness and overcrowding at the end of WORLD WAR II. Over 150,000 were built between 1945 and 1950. The single-storey dwellings proved surprisingly popular and thousands remained in use – some to the present day – long after their expected life, because of continuing shortages in HOUSING.

Prelate, ecclesiastical dignitary: often applied to the PEERS spiritual in the House of LORDS – i.e. bishops and (formerly) abbots. Used in a derogatory sense by those suspicious of clerical pretension.

Premonstratensians, order of CANONS REGULAR, also known as 'Norbertines' from their founder St Norbert (*c.*1080–1134). Their Rule was a development of the AUGUSTINIAN Rule to emphasize austerity. Norbert founded their first house at Prémontré in 1120, and their first English house was established *c.*1143.

Pre-Raphaelites, group of artists, together with critics and poets, founded in 1848, who admired the art of *quattrocento* (15th-century) Italy, and hence rejected both the authority given to Raphael as the ultimate master of painting, and the 19th-century academic school of painting. The Pre-Raphaelite Brotherhood was originally formed by John Everett Millais (1829–96), William Holman Hunt (1827–1910) and Dante Gabriel Rossetti (1828–82), and their work, with that of their followers, relied heavily for its subjects on illustration of poetry, especially that of Keats, and was characterized by adherence to nature, with clear light, strong colours and close observation of flora, and a high moral tone. Many of the group's paintings were religious, such as Hunt's *The Light of the World* or Millais' *Christ in the House of his Parents* (1850); others illustrated medieval life. The members were heavily influenced by John Ruskin (1819–1900); like the later ARTS AND CRAFTS movement, the Pre-Raphaelites reacted against what they saw as the ugliness of contemporary life and dress. The movement's most influential member was William Morris (1834–96), who transformed the Brotherhood's message into his personal brand of Utopian socialism. The Brotherhood itself dissolved in the course of the 1850s, but the distinctive style remains an enduringly popular variety of Victorian art.

Prerogative Courts, those outside the COMMON LAW system, set up by the crown in the late 15th and 16th centuries to obtain more effective government and justice – e.g. the courts of REQUESTS, STAR CHAMBER and HIGH COMMISSION and regional COUNCILS – all abolished in the 17th century.

Prerogative, Royal, the discretionary powers and rights of the crown. Its vague boundaries prompted large claims by RICHARD II, the Tudors and Stuarts, culminating in the confrontation between CHARLES I and PARLIAMENT that led to legislative curbs from 1641. These were reinforced at the RESTORATION and by the BILL OF RIGHTS (1689). *See also* SUSPENDING AND DISPENSING POWERS.

Presbyterianism John Calvin (*see* CALVINISM) claimed that church government in the New Testament gave no special hierarchical status to individuals, but that ministers (presbyters) of equal status made decisions together in councils (presbyteries or synods). Presbyterianism involves tiers of these councils at national and local level, usually with lay elders taking part; charity is undertaken by deacons, and theological education by 'doctors' (teachers).

The Established Churches of the Netherlands and Scotland became Presbyterian, and many PURITANS wanted to imitate this in England (*see* CLASSICAL MOVEMENT). (For CIVIL WAR and INTERREGNUM use of the term in politics and religion, *see* INDEPENDENTS.) After the RESTORATION, Presbyterian congregations survived as DISSENTERS, but many became UNITARIAN in the 18th century. The Presbyterian Church of England – which united with the CONGREGATIONALISTS in 1972 to become the United Reformed Church – was largely composed of later Scots immigrant congregations.

Press Gang, a body of sailors employed by the NAVY to impress (i.e. force) men into naval service. This traditional method of recruiting merchant seamen for naval service was largely abandoned after the FRENCH REVOLUTIONARY and NAPOLEONIC WARS (1793–1815). The introduction of the Continuous Service Act in 1853, which enabled ratings to receive permanent engagements, made the press gang redundant.

Pretender, Old, *see* STUART, JAMES EDWARD

Pretender, Young, *see* STUART, CHARLES EDWARD

Prevention of Crimes Act 1882 Passed in response to the PHOENIX PARK MURDERS, and limited to Ireland, it created a special tribunal of three judges to try cases without juries, extended the summary jurisdiction of magistrates and authorized the lord lieutenant to prohibit meetings where necessary.

Prevention of Terrorism Act 1974 Intended as a temporary measure, the Act was passed rapidly by the LABOUR government in 1974 in the wake of the BIRMINGHAM PUB BOMBINGS by IRA terrorists. It gave the police wide powers to hold suspects for up to five days and exclude them from the British mainland.

Price-Fixing Term used by historians to denote one of the courses of action crowds sometimes adopted during GRAIN RIOTS: coercive insistence that grain be sold at a designated (lower) price. Local magistrates had authority to set the bread prices, by an Assize of Bread; in the face of crowd demands, they would sometimes adjudicate prices of other foodstuffs.

In the 20th century there are two possible reasons for attempts to fix prices. Governments have frequently used it as a way of coping with inflation and/or protecting particular interest groups. Thus rent controls have been a clear case of protecting tenants against potential exploitation from landlords; and the Common Agricultural Policy, a key feature of the EEC (*see* EUROPEAN UNION), fixed agricultural prices in order to protect the incomes of farmers. However, price-fixing has not been confined to governments, but has been implemented by industrial and commercial interests as a way of limiting competition. Competition is frequently viewed as potentially ruinous to individual firms which comprise an industry and agreements to fix prices are seen as bringing stability to the industry in question. The practice was explicitly promoted in the UK during the 1930s in an attempt to deal with the worst effects of the DEPRESSION, and many of the agreements persisted after World War II. In 1964, however, the government introduced an Act abolishing what was then called resale price maintenance, a practice whereby producers would dictate the price at which their goods could be sold by retailers. Nevertheless price-fixing may still occur in a clandestine form and as a consequence the government may refer suspicious cases to the Office of Fair Trading, to adjudicate whether there is indeed a case of price-fixing against the public interest.

Prices and Incomes Board, introduced by George Brown under the WILSON government in Feb. 1965 in order to provide machinery for reviewing prices and incomes. All price increases and wage claims were to be referred to the Board. Its attempt to regulate them had to be replaced by a prices and incomes 'freeze' for six months in 1966. The Board was abolished by the newly elected HEATH government in Nov. 1970 as part of its attempt to deregulate the economy. *See also* INCOMES POLICIES.

Pride's Purge, Dec. 1648, the inevitable outcome of a trial of strength between Parliament and the army. After increasing tension, which had included an attempted coup by PARLIAMENT against the army in summer 1647, and which had contributed to the second CIVIL WAR (summer 1648), Col. Thomas Pride's troops expelled from the COMMONS those MPs (mostly PRESBYTERIANS) who favoured further negotiations with CHARLES I. The remaining MPs, mainly INDEPENDENTS, formed the RUMP PARLIAMENT.

Priestley Riots, 14–18 July 1791, RIOTS that broke out in BIRMINGHAM following a dinner commemorating the second anniversary of the fall of the Bastille, which was seen as a provocative assertion of disloyalty to the established order. Crowds wrecked the tavern where the dinner had been held, as well as DISSENTING chapels and the shops and houses of prominent Dissenters, notably the house, chapel and laboratory of Joseph Priestley (1733–1804) the scientist and political and theological writer, who was sympathetic to the French Revolution and had published a reply to BURKE's hostile *REFLECTIONS*. Local authorities were criticized for their slow and ineffective response; it was suggested that they had colluded with or even incited the crowds. Troops arrived four days after the start of the disturbances. Subsequently 17 rioters were tried, four were convicted and two executed.

Prime Minister, term (originally abusive) in modern British politics for the chief minister of the CROWN and effective head of the government. It was applied to GODOLPHIN and HARLEY, dominant ministers under ANNE. However, the first minister fully to warrant the title by his unchallengeable ascendancy in government was Robert WALPOLE who, from 1722 onwards, built up his power not simply by exploiting his post as FIRST LORD OF THE TREASURY, but also by declining translation to the LORDS, thereby retaining a firm grip on the COMMONS and so distinguishing himself from such precursors as Danby (*see* OSBORNE, THOMAS) and HARLEY. Henry PELHAM achieved a similar status to Walpole as first lord in 1743, but thereafter the evolution of the office through the 18th century was dependent on the individual personalities and talents of first lords; it was only firmly established by the successive periods in power of PITT THE YOUNGER. The office of prime minister is by convention conferred when the new prime minister kisses hands with the monarch. Its first formal recognition in Britain only came with the Ministers of the Crown Act (1937). The term has been exported worldwide, both to constitutions descended from British practice in the former BRITISH EMPIRE and to quite different political systems.

Primitive Methodists, *see* METHODISM

Primogeniture, the custom of land INHERITANCE whereby the entire estate passes to the eldest son. The custom spread from Europe to Britain from the 11th century, starting with the largest ARISTOCRATIC estates, but it was not established as the universal basis for the transmission of estates until 1926. *See also* BOROUGH-ENGLISH; FEE SIMPLE; GAVEL-KIND; USE; WILLS.

Primrose, Archibald (5th Earl of

Rosebery) (1847–1929), Liberal politician and Prime Minister (1894–5). An aristocrat who married a Rothschild heiress, Rosebery succeeded his grandfather as earl in 1868. He first held office as under-secretary in the home office with responsibility for Scottish affairs (1881–3), and was subsequently appointed commissioner of works and lord Privy Seal, in which capacity he was largely responsible for the creation of the Scottish office. He was the first chairman of the LONDON COUNTY COUNCIL (LCC) and served as foreign secretary in GLADSTONE's 1886 LIBERAL government, and again in 1892. He succeeded Gladstone as prime minister in March 1894, resigning in June 1895 after endless CABINET disputes and defeat in the COMMONS. As prime minister he had failed to carry the Liberal legislative programme through the LORDS – other than the budget which introduced death duties for the first time. As Liberal leader he failed to give the party leadership in its internecine struggles, or a way forward as a credible party of the left. He resigned from the leadership in 1896.

Primrose League, founded in 1883 to commemorate DISRAELI's politics and promote the principles of TORY Democracy which he advocated. The primrose was Disraeli, Lord Beaconsfield's floral emblem, and the anniversary of his death (9 April) became known as Primrose Day. It developed into a mass political organization which was particularly active in mobilizing women to work on behalf of the CONSERVATIVE PARTY.

Prince Edward Island Smallest of the provinces of CANADA, the island was discovered by the French in 1534 and ceded to Britain in 1763. Charlottetown, the island's capital, was the venue for the meeting of the 'Fathers of Confederation' in 1864 which passed the resolutions leading to the BRITISH NORTH AMERICA ACT. The farming and fishing community is known throughout the world from the *Anne of Green Gables* stories by L. M. Montgomery.

Prince of Wales, *see* WALES, PRINCE OF

Prince Regent, *see* GEORGE IV

Princes in the Tower, *see* EDWARD V

Printing in Britain That printing sparked a revolution is no less true for being a cliché. Together with the spread of paper manufacture to western Europe in the 13th century, it represented the only major advance in information technology between the 1st/2nd-century AD invention of the book-form and 19th-century innovations.

In 1476, William CAXTON set up his press in Westminster, soon to be followed by other presses in London and in Oxford and St Albans. In 1507, Walter Chepman and Andrew Myllar received a licence for printing in Edinburgh. English privileges for foreign-born printers were withdrawn in 1534, and henceforth, natives dominated the trade, which greatly expanded after restrictions on setting up printing businesses were eased in 1695.

With cheap and quick transmission of words on paper, the acquisition of LITERACY skills became much more attractive – individuals could afford to own books. Although the first printed books were very traditional texts (which made sound commercial sense – they had a ready-made market), the rapid spread of ideas that caused the upheavals of the REFORMATION would have been impossible without printing. For instance, compare this with the limited impact made by the earlier LOLLARDS, a number of whose ideas were the same as those of the 16th-century reformers. *See also* CENSORSHIP.

Printing equipment was relatively simple, and despite an ever-growing volume of books and pamphlets, from CHAPBOOKS and ALMANACS to BIBLES and multi-volume novels, there were few technical advances until the end of the 18th century. The mechanization of paper manufacture in 1798 rapidly reduced its cost, while the replacement of the wooden bed of the press with iron, the making of pages of type in one mould, and much faster type-founding had all vastly increased printers' rate of production by the 1830s. The adoption of lithography, printing from the surface of a specially prepared stone, took illustration a stage further from the old woodcuts and Thomas Bewick's wood engravings, while the invention of new machines from the 1860s, culminating in the Linotype and Monotype of the 1880s, greatly speeded up typesetting.

As the mechanical processes were taking over volume-printing, hand-printing was being revived, notably by William Morris and his Kelmscott Press, which produced some of the finest books ever made. The craftsmanship associated with the private press has continued to have a place in the modern world, while since the 1960s photo-reproduction and other technological advances have once more transformed the world of printing. Yet, over more than five centuries, the end product has remained basically unchanged. *See also* NEWSPAPERS.

Priories, Alien, *see* ALIEN PRIORIES

Prison Commission, 1878. Under Edmund Du Cane (1830–1903) the commission closed 38 local prisons and phased out many more so that by 1894 only 56 local prisons were left. A prison staff structure on military lines and meritocracy replaced the patronage system of earlier years. The hierarchy consisted of governor, chief warder, principal warders, warders and assistant warders. A strict rule book was enforced and warders who ill-treated prisoners were to be severely dealt with. The practice of appointing prisoners as guards was discontinued. Prisoners wore uniforms and were subjected to a progressively strict regime: 'Hard bed, hard fare, hard labour.' However, this obsession with uniformity and the application of a deterrent system seems to have had no discernible effect on the prisoner's propensity to re-offend. *See also* PENTONVILLE.

Prison Reform The proper keeping of prisoners in gaols, HOUSES OF CORRECTION and other prisons was an object of concern to SHERIFFS, JUSTICES OF THE PEACE and others throughout the medieval and early modern periods. Only from the 1770s, however, did prison reform acquire the status of a cause, mainly due to the efforts of John Howard, after whom the Howard League for Penal Reform is named, whose exposé *The State of the Prisons* was first published in 1777. Many counties rebuilt their prisons on more ambitious lines and at great expense in the following decades; Jeremy BENTHAM suggested that the ideal prison might take the form of a PANOPTICON. Pressure for continuing effort and innovation was maintained by the increasing use made of imprisonment (as opposed to TRANSPORTATION, whipping or fines) in punishment. The first national prison for convict prisoners, Millbank, opened in 1816. In the same year, QUAKER Elizabeth Fry initiated ladies' prison visiting, an activity which became popular among the philanthropic. PEEL's 1823 Prison Act consolidated earlier legislation and required justices to send to the home secretary quarterly reports on the state of the prisons. *See also* PRISONS ACT 1865; PRISONS ACT 1877.

Prisons Act 1865 An expression of the contemporary confusion over the retributory deterrent or reforming purposes of punishment, it was designed to make imprisonment more uncomfortable and to emphasize deterrence at the expense of education or moral reform. Local authorities were ordered to construct separate cells for all prisoners. Hard labour was divided into two classes. First-class labour included treadwheel, crank and stone breaking; second-class labour consisted of any kind of hard physical exertion ordered by the home secretary. Prison governors received discretionary power to order solitary confinement for three days and nights on bread and water; and visiting JUSTICES OF THE PEACE could order a month in a punishment cell or a flogging. Chains, irons and other restraints were specifically authorized. There were uniform codes of rules, uniform dietary standards and uniform spiritual and health provision (an Anglican chaplain and a doctor). A coroner's inquest was to be held for all prisoners who died in gaol. Grants were to be made to aid discharged prisoners. The Act led to the closure of many small gaols which could not afford to meet the new standards.

Prisons Act 1877 It brought prisons in England and Wales under central government control and made co-ordinated prison policy possible. By this Act the ownership of all the local prisons was vested in the home secretary and their general superintendence was committed to a body of commissioners appointed by him. The centralization of prison administration represented a landmark in the history of penal policy.

Private Eye, satirical weekly magazine, founded in 1961, and part of the 'satire boom' of the early 1960s. It helped to discredit the CONSERVATIVE governments of MACMILLAN and DOUGLAS-HOME and has continued to show a lively irreverence towards the establishment and thus acquire a succession of writs for libel.

Privateering, private war at sea, licensed by the state. Generally it involved the fitting out of a ship to take vessels of other nationalities (usually those at war with the home state) for profit. There were two types of licence for this activity: 'letters of reprisal' which were issued to individual merchants to take forcible steps to obtain compensation for injuries done them by foreigners or foreign countries; and 'Letters of marque' which were more generally used, and were given out against ships of particular nationalities with which Britain was at war. Both were issued by the lord high admiral, and the ships taken 'prize' as a result were 'condemned' as such in the ADMIRALTY Courts.

The practice had its origins in the middle ages. The first major period of English privateering was against Spain in the reign of ELIZABETH I, and DRAKE's round-the-world voyage was a privateering one. Despite the West Country legend, the most successful and intensive privateering was done by LONDON ships. In the earlier 17th century, on balance, England seems to have suffered more from privateering than it gained; raids by the North African privateers known as 'Barbary corsairs' took ships and slaves in the Channel, the eastern end of which was terrorized by Dunkirk privateers. The latter half of the century saw the second great period of privateering in the WEST INDIES, though privateering often shaded into piracy as practised by the 'buccaneers', culminating in Henry Morgan's sack of the city of Panama.

As English naval and mercantile strength grew, so the available target for foreign raiders also enlarged. In the latter part of KING WILLIAM'S WAR France adopted commerce raiding as its main weapon against England, and French warships were lent to privateering consortia. Though great damage was done to English trade, commerce raiding alone did not bring victory to France, nor did it do so in the succeeding Anglo-French wars of the 18th century (*see* FRENCH REVOLUTIONARY WARS). The other side of the picture is that British privateers were very active, particularly ships from BRISTOL and LIVERPOOL, whilst the CHANNEL ISLANDS, close in to the French coast, specialized in privateering and scored many successes. British privateers continued to sail until the end of the NAPOLEONIC WARS. In 1856, at the Peace of Paris, Britain signed an agreement ending privateering. Although some nations, particularly the United States, did not sign, this form of private war had effectively finished.

Privatization As part of its free market policies to reduce the influence of the State, the post-THATCHER Conservative government in 1979 started to sell nationalized (*see* NATIONALIZATION) industries and other public sector activities to private businesses and individuals. BP (British Petroleum) (1979), British Aerospace (1980), British Telecom (1984), National Bus, British Nuclear Fuels, British Steel (1984-5 and 1988), British Gas (1986), British Airways (1986–8), the Trustee Savings Bank (1986), Regional Water Authorities (1989–92), and British Rail (completed 1997) were amongst those wholly or partly sold off, making a new cohort of shareholders among the British public. In addition, local authorities were required to 'contract out' services to private employment and an 'internal market' was established in the NATIONAL HEALTH SERVICE. Privatization was not immediately welcomed even by all those in the Conservative party (Harold MACMILLAN complained of 'selling the family silver'), unease was expressed about the low prices paid, the deterioration of service, the lack of investment and limited powers of the regulators in some industries, but, by 1997 the political consensus was that privatization as a policy was a good thing, bringing greater efficiency and lower consumer costs and, in government, the LABOUR PARTY has given no commitment to roll back the frontiers of the private sector (*see also* ECONOMY; ELECTRICITY INDUSTRY; GAS INDUSTRY; RAILWAYS; TELECOMMUNICATIONS).

Privy Chamber Originally the suite of private apartments at COURT, which evolved for the monarch's greater privacy behind the CHAMBER, the term came to refer to the staff who looked after the monarch in those apartments. Recent research recognizes its political significance. Although HENRY VII had staffed it with the politically innocuous to preserve his political distance, HENRY VIII's extrovert style transformed the institution so that service within it became a political prize. EDWARD VI's Privy Chamber was the scene of struggles for access to and therefore control of the boy-king, but the subsequent reigns of two women reduced its influence. Under JAMES I, the Royal Bedchamber took on similar political importance.

Privy Council The emergence of the Privy Council is complex and controversial (*see*

TUDOR REVOLUTION IN GOVERNMENT). Confusingly, some especially favoured 15th-century royal councillors were called 'privy councillors', but at that date there was no Privy Council as such. However, a small powerful council did emerge from the larger KING'S COUNCIL under HENRY VIII.

Two models of government alternated in his reign: a consortium of advisers, often ill-assorted and quarrelsome; and a single strong minister, such as WOLSEY or Thomas CROMWELL. In 1509, a small group of councillors (not a 'privy council') tried to direct the young king until Wolsey took control. The latter's fall caused confusion which Cromwell never resolved; his schemes for reconstructing the council were complicated by struggles with rivals. After 1537, a small group of leading councillors – several of them Cromwell's enemies – were commonly credited with the title 'privy councillors'; however, it was not until 1540, in reaction to his fall, that a Privy Council was formally set up, initially designed to curb any future Cromwell in the interests of the nobility, who regarded themselves as the king's natural councillors. Except for a brief interval when Somerset (*see* SEYMOUR, EDWARD) monopolized power (1547–9), this remained the main executive body until CHARLES I's reign, when it became too large for effective decision-making. After the RESTORATION power increasingly devolved to specialized departments, such as the TREASURY and ADMIRALTY. The CABINET emerged as an effective inner council within the Privy Council.

The Privy Council still exists, advising the sovereign on the approval of 'ORDERS IN COUNCIL' and on the issuing of royal proclamations; various committees undertake legislative and legal duties for overseas territories of the crown and for certain universities. Membership (which is for life) now consists of all those chosen as British CABINET ministers, and an assortment of eminent people from monarchical countries within the COMMONWEALTH.

Privy Council's Committee on Education Specially created in 1839 to oversee the distribution of the educational grant made to assist the denominational societies in the provision of schools, it was symptomatic of the piecemeal development and supervisory basis of state involvement in EDUCATION. In 1846 the committee proposed the replacement of the MONITORIAL SYSTEM by trained PUPIL-TEACHERS; in that year, too, the parliamentary grant was raised to £100,000, and in 1857 it was further raised to £541,233. The growing role of the state in education was deemed sufficient to justify direct representation in the House of COMMONS. A new office was created under the crown; the holder, who was entitled Vice-President of the Committee of the Privy Council for Education, was in effect the minister for education.

Privy Seal, originally a private seal for the monarch, a replacement for the bureaucratized GREAT SEAL; there is mention of one in JOHN's reign, and even in the earliest extant examples it is one-sided. It was used to seal informal documents, and during the 15th century was increasingly associated with the miscellaneous business of the KING'S COUNCIL. From the reign of EDWARD I it was in the care of a keeper of the Privy Seal, who was first known as lord Privy Seal when Thomas CROMWELL held the office. From his time, it was used for PRIVY COUNCIL business.

Probate, *see* WILLS

Prodigy Houses, an architectural phenomenon of ELIZABETH I's reign: houses built with an eye to royal PROGRESSES. Medieval monarchs had relied much for hospitality on monasteries, and leading gentry and aristocratic families who had benefited from the DISSOLUTION were now expected to shoulder the burden. House layout reflected the needs of a visiting court grafted on to a normal household, and every architectural device was used to express lavish display and grandeur. The architect who set the standards and designed many such houses – e.g. Longleat House, Wilts. and HARDWICK Hall, Derbys. – was Robert Smythson (1535–1614). The term 'prodigy' in this sense comes from the Latin *prodigium*, which originally meant 'portent' and developed to signify something monstrous, out of the ordinary.

Profumo Affair, sexual and espionage scandal in 1962 which was a factor in the demise of MACMILLAN'S CONSERVATIVE government. John Profumo, the minister for war, denied in the COMMONS having had an affair with Christine Keeler; when it was revealed that not only he but also a Russian military attaché had had affairs with her simultaneously, Profumo was forced to resign and the Conservative party suffered long-term damage.

Progresses, Royal, summer tours by the monarch with the aim of meeting the kingdom's subjects. Primitive domestic sewage systems encouraged great medieval and early modern households to keep on the move, while the equally elementary state of royal military force was an incentive for monarchs to pre-empt trouble by making regular royal visits. Progresses – which exported the splendour of the court to impress the provinces (usually at the provinces' expense) – could unite the realm and give people a chance to affirm their loyalty to the monarch.

HENRY VII, ELIZABETH I and JAMES I were assiduous in exploiting progresses. However, EDWARD VI and MARY I were reluctant to make them in the fragile state of provincial order; and HENRY VIII, surprisingly, did not travel north until 1541 – an earlier progress might well have defused the tensions behind the PILGRIMAGE OF GRACE. After the interruption of the CIVIL WARS, progresses resumed, but generally on a more modest scale, and royal visits remain a feature of British ceremonial life. *See also* GIESTS; PRODIGY HOUSES.

Progressive Party, a LIBERAL political organization formed to contest local elections for the LONDON COUNTY COUNCIL in 1889 on a programme of municipal socialism that was calculated to bring working-class supporters closer to Liberalism and Liberalism closer to collectivism. The Progressives held power in the London County Council from 1889–1907, but subsequently fragmented and returned to their Liberal identity as the LABOUR PARTY became the largest party in the capital.

Proletarianization, both a cause and effect of the industrialization process (*see* ECONOMY; INDUSTRIAL REVOLUTION), whereby the population is increasingly divorced from landholding or landownership and becomes largely dependent on the income from waged work in the secondary and tertiary sectors of the economy, often in an urban rather than a rural setting. Proletarianization was a major result of the changes occurring in British AGRICULTURE from the later 17th century and can be seen to have had a major impact upon the supply of labour for industrialization, upon urbanization, the growth of an internal market for manufactured goods, and in influencing the age and rate of MARRIAGE.

Prophesyings, *see* EXERCISES OF PREACHING

Prosopography, the systematic study of a group of individuals' lives and careers, a method developed by Charles A. Beard, an American historian interested in the social basis of American politics, as an alternative to the random accumulation of examples. In an English context, the technique is especially associated with the work of Sir Lewis Namier, and the History of Parliament Trust on the biographies of members of the House of COMMONS.

Prostitution Often now termed 'the sex industry', and in a more traditional cliché, 'the oldest profession', the provision of sexual favours for payment is probably indeed as old as the invention of money. Attitudes to prostitution have varied over time, just as much as general attitudes to gender and sexual identity. Particularly in societies such as the pagan classical West, where women and children were regarded as almost totally passive sexual objects, payment by men for sex with these categories of people had little moral stigma attached to it for either side in the transaction. Once Christianity became the main established religion in the Roman Empire in the 4th century, it exported its more restrictive sexual attitudes to a wider society, but the Church quickly came to establish a paradoxical toleration of prostitution by adult females of low social status. It regarded them as performing a service, contributing to the stability of married life which Christianity prized so much, by diverting men from seduction, rape and HOMOSEXUALITY. The theologian Thomas Aquinas (*c.*1225–74) therefore compared brothels to sewers in a palace: indispensable, but not to be visited if one could possibly help it. As a result, medieval cities possessed brothels with a recognized legal status and official regulation in certain designated localities (*see* STEWS). This toleration ended throughout PROTESTANT and CATHOLIC Europe in the 16th century, as a result of increased official desire to regulate people's lives, and in particular, new anxiety about sexual contact, thanks especially to the series of syphilis EPIDEMICS (*see* VENEREAL DISEASE). Brothels were driven further to the margins of society.

Renewed anxiety was sparked by the rapid expansion of urban life as a result of the INDUSTRIAL REVOLUTION, and by the creation of ever larger STANDING ARMIES (military organizations always providing a ready market for casual sex, both as customer and supplier). This resulted in renewed attempts at regulation, and the passing of the CONTAGIOUS DISEASES ACTS, of 1864, 1866 and 1869, finally repealed in 1886 after prolonged moral agitation by Josephine Butler and other campaigners. Their success was a curious alliance between campaigners for sexual repressiveness, early forms of feminism, socialism, and public anxiety about the exploitation of children. The highly important legislative replacement, the CRIMINAL LAW AMENDMENT ACT 1885, was an attempt to outlaw brothels, but it also raised the female age of consent for sexual intercourse to 16 and introduced new penalties against male homosexual behaviour. This connection between legislation on prostitution and homosexuality would persist into 20th-century Britain. The 1885 Act's effect was to disperse rather than destroy prostitution, both female and male. The Street Offences Act 1959 was one of the most prominent in a series of feeble legislative attempts to deal with this by drastically raising penalties for prostitution in public; but once more it merely led to a reorganization of the industry. The ambivalence of feminism towards female prostitution has continued, with disagreement as to whether it is a form of male exploitation or an assertion of female earning power.

Protectionists, a dissident CONSERVATIVE political grouping that derived its name from a society for the protection of AGRICULTURE established in 1844 in opposition to the ANTI-CORN LAW LEAGUE. It was led by Lord George Bentinck and DISRAELI but lacked cohesion and commitment. The Protectionists, following the disruption of the party over the abandonment of the CORN LAWS, quickly came to accept the finality of repeal. Disraeli and Edward STANLEY, Earl of Derby, both recognized that it had become a serious obstacle to a Conservative electoral revival.

Protector, Lord, title adopted in royal minorities, designed to avoid the granting of virtually full royal powers that would be involved in the creation of a regency. Lord protectorship was exercised by HUMPHREY OF GLOUCESTER (1422–9), RICHARD OF YORK (1454–5), Richard of Gloucester (the future RICHARD III) (1483) and Edward SEYMOUR, Duke of Somerset (1547–9). Despite these mostly dismal precedents, the title was also adopted by Oliver CROMWELL from 1654–9 (hence the designation of this period the Protectorate) to resolve the conundrum of government during the INTERREGNUM.

Protectorate, *see* INTERREGNUM; PROTECTOR, LORD

Protestant, *see* PROTESTANTISM

Protestant Ascendancy, term retrospectively applied to the Anglo-Irish ruling class, who dominated the Irish PARLIAMENT during its heyday, 1692–1800. The term was first popularized by the corporation of Dublin in the early 1790s – then denoting a political order privileging Protestants, which the incorporated tradesmen and artisans of Dublin were anxious to defend against Catholic counterclaims. Subsequently (and now commonly in the historiography) it came to be applied to the ruling class within that order. Successive waves of settlement from England and Scotland in the 16th and 17th centuries determined that by 1700 some quarter of the Irish population was of relatively recent English or Scottish origin. Unlike the native Irish and 'Old English', these New English (*see* PLANTATIONS IN IRELAND) settlers were overwhelmingly Protestant: chiefly adherents of the 'Anglican' CHURCH OF IRELAND, or PRESBYTERIANS. They constituted a majority of the population of ULSTER, and diminishingly significant minorities in LEINSTER, MUNSTER and CONNACHT. Their share of Irish land had been greatly increased by CROMWELL's land grants, diminished somewhat by the 1662 Act of SETTLEMENT, then increased again by land confiscations arising from KING WILLIAM'S WAR, stabilizing at about 86 per cent. Major landowners comprised some 5,000 major gentry families. The structure of Irish rural society was different from that of contemporary England. At its base, smallholders often subsisted on tiny parcels of land; 'middlemen' often interpolated between landlords and subletting smallholders. Many landowners, including some of the largest, were absentees, resident in England. English observers judged Irish GENTRY (in a broad sense) sociable but uncouth; some blamed them for the underdevelopment of the country, and were horrified by incidents of casual brutality to inferiors. In fact 'improvers' were by no means absent: the DUBLIN SOCIETY was pioneering in its interest in schemes for economic and social development.

Though its hegemony was in large part a function of property ownership, the Anglo-Irish élite also benefited from an array of laws and practices excluding the mass of the population, including propertied Catholics and DISSENTERS, from political power and limiting their civil rights. Catholics were excluded from Irish parliaments after WILLIAM III's victory over the Catholic JAMES II. Triumphant Protestants then consolidated their position with a battery of PENAL LAWS, barring Catholics from public office and depriving them of the vote, as well as limiting their rights to hold property and to educate their children, and imposing severe restraints and penalties on Catholic clergy. Legal restrictions played an important part in making towns a Protestant power base: Catholic rights to own urban property and hold civic office were both restricted. Ulster Presbyterians also received short shrift from overwhelmingly Church of Ireland MPs mindful of the levelling inclinations sometimes shown by radical Protestants: their rights to hold public office were also limited by a sacramental test.

In the 18th century, Irish parliaments usually met biennially, whereas previously they had met rarely. The enhanced role of parliament increased the power of the Anglo-Irish gentry, the largest group within it, in national affairs. Until the 1760s, the lord lieutenant was an absentee, and Irish politics was dominated by a group of political managers called UNDERTAKERS – though self-government was limited by POYNINGS' LAW and the British Parliament's claim of power to legislate for Ireland, affirmed in the DECLARATORY ACT. Resentment at such subordination, and at the allied subordination of Irish to British economic interests, recurrently sparked controversy, as over WOOD'S HALFPENCE, or in the IRISH CRISIS OF 1753–6. The triumph of the campaign for Irish LEGISLATIVE INDEPENDENCE in 1782 fell short of meeting all Anglo-Irish aspirations – frustrated by the lord lieutenant's continuing ability to influence parliament, some agitated for PARLIAMENTARY REFORM. The Ascendancy also divided in this period in their attitudes to Catholic pressure for relief from penal laws. Some were happy to incorporate CATHOLIC EMANCIPATION into their reforming vision; others were rather more worried that Catholics in power might undermine the position of the Church of Ireland, and Protestant titles to Irish land. Protestant townsmen, though vigorous 'PATRIOTS', were often equally fiercely dedicated to upholding the Protestant regime.

After the FRENCH REVOLUTION, a growing tide of rural unrest, manifest once in WHITEBOY, more recently in the DEFENDER movement, fused with political radicalism under the leadership of originally largely Protestant UNITED IRISHMEN. Catholics were dominant in the risings, as in the population at large, but there were also risings in Ulster, and Protestant supporters elsewhere. A few scions of the Anglo-Irish gentry, notably Lord Edward FITZGERALD, promoted rebellion in 1798 (*see* IRISH REBELLION), but more supported yeomanry forces and troops which quelled risings at the cost of some 20,000 dead. A majority of MPs, and the class they represented, probably opposed the Act of UNION which amalgamated the Irish into a new imperial parliament in 1801, but the Anglo-Irish élite had failed to demonstrate to the British government's satisfaction their ability semi-autonomously to rule a changing Ireland within the framework of the British imperial system.

Protestant Association, formed in 1780 to resist any measure of CATHOLIC EMANCIPATION in Scotland, and to campaign for the repeal of the English 1778 Catholic Relief Act, which had itself repealed only certain exceptionally repressive laws. Lord George Gordon was elected president in Nov. In 1780 the Association organized a petitioning campaign; its march to Parliament to present the petition precipitated the GORDON RIOTS. Although the Association itself survived this cataclysm, it had no further influence on public events.

Protestant Methodists, *see* METHODISM

Protestant Succession, descent of the crown through Protestant heirs only. After the GLORIOUS REVOLUTION of 1688–9, the coronation oath was amended to incorporate a promise to uphold the 'Protestant reformed religion established by law'. The 1701 Act of SETTLEMENT provided that, on the death of Queen ANNE, the crown should pass to her nearest Protestant relative: failing the survival of an heir of her body, to Sophia, Electress of Hanover, or her descendants. This legislation provided the basis for the HANOVERIAN SUCCESSION.

Protestantism, the view of Christian belief derived from the 16th-century REFORMATION. It stresses the central place of the Bible as the only source of God's revealed truth, and is suspicious of anything which represents a possible alternative route to salvation, such as the powers of clergy and of church institutional structures, ritual or the aesthetic contemplation of beauty. The name derives from the formal 'Protestation' made by a minority of LUTHERAN-sympathizing princes at the Imperial Diet of Speyer in 1529 against decisions taken by the CATHOLIC majority. The CHURCH OF SCOTLAND and the FREE CHURCHes have always proclaimed their Protestant belief; the ANGLICAN tradition has been more hesitant, at least since the influence of the OXFORD MOVEMENT. However, such was the force of ANTI-CATHOLICISM in England before 1800 that most contemporaries were uninhibited about referring to the CHURCH OF ENGLAND as Protestant. *See also* EVANGELICALISM.

Protestantism, Magisterial, *see* MAGISTERIAL PROTESTANTISM

Proto-Industrialization, historian's term for a supposed stage in economic development when manufacturing industries – chiefly textiles and metalwork – were carried on in workers' homes, sometimes in conjunction with farming activity, but products were intended for distant markets (*see* PUTTING OUT). It has been hypothesized that this phase of industrial development brought forward the conditions necessary for the development of FACTORY-based industries. These included the accumulation of capital, skills and knowledge of markets as well as a growing labour supply through population growth encouraged by rising incomes. Especially associated with the 17th and 18th centuries, proto-industry was concentrated in particular regions. Examples include: weaving in East Anglia, parts of the West Country, Yorks., Lancs. and Ulster; and metalworking in the Birmingham region.

Historians of proto-industrialization have taken a broad view of its causes and effects, exploring its association with particular kinds of terrain, patterns of cultivation, tenurial regimes and rates of POPULATION growth. Attempts to develop simple models of the proto-industrialization process have failed – proto-industry flourished in diverse conditions and had diverse effects – but the attempt to devise and test such models has stimulated fruitful research.

Provence, Eleanor of, *see* ELEANOR OF PROVENCE

Providence Island Company, founded in 1629 by PURITAN aristocrats – Robert RICH, Earl of Warwick, Francis Russell, Earl of Bedford, and William Fiennes, Viscount Saye and Sele – to settle Providence Island (off the coast of modern Nicaragua) as a PRIVATEERING base against Spain. Business meetings provided a useful liaison for the 1630s' opposition to CHARLES I. The island was captured by the Spanish in 1642, and the company went bankrupt; its last meeting took place in 1650.

Provisional IRA, *see* IRISH REPUBLICAN ARMY

Provisions of Oxford, 1258, a set of reform proposals imposed on HENRY III by a group of magnates irritated by his incompetence, who took advantage of his mismanagement of the SICILIAN ADVENTURE. The effect of the Provisions was to take power out of the king's hands and establish instead a governing council responsible to the baronage in Parliament. In 1261, Henry – taking advantage of dissension caused by the PROVISIONS OF WESTMINSTER – repudiated his oath to abide by the Oxford Provisions.

Provisions of Westminster, 1259. A set of reforms principally concerned with English local administration, they marked the obvious next step in the baronial reform programme once the PROVISIONS OF OXFORD had dealt with central government. But whereas most magnates were happy to see royal administration (both central and local) overhauled, many were disturbed by the prospect of interference with seigneurial (i.e. their own) administration. Thus although these provisions were, as Simon de MONTFORT recognized, popular with the gentry, they tended to split the ranks of the aristocracy. This division of magnate opinion enabled HENRY III to undermine the Provisions in 1261 and so set in train the sequence of events that led to the BARONS' WAR.

Provisors, Statutes of, 1351, 1390, enactments intended to curb the pope's practice of providing his own nominees to lucrative BENEFICES in the English CHURCH. Petitions to PARLIAMENT indicate the widespread unpopularity of these 'provisions'. Both EDWARD III and RICHARD II exploited this to bring diplomatic pressure on the papacy. *See also* PRAEMUNIRE, STATUTES OF.

Provost (from Latin *praepositus*). A term used in Scotland for the presiding officer in BURGHS, equivalent to the English or Irish MAYOR; in England certain heads of UNIVERSITY colleges, and the head of Eton College, use the title. In the CHURCH OF ENGLAND the word is used to describe the presiding clergyman in the CATHEDRALS of DIOCESES where the cathedral also remains a PARISH church; his equivalent in older non-parochial cathedrals is the DEAN.

Pseudo-Gentry, a term coined by the historian Alan Everitt to describe town dwellers who lived in the style of the GENTRY, but without a substantial landed base. They might include impoverished landowners, retired merchants, officers on half-pay, substantial clergy, lawyers, doctors, widows of wealthy tradesmen, or independent women with private incomes. The term has commended itself to other historians largely because it seems to capture such people's self-image better than the term middle class.

Public Accounts, Commissioners for Examining the Building on previous attempts to enhance parliamentary control over public expenditure, PARLIAMENT elected a public accounts committee during every session from 1690–7. Those elected were chiefly opposition MPs. They were paid a salary of £500, and empowered to examine on oath. Their inquiries fuelled COUNTRY PARTY hostility to the executive. Further such appointments were made in 1702 and 1711–14.

In 1781, NORTH tried to deflect parliamentary demand for ECONOMICAL REFORM by appointing commissioners to audit the public accounts. These commissioners were asked not merely to look for abuses, but also to recommend better methods of keeping accounts, so that more accurate statements could be made to Parliament. The commission issued 15 reports, recommending restructuring in various government departments, before it lapsed in 1786. PITT THE YOUNGER acted on their recommendations, but because he did not wish to deprive living office-holders of their posts, the pace of change was slow, though much had been achieved by the time of Pitt's death in 1806.

Public Health The public health movement developed out of a growing concern about the rise in POPULATION and the rapid movement of rural workers to fast industrializing cities that lacked basic services and amenities. EPIDEMIC disease, high DEATH RATES and low LIFE EXPECTANCY, and degradation, physical and moral, underlined the inadequacies of existing arrangements. Fears of disorder gave the concerns of the propertied classes a political dimension which made reform urgent as well as desirable. It was this mood which was so successfully exploited by Edwin Chadwick and the BENTHAMITE reformers – doctors, statisticians and social reformers – during the 1830s and 40s. The revelations contained in his *REPORT ON THE SANITARY CONDITION OF THE LABOURING POPULATION* in 1842 provoked an outcry which prompted the PUBLIC HEALTH ACT 1848. Opinion in favour of centrally administered preventative medicine, checked by Chadwick's excesses as secretary to the Board of Public Health, recovered under the impetus of the social reformer Sir John Simon (1816–1904) and found expression in the development of a unified public health administration with the LOCAL GOVERNMENT ACT 1871, the PUBLIC HEALTH

ACT 1872 and in the further consolidation sanctioned by the PUBLIC HEALTH ACT 1875. Theirs was no unqualified victory. Overall the public health did improve in the last quarter of the 19th century. Nevertheless, the votaries of dirt and disease, usually in the guise of defenders of local rights against state CENTRALIZATION, were skilful and resourceful and capable of protracted guerilla warfare. There is also a class-specific aspect to the public health movement to consider. Piped water and sewerage systems came to wealthy suburbs a generation before they were introduced among the urban poor. The historian F. B. Smith argues that the channelling of the refuse of the rich into rivers which supplied water for the poor may have maintained the high typhoid, CHOLERA, diptheria and gastro-enteritis rate among the latter. The 20th-century PLANNING movement subsequently grew out of the 19th-century public health movement. *See also* HOUSING; POVERTY; SANITARY REFORM MOVEMENT; SLUM CLEARANCE; WELFARE STATE.

Public Health Acts 1848, 1872, 1875, designed to improve sanitary administration. An outgrowth of the SANITARY REFORM MOVEMENT, the Public Health Act of 1848 provided for the formation of a central board of health analogous to the POOR LAW Board, with powers to create local boards to oversee street cleansing, refuse collection, water supply and sewerage systems. Permissive in character and preventative in method, the Act offended the interests of ratepayers, was considered suspect by local authorities resentful of any form of centralized interference, and alienated medical opinion by its inattention to contagionist theories or curative measures. The Public Health Act of 1872 transferred the responsibilities of the local board of health and IMPROVEMENT commissioners to newly created urban sanitary authorities who were required to appoint one or more medical officers of health and inspectors of nuisances. In 1875, a further Public Health Act amended and consolidated the earlier acts and gave local sanitary authorities wider powers of enforcement in relation to drainage, sanitation and water supplies; for this purpose all authorities were required to employ health inspectors. Sanitary reformers, however, were disappointed in the failure to provide for the creation of a central ministry of health.

Public Order Act 1936 Passed in the wake of the 'battle' of CABLE STREET, the Act was designed to limit disorder caused by the activities of the British Union of FASCISTS. It gave the home secretary the power to ban marches in the London area and police chief constables could apply to him for bans elsewhere. The Act made it an offence to wear political uniforms, and tightened up the law on threatening and abusive words or behaviour.

Public Record Office (PRO), central state and official archive for England and Wales, established in 1838 and housed in Chancery Lane, London. The office was built between 1851 and 1896, appropriately on the site of the Rolls Chapel since the Master of the Rolls, the senior judge in CIVIL LAW, had official guardianship of the records of the state. A new building for the PRO's post-1800 holdings was built at Kew in 1973–7 and the entire holdings were moved there in 1996. The equivalent archive for Scotland is housed in the General Register Office, Edinburgh. The Public Record Office for Ireland was burned in 1922 during the IRISH CIVIL WAR, thus destroying many of the nation's earlier archives.

Public Schools, in the British tradition, at least since the 18th century, fee-paying schools catering for the sons (and much later daughters) of the landed and wealthy. Many schools have ancient foundations, e.g. Winchester, founded by WILLIAM OF WYKEHAM, or Eton, founded by HENRY VI; many more were established as a result of local initiatives in the Tudor period. The curricular diet of the classics, and a noted regime of bullying and violent punishment, scarred many pupils both emotionally and physically. Reform of public schools, in ethos, discipline, and study, is particularly associated with the 'muscular Christianity' of Thomas Arnold at Rugby, and the network of ANGLICAN 'proprietary' boarding schools launched by the Revd Nathaniel Woodard in the late 1840s, of which Lancing, Sussex was the prototype and focus. Old charitable foundations were relaunched, while charitable organizations like the Girls Public Day

Schools' Company (later Trust) promoted public school education for girls from the 1860s. Public schools in the 20th century have come to be associated with the establishment, that amorphous institution which is usually supposed to ensure that the 'right people', from the best schools, universities, army regiments, etc., secure the best positions. The 1964–70 LABOUR government appointed a royal commission on public schools and also phased out the direct grant system which linked many endowed schools to the state system. This did not, however, have the effect of shrinking the private education sector, and issues of private education and the abolition of public schools remain divisive political questions. *See also* EDUCATION.

Public Utilities, industries which are regarded as particularly significant because their outputs are considered essential. Thus GAS and water were originally the industries which were seen as 'the public utilities', later joined by ELECTRICITY. Gas and water were largely developed in the 19th century by municipal and local authorities, hence the expression public utilities carries two sorts of meaning: that they should be widely available and that they derive from the public domain. The technology of production and distribution of these goods tends to produce natural MONOPOLIES, so that public ownership was seen as a solution to the possible exploitation which monopoly might bring about. However, in the United States and since the 1980s in many European countries, including Britain, these industries have been privatized. The significant market power enjoyed by the utilities in these cases is supposedly constrained by legal regulation.

Public Works Loan Board Created in 1817, the Board's purpose was to advance money, subject to the approval of the Treasury, to municipal authorities for public works such as housing schemes. Public utility societies were also eligible for such assistance. Local authority take-up was limited because of the onerous repayment conditions that were imposed.

Puddling and Rolling These processes, developed by Henry Cort in the 1770s–80s, allowed the conversion of large quantities of pig iron into refined bar iron. Whereas open-hearth refining required the use of charcoal, puddling could be coal-fuelled, an advantage when timber supplies were limited but COAL mining was developing. Puddling involved the decarbonizing of pig iron in a reverberatory furnace: carbon from the iron combined with oxygen from clinkers rich in iron oxide, and the malleable iron thus produced was drawn out in a rolling mill, after which it could be cut into bars. The chemistry underlying these operations was not understood until the 19th century. *See also* IRON AND STEEL INDUSTRY.

Punishment The type of punishment handed out to criminals has changed markedly over time. From the 18th century there was a decline in the old shaming punishments (e.g. stocks, the ducking stool) used to inflict humiliation on offenders. These were most effective in stable face-to-face communities, although they were also seen as less appropriate with new ideas about individual bodily rights, and about reform and rehabilitation rather than retribution. There was a decline in retributive punishments designed to fit the precise offence, and wider use of pardons and TRANSPORTATION instead of hanging. The major shift in the nature and idea of punishment in modern times came with the rise of the prison system. There were precursors from the late 16th century but the classic period of design and construction of the national prison network came in the 19th century (*see* PRISON REFORM). The idea behind the prison was that of reform through labour discipline and solitary contemplation, and some historians have seen a marked association between the development of the coercive prison and of the FACTORY and the inculcation of industrial work habits and labour discipline in wider society. Prisons never appear to have achieved the desired effect of reform of individuals, and experience of prison is often associated with the hardening of the criminal class. The tensions between retribution and reform which prison represents have also never been resolved, despite abolition of the death penalty in 1965 (*see* CAPITAL PUNISHMENT).

Punks, name given to fashionable youth group of the 1970s who were followers of the crude, self-consciously discordant music known as 'punk' rock, played by such groups as the Sex Pistols. Punks developed a style of dress characterized by black leather, dyed and outlandish hairstyles, and sado-masochistic accessories such as zips, safety-pins, and studs on both the body and clothing. The movement, which was oppositional both in terms of class and cultural politics, was an extravagant outgrowth from the 'biker' gear of the ROCKERS, without the motor-bikes.

Pupil-Teacher System, a method of training teachers developed by Sir James Kay-Shuttleworth, secretary to the PRIVY COUNCIL'S COMMITTEE ON EDUCATION, who had seen a variant operating in Holland and considered it superior to the MONITORIAL SYSTEM developed by Andrew Bell and Joseph Lancaster. It was officially introduced into the education system in 1846. Potential recruits selected from amongst pupils had to be at least 13 years old before they could begin their training. Apprentices were required to assist the teacher in the classroom during the day and study in the evenings. After five years and the successful passage of an entrance examination, they enrolled at a teacher-training college with a Queen's scholarship to finance further study. Pupil-teachers who failed the examination became assistant teachers.

Purgatory, the intermediate state between heaven and hell that provides an opportunity for further purging of sin after death. Based on 3rd-century AD Alexandrian scholarly speculation, the idea offered a welcome second chance in the afterlife, and prayers for souls in purgatory became a dominant cult in medieval western theology (*see* CHANTRIES); accordingly the 16th-century PROTESTANT reformers made purgatory a chief target of hatred. It plays a much diminished role in modern CATHOLIC theology.

Puritanism This term is difficult to define, but Puritans are easy to recognize; the difficulty arises because the word 'Puritan' was appropriated in the mid-1560s as a term of abuse and was rarely used by the subjects of the description.

Under ELIZABETH I, Puritans comprised those in the Church of England unhappy with the limitations of the ELIZABETHAN SETTLEMENT; some were PRESBYTERIANS, and all were to some extent CALVINISTS (though not all Calvinists were Puritans). They tended to favour plain styles of dress, and lived lives of strict morality. Common features of their attitudes towards the Church were their insistence on the urgency of re-creating the clergy as a preaching body, and their suspicion of ceremony in worship (*see* VESTIARIAN CONTROVERSIES); confusingly, many of their opponents in the Church hierarchy sympathized with these concerns.

Later, LAUDIANS extended the word to describe anyone who opposed their views, including SEPARATISTS who would not have been termed Puritans under Elizabeth; it became a convenient catch-all label for the disparate groups who led much NEW WORLD colonization and won the English CIVIL WARS. Given that success, a great puzzle of the 17th century is the collapse of Puritan militancy after the RESTORATION. *See also* SABBATARIANISM.

Purveyance, the crown's right to provisions from subjects. Corruption by the officials (purveyors) who collected these provisions was a constant medieval and early modern grievance, and although ELIZABETH I'S government negotiated local agreements ('compositions'), trouble predictably flared up again under JAMES I and CHARLES I. Modern wartime conditions saw the revival of similar compulsory purchase schemes.

Putney Debates, the discussions about reconstructing post-war England held at Putney Church and Whitehall in London by the victorious NEW MODEL ARMY in 1647–8. Those involved included senior officers and rank-and-file representatives (confusingly called 'agitators', meaning 'agents'). LEVELLER proposals were among those considered. There was little concrete outcome.

Putting-Out Industrial work was said to be 'put out' when merchant-manufacturers retained ownership of the raw materials – such as iron, wool or yarn – but consigned them to workers working in their homes or small workshops at one or more stages in the production process, such as in nailmaking, spinning or weaving. It represented an alternative to the form of 'domestic industry' in which small producers purchased their own materials, and sold their own products. Putting-out developed from the 14th and 15th centuries; it was common in the West Country WOOLLEN INDUSTRY, and the Yorks. worsted industry by the late 17th century; in the Yorks. woollen industry, by contrast, independent small producers remained the norm until the rise of the FACTORY. *See also* PROTO-INDUSTRIALIZATION.

Pym, John (?1584–1643), politician. An Oxford-educated Somerset man, he was – as an MP in the Parliaments of the 1620s – bitterly critical of government. In the LONG PARLIAMENT, he was a leading militant against CHARLES I, spearheading LAUD's and WENTWORTH's IMPEACHMENTS and eventually rejecting conciliatory offers of the chancellorship of the Exchequer.

He backed the ROOT AND BRANCH Bill and helped draft the GRAND REMONSTRANCE of 1641. Named first amongst the FIVE MEMBERS Charles tried to seize in 1642, he directed the setting-up of governmental, military and financial administrations to support the war against Charles, and determinedly pursued alliance with the Scots before his early death from cancer.

Pytheas of Marseilles (*fl. c.*310 BC), Greek navigator. His account of a voyage from Greece to the coasts of Spain, France and Britain supplies the earliest written evidence of the existence of the British Isles. His dramatic story of cold and fog may indicate that he sailed as far as the Arctic. The mysterious island of 'Thule', which he mentions finding to the north, was generally equated with Iceland during the Middle Ages, but it is possible that he travelled no further than the Shetlands.

Q

Quadruple Alliance Britain, France and the United Provinces, having formed the TRIPLE ALLIANCE in 1717 to maintain the settlement made by the peace of UTRECHT, were joined by the Holy Roman Emperor the following year. The four agreed on 2 Aug. 1718 that the king of Spain should return Sardinia, which Spain had invaded in 1717, to the emperor and renounce his claim to the French succession. Britain and France promised aid to the emperor to capture Sicily, which he was then to be assigned in exchange for Sardinia. France and the emperor guaranteed the PROTESTANT SUCCESSION in Britain, and the four powers agreed to assist one another in the event of attack. With the Spanish preparing for an Italian war, Admiral George Byng was sent in 1718 to try to stop the Spanish fleet from joining in, and France declared war in 1719. The Spanish responded by backing a JACOBITE invasion force but this was stopped by storms. With the dismissal of Cardinal Alberoni in Dec. 1719 Spanish policy changed, and in Jan. 1720 Spain joined the Quadruple Alliance under terms which provided for a congress to discuss territorial disputes.

Quadruple Treaty, 1834, a treaty which arose out of dynastic disturbances in Spain and Portugal and from Palmerston's (*see* TEMPLE, HENRY) concern to prevent French interference therein. Signed in London by representatives of Great Britain, France, Spain and Portugal, the treaty secured the Spanish throne for Isabella II. Palmerston, who had sent troops to help expel the Miguelists from Portugal and the Carlists from Spain, regarded it as a useful means of preventing France from taking unilateral action in Spain as well as an unqualified triumph for his personal diplomacy.

Quaker Act 1662 The Act imposed penalties on anyone who maintained that the taking of an OATH was unlawful or contrary to God, refused to take an oath or tried to persuade another to refuse. It was also made an offence for more than five adult QUAKERS to assemble under pretence of worship not authorized by law; a third conviction could be punished by TRANSPORTATION.

Quakers A religious grouping founded in the 1650s by George FOX, which gained its nickname after Fox told a judge to tremble at the name of the Lord. He called them 'Friends of the Truth', and the sect itself adopted the name 'Religious Society of Friends' in the late 18th century. Friends shun liturgical and sacramental worship, spending their time in their meetings in 'waiting on the Lord'; they reject a professional ministry, seeking God's inner light in the individual. As part of the INTERREGNUM's radical fringe, and because of their association with FIFTH MONARCHISTS, they attracted much alarm and persecution in Britain and the New World; this continued until the 1689 TOLERATION ACT, particularly because of their distinctive code of dress and manners and their refusal to observe contemporary status distinctions, to swear OATHS or to pay TITHES to the Established Church. William Penn, himself a Quaker, founded PENNSYLVANIA as a NEW WORLD refuge in 1682.

Many Friends – including the banking families of Lloyd, Barclay, Hoare and Gurney – prospered in commerce, quickly gaining respect for their honesty in business; in the late 18th and early 19th centuries they were prominent in philanthropic and reform movements, particularly in the ANTI-SLAVERY and PRISON REFORM campaigns. During the 19th century they abandoned some of their outward conventions such as distinctive dress. In the 20th century, their pacifist commitment (*see also* CONSCIEN-

TIOUS OBJECTORS) is reminiscent of their original radicalism.

Quebec, originally a French colony in North America, which was taken by WOLFE in 1759 during the SEVEN YEARS WAR. It became a part of Britain's possessions within CANADA, for a period known as Lower Canada, and eventually a province within the DOMINION. Quebec remains a strongly Francophone region, and there have been many movements for its independence. *See also* CANADA ACTS; QUEBEC ACT 1774.

Quebec Act 1774 This laid down the terms by which the colony of QUEBEC – conquered from the French in 1759, and definitively delivered into British hands in 1763 – was to be governed. The Act was intended to help reconcile the French *habitants* of Quebec to British rule: it provided for the retention of French civil (but not criminal) law, and the payment of tithes to the Catholic Church. But these very provisions, and the Act's failure to establish an elected assembly, alienated sections of British, American and Canadian feeling. Opponents of the government sometimes classed the Act among the INTOLERABLE ACTS that precipitated the War of AMERICAN INDEPENDENCE. The fact that the *habitants* remained, by and large, loyal to the British during the war suggests, however, that the Act was not entirely misjudged. *See also* CANADA.

Quebec Conferences, Anglo-American summit conferences between CHURCHILL and Roosevelt during WORLD WAR II. The first was held in Aug. 1943 and agreed the date for the opening of the Second Front in France as May 1944 (*see* D-DAY; OVERLORD, OPERATION). It also established Anglo-American co-operation in the Manhattan Project to develop an atomic bomb, and created a South-east Asia Command to co-ordinate the war in BURMA. The second, less important, Quebec conference was held in Sept. 1944 in the run-up to the YALTA conference. There was inconclusive discussion about the future of Germany, and Britain agreed to send a fleet to assist in the Pacific war against Japan.

Queen Anne's Bounty, a fund established in 1704 for the relief of the poorer ANGLICAN clergy, by making grants to livings with an income of less than £10 p.a. (raised in 1788 to £35). The fund was fed by the proceeds of the FIRST FRUITS AND TENTHS, allocated to it by Queen ANNE; from 1809, it was augmented by parliamentary grants. In 1948, the managers of the fund and the ECCLESIASTICAL COMMISSION were merged to form the Church Commissioners.

Queen's Bench, *see* KING'S BENCH

Queen's Counsel, *see* BARRISTER

Queensland Discovered by COOK in 1770 and first explored from NEW SOUTH WALES in the 1810s, Queensland became a new convict colony in AUSTRALIA from 1823 (*see* TRANSPORTATION). Hesitant early growth was followed by substantial migration from Britain after 1850, aided by the GOLD RUSH. SUGAR, planted from the 1860s, joined ranching as the economic mainstay. The 1890s depression fostered radical labour politics, although in recent times Queensland has been more noted for conservatism.

Quit Claim of Canterbury, *see* FALAISE, TREATY OF

Quo Warranto Latin term meaning 'By what warrant?', used to refer to a royal WRIT inquiring into the basis of claims of privilege, such as those of FRANCHISES. The writ was much employed in the 13th century; many of the most powerful English nobles regarded these inquiries as aggressive intrusions into their traditional rights, and they significantly contributed to the sometimes tense relationship between crown and aristocracy during the reigns of HENRY III and EDWARD I. The resentment was addressed in the Statute of *Quo Warranto* (1290), which allowed that a claim of long use for a privilege was acceptable.

CHARLES II and JAMES II revived the writ in order to attack the independence of BOROUGHS. It was easy for the monarchy to detect some technical infringement of the terms of the corporation's CHARTER; this could then be confiscated, and a new charter issued with provisions for the corporation and the electoral franchise to be more closely controlled by central authority. These reissued charters were overturned and nearly all the old ones restored after the GLORIOUS REVOLUTION.

R

Race Relations Acts 1965, 1968, 1976 The 1965 Act, introduced by the WILSON government, against a background of increased IMMIGRATION from the Caribbean and Indian subcontinent in the 1950s, banned discrimination against any national or racial group in hotels or public places and set up a Race Relations Board to investigate complaints. Incitement to racial hatred by written or spoken words was made an offence. Further Acts in 1968 and 1976 made racial discrimination illegal in housing, employment and insurance or financial services. A permanent Race Relations Commission was established in 1976 to promote equality of opportunity and multicultural activities. In addition, the Public Order Act (1986) made it a criminal offence to incite racial hatred, while the Crime and Disorder Act (1998) created new offences of racial harrassment and racially motivated violence.

Rachmanism, name coined in the late 1950s for the policy of intimidating tenants or charging extortionate rents to secure their removal, associated with property developer Peter Rachman. Shortage of rented accommodation and decontrol of rents in the 1957 RENT ACT were widely blamed for Rachmanism and other malpractices. The LABOUR government elected in 1964 brought in a new Rent Act in 1965 which reintroduced controls over most privately owned unfurnished accommodation.

Radar (radio detecting and ranging), a system for detecting distant objects, such as aircraft. Pioneered by Sir Robert Watson Watt, it works by sending out a radio signal, which is reflected back by solid objects and picked up as a blip on the screen of a cathode-ray tube. In 1936 a system of radar location stations was begun around the southern and eastern coasts of England which was completed in time for use during WORLD WAR II. Early location of incoming enemy planes proved of decisive assistance during the Battle of BRITAIN. The development of airborne and shipborne radar also proved of immense value in the Battle of the ATLANTIC and as directional aids for the BOMBING OFFENSIVE against Germany. Although developed independently by the Germans, the British (and American) lead in radar proved a major factor in their ultimate victory. After the war it became standard equipment, with both military and civil applications.

Radicals and Radicalism The term 'radicalism' was first used in the 1820s to describe the movement for fundamental political reform, especially PARLIAMENTARY REFORM, which had developed in the previous century, associated with such men as WILKES, Wyvill and Burdett, and such organizations as the SOCIETY FOR CONSTITUTIONAL INFORMATION and the LONDON CORRESPONDING SOCIETY. Radicals also agitated for the preservation and extension of civil liberties, and opposed what they saw as unjust legislation, such as the GAME LAWS; from the late 1780s, they were also associated with the campaign for the abolition of the SLAVE TRADE.

The economic disruption of the early 19th century led Radicals to concentrate on campaigns for electoral reform to alleviate economic and social distress. In contrast to 'moderate' parliamentary reformers, the radical agenda was for manhood suffrage and annual parliaments as surety that their demands would be met by parliamentary action. The most prominent Radicals were Henry Hunt, Francis BURDETT, William COBBETT and Thomas Attwood. Increasingly, the old-style Radicalism of the CORRESPON-

DING SOCIETIES was becoming a mass movement and drawing support from new areas of industrial growth. By 1829 every major industrial city had its own political union, based on Thomas Attwood's Birmingham Political Union, and the growing economic distress swelled their ranks. After the disappointment of the 1832 REFORM ACT, which had satisfied none of the Radicals' demands, support realigned behind William LOVETT's *People's Charter*, and it was the CHARTIST movement that largely absorbed the Radicals until its collapse in 1848 and 1849. In the later 19th century, Radicals were an important element of the LIBERAL party, particularly its NONCONFORMITY-associated policy and Joseph CHAMBERLAIN's programme of 'municipal socialism' in Birmingham in the 1870s, culminating in the 1885 Unauthorized Programme. Chamberlain carried this tradition into the LIBERAL UNIONIST Conservative Alliance where it found echo with Randolph Churchill's ideas of TORY DEMOCRACY. LLOYD GEORGE's social reform programme of 1906–11 seemed to fulfil radical intentions, but by World War I, the politically-conscious working-class vote sought not just measures of social reform but a fundamental restructuring of the economic and social system.

Radio, *see* BBC; TELECOMMUNICATIONS

Radmen, an Anglo-Saxon category of men, found only in *DOMESDAY BOOK* survey of the English counties bordering Wales. They owed services to their lords as riders and messengers, and seem also to have been required to plough.

RAF, *see* ROYAL AIR FORCE

Ragged Schools Developed from the initiative of John Pounds, a Portsmouth shoemaker who from 1818 had undertaken the teaching of deprived children, these schools charged no fees and gave the poorest vagabond children a basic education with practical skills. The Ragged School Union, formed in 1844, brought the movement together under the patronage of Anthony Ashley Cooper, Lord Shaftesbury. In 1852 there were 132 ragged schools in LONDON (with 26,000 children) and 70 in other large urban centres. By 1870 there were 250 such schools in London and over 100 in the provinces. They were absorbed into the BOARD SCHOOLS thereafter but in the interval had exerted a beneficial influence in the fight for basic LITERACY.

Ragnall (?–921), King of York. A grandson of IVAR THE BONELESS with connections with DUBLIN, Ragnall appeared in northern England in the early 910s, won the two battles of CORBRIDGE and had, by 919, established himself as king of YORK. Although, the following year, he acknowledged the overlordship of EDWARD THE ELDER, his whole career demonstrates the enduring capacity for renewal of the VIKING colony at York.

Ragnar Lothbrok (?–850s), VIKING warrior. A mixture of historical and legendary sources suggest that his piratical activities took him to Ireland, France and NORTHUMBRIA, and that it was in the last that he was killed. He may well have established a pattern of activity followed by his sons HALFDAN and IVAR THE BONELESS who led the GREAT ARMY of 865.

Raid of Ruthven, *see* RUTHVEN RAID

Railway Act 1844, *see* RAILWAY MANIA

Railway Clearing House Set up by the railway speculator George Hudson in 1842, it was a partial solution to the inefficiencies of a privately managed and unregulated rail system. Having created a 'through system' whereby the separate companies allowed each other's rolling stock to run along all their lines, he organized a clearing house where companies could settle the debts arising from this traffic. It constituted the basis of the modern railway network.

Railway Mania, a term used to describe the extraordinary burst of speculation and construction which created the basis of the railway network. It had three high points – 1836–7, 1840 and 1844–8. In 1838 LONDON was connected with BIRMINGHAM and in 1840 Birmingham with LIVERPOOL. By 1843 lines ran from London to BRISTOL and from SOUTHAMPTON, BRIGHTON and Dover, and by the close of the 1840s there were two routes from London to Scotland. From these frenzied bursts of activity mid-Victorian Britain received nearly 7,000 miles of track. Only the hilly areas of mid- Wales and south-west England remained untouched by the mania. The Railway Act (1844) provided for a measure of public control over the privately run railway system. It empowered the government to purchase the railway companies after 21 years and required each railway company to provide at least one train a day with a third-class fare of one penny (1d) a mile – 'the parliamentary train' – to encourage travel for the labouring classes.

The rhythm of construction moved in cycles that depended upon the state of the capital market, the availability and cost of money and the level of business confidence. In prosperous times, when credit was easy to obtain and interest rates low, new railway companies found a ready market for their shares. At their peaks these promotions became speculative ventures – far more lines were promoted than were ever built and many were never profitable – inciting dubious projects such as those associated with the speculator George Hudson (1800–71). Recessions brought a sharp fall in railway shares and company failures as money became dear, confidence collapsed and the mania subsided.

Railways, a principal mode of inland transport developed in Britain after 1830, growing out of two technological developments – the tramway and the STEAM engine. By the late 17th century tramways were widely used in many mining areas of the country for transporting COAL and IRON. From the late 18th century cast and later wrought iron replaced wooden rails. Although James Watt developed rotary motion in 1781, this was slow to be applied to traction other than via stationary engines used to haul wagons on a cable. George Stephenson brought locomotives and railways to public attention. He was employed to engineer the first public railway, the Stockton–Darlington line, which opened in 1825. In 1826 he and his son Robert Stephenson had taken on the construction of the Liverpool–Manchester line which, following the Rainhill Trials, was opened in 1830 using Stephenson's *Rocket*. William Huskisson, MP for Liverpool and former president of the Board of Trade and colonial secretary, was killed when he stepped in front of the *Rocket* at the opening, supposedly misjudging both its speed and braking distance.

By 1852 there were over 7,000 miles of track in Britain, with two through routes to Scotland, lines from London to the coast of north and south Wales, and regional networks in the Midlands, Yorks., and Lancs. The development of through routes was aided by the RAILWAY CLEARING HOUSE. A large mileage of more speculative construction followed in the 1860s–70s and included the building of lines which were never profitable. The dense network spawned problems for operators in the 20th century which saw the gradual closure of some of the least used lines and those most affected by the growing ROAD transport system. In the 1930s and during WORLD WAR II there was virtually no net new investment and the system was in a very poor state. NATIONALIZATION and rationalization followed in 1947 but this was unable to restore sufficient profitability and was followed by a further major contraction after the BEECHING REPORT of 1963.

Railways from their inception required new forms of state intervention. They needed parliamentary approval for the compulsory purchase of land, and the state also became involved over the regulation of safety (via the railway department of the BOARD OF TRADE) and of MONOPOLISTIC practices.

However, under the CONSERVATIVE government, railway services throughout the British Isles were privatized by 1997. Railtrack is responsible for operating all track and infrastructure; there are three rolling stock companies which lease locomotives and passenger carriages, 25 passenger train operating companies, four freight service providers; and a number of infrastructure maintenance companies. Unsurprisingly, given this fragmentation of services, there have been considerable concerns about safety, fare structures, efficiency and reliability. The BLAIR government has proposed the establishment of a Strategic Railway Authority (SRA) to support and integrate transport policy for both passengers and freight, and monitor the franchise for operating rail services.

The opening of the Channel Tunnel, a private-sector financed link, in 1994, has connected the UK to the rest of Europe by a rail link for both passengers and freight.

Railways and Economic Growth Railways were important in the development of the British economy in the 19th century although some accounts exaggerate their impact. They stimulated the COAL, IRON and ENGINEERING industries and created employment and income flows. They also formed a new EXPORT sector of major importance and provided a dynamic outlet for private investment. The historians Hobsbawm and Checkland have argued that the railway was the saviour of British capitalism: that the depression of the 1840s was terminal and that railway development came at a critical moment when the exhaustion of investment opportunities seemed to presage the demise of free enterprise capital. Railways ushered in the diversification of the ECONOMY attendant upon the growth of the capital goods sector and ended a dangerous dependence on textiles. Railways also of course influenced the efficiency and cost of transport, but the impact of this in the shorter term, especially in the freight market, was limited. CANALS remained cheaper for the transport of many bulky low-value commodities until the later 19th century, and were only eclipsed after this in these trades because railway companies bought up canals to limit competition and to create MONOPOLIES. It was only in the transport of lighter-weight valuable and perishable goods that railways excelled in the freight market in the 19th century, and most railway profits (unexpectedly) came initially from the transport of passengers; freight receipts did not exceed the income from passengers on the system as a whole until the mid-1850s.

The importance of railways to ECONOMIC GROWTH has become a testing ground for the application of 'counterfactual history'. The key English study undertaken by G.R. Hawke examined the social saving created by railways in 1865 (the savings which accrued from not using the alternative of ROADS and canals for the transport of goods and passengers): he concluded that railways contributed between 7 and 11 per cent of national income in England and Wales in 1865. He also argued that railways consumed under 10 per cent of pig-iron output between 1835 and 1869 – less than previously thought. Hawke's counterfactual approach only provides a snapshot view and ignores longer-term benefits of the railway sector; he also fails to specify the modifications in economic behaviour which may have been present in a world without railways. Nevertheless his work is a powerful antidote to the view that railways were of overriding importance in the British economy.

Less researched is the social and cultural impact of railways: the widening of geographical horizons; the speedier movement of people and information; the nutritional and social effects of efficient movement of perishable foodstuffs such as fish, milk, fruit and vegetables; the development of excursions, seaside holidays and trips, commuters and suburbs.

Raleigh, Sir Walter (1554–1618), courtier, writer and colony founder. Devon-born, Raleigh (or Ralegh) studied at Oxford and then fought in the French civil wars (1569–72). While embarking on a court career and winning ELIZABETH I's affection, he became involved in overseas voyaging and colonial ventures and fought in Ireland in 1580–1. Although Elizabeth insisted that he remain at home, he backed Humphrey Gilbert's 1583 NEWFOUNDLAND expedition, and between 1584 and 1586 masterminded a number of abortive attempts to colonize ROANOKE Island.

Essex (*see* DEVEREUX, ROBERT) became a detested court rival and undercut his position; the exposure of Raleigh's secret marriage to the royal maid-of-honour Bess Throckmorton in 1591 provoked the queen's rage. Four years later, Raleigh sought to revive his career by his expedition to Guiana to search for the fabled Eldorado. Unusually among contemporary explorers, he made a good impression on the native population, but Elizabeth was not so impressed, despite the publishing success of his description of his exploits. Further military adventuring against the Spaniards did not fully rescue him.

The pursuit of peace by JAMES I with Spain inflicted further humiliation, and Raleigh's involvement in the MAIN PLOT of 1603 brought a death sentence. Spared for the time being, he lived in the Tower, occupying himself with writing, including the *History of the World*. The death of his patron Prince HENRY was yet another blow, but in 1616, James was persuaded to release him for another Guiana expedition. This proved a disaster, involving clashes with the Spaniards that led to Raleigh's long-postponed execution when he returned. His brilliant and varied talents never redeemed a career of unfulfilled promise and unsuccessful playing of the courtly game.

Ralph of Coggeshall (*fl. c.*1210), chronicler. Abbot of the CISTERCIAN abbey of

Coggeshall, Essex from 1207 until he resigned in 1218, he was the author of a lively account of events chiefly in England and on CRUSADE between 1187 and 1224.

Ramsey Abbey, Cambs. Founded by St OSWALD in *c*.969, it was one of the great abbeys of the TENTH-CENTURY REFORM. It was colonized from Oswald's first monastery at Westbury-on-Trym, near Bristol, which faded away as a result. It was dissolved in 1539.

Ranelagh, formal gardens originally laid out at the private house of the paymaster-general, Richard, Viscount Ranelagh, in *c*.1690, east of Chelsea Hospital in London. From 1742, they were opened as a profit-making entertainment centre, where concerts, balls, gaming, fireworks and masquerades were popular. However, the principal attraction was promenading in the Rotunda, a vast circular building lined with dining boxes and supplied with an orchestra. The house and rotunda were demolished in 1805.

Ranters, a grouping of ANTINOMIAN exhibitionists during the INTERREGNUM: their antics included ostentatious swearing, fornication and public nudity. Acute controversy has raged as to whether they existed at all; it is likely that an assortment of like-minded radical individuals sparked popular fears because of their wild behaviour, and attracted the collective label with the help of some scaremongering journalism. Early QUAKERS suffered by being confused with them. Folk memory later labelled Primitive METHODISTS 'Ranters'.

Rates, Books of, *see* BOOKS OF RATES

Rational Dissenters Following the failure of moves at the SALTERS' HALL synod of 1719 to impose trinitarian tests on Dissenting ministers, many PRESBYTERIANS gradually abandoned Arianism in favour of Socinianism or UNITARIANISM. After the failure of the FEATHERS' TAVERN PETITION, rational dissent gained new recruits from the Established Church. Emphasizing not depravity and salvation, but human capacity for improvement in accordance with the designs of a benevolent God, such ministers and their congregations supported a variety of political and humanitarian reforming causes, being prominent in, for example, the SOCIETY FOR CONSTITUTIONAL INFORMATION.

Rationing This was introduced in Britain during both WORLD WAR I and WORLD WAR II to cope with shortages of food supplies caused by enemy submarine action. As a major food importer in peacetime, Britain was vulnerable to any interruption of supply. SUGAR was the first foodstuff rationed in World War I; this was followed in 1918 by a more extensive system of rationing covering most major foodstuffs. In World War II rationing was introduced in Jan. 1940 for foods including butter, bacon and sugar; meat followed in March as did other items in short supply. A general 'points' system for clothes was introduced in June 1942. Rationing worked reasonably fairly with minimum complaint, but incurred greater unpopularity when it was continued into peacetime under the AUSTERITY programme of the ATTLEE government, with bread being rationed for the first time in 1946. Rationing was almost entirely removed between 1950 and 1953 though sweets remained rationed until 1953. Petrol rationing was briefly reintroduced during the SUEZ CRISIS in 1956 and was planned but not implemented during the Arab oil boycott of 1973–4.

Readeption, name given to the brief second reign of HENRY VI, Oct. 1470–April 1471. *See also* EDWARD IV; WARS OF THE ROSES.

Reading, an aspect of LITERACY to which historians are giving increased attention. School curricula, autobiographical evidence and the volume of often ephemeral printed books suggest that until the mid-19th century there was a far higher degree of reading attainment than writing ability, since reading was taught in advance of, rather than simultaneously with, writing. Many who could read employed other people to do their writing for them. Many poorer people learned to read in later life. The teaching of reading in schools has gone through various fashions, from rote-learning to free expression, especially in the 20th century as fears about the low levels of literacy among some parts of the school and adult populations have been addressed. The initial teaching alphabet, i.t.a., for example, first used in 1961 and devised by Sir James

Pitman to eradicate the idiosyncrasies of English spelling, had a short but prominent lease of life as a first stage for reading attainment. The progressive 1975 BULLOCK REPORT also had a long-term effect on the teaching of reading. *See also* PRINTING.

Rebecca Riots, 1842–3. Led by a secret Welsh organization whose object was to destroy toll gates in order to relieve an economically depressed population, the rioters disguised themselves in women's clothes and called themselves 'Rebecca's daughters', as if in fulfilment of the prophecy (Genesis 24: 60) that Rebecca's seed should possess 'the gate of those which hate them'. Their nocturnal activities did much damage. A general relief from highway tolls followed after a commission of inquiry. The imposition of the POOR LAW AMENDMENT ACT 1834 was a contributory cause of the riots.

Reception, *see* COMMON LAW

Reception of Roman Law, *see* CIVIL LAW

Reciprocity of Duties Act 1823, one of a number of reforms promoted by William Huskisson, president of the Board of Trade (1823–7), which brought Britain a little closer to the status of a FREE TRADE nation. It enabled governments to negotiate trading terms with individual nations, encouraging the flow of trade and improving international relations.

Recognizance, a sum of money pledged as security for the performance of an act or for loyal service, the sum being due in the event of failure to perform. Some English kings – e.g. JOHN and HENRY VII – tended to use recognizance almost as the basis of their government. Today, individuals are still released from custody 'on their own recognizance' – i.e. by pledging a bond to reappear when summoned.

Recoinage of 1696 This was undertaken to stabilize and re-establish confidence in the currency. In the early 1690s, the high demand for bullion associated with KING WILLIAM'S WAR had stimulated much 'clipping' of silver coins (*see* COIN CLIPPING), and a Recoinage Act provided for the recoining of all clipped coin handed in. The exercise disrupted both the domestic economy and foreign payments. The face value of the new silver COINAGE quickly proved to understate its bullion value, encouraging further clipping. In the 18th century, gold coins were vastly more numerous than silver.

Reconstruction, the term applied to the broad social reforms enacted as a consequence of both world wars in the 20th century. It is often seen as an indirect effect of total war which necessitated concessions to significant sectors of the population to keep up wartime morale. LLOYD GEORGE'S housing, education, national insurance and franchise Acts of 1918–20 were part of a programme of fulfilling pledges made and aspirations encouraged during WORLD WAR I. WORLD WAR II similarly gave rise to the BEVERIDGE REPORT, the EDUCATION ACT of 1944 and the creation of a WELFARE STATE after 1945.

Recruiter MPs, MPs elected to the LONG PARLIAMENT from 1645 to fill seats left vacant by death or the purge of ROYALISTS; by the end of 1646, they comprised almost half the COMMONS. Reflecting war-weariness in the country at large, they increasingly reinforced the peace party against the army. *See also* CIVIL WARS.

Rectitudines Singularum Personarum, an early 11th-century tract that is an important source for late Anglo-Saxon rural society. It sets out the various categories of tenants living on an estate (probably in WESSEX), along with their obligations and rights. *See also* CEORL; THEGN.

Rector, Latin for 'governor'. When the PARISH system was organized, from the 7th century onwards, the title was applied to parish priests receiving the greater TITHES of grain. Many rectories became APPROPRIATED to monasteries, which then installed substitutes to perform the former rectors' duties. These priests received only the lesser tithes of cheese and eggs, etc. (Latin *vicarius*, 'substitute', hence 'vicar'). Monastic rectories were impropriated to lay people at the DISSOLUTION (*see* FEOFFEES FOR IMPROPRIATIONS). A 'rector' is also a senior governor in Scottish and many European universities.

Recusancy In general, this means refusal (Latin *recuso*, 'I refuse') to obey government orders, but – from EDWARD VI's reign – it became the term for the specific refusal to attend services of the Church of England, mostly by Roman CATHOLICS, but also by SEPARATISTS ('sectary recusants'). There was legislation against recusancy from 1549, especially under ELIZABETH I; an increasingly savage range of penalties was laid down, including fines, forfeiture of property, life imprisonment, banishment and death, although enforcement varied in proportion to ANTI-CATHOLIC feeling. (Catholics maintaining minimum attendance at parish churches to avoid penalties were called 'church papists'.) Repeal of the legislation took place in stages from 1778. *See also* CATHOLIC EMANCIPATION.

Red Comyn, *see* COMYN, JOHN

Red Cross, *see* GENEVA CONVENTION

Redundancy Payments Act 1965 Passed by the WILSON government in 1965, the Act gave statutory rights to redundancy payments according to length of service beyond a minimum period. The Act was intended to facilitate industrial restructuring and reduce the fear of temporary UNEMPLOYMENT. It has since been supplemented by special, more generous, schemes for particular industries, notably the COAL INDUSTRY, and also in the armed forces and amongst university teachers.

Redwald (?–*c.* 627), King of EAST ANGLIA. Named by BEDE as one of the seven kings who had exercised overlordship south of the Humber (*see BRETWALDA*), his eminence presumably stemmed from his defeat of Ethelfrith of NORTHUMBRIA in 616 and the restoration of EDWIN that followed. He occupies a notably ambiguous place in the history of the CONVERSION to Christianity, since he is said to have erected Christian and pagan altars in the same building. He is the best available candidate to have been buried at SUTTON HOO. *See also* PAGANISM.

Re-Exports, goods imported into Britain and then re-exported. Under the NAVIGATION ACTS, ENUMERATED GOODS (those listed in the Acts) produced in English colonies and bound for European markets had to be carried via England; English ships also carried Asian produce to Europe. Re-exports – especially in such goods as SUGAR, TOBACCO, coffee and dyestuffs – provided the most dynamic element in English overseas commerce in the late 17th century, and played a significant part in the so-called COMMERCIAL REVOLUTION. By 1700, re-exports made up about one-third of all EXPORTS; thereafter they maintained but did not much increase their share until the 1770s. After the loss of the American colonies, their significance declined; their composition also changed, foodstuffs becoming less important, industrial raw materials more so.

Reform Act 1832, the first parliamentary reform legislation since the defeat of PITT THE YOUNGER's proposals in 1785 and since the fears engendered by the FRENCH REVOLUTION arrested the development of the PARLIAMENTARY REFORM movement. Passed against the background of widespread unrest, and a fierce TORY opposition that was only overcome by WILLIAM IV's willingness to create sufficient peers to ensure its passage through the House of LORDS, the Reform Act extended the vote, hitherto the preserve of the landed interest, to the more prosperous middle classes. Under its provisions, 56 ROTTEN and POCKET BOROUGHS were abolished and 30 BOROUGHS with fewer than 4,000 inhabitants each lost one member. The net effect was to release 143 seats of the total of 658, for redistribution: 65 were allocated to the counties; 44 were given to large towns (the new industrial cities such as BIRMINGHAM, MANCHESTER, LEEDS and SHEFFIELD each received two); 21 were given to smaller towns, each receiving one; eight were given to Scotland and five to Ireland.

The Act, which conferred votes on propertied adult males, created a uniform voting qualification extended to borough householders paying an annual rent of £10. In the counties, the 40s freeholders retained the FRANCHISE, and it was also extended to copyholders, so called because they based their right to the land they held on copies of the rolls of a MANOR made by a steward of the lord's court (*see* COPYHOLD TENURE), paying £10 a year in rent; to leaseholders for 20 years paying £50 rent; and to tenants at will paying the same.

The Reform Act, on one calculation, increased the electorate from 435,000 to 652,000. It gave greater political importance to the industrial centres of the North and the Midlands, but left the counties under aristocratic control. Nobility and GENTRY continued to dominate PARLIAMENT and public life. The Act mitigated the electoral grievances of the middle classes; but Lord John RUSSELL, the principal architect of the legislation, who was known as 'Finality Jack' because he hoped it would render further reform superfluous, had underestimated the strength of popular feeling. The exclusion of an embittered working class meant that the settlement of 1832 would in due course require revision. *See also* REFORM ACT 1867; REFORM ACT 1884.

Reform Act 1867 An inevitable sequel to the REFORM ACT 1832, it was passed against the background of renewed working-class agitation for PARLIAMENTARY REFORM and reawakened fears of social disorder. Fifty-three seats were made available for redistribution to the large population centres. Nine new BOROUGHS and London University were enfranchised with one member each; five seats were awarded to increase the representation of BIRMINGHAM, MANCHESTER, Salford, LEEDS and LIVERPOOL; Chelsea and Hackney each became two-member constituencies; 25 seats were allocated to the English counties; Wales received one extra seat and Merthyr Tydfil became a two-member constituency; Scottish boroughs secured five additional seats; and Scottish counties three.

FRANCHISE qualifications were also amended with the intention of giving the vote to skilled workers. Borough franchises were extended to all householders paying rates and to lodgers paying a £10 rental who had been resident for 12 months. The COUNTY franchise was extended to occupiers of property rated at £12 per annum (£14 in Scotland) and to those with lands worth £5 per annum. The age of mass democracy, though, had not yet dawned. The electorate increased but its growth was restricted by registration technicalities and inadequate measures to combat corrupt practices. In 1869 only a third of all adult males were eligible to vote, and no women. Universal suffrage had to await the passage of the REPRESENTATION OF THE PEOPLE ACTS in 1918 and 1928.

Reform Act 1884 This Act corrected the deficiency of the REFORM ACT 1867 by extending the terms of the FRANCHISE in the BOROUGHS to the countryside. The legislation provided that the COUNTY franchise, like the borough franchise, should be extended to all occupiers and to lodgers paying a £10 annual rental, subject to a 12 months' residential qualification. It also included a service or occupation franchise for those with lands or tenements worth £10 per year.

A separate Redistribution Act, passed in June 1885, made 138 seats available for redistribution. In the reallocation, LONDON members were increased from 22 to 62; provincial English boroughs received 26 additional seats; six new provincial boroughs were created in England and Wales returning one member each; English and Welsh counties secured 66 additional members; seven seats were added to Scottish counties and seven more to ABERDEEN, EDINBURGH and GLASGOW; Irish counties gained 21 extra seats, and two seats were awarded to BELFAST and DUBLIN. Although the electorate was enlarged by this legislation, large numbers of the population were still disfranchised under its provisions. There were only 5.6 million electors out of a population of some 36 million in the UK. Until the passing of the REPRESENTATION OF THE PEOPLE ACT in 1918 an estimated 40 per cent of all adult males were not registered to vote and women were excluded entirely.

Reformatio Legum ('Reformation of Laws'), the name given by John FOXE to a replacement of medieval CANON LAW along REFORMED lines, prepared in 1551–3 under CRANMER's chairmanship after two decades of procrastination. Politicking and EDWARD VI's death prevented implementation, and ELIZABETH I did not respond to efforts at revival.

Reformation, a term used particularly to describe the religious renewal movement that, in the 16th century, resulted in the fragmentation of the medieval Western Church and the creation of Magisterial Protestant and ANGLICAN Churches alongside the Roman CATHOLIC church. It also saw the emergence of new movements of radical Christianity – for instance, ANABAPTISM. *See also* BIBLE; CALVINISM; CHURCHES: ENGLAND, IRELAND, SCOTLAND, WALES; LUTHERANISM; PRAYER BOOKS; PRESBYTERIANISM; REFORMED CHURCHES; REVISIONISM.

Reformation of Manners Movement, a campaign against 'vice and immorality' waged c.1690–1738. Reformation of manners societies, characteristically composed mainly of tradesmen, raised funds to hire 'informing constables', to bring prosecutions for such offences as streetwalking, swearing and breach of sabbatarian regulations. Royal proclamations against vice and immorality, issued repeatedly in the 1690s and early in the 18th century, testified to royal concern (MARY II took an especial interest); and the SPCK gave cautious backing to the campaign. Critics, including Henry Sacheverell (*see* SACHEVERELL AFFAIR), denounced this puritanical assault on English liberty, so easily degenerating into a protection racket if constables succumbed to the temptation to take bribes not to bring charges. Enthusiasm for such efforts revived briefly in the late 1750s, and again in the mid-1780s. GEORGE III was persuaded to issue a new proclamation in 1787, and WILBERFORCE instituted a Proclamation Society to co-ordinate reforming effort, later superseded by the VICE SOCIETY.

Reformation Parliament, label probably first used in 1859 for the 1529–36 Parliament. This passed the legislation breaking with Rome that still defines the CHURCH OF ENGLAND, especially the Acts in RESTRAINT OF APPEALS (1533), of Supremacy (1534; *see* ROYAL SUPREMACY), and for DISSOLUTION of the lesser monasteries (1536).

The name is also used for the Convention of Scottish Estates (Aug. 1560), an informal meeting of the Scots PARLIAMENT, which broke with Rome and accepted a REFORMED Confession of Faith.

Reformed Churches This term should not be used indiscriminately to describe PROTESTANT Churches created as a result of the 16th-century REFORMATION, and especially not for those created by Martin Luther. It refers to those Churches inspired by the Swiss Reformation, pioneered in Zürich by Huldrych Zwingli (1484–1531), influenced by Martin Bucer's (1491–1551) leadership in Strasbourg, and later developed in Geneva by John Calvin, whose theology shaped Reformed beliefs. The English Reformation under EDWARD VI and ELIZABETH I was more influenced by the Reformed than the LUTHERAN tradition, although the government resisted CALVINIST ideas on PRESBYTERIANISM.

Refugees, those fleeing from war or persecution in another country. Britain has frequently been ready to receive refugees, and to take advantage of their particular skills. Protestant incomers from the Flemish Low Countries in the mid- and late-16th century brought industrial skills important to the CLOTH INDUSTRY in the introduction of the NEW DRAPERIES, especially in East Anglia. After 1685, when religious toleration was no longer permitted to French Protestants, huge numbers came to Britain and Ireland, and often went on to the colonies (*see* PALATINES). The high-class skills they brought – in gold and silver work, weaving, and design – were of immense importance in the Georgian economy, and in some cases, notably Courtaulds, their influence survives. During the 19th century, political exiles like MARX, and nationalists plotting the revolutions that shook Europe, worked from Britain, and Jews (*see* JEWS IN BRITAIN) from eastern Europe and Russia, fleeing the pogroms and their persecutors, congregated in the East End of LONDON, GLASGOW, MANCHESTER and elsewhere during the 1870s to 1890s. A further influx of Jews, as well as other Germans, occurred in the 1930s with the rise of Hitler and Nazism, and children were also evacuated to England from the Basque country of Spain in 1936 in the face of Franco's advance in the Spanish Civil War. The 30,000 UGANDAN Asians, expelled by Idi Amin in 1972, were far from the last in the line. Britain's long imperial traditions – many refugees in the 20th century have held British passports – a lasting tradition of liberalism, more so in the 19th century than the 20th, and the fact that refugees have been economically useful or co-religionists, have all contributed to this reception (but *see also* IMMIGRATION).

Regality, *see* PALATINATE

Regency Act 1811 Passed in the reign of GEORGE III, who had suffered severe illness in 1788 and 1801 and complete breakdown in 1810, the Act appointed the Prince of Wales (afterwards GEORGE IV) to the regency during his father's mental incapacity.

Regency Crises, 18th-century. The need to provide for what should happen if the monarch or his or her heir should be incapacitated gave rise to several serious political disputes in the 18th century. First in 1751 on the death of Frederick, Prince of Wales; again in 1765 when GEORGE III suffered an incapacitating illness, and then most seriously in 1788, when the king had another attack and became temporarily insane, FOX and Richard Sheridan hoped to secure the regency for the future GEORGE IV. PITT THE YOUNGER brought in a Bill that limited the regent's powers, to prevent the Foxite WHIGS from entrenching themselves, but then the Irish Parliament invited the prince to assume royal functions without conditions. The king made a dramatic recovery before the English Bill had passed. *See also* REGENCY ACT 1811.

Regional Policy, *see* ASSISTED AREAS; PLANNING

Regionalism, both a sense of regional identity and an economic policy which lays emphasis upon the positive assistance of depressed regions, often using both direct public investment and a range of financial incentives to attract firms. Regional identities can be traced in many periods of Britain's past, often based on shared experiences of topography, soils, farming type and political or institutional histories. It has been argued that industrialization reinforced a sense of regional identity because of the sectoral specialization of the economy by region (for example, COTTON in Lancs., WOOLLENS in Yorks., the IRON AND STEEL INDUSTRY in the north-east, south Wales and elsewhere). This encouraged regionally-based social structures and cultural patterns associated with various dominant employment and trading structures and reflected in regionally-based employers' associations and TRADE UNIONS. The regional focus of transport developments and industrial capital markets before the late 19th century reinforced regional cohesions. Regional intervention in the economy (regionalism or regional policy) came to the fore in the 1930s when the worst effects of the DEPRESSION produced very pronounced regional disparities in UNEMPLOYMENT; the decline in the SHIPBUILDING, textiles and COAL industries had highly localized effects in Wales, the North and Scotland. After World War II a wider range of policy measures was introduced. Some were designed to facilitate greater labour mobility via skill retraining or helping to finance a move. Others (e.g. industrial development certificates) prevented firms from locating in particular areas. Similarly, tax incentives were deployed to encourage firms to locate new investment in specific areas – for example, from 1972 into the 1980s regional development grants were paid to manufacturing firms locating new plant in the areas needing help. Finally, in an attempt to reduce the costs of labour over the period 1967–76, a regional employment premium was paid on all employees in selected areas. *See also* CENTRALIZATION.

Registers, Parish Records of baptisms, marriages and burials were made compulsory for each English PARISH by Thomas CROMWELL in 1538, although a few earlier examples exist. Despite patchy survival, particularly before a 1598 order to copy earlier registers, they remain invaluable especially for GENEALOGY and HISTORICAL DEMOGRAPHY (*see also* FAMILY RECONSTITUTION). The fullness of registration declined markedly in the 18th and early 19th centuries; in 1837 the advent of civil registration under the registrar-general John Rickman ushered in a new age of record-keeping. NONCONFORMIST and FREE CHURCH congregations also keep registers, the older of which are at the PUBLIC RECORD OFFICE in London. Neither these nor parish registers should be confused with bishops' registers, the main record of episcopal business. *See also* PARISH REGISTER ABSTRACTS.

Registrar-General, chief public official responsible for the CIVIL REGISTRATION of births, marriages and deaths and for the decennial CENSUS. The investigations in the published annual reports of the 19th century office, by John Rickman and William Farr (who as deputy was Registrar-General in all but title), are of immense importance in understanding the dynamics of the POPULATION, and especially MORTALITY, of that era.

Regrating, *see* MORAL ECONOMY

Regular and Secular Clergy *Regular* clergy comprise monks, nuns and FRIARS who live under a Rule (*regula*). *Secular* (i.e. non-monastic) clergy live in the world (*saeculum*).

Regularis Concordia (Agreement about the Rule), one of the fundamental texts of English medieval monasticism, completed in c.970 under the direction of St Ethelwold. Aiming to establish a common pattern of observance throughout the English monasteries established during the TENTH-CENTURY REFORM, it drew on the customs of reformed abbeys on the Continent.

Regulation of Railway Act 1889 Passed in response to the Armagh crash of 12 June 1889 which left 80 fatalities and 250 injured, the Act recognized the need for improvements in locomotive brakes and signalling systems to cope with the increase in RAILWAY traffic. It made block signalling, continuous brakes and interlocking points compulsory.

Relay System, *see* TEN HOURS MOVEMENT

Relics, *see* PILGRIMAGE

Relief, the payment made by a tenant to his lord on entry to the tenancy. In most cases, it was paid by an heir to obtain his inheritance and, in effect, was so similar to the Anglo-Saxon HERIOT that Anglo-Norman writers regarded it as a new name for an old institution. After the NORMAN CONQUEST, when familial claims to particular estates were recent and weak, kings of England were able to demand very high reliefs. HENRY I's CORONATION CHARTER shows that, by 1100, relief levels had become a thorny issue between king and barons; they remained so until MAGNA CARTA fixed the relief payable by the heir to a barony at £100.

Religious Attendance, Census of, 1851. The CENSUS-takers uniquely included in their counting attendance at churches and places of worship on the last Sunday in March of that year. They listed 37 separate denominations apart from the CHURCH OF ENGLAND, plus 'isolated congregations'. Some 60 per cent of the population attended a place of worship on Census Sunday, and less than half of those went to an ANGLICAN church.

Religious Society of Friends, *see* QUAKERS

Remainders, *see* STRICT SETTLEMENT

Remembrance Sunday, *see* ARMISTICE DAY

Remodelling of Corporations, *see* CORPORATIONS, REMODELLING OF

Remonstrance of the Irish Princes, 1317–18, a protest against the injustices of English rule, composed on behalf of Donal O Neill and other Irish chiefs in justification of their support for Edward BRUCE. Sent to Pope John XXII, it accused the English of disregarding the terms of an earlier papal bull, *LAUDABILITER*.

Renaissance and Renaissance Humanism The term was first used as *Renascenza* ('rebirth') by Francesco Petrarca ('Petrarch', 1304–74) to celebrate the literary achievements of Dante Alighieri (1265–1321). Its French form was used by 19th-century scholars to describe the western European upsurge in creativity inspired by a passion for classical Greece and Rome: a period from the 14th to the 17th centuries (though the word is also used for similar movements in the 9th and 12th centuries).

HUMANISM, another 19th-century term, describes the scholarly impulse in the Renaissance: rediscovering and editing ancient texts (*humanae litterae*, 'civilized literature') in order to apply them to contemporary education and life. Humanism began to affect northern European universities in the 15th century; its ideas were given speedier currency by PRINTING, and ERASMUS emerged as a distinctive northern genius.

Renaissance literature and even music were shaped by classical models; slower to arrive in the north was classicism in art and architecture. Classical buildings were rare in 16th-century England and Scotland, and even in the 17th century, GOTHIC architecture was never completely ousted.

Renovatio Monete, the practice whereby the English COINAGE was renewed every few years from the time of King EDGAR's reform onwards. The changes could involve an increase or decrease in weight and silver content, a procedure that could be used by the kings as a form of taxation.

Rent Acts The cost of HOUSING is one of the most significant items in the family budget. Hence any increase in housing costs through rising rents or MORTGAGE repayments tends to be very sensitive politically, and governments frequently look to defray the cost of housing. The imposition of maximum levels of rent by government had its origins in 1915, when rapidly rising rents in GLASGOW sparked a series of rent strikes and civil unrest. The government's response was to introduce a ceiling on rents which was to be applied on a 'temporary basis'. However, after this first intervention there was an almost continuous form of rent control of one sort or another, supplemented by a variety of legal measures aimed at strengthening the security of tenure of the sitting tenant. There were some 15 different legislative measures relating to rent control and tenure between 1915 and 1980. By 1957 there were 5 million properties with controlled rents, almost a million of which were set at a very low level. The Rent Act (1957) abolished rent control on a large number of houses and flats owned by private landlords with the aim of stimulating the rapidly dwindling private sector. However, the absence of controls led to reports of abuse by private landlords forcing tenants to pay extortionate rents or practicing intimidation, which became known as RACHMANISM. In the Rent Act (1965) the LABOUR government reintroduced the rent controls abolished by the 1957 Act over most unfurnished privately rented property. However, the overall effect of the various Acts was to depress the economic return to the private rental sector of the housing market, and as a consequence this form of tenure has seen a spectacular decline. The withdrawal of private accommodation from the supply of housing resulted in local authorities filling the void, so that prior to WORLD WAR II and particularly in its aftermath there was a considerable expansion of COUNCIL HOUSING. Before the war some 90 per cent of households were tenants of essentially unfurnished private accommodation and by 1980 this figure had fallen to 12.5 per cent. The tax advantages of home ownership clearly exacerbated this contraction and by the 1980s with extensive privatization of council stock the figure for private rental accommodation was less than 8 per cent.

Renunciation Act 1783 It completed the sequence of Acts establishing Irish LEGISLATIVE INDEPENDENCE. The Irish politician Henry Flood argued that it was insufficient for the British Parliament just to repeal the DECLARATORY ACT, since that arguably left intact the British Parliament's right to legislate for Ireland which the Act had merely 'declared': he suggested that the British must formally renounce any such claim. To remove any doubt as to British good faith, Parliament did so.

Reparations, payments imposed on Germany in 1919 by the victorious powers in the treaty of Versailles (*see* PARIS PEACE CONFERENCE) to pay for damages and losses incurred in WORLD WAR I. These were fixed by the London Conference (1921) at £6,600 million. However, rampant inflation rendered Germany unable to pay this unrealistic figure. Reductions were made in 1924 and 1929 and finally the reparation payments were cancelled in 1932, largely because of the DEPRESSION. The POTSDAM CONFERENCE after the end of WORLD WAR II in Europe decreed that this time reparations should be exacted not in the form of money, but of capital equipment, to enable the allies to rebuild their industries.

Report on the Sanitary Condition of the Labouring Population of Great Britain, 1842, a key primary source on the mid-Victorian urban environment, written by Sir Edwin Chadwick, secretary to the POOR LAW COMMISSIONERS. It showed with a wealth of graphic illustration that POVERTY was closely connected with the ill-health caused by squalid sanitary conditions. Thirty thousand copies were initially printed of what, in effect, was the charter of the SANITARY REFORM MOVEMENT. The PUBLIC HEALTH ACT of 1848 and the establishment of local boards of health were a direct outcome of its findings.

Reports, Law, *see* YEAR BOOKS

Representation of the People Acts 1918, 1928, 1948, 1969, a succession of 20th-century Acts which have broadened the FRANCHISE from its restricted 19th-century base. The Act of 1918, sometimes known as the 'Fourth Reform Act' (*see* REFORM ACTS 1832, 1867, 1884), enfranchised the largest number of people of all the major parliamentary reforms. It gave the vote to all men over 21 – enfranchising the 60 per cent of men who had previously been without the vote – and all women over 30 who were ratepayers or wives of ratepayers, representing a triumph for the WOMEN'S SUFFRAGE CAMPAIGN. The combined effect of the Act was virtually to treble the electorate to around 21 million people. Widely regarded as the result of the democratizing effect of WORLD WAR I and the recognition of the part women had played in the war effort, its impact on party politics has been hotly debated. By enfranchising a large section of the working class and their wives it assisted the rise of the LABOUR PARTY and the eclipse of the LIBERAL PARTY, although its full effects in this respect were not felt until the general elections of 1922–4.

The Representation of the People (Equal Franchise) Act 1928, passed by the BALDWIN government, completed the enfranchisement of women begun in 1918 by giving the remaining women between the ages of 21 and 30 the vote. A further minor reform was enacted in the Representation of the People Act 1948, which abolished plural voting: the university vote, the right of people to vote both where they resided and where they had their business, and the remaining 12 double-member constituencies. Finally the Representation of the People Act 1969 further extended the franchise by reducing the minimum age for voting from 21 to 18, allowing that age group to vote for the first time in the June 1970 election. The change was partly influenced by the growth of youth culture since WORLD WAR II and the increasing attention being paid to the opinions of the young. After this Act, the electorate stood at approximately 40 million.

Repton, Derbys. A double monastery (i.e. for men and women) was founded here in the 7th century, and the church, of which the splendid crypt still survives, was the burial place of several MERCIAN kings. The monastery was destroyed by the VIKINGS, and recent excavations in the vicinity have uncovered a fortified camp and a large number of burials, including the remains of a ship-burial. It was dissolved in 1538.

Repugnancy, a legal doctrine important in the development of self-government within the BRITISH EMPIRE. It was founded on the assumptions that the British Parliament possessed full powers to legislate for the colonies and that, as the colonists had taken English law with them, colonial legislatures could not pass laws that were in conflict with or repugnant to English law. It was abolished by the Statute of WESTMINSTER in 1931.

Requests, Court of Set up by WOLSEY at WHITEHALL in 1519 with a specialist staff of royal councillors, the Court's purpose was to provide cheap and speedy justice in cases which would otherwise take up the time of councillors attendant on the king. Further moves in 1529 and 1538 completed its formal status. It did not sit after 1642.

Responsible Government, an early Victorian concept embodying the demands of the colonial settler population, for control of local officers by local men. It was more a claim for local autonomy than for independence, and was in general satisfied by the creation of an executive responsible to an elected assembly and by giving the elected assembly financial control. *See also* BRITISH EMPIRE; DECOLONIZATION.

Restoration, the restoration of the Stuart dynasty with the return of CHARLES II to England in 1660, 11 years after his father's execution, and of traditional Parliaments (that is, of parliaments consisting of LORDS and COMMONS elected on the old FRANCHISE): contemporaries were careful to associate the two. Historians also apply the term to the period between the Restoration and the GLORIOUS REVOLUTION of 1688–9.

Oliver CROMWELL's ability to maintain the confidence of both the ARMY and civil government eluded his successors: his son Richard CROMWELL, then the reconvened RUMP. It fell to General MONCK to tilt the balance of power away from the army, to ensure that members excluded in PRIDE'S PURGE were readmitted to Parliament, and that it should be Parliament that decided the future form of government. In March 1660, the LONG PARLIAMENT finally dissolved itself, providing for the election of a CONVENTION PARLIAMENT. Charles issued a conciliatory declaration of his intentions from BREDA in April, and was accepted by Parliament without conditions. He was proclaimed king on 8 May and arrived in London on 29 May; the RESTORATION SETTLEMENT provided the constitutional and legal framework for the restitution of the monarchy.

Restoration Settlement, the constitutional and legal framework of the RESTORATION, as agreed by the reinstituted separate Parliaments of England, Scotland and Ireland. CHARLES II was granted revenues expected to amount to £1.2m for life: an apparently generous financial settlement that was to prove inadequate in practice. His reign was formally backdated to his father's execution, and all acts and ordinances passed since 1641 (in Scotland, since 1640) were removed from the statute book. Some reforms of the preceding period were undone – for instance, Latin replaced English in legal documents – but others were in practice continued, and many who had held authority during the INTERREGNUM, at all levels, were given office. An Act of Indemnity and Oblivion restricted scope for vengeance: only the regicides and three others were executed. An Act confirming Judicial Proceedings confirmed the validity of land sales to which the vendors had consented – even if under pressure of penury or following confiscation; other confiscated lands, including crown and church lands, were restored. In the Declaration of BREDA, and again in the Worcester House Declaration, Charles had indicated that a relatively liberal religious settlement might be anticipated; in the event parliamentary measures, embodied in the CLARENDON CODE, were more restrictive than many PRESBYTERIANS had hoped and than some moderate ANGLICANS thought wise.

In Ireland, the Cromwellian regime was overthrown by a coup in Dec. 1659, and a convention was summoned. As in England, the settlement finally agreed was selective in what it restored. The Act of SETTLEMENT of 1662 confirmed Protestants in their hold on the mass of land seized from Catholics in the 1650s – with the important qualification that Catholics innocent of rebellion could petition to have their lands returned, which many successfully did. Hopes that the religious settlement would recognize the range of Protestant belief were frustrated: the CHURCH OF IRELAND was re-established on a narrowly ANGLICAN basis, and Presbyterian ministers purged.

Restraint of Appeals, Act in, 1533, an Act of Parliament forbidding all appeals to authorities outside the realm except in cases of heresy. It was intended to stop CATHERINE OF ARAGON appealing to the pope and obstructing HENRY VIII's quest for an annulment of their marriage. It was an important step in creating ROYAL SUPREMACY over the Church. *See also* CROMWELL, THOMAS; PRAEMUNIRE; REFORMATION PARLIAMENT.

Resumption, Acts of, the recall of previous royal grants. This was a major issue in 15th-century England: weak or insecure monarchs were inclined to grant away royal lands, causing indignation from taxpayers, who had to make up the resulting shortfall in revenue, and provoking pressure for resumptions. The large-scale confiscations of Church lands from the 1530s (*see* DISSOLUTION) were often presented as legitimate resumptions of ancient royal grants to the Church. In early 17th-century Ireland and Scotland, threatened and actual royal resumptions (revocations) of former Church lands obtained by private individuals caused a storm of fury and apprehension among landowners, which spread to England.

Resurrectionists, popular name given to those who during the decades around 1800 illicitly dug up freshly buried corpses, mainly to provide bodies for dissection in the medical schools. Laurence Sterne, the author of *The Life and Opinions of Tristram Shandy, Gentleman* (1760–7), was perhaps the most famous such corpse, which was recognized at a Cambridge anatomy lecture. The notorious activities in 1828–9 of the murderers Burke and Hare, who sold corpses to the Edinburgh anatomists, and the fears aroused by the activities of the resurrectionists – out of all proportion to their real effect – prompted the passing of the ANATOMY ACT 1832.

Return of the Owners of Land, survey of landownership carried out in 1872–3. The Return, or 'New Domesday', prompted by debate on whether landownership was being concentrated in fewer hands, was the first comprehensive investigation since 1086. The result astonished even those who thought concentration was marked. Although more than one million people did own land in England and Wales, four-fifths of the total acreage was owned by fewer than 7,000 people, with 363 of them owning estates over 10,000 acres, and 44 owning over 100,000 acres. The dominance of a few could not be gainsaid, and all the indicators were that their grip had been increasing remorselessly over time, so extinguishing many small owners.

Reversionary Interest, a term used by historians to denote political groupings associated with heirs to the throne, who might hope to come to power on the coat-tails of the heir. Reversionary interests were a common feature of 18th-century politics: relations between Hanoverian kings and their eldest sons were consistently bad, and the Prince of Wales was usually a focus for opposition.

Revisionism Historians are by nature revisionists, constantly modifying previous work by research in new sources or reinterpretation of old ones; however, some recent historians have been labelled 'revisionists' by themselves or others. They frequently disagree with each other even if they are seeking to reinterpret the same period. If anything unites them, it is a general (and healthy) distrust of preconceived schemes and received overall views in historical writing.

Naturally, Marxist historical research is a prime target, but there are others. These include views of the English REFORMATION that (in the tradition of John FOXE) have seen early popular pressure for religious change as significant; and views of the British CIVIL WARS that have stressed long-term conflicts, particularly in PARLIAMENT. One revisionist view of 18th-century England stresses the enduring strength of traditional values and of the ANGLICAN Church, where previous historians concentrated on the social changes brought about by commercial and industrial growth.

As a reminder of the historian's duty to challenge simplified assumptions, revisionism performs a service, although many revisionist conclusions are themselves being revised where they have settled down into a new orthodoxy.

Revocation, Acts of, *see* RESUMPTION, ACTS OF

Revolt of the Field, name given to the widespread strike in 1874 of agricultural labourers in the TRADE UNION led by Joseph Arch (1826–1919). Agricultural workers' unions had been formed throughout the country in the early 1870s; most affiliated to what became Arch's National Agricultural Labourers' Union with 86,000 members, plus another 49,000 in other unions. In Feb. 1874 a lockout of Suffolk men demanding higher wages demonstrated farmers' opposition, and the response was a widespread strike of 6,000 men, 'The Revolt of the Field'; by July the strike had died. The NALU declined thereafter – farmworkers were hard to mobilize – and the number of workers on the land was already beginning to fall.

Revolution Settlement, the constitutional settlement agreed in the aftermath of the GLORIOUS REVOLUTION of 1688–9, devised by the CONVENTION PARLIAMENT in consultation with WILLIAM III and MARY II (as they became). Agreement as to the terms upon which the crown was to be conferred proved difficult to achieve: the final English formula was that JAMES II had left the throne vacant, while the Scots said he had forfeited it. The LORDS would have preferred to make William regent, with Mary as sole monarch; but, under pressure from the COMMONS, London WHIG activists and William himself, they agreed to offer him the crown, jointly with Mary, and to give ANNE and her children preference over any of his own by subsequent marriage. The offer of the crown in Feb. 1689 was accompanied by the DECLARATION OF RIGHTS, but William refused to regard the offer as conditional. A TOLERATION ACT was passed in May, though the Comprehension Act (*see* COMPREHENSION) that was to have accompanied it was defeated; in the same month, the Scots parliament abolished 'prelacy', subsequently re-establishing PRESBYTERIANISM. The BILL OF RIGHTS, incorporating much of the Declaration, was passed in Dec.

Other measures determining the character of the post-revolutionary regime were adopted in the course of the reign, under the shadow of KING WILLIAM'S WAR. In 1694, the establishment of the BANK OF ENGLAND facilitated deficit finance, and the TRIENNIAL ACT laid down that elections must be held at no longer than three-year intervals. In 1695 the LICENSING ACT was allowed to lapse; in 1697–8 it was accepted after controversy that a STANDING ARMY should be maintained in peacetime; and in 1698, the CIVIL LIST Act placed only restricted funds at royal disposal, making the remainder dependent on annual parliamentary grants. Finally, the Act of SETTLEMENT (1701) dictated the form of the PROTESTANT SUCCESSION, and imposed new restrictions on the royal prerogative, some of which were repealed before they came into effect.

Rheged, British kingdom of the post-Roman period. Its extent is unclear; it lay around the Solway Firth and may occasionally have stretched as far south as Lancs. Possibly representing the results of a reorganization of a section of the BRIGANTES, it was eventually absorbed – probably by force – into NORTHUMBRIA during the 7th century.

Rhode Island, *see* MASSACHUSETTS; NEW WORLD

Rhodes, Cecil (1853–1902), imperial statesman. Born into an East Anglian clergyman's family, Rhodes was sent to Southern Africa because he suffered from a weak chest. By the age of 30 he was one of the world's wealthiest men having made a fortune from diamond mining in Kimberley with the company he founded, De Beers. He then moved into gold, founding Consolidated Gold Fields in 1887. His ambitions had become political and territorial; he was instrumental in acquiring BECHUANALAND for the CAPE COLONY in 1884 and in inducing the Matabele king to cede mineral rights, and in 1887 he founded the British South Africa Company, which received its royal charter in 1889. Its extensive territory – some of it acquired from African kings by dubious means – was to bear the name RHODESIA. In 1890 Rhodes became prime minister of the CAPE COLONY, but was forced to resign in 1896 after being found guilty of complicity in the JAMESON RAID.

In his will he endowed the 170 distinguished scholarships which bear his name at Oxford where he had studied, for students from the colonies, the USA and Germany.

Rhodesia, Northern, former British colony in East Africa, now Zambia. British sovereignty over the area was recognized by treaty with Germany in 1890 (*see* SCRAMBLE FOR AFRICA). In 1891 RHODES' Royal South Africa Company was allowed to extend from what became Southern Rhodesia to the area north of the Zambezi. White settlement was less extensive than in Southern Rhodesia, except in the areas of copper exploitation; the country became a major source of migrant workers for southern Africa. The hydroelectric dam schemes on the Zambezi in the early 1950s were among the first stages of British attempts at modernization and development, which would ultimately result in independence.

Separate nationhood was achieved under President Kenneth Kaunda (1924–), a one-time leader of the proscribed nationalist Zambian African National Congress, in 1964. *See also* RHODESIA, SOUTHERN.

Rhodesia, Southern, former British colony in East Africa, now Zimbabwe. After missionary and trading expansion up the Zambezi, RHODES and other British exploiters saw that a second Rand could be developed above the Limpopo river, and in 1890 white settlers under the Royal South Africa Company, moved north through BECHUANALAND. The early years of white settlement were marked by prolonged fighting with the African peoples, and the eventual confiscation after 1896 of the lands of the rebellious Ndebele and Mashona tribes.

The dominant white population in Southern Rhodesia – the most extensive in southern Africa outside SOUTH AFRICA – promoted a Central Africa Federation of the two Rhodesias and NYASALAND; it was split by states of emergency caused by nationalist resurgence in 1959, and then by the independence of the new states of Zambia and Malawi in 1963. Resistance to independence movements led to Ian Smith's Unilateral Declaration of Independence (UDI) in 1965. After a long struggle, independence was finally achieved under Robert Mugabe in 1980 (*see* LANCASTER HOUSE AGREEMENT).

Rhodri Mawr ('Rhodri the Great'; Rhodri ap Merfyn) (?–878), King of Gwynedd. One of the most powerful kings of GWYNEDD, he was a member of a relatively new ruling family who brought new vigour to the kingdom. His military successes included the absorption of CEREDIGION and POWYS, and the defeat of a VIKING war band in 856. He was driven from his kingdom by the Norsemen in 877 and, on his return, was killed by an alliance of MERCIANS and Vikings. His military achievements and dynastic marriages meant that his descendants had an interest in most of the other Welsh kingdoms, which in turn underpinned Gwynedd's predominance in pre-Norman Welsh political life.

Rhuddlan, Statute of, 1284, the proclamation by EDWARD I which set up colonial governmental institutions for the Principality of Wales. It created English-style SHIRES in the north (Flint, Anglesey, Merioneth and Caernarfon), and extended the existing counties of Cardigan and Carmarthen. The MARCHER LORDSHIPS remained unaffected. Welsh customary law and certain institutions were allowed to survive alongside the introduction of English COMMON LAW and law courts for criminal cases, but the Welsh were excluded from chartered BOROUGHS, which were settled with English immigrants. The Statute was taken as the limit of legal memory in north Wales, but was otherwise superseded by the parliamentary legislation of 1536–43. *See also* UNION OF WALES AND ENGLAND; WALES, PRINCE OF.

Rhys ap Gruffudd (also 'Gruffydd') (*c.*1130–97), generally known as 'the Lord Rhys', ruler of Deheubarth (*see* DYFED). He led the resistance against HENRY II's invasions of Wales between 1157 and 1165, and was then able to acquire a 30-year ascendancy over all the Welsh princes of south Wales. In 1171–2, Henry accepted Rhys's territorial gains, and in return, Rhys recognized Henry's overlordship. During the relative peace that lasted until 1189, Rhys overhauled the government of Deheubarth, patronized churches and poets, and was probably responsible for the compilation of the laws of HYWEL DDA. In the last years of his life, diplomacy once more gave way to war, both between the Welsh and the English, and between members of Rhys's own family angling for the succession. After his death, Deheubarth fragmented and was never reconstructed as the premier Welsh kingdom.

Ribbonism Initially religious associations to protect CATHOLICS against Orangemen (*see* ORANGE ORDER), the secret Ribbon or Riband societies began to spread from ULSTER to Sligo around 1820. Between 1835 and 1849, Ribbonism became a form of agrarian terrorism, practised by the Irish Catholic peasantry to prevent eviction by their often PROTESTANT landlords, determined to secure their rents. The British Parliament, unwilling to contemplate large-scale interference with Irish property rights, fell back upon a mix of coercion and conciliation. GLADSTONE's programme of pacification marked the most significant attempt to tackle the IRISH QUESTION in the 19th century. *See also* WHITEBOYS.

Ricardo, David (1772–1823), political economist. Apart from Adam SMITH, he was the dominant influence upon the aims and methods of 19th-century economics. Ricardo's law of rent, based on the observation that the differing fertility of land yielded unequal profits to the capital and labour applied to it, was his most notable formulation. His law of comparative cost, demonstrating the advantages of international specialization, lay at the heart of the FREE TRADE argument (*see also* MALTHUS). Using what economists would now refer to as a model of the economic process, he demonstrated that the Corn Laws (*see* CORN LAW ACT 1815) had the effect of increasing the price of corn and hence increasing the incomes of landowners and the ARISTOCRACY at the expense of the working class and the rising industrial class. Thus he argued for the abolition of the Corn Laws as this would help to distribute the National Income toward the more productive and innovative group in society. Ricardo also developed the Labour Theory of Value to explain the determination of prices, and this was a central idea in MARX's theories about the evolution of capitalism. His abstract deductive methods fell out of favour in the 1870s as the discrepancy between political economy and the real world became embarrassing and politically dangerous.

Riccardi, the company of Italian merchant bankers based in Lucca whose cash advances – nearly £400,000 between 1272 and 1294 – were the mainstay of English royal finance during the early years of EDWARD I's reign.

Rich, Edmund (St Edmund of Abingdon) (*c.*1170–1240). Archbishop of Canterbury (1233–40). Born at Abingdon and educated at Oxford and Paris, he taught theology at Oxford before being elected Archbishop of Canterbury in 1233. A scholar and ascetic, he was the author of the widely read spiritual treatise *Speculum Ecclesie* ('Mirror of the Church'). Quarrels with HENRY III and the monks of Christ Church, CANTERBURY took him to Rome, but he died en route. He was formally declared a saint in 1246 after a canonization campaign efficiently led by the CISTERCIAN house of Pontigny (which possessed his body).

Rich, Robert (23rd [2nd Rich] Earl of Warwick) (1587–1658), seafarer and politician. Cambridge educated, he was one of the leading PURITAN peers before the CIVIL WARS. His pre-war PRIVATEERING and colonizing experience won him command of Parliament's navy in 1642; he retired under the SELF-DENYING ORDINANCE in 1645, but again took command in 1648–9. CHARLES I's execution led to him quitting politics, but he took a leading part in the inauguration ceremony of the Protectorate (*see* INTERREGNUM) in 1657.

Richard I, Coeur de Lion ('the Lionheart') (1157–99), King of England (1189–99). The third son of HENRY II and ELEANOR OF AQUITAINE, he was intended from an early age to inherit his mother's duchy. In 1173–4, he joined his mother's revolt against his father, but was pardoned and entrusted with AQUITAINE, where he rapidly gained a formidable reputation. In 1183, Henry helped him to put down a rebellion involving his elder brother, HENRY THE YOUNG KING. However, as Henry II became increasingly concerned to provide for his youngest son JOHN, apparently at Richard's expense, so Richard turned to Philip II Augustus of France. This alliance ensured Richard's undisputed succession to virtually the whole ANGEVIN EMPIRE in 1189.

In 1190, he set out on the Third CRUSADE, conquering CYPRUS (May 1191) en route. At Limassol, he married Berengaria, sealing the alliance with her father, Sancho VI of Navarre, which ensured the safety of Richard's southern dominions during his absence. The marriage also meant breaking with Philip, to whose sister he had been betrothed since 1169 – she had been in Henry II's custody for 20 years, and it was widely believed that he had seduced her. In July 1191, Muslim Acre capitulated soon after Richard's arrival, but Philip immediately left, leaving Richard with overall responsibility for subsequent events: the massacre of the prisoners of Acre; the victory over Saladin at Arsuf; the decision, taken largely on logistical grounds, not to besiege Jerusalem; the grant of Cyprus to Guy of Lusignan; and the selection of a new king of Jerusalem. Despite the failure to recover the Holy City itself, Richard negotiated terms with Saladin in Sept. 1192 which enabled the hard-pressed crusader states to survive for another century.

Returning home, he was seized (Dec. 1192) and held to ransom by Leopold of Austria, with whom he had quarrelled at Acre. The arrangements Richard had made for the governing of his kingdom during his absence stood up well to this unforeseeable turn of events; John's rebellion was contained and the king's ransom paid. But Philip was able to capture some important frontier castles, and after Richard was freed in Feb. 1194, he devoted the remainder of his life to their recovery. This task, which involved building the great fortress of Château-Gaillard, south-east of Rouen, was almost complete when he was fatally wounded at Chalus, a castle belonging to the rebellious Viscount of Limoges.

Contemporaries saw in Richard a masterful ruler and a fine soldier. Indeed he became a legend in his own lifetime, in part because, as a songwriter and a highly educated man who understood the power of words, he deliberately cultivated the King ARTHUR-like image of the Lionheart, which has remained attached to him ever since. Other legends are later accretions: in the 16th century, his story became entangled with that of Robin HOOD; in the 20th, he became a homosexual. Most widespread has been the view of him that developed in the 17th century and gradually became dominant: that he was a negligent ruler. True, he spent little time in England, but England was only one – and the least threatened – of his dominions. He had much wider responsibilities and was regarded by his contemporaries as living up to them. Indeed, no other king of England played so important a role on the world stage.

Richard II (996–1026), Duke of the Normans. He is important in British history because of the asylum he gave in 1013 to his sister EMMA's children, including the future king EDWARD THE CONFESSOR. Although Richard personally came to terms with King CNUT in 1017, his earlier actions established the links between NORMANDY and England that were later to have such fateful consequences (*see* ROBERT I; SUCCESSION, ENGLISH, IN 1066).

Richard II (1367–1400), King of England (1377–99). Son of EDWARD THE BLACK PRINCE and Joan of Kent, the fact that he was still a boy at his accession in 1377 evokes sympathy, even from historians. So does the image of Richard grieving over the death of his wife ANNE OF BOHEMIA in 1394, as does the tragic finale portrayed in SHAKESPEARE's *Richard II*. But most – though not all – historians follow

Jean Froissart in criticizing the king while sympathizing with the man.

After displaying courage in the face of the PEASANTS' REVOLT, in the next few years the youthful king became difficult for the senior politicians around him, notably JOHN OF GAUNT, to deal with. In particular, his distribution of patronage, especially his generosity to Robert de Vere, was ill judged. In 1386, he tried to defy PARLIAMENT, but was forced to yield and watch while his minister Michael de la Pole was impeached and a commission was appointed to control the following year's expenditure and patronage. His response was to elicit from a panel of judges a definition of the royal PREROGATIVE in terms that declared that the parliamentary proceedings of 1386 had been illegal and that those who had promoted them should be punished as traitors. When the judges' opinions were leaked, a brief civil war followed, culminating in the battle of Radcot Bridge.

In consequence, Richard found himself at the mercy of the APPELLANTS, and had to endure the humiliation of the MERCILESS PARLIAMENT (Feb. 1388) – but at least he avoided deposition. In 1389, he formally resumed control of government and, with Gaunt's help, ruled peacefully for eight years; in 1396, he made a 28-year truce with France. The war over, he set himself the task of making the crown independent of the COMMONS in Parliament. Some historians see this as a 'progressive' policy, but it went hand in hand with the pursuit of vengeance for what had happened in 1388. By 1399, he was indeed a very wealthy king, but he had dispossessed a third of the upper nobility and had hounded to death his old enemies (including his uncle Thomas of Woodstock).

At this stage, having alarmed all his subjects, he went to Ireland, and when Bolingbroke (*see* HENRY IV) and the PERCYS struck, no one would lift a finger to save him. He lost two armies in two weeks and surrendered at Conway, perhaps hoping for a repeat of 1387–9. Instead he was coerced into abdicating on 29 Sept. 1399 and then imprisoned. The following Jan., a plot to rescue him only revealed how little support he had and probably precipitated Henry IV's decision to have him murdered. His body remained at King's Langley (Herts.) until HENRY V had it reburied in WESTMINSTER ABBEY.

Richard III (1452–5), King of England (1483–85). The fourth son of RICHARD OF YORK, he was created Duke of Gloucester in 1461 soon after his eldest brother became EDWARD IV. Compared with another brother, George Plantagenet, Duke of Clarence, Richard remained conspicuously loyal, sharing Edward's exile in 1470 and the dangers and triumphs of 1471 – and he was conspicuously well rewarded. To Clarence's chagrin, he married Anne Neville and, in consequence, obtained the northern half of the Warwick (*see* NEVILLE, RICHARD) inheritance. On this foundation, he engineered a commanding position for himself as Edward's lieutenant in the north. In 1482, he commanded the invasion of Scotland, which resulted in the recapture of BERWICK, and in Feb. 1483, he was given authority to keep whatever he could conquer in south-west Scotland.

Thus far, his career had been – for a royal duke – fairly unremarkable. He had been overbearing and acquisitive, but not the murderer and schemer portrayed by SHAKESPEARE. After Edward's death in April 1483, however, Richard's actions were, to say the least, extraordinary. On 30 April, claiming he was forestalling a Woodville conspiracy against him, he arrested Anthony Woodville, Earl Rivers, took possession of young EDWARD V and was subsequently appointed PROTECTOR. On 26 June, the boy was deposed and Richard proclaimed king.

Richard's defenders incline to the belief that he took this step only after learning (on or about 22 June) that Edward V and his brothers and sisters were illegitimate. Others believe that he had made up his mind earlier and that the bastardization of his nephews and nieces was a political manoeuvre designed to clear his path to the throne. Undoubtedly other potential obstacles – the royal servant William Hastings, and Earl Rivers, for example – were removed by the simple expedient of summary execution, and by the autumn, it was rumoured that the ex-king and his younger brother – the 'princes in the Tower' – had also been removed. Richard made no attempt to prove that they were still alive.

In Oct.–Nov. 1483, many former servants of Edward IV risked life and property by joining BUCKINGHAM'S REBELLION (*see also* STAFFORD, HENRY) against a king whom, a few months earlier, they had assisted in his programme of cutting the Woodvilles down to size. Richard suppressed the revolt, but grants of rebel property to his own loyal supporters reinforced the impression that his was a northern regime imposed upon a reluctant south. Moreover, the conviction that the princes were dead now focused attention on a hitherto insignificant exile: Henry Tudor (*see* HENRY VII).

Although Richard adopted a high moral tone in presenting himself as a God-fearing king opposed to the licentiousness that had, he proclaimed, characterized his brother's court, very little went right for him during the remainder of his short reign. His only legitimate son died in 1484, followed by his wife in March 1485, and he had to deny the story that he had caused her death in order to marry his niece. In Aug., he was able to muster enough troops to outnumber Henry's largely French army, but at BOSWORTH, many of his 'followers' either stood by or joined the invaders. He died fighting, believing that he had been betrayed.

The instinct to leap to the defence of anyone who has had the monumental misfortune to have their character assassinated by Shakespeare has resulted in Richard III becoming the most controversial of English kings. Particularly in recent times – and partly thanks to the work of the Richard III Society – he has found many admirers, and this despite his total failure to live up to a king's most basic responsibilities: to ensure the survival of himself, his dynasty and his followers.

Richard of York (1411–60), dynast. He became Duke of York at the age of four when his uncle Edward was killed at AGINCOURT. He served as HENRY VI's lieutenant in France in 1436–7, then as governor of France and Normandy (1440–5), but by the latter part of the 1440s, the court regarded him with suspicion. As son of Anne Mortimer and Richard, Earl of Cambridge (executed for his part in the SOUTHAMPTON PLOT), he was descended on both sides from EDWARD III, and had Henry died childless, his claim to the English throne would have been virtually unassailable.

In 1447, instead of the command in France he wanted, he was made lieutenant of Ireland. His delay in taking this up suggests that he shared the view that the appointment was tantamount to exile. Although his estates in England, Ireland and Normandy made him the greatest of the king's TENANTS-IN-CHIEF, the EXCHEQUER was slow in paying the wages due to him as governor; by 1449–50, he was in financial difficulty and was forced to sell some of his manors. At the same time, the fall of Normandy meant, in his case, the loss of valuable lordships as well as national humiliation.

In Sept. 1450, he returned from Ireland blaming Edmund BEAUFORT, Duke of Somerset, for the débâcle and determined to replace him in the king's counsels. But Henry, still reeling from the shock of CADE'S REBELLION – with its YORKIST overtones – had no intention of allowing Richard to be foisted upon him. Nor was he mollified by a parliamentary Bill seeking Richard's recognition as heir presumptive. In an attempt to force Henry's hand, Richard took up arms in 1452, but soon had to back down. However, after the king's breakdown, the court found Richard's demands hard to resist, and in March 1454, he was appointed PROTECTOR. Henry's recovery led directly to the WARS OF THE ROSES.

Deprived of authority, Richard resorted to force, and with Neville support – his wife was Cecily Neville (*see also* Richard NEVILLE, Earl of Warwick) – he won the first battle of ST ALBANS (1455). In Nov., he was reappointed protector, only for the king to relieve him of the office three months later.

By 1459, it was clear that the queen, MARGARET OF ANJOU, was out to break anyone who appeared to threaten her son's prospects. Richard's response was to renew his appeal to arms, but this ended at Ludlow, Salop, in Oct. when he and the Nevilles failed to persuade their troops to fight against the king. Richard fled to Ireland, but in 1460, after Warwick had captured Henry at NORTHAMPTON, he returned and claimed the throne. Reluctantly the Oct. Parliament recognized him as Henry's heir and granted him the heir's estates: Wales, Cornwall and Chester. He marched to challenge the LANCASTRIAN hold on the north, and was met at WAKEFIELD by the sons of the men killed at St Albans. He was himself killed and his head displayed at YORK, embellished with a paper crown. The real crown would be worn by two of his sons: EDWARD IV and RICHARD III.

Richborough (*Rutupiae*), Kent. Lying as it then did on the Wantsum Channel that separated Kent from the island of Thanet, this was an important port in Roman times. It was the place where the majority of the Emperor CLAUDIUS' invasion force established its base (*see also* AULUS PLAUTIUS), the site of a SAXON SHORE fort, and the main harbour for Channel crossings throughout the Roman period.

Ridolfi Plot, 1570, organized by Roberto Ridolfi (1531–1612), a Florentine banker resident in London, to depose ELIZABETH I with the aid of a Spanish invasion. Thomas Howard, 9th Duke of Norfolk, was half-heartedly involved and, as a result, was executed.

Rightboys, *see* WHITEBOYS

Ring Forts, Irish (*raith*) The normal residence for a family of any substance in early medieval Ireland, these usually consisted of a circular enclosure surrounded by a high bank of earth and a ditch, and would have contained one or more wooden buildings. Some were built as early as the Bronze Age, but archaeological excavation suggests that the majority were constructed during the early Middle Ages. Their defensive capabilities were presumably necessary in the violent conditions of early Irish society (*see* KINGSHIP). Some ring forts – such as TARA, the residence of the UÍ NÉILL kings – were exceptionally elaborate structures.

Riot Act 1715 Passed under threat of a JACOBITE invasion, at a time when anti-Hanoverian mobs were attacking DISSENTING meeting houses, the Act was designed to strengthen the hand of the civil power in the face of riotous crowds. It made it a FELONY for members of a crowd of 12 people or more to refuse to disperse within an hour of being ordered to do so by a MAGISTRATE: hence, the phrase 'being read the Riot Act'. The Act was recurrently criticized as a repressive measure, although, in practice, magistrates and troops were often apparently constrained rather than emboldened by its provisions.

Riots, legally, acts of collective violence by three or more people in pursuit of a common purpose. The medieval English tradition of popular risings effectively ended with KETT'S REBELLION in 1549 (though *see also* MIDLAND RISING; OXFORDSHIRE RISING), but thereafter, until the late 19th-century mass extensions of the electoral franchise, riots on local and particular issues remained a normal part of popular political expression.

Generally not life-threatening, they operated under certain unwritten rules reflecting notions of order and morality (*see* MORAL ECONOMY). Food rioters seized food to sell at equitable prices (*see* GRAIN RIOTS; PRICE-FIXING); traditional rights were defended against such changes as ENCLOSURES and FEN DRAINAGE; and attacks were made on social enemies such as homosexuals, METHODISTS or CATHOLICS (*see* GORDON RIOTS). In the 18th century, riots often reflected party conflicts.

Official responses were frequently conciliatory, since the means of coercion were weak (the RIOT ACT 1715 was meant to remedy this). Moreover, the GENTRY often recognized the legitimacy of the complaints being expressed and so produced remedies.

Riot remained a potent weapon for the disadvantaged or disenfranchised, although its incidence has certainly diminished and the seriousness with which it is viewed has increased. The momentous changes of the 1830s and 1840s saw a range of riots (*see* ANTI-POOR LAW RIOTS; REBECCA RIOTS; SWING RIOTS); and the coming of the industrial age brought more rioting in its wake (*see* PLUG RIOTS; PETERLOO MASSACRE). In the 1980s, a distinctive wave of riots affected low-income urban and suburban areas. Notably, destructiveness was directed towards the rioters' own depressing surroundings rather than outwards into more prosperous areas.

Ripon, 1st Earl of, *see* ROBINSON, FREDERICK

Ritualism, a hostile term for a 19th-century religious movement within the Church of England in which clergy and laity succeeded in reviving liturgical practices associated with a more CATHOLIC interpretation of Christianity. Sympathizers labelled themselves ANGLO-CATHOLICS. Ritualism was an outgrowth of the OXFORD MOVEMENT, which originally had concerned itself little with the outward appearance of worship; the development was linked with the intense interest general throughout Victorian educated society in medieval architecture, and one of its earliest manifestations was the foundation (1839) of the Cambridge Camden Society (from 1846 the Ecclesiological Society), which aimed to study pre-REFORMATION churches and promote interest in their restoration to medieval splendour. Soon ritualists attracted PROTESTANT alarm already aroused by the Oxford Movement, and there were even RIOTS at some churches which were strongholds of liturgical innovation. EVANGELICALS and LOW CHURCHMEN attempted to use the law to curb ritualism, but the Public Worship Regulation Act (1874) spectacularly backfired when successive prosecutions resulted in the imprisonment of respectable and respected priests; public sympathies shifted cautiously to the ritualists. Thereafter, attempts to rid the Church of ritualism were doomed to failure, and Anglo-Catholics produced some exuberant elaborations of liturgy. Their influence, however, was diffused in Anglican worship far more widely than their own grouping, coming to fruition from the 1960s in liturgical changes culminating in the Alternative Service Book (1980); they also affected the liturgical practice of the initially hostile Church of Scotland and FREE CHURCHES. The ritualist impulse was upstaged by the Roman Catholic Church's sudden conversion to simple liturgy in the vernacular after the Second Vatican Council of 1962–5.

River Plate, Battle of the, early British naval success in WORLD WAR II when the German 'pocket battleship' *Admiral Graf Spee* was engaged by two British and one New Zealand CRUISER off the coast of Uruguay in Dec. 1939. Although outgunned and severely damaged, the cruisers forced the *Graf Spee* into neutral Montevideo on the River Plate estuary for repairs. Believing that a much stronger British fleet was at hand, Captain Langsdorff took orders from Berlin and scuttled his ship rather than face defeat or surrender.

Roads Purpose-made roadways have been found dating back to Bronze Age and Celtic Britain, but the first roads to have been formed into a national network were constructed by the Romans in their years of occupation, principally centred upon LONDON (*see* ROMAN ROADS). The routes, e.g. the FOSSE WAY from Devon to Lincs., WATLING STREET from London to North Wales, and occasionally even the roadways themselves, survive. The major roads, which were remarkably straight, connected principal urban centres (*see CIVITAS*) and LEGIONARY FORTRESSES, and were designed mainly for military purposes; they remained in use through medieval times. In the Anglo-Saxon period the concept of the 'king's highway' was securely established, and repair of bridges was a central feature of the COMMON BURDENS. Maintenance of roads and bridges remained a function of local, parish or county, authorities through the succeeding centuries, and largely does still.

Historians have come to revise their opinion of early modern English roads, which were commonly held to have largely been impassable mud-baths, by pointing to the volume and increasing sophistication of wheeled traffic, especially in the 17th century when virtually every part of the country came to be connected to the capital by regular carrying services. On the whole, however, transportation was arranged by water if possible rather than road, either by river or coastal shipping, since it was cheaper and easier to move bulk goods on water than on land and roads were frequently poorly maintained, as the acerbic comments of the traveller and diarist Celia Fiennes (1662–1741) indicate.

The principal means of road improvement in the 18th century was the TURNPIKE trust. Turnpiked roads, charging tolls, covered some 15,000 miles of England and Wales by 1770, their distribution reflecting the pace of economic change in 18th-century England. The system had grown to 22,000 miles by 1830, when the day of the turnpike was coming to its end. The improved methods of road construction associated with John Metcalf (known as 'Blind Jack of Knaresborough', 1717–1810), John Macadam (1756–1836), George Wade (1673–1748) and Thomas Telford (1757–1834), promoted the growth of stagecoach services, substantially reducing travelling time. The two-day road journey from London to Cambridge of 1750 had become a seven-hour trip by 1820. In Scotland, the roads which General Wade's engineers put through the Highlands in the wake of the 1745 JACOBITE rebellion opened the depths of Scotland to the outside world; the road network which crossed Wales was primarily directed towards the western ports which traded with Ireland, although the growing significance of the coalfields and ironworks of south Wales was a further spur to road improvement.

Although the coaching trade experienced a huge boom between *c.*1810 and 1830, with more than 3,000 coaches in use supported by an army of helpers in inns and roadside stations, it could not compete with the CANALS and then RAILWAYS for the movement of bulk and finished goods, while the railways became the principal mode of passenger transport. The heyday of the roads came again in the 20th century as the motor car and then motor lorry grew in importance. If the roads were fairly empty in the 1920s, they were soon filling up, and concerted efforts of improvement were made. The super highways envisaged by Sir Patrick Abercrombie and other post-war planners, the Preston bypass of 1959 and the opening of the first stretch of motorway ushered in a new age of the road, finally superseding the network laid down in the 1st and 2nd centuries AD.

Roanoke, abortive first English attempt at colonization in North America, in a scheme of 1584 under Sir Walter RALEIGH. Six hundred colonists were established on Roanoke Island on the CAROLINA Outer Banks in June 1585, and evacuated a year later. A second colony, of 110 people including women and children, was established in VIRGINIA in July 1587, but was not resupplied – the advent of the Spanish ARMADA had made that impossible. When an expedition returned in 1590 it found the colonists had gone, leaving a cryptic message; it was supposed that they had been murdered by natives, assimilated with them, or had wandered away and perished. The 'lost colonists' are one of the enduring items of interest in the popular history of early America.

Robbins Report, *see* NEW UNIVERSITIES

Robert I (*c.*1010–35), Duke of Normandy (1027–35). The father of WILLIAM I THE CONQUEROR, he was the Norman duke who decided to give positive support to the exiled EDWARD THE CONFESSOR's claim to the English throne, in opposition to CNUT who had supplanted Edward's father ETHELRED II THE UNREADY. It is possible – although the matter is controversial – that Robert even attempted an invasion on Edward's behalf.

Robert I, King of Scots, *see* BRUCE, ROBERT

Robert II (Robert Curthose [Short Boots]) (*c.*1053–1134), Duke of Normandy. Eldest son of WILLIAM I THE CONQUEROR, he inherited Normandy after his father's death in 1087 and was expected by many to become king of England. In the event, the Conqueror's choice for the throne, WILLIAM II RUFUS, defeated the rebellion raised on Robert's behalf by his father's half-brother, ODO OF BAYEUX. In 1096, Robert joined the First CRUSADE, mortgaging his duchy to William Rufus for 10,000 MARKS to finance the expedition; as one of the conquerors of Jerusalem, he returned with his reputation much enhanced. William Rufus's death in 1100 gave Robert a second opportunity to take the English throne, and the following year, he invaded, but withdrew rather than risk battle. At Tinchebrai in Normandy in 1106, he was captured by another brother, HENRY I, and remained his prisoner until he died in 1134. He is buried in GLOUCESTER Cathedral.

Robert II (1316–90), King of Scots (1371–90). As son of Walter the Steward and of Marjory, daughter of Robert BRUCE, 'Robert the Steward' was recognized as heir presumptive in 1318, but the birth of David Bruce (the future DAVID II) meant he had to wait more than 50 years before finally becoming the first Stewart king in 1371.

In the meantime, he was made guardian of Scotland in David's absence in 1338, and again following the king's capture at the battle of NEVILLE'S CROSS in 1346 until he was freed in 1357. Not surprisingly, relations between king and heir presumptive – who had fled from Neville's Cross – remained troubled, but after the abortive rising of 1363, Robert bided his time.

After his succession at the age of 55, he proved to be a lax ruler, whose lack of interest in soldiering made him an ineffective leader once border warfare had been renewed on the death of EDWARD III in 1377. In 1384, he handed over responsibility for law and order to his eldest son John (later ROBERT III), but four years later he acquiesced in the appointment of his more energetic second son Robert, Earl of Fife, as guardian of the realm. He fathered at least 21 children, but only four of them were indisputably legitimate.

Robert III (?1336–1406), King of Scots (1390–1406). When he succeeded to the throne, he took the name Robert in preference to his given name John. As king, he continued to play the prominent yet ineffective role he had already, as Earl of Carrick, played during the reign of his father ROBERT II. In 1399, this led to his eldest son David, Duke of Rothesay, being given a three-year appointment as the king's lieutenant, and to quarrels between Rothesay and the latter's uncle, Robert, Duke of Albany. Rothesay's arrest and death in 1402 resulted in rumours that Albany, who succeeded him as lieutenant, had also been responsible for his murder. In 1406, Robert decided to send his heir (later JAMES I) to France, but the boy was captured by the English and sent to the Tower. The following month, Robert died. According to the poet Gower, he asked that he be buried in a midden (dunghill) as 'the worst of kings and most wretched of men'.

Robert Curthose, *see* ROBERT II (Robert Curthose)

Robert of Bellême (*fl.* late 11th century). The most notorious of the Anglo-Norman magnates, with a fearsome reputation for cruelty, he was the eldest son of Earl Roger of Shrewsbury and heir to the Montgomery estates. Robert of Bellême was usually a loyal supporter of ROBERT II, Duke of Normandy (Robert Curthose), supporting him against, in their turn, WILLIAM I THE CONQUEROR in 1077, WILLIAM II RUFUS in 1087 and HENRY I in 1101–6. He did manage to co-operate with William Rufus after Robert Curthose's departure for the First CRUSADE, but fell foul of Henry and was seized by him in 1112, remaining in prison until his death (date unknown).

Robert of Gloucester (*c.*1090–1147), illegitimate son of HENRY I. Created Earl of Gloucester in 1122, he became one of his father's most trusted advisers and the richest landowner in England. There is no evidence to support the theory that he was a candidate for the throne in 1135. Initially, he recognized STEPHEN, then in 1138 transferred his allegiance to his half-sister, the Empress MATILDA; from then until his death, he remained the mainstay of her party in England. His importance can be judged from the fact that Stephen was exchanged for him after they had both been captured in battle, Stephen at LINCOLN (Feb. 1141), Robert a few months later at the rout of Winchester. A cultivated man, he was the patron of two of the greatest writers of 12th-century Britain: GEOFFREY OF MONMOUTH and WILLIAM OF MALMESBURY.

Robinocracy, also known as 'Robinarchy': the regime of Sir Robert ('Robin') WALPOLE.

Robinson, Frederick (Viscount Goderich, 1st Earl of Ripon) (1782–1859), politician and Prime Minister (1827–8). He entered Parliament in 1806 as a liberal TORY, and held office as under secretary for the colonies (1809), vice-president of the Board of Trade (1819–22), and chancellor of the Exchequer (1823–7). He served as prime minister following the death of CANNING in Aug. 1827, but was indecisive and incapable of preserving the frail coalition of Canningite Tories and aristocratic WHIGS. He resigned in Jan. 1828 after less than five months in office. He subsequently served under GREY and PEEL as colonial secretary, lord Privy Seal and president of the Board of Trade.

Robinson, John (1727–1802), proto-civil servant. As secretary to the TREASURY from 1770–82, Robinson, who also sat as an MP, occupied a crucial place within the government's patronage machine. His elaborate lists, analysing the likely outcomes of general elections, have for modern historians shed light on both the extent and limits of the political influence of 18th-century administrations. The phrase 'before you can say Jack Robinson' has its origins in a parliamentary joke at Robinson's expense: asked in debate to name the man he had charged with seducing opposition members into government ranks, the WHIG Robert Brinsley Sheridan retorted that he could name the man 'as soon as I could say Jack Robinson'. Robinson can be seen as a prototypical civil servant; he probably regarded himself as, above all, a loyal servant of the king.

Rochdale Pioneers, *see* CO-OPERATIVE MOVEMENT

Rochester, 4th Earl of, *see* HYDE, LAURENCE

Rockers, name given to leather-clad motorcycle gangs in the 1960s, allegedly fans of 'rock' music. They attracted unfavourable publicity for their fights with rival groups of MODS at holiday resorts during the decade.

Rockingham, 2nd Marquess of, *see* WENTWORTH, CHARLES

Rockinghamite Whigs, a group of politicians who accepted the leadership of Charles WENTWORTH, Marquess of Rockingham from his administration of 1765 to his death in 1782. Critical of the policies of GEORGE III and his favoured ministers, they claimed to be the only true heirs to the WHIG tradition. Though membership of the group was ill-defined at the margins – some wavered between Rockingham and PITT THE ELDER – they were proud of their cohesiveness, and, flying in the face of contemporary suspicion of FACTION, publicly defended the value of party allegiance under the name of 'honourable connections'. The historian, Sir Lewis Namier credited them with having brought about the 'birth of party'. The group drew support from members of great Whig dynasties, such as the Portlands (*see* BENTINCK) and Devonshires (*see* CAVENDISH); Edmund BURKE was its ideologist. Charles James FOX, who became associated with the group in the course of the 1770s, took over its leadership upon Rockingham's death.

Rockites, *see* WHITEBOYS

Rococo, an ornamental style of decoration, fashionable in France and Germany in the early 18th century, and subsequently in Britain. Characterized by undulating line and movement, counterbalancing curves and the use of *rocaille* (coral and seashell motifs), it was employed in the interior decoration of PALLADIAN buildings, notably Chesterfield House in London and the chapel of the Rotunda Hospital, Dublin, as well as in silverware and in the painted decoration on teapots and other domestic ware. Thomas Chippendale's *Gentleman and Cabinet-Maker's Director* (1754) popularized rococo furniture designs. The style was championed by the artist William Hogarth who, with others, associated it with a loosely oppositional, 'PATRIOT' stance primarily because it represented an alternative to the dominant Palladianism.

Roger of Howden (?–*c.*1202), chronicler. The crusading parson of Howden, Yorks., his writings – which include the *Gesta Regis*, formerly attributed to Benedict of Peterborough – comprise the most detailed narrative of events in England and on CRUSADE between 1170 and 1201. His years in government service as a royal judge and diplomat gave him access to official letters; without his habit of giving texts in full, very little would be known of the ASSIZES of HENRY II and RICHARD I.

Roger of Salisbury (?–1139), chief minister. A Norman clerk in HENRY I's household, by 1101 he had become CHANCELLOR and was nominated bishop of SALISBURY the following year. As an embryonic JUSTICIAR, he had general charge of financial and judicial business, and in the 1120s headed the council while Henry was in NORMANDY; he is often credited with the development of the EXCHEQUER. He supported STEPHEN's succession, but in 1139 the king suspected him of disloyalty and he and his family were arrested. He died a broken man, deprived of his wealth and castles.

Roger of Wendover (?–1236), monk of ST ALBANS abbey and founder of the St Albans school of English history. After being dismissed from office as prior of Belvoir for squandering the priory's resources, he concentrated on writing his *Flores Historiarum*, a chronicle of the period from the Creation to 1234. His work was continued by Matthew PARIS.

Rognvald of Moer (*fl.* 9th century), Earl of Orkney. The saga tradition of the 13th century indicates that, in the second half of the 9th, he received ORKNEY from the Norwegian king, Harold Finehair. However, modern opinion generally rejects this view, seeing it as a late tradition designed to demonstrate long-standing Norwegian authority over the islands. It is more plausible that Rognvald independently established his family's power there, perhaps in alliance with a Norse warrior from DUBLIN, such as OLAF THE WHITE. Rognvald's son Rollo founded what became the duchy of NORMANDY.

Rolls-Royce, *see* MOTOR INDUSTRY

Roman Conquest of Britain The period of military conquest can reasonably be said to have begun with the landing of the armies of the Emperor CLAUDIUS in AD 43 and to have ended after AGRICOLA's attack on the Highland tribes in AD 84. It had been preceded by JULIUS CAESAR's two invasions in

55 and 54 BC, but these had done no more than establish a Roman interest in Britain that his historically minded successor decided to follow up. Roman rule finally collapsed in the 5th century.

The first stage of conquest was distinguished by steady military advance (*see* AULUS PLAUTIUS; OSTORIUS SCAPULA; CARATACUS), the defeat of some British tribes (*see* CATUVELLAUNI; TRINOVANTES; DUROTRIGES; DOBUNNI) and the establishment of CLIENT KINGDOM relations with others (*see* ATREBATES; BRIGANTES; ICENI; COGIDUBNUS). The progress of Roman power was rudely interrupted by BOUDICCA's revolt in AD 61, which was followed by a decade of consolidation.

In the early 70s, military advance was resumed (*see* PETILLIUS CERIALIS; JULIUS FRONTINUS), client kingdoms were taken over and the Welsh tribes crushed (*see* DECEANGLI; ORDOVICES; SILURES). Agricola's campaigns in northern Britain culminated in the great victory of MONS GRAUPIUS in AD 84, but plans to subdue the Highlands were rapidly abandoned after his recall to Rome (*see* INCHTUTHIL; SCOTTISH LOWLANDS).

Roman success was based on overwhelming military power, flexibly deployed as the immediate demands of war required (*see* LEGIONARY FORTRESSES; VEXILLATION FORTRESSES). Four legions took part in the original conquest, supported by an equivalent number of auxiliary troops – around 40,000 men in all. The innate discipline of the Romans proved too much for the British, despite the ferocity of their assaults on the conquerors and their fearsome war chariots. The British tribes were only occasionally able to group under a single leader (e.g. CASSIVELLAUNUS, Caratacus, Boudicca), and most of their victories were gained against isolated or reduced Roman forces.

The latter's military successes were supported by a form of organization that accorded with a long-established Roman formula. Most tribal territories became self-governing units known as *CIVITATES* focused on an urban centre, either an existing British town or a new Roman one. These centres comprised all the typical features of a Roman town and were intended to accustom the natives to Roman civilization. Tacitus tells something of how the British aristocracies adopted Roman manners; their acquiescence in Roman rule is everywhere evident.

Nevertheless, the conquest remained incomplete, which posed permanent problems for the Romans. Despite all their attempts, the northern frontier was never truly stabilized, and the succeeding centuries were typified by efforts to define a frontier (*see* HADRIAN'S WALL; ANTONINE WALL). In addition, there were assaults by northern tribes (*see* CALEDONII; MAEATAE; PICTS) and Roman campaigns north of Hadrian's Wall (*see* CONSTANTIUS I; SEPTIMIUS SEVERUS).

The famous proclamation of AD 410 by the Emperor HONORIUS – that the British province should henceforth fend for itself – did not follow a military defeat, and was probably not intended to be a permanent withdrawal. The Romans were not driven from Britain; they abandoned it.

As well as the trouble they encountered along the northern frontier, a number of other things led the Romans to this point. There was the mounting pressure of raids on the entire empire by peoples from outside, which had begun in earnest in the 3rd century and seem to have been regarded as more dangerous in regions other than Britain. Therefore, while the Roman defences in Britain were impressive (*see NOTITIA DIGNITATUM*; SAXON SHORE), the best troops were withdrawn to prop up the empire elsewhere. Britain's defences were also weakened by the frequency with which rival emperors were proclaimed there. These usurpers – the last of whom was CONSTANTINE III in 407 – all took troops to the Continent to fight their wars.

Following the withdrawal, aspects of Roman life continued (*see* GERMANUS; ANGLO-SAXON SETTLEMENT; TOWNS), but disintegration was none the less swift during the 5th century.

CHRONOLOGY

55 BC JULIUS CAESAR's first invasion of Britain.

54 BC Julius Caesar's second invasion of Britain.

AD 43 Landing of the armies of Emperor CLAUDIUS; start of Roman conquest.

AD 47 Roman power extended roughly to line of FOSSE WAY. Defeat of British chieftain CARATACUS.

AD 61 Revolt of Queen BOUDICCA and the Iceni.

AD 71–4 Roman subjugation of BRIGANTES completes Roman conquest of northern England.

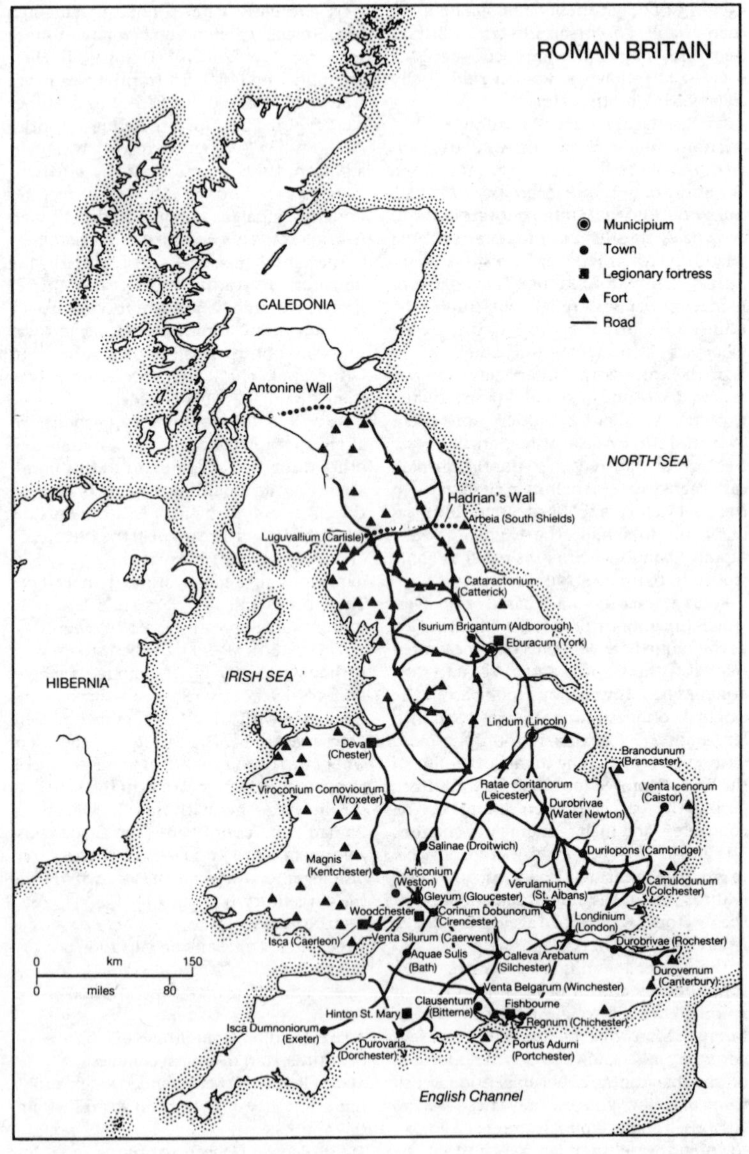
ROMAN BRITAIN
Municipium
Town
Legionary fortress
Fort
Road
CALEDONIA
Antonine Wall
NORTH SEA
Hadrian's Wall
Arbeia (South Shields)
Luguvallium (Carlisle)
Cataractonium (Catterick)
Isurium Brigantum (Aldborough)
Eburacum (York)
HIBERNIA
IRISH SEA
Lindum (Lincoln)
Deva (Chester)
Branodunum (Brancaster)
Ratae Coritanorum (Leicester)
Venta Icenorum (Caistor)
Viroconium Cornoviourum (Wroxeter)
Durobrivae (Water Newton)
Salinae (Droitwich)
Durilopons (Cambridge)
Magnis (Kentchester)
Ariconium (Weston)
Verulamium (St. Albans)
Camulodunum (Colchester)
Gleyum (Gloucester)
Woodchester
Corinum Dobunorum (Cirencester)
Londinium (London)
Isca (Caerleon)
Venta Silurum (Caerwent)
Durobrivae (Rochester)
Aquae Sulis (Bath)
Calleva Arebatum (Silchester)
Durovernum (Canterbury)
0 km 150
0 miles 80
Venta Belgarum (Winchester)
Clausentum (Bitterne)
Fishbourne
Hinton St. Mary
Regnum (Chichester)
Isca Dumnoniorum (Exeter)
Durovaria (Dorchester)
Portus Adurni (Portchester)
English Channel

AD 78–84 Governorship of AGRICOLA: subjugation of Welsh tribes completed and victory over northern British tribes at MONS GRAUPIUS. Romans abandon Scottish Highlands soon after Agricola's departure.
AD 122 Visit to Britain by Emperor HADRIAN; start of construction of HADRIAN'S WALL.
***c.*AD 140** Construction of ANTONINE WALL.
***c.*AD 160** Final abandonment of Antonine Wall; northern Roman frontier henceforth Hadrian's Wall.
***c.*AD 200** Approximate date for earliest raids on eastern Britain by Franks and Saxons; Romans start construction of increasingly elaborate system of coastal defences.
AD 208 Invasion of Scotland by Emperor SEPTIMIUS SEVERUS.
AD 260–73 Period of the GALLIC EMPIRE: Gaul, Germany, Spain and Britain temporarily secede from Roman Empire.
AD 287–96 Second period of temporary separation from Roman Empire under rule of CARAUSIUS and Allectus.
AD 306 CONSTANTINE I THE GREAT proclaimed emperor at YORK.
AD 383–8 MAGNUS MAXIMUS establishes himself as Emperor in Britain.
AD 407 CONSTANTINE III proclaims himself emperor and removes most of remaining Roman troops from Britain.
AD 410 Emperor HONORIUS proclaims that inhabitants of Britain should henceforth fend for themselves.
AD 429 Visit by GERMANUS: Britain still largely Christian and resisting invaders.

Roman Law, *see* CIVIL LAW

Roman Roads The network of ROADS that the Romans constructed in Britain were to have a profound long-term effect on the island's history. LONDON was the hub of the system, testimony to its importance as provincial capital. The main roads, which were remarkably straight (lesser ones were not), connected major urban centres (*see CIVITAS*; LEGIONARY FORTRESSES) and were clearly intended to assist military operations. Roman roads frequently remained in use into the medieval period and were the basis of Britain's road system right up to the construction of the motorways (*see* FOSSE WAY; WATLING STREET). The notion of special protection for travellers on the 'king's highway', which appears in Anglo-Saxon LAW CODES, may well be a legacy of Roman rule. *See also* ANTONINE ITINERARY.

Romanesque, architectural style found across Europe from the 8th to the 12th centuries, as both a half-remembered survival and a poorly understood revival of Roman classicism. The English Romanesque style is often called NORMAN, since its introduction is associated with the Conquest.

'Root and Branch', catchphrase of a Dec. 1640 London petition and June 1641 parliamentary Bill seeking to abolish EPISCOPACY outright. It divided the opposition to CHARLES I and was therefore dropped; episcopacy was not abolished until 1646.

Rory O'Connor (Ruaidri O Conchobhair) (?–1198), High-King of Ireland (1166–83). In 1156, he succeeded his father TURLOCH as king of CONNACHT; within ten years, he was well enough established there to be able to exploit the sudden collapse of Muirchertach O mac Lochlainn's power. As the last high-king of an independent Ireland, he drove out DERMOT MAC MURROUGH, with the unforeseen consequence that he had to face far more formidable foes: Strongbow (*see* CLARE, RICHARD DE) and HENRY II. In 1171–2, he was one of the few Irish kings not to submit to the English, but by 1175 he was prepared to acknowledge Henry II's overlordship (*see* WINDSOR, TREATY OF). In 1183, he retired to a monastery; his re-emergence two years later only resulted in a long power struggle in Connacht.

Rosebery, 5th Earl of, *see* PRIMROSE, ARCHIBALD

Rose-Noble, *see* NOBLE

Rose's Act 1793, legislation promoted by George Rose, secretary to the TREASURY, giving legal recognition and status to FRIENDLY SOCIETIES which registered with JUSTICES OF THE PEACE. In the context of official fears of CORRESPONDING SOCIETIES, this Act sought to distinguish, protect and control respectable popular societies.

Roses, Wars of the, *see* WARS OF THE ROSES

Ross, earldom in northern Scotland. The first Earl of Ross was Malcolm mac Heth, who was probably an illegitimate son of ALEXANDER I. His challenge to the kingship of DAVID I led to his imprisonment from

1134–57, when he was released and granted the earldom. At his death in 1168, Ross was taken back into direct royal control. After helping ALEXANDER II to eliminate the rival MACWILLIAM dynasty, Farquhar mac Taggart was created Earl of Ross in *c.*1230; the earldom generally remained in the hands of his descendants until the late 15th century.

Rotation, change (usually annual) in the use of fields, primarily to promote better growth and at the same time not exhaust the soil's fertility. Fixed rotations were an integral part of traditional systems of farming in OPEN FIELDS, with each field in turn being allowed to lie fallow for a year to recover. One element in the agricultural productivity changes from the 17th century was the improved forms of arable rotations, which ENCLOSURE often made easier for individual farmers to undertake. Many new rotations involved growing clover and turnips, which first became important in eastern England by the mid-17th century, raising the ability to keep livestock which then manured the land and improved productivity. Clover also has the advantage, not recognized initially, of helping fix nitrogen in the soil. Turnips were later publicized by Charles, Viscount 'Turnip' Townshend from 1730, commonly but erroneously called one of the pioneers of the AGRICULTURAL REVOLUTION. The Norfolk four-course rotation, of wheat, turnips, barley, and clover was the ultimate expression of these developments, eliminating fallow, although it was usually only practised in this pure form on lighter lands. It underpinned the HIGH FARMING of the mid-19th century, but cropping rotations became less prominent thereafter, particularly with the increasing use of artificial fertilizers. *See also* AGRICULTURE.

Rothschild, European banking family originating from Frankfurt in the late 18th century, founded by Mayer Amschel Rothschild and his five sons. By the middle of the 19th century an interlocking, and intermarried, network of Rothschild family members stretched across Europe, with BANKS based in London, Frankfurt, Paris and Vienna. The super-wealthy members of the banking family in England virtually colonized Bucks. in the mid- and late 19th century, acquiring considerable tracts of land and building great houses, of which the first was Mentmore Towers (1852–4) and the grandest of all Waddesdon (1875–80).

Rotten Boroughs, term adapted from PITT THE ELDER's remark that BOROUGH representation was 'the rotten part of the constitution'. Depending on the vantage point of the speaker, the term might be confined to those twenty or so venal boroughs whose members (or their backers) secured their election by outright bribery – e.g. Dunwich – and in which no patron had any continuing influence. Or the term might be extended to embrace POCKET BOROUGHS as well. The REFORM ACT 1832 began the process of reducing both patronage and venality by redistribution of parliamentary seats and changes in the FRANCHISE.

Rotunda Parliament, 1783. Delegates from Irish VOLUNTEER corps, having previously assembled in provincial conventions, at DUNGANNON and elsewhere, met in Nov. at the 'Rotunda' Assembly Rooms in Dublin to promote a measure of PARLIAMENTARY REFORM, argued to be the necessary final step in the campaign for Irish LEGISLATIVE INDEPENDENCE. Henry Flood carried into Parliament a bill whose provisions included triennial parliaments and the addition of neighbouring rural electors to decayed BOROUGHS (but which remained silent on the controversial issue of removing the bar on CATHOLIC voting); it was voted down by more than 2–1. This GENTRY-dominated convention represented the high point of reforming agitation; radicalization of the issue, and the rise of a more radical urban leadership in the following year, alienated country gentry.

'Rough Wooing', *see* GORDON, GEORGE (4TH EARL OF HUNTLY); PINKIE, BATTLE OF

Roundheads, normally abusive nickname for those fighting CHARLES I in the first English CIVIL WAR (1642–6), supposedly from a remark about a severe pre-war PURITAN haircut. Exactly who first said it about whom is controversial, although the first usages are from 1641. *See also* ROYALISTS.

Roundway Down, Battle of, 13 July 1643, ROYALIST victory in Wilts. over the western Parliamentary commander Sir William Waller, ending his run of success. The victory gave CHARLES I control over most of south-west England, leading on to the capture of the strategic port of BRISTOL. *See also* CIVIL WARS.

Roy's Military Survey, mapping of Scotland by William Roy during the 1750s, in the aftermath of the '45 JACOBITE Rebellion. The maps were exceptionally detailed, and developed forms of shading and use of symbols which were influential in the subsequent formation of the ORDNANCE SURVEY. The maps are of particular interest in showing Scotland on the verge of considerable economic change, and are frequently studied in combination with the near-contemporary Webster's POPULATION estimate and *STATISTICAL ACCOUNT*.

Royal Academy Founded in 1768, following a memorial by 22 leading artists encouraged by GEORGE III, it was intended to promote arts and design. (The absence in Britain of institutional support for the arts comparable to that which existed in France had previously been the subject of complaint.) The Instrument of Foundation stipulated that there should be 40 royal academicians, to be chosen from among painters, sculptors and architects resident in Great Britain. Vacancies were to be filled by election from among those who exhibited at the Academy. Initial members included two women, Angelica Kauffman and Mary Moser, who were considered full members but not expected to attend meetings. The Academy organized an annual exhibition, whose proceeds were used to support indigent artists, and ran a free school. Sir Joshua Reynolds (1723–92) was first president. Initially located in Pall Mall, London, the Academy moved in 1771 to old Somerset House in the Strand, and in 1867 to Burlington House, Piccadilly, where it remains.

Royal African Company The Royal Adventurers of England trading into Africa were chartered in 1662, with the exclusive right of trade with the coast from Sallee to the Cape of Good Hope. When they ran into financial difficulties in 1672, creditors and some shareholders were incorporated as the Royal African Company. Initially highly successful, the company traded in slaves, gold, silver and redwood. Its monopoly was attacked in 1692–4; the trade was opened to independent traders, who had to pay fees to the company; and in 1712 a proposal to open the trade to all was successfully resisted. Yet the Company did not prosper. The ASIENTO slave contract was assigned to the SOUTH SEA COMPANY. The JOINT STOCK was dissolved in 1750, and in 1752 the Company's African forts were transferred to the crown.

Royal Air Force (RAF), the youngest of Britain's armed services, formed in April 1918 from an amalgamation of the ROYAL FLYING CORPS and the Royal Naval Air Service. It was created following the public outcry over ZEPPELIN and other air raids during WORLD WAR I. Under its first chief of air staff, Hugh TRENCHARD, the RAF built up an independent bomber force and from 1936 placed orders for new monoplane fighters and began work on a ground-control system based on RADAR.

During WORLD WAR II, the RAF was the decisive instrument in countering the threat of invasion by its victory in the Battle of BRITAIN, and under HARRIS carried out the sustained BOMBING OFFENSIVE against Germany. After 1945, the RAF was equipped with modern jet aircraft, becoming the mainstay of Britain's nuclear forces with the V BOMBER FORCE in the 1950s. After the introduction of the POLARIS submarine-launched nuclear missiles, the RAF continued to deploy tactical nuclear bombers, as well as aircraft for air defence, ground support, and transport. *See also* WARFARE, AIR.

Royal Commission on Labour, 1891–4. A response to the growth of the NEW UNIONS, its membership included some half-dozen TRADE UNIONISTS and several labour sympathizers under the chairmanship of Spencer Cavendish, Duke of Devonshire. The outcome of its deliberations, the CONCILIATION ACT of 1896, seemed hardly commensurate with the depth and thoroughness of its inquiry into the state of industrial relations. Its value as a document however is enormous. It is an indispensable resource for industrial conditions and working-class attitudes in the generation before WORLD WAR I.

Royal Commission on Trade Unions, 1866–9. Appointed in the aftermath of the SHEFFIELD 'OUTRAGES', it was the subject of intensive lobbying on the part of the JUNTA and their POSITIVIST allies. The Commissioners accepted the case advanced by William Allan and Robert Applegarth that strong and effective TRADE UNIONS reduced STRIKES and violence and made for better industrial relations. The TRADE UNION ACT 1871, which gave trade unions legal recognition and the right to protect their funds, was the direct outcome of their efforts.

Royal Flying Corps (RFC) The predecessor of the ROYAL AIR FORCE, the RFC was established in April 1912 with a naval and an army wing, primarily intended for scouting. The navy wing split off to form the Royal Naval Air Service (RNAS), and by 1914 the RFC had 63 operational aircraft and the RNAS 66. With the outbreak of WORLD WAR I the uses and number of aeroplanes multiplied enormously, increasing the RFC to several thousand aircraft. The RFC was still under nominal ARMY control, but there were growing demands for an independent air service, especially to deal with ZEPPELIN and air raids on Britain. A committee set up in 1917 concluded that the Royal Air Force should come into being in 1918 by amalgamating the RFC and the RNAS.

Royal Navy, *see* NAVY; WARFARE, NAVAL

Royal Prerogative, *see* PREROGATIVE, ROYAL

Royal Society In full, the Royal Society for the Promotion of Natural Knowledge, founded 1660, and surviving until the present as a scientific club. Developed out of INTERREGNUM scientific groups, modelling its rules on those adopted by Oxford experimental philosophers in 1651, it was also influenced by the French *académies privées*. It received a royal charter in 1662. Scientific ideas were discussed at its meetings; it also promoted research and experiment, and published reports in its journal, *Philosophical Transactions*, from 1695. Unlike its continental counterparts, it had no endowment, and depended on members' subscriptions.

Royal Society of Arts, *see* SOCIETY FOR THE ENCOURAGEMENT OF ARTS

Royal Supremacy The centrepiece of HENRY VIII's break with Rome, supremacy was implied by the 1532 SUBMISSION OF THE CLERGY, then established over the CHURCH OF ENGLAND by the 1534 Act of Supremacy, repealed by MARY I's 1554 Parliament and restored in 1559. In Ireland, there was parallel legislation, repealed in 1869.

The powers of 'headship' of the Church were declared to be God-given, having been usurped by the Pope in previous centuries. The 1559 Act declared the monarch supreme governor, not supreme head – probably as a concession to male chauvinism, since the then monarch was ELIZABETH I – but the change made no practical difference. The royal supremacy has never operated in Scotland, where the Established Church has jealously preserved its CALVINIST independence. *See also* VICE-GERENCY.

Royal Title Act 1876 An example of DISRAELIAN imperialism, by this legislation Queen VICTORIA received the title Empress of INDIA. The monarchy was thereby glorified, and the importance of the Indian Empire enhanced.

Royalists, the term commonly used for those who fought for CHARLES I in the first English CIVIL WAR (1642–6), and in general for those who sustained the royal cause through the INTERREGNUM. They were also known as Cavaliers, an initially abusive term coined by 1641, and originally used in the form 'cavallero' or similar Spanish, Portuguese or Italian forms for a knightly horseman. The overtones of this usage were various but all initially hostile: they implied that the king's supporters were military-minded courtiers, and were seeking the sort of arbitrary government backed by brute force which patriotic (or xenophobic) Englishmen associated with Roman Catholic and down-trodden Mediterranean Europe. Gradually Royalists adopted the term, liking its implications of dashing gallantry.

Rufus, *see* WILLIAM II RUFUS

Rump Parliament, the name given to the Parliament which consisted of the rump of the LONG PARLIAMENT MPs (largely INDEPENDENTS) left after PRIDE'S PURGE in 1648; also known as the 'Purged Parliament'. Ejected by Oliver CROMWELL in April 1653, they were recalled for a session from May to Oct., 1659 and then (with surviving purged members) from Dec. 1659 to March 1660.

Runic Inscriptions These survive from many parts of Europe from the first millennium AD and after. Among Germanic peoples, the runic alphabet was associated with ritual and magic, and most surviving examples appear on objects of some special significance. Among the English ones are the RUTHWELL CROSS, the Franks Casket and the Mortain Casket, as well as assorted coins and weapons. Runes were also used in VIKING Scandinavia; specimens in Britain include a stone found in St Paul's churchyard in London. The sword described in the great poem *BEOWULF* illustrates well the magical powers attributed to runes.

Rupert of the Rhine, Prince (1619–82), soldier. JAMES I's grandson, he fled to England on his father Frederick's loss of the Palatine Electorate. With the outbreak of CIVIL WAR, he was made ROYALIST general of the horse, then commander-in-chief, also receiving the titles of Earl of Holderness and Duke of Cumberland (1644). His military talents and his experience gained in the THIRTY YEARS WAR were offset by his quarrelsomeness, and CHARLES I finally became disillusioned after the loss of BRISTOL, the last major Royalist asset, in 1645. Rupert then took command of the part of the NAVY that had come over to the Royalists, until it was dispersed by BLAKE. After the RESTORATION he commanded fleets against the Dutch. A man with an enquiring mind and artistic talent, he was an early member of the ROYAL SOCIETY.

Rural District Councils (RDCs), *see* DISTRICT AND PARISH COUNCILS ACT 1894

Russell, Lord John (1st Earl Russell) (1792–1878), politician and Prime Minister (1846–52, 1865–6). A WHIG MP from 1813, he represented the City of Westminster 1843–61, when he was created Earl Russell. A promoter of the abolition of the TEST AND CORPORATION ACTS 1828 and an ardent advocate of PARLIAMENTARY REFORM, he was largely responsible for drafting the 1832 REFORM ACT during his time as paymaster-general (1830–4), and he advocated further measures as a member of Aberdeen's (*see* GORDON, GEORGE) coalition government in 1852. He was home and then colonial secretary before becoming leader of the COMMONS in Melbourne's (*see* LAMB, WILLIAM) administration (1835–41). On PEEL's resignation in 1846 after the repeal of the CORN LAWS, Russell became prime minister. Twice foreign secretary (under Aberdeen and Henry TEMPLE, Viscount Palmerston), he had an uneasy relationship with Palmerston, whom he had dismissed in 1852 over the latter's unauthorized recognition of Louis Napoleon's overthrow of the French Second Republic. Russell's record in foreign affairs, however, was chequered: he initially supported Britain's role in the CRIMEAN WAR, but then resigned over its mismanagement; he was behind Piedmont in the struggle for Italian unification, aided Richard Cobden in his efforts to conclude a FREE TRADE treaty with France, and introduced reforms in the foreign service in 1861. However, his handling, with Palmerston, of the *ALABAMA* affair during the American Civil War, when a British-built ship was allowed to fall into US Confederate hands, was potentially damaging to British–US relations. He became prime minister for a second time on Palmerston's death in 1865, but resigned in the same year when his government's proposals for further reform of the FRANCHISE were defeated by the revolt of the ADULLAMITES led by Robert Lowe. A man of short stature and wide learning, 'Johnny Russell' was once reproved by his father, the 9th Duke of Bedford, for 'giving great offence to your followers in the House of Commons by not being courteous to them, by treating them superciliously, and *de haut en bas*, by not listening with sufficient patience to their solicitations or remonstrances'.

Russia Company Chartered in 1555, following an expedition of London merchants to Moscow the previous year, the company was given exclusive rights of trade with Russia. It was incorporated as a JOINT-STOCK company of more than 200 members, aiming to export English cloth and import NAVAL STORES as well as furs and other cold-climate products. However, its most profitable trade came to be that with Persia, where it competed with the LEVANT COMPANY. Suffering from Dutch competition in the late 17th century, it was reconstructed as a loose trade association, with a mere £5 entry fee, admitting retailers as well as merchants. It flourished on this basis and, by the mid-18th century, dominated Russia's foreign trade.

The company was exceptionally well represented on 18th-century charitable governing bodies, and proved a seedbed of EVANGELICALISM. Members included Jonas Hanway, Robert Wilberforce (father of William) and Thomas Raikes (brother of Robert).

Ruthven Raid, Aug. 1582, the seizure of JAMES VI by PROTESTANT aristocrats led by John Erskine, 19th Earl of Mar, and William Ruthven, Earl of Gowrie, with the intention of ending the power of Esmé Stuart and James Stewart, 5th Earl of Arran. The Scottish king escaped from Ruthven Castle in June 1583, his prejudice against PRESBYTERIANISM confirmed. Gowrie was executed in 1584; Mar was banished, but in 1585 wormed his way back into James's favour.

Ruthwell Cross, Dumfries. The most famous of the surviving Anglo-Saxon crosses, this was reconstructed after being broken up at the REFORMATION and now stands to a height of over 5 m (16 ft). Its decoration includes a RUNIC version of the poem 'The *DREAM OF THE ROOD*'. It dates from either the 7th or 8th century and can be compared to other great crosses at Hexham, Northumb., or Bewcastle, Cumbria.

Ryal, *see* NOBLE

Rye House Plot, 1683, a plan to assassinate CHARLES II and the Duke of York (the future JAMES II) on their return from Newmarket to London, by blocking the road at a narrow passage at the Rye House near Hoddesdon, Herts. The attempt was accidentally foiled by their early departure. Although the plot was probably the work of minor figures, the government took the opportunity to implicate others. Some of those defeated in the EXCLUSION CRISIS – including Monmouth (*see* SCOTT, JAMES), Shaftesbury (*see* COOPER, ANTHONY ASHLEY) and other WHIGS and Archibald CAMPBELL, 9th Earl of Argyll – had apparently considered organizing risings in England and Scotland. Algernon Sidney, William Russell and the Earl of Essex were charged with complicity in the assassination attempt. Essex committed suicide in gaol; Sidney and Russell were executed on 21 July 1683.

Ryswick, Treaty of, Sept. 1697. This ended KING WILLIAM'S WAR between France, on the one hand, and the Holy Roman Empire, Spain, England, Brandenburg and Holland on the other. France acknowledged WILLIAM III as king of England 'by the grace of God', promised peace and friendship with him and his successors (taken in England to constitute a guarantee of the PROTESTANT SUCCESSION) and withdrew aid from JAMES II. France also surrendered all its conquests except Strasbourg. By agreement between the Spanish Netherlands and the Dutch, Dutch garrisons were installed in all the Low Country fortresses, creating a 'barrier' against French aggression (*see* BARRIER FORTRESSES).

S

Sabbatarianism, Christian belief that Sunday should be kept especially holy (taken from the biblical commandment about the Jewish Sabbath on Saturday). It was strong during the REFORMATION of the 16th century, although in the 17th, it became a mark of PURITANISM. Occasional attempts have been made to bring Christianity back to Saturday observance, particularly by some 17th-century fundamentalist sects and, from the 19th century, the Seventh-Day Adventists.

Sunday observance still affects British law: certain areas of Wales hold referenda, which keep pubs closed on Sundays; English Sunday trading legislation, a complex mess of contradictions, remained unreformed until 1994 while various interest groups squabbled.

Sacheverell Affair, a storm of 1709–10 provoked by the provocative preaching of Tory HIGH CHURCHMAN Henry Sacheverell, who claimed that DISSENTERS threatened the Church, and that WHIGS and moderate TORIES were failing to defend it. When he combined these charges with an attack on the Whig JUNTO ministry – in an assize sermon at Derby and again in a sermon at St Paul's in 1709 – the government started IMPEACHMENT proceedings. This provoked riots in his favour, during which Dissenting meeting houses were attacked.

Sacheverell was suspended from preaching for three years, but allowed to perform other clerical functions. He was hailed as a martyr; the ill-advised impeachment contributed to Queen ANNE's dismissal of GODOLPHIN and the latter's replacement with a Tory-oriented ministry under HARLEY. *See also* 'CHURCH IN DANGER'.

St Albans, *see* VERULAMIUM

St Albans, 1st Viscount, *see* BACON, FRANCIS

St Albans, Battles of There were two. The first, on 22 May 1455, is traditionally regarded as the initial battle of the WARS OF THE ROSES. Richard NEVILLE, Earl of Warwick, fought his way into the LANCASTRIAN-held town when HENRY VI refused RICHARD OF YORK's demand that Edmund BEAUFORT, Duke of Somerset, be imprisoned. The victorious YORKISTS, while insisting that they were entirely loyal to the king, used the opportunity to kill their principal enemies: Somerset, Northumberland and Clifford.

The second battle (17 Feb. 1461) resulted in victory for MARGARET OF ANJOU'S Lancastrian army over the Earl of Warwick, who was defending the Yorkists' possession of London and HENRY VI. Warwick was taken by surprise, and the confusion in his ranks was such that, when he fled, he failed to take the king with him.

St Andrews, Fife. The place once known simply as 'Andrews' became important in the early 8th century when relics of the apostle St Andrew were translated there (exactly how is the subject of varying legends). The town became a bishopric in the 10th century, and by the later 12th, its saint had been recognized as the patron saint of the Scots. Because of St Andrews' special religious status among the Scots in the medieval period, there were periodic attempts to elevate it to an archbishopric, which finally succeeded in 1476. The CATHEDRAL, served by AUGUSTINIAN canons, was begun *c.*1162 and was from the beginning conceived as the largest church in Scotland. Deliberate destruction began soon after the national revolution of 1560, and the Fife weather continued the work, leaving today only sad fragments, together with the remarkable 11th-century tower of the cathedral's predecessor, St Regulus. Scotland's first UNIVERSITY was founded in the town in 1411.

St Brice's Day Massacre According to the *ANGLO-SAXON CHRONICLE*, ETHELRED II THE UNREADY ordered that all Danish men in England should be killed on 13 Nov. 1002 because 'they intended to kill him and his counsellors'. It is uncertain how far this order was actually carried out or what its results were. The probability is that the targets were Danes recently settled in England whose loyalty was suspect (*see* SCANDINAVIAN SETTLEMENT). It certainly did not stop the Danish onslaught, since another expedition arrived from the Continent in 1003.

St David's, Dyfed. Because of its association with St DAVID, this became the most prestigious religious centre in Wales. The present St David's Cathedral is built on the site of an 8th-century monastery, the prestige of which was such that WILLIAM I THE CONQUEROR made a pilgrimage there in 1081. A century later, determined – but ultimately unsuccessful – attempts were made to exploit its traditional importance and create a Welsh archbishopric there. *See also* BARRI, GERALD DE.

St George's Field Massacre, May 1768, the shooting by soldiers of several members of a crowd that had gathered in Southwark, south London, to acclaim the radical WILKES after his incarceration in the King's Bench prison. The incident was exploited by Wilkes' supporters to dramatize the dangers of rule by an unpopular ministry.

St Helena, remote Atlantic island and British colony. It was discovered by the Portuguese in 1502 and claimed by the Dutch in 1633. Annexed in 1651 by the EAST INDIA COMPANY, whose rights were confirmed in 1673 after Dutch attacks were repulsed, the British government assumed full responsibility in 1834. St Helena's fame came as Napoleon's place of exile after 1815; he died there in 1821.

St John, Henry (1st Viscount Bolingbroke) (1678–1751), freethinker and politician. Although a notorious freethinker, he was a key figure in the (assertively Anglican) TORY party of ANNE's reign, and was made secretary of state in 1710. An opponent of the HANOVERIAN SUCCESSION, he fled to France after the defeat of the 1715 JACOBITE rebellion, and served as the Old Pretender's (*see* STUART, JAMES EDWARD) secretary of state. Returning to England in 1723, he disclaimed his former Toryism, but threw himself into the cause of opposition, contributing to the journal *The CRAFTSMAN* and attempting to rally Tory and opposition WHIG forces under the banner of 'country' ideology (*see* COUNTRY PARTY). His pamphlet *The Idea of a Patriot King*, published in 1749 but written over a decade earlier, was alleged to have helped shape the future GEORGE III's political ideas, but that monarch's most recent biographer is dismissive of the notion.

St Kitts and Nevis St Kitts (or St Christopher) was Britain's first settlement in the WEST INDIES, colonized in 1623. From the 1650s, together with neighbouring Nevis, it was an important SUGAR producer. Partitioned with France until the 1713 Treaty of UTRECHT, they became British colonies in 1783, run in joint administration with ANGUILLA and the BRITISH VIRGIN ISLANDS from 1816, then within the LEEWARD ISLANDS FEDERATION. Forming with Anguilla the West Indies Federation 1958–62, the pair of islands achieved independence in 1983.

St Lucia Possession of St Lucia was continually fought over between the British, French and Caribs after 1638. Until becoming a British crown colony in 1763 under the Treaty of PARIS, the Caribbean island had changed hands 14 times. Included in the WINDWARD ISLANDS FEDERATION after 1838, independence was gained in 1979.

Saint Monday, popular term in the 18th century for choosing not to work on a particular weekday, and a relic of a lax pre-industrial approach to time discipline which 19th-century employers attempted to eradicate.

Saint-Sardos, War of, 1324–5, a war fought in south-west France between France and England precipitated by the ineptitude of EDWARD II's handling of the furore caused when one of his Gascon vassals destroyed the newly built French fortress of Saint-Sardos in the Agenais. Declaring AQUITAINE confiscated, Charles IV invaded the duchy, but in 1325, he agreed to restore it under peace terms arranged by his sister, Edward's wife ISABELLA OF FRANCE. The negotiations led directly to Edward's downfall, since they had taken both the queen and her son, the future EDWARD III, to Paris, from which she refused to return and where she took Roger MORTIMER as her lover.

St Vincent and the Grenadines Caribs prevented early settlement of these Caribbean islands, and Britain and France wrestled for control between 1722 and final ceding to Britain under the 1783 Treaty of VERSAILLES. Conflict continued with local inhabitants, descendants of slaves shipwrecked in 1675, until they were crushed in 1796; labour was provided by Portuguese and East Indian immigration in the 19th century. Within the WINDWARD ISLANDS FEDERATION from 1838, and then the West Indies Federation 1958–62, the islands gained full independence in 1979.

Saints, exceptional religious figures recognized either officially or unofficially as being particularly close to God, and therefore having an assured place in the afterlife. All religions honour holy men, and several varieties of Judaism were developing traditions of especially honoured figures in the two or three centuries before the coming of Christianity. However the image of the austere, world-denying figure familiar in the later history of the Church is first found in developed form in 2nd-century AD versions of Christianity which the Church declared heretical, collectively known as Gnosticism. The mainstream Church concentrated its honour on those Christians who had died for the faith ('witnesses' or martyrs). Hence the earliest saint associated with Britain is ALBAN, a Roman soldier who was executed because of his Christian belief either in the 3rd or 4th centuries; the cult at his tomb at VERULAMIUM (St Albans) survived the end of Roman rule. Another Roman Christian cult tomb which survived into the ANGLO-SAXON period has recently been excavated at Wells (Som.).

During the 4th century, the cult of the saints rapidly expanded throughout the Church to include a variety of categories: those who suffered but were not killed for their faith ('confessors', from the Roman legal term for someone who pleads guilty in a trial); virgins (martyrs to chastity); and even, in the end, theologians. Sainthood in CELTIC Christianity was informally conferred on the founders of new missions, churches and monasteries, accounting for the number of placenames with references to local saints in Cornwall, Ireland, Scotland and Wales. Throughout Europe pilgrimage to SHRINES became a major component of medieval devotion, particularly as sponsored by BENEDICTINE and CLUNIAC monasteries. The medieval Western Church, with its bureaucratic approach to faith, instituted a formal process of canonization by the papacy, especially from the 13th century onwards.

PROTESTANTS in the 16th-century REFORMATION rebelled strongly against the idea of any human being having an assured place in heaven, and suppressed cults of saints and their shrines. However, it proved more difficult in England to remove the memory of saints' feast-days, since they were the occasions for leisure and fun (holy days, which become HOLIDAYS), and since they also structured the legal year of the COMMON LAW courts. The PRAYER BOOK retained many holidays, and later ANGLICANISM remained in general hospitable to the notion of saints, particularly under the influence of the 19th-century OXFORD MOVEMENT. The CHURCH OF ENGLAND has not revived any formal procedure for canonization, but its Alternative Service Book (1980) provides an interesting new list of special days for particularly outstanding heroes of English church history, mostly male and clerical. Meanwhile the Roman Catholic Church has canonized various men and women from Britain, notably MORE, FISHER and others executed in the religious upheaval of the Reformation.

Saintes, Battle of the, 12 April 1782, a British naval victory in the War of AMERICAN INDEPENDENCE. The largest naval battle of the 18th century, it was fought off the Iles des Saintes between Guadeloupe and DOMINICA in the WEST INDIES, between a British fleet under Admiral Rodney and a French fleet under Admiral de Grasse. De Grasse had captured ST KITTS, MONTSERRAT and NEVIS, and was escorting an invasion convoy to join the Spanish in an attack on JAMAICA. After the battle, in which the French flagship surrendered, the invasion was abandoned and British possessions in the West Indies were secured. But news of the victory arrived too late to save NORTH's ministry, which collapsed after the defeat at YORKTOWN.

Sake and Soke, a common formula in grants of property made in late Anglo-Saxon and Norman times. It literally means 'suit and cause' and can usually be taken to infer a right to hold a court and exercise jurisdiction within the property granted. By the 11th century, it frequently implied that a HUNDRED-court had been transferred from royal to private hands.

Saladin Tithe, 1188, tax levied by HENRY II to finance the Third CRUSADE, called in response to the capture of Jerusalem in 1187 by Saladin, sultan of Egypt. Paid by those who did not 'take the cross' and at a rate of one-tenth of a valuation of their revenues and moveables, its yield proved so great that it became the precedent for the system of direct taxation central to English royal finance for the next three centuries.

Sale of Food and Drugs Act 1875 This Act addressed the problems posed by the adulteration of food, and provided for the appointment of public analysts, but it was not until such appointments were made compulsory in 1879 that effective action was possible.

Salisbury (New Sarum), CATHEDRAL city in Wilts., established as a new town on a rectilinear plan beside the River Avon in 1219. The town and cathedral were established on the abandonment of the nearby hill site of Old Sarum, and the cathedral is one of the most complete examples of EARLY ENGLISH architecture. Its spire, at 404 feet (123 m), is the tallest in Britain. The principal liturgy of the medieval English church – the USE of Sarum – derived from Salisbury, supposedly introduced by its saint and founder bishop, Osmund. Salisbury became an important centre of the WOOLLEN INDUSTRY in late medieval and early modern times, and was the model for Anthony Trollope's fictional Barchester. The uninhabited site of Old Sarum remained a parliamentary seat until the REFORM ACT 1832, and was a notorious POCKET BOROUGH.

Salisbury, Roger of, *see* ROGER OF SALISBURY

Salisbury, 15th Earl and 3rd Marquess of, *see* CECIL, ROBERT GASCOYNE

Salt Industry Salt was important in early economies as a food preservative. Not surprisingly, there is an exceptionally large amount of archaeological and documentary evidence of salt production all around the English coasts and of the intensive exploitation of the inland brine springs at Droitwich and Nantwich from Anglo-Saxon times. Later, intensive development of the Ches. salt plain came with the construction of the Weaver-Sankey and St Helens CANALS, the latter solving a threatened fuel crisis in the Mersey salt refineries. From the later 19th century, the Ches. salt deposits formed the basis of the early CHEMICAL INDUSTRY.

Salters' Hall Controversy This City of London hall was the meeting place of the Protestant DISSENTING DEPUTIES. In 1719, the deputies were riven by disputes over the necessity of belief in the Trinity. 'Subscribers' to a Trinitarian declaration comprised mainly INDEPENDENTS and Particular BAPTISTS; the 'Non-Subscribers', who refused to condemn any whose beliefs conformed to the Scriptures, consisted of PRESBYTERIANS and General Baptists. The debates took place against the background of attempts to secure repeal of the OCCASIONAL CONFORMITY and SCHISM Acts, and the BANGORIAN CONTROVERSY among churchmen: the cleric Benjamin Hoadly (1676–1761) welcomed the victory of the Non-Subscribers, which he saw as a triumph 'for liberty'. Doctrinal differences were not healed: by the end of the century, Presbyterian and General Baptist meetings were commonly UNITARIAN; Independents and Particular Baptists, Trinitarian.

Salvation Army A Christian organization for evangelistic and social work, it was founded by William Booth in 1865 but received its present form and name in 1878. It is organized on a military basis and is international in scope. 'General' William Booth died in 1912 and was succeeded by his son, William Bramwell Booth, but since 1931 the 'General' has been elected by the high council. The Army rejected all belief in 'sacraments' although its teaching was in other ways consistent with most EVANGELICAL belief. In the 19th century it stressed the moral aspects of Christianity. Open-air meetings, brass bands and banners; aggressive and emotional public conversions; public testimony and penance characterized its worship. It remains involved in social work on a large scale, especially in rescue work among alcoholics, drug addicts, prisoners, young people and the homeless. Although its headquarters have always been in London, its most spectacular growth has been in the United States of America. Its style has changed, but its mission continues.

Samson of Bury St Edmunds, *see* JOCELIN OF BRAKELOND

Samuel Commission, ROYAL COMMISSION into the COAL INDUSTRY which preceded the GENERAL STRIKE. Set up by BALDWIN under Sir Herbert Samuel in 1925, it was intended to avert a looming clash in the industry between the miners and the coal-owners. Although the appointment of the Commission was welcomed by the miners, they rejected its report in March 1926 when it recommended wage cuts as the only means of creating a profitable industry, and appealed to the TRADES UNION CONGRESS for assistance, leading to the calling of the General Strike. Samuel's talks with a negotiating committee of the TUC, offering terms for a settlement along the lines of his report, encouraged the TUC to call off the strike; but the miners refused to compromise and continued their industrial action until forced back to work in the autumn on even more unfavourable terms.

Sancroft, William (1617–93), Archbishop of Canterbury (1678–89). A fellow of Emmanuel College, Cambridge, he was ejected for refusing to take an oath of loyalty to the Commonwealth (*see* INTERREGNUM), and subsequently travelled on the Continent. He was dean of St Paul's between 1664 and 1677, and archbishop from 1678. Following an unsuccessful attempt to convert JAMES II to ANGLICANISM, he and the king fell into open dispute in 1688, when Sancroft headed the SEVEN BISHOPS in defying royal orders. He played no part in the GLORIOUS REVOLUTION, arguing that the OATH he had taken to James precluded his taking another to WILLIAM III and MARY II. As a result, he was suspended from office in 1689, becoming the most eminent of the NON-JURORS. Contemporaries agreed in judging him a man of integrity; he was noted for abstemiousness and for the scale of his charitable giving. However, the staunch WHIG Gilbert BURNET condemned him as cold and weak.

Sanctions, coercive restrictions on trade used as an alternative to military action. They were espoused by the LEAGUE OF NATIONS between the two World Wars and Britain supported their employment against Italy during the invasion and conquest of Abyssinia in 1935–6, though they proved ineffective. Britain applied oil sanctions on Southern RHODESIA following the Unilateral Declaration of Independence, though 'sanctions busting' limited their effects. Sanctions were also applied in the 1990s by the UNITED NATIONS on Iraq up to and following the Gulf War of 1991 and on Serbia during the conflict in the former Yugoslavia. Their effectiveness in bringing about decisive political results has often been questioned.

Sanctuary, a refuge to fugitives offered by the Church. Certain sacred places, monasteries and churches conferred sanctuary on anyone in need coming within their precincts. Criminals had to leave the country or stand trial after 40 days in sanctuary, although some liberties (i.e. jurisdictions exempt from the crown's normal authority), such as DURHAM, provided permanent sanctuary. *See also* FRANCHISE.

From 1486, treason and second offences were excepted; a 1540 Act further limited the privilege, naming only eight places of refuge. These sanctuaries were abolished in 1603, leading to the re-establishment of COMMON LAW sanctuary rights. However, abolition for criminal offences came in 1624 and for civil offences in 1697 and 1723.

Sandwich Now a small, well-preserved town on the River Stour in Kent, it was described as the greatest port of the English kingdom by an 11th-century writer. It owed its importance to the Wantsum Channel between the Isle of Thanet and Kent, which silted up later in the medieval period. Other 11th-century sources also show that it was a major harbour for the Anglo-Saxon NAVY.

Sanitary Reform Movement Established in the 1830s, the movement was at its most effective in the 1840s. BENTHAMite in origin and empirical in method, it brought together a number of influential clergymen, medical men, philanthropists and parliamentarians in a campaign against the waste and inefficiency caused by the pollution of the urban environment. One of its key achievements was the publication of the seminal *REPORT ON THE SANITARY CONDITION OF THE LABOURING POPULATION OF GREAT BRITAIN* (1842). Preventative rather than curative in approach, the movement insisted upon improved sanitation and the reform of urban administration as the way forward. Its message was promoted by the Health of Towns Association, formed in 1844, with branches and news-sheets throughout the country. Opinion was mobilized both for and against PUBLIC HEALTH reform. Opponents of centrally directed sewerage and drainage schemes conducted a formidable defence of local freedoms.

Sanquhar Declaration, *see* CAMERONIANS

Saratoga, Convention of, 17 Oct. 1777. This marked the defeat of a crucial aspect of British strategy in the War of AMERICAN INDEPENDENCE. Burgoyne's army, heading south from CANADA and intending to meet up with British troops advancing from NEW YORK, split the American forces and gave the British decisive advantage. But American forces under General Gates blocked their advance and surrounded the army at Saratoga. The British surrendered and signed a convention by which they were to be disarmed and sent home. This first major American victory induced France to recognize the United States and conclude treaties of alliance and commerce. Defeat changed Britain's war policy: all bases but New York and Rhode Island were evacuated, and attention switched to an attempt to capitalize on loyalty in the south, a peace mission being dispatched under the Earl of Carlisle. The French formally allied with the Americans in Feb. 1778; their engagement transformed a colonial war into a conflict of empires.

Sarum, *see* SALISBURY

Saskatchewan, prairie province of CANADA founded in 1905, along with ALBERTA, out of the former NORTHWEST TERRITORIES. The Europeans arrived in 1671 in the shape of traders from the HUDSON'S BAY COMPANY, and like neighbouring MANITOBA the early history of the province is filled with feuding between the rival Hudson's Bay and North West Companies, and with uprisings by the mixed white and Indian Métis. The region was opened up with the railway and the establishment of grain growing from the 1880s, while it was one of the sorriest victims of the Depression of the 1930s.

Savile, George (1st Marquess of Halifax) (1633–95), politician. Son of the ROYALIST governor of CIVIL WAR Sheffield and York, Halifax played a prominent though not a leading part in political life in the 1660s and 1670s, being most notable for his consistent efforts to maintain a moderate stance in those difficult times. Although an opponent of Danby's (*see* OSBORNE, THOMAS), and restored to office on the latter's fall in 1679, he also opposed EXCLUSION. Briefly lord president of the Council under JAMES II, he was dismissed for failing to support the repeal of the TEST and CORPORATION ACTS. He joined the moderate opposition and, in the privately circulated *Character of a Trimmer*, argued the cause of moderation. He remained neutral in the early stages of the GLORIOUS REVOLUTION, supporting William of Orange (the future WILLIAM III) only after James's flight. Halifax chaired the meeting of peers which tried to cope with the power vacuum. Having played a prominent part in debate in the LORDS about the constitutional settlement, when he opposed the proposal for a regency, he was chosen to offer William and MARY the crown. Appointed lord Privy Seal in Feb. 1689, he tried to form a broadly-based government, but was unable to rally support from either side. Resigning in 1690, he remained in opposition thereafter.

Savoy Conference, 1661, series of meetings held at the Savoy Hospital, London, between ANGLICAN and PRESBYTERIAN commissioners from April to July 1661 to try to find a consensual foundation for the religious dimension of the RESTORATION SETTLEMENT. Chaired by Archbishop SHELDON with Richard Baxter as the leading Presbyterian, the conference failed to produce agreement about the revision of the Book of Common Prayer (*see* PRAYER BOOKS). The failure opened the way for the rigorously Anglican settlement embodied in the CLARENDON CODE. Historians have debated the inevitability or otherwise of this outcome. This meeting is not to be confused with the meeting of 1658, also at the Savoy Hospital, which resulted in the Savoy Declaration of CONGREGATIONALIST principles.

Savoy Declaration, *see* CONGREGATIONALISTS; INDEPENDENTS

Saxon Shore (*Litus Saxonicum*). The Latin term first occurs in the *NOTITIA DIGNITATUM* of *c*.408, which mentions ten coastal forts in eastern and south-eastern England under the control of a single commander (the *comes litoris Saxonici*). However, the different styles of construction employed and archaeological finds have demonstrated that the forts did not originate as a unified response to Saxon invasions. Some, such as Reculver in Kent and Brancaster in Norfolk, must date from the 2nd century, and RICHBOROUGH was important even earlier. The forts were probably built separately to support the Roman fleet. It is not known when they were formed into a single command to resist invasion; the later 3rd century is normally thought to be the earliest possible moment.

Saxons, one of the three peoples identified by BEDE as taking part in the migration of Germanic peoples that overwhelmed Britain in the 5th century. The Saxons came from north Germany and, according to Bede, took over ESSEX, SUSSEX and WESSEX. Extensive archaeological work has confirmed Bede's statement in its broad outline, but also suggests that the ANGLES and Saxons were more intermingled than he believed (*see* ANGLO-SAXON SETTLEMENT).

Saxons, South, *see* SUSSEX

Scandinavian Settlement in England The question of whether, from the mid-9th to the mid-11th centuries, Scandinavians settled in large or small numbers has been fiercely debated in recent years, with chronicles, PLACE NAMES, institutions, archaeology and language used as evidence for one side or the other.

At the least, it is obvious that the majority of immigrants settled in the northern and eastern counties. The most powerful evidence in favour of extensive settlement is supplied by place names and language. Both require sensitive analysis, but the range of the changes is none the less remarkable. The institutional evidence – supplied by terms such as SOKEMAN, *WAPENTAKE* and *CARUCATE* – is now considered less important than once thought, but it should still be recognized that the impact of institutions was sufficient to mould an already well-formed society into patterns that were significantly different from those of the south and west. Discoveries in towns such as YORK and LINCOLN are revealing an ECONOMY that received a powerful stimulus from the settlement. Scandinavian warriors (*see* VIKINGS) came to England in some numbers; whether or not they settled, their indirect effect is likely to have been great.

Sceattas, the name given by numismatists to the silver COINAGE widely used in England from the end of the 7th century until the end of the 8th, when it began to be replaced by the PENNY. There was a profusion of designs, and silver content generally deteriorated over time. Scholars dispute whether the minting of *sceattas* was under royal control.

Schiltrons, *see* FALKIRK, BATTLE OF

School Meals Under the EDUCATION (PROVISION OF MEALS) ACT 1906 local authorities were permitted to provide school meals. Initially the local authorities which chose to do so, usually LABOUR-controlled, were concentrated in the poorest areas. By 1939 half of all education authorities were providing school meals but provision was greatly extended during WORLD WAR II to ensure adequate nutrition for young children and to facilitate women taking on war work while their children stayed at school. The service continued after the war and by 1970 two-thirds of English and just under half of Scottish children were taking schools meals, many of them free. The proportion fell as the price of meals was raised from 1971, and in 1980 local education authorities were given greater discretion in setting prices and providing school meals, leading many to abandon them altogether. School meals and (from 1934 until 1971, when it was withdrawn for children over seven) free or subsidized milk played a significant part in improving the health and stature of schoolchildren in the post-war period, especially amongst the poor. Their importance was contested in the more affluent years from the 1960s.

School-Leaving Age The ELEMENTARY EDUCATION ACT of 1880 made school attendance compulsory to the age of 10. The minimum age for ending full-time education was raised to 11 in 1893, and 12 in 1899, though children who had reached a certain educational standard were allowed to work in factories half-time and to go to school for the rest of the day. The half-time system was abolished in the 1918 EDUCATION ACT, which also raised the minimum age for leaving to 14. Raising the school-leaving age remained an objective of progressive educationalists but was delayed by the DEPRESSION of the 1930s. The leaving age was finally raised to 15 in 1944 and, after further delay due to economic circumstances, to 16 in 1973.

Scone, near Perth, the original site of the 'Stone of Destiny' on which Scottish kings since the time of KENNETH MAC ALPIN were seated on the occasion of their inauguration. Until 1331, when DAVID II was anointed, the ceremony was a secular one. It involved a lengthy recital – in GAELIC – of the new ruler's genealogy, as well as other, unknown features (possibly including animal sacrifice), which the English-educated DAVID I is said to have found distasteful. In 1296, EDWARD I took the Stone (a block of reddish-grey sandstone) from Scone Abbey to WESTMINSTER where it was placed under the Coronation Chair, since when all newly enthroned English sovereigns have sat upon it. It was returned to Scotland in 1996 and is now in Edinburgh Castle.

Scots Originating in Ireland, they began to raid the west coast of what is now called Scotland in the 3rd century AD. By the 5th century, they were settling in modern ARGYLL and, a century later, had formed the kingdom of DALRIADA. Their interests on both sides of the Irish Sea were important in bringing St COLUMBA and other Irish churchmen to Scotland. There was a period of great military strength in the time of Aidan mac Gabhráin in the late 6th century, but after the battle of MAG RATH in 637, the political connection with Ireland was cut. The Scots and the PICTS – their neighbours and rivals – were permanently unified in a single kingdom from the time of KENNETH MAC ALPIN in the 9th century. *See also* KINGSHIP; STRATHCLYDE.

Scots Guards, *see* GUARDS

Scott, James (1st Duke of Monmouth) (1649–85), nobleman. The illegitimate son of CHARLES II and Lucy Walter, he was recognized by the king and created duke in 1663. In 1670, he was made captain general of the royal forces, and participated in the Third DUTCH WAR. He took the WHIG side in the EXCLUSION CRISIS, but in 1679 put down the revolt of the COVENANTERS at BOTHWELL BRIDGE. Exiled to Holland to prevent his intrigues to be made heir to the throne, he returned in 1680 to popular acclaim. He was arrested, and in 1683 was exiled once more.

What came to be known as 'Monmouth's Rebellion' – the rising in support of Monmouth in preference to the Catholic James, Duke of York – had its roots in the abortive 1683 RYE HOUSE PLOT and involved the same group of conspirators. A new scheme was already in hand when Charles's death brought James to the throne as JAMES II. Argyll (*see* CAMPBELL, ARCHIBALD) strove to stir up a rising in Scotland, but was defeated. Monmouth, having been expelled from Holland on James's accession, landed at Lyme Regis in Dorset on 11 June 1685, and issued a proclamation asserting his claim to the throne. He collected a following of between 3,000 and 4,000 – apparently chiefly men of middling social status, some of them DISSENTERS and supposedly including Daniel DEFOE. They succeeded in capturing Taunton, Som., but were defeated by royal troops (their number augmented by special parliamentary grant) at SEDGEMOOR on 5 July. Found in hiding after the defeat, Monmouth was taken to London and executed on 15 July. Other captured rebels were tried at the BLOODY ASSIZES.

Scottish Church, Disruption of, *see* DISRUPTION OF THE CHURCH OF SCOTLAND

Scottish Enlightenment Historians' term for the appearance in mid-18th-century Scotland of a group of thinkers and writers, mainly based in Scottish universities, whose writings on ethics, jurisprudence, history and what would later be termed economics and sociology commanded international respect and influence. Notable figures of the Scottish Enlightenment included the moralist Francis Hutcheson, the historian William Robertson, pioneering sociologist Adam Ferguson, the jurist Henry Home (Lord Kames) and the economist Dugald Stewart, as well as the more polymathic and enduringly famous David HUME and Adam SMITH.

Scottish Independence, Wars of In 1291, EDWARD I declared that, if the Scots wanted to oppose his claims to lordship over their country, they would have to do so by force of arms. From 1296 (when Edward invaded and sacked BERWICK) to the mid-14th century, this is precisely what they did. Against a series of assaults launched by their much richer neighbour, resistance leaders such as William WALLACE and Robert BRUCE – encouraging and encouraged by the patriotism that would be expressed in the Declaration of ARBROATH of 1320 – managed to organize a costly but ultimately successful defence of the tradition of an independent Scottish kingdom.

The wars began when Edward I took advantage of the fact that he had been asked to settle the GREAT CAUSE. He subsequently treated the new Scottish king John BALLIOL in so overbearing a way as to drive him into opposition, which Edward then chose to interpret as rebellion.

He and his successors had at their disposal much greater resources than the Scots – but not so great that they could afford to fortify and garrison Scotland in the way that Edward I had done to north Wales. The English could normally win pitched battles, as when Edward defeated Balliol at DUNBAR and Wallace at FALKIRK – though sometimes English over-confidence led to defeat, as at STIRLING BRIDGE and BANNOCKBURN. But what they could not do was persuade the Scottish people to accept their rule. Indeed, Edward's policy of treating the Scots as rebels instead of as foreign enemies, and thus punishing them ferociously when captured, was generally counter-productive, as it strengthened their patriotism and resolve. Even so, in the face of Edward's unrelenting determination, there were times, as after Bruce's defeat at Methven, when Scottish prospects looked bleak. Luckily for them, the succession of the ineffective EDWARD II in 1307 created opportunities that Bruce exploited tirelessly, finally in 1328 forcing the English to recognize his kingship.

However, his death the following year allowed a new and vigorous English king, EDWARD III, to ally with the DISINHERITED. For a few years after their victories at DUPPLIN MOOR and Halidon Hill, the English governed much of south-east Scotland, but as war with France loomed ever larger in Edward's mind, so he let Scotland slip from his grasp. After some 50 years of attempted conquest, only the Isle of MAN and Berwick (except for 1461–82) were to remain in English hands, but the hostilities engendered were to make the Anglo-Scottish border a dangerous place for more than two centuries.

CHRONOLOGY: BATTLES

E=English victory S=Scottish victory

1296 Battle of DUNBAR (E)
1297 Battle of STIRLING BRIDGE (S)
1298 Battle of FALKIRK (E)
1304 Fall of Stirling Castle (E)
1305 Execution of William WALLACE
1306 Battle of Methven (E)
1314 Battle of BANNOCKBURN (S)
1318 Capture of BERWICK (S)
1320 Declaration of ARBROATH
1328 Treaty of NORTHAMPTON
1329 Death of Robert BRUCE
1332 Battle of DUPPLIN MOOR (E)
1333 Battle of Halidon Hill (E)

Scottish Lowlands, Roman Occupation of From AGRICOLA's victory at MONS GRAUPIUS in AD 83 to the final abandonment of the ANTONINE WALL in *c.*160, the Romans occupied parts of Lowland Scotland. They normally travelled along the two roads that passed northwards through, respectively, Carlisle and CORBRIDGE, along which numerous forts and temporary camps have been found.

After the Romans gave up their attempts at permanent control, Lowland tribes such as the MAEATAE occasionally launched attacks across HADRIAN'S WALL, provoking retaliatory campaigns (*see* SEPTIMIUS SEVERUS; CONSTANTIUS). However, the Romans' retreat from the Scottish Lowlands was undoubtedly primarily the result of their inability to establish a tenable frontier on the Forth–Clyde line against the tribes to the north (*see* PICTS). *See also* ROMAN CONQUEST OF BRITAIN.

Scottish Missionary Society, *see* MISSIONARY SOCIETIES

Scottish National Covenant, *see* COVENANT

Scottish National Party (SNP), formed in 1934 from a merger of the National Party of Scotland (1928) and the Scottish Party (1930). In 1945 the SNP won its first parliamentary seat in a by-election, though this was lost again three months later. Despite contesting seats at subsequent general elections, the SNP did not win another seat until Winifred Ewing's victory at the Hamilton by-election in 1967. In 1970 the SNP fielded almost a full slate of candidates in Scottish constituencies, and returned 11 MPs in Oct. 1974 at the height of the campaign for Scottish DEVOLUTION. After the narrow defeat on the devolution issue in the referendum of 1979 the SNP went into decline, obtaining only two seats in 1979. However, support for the party revived as a result of opposition to the THATCHER government's poll tax, culminating in a by-election victory at Glasgow Govan in 1989 and three seats at the 1992 general election. In the May 1999 elections to the Scottish parliament, set up after the referendum on the LABOUR government's proposals for DEVOLUTION, the SNP (which had won 6 seats in the 1997 General Election) returned a total of 35 MSPs compared to 56 Labour. As the oldest member of the new Parliament, Winnie Ewing welcomed the parliament back to Scotland after 300 years.

Scout Movement, founded by Robert Baden-Powell, the 'hero of MAFEKING' in the Transvaal during the BOER WAR. After his retirement from the army in 1910, 'B-P' devoted his life to the youth movement which he founded. The first Scout camp for boys was held on Brownsea Island in Poole (Dorset) harbour in 1907, and the next year the fortnightly *Scouting for Boys* was published. The Boy Scout movement, and the Girl Guide movement which involved Baden-Powell's sister, and later his wife Olave, whom he married in 1912, laid stress on individual responsibility, the outdoors, and particularly the closed world of camp routine to engender ideals of discipline, self-reliance and a robust community spirit. From the 1920s huge international camps or 'jamborees' were held regularly. There are now some 160 million members of the scouting movement in 150 countries.

Scramble for Africa A phase in European IMPERIALISM between *c.*1875 and 1900, which marked the increasingly rapid acquisition and division of territory in AFRICA among the European powers. In the 1870s other nations moved in upon Africa, which Britain had tended to regard as its private enclave, beginning with the French building a trans-Saharan railway; while Leopold, king of the Belgians, the French, Germans and British squared up in west Africa to command the co-operation of native people, especially in the Congo and Niger regions. The ensuing Congress of BERLIN in 1878 reduced the antagonism. A second scramble was marked by the Brussels Congress of 1890, when European nations divided up the spoils of Africa and began to fight to subdue African peoples, the French in the upper Niger and Guinea, the British in Sierra Leone and what became Nigeria. British interest in southern Africa was also designed to drive a wedge between other nations' spheres of interest, while the rush for gold and diamonds opened the interior further. *See also* under individual countries.

Scriblerus Club Founded in the winter of 1713–14, its members included Jonathan SWIFT, Alexander Pope, John Gay, John Arbuthnot and Thomas Parnell. These authors' central light-hearted project was to compose the fictional *Memoirs of ... Martinus Scriblerus*, an archetypal pedant of WHIG political inclinations. However, before that work was finally published in 1741, their discussions influenced such diverse creations as Gay's *Beggar's Opera*, Pope's *The Dunciad* and Swift's *Gulliver's Travels*.

Scrivener, quasi-legal practitioners and financial intermediaries from at least the 14th century onward. In London, their company (the Company of Writers of the Court Letter, whose records date from as early as 1392) was incorporated in 1616. While the writing of bonds and deeds made up the bulk of their work, the nature of their tasks led many to act as money lenders; some scriveners also practised in central and local courts as attorneys. Perhaps the most successful scriveners of the 17th century were Robert Abbot and his successors John Morris and Sir Robert Clayton; they received money on deposit for their landed clients, held their documents in their vaults for safe-keeping, and acted as brokers for mortgages and conveyancers for land sales. In the 18th century, however, scriveners were increasingly superseded in their functions by accountants, bankers, and legal professionals.

Scutage, a money payment demanded of a tenant by his lord in lieu of the military service (KNIGHT SERVICE), which otherwise would have been due. When the king imposed a scutage, his TENANTS-IN-CHIEF were entitled to do the same to their tenants – and they could make a profit if the knight service owed by these added up to more than their required quota. The earliest reference to scutage dates from 1100 – although some forms of commutation of military service are certainly much older than this. *See also* FEUDALISM.

Seafarer, The, one of the best-known Old

English poems, which was included in the late 10th-century anthology, the EXETER BOOK. It celebrates the joys of life at sea, but also reflects upon the dangers and advantages of life on land. Its content is also significant for what it reveals of the importance of the sea in early English life.

Sealed Knot, English ROYALIST secret society operating during the Protectorate (*see* INTERREGNUM). It initiated no significant military action, and collapsed after BOOTH'S RISING. Its modern namesake, the most prominent organization devoted to re-enacting the British CIVIL WARS, cuts more of a dash.

SEALION, OPERATION (*Seelöwe*), code-name for the German plan to invade Britain during WORLD WAR II following the fall of France and Britain's refusal of peace negotiations. The scheme required German command of the air and sea; the *Luftwaffe's* losses in the air during the Battle of BRITAIN in 1940 convinced Hitler that command of the air had not been obtained and the weak German navy knew it would be nearly impossible to sustain a landing against British naval superiority even with command of the air, despite assembling a large fleet of improvised landing barges in the Channel ports. The invasion forces were finally dispersed in Sept. 1940.

Seals The earliest surviving seal of an English king is the double-sided seal of EDWARD THE CONFESSOR, which was attached to WRITS issued in his name. Evidence that kings may have used a seal to authenticate their orders exists in documents from as early as the reign of ALFRED THE GREAT, and laymen's seals have been discovered that suggest that they were widely used by the time of ETHELRED II THE UNREADY. Whether they were used to authenticate documents or verbal messages remains uncertain. *See also* GREAT SEAL; PRIVY SEAL; SIGNET.

SEATO, *see* SOUTH EAST ASIA TREATY ORGANIZATION

Sebastopol, Battle of, *see* CRIMEAN WAR

Second British Empire, *see* BRITISH EMPIRE, SECOND

Second Front, term used for the cross-Channel invasion of the German-occupied Continent during WORLD WAR II. The American High Command and the Soviet leader, Stalin, urged a cross-Channel invasion as early as 1942, but the British chiefs of staff argued strongly for delay, especially after the heavy casualties in the DIEPPE RAID. The alternative strategy of clearing North Africa of Axis forces was pursued, followed in 1943 by the invasion of Sicily and Italy. This postponed a cross-Channel invasion until June 1944. Delay in opening a second front was a major irritant in Allied–Soviet relations, fostering Soviet suspicions that the Russian forces were deliberately being allowed to bear the brunt of the land fighting. In fact, Allied calculations were dictated by caution about the difficulties of mounting a highly complex amphibious landing against a defended coastline. *See also* D-DAY; OVERLORD, OPERATION.

Second World War, *see* WORLD WAR II

Secondary Picketing, picketing of places of work by workers not directly involved in an industrial dispute themselves. Secondary picketing was a powerful weapon used by TRADE UNIONS in industrial disputes in the 1970s to maximize the effect of STRIKE action. It was used extensively during the miners' strikes of 1972 and 1974 and during the 1979 'WINTER OF DISCONTENT'. The Employment Act 1980 of the THATCHER government outlawed the practice.

Secretary, Royal The late medieval principal secretary was a clerk who was in charge of confidential royal correspondence and controlled either the PRIVY SEAL or the SIGNET. The first lay secretary, Thomas CROMWELL, transformed the office's power; the appointment of two principal secretaries after his fall in 1540 was an attempt to stop this happening again by dividing the responsibility. However, the secretaryship regained its leading role under ELIZABETH I, when William CECIL and Francis WALSINGHAM became joint chief royal executive officers with a permanent staff. In the 17th century, secretaries (styled 'secretaries of state') were often leading royal ministers; in the 1780s, the two secretaries were assigned discrete responsibilities as secretary for home affairs and for foreign affairs.

Sectaries, a 16th- and 17th-century label for Protestant DISSENTERS wishing to separate from the Established Church. Applied as vaguely as most terms of religious and political abuse, it included ANABAPTISTS, BAPTISTS and SEPARATISTS.

Secular Clergy, *see* REGULAR AND SECULAR CLERGY

Secularism, a term first used around 1850 to describe an attitude which interprets life wholly in terms of this world, without reference to a belief in God or an afterlife. Secularists tended to adopt a militantly anti-religious, and particularly anti-Christian, position and a style which was itself almost religious in character. Socially progressive, secularists were preoccupied with the extension and improvement of working-class rights and conditions. The organized secularist movement, under the leadership of the radical politician, Charles Bradlaugh (1833–91), peaked in the 1880s and declined steadily until 1914.

Secularization, a contested and controversial concept, used from the 18th century until the present, which claims to describe the process by which religion and religious activity lost ground to non-religious influences and came to occupy a marginal rather than a central position in culture and society.

Sedgemoor, Battle of, 1685, the engagement which brought about the defeat of Monmouth's (*see* SCOTT, JAMES) Rebellion against his uncle JAMES II. Royal troops, augmented by a special parliamentary grant, were dispatched to meet the rebels. Monmouth launched a surprise attack at Sedgemoor in Som., but was outmanoeuvred. Some 1,300 rebels were killed, and a similar number captured.

Self-Denying Ordinance, 1644–5, adroit response by Oliver CROMWELL's circle to the growing disarray in the Parliamentary war effort against CHARLES I. Cromwell prompted Zouch Tate to propose that membership of either house of Parliament should be incompatible with military or naval commands, and that this should be combined with the formation of a NEW MODEL ARMY. Senior commanders such as Robert DEVEREUX, Earl of Essex, and Edward Montagu, Earl of Manchester, complied with ill grace and resigned their military commands; Cromwell and others were reinstated where convenient. *See also* CIVIL WARS.

Self-help, published in 1859. The book made Samuel Smiles' (1812–1904) name and came to sum up an age of Victorian bourgeois values. In it Smiles advocated political, social and personal reform along the *LAISSEZ-FAIRE* lines of the MANCHESTER SCHOOL, and wrote biographies of those who suited his outlook. He preached industry, thrift and self-improvement as the path to progress, and attacked over-government. The work struck a significant chord, rapidly became immensely successful and was translated into many languages. Smiles' message has consistently been derided in the 20th century, although it saw a revival in the selective espousal of traditional 'Victorian values' by THATCHER in the 1970s and 1980s. Studies of ENTREPRENEURS have shown that successful 19th-century men usually had much greater initial advantages than Smiles ever allowed, and that the impact of self-help was considerably less than the publicity suggested.

Selgovae, an Iron Age tribe that inhabited the central Scottish Lowlands. They came under Roman rule during the 1st century AD (*see* SCOTTISH LOWLANDS, ROMAN OCCUPATION OF), but thereafter regained their independence. They appear to have been absorbed into the Northumbrian kingdom of BERNICIA in the 5th or 6th century.

Sempringham, Gilbert of, *see* GILBERT OF SEMPRINGHAM

Senchus Fer Nalban ('Tradition of the Men of Scotland'). This document, which survives in a 10th-century copy, provides two assessments of the military strength of the kingdom of DALRIADA, one from the middle of the 7th century and one from the end. A unique record, it shows that the kingdom could raise a military force of over 1,000 men, and illuminates the almost entirely unknown organization of this 'Dark Age' kingdom.

Separatists, a term used in the 16th and 17th centuries for INDEPENDENTS and CONGREGATIONALISTS. *See also* SECTARIES.

Septennial Act 1716 This extended the maximum term between parliamentary elections from three to seven years, and was passed by the WHIGS to prolong the tenure of the Parliament elected in the backlash against the JACOBITE rebellion of 1715. Critics – from early 18th-century TORIES to mid-

19th-century CHARTISTS – argued that shorter Parliaments would be more respectful of the electorate, but the Act remained in force until 1911, when the PARLIAMENT ACT set the maximum at five years.

Septimius Severus, Roman Emperor (193–211). In 208, 11 years after he became uncontested emperor following his defeat of CLODIUS ALBINUS, Severus brought a large army to Britain. He campaigned far into Scotland against tribes such as the MAEATAE and CALEDONII, who seem to have been especially restive at this time. He died at YORK while preparing for another campaign with the possible aim of a complete conquest of Britain; civil war in Rome meant that his son Caracalla had to abandon the project.

Serfdom, modern word for villeinage, the legal condition of personal servitude into which 13th- and 14th-century lawyers consigned roughly half the population of rural England, the serfs. Although by this date 'serf' (Latin *servus*) and 'VILLEIN' were equivalent terms, and the former had once meant 'slave', serfdom has to be distinguished from SLAVERY because the services due to the serf's lord were more or less limited by law or custom. Serfs usually held small holdings in return for rent and labour services, and were chiefly distinguished from free tenants by the theory and occasional fact that the latter could plead in the royal courts, from which the former were excluded. Thus although serfs were protected by law, it was the law of their lord's MANORial court; hence their status remained both vulnerable and servile. Typically the serf was 'attached to the soil' (Latin *adscriptus glebae*), and was transferred with the lord's land when it passed to another owner. Under a variety of names unfree tenants could be found throughout the British Isles: in Ireland they were called 'betaghs', in Scotland 'neyfs'; in Wales modern historians usually refer to them as 'bondmen'.

Grants of freedom by the lord – called manumissions (i.e. 'letting go by hand') – were always possible. The labour shortages of the late 14th century (one result of the BLACK DEATH) made it easy for serfs to flee their lords' estates, and many who stayed found it possible to make deals with lords, gaining freedom and commonly becoming COPYHOLD tenants.

Serfdom was always seen as a personal humiliation, and in the 15th and 16th centuries, most remaining serfs – often prosperous farmers – bought their freedom. In England this was frequently achieved by the employment of a bizarre LEGAL FICTION in the law courts: certification of bastardy. Since serfdom passes through the male line, a serf could win absolute and secure freedom by being legally recognized as illegitimate – in law, a bastard had no certain father. A serf would (illegally) set up a collusive legal action with his lord, about the ownership of a piece of land; the lord would point out in court that the other party was a serf; the procedure then involved a white lie about the illegitimacy, agreed on for a fat fee paid by the serf to the lord, as well as to the clergy and lawyers involved.

Serfdom has never been abolished in Britain. However, its theoretical existence means that all other forms of slavery are illegal on British soil (*see* SOMERSET CASE).

Serjeants at Arms, ceremonial guards in the royal household and in the two Houses of PARLIAMENT.

Serjeants at Law, the group of senior advocates in the COMMON LAW courts which developed in the 13th century and was organized as an order or GUILD in the 14th century, with its own robes and distinctive coif (hat), and two Inns among the INNS OF COURT. Serjeants lost their exclusive rights of pleading in COMMON PLEAS in 1846, and the order was dissolved in 1877 in England; the last serjeant of the Irish bar died in 1959.

'Sermo Lupi ad Anglos' (The Sermon of the Wolf to the English), the great homily of Archbishop WULFSTAN of York, probably composed in 1014, in which he castigated his fellow English for their sins, which he blamed for the disasters of the reign of ETHELRED II THE UNREADY.

Servants in Husbandry, farm servants, one of the most important forms of agricultural labour common in most rural areas until at least the 19th century. Service, in AGRICULTURE as well as DOMESTIC SERVICE, was a common pattern in the pre-industrial past, when young people left home in their teens and moved around within a fairly narrow circuit until they married and settled. Servants in husbandry were employed on (usually annual) contracts at relatively young ages, and lived in their master's household; the word FAMILY, indeed, usually encompassed servants who were not themselves relations. Service was one of the criteria used under the SETTLEMENT ACTS to define place of settlement in the 17th and 18th centuries. Service in husbandry began to die out from the late 18th century, the process beginning in south-eastern England, in the face of changing social attitudes and the growing cost of POOR RELIEF; it persisted in many upland areas of England, Wales and Scotland, and in rural Ireland, into the 20th century.

Servia, the first ocean-going LINER to be constructed from steel. It was built on Clydeside in 1881 for the CUNARD LINE and could accommodate 1,250 passengers. She demonstrated the superiority of steel over iron as a SHIPBUILDING material.

Service, Domestic, *see* DOMESTIC SERVICE

Servitium Debitum, *see* KNIGHT SERVICE

Settlement, *see* ELIZABETHAN SETTLEMENT; GLORIOUS REVOLUTION; RESTORATION SETTLEMENT; REVOLUTION SETTLEMENT; SETTLEMENT ACTS; SETTLEMENT, ACT OF (IRISH), 1662; SETTLEMENT, ACT OF, 1701

Settlement Acts, 1662, 1692, 1697, a set of laws which defined a place of 'settlement', thereby conferring right to POOR RELIEF under the Old POOR LAW. The laws were instituted to marry the need to provide assistance when required with the realities of everyday life and MIGRATION. All the laws provided ways of qualifying for relief. The first Settlement Act (1662) conferred the right through residence or participating in the local community through ratepaying or office-holding, while a system of certificates was developed stating a person's settlement and right to relief in a particular parish. The later enactments, notably of 1692 and 1697, replaced residence qualifications with serving as a covenanted SERVANT for a full year or serving out an APPRENTICESHIP, with a system of examination before a JUSTICE OF THE PEACE to determine the PARISH of settlement and the right to remove the pauper to his or her place of settlement (or receive payment from it). The settlement system, although often criticized for being intended to curb mobility, was designed to codify existing forms of movement, but came to be increasingly out of step with reality in the 18th century as POPULATION, POVERTY, INDUSTRY and TOWNS grew. Settlement continued to be an issue under the New POOR LAW after 1834, but without the overwhelming importance it had had previously.

Settlement, Act of (Irish), 1662, Act passed by the Irish parliament as part of the RESTORATION SETTLEMENT, dealing with the allocation of land. The Catholic share of Irish land, which had shrunk from about 60 per cent in 1640 to 8 per cent by 1659, rose again to some 20 per cent. The 1689 JACOBITE PARLIAMENT favoured a return to the status quo of 1641: the Treaty of LIMERICK (1691) stabilized Catholic landowning at about 14 per cent of the total.

Settlement, Act of, 1701 The Act provided for the succession of a PROTESTANT to the throne, in case WILLIAM III or ANNE died without a child surviving, by determining that the crown should then pass to Sophia, Electress of Hanover (a granddaughter of JAMES I) and her heirs. The Act ensured the HANOVERIAN SUCCESSION by passing over the superior hereditary rights of the Stuarts. It required the sovereign to be an ANGLICAN, and to seek the consent of PARLIAMENT before engaging in wars for the defence of possessions abroad not belonging to the crown of England. Other clauses stipulated that only natives of Britain were eligible to hold office or receive grants of crown lands; that judges were removable only by address by both Houses of Parliament; and that royal pardons were powerless to bar IMPEACHMENTS. Clauses requiring all advice to the crown to be signed, and barring placemen (*see* PLACE BILLS) from serving in the COMMONS were repealed in 1706.

Seven Bishops Case, 1688, the trial of seven bishops, led by SANCROFT, archbishop of Canterbury, for seditious libel as a result of presenting a petition to JAMES II asking not to be required to order clergy to read the second DECLARATION OF INDULGENCE to their congregations, and arguing that the king's claim of a SUSPENDING POWER had no legal foundation. The trial provided a focus for opposition. The bishops were acquitted.

Seven Years War, 1756–63. Undertaken in pursuit of ambitions left unfulfilled by the

War of the AUSTRIAN SUCCESSION, it was preceded by the escalation of conflict between France and Britain in North America. In 1755 the British attacked French commercial shipping. Then, having by a DIPLOMATIC REVOLUTION discarded their old ally Austria in favour of Prussia in Jan. 1756, they declared war on France in May. The French seized Minorca, held by Britain since the Peace of UTRECHT and highly valued as a Mediterranean base; Admiral BYNG was executed for failing to protect it. Clamour arising from its loss toppled the Newcastle (*see* PELHAM-HOLLES, THOMAS) ministry and brought PITT THE ELDER to office in Dec.

Imperial conflict played an unprecedentedly large part in this war. In INDIA, British troops faced both Indian and French forces: the Nawab of Bengal had seized Calcutta in June 1756 and put British prisoners in the notorious Black Hole of Calcutta; in Jan. 1757 CLIVE retook Calcutta and in June, after a great victory at PLASSEY, became governor of Bengal. There was also fighting in CANADA: in July 1758 the British captured Louisbourg on Cape Breton Island (also captured in the previous war).

Meanwhile the continental war had escalated: Frederick of Prussia had attacked Saxony in Aug. 1756; in response, the French and Austrians converted their defensive alliance of the previous May into an offensive alliance in May 1757. In June Newcastle was readmitted to the ministry and assumed responsibility for financing the war, while Pitt oversaw its military aspects. Though previously a critic of continental entanglements, in this war Pitt pursued the traditional policy of trying to keep France sufficiently embroiled on the Continent to advantage the British elsewhere. Embarrassingly, in Sept. WILLIAM AUGUSTUS, Duke of Cumberland, was defeated by the French and was forced to sign the Convention of KLOSTERZEVEN. Frederick of Prussia's uneven fortunes improved at the end of the year; in April 1758 the British signed a second Convention of Westminster with him. Choiseul had become French foreign minister in 1758; in 1759, he pursued a vigorous pro-Austrian policy. That year, however, was Britain's *annus mirabilis*. Though Russians and Austrians annihilated Frederick's army at Kunersdorf, British and German troops defeated the French at Minden; high points outside Europe were the capture of Guadeloupe from the French in May, and of QUEBEC by WOLFE in Sept. In Nov. Hawke's victory over the French fleet at Quiberon Bay gave the British complete command of the sea. In Jan. 1760 the British decisively defeated the French in southern India. The Prussians continued to struggle between victory and defeat.

GEORGE III, who succeeded his grandfather in Oct. 1760, had been raised by his tutor Bute (*see* STUART, JOHN) with a traditional 'COUNTRY' suspicion of onerous military endeavour. He planned his speech on the opening of Parliament to refer to a 'bloody and expensive war', but was persuaded to change it to 'just and necessary'. In Aug. 1761, John Russell, Duke of Bedford, was sent to France to open peace negotiations. However, when France formed an alliance with Spain (whose king was alarmed by the scale of British success), these negotiations were broken off. Pitt, having failed to win others to his proposal for war with Spain, resigned in Oct. – only to find Spain herself declaring war in Dec.

The next year saw significant British victories in the WEST INDIES: French islands Martinique, ST LUCIA, ST VINCENT and GRENADA were occupied; Havana, Cuba and also Manila in the Philippines were captured from Spain. Peace negotiations, however, had been secretly reopened in March 1762. Preliminaries were signed in Nov., and the Treaty of PARIS itself in Feb. 1763. Though the treaty brought Britain access to new territories – including Quebec, Florida, several West Indian islands and Minorca, as well as the territories conquered by Clive in India – it was attacked in PARLIAMENT as insufficiently reflecting Britain's success at arms. Pitt and followers of Newcastle, who had followed him from office in May 1762, attacked Bute who had succeeded them; faced with a storm of criticism from both Parliament and press, he resigned in April.

The war made Britain the leading world power, but success had its costs. Notably expensive, this war almost doubled the size of the national debt, from £76 million to £133 million. The desire to recoup the costs of imperial conflict led GRENVILLE to initiate what was to prove the disastrous policy of trying to raise tax revenues in America with the STAMP ACT of 1763. Fear of Britain's growing power had led traditional allies, the Dutch, to remain aloof in this war; the War of AMERICAN INDEPENDENCE was to see Britain entirely bereft of European allies. Success in war fostered a bellicose nationalism, which made the losses in that next war all the more shocking.

Severalty, a term employed from at least the 15th century to describe privately held land, not subject to any form of common right. Land in severalty was not necessarily enclosed, but the extinction of common rights and the establishment of landholding in severalty was often associated with ENCLOSURES.

Sex Discrimination Act 1975 The Act made discrimination on grounds of sex unlawful in employment, education and training, and the provision of housing, goods, facilities and services. Discriminatory advertisements were also made illegal. An EQUAL OPPORTUNITIES COMMISSION was set up to assist enforcement of this Act and the earlier EQUAL PAY ACT.

An amendment to the Act in 1984 entitles women to equal pay with men when doing work which is the same, broadly similar, or of equal value. The Sex Discrimination Act 1987 bought the 1975 Act into line with various EC (*see* EUROPEAN UNION) directives including one which gave women the right to continue working until the same age as men.

Sex Disqualification Removal Act 1919 The Act opened all professions (except the Church) to women, though it took no steps to end informal discrimination. *See also* WOMEN, LEGAL STATUS OF.

Sextant Conference, *see* CAIRO CONFERENCE

Seychelles, *see* MAURITIUS

Seymour, Edward (Viscount Beauchamp, 8th [1st Seymour] Earl of Hertford, 5th [1st Seymour] Duke of Somerset) (?1500–52), politician. Of Wolf Hall, Wilts., he served at court in his teens. His career blossomed when his sister JANE SEYMOUR married HENRY VIII in 1536; a year later he gained his earldom of Hertford. He was prominent in Henry's Franco-Scottish wars in the 1540s, and led the destruction of the HOWARDS in 1546. The following year, soon after Henry's death, he staged a quiet coup (with William Paget's aid) against the conservatives among the other royal executors. He was named lord PROTECTOR of his nephew EDWARD VI and was raised to Duke of Somerset.

His reputation among historians has declined: he monopolized power, ignoring his fellow councillors, and financed his single-minded pursuit of the Scottish war by a continuing disastrous debasement of the COINAGE. He attacked the old religion, completing the CHANTRY dissolutions, ordering the destruction of Catholic church fittings (*see* ICONOCLASM) and authorizing English liturgies (*see* PRAYER BOOKS). In March 1549, he reluctantly allowed the execution of his treacherous brother Lord Thomas Seymour, provoking widespread criticism. That year also saw an outbreak of popular unrest encouraged by Somerset's sponsorship of ENCLOSURE investigations (*see* KETT'S REBELLION). Coupled with the WESTERN REBELLION, this prompted his fellow councillors, led by John DUDLEY, to stage a coup in Oct. 1549. Pardoned and released from the Tower in 1550, Somerset was readmitted to the KING'S COUNCIL, but Dudley remained suspicious of his popularity and he was executed on flimsy charges of treason. His extensive (unfinished) building projects were among the first pure RENAISSANCE designs in England.

Seymour, Jane, *see* JANE SEYMOUR

Shaftesbury, 1st Earl of, *see* COOPER, ANTHONY ASHLEY

Shaftesbury Abbey, Dorset, a nunnery founded by ALFRED THE GREAT in the late 9th century and placed under the rule of his daughter Aethelfgifu. It was later the burial place and centre of the cult of EDWARD THE MARTYR. One of the wealthiest abbeys in medieval England, it was dissolved in 1539.

Shakespeare, William (1564–1616), dramatist and poet. Son of a wool-dealer and glover in STRATFORD-UPON-AVON, Warwicks., in the late 1580s he began his theatrical career in London, and probably started writing plays *c.*1588. He attracted patronage from Henry Wriothesley, Earl of Southampton, to whom he dedicated much of his poetry. He spent his acting career from 1594 with the Lord Chamberlain's Company (renamed the King's Company in 1603), and acquired interests in the Globe and

Blackfriars theatres; he became a groom of the CHAMBER in 1603.

The chronology and scope of Shakespeare's writing is more uncertain than standard editions pretend. Subsequent forgeries are easy to detect, but throughout his career, he wrote some plays in collaboration with others, and in retirement at Stratford from *c.*1613, he revised many of his plays for publication. The first collected edition of his works – the First Folio – was only published posthumously in 1623. The undramatic nature of his life has provoked fantasy and various snobbish reassignments of his work, the least deranged of which are to Francis BACON and to Edward de Vere, 17th Earl of Oxford.

Shakespeare's cultural influence both on the English language and on European culture has been immense. Soon after his death, his work was already being esteemed above that of his English contemporaries as dramatists, with three folio editions of his work published between 1623 and 1664. During the 17th and 18th centuries his work was frequently edited in order to smooth down what was considered its unacceptable roughness for contemporary audiences; in the 19th century, while the language was restored, many sexual and scatological elements in the plays were omitted, notoriously in the edition of 1818 by Thomas Bowdler (hence 'bowdlerization'). Translations into major European languages (e.g. German 1762, French 1776, Italian 1814, Russian 1841) played a great part in the Romantic movement and stimulated the search for similar symbolically dominant literary figures for other national cultures. In the history plays, Shakespeare drew on the commonplace historical sources of his day, especially HOLINSHED's *Chronicles*; as a result, the triumphalist dynastic propaganda of the Tudors about themselves and previous monarchs became deeply embedded in English consciousness, distorting in particular assessment of Shakespeare's arch-villain, RICHARD III.

Overall, his works, and phrases remembered from them, have shaped the development of English as decisively as the almost contemporary English translations of the BIBLE and CRANMER'S PRAYER BOOK. The widespread interest in the recent unearthing of the sites in Southwark of theatres associated with him, the Rose and the Globe, illustrates the continuing English fascination with Shakespeare as a national symbol.

Sheffield, Yorks., town most famous for its place in the steel and cutlery industries. It acquired its speciality in cutlery in the 16th century if not earlier, with supplies of iron and fast-flowing Pennine streams providing the basis for the industry. In the mid-18th century silver plating and steelmaking in clay crucibles brought considerable advance to the local economy; a population of *c.*5,500 in 1700 had become 31,000 in 1801, and was to rise to 300,000 by the end of the 19th century. In the mid-19th century the small-scale steelmaking and cutlery enterprises were rapidly replaced by large enterprises, led by Spear & Jackson. Sheffield saw considerable reconstruction of its centre in the PLANNING boom of the 1950s and 1960s, but its economic fortunes mirrored those of the IRON AND STEEL INDUSTRY.

Sheffield 'Outrages', 1866–7, a series of violent incidents, including arson and murder, committed by TRADE UNIONISTS in the regions of SHEFFIELD and MANCHESTER to coerce non-unionists. They provoked a good deal of concern and a public inquiry which showed that such practices were in decline and prevailed only among a few backward unions. It was argued that the best way to improve industrial relations was to remove legal constraints upon the status and funds of superior formations like the eminently respectable NEW MODEL UNIONS.

Shelburne, 3rd Earl of, *see* PETTY, WILLIAM

Sheldon, Gilbert (1598–1677), cleric, Archbishop of Canterbury (1663–77). Educated at Oxford, ordained, and appointed warden of All Souls in 1626, he associated with the Great Tew Circle. He was confidential adviser to CHARLES I in 1646–7 and during the Isle of Wight treaty negotiations. In 1648, he was ejected from his wardenship and imprisoned for a year.

Reinstated in 1659, he was made bishop of London the following year. He was prominent in royal favour, and was a member of the PRIVY COUNCIL. He presided over the SAVOY CONFERENCE, where his disinclination to allow variety in practice within the Church contributed to the thwarting of proposals for COMPREHENSION. In 1663, he was made archbishop of Canterbury and, as such, oversaw much of the practical work of re-establishing the Church. The year after his appointment, he agreed that the clergy should henceforth be subject to parliamentary taxation.

Sheldon has been criticized for his narrowness of vision, but must be given credit for the energy with which he achieved the re-establishment of a united and disciplined Church.

Shells Scandal, political crisis during WORLD WAR I in May 1915, over a shortage of munitions amongst British forces in France. The crisis broke on 14 May following articles in *The Times* about British troops being left short of shells – reports encouraged by the British commander FRENCH, who felt the war effort was being poorly served by Asquith's LIBERAL government. Presented with a virtual ultimatum on the issue by LLOYD GEORGE and the CONSERVATIVE leader, Bonar LAW, ASQUITH formed a coalition government on 18 May with Conservatives taking senior Cabinet positions and Lloyd George taking on the task of reorganizing war production under the new MINISTRY OF MUNITIONS.

Sherborne, Dorset, the seat of an Anglo-Saxon BISHOPRIC, established in 705, which originally comprised most of western England, but which was reduced in the early 10th century when the dioceses of Crediton and Wells were created. The centre of the diocese was moved to Old Sarum (Salisbury) after the NORMAN CONQUEST. The BENEDICTINE monastery, founded *c.*993, was dissolved in 1539; its beautiful church survives.

Sheriff In England, control of the SHIRES was from the early 11th century delegated by the earls to 'shire-reeves', an office retained by the Normans. From the 12th century, what came to be called 'sheriffs' were generally chosen annually by the CROWN, to prevent them building excessive local powerbases. Gradually other officials – such as CORONERS, ESCHEATORS and JUSTICES OF THE PEACE – took much of their authority, and during the 16th century, sheriffs' courts (tourns) lost significance. The English sheriff – commonly called the 'high sheriff' – retains considerable social cachet and, up to the 19th century, remained important through his control of shire elections. *See also* SHIP MONEY.

In Scotland, sheriffs were introduced in the 12th century, and because the office continued to be an hereditary honour without annual election, they remained more powerful than their English counterparts. Reforms in the 18th century remodelled the office and preserved its significant legal powers in criminal and civil cases. The sheriff's jurisdiction is called the shrievalty.

Sheriffmuir, Battle of, 13 Nov. 1715. Fought near Stirling between John Erskine, 23rd Earl of Mar, with 10,000 Highland clansmen raised at Perth for James Edward STUART, the Old Pretender, and 35,000 government soldiers under the Duke of Argyll (*see* CAMPBELL, JOHN). Although the Highlanders forced the government troops to retreat, the clansmen's advance was halted, Mar retreated to the north and his force disintegrated. The arrival in Scotland of the Pretender at Christmas 1715 brought no reverse; James and Mar left in Feb. 1716.

Shetland, *see* VIKINGS

Shilling, unit of currency and COIN worth 12 PENNIES. The silver coin was first minted by HENRY VII in 1504 and was generally known as a 'testoon', from Italian coins which anticipated its introduction of a profile portrait (the first on an English coin since the 12th century). The shilling was replaced by the 5p piece at DECIMALIZATION.

Ship Money, a levy on certain port towns in time of war (in lieu of the provision of ships for the king's NAVY); it was first extended to inland areas in the 1590s to help finance the long and costly war against Spain. However, the protests of the 1590s were ignored by the government of CHARLES I in reviving the collection of this levy in 1634, and high collection rates were maintained by making SHERIFFS responsible for each county's entire sum. Charles I spent much of the collected money on naval improvements (the navy showed its ingratitude by mostly siding with Parliament in the CIVIL WARS). HAMPDEN'S test case in 1637 failed to halt collection, which only crumbled after royal defeat in the BISHOPS' WARS. Ship money was declared illegal in 1641.

Shipbuilding There is archaeological evidence of ship- (or at least boat-) building in Britain from the Neolithic period. The oldest planked crafts yet found in Europe have been dug up on the banks of the Humber and at Dover. Ships of the Roman period found in the Thames and a SAXON vessel found in North Kent are solid indications of local traditions of wooden shipbuilding about which we need to learn much more, but are clearly different from those of the Mediterranean on the one hand and Scandinavia on the other (though many of the local boat types of Scotland and of some parts of England were very much in the VIKING style).

Building ships from wood (there had also been a separate tradition of skin boat building – surviving in the Irish curragh and the Welsh coracle) had, from the beginning, involved the joining together of the shell of planking first, then putting in a skeleton of ribs. It is perhaps no accident that the introduction, from the Mediterranean, of the skeleton-first method of building ('carvel' as opposed to the native 'clinker') coincided with the first use of large guns firing through ports in the hull. This happened about 1500, just after the three masted 'ship' rig had replaced the traditional single mast of sailing ships in north-western Europe. The next century seems to have witnessed the first use of plans in shipbuilding. Leading shipwrights began to transfer their craft from a matter of traditional, intuitive skill, with carefully guarded trade secrets, to the scientific, educated, numerate engineering skill of the naval architect. This process could only be completed once steam propulsion and metal hulls had completely altered the business of shipbuilding in the second half of the 19th century.

Shipbuilding was done all round the coasts, but in the 17th century the chief centres of building larger ships were East Anglia, the Thames and Medway, the Solent, Bristol and Hull. Towards the end of the century East Anglia declined, and the shipyards of the north-east of England began their rise by copying the captured Dutch types of efficient, cheap and capacious cargo-carriers. LIVERPOOL also became more important. Most yards were fairly small, but the Royal DOCKYARDS and also the Blackwall yard of the EAST INDIA COMPANY showed the way forward as the largest industrial organizations in the country, and also, because of the size of their workforce, the places in which STRIKES and other forms of industrial struggle began.

The real changes in British shipbuilding came with the technological advances of the 19th century. First steam propulsion and then metal hulls made ships more complex and larger, and the building of them moved from a craft to an INDUSTRY. Here the Clyde showed the way: most iron shipbuilding firms were founded by Scots, or men trained in Scottish yards. The North East and (at first) the Thames adapted well to the new shipbuilding techniques. Liverpool maintained its prominence for a while, but eventually Merseyside would be represented by one, very important, firm, Laird (later Cammell–Laird) of Birkenhead. Later Belfast (Harland and Wolff) and Barrow (Vickers) were of great importance because of individual firms. In the later 18th and early 19th centuries Britain had been an importer of ships, up to one third of the Merchant Navy being built in North America. Steam and iron totally changed this. Britain exported techniques, experts and ships. Towards the end of the 19th century over half the world's total tonnage was built in Britain. The Royal and Merchant Navies were both by far the biggest in the world and virtually entirely built in home yards. Warships as well as merchantmen were exported.

Britain remained the world's shipbuilder until around 1960, though with diminishing success. This century of dominance cannot be equalled by any other country or industry. Though the technological lead was reduced, it was still evident well into the 20th century. The 'Liberty Ship' of WORLD WAR II, for example, was a British design (but adapted for American production techniques), as was the concept of wartime 'standard ships'. Much damage was done to the industry by the DEPRESSIONS which followed WORLD WAR I. The yards which survived were handicapped by under-investment and poor labour relations (an old problem in this industry). British shipbuilders failed to take advantage of the developments in bulk carriers, particularly oil tankers, in the 1960s when the Japanese took over, and were eliminated one by one in a welter of mergers, failures, social experiments and strikes.

Ship-Soke, Anglo-Saxon territorial districts responsible for the fitting-out and manning of ships. An entry in the *ANGLO-SAXON CHRONICLE* for 1008 has been interpreted as showing that each ship-soke consisted of 300 HIDES and supported a ship with 60 oars, but it is now thought that both sokes and ships were much more variable in size. The ship-soke may have been imposed on the English kingdom in 1008, but it is probably of earlier origin. *See also FYRD*; NAVY.

Shire-Court The meeting of the most prominent individuals within a single shire, the shire-court was the heart of English local government from the 10th century onwards. The earliest reference to it – in a law code dating from EDGAR's reign – implies a gathering whose existence was already well established, and it is assumed to have evolved out of a popular folk-court. Meeting twice a year, it was a great occasion where matters of major legal and social importance for the region were dealt with. Although subject to occasional royal interventions, its jurisdiction was theoretically unlimited, and its personnel comprised all free men of the shire. It only became integrated into a national framework with the frequent dispatch of itinerant royal justices under HENRY II. *See also* COUNTY COURT.

Shires, Origins of England was divided into shires during the 9th–11th centuries, and by 1066 had assumed, with some exceptions, the pattern familiar until the LOCAL GOVERNMENT REORGANIZATION ACT 1972. The actual process by which shires were created is obscure, although it was clearly a consequence of the extension of the authority of the kings of WESSEX over the rest of England during the 9th and 10th centuries. Within Wessex, some shires, such as KENT, were ancient kingdoms, while others, such as Dorset, were territorial creations around a central *BURH*. It is generally accepted that the shires of MERCIA were artificial units that were probably imposed, since they cut across the boundaries of earlier kingdoms. The large shires to the north of a line from the Humber to the Mersey resemble large EARLDOMS rather than compact units. The 'shiring' of Wales, Scotland and Ireland was a later process. *See also* UNION OF WALES AND ENGLAND.

Shirley v. Fagg In 1675, Dr Shirley lost a suit in CHANCERY against the MP, Sir John Fagg, and appealed to the LORDS. The COMMONS voted this a breach of privilege, and had Fagg imprisoned for appearing to answer the appeal. A constitutional dispute ensued. The Commons did not again contest the Lords' right to act as final court of appeal even in cases involving MPs.

Shop Hours Act 1886 An attempt to ensure a modicum of leisure for notoriously overworked shop assistants, it imposed a maximum of 74 hours a working week. However, its provisions remained ineffectual until their enforcement was entrusted to the local authorities in 1912.

Shop Stewards' Movement, term for the growth of shop-floor TRADE UNION organization, particularly in the ENGINEERING INDUSTRY, before, during and after WORLD WAR I. Committees of shop stewards were formed by skilled workers distrustful of deals made by trade union leaders at national level. They were active in opposition to DILUTION and during the strikes and unrest of Red Clydeside.

Short Cross Coinage, name given to the silver PENNIES issued for the English monarchy between 1180 and 1247. Its name comes from the fact that the cross shown on the reverse did not reach to the edge of the COINS. Although this design defect made it vulnerable to CLIPPING, HENRY II's penny, still bearing the name *Henricus*, continued to be issued in huge numbers during the reigns of RICHARD I and JOHN, as well as that of HENRY III. *See also* LONG CROSS COINAGE.

Short Parliament, named in contrast to the subsequent LONG PARLIAMENT. Called during the crisis caused by the first BISHOPS' WAR, it sat from 13 April to 5 May 1640, when CHARLES I dissolved it, unnerved by the barrage of criticism emanating from it.

Short Title Catalogue, catalogue of English books, an invaluable aid to scholarship. The first catalogue, for books published between 1475 and 1640, was issued in 1926, and has since 1976 been revised and enlarged. Its continuation for the years 1641–1700, usually known as Wing after its editor, D. G. Wing, was published in 1945, with a second edition in 1972. The 18th-century *Short Title Catalogue* is still in progress. The catalogues bear witness to changing technology: all are available on-line and as computer disks.

Shrewsbury, Salop, historically important

Welsh border town. The CASTLE commanding the loop in the River Severn in which the town grew up was begun in 1102, and it was there in 1283 that the first PARLIAMENT in which the COMMONS were properly represented was held. The battle of SHREWSBURY was fought in 1403, by which time the town was becoming an increasingly important centre of the CLOTH INDUSTRY and boasted a large number of churches, as well as the Abbey founded in 1080. From 1500 Shrewsbury was one of the seats of the COUNCIL IN THE MARCHES, and the 16th century was the period of its greatest wealth and prosperity. CHARLES I and Prince RUPERT resided there in 1642, and the town was taken for the PARLIAMENTARIANS in 1645. The town is most remarkable for the survival of considerable numbers of exuberant half-timbered buildings and for its many churches, although the Abbey precincts were destroyed in 1836 when Thomas Telford built the London–Holyhead road.

Shrewsbury, Battle of, 21 July 1403, victory for HENRY IV and the Prince of Wales (later HENRY V) over the forces of Hotspur (Henry Percy) and Thomas Percy (*see* PERCY REBELLION). By forced marches to Shrewsbury, the king saved his son from falling into rebel hands, but the subsequent battle was hard fought, with the issue in doubt until Hotspur was killed by an arrow at nightfall.

Shrievalties, *see* SHERIFF

Shrines As focuses for the cults of SAINTS, these were an obvious target for reforming hatred in the 16th century. Thomas CROMWELL encouraged propaganda against them and in 1538 ordered the destruction of the leading shrines, particularly Thomas BECKET's in CANTERBURY; HENRY VIII continued the process after Cromwell's fall. MARY I's regime did little to revive the past in this respect. Many shrines have since been restored on old sites and are maintained by ANGLICANS and Roman CATHOLICS. *See also* PILGRIMAGE.

Shrove Tuesday, day before Ash Wednesday, the first day of Lent (the period of fasting before Easter), and hence traditionally a day of celebration and of eating foods which would be proscribed for the next six weeks. Many CALENDAR CUSTOMS are associated with Shrove Tuesday, especially involving pancakes and other food. However, the British Isles rarely sees the scale of carnival or *mardi gras* festivities common in Europe and elsewhere. The word 'Shrove' derives from the medieval requirement for the laity to be shriven, or confess their sins, before Lent.

Sicilian Adventure, the term used by historians critical of HENRY III's plan to make his second son, Edmund, king of Sicily. (Those who judge the scheme more sympathetically call it the 'Sicilian business'.) In 1255, Henry agreed to pay Pope Alexander IV more than 135,000 MARKS for Sicily. However, since, in practice, this simply meant paying for the right to send an army to wrest the kingdom from Manfred, the ruler in residence, it was a high price for what was, at best, an expensive gamble: Richard of Cornwall, when offered Sicily on these terms, had said it was like being invited to buy the moon. Practical considerations did not deter Henry, but when he tried to raise the money, he found himself compelled to accept both the PROVISIONS OF OXFORD of 1258 and the cancellation of his agreement with the pope.

Sidmouth, 1st Viscount, *see* ADDINGTON, HENRY

Sign Manual, the monarch's signature, necessary for warrants; occasionally replaced by the DRY STAMP.

Signet, attempt by the English monarchy to provide itself with a private SEAL after the bureaucratization of the GREAT SEAL and PRIVY SEAL. It was one-sided, and was first used by EDWARD II; it was kept at first by royal SECRETARIES, later by the secretaries of state.

Sigurd the Mighty, Earl of Orkney (*c.*850–70). He was the brother of ROGNVALD OF MOER who, it is said, established him in ORKNEY, although the sources relating to Sigurd's career are generally late ones, and even the dates of his activities are uncertain. It is known that, in alliance with THORSTEIN THE RED, he used the islands as a base from which to conquer Caithness and Sutherland, and it is likely that his wars established the earldom of Orkney.

Sigurd the Stout, Earl of Orkney (*c.*985–1014). One of the greatest of the earls of ORKNEY, he was successful not only in defending the mainland territories of the earldom against Scottish encroachments, but also in extending his authority to include overlordship of the Scandinavian settlements in the HEBRIDES. He was supposedly converted to Christianity by force by Olaf Tryggvason, King of Norway, in 995. His great power involved him in the politics of western and northern Britain, and he died fighting alongside the Scandinavian king of DUBLIN at the battle of CLONTARF.

Silchester (*Calleva Atrebatum*), Hants. Formerly the chief centre of the northern ATREBATES, it subsequently became the capital of a Roman *CIVITAS*. The later disappearance of urban life there has meant that the Roman town plan is still exceptionally well preserved; it includes such expected features as an amphitheatre, forum, baths and temples, as well as a Christian church. Silchester's decline probably coincided with that in the use of ROAD transport after the 6th century, and it was replaced by nearby Reading, Berks.

Silures, the pre-Roman British tribe that inhabited the modern counties of Glam. and Gwent. They fought with CARATACUS against the Romans in AD 51 (*see* CAER CARADOG) and, although defeated there, continued to be difficult opponents. They inflicted several defeats on legionary troops, and were not finally subdued until the governorship of JULIUS FRONTINUS. It is likely that he began the construction of a new capital for the *CIVITAS* of the Silures at CAERWENT, Gwent, which also contained the LEGIONARY FORTRESS of CAERLEON.

Simnel, Lambert (?1475–1525), conspirator. This Oxford-born youth was taken to Ireland in 1487 and promoted by YORKIST plotters (including Gerald FITZGERALD, 8th Earl of Kildare, and the Archbishop of Dublin) as Edward Plantagenet, Earl of Warwick, the imprisoned nephew of EDWARD IV. Recognized by MARGARET OF ANJOU, he was crowned as Edward VI. Captured after the battle of STOKE, he was pardoned as harmless and allowed to survive as a servant.

Simon Commission, commission appointed in 1927 under the Liberal politician Sir J. A. Simon (1873–1954) to investigate the workings of the INDIA Act of 1919 and the MONTAGU-CHELMSFORD REFORMS, and to determine India's future development. The Commission did not report until June 1930, recommending the establishment of fully RESPONSIBLE GOVERNMENT in the provinces, and negotiations between the British government, the Indian politicians, and the native princes about the future of the central government. The Government of India Act of 1935 embodied the recommendations on provincial government but left the central government still effectively under the viceroy's control, failing to satisfy India's aspirations.

Singapore, former British island colony in the Malay archipelago, founded in 1819 by Thomas Stamford Raffles (1781–1826), officer of the EAST INDIA COMPANY. Raffles had become lieutenant-governor of Java in 1811, when it had been taken from the French-controlled Netherlands; after it was restored to the Dutch in 1816, Raffles persuaded the Company to seek another site and so established Singapore. British and Dutch interests in the region were settled by treaty in 1824. Although the East India Company tended to ignore Singapore and its attendant STRAITS SETTLEMENTS, especially after it had lost its trade monopoly in the Far East in 1833, the settlement prospered with growing trade and in 1867 applied to become a crown colony. By 1900, as a result of treaties with sultans and chiefs in the various Malay States, all had come under Britain's control; British enterprise exploited the rubber and tin reserves. Singapore was seen as of strategic importance in South-east Asia, and was garrisoned accordingly. Its swift fall in 1942 to the Japanese, who launched their final assault from the mainland rather than attempting the anticipated landing from the sea, was one of the great blows to British morale, as well as a cause of great loss of life, in the early stages of the Pacific war (*see* WORLD WAR II). Singapore gained its independence from Britain in 1965 under Prime Minister Lee Kuan Yew, who forged it into an international commercial centre. *See also* MALAYA.

Sinn Féin, Irish political party dedicated to the cause of Irish nationalism, whose fortunes have been closely linked to the paramilitary terrorist organization, the IRISH REPUBLICAN ARMY or IRA. The party was formed in 1907 under the Gaelic title meaning 'for ourselves'. In the first post-war

British general election in Dec. 1918 the party won 73 seats (*see also* Countess de MARKIEWICZ), and, refusing to take its seats at WESTMINSTER, seceded to form the DÁIL in Dublin, proclaiming Ireland's independence in Jan. 1919. Sinn Féin refused to accept the partition of Ireland, supporting the struggle of the IRA in the ensuing civil war, and thereafter abstaining from the Dáil. It returned to prominence with the troubles in ULSTER in 1969, and split with the IRA into the two separate organizations, Official and Provisional. Provisional Sinn Féin, based in Belfast, has taken a more active political role since the 1970s, including standing for local and national election while acting as the political wing of the IRA. The Official wing dropped its abstentionist approach in Dublin, moved progressively to the left, and in 1982 changed its name to the Workers Party (and, more recently, to the Democratic Left).

Sinn Féin was further isolated by public revulsion at the intensification of violence in the late 1980s, but gained electoral support for their part in the peace process and the involvement of Sinn Féin's leader Gerry ADAMS in the IRA ceasefire negotiations in the 1990s. Sinn Féin signed the Good Friday Agreement in 1998 (*see* ULSTER) as a step towards a United Ireland and took 18 seats in the Northern Ireland Assembly, but its position was weakened while the IRA refused to begin to give up its weapons.

Sion Abbey, *see* SYON ABBEY

Six Acts, 1819. A response to the PETERLOO MASSACRE by a frightened Liverpool (*see* JENKINSON, ROBERT) ministry that equated PARLIAMENTARY REFORM with treason, the SIX ACTS prohibited meetings of more than 50 people, increased stamp duties on NEWSPAPERS, made the publication of blasphemous and seditious libels a transportable offence, and extended the summary powers of JUSTICES OF THE PEACE.

Six Articles, Act of, 1539, a measure promoted by HENRY VIII and Thomas CROMWELL's enemies, which spelled out traditional views on the miracle of the MASS and that laity should receive bread only in the mass. It also reaffirmed clerical and lay vows of CELIBACY, and the value of intercessory masses and of confession to a priest. Penalties for dissent were savage. The Act was repealed in 1547 but temporarily revived under MARY I.

Skinheads, youth movement originating in the 1970s mainly associated with white working-class youths distinguished by close-cropped hair and large 'Doc Marten' boots. Skinheads were associated with racist attacks on members of the Asian community in London and elsewhere.

Skinner v. East India Company, 1668, a case which helped to define the judicial role of the House of LORDS. Skinner claimed that although he had been wronged by the EAST INDIA COMPANY, because the wrong had been committed abroad he was having difficulty getting his case heard in the lower courts. The king on the advice of some PRIVY COUNCILLORS referred the case to the Lords. It awarded Skinner damages, but the Company petitioned the COMMONS, arguing that the case should have gone to the ordinary courts. The Commons declared that the Lords had no original jurisdiction in civil cases; the Lords, that there were no limits to its jurisdiction. The quarrel which ensued was interrupted by the prorogation of PARLIAMENT. When Parliament reassembled in 1670 the king suggested that all references to the case be removed from the journals of both Houses. The Lords never again attempted to exercise original jurisdiction in civil cases.

Slave Trade The trade in human cargoes was one of the underpinnings of the great Atlantic commercial system, associated especially with the Iberian nations in the 16th century, and with Britain and her empire from the 17th century, while this great migration transformed the culture and society of many NEW WORLD territories. The origins of Europeans trading for slaves in Africa lie in the mid-15th century, when the Portuguese first imported Moors from north Africa – hence the common 18th-century English term 'blackamoor'. Slaves from west Africa (*see*, e.g., NIGERIA, GAMBIA) became important with the need to provide labour for the growing Spanish and Portuguese empires in the New World, both in the Caribbean and on the mainland, especially since native populations were severely reduced by disease or proved less than manageable. English attempts by John HAWKINS from 1578 to take a part of the lucrative Spanish trade in slaves were rebuffed, but the British gained their advantage in slave-trading in the following century.

The establishment in the 17th century of the great staple commodities, notably SUGAR in Brazil and then in the Caribbean, and subsequently TOBACCO in mainland North America, intensified the demand for slave labour. Whereas labour requirements were initially met by the employment of INDENTURED SERVANTS, these free white workers were rapidly supplanted by unfree black workers. Although the sugar colonies with their vast wealth rapidly moved to slave labour, the lower level of profitability in tobacco-growing meant that slaves were slow to be employed in VIRGINIA and the other southern colonies, although they came to dominate the population and labour force. There were some 2,000 negro slaves in Virginia in 1681; but by 1754 there were over a quarter of a million.

The trade in slaves to British possessions was granted exclusively to British ships in the ASIENTO clause secured in the 1713 Peace of UTRECHT. The cruel and degrading transatlantic slave trade was an integral part of the so-called TRIANGULAR TRADE between North America, Britain (especially LONDON, LIVERPOOL, BRISTOL and GLASGOW) and west Africa, secured by the NAVIGATION ACTS. Estimates of the volume of slave imports into the Americas have been hotly debated, but recent figures suggest the following broad outline:

1551–1600 0.7 million
1601–50 1.0 million
1651–1700 1.7 million
1701–50 3.0 million
1751–1800 3.8 million
1801–50 3.2 million

Of the destinations, over the long term Brazil had by far the highest number of slaves, over 4 million, with the British Caribbean receiving some 2.4 million slaves, the French Caribbean and Spanish America some 1.7 million each, and British North America 0.5 million.

All these estimates cover importations; there was often swingeing mortality, especially in the early years, among those carried in the slave ships. The 18th-century slave trade was dominated by Britain, which in the years 1781–1807 alone carried over 1 million slaves from Africa to the Americas, followed by the Portuguese who carried some 700,000, and the French who had carried about 400,000 before they abolished slavery at the Revolution. The introduction of COTTON-growing to the southern USA in the 1790s was a further boost to demand. By the time of the American Civil War there were some 4 million slaves (mainly native-born) in the USA; American ships had continued to carry slaves after the abolition in 1807 of the slave trade within the British empire, and also abolition by other nations, which was followed by the abolition of the institution of slavery itself.

There had been little mass opposition to the slave trade until the very early 19th century, although certain radical and religious groups, notably the QUAKERS, were active in the nascent ANTI-SLAVERY MOVEMENT in the 18th century. The remarkable published testimony of Olaudiah Equiano (*c.* 1750–97), a Nigerian-born former slave who wrote about his experiences and privations, was an influential document in the early stages of agitation. *See also* CLAPHAM SECT; WILBERFORCE, WILLIAM.

Slavery has had an important position in the society and economy of the British Isles and of Britain's imperial possessions from time immemorial until the relatively recent past. It was an integral institution in Roman society. It played a large part in CELTIC societies, and was important in Irish society until the 12th century. The Irish were particularly assiduous slave traders, while prisoners taken in battle were frequently enslaved; there was also a flourishing trade in slaves between BRISTOL and DUBLIN against which Wulfstan, bishop of Worcester preached. Slavery had been an important institution for the Anglo-Saxons in England; slaves could be bought and sold, and slavery was an inherited condition or could be imposed as a legal punishment. Ten per cent of the population recorded in *DOMESDAY BOOK* were slaves. The disappearance of slavery in England in the early 12th century remains a mysterious process.

Only with the short-lived Vagrancy Act under EDWARD VI was there again an attempt to enslave people at home. Within a short space of time Britain came to be involved in the SLAVE TRADE from AFRICA to the plantation economies of the NEW WORLD and by the 18th century held a virtual monopoly on transatlantic traffic.

The growing sense of the iniquity of owning another person resulted in the lengthy campaigning of the ANTI-SLAVERY movement, and at least in part to the conflict of the American Civil War. The SOMERSET CASE (1772) had established that a person could not be a slave in Britain; the slave trade was abolished in 1807, and emancipation eventually followed in 1833. Meanwhile Britain had undertaken a prolonged naval and diplomatic campaign against the international slave trade. The victory of the North in the American Civil War and the gradual elimination of slavery by imperial expansion in Africa itself finally bought the need for this campaign to an end. *See also* SERFDOM.

Slum Clearance Clearance of insanitary and unfit dwellings became a major feature of PUBLIC HEALTH and HOUSING policy between the two WORLD WARS. Under the HOUSING ACT 1930 local authorities were given graduated subsidies according to the number of people rehoused and the cost of clearance. Local authorities were obliged to draw up five-year plans for slum clearance. The Housing Act 1933 drew up fresh plans, aiming to clear 266,000 slum dwellings and rehouse one and a quarter million people. By 1939 over two million slum dwellers had been rehoused. Further large-scale slum clearance took place after 1945 with over four million slum properties demolished by 1985.

Sluys, Battle of, 24 June 1340, the bloodiest naval battle of the HUNDRED YEARS WAR. EDWARD III's fleet defeated a French force that had been moored in the Zwin estuary, Flanders, to oppose his landing in support of his Flemish allies. A total of 190 French ships were captured.

Small Holdings Act 1892 A measure to check rural depopulation, it arose from the agitation of RADICALS like Joseph CHAMBERLAIN and Jesse Collings and empowered the county councils created under the LOCAL GOVERNMENT ACT of 1888 to purchase land for the provision of small holdings for sale or rent on easy terms. Under the Small Holdings and Allotments Act of 1907, county councils received new compulsory powers where the land required for the provision of small holdings could not be obtained by agreement. Special commissioners were appointed by the BOARD OF AGRICULTURE to press the county councils to make use of their powers. Seven years after the passage of the legislation, 200,000 acres had been acquired and 14,000 small holdings created.

Small Tenements Recovery Act 1838 provided a cheap and expeditious mode of recovering houses let to the working classes. It was passed in response to a campaign by small property owners' associations, whose members were aggrieved at having to resort to expensive and/or violent means to recover property. Property managers thenceforth had merely to apply to a local magistrate for an order for possession, a process which from initiation to completion took a matter of weeks. Although little noticed by historians, it remained a defining feature of tenure relations until the late 20th century.

Smallpox, *see* EPIDEMICS; INOCULATION

Smith, Adam (1723–90), economist. He was educated at Glasgow University and at Oxford, and was elected professor of logic at Glasgow in 1751 and of moral philosophy the following year. In 1759, he published a *Theory of Moral Sentiments* and travelled in France as tutor to the Duke of Buccleuch. Elected to the ROYAL SOCIETY in 1767 he returned to Scotland to write; his best-known work *The Wealth of Nations* – an outstandingly effective systematization of ideas about the workings of economies, and the logic of economic development – was published in 1776. Renowned especially for its reasoned advocacy of FREE TRADE, it was widely cited, and translated into several European languages. It has subsequently been regarded as a founding text of the modern discipline of economics. Smith was consulted by PITT THE ELDER on economic matters; in 1777 he was appointed a commissioner of customs, and in 1787 he was elected lord rector of Glasgow University. His ideas are frequently misrepresented in the 20th century and have often been used to justify the free market ideology of recent decades.

Smith, John (1938–94), politician. A Scottish solicitor from a radical Presbyterian family, elected Labour MP for Lanarks. North (1970–83) and Monklands East (1983–94), Smith was shadow chancellor of the Exchequer (1992) and then leader of the

LABOUR PARTY after the resignation of Neil KINNOCK whose work of modernizing Labour and making it electable he continued, most notably in ending the Trade Union block vote on party policy. A bank-manager like figure he gave economic solidity and integrity but hardly charisma to the party, and his untimely death from a heart attack in May 1994 leaves unanswered the question of whether he would have been able to lead Labour to victory in 1997, and if so, how different its policies in power might have been.

Smuggling, *see* CONTRABAND

Socage, *see* FREEHOLD; SOKEMAN

Social Contract, informal system of co-operation between the TRADE UNIONS and the WILSON LABOUR government of 1974. In an attempt to control the surge in inflation caused by the OIL CRISIS, without causing large rises in unemployment, the government agreed to repeal the restrictions on trade union activity imposed by the HEATH government, in return for voluntary pay restraint. However, the Social Contract broke down in autumn 1978 when the unions rejected a 5 per cent pay norm. The attempt by CALLAGHAN's government to apply the norm sparked the industrial unrest known as the 'WINTER OF DISCONTENT', which severely tarnished the Labour government's image and contributed to a CONSERVATIVE victory at the May 1979 general election.

Social Crime, activity which is illegal but which appears to have been widely accepted as legitimate by a broader popular consensus and is often carried out as a protest against formal judicial authority and the propertied classes which this authority represents. Thus historians, notably E. P. Thompson, have argued that in the 17th and 18th centuries activities such as poaching, trespass and the capturing of grain stores reflected protest against ENCLOSURE and the free market, rather than simply the activities of criminals and/or the hungry. Similarly machine-wrecking during industrialization can be viewed as a concerted effort both to put pressure on employers to improve conditions and to express widespread opposition to machines which destroyed older hierarchies of labour, and control by workers over the pace and nature of production. It is notable that whole communities often supported the perpetrators and closed ranks against attempts by the authorities to isolate and punish offenders. Petty pilfering and attempts to sabotage production lines in later industrial contexts can also be seen as social crime (widely regarded as legitimate), but the problem with the concept applied in all contexts is that it is difficult for historians to identify and to attribute motives where social crime is inextricably linked with more straightforward theft, mere avarice, or even with organized crime on a large scale. *See also* CRIME; MORAL ECONOMY.

Social Democratic and Labour Party (SDLP), moderate Northern Irish political party formed in 1970 by civil rights activists amongst the CATHOLIC population. Led first by Gerry Fitt, and after 1983 by John Hume, it co-operated with attempts to create a power-sharing executive in the early 1970s and supported the Anglo-Irish Agreement of 1985. Though under electoral pressure from SINN FÉIN in the early 1980s, it established itself as the main political vehicle for the non-violent nationalist movement in ULSTER. Though non-sectarian by its own constitution, its support has been overwhelmingly from the Roman Catholic community.

In the elections to the Northern Ireland Assembly in June 1998 following the Good Friday Agreement (*see* ULSTER) the SDLP emerged as the second largest party after the UUP (*see* ULSTER UNIONIST PARTY), and the SDLP member Seamus Mallon was elected Deputy First Minister.

Social Democratic Federation, Britain's first Marxist political party. Formed in 1881 by H. M. Hyndman as the Democratic Federation, it recruited many members but retained few. It organized large meetings of the unemployed in the 1880s, and was active in every phase of labour politics down to 1914, but its sectarianism, chauvinism and lack of leadership reduced any limited electoral appeal it might have possessed. Many of its members found a home in the newly formed COMMUNIST PARTY OF GREAT BRITAIN after World War I, by which time it had ceased to exert any political influence.

Social History Historical writing about the place of 'ordinary' people rather than privileged élites and rulers began as early as the late 19th century with works such as J. R. Green's *Short History of the English People* (1874), while the growth of ECONOMIC HISTORY provided an umbrella under which the social repercussions of economic change were examined by historians such as B. L. Hammond and G. D. H. Cole. The early emphasis on the consequences of industrialization was given broader shape by G. M. Trevelyan's *English Social History* (1944), which examined social life from the 14th to the 20th centuries. One of the great historical best-sellers of all time, it offered the famous definition of social history as 'history with the politics left out', though Trevelyan argued strongly for the importance and vital interrelation of all branches of history. From the 1950s, the opening of local records gave further impetus to a flourishing tradition of local history to develop regional, county and urban studies which examined in more detail aspects of county communities and urban life. At another level, a prominent part was played by Marxist historians such as C. Hill, E. J. Hobsbawm, and E. P. Thompson, who examined the popular dimensions of political and economic upheavals from the 17th century to the emergence of the LABOUR movement at the end of the 19th century. A growing interest in the social sciences, notably social anthropology, sociology and psychology, and in cross-cultural comparisons, was reflected in the journal *Past and Present* and such studies as L. Stone's *Family, Sex and Marriage* (1977), A. MacFarlane's *The Family Life of Ralph Josselin* (1970) and K. Thomas's *Religion and the Decline of Magic* (1971). Social history also assimilated the radical influences of the 1960s with increasing interests in labour history and social protest. With an increasing emphasis on theoretical issues, social history by the 1970s and 1980s was far removed from being merely 'history with the politics left out'. Groups and disciplines such as the Society for the Study of Labour History, HISTORY WORKSHOP, ORAL HISTORY, and WOMEN'S HISTORY have developed their own journals and conferences since the 1970s, and many of their contributions have become part of the mainstream of a broader history curriculum.

Social Mobility, the movement of individuals or families from one social group to another, especially upwards or downwards in the social scale. In the modern era social mobility, especially upward mobility and the so-called 'meritocracy', is a function of education and occupational mobility, and also of the diminishing importance of low-skill manual occupations. Social mobility (whether articulated in those terms or not) has always been a key area of study for historians, assessing whether a particular social group has risen or fallen *vis-à-vis* another (*see* GENTRY), or whether MARRIAGE, INHERITANCE, MIGRATION, chance, urban living, opportunities resulting from the BLACK DEATH, etc., have been a key ingredient in social change.

Social Order, term for social stratification, commonly used by historians, especially for the 16th and 17th centuries when contemporaries were themselves occupied with the definitions and problems of order and social gradation from the PEERAGE through the GENTRY, yeomen and husbandmen to labourers. The term has a sense both of hierarchy and of harmony.

Socialist League, a splinter from the SOCIAL DEMOCRATIC FEDERATION, it was formed by the craftsman and poet William Morris (1834–96) and Eleanor Marx-Aveling (1855–98), the writer and trade unionist daughter of Karl MARX, in 1885 and others who were disillusioned with Hyndman's autocratic leadership. Its most permanent achievement was *Commonweal*, an informative weekly, which advocated revolutionary international socialism until captured by the even more marginal anarchists at the beginning of the 1890s.

Society for Constitutional Information (SCI), established in London in 1780 to sustain knowledge of constitutional rights, and advance the cause of PARLIAMENTARY REFORM. John Cartwright was prominent among its founders. It printed and reprinted tracts for distribution in London and the provinces. It sponsored an inquiry into inequities in parliamentary representation, which provided the foundation for Thomas Oldfield's 1792 *History of the Boroughs*. Quiescent in the mid-1780s, it revived with the campaign of 1787–90 for the repeal of the TEST and CORPORATION ACTS. In spring 1792 it assumed leadership of the growing popular RADICAL movement, co-operating with the CORRESPONDING SOCIETIES in organizing the British Convention in Edinburgh, and petitions for parliamentary reform in 1793. In May 1794 six of its leaders were charged with sedition; after the treason trials of that year it largely ceased to meet, though it revived temporarily to oppose the TWO ACTS of 1795, which were directed against the popular radical societies.

Society for Psychical Research, founded in 1882 to investigate such phenomena as are included in the terms mesmerism, psychology and spiritualism. It attracted serious intellectuals and sober-minded rationalists as well as a number of cranks. It continues to flourish.

Society for the Encouragement of Arts, Manufactures and Commerce, founded in London in 1754 on the model of the DUBLIN SOCIETY. It sought to encourage innovations and improvements by offering prizes in six subjects: the polite and liberal arts; agriculture; manufactures; mechanics; chemistry, dyeing and mineralogy; and trade and colonies. Prizes were given only to unpatented inventions, to encourage the diffusion of new ideas. The society also offered drawing classes to improve the skill of British designers. It carried out and supervised experiments, and printed its *Transactions*. It survives today as the Royal Society of Arts.

Society for the Promotion of Christian Knowledge (SPCK) Founded by a group of MPs and pious laymen in London in 1698, it produced cheap religious publications that were circulated to a network of largely clerical members throughout England and Wales. (A similar body was established in Scotland in 1709.) In its first decades, the SPCK also acted as a ginger group, promoting religious, moral and socially improving projects – for example, the establishment of CHARITY SCHOOLS and WORKHOUSES. An overwhelmingly ANGLICAN body, it was not hostile to respectable DISSENT, but was initially so to the QUAKERS and more persistently to Catholicism. It represented a creative ANGLICAN response to the development of religious pluralism following the TOLERATION ACT 1689. It survives as a religious publishing house.

Society for the Propagation of the Gospel (SPG) Founded in 1701 at the instigation of Thomas Bray, with the support of the archbishop of Canterbury and several bishops, it was in effect a specialized offshoot of the SOCIETY FOR THE PROMOTION OF CHRISTIAN KNOWLEDGE (SPCK), intended to promote Church of England Christianity among English settlers in the colonies, and subsequently to convert indigenous inhabitants and to create a diligent, religious labouring class. In the 18th century, it was most active in New England and the West Indies and continues to publish today. *See also* MISSIONARY SOCIETIES.

Society for the Protection of Ancient Buildings (SPAB), pressure group formed by the craftsman and poet William Morris , in 1877, dedicated to protecting historic buildings from over-zealous restoration, often known as 'antiscrape'. The *cause célèbre* which prompted Morris to act was the proposed restoration of Tewkesbury Abbey, Glos. The Society remains active, and is a leading voice in the lobby for the CONSERVATION of historic buildings, with a particular emphasis on traditional techniques and non-interventionist repair.

Society of Antiquaries of London, *see* ANTIQUARIES AND ANTIQUARIANISM

Society of Dilettanti Initially a convivial dining club formed in London in 1754 by a group of young gentlemen who had recently visited Italy on the GRAND TOUR, it later sponsored artistic and scholarly works. Founding members included Sir Francis Dashwood (probably the moving spirit) and the Dukes of Dorset, Manchester and Northumberland; later members included Rockingham (*see* WENTWORTH, CHARLES) (1755), the artist Sir Joshua Reynolds (1766), FOX (1769), the actor-manager David Garrick (1777) and the theorists of the PICTURESQUE Uvedale Price (1770) and Richard Payne Knight (1781).

Each member was expected to pay 4 per cent of additional income in the first year of an inheritance, marriage or preferment; the society thus became very wealthy. In the 1740s, it raised a subscription for the support of Italian opera; in the 1750s, it was engaged in planning a ROYAL ACADEMY of arts – a plan realized in the next decade. It funded annual scholarships to send Academy students to Italy or Greece, and sponsored Richard Chandler, William Pars and Nicholas Revett's expedition to Greece and Asia Minor in 1764, and the publication of their *Ionian Antiquities* (1769–97), which influenced the development of NEO-CLASSICISM.

Society of Friends, *see* QUAKERS

Society of Supporters of the Bill of Rights (SSBR), a London-based political campaigning society formed in Feb. 1769 to 'defend and maintain the constitutional liberty of the subject', especially by promoting the cause of John WILKES. Its members – who included MPs, lawyers, merchants and country gentlemen – appealed for funds to pay off Wilkes' debts (they collected some £20,000), and promoted a nationwide petitioning campaign against the Grafton (*see* FITZROY, AUGUSTUS) ministry. In 1771, the society devised and publicized a comprehensive plan for PARLIAMENTARY REFORM, advocating shorter parliaments, a reduction in placemen and pensioners (*see* PLACE BILLS) and a reform in representation. They urged electors to press parliamentary candidates to pledge support for this programme, and in the 1774 election, 12 did so.

Society of the Friends of the People, society formed in 1792 by Charles GREY and Richard Brinsley Sheridan, to recruit liberal WHIG support for PARLIAMENTARY REFORM. Charles James FOX doubted the wisdom of flirtation with popular RADICALISM at this point, but ultimately aligned himself with the radical young as against the more conservative Portland (*see* BENTINCK, WILLIAM CAVENDISH) Whigs. The Scottish Friends of the People included aristocratic members, but also had a popular membership. They organized the British Convention of 1792 in EDINBURGH. Three delegates, Joseph Gerrald, Maurice Margarot and William Skirving, were TRANSPORTED for their part in this, leading to the disintegration of the Scottish society.

Socinianism, *see* UNITARIANS

SOE, *see* SPECIAL OPERATIONS EXECUTIVE

Soke, an Anglo-Saxon term for land over which jurisdiction is exercised. *DOMESDAY BOOK* shows that some sokes in the eastern counties also included many villages. A soke (such as the Soke of Peterborough, which survived into modern times) could be a compact area created by grants of special jurisdiction. In eastern and northern England, it might also represent a pre-manorial organism that originated in the exercise of lordship over individuals, rather than over an area of land. *See also* SAKE AND SOKE; MANOR.

Sokeman, a category of peasant recorded from the 10th century onwards, occurring almost exclusively in the DANELAW counties of northern and eastern England. Such peasants generally owed lighter services to a lord than did a VILLEIN. The sokemen, once believed to be the descendants of the Scandinavian armies that settled in the Danelaw, are now regarded as an older, less manorialized part of society.

Solemn League and Covenant, *see under* COVENANT

Solicitor, a lawyer undertaking general legal work for a client, usually in a court of EQUITY. After Parliament provided for formal registration of ATTORNEYS (those practising in the courts of COMMON LAW) and solicitors in 1729, some London members of both 'the lower branches' of the profession joined in the next decade to form The Society of Gentlemen Practisers in the Courts of Law and Equity, a precursor of the Law Society (incorporated in 1826).

Solicitor-General, with the ATTORNEY-GENERAL, one of the two senior legal advisers of the CROWN. The first was appointed in 1461, and from the 1530s he has regularly gone on to be attorney-general.

Solomon Islands, island group in Polynesia and former British protectorate. Discovered by the Spanish in the late 16th century, and rediscovered by the British in 1767, the islands were evangelized by Catholics and the NEW ZEALAND Anglicans in the 1840s and 50s. By the 1870s copra production was important, while many islanders were being enticed to the SUGAR cane fields of QUEENSLAND and FIJI. A protectorate was declared over the islands in 1884, in response to Germany's growing territorial ambitions in the Pacific, and other islands were added to the territory in 1898–1900.

One of the most fiercely-fought Pacific battles of WORLD WAR II raged through the islands in 1942–3, centred upon Guadalcanal. After the defeat of Japan, some of the islands were gripped by powerful cargo cults, which were curbed by heavy-handed police action in 1948. With the people united against them, the British responded with ever-growing local government, which resulted finally in self-government in 1976 and independence in 1978.

Solway Moss, Battle of, 25 Nov. 1542, chief battle, fought in Dumfries., of a short Anglo-Scots war resulting from a build-up of tension over religious differences, and from Scotland's alliance with France. When an unenthusiastic Scots army was routed by the English under Thomas Howard, Duke of Norfolk, the shock of the news killed JAMES V. The defeat led to the treaty of Greenwich, which envisaged a marriage between the infant MARY QUEEN OF SCOTS and the future EDWARD VI.

Somerled (?–1164), King of Argyll. Of Norse-Gaelic descent (Somerled means 'summer voyager' in Norse), he was a powerful figure in Scottish politics. Only rarely did he recognize the authority of MALCOLM IV – though, as the result of one short-lived reconciliation with him, he acquired the nickname 'Sit-by-the-king'. In the late 1150s, he defeated the King of MAN and conquered much of the Western Isles, becoming an important patron of IONA. He was killed in 1164 while leading an attack on Glasgow. His sons divided his territories between them, and it is from them that the numerous MacDougalls, MacRorys, Macdonnells and Macdonalds of the Isles claim descent. *See also* ARGYLL.

Somers, John (1st Baron Somers) (1651–1716), lawyer and politician. Educated at Oxford and called to the Bar in 1676, he was junior counsel for the defence at the SEVEN BISHOPS trial. Elected MP for Worcester in 1689, he played a very active part in the CONVENTION PARLIAMENT, and presided over the drafting of the DECLARATION OF RIGHTS. A firm WHIG, he was also concerned to protect constitutional balance.

Becoming lord keeper in 1693 and lord chancellor in 1697, he increased the efficiency of the House of LORDS as a legal tribunal by compelling the judges to sit as assessors, and he played a key part in bringing about Anglo-Scottish UNION in 1707. Accumulated experience and dedication to public business and learning made him pre-eminent among the JUNTO Whigs; he was also noted for his charm, which won him many friends among MPs. State papers from his library were published in 1748 as the *Somers Tracts*.

Somerset, 2nd Duke of, *see* BEAUFORT, EDMUND

Somerset, 5th Duke of, *see* SEYMOUR, EDWARD

Somerset Case, 1772. William Murray, Lord Mansfield's judgment in the case *Somerset v. Stewart* affirmed that black slaves in England might not forcefully be sold abroad by their masters; in effect, the decision established that English courts would not view SLAVERY as an enforceable contractual arrangement. The decision received much press attention, and was widely regarded as ending slavery in England. *Knight v. Wedderburn*, 1778, established the plainer precedent that Scottish courts would not uphold a master's claim to a runaway slave.

Somme, Battle of the, northern France, 1 July–18 Nov. 1916. This WORLD WAR I Anglo-French battle to break the German trench lines was the first major use of the new British volunteer armies raised by Kitchener, and the first Western Front offensive in which the British took the dominant role. The disaster for the British on the first day (57,000 casualties), in contrast to the high expectations of success, had a deep cultural impact on their perceptions of warfare and the Western Front for the rest of the century. The first use of TANKS took place in Sept. The attacks on both sides continued through into Nov. in appalling conditions. Casualties have been disputed, but were probably about 400,000 each, Germans and British, and 200,000 French. The experience confirmed LLOYD GEORGE in his hostility to HAIG just as he became prime minister in Dec. 1916. The contribution of the battle to the allied victory two years later may have been much greater than was apparent at the time.

Soul-Scot, *see* TITHES

South Africa The Union of South Africa was formed in 1910 and included the formerly self-governing colonies of CAPE COLONY, NATAL, the Transvaal and the Orange River (*see* BOER WARS). The two British colonies, Cape Colony (with responsible government since 1872) and Natal (self-governing since 1893) were joined with the former Boer Republics of Transvaal and the Orange Free State, which had secured self-government in 1907. All four states adopted common policies on customs, railways, and attitudes towards the black population, who were subject to economic exploitation, social discrimination and denied voting rights. In order better to preserve white minority rule South Africa proclaimed itself a republic and left the COMMONWEALTH in 1961, having built the system of *apartheid*. South Africa became increasingly isolated in the international community because of its racial policies and their often bloody repercussions. The repressive regime, which exiled, executed or gaoled its critics (including the icon of the struggle against *apartheid*, Nelson Mandela), was met by stiff resistance from its newly independent neighbours, against whom it waged military and economic warfare through the 1970s and 1980s. It was not until 1991 that Mandela was released and 1994 that one person one vote was introduced and Mandela, leader of the African National Congress, was elected president.

South African War, *see* BOER WARS

South Bank, area within Southwark and Lambeth on the southern side of the River Thames in LONDON. The term Bankside was used in the 16th and 17th centuries, especially for the area opposite the City of LONDON, where publicly sanctioned PROSTITUTION in the STEWS was commonplace until their closure in 1546, and where SHAKESPEARE and other artists built their THEATRES in the years around 1600. This area was noted for its 'liberties', or districts outside normal judicial control, and it was also here that many prisons were established, e.g. CLINK and MARSHALSEA. The term South Bank is now commonly applied to the area across the Thames from the Strand, where the FESTIVAL OF BRITAIN was held in 1951, and to the arts complex comprising the Royal Festival Hall (the principal survivor from the Festival site), the National Theatre and other galleries and concert halls subsequently built in the 1960s. The London Eye, the millennium ferris wheel, is situated on the South Bank.

South Cadbury, *see* CADBURY, SOUTH

South East Asia Treaty Organization (SEATO), Western-orientated defensive alliance in South-east Asia formed in 1954 by Britain, the United States, France, PAKISTAN, AUSTRALIA, NEW ZEALAND, the Philippines and Thailand, which guaranteed collective action against internal as well as external aggression. The treaty was part of the COLD WAR 'containment' of Communist advance or subversion by a series of major western alliances, including NATO and the BAGHDAD PACT.

South Sea Bubble, a speculative boom that reached its height in July 1720. It was especially stimulated by the rapid rise in the price of SOUTH SEA COMPANY stock, following parliamentary approval of a scheme designed to encourage holders of government stock to trade it in for company stock. The company had agreed to charge the government a lower rate of interest than that to which it had committed itself under wartime borrowing conditions. Bribes to prominent politicians and courtiers, in the form of notional stock holdings, helped the company secure the deal despite competition from the BANK OF ENGLAND.

The 'BUBBLE COMPANIES ACT' – passed in the early stages of the boom and prohibiting trading in the stock by any but chartered companies – helped to focus speculative attention on South Sea stock. The bubble 'burst' in mid-Sept., as investors concluded that the price ceiling had been reached, and confidence collapsed rapidly. GEORGE I and many other prominent people lost heavily; some of the politicians and financiers most involved fled or committed suicide.

South Sea Company Chartered in 1711 to trade with South America, the company was intended also to rival the WHIG-dominated BANK OF ENGLAND and EAST INDIA COMPANY as a source of loan funds for the government. HARLEY first proposed its formation in 1710. Holders of government securities were compelled to exchange them for shares at par in the new company, which was given a monopoly on trade with South America, the west coast of North America and all Spanish colonies. The Company was guaranteed an annual payment from the EXCHEQUER equivalent to 6 per cent of the stock it took over. Harley was its first governor; nine of the 30 directors were political nominees. In 1713, under the terms of the Treaty of UTRECHT, the Company was awarded the ASIENTO contract to supply slaves to Spanish colonies. In 1719 a scheme for the Company to assume more of the national debt provoked the SOUTH SEA BUBBLE crisis, which the Company itself survived. In 1750 the Company surrendered the Asiento and other trading privileges to the Spanish crown in return for £100,000. Its only function thereafter was to distribute dividends arising from interest payments on its diminishing share of the national debt. It was wound up in 1854, its remaining capital being converted into consols.

Southampton, Hants., port city. The Anglo-Saxon town was founded on the spur of land between the Rivers Test and Itchen, and the walled Norman town became one of the wealthiest settlements in medieval England, largely through its port activities and the CLOTH and WINE trades. The walls still largely survive, refortified in response to repeated attacks by the French, especially in the 14th century. Southampton had gone into the economic doldrums by the 17th century; it began to revive as a SPA in the late 18th century, but its second major lease of life came in the 19th century when the modern deep-water docks were developed. It also became the major port for the CUNARD LINERS. The town was heavily bombed in WORLD WAR II, and substantial portions were rebuilt. The docks have continued to give it its economic focus.

Sovereign, a gold coin worth 20 SHILLINGS, first issued by HENRY VII in 1489; it was distinguished by a full-figure portrait of the monarch, from which it took its name. It remained in common circulation until 1914.

SPAB, *see* SOCIETY FOR THE PROTECTION OF ANCIENT BUILDINGS

Spa Fields Riot, 2 Dec. 1816. After a meeting calling for PARLIAMENTARY REFORM in Spa Fields, Clerkenwell, had degenerated into a riot, the participants pillaged local gunsmiths and attempted to march on the TOWER OF LONDON to proclaim the creation of a committee of public safety. The crowd was dispersed at the Royal Exchange. The riot was a dramatic illustration of the economic dislocation and political unrest that followed the termination of the FRENCH REVOLUTIONARY and NAPOLEONIC WARS (1793–1815). *See also* BLANKETEERS; PETERLOO MASSACRE; SIX ACTS; SUSPENSION OF *HABEAS CORPUS* ACT.

Spanish Succession, War of the, 1702–13. The death of Charles II, the last Spanish Habsburg king, in Oct. 1700 set the scene for war, as the PARTITION TREATIES (1698, 1700) among the European powers had failed to maintain consensus as to how the Spanish dominions were to be distributed on his death. In Jan. 1701 the French seized Dutch BARRIER FORTRESSES in the Spanish Netherlands and began to occupy key ports and cities. In June, John CHURCHILL, Duke of Marlborough, was sent as plenipotentiary to the Hague to negotiate an anti-Bourbon alliance, on the lines of that formed to fight KING WILLIAM'S WAR. A new treaty of Grand Alliance was signed in Aug., the English, Dutch and Holy Roman Empire being signatories. In 1702 unofficial conflict between Austria and France broke out in Italy; in May members of the Grand Alliance declared war on France, championing the claims of the Habsburg 'Charles III' to the Spanish throne; Bavaria joined the Franco-Spanish alliance in Sept. In Aug. Marlborough opened a campaign in the Netherlands, while the English fleet harried the French and Spanish. In May 1703 the first METHUEN TREATY brought Portugal into the war, securing naval bases for the English, but at the price of an English commitment to 'No peace without Spain'. The first Anglo-Dutch troops arrived in the Peninsula in 1704; GIBRALTAR was captured in July. In Aug. Marlborough, now in Germany with imperial forces, crushed Franco-Bavarian troops at BLENHEIM; Bavaria was occupied and taken out of the war, and French troops driven back across the Rhine. In 1705 Barcelona fell to forces under Lord Peterborough; Catalonia backed the Alliance. Marlborough failed to make significant inroads into French positions, but in 1706, after victory at RAMILLIES in May, drove them out of the Spanish Netherlands. Anglo-Portuguese forces briefly captured Madrid; a decisive Austrian victory at Turin broke the French hold on northern Italy.

The next year, by contrast, saw a series of setbacks: the allied army in Spain was disastrously defeated at Almanza in April 1707; imperial forces were defeated in Germany; and an attempt to capture Toulon failed, though the French grand fleet was scuttled. The conduct of the war became the subject of parliamentary debate, with TORIES and dissident WHIGS on the attack, but SOMERS succeeded in carrying a motion for 'No peace without Spain'. In March 1708 a Franco-JACOBITE attempt to invade Scotland and exploit domestic discontent failed – prompting a swing to the Whigs in the May general election. In June Marlborough won a further major victory at Oudenarde in the Netherlands; Sardinia was captured for the Habsburgs and Minorca for the British; the fortress of Lille was taken after a bitter siege. In 1709, with France desperate for peace, negotiations began at the Hague, Marlborough and TOWNSHEND representing Britain. Their insistence that Louis XIV not only abandon all Bourbon claims to Spain but also remove Philip V within two months was, however, too much for French pride, and talks broke down.

MALPLAQUET in Aug. was technically a victory for the Allies, but at such cost as to fuel desire for peace. Townshend negotiated the first BARRIER TREATY to keep the Dutch in the war. In 1710 fresh peace negotiations stalled. GODOLPHIN's and the Whig JUNTO's hold on power, loosened by war-weariness and the SACHEVERELL AFFAIR, was undermined by Robert HARLEY's growing favour with Queen ANNE, and a change of ministry followed. Harley became first commissioner of the Treasury in Godolphin's stead and the Whigs suffered a sweeping defeat in the elections that autumn. Meanwhile victories by James STANHOPE and imperial forces in Spain briefly revived the allied cause, and in Sept. NOVA SCOTIA was captured by British and American forces, but in Dec. British forces in Spain surrendered at Brihuega.

In 1711 the Habsburg claimant to the Spanish throne succeeded the suddenly deceased Holy Roman Emperor as Charles VI. There were further peace talks. In Sept. Franco-British peace preliminaries were signed; the proposal that Spain be left in Bourbon hands was leaked to the press by the imperial envoy. SWIFT attacked the government in a famous pamphlet, *The Conduct of the Allies*; in Dec. the government was defeated in the LORDS. The political crisis was resolved in the government's favour by the creation of twelve new Tory peers and the dismissal of Marlborough. Peace negotiations were opened at UTRECHT in Jan. 1712, and concluded a year later with the signing of the Treaty of Utrecht; articles designed to promote commerce between Britain and France were defeated in the COMMONS.

This war was not as disruptive of British trade and finance as King William's War had been, although the post-war attempt to renegotiate interest rates on the war debt set the scene for the SOUTH SEA BUBBLE. Belief that the Whigs were pursuing the war at the expense of the national interest helped to bring the Tories to power in 1710, but by 1712 differences as to how best to proceed were creating strain between Harley and Bolingbroke (*see* ST JOHN, HENRY), and the Tories lost support in 1713 when they were thought to be conceding too much to France.

Spas, mineral water resorts. The taking of waters for medicinal purposes has an ancient history, but the 18th and early 19th centuries were the golden age of spas. BATH, *Aquae Sulis* to the Romans, was the most ancient of English spas, and rose to social prominence again from the later 17th century, especially with its great classical rebuilding and social cachet under John Wood and Beau Nash. Its success was emulated across the country – spas were among the fastest-growing type of town in the Georgian age. Visiting a spa was a mark of gentility, and the social season commonly involved a sojourn in Cheltenham or Bath, and later Scarborough, Harrogate or Leamington. Even quite obscure places – e.g. Melksham, Wilts. – or unexpected towns, like SOUTHAMPTON, had a brief blaze of glory as spas. The importance of spa towns as places of general resort was supplanted by the rise of the seaside, beginning in towns like BRIGHTON and Margate and continuing in Bournemouth or Blackpool. Many spas, such as Royal Leamington Spa, continued in importance thereafter as retirement centres.

SPCK, *see* SOCIETY FOR THE PROMOTION OF CHRISTIAN KNOWLEDGE

Speaker, the presiding officer in either House of PARLIAMENT. The lord chancellor acts as Speaker in the House of LORDS; the COMMONS Speaker is chosen by his or her fellow-members and acts as the guardian of their PARLIAMENTARY PRIVILEGES. The first Commons Speaker was chosen in 1376; early Speakers were royal officials, but during the 17th and 18th centuries the CROWN ceased to interfere with the choice. The principle was finally established when the Commons rejected the royal recommendation of Sir Thomas Littleton in 1695, after which the choice was made by majority vote. Since 1742, no Speaker has held ministerial office; however, it was not until the mid-19th century that Speakers accepted the convention that they were impartial in debate.

Special Areas Act 1934, Act in which the NATIONAL GOVERNMENT gave grants of up to £2 million in total to 'Special Areas' – those designated as suffering from especially high unemployment and problems of economic restructuring. The Act was criticized as a pre-election gimmick; it did, however, recognize the need for government assistance to the most depressed regions and produced some useful investment in the infrastructure of the regions concerned.

Special Branch, department of the Metropolitan POLICE with responsibility for political security, under the home office. Founded in 1881 as a 'Fenian Office' to deal with Irish terrorism, the organization took on surveillance of anarchists, left-wing groups and foreigners before WORLD WAR I. Between the wars it collected information on left-wing and fascist groups. It continued and expanded its 'anti-subversive' role after 1945. *See also* MI5.

Special Operations Executive (SOE), British secret service organization set up in July 1940 to support and stimulate resistance activity in occupied countries during WORLD WAR II. At its peak it employed over 10,000 men and over 3,200 women, many of them involved with resistance groups in Europe and the Far East. SOE was officially closed down in Jan. 1946, when some of its personnel joined parallel secret organizations such as MI6.

Special Relationship, term widely used to describe Anglo-American relations during the 20th century, based upon the shared language, culture and political outlook of Britain and the USA. The relationship has been at its closest during war, especially WORLD WAR II after the USA joined the Allies in 1941, and during the COLD WAR of confrontation and then *détente* with the Soviet Union; relations were at their weakest during the SUEZ CRISIS. The perceived value of the transatlantic relationship was one element which long kept Britain aloof from European integration; most commentators now regard efforts to keep the relationship separate from USA–Europe relations as doomed. The relationship has usually flourished at times when the president of the USA and the British prime minister have enjoyed a personal friendship, as in the Kennedy–MACMILLAN era and latterly in the Reagan–THATCHER years, although the partnership – given Britain's relative economic and political decline in the 20th century – has never been remotely equal.

Spectator, a literary periodical edited by Richard Steele and Joseph Addison as a successor to the *Tatler*, which appeared daily from 1 March 1711 to 6 Dec. 1712. Addison revived it on his own for 80 issues in 1714. Mainly concerned with literature, manners and morals, it advocated moderation and toleration in politics and religion, and attempted to disseminate the values of a liberal 'polite' culture to a wide readership. The issues were frequently republished, in collected form, during the remainder of the century.

Speenhamland, name given to the POOR RELIEF system developed by a meeting of Berks. magistrates at Speen near Reading in 1795. Responding to a poor harvest and high food prices, they drew up a scale to regulate payments to the poor, taking account of the size of the claimant's family, and the price of bread. Many other counties in southern England followed suit. Such practices were criticized in Parliament in 1817–24, and again by the Royal Commission on the Poor Laws in 1832–4. It was argued that allowances in aid of wages depressed wage levels, and reduced incentives to save or delay marriage, thus further increasing the burden of the Old POOR LAW, but there is insufficient evidence to suggest that this was more than UTILITARIAN-inspired prejudice.

Spencer, Charles (3rd Earl of Sunderland) (1674–1722), politician. Second son of the

2nd Earl, he entered Parliament in 1695; his second marriage, to Marlborough's (*see* CHURCHILL, JOHN) daughter in 1700, brought him important WHIG connections. Although disliked by Queen ANNE, he became secretary of state in 1706, and was one of the Whig JUNTO that dominated the government from 1708–10, when he was dismissed for his part in attempting to impeach SACHEVERELL. His career revived after the accession of GEORGE I, and he rose through a series of offices to become first lord of the TREASURY in 1718, controlling internal affairs while STANHOPE dealt with foreign policy. The SOUTH SEA BUBBLE had its origins in his schemes to reduce the burden of the national debt; after the Bubble burst, he ceded the effective headship of the Treasury to WALPOLE (who ably defended him in the COMMONS). But as groom of the stole he retained personal access to George I, and only Spencer's unexpected death on 19 April 1722 forestalled his new bid for ascendancy at court.

Spencer, Robert (2nd Earl of Sunderland) (1640–1702), politician. Son of the 1st Earl (killed in the CIVIL WAR in 1643), he went to Oxford in 1661, but left with William Penn and others who objected to the clergy having to wear surplices. He was sent on several diplomatic missions in the 1670s, and was made a privy councillor in 1674 and, five years later, northern secretary of state. When he voted for the EXCLUSION Bill 1680, he was dismissed from the PRIVY COUNCIL, but in 1682 was reconciled with the king.

Not initially favoured by JAMES II, he was appointed lord president in succession to Charles Montagu, Earl of Halifax when he supported the repeal of the TEST ACT, which Halifax did not. Unlike most of his contemporaries, Sunderland was willing to go further with James: he was indeed the only significant political figure to remain in his inner circle to the end. In 1686, he was appointed to the ECCLESIASTICAL COMMISSION, and two years later, he gave evidence against the SEVEN BISHOPS and renounced Protestantism for Catholicism. He advised the king to seek French support, but in Oct. 1688, a draft of an Anglo-French naval treaty was lost while in his care; he was pardoned but dismissed, and fled to Rotterdam in disguise.

In 1689, he published a pamphlet justifying his conduct as an attempt to moderate James's policies. He was excluded from both the INDEMNITY ACT 1689 and James's offer in 1692 of a pardon in the event of his reinstatement as king. In 1691, Sunderland returned to England and reappeared in Parliament; by 1692, WILLIAM III was regularly consulting him on ministerial changes, and during the next four years he functioned as 'minister behind the curtain' – fearing parliamentary condemnation should he accept office. However, in the spring of 1697 he did accept appointment as lord chamberlain, only to resign hastily the following winter when he came under fire in the COMMONS.

In a period in which the uncertain course of politics produced many complicated and apparently inconsistent careers, Sunderland gained a reputation for exceptional cynicism.

SPG, *see* SOCIETY FOR THE PROPAGATION OF THE GOSPEL

Spinning Jenny, spinning machinery developed by James Hargreaves in the early 1760s and refined by John Kay, allowing spinners to spin more than one thread at a time. Jenny-spun yarn was soft and therefore suitable only for weft: Richard Arkwright's frame by contrast could produce strong warp thread. Jennies were cheap to construct, and models with few spindles were small enough to be housed in cottages. Models with more than 20 spindles were used in factories. By 1788 there were estimated to be 20,000 in use. *See also* CLOTH INDUSTRY; COTTON INDUSTRY; MULE.

Spitalfields, area immediately to the east of the City of LONDON, taking its name from the medieval hospital foundation of St Mary Spital, which became one of the leading craft areas of 18th-century London. Occupied by HUGUENOT silk weavers and other fine craftsmen, and dominated by Nicholas Hawksmoor's (1661–1736) mighty Christ Church, it was a wealthy area which subsequently went into long-term decline. The Huguenots' places were taken by Jewish immigrants from Eastern Europe and Russia, who continued the tradition of textiles and garment-making; the area became synonymous with POVERTY, and was the scene for the notorious 'Jack the Ripper' murders in 1888. Since the 1960s Spitalfields has become home to another immigrant group, largely from Bangladesh; they too have frequently been involved in the garment trade. The survival of handsome but sorely-neglected streets and houses from the Huguenot era was a spur to the CONSERVATION movement led by the Spitalfields Trust, which was founded in 1977. The removal of the fruit and vegetable market from Spitalfields in the 1990s has rejuvenated the area as part of the East London art and design efflorescence.

Spithead Mutiny, *see* NORE MUTINY

Squadrone, a Scottish political grouping formed in 1704, known as the 'Squadrone Volante', or 'flying squadron', because of their preference for impermanent alliances with other groups. Formed from members of the Scots COUNTRY opposition, they supported the PROTESTANT SUCCESSION, opposed the JACOBITES, and provided vital support for the UNION of Scottish and English parliaments in 1707. In the following year's election, they allied with the Jacobites in an attempt to take over the management of Scottish affairs from the Queensberry connection. From 1714, they lost ground to Argyll's (*see* CAMPBELL, JOHN) court faction.

Squarson, a term coined in the early 19th century to denote a clergyman (parson) who was also a country squire, and well connected with the PEERAGE or GENTRY. More clergy came to hold substantial amounts of land in the later 18th century, when parliamentary ENCLOSURE ACTS converted TITHE claims into landholdings, and the value of land rose. These years also saw increasing numbers of clerical magistrates. In the early 19th century, these clergy, whose social role was as much secular as spiritual, attracted criticism from EVANGELICALS and Church reformers.

Sri Lanka, *see* CEYLON

Staller, the title given to members of the English royal household who seem to have been employed when required on specific royal business. First appearing in the reign of CNUT, by the time of EDWARD THE CONFESSOR they held extensive landed estates and had something of the character of 'trouble-shooters'. The title disappeared after the NORMAN CONQUEST.

Stamfordbridge, Battle of, 25 Sept. 1066, a victory in Yorks. for HAROLD II of England over HARALD HARDRAADA, king of Norway, and his own brother TOSTIG. Harold II was able to take by surprise opponents already weakened by the earlier battle at FULFORD GATE. However, while the English king was occupied in the North, the Norman army landed at Pevensey on 28 Sept.

Stamp Acts, Acts requiring that certain goods be stamped: the fee charged for the stamp generated revenue for the government, and the stamping requirement gave oversight over certain products – inasmuch as the tax raised prices, it might also be expected to restrict use. Stamp taxes were levied on NEWSPAPERS and pamphlets from 1712, being recurrently modified. In 1815, this tax stood at a level of four pence a copy. Agitation against 'taxes on knowledge' led to its reduction to one penny in 1836, and finally to its abolition in 1855. 'Unstamped' newspapers, sold at a cheaper price and characteristically stridently oppositional in content, were a feature both of the period 1720–50 and of the early 19th century.

The 1765 Stamp Act, a measure introduced by GRENVILLE, was designed to raise revenue from the WEST INDIES and North American colonies to defray the cost of defending them. All official and legal papers, newspapers, pamphlets, playing cards and dice were to carry duties similar to those already payable in Britain. Expected to raise £40,000–£100,000 a year, the taxes met unexpectedly determined resistance. Americans were accustomed to the imperial Parliament imposing customs duties, but not internal taxes; many colonists argued that the Act was unconstitutional, saying that there should be 'no taxation without representation'. It was repealed by the Rockingham (*see* WENTWORTH, CHARLES) ministry in 1766, but good relations with the colonies were not to be re-established: the War of AMERICAN INDEPENDENCE broke out 10 years later.

Standard, Battle of the, 22 Aug. 1138, an engagement near Northallerton, Yorks., between DAVID I of Scotland and an English army organized by Thurstan, Archbishop of York. As the Empress MATILDA's uncle, David took her side against STEPHEN and launched attacks on northern England in 1136, 1137 and 1138. The 'native' Scots in his army, Galwegians and Highlanders, treated these campaigns as slave hunts. This shocked the English – who had recently given up SLAVERY – and in consequence, Archbishop Thurstan and some northern barons initiated a 'holy war' against a barbarous invader.

They marched with the banners of St Peter of York, St John of Beverley and St Wilfrid of Ripon flying from a mast mounted on a cart (the 'standard' from which the battle takes its name). The Scots, though they may have outnumbered the English, were no match for them in terms of armour and ammunition. They suffered heavy losses at the hands of the English archers and fled in disarray.

Standard-of-Living Debate One of the longest-running and most inconclusive of historical controversies, it is primarily concerned with the nature of industrial capitalism, and the social costs arising from its formation, during the period 1790–1850. The 'optimistic' school of historians, who believe that it brought an increase in the standard of living of the working population, rest their argument principally upon a study of real wages and increased job opportunities. The 'pessimists' deny the validity of the wages data and insist that the early period of industrial capitalism reduced the standard of living, debased the quality of life and, indeed, was experienced by the common people as a social catastrophe. The arguments, though sustained by the deficiencies in the evidence, are at bottom ideological and reflect the differing political standpoints of historians and their conceptions of the character of capitalism.

Standing Army, a military force permanently embodied. The NEW MODEL ARMY of 1645 broke with previous practice in that it was maintained in peacetime. This experience, and contemporary continental developments, were subsequently cited to demonstrate that standing ARMIES were instruments of executive tyranny. The royal guards maintained by CHARLES II and JAMES II attracted criticism as a form of standing army (*see* GUARDS AND GARRISONS), and the 1689 BILL OF RIGHTS stated that there should be no peacetime standing army without parliamentary consent. The decision only partially to demobilize the army after the Treaty of RYSWICK (1697) provoked controversy, but received parliamentary sanction. Critics of government continued to employ the phrase throughout the 18th century. *See also* ARMY.

Stanhope, James (1st Earl Stanhope) (1673–1721), politician. Grandson of the 1st Earl of Chesterfield, he fought in the wars of the 1690s and early 18th century, ultimately becoming commander of the British forces in Spain. Elected MP in 1701, he was a strong WHIG and played a major part in the IMPEACHMENT of SACHEVERELL. He helped suppress the JACOBITE rising of 1715, was made southern secretary of state, served briefly as first lord of the TREASURY in 1717, but returned to the secretaryship. His main political achievements were in foreign policy, helping to secure the treaty of Westminster (1716) and the TRIPLE ALLIANCE (1717). As a leading minister, he shared the blame for the bursting of the SOUTH SEA BUBBLE in 1720, which effectively ended his political career.

Stanley, Edward (23rd [14th Stanley] Earl of Derby) (1799–1869), Conservative politician and Prime Minister (1852, 1858–9, 1866–8). His political loyalties were fluid in the early stage of his career. Identified with the WHIGS from 1820, he nevertheless served in the liberal TORY administration of CANNING and Goderich (*see* ROBINSON, FREDERICK). He established his reputation as an able parliamentary orator in GREY's Whig ministry in which, as secretary for Ireland, he carried the Irish Education Act of 1831, and, as secretary for war and the colonies (1833–4), brought about the abolition of SLAVERY in the WEST INDIES. In 1835 he resigned over Lord John RUSSELL's plan to use Irish church revenues for secular purposes, and thereafter allied himself with PEEL, whom he served as colonial secretary (1844–5), resigning the following year over the repeal of the CORN LAWS. During the 1850s and 1860s he led the PROTECTIONIST wing of the CONSERVATIVES and co-operated with DISRAELI in the rebuilding of the party. Thrice prime minister of minority governments, his principal aim was to establish the Conservatives as a credible party of government in a fast-growing democracy. The extension of the FRANCHISE in his final administration seems to have been prompted by this attempt to establish Conservative credibility. *See also* REFORM ACT 1867.

Stannary Parliament, *see* TIN INDUSTRY

Staple, a fixed place through which medieval wool exports were channelled. The staple system was developed by the English crown in the early 14th century to control and tax the export trade in a commodity that was indispensable to the cloth manufacturing towns of Flanders. The first compulsory staple, established in 1313, was at St Omer, south-east of Calais; in 1326, 14 'home staples' were set up in England, Ireland and Wales. However, after further experimentation, the staple was established at CALAIS in 1363 and remained there until 1558 (when the town was lost); it was then moved to Bruges and later to Middelburg, although by then exports of manufactured cloth were more important. Hence, from the 16th century onwards, we have used terms such as 'staple commodity'. *See also* WOOL INDUSTRY.

Staple, Company of the, a company of wool exporters established in 1343 and normally based at the STAPLE at CALAIS. Dominated by a small group of wealthy London businessmen, the company became an important part of the system of English government finance, making loans to the crown out of the profits of their near monopoly of the wool trade and obtaining repayment from the revenues of the WOOL SUBSIDY.

Staple Economies, *see* PLANTATION

Staple Industries, Old, the name given to the textile, IRON AND STEEL, SHIPBUILDING and COAL-mining sectors of the British economy in the first half of the 20th century. These were the industrial sectors which had been of central importance to the ECONOMY since the INDUSTRIAL REVOLUTION but which, by the inter-war period, were experiencing major international competition, contraction and loss of employment. Depression in these industries was responsible for the bulk of inter-war UNEMPLOYMENT, felt heavily in the provincial industrial areas where they were concentrated. The Old Staples enjoyed a brief respite during WORLD WAR II but have suffered terminal decline since then – with the exception of a few specialist firms which have secured a niche in markets despite the competition, largely from Japan and the Far East but also from Western Europe, and (in the case of coal) from alternative sources of power, especially ATOMIC ENERGY.

Star Chamber, Court of, the KING'S COUNCIL sitting as a court of law in the Star Chamber, a room in the palace of WESTMINSTER whose ceiling was decorated with stars. Its 15th-century origins have been confused by the setting up in 1487 of a small, short-lived tribunal that used the same room. From 1516, WOLSEY greatly developed it as his personal agency for enforcing justice, creating a flow of business that necessitated reorganization in the 1530s and 1540s; thereafter the court consisted of the PRIVY COUNCIL and the chief justices. Originally dealing with public disorder, the range of its work was much extended by LEGAL FICTIONS. Generally esteemed for its decisive action, it was discredited when CHARLES I and the ARMINIANS used it against their opponents in the 1630s, and it was abolished in 1641. Contrary to popular myth, it never used TORTURE.

Statistical Account, survey of all Scottish PARISHES, published in 21 volumes 1791–8; a *New Statistical Account* was published from 1834–45. The relatively novel term 'statistical', borrowed from German usage, meant information about or of use to the state. The survey was promoted by the MP Sir John Sinclair, who persuaded the General Assembly of the Church of Scotland to support it. Questionnaires sent to ministers enquired into parish resources, disease, MIGRATION, POPULATION, production, rents, antiquities, ROADS, bridges, ENCLOSURES, the effects of the 1782–3 famine, changes in manners and dress, morals, crime and EDUCATION. The published volumes are a mine of information for historians.

Statute of Artificers, *see* ARTIFICERS, STATUTE OF

Statute of Labourers, *see* LABOURERS, STATUTE OF

Statute of Ruddlan, *see* RUDDLAN, STATUTE OF

Statute of Westminster, *see* WESTMINSTER, STATUTE OF

Steam Hammer Invented by James Nasmyth in 1839, it proved of great utility in the development of the IRON AND STEEL INDUSTRY. The hammer was so designed and so perfectly controlled by STEAM POWER that its action could be gauged with great accuracy: it could be made to crack the glass of a watch without actually breaking it, or brought down upon a mass of molten iron with a force representing many hundreds of tons.

Steam Power 'Steam', wrote the historian T. S. Ashton, 'was the pivot on which industry swung into the modern age.' Steam supplied the reliable source of motive power that was central to the development of mechanical mass production.

The replacement of wind, water and animal power did not happen overnight, however, and it was not until the mid-19th century that steam became the main source of industrial power. The economic and social effects were enormous. Steam engine manufacture stimulated the growth of the COAL and IRON AND STEEL INDUSTRIES, led to the development of a machine tool industry, and promoted mechanical engineering with specialization in civil, marine and (later) electrical engineering (*see* ENGINEERING INDUSTRY). The application of steam power was central to the development of the FACTORY SYSTEM, the relocation of industry to the coalfields, and to new patterns of urban settlement, as well as to new forms of transport, especially the RAILWAYS and STEAMSHIPS.

CHRONOLOGY: EARLY DEVELOPMENT

1712 Thomas Newcomen's first engine, a vast improvement on Thomas Savery's, erected at Dudley colliery.

1775 100 Newcomen engines at work collieries in the north-east alone; but these engines consume large amounts of coal and are only capable of lifting water out of mines.

1769 Condenser, devised and patented by James Watt, reduces fuel consumption and makes the application of steam power more commercially attractive.

1776 Watt's improved engine, with accurately bored cylinders, installed at Blomfield colliery near Tipton.

1781 Watt and Murdoch, encouraged by Matthew Boulton, construct first commercial rotative engine to drive machinery in factories and mills.

1782 Double action added. Previously a piston could only be driven by compression from above; the improved version allows steam into the cylinder at both ends by means of two valves.

1788 Watt perfects steam engine by addition of a centrifugal governor to maintain an even running speed. In the 1780s he also adds automatic regulators, steam jacketing and lagging, and improves transmission gears.

1800 Approximately 2,500 steam engines in production with about a third of these produced and installed by Boulton and Watt from the late 1790s on. Engines are increasingly used in textile mills from the mid 1780s, at first largely as a supplement to water power but increasingly as the major source of power by the late 1790s.

1802 Invention of high pressure engine by Richard Trevithick, soon applied to transportation and mining. Watt's low pressure engine remains the prime form of steam power in manufacturing until the 1860s when high pressure becomes widespread, resulting in the most substantial reduction in power costs since the 1790s.

1884 Invention of the steam turbine by Charles Parsons.

Steamships The first successful uses of steam engines afloat in Britain were in a dredger for Portsmouth Dockyard (1801 – powering the bucket train), and to propel a vessel, the canal tug *charlotte Dundas*, in the Forth and Clyde Canal. However, Henry Bell's *Comet* of 1812, the first successful British seagoing steamer and the first of many Clyde paddlers, marks the real beginning of the steamer in these islands. All the earliest steamers were built on the Clyde, including Denny's *Tug* which gave her name to their main activity apart from carrying passengers. Early engines were both unreliable and very uneconomic in fuel, restricting the steamers to river traffic and cross-channel work – those that went further afield did so mostly under sail.

By the early 1820s Britain was exporting steamships, engines and engineers to the rest of Europe and further afield, and, at the same time, the NAVY built its first steamers for towing and general duties. Within a decade the Navy was building steamships intended to fight, armed with heavy guns, and by the early 1840s the steam transatlantic LINER had become a practicality, when scientific developments with compasses made it possible to use iron for the hulls of seagoing ships. Simultaneously John Ericsson and Sir Francis

Pettit Smith proved the concept of screw propulsion, a development seized on by the ADMIRALTY to enable it to provide steam power without compromising the broadsides or sailing abilities of its ships of the line. Iron did not initially prove very suitable for warship hulls, but developments in iron production made it possible to build ironclads during the CRIMEAN WAR (1854–5) and by the end of that war no sailing warships were left in first-line service.

In 1860 the first seagoing iron-hulled ironclad (*Warrior*) was being built and soon afterwards production of wooden warships all but ceased, though for a time composite construction (wooden planking on iron frames, producing a hull that could be copper-sheathed) was popular for warships and merchantmen which had to make long voyages. Meanwhile developments in marine engineering by John Elder and others were producing much more economical engines and, for the first time, steamships began to carry cargo (though only high-value or perishable cargo) over long distances.

In the 1870s the Navy and torpedo boat builders began to use steel for steamers, though it was not until the early 1880s that the introduction of mild steel made it very rapidly into the standard material for merchantmen. At the same time the development of the triple-expansion engine improved steaming economy to the extent that steam became preferable to sail for most cargoes on all except the longest routes. In the same decade the oil tanker and the refrigerated cargo vessel came into service, and engines had become reliable enough for seagoing steamers to dispense with the masts and sails that they had carried as an emergency standby.

With the 20th century came new propulsion systems such as the turbine and the diesel which gradually replaced steam power. Warship development was rapid and complex, but for merchantmen the most dramatic changes were not till the revolution in shipping of the 1960s and 1970s, with huge supertankers, containerization, 'roll-on, roll-off' ferries and the like, very few of them any longer powered by steam, replacing the preceeding types of ship.

Steel, Sir David (1938–), Liberal politician and party leader. Britain's youngest MP when he was elected in 1965, he sponsored the 1967 ABORTION Bill. He helped the LIBERAL PARTY recover from the THORPE affair and became its leader, 1976–88. The LIB-LAB PACT of 1977–8 maintained the minority LABOUR government in power during the DEVOLUTION referendum campaigns. In 1981, he led the Liberal Party into an alliance with the newly founded Social Democratic Party and was instrumental in bringing about a merger of the two parties to form the Liberal Democrats in 1988. As well as sitting in the Lords, Steel is also the elected presiding officer of the Scottish parliament in Edinburgh (*see* DEVOLUTION).

Steel Industry, *see* IRON AND STEEL INDUSTRY; SHEFFIELD

Steelyard, from the 13th to the 17th century, the enclosed site of the London *Kontor*, the privileged and largely self-governing community of HANSEATIC merchants.

Stephen (*c.*1096–1154), King of England (1135–54). The younger son of Stephen, Count of Blois, and Adela, daughter of WILLIAM I THE CONQUEROR, thanks to the generosity of his uncle HENRY I, Stephen became the wealthiest Anglo-Norman magnate, and in 1125 he married MATILDA OF BOULOGNE, heiress to that French county. Although, in 1127, he had sworn an oath recognizing his cousin the Empress MATILDA as her father's heir, when Henry died on 1 Dec. 1135, Stephen wasted no time in getting himself crowned king at WESTMINSTER on 22 Dec., and then recognized as Duke of Normandy.

While the Empress Matilda and her husband, Geoffrey of Anjou, concentrated on invasions of Normandy, Stephen first dealt successfully with challenges to his authority in England. But from 1139, the year in which Matilda landed in England, he was in serious difficulties. Although the fact that his rival was a woman had allowed him to seize the throne in the first place, it also meant he now faced an opponent whom it was hard to eliminate without offending against CHIVALRY.

In Feb. 1141, he was captured at the battle of LINCOLN, and for several months, his cause seemed lost. In Normandy, Geoffrey made crucial advances; in England, Stephen's brother, HENRY OF BLOIS, was prepared to accept the verdict of battle. But the empress overplayed a winning hand, allowing Stephen's queen to organize a comeback. When the empress's half-brother, ROBERT OF GLOUCESTER, was captured, an exchange of prisoners was agreed: Robert for Stephen. Stephen retained control of LONDON and much of eastern England, but he never returned to Normandy, and by 1145, Geoffrey had completed his conquest of the duchy.

From then on, Stephen's supporters with major connections in Normandy could give him, at best, half-hearted allegiance. He fought on, however, until disheartened by the deaths of his wife and his eldest son Eustace, both in 1153. By the treaty of Winchester in Nov. of that year, he recognized Matilda's eldest son Henry as his heir in return for life possession of the throne and a guarantee that his own second-born son, William, would be allowed to keep all his family lands in England and Normandy. After 14 years of civil war, no one was prepared to dispute HENRY II's right to the throne when Stephen died the following Oct.

Stephen has to take some responsibility for the troubles of his reign. Above all, the fact that he visited Normandy only once, in 1137, meant that he failed to take proper account of the cross-Channel structure of the ANGLO-NORMAN REALM. In addition, he was perhaps too chivalrous and gallant for his own good – at Lincoln, for example. On the other hand, these were the very qualities that had made him an attractive candidate for the throne and enabled his wife to campaign on his behalf in the crisis of 1141.

Sterling, principal money of the United Kingdom; English, Scottish or British money of standard value, hence the pound sterling (and sterling silver). The name probably derives from the NORMAN coin bearing a star. *See also* BRETTON WOODS; DEVALUATION; STERLING AREA.

Sterling Area, term applied to the group of countries, especially (but not exclusively) those of the BRITISH EMPIRE and subsequently the COMMONWEALTH, which have used the pound sterling as their principal reserve currency and as a major trading currency, most frequently settling transactions among themselves through the City of LONDON markets. From WORLD WAR II and the BRETTON WOODS agreements, the grouping was formalized into the Scheduled Territories for the maintenance of foreign exchange controls; CANADA with its dollar closely tied to the USA was excluded. Since the early 1970s floating exchange rates have broken the ties, with only the UK, CHANNEL ISLANDS, GIBRALTAR and Isle of MAN remaining within the Sterling Area.

Stewart, *see* STUART FAMILY NAME

Stewart, Henry (styled Lord Darnley) (1545–67), King of Scots. Born in Yorks. to Matthew Stewart, Earl of Lennox, and Lady Margaret Douglas, his mother's incessant scheming for his dynastic advancement finally succeeded when, having been allowed to leave England in 1565 by an exasperated ELIZABETH I, he captivated MARY QUEEN OF SCOTS with his vacant good looks – and perhaps his Catholicism. Showering him with titles, she married him and pronounced him king of Scots in July 1565, but soon even she could see that he was utterly untrustworthy.

In 1566, furious that she had turned to David Rizzio, he collaborated in the Italian's murder. After Mary gave birth to Darnley's son (the future JAMES VI AND I) later the same year, the couple separated; by now Mary was involved with Bothwell (*see* HEPBURN, JAMES). She persuaded Darnley to return to Edinburgh; he was found strangled after his lodging, Kirk o' Field, had been blown up. The murder proved the downfall of both Mary and Bothwell.

Stewart, Robert (styled Viscount Castlereagh, 2nd Marquess of Londonderry) (1769–1822), politician. He played a significant part in promoting the UNION of the English and Irish parliaments under PITT THE YOUNGER, was blamed for the WALCHEREN fiasco, but achieved considerable success as foreign secretary (1812–22), with a major role in shaping the post-NAPOLEONIC WAR settlement that gave Europe long years of peace. His diplomacy was critical in bringing Russia, Austria and Prussia together in a single confederacy to defeat Napoleon. As British plenipotentiary on the Continent he negotiated the treaty of Chaumont (1814) in which the allies reaffirmed their decision not to make a separate peace and to remain in alliance for 20 years after the war to ensure stability. At the Congress of VIENNA (1815) he was instrumental in preventing the imposition of a vindictive peace on France, and in limiting Prussian and Russian ambitions in the interest of a viable BALANCE OF POWER. Liberal abroad, he was reactionary at home, and identified with the sternest repression of popular RADICALISM. His suicide, brought about by derangement of the mind as a result of overwork, was celebrated by the London mob, who cheered at his funeral.

Stews, medieval brothels located in Southwark and licensed by the bishop of WINCHESTER, their landlord. HENRY VIII closed them down by royal proclamation in 1546, reflecting a moral panic which affected most of Europe during the 16th century; the effect was to spread the sex industry more widely through LONDON. *See also* PROSTITUTION.

Stigand, Archbishop of Canterbury (1052–70), a worldly and very wealthy prelate whose failings typify the weaknesses of the English Church before 1066. Stigand was an unashamed careerist who held CANTERBURY and WINCHESTER – the two richest dioceses in England – in plurality after 1052, as well as a large private estate. He was intruded into Canterbury after the expulsion of Archbishop Robert of Jumièges and, for this reason, his position was always regarded as uncanonical by the papacy. He was apparently at first accepted by WILLIAM I THE CONQUEROR, but in 1070 was abandoned and deposed by a papal legate.

Stirling Bridge, Battle of, 11 Sept. 1297, the first great Scottish victory in the Wars of SCOTTISH INDEPENDENCE. When the vanguard of an overconfident English army crossed the bridge to the north bank of the Forth, it was slaughtered by the Scottish resistance forces raised by William WALLACE and Andrew Moray. One of the English commanders, Cressingham, was killed and skinned.

Stock Exchange, market in securities – government bills, orders and the stocks and bonds of chartered companies – semi-formalized in the late 17th century in a series of London COFFEE HOUSES, especially Jonathan's and Garraway's, in Exchange Alley near the Royal Exchange, in the City of LONDON. An Act of 1697 limited to 100 the number of licensed brokers (*see* SOUTH SEA BUBBLE). The first purpose-built Stock Exchange opened in 1802.

After the collapse of the 1930s and in the period following WORLD WAR II, the London Stock Exchange was constrained by the small size of the domestic economy. Its dealings were dominated by the trading of UK government bonds rather than equities. From the late 1940s through the 1950s, the Stock Exchange stagnated; but with the revival of the international banking activities of the City in the 1960s and 70s, as London became a global centre for the trading of foreign currencies and EUROBONDS, the Stock Exchange also prospered. In particular the Stock Exchange began to deal not only in the shares of domestic companies but also of many foreign companies. By the 1980s shares in European companies such as Fiat, Volvo and Electrolux were being traded in larger volumes in London than in their domestic markets.

In Oct. 1986 the so-called 'Big Bang' revolutionized the Stock Exchange with the introduction of computerized trading, and in Oct. 1987 'Black Monday' saw £50 billion wiped off share values as the world stock markets recorded the largest fall since the crash of 1929.

As a result of the privatization of state industries and the demutualization of BUILDING SOCIETIES etc., the number of investors has increased considerably during the 1990s, and in 2000, the number of investors totalled 12.5 million.

Stockton, 1st Earl of, *see* MACMILLAN, HAROLD

Stoke, Battle of, near Newark, Notts., 16 June 1487, the defeat of the impostor Lambert SIMNEL's forces by HENRY VII. Often seen as ending the WARS OF THE ROSES.

Stonehenge, prehistoric stone circle or henge monument on Salisbury Plain, Wilts., and the focus of archaeological and mystical interest since the 17th century. *See also* AVEBURY.

Stop of the Exchequer, 1672, partial repudiation of a part of the crown's debts. Orders of Payment had been introduced in 1665 to authorize EXCHEQUER payments; they circulated like BANK NOTES. In Jan. 1672 a moratorium on certain of these payments was ordered; the crown undertook to pay 6 per cent interest. London bankers, the most important holders of the Orders, instituted a protracted lawsuit; their claim was settled by the creation of 'Bankers Annuities' carrying only 3 per cent interest, payment of which was however guaranteed. The Stop was long remembered to CHARLES II's discredit.

Stop-Go, name given to swings in government economic policies in the 1950s and 1960s aimed, under the influence of KEYNES-ianism, at coping with the extremes of the business cycle. Changes in taxes, government spending, interest rates, the regulations governing hire purchase and other policies were used in attempts to control a boom or start a recovery. By the 1960s, these sharp swings in policy were becoming discredited because the impact of intervention could not be controlled, the extremes of the cycle were sometimes exacerbated, and frequent policy changes proved very damaging to business confidence and to longterm business planning and investment.

Stormont, name commonly given to the parliament for Northern Ireland after partition, which sat in Stormont Castle outside BELFAST. The assembly at Stormont did not sit after DIRECT RULE was introduced in 1972 until the brief period of devolved government 2 Dec. 1999 to 11 Feb. 2000 following the Good Friday Agreement. *See also* ULSTER.

Stow, John (*c.*1525–1605), historian. A self-educated London tailor of conservative religious sympathies, from the 1560s he devoted himself to gathering manuscripts and producing chronicles, activities which exposed him to the jealousy and attack of a rival and staunchly PROTESTANT chronicler, the printer Richard Grafton (*c.*1507–73). He escaped serious trouble for possession of CATHOLIC writings after repeated official examinations between 1568 and 1570, and retained the friendship of his fellow-historian Archbishop Matthew PARKER. His devotion to scholarship dispersed his commercial fortune and left him dependent on the charity of admirers. His works include an edition of CHAUCER's works (1561), various medieval chronicles, his own *Chronicles of England* compilation (1580) and a revision of HOLIN-SHED's *Chronicles* (1585–7), but his lasting achievement is *A Survey of London* (1598), a loving and detailed account of his native city.

Strafford, 1st Earl of, *see* WENTWORTH, THOMAS

Straits Settlements, former British colony, subsequently absorbed into MALAYA, created in 1824 under the Anglo-Dutch Treaty of London, comprising Penang, Melaka and SINGAPORE. It became a crown colony in 1867 and was dissolved in 1946.

Stranger Churches, churches set up in England for congregations of exiled PROTES-TANTS, chiefly Dutch and French (*see* HUGUENOTS), but also initially Italian. They were first founded in 1550, with the encouragement of EDWARD VI's government, but were forced to flee abroad once more by MARY I; ELIZABETH I allowed them to return in 1559. Some of these churches still survive – e.g. in LONDON and NORWICH.

Strangford Lough, Battle of, Co. Down, 877. One of the many engagements between the VIKINGS and the Irish, it demonstrated that the Irish were capable of tackling the raiders on water, and is also important for the death of the great chieftain HALFDAN. The battle was one reason why Viking settlement in Ireland remained restricted to the coastal towns (*see* DUBLIN).

Stratford-Upon-Avon, Warwicks., birthplace of SHAKESPEARE and centre of the 'Shakespeare industry'. The wealth of the medieval and early modern CLOTH trade is evident in the parish church, Guild Chapel, and the former Guild Hall, as well as in the survival of half-timbered houses for which Stratford is famous. Stratford also enjoyed Georgian prosperity, of which the town hall and the nearby canal are testimony. The increasing veneration for Shakespeare is evident in the memorial erected by the actor-manager, David Garrick (1717–79), then the theatre of 1874–7 (which was destroyed by fire, and only restored in the 1980s as the Swan Theatre), the Shakespeare Memorial Theatre of 1928–32, and the very modernist Shakespeare Centre of 1963–4.

Strathclyde, British kingdom in south-west Scotland. It first appeared in the 5th century and retained a separate identity until incorporated into the kingdom of the SCOTS in the first half of the 11th century during the reign of MALCOLM II. Along with the kingdoms of the PICTS and the Scots, it was one of the three dominant powers in early medieval Scotland. As well as periods of weakness, it enjoyed periods of domination over the other two, notably during the 7th century and during the reign of OWEN MAP BILI.

The last independent king of Strathclyde was Eochaid (died *c.*889), after whom the kingdom was ruled by descendants of KENNETH MAC ALPIN (*see also* DUMBARTON ROCK; KINGSHIP). These kings achieved a notable extension of territory in the 10th century, advancing as far south as Penrith, Cumbria, before being repulsed by the English king ATHELSTAN (*see* BRUNANBURH; CONSTANTINE II).

Strict Settlement, COMMON LAW arrangements of fiendish complexity devised by mid-17th century lawyers in order to keep landed estates intact, against the natural wish of many young heirs to sell their lands and enjoy the proceeds. The settlor set up trustees for the land, giving himself and his heirs merely a life estate in it, with no right to sell it; remainders (a legal term for a specified succession of heirs) were made to the children of the life tenant in order of seniority. The settlement would be reconstructed in every generation. By the 19th century such settlements were increasingly felt to be undesirable, since they restricted the land market, and legislation provided ways of introducing flexibility. The end of strict settlements was given added momentum in the 20th century by the increasingly high level of death duties aimed precisely at the destruction of hereditary landed wealth. *See also* LANDOWNERSHIP.

Strikes These occur when workers withhold their labour as a way of putting pressure upon employers to improve conditions of work or remuneration. They can also be used to put pressure on the state where the state is the employer or where a legislative solution to labour problems is sought. Strikes are usually used only when discussion or negotiation fails because, even if trade union finances are available and used, strikers usually have to face serious loss of income during a dispute with no guarantee of a successful outcome. The history of strikes is thus a history of the development of TRADE UNIONS, trade union finance, policy and machinery for collective bargaining: the evolution of alternative methods for, and approaches to, the resolution of disagreements over pay or conditions of work. It is also a history of changing attitudes on the part of employers and the state to the role of strikes as an industrial and political tool of the labour movement.

Before the INDUSTRIAL REVOLUTION and the centralization and mechanization of work in many sectors of the ECONOMY, strikes were relatively rare. Trade unions as institutions for local and, later, national collective bargaining and negotiation were not yet common but neither was the separation of work from the home or employers from the employed. Most people worked in small workshops or in their own homes, and either worked alongside their immediate employer or were so geographically separated from their fellow workers that strikes were difficult to organize. Rapid POPULATION growth from the later 18th century and the absence of trade unions meant that employers could find new workers relatively easily if a strike was threatened, and employers in the textile districts made agreements with one another not to employ troublesome workers. The growth of larger firms and of larger workforces under one roof, often experiencing similar conditions of work and pay, encouraged trade union organization and made use of the strike more attractive to workers and very unattractive to employers who now ran the risk of expensive fixed capital lying idle. Strikes in the first half of the 19th century were mainly localized and short-lived, although the social unrest of the period made the authorities deeply suspicious of strike actions, linked, as they sometimes were, to attacks on property and machine-wrecking (*see* LUDDITES; SWING RIOTS) and to wider political activities. This was particularly the case during the NAPOLEONIC WAR period when insurrection on the French model was feared. Strikes were outlawed by the COMBINATION ACTS and agents provocateurs were employed by the government to infiltrate organized labour groups. Again during the CHARTIST agitation strikes occurred, notably the PLUG RIOTS when boilers were sabotaged across northern industrial districts, property was attacked and large sections of the textile industry were brought to a standstill.

The third quarter of the 19th century used to be seen as a peaceable, relatively strike-free period associated with the rise of nationally organized NEW MODEL UNIONS of skilled workers who were concerned to create a respectable face to win full legal recognition and thus viewed strikes as a last resort. More recently, historians viewing the whole of the labour movement argue that there were more continuities than discontinuities in trade union action and policy and in the nature of industrial relations, including violence and strikes, between the early and late 19th centuries. The last two decades of the 19th century, which saw increasing unionization of unskilled groups, were marked by many large and significant strikes in New Unions, as were the years leading up to WORLD WAR I which saw strikes of miners, dockers, seamen and railway workers, the formation of the TRIPLE ALLIANCE of miners, dockers and railwaymen, and the growth of syndicalism. The collapse of the short-lived post-war boom, the onset of mass UNEMPLOYMENT and the deflationary policies of the government pursuing a return to pre-war parity under the GOLD STANDARD ushered in renewed industrial conflict which was met with concerted employer and state reaction culminating in the defeat of the GENERAL STRIKE of 1926.

New and generally successful waves of strike activity occurred from the 1950s when high and rising employment gave labour increased power in extracting concessions from employers. In the late 1960s and 1970s widespread strikes in the public as well as the private sector destroyed the credibility of the WILSON and HEATH governments and undermined the CALLAGHAN administration. Powerful trade unions and strikes were increasingly seen as responsible for low productivity, successful foreign competition, especially in manufactured goods, and rising unemployment, a view encouraged by the THATCHER government, enabling it to take a severe anti-union stance in legislation and a repressive and violent position in combating strike action – as in the defeat of the miners' strike of 1984. In the 1980s government policy regarding strikes was inflamed by the notion that they were motivated by political as well as economic considerations, and the state reacted accordingly, with widespread use of the POLICE and the ARMY and including the use of covert operations to discredit the integrity of union leaders such as Arthur Scargill of the NUM during the year-long miner's strike (March 1984–5), though overall, strike activity declined by over half between 1979–80 and 1989–90. *See also chronology under* TRADE UNIONS.

Strongbow, *see* CLARE, RICHARD DE

Stuart, Charles Edward ('Charles III', 'Bonnie Prince Charlie', 'Young Pretender') (1720–88), royal pretender. Eldest son of the 'Old Pretender' (James Edward STUART), he was born in exile in Rome. In 1744–5, Louis XV of France, then at war with the British, encouraged his attempt to retake the British throne for the Stuarts. Landing in the Hebrides in July 1745, he reached Edinburgh in Sept. He defeated government forces at Prestonpans, and advanced southwards, but was turned back at Derby in Dec., and was defeated at CULLODEN on 16 April 1746. Thereafter he spent five months as a fugitive in the Highlands before escaping to France with the help of Flora Macdonald.

The treaty of AIX-LA-CHAPELLE provided that he should be removed from France to Avignon (then a papal state). In 1750, he made a secret visit to London and converted to ANGLICANISM; however, plans for another rising in 1752–3 came to nothing. When his father died in 1766, Pope Clement XIII, keen to improve relations with Britain, withheld recognition from Charles. He married Princess Louise of Stolberg in 1772, but produced no heirs; his brother Henry, Cardinal Duke of York, who survived him, made no formal claim to the throne.

Charles's youth, early success and ultimate failure in 1745 gave him an aura of romance that stirred contemporary imaginations, though to little or no serious political effect. In later life, jaded and drunken, he failed to impress.

Stuart Family Name Conventions about the spelling of this important surname are not consistent. In general, representatives of the family, including the Scottish royal family, are styled 'Stewart' before JAMES VI became James I of England in 1603 (apart from the French Stuarts). Thereafter, and especially in an English context, the royal family's name is spelled 'Stuart'; other branches make their own decisions.

Stuart, James Edward ('James VIII and III', 'Old Pretender') (1688–1766), royal pretender. The only surviving son of JAMES II, his birth provided the king with a presumptively

CATHOLIC heir, and helped to spark the GLORIOUS REVOLUTION. Some found his birth too convenient to the king to be plausible, and suggested that he had not, in fact, been born to the queen, but had been smuggled in in a WARMING PAN.

He grew up in the JACOBITE court at St Germain in France. He was excluded from the succession by the Act of SETTLEMENT but, on James II's death in 1701, was acknowledged king by Louis XIV. Although he fought in the French army in the War of the SPANISH SUCCESSION, he was exiled from France under the terms of the peace of UTRECHT. He landed in Scotland in 1715, in the context of a Jacobite rising organized by the 6th ERSKINE Earl of Mar, but government forces impelled his troops to retreat, and James fled to France.

His court moved from St Germain to Rome, then in 1719 to Madrid, where another rising was planned with Spanish help. Bad weather drove back the bulk of the force; the remainder surrendered after a brief encounter at Galashiels. When correspondence with Bishop ATTERBURY relating to plans for further risings was discovered by the British government, James dismissed Mar on suspicion of treachery. Hopes for a restoration increasingly focused on James's son Charles STUART, whose departure for Scotland in 1745 was kept from James until after the event. He died in Rome.

Stuart, John (3rd Earl of Bute) (1713–92), courtier, politician and Prime Minister (1762–3). Elected a Scottish representative peer in 1737, he became acquainted with FREDERICK, Prince of Wales after moving to London in 1745, and was made gentleman of the bedchamber to him in 1750. After Frederick's death, he served as tutor and companion to the young Prince George (later GEORGE III); his friendship with the princess dowager attracted scandalous gossip. On George's accession in 1760, Bute was made groom of the stole – a court office which entailed the closest attendance on the monarch – and six months later was brought into the ministry as northern secretary of state.

When both PITT THE ELDER and Newcastle (*see* PELHAM-HOLLES, THOMAS) resigned in 1762, he was made first lord of the Treasury. His ministry concluded the widely unpopular peace of PARIS in 1763; a new cider EXCISE also attracted criticism. Bute was attacked by politicians and pamphleteers (*see NORTH BRITON*) and lampooned by demonstrating crowds as a royal favourite; it was suggested that he was encouraging the king to extend monarchical power.

Bute resigned in 1763 but continued to advise the king against his successor GRENVILLE's wishes; only in 1765 did George promise not to consult him. Although Bute opposed the repeal of the STAMP ACT 1766, he had by then largely withdrawn from political life, though the OLD CORPS WHIGS continued to attack him and to suggest that he was a power behind the scene.

Stycas, the name given by numismatists to the type of *SCEATTAS* that continued to be minted by the NORTHUMBRIAN kings until the kingdom's destruction in 867. Some of the later examples contain no silver at all. *See also* COINAGE.

Submission of the Clergy, an agreement extracted by HENRY VIII from the CONVOCATION of Canterbury on 15 May 1532, which surrendered to the CROWN the English Church's freedom to legislate. It triggered Thomas MORE's resignation as lord chancellor.

Subscribers, *see* SALTERS' HALL CONTROVERSY

Subscription Charities, charities financed not by individual gift or bequest, but by the amassing of large numbers of contributions, sometimes regularized in the form of regular annual subscriptions. They were characteristically organized by a group of enthusiasts, formalized as a committee or board of governors, who had first to arouse the interest of a broader public through publicity, then to sustain their interest and trust, usually through a combination of regular reporting and constitutional devices. Subscription charities first became a popular form of charitable organization in the 18th century: for example, the voluntary hospitals which proliferated from the 1730s were commonly financed by a mixture of endowed moneys and subscriptions.

Subscription Controversy, *see* FEATHERS' TAVERN PETITION

Subsidy, a financial grant to the crown. The term was used especially for the customs levy on wool (*see* WOOL SUBSIDY), and for the tax introduced in 1513 which supplemented the FIFTEENTHS AND TENTHS and was distinguished from them by being a tax on personal property (land and goods).

Succession, English, in 1066 To become king, a man usually had to have a blood relationship with previous rulers and to have been acknowledged by the chief nobles and designated by his predecessor. Many of the claimants to the English throne in 1066 had one or more of these factors in their favour.

The dispute over who would succeed on the death of EDWARD THE CONFESSOR, finally resolved by the battle of HASTINGS, had its origins in the Danish conquest of England in the early 11th century by SVEIN FORKBEARD and CNUT. It was exacerbated by the childlessness of a number of kings – notably Edward – and notions of succession that were open to exploitation.

The gratitude felt by Edward for the generous treatment shown him during his long exile in Normandy (*see* RICHARD II; ROBERT I) caused him to promise the succession to Duke William of Normandy (the future WILLIAM I THE CONQUEROR) in 1051; he then had Earl HAROLD of WESSEX repeat the promise, probably in 1064. However, fears of another invasion from Scandinavia appear to have caused Edward to make another vague promise to SVEIN ESTRITHSSON of Denmark. Then the wish of the English nobles to be ruled by someone of English stock led to the recall of Edward's nephew EDWARD THE EXILE from Hungary in 1057, presumably as a potential successor (he died soon after). HARALD HARDRAADA of Norway also claimed the kingdom on the supposed basis of a promise by CNUT's son HARTHACNUT. By blood, the nearest heir was the young EDGAR THE ÆTHELING, son of Edward the Exile, but he was thrust to one side as the issue was settled by force.

On his death-bed, Edward bowed to immediate pressures and chose Harold of Wessex to succeed him. *See also* NORMAN CONQUEST.

Succession, Law of, *see* SETTLEMENT, ACT OF, 1701

Sudan, Africa's largest country, and a meeting-point for 'Black' Africa and the Muslim world. The Islamic sultanates had acquired power in central Sudan in 1504, extinguishing the last of the Christian kingdoms; in 1820–2 the conquest of Sudan from EGYPT began. Egyptian rule was guaranteed in 1840–1 under the Convention and Treaty of London, and Egypt introduced ANTI-SLAVERY measures between 1863 and 1879, but the forces for Islamic reform were swelling. Meanwhile, Britain and other European powers had achieved considerable sway over Egypt's (and hence Sudan's) affairs. The reconquest of the Sudan under the MAHDI (Muhammad Ahmad al-Mahdi) began in 1881, culminating in the capture of Khartoum in 1885 and the controversial General Charles GORDON's death. The Mahdist forces' moves towards Egypt were rebuffed in 1889, and in 1898 the Anglo-Egyptian recapture of Sudan was achieved, culminating at OMDURMAN. British and French forces almost fought at Fashoda in 1899 in their imperialist rivalry for control of the Upper Nile, and thereafter a condominium rule of Sudan between Britain and Egypt was established. Anti-colonial revolts in 1900–12, and full-scale nationalist outbreaks in 1924 during which the British governor-general was assassinated, showed the depth of anti-imperialist feeling. In the 1930s, policies of separating the Islamic north and more Christianized south of Sudan were put in train which, though ultimately rejected by the native political leaders, showed the way towards later conflict. Although during WORLD WAR II Britain rejected the growing independence movement and rebuffed the emerging political parties, the 1952 Self-Government Statute placed Sudan on the road to self-rule, which was finally achieved in 1956.

Sudbury, Simon (?–1381), Archbishop of Canterbury (1375–81). Having studied at Paris, he had entered the papal administration before becoming a capable diocesan. Bishop of London from 1361, 14 years later he was raised to Canterbury, where he paid for YEVELE's rebuilding of the nave.

He had the misfortune to have been recently appointed CHANCELLOR of England at the time of the PEASANTS' REVOLT and was consequently blamed for government mismanagement and unjust taxation. Although he resigned the GREAT SEAL on 12 June 1381, two days later the rebels dragged him from the Tower and beheaded him. His mummified head is displayed in the vestry of St Gregory's church, Sudbury (Suff.).

Suetonius Paulinus, Gaius (*fl.* AD 60s), Roman governor. He was trying to extend the ROMAN CONQUEST in north Wales when BOUDICCA's revolt broke out in 61; he returned to defeat her army at an unknown site in the Midlands. His subsequent repressive policies led to clashes with other Roman officials who favoured more conciliatory measures, and later in the same year, he was recalled to Rome where he subsequently prospered.

Suez Canal, originated as a Franco-Turkish project in 1859 and opened to shipping ten years later. The construction of the canal, with contemporary advances in the efficiency of steam propulsion, signalled the triumph of the latter over sail in the higher-value long-range trades to Asia and Australasia. The canal shortened voyages to INDIA, for example, from about three months to some three weeks but only for STEAMSHIPS; sailing ships could not use the canal because of unfavourable conditions in the Red Sea. In 1875 DISRAELI, in a dramatic stroke of imperial policy, purchased from the spendthrift Khedive (viceroy) Ismail about half the shares in the Suez Canal Company. By this purchase Britain secured a control of the road to India and an active interest in EGYPT. An anti-European nationalist rising led to British military intervention in 1882, which, unlike the SUEZ CRISIS of 1956, was executed without foreign interference. Britain thereby secured a controlling hand in Egypt. Evelyn Baring (1841–1917) 1st Earl of Cromer (1901) was made consul-general and 'advised' the khedive from 1884–1907.

Suez Crisis, major crisis in British post-war diplomacy in the Middle East which ultimately destroyed the EDEN premiership. Following the withdrawal of American and British funding the Aswan High Dam, triggered by an Egyptian arms deal with the Soviet Union, EGYPT's leader Colonel Nasser (1918–70) retaliated by nationalizing the SUEZ CANAL on 26 July 1956. Protracted negotiations for a diplomatic settlement got nowhere and Britain, France, and Israel agreed secretly for Israel to attack Egypt after which Britain and France would occupy the canal zone on the pretext of separating the combatants in order to keep the canal open. Israel duly attacked Egypt on 29 Oct., a move followed by full-scale intervention by over 8,000 British and French troops on 5–6 Nov. The attack provoked intense political controversy in Britain and widespread opposition amongst the wider international community, including the United States. Increasingly isolated, Britain and France halted the invasion on 6 Nov. Faced with a massive international run on STERLING and pressure from the United States, they were forced to accept a UNITED NATIONS peacekeeping contingent and to agree to an unconditional withdrawal. Eden's humiliation destroyed his reputation and contributed to his declining health, leading to his resignation as prime minister in Jan. 1957. The Suez débâcle emphasized American dominance in the Anglo-American SPECIAL RELATIONSHIP, and demonstrated at home and abroad that the era of Britain's great power status was at an end.

Suffragan Bishops, assistants to a diocesan bishop. Active in England from the 13th century, they usually held an episcopal title from former Christian cities occupied by Islam ('*in partibus infidelium*'), or an almost equally fictional Irish diocesan dignity. An Act of Parliament of 1534 substituted titles from 26 named English towns, but the last such suffragan died in 1608. When ANGLICAN diocesan bishops were made to work harder by the Victorians, suffragan titles were revived (1870), and more have been created to the present day.

Suffrage Campaign, Women's, *see* WOMEN'S SUFFRAGE CAMPAIGN

Suffragettes, appellation first hurled as an insult by the *Daily Mail* which came to be used for the militant, activist suffragists of the WOMEN'S SOCIAL AND POLITICAL UNION who favoured direct action in the campaign to get the vote for women, to distinguish them from the suffragists who favoured working through constitutional channels for the same end. *See also* WOMEN'S SUFFRAGE CAMPAIGN.

Suffragists, Radical, a concept formulated by Jill Liddington and Jill Norris in the 1970s to emphasize the contribution of the female cotton workers in Lancs. who objected to the violence of the WOMEN'S SOCIAL AND

POLITICAL UNION and the middle-class domination of the NATIONAL UNION OF WOMEN'S SUFFRAGE SOCIETIES. The radical suffragists are presented by Liddington and Norris as a splinter group from the NUWSS with strong TRADE UNION connections, allied to the LABOUR PARTY, and concerned with winning votes for women as the prelude to securing equal pay and full sexual equality.

Sugar, staple PLANTATION crop which was one of the economic underpinnings of the BRITISH EMPIRE. Before the importation of cane-derived sugar from the NEW WORLD in the 16th century and after, sugars had been derived either from honey or from sweet roots; sweetness was an expensively acquired taste. Large-scale importation of sugar began in the mid-17th century; the opportunity afforded to British merchants by the DUTCH WARS opened the Brazilian sugar trade to them, and from the early 1650s BARBADOS and then other Caribbean islands switched to intensive sugar cultivation. JAMAICA and TRINIDAD, the largest British possessions in the WEST INDIES, dominated the trade, and rapidly expanded production on large plantations with the use of SLAVES; BRISTOL and LIVERPOOL were the most important British sugar ports. Sugar-based wealth was an important element in 18th-century British economy and society: imports of sugar helped to underpin the expansion of British manufactured exports and was a vital element in re-exports as well as creating wealth amongst merchants and planters and new dietary and social habits through much of society. Sugar production subsequently spread to other colonies, notably QUEENSLAND. Competition from other sugar producers, exhaustion of the soil, and then the international collapse of sugar prices after WORLD WAR II, reinforced by the protectionism of the EEC (*see* EUROPEAN UNION), proved fatal to many Caribbean sugar economies by the 1960s.

Suicide The incidence of and attitudes to suicide have varied over the centuries. Research into its history is complicated by the fact that, under Christian influence and until modern times, suicide remained a crime – self-murder (*felo de se*) – involving ESCHEAT of property; as a result, kindly witnesses often concealed suicides. From *c.*1500 to *c.*1600, there was a decline in sympathy for suicides, and therefore more frequent court suicide verdicts – a change that is probably associated with the Protestant REFORMATION. Thereafter, attitudes softened, and by the late 18th century, aided by a certain vogue in the Romantic movement, suicide was being seen as a medical or emotional problem. Even so, until 1961 it was still legally considered a crime to attempt suicide.

Summary Jurisdiction (Married Women) Act 1895, *see* WOMEN, LEGAL STATUS OF

Sumptuary Laws, attempts to legislate against forms of personal expenditure, particularly on clothing, or to limit it to certain social groups; after 1363, repeated efforts were made in status-conscious medieval and Tudor societies. Tudor statutes for financing military expenditure by taxation that was estimated on the contents of female wardrobes were particularly ludicrous but busily enforced up to the 1560s. Thereafter enthusiasm faded.

Sunday School Movement Gloucester newspaper proprietor Robert Raikes (1735–1811) tackled the problem of disorderly and idle children on the Sabbath by gathering a group together and teaching them in a 'Sunday School' in church in 1780. Raikes' idea caught on, especially in industrial districts, where children worked through the week. ANGLICANS and DISSENTERS initially co-operated in setting them up, but from the 1790s they were increasingly founded on a sectarian basis. By 1795 there were an estimated 250,000 children learning the three 'Rs' and hearing the Bible read to them at Sunday School. By 1801 there were 2,290 such schools and by 1851 23,135. By then an estimated two-thirds of working-class children aged 5 to 15 were attending these institutions. While many ceased to teach writing in the 1790s, they probably did prevent a fall in LITERACY levels, offered some useful education, provided a social life for the children and enabled parents to develop one on their own.

Sunderland, 2nd Earl of, *see* SPENCER, ROBERT

Sunderland, 3rd Earl of, *see* SPENCER, CHARLES

Sunningdale Agreement, signed between the British and Irish governments over

Northern Ireland in 1973 for the setting-up of a power-sharing executive. The talks also agreed to set up a Council of Ireland to deal with matters of common concern and agreed to preserve the status of Northern Ireland as part of the United Kingdom as long as a majority wished it to remain so. The power-sharing executive was formed in Jan. 1974 but was brought down within five months by a strike organized by the Protestant ULSTER WORKERS' COUNCIL. *See also* IRISH QUESTION.

Suppression of the Monasteries, *see* DISSOLUTION OF THE MONASTERIES

Supremacy, Act of, *see* ROYAL SUPREMACY

Surrey, 14th and 15th Earls of, *see* HOWARD, THOMAS

Suspending and Dispensing Powers The suspension of legislation makes it completely inoperative; a dispensation allows the commission of an act otherwise illegal. Both powers were traditionally reckoned part of the royal PREROGATIVE, and were employed in a variety of contexts. There were 16th- and early 17th-century instances of their use in a religious context: ELIZABETH I and JAMES I both gave some Catholic RECUSANTS dispensation from penal laws. When CHARLES II and JAMES II attempted to employ them, questions were raised about their legality. Protests from the COMMONS and LORDS led Charles to withdraw the 1672 DECLARATION OF INDULGENCE, suspending laws penalizing DISSENT and Catholic recusancy. James dismissed half the judges to ensure that the bench would support the dispensing power in the test case *GODDEN v. HALES*, and issued his own Declaration of Indulgence in 1687 and 1688. The DECLARATION OF RIGHTS 1689 stated that the suspending power 'as it hath been exercised of late' was illegal; the BILL OF RIGHTS ruled that all dispensations were void unless permitted by Act of PARLIAMENT.

Sussex The kingdom of the South Saxons originated in the 5th century and is associated with King ÆLLE. It roughly comprised the modern county of Sussex, and at times may well have been divided among several kings. It was apparently still largely PAGAN in the late 7th century. The line of Sussex kings was suppressed in the time of OFFA of MERCIA.

Sutton Hoo The unique treasures of the great ship-burial discovered in 1939 at Sutton Hoo near Woodbridge, Suff. – and now in the British Museum – have made a massive contribution to our knowledge of 'Dark Age' society. They show not only the great wealth of a 7th-century king or nobleman, but also the extensive range of contacts that such an individual would have possessed – not only with Scandinavia, France and the Celtic north, but also with Byzantium and the Mediterranean. The presence of Christian objects in a burial whose ethos is utterly pagan demonstrates the manner in which Christianity and Anglo-Saxon heathenism intermingled during this fluid period (*see* CONVERSION; PAGANISM). Exactly who was buried in the tomb remains uncertain and controversial; the favoured candidate is normally an East Anglian king, with REDWALD the most convincing possibility.

Svein Estrithsson, King of Denmark (1047–76). The son of a sister of King CNUT, he represented another strand of the Scandinavian interest in the English SUCCESSION in 1066; Scandinavian sources claim that he was promised the English throne by EDWARD THE CONFESSOR. His eventual invasion of England in 1069–70 was defeated rather easily by WILLIAM I THE CONQUEROR.

Svein Forkbeard, King of Denmark (988–1014). He displaced his father Harold Bluetooth as king in 988, and from 994 (at the latest), he devoted a great amount of time to attacking and exploiting ETHELRED II THE UNREADY's England. Archaeological exploration of great Scandinavian camps such as Trelleborg has shown that the Danish kingdom possessed a formidable military organization. In 1013, Svein launched a campaign to conquer England, which had largely succeeded at the time of his sudden death. His work was continued by his son CNUT.

Swaziland, a small independent state and former British colony, which is surrounded by SOUTH AFRICA. The native lands were gradually lost to encroachment by South Africa between the 1830s and 1880s, until Swaziland was placed under the civil administration of the Transvaal in 1895. Following the BOER WAR, Britain took over administration in 1903, making it a High Commission of

South Africa in 1906. Only minimal control was ever exercised, and no form of government institution was put in place until the 1950s. The independence movement which grew up in 1960 was rewarded in 1968; Swaziland has essentially remained a tourist centre for South Africa, and had an uneasy relationship with it during the apartheid years.

Sweated Trades The low-wage, unregulated and dispersed sectors of the later 19th-century ECONOMY, they employed mostly women working long hours under poor conditions in their own homes or in small workshops. Sweating proliferated with the growth of subcontracting, especially in the garment trades, metal goods manufactures, envelope and box manufacture. The centrifugal nature of sweating was encouraged by family POVERTY, a ready supply of cheap female labour, fluctuations in the TRADE CYCLE, urban growth (and high inner-city rents for factory buildings), and by poorly policed FACTORIES AND WORKSHOPS ACTS, which imposed additional costs on employers and encouraged every effort to utilize the lower-cost unregulated sector. Sweating was also attractive to employers as a hedge against TRADE UNIONS. Outwork, homeworking and sweating remain features of the 20th-century economy, but their worst excesses have been ameliorated by tighter government controls, by state welfare provisions for destitute women, and by a new international division of labour which has shifted some of this sort of employment to the Third World, where wages are lower and where there are fewer government controls.

Swift, Jonathan (1667–1745), writer. Son of a Dublin lawyer, he first served as secretary to the diplomat Sir William Temple. In 1695, he was ordained, and shortly acquired three Irish livings, which gave him financial independence. His prose satire *The Tale of a Tub* (1704) got him noticed, and he became a leading WHIG pamphleteer. His commitment to the Established Church, which led him to write against the repeal of the TEST ACT, ended this relationship. He joined the SCRIBLEURS CLUB and edited the TORY *Examiner*, in which he attacked the Whig ministers' war policies. Made dean of St Patrick's Cathedral, Dublin, in 1713, he left England on the death of Queen ANNE and the fall of the Tory ministry. His *Drapier's Letters* (1724) fuelled the campaign against WOOD'S HALFPENCE, and the satirical *Gulliver's Travels* (1726) was an instant success. Swift represents a generation of writers whose careers were shaped by the advent of vigorous party conflict.

Swing Riots, 1830. Provoked by the harvest failure of 1829 and the widespread introduction of threshing-machines, they were the product of overpopulation and underemployment generated by economic change. Letters signed by one 'Captain Swing' warned farmers of the wrath to come, which duly began in Kent in June 1830 and by Nov. had spread into Sussex, Hants., Dorset, Wilts., Berks. and north into the Midlands and East Anglia. Hayricks and barns were burnt, machines destroyed and unpopular POOR LAW officials attacked. The riots were spontaneous and without central direction. The savage official response resulted in 19 executions, 505 TRANSPORTATIONS, 644 imprisonments, seven fines and one whipping, but in southern England at least the introduction of the labour-saving threshing-machine was considerably delayed.

Swithun, St (?–862), Bishop of Winchester (852–62). Almost nothing is known about Swithun's life. There may have been a local cult of sanctity soon after his death, but his reputation as a saint was forcefully propagated only in the time of his successor St Ethelwold. The notion that rain on St Swithun's Day (15 July) will be followed by another 40 days of precipitation seems to have been invented in the 16th century.

Sykes-Picot Agreement, 16 May 1916, secret agreement during WORLD WAR I signed by representatives of the British and French governments, over the fate of the Ottoman Empire, an ally of Germany, in the event of her defeat. It defined respective spheres of influence for Britain and France both in the non-Turkish parts of the Turkish Empire and in parts of mainland Turkey, which would have left the Turks reduced to a rump state in northern and central Anatolia. Although the agreement was not fully implemented, its harsh provisions were reflected in the allocation of MANDATES to France and Britain in non-Turkish territory in the Middle East.

Syndicalism, from the French *syndicat* ('TRADE UNION'), a tendency within socialist thought supporting the principle of the direct ownership and control of INDUSTRY by the workers themselves. It was first developed in France and the United States and came to Britain in 1910. Its aims included the consolidation of union strength in large federations and great industrial unions, the progressive weakening of capitalist employers by industrial aggression, and their eventual dispossession. Syndicalists were critical of the sectionalism and fragmentation encouraged by the existing trade union structure, considered state socialism no better than capitalism, and parliamentary methods inferior to direct action on the factory floor. In Britain these ideas found their chief exponent in Tom Mann and his monthly journal the *Industrial Syndicalist*. Syndicalism affected the temper of the pre-war labour unrest in the mining and transport industries, where it was also influential in the genesis of the National Union of Railwaymen, the Transport Workers' Federation and the TRIPLE ALLIANCE. Syndicalist ideas exerted a considerable influence upon the SHOP STEWARDS' MOVEMENT, but waned rapidly after World War I.

Synod of Whitby, *see* WHITBY, SYNOD OF

Syon Abbey, Middx., founded by HENRY V in 1415 at Twickenham and moved to Syon in 1431. It was a self-conscious standard-bearer of renewed MONASTICISM, with an abbey for nuns and an associated community of monks following the Bridgettine rule of the 14th-century St Bridget of Sweden. It remained much patronized by the royal family, the GENTRY and aristocracy, and the mercantile élite of London; it was one of the chief focuses of devotional writing and publishing in the early 16th century. One of its monks, Richard Reynolds, was executed in 1535 for refusing the oath of ROYAL SUPREMACY; many nuns went into exile at the DISSOLUTION, returning when MARY I refounded the house in 1557. ELIZABETH I's accession forced them abroad once more, but the community has remained together ever since, and has now returned to South Brent, Devon.

T

Tacking, parliamentary practice of attaching other measures to money Bills in an attempt to ensure their passage through the LORDS – the COMMONS claimed that the Lords had no right to amend such Bills. Although the Lords did not concede this, by the early 18th century it was clear that, if they did amend such a Bill, they could expect vigorous protests on constitutional grounds. This circumstance, combined with the tension between a WHIG-dominated Lords and a TORY-dominated Commons, made the first few years of the 18th century the golden age of tacking.

The term 'tacker' was more specifically applied to those who advocated tacking a clause against OCCASIONAL CONFORMITY to a Bill of supply in 1704.

Tacksman or Woman, Scottish term, in use from at least the 16th century, for someone holding a lease or 'tack' of land, tithes, customs, or anything else farmed or leased. In the Scottish Highlands, the term was especially used of those who leased land from large proprietors for subletting in small farms. Great proprietors provided for their supporters in this manner. Tacksmen were in effect clan GENTRY, playing an important role in clan administration.

Taexali, one of the tribes that inhabited Scotland in the 1st century AD. Their settlements were located in the valley of the River Dee to the west of Aberdeen. By the 3rd and 4th centuries, they had apparently been absorbed into the larger Celtic confederation of tribes known as the PICTS.

Taff Vale Decision, 1901. The culmination of a series of legal decisions that adversely affected the status of TRADE UNIONS, it determined that trade unions could be sued for damages caused by the action of their officers. The Taff Vale Railway company sued the Amalgamated Society of Railway Servants for losses during a STRIKE and was awarded £23,000. It had hitherto been supposed that, although trade unions had certain legal rights, they were not legal corporations and could not be sued for the tortious acts of their members. The court's contrary ruling exposed trade unions to crippling actions for damages whenever they were involved in a trade dispute. Trade unions, in the light of this decision, began to reconsider their alliance with a LIBERAL PARTY which seemed evasive in its approach to the unions' campaign to safeguard their funds and functions. The Taff Vale decision was thus significant in converting the unions to independent LABOUR representation.

Tail, *see* ENTAIL

Tait, Archibald (1811–82), Anglican prelate and Archbishop of Canterbury (1869–82). A vigorous opponent of the OXFORD MOVEMENT, and Thomas Arnold's successor as headmaster at Rugby, he became bishop of London in 1856. Firm but tactful in relation to RITUALISM and the controversies raised by biblical criticism, he was transferred to Canterbury in 1869, where he did much to reduce the unrest caused by Irish Disestablishment and improve Church organization in the colonies.

Talbot, Charles (15th [12th Talbot] Earl and 1st Duke of Shrewsbury) (1660–1718), politician. He was educated a Catholic, but in 1679 converted to ANGLICANISM. Rank and talent favoured his political career, but indifferent health and indecisiveness limited his accomplishments. One of the 'immortal seven' who signed the letter of invitation to William of Orange (the future WILLIAM III), he was briefly in office from 1689–90, and again from 1694, when he became secretary of state in the JUNTO ministry and was made a duke. He resigned in 1700, pleading ill health, and spent several years abroad, initially in Rome. Returning to England, he was made lord chamberlain and became involved in peace negotiations with France (1711–12); in 1713, he was made lord lieutenant of Ireland, then lord treasurer shortly before ANNE's death. He helped make arrangements for the beginning of GEORGE I's reign. He resigned as lord chamberlain in 1715.

Talbot, Richard (3rd [1st Talbot] Earl of Tyrconnell) (1630–91), soldier and politician. Younger son of an Irish baronet, he fought in Ireland during the CIVIL WARS, fled to the Continent, where he met the Duke of York (the future JAMES II), went to England as a ROYALIST agent, was imprisoned and escaped. Made a gentleman of the bedchamber to the duke at the RESTORATION, he was imprisoned for supposed involvement in the POPISH PLOT in 1678. On James's accession, he was made an earl and given command of the army in Ireland, which he sought to Catholicize. Made lord deputy in 1687, he introduced dramatic changes across a broader front: Catholics were admitted to office in courts of law and CORPORATIONS; money from vacant Anglican BENEFICES was channelled into the Catholic Church. The proceedings of the JACOBITE PARLIAMENT of 1689 revealed divisions between Tyrconnell's followers and James's. His role in the JACOBITE defeat at the battle of the BOYNE was controversial, since he appeared indecisive and lethargic. He returned to Ireland in 1691 as lord lieutenant and commander-in-chief, and died suddenly a month after the Jacobite defeat at AUGHRIM.

Tallies, uniquely notched lengths of wood, split to provide two identical pieces, which were used as receipts in the EXCHEQUER and other departments of state from the Middle Ages through to the late 18th century. Tallies on forthcoming tax revenues were traded at discounts, especially in the late 17th century, as other stocks were, and were important in the development of government stock markets. Paper transactions superseded the wooden ones; the decision to burn the accumulated wooden tallies of the centuries accidentally resulted in the fire in 1834 which destroyed the old Palace of WESTMINSTER.

Tamworth, Staffs., the most important centre in the kingdom of MERCIA. Located on the Middle Trent, the people later identified as the Mercians settled there, and it is where kings such as OFFA are known to have celebrated many of the great religious festivals. ARCHAEOLOGY has revealed early evidence of fortification. The town's importance was also reflected by the proximity of the Mercian bishopric at LICHFIELD.

Tamworth Manifesto, 1834, Sir Robert PEEL's election address, often described as the charter of the CONSERVATIVE PARTY. It recognized the new conditions created by the INDUSTRIAL REVOLUTION and the REFORM ACT of 1832 and asserted principles of reform consistent with established rights.

Tanganyika, former British protectorate and colony in east Africa, which united with ZANZIBAR to form Tanzania after independence. When Germany was defeated in WORLD WAR I, Britain assumed the MANDATE over most of German East Africa as Tanganyika, with control of the territories of Rwanda and Urundi (later Burundi) assumed by Belgium. The independence movements rose, especially after 1945, when improvements in education, communications and government institutions were put in place. Tanganyika was given self-government in May 1961, and independence that Dec. In April 1964 the new nation, under Julius Nyerere who had led it to independence, was united with Zanzibar.

Tangier, acquired by CHARLES II in 1662 as part of the dowry of his queen, Catherine of Braganza. Valued as a military base in the Mediterranean which it was hoped might advantage English trade, much effort was expended in improving the harbour. But it was never satisfactory, being constantly threatened by the Moors, and it was abandoned in 1684.

Tanist, the term for someone who is second in rank to a king or chief, commonly used of an heir apparent, usually the eldest or worthiest kinsman. The word derives from the Irish *tanaiste,* meaning 'second'. 'Tanistry' usually refers to a system of succession that recognizes the claims of the tanist; it is widely believed to have been the custom in early medieval Ireland and Scotland.

Tanks The idea of the tank has been traced back to sketches by Leonardo da Vinci, and it featured in writings by H. G. Wells before WORLD WAR I. Its exact inventor is disputed, but part of the credit for its development goes to Winston CHURCHILL. The first British tanks saw action in small numbers on 15 Sept. 1916 at Flers-Courcelette, part of the SOMME battle, joined soon afterwards by separately invented French tanks. By 1918 the British and French employed tanks in their hundreds, and they played an important part in breaking the trench deadlock (*see* AMIENS, BATTLE OF; CAMBRAI, BATTLE OF). The Germans also had a handful of very large tanks, and the first tank against tank action took place in April 1918. The development of mechanically reliable tanks capable of more than a few miles an hour in the 1920s made the tank the main weapon of land WARFARE in WORLD WAR II.

Tanzania, *see* TANGANYIKA

Tara, Co. Meath, the site from which the UÍ NÉILL kings of early medieval Ireland traditionally exercised their power. Tara is associated with numerous legendary and historical events in early Irish history, such as pagan inauguration rituals for kings and the conversion of a Uí Néill king by St PATRICK. The site is now represented by a splendid triple-ramparted hill-fort (*see* RING FORTS).

Tariff Reform League, 1903–6. Inspired by Joseph CHAMBERLAIN, it sought to transform the BRITISH EMPIRE into a unified trading bloc, enlarging the market for industrial goods and to generate cash for social reform and HOUSING programmes. The CONSERVATIVE Cabinet, whom Chamberlain hoped to convert, rejected his ideas and he resigned his position as colonial secretary to mobilize public support for his policy. Ironically, the issues which divided the Tories united the LIBERALS, whose defence of FREE TRADE and cheap food helped them to their landslide victory in the general election of 1906. *See also* IMPERIAL PREFERENCE.

Tasmania Originally Van Diemen's Land, after its Dutch discoverer, this was the second colony in AUSTRALIA. Convicts and other settlers came in 1804; self-government was granted in 1825. The early years were marked by determined destruction of the Aboriginal population; prosperity from wheat-growing was followed by severe depression, saved after the 1880s by mining and forestry.

Taunton Commission, 1864–7, the third of the three great mid-Victorian reviews of the educational system, following the NEWCASTLE and the CLARENDON COMMISSIONS. Its recommendations in favour of rate-aided secondary schools to improve EDUCATION for the middle classes, though stillborn, were indicative of the deeply rooted caste system in English education.

Tea, beverage from the dried leaves of the plant *Camellia sinensis*. As the botanical name suggests, the drink originated from China; it was introduced to Europe by the Dutch in 1606, and was first brought to England in the 1650s and 1660s. Originally prized for medicinal properties, it rapidly became a fashionable drink, and as such was subject to duty from 1660 until the 1780s. Demand produced both a huge rise in imports and a significant CONTRABAND trade. Tea-planting was introduced to INDIA, where conditions were good, in 1834, when the Tea Committee was established by Lord William Bentinck, and seeds collected by J.C. Gordon in China were grown in special nurseries in Calcutta. The India tea trade, growing both the plants from China and cultivating the wild tea of Assam, was established by 1838. After 1860 tea-planting was extended to CEYLON. India and Sri Lanka now account for over 80 per cent of world tea exports. The British tea trade expanded enormously from the 1880s, when branding and brand loyalty (e.g. Twining and Lipton) were firmly established and tea became the national British drink.

Tea has had an importance out of all proportion to its relatively insignificant appearance: as a factor in diplomacy; as a stimulus to design and industrial production, with teacups, dishes and pots; as a major contribution to international trade and local economies; and as a form of social expression, afternoon tea being devised in the 19th century to fill the lengthening hours between lunch and dinner, with an appropriate ritual to accompany it.

Tealby Coinage, name given to the silver PENNIES issued under HENRY II's name between 1158 and 1180, and so called because thousands of the COINS were found in the Tealby hoard (Lincs.).

Technical Education Act 1889 It authorized certain local authorities to aid or supply higher EDUCATION at a cost limited to a rate of 1d in the £. It represented a belated and inadequate response to Britain's labour force requirements in a period of intensifying foreign competition. The failure to devote resources to technical education is sometimes identified by historians as an important element in Britain's slow but steady relative economic decline.

Teddy Boys The first of the distinctive post-WORLD WAR II youth movements, they took their name from the adoption of supposedly 'Edwardian' fashions, including fur and velvet collars, tight 'drainpipe' trousers, and heavily oiled hair. Teddy boys were associated with the popular rock-and-roll music of the 1950s and attracted some unfavourable publicity over teenage rebellion and violence at dance halls.

Teetotallers, name given to the originators of the first British TEMPERANCE SOCIETY in 1831 and since applied to anyone practising abstinence from alcoholic drink. It arose from the quaint assertion of a Preston working man, when the question of partial or total abstinence was discussed, that nothing but 'T-total' would do.

Tehran Conference, first meeting of the 'Big Three', CHURCHILL, US President Roosevelt and Soviet leader Stalin, during WORLD WAR II, from 28 Nov. to 1 Dec. 1943 at Tehran in Iran. They discussed arrangements for the opening of the SECOND FRONT in May 1944, and co-ordination with a renewed Soviet offensive against Germany. The main lines of the post-war territorial settlement in Europe were discussed, including the Polish frontiers. No agreement was reached on the future of Germany, although there was preliminary discussion of its possible dismemberment. The final arrangements were left until later conferences.

Teinds, *see* TITHES

Telecommunications The invention and spread of the telegraph and later of the telephone have been among the most significant examples of progress towards speeding communications. Signalling, by bonfires and later by semaphore or flags, had a long history. W. F. Cooke and Charles Wheatstone's telegraph patent in 1837, with electro-magnetic signals causing a needle to point to letters of the alphabet, is taken as the beginning of electric telegraphic communication. The Morse code of 1838 quickly passed into international use. Telegraph communication spread quickly on both sides of the Atlantic, and could cross the ocean after the laying of the first viable transatlantic submarine cable in 1866. The 1850s saw the proliferation of news by telegraph: Reuters was founded in 1859, and the racing news from Newmarket had first arrived five years before. In 1870 the telegraph system was taken into state ownership under the Post Office (*see* POSTAL SERVICES).

In 1876 Alexander Graham Bell patented the telephone in the USA. His was a one-way instrument; Edison's telephone of the following year was already more sophisticated. The growth of the telephone industry was considerably faster in the USA than in Britain, although the first telephone exchange was opened, in the City of LONDON, in 1879. The Post Office soon imposed controls over telephones, since it had control of the telegraph; by 1897 it owned and managed all trunk lines. By 1900 there were 210,000 telephones in Britain; in 1912 when the system was nationalized there were 700,000; and by the outbreak of war in 1939 there were 3.3 million subscribers. Special efforts were made to extend the network into the countryside. Meanwhile, the telegraph service went into sustained decline, driven out by the telephone and wireless communication. Guglielmo Marconi's first radio patent was taken out in 1896, and was to link ship to shore and eventually continent to continent across the Atlantic. The Marconi company, formed in 1900, dominated the business; in 1924 it announced directed short-wave radio transmission, the 'beam' which could cross the great inter-continental divides. (For radio broadcasting, *see* BBC.)

The telephone increased its hold inexorably in post-1945 Britain. By 1978 there were 8 million private subscribers. Subscriber trunk dialling, bypassing the traditional operator, was introduced in Bristol in 1958, in London in 1961, and was extended throughout the UK by the early 1970s. The advent of satellite communication came with the launch of Telstar, the first British telecommunications satellite, in 1957. The Post Office's control over telecommunications was removed with the separate formation of British Telecom in 1981, which was privatized in 1984, and the subsequent proliferation of commercial providers.

Television, *see* BBC; ITV

Temperance Societies first began in the United States in 1826 and crossed the Atlantic in 1831 when the British and Foreign Temperance Society was established. Apart from the campaign against excessive drinking, the temperance societies played a key role in the improvement of manners and morals and in the formation of a distinct working-class culture of respectability. The Temperance Acts of 1853 (in Scotland), 1869 and 1904 which controlled licensing laws helped diminish their support.

Temple, Frederick (1821–1902), Archbishop of Canterbury (1896–1902). Educated at Balliol College, Oxford, after his ordination as priest in 1847 he taught for a while at Balliol, becoming an advocate of educational reform. He was headmaster of Rugby from 1857–69, doing much to increase the school's reputation and becoming prominent in the arena of education. As bishop of Exeter (1869–85) he fostered Church schools and the work of the temperance movement. After he became bishop of London in 1885 he played an important role in the 1887 jubilee celebrations and in the Lincoln Judgement of 1892. He was in constant conflict with the HIGH CHURCH Party and his translation to Canterbury in 1897 (which coincided with the queen's diamond jubilee) was a political statement, echoed by the Lambeth Conference (1897) and the Lambeth Opinions (1899–1900).

Temple, Henry (3rd Viscount Palmerston) (1784–1865), Whig politician and Prime Minister (1855–8, 1859–65). An Irish peer who sat in the COMMONS for 58 years and held office for 48, as a Canningite TORY he served under PERCEVAL, Liverpool (*see* JENKINSON, ROBERT), CANNING, Goderich (*see* ROBINSON, FREDERICK) and Wellington (*see* WELLESLEY, ARTHUR) before transferring his party allegiance from the Tories, over their opposition to any PARLIAMENTARY REFORM, to GREY's government. As WHIG foreign secretary (1830–41) he strengthened British influence in Europe without dangerous involvements. He guaranteed the neutrality of the newly-formed state of Belgium by the Treaty of London (1839), supported liberalism abroad, including defending the Spanish and Portuguese queens against absolutist pretenders, supported Greek independence, upheld Turkey against Russian and then Egyptian expansionism, and prosecuted the OPIUM WAR against China.

Out of office during PEEL's premiership, Palmerston was back at the foreign office from 1846–51 when he again generally supported European independence movements whilst maintaining a policy of non-intervention, though his stance became increasingly high-handed and inconsistent and he was always ready to defend the rights of Englishmen by force (*see* DON PACIFICO INCIDENT). In 1851, at Queen VICTORIA's urging, RUSSELL dismissed him when he unreservedly, but on no authority, welcomed the *coup d'état* by which Louis Napoleon (Napoleon III) overthrew the constitution of the Second French Republic. The following year, however, Palmerston agreed to become home secretary in Aberdeen's (*see* GORDON, GEORGE) Whig-PEELITE coalition where, encouraged by his son-in-law, Anthony Ashley Cooper, 7th Earl of Shaftesbury, he was persuaded to introduce penal reform and legislation governing working and safety conditions, in FACTORIES. The Aberdeen ministry took Britain into the CRIMEAN WAR in 1854, though the prime minister was careful to keep Palmerston, who had more belligerent war aims than those of the government, away from direct intervention in the war.

The fall of Aberdeen's coalition in 1855 over the conduct of the Crimean War brought Palmerston the premiership. He concluded the war and suppressed the INDIAN MUTINY. He was defeated in the Commons in Feb. 1858 by a combination of CONSERVATIVES and RADICALS, but their disunity meant that Derby's (*see* STANLEY, EDWARD) precarious Conservative government was short-lived and fell in June 1859, and Palmerston once again resumed the premiership, heading a powerful CABINET that included Russell as foreign secretary and GLADSTONE as chancellor of the Exchequer. His second ministry, a mixture of Whigs, Peelites and RADICALS, is often credited with consolidating a modern

LIBERAL PARTY: it cut government expenditure, reduced taxes and duties at home, promoted FREE TRADE, and abroad recognized Italian unification and managed to maintain a position of neutrality during the American civil war. But it was not a reforming ministry: despite increasing pressure for parliamentary and EDUCATION reforms, Palmerston was adamant: 'There is really nothing to be done. We cannot go on adding to the Statute Book *ad infinitum*,' he said, rejecting calls for the extension of the FRANCHISE, for Irish land reforms, and the reform of the CIVIL SERVICE. He died in office aged 81.

A would-be Casanova in his private life – as a young man he earned the sobriquet 'Lord Cupid' – Palmerston was an instinctive, hugely experienced, pragmatic, pugnacious, energetic, improvising, exceptionally industrious and charismatic politician, who tapped a vein of British patriotism and JINGOISM that delighted the British public as it often appalled his colleagues, his queen and later historians. But though he usually acted with more caution than his rhetoric suggested, Palmerston's foreign policy, whilst frequently skillful, was informed by few abiding principles other than 'British interests', of which he took a short-term view. The reputation of his domestic policy, which moved away from the reforming tendencies of his youth to a resistance to change, has recently undergone some reassessment, acknowledging that he did develop an accommodation with mass politics and a style of platform oratory that Gladstone was later to perfect.

Ten Hours Movement, a popular movement in the 19th century to reduce working hours in INDUSTRY. It was led by a curious combination of working-class RADICALS, including Chartists (*see* CHARTISM), and paternalistic TORY employers and landowners, such as J. R. Stephens, Richard Oastler and John Fielden, and gained momentum during the 1830s. The parliamentary campaign was led by the evangelical 3rd Earl of Shaftesbury, provided with information by local committees in the textile areas of Lancs. and Yorks. Their first success, the FACTORY ACT of 1833, was limited to child employment, whereas the reformers sought a measure that would regulate the hours of both women and children on the assumption that mill-owners would find it unprofitable to run their machines for longer than they could keep the female workers to their task. It proved to be a shrewd calculation: political opposition was weakened; and the gains of the female operatives were shared by the male. The culmination of the movement came with the Ten Hours Act of 1847, but the triumph was short-lived. Poor drafting meant that employers could easily side-step the new laws, and further legislation was required to remedy the defects. There were further compromises, and the clear ten hours were only secured in 1874.

Tenant-in-Chief, a tenant holding his estate directly from the crown. In return for their land, tenants-in-chief were expected to give the king political service and, in time of war, military or financial aid. Heirs of tenants-in-chief had to pay a duty, known as 'RELIEF', in order to enter their inheritances; if they were under age, the king took them into his WARDSHIP and their estates into his custody, a practice that continued until the 17th century. *DOMESDAY BOOK* provides the earliest extant list of tenants-in-chief. *See also* FEUDALISM.

Tenth-Century Reform, a movement that radically changed the organization and ideals of the English Church in the second half of the 10th century. The beginnings lie in the reign of ATHELSTAN, but the dominant figures were saints DUNSTAN, Ethelwold and Oswald and King EDGAR.

All the reformers were men from aristocratic backgrounds who came under the influence of similar reforming movements on the Continent. Their aim was to set up monasteries that followed the rule of St Benedict (*see* BENEDICTINE MONASTICISM) and to improve the moral state of the Church through the advancement of monks and monasticism. Many new abbeys were founded, and the promotion of monks to bishoprics became common in England up to and beyond 1066. Royal authority was one of the chief agencies through which reform was effected, and the religious standing of the king was elevated to a high level. The greatest single document of the Reform is the *REGULARIS CONCORDIA*.

The reformers offended many vested interests because of their attacks on existing religious communities and their single-minded pursuit of reform allied to property and power. At the same time, they contributed to the advance of royal authority because the new abbeys received extensive lands and jurisdiction in their localities. The northernmost point reached by the Reform was BURTON-upon-Trent, a sign of the limitations of late Anglo-Saxon royal power. *See also* KINGSHIP; UNIFICATION.

Ten-Year Rule, ruling first adopted in 1919 that British defence policy should operate on the assumption that there would be no major war for the following ten years. It formed the basis for heavy cuts in defence expenditure during the 1920s and the naval restrictions of the WASHINGTON NAVAL AGREEMENT. Reaffirmed in 1926 and 1927 and on a rolling basis from 1928, it was abandoned in 1932 as a result of growing tension in the Far East and elsewhere.

Territorial Army Part of the reforms of Richard Haldane, secretary of state for war (1905–12), the 1907 Territorial and Reserve Forces Act amalgamated all voluntary military organizations such as the MILITIA into the Territorial Force. Intended for home defence only, Territorial Force units fought overseas in WORLD WARS I and II. Renamed Territorial Army in 1921, its size was greatly reduced in 1966.

Test Acts 1673, 1678 The Act of 1673 required all civil and military officeholders to take the OATHS of allegiance and supremacy, sign a declaration against TRANSUBSTANTIATION, and receive the sacrament after the forms of the Church of England. Passed in the context of fear of popish conspiracies, it was intended to exclude CATHOLICS from office. CHARLES II's financial needs obliged him to accept the measure, although it meant that his brother, the Duke of York (the future JAMES II), had to resign as lord high admiral. The Catholic minister Thomas Clifford also resigned, and the CABAL disintegrated. A second Test Act, passed in the context of the furore engendered by the supposed POPISH PLOT, provided that members of the Lords and Commons must take oaths of supremacy and allegiance and make an anti-Catholic declaration before taking their seats; the Duke of York was explicitly exempted. From 1727, the provisions of the first Test Act were mitigated by the passage of INDEMNITY ACTS, protecting those not prosecuted within a set period, but despite several earlier attempts at repeal, it remained on the statute book until 1828.

Test Act, Scottish, 1681 This marked the reversal of Lauderdale's (*see* MAITLAND, JOHN) policy of concessions to DISSENTERS. It required all officeholders to accept the Church of Scotland's Confession of 1560, and to recognize the supremacy of the king in spiritual as well as temporal matters. Among those who left Scotland in consequence were the jurist Sir James Dalrymple of Stair, and the political theorist Andrew Fletcher of Saltoun. Some argued that royal spiritual supremacy was itself inconsistent with the 1560 Confession. Archibald Campbell, 9th Earl of Argyll (1629–85) was sentenced to death after raising doubts on this score.

Test and Corporation Acts 1828 They repealed discriminatory legislation in the TEST ACT of 1673 directed at NONCONFORMISTS who were henceforth allowed to hold municipal and state office. It made the case against CATHOLIC EMANCIPATION more difficult to justify.

Testoon, *see* SHILLING

Tettenhall, Battle of, Staffs., 910, decisive victory gained by King EDWARD THE ELDER against a Scandinavian army from NORTHUMBRIA, which opened the way for Edward's later subjugation of the Danish districts south of the Humber (*see* YORK).

Tewkesbury, Battle of, Glos., 4 May 1471, YORKIST victory in the WARS OF THE ROSES. EDWARD IV defeated MARGARET OF ANJOU'S army just before it could cross the Severn and join up with Welsh troops raised by Jasper Tudor. The death of Margaret's son, Prince Edward, as he fled the field meant the extinction of the house of Lancaster.

Texel, Battle of, *see* DUTCH WAR, THIRD

Textus Roffensis, an early 12th-century manuscript, written at Rochester cathedral, which is one of the fundamental sources for our knowledge of Anglo-Saxon LAW CODES.

Thatcher, Margaret (née Roberts; Baroness Thatcher) (1925 –), Conservative politician and Prime Minister (1979–90). The daughter of a grocer at Grantham, Lincs., she studied chemistry at Oxford university, then after becoming a lawyer she was elected MP for Finchley in 1959. She served as education secretary in the HEATH government (1970–4), tasting controversy for the first time when she ended the provision of free school milk (*see* SCHOOL MEALS). After the 1974 general election defeat, she aligned herself with right-wing critics of Heath's approach, particularly Sir Keith Joseph, and defeated Heath for the leadership in 1975. Initially constrained by the views of her Heathite senior colleagues, she began to move away from Heath's centrist policies and embraced monetarism in her economic policy. She also advocated a tough line on law and order, defence and immigration. She capitalized on the CALLAGHAN government's difficulties in the 'WINTER OF DISCONTENT' and won a 45-seat majority in the 1979 general election, making her Britain's first woman prime minister. Her popularity increased hugely after the 1982 Falklands War and in 1983 the CONSERVATIVE PARTY won its largest number of seats since the 1935 election. Thatcher won a third electoral victory in 1987, but falling support in the Conservative Party led to a Conservative leadership election and to her replacement by John MAJOR, in 1990. From the back benches and then from 1992 from the LORDS she has remained a forceful critic of European integration and an idol to those of the right of the party.

Theatres, permanent or temporary structures for the production of plays and other dramatic entertainments. Plays were frequently presented in inn yards in the 16th century, and their enclosed gallery structure influenced the first purpose-built theatres, notably those associated with SHAKESPEARE and his contemporaries on the SOUTH BANK of the Thames in London. These, the Globe, Rose and Curtain among them, were outdoor theatres with roofed galleries encircling a central open area. The MASQUE and courtly entertainments associated with CHARLES I produced significant developments in indoor staging with scenery, and although theatres were officially proscribed during the Commonwealth, private indoor entertainments paved the way for RESTORATION drama and opera.

The first indoor theatre was built in the 1660s at Dorset Gardens, and other theatres followed; by the mid-18th century, when great actors like David Garrick were the toast of society, the most fashionable new London theatres were being built in COVENT GARDEN. In the regions by that date, and through until the early 19th century, many new theatres were going up, often to accommodate touring companies of actors (the Georgian theatre in Richmond, Yorks., is the finest surviving example). As these local venues waned in popularity and influence, so theatres in major towns and cities grew in size and attractiveness, with the 19th-century growth of melodrama occurring alongside the presentation of the classics. Beside them, the MUSIC HALL also flourished. By the end of the Victorian age, architects like Frank Matcham could specialize almost exclusively in theatre design, while promoters built chains of baroque, florid theatres throughout Britain. The reaction against late Victorian excess in both staging and theatre design brought a sparer style, particularly when new theatres came to be built in substantial numbers in the 1950s. Theatrical presentation today ranges from the institutionalized in buildings such as the National Theatre on the South Bank (*see* ROYAL NATIONAL THEATRE) or the Shakespeare Memorial Theatre in STRATFORD-UPON-AVON, to fringe events in London pubs or at the EDINBURGH FESTIVAL.

Thegn, a complex term used mostly between the 9th and 11th centuries to describe an Anglo-Saxon noble retainer with specific duties in a royal or noble household, who had a fortified residence of his own and at least five HIDES of land. A *thegn* also played a fundamental role in royal military service and the administration of SHIRE-COURTS and HUNDRED-courts.

Theodore of Tarsus, St (*c*.602–90), Archbishop of Canterbury (668–90). The Greek theologian Theodore must be given credit for three achievements. Beginning at the synod of HERTFORD, he undertook a major reorganization of the English Church during which a diocesan structure was created that, in broad terms, lasted for the rest of the medieval period (*see* BISHOPRICS). He established a school at Canterbury – with pupils that included Aldhelm – which did a great deal to raise the educational standards of the higher clergy in southern England.

Finally, he asserted the authority of the archbishopric of CANTERBURY in such a way as to produce for the first time a unitary English Church. This undoubtedly acted as a stimulus to a sense of unity among the English peoples.

Texts such as the *Penitential* reveal a great deal about Theodore's pastoral methods. His success is all the more surprising since he was already in his 60s when he was sent to England by Pope Vitalian.

Thirty Years War This began in 1618–19 after the Habsburgs overthrew the newly elected king of Bohemia (JAMES I's son-in-law Frederick, Elector Palatine), and ended in 1648, with the treaty of Westphalia. It drew in most of continental Europe in a struggle to contain the ambitions of the Habsburgs, with Catholic France fighting alongside Protestant powers.

The war was a political issue in England, first because of James's pacifism, then because of the Duke of Buckingham's (*see* VILLIERS, GEORGE) failure as a military leader when CHARLES I did go to war. Opposition to forced loans and arbitrary imprisonment of resisters culminated in the PETITION OF RIGHT in 1628. After Buckingham's assassination later that year, the king withdrew from the conflict and remained thereafter at least nominally neutral.

Thirty-Nine Articles, the doctrinal standard of the CHURCH OF ENGLAND, slightly modified from the Forty-two Articles (1553) and so a statement of moderate REFORMED theology. Passed by CONVOCATIONS in 1563 (with revisions in 1571), PARLIAMENT gave this formulary its sanction by statute in 1571 by requiring that all those clergy not ordained under the Edwardian ordinal subscribe to the articles.

Thomas of Lancaster (1278–1322), EDWARD II's cousin. By far the richest earl of the day, he was able to play a dominating political role, which, because of his consistent opposition to the king, was also highly controversial. His enormous wealth was based on the Lancaster, Leicester and Ferrers earldoms, which he inherited from his father Edmund of Lancaster (Edmund Crouchback) in 1296, and the inheritance of the earldom of Lincoln by his wife, Alice de Lacey, in 1311. He became an ORDAINER in 1310 and, two years later, took a leading part in the quasi-judicial murder of GAVESTON. During 1315 and 1316, after Edward II's humiliation at BANNOCKBURN, Thomas dominated the KING'S COUNCIL, insisting that the ORDINANCES be observed.

However, his personality gradually alienated some of his supporters – and led his wife to leave him. In 1317, Edward recovered control, and only the rise of a new royal favourite – Hugh Despenser – enabled Thomas to re-form an opposition group in 1321. But his popularity was already waning again – he had made the political error of seeking Scottish aid – when he was brought to battle and defeated at BOROUGHBRIDGE. Six days later, he was executed for treason. Not since the execution of Waltheof in 1076 had a man of his rank been put to death for rebellion, but Edward, determined to avenge Gaveston, would not be stopped. Whatever his flaws, Thomas's presentation of himself as another Simon de MONTFORT and Edward's continuing unpopularity led to a movement that sought the earl's canonization, and his tomb in Pontefract priory became the focus of a short-lived cult.

Thorfinn the Mighty (*c.*1020–65), Earl of Orkney. A son of SIGURD THE STOUT, he eventually emerged as sole ruler of ORKNEY after sharing power there with various relatives. Like his father, he was a conqueror, securing control over the Shetlands, re-establishing lordship over the HEBRIDES and, according to saga tradition, launching a raid against England. Having been brought up at the court of MALCOLM II, king of Scots, he was more cosmopolitan than his predecessors; he later converted to Christianity and went on a pilgrimage to Rome, during which he visited the courts of the kings of Germany and Norway. His reign also saw the establishment of a bishopric in Orkney and a rudimentary governmental administration.

Thorney Abbey, Cambs., one of the fenland abbeys established during the TENTH-CENTURY REFORM. It was founded by St Ethelwold in 972 or 973 with monks from the abbey of ABINGDON; it was dissolved in 1539.

Thornhill, Sir James (1675–1734), painter. The only major English decorative painter at a time when the field was dominated by foreign craftsmen, Thornhill was made history painter to GEORGE I in 1718. His more prestigious commissions included work at St Paul's cathedral, Hampton Court, Blenheim Palace and Greenwich Hospital. His BAROQUE *trompe l'oeil* style, influenced by Verrio and Laguerre, fell out of fashion in the 1720s. His daughter married William Hogarth.

Thorough, the nickname given to CHARLES I's personal rule (1629–40), more abusively known as the 'Eleven Years' Tyranny'. 'Thorough' referred to the intention – particularly of LAUD and WENTWORTH – to provide newly efficient government; the reality was more chaotic.

Thorpe, Jeremy (1929–), politician and leader of the Liberal Party (1967–76). Oxford educated, he served as MP for North Devon (1959–79), achieving the leadership, aged only 38, at a time when the first LIBERAL revival under GRIMOND appeared to have faltered in the 1966 general election with a fall in the overall Liberal vote. Thorpe was unable to prevent a halving of the party's representation at the 1970 general election, from 12 to 6 seats, but presided over another mini-revival in 1972–3 as the HEATH government ran out of steam, securing 5 by-election victories. In the Feb. 1974 general election under his leadership the party obtained its largest share of the vote since 1928 and 14 seats. Allegations of his relationship with male model Norman Scott and other bizarre accusations forced his resignation as leader in May 1976. Although subsequently acquitted of any criminal activity, his political career never recovered.

Thorstein the Red, Scandinavian warrior (*c.*855–75). The son of OLAF THE WHITE, King of DUBLIN, and Auld, daughter of KETIL FLATNOSE, he was associated with SIGURD THE MIGHTY, Earl of ORKNEY, in the conquest of Caithness and parts of Sutherland. When he was killed by the Scots in 875, his family's fortunes collapsed, and his mother and other relatives left Britain to play an important role in the colonization of Iceland (*see* HEBRIDES).

Thrashers, *see* WHITEBOYS

Three Choirs Festival, pioneering music festival, based on the annual meeting of the three choirs of Hereford, WORCESTER and GLOUCESTER cathedrals, held at each city in rotation since at least 1724, initially to raise money for clerical widows and orphans.

Three-Day Week, emergency measure to restrict production to three days a week by the HEATH government in Dec. 1973 during a miners' overtime ban and following a major rise in oil prices by OPEC the previous month (*see* OIL CRISIS). Other restrictions to conserve fuel were a 50 mph speed limit, reductions in street lighting, and cuts in hours broadcast by television. The three-day week was ended in March 1974 following the defeat of Heath's government in the general election and the coming into office of a LABOUR government under WILSON. To everyone's surprise, output remained virtually unaffected during the period of enforced short-time working.

Throckmorton, Elizabeth, *see* RALEIGH, SIR WALTER

Throckmorton, Job, *see* MARPRELATE SCANDAL

Thrymsas, gold COINS first minted in England in the second quarter of the 7th century in imitation of the Merovingian *tremissi*. They were replaced by the silver *SCEATTAS* towards the end of the 7th century.

Thule, *see* PYTHEAS OF MARSEILLES

Tilbury, Gervase of, *see* GERVASE OF TILBURY

Tillotson, John (1630–94), theologian, Archbishop of Canterbury (1691–4). Having gone to Cambridge in 1647, he was made a fellow of Clare Hall in 1651 but was ejected ten years later (*see* EJECTED CLERGY). In 1664, he married a niece of Oliver CROMWELL. He was influenced by the Cambridge PLATONISTS and became a leading LATITUDINARIAN. By 1675, he had been appointed dean of Canterbury and a PREBENDARY of St Paul's. In 1691, he succeeded SANCROFT as archbishop of Canterbury, having carried out the duties of the office since 1689, when Sancroft, as a NON-JUROR, was disabled from acting. Tillotson's 'His Commandments Are Not Grievous' is said to have remained the most popular sermon throughout the 18th century.

Tin Industry Tin mining is attested in the south-west peninsula of Devon and Cornwall in prehistoric times, and tin was already a

British export before the ROMAN CONQUEST, which naturally intensified its exploitation. There is documentary evidence of mining in Devon from the 12th century, and signs of a major resumption in Cornwall from the 13th century, from which time Cornwall remained the centre of British tin production. The exceptional importance of the industry was recognized by a charter of EDWARD I (1305), which confirmed the tinners' existing organization and privileges of exemption from ordinary taxation. The mines were administered in area jurisdictions known as Stannaries over which a warden presided: four in Devon and five in Cornwall. The presiding court of the whole jurisdiction was called the Stannary Parliament; it last met at Truro in 1752, and was formally abolished in 1896, although it has been unofficially revived in recent years for the purposes of fostering local identity and attempted tax evasion.

Shaft mining in place of ecologically disastrous surface-stripping was introduced during the 15th century. The next major technical advance was the application of STEAM POWER to drainage pumps in the shafts by the Devonian Thomas Newcomen (1663–1729) in the early 18th century; this technology has bequeathed west Cornwall the engine house as a characteristic landscape element. Production was at the same time given a major incentive by the founding of a native British tin-plating industry, thanks to the solving of technological problems by the South Wales ironmaster John Hanbury (1666–1734); the plating industry, concentrated round Cardiff, soon effectively displaced imports of tin plate in favour of Cornish tin. Tin-mining flourished in Cornwall through the 18th, 19th and early 20th centuries, but a fall in world prices destroyed all but one of the last commercially-operated mines in the 1980s.

Tintagel, clifftop location in north Cornwall, with a dramatic situation and remains of a medieval CASTLE on a site traditionally associated with ARTHUR. The association only goes back to the retelling of the Arthur story in *c.*1140 by GEOFFREY OF MONMOUTH who placed Arthur's conception there, but the castle site has clear Celtic antecedents.

Titanic Then the world's largest ship, of 46,382 tons, and built in BELFAST, the *Titanic* sank on her maiden voyage in 1912 after colliding with an iceberg in mid-Atlantic. Her distress signals by wireless were an early example of the power of TELECOMMUNICATION, since a fleet of vessels was called to her rescue. The ship and 1,635 passengers and crew were lost, but another 732 were saved who would otherwise have perished. The *Titanic* disaster has lived on in the popular imagination, and in recent years the wreck has been located and items recovered from the seabed.

Tithes The idea that all should pay tithes – 10 per cent of the annual produce of land or labour – to support their local MINSTER or PARISH church – was first stated as a universal obligation in England in the legislation of the synod of Clovesho (787). The 10th-century LAW CODES show that kings had started to impose heavy penalties for non-payment. In general, it appears certain that, from the 7th century onwards, the Church required payments such as church-scot, soul-scot and tithe from its flock. From the 11th century much tithe was being appropriated to monastic and college foundations, the corporations becoming the nominal RECTORS, merely leaving the lesser tithes to vicars ('substitutes'). Much of this was 'impropriated' to lay owners at the DISSOLUTION OF THE MONASTERIES (*see* FEOFFEES FOR IMPROPRIATIONS). The INTERREGNUM regimes failed to abolish tithe (much to the disgust of radical reformers), not being able to agree on an alternative system of church finance. By the 19th century, tithes, payable irrespective of denomination, were a major source of ill-feeling in Ireland for the non-Anglican majority, and in England and Wales for NONCONFORMISTS; SECULARISTS also seized on the issue to inflame ANTI-CLERICALISM. In Ireland they were commuted in 1838, and in England and Wales from 1836; the detailed and intricate mid-19th century maps produced in connection with this commutation are a major source for local and agricultural historians. Nevertheless, there were still some well-publicized conflicts over the payment of tithe in the 1920s and 1930s, and a final plan of liquidation was not worked out until 1951. Similarly in the CHURCH OF SCOTLAND, the payment of tithe, or 'teinds', remained an issue of conflict until legislation of 1925.

Tithing First mentioned in a 10th-century LAW CODE of King ATHELSTAN, a tithing was a unit of ten men and part of the sub-structure of a HUNDRED-court. By CNUT's time, it had become (ideally, at least) a mechanism to ensure that all male members of the community performed their legal responsibilities within local society. Tithings, which probably did not extend into NORTHUMBRIA, were regularly inspected by the SHERIFF, a practice that evolved into the system known as 'view of frankpledge' after 1066.

Titles, Peerages, *see* DUKE; MARQUESS; EARL; VISCOUNT; BARON

Tobago, *see* TRINIDAD AND TOBAGO

Tobacco, leaf of the *nicotiana* plant which is smoked, chewed or sniffed, providing an addictive nicotine boost. It was first imported as a plant from Mexico during the 16th century by a Spanish physician, Francisco Fernandes, but it was English explorers who brought back the habit of smoking, an early practitioner being RALEIGH. Government disapproval, including severe punishments such as flogging in some countries, and the eloquence of JAMES I, did nothing to stop the rapid spread of the habit through western Europe, and fragments of clay pipes are one of the most common finds in early modern archaeology. Tobacco-growing proved ideal for conditions in southern England and quickly became a favourite and profitable crop for small farmers, but from the time of CHARLES II this industry was completely destroyed by government intervention in order to protect the large plantations of the North American colonies, especially VIRGINIA, where tobacco exports from 1614 had proved the salvation of a settlement which had at first appeared to be a commercial disaster. By 1700 England was importing 38 million pounds of tobacco from the NEW WORLD, two-thirds of which was re-exported to the Continent, even though there was large-scale farming there, and the English government made comfortable sums from high EXCISE duties (as it still does).

Cigar-making was at first a New World domestic industry, and as such was dominated by women, but from the imposition of systematic taxation in the United States in 1861, it began to be industrialized. After the popularization of commercially prepared cigarettes in the 19th century, their manufacture in England from imported tobacco became concentrated in the hands of large companies, particularly in BRISTOL, LIVERPOOL and LONDON. Both cigarette and cigar manufacture remained notable, like the COTTON INDUSTRY, for providing major opportunities for female labour, despite initial male opposition.

The puncturing of myths about tobacco's health-giving properties began in the 1960s, with the introduction of official health warnings in cigarette packaging and advertising; but the subsequent decline in British consumption has been notably concentrated in the more affluent sections of society. From the late 1980s health scares about 'passive smoking', the danger of the non voluntary inhalation of smoke by non smokers, has led to a considerable increase in the places where smoking is banned – most notably public transport, cinemas, work places, large sections of restaurants etc.

Tolbooth, originally the hut from which a collector of taxes operated, hence in TOWNS the centre of administration. In Scotland, it remains a common name for a town hall.

Toleration Act 1689 Modifying but not abolishing penal laws against DISSENTERS, the Act provided that those who took the OATHS of allegiance and supremacy, and subscribed to a declaration against TRANSUBSTANTIATION, would escape the penalties for not attending church, and for attending CONVENTICLES. Those Dissenting ministers who signed the doctrinal parts of the THIRTY-NINE ARTICLES, though not those parts pertaining to church order, were exempted from penalties under the Act of UNIFORMITY, FIVE MILE ACT and Conventicle Act. QUAKERS, who conscientiously objected to oaths, were allowed instead to declare their allegiance and belief in the doctrine of the Trinity and inspiration of the Bible. Non-Trinitarian Dissenters and Catholics were specifically excluded. Daniel Finch, Earl of Nottingham who introduced the Bill, had hoped to join it with a COMPREHENSION Act, but that was defeated. In practice, the Act inaugurated an era in which toleration extended much more widely than the Act formally guaranteed.

Toll and Team, one of the powers most frequently granted to lords of estates in late Anglo-Saxon and early Norman England. 'Toll' signified the right to take tolls on goods sold within an estate and to settle disputes connected with this right. 'Team' involved supervision of 'vouching to warranty' – that is, ensuring that goods sold belonged to the vendor.

Tolpuddle Martyrs, the name given to the six Dorset farmworkers who in 1834 were sentenced to TRANSPORTATION to AUSTRALIA for having sworn an oath of loyalty to the labourers' union in the village of Tolpuddle. Although prosecution was meant to overawe the nascent labour movement, the vindictive action of a frightened WHIG government outraged public opinion. The condemned men, who were pardoned in 1836 and returned to England, became a symbol for defenders of the right of free association.

Tone, Wolfe (1763–98), Irish radical. He studied at Trinity College, Dublin, and at the Middle Temple, London, qualifying as a barrister in Dublin in 1789. Although an Episcopalian, he supported CATHOLIC EMANCIPATION, publishing *An Argument on behalf of the Catholics of Ireland* (1791). One of the founders of the UNITED IRISHMEN, in 1795 he visited Philadelphia and then France to solicit an invasion of Ireland. He joined the French army and, in Dec. 1796, accompanied Hoche's abortive invasion expedition. After the failure of the IRISH REBELLION, he returned with a much smaller force in Sept. 1798 and was captured. He was tried before a British military court and sentenced to death for treason, but apparently committed suicide before his execution.

Tonga, island group in the South Pacific, kingdom and former British protectorate. First visited by the Dutch explorer Tasman in 1643, Tonga was revisited in 1773, 1774, 1777 by James COOK, who gave it the title 'Friendly Islands'. Missionaries soon arrived; the Tongan kings progressively introduced reforms on European lines, resulting in the Constitution of 1875. Treaties were signed with Germany, Britain and the USA in 1876–88. Tonga was never colonized, although a Treaty of Friendship was signed with Britain in 1900 to stave off German expansion; the treaty lasted until 1970 when British protection, especially in foreign affairs, came to an end. Salote, Queen of Tonga 1918–65, was the almost larger-than-life embodiment of the continuity of rule of the Tongan royal family.

Tonnage and Poundage, Customs revenues levied by the English crown from the early 14th century onwards. Tonnage (or 'tunnage') was a payment on each tun of wine imported; poundage was a money levy on the pound sterling value of all imported and exported goods. In 1625, these revenues were granted to CHARLES I for one year only as a sign of the opposition's unhappiness with royal revenue collection. Charles persisted in collecting them, aggravating confrontation, and in 1641, PARLIAMENT ordered that they could be collected only with parliamentary consent.

TORCH, OPERATION North Africa, 8–11 Nov. 1942, codename for Anglo-American amphibious landings in French North Africa during WORLD WAR II. The landings were by no means bloodless, but the Vichy French forces surrendered within three days. The landings also hastened Rommel's retreat after his defeat at EL ALAMEIN a week before. Axis forces in Tunisia were not finally defeated until May 1943.

Torrens Act 1868 More concerned with SANITARY REFORM than housing reform, it gave local authorities the power to demolish individual dwellings which had no drainage or water closet. Although designed as an enlightened measure, in the short run, it probably aggravated the condition of the urban poor by dispossession without the provision of alternative accommodation.

Torture Most legal systems based on Roman law (*see* CIVIL LAW) routinely employed torture for investigation, and it was used by ecclesiastical INQUISITIONS in continental Europe. English COMMON LAW was exceptional in avoiding it. Contrary to popular myth, the 16th- and 17th-century STAR CHAMBER had nothing to do with it; only the English PRIVY COUNCIL and the COUNCIL IN THE MARCHES OF WALES could officially authorize torture. Scottish law followed the Continent, and the CHURCH OF SCOTLAND can claim credit for inventing sleep deprivation, part of its procedure for interrogating WITCHES. Torture disappeared from Western legal procedures during the 19th century, encouraged by the Napoleonic legal system, but has made a widespread if shamefaced comeback in the interrogation practice of the 20th century. One of the many countries which have been accused by human rights organizations of unofficially reviving methods equivalent to torture is Great Britain, mainly in relation to security operations in Northern Ireland after 1969.

Tory, from *Toraidhe,* Irish for bandit, cattle thief or outlaw, applied, originally abusively, to supporters of the Duke of York (the future JAMES II) in the EXCLUSION CRISIS, and subsequently by common acceptance to those whose focal loyalties were to 'Church and King'. Tories were divided by the GLORIOUS REVOLUTION. Though most had disliked the policies of James II, many were unhappy with any suggestion that PARLIAMENT might be sovereign even over the crown. Widespread unhappiness with what was seen as the power-hungry Whig JUNTO helped to give them a new focus – somewhat paradoxically, they began to win support as defenders of popular liberties. In the early 18th century HARLEY and other WHIGS disaffected with the Junto helped form a New Tory Party. Early 18th-century Tories were caricatured as backwoods squires; they did include many such, especially from the south-west and west Midlands, but also large landowners, merchants and lawyers. Some of their support came from LONDON and other towns. High Tories under ANNE rallied those fearful of what they saw as the excessive strength of DISSENT. From that time, however, division over religious issues and the succession, rivalry between Harley and Bolingbroke (*see* ST JOHN, HENRY), and discredit arising from the support some gave to the JACOBITE rising of 1715, all exploited by the Whigs, crippled the party for two generations.

Though they retained sizeable numbers of MPs, and a following in the country, they were excluded from high office by both GEORGE I and GEORGE II. At most, they were able to tilt the political balance, contributing to the fall of WALPOLE and assisting the rise of PITT THE ELDER. GEORGE III on his accession pronounced an end to Tory exclusion; many seized the chance to drop a discredited name, though the term continued to be employed abusively by ROCKINGHAMITE WHIGS and others, who extended it to cover all who supported the supposedly authoritarian king. Reaction against the FRENCH REVOLUTION helped relegitimate traditional Tory values; the name was applied retrospectively to PITT THE YOUNGER, and to Liverpool (*see* JENKINSON, ROBERT), Wellington (*see* WELLESLEY, ARTHUR) and PEEL, though not favoured by them; DISRAELI was the first leading politician to favour the term.

The CONSERVATIVE PARTY emerged from the Tory grouping of the 1830s. Peel used the term in his TAMWORTH MANIFESTO since he thought that Tory had resonances of illiberality and would be a handicap in winning the middle ground in politics. In common parlance today the terms are interchangeable, though the right wing of the Conservative Party is more attached to the historical associations of 'Tory' and frequently uses it in naming their groupings – often when critical of the party leadership.

Tory Democracy, a controversial concept, proclaimed as one of the organizing principles of modern CONSERVATISM from DISRAELI to THATCHER. It represents the search for a political style that would convince working-class voters that the advancement of their interests lay in the reinforcement, rather than the destruction of the institutions, interests, and structures of the polity. Some historians dismiss it as an empty vessel; others see it as the basis of a prudent progressivism that has made for economic progress and social reform without a fundamental change in the distribution of wealth.

Tory Reaction, name given by historians to the period following the EXCLUSION CRISIS of 1679–81, when ministers including Rochester (*see* HYDE, LAURENCE), Sunderland (*see* SPENCER, HENRY) and the lord keeper Lord Guilford took vigorous measures to suppress disloyalty and religious DISSENT. They were assisted – indeed perhaps outstripped in vigour – by many of the GENTRY and by urban Tories, who had apparently been alienated by WHIG extremism, most strikingly manifested, as it seemed, in the RYE HOUSE PLOT. Local government was thoroughly purged: commissions of the peace were revised, and numerous CORPORATIONS REMODELLED. The CLARENDON CODE was vigorously implemented. Leaders of the 'reaction' were not all of one mind; conservative figures, such as lord keeper Guildford, were wary of such zealots as Judge Jeffreys. Under the provisions of the TRIENNIAL ACT, CHARLES II could legally dispense with PARLIAMENT from 1681–4; but when he failed to summon a Parliament in 1684, some of his close advisers, such as the 1st Marquess of Halifax (*see* SAVILE, GEORGE), were dismayed.

Tostig (?–1066), Earl of Northumbria (1055–66). The third son of Earl GODWINE of WESSEX, his appointment to the earldom of NORTHUMBRIA in 1055, in contravention of the claims of the family of Earl SIWARD, seemed to cement the dominance of Godwine's sons over the English kingdom. Tostig, however, was unpopular and provoked a rebellion within his earldom in 1065; when his brother HAROLD did not support him militarily, he went into exile and joined Harold's enemies. Harold became king soon after; Tostig was killed alongside HARALD HARDRAADA, king of Norway, at the battle of STAMFORDBRIDGE.

Tournament, a form of mock battle between teams of knights fought out within a precisely defined (but often very large) area of ground. As in a real battle it was usually the better disciplined team which won – and earned the applause of the spectators, male and female. Typically early tournaments began with a JOUST, but once the lances were broken most of the fighting was done with mace and sword; thus the tournament emerged in the early 12th century when good-quality body armour became available on a scale sufficient to make so realistic a sport possible. Even so, as a game it always remained expensive (and thus exclusively high status) as well as highly dangerous. Captured knights lost their horses and had to pay ransoms, enabling tournament 'stars' such as William Marshal to earn fortune as well as fame. In England, tournaments were banned by HENRY II, then reintroduced (under licence) by RICHARD I. From then on most English kings (and in this they were to be followed by the Scottish kings) regarded the patronage of tournaments as a way of showing off their power, wealth, CHIVALRY and interest in military matters. Hence the keenest patrons tended to be warlike kings such as EDWARD I, EDWARD III, JAMES IV and HENRY VIII.

Despite the decay of the feudal and knightly culture which had created them, tournaments flourished in the Tudor age as a formalized and rule-bound élite sport controlled by the monarchy. Combats on foot and mounted contests in teams remained common, but central was the matching across a tilt barrier of two armoured knights on horses with couched lances: the JOUSTS. Participation in these ritualized fights was a convenient way of disguising the fact that the nobility increasingly owed their position and power to royal service rather than military prowess, and it worked off the surplus aggression of bored young men at court. Expenditure on tournaments increased dramatically under Henry VIII, with the king not merely a spectator but an enthusiastic participant (*see* FIELD OF THE CLOTH OF GOLD). Several prominent aristocratic politicians, particularly Charles Brandon, Duke of Suffolk, owed advancement in their careers under Henry to their jousting skills. Under ELIZABETH I, an important development were her celebratory ACCESSION DAY TILTS, and in general ritual and symbolic elements were greatly developed. Tournaments remained occasional features of court life after her death, but the early Stuarts preferred the alternative ritual of MASQUES as the centre of court entertainment, and the tournament of 1624 seems to have been the last. Tournaments would have appeared absurd after the RESTORATION (whose settlement included the abolition of feudal dues), and were not revived. The Eglinton tournament of 1839 (staged by the private enterprise of Archibald Montgomerie, 13th Earl of Eglinton) was an important moment in the GOTHIC Revival, despite disruptions by rain and widespread national ridicule.

Tower of London Soon after 1077 WILLIAM I THE CONQUEROR began a CASTLE straddling the south-east corner of the Roman wall of the city of LONDON; it was completed in 1097. From this initial phase of building there remains the White Tower (originally whitewashed, hence its name), the second largest Norman fortification in England after COLCHESTER keep. There are major remains of all periods from the 13th century, the two concentric defensive enclosures being built for HENRY III and EDWARD I. The Tower remained in regular use as a royal residence until the reign of CHARLES I, particularly in times of unrest. From early on it has also been used as a state prison, being last so employed for Rudolf Hess during WORLD WAR II, and it has been the scene of many political executions (*see also* EDWARD V). Its other occupants have included the medieval and early modern royal zoo, and still include the crown jewels.

Town and Country Planning Act 1947, the first Act to control the use and development of land and buildings in the interests of the nation as a whole, along the lines advocated by pre-WORLD WAR II and wartime reports. County councils had to prepare development plans, revised quinquennially, and were given powers of compulsory purchase. Planning permission was required by property owners for changes of use or alterations to buildings. The Act created the framework for post-war planning controls over land use and building, and remains operative in its essential elements.

Towns Early urban growth in England effectively had two beginnings. The Romans introduced an urban society and culture (*see CIVITAS* and under the names of individual towns), but despite some evidence of continuity, there was generally a serious decline during the 5th and 6th centuries (*see* ANGLO-SAXON SETTLEMENT). In many places, the presence of buildings and fortified walls ensured the survival of towns into the medieval and modern period, but some major Roman towns such as SILCHESTER and WROXETER actually disappeared.

The establishment of *BURHS* in the late 9th and 10th centuries gave an economic and social kick-start to an urban revival, and it is clear that municipal government began in a number of centres. The presence of MINTS and markets also played a key role, and by the time of *DOMESDAY BOOK*, it is estimated that 10 per cent of England's inhabitants lived in towns – as high a proportion as 500 years later. Uniquely urban forms of tenure also gave the emerging towns a distinctiveness that differentiated them from the countryside.

Towns frequently acquired walls and defences in medieval times and earlier, as a stronghold, while many towns in Norman England had their origins within the protection of a CASTLE or to serve a great religious institution. Market functions, specialized economic activities, and frequently industrial production, increasingly set towns apart from the rural settlements in their hinterland. Architectural differences, with closely set houses fronting streets, and often BURGAGE plots of land running behind them, also distinguished town from country. Tax returns from the medieval and early modern periods demonstrate the considerable wealth of many towns, some of which are now little more than villages. The restrictions upon industry imposed by many urban authorities, especially the hold of the craft GUILDS upon certain trades, probably contributed to the 16th-century trend for domestic industry to relocate or expand in the countryside. Historians talk of an urban crisis in the late 16th century as the pressures of POPULATION growth, falling trade, VAGRANCY and POVERTY all had a negative impact.

The proportion of people living in towns, in Scotland and possibly in Ireland and Wales as well as in England, continued to rise from the late 16th century, and although there were casualties most towns grew inexorably. The place of LONDON within the urban sector was always overwhelming; until the 18th century, its population was larger than that of all other towns in Britain put together. The Georgian age was one of greater differentiation between towns, some experiencing an URBAN RENAISSANCE in which they transformed themselves into resorts of pleasure, while ports, and later manufacturing centres, flourished and began to outstrip the rest of the urban sector in terms of growth. By the start of the 19th century, the situation which had persisted for centuries in which, with the exception of YORK, the major urban centres – London, NORWICH, BRISTOL – were predominantly in the south and east had been firmly eclipsed. The densest urban concentration was in the north-west centred on MANCHESTER and LIVERPOOL, with the north-east, the west Midlands, EDINBURGH and GLASGOW the other most important centres. That pattern intensified through the 19th century, with towns in south Wales also joining the league and London's dominant position continuing to slip (although it was never less than 5.5 times the size of its nearest rival). The proportion of the population living in towns increased inexorably: in 1851 just over half the population were living in towns; by 1901 it was more than three-quarters.

The crowding and disamenities of urban living were gradually ameliorated by reform of LOCAL GOVERNMENT, sanitation, HOUSING improvements and SLUM CLEARANCE; but the wish to escape the worst aspects of urban living resulted in the GARDEN CITY movement and later the establishment of the NEW TOWNS. The continuing growth of towns in the 20th century has also been accompanied by the expansion of suburban living, and in the number of those commuting to work from the surrounding countryside, thus arresting the slide in rural populations. The decline of the staple industries of COTTON, WOOL and IRON AND STEEL has also, especially since WORLD WAR II, caused the relative or absolute decline of the populations of those towns which relied upon them. There has been a corresponding rise of towns based upon new, lighter industries or service functions, particularly in the south and east, so reversing the trend of the 19th century.

Townshend, Charles (2nd Viscount Townshend) (1675–1738), politician. A childhood friend of WALPOLE's, whose sister he married, he became the future prime minister's close ally. Taking his seat in the Lords in 1697, Townshend supported the JUNTO WHIGS, and helped negotiate the UNION with Scotland and the BARRIER TREATIES. When Sunderland (*see* SPENCER, CHARLES) and STANHOPE persuaded GEORGE I to dismiss him in 1717, Walpole also resigned, and the two harried the ministry. Returned to office in 1720 and becoming secretary of state in 1721, Townshend pursued an aggressive foreign policy; in 1725, he abandoned an agreement with Austria and Spain in favour of a new alliance system, the League of Hanover with France and Prussia. Having tried and failed to jettison the more pacific Newcastle (*see* PELHAM-HOLLES, THOMAS), he resigned in 1730. A keen agricultural improver, he was nicknamed 'Turnip Townshend'.

Townshend Act 1767, legislation introduced by Charles Townshend (1725–67) as chancellor of the EXCHEQUER, which applied customs duties to a range of goods upon their importation into America, including lead, paper, glass, painters' colours and TEA. It was expected that some £40,000 a year would be raised, which was to be used to pay royal governors and certain officials (previously dependent on colonial assemblies for their salaries) and to support the expense of troops. Seen as part of a plan to strengthen British authority, the duties provoked a colonial campaign of, first, non-importation and then non-exportation. In 1770, NORTH repealed all the duties except that on tea; resistance to this duty was expressed in the BOSTON TEA PARTY (*see* INTOLERABLE ACTS 1774). The episode strengthened animosities aroused by the STAMP ACT 1765, and helped prepare the ground for rebellion.

Towton, Battle of, Yorks., 29 March 1461, the bloodiest battle of the WARS OF THE ROSES and the victory that gave EDWARD IV the throne. Although the LANCASTRIANS probably outnumbered the YORKISTS, they lacked a royal leader to match Edward in prowess; in a fiercely contested engagement, this counted. During and immediately after the battle, six Lancastrian peers and over 40 knights were killed. These heavy losses meant that it was to be years before MARGARET OF ANJOU could mount an effective challenge to the Yorkist regime.

Toynbee Hall Situated in Commercial Street, Whitechapel, in the East End of London, it was the first university settlement. Founded in 1884, it was the product of a movement designed to enable resident university graduates to work among, and improve the lives of, the poor. Its first warden was Samuel Barnett, vicar of St Jude's, Whitechapel. It served as a work station for Charles BOOTH's study of *Life and Labour of the People in London* in the 1880s and 90s. Many individuals prominent in public life in the 19th and 20th centuries were associated with its work, including Clement ATTLEE, William Beveridge (*see* BEVERIDGE REPORT), Alfred Milner and John Profumo (*see* PROFUMO AFFAIR). It promoted the introduction of free legal advice; the provision of affordable workers' HOUSING; the WORKERS' EDUCATION ASSOCIATION; the Whitechapel Art Gallery; and a varied menu of lecture programmes and classes.

Tractarianism, *see* OXFORD MOVEMENT

Trade Boards Act 1909 Passed in response to the anti-sweating campaign, it marked an abandonment of the doctrinaire belief in the necessary perfection of an unregulated market. In four trades – chain-making, ready-made and wholesale bespoke tailoring, paper-box making and lace-finishing – wages were to be regulated by Trade Boards, consisting of equal members of representatives of employers and employed, together with certain independent appointed members. After confirmation by the BOARD OF TRADE the wage rates fixed by these Boards became the legal minima.

Trade Boards Act 1913 Provided for the extension of the Trades Boards system, since on the basis of the evidence supplied by the experimental legislation of 1909, the application of the legal minimum wage seemed to promote improved industrial efficiency rather than the widespread ruin predicted by critics.

Trade Disputes Act 1906 By removing TRADE UNION liability for damage by strike action, the Act undid the damage caused by the TAFF VALE DECISION of 1901.

Trade Disputes and Trade Unions Act 1927 Passed following the GENERAL STRIKE, the Act outlawed general strikes and sympathetic strikes, and banned civil servants from joining unions affiliated to the TRADES UNION CONGRESS. It also attacked the link between the unions and the LABOUR PARTY by forcing union members to make a positive decision to pay a levy to a political party ('contracting in') rather than letting them 'contract out' only if they did not want to pay the levy. The effect was to deprive the Labour Party of about one-third of its subscriptions. Regarding it as vindictive and anti-Labour, the Labour Party was committed to the Act's alteration, achieved in 1946 when 'contracting out' was restored and sympathetic and general STRIKES were again made legal.

Trade Union Act 1913, provided that before engaging in political activities a TRADE UNION must secure the approval of a majority of the members voting in a special ballot. It also nullified the effects of the OSBORNE JUDGMENT by enabling a trade union to divide its subscriptions into a political fund and a social fund with the consent of the members. Union members objecting to the political contribution could 'contract out', if they were prepared to resist peer pressure, without losing any of their ordinary rights as members.

Trade Unions, continuous associations of wage earners which exist to maintain or improve the conditions of work and rates of pay of their members. At the same time, and especially since the late 19th century, they can also be seen in a more political light, especially in their role as an arm of the labour movement and an important element behind the formation, finance and functioning of the LABOUR party. Unions originated in the late 18th century as associations of skilled workers and were formed partly as social clubs and for MUTUAL INSURANCE such as the accumulation of funds to cover sickness and burial. Widespread unionization was impossible in the pre-factory period because most workers were geographically scattered in small workshops, worked alongside their immediate employer and shared his interests, and/or earned too little to join an organization which demanded regular subscriptions. Rapid POPULATION growth from the later 18th century, the consequent ready supply of labour and the absence of protective legislation also meant that employers could choose only unorganized workers, including women and children. The centralization of work and the employment of larger workforces encouraged union organization, but this was hampered in the 19th century by the attitudes of most employers and the state, who identified combinations of workers with attacks on property and political insurrection and adopted repressive policies as with the COMBINATION ACTS. Trade union organization and personnel in the first half of the 19th century did spill over into social and political protest, as in LUDDISM, CHARTISM and Owenism. Because of this it took the whole of the 19th century to establish a satisfactory legal basis for trade union activity.

Early trade unions were generally small and localized with the exception of Robert OWEN's Grand National Consolidated Trades Union (GNCTU). But the rise of nationally organized NEW MODEL UNIONS of skilled workers in the third quarter of the 19th century ushered in a new phase. New Model Unions were concerned to create a respectable face to win full legal recognition; they viewed STRIKES as a last resort and stressed mutual improvement and self-help activities. The WEBBS saw this as part of a progression whereby trade unions became recognized as civilized and civilizing institutions playing a role in social betterment and moral improvement with the accent on patience, self control and negotiation.

More recently, historians viewing the whole of the labour movement argue that there were more continuities than discontinuities in trade union action, and policy between the early and late 19th century, especially after the growth of unskilled unionism in the New Unions and associated strikes from the 1880s to 1914. In 1910 trade union membership was 2,564,000, three times that of 1888 and much wider in scope. Membership rose from just over 4 million in 1914 to 8.3 million in 1920. Much of the growth in its strength and membership took place in periods of high employment and demand (e.g. 1833–5, 1872–4, 1889–90) when workers were in a powerful position to press their claims. Recruitment and strength is always weaker during economic DEPRESSIONS when there is less to gain, more UNEMPLOYMENT and employers have most to lose. Union strength and activity was thus weak during the inter-war slump following the defeat of the GENERAL STRIKE of 1926. It picked up in the 1950s and 1960s and became a thorn in the side of successive governments struggling to control INFLATION and to improve the competitiveness of INDUSTRY. In 1976–7 the largest union was the TGWU with over two million members; the next largest AUEW with 1,428,319 members. The GMWU had 916,438; NALGO 683,011; NUPE 650,530. In the same period ASTMS had 396,000 members; COHSE 200,450; NUM 259,966; NUR 180,000 (ASLEF 28,189); NUT 289,107; and USDAW 412,627. By 1978 there were 115 organizations affiliated to the TRADES UNION CONGRESS (TUC), together representing about 11.5 million workers. Union membership began to decline in 1979 hastened by rising unemployment, legal changes which stripped unions of many of their old rights, and political repression of strikes, especially the year-long miners' strike of 1984.

Between 1963 and 1978 the number of TUC affiliated unions dropped by 86 through mergers, but membership increased by over 3 million; 62 unions were affiliated to the Labour Party in 1974 and over 5 million trade unionists were members of the party through their unions' affiliation. The unions provided the bulk of the Labour Party's central finances but union members could contract out of contributions to the unions' political funds. The TUC itself is not affiliated to the Labour Party.

CHRONOLOGY

1799 COMBINATION ACT outlawed combinations in trade. Workmen could be given prison sentences for combining to improve working conditions or wages or other acts that made this possible.

1800 Combination Act modified some of the features of the 1799 Act, namely that provision for arbitration was introduced, magistrates trying cases could not be employers in that trade, and masters were prohibited from combining to reduce wages or increase hours.

1801–24 STRIKES in SHIPBUILDING industries, COTTON weaving and spinning, WOOLLEN INDUSTRY. LUDDITE campaign (starts 1811) and frame breaking, lay-offs and wage reductions in IRON-working industries.

1824 Repeal of COMBINATION ACT: largely as a result of the campaign orchestrated by Francis PLACE and Joseph Hume, 1800 Act repealed almost in its entirety. Combinations for the purpose of improving working conditions and wages now legal.

1825 Outbreak of STRIKES and intensification of Trade Union activity resulted in a new COMBINATION ACT. This narrowly defined the rights of Trade Unions as meeting to bargain over wages and conditions. Anything outside these limits was liable to prosecution as criminal conspiracy in restraint of trade.

1829 Union of Trades launched and General Union of Spinners formed.

1830 Union of Trades changes name to National Association for the Protection of Labour, with branches in cotton-spinning areas of North and Midlands.

1831 Spinners Union collapses.

1832 Robert OWEN starts the Grand National Consolidated Trades Union (GNCTU) with the object of linking all British trade unions to his co-operative and socialist movement; 16,000 members mainly in London and among skilled trades, but little support among cotton and cloth workers, etc. National Association collapses. Industrial unrest among coalminers of Wales and building workers who want new terms of employment.

1834 Failure of GNCTU and Builders' Union. TOLPUDDLE MARTYRS sentenced to TRANSPORTATION. Widespread protests throughout the country.
1841 National Miners' Association of Great Britain and Ireland formed – soon split into a number of separate county associations.
1842 PLUG RIOTS.
1851 Amalgamated Society of Engineers formed; regarded as a new 'model union' and copied by other groups of skilled workers. Initial membership of 12,000 rises to 71,000 by 1891.
1853 Amalgamated Association of Operative Cotton Spinners formed.
1855 Friendly Societies Act protects unions' funds.
1859 Molestation of Workmen Act allows peaceful picketing.
1860 COAL MINES REGULATION ACT regulates conditions of employment. London Trades Council and Amalgamated Society of Carpenters and Joiners formed.
1864 First national conference of trade union delegates.
1866 SHEFFIELD OUTRAGES, resulting in setting up of ROYAL COMMISSION on Trade Unions. *HORNBY V. CLOSE* case calls into question degree of protection really given by Friendly Societies Act (1855).
1867 Master and Servant Act. Strikers can only be prosecuted for breach of contract, but criminal action can still be brought for 'aggravated cases'. Royal Commission recommends legislation on trade unions.
1868 First TRADES UNION CONGRESS in Manchester; 34 delegates attend.
1869 Second TUC at Manchester; 40 delegates attend, representing 250,000 members.
1870 National Union of Teachers (NUT) established; reformed in 1889.
1871 Trade Union Act and CRIMINAL LAW AMENDMENT ACT. Unions given legal recognition and right to protect funds. Picketing made illegal.
1872 National Agricultural Union formed by Joseph Arch.
1874 First Trade Unionist MPs elected (Alexander MACDONALD and Thomas Burt).
1875 CONSPIRACY AND PROTECTION OF PROPERTY ACT allows peaceful picketing. EMPLOYERS AND WORKMEN ACT states that breach of contract is no longer a criminal offence.
1880 EMPLOYER'S LIABILITY ACT.
1888 MATCH GIRLS STRIKE. Miners' Federation of Great Britain founded. Start of mass NEW UNIONISM of unskilled workers.
1889 London DOCK STRIKE won wage rise and the Dock, Wharf, Riverside and General Labourers' Union formed under Ben Tillet (1860–1943). Gas workers win reduction in working day from 12 to 8 hours. National Union of Public Employees (NUPE) founded.
1893 INDEPENDENT LABOUR PARTY (ILP) established.
1896 *LYONS V. WILKINS* case prevents members of Leather Workers' Union from picketing. Employers Federation of Engineering Associations formed.
1897 July–1898 Jan. National lock-out in ENGINEERING INDUSTRY ends in success for employers.
1898 Scottish TUC formed.
1899 General Federation of Trade Unions formed, to control a fund for support of trade unionists in the event of a strike.
1900 LABOUR REPRESENTATION COMMITTEE (LRC) formed.
1901 TAFF VALE DECISION established the principal that a trade union could be sued for damages incurred as result of a strike.
1905 National and Local Government Officers' Association (NALGO) formed.
1906 TRADE DISPUTES ACT reverses Taff Vale decision. 26 Labour MPs elected. Parliamentary LABOUR PARTY formed.
1909 OSBORNE JUDGMENT prevents trades unions using their funds for political purposes. Trade Boards Act sets up mechanism to regulate wages in industries employing cheap labour.
1910 National Transport Workers' Federation set up by Ben Tillet, Tom Mann and Havelock Wilson. Miners' strike in South Wales lasts nearly a year. Confederation of Health Service Employees (COHSE) founded.
1911 Dockers, seamen and railway union strike.
1912 Three-month strike by miners for minimum wage: achieved. Blackleg labour used to break London Dock strike.
1913 TRADE UNION ACT reversed Osborne Judgment: trade union funds can, under certain circumstances, be used for political purposes. National Union of Railwaymen (NUR) formed by amalgamation of ASRS and other unions. Association of Locomotive

Engineers and Firemen (ASLEF), founded in 1880, remains independent.
1914 Attempt to organize TRIPLE ALLIANCE of miners, railwaymen and transport workers. Truce declared on outbreak of war. Trade Union membership stands at around 4 million.
1915 Clydeside movement against wartime DILUTION of skilled by unskilled labour.
1917 Strikes and unrest in munitions and other factories over dilution, CONSCRIPTION of skilled workers, and rising prices. WHITLEY COUNCILS established.
1918 Largest number of days lost in strikes during the war – including POLICE strikes in London and Merseyside.
1919 Scottish TUC and Clyde Workers' Committee call for 40-hour strike on 27 Jan. 'Bloody Friday' (30 Jan.) when strikers clash with police: troops called in; strike leaders arrested: strike collapses.

Industrial Courts Act establishes a permanent advisory arbitration tribunal. Sankey Commission investigates wages and management of mines after threatened miners' strike: recommends NATIONALIZATION, but government and mine owners reject. National railway strike in opposition to GEDDES 'AXE'. RIOTS in Liverpool as a result of police strike, but similar strikes fail in rest of country.
1920 London dock strike and continuing industrial unrest among miners and railwaymen. Dockers block loading of arms for Soviet Union to crush the Russian Revolution.
1921 'Black Friday' 15 April: of Triple Alliance unions, only miners strike.
1921–4 Amalgamated Engineering Union (AEU), Transport and General Workers Union (TGWU) and National Union of General and Municipal Workers (GMWU) formed.
1925–6 Miners strike, leading to GENERAL STRIKE.
1927 TRADE DISPUTES AND TRADE UNIONS ACT: general strikes and sympathetic strikes made illegal and imposes system of 'contracting in' for political levy.
1928 Amalgamation of TGWU with Workers' Union. MOND-TURNER TALKS.
1931 Fall of second Labour government: General Council of the TUC refuses to accept spending cuts. Ramsay MACDONALD forms a NATIONAL GOVERNMENT. TUC continues to support LABOUR PARTY.
1931–2 National Council of Labour (reconstructed from National Joint Council) set up, with formalized links to Labour Party and thus greater political power.
1930–5 Economic DEPRESSION reduces membership of some unions: from a peak of 8.3 million in 1920 membership plummets to around 3.5 million in 1935 (miners fall from 804,236 members in 1929 to 588,321 in 1939). Largest union now TGWU; AEU and Electrical Trades Union (ETU) and General and Municipal Workers (GMW) grow.
1940–5 Ernest BEVIN becomes minister of labour. Control of Employment Act gives government power to direct labour: Order 1305 legally restricts strikes and lock-outs and makes arbitration compulsory. Membership of most unions increases during war.
1944 National Union of Mineworkers (NUM) formed to replace MFGB.
1946 Repeal of 1927 Trade Disputes and Trade Unions Act means union members now able to opt out of political levy.
1947 Union of Shop, Distributive and Allied Workers (USDAW) established.
1951 Wartime Order 1305 withdrawn after unsuccessful prosecution of some dockworkers.
1956–62 ETU struggles over alleged malpractices and Communist leadership; union expelled from TUC and Labour Party; moderates win.
1958 Wartime National Arbitration Tribunal – popular with the unions – disbanded. London busmen's strike.
1959 Terms and Conditions of Employment Act.
1962 National Economic Development Council formed with TUC participation.
1964 Department of ECONOMIC AFFAIRS set up under George BROWN and PRICES AND INCOMES BOARD. *Rookes v. Barnard* case made threat to strike to injure a third party illegal, even if in furtherance of a trade dispute. *Stratford v. Lindley* case determined that strike action not in furtherance of a trade dispute was not protected by 1906 Act.
1965 Trade Disputes Act reversed *Rookes v. Barnard* and gave trade unions further legal immunities.
1966 Prices and Incomes Bill passed. National seamen's strike defeated.
1968 Report to Donovan Committee on Industrial Relations argues against legal

intervention and in favour of voluntary agreements in industrial relations. Association of Scientific, Technical and Managerial Staffs (ASTMS) established.
1968 ETU re-formed as Electrical, Electronic, Telecommunication and Plumbing Union under leadership of Frank Chapple.
1969 Labour government White Paper *IN PLACE OF STRIFE*. Opposition from TUC: proposals dropped.
1970–1 CONSERVATIVE government passes INDUSTRIAL RELATIONS ACT (Aug. 1971) which gives government wide-ranging and unprecedented powers over trade unions. National Industrial Relations Court established. Massive TUC opposition to proposals. Amalgamated Union of Engineering Workers (AUEW), embracing Foundry Workers' Union, Constructional Engineering Union and Draughtsmen's and Allied Technicians' Association, formed.
1972 Highest number of days lost in strikes since 1926. Miners' strike begins in Jan. – widespread power cuts; Feb.: state of emergency declared as power crisis intensifies. Report of Wilberforce Committee recommends acceptance of many of miners' demands; strike called off. National Industrial Relations Court set up under terms of Act. TGWU and, later, AUEW refuse to recognize its powers and are heavily fined. National dock strike after the imprisonment of the 'Pentonville Five', who ignored an order by the NIRC to stop blacking containers. Contracts of Employment Act.
1973 Escalating industrial action begins in autumn by firemen, Electrical Power Engineers Association, miners and ASLEF. Government takes emergency measures; 3 day working week announced from 31 Dec.
1974 Poll shows 81 per cent of miners in favour of strike. HEATH calls 'Who Governs Britain?' election on union power; defeated. Trade Union and Labour Relations Act revokes most of the provisions of Industrial Relations Act. NIRC abolished in July after sequestering £280,000 of AEU's funds for non-payment of fines; fines paid anonymously. SOCIAL CONTRACT initiated between trade unions and government. Welsh Trade Union Council created.
1975 Employment Protection Act invests Advisory, Conciliation and Arbitration Service (ACAS) with authority to arbitrate, if requested, in industrial disputes, and extends the rights of individual employees and trade unions. TUC accepts flat-rate pay increase norm.
1976 Employment Protection Act comes into force.
1977 Firemen's strike: troops called in to deal with fires.
1978 Unions reject 5 per cent wages norm. Widespread industrial action throughout 'WINTER OF DISCONTENT' by hospital and municipal workers, etc.
1979 Conservative government elected, committed to reform trade union law, e.g. 'closed shop' agreements, secondary picketing and the use of secret ballots to call strikes.
1980s Legislation throughout the 1980s implemented by Conservatives further restricting union rights and encouraging workplace independence from union organization.
1999 The Employment Relations Act introduced provisions concerning the recognition by employers of trade unions. These apply to firms with over 20 employees and strengthen the rights of collective bargaining, protection from dismissal as a result of lawfully organized official industrial action, protection for workers in the event of take overs and mergers, and consultation over redundancies, as well as 'family friendly' employment rights concerning parental leave.

Trades Councils, local organizations of TRADE UNIONS representing the major unions in particular areas. They have usually acted as spokespersons for the workers' side of local industry against local chambers of commerce.

Trades Union Congress (TUC), umbrella organization of the British TRADE UNION movement, founded in Manchester in 1868 to co-ordinate union action by means of annual conferences. Initially a small body, representing primarily the skilled craft unions, in 1871 the TUC set up a 'parliamentary committee' to represent union interests. The TUC grew with the development of NEW UNIONISM in the late 19th century to represent over a million workers by 1900. The same year it supported the setting up of the LABOUR REPRESENTATION COMMITTEE to sponsor trade union issues in Parliament and to elect its own MPs. By 1914 union affiliation to the early LABOUR PARTY was growing and the TUC had over 2.5 million members.

The TUC was responsible for organizing a 'strike truce' at the outbreak of WORLD WAR I, during which its influence extended considerably as TUC membership reached a peak of over 6 million by 1920. The following year a 30-strong General Council was set up to co-ordinate industrial action, settle inter-union disputes, and forge international links, though without formally affecting the autonomy of individual unions. The TUC leadership suffered a major defeat through its role in calling and then abandoning the GENERAL STRIKE in 1926 leading it to concentrate increasingly on support for the Labour Party. From 1932 it exercised virtually total control of Labour Party policy through its representation on the National Joint Council which co-ordinated Labour and TUC activity, and from 1933 even had a formal veto on any future Labour leader. During the 1930s the TUC remained strongly opposed to communism, forbidding communists from becoming officials in 1934 by the 'Black Circular' while also becoming increasingly active in the opposition to fascism, supporting a rearmament policy in 1936.

During WORLD WAR II the TUC's influence expanded rapidly; senior officials and union leaders co-operated with the war effort and saw TUC membership once again reach a record level – of over 8 million by 1951. The implementation by the ATTLEE governments of much of the welfare and NATIONALIZATION programme agreed with the TUC before 1939 was followed by a lengthy period in which the TUC enjoyed the position of a major estate of the realm, represented on tripartite bodies with employers' organizations in what was seen as an increasingly corporatist relationship with governments of all complexions. The TUC, however, retained its special links with the Labour Party through its traditional role in Labour politics at grass roots and parliamentary levels, its powerful block vote at Labour conferences, its sponsorship of MPs, and its role in funding Labour Party election campaigns.

Scottish Trade Unions have their own central body (STUC) which is similar in constitution and functions to the TUC; unions whose members include Scottish workers could affiliate to both the STUC and the TUC. Trade Unions in Northern Ireland are represented by the Northern Ireland Committee of the Irish Congress of Trade Unions (ICTU), though the majority of trade unionists in Northern Ireland belong to British-based unions.

In spite of growing criticism of British industrial relations, the TUC successfully opposed an attempt by the WILSON government in its White Paper *IN PLACE OF STRIFE* (1969) to introduce a legal framework for industrial bargaining. It also resisted the INDUSTRIAL RELATIONS ACT introduced by HEATH in 1971. During the Wilson and CALLAGHAN period from 1974–9 the TUC attempted to secure voluntary agreements from unions to pay norms during a period which saw TUC membership rise to a new peak of over 12 million members by 1979.

By 1999 there were approximately 6.8 million members of Trade Unions affiliated to the TUC – around 20 per cent less than 10 years earlier – but stable since 1998. In total there were 7.1 million Trade Union members with UNISON, the public sector union being the largest with some 1.3 million members.

Trafalgar, Battle of, 21 Oct. 1805, decisive naval battle of the NAPOLEONIC WARS in which NELSON, commanding from the *Victory*, destroyed the combined French and Spanish fleet under Villeneuve as it sailed from Cadiz towards the Mediterranean. Nelson attacked the French column at right angles with two divisions, split their line in two and engaged in a close-quarters attack in which 18 French ships were taken with no British losses. Although killed by a sniper from the *Redoubtable* during the battle, Nelson's tactical and strategic brilliance ensured both the immediate victory and British naval domination for the following century.

Tramping System, term used to describe the means whereby members of particular industrial or craft trades travelled around the country in search of work or to receive financial assistance from other members of their trade. 'Houses of call', frequently inns or public houses where the trade groups met, operated as staging-posts on a tramping artisan's route. The system had ancient origins, especially for masons, but came to prominence in the later 18th century and flourished until the mid-19th century, often under the aegis of the early TRADE UNIONS in

ENGINEERING and similar industries. The growing regularity of a national TRADE CYCLE, in which booms and slumps occurred throughout the economy, was one of the reasons for its demise and replacement by locally based forms of assistance and relief.

Trams, public transport vehicles running on rails let into the surface of the road. The first English tramway was opened in Birkenhead in 1860 and the first London tramway at Bayswater, in 1861. It was not until after 1870, however, when an Act to facilitate the construction of tramways was passed, that any great extension took place. Between 1870 and 1880, 233 miles of tramways were constructed in England and Wales. By 1910, when horse-drawn trams had been superseded first by STEAM POWER and then by electric traction, there were about 3,000 miles of tramways in the United Kingdom.

The cheap and efficient service the tramcars provided enabled some people to remove from congested central districts to more salubrious suburbs, but by the late 1920s electric tramways were under severe pressure from motor-bus services. During the 1930s local authorities began to abandon their tramway systems and after World War II the process was rapidly completed. The last tram left London for the scrapyard in 1952. There was no overwhelming technical or economic case for the downfall of the tram; it was associated with a decaying world of working-class poverty, and particularly in the post-war mood of structural reform and the erosion of social inequalities, this spelled its doom. The folly of destroying tram systems has been realized in recent years, and many cities (e.g. MANCHESTER and NEWCASTLE-UPON-TYNE) have reinstated systems; others are planning to do so.

Transitional, term used for the hybrid architectural style of the late 11th and early 12th centuries, characterized by a combination of NORMAN and EARLY ENGLISH styles, and especially by the early use of pointed arches.

Transportation The transportation of convicts, as a condition of pardon from a death sentence, was inaugurated in 1614–15. VIRGINIA was the initial, and long remained a favourite, destination. In the late 17th–early 18th centuries, some convicts were sent to the WEST INDIES. The Transportation Act of 1718 gave the courts the power to sentence those convicted of certain felonies and lesser crimes to terms of transportation to the North American colonies (respectively of 14 and 7 years). Thus transportation afforded a secondary punishment that, unlike BENEFIT OF CLERGY, removed offenders from British society without recourse to the ultimate sanction of the gallows (*see* CAPITAL PUNISHMENT). The shipping of convicts was managed by contractors, who recouped their costs by selling convicts as INDENTURED SERVANTS to American employers. Scottish and Irish convicts were also transported, but on a different legal basis. By 1776 about 1,000 convicts a year were sent to America.

The War of AMERICAN INDEPENDENCE ended this; prison HULKS moored in the Thames offered a temporary solution. By 1790 transportation to AUSTRALIA – principally to BOTANY BAY – was well under way. The convicts in NEW SOUTH WALES worked in strictly disciplined gangs in government employ, clearing the land, building the houses and the docks, or as labourers and servants to the free population. Criticism of the system grew in the 19th century. In 1840 transportation to New South Wales was ended; in 1846 transportation to Van Diemen's land (now TASMANIA) was suspended for two years. The colonial secretary, Earl Grey, introduced a three-stage plan to cope with the problem: those sentenced to transportation would serve a period in a prison cell in Britain, then a period of hard labour either in Britain or a colony, and then an indefinite exile in a colony. Grey's exiles were extremely unpopular with the colonies who wanted an end to the system altogether. And in the 1850s the British public also turned against transportation as both an incitement to commit crime and an expensive alternative to serving a prison sentence at home. In 1853 Van Diemen's land ceased to be a penal colony; Norfolk Island penal settlement was closed in 1856. Transportation to Western Australia alone continued until 1867. The prison hulks were gone by 1857, when the last ship used for the purpose, *Defence*, was destroyed by fire.

Transportation Act 1718, *see* TRANSPORTATION

Transubstantiation, theory which seeks

to explain how the miracle of the MASS takes place, in terms of the scientific language of 'substance' and 'accidents' evolved by the ancient Greek philosopher Aristotle. It suggests that the substance of bread and wine in the eucharist are replaced by the substance of the body and blood of Christ, while the accidents (i.e. outward appearance) of bread and wine remain unchanged. Transubstantiation was only one scholastic theory, without full official status during the medieval period, although this did not stop the Church burning as heretics (*see* HERESY) those who denied its truth. It was made an official doctrine of the Roman CATHOLIC Church at the Council of Trent in 1551 (*see* COUNTER-REFORMATION).

Treason, one of the first crimes to receive statutory definition: the 1351 Treason Act included violence against the royal family or senior officials and forgery of COINAGE or the GREAT SEAL. Petty treason was also defined, as the killing of a superior by an inferior (reduced to murder in 1828). Tudor legislation, particularly that passed in 1534 in the tense aftermath of HENRY VIII's marriage to ANNE BOLEYN, extended high treason to include treason by words as well as deeds, to deal with opponents of government religious policy. Treason remains one of the few capital crimes (*see* CAPITAL PUNISHMENT) still on the statute-book of English law. *See also* TWO ACTS.

Treasury As an informal usage from an early date, it was a place of deposit for treasure and coin, and the word was used in this sense by medieval English monarchs. The modern institution of government so called originated as the private office of the lord high treasurer of England, the presiding officer in the EXCHEQUER. It was developed by successive Tudor and early Stuart treasurers, William Paulet, and William and Robert CECIL: one reason for this was that administering money within a private setting avoided the formal audit procedures in the established government financial departments. On Robert Cecil's death, JAMES I wished to avoid creating a similar dominant role for any other individual, and so he appointed a set of commissioners in his place. A commission could not work in the same informal way as a single great minister, and increasingly the work of the Treasury became formalized, while the Exchequer's financial responsibilities atrophied. In the later 17th century the appointment of a single lord treasurer became infrequent, lapsing altogether in 1714, and the lords commissioners assumed a permanent role at the Treasury Board, particularly if the monarch was not present to preside; from them, the FIRST LORD OF THE TREASURY emerged as PRIME MINISTER, thanks to Robert WALPOLE. After the abolition of the ancient official structure of the Exchequer in 1833 the Treasury finally emerged as a ministerial department and its normal presiding officer, the chancellor of the Exchequer, became a figure of CABINET rank. The powers of the lords commissioners are now purely formal. The usage retains an informal aspect, as a label for those departments and ministers of government whose responsibilities are primarily the management of finance, and whose approach to government policy is dominated by this consideration.

By the 20th century the Treasury was becoming the most important department of the government and the chancellor of the Exchequer the second most powerful figure in the Cabinet. With the increased economic role and responsibilities for governments implied in KEYNESian ideas of macroeconomic management the powers of the Treasury were enhanced. It was no longer simply a question of looking after the fiscal position of the government, the Treasury became involved in the management of the overall ECONOMY. In 1961 the Treasury became involved in new methods for controlling public expenditure – the Public Expenditure Survey Committee (PESC). In addition, economic management required the development of statistical forecasting models of the economy so as to determine the short-run outlook, and this too was entrusted to the Treasury. Finally, decisions about monetary policy and interest rates (an area which had traditionally been regarded as the domain of the BANK OF ENGLAND) became the province of Treasury ministers until the incoming LABOUR government returned powers over setting interest rates to the Bank in 1997.

Treaties, *see under their locations*

Trenchard, Hugh (1st Viscount Trenchard)

(1873–1956), Marshal and 'father' of the RAF. He joined the army in 1893 rising to major-general, and in 1912 was seconded to the ROYAL FLYING CORPS, commanding its forces on the Western Front in WORLD WAR I. He fought for the establishment of the ROYAL AIR FORCE as a separate service, which was achieved in April 1918. Temperamental by nature, he resigned more than once, but effectively served as chief of the air staff (1919–29), establishing the offensive bomber force which he saw as essential for an independent RAF (*see* WARFARE, AIR). After retiring from the RAF, he was commissioner of the Metropolitan POLICE (1931–5), during which time he dealt toughly with hunger marches and anti-fascist demonstrations. During WORLD WAR II he was a strong advocate of the BOMBING OFFENSIVE against Germany.

Trent, Council of, *see* COUNTER-REFORMATION

Trespass, *see* FELONY

Trespass, Mass, phrase used particularly to describe the collective action taken by some 400 walkers on Kinder Scout, in the Derbys. Peak District, on 24 April 1932. The explosion of interest in rambling and walking in the 1920s and 1930s was often thwarted by the extent of land privately owned for shooting to which access was forbidden. This demonstration and others that followed were of importance in the continuing battle over rights of way and common land, and the establishment of the NATIONAL PARKS provided for much freer public access where previously it had often been denied.

Trial by Battle, or trial by combat, a COMMON LAW method for an aggrieved party to seek retribution for a FELONY, probably introduced to English legal custom by the Normans. It was condemned by GLANVILL as early as 1190. Long obsolete, thanks to the success of the JURY system, it was formally abolished in 1833, after an alarming attempt at revival by a litigant in KING'S BENCH in 1818. *See also* BLOOD FEUD.

Trial by Jury, *see* JURY

Trial by Ordeal, a system of trying disputes at law which relied on the assumption that God has knowledge about human disputes and is prepared to make direct intervention. Some methods required proof of rapid healing after the accused was put into contact with heated iron or water. Another approach was to throw the accused into deep water: immediate sinking was adjudged a proof of innocence, since the pure water was prepared to accept the suspect. Prompt rescue was then both desirable and justified. Trial by ordeal was used in Anglo-Saxon customary law, and survived into COMMON LAW, but its patently arbitrary nature aroused unease; the Church took the lead in undermining it, and in 1215 the Lateran Council banned the participation of clergy. *See also* COMPURGATION; JURY; TRIAL BY BATTLE.

Triangular Trade, term used to describe the trading connections in the 18th century between North America, the British Isles, and the west coast of AFRICA. Cargoes of British manufactured goods, especially small arms and fancy goods from the West Midlands, together with Far Eastern products such as spices, textiles and cowrie shells, were dispatched to West Africa, where they were sold in exchange for SLAVES. In turn Negro slaves were then transported in densely-packed holds from West Africa to the WEST INDIES and mainland North America. Most often by the mid-18th century they were sold for cash or bills, and slave ships returned to England, notably LIVERPOOL and BRISTOL, in ballast. An often entirely separate two-way transatlantic trade of British manufacturers in exchange for colonial products, notably COTTON and SUGAR, existed. The term triangular, denoting an integrated pattern of trade between the three regions, is thus something of a misnomer.

Tribal Hideage A mysterious and much discussed document, it survives in no manuscript earlier than the 11th century, but has the appearance of being an ancient administrative record – possibly a sort of tribute list – dating probably from the 7th or 8th century. It consists of a list of over 30 peoples to each of which is assigned a number of HIDES.

Some of the entries describe easily identifiable peoples and clearly relate to early English kingdoms, whereas others describe smaller groupings, and some cannot be readily located. Thus, 30,000 hides are assigned to the MERCIANS and the ANGLES, 7,000 to the South Saxons (*see* SUSSEX), 7,000 to dwellers in The Wrekin, Staffs., and 600 to the people of Spalding, Lincs. The omission of the NORTHUMBRIANS suggests that the text may belong to the period of Mercian supremacy over southern and central England, although the possibility that it was drawn up in the time of the Northumbrian *BRETWALDAS* cannot be entirely dismissed.

The document is also important as a record of the social groupings that came to England during the ANGLO-SAXON SETTLEMENT and were gradually absorbed into the kingdoms of the HEPTARCHY.

Tribune Group, Labour Party grouping, named after the left-wing weekly, *Tribune*, founded in 1937. In the years after 1945, the group provided a caucus for left-wing opinion in the party advocating further NATIONALIZATION, UNILATERAL nuclear disarmament, and opposition to entry to the EEC (*see* EUROPEAN UNION). Influential members included Aneurin BEVAN, Harold WILSON, Michael FOOT and Richard Crossman. The group remains an active force in the LABOUR PARTY, although its influence over appointments to the party's National Executive and party policy waned during the 1980s.

Tridentine Catholicism, *see* COUNTER-REFORMATION

Triennial Acts 1641, 1664, 1694 The Act of 1641, designed by the LONG PARLIAMENT to prevent a recurrence of the long absence of Parliaments between 1629 and 1640, stipulated that a new parliament be called no later than three years after the dissolution of its predecessor. It incorporated an elaborate procedure for holding elections and convening the House of LORDS and the House of COMMONS should the monarch fail to observe the terms of the statute. In 1664 an amendment provided for parliamentary sessions rather than new elections at least once in three years, but this did not prevent Charles II from ruling without meeting Parliament from 1681–5. A new Act of 1694, passed after WILLIAM III had vetoed an earlier version, further provided that no parliament could last longer than three years (as a means of preventing any recurrence of the long-lived CAVALIER PARLIAMENT of Charles II). The 1694 Triennial Act was superseded in 1716 by the SEPTENNIAL ACT, but during its lifetime no less than 10 general elections were held.

Triers and Ejectors The Triers were a London-based commission set up in March 1654, during the INTERREGNUM, to examine candidates for the PARISH ministry and all other preaching posts. The following Aug., the Ejectors were formed on a county basis to remove unsuitable clergy or schoolmasters. The membership of these bodies was drawn from both laity and clergy, and was recruited broadly from among non-ANGLICAN Protestants. The RESTORATION ended their work. They are commonly linked by historians since the work of both aimed to ensure the political and religious reliability of the clergy.

Trimble, David (1944–), politician. In the 1970s Trimble was prominent in Vanguard, a hard-line Unionist movement which advocated an independent Protestant-dominated Northern Ireland, opposed to power-sharing. In 1975 he was briefly deputy leader of Vanguard, but for the next decade he was relatively politically inactive as he built his career as a law lecturer at the Queen's University, Belfast. Elected ULSTER UNIONIST MP for Upper Bann in 1990, he rapidly emerged as an articulate spokesman for the party. Leader of the UUP since 1995, Trimble signed the Good Friday Agreement in April 1998 (see ULSTER), despite vociferous opposition from Ian PAISLEY and other members of his party, and after its ratification, he became First Minister designate of the Northern Ireland executive. Awarded the Nobel Peace Prize in 1998, his generally moderate leadership was threatened both by challenges in his own party to his continuing commitment to a power-sharing executive, and from the refusal of the IRISH REPUBLICAN ARMY (IRA) to start the processes of decommissioning arms.

Trinidad and Tobago Neighbouring Caribbean islands, Trinidad and Tobago have been united since 1888. Trinidad, discovered by Columbus in 1498, but only settled by Spain from 1783, was captured for Britain in 1797 by Sir Ralph Abercromby. Spain ceded possession under the Treaty of AMIENS 1802. Labour immigration came principally from the East Indies, China and INDIA between 1844 and 1917, frequently through INDENTURED SERVICE. Tobago was colonized by Britain in 1641, although it was occupied by the Dutch between 1658 and 1662, and frequently held by both the Dutch and the

French until British possession was secured under the Treaty of PARIS 1763, confirmed by the Treaty of Amiens. Tobago became a crown colony in 1877. A joint colony from 1888, Trinidad and Tobago became part of the Federation of the West Indies in 1958, with independence in 1962. It became a republic in 1976. Its first prime minister, Dr Eric Williams, was a distinguished historian of the WEST INDIES.

Trinity House, situated on Tower Hill, London. Originally incorporated as a piloting association in 1514, it is principally concerned with the regulation of all matters concerned with navigation in coastal waters. In 1836 it assumed responsibility for the supervision of the nation's lighthouses, and it remains the principal lighting, buoying and pilotage authority in Britain.

Trinoda Necessitas, *see* COMMON BURDENS

Trinovantes, pre-Roman British tribe, whose territory lay in modern Essex and the southern parts of Suffolk. From the 1st century BC, they were involved in a long struggle with their neighbours, the CATUVELLAUNI, during which they invited JULIUS CAESAR to come to their assistance – one cause of his invasions in 55 and 54 BC. Nevertheless, they fell under Catuvellaunian domination during the rule of CUNOBELIN, and in consequence their chief town, COLCHESTER, received the ceremonial entry of the emperor CLAUDIUS at the head of his victorious army in AD 43. The Trinovantes did not submit easily to Roman rule, and great numbers took part in BOUDICCA's revolt. Chelmsford became the capital of the *CIVITAS* of the Trinovantes, but the chief town continued to be Colchester, the Roman provincial capital. *See also* BOROUGH.

Triple Alliance, 1668. After the Treaty of BREDA, the English sought reconciliation with the Dutch because of fear of the growing power of France. In Jan. 1668 an Anglo-Dutch treaty was concluded in which they agreed to mediate between France and Spain in an attempt to end the 'War of Devolution', in which France had already seized the Spanish Netherlands and the Franche-Comte. The alliance became Triple when Sweden joined shortly thereafter, and was formalized by the Treaty of AIX-LA-CHAPELLE. The alliance united the then principal PROTESTANT powers against France. CHARLES II told Louis XIV he regretted the Alliance, and soon after began the negotiations which led to the Treaty of DOVER.

Triple Alliance, 1716/17. An alliance between Britain and France agreed in Sept. 1716 was joined by the United Provinces at the end of the year. This dramatic reversal of a quarter of a century's Anglo-French hostility has been termed a 'Diplomatic Revolution'. It continued formally to structure Anglo-French relations until 1744. Each government was motivated by worries about the stability of its dynasty: the British feared JACOBITE risings; in France a regent ruled for the minor Louis XV. GEORGE I was also keen to keep the French out of the Baltic; the French wanted support for their rivalry with Philip V of Spain. All parties agreed to uphold the UTRECHT settlement, and to aid each other in the face of internal uprisings. The treaty helped to split the WHIGS: TOWNSHEND and WALPOLE disapproved of what they saw as the excessively Hanoverian policies of STANHOPE and Sunderland (*see* SPENCER, CHARLES), and went into opposition in 1717.

Triple Alliance, agreement for mutual support between the three most powerful British TRADE UNIONS – the miners, dockers, and railwaymen – carrying with it a challenge to the authority of the state through the implicit threat of a virtual general strike. Seen as part of the crisis of the LIBERAL government in 1914 when negotiations on the Alliance were started, it was interrupted by the outbreak of WORLD WAR I and the temporary cessation of union militancy. The attempt to put the Alliance into operation in April 1921 broke down on BLACK FRIDAY, when the dockers and railwaymen failed to call sympathetic STRIKES in support of a miners' strike.

Tristan Da Cunha, southern Atlantic volcanic island and British colony, acquired by Britain in 1815 to guard against any French attempts to free Napoleon from ST HELENA. When the principal volcano erupted in 1961, the 264 islanders were evacuated to Britain; almost all subsequently elected to return. Tristan's principal importance has always been as a fishing station and a revictualling point.

Troops Out, slogan used by those, especially on the left in British politics and nationalists in Northern Ireland, who have demanded the withdrawal of British troops from ULSTER following their introduction in 1969. The term is also applied to a general political movement with this aim.

Troubles, name commonly given to the post-1968 terrorist and political upheaval in Northern Ireland (*see* ULSTER).

Troyes, Treaty of, 21 May 1420, the treaty whereby HENRY V married CATHERINE OF VALOIS, daughter of Charles VI, and was made heir to the throne of France. In future, England and France were to be ruled by one person, but it was stipulated that each kingdom would retain its own laws and separate administration. The terms of the treaty reflected not only Henry V's military dominance in northern France, but also the determination of the Burgundian party to punish Charles VI's son – the Dauphin – for his part in the murder of Duke John the Fearless of Burgundy in 1419.

Troyes, Treaty of, 1564, a treaty between England and France, ending the disastrous English military intervention in northern France (1562–4) on behalf of the HUGUENOTS. It effectively killed English hopes of regaining CALAIS.

Truck, payment of workers in goods rather than money. Employer preference for payment in kind, given in the form of coupons or tokens that were exchangeable for goods in shops owned by the employer (called 'tommy shops' by the workers), was an extension of labour discipline beyond the workplace. Workers were often also paid directly in groceries, coal or faulty goods which had to be resold to realize cash. To some extent these forms of payment resulted from a severe shortage of small denomination coins in circulation, especially in the 18th century. But there were abuses and employers stood to gain from the profits of truck shops and overpricing. Workers maintained that the truck system not only gave them inferior goods at inflated prices, but was a practice that was inconsistent with political liberty and political economy. Payment in truck was outlawed in numerous trades and industries by clauses in 18th-century Acts primarily devoted to restricting workers' combinations in those trades. The Truck Act 1831 was the culmination of a long-running campaign for legislation; it prohibited the payment of wages other than in cash but abuses continued and were prevalent in the HUNGRY FORTIES.

Truck Act 1831, *see* TRUCK

Tuberculosis (TB), infectious disease caused by tubercle bacilli, present in western Europe from earliest times. Encouraged by poverty, poor ventilation and overcrowding, it was a major cause of death especially amongst the poor, but claimed victims of all classes (including, for example, EDWARD VI). Estimates of deaths vary, but at least 50,000 people per annum died in England and Wales from the disease in the mid-19th century, more than all other infectious diseases put together. Pulmonary tuberculosis (of the lungs) was the greatest killer. Until World War II, the main cures were rest, sunlight, fresh air and good food provided by sanitoria. The NATIONAL INSURANCE ACT 1911 provided £1.5 million for their provision and by 1930 there were 500 institutions with 25,000 beds. The incidence of the disease was eventually reduced by pasteurization of milk to kill the tubercle bacillus, and the introduction of the BCG vaccine after 1945. The use of X-ray diagnosis and of a combination of antibiotic drugs to kill the bacillus led to its virtual elimination by the 1950s. However, the advent of AIDS, insanitary conditions associated with water disconnections and increased homelessness have led to a rising incidence of TB in the 1990s.

TUC, *see* TRADES UNION CONGRESS

Tudor, Henry, *see* HENRY VII

Tudor Revolution in Government, The, the title of a 1953 book by Sir Geoffrey Elton (1921–94), which argued that Thomas CROMWELL consciously weakened the royal household's role in government and its control of the national treasure, building instead a central bureaucratic administration divided into 'courts' (ministries) and controlled by a new PRIVY COUNCIL.

The thesis was attacked by medievalists – who pointed out that medieval England already had the most complex bureaucracy of any European state – and by Stuart historians, who showed that government finance and policy-making became personalized once more under the early Stuarts. There has been a reassessment of the Tudor court, emphasizing its continuing importance in government – not just in spite of all its showy ceremony, but because of it. Other research has revealed that many Cromwellian reforms in the structure of law courts, finance and LOCAL GOVERNMENT had precedents in the years of Thomas WOLSEY's ascendancy (*see* CHAMBER, ROYAL, AND FINANCE; COURT, ROYAL; STAR CHAMBER).

Nevertheless, historians constantly rediscover the 1530s as a crucial decade in bringing major change in English politics and in central and local government. Moreover, the revolution in the government and theology of the English Church, which was not Elton's prime concern, was launched in the 1530s (*see* REFORMATION PARLIAMENT; ROYAL SUPREMACY).

Tumultuous Petitioning, Act Against, 1661 was intended to prevent petitions from becoming an instrument of organized political dissent, as had been the case in 1640–2. Petitions might be signed by no more than 20 people, unless the subject had been agreed to by the grand JURY at quarter sessions or assizes, or in London by the lord mayor and common council. No more than ten people were to be present at the presentation of the petition.

Tunnage and Poundage, *see* TONNAGE AND POUNDAGE

Turgesius (?–845), Viking chieftain. Along with IVAR THE BONELESS and OLAF THE WHITE, he was one of the most prominent chieftains in the early VIKING raids on Ireland. A 12th-century source credits him not only with the founding of DUBLIN, but also with seeking to conquer all Ireland. Early documents record only his defeat and death at the hands of the king of the UÍ NÉILL.

Turks and Caicos Islands, a group of northern Caribbean islands which continually switched between Spanish, French and British control until becoming part of the BAHAMAS colony in 1766. Annexed to JAMAICA in 1874, the islands became a crown colony in 1962.

Turloch O Connor (Toirrdelbach Ua Conchobair) (*c.*1088–1156), King of Connacht. Installed in 1106 as king in the O Connor kingdom of CONNACHT – which he was to rule for 50 years – by Muirchertach O Brien, by 1114 he was ready to seize the opportunity presented by the collapse of the O Brien high-kingship. Famous as a commander of fleets and builder of CASTLES and bridges, he fought and ruthlessly intrigued his way to predominance. After 1131, when his enemies began to combine more effectively against him, his fortunes fluctuated, and from 1150, he had to recognize the greater power of Muirchertach O mac Lochlainn. Even so, the 1152 elevation of Tuam in Galway to an archbishopric was an acknowledgment of what his long reign had done for the Connacht kingship.

Turnpikes, roads maintained by tolls collected from travellers. From 1663, responsibility for maintaining ROADS in certain regions was sometimes vested in local magistrates by special acts of parliament; from 1706, it became common to vest these powers in nominated trustees. Trustees were allowed to mortgage the proceeds of tolls to pay for road improvements. In the early 18th century, turnpikes sometimes evoked opposition on the grounds that landowners, who would otherwise have had to bear road maintenance costs on the rates, were evading their responsibilities; new penal statutes, passed in response to rioting, increased penalties for attacks on turnpikes. By the 1750s most of the main trunk roads to London, main roads near London, and many important inter-provincial roads had been turnpiked. By the mid-1830s, over 1,000 trusts controlled more than 20,000 miles of roads, collecting tolls worth £1.5m annually; 80 per cent of the nation's roads, however, remained untouched by the trusts. The RAILWAYS attracted away much of their traffic, and destroyed their financial base. Gradually the trusts were liquidated, and responsibility for the public highways was transferred to the local authorities.

Two Acts, 1795. The Treasonable Practices Act, extending the scope of the TREASON laws, and Seditious Meetings Act, limiting freedom to hold public meetings or lectures on political subjects, were directed against the activities of popular RADICAL societies, and passed after GEORGE III's coach was apparently attacked as he went to open Parliament in Oct. 1795 (though the 'popgun' attack may have involved no more than a stone). Moderate and radical reformers temporarily combined to campaign against these so-called 'Gagging Acts'. The Acts made it difficult, but not impossible, for popular radical societies to operate: on the advice of the SOCIETY FOR CONSTITUTIONAL INFORMATION, for example, the LONDON CORRESPONDING SOCIETY reorganized itself into divisions of limited size, so evading the legislation.

Tyburn, the place of public execution in London until it was moved to NEWGATE in 1783. 'Tyburn tree' was a triangular gallows that stood near present-day Marble Arch, at the north-east edge of Hyde Park, which until the late 18th century marked the western end of the built-up area.

'Tyburn tickets' were a certificate given to those who had helped secure convictions for capital offences. Introduced in 1698 and abolished in 1818, they conferred exemption from service in PARISH and ward offices, and commanded a high market price.

Tyler, Wat (?–1381), rebel. His identity is uncertain, but he was undoubtedly of humble origin (he may have been an Essex tiler), yet for a week in June 1381, he dominated English politics. He rose to command the Kentish section of the PEASANTS' REVOLT, led their march on London and then acted as their chief and possibly most radical spokesman in the attempt to extract general concessions from RICHARD II. During a confrontation with the king at Smithfield on 15 June, he was mortally wounded by Mayor Walworth. According to the alleged confession of Jack Straw, Tyler's aim was to become king of Kent. Whatever his intentions, his death was swiftly followed by the collapse of the revolt.

Tyndale, William (?1494–1536), Bible translator. Oxford-educated, he taught in his native Glos. before embarking on the first large-scale English BIBLE translation since the LOLLARDS. His unauthorized initiative quickly earned disapproval and suspicion from the Church hierarchy, recently thrown on the defensive by Luther's revolt, so Tyndale settled in Germany, and in 1525 began printing his work. In 1535, he was arrested by the imperial authorities, and executed near Brussels. His incomplete translation lies behind all subsequent work.

Tynwald, *see* MAN, ISLE OF

Tyrconnell, 3rd Earl of, *see* TALBOT, RICHARD

Tyrone, 1st Earl of, *see* O'NEILL, CON BACACH

Tyrone, 3rd Earl of, *see* O'NEILL, HUGH

U

Uganda, independent COMMONWEALTH state and former British protectorate in east Africa. The territory was opened up by the British East Africa Company after Sir Frederick Lugard's treaties with native rulers in 1890–1. Uganda was declared a British protectorate in June 1894, since the government wished to safeguard the approach to the sources of the River Nile. The rule of native monarchs continued, while in 1955 a full ministerial system was instituted; independence was granted in 1962. During the tyrannical rule of Idi Amin (1971–9), 30,000 Ugandans of Asian origin were expelled and became REFUGEES to the UK.

Uí Néill, the most powerful royal family of early medieval Ireland. They originated in CONNACHT and from there expanded their power during the 5th and early 6th centuries to exercise hegemony over other kings in the northern half of Ireland (*see* TARA; ULAID). The founder of the dynasty's fortunes in the 5th century was Niall Noígiallach ('Niall of the Nine Hostages'). KINGSHIP was usually divided between the northern and southern Uí Néill, and feuds within the family were frequent. Their pre-eminence lasted until the early 11th century, when they were briefly subjugated by BRIAN BORU, king of MUNSTER, and subsequently by other southern Irish kings (*see* DIARMIT MAC MÁEL NA MBÓ).

Ulaid, a people that dominated a region approximating modern Northern Ireland until the mid-5th century. They were then defeated by the UÍ NÉILL and subjugated by them. Thereafter their power was restricted to eastern ULSTER where they retained their independence until the English conquests of the 12th century. The centre of the kingdom lay near ARMAGH. *See also* KINGSHIP.

Ulster, ancient Irish kingdom, and name commonly given to the province of Northern Ireland since its creation in 1920.

The UÍ NÉILL dynasty thrust upwards from CONNACHT to control many of the areas of Ulster at the time of the collapse of the Roman Empire elsewhere in Europe, while ARMAGH was to be a great centre of Irish Christianity from the mid-5th century, possibly connected with the conversion work of St PATRICK; its missionaries were to penetrate into the heart of Europe. Under Uí Néill patronage Armagh became Ireland's most important town. Ulster was also the launching pad for the Gaelic colonization of Scotland at the end of the 5th century (*see* DALRIADA). In the 10th century it was the prey of invading VIKINGS. The eclipse of the Uí Néill from the time of BRIAN BORU onwards led to long years of warfare, and Ulster was taken by surprise in 1177 in the second phase of the English invasion of Ireland.

The English rule of Ulster ended with the Scots invasion of 1315; thereafter Ulster reverted to being the most turbulent and inaccessible part of the island. Its tempestuous Tudor history came to an end with the defeat of the rebels of 1603, the subsequent FLIGHT OF THE EARLS (1607) and the initiative for the PLANTATION of Ulster. This most Catholic of regions became intensely PROTESTANT as Scotsmen, and men appointed by the City of LONDON companies, were given the lands forfeited to the crown. Ulster played its momentous part in the aftermath of the GLORIOUS REVOLUTION, with the long siege of LONDONDERRY and the defeat of the Catholic JAMES II's army at the BOYNE.

Ulster was now strongly Protestant, and was in the 18th and 19th centuries the most industrialized part of Ireland, especially with the linen industry centred on BELFAST. Heavy industry, notably SHIPBUILDING, had also come to Belfast by the later 19th century. Although its agriculture was backward by English standards, the region suffered the least in the POTATO FAMINE and had the lowest levels of emigration in the 19th century. The scene was set for LOYALIST Ulster Protestantism's stand against HOME RULE for Ireland, and the militant advocacy of Randolph CHURCHILL and then Edward Carson. The division of Ireland came in the GOVERNMENT OF IRELAND ACT 1920, legislating for a Belfast parliament for the six counties – Fermanagh, Armagh, Tyrone, Londonderry, Antrim and Down – that were to constitute Northern Ireland. (The other three counties of the ancient Ulster, with their substantial Catholic majority, were included in southern Ireland.) Plans for a devolved southern parliament were overtaken by events: the ANGLO-IRISH WAR and the creation of the IRISH FREE STATE. The BOUNDARY COMMISSION fixed the border between the two new states in 1925.

The new Ulster's politics were heavily determined by fear of southern claims to its territory, enshrined in the 1937 constitution, by sporadic IRA activity across the border and by the large Catholic minority within the borders. The grip of UNIONIST, Protestant rule, dominating the Northern Irish parliament at Stormont and backed up by the paramilitary 'B' specials, with active discrimination against Catholics in housing, jobs and voting, was loosened both by the attempts of Terence O'NEILL to forge better relations with the south and with the CIVIL RIGHTS ASSOCIATION's activism. When civil rights marches turned into riots in 1968 and 1969, British troops were called in, Ulster politics were shattered and the Provisional IRA took advantage of the vacuum to regroup and mount an active terrorist campaign. British attempts at reform in the early 1970s, including anti-discrimination laws and the disbandment of the 'B' Specials, were caught between nationalist terrorism and Loyalist militancy. Internment of suspected terrorists was introduced, and further polarized the situation. The Northern Ireland government was suspended in 1972 and DIRECT RULE from Westminster substituted; attempts in 1974 and 1975–6 to create an executive where Catholics and Protestants shared power were brought down each time by Loyalist strikes. Direct rule and violence have continued; the death toll since the late 1960s passed the 3,000 mark in 1992. A cease-fire in Aug. 1994 followed the Downing Street Declaration of Dec. 1993 between the British and Irish governments, promising political talks to end the 'troubles'.

In 1995 an Anglo-Irish 'framework' document was published and all-party talks resumed in 1997 which established a political structure based on a six-county power-sharing assembly elected on proportional representation with cross-border institutions charged with executive powers. The 'Good Friday' Agreement (April 1998) brokered by the former US senator George Mitchell, embodied this and elections to the Assembly were held in June. The ULSTER UNIONIST PARTY (UUP) emerged as the largest party with its leader David TRIMBLE elected as First Minister designate. Little progress was made to begin the decommissioning of paramilitary arms, a condition of the Assembly's operation, and in Jan. 2000 DIRECT RULE was again imposed from Westminster. However, the often-voiced desire for peace of the majority of the population of Northern Ireland ensures that however fragile such attempts have proved so far, the Northern Irish political parties are obliged to continue to seek a workable solution. *See also* SUNNINGDALE AGREEMENT; ULSTER WORKERS' COUNCIL.

Ulster Custom, tenant right prevailing in ULSTER. It recognized the right of a yearly tenant to remain in occupation so long as a fair rent was paid, and secured for lessees compensation for improvement or disturbance. The IRISH QUESTION in the 19th century in large part revolved around the extension of comparable security of tenure and a right to compensation throughout the country.

Ulster Defence Association (UDA), largest of the Protestant and LOYALIST paramilitary groups in Northern Ireland. It emerged in 1971 as the co-ordinating body for the various 'Defence Associations' which had arisen in response to the activities of the CIVIL RIGHTS ASSOCIATION and the re-emergence of the IRA. The UDA's members have been implicated in many terrorist activities, and its many offshoots have pursued violent tactics; but the UDA remained unproscribed until 1992. Its most significant success was in mobilizing Protestant support to organize the Loyalist strike of 1974 which brought down the power-sharing executive (*see* SUNNINGDALE AGREEMENT; ULSTER WORKERS' COUNCIL).

Ulster Defence Regiment (UDR), part-time regiment set up in ULSTER in 1970 to replace the discredited 'B' SPECIALS, widely regarded as a partisan, pro-Protestant force. The UDR was intended to be non-denominational, but had considerable difficulties in recruiting Catholics in large numbers because of intimidation and persistent attacks by Republican terrorists on UDR members. With a peak strength of almost 9,000, it has played a major part in security operations during the Ulster crisis, suffering almost 200 fatalities. Allegations of UDR involvement in sectarian killings led to its merger with the Royal Irish Regiment in 1992.

Ulster Unionist Party, Protestant LOYALIST party of Northern Ireland which dominated parliamentary and local representation in ULSTER from the creation of a self-governing Northern Ireland in 1921 until the 1970s. The Unionists conventionally took the CONSERVATIVE Whip at Westminster, adding to its voting strength in the Commons. Terence O'NEILL's attempts to achieve a dialogue with the Catholic minority in the 1960s began to provoke an extreme Protestant backlash, leading to the creation of PAISLEY'S breakaway DEMOCRATIC UNIONIST PARTY in 1971. During the 1980s the two unionist parties came closer together to oppose the Anglo-Irish Agreement of 1985 and to represent Protestant interests in negotiations with the British government; both parties resigned their Westminster seats to fight by-elections as a protest against the agreement. The UUP retains the larger share of Northern Irish seats: in the 1997 election it returned 10 MPs to Westminster and in the elections to the Northern Ireland Assembly in June 1998 following the Good Friday Agreement was the largest party, and on 1 July the UUP leader David TRIMBLE was elected as the First Minister designate and has worked to enforce the terms of the Agreement, despite opposition from both Loyalist and Republican groups (see ULSTER).

Ulster Volunteer Force (UVF), Loyalist paramilitary organization raised by Sir Edward Carson in ULSTER in 1912 to resist HOME RULE. The name was revived by Protestant extremists in 1966 for a group designed to counter with violence the activities of the CIVIL RIGHTS movement. It was almost immediately proscribed by Terence O'NEILL, and remains illegal; until 1980, by which time most of its leaders had been gaoled, the UVF was the foremost LOYALIST terrorist group in Northern Ireland, responsible for hundreds of murders.

Ulster Workers' Council (UWC), grouping of Protestant trade unionists which organized the strike of May 1974 that brought down the power-sharing executive set up in the previous Jan. under the SUNNINGDALE AGREEMENT. The UWC attempted a less successful 'constitutional stoppage' in 1977, but has failed to repeat the decisive impact of its actions in 1974.

Ultimogeniture, *see* BOROUGH, ENGLISH

Ultra Secret, The, codename for a secret British codebreaking operation in WORLD WAR II. Before the war the Germans had adopted the Enigma machine, a typewriter-like device, to encode mechanically all radio telegraph transmissions. Believed to be unbreakable, the Engima codes were used by German diplomats and armed forces. Building on work by the Poles and the French, by 1940 the British had devised a primitive electronic computer to break the Enigma codes, partly the work of mathematician Alan Turing. Ultra gave the Allies at least partial understanding of German intentions throughout the war, and together with the Doublecross system played a major part in victory, particularly in the Battle of the ATLANTIC and Operation OVERLORD. Ultra was known only to senior Allied commanders, and was not made public until the 1970s.

Ultramontane Literally 'lying beyond the mountain', i.e. the Alps, it describes the tendency of certain Northern European Catholics to look for leadership in all matters of doctrine and morals to the papacy. Ultramontane hostility to modernism and theological liberalism was an important source of cleavage within the Catholic community in Victorian Britain.

Undertakers, a group of leading Irish politicians, notably the PONSONBY FAMILY, who acted as political managers in the mid-18th century. The name refers to their having undertaken to carry government business through Parliament in return for the disposal of much crown patronage. Until 1767, Irish lords lieutenant were not permanently resident in Ireland, and the undertakers' role was crucial.

Unearned Increment, the economic term applied to the increase in the value of land or building which arose from causes other than the efforts or exertion of the owner. It was a central feature of the 19th-century Liberal-RADICAL critique of aristocratic landownership and an important source of finance for the social reform proposals of the NEW LIBERALISM. It was first brought within the range of taxation in the PEOPLE'S BUDGET (1909).

Unemployed Workmen Act 1905 The Act established distress committees in BOROUGHS and urban districts with populations of not less than 50,000. They were empowered to aid emigration and MIGRATION, and to assist with the provision of temporary work for the UNEMPLOYED. It made little impression upon the unemployment problem and underscored the need for a comprehensive reorganization of the labour market.

Unemployment, being without paid work. The term, although applicable to individuals, is more usually applied to the state of the workforce as a whole, hence, e.g., 10 per cent unemployment – 1 person in 10 in the productive adult labour force being without a job or, more commonly, being registered as seeking work and drawing some state benefit. The level of unemployment has been seen in the 20th century as a crucial measure of the well-being of the economy.

Economists divide unemployment into *voluntary*, for those not wishing to work, and *involuntary*, for those willing to work at the prevailing WAGE rate but who cannot find work. *Frictional* unemployment occurs when the labour market is temporarily out of equilibrium, during the slump period in the TRADE CYCLE; *structural* unemployment refers to long-term disequilibrium, with the decline of a traditional industry, as may be seen in former COAL-mining or SHIPBUILDING districts.

The official definition of unemployment has repeatedly changed, and the sophistication of statistical collection improved, in the course of the 20th century. Unemployment statistics are notoriously unreliable for women within the productive labour force. Official unemployment percentages have varied (with the exception of the artificially low unemployment levels of wartime and conscription) from less than 2 per cent in the early 1960s to over 10 per cent in 1920, the DEPRESSION years of 1930–5, and the period after 1980.

The concept of unemployment has evolved only very gradually over time. It was unknown, at least in the framing of statutes, in the 16th century, when being without work was considered to be voluntary idleness (*see* POOR RELIEF; VAGRANCY). In reality, there was increasing recognition that unemployment could occur structurally in the early modern economy, through the decline of industrial employment in certain regions (*see* OLD DRAPERIES) or pressure of POPULATION, and this was met through, e.g., town work schemes and CORPORATIONS OF THE POOR. Underemployment was endemic in many sectors of the pre-industrial economy. The antagonism against those out of work has continued (reinforced by, e.g., the Victorian gospel of *SELF-HELP*), as has resentment of newcomers, who may be seen as taking work away from local people at times of economic difficulty.

Unemployment Assistance Board Act 1934–5, an Act passed by the NATIONAL GOVERNMENT which rationalized the administration and payment of UNEMPLOYMENT assistance, and which was the cause of serious protests in 1935. Part 1 of the Act, passed in 1934, set up an Unemployment Assistance Board to take over payments to the unemployed. Part 2, which followed early in 1935, implemented new relief scales, which caused widespread demonstrations and disorder when it was discovered that payments were sometimes lower than before, contrary to what had been promised. After considerable uproar, the government was forced to issue a standstill order guaranteeing existing levels of benefit and phasing in its reform more gradually.

Unfederated Malay States, *see* FEDERATED AND UNFEDERATED MALAY STATES

Unification, English The unification of the English under a single king took place in the 10th century. The chief cause was the VIKINGS, whose conquests in the 9th century destroyed all English kingdoms except WESSEX, and whose menacing presence in the 10th influenced the kings of Wessex to undertake the conquest of the North. The idea of unity was first given written expression by BEDE and appears as an occasional possibility during the 8th-century hegemony of the kings of MERCIA. The decisive moment came in the 880s when ALFRED THE GREAT proclaimed himself king of all the English not under Danish rule, a status that his successors used to justify their assimilation of former kingdoms.

Unity was obviously not pre-ordained and, in the 10th century, was not very secure. First achieved under King ATHELSTAN from 927, it was temporarily destroyed in the reigns of his brothers EDMUND and EADRED by a resurgence of the Scandinavian kingdom of YORK under OLAF GUTHRICSSON, OLAF SIHTRICSSON and ERIC BLOODAXE. The kingdom of the English was partitioned between EADWIG and EDGAR during the period 957–9, and again between CNUT and EDMUND IRONSIDE for a short time during 1016; as late as the time of EDWARD THE CONFESSOR, the title 'King of the Angles and Saxons' was still sometimes used. The frontier with the kingdom of the Scots was not defined until the 13th century.

Uniformity, Act of, 1662 It replaced the synonymous Act of 1559 (*see* ELIZABETHAN SETTLEMENT), and set the doctrinal and liturgical character of the RESTORATION Church. It required all clergy to declare their consent to everything in the Book of Common Prayer, to renounce the SOLEMN LEAGUE AND COVENANT, to be ordained according to the rites of the Church of England, and to subscribe to all its doctrinal articles. It expressed the wishes of the more intolerant ANGLICANS in the Commons, though votes on some clauses were only very narrowly won. Clarendon (*see* HYDE, EDWARD) was unhappy with the Act, but SHELDON would not countenance concessions. The Act led to the ejection of 960 ministers (*see* EJECTED CLERGY).

Unilateral Declaration of Independence (UDI), *see* RHODESIA, SOUTHERN

Unilateralism, belief in the need for one-sided cuts in armaments, in particular NUCLEAR WEAPONS, to encourage disarmament, as opposed to MULTILATERALISM. From the 1950s onwards, unilateralism was strongly supported within the CAMPAIGN FOR NUCLEAR DISARMAMENT (CND) and caused serious splits within the LABOUR PARTY. The unilateralists won the support of the Labour Party conference in 1960 against the opposition of the Labour leader GAITSKELL, but the decision was reversed in subsequent years. Unilateralist sentiment remained strong, however, and the Labour Party adopted a unilateral manifesto in the 1983 and 1987 general elections, but abandoned it thereafter, having become convinced that it was a fatal electoral liability. The issue has lost some of its potency with the ending of the COLD WAR.

Union (Britain and Ireland), Act of, 1800 Legislative union between Britain and Ireland was a recurrent talking point in the 18th century. Some British statesmen were particularly uneasy with the situation that prevailed after the repeal of POYNINGS' LAW in 1782, and the IRISH REBELLION of 1798 persuaded many of the urgency of gaining effective control. It was also increasingly felt to be unjust to limit Catholics' political rights – but impossible to allow them to dominate the Irish PARLIAMENT. However, if the Irish were to return MPs to the British Parliament, Catholics could be at once emancipated and contained (*see* CATHOLIC EMANCIPATION).

Although proposals to this effect were widely opposed within IRELAND, such an Act came into effect on 1 Jan. 1801. Some of the smaller boroughs were disfranchised to ensure that Ireland had no more than 100 MPs. The Irish, like the Scots, were allowed to send only representative peers (those chosen by their fellow peers) to the LORDS, but unlike the Scots, these sat for life; in addition, four Irish bishops sat in the Lords by rotation. The Churches of England and Ireland were also united until the Irish Church's disestablishment in 1869.

Union (England and Scotland), Act of, 1707 The return of traditional government at the RESTORATION brought Anglo-Scottish constitutional relations back to the state in which they had existed before the CIVIL WARS: although the crowns were united, the kingdoms each had their own PRIVY COUNCILS, PARLIAMENTS, Churches and laws.

The JUNTO WHIGS were impelled to consider union because of their concern to secure the succession: passage of the Scottish Act of SETTLEMENT 1704 had raised the spectre of a separate Scottish settlement of the crown upon the Stuart line at the death of ANNE. On the Scottish side, the prospect of being brought within the scope of the NAVIGATION LAWS, and given free access to England's trading system, was a key consideration. However, JACOBITES and PRESBYTERIANS each feared that a union would weaken their position, and some believed that the removal of trade barriers would disadvantage Scotland. In consequence there was both popular opposition to union and hard battles in the Scottish parliament.

The 1707 Act as finally agreed eliminated the separate Scottish Parliament and converted the English into a British Parliament; henceforth Scots were to return MPs to Westminster and Scottish representative peers would be summoned to the LORDS. The Scots were compensated for taking on part of the English national debt by the payment of the EQUIVALENT. They retained their own laws and their own religious establishment, but the Scottish Privy Council was abolished by an Act of 1708, which grew out of a struggle for power between groups within Scotland; its passage was a victory for the SQUADRONE.

Union Movement, *see* MOSLEY, SIR OSWALD

Union of Wales and England A tidying-up of the administrative confusion of late medieval Wales was initiated by Thomas CROMWELL and continued after his fall. Acts of Parliament in 1536 and 1543 were the most important elements of a union with England that abolished the MARCHER LORDSHIPS and set up counties and JUSTICES OF THE PEACE on the English model – a process called the 'shiring of Wales'. The COUNCIL IN THE MARCHES OF WALES was retained and its powers enhanced. English was made the language of administration. For better or worse, the union endures. *See also* GREAT SESSIONS; RHUDDLAN, STATUTE OF; WALES, PRINCE OF.

Unionist, in the 19th and early 20th centuries a supporter of the constitutional link between Ireland and Great Britain formed by the Act of UNION of 1800. Unionists were usually, but not exclusively, Protestants. Adopted by the opponents of HOME RULE and part of political nomenclature, as in LIBERAL UNIONIST and the Conservative and Unionist Party, it was once the term frequently employed as a general party appellation for the CONSERVATIVES. After the creation of the IRISH FREE STATE in 1922, the term was used to describe supporters of the link between Northern Ireland and Britain, as in the ULSTER UNIONIST PARTY and more generally.

Unitarians, Christian groups who deny the Trinity, and usually the divinity of Christ. Some 16th-century ANABAPTISTS who felt the Trinity was an unscriptural doctrine were burned for this. From the 17th century, many intellectual Christians found Trinitarian belief increasingly difficult to swallow, attracting the label 'Socinian' – from two 16th-century Italian Unitarians (uncle and nephew) called Sozzini or Sozini (Socinus in Latin) – which was often used indiscriminately to abuse undogmatic Christians. During the 18th century, quite a number of well-educated DISSENTER congregations, especially PRESBYTERIANS, became Unitarian, causing many disputes about chapel ownership in the following century. Unitarianism, like QUAKERism, was an important link between early FACTORY owners and industrialists, and in the first half of the 19th century the denomination looked set to become the readiest alternative to the Established Church, especially in northern England.

United Company, *see* EAST INDIA COMPANY

United Irishmen The United Irish Society was formed in 1791 as one of the most advanced reform associations. Initially led by Protestant merchants and professionals from Belfast and Dublin, its members included both Protestants and Catholics. Later it became militantly anti-English and republican, and in 1795 was driven underground. During 1795–8 United Irishmen helped to organize the politically disaffected in England, spawning the 'United Englishmen'; they negotiated for foreign military support, but collapsed as an organized movement after the suppression of the IRISH REBELLION of 1798. The 1798 Banishment Act excluded them from Ireland; thenceforth they operated in exile in England, France and Hamburg. Many others left for America.

United Methodist Church, *see* METHODISM

United Methodist Free Churches, *see* METHODISM

United Nations, international organization intended to ensure world peace and security. Plans for the new organization were first formulated by the wartime Allies at Moscow in Oct. 1943. The UN was intended as a more effective replacement for the failed LEAGUE OF NATIONS. Following detailed talks at the Dumbarton Oaks Conference in 1944, the UN was founded at a conference at San Francisco, April–June 1945. Fifty nations signed the UN Charter. The organization, consisting of a General Assembly of all members and an inner core in a Security Council, was and is based in New York. The United States, Soviet Union, Nationalist China (replaced by the People's Republic of China in 1971), Britain and France made up the permanent membership of the Security Council, each with a right of veto. The Security Council had, in theory, wide powers to act in the name of world order, but in fact, the UN has for much of its existence been rendered largely ineffective by the stalemate of the COLD WAR. It fell to successive secretary-generals to attempt to facilitate delicate international diplomacy. But on occasions the UN did authorize the use of force, as in 1950 when a Soviet boycott enabled the other members to vote for UN action in the KOREAN WAR. Following the ending of the Cold War, the UN has become more active – and more criticized – for its peacekeeping role in areas of international tension. It has also engaged in a wide range of activities through its associated organizations, such as the UN High Commission for Refugees and the International Court of Justice. There is increasing pressure for Britain to surrender its permanent seat on the Security Council in recognition of its diminished world status.

United Reformed Church, *see* CONGREGATIONALISTS; PRESBYTERIANISM

United Society for the Propagation of the Gospel, *see* MISSIONARY SOCIETIES

United Ulster Unionist Council (UUUC), umbrella organization of UNIONIST parties, including Ian PAISLEY'S DEMOCRATIC UNIONIST PARTY, which opposed the setting up of the power-sharing executive under Brian Faulkner in Jan. 1974 (*see* SUNNINGDALE AGREEMENT). In the Feb. 1974 general election, UUUC candidates won 11 of the 12 Northern Irish seats, encouraging the extra-parliamentary actions of the ULSTER WORKERS' COUNCIL in calling the strike in May 1974 which brought down the power-sharing executive. The UUUC survived until 1977, when it collapsed amid disagreements about a further wave of strikes.

Universities The history of universities takes a very different path in each of the four parts of the British Isles. England was monopolized by OXFORD and CAMBRIDGE down to the 19th century, despite abortive attempts to found universities at LONDON by Sir Thomas GRESHAM (in his will of 1575) and at DURHAM by Oliver CROMWELL (1657). Wales established institutions in parallel with the 19th-century expansion of English higher education.

Ireland's medieval political situation was not conducive to university foundation, and after the REFORMATION, matters were complicated by England's efforts to impose its culture on Ireland and eliminate Roman CATHOLICISM. These aims lay behind the foundation of Trinity College, DUBLIN – to this day an independent university college. In the 19th century, government efforts to establish non-denominational higher education in Ireland were hampered by the suspicions of both the Roman Catholic Church and Trinity College, while until the late 1960s, the Catholic hierarchy remained hostile to the PROTESTANT foundation of Trinity.

In Scotland, a university system was established in the 15th century, looking to the Continental model rather than the English. During the Scottish Reformation, the universities were quickly taken over by the newly established Protestant Church, and retain close links in their theological training with the CHURCH OF SCOTLAND.

In the 20th century, higher education has continued to expand and institutions have proliferated throughout the British Isles (*see* NEW UNIVERSITIES). During 1992 and 1993, polytechnic institutions and other colleges took the opportunity afforded by government legislation to assume university status.

University Test Acts 1871 A meritocratic measure, typical of GLADSTONIAN LIBERALISM, it broke the ANGLICAN monopoly on teaching posts at the universities of OXFORD and CAMBRIDGE and opened the door of opportunity to men of all creeds.

Urban District Councils (UDCs), *see* DISTRICT AND PARISH COUNCILS ACT 1894

Urban Renaissance, a term used by historians to characterize the revitalization of urban culture in the late 17th and 18th centuries. Provincial capitals and some other larger TOWNS found a new role for themselves as providers of social amenities to the GENTRY and moneyed classes. There was much new building, often in a fashionable PALLADIAN or NEO-CLASSICAL style, and improvements in water supply, paving and street lighting. Characteristic features of the new urban scene included assembly rooms, COFFEE HOUSES, LIBRARIES, bowling greens, NEWSPAPERS, concerts and THEATRES.

Use, in law, a trust. From the 14th century, uses became a favourite English device to bequeath land freely and secondarily to avoid the crown's rights over TENANTS-IN-CHIEF. Land was conveyed to trustees ('feoffees to uses') for the benefit of the real owner, the *cestuy que use*; new appointments could ensure that the body of trustees continued in existence, and therefore the crown's feudal rights ('incidents') were never due. Alarmed at the financial loss, HENRY VIII sponsored a legal attack that culminated in the Statute of Uses (1536), which transferred title in the land from the feoffees to the *cestuy que use*. Subsequent unrest fuelled the PILGRIMAGE OF GRACE, and in 1540, the crown compromised in the Statute of Wills, which conferred for the first time the legal power to dispose of freeholds by WILL (save for one-third of any land held by KNIGHT SERVICE) (*see* PRIMOGENITURE).

A *liturgical use* is the term used for local traditions in Christian worship, often named after the cathedral that developed them. *See also* OSMUND OF SALISBURY; SALISBURY.

Usk, Gwent. The discovery of a pre-AD 54 Roman fort at Usk has added an important dimension to our knowledge of the extent of the early Roman advance into Wales. The excavation there has revealed an extensive fortress, the function of which would later have been taken over by the LEGIONARY FORTRESS at CAERLEON.

Usk, Adam, *see* ADAM OF USK

Utilitarianism, ethical system based upon the principle of morality and society being organized to secure the greatest happiness for the greatest number, and defining the rightness of actions in terms of their contribution to the general happiness, associated particularly with Jeremy BENTHAM. The doctrine of social usefulness became one of the underpinnings of society and reform in the first half of the 19th century, and saw its practical application in the design of prisons and other public institutions, the framing of the New POOR LAW and SANITARY REFORM under Edwin Chadwick, and the collection of statistics with which to determine how best to reform the world. The doctrine of utilitarianism was mocked in Dickens' *Hard Times* (1854), with Thomas Gradgrind portrayed as a deeply misguided utilitarian, and was redefined by J. S. MILL in an essay of 1863, which maintained that pleasures differ in quality as well as in quantity.

Utrecht, Peace of, April, July 1713. Treaties between Britain and France on the one hand, Spain on the other, concluded British involvement in the War of the SPANISH SUCCESSION, and marked the successful containment of French ambition. (France and the Empire did not make peace until 1714, at Rastatt.) The Treaties provided that the Spanish inheritance should be divided. The PROTESTANT SUCCESSION in Britain was secured and the Pretender (*see* STUART, JAMES EDWARD) compelled to leave France. Britain received NEWFOUNDLAND, Acadia (NOVA SCOTIA), ST KITTS and the Hudson's Bay territory from France, and Minorca and GIBRALTAR from Spain. By the *ASIENTO des negros*, Spain transferred the contract for the SLAVE TRADE from France to England. Philip V was recognized as king of Spain and the Emperor Charles was compensated for the disappointment of his hopes with Milan, Naples, Sardinia and the Austrian Netherlands. The treaty was the first major international treaty to be composed in

French (rather than Latin), and to invoke the concept of the BALANCE OF POWER. Articles endorsing reciprocal 'most favoured nation' arrangements between Britain and France were defeated in the COMMONS by a combination of WHIGS and dissident TORIES; legal trade between the two countries was to run at a very low ebb until the EDEN TREATY of 1786.

Utrecht, Treaty of, 1474, *see* HANSEATIC LEAGUE

UVF, *see* ULSTER VOLUNTEER FORCE

V

V Bomber Force, aircraft which provided the ROYAL AIR FORCE's strike force of strategic nuclear bombers, the Valiants, Victors and Vulcans, during the 1950s and 1960s. The fleet of bombers was recognized as increasingly vulnerable to missile attacks and was replaced as the nuclear strike force by the POLARIS submarines, secured under the NASSAU AGREEMENT of 1962.

V-Weapons, from *Vergeltungswaffe* ('retaliation weapons'), new German weapons used chiefly against the British HOME FRONT after the D-DAY landings in WORLD WAR II. The 'V-1' was a small pilotless jet aircraft with a range of 130 miles, carrying an explosive warhead of two-thirds of a ton, first used in June 1944. About 16,000 were fired, over a quarter at northern France and Holland after Allied liberation and the rest at Britain. Nearly half were shot down, but the remainder caused over 45,000 casualties. The 'V-2', first launched in Sept. 1944 with a range of 200 miles and a payload of one ton of explosive, was impossible to intercept. About 2,000 were fired at Britain causing 9,000 casualties. The 'V-3' was a giant gun with a range of 175 miles, of which the only complete example, built into a hillside near Calais, was overrun by Allied troops before its completion.

Vaccination, term coined by Edward Jenner (from the Latin for 'cow': *vacca*) in 1798 to describe his new process of protection against smallpox through INOCULATION with cowpox. Cowpox, a mild disease of cows, provides humans with immunity to the closely related – and much more serious – smallpox. Free provision was made available from 1840 and it was made compulsory for all school-age children in 1853. The last serious smallpox epidemic in Britain occurred in 1871–2. Compulsory vaccination ended in 1948, and smallpox was eradicated from the globe in 1979. 'Vaccination' has become a generic term for procedures that provide immunity to various diseases such as rabies, diphtheria, poliomyelitis and TUBERCULOSIS.

Vacomagi, a Celtic tribe recorded in the 1st century AD as living south of the Moray Firth, to the north-east of modern Aberdeen. Little is known about them; in the 3rd and 4th centuries, they were absorbed into the tribal grouping known as the PICTS.

Vagrancy In 1536, the Beggars' Act was the first attempt to regulate the raising of money to relieve vagrants, with the provision that sturdy beggars should be put to work. The most draconian of all pieces of legislation was the 1547 Act introducing SLAVERY for persistent vagrancy, which proved unworkable and was quickly repealed, but showed the desperation of authorities in the face of a growing phenomenon they could not understand. Vagrancy provisions continued to be enforced through the 16th century, in the face of a growing tide; vagrants were apprehended if they begged without licence or refused work, and were frequently whipped, sometimes branded, and returned to their place of birth. There was a general fear of vagrants in the years around 1600, partly exaggerated by semi-imaginative literature about this underworld. Vagrancy legislation continued to be separate from the ordinary POOR LAW and SETTLEMENT provisions, and the evidence is that the amount of vagrancy grew markedly in the 18th and early 19th centuries with the growth of POPULATION and the greater chance of economic dislocation. The Irish were always heavily represented, both before the POTATO FAMINE and after.

Vagrants were supposed to be given overnight accommodation and to do hard work in return in the WORKHOUSES of the New POOR LAW; and the tramp became an object of interest and curiosity to social investigators like Henry Mayhew (1812–87). The 19th-century image of the vagrant gradually turned from one of fear to a mixture of envy, humour and disdain – they were the 'gentlemen of the road'. In the later 20th century the word vagrant is less used: the homeless, however, are unfortunately still present.

Valor Ecclesiasticus, an inventory of ecclesiastical lands made by commissioners in 1534–5 to facilitate the collection of taxes newly due to the CROWN. It is as useful to historians as it was to HENRY VIII in his confiscation of Church wealth.

Van Diemen's Land, *see* TASMANIA

Vanuatu, formerly the New Hebrides, an Anglo-French condominium island territory in the South Pacific. The British and French were both making significant inroads into the New Hebrides and other islands by the later 19th century. The fears of AUSTRALIA were aroused, and ultimately by 1878 Britain and France jointly agreed not to annex the islands without consulting one another. A joint naval commission was established in 1878, and in 1906 – following increasing German interest in the region – a condominium was established, formally proclaimed in 1926. The islands were used as a base for the American campaign in the SOLOMON ISLANDS in WORLD WAR II. Freedom and, finally, independence (1981) was only attained after a sustained struggle against stiff French opposition.

Variolation, *see* INOCULATION

Vauxhall, South London 'pleasure grounds' of late 17th to early 19th centuries. In the 1660s, Sir Samuel Morland, owner of a south London estate, opened his grounds to the public under the name of Spring Garden. In the late 1720s a new proprietor further developed the area, providing formal tree-lined gravel walks, statues, buildings and paintings. From the 1730s, a high entrance fee of a shilling was charged. Vauxhall, however, continued to have a rowdier reputation than its rival RANELAGH. The gardens were partly redesigned in 1810–11, and in 1859 the land was sold and built over. In its heyday Vauxhall was the premier pleasure grounds of 18th-century London.

Vegetarianism, the theory that vegetables are the only proper food for human beings and supply all the nutrients that are necessary for a healthy existence. A Vegetarian Society was founded in London in 1847, and vegetarian restaurants established across the country with some success. Although vegetarianism was sometimes identified with cranks, faddists and political dissidents, it has become increasingly common in the latter half of the 20th century to decline to eat animals. It appears to remain a subject in search of a historian.

Venerable Bede, *see* BEDE, ST

Venereal Disease (VD), infectious disease which is contracted through sexual intercourse. Historically the principal sexually transmitted diseases have been syphilis, gonorrhoea and chancroid, the first two of which may also be transmitted to babies during pregnancy or delivery. In the 20th century it has come to be realized that there are many more sexually transmissible diseases, from genital herpes to AIDS, for which sexual contact may be the most important but not the sole means of infection, and the term venereal disease has passed out of general medical use. The 20th century has also seen the effective treatment and partial conquest of some of these diseases, notably syphilis, especially with the introduction of sulphonamide drugs from the late 1930s.

The widespread introduction of syphilis – traditionally supposed to have come from the NEW WORLD, although that belief has come to be questioned – traumatized late 15th- and early 16th-century Europe, and fears of syphilis and its inherited characteristics have been a recurring theme, notably in late 19th-century Europe and in the USA in the inter-war years. Condoms, and other artificial forms of BIRTH CONTROL, were frequently originally intended to guard against disease. Sexually transmitted diseases have always been particularly associated with PROSTITUTES and their clients, of whom James Boswell is probably the most noted Georgian example, from the evidence of his sexually explicit private diaries. The CONTAGIOUS

DISEASES ACTS were a mid-Victorian response to the widespread incidence of venereal disease among troops, and the campaign for their repeal was a watershed both in feminist political agitation and in the definition of sexual double standards. *See also* EPIDEMICS.

Venicomes, a tribe recorded in the 1st century AD as living in the region of modern Fife and Strathmore. They were probably of Celtic origin and, in the 3rd and 4th centuries, were absorbed into the larger tribal grouping known as the PICTS.

Venner's Rising, Jan. 1661, radical MILLENARIAN rebellion following the RESTORATION. The wine cooper James Venner was a FIFTH MONARCHIST, believing that the Godly Saints must seize civil power so that Christ might return. On 6 Jan. 1661, he led a group of about 50 to recover the regicides' heads on display at Westminster Hall and on London Bridge. Two days' skirmishing with the MILITIA led to about 20 losses on each side; Venner and 16 others were executed for murder and high treason on 19 Jan. Although less radical DISSENTERS condemned the uprising, the affair precipitated a variety of repressive moves. About 100 Fifth Monarchists and 4,000 QUAKERS were imprisoned, and the crown argued that the incident demonstrated the need for a permanent military force, and for new legislation restricting Dissenting activity. These needs were met in part by the establishment of the GUARDS and subsequently by the passage of the CLARENDON CODE.

Vere, Robert de, *see* DE VERE, ROBERT

Vermuyden, Cornelius, *see* FEN DRAINAGE

Vernacular Buildings, native, local or regional style of building, usually devoid of conscious architectural style, employing traditional techniques of construction and commonly available materials. Until the 19th century, all but the most substantial structures – grand houses, churches and public buildings – would usually be considered vernacular, but the 19th-century introduction of mass-produced or readily transported materials, such as tiles and Welsh slates, considerably reduced local variability in buildings. There have been self-conscious attempts to incorporate vernacular building methods and features into architectural design, e.g. in the ARTS AND CRAFTS movement and some works by Edwin Lutyens, and latterly into volume house-building and supermarket design. Recognition of the uniqueness and local importance of vernacular buildings has been an important element in building CONSERVATION.

Verneuil, Battle of, 17 Aug. 1424, victory in Normandy for JOHN OF LANCASTER, Duke of Bedford, over a French counter-attacking force. It consolidated HENRY V's conquest of Normandy, and marked a high point of English success in the HUNDRED YEARS WAR.

Verona, Congress of, 1822, one of the periodic meetings provided for by the Congress of VIENNA (1815). By the time the diplomats assembled, the collaboration between Great Britain and the powers of the HOLY ALLIANCE (Russia, Prussia and Austria) had broken down. CANNING's refusal to approve French military intervention in defence of the reactionary Spanish monarch, Ferdinand VII, and his protest against the moral support which the continental powers were willing to extend to France, signified the end of British participation in the congress system. The attempt to regulate international relations, embodied in the Congress of Vienna and the successor Congresses of AIX-LA-CHAPELLE, and LAIBACH, had collapsed.

Versailles, Peace of, 3 Sept. 1783, ended the War of AMERICAN INDEPENDENCE. The preliminaries were signed with America in Nov. 1782, and with France and Spain in Jan. 1783, but the definitive treaty only later. Its terms, particularly its failure to secure property confiscated from American loyalists, were censured in Parliament, as were Shelburne's (*see* PETTY, WILLIAM) plans for Anglo-American commercial co-operation. The British recognized American independence and renounced the north-west territory. European powers mutually restored captured territories. In Africa, the French were to have Senegal and the British the Gambia river as trading bases. In exchange for the return of Trincomalee in CEYLON and other conquests, the Dutch gave the British Negapatam near Madras, and freedom of navigation among the Dutch spice islands. In return for the recovery of WEST INDIAN islands, the British gave Minorca and Florida (but not GIBRALTAR) to Spain, and TOBAGO and fishing rights off the coast of NEWFOUNDLAND to France. French hopes of reversing the 1763 Treaty of PARIS had not been realized.

Versailles, Treaty of, 28 June 1919, *see* PARIS PEACE CONFERENCE

Verulamium (St Albans, Herts.), the chief centre of the territory of the CATUVELLAUNI, which was taken over by the Romans and made capital of the Catuvellaunan *CIVITAS*. It appears to have been especially favoured by the Romans, since archaeological evidence has shown substantial signs of Roman-style development before its destruction during BOUDICCA's rebellion in AD 61; it thereafter developed all the normal features of a Roman town. The record of the 5th-century visit by GERMANUS of Auxerre shows that the town remained prosperous for some time after the Romans' departure; its medieval revival owed a great deal to the cult that developed around the martyrdom of St ALBAN (which also indicates the existence of an early Christian community).

Verulam, 1st Baron, *see* BACON, FRANCIS

Vestiarian Controversies, REFORMATION arguments about whether clergy should adopt distinctive dress in public or in worship – important because separate dress implied a separate clerical order, which most PROTESTANTS wished to deny. John Hooper made an unsuccessful stand on the issue in 1550–1, and there was fresh trouble in 1564–6, when ELIZABETH I determined to make the clergy conform to dress requirements. Typically, she sidestepped unpopularity by leaving Archbishop PARKER to work out how to do this: his attempt to do her bidding by issuing a personal order (his 'advertisements') met with only partial success. His hardline opponents were the first to be called PURITANS.

Vexillation Fortresses, structures that were usually approximately half the size of LEGIONARY FORTRESSES, and which played a key role in the ROMAN CONQUEST of Britain. Archaeological excavation suggests that the majority date from between AD 43 and 77, and their location on the main ROADS leading westwards and northwards indicates a flexible role in the process of expansion and conquest.

Vicar, *see* RECTOR

Vice Society, an Anglican society founded in 1802 to encourage the prosecution of people indulging in such vices as swearing, profanation of the Sabbath, publication of blasphemous, licentious or obscene books and prints, selling by false weights and measures, the keeping of brothels or disorderly houses, the running of illegal lotteries, and cruelty to animals. The subscriptions of a lesser-gentry and middle-class membership offset the costs of private prosecutions. It was criticized for operating a social double standard, usurping the role of authority, and encouraging religious fanaticism. Following the NAPOLEONIC WARS, it became involved in the attempt to suppress RADICALISM, launching a series of well-publicized prosecutions for blasphemy against Thomas Carlyle (1795–1881) and others. In the Victorian period its wider concerns largely dropped away and it became increasingly preoccupied with literary decency, merging with the National Vigilance Association in 1886. *See also* REFORMATION OF MANNERS MOVEMENT.

Vice-Gerency, powers of the ROYAL SUPREMACY in the Church deputed by HENRY VIII to Thomas CROMWELL as vice-gerent in spirituals from 1535-40. Cromwell held his own national VISITATION and was developing a bureaucracy when he died, but he had no successors. Not to be misspelled as 'vice-regency'.

Victoria (1819–1901), Queen of Great Britain and Ireland (1837–1901) and Empress of India (1877–1901). The longest-reigning monarch in British history, Victoria was born on 24 May 1819, the only child of GEORGE III's fourth son, the Duke of Kent, and Princess Victoria of Saxe-Coburg-Gotha. Her father died when she was eight months old and on the death of her uncle, WILLIAM IV, in 1837, she ascended the throne at the age of 18.

Her friend and mentor Lord Melbourne (*see* LAMB, WILLIAM), the WHIG prime minister, was a fatherly guiding influence in the early years of her reign, but in 1840 she married her first cousin Prince ALBERT of Saxe-Coburg-Gotha and for the next 20 years they were inseparable in domestic, as in constitutional, matters. Victoria bore nine children, and her descendants were to succeed to the thrones of Germany, Russia, Sweden, Denmark, Spain, Greece, Romania and Yugoslavia, as well as Britain. Her attitude to foreign policy was coloured by concern for the dynasties into which her children had married, especially the German royal families, and this led to conflict with her ministers on several occasions.

Victoria and Albert's ideal of a constitutional monarchy that transcended transient political parties but exerted an independent influence on the nation was realized to a considerable extent during the years 1846–59, when no single party could command an overall majority in the House of COMMONS. The Queen thus determined the composition of several ministries; she was successful in ensuring the dismissal of her errant foreign secretary Palmerston (*see* TEMPLE, HENRY) in 1851, and Aberdeen (*see* GORDON, GEORGE) and Rosebery (*see* PRIMROSE, ARCHIBALD) were effectively her personal appointments.

When Albert died from typhoid fever in Dec. 1861, Victoria's overwhelming grief made her almost entirely withdraw from public life for more than a decade, confining her duties to advising her ministers (largely by post) and unveiling a series of memorials to her departed husband. This perceived dereliction of public duty – the queen had refused to open Parliament personally on more than seven occasions since Albert's death – coupled with unsubstantiated rumours about her relationship with her Scottish ghillie, John Brown, led to increasing criticism, but by the late 1870s the prime minister DISRAELI had coaxed her back into public view. Although she described herself as a liberal and was an advocate of constitutional government, FREE TRADE and religious tolerance, Victoria's greatest rapport – both personal and political – was with the CONSERVATIVE Disraeli, who made her Empress of INDIA in 1877, rather than the LIBERAL leader GLADSTONE, whose policies, particularly on Irish HOME RULE, she frequently opposed.

In the last decades of her life, Victoria resumed her political and constitutional interest with vigour, to the detriment of her somewhat wayward son and heir to the throne, who later became EDWARD VII and who was denied access to many vital state papers until 1892. The queen herself was indefatigable in studying voluminous numbers of state papers and corresponding with her ministers, with whom she insisted on frequent consultation. By the time of her national jubilees – Golden in 1887 and Diamond in 1897 – her popularity was assured and the almost entirely ceremonial role of the British monarchy firmly established.

When Victoria died at Osborne House on the Isle of Wight, on 22 Jan. 1901, she was the matriarch of European royalty, had transformed the standing of the monarchy, and had made it the single most obvious link holding together the world's largest empire – by the 1890s, one person in four on earth was a subject of Queen Victoria. Her name is synonymous with the 19th century in style as in achievement.

Victoria After initial failure to settle this region of AUSTRALIA with convicts in 1803, farmers moved in from NEW SOUTH WALES and TASMANIA after 1820. Separate colonial status came in 1851. The GOLD RUSH immediately followed, with depression in its wake. Economic boom and bust ensued, mainly in agriculture; Victoria established a reputation for arch-conservatism.

Vienna, Congress of, 1815, assembled after the defeat of Napoleon to restore order to a Continent shaken by war and revolution. Under the guiding principle of legitimacy, the old dynasties in France, Spain, Naples, the Papal States and the Italian duchies were restored. To prevent a renewal of French aggression, Belgium was merged with Holland to form the Kingdom of the Netherlands; Prussia was given territory on the Rhine; and Genoa assimilated to Piedmont. Napoleon's Confederation of the Rhine was replaced by a German Confederation under Austrian leadership; Prussia received Swedish Pomerania and parts of Saxony. Russian control of Finland and Bessarabia was recognized, as was Poland's status as a province of the Russian Empire shortly afterwards. Norway was transferred from Denmark to Sweden. France retained her frontiers of 1790 and had to endure an army of occupation until an indemnity of 700 million francs was paid. Britain, with few territorial ambitions in Europe, gained additional colonies and secured permanent control over various wartime seizures. Her acquisitions included the Cape of Good Hope, CEYLON, MAURITIUS, GUIANA, TRINIDAD, TOBAGO, MALTA, and HELIGOLAND.

Apart from the allocation of territory and redrawing of frontiers, the victorious powers sought to maintain peace by combined action, establishing a Concert of Europe. Britain, Russia, Prussia and Austria bound themselves together in the QUADRUPLE ALLIANCE and undertook to confer regularly on the international situation and the best means of preserving the peace – the famous congress system. For all its defects, the territorial settlement agreed at Vienna lasted for 40 years.

Vienna, Treaty of, March 1731. By this treaty Britain, the Austrian Netherlands and Holland recognized the 'Pragmatic Sanction', which allowed Maria Theresa of Austria to inherit the Habsburg lands. Austria, in return, was to abandon the Ostend Company; Spain was to occupy Parma and Piacenza. This agreement isolated France and frustrated French attempts to exploit uncertainty over the Polish succession to strengthen French power in central and eastern Europe.

Vietnam War, the biggest, most destructive and prolonged conflict of the COLD WAR era. The war had its roots in the partition of French Indo-China in July 1954, when the country was divided at the 17th parallel. The Americans and British, fearing that Ho Chi Minh's republic in the North would spread communism to the South, backed the regime based in the southern capital Saigon. From 1960 onwards, North Vietnam fought a guerrilla war against the South, which was forced to draw on ever greater American assistance, with escalating numbers of combat troops being sent from Aug. 1964. The war ended only with the fall of South Vietnam in April 1975.

In Britain, US involvement in the war became a rallying point for left-wing opinion, especially among the young. Large protests took place outside the American embassy in Grosvenor Square, in Oct. 1967 and March 1968.

The WILSON government refused American requests to send troops to Vietnam, causing strain in Anglo–US relations, but the government's unwillingness to condemn the war led to friction within the LABOUR PARTY, and to a growth of left-wing groups outside it.

View of Frankpledge, *see* COURT BARON; MANOR; TITHING

Vikings The Vikings is a collective description of peoples from Scandinavia who raided and traded with much of northern and western Europe during the period from the 8th to the 11th centuries.

IMPACT ON ENGLAND

The earliest reference to a Viking raid on England dates from 789, followed by the dramatic attack on the island monastery of LINDISFARNE in 793. From the 830s, the intensity of the raids grew, alongside increased activity in Ireland, Scotland and France. Thereafter England and much of north-western Europe were victims of both systematic and piecemeal exploitation by war bands who sometimes joined together to form large armies. Such attacks continued intermittently until the late 11th century, when Scandinavian interest in England finally declined.

The main events in this long period were: the invasion of the GREAT ARMY in 865, which destroyed all the ancient English kingdoms except WESSEX, and whose attempt at total conquest was thwarted by ALFRED THE GREAT; the reconquest by Wessex of the kingdom of YORK, which was completed in 954; the renewal of the attacks by SVEIN FORKBEARD and CNUT and the completion of conquest in 1016; the return of the English king EDWARD THE CONFESSOR in 1042; and the defeat of the invasions of the 1060s by kings HAROLD II and WILLIAM I THE CONQUEROR.

The causes for the Viking assaults are much debated. It is probably best to think in terms of exceptionally skilful seafarers who found that their military and acquisitive skills could be well rewarded – in much the same way that earlier raiders, such as the ANGLES and SAXONS, had done. It also needs to be emphasized that contacts between England and Scandinavia extended far back, beyond the time of the first raids, and that the raids were in some respects only an extension of existing activity.

Their continuation over a period of two centuries did have profound consequences. The Vikings indirectly caused the UNIFICATION of England by destroying all rivals to the kings of Wessex. The ENGLISH LANGUAGE, PLACE-NAME structure and economy were each greatly affected, the last by the establishment of major settlements such as York. (The scale of settlement is controversial and is discussed elsewhere; *see* SCANDINAVIAN SETTLEMENT.) Although the 10th-century reconquest of the Scandinavian parts of England was followed by the steady assimilation of the settlers into English governmental structures and the Christian religion, it is certainly correct to describe much of English society as Anglo-Scandinavian. Another consequence of Viking activity – the duchy of NORMANDY – produced the invasion force of 1066. A further element in the importance of Scandinavia for England's history was the fear of further attacks, which affected the policies of both Edward the Confessor and William the Conqueror. Another was the major role played by English MISSIONARIES in converting Scandinavia to Christianity.

IMPACT ON IRELAND

The first recorded Viking raid on Ireland took place in 795. The raids continued until the 830s, after which the coastal settlements of DUBLIN, Waterford, Cork and Limerick were established. Scandinavian settlement within Ireland was largely confined to these coastal towns and their environs, and because of this, their impact, though often disruptive, was restricted in many respects. However, there is no doubt that the Irish economy was stimulated by Viking trading activities and the wide-ranging contacts that their seafaring life supplied – some Scandinavian maritime terms were even incorporated into the Irish language.

The coastal settlements were frequently used by the Vikings in the 9th and 10th centuries as bases from which to launch attacks on England and Scotland (*see* IVAR THE BONELESS; OLAF SIHTRICSSON; YORK), and the Norsemen soon totally dominated the Irish Sea (*see* MAN, ISLE OF). In the later 10th century, their settlements were one further complicating factor in the wars between the Irish kings (*see* CLONTARF; KINGSHIP). Intermittently subjected by neighbouring Irish rulers, they endured until the English conquest of Ireland in the 1170s.

IMPACT ON SCOTLAND

The whole of Scotland was directly or indirectly affected by the Vikings' activities in the 9th and 10th centuries. Their interventions both as predatory enemies and as allies in native feuds, undoubtedly influenced the political fortunes of the main Scottish kingdoms and contributed to the first stages of unification (*see* BRUNANBURGH; CONSTANTINE II; DUMBARTON ROCK; KENNETH MAC ALPIN; PICTS; SCOTS; STRATHCLYDE).

The HEBRIDES, ORKNEY and Shetland passed into the political control of Viking dynasties, who held on to the first until 1266 and the second and third into the 15th century. PLACE-NAME and linguistic evidence suggests that ORKNEY and Shetland became Scandinavian in all fundamental respects, with the Norn dialect of Old Norse still widely spoken there as late as the 18th century. Gaelic ultimately prevailed in the Hebrides, but again place-name evidence points to a strong Scandinavian impact (*see also* OUNCELAND).

Conversion to Christianity, which started in the 10th century, is one sign that the newcomers gradually reached an accommodation with native values. Small settlements appear to have been created in the western Scottish Lowlands and elsewhere, and Scandinavian language had a small effect on Scottish legal terminology.

Although much of the topic remains controversial, it is safe to conclude that the Viking impact on Scotland was considerable, with the northern and western islands thereby acquiring their distinctive characters.

IMPACT ON WALES

There were many Viking raids on the Welsh coast from the mid-8th to the end of the 11th centuries. The raiders almost invariably came from the Scandinavian settlements in Ireland, with the clear motive of seizing booty. For example, ST DAVID'S was sacked at least seven times, and other monasteries also suffered badly.

However, the Vikings had little or no long-term impact and the Welsh language remained virtually untouched. Although there are Scandinavian place names all along the south coast of Wales, they are best regarded as having been coastal stations rather than significant settlements.

Villa, Roman This was an important form of rural organization imported into Britain by the Romans (although a continuity of a sort can be seen in those built on Iron Age sites), comprising a house at the centre of an estate purposefully geared to agricultural production. There are around 600 identified villa sites in Britain, the vast majority in the south and east. The apparent correlation between the siting of villas and urban growth indicates that their primary purpose was to sell agricultural produce to the TOWNS.

The houses varied enormously in size and style – from a palace such as FISHBOURNE to buildings that were no more than farm-houses. Excavations have revealed that, usually in the 3rd and 4th centuries AD, many were enlarged to increase the comfort of their owners, a large number of whom must have been British aristocrats rather than Romans. Examination of domestic buildings has shown that the villa ECONOMY was one of mixed arable and pastoral farming. The houses were invariably abandoned as the Roman Empire collapsed. However, some of the villa estates and many more of the farms that belonged to them survived into the medieval period. *See also* MANOR.

Villages, English, Origins of Study of the origins of English villages has been one of the most fruitful areas for collaboration between historians and archaeologists over recent years. The result has been to erode the 19th-century belief that the nucleated villages typical of the English landscape were imported as a social and cultural form by the Anglo-Saxons (*see* ANGLO-SAXON SETTLEMENT). Numerous individual studies have shown instead that the typical village, with its associated fields, was frequently a creation of the period between the 8th and 12th centuries. The earlier English landscape was much more of a Celtic one, comprising dispersed settlements and hamlets.

Villein This word, derived from the Latin *villanus*, usually means a tenant-farmer owing onerous rents and services to his landlord. More than 40 per cent of the households recorded in *DOMESDAY BOOK* belonged to *villani*; comprising the largest group in the country, they were the backbone of the rural economy. In 1086, they were treated as freemen, but in about 1200, they were denied access to the king's courts. From then on, a villein's disputes had to be adjudicated in his lord's manorial court. Thus 'villein' in the 13th century and later means a serf, an unfree tenant (*see* SERFDOM). However, when the rural population declined in the aftermath of the BLACK DEATH, landlords were no longer able to fill vacant tenancies on such burdensome terms, and serfdom and villeinage gradually died out.

Villeinage, *see* SERFDOM

Villiers, George (4th [1st Villiers] Duke of Buckingham) (1592–1628), politician. A Leics. gentleman, his career was built on JAMES I's love. Within four years of their meeting in 1614, he was a marquess and main rival of the Howard family, becoming lord admiral in 1619 and duke in 1623. His commitment to reform and vigorous government was compromised by massive and blatant corruption, accumulating wealth for himself and his insatiable relatives, and his inept and contradictory interventions in foreign policy. He became massively unpopular.

In 1623, he persuaded James to sanction an expedition to Spain with Prince Charles (the future CHARLES I) to win the latter a Spanish princess, causing national dismay until they returned empty-handed. Puzzlingly, Charles allied himself with his father's favourite, and despite determined parliamentary attacks in 1626, Buckingham's power only ended when he was assassinated by a PURITAN, John Felton.

Vinegar Hill, Battle of, 21 June 1798. During the final stage of the IRISH REBELLION of 1798, a rebel force of 16,000 led by Father John Murphy established a camp at Vinegar Hill, near Enniscorthy, Co. Wexford. 13,000 British troops commanded by General Gerard Lake attacked from five sides and captured the camp with little fighting, although 400 of the rebels were killed. Murphy fled to Wexford, where he was captured and hanged. The battle virtually ended the rebellion.

Vineyards *DOMESDAY BOOK* reveals a considerable number of vineyards in southern and eastern England. Some may have been constructed by the Normans, but vineyards are recorded in English sources from the 8th century onwards. Evidence suggests that, during this period, the climate was warmer than in later medieval and early modern times. Further climatic change has made it possible to re-establish vineyards in the same areas in the 20th century. *See also* WINE TRADE.

Virginia, first permanent British colony in North America, and one of the 13 original states of the USA. Named to honour ELIZABETH I, it was founded in 1607 as a military base under Captain John Smith, on the same model as that being used to quell Ireland. The difficulties of military discipline, disease and high MORTALITY, and the unwelcome and increasingly hostile attentions of the natives, almost brought the infant colony to its knees. Its salvation was TOBACCO-growing, which soon brought wealth to the colonists and encouraged incomers to settle further areas; Virginia became (and remains) a synonym for tobacco. The colony was able to withstand attacks from the Indian nations in 1622, and to continue to prosper. It was one of the most important destinations of INDENTURED SERVANTS in the 17th century, and by the early 18th century was able to afford the mass importation of Negro SLAVES. Virginia's former capital, Williamsburg, survived and has been restored to its 18th-century appearance, which demonstrates the gentility and wealth of the colonists. Virginian gentlemen, notably George WASHINGTON and Thomas Jefferson, were prominent among the leaders of the 13 colonies' struggle against Britain in the War of AMERICAN INDEPENDENCE, and it was at YORKTOWN, Virginia that CORNWALLIS surrendered. *See also* NEW WORLD.

Viscount PEERAGE title, fourth in rank between EARL and BARON, first created by HENRY VI in 1440.

Visitations, inspections of Church affairs made by bishops and also, in England during the REFORMATION, by the crown. The records of these – articles of enquiry, returns to articles and subsequent injunctions – provide valuable information. For heraldic visitations, *see* HERALDRY.

Vita Aedwardi Regis (The Life of King Edward), a crucial source for the reign of EDWARD THE CONFESSOR. Probably written in 1065–7 by an anonymous Flemish monk for Edward's widow EDITH, it sets out to narrate the triumphs of Edward and of Edith's father Earl GODWINE and her brothers HAROLD and TOSTIG. The NORMAN CONQUEST destroyed its initial purpose, and its second part (which seems to have been written after 1066) celebrates Edward's religious life.

Volunteers, armed forces raised by an extraordinary appeal for volunteers, and funded partly or wholly by private gifts or public subscription. In the 18th century, the term applied both to supplementary regiments raised to augment the regular ARMY, and to voluntary associations of armed civilians formed to maintain public order and repel invasion, in effect augmenting the MILITIA. Volunteer associations were formed in many English counties in the face of JACOBITE rebellion in 1745, and in both IRELAND and England in 1778, when the French, having entered the War of AMERICAN INDEPENDENCE, threatened to invade. During the FRENCH REVOLUTIONARY WAR volunteer infantry, cavalry and artillery were raised, distinct from both army and militia; local 'armed associations' were formed for neighbourhood civil defence and a maritime first line of defence was provided by the Sea Fencibles, recruited from watermen and fishermen. In the first phase (1793–4), more than 40,000 joined; by 1803, almost a fifth of men of military age may have belonged. Subsequently brought under tighter governmental control, in 1807 these forces were largely replaced by the new local militia. Generally patriotic in ethos, volunteer corps none the less brought together men of diverse political views and social standing.

The invasion scare of 1859, also of a Franco-phobic character, prompted the formation of the Volunteer force which, in 1901, reached a peak membership of 288,476. These part-time soldiers, though regarded as a measure of popular patriotism, were as much concerned with recreation as with national defence. The volunteers were reformed as the Territorials in 1908. The naval equivalents, the Royal Naval Coast Volunteers (1853–73) and the Royal Naval Artillery Volunteers (1873–92), were eventually replaced by the Royal Naval Volunteer Reserve in 1903. After making vital contributions to the strength of the NAVY in both world wars, the RNVR (known as the 'wavy Navy' from the form of the gold rings showing officers' ranks) was merged with the Royal Naval Reserve in 1956. *See also* TERRITORIAL ARMY.

Vortigern, the name given by BEDE to a British ruler said by GILDAS (who did not name him) to have invited Germanic tribesmen to fight on his behalf against the PICTS and SCOTS, and who was overwhelmed and defeated by these newcomers. By the time of NENNIUS, many legends had developed around Vortigern's career, all concerned with weakness and treachery. The pattern of events in which he was supposedly involved is a plausible one, and if he did exist, it must have been at some time during the 5th century. *See also* ANGLO-SAXON SETTLEMENT.

Votadini, a tribe of the eastern SCOTTISH LOWLANDS that was briefly subjected to Roman rule (*see* ANTONINE WALL), but thereafter re-emerged as an independent people. Numerous Roman artefacts have been discovered in archaeological excavations in their territory, probably indicating friendly relations across HADRIAN'S WALL. The Votadini subsequently created the post-Roman British kingdom of GODODDIN.

Wace (*fl.*1160), poet. A Norman court poet patronized by HENRY II, it was his *Roman de Brut* – a version of GEOFFREY OF MONMOUTH's *Historia Regum Britanniae*, written in ANGLO-NORMAN verse and completed by 1155 – that took the story of King ARTHUR and the Round Table (a detail that first appears in Wace) to the wider world. He left unfinished his verse chronicle of the dukes of Normandy – the *Roman de Rou* – when he lost his role as the Henrician court's vernacular chronicler to Benoit de Sainte-Maure.

Wager of Law, *see* COMPURGATION

Wages Board Councils, bodies set up by the Wages Council Act of 1945, to arbitrate on wages and conditions in a number of industries, including catering, road haulage, the distributive trades and agriculture. Their intention was to provide a degree of protection for workers in trades whose structure inhibited collective bargaining. Many wages councils were abolished by legislation in 1992, though retained in agriculture.

Wakefield, Battle of, 30 Dec. 1460. Little is known about this battle, only that RICHARD OF YORK made a sortie out of Sandal castle, Yorks., that the LANCASTRIANS under Henry Percy, Earl of Northumberland, won, and that it resulted in the deaths of the YORKIST leaders: Richard of York himself, his second son Edmund, and the Earl of Salisbury.

Walcheren Expedition, 1809, ultimately unsuccessful amphibious attack during the NAPOLEONIC WARS. The aim was to destroy shipyards and ships at Antwerp, and ultimately to encourage an uprising in Germany. However the leisurely approach of the army commander, the Earl of Chatham, ensured that only the initial objective, the island of Walcheren in the mouth of the Rhine, was taken. By the time it withdrew 4,000 of the 40,000 strong army were dead of malaria and nearly as many again permanently invalided by the disease.

Wales, Gerald of, *see* BARRI, GERALD DE

Wales, Prince of LLYWELYN AP GRUFFUDD was the first ruler in Wales to use the title Prince of Wales, and he was recognized as such by HENRY III in the treaty of MONTGOMERY (1267). After his death in battle near Builth (1282), his principality was annexed to the English CROWN as its direct possession, unlike the MARCHER LORDSHIPS (*see* RHUDDLAN, STATUTE OF). Later, in 1301, EDWARD I created his son (the future EDWARD II) Prince of Wales as a nominal royal representative in the territory: the story of the king presenting the Welsh with an infant son who could speak no English is apocryphal. EDWARD III created the Black Prince Prince of Wales (*see* EDWARD THE BLACK PRINCE) in 1343, and when the latter died (having never visited the Principality) in 1376, Edward conferred the title on the future RICHARD II, the king's grandson. Owain GLYN DWR styled himself Prince of Wales, but the honour has since been given by the English monarch to his or her eldest son. Medieval-style ceremonies were invented for the investiture as Prince of the future EDWARD VIII at Caernarfon Castle in 1911, and these were revamped for Prince Charles in 1969. The term Principality is now informally used for the whole of the territory of Wales, including the former Marcher lands (*see* UNION OF WALES AND ENGLAND).

Wales, Statute of, *see* RHUDDLAN, STATUTE OF

Wales, Union of, and England, *see* UNION OF WALES AND ENGLAND

Wallace, William (?–1305), Scottish leader. He was a hero of the Wars of SCOTTISH INDEPENDENCE, who came to prominence in 1296–7 after the defeat of John BALLIOL, at a time when the Scottish aristocracy was prepared to capitulate to EDWARD I. At this critical moment, the fierce resistance of two esquires – Wallace and Andrew Moray – enabled them to raise an army capable of inflicting a humiliating defeat upon the English at STIRLING BRIDGE in Sept. 1297. Moray was mortally wounded, and for the next ten months, Wallace was the unrivalled leader of the Scots until he unwisely engaged Edward I's army at FALKIRK. He fought on, once again in relative obscurity, until 1305 when he was betrayed to the English and executed at Smithfield. But he had inspired a patriotic resistance that outlasted his defeat and death.

Walpole, Sir Robert (2nd [1st Walpole] Earl of Orford) (1676–1745), politician, Prime Minister (1721–42). Sometimes called the first PRIME MINISTER, Walpole commanded the heights of politics for longer than any other 18th-century politician. Younger son of a well-established Norfolk county family, he entered Parliament in 1701, associating with the WHIGS. He served his political apprenticeship in a period of violent party conflict: in 1712, he was impeached by HARLEY and Bolingbroke (*see* ST JOHN, HENRY) for corruption during his time as secretary at war (1708–10) (*see* IMPEACHMENT); returned to office in 1714, he in turn impeached them for TREASON. Becoming FIRST LORD OF THE TREASURY in 1715, he resigned two years later when his brother-in-law and ally, the 2nd Viscount TOWNSHEND, was dismissed; after a period in which they joined with the TORIES to harry the ministry, the two returned to office in 1720, Walpole as paymaster-general.

His part in restoring public confidence after the bursting of the SOUTH SEA BUBBLE earned him credit and in 1722, he exploited the discovery of the ATTERBURY PLOT to consolidate his position. As first lord of the Treasury for the next 20 years, he distinguished himself by his effective financial management, and his close control of parliamentary business and of patronage. He had the confidence of GEORGE I and won that of GEORGE II, partly through the support of Queen Caroline. Although he maintained his hostility to self-confessed Tories, he pursued policies – of peace abroad and consequent economy – that were attractive to many of them. His ministry was termed the 'Robinocracy' by opponents, who portrayed him as corrupt, self-serving, partial and oppressive (*see CRAFTSMAN, THE*).

Townshend's resignation in 1730 left Walpole without any colleague of equal stature in the Cabinet, but it was only the clamour over his proposed extension of the EXCISE in 1733 that exposed potential weaknesses in his position. However, after abandoning the scheme, Walpole fought back determinedly, successfully appealing to Whig party loyalties against the 'PATRIOT' opposition led by Bolingbroke and William Pulteney. Thus it was only when chauvinistic extra-parliamentary pressure and the urgings of his colleagues pushed a reluctant Walpole in 1739 into a mismanaged war against Spain, that his political mastery dissolved. The 1741 election further undermined him, and despite the pleas of George II he resigned in early 1742. He accepted a peerage as Earl of Orford, and continued to advise his former colleagues, the PELHAM brothers, until his death.

Walsingham, Sir Francis (?1532–90), politician. Cambridge-educated and from a London family with early PROTESTANT sympathies, he travelled abroad during EDWARD VI and MARY I's reigns. By 1568, he was being used by his friend William CECIL and ELIZABETH I in diplomacy and foreign affairs, often loyally restraining his PURITAN instincts; he became principal royal SECRETARY in 1573. He developed a network of agents and informants abroad and at home, combating conspiracies against Elizabeth, including those of MARY QUEEN OF SCOTS. He was one of the ablest and most reliable of Elizabeth's advisers, and much esteemed by the queen, even though she frequently disregarded his advice.

Walsingham, Thomas (?–*c*.1422), chronicler. A BENEDICTINE monk of ST ALBANS, he revived the abbey's tradition of history writing. His main work was a massive history of England conceived as a continuation of Matthew PARIS's *Chronica Majora*. Walsingham's strong views on prominent contemporaries – JOHN OF GAUNT, WYCLIF, PERRERS and the leaders of the PEASANTS'

REVOLT, for example – were expressed freely in his original version, completed *c*.1392. However, when he returned to writing history after the deposition of RICHARD II, his new enthusiasm for the LANCASTRIAN dynasty made him extensively revise his earlier work as well as continue it to 1420.

Walter, Hubert (*c*.1140–1205), Archbishop of Canterbury (1193–1205). Being a nephew of the justiciar Ranulf Glanvil eased his path into HENRY II's service, but it was under RICHARD I that his career really flourished. Richard made him bishop of Salisbury in 1189, employed him as chief of staff on CRUSADE and was so impressed by his performance in these challenging circumstances that, in 1193, he promoted him to take charge of both secular and ecclesiastical government in England as JUSTICIAR and archbishop of Canterbury. While the king was in France, he governed England; he would later rightly be called 'one of the greatest royal ministers of all time'.

In 1195 he was made papal legate and, on JOHN's accession, was appointed CHANCELLOR – the great series of CHANCERY rolls, for centuries the central records of English government, date from his period in office (*see* LETTERS PATENT). As archbishop, although clearly appointed for entirely secular reasons, he proved to be an active and responsible head of the English Church who found time to summon and preside over reforming provincial and legatine councils.

Wanderer, The, a poem of 115 lines that survives in the late 10th-century collection known as the *EXETER BOOK*. It describes the feelings of a young exile of noble birth and his search for a noble war band to join. It not only reveals a great deal about the attitudes of an Anglo-Saxon warrior, but also provides important information about the structure of Anglo-Saxon society (*see* HOUSECARLS; MALDON). The ruined citadel visited by the hero is often seen as a description of a derelict Roman centre.

Wapentake, the equivalent of the Anglo-Saxon HUNDRED in the Danish eastern and northern regions of England. Although the name *wapentake* ('vápnatak': brandishing of weapons) reflects Scandinavian linguistic influence, its function and that of the hundred were virtually identical.

War Artists, name for artists given official status in the two world wars and later conflicts to record images of war both at home and abroad. Thousands of works were commissioned in both wars. Many WORLD WAR I artists, including C. R. W. Nevinson, Wyndham Lewis, and Paul Nash, displayed increasingly strong influences from contemporary artistic movements such as Vorticism, Futurism and Cubism. Official war artists in WORLD WAR II included Stanley Spencer, Eric Ravilious, Graham Sutherland, and Henry Moore. Many of their memorable and striking images of modern war hang in the Imperial War Museum, London.

War of 1812, *see* ANGLO-AMERICAN WAR

War Poets, collective name given to the poets of WORLD WAR I, most notably Rupert Brooke, Siegfried Sassoon, Ivor Gurney and Wilfred Owen. Although 'war poetry' was also produced in WORLD WAR II, the poets of World War I have had a lasting impact through their evocation of romantic patriotism, lost innocence, and the horror and bitterness induced by the reality of modern warfare.

Warbeck, Perkin (?1474–99), conspirator. A possible bastard of EDWARD IV, he was apparently from Flanders, where YORKIST conspirators discovered his acting abilities. In 1491, he was taken to Ireland, where his career of impersonation began, first as Edward Plantagenet, Earl of Warwick (the nephew of EDWARD IV), then as Richard, the younger prince in the Tower (*see* EDWARD V). A Europe-wide network of plots against HENRY VII and two failed invasion attempts ended in capture in 1497 after a third landing in Cornwall. Comfortably imprisoned in the Tower, he made escape attempts and was executed with the real Earl of Warwick.

Ward, a subdivision supervised by an ALDERMAN in the City of LONDON and other early urban centres for administrative and policing purposes. The urban equivalent of the HUNDRED, it was also the usage for hundreds in Northumb. and Cumb. Under modern local electoral arrangements, it has become a subdivision which elects councillors. In the small area of the City of London, the ward system with aldermen survives today.

Wardrobe In the course of the 13th century the wardrobe took over the CHAMBER's role as the chief spending department attached to the English royal household. Its administrative significance derived from the fact that one of the wardrobe officials, the controller, had charge of the PRIVY SEAL. EDWARD I found that the greater flexibility of the wardrobe's procedures made it a more convenient instrument of war finance than the EXCHEQUER, but by the end of his reign the result of this was that he was deep in debt, and in EDWARD II's reign measures were taken to limit the wardrobe's freedom of action.

Wardship, the right whereby a landlord took control of a tenant's estate during the minority of the tenant's heir, including normally the right to arrange the heir's marriage. Wardship of TENANTS-IN-CHIEF was a revenue device for medieval and Tudor monarchs (part of the surviving financial aspects of FEUDAL rights known as 'fiscal feudalism'), and in 1540, a Court of Wards and Liveries was formalized to manage the business. Wardships were sold to the highest bidders, who often acted more in their own interests than in their wards'. The system was hated by landowners, and was the main reason for the abolition of feudal dues in the RESTORATION settlement.

The necessity for the wardship of orphaned children has continued, guardians being appointed by the will of the parent(s) or, in default of this, by a court. Children can also be made 'wards of court' in the event of one or both parents abusing their rights or inflicting serious cruelty. Jurisdiction was traditionally in the hands of the Court of CHANCERY, but is now exercised by its successor, the High Court of Justice.

Warfare, Air Tethered balloons for observation etc. were first used by armies in the FRENCH REVOLUTIONARY WAR, and continued in use to the end of WORLD WAR I, while barrage balloons were still in use in WORLD WAR II (*see* AIR RAID PRECAUTIONS). The phenomenally rapid development of AIRCRAFT and powered flight in the 20th century (from the Wright brothers in 1903 to the moon landings in 1969) was stimulated chiefly by their military potential. Aircraft were first used in colonial campaigns as early as 1912, and were promoted as a cheap form of imperial policing, by the British in particular, until after World War II.

Air warfare made major strides in World War I. At its start, most armies had a few unarmed aircraft for scouting, and these played a small but important role in the first battle of the MARNE. By early 1917 both sides possessed thousands of aircraft, and control of the air had become crucial to success in land battles (*see* WARFARE, LAND). At sea, British aircraft armed with torpedoes first sank enemy ships in 1915, a seaplane-carrier took part in the battle of JUTLAND, and the first aircraft-carriers were completed by the end of the war (*see* WARFARE, NAVAL). The Germans first used ZEPPELIN rigid airships to bomb British cities in 1915, and by 1917 all sides possessed primitive long-range bomber aircraft. In April 1918 the British established the ROYAL AIR FORCE (RAF), the world's first institutionally independent air force.

Between the wars theorists of air power, including John Trenchard, argued that air warfare made fleets and armies obsolete, that there was no defence against the bomber, and that a strategy of bombing cities would cause enemy society to collapse. Fear of the bomber was an important factor in APPEASEMENT in the 1930s.

By World War II air power was fundamental to all aspects of land and sea warfare, with fighter, bomber and transport aircraft all playing a major role. World War II also saw the first use of paratroops and glider troops (at, *e.g.*, ARNHEM), and of jet aircraft and helicopters at the very end of the war. The failure of Germany to win the Battle of BRITAIN ended plans for Operation SEALION, the projected invasion of Britain. Both the German BLITZ and the much greater British and American BOMBING OFFENSIVE did massive damage to cities, but strategic bombing proved both morally controversial and less militarily successful than had been claimed. At sea during World War II the aircraft-carrier eclipsed the battleship as the principal capital ship of naval warfare.

Following World War II air warfare continued to increase in importance. The use of the atomic bomb in 1945 and the development of NUCLEAR WEAPONS provided a new dimension, with increased emphasis on attacking enemy cities, for which the RAF developed its V BOMBER FORCE in the 1950s. America in particular used limited conventional strategic bombing rather than land forces to attack enemy homelands in the

KOREAN WAR and the VIETNAM WAR, which also saw a greatly increased use of helicopters. Rapid developments in military aircraft and rocket technology during and after World War II (*see* V-WEAPONS) also led to the space race and ultimately to the moon landings.

Warfare, Land Until very recent times, most adult males throughout the world have at least carried weapons and engaged in small-scale or localized warfare (e.g. cattle raids) as a matter of course. On rare occasions entire societies might mobilize for war. This has produced a very ancient obligation on all men to fight (*see* MILITIA), which formed the basis of much medieval and early modern military service, and of later systems of CONSCRIPTION. However, this tradition of improvised or irregular forces, often called 'guerrillas' after the Spanish popular forces of the NAPOLEONIC WARS, has progressively diminished in importance and legitimacy since medieval times, becoming associated with dissidents against the state, or with opposition to an invader or imperial power. In Europe in particular, it has also co-existed with a tradition of exclusive or select armed forces under some central authority. Although classical Greece and Rome formed important models for this tradition, it did not achieve dominance in Europe until the growth of state authority in the 17th century. Such specially raised armies represented a valuable and temporary asset, only to be risked in battle for the most compelling reasons, and until the 20th century deaths from disease, starvation and poor hygiene far outnumbered those from actual fighting.

Despite great cultural variations in armies over the centuries, the actual conduct of war prior to the industrial era changed hardly at all, to the extent that JULIUS CEASAR could have commanded at AGINCOURT, and probably at WATERLOO. In medieval warfare the defence dominated in the form of CASTLES of increasing sophistication, each with a 'range' equivalent to the distance a mounted man could ride out and back before nightfall, which could usually only be taken by assault or an equally costly protracted siege. War and ritualized practice for war dominated the behaviour of the medieval ARISTOCRACY. An individual knight in armour was almost invulnerable except to an equal, and repeated attempts were made to outlaw weapons which threatened this status (such as the crossbow). But the assembly and control of a field army of more than a few thousand knights and men-at-arms was almost impossible. An army required to advance only a short distance into battle could fall apart through divided command and tactical ineptitude, as happened to the French at CRÉCY.

The first impact of gunpowder weapons on warfare came in the 14th century in the form of siege artillery capable of defeating the walls of castles, culminating in the fall of the great walls of Constantinople to Turkish cannon in 1453. This technological development began a shift of power from individual aristocrats towards central government, by limiting the value both of the castle (particularly in rebellion) and the armoured knight. Artillery on the battlefield was followed by primitive infantry matchlock muskets, and in combination with pikes these became increasingly capable of resisting the knightly charge. By the early 16th century the medieval custom of paying troops had combined with their growing professionalization into the widespread use of mercenary forces. Together with the separation of warfare from other trades, this brought the word 'soldier' into use for the first time. Equally, although the aristocratic tradition of fighting continued, the individual warrior accepted authority and responsibility as an 'officer'.

Foreign mercenaries, either as individual soldiers or formed units for hire (often from smaller states), remained an important part of most European armies until the 19th century. However, the gradual emergence of the sovereign state by the end of the 17th century, partly from the crucible of the THIRTY YEARS WAR (1613–48), led to a general decline in reliance on mercenaries and the establishment of permanent STANDING ARMIES. Uniforms, regulation and training, and regular payment all fostered patriotism as well as professionalism. Infantry pikes or other cutting or stabbing weapons became obsolete, and bayonets were introduced for the new flintlock muskets. Cavalry shed their knightly origins and in most cases their armour, although still relying on the mounted charge for their principal effect. Cannon became more mobile and employable on the battlefield.

In the face of improved siege artillery, after

centuries of fortification based on high walls a new science of military engineering based on open and interlocking fields of fire transformed fortified frontier towns and cities, and engineers or trench-digging 'sappers' emerged as the fourth main arm of land warfare. Progressively, as firepower increased, fortifications sank underground, culminating in defensive systems of WORLD WAR II like the French Maginot Line. Battle remained a bloody and uncertain experience, and even a victory would usually cost a commander up to a third of his men. In 11 campaigns the Duke of Marlborough (*see* CHURCHILL, JOHN), regarded as an unusually aggressive commander, fought only four major battles but conducted over 30 sieges.

The 18th century also saw a distinction emerge between European and non-European warfare. The cultural separation between the professional soldier and the civilian reached its apogee with the idea (never achieved in practice) that a war might be fought between European armies without the population being affected in any way. Except as deliberate terror weapons, states were increasingly reluctant to employ within Europe techniques of warfare which remained accepted practice in colonial war until much later. Up to WORLD WAR I and even beyond, European powers would fight to defeat their enemies, not to destroy them, in the knowledge that next time they could be allies.

The introduction of formal drill and marching in step in the middle of the 18th century greatly improved tactical mobility, particularly in the Prussian army of Frederick the Great. Most states also recruited semi-guerrillas or 'light troops' from the fringes of European civilization (e.g. Cossacks, Highlanders, Croats). As armies grew in size to almost 100,000 men, their movement and feeding became matters of genuine military science, leading to the establishment of the first military training schools. However, the more radical ideas of 18th-century warfare were only first applied by the French armies of the FRENCH REVOLUTIONARY and NAPOLEONIC WARS. These included an emphasis on manoeuvre and shock in battle, and strategic movement by 'divisions' or 'corps', miniature armies in themselves, able to march separated but combine on the battlefield, mixing traditional supply with scavenging and so avoiding the problem of fortresses. This was only possible through improvements in European agriculture which made 'living off the land' feasible, and for armies motivated by a new spirit of nationalism. In 1793 Revolutionary France introduced conscription for the first time in modern history, mobilizing the French nation for war. The army which invaded Russia in 1812 numbered over 600,000 troops, about half of them French. It was this combination, together with the military genius of Napoleon, which gave France its early victories.

The technological base of Napoleonic warfare was still largely pre-industrial. Despite the increased size of armies, the largest number that could normally be brought together in a single day for battle was still under 100,000, as at Waterloo. The exceptional battle of Leipzig of 1813 (the 'battle of the nations'), involving almost 500,000 troops over three days, was beyond even Napoleon's ability to control. Particularly in Russia and Spain, on the fringes of European agricultural reform, the French system of supply broke down, while their strategic manoeuvres could be defeated by avoiding battle and even using lines of fortification like those built by Wellington (*see* WELLESLEY, ARTHUR) at Torres Vedras. As the Napoleonic Wars continued, other states, particularly Prussia after 1812, also learned to copy French tactics, to mobilize their populations and to inspire their soldiers with a new nationalism.

The impact of the INDUSTRIAL REVOLUTION on land warfare came almost entirely after the Napoleonic Wars, during a period of relative peace in Europe. The first major change was the development of RAILWAYS and the electric telegraph, making it possible to move large armies over considerable distances in days. Weapons also improved with the introduction of rifled cannon and percussion-cap rifled muskets (with effectively twice the range of an old smooth-bore musket), and the first breech-loading rifles in the 1840s. As infantry and artillery firepower increased, the value of cavalry declined except for scouting. Nevertheless, battles of the CRIMEAN WAR and even the American Civil War (fought by European-style armies) remained very Napoleonic in appearance. In colonial warfare, a marginal European superiority in organization and weapons gradually became an absolute dominance by the end of the century, helping foster a conservative approach to tactics and the retention of almost Napoleonic formations.

Except for Britain, Europe faced the problem of how to retain mass armies by conscription that were also politically reliable, something which proved critical in the revolutions of 1848 and the wars of unification which followed. Most countries used some form of limited long-service conscription until the Franco-Prussian War (1870–1) when, by using universal short-service conscription, Prussia and its associated states produced a field army of over a million men, greatly outnumbering the French. The Prussian (subsequently German) victory was seen chiefly as the product of superior professional staffwork and organization rather than traditional battlefield virtues. Almost all European countries copied the German conscription system, and in the late 19th century factors such as birthrate, education and popular health became military issues. In 1914 Germany itself could mobilize almost 3.5 million men.

The quarter-century before World War I, a period of almost unprecedented peace in Europe and colonial expansion outside it, also saw the effects of industrialization reach the battlefield in the form of new artillery, magazine rifles and machine-guns with ranges and rates of fire far exceeding anything previously known, and which remained in service until the late 20th century. The combination of this new firepower technology with enthusiastic and well-organized armies in their millions represented a genuine revolution in land warfare, utterly unlike anything in previous history. However, strategic mobility and communication had not been matched by any equivalent improvement at the tactical level, where transport was still largely by horse and foot.

The failure of the various plans for victory by manoeuvre in 1914 produced the trench stalemate of which most European commanders had been at least dimly aware before the war and had hoped to avoid. The mobilization of the 'nation in arms' on all sides, and the establishment of a HOME FRONT to provide and support the mass armies, also made it politically virtually impossible to seek a compromise peace. 'Battles' resembled earlier sieges, very heavy in casualties and continuing for months in an attempt to break through trench systems only a few miles deep. Siege techniques dating from the 17th century were revived both for attack and defence, including the use of mining to plant explosives under enemy positions, and the reintroduction of the hand grenade and body armour.

The solution to this stalemate was successfully sought in more technology. The old division into infantry, cavalry and artillery was transformed into innumerable separate military functions. New weapons such as flame-throwers and the TANK were invented, and others such as aircraft and poison gas greatly improved. Most importantly, artillery underwent a complete transformation, less in the nature of the guns than in methods of using them in great mass bombardments. For the first time, the supply of ammunition became more important than food. By 1918 armies using these methods could achieve at least semi-mobile warfare, breaking through the trench defences. The restoration of mobility to the battlefield was completed in the 1920s when portable radios restored effective command, tanks became sufficiently fast and reliable to replace cavalry, and lorries replaced horses for transport.

World War II saw almost all the features of industrialized mass warfare associated with World War I on an even greater scale, including the use of new technologies and weapons (although not poison gas). The nature of land warfare in particular had not changed significantly in 20 years, despite some early successes achieved by the tank, which assumed the central role in fighting by the war's end. The Eastern Front (1941–5) was a far more violent and destructive conflict than the Western Front (1914–18). Fuel had now joined ammunition as the most important supply priority, and the vast majority of troops served as a transport and supply system behind the lines, rather than fighting. With the global nature of the war and the use of air power it also became increasingly unrealistic to distinguish land warfare from air and naval warfare (*see* WARFARE, AIR; WARFARE, NAVAL), or even from civilian life. Guerrilla war was again legitimized in the form of resistance movements, and cities were subject to mass bombing including the final use of atomic bombs. World War II continued to dominate military thinking well into the second half of the 20th century. However, the invention of NUCLEAR WEAPONS and the wide employment of guerrilla strategies, particularly by anti-colonial or revolutionary movements, cast doubts on the continuing value of armies. Increasingly, industrialized mass land warfare was viewed as something to be prevented and deterred rather than fought.

Warfare, Naval The Romans had a British-based fleet, the *Classis Britannicus*, which used rowing warships (galleys) of some kind; although very little is known, it is likely that, as in the Mediterranean, the ram was used as well as missiles projected by the crew, and perhaps some form of catapult. Equally little is known about the way the substantial Anglo-Saxon fleet of rowing and sailing ships created by ALFRED THE GREAT fought, though it is probable that the ships were merely means of transport and fighting platforms for crews armed with bows, spears and hand weapons. The same would seem to be true of the most important navy of medieval Britain, the galleys of the Lords of the Isles.

The fleets intermittently collected in the later middle ages by the kings of England mostly consisted of conversions of merchantmen used as floating fortresses with built-up 'castles' fore and aft, to fight what was, in effect, an infantry battle at sea. Guns were first used as an addition to the individual projectile weapons of archers and javelin-men in the 'castles'. It was probably the English fleet in the later 16th century that introduced the idea that repeated salvoes from larger guns, now mounted to fire through 'ports' cut in the side of the hull, could become a battle-winning weapon in their own right. The idea was, and remained until the late 19th century, not so much to sink enemy ships (a very rare event) but to disable them ,by killing, wounding or demoralizing the crew, crippling the motive power (by destroying sails and rigging and knocking down masts), and dismounting and disabling the armament – the end result, with or without boarding, to be the capture of the enemy.

Ahead or astern fire was both difficult to arrange and weak in any sailing ship; almost all the guns had to be carried pointing out from the sides of a ship. During the First DUTCH WAR artillery warfare between fleets under sail produced the inevitable result of fighting in line astern, broadside to broadside. A concomitant of this was that only the most powerful ships were capable of being 'ships of the line' – the origins of the BATTLESHIP. Until the early 19th century sea battles were fought in line unless the enemy was significantly weaker or less competent, when the line could be broken and individual enemy ships overwhelmed by superior numbers or fighting power. From the early 18th century British crews usually had an advantage in rate of fire over most enemies – partly due to superior training, partly for technical reasons; and the problem of battle with the chief opponent, the French, was to force action on an increasingly unwilling opponent. The Dutch had been fighting for predominance at sea in north European waters; the French usually had particular missions to perform, and their concentration on these handicapped them in battle. However, battles became much rarer, and very often fleets missed each other in the vastness of the ocean, particularly as European wars spread to other parts of the world. This placed greater emphasis on the seaworthiness of ships, the endurance of their crews, and improved supply and repair organizations with overseas bases. Prevention of infectious and deficiency diseases acquired greater importance, as did better navigational techniques.

During KING WILLIAM'S WAR the French turned increasingly to commerce raiding against the growing English merchant fleet. This made the English turn from fighting fleet actions to the problems of trade protection. CONVOYS had to be organized, and increasing numbers of smaller vessels to be built for escort and other sea-control tasks, to supplement the ships of the line. During the 18th century increasing use was made of BLOCKADE against enemy fleets, and then as a measure of economic warfare against enemy trade.

The technical advances of the 19th century – steam propulsion, metal hulls, bigger guns, armour, etc. – produced a massive increase in the size, fighting power and cost of individual ships. Meanwhile underwater attack, made possible by the development of mines and torpedoes, together with the use of explosive projectiles, made the destruction or sinking of an opponent the usual result of a successful action. The torpedo for the first time (except for the self-destructive use of a fireship) made it possible for a much smaller vessel to destroy a larger one. At the end of the 19th century developments in explosives, gun manufacture and torpedoes suddenly opened out the ranges at which action was possible, from a mile or so to the limits of visibility. This made fire-control a vital element – not only finding the range of the enemy ship but predicting where he would be in the time the projectiles took to cover the distance. Early forms of computer were developed to cope with these problems. Already the introduction of radio (in whose development the Royal NAVY had played a pioneering part) had completely altered the control of naval warfare by permitting direct contact between headquarters and fleets and ships at sea. The first practical submarines and aircraft began to put an emphasis on warfare in three dimensions even before the outbreak of WORLD WAR I in 1914. There had been no serious experience of naval war to match technological development and many mistakes were made, most notably the extraordinary refusal to accept that convoy was the answer to submarine attack until almost too late. During WORLD WAR II air and anti-submarine warfare were even more important, with the aircraft-carrier replacing the battleship, and new types of escort ship (FRIGATES) coming into service. A new dimension was added to warfare by the introduction of RADAR and electronic warfare, and the involvement of scientists went further with the development of the techniques of operational research to cope with the problems of the Battle of the ATLANTIC. The post-war development of atomic submarines has thrown even more emphasis onto the importance of undersea warfare. Sensors, computers and sophisticated communications have become more and more important, making ships and navies more expensive than ever.

Warham, William (*c.* 1456–1532), Archbishop of Canterbury (1503–32). A civil lawyer trained at Oxford, he was a useful diplomat under HENRY VII and was rewarded with the bishopric of London (1502) and the archbishopric of Canterbury (1503), becoming CHANCELLOR in 1504. He expressed doubts about the wisdom of HENRY VIII marrying CATHERINE OF ARAGON, the widow of Prince ARTHUR, but presided at their coronation. WOLSEY replaced him as lord chancellor in 1515, and when he was also made LEGATE *a latere* in 1518, this encroached on Warham's legatine position as primate of All England; relations remained cool but correct between them. Warham did nothing to assist Catherine against Henry's efforts from 1527 to have their marriage declared null, but he became increasingly unhappy with the radically anti-papal turn of royal policy after 1530. In 1532 he made a formal but secret protest against royal moves to curb the independence of the Church, and was contemplating speaking out openly. However, he drew back from such defiance of the monarchy which he had served all his life, and agreed to the SUBMISSION OF THE CLERGY. His death soon after enabled Henry to appoint Thomas CRANMER as archbishop, to act as a reliable agent of royal policy. Warham was a good example of the late medieval English church hierarchy: pious, energetic and a great builder, generous patron of HUMANISTS including ERASMUS, and deeply hostile to those who wanted radical change in the Church. His archdeacon of Canterbury, William Warham, was probably his illegitimate son.

Warming Pan, an anti-JACOBITE symbol. JAMES II's two marriages had failed to produce a living male heir, making his son-in-law, William of Orange (the future WILLIAM III), heir-presumptive. Then, in the winter of 1687, it was reported that Queen Mary (of Modena) was again pregnant, and on 10 June 1688, the birth of a son, James Edward STUART (the future Pretender), was announced. The king's opponents suggested that the child had, in fact, been smuggled into the queen's room in a warming pan, to secure a Catholic succession.

Wars of the Roses, 1455–87, English civil wars fought for possession of the crown. After BOSWORTH, one contemporary commented that the red rose (HENRY VII) had avenged the white (the sons of EDWARD IV) – an allusion to the fact that the red rose was one of the badges used by the house of Lancaster, and the white one of the badges used by the house of York. The symbolism originally referred just to the events of 1483–5, but by the 17th century, it was being applied to the 15th-century civil wars in general. The term

ENGLAND AND WALES DURING THE WARS OF THE ROSES
Battle
Castle
Frontier in 1470
R. Tay
SCOTLAND
Edinburgh
R. Clyde
Berwick
Bamburgh
Hedgeley Moor 1464
Alnwick
NORTH SEA
Hexham 1464
R. Ouse
Middleham
Lancaster
1461 Towton
York
Pontefract
Wakefield 1460
IRISH SEA
IRELAND
Dublin
R. Trent
1487 Stoke
Conway
Flint
Chester
Blore Heath 1459
Nottingham
Harlech
R. Severn
Shrewsbury
1470 Empingham (Losecoat Field)
Caister
1485 Bosworth
Kenilworth
R. Ouse
Ludlow
Ludford Bridge 1459
Warwick
1460 Northampton
Mortimer's Cross 1461
1469 Edgcote
1471 Tewkesbury
1455 St. Albans 1461
1471 Barnet
Milford Haven
Pembroke
R. Thames
London
Cardiff
Bristol
Windsor
Leeds
Sandwich
Dover
Calais
0 km 150
0 miles 80
Exeter
Plymouth
English Channel
St. Michael's Mount
FRANCE

'Wars of the Roses', first used by Sir Walter Scott (1771–1832), is misleading in that it has tended to create the impression of an unbroken series of wars from 1455–87, caused by a single problem – the dynastic quarrel between the houses of Lancaster and York.

In reality, there were a number of separate wars. The first was caused by HENRY VI's complete inadequacy as a ruler. The humiliating loss of Normandy in 1449–50, swiftly followed by Jack CADE'S REBELLION, ushered in a period of demoralized government when quarrels between magnates escalated into private wars and encouraged the ambitions of RICHARD OF YORK. This conflict came to a crisis in 1459–61 and, although it continued to simmer in the North until 1464, was effectively settled when Edward IV won the fiercely contested battle of TOWTON.

The second war (1469–71) was caused by the discontent of Richard NEVILLE, Earl of Warwick. The extraordinary alliance between the 'Kingmaker' and MARGARET OF ANJOU, hitherto his greatest enemy, gave the LANCASTRIAN cause an unexpected new lease of life – but one that ended in 1471 when Edward IV killed off the surviving Lancastrians. He then ruled in peace until his death in 1483.

The third war (1483–7) was triggered by RICHARD III's coup, which shattered the YORKIST establishment and allowed the obscure exile, Henry Tudor (who was to become Henry VII), to return as champion of Lancaster and York alike.

SHAKESPEARE's portrayal of these years did much to instil the long-dominant interpretation of the wars as nasty, brutish and long. In the minds of historians in the 19th and first half of the 20th centuries, this suggested a deep-seated cause. They invented the concept of BASTARD FEUDALISM and portrayed it as a malignant disease of the body politic, with an allegedly 'weak crown' confronted by a number of 'overmighty subjects'. But since K. B. McFarlane's revised interpretation of bastard feudalism, historians have been much more inclined to emphasize the 'accidents' of personality and 'events' in explaining the outbreak and renewal of civil war.

Although there is no precise agreement among historians as to when the wars started and ended, it is generally accepted that, in a period of over 30 years, the total time spent at war was, at most, 15 months. The armies were fairly small (except at Towton), and in terms of material damage and loss of life, these civil wars did relatively little harm; however, the war-makers among the aristocracy suffered disproportionately heavy casualties. This left the governing class with an abiding memory of the horrors of civil war, one that, cultivated by the Tudors, was vividly reflected in Shakespeare's history plays.

CHRONOLOGY: BATTLES

Y=Yorkist victory L=Lancastrian victory

1455 First battle of ST ALBANS (Y).

1459 Battle of Blore Heath (Y). Flight from Ludford Bridge (L).

1460 Battle of Northampton (Y). Richard of York claims throne. Battle of WAKEFIELD (L). RICHARD OF YORK killed.

1461 Battle of Mortimer's Cross (Y). Second battle of St Albans (L). Battle of TOWTON (Y). EDWARD IV crowned.

1461–4 Struggle for control of Northumbrian castles (Y).

1469 Warwick rebels and wins victory at Edgecote, Northants.

1470 Edward defeats LINCOLNSHIRE RISING at Losecoat Field. Warwick and Clarence flee to MARGARET OF ANJOU in France. Warwick and Lancastrians invade. Edward escapes to Holland. Restoration (READEPTION) of HENRY VI.

1471 Edward invades and is joined by Clarence. Battle of BARNET (Y). Battle of TEWKESBURY (Y). Henry VI murdered.

1483 RICHARD III seizes throne. Princes in Tower disappear, presumed murdered. Rebellion and execution of Henry STAFFORD, Duke of Buckingham.

1485 HENRY VII wins battle of BOSWORTH. Richard killed.

1487 Battle of STOKE.

Warwick, county town of Warwicks., founded as a BURH in 914. The town is built on a rocky outcrop above the River Avon, on which is situated one of the most impressive of all English CASTLES, begun in 1068 but with most of the grandest work dating from the 14th century. Much of the town was rebuilt on an ordered pattern after a fire in 1694, an early example of self-conscious and genteel renewal in the URBAN RENAISSANCE. Warwick's lack of significant growth from the 18th century is principally a result of the expansion of its immediate neighbour, Leamington SPA.

Warwick, 16th Earl of, *see* NEVILLE, RICHARD

Warwick, 19th Earl of, *see* DUDLEY, JOHN

Warwick, 23rd Earl of, *see* RICH, ROBERT

Washington Naval Agreement, an exercise in armament limitation after WORLD WAR I, and a successful attempt to prevent a shipbuilding-race between the USA and Japan. The treaty imposed a ten-year moratorium on the building of capital ships and Britain, the USA and Japan agreed to a 5:5:3 ratio in them, with France and Italy each at half the Japanese level. This represented a diplomatic triumph for Britain, which, with her finances shattered by war, could never have kept up in a building race. The treaty did, however, formally recognize the end of two centuries of the British fleet being the largest in the world.

Water Frame, *see* COTTON INDUSTRY

Water Power The power of a river or head of water to turn a wheel, and thus drive machinery, was the greatest that men could muster before the advent of steam. Water power was therefore crucial to the workings of the pre-industrial and early industrial ECONOMIES. Watermills for grinding corn were the most important; under the MANORIAL economy mill rights were jealously guarded, and dues exacted for the compulsory use of the lord's mill. The earliest reference to a watermill dates from the 8th century, and thousands are recorded in *DOMESDAY BOOK*. Larger waterwheels and improvements to the way in which the water was sent round them produced ever-greater power, and the early FACTORIES were water-powered, often with huge wheels. Arkwright and other early industrialists chose to site their mills – the word is significant – alongside suitable water-courses. Even with the introduction of STEAM POWER, improvements in waterwheels continued to be made, and only after 1850 could steam-driven mills compete with the power of the largest water-driven ones. Thereafter, water power went into rapid decline, although its use continued in a few places. The harnessing of water for electricity began to become a serious option from the 1880s; William Armstrong (1810–1900) and others experimented, and hydro-electric power schemes were introduced in northern Scotland from the 1930s.

Waterloo, Battle of, south of Brussels, Belgium, 18 June 1815, the climax of the FRENCH REVOLUTIONARY and NAPOLEONIC WARS (1793–1815). Napoleon, having returned from Elba, sought to surprise the coalition forces ranged against him. He attacked and defeated the Prussian army at Ligny while holding part of the British force at Quatre Bras. The British under Wellington (*see* WELLESLEY, ARTHUR) retreated in an orderly manner to the Waterloo battlefield, just south of the town. Napoleon with 72,000 men and 226 guns outnumbered Wellington with 66,700 men and 156 guns, but the contingent which he had detached to harry the Prussians failed to do so effectively. From late morning Napoleon tried and failed to break Wellington's line, until the arrival of the Prussians late in the afternoon enabled the Allies to sweep the French from the field.

Watling Street, one of the great roads built by the Romans, which ran from London to Holyhead on Anglesey. The many sites of camps and fortresses found along the road – e.g. WROXETER and Mancetter – are evidence of the important military role it played in the defeat of Welsh tribes such as the ORDOVICES, as well as in SUETONIUS PAULINUS' rapid return to southern Britain to defeat BOUDICCA's rebels. *See also* FOSSE WAY; ROADS; ROMAN ROADS.

WEA, *see* WORKERS' EDUCATIONAL ASSOCIATION

Webb, Beatrice (née Potter; Baroness Passfield) (1858–1943) and Sidney (1st Baron Passfield) (1859–1947), social investigators, reformers and pioneer socialists. Together they devoted their prodigious energy to studies of TRADE UNIONISM, industrial democracy, and LOCAL GOVERNMENT, their unique partnership providing the research with which they aimed to influence society in a socialist direction rather than through revolutionary action. Active FABIANS, they also founded the London School of Economics and Political Science (1895) and the *NEW STATESMAN* (1913). As members of the Royal Commission on the POOR LAWS (1905–9), they produced a minority report that foreshadowed aspects of the later WELFARE STATE, while Sidney served on the executive of the LABOUR PARTY (1915–25), in 1918 drafting its new constitution and, with Beatrice, writing the policy statement *Labour and the New Social Order*.

As MP for Seaham (1922–9), Sidney served as president of the Board of Trade in 1924 in MACDONALD's government and as secretary for dominions and colonies (1929–30) and for colonies (1930–1). Following a visit to the Soviet Union in 1932, the Webbs published their enthusiastic impressions in *Soviet Communism: A New Civilization?* (1935) – the question mark disappeared from subsequent editions. Major influences on British socialism in a non-revolutionary 'gradualist' direction, they also made a lasting impact on the character of British social investigation and perhaps on the Labour Party.

Wedmore, Peace of, Som., 878, a decisive moment in ALFRED THE GREAT's resistance to the VIKINGS, which followed his military victory at EDINGTON. In the treaty, between Alfred and the Scandinavian king GUTHRUM, the Vikings agreed to give Alfred hostages, to leave WESSEX and to convert to Christianity.

'Wee Frees', derogatory name for the group of 'independent' LIBERALS, supporters of ASQUITH, who opposed the Coalition Liberals led by LLOYD GEORGE. Only 28 were elected in the 'COUPON' ELECTION of 1918 when Asquith was also defeated. They eventually reunited with the former Coalition Liberals to fight the 1923 election, although by that time the separation of the Liberals into rival factions had done lasting damage to the party. The name derives from the jocular Scots nickname for the section of the Free Church of Scotland which continued to go it alone after church reunions from 1900 onwards.

Welfare State, term used to denote the provision of extensive social welfare by the state, coined in the 1930s to contrast with the 'warfare state' devoting itself to armaments. The phrase has been used retrospectively to describe the introduction of extensive welfare legislation by the pre-1914 LIBERAL governments of ASQUITH, which provided OLD AGE PENSIONS in 1908 and national insurance in 1911, covering workers for UNEMPLOYMENT, sickness, and accidents – the so-called 'Liberal Welfare State'. These policies were extended between the wars with the widening of national insurance in 1920, the introduction of widows' pensions in 1925, and the rationalization of unemployment insurance under the UNEMPLOYMENT ASSISTANCE BOARD ACT in 1934–5. State HOUSING, EDUCATION, and the provision of services such as SCHOOL MEALS and milk were accepted parts of welfare provision by the outbreak of WORLD WAR II (*see* POOR LAW, NEW).

The BEVERIDGE REPORT of 1942 and the pressures for post-war reconstruction brought about proposals for comprehensive social insurance for all, a free health service, family allowances, and free secondary education: welfare from the cradle to the grave. The principal legislation comprised the EDUCATION ACT 1944, the FAMILY ALLOWANCES ACT 1945, the NATIONAL INSURANCE ACT 1946, the NATIONAL ASSISTANCE ACT 1948, and the NATIONAL HEALTH SERVICE ACT 1946.

Although the costs were partly met by compulsory contributions by employees and employers, the welfare state established after 1945 required an increasing level of support from general taxation. Welfare benefits were extended to include supplementary benefits, invalidity benefits, housing benefits, and discretionary payments under the Social Fund. By 1990 social security, excluding education and housing, made up almost 40 per cent of government spending. The welfare state had considerable cross-party support for much of the period after 1945, but as the post-war political consensus started to break down in the 1970s it became more contentious. Thus on the right the notion of the welfare state or welfarism was identified as causing the emergence of a culture of dependency, and acting as a stifling burden on free enterprise undermining ECONOMIC GROWTH. On the left the welfare state was seen as a mechanism for helping to redistribute the wealth of society and protecting vulnerable groups from the effects of economic change. The debate on the welfare state has recently been sharpened by public perception of increasing expenditure on state welfare and the higher costs imposed by an ageing population and higher demands for health care.

Wellesley, Sir Arthur 'The Iron Duke' (1st Duke of Wellington) (1769–1852), soldier, politician and Prime Minister (1828–30). Born into the Irish aristocracy, he commanded the 33rd Foot in INDIA (1797), was governor of Mysore in 1799 and became a major-general in 1802, after which he fought in the second Maratha War (1803–5). After returning to England he became MP for Rye in 1806. As chief secretary for Ireland (1807–9) he was firm but fair-minded, criticizing absentee landlords and prohibiting triumphalist processions on the anniversary of the defeat of the UNITED IRISHMEN.

It was the PENINSULAR WAR that confirmed Wellesley's military reputation. After Sir John Moore's abortive Corunna campaign, Wellesley led the British ARMY and its Portuguese allies into a five-year campaign against the French in the Peninsula. His success was largely due to the British NAVY which supplied him with provisions or the wherewithal to obtain them from the local population, whereas the much larger French armies were forced to scavenge from the land. He won a series of battles against the French – Talavera (28 July 1809); Busaco (26 Sept.); Albuera (16 May 1811) – and was able to sit out a French onslaught ensconced in a coastal stronghold in the Torres Vedras campaign of 1811–12. He conducted successful sieges against French-held fortresses at Ciudad Rodrigo (8–9 Jan. 1812) and Badajoz (16 March–6 April), caught the retreating French forces at the battle of Salamanca on 23 July 1812 and moved to capture Madrid on 12 Aug. Napoleon's withdrawal of forces for the Russian campaign allowed Wellesley to regroup and pursue the French back into their own soil, winning the victories at Orthez (27 Feb. 1814) and Toulouse (10 April). Napoleon then abdicated and departed for Elba.

In acknowledgment of his services Wellesley was created 1st Duke of Wellington and appointed ambassador to the French court, attending the Congress of VIENNA. Shortly afterwards, Napoleon, who had escaped from Elba, re-entered Paris. Wellington was made commander-in-chief of the British forces in March 1815, and began to assemble an allied army to defeat the Corsican. He marched his army to meet Napoleon, intervening in the Franco-Prussian battle of Ligny on 16 June at Quatre Bras. But it was not until 18 June that the British encountered the full French army at WATERLOO. Wellington's army, disposed just behind the crest of a long ridge with two fortified positions, held firm against five major attacks by the French forces. Finally Wellington ordered the counter-attack, and sweeping down drove the French armies from the field, pushing them back to Paris, from where Napoleon was again sent into exile, this time to ST HELENA, and Wellington was put in charge of the allied army of occupation. His military success was largely due to his brilliance as a defensive tactician, stringent in the conservation of his forces, always poised to take advantage of the enemy's mistakes or weakness, and able to judge exactly when to counter-attack without unnecessary loss of life.

Wellington became prime minister at the beginning of 1828 when the demand for CATHOLIC EMANCIPATION was at its height. Supported by his home secretary Sir Robert PEEL, he agreed to the conditions laid down by GEORGE IV that emancipation should not become a government issue. But after the Clare by-election he recognized that further deferment could only result in civil war. The king was won round only after Wellington and Peel threatened to resign. Catholic emancipation split the Tories and brought the WHIGS to power in 1830, after which Wellington became the elder statesman of the TORY party. He served briefly as foreign secretary in Peel's minority government of 1834–5 and was minister without portfolio during Peel's second ministry of 1841–6. His sense of duty and discipline and concern for order gave his Toryism a pragmatism that was lacking among the ultra-Tories with whom he tended to identify.

Wellington, 1st Duke of, *see* WELLESLEY, SIR ARTHUR

Welsh Nationalist Party, *see* PLAID CYMRU

Wendover, Roger of, *see* ROGER OF WENDOVER

Wentworth, Charles Watson (2nd Marquess of Rockingham) (1730–82), politician and Prime Minister (1765–6, 1782). Only surviving son of the first marquess, in 1750 he succeeded to his father's title and, with it, a substantial political interest in Yorks. The following year, he became a lord of the bedchamber. However, much disturbed by the admission of former TORIES to court positions at the accession of GEORGE III in 1760, he resigned over the preliminaries to the

Peace of PARIS two years later. He was not naturally assertive – he hardly ever spoke in Parliament – but veteran politicians such as Newcastle (*see* PELHAM-HOLLES, THOMAS) and Hardwicke were aged and/or dying, and many of those who shared his deep distrust of the new king were too young and inexperienced to take the lead. These circumstances determined that Rockingham emerged as leader of a group of disgruntled OLD CORPS WHIGS, consequently known as the ROCKINGHAMITE WHIGS.

Rockingham came to the fore when he was made FIRST LORD OF THE TREASURY in the ministry put together by Cumberland (*see* WILLIAM AUGUSTUS) in 1765, which courted popularity at home and in the colonies by repealing Bute's (*see* STUART, JOHN) cider EXCISE and GRENVILLE'S STAMP ACT. A quarrel with the king over appointments led to Rockingham's dismissal in 1766; those who left with him became his core followers. He presided over fierce opposition to Grafton (*see* FITZROY, AUGUSTUS), and somewhat more intermittent opposition to NORTH. In 1780, an attempt was made to incorporate him in a reconstructed ministry, but by then he was making both recognition of AMERICAN INDEPENDENCE and ECONOMICAL REFORMS conditions for accepting office.

On North's resignation in 1782, he returned to the Treasury, presiding over a mixture of his followers and those of the recently deceased PITT THE ELDER. His second ministry made the first moves towards ending the war in America, gave Ireland LEGISLATIVE INDEPENDENCE by repealing the DECLARATORY ACT 1720 and encouraging the Irish PARLIAMENT to repeal POYNINGS' LAW, and enacted certain measures of economical reform. His sudden death in July 1782 precipitated a latent split among his colleagues. Though Rockingham was not an assertive figure, some political skill is suggested by his nurturing of the Yorks. interest, and his ability to hold together a group of talented but independent-minded followers.

Wentworth, Thomas (Baron and Viscount Wentworth; 1st Earl of Strafford) (1593–1641), politician. A Yorks. gentleman, he was prominent in the parliamentary opposition (including that to the FORCED LOAN) until 1628, when CHARLES I gave him a barony and the presidency of the COUNCIL OF THE NORTH. He became increasingly prominent on the Irish committee of the PRIVY COUNCIL, and in 1632 was made lord deputy in Ireland, charged with increasing royal revenue and bringing an end to corruption and waste. To do so, he ruthlessly and tactlessly promoted THOROUGH, first making an unexpected alliance with the Old English against the NEW ENGLISH settlers. However, in turn he alienated the Old English by his investigation of insecure land titles in the interests of the crown. Such was his success in the short term that in 1634 he gained Charles's permission to hold a PARLIAMENT (in contrast to its complete abeyance in England; it was dissolved in 1635); in this he exploited the rivalry of New and Old English for the crown's benefit. His backing of a new PLANTATION scheme in CONNACHT (1635) aroused fury among the Old English for its threat to their interests, while the simultaneous crown seizure of LONDONDERRY appalled the New English and their contacts in England. Wentworth allowed a good deal of latitude to Roman CATHOLIC clergy; he also backed moves to bring the CHURCH OF IRELAND into line with the policies of William LAUD in the CHURCH OF ENGLAND, in opposition to its generally CALVINIST-sympathizing leadership. He was as energetic in reclaiming lands for the Church as for the crown, but additionally he made a huge profit for himself in lands and revenues from his lease of the CUSTOMS.

Wentworth was recalled to England in 1639 to help the king in the gathering crisis. On the collapse of Charles's regime in 1640, he was a prime target for revenge, particularly from the champion of the New English, Richard Boyle, Earl of Cork. The king at first showed his defiance of his critics by conferring an earldom on Wentworth, one of his few resolute and decisive supporters, but then he abandoned him, assenting to his ATTAINDER and execution in 1641. Wentworth was a man of energy and efficiency who had little belief in compromise and little respect for the judgement of his opponents.

Wergeld, the term used in Anglo-Saxon LAW CODES to describe the price that a kindred was obliged to pay to compensate the kindred of anyone murdered by one of its members. It was associated with one of the most fundamental of all institutions of early societies: the kindred's responsibility to seek revenge for murder (*see* BLOOD FEUD).

The mention of *wergelds* in early law codes, such as those of kings ETHELBERT and INE, indicates that 7th-century English society was already seeking a means of reducing violence through mechanisms of compensation and social control. The law codes ultimately developed a complex set of *wergeld* payments that were directly related to social status. Although *wergelds* feature in a 12th-century text – the *Laws of King Henry I* – other evidence from that period and earlier shows English government taking over responsibility for the punishment of violent crime. *See also* GALANAS.

Wesley, John (1703–91), founder of Methodism. Educated at Oxford, he became a college tutor there and, together with his brother Charles, was a member of the HIGH CHURCH 'Holy Club' for religious study and devotion as well as pastoral work among prisoners and the poor. In 1735 he was appointed to minister to colonists in Georgia, but having aroused antagonism, he returned two years later. Contact with the MORAVIAN brethren and their devotional practices provided the context for a religious experience at a meeting in Aldersgate, London in 1738, which fired his interest in the relationship between conversion and faith.

Following the example of George Whitefield, whom he had first encountered in the Holy Club, Wesley began to travel and preach in the open air, attracting large crowds. He encouraged the formation of METHODIST societies for devotional purposes, and devised an organizational structure that effectively bound these bodies together; the first of a series of annual conferences was held in 1744. He claimed that his efforts were intended to strengthen the Established Church, but in practice, his network of lay preachers – humble men by the standards of the ANGLICAN clergy – was not easily accommodated within the establishment. After his death, a formal separation took place.

In some ways very much a man of his age, with an interest in science and the systematic study of religious experience, Wesley was an inspired popularizer, warily sympathetic to the ways in which poorer people spontaneously expressed their fears, hopes and beliefs. A very effective orator and prolific writer, he tried to make suitable contemporary works of fiction and non-fiction accessible to a wide audience by abridging and rewriting them.

Wesleyan Methodism, *see* METHODISM

Wessex This was ultimately the most successful of the early English kingdoms, since the 10th-century 'West Saxon' kings were able to build on ALFRED THE GREAT's defiance of the Vikings' GREAT ARMY to bring about the UNIFICATION of the English peoples. *See also* ENGLISH, ORIGINS OF THE.

The apparently clear account of the kingdom's origins in the *ANGLO-SAXON CHRONICLE* is now regarded with suspicion and its beginnings must be considered obscure. The likely location of the dynasty's earliest lands is the upper Thames valley, and the first king was probably CERDIC, who reigned in either the late 5th or the early 6th century.

The kingdom's fortunes fluctuated during the following centuries. King CEAWLIN – listed among the seven kings said by BEDE to have exercised overlordship south of the Humber (*see BRETWALDA*) – was successful in pushing West Saxon power westwards at the expense of the Britons. CADWALLA and INE defeated the English peoples to the south and east. However, the 8th century was dominated by MERCIA, and no Wessex king achieved much success until the time of EGBERT, who not only ended Mercian hegemony for ever, but also extended his authority into Cornwall, creating a kingdom that covered all England south of the Thames.

The organization of the kingdom before the time of Alfred the Great appears to have been much the same as that of any other early kingdom; Ine, for example, issued a LAW CODE, and there is also clear evidence of the development of the COMMON BURDENS. Major reforms took place in Alfred's time, to be followed under his successors by the development of a formidably effective system of government.

The rise of the Wessex dynasty to the throne of England owed much to the VIKINGS, whose elimination of all the other major kingdoms left the field open to the one remaining line of English kings. As the kings of Wessex became kings of the English, Wessex itself became the responsibility of a number of EALDORMEN (*see also* EARLDOMS, ANGLO-SAXON). This changed in the reign of CNUT, when a single earldom of Wessex was created for GODWINE, whose family dominated English politics until 1066, when his son HAROLD II was briefly king.

Wessex, Earl of, *see* GODWINE

West Indies, general term for the islands in the Caribbean, many of which were (and a few of which remain) British colonies. BARBADOS was the first island to become a British possession; JAMAICA, acquired in the war against Spain under Oliver CROMWELL, was the largest and most important. Most of the islands came to specialize in SUGAR cultivation, and to become labour cultures (*see* SLAVE TRADE); West Indian wealth underpinned many political careers and artistic endeavours in 18th-century England. The islands remained colonies when the 13 colonies on the mainland broke away from Britain in the War of AMERICAN INDEPENDENCE, and they were an important element in the continuing wars against France in the 18th and early 19th centuries. With declining sugar prices and productivity, and the continuing poverty of the islands, many islanders left in the considerable MIGRATION to Britain in the 1950s and 1960s.

Western Australia Fears of French incursions prompted Britain's first settlement of west AUSTRALIA in 1826. Convict labour sustained the struggling colony (*see* TRANSPORTATION), but success only came with GOLD discoveries from 1888. Self-governing from 1890, there was a strong movement for secession from the new post-1901 federation, overruled by Britain after a 1933 referendum.

Western European Union, *see* BRUSSELS, TREATY OF

Western Rebellion, 1549. Two years of unrest in the West Country exploded into open conflict throughout Devon and Cornwall around Whitsunday (9 June) 1549, the day specified for the first use of the English PRAYER BOOK. The rebels were delayed by an unsuccessful siege of EXETER, and were eventually defeated by a royal army under John Russell. Besides the religious motive, recent research points to the role of the clientage of the disgraced Courtenay family, and of economic grievances.

Westminster There is evidence of Roman settlement on the site of Westminster Abbey, but the origins of the Abbey itself, at a place called Thorney by the Anglo-Saxons, are obscure; the earliest authentic mentions are from the time of the TENTH-CENTURY REFORM. Westminster Abbey, the principal burial place of royalty and distinguished persons, was already associated with royalty before the NORMAN CONQUEST, being the site of HAROLD I HAREFOOT's burial (1040), and EDWARD THE CONFESSOR undertook a spectacular rebuilding of the church from *c.*1050; this indicates a change of residence by the Anglo-Saxon royal family from their traditional main home at WINCHESTER. The palace, with which the abbey remained closely associated, remained a favourite of the ANGEVIN monarchs, and hence it became a centre of government thanks to the administrative innovations of HENRY II; the abbey church was lavishly rebuilt in the French style under HENRY III and his successors, with the CORONATION space and the shrine of the canonized Confessor at its heart. The last main extension was HENRY VII's chapel at the east end, originally intended as a shrine for HENRY VI who was, in the event, never canonized.

By the 16th century, the palace had ceased to be a royal residence, having been completely colonized by the institutions of central bureaucracy, the COMMON LAW courts (housed in WILLIAM II RUFUS's Westminster Hall) and PARLIAMENT; hence one still refers informally to 'Westminster' when talking about these institutions (*see also* CROWN; WHITEHALL). New residential palaces were built by HENRY VIII immediately to the north – St James's and Whitehall (the former York Place, confiscated from WOLSEY). Henry also spared the former abbey at its dissolution, making it into a CATHEDRAL in 1540; however, the DIOCESE was dissolved and reabsorbed into London in 1550, and the church became COLLEGIATE with PECULIAR status which it has retained to the present day, apart from a brief restoration of the monks under MARY I.

The rambling complex of palaces was subject to frequent fires, the two most serious of which were those of 1698, which destroyed most of Whitehall, and of 1834 (*see* TALLIES), which affected the Palace of Westminster except for Westminster Hall and some minor buildings. The rebuilding after 1835 of the Houses of Parliament by Charles Barry (1795–1860) and Augustus Pugin (1812–52) was a major triumph for the GOTHIC Revival style. Westminster was created a city, consisting of inner west London north of the Thames, in 1900. Of its many major buildings, the Roman Catholic Westminster Cathedral (1895–1903, in a free Byzantine style by J. F. Bentley) complements rather than rivals the Abbey.

Westminster Assembly, gathering of laity and clergy with Scots representatives, established by PARLIAMENT in June 1643 to plan Church reform. Although hampered by quarrels between strict PRESBYTERIANS and pragmatists, in 1645 it produced a Directory of Worship to replace the PRAYER BOOK and, the following year, the Westminster Confession, based on the Solemn League and COVENANT. The Confession remains a doctrinal standard in Presbyterian churches, and has influenced many CALVINIST Confessions. Assembly meetings petered out in 1653.

Westminster Confession, *see* WESTMINSTER ASSEMBLY

Westminster, Provisions of, *see* PROVISIONS OF WESTMINSTER

Westminster, Statute of, 1931, Act which gave the self-governing DOMINIONS within the BRITISH EMPIRE legislative independence from the United Kingdom. The Imperial Conference of 1926 had defined the Dominions as 'autonomous communities within the British Empire' and the Statute of 1931 enacted the full sovereignty of the Parliaments of CANADA, AUSTRALIA, NEW ZEALAND, the Union of SOUTH AFRICA, the IRISH FREE STATE and NEWFOUNDLAND. It was regarded at the time as a milestone in the constitutional development of the British Empire into a COMMONWEALTH of independent states.

Westminster, Treaty of, 1654, *see* DUTCH WARS

Whig, term applied – initially in the extended form 'whiggamore' – to Scots COVENANTERS, and thence to those who opposed the Duke of York (the future JAMES II) in the EXCLUSION CRISIS. Civil and political liberty were key Whig values. The GLORIOUS REVOLUTION brought the Whigs into favour, and inaugurated decades of tension between the attractions of power and the Whigs' oppositional ideological heritage. Disillusioned with the JUNTO, some alienated Whigs followed HARLEY to form the NEW TORY Party in the early 18th century. Early 18th-century Whigs presented themselves as archetypically merchants; their critics represented them as archetypically speculators and profiteers. They were well represented among the directors of the BANK OF ENGLAND and EAST INDIA COMPANY, but also included many landowners, especially from the west and north-west of England, and, at their core, some of the greatest landowners of England and Ireland. More consistent than the TORIES in supporting the HANOVERIAN SUCCESSION, the Whigs persuaded both GEORGE I and GEORGE II that only they could be trusted in office, and thus established a WHIG OLIGARCHY. Dissident Whigs joined with Tories in a COUNTRY alliance that helped bring down WALPOLE'S ministry in 1742, but the OLD CORPS WHIGS effectively regrouped and reasserted themselves under the PELHAM brothers.

The cohesion of the traditional Whig party was permanently shattered only when GEORGE III pronounced an end to Tory exclusion, and drove first PITT THE ELDER, then Newcastle (*see* PELHAM-HOLLES, THOMAS) from power. Some Whigs, e.g. NORTH, were happy to serve the new king on his terms, but others rallied under Rockingham (*see* WENTWORTH, CHARLES) and Pitt, ennobled as Chatham, and questioned the constitutionality both of his style of rule and of the policies of his ministers. The ROCKINGHAMITE WHIGS especially proclaimed themselves the only true Whigs, and also laid proud claim to the name of 'party', construed by their ideologist BURKE to denote 'honourable connexion'. Deeply reluctant to appoint these Whigs to office after the fall of North, George seized the chance to dismiss the FOX–North coalition when it offered; his preferred PITT THE YOUNGER saw himself as a Whig, but was labelled a Tory by his critics, and retrospectively claimed as such by early 19th-century admirers.

Divided in their responses to the French

Revolution, the Whigs split in 1794 between a group under Portland (*see* BENTINCK, WILLIAM CAVENDISH) who joined Pitt's ministry, and an oppositional group under Fox: some of those who left with Portland drifted back later in the decade, and especially after Pitt's fall. Fox's stance in the 1790s helped to ensure that the Whigs were henceforth associated with the causes of political and religious reform; distinguishing themselves from the populist RADICALS, they also became increasingly ready to endorse the notion that they were a distinctively 'aristocratic party', initially a charge levelled against them.

By the end of 1829, with the disintegration of parties, the demise of the Whigs as a separate party seemed a certainty, and they seemed doomed to 'do the only good things Whigs ever do, by acting separately and watching the government', as the Marquess of Tavistock expressed it. However, the debates around the 1832 REFORM ACT made 'Whiggery' relevant again as a 'body of men connected with high rank and property, bound together by hereditary feelings, party ties, who when the people are roused, stand between the Constitution and revolution, and go with the people, but not to *extremities*'. But it was a brief revival: by the end of the 1850s the party was a LIBERAL PARTY not a Whig one. The 1867 REFORM ACT, with its move towards the democratization of the representative system, was the final death-knell to a party which believed itself to have the prerogative to govern and to control reform, not to see that right pass into the hands of the people. Unlike the term Tory, the name Whig is not recalled by the Liberal Party, nor used by anyone in political discourse.

Whig Oligarchy, historians' term for the political system under which, between 1715 and 1760, public life at almost all levels was effectively monopolized by WHIGS.

The HANOVERIAN SUCCESSION, defeat of the 1715 JACOBITE rising, and the Whig election victory in the same year were accompanied by the removal of TORIES from government and household offices, and unusually thorough purges of the army, the law, higher clergy, minor office holders, county lieutenancies and commissions of the peace. More far-reaching measures planned for the 1719 parliamentary session – a Peerage Bill, repeal of the SEPTENNIAL ACT's requirement that new Parliaments be summoned every seven years, and a plan to secure more effective political control of universities – were, however, defeated or dropped. Sir Robert WALPOLE treated all Tories as crypto-Jacobites; men of ambition in the 1720s and 1730s converted to Whiggery to advance their careers.

From the 1740s, more Tories were made magistrates; in the 1750s, they were given commissions in the revived MILITIA; and Henry PELHAM and PITT THE ELDER showed some willingness to co-operate with them on their own terms. GEORGE III refused to discriminate between loyal subjects, admitting Tories to posts in the household, welcoming them to court, and decimating the ranks of Whig placemen in the 'massacre of the Pelhamite Innocents'. The name 'Tory' did not regain popularity until the early 19th century: in a sense, Whiggery remained a ruling force, but thenceforth on a more consensual basis.

Whimsical (or Hanoverian) Tories, TORIES who broke ranks to vote with the WHIGS on certain key measures in 1713–14, apparently because they thought the Oxford ministry (*see* HARLEY) was taking insufficient care of PROTESTANT interests. Sir Thomas Hanmer was their most prominent member in the Commons, the Earl of Anglesey in the Lords. In 1713, they helped vote down a commercial treaty with France, intended to complement the Peace of UTRECHT; in 1714, they several times voted with Whigs to secure the HANOVERIAN SUCCESSION, in this way helping to establish Whig ascendancy.

Whisky Money A popular term, it described the provisions of the Local Taxation (Customs and Excise) Act 1899, relating to the assignment of a portion of the EXCISE duty as a grant in aid of TECHNICAL EDUCATION.

Whitby Abbey, Yorks. Founded by King OSWY of NORTHUMBRIA in 657, this was one of the most important of the abbeys of the CONVERSION period (*see also* JARROW; LINDISFARNE; MONKWEARMOUTH). Its first abbess was St Hilda, a member of the Northumbrian royal house, a fact that reflects the aristocratic nature of many of these early monasteries and the uniquely English prominence of women in their governing. Like others, Whitby was a 'double monastery', comprising segregated communities of men and women. It was destroyed during the VIKING invasions; refounded in the 11th century, it was dissolved in 1539, but its splendid remains can still be seen.

Whitby, Synod of, 664, the occasion when disputes between the Roman and Irish missions over the correct date of EASTER were resolved. The synod is currently regarded more as a consequence of the manipulations of NORTHUMBRIAN court politics and the forceful Romanizing influence of WILFRID than as an indication of a long-standing bitter disagreement between Roman and Irish clerics. The debate – and King OSWY's decision in favour of Roman usage – are, none the less, important moments in the recognition by the churches of the British Isles of their place in the wider European ecclesiastical scene. *See also* CONVERSION.

White Rose, a badge adopted by the YORKISTS in the 15th century (*see* WARS OF THE ROSES). It was also used by the 18th-century JACOBITES as an emblem of the Pretender (*see* STUART, JAMES EDWARD), apparently because they were obliged to support him *sub rosa* ('under the rose') – i.e. secretly.

White Ship This ship and the lives of nearly all on board were lost – allegedly because the crew was drunk – on 25 Nov. 1120, shortly after leaving the Norman port of Barfleur on one of the routine cross-Channel voyages characteristic of the ANGLO-NORMAN REALM. This disaster precipitated a dynastic crisis since among those drowned was HENRY I's only legitimate son, William.

Whiteboys, the name given to Irish smallholders and the like who protested against ENCLOSURES, land-jobbing (the leasing of land involving the displacement of the sitting tenant at the expiry of a lease), evictions, high rents and tithes in MUNSTER in 1761–2 and again in 1769–75. They took oaths of secrecy, destroyed enclosures and houses, and rode in groups at night blowing horns. Some landowners suspected a French-backed Catholic conspiracy, and a parliamentary inquiry of 1764 concluded that the disorders had been planned. The name 'Whiteboys', which initially referred to the white shirts or smocks worn by the protesters, was later applied generically to all forms of Irish agrarian discontent associated with secret societies, oaths and violence. Later protesters were also known as Rightboys (1785–7), Peep O'Day Boys, Thrashers (1806–7) and Rockites (1821–4).

Whitehall, street in London running from Trafalgar Square (once the Royal Mews) to the palace of WESTMINSTER, and the site of the palace of Whitehall, formerly known as York Place, which was seized from WOLSEY BY HENRY VIII in 1529. The palace burned down in 1698 and thereafter ceased to be a royal residence; the only substantial survival is Inigo Jones's Banqueting House, the venue for the execution of CHARLES I. From the 18th century onwards, Whitehall has become the seat of many departments of state, which adapted existing houses or acquired purpose-built offices, beginning with Thomas Ripley and Robert Adam's Admiralty building (1722 and 1759). The TREASURY and Gilbert Scott's Foreign Office are the most substantial buildings, while the prime minister's and other official residences are situated on Downing Street leading off Whitehall. Whitehall is also a ceremonial route, with Horse Guards Parade leading off it through to the Mall, and the CENOTAPH placed in the centre of the street. Official plans in the 1960s for the area's wholesale redevelopment and demolition to provide a modern, purpose-built centre for government administration were thwarted by successful CONSERVATION campaigning.

By extension from its functions, 'Whitehall' has come to be a generic term for the CIVIL SERVICE and the workings of the departments of state.

Whitehaven, Cumbria, coastal port town, which was developed on a grid plan from the 1690s on land owned by the earls of Lonsdale, and which flourished in the 18th century as a centre for the colonial and Irish trades, specializing in TOBACCO, cattle and COAL. It was subsequently eclipsed by both LIVERPOOL and GLASGOW, and became progressively poorer. Its many surviving Georgian buildings have made it a focus of CONSERVATION activity in recent decades.

Whitgift, John (1532–1604), Archbishop of Canterbury (1583–1604). Born in Lincs., Whitgift was a CAMBRIDGE don with

CALVINIST sympathies, but he was nevertheless very concerned to enforce Church order. His brisk disciplining of PURITANS attracted ELIZABETH I and led to the bishopric of Worcester in 1577, and in 1583 the archbishopric of Canterbury. He immediately confronted the Puritan clergy. Although government nervousness at the ensuing rows somewhat restrained him, he relied on Christopher Hatton's support against the discreet hostility of William CECIL, and encouraged much gradual reform in the Church.

Whitley Councils, important attempt at industrial arbitration, the product of the Whitley Report of 1917. The report aimed to resolve labour disputes by setting up Joint Industrial Councils made up of representatives of employers and workers at national, district, and works level. By 1920 JICs or 'Whitley' Councils covered almost 3.5 million workers. Though they went into decline between the two world wars and were never as extensive as anticipated, they remained important in areas of government employment, especially the CIVIL SERVICE. During WORLD WAR II further councils were set up to cover the distributive trades.

Whitsun, popular name for the Christian movable festival of Pentecost in late spring. Whitsun was the occasion for many CALENDAR CUSTOMS, and a particularly popular day from the 16th to the 19th centuries for fairs, village sports, and the like. It remained a Bank Holiday until the 1960s, when it was replaced by the late spring holiday.

Wiener Thesis, *see* GENTLEMANLY CAPITALISM

Wife's Lament, The, a short poem of 53 lines contained in the 10th-century anthology known as the EXETER BOOK. Describing a wife's grief during a husband's deliberate absence, it is one of the earliest surviving love poems in the English language.

Wigstan, St, *see* WYSTAN

Wihtred, King of Kent (691–725). A ruler of some importance, he freed KENT from the domination of neighbouring kingdoms, issued a LAW CODE that gave especially privileged treatment to the Church, and had an extensive COINAGE of *SCEATTAS* minted on his behalf.

Wihtred's career illustrates well the achievements of the lesser kingdoms of the HEPTARCHY in the years before the domination of southern England by MERCIA and WESSEX.

Wilberforce, William (1759–1833), evangelical philanthropist. Son of a prosperous Hull merchant, in 1776 he was sent to Cambridge, where he became a friend of PITT THE YOUNGER. From 1780–4 he served as MP for Hull, then for Yorks. In 1785, while on a continental tour, he experienced religious conversion, as a result of which an already promising political career developed in unconventional fashion.

He took as his initial objects the REFORMATION OF MANNERS and the abolition of slavery (*see* ANTI-SLAVERY). In 1807, he was instrumental in securing the abolition of the SLAVE TRADE in Britain, and subsequently worked, through the African Society, for its international abolition. His religious associates became known as the CLAPHAM SECT, his parliamentary allies as 'the SAINTS'. Among the many other philanthropic and improving causes with which he was associated were the Society for Bettering the Condition and Increasing the Comforts of the Poor, the BRITISH AND FOREIGN BIBLE SOCIETY and the London Missionary Society.

He was too radical for conservatives of his day, and too conservative for the radicals. He supported DISSENT, but encouraged the prosecution of Thomas PAINE's *Age of Reason*; he criticized the beliefs and conduct of the rich and educated – notably in his 1797 *Practical View of the Prevailing Religious System of Professed Christians* – but did not wish to see the social order overturned.

He resigned his populous and demanding Yorks. seat in 1812 because of failing health, becoming MP for Bramber. His sons distanced themselves from their father's EVANGELICALISM; one, Samuel, became an Anglican bishop.

Wild Geese, Irish soldiers serving in foreign, especially CATHOLIC, armies. The name was established by the 1720s; KING WILLIAM'S WAR had provided the occasion for large-scale movements of Irish troops to France. During the time of both James Edward and Charles Edward STUART, the Old and Young Pretenders, the Stuart cause continued to attract a steady stream of Irish recruits to foreign armies. They contributed significantly to French military effort in several wars, perhaps most notably at the battle of FONTENOY in 1745. When the FRENCH REVOLUTION overthrew the Bourbon monarchy, Irish soldiers divided their loyalties between the royalist and revolutionary causes. Some returned to Ireland; others accepted GEORGE III's 1794 invitation to join the British army – including among their senior officers Daniel Count O'Connell, uncle of 'Liberator' Daniel O'CONNELL.

Wilfrid, St (634–709), Bishop of York (665–709). Of Northumbrian descent, he was one of the most important and controversial figures of the CONVERSION period. A great deal is known about his career from the biography composed by his chaplain Eddius and from BEDE. Having spent important formative years in France and at Rome, he returned to England imbued with Gaulish ideas on episcopal dignity and with a strong devotion to the papacy. As a result, he was the leading protagonist on the Roman side at the synod of WHITBY in 664, and his habit of appealing for papal support was to reinforce England's strong connections with Rome.

Appointed bishop of York in 665, for the rest of his life he was involved in disputes with kings ECGFRITH and ALDFRITH of NORTHUMBRIA, and with Archbishop THEODORE of CANTERBURY, who sought, successfully, to divide Wilfrid's large diocese (*see* BISHOPRICS). During his exiles from Northumbria in 678 and 680, which resulted from his quarrels with Ecgfrith, he undertook missionary work in southern England, becoming the head of a confederation of monasteries in several kingdoms. He was a great builder, although now only the crypts of his churches at Hexham and Ripon survive.

Wilkes, John (1727–97), radical. Son of a London distiller and educated at Leiden, he was flamboyantly rakish in conduct. Elected MP in 1757, he supported PITT THE ELDER and, between 1762 and 1763, attacked Bute's (*see* STUART, JOHN) ministry in his weekly essay paper, the *NORTH BRITON*. Charged with libel on the king's speech in issue NUMBER 45, he was expelled from PARLIAMENT; the episode was highly controversial, and the GENERAL WARRANTS issued for the arrest of those involved in publishing the paper were argued and later judged unconstitutional. Wilkes was widely identified with the cause of 'liberty', and became a popular hero, at least in England – the violently anti-Scottish rhetoric he had directed against Bute and others earned him hatred north of the border.

Found guilty (in his absence) of obscene libel for the poem 'Essay on Woman', he took refuge abroad. Returning in 1767, he was elected MP for Middlesex; he then surrendered to the court of KING'S BENCH and was imprisoned for two years. He was expelled from Parliament once more for a libel in relation to the ST GEORGE'S FIELD MASSACRE, but was three times re-elected despite Parliament's repeated refusal to seat him. The SOCIETY OF SUPPORTERS OF THE BILL OF RIGHTS and ROCKINGHAMITE WHIGS organized petitions in his favour.

Released in 1770, he was elected an alderman of London, becoming lord mayor in 1774. In the same year, he was again elected MP for Middlesex and this time he was seated. He opposed the War of AMERICAN INDEPENDENCE and supported the ASSOCIATION MOVEMENT. An avowed DEIST and advocate of religious toleration, he opposed the crowd in the GORDON RIOTS. However, his support for PITT THE YOUNGER increasingly estranged him from radical causes.

Wilkes's devil-may-care style seems to have enhanced his popular appeal, though it alienated more respectable radicals. In latter days, he told GEORGE III that he 'was never a Wilkite'.

William I the Conqueror (1027/8–87), King of England (1066–87) and Duke of Normandy. As the organizing genius of the NORMAN CONQUEST, he pushed through a more brutal transformation of English society than any ruler before or since. Although of illegitimate birth, as his father's only son he succeeded him as duke in 1035. He somehow survived the turmoil of his minority; then, in the late 1040s and 1050s, he defeated rebellions led by rival claimants to the duchy and invasions launched by neighbouring French princes. On the deaths in 1060 of his two principal enemies, Henry I of France and Count Geoffrey Martel of Anjou, William seized the initiative in devastating fashion.

In 1063, he conquered Maine. Then, after the death of EDWARD THE CONFESSOR in Jan. 1066, he claimed the English throne in opposition to HAROLD II (*see* SUCCESSION, ENGLISH, IN 1066). Brilliant generalship and luck enabled him to win the battle of HASTINGS, and he was crowned king on Christmas Day 1066. He then had to overcome an English resistance movement that held out until 1071, and which was particularly strong in the north of England: in 1069–70, this led him to order the notorious HARRYING OF THE NORTH. He built CASTLES in all the major English TOWNS, and by confiscating opponents' estates and transferring them to those whom he regarded as reliable (nearly all Frenchmen), he established an entirely new, French-speaking ruling class. A seal was set on this process when, in 1085, he set in motion the great inquiry that led to the drawing up of *DOMESDAY BOOK*.

His marriage to MATILDA OF FLANDERS produced nine children, but his last few years were darkened by quarrels with his eldest son, the future duke, ROBERT II (Robert Curthose). There was also constant, and again defensive, warfare against neighbouring princes, who were, rightly, alarmed by his astonishing success. In Sept. 1087, he died after a fall from his horse. He had been tempted to disinherit Robert altogether, but in the end agreed that the ancestral lands (Normandy) should go to the eldest son, leaving his conquest to his second son WILLIAM II RUFUS. The Conqueror was buried in his own foundation, St Stephen's in Caen; his corpulent body was too big for the stone sarcophagus that had been prepared, and burst when they tried to force it in.

William I the Lion (?1142–1214), King of Scots (1165–1214). The second son of Henry, Earl of Northumbria, after his father's death in 1152, while he was still a child. William was invested with the earldom, but his older brother MALCOLM IV was unable to prevent HENRY II from reclaiming it for the English crown. William succeeded to the Scottish throne following Malcolm's death in 1165.

The rebellion of 1173–4 against Henry gave William his opportunity to retake NORTHUMBRIA, but his invasions ended disastrously when he was taken by surprise at Alnwick and captured. To obtain his freedom, he had to accept the treaty of FALAISE, but in 1189, by the agreement known as the Quit Claim of Canterbury, RICHARD I released him from its terms. For much of his time on the throne, William's right to it was challenged by the MACWILLIAM dynasty. Despite these difficulties, the reign witnessed the extension of royal authority northwards across the Moray Firth.

William was succeeded by ALEXANDER II, his son by Ermengarde of Beaumont, whom he had married in 1186. Why later writers called him 'the Lion' is unclear; possibly it was because, in one obituary, he was referred to as 'the lion of justice'.

William II Rufus (*c.*1058–1100), King of England (1087–1100). The name 'Rufus' by which he is – and was – familiarly known derived from either his red hair or his ruddy complexion. The second son of WILLIAM I THE CONQUEROR, William Rufus was able to remain on good terms with his father, an advantage that eventually allowed him to succeed as king of England in 1087. However, his elder brother, ROBERT II (Robert Curthose), having secured NORMANDY, disputed his title to England. In consequence, William Rufus faced revolts in 1088 and 1095, as well as a war of succession that lasted until 1096 when Robert joined the First CRUSADE. To finance this enterprise, he mortgaged his duchy to Rufus.

Over the next few years, Rufus established a formidable military reputation during the near-permanent warfare among the princes of northern France. He also came to be known as a chivalrous and generous leader of knights. But these secular qualities cut no ice with churchmen; moreover, most of these were appalled by what they regarded as William Rufus's rapacious disregard for their property rights. His quarrels with Archbishop ANSELM of Canterbury were fierce enough to drive the archbishop into exile. In an age when most chroniclers were monks, this inevitably meant that William Rufus got a very bad press, and his sudden death in the New Forest, probably in a hunting accident, was readily interpreted as God's punishment of an irreligious man. (This was felt to be especially true when the tower of Winchester Cathedral fell down after he was buried under it.)

William Rufus died unmarried and with no acknowledged illegitimate children. This has sometimes inclined modern historians to interpret contemporary denunciations of the 'effeminate' long hair and fashionable styles of dress of his courtiers as evidence of the king's own homosexuality. This is to read a great deal into the words of monks profoundly out of sympathy with the worldly life-style enjoyed at Rufus's court. GAIMAR, by contrast, remembered William as a fine, generous and good-tempered king. One of his buildings still stands: Westminster Hall, in its day by far the greatest royal hall in Europe.

William III ('William of Orange') (1650–1702), King of England and Scotland (1689–1702) and Ireland (1691–1702). The posthumous and only son of William II, Prince of Orange, and Mary, daughter of CHARLES I, William's power within the Netherlands was initially constrained by the states general and the de Witt brothers. In the face of French threats he was made captain-general and admiral-general in 1672, and in 1673 was appointed to the newly revived office of stadholder, that office being made hereditary in 1674. War with France continued until the Treaty of Nijmegen, 1678, but a separate peace with Britain was made in 1674, and in 1677 William married his cousin MARY II, daughter of James, Duke of York, later JAMES II.

In 1685 William sent British regiments in Dutch service to help James to quell Monmouth's Rebellion (*see* SCOTT, JAMES), but when in 1688 he was approached by William Russell and asked to lead an expedition to England to put pressure on James, he agreed on condition an invitation was arranged. He landed on 5 Nov. 1688. His motives are disputed: he was certainly anxious to secure consistent British support against the French, but it is not clear to what lengths he was prepared to go to achieve this. As it was, James fled, thus opening the way for the GLORIOUS REVOLUTION. William was unwilling to serve as regent or to let Mary reign alone (which Mary also did not wish); a CONVENTION PARLIAMENT offered the crown to them as joint monarchs in Feb. 1689. The Scots parliament followed suit, and they were crowned in April. A DECLARATION OF RIGHTS settled the succession in favour of Mary's children, then ANNE and her children, then William's children by any later marriage. The REVOLUTION SETTLEMENT which accompanied William's accession did not of itself significantly constrain royal power.

William proved a vigorous and assertive monarch, disinclined to allow the crown to become the pawn of any party. An active military leader in a war-torn decade, he was inevitably often out of the country. The needs of war persuaded PARLIAMENT to grant him substantial resources; however, anxiety lest they lose their regained liberty at the same time spurred them to search for ways of controlling the king. This recurrently led to conflict.

William defeated JACOBITE forces in Ireland at the battle of the BOYNE in 1690. Britain, the United Provinces and the Holy Roman Empire had jointly declared KING WILLIAM'S WAR on France in 1689; under the terms of the treaty of RYSWICK in 1697 France effectively recognized him as king of Great Britain and Ireland (Mary had died in 1694). Peace did not resolve the differences between the king and the English Parliament, however. MPs opposed William's plans for fuller union with Scotland, and invalidated his Irish land settlement.

On the death of James II in 1700, the French recognized his son James Edward STUART as his heir. The death of Anne's only surviving child in 1701 made alternative provision for a PROTESTANT SUCCESSION necessary: this was effected by the Act of SETTLEMENT. William died in March 1702 from complications resulting from a fall from his horse, which stumbled on a mole-hill at Hampton Court, giving rise to the Jacobite toast to 'the little gentleman in black velvet'.

William IV (1765–1837), King of Great Britain and Ireland (1830–7), the 'sailor king'. The third son of GEORGE III, he joined the Royal NAVY in 1779 and served in America and the WEST INDIES. In 1789 he was made Duke of Clarence, and was promoted admiral of the fleet in 1811 and lord high admiral in 1827. A popular if somewhat eccentric figure, he married Princess Adelaide, daughter of the Duke of Saxe-Meiningen, in 1818, but their two daughters both died in infancy. He had previously lived with the actress Dorothy

Jordan from 1790–1811 and they had 10 children. The death of the Duke of York in 1827 made him heir presumptive to the throne, to which he succeeded three years later. As king his most important public act related to the crisis that preceded the passage of the 1832 REFORM ACT; the king's hostility to reform was, indeed, a key element in the crisis. From 1830–2 the House of LORDS, with the crown's encouragement, resisted the Reform Bill, twice rejecting the measure. After a dissolution the WHIGS returned to power under GREY with a huge majority and persuaded the king to create sufficient peers to pass the Bill if it were rejected in the Lords again. When opposition was renewed in the upper house, the king changed his mind and tried to withdraw from his undertaking to create 50 new peerages; the ministry resigned. The king tried to form another ministry under Wellington (*see* WELLESLEY, ARTHUR), but failing to do so surrendered. In doing so he avoided internal disorder but set in motion the transformation of the constitutional balance between crown and PARLIAMENT. When in 1834 he ignored parliamentary support for PEEL and replaced him with Melbourne (*see* LAMB, WILLIAM), he was the last British monarch to try to choose the prime minister in opposition to the wishes of Parliament. Dying without a legitimate heir, the crown passed to William's niece, VICTORIA.

William Augustus, Prince (3rd Duke of Cumberland) (1721–65), second son of GEORGE II. He defeated the JACOBITE army at CULLODEN in 1745, acquiring the nickname 'The Butcher' for the cruelty he displayed. After surrendering the British and allied forces at KLOSTER-ZEVEN in 1757, he retired from his military career. He had considerable influence as a political patron, being an early backer of PITT THE ELDER and Henry FOX, and playing a crucial part in the formation of the first Rockingham (*see* WENTWORTH, CHARLES) ministry.

William of Malmesbury (*c.*1095–?1143), historian. A monk of Malmesbury, Wilts., his breadth of reading, devotion to classical culture, acute sense of style and textual criticism all combined with his patriotism to make him – as he well knew – the greatest English historian since BEDE. After extensive research in the libraries of the CATHEDRALS and major abbeys of the land, he composed what remained for some centuries the standard history of England from Bede to his own day.

He did this in two complementary works – the *Gesta Regum Anglorum* ('The Deeds of the English Kings') and the *Gesta Pontificum* ('The Deeds of the Bishops') – both completed by 1125. The latter work – a diocese-by-diocese history cum topographical survey – was a wholly original concept that showed that he had used his travels to observe buildings as well as to read manuscripts. He also wrote a remarkable research monograph – *The History of Glastonbury* – a book of miracles and lives of Wulfstan (Bishop of Worcester) and other saints, before carrying the national history up to 1142 in his *Historia Novella* ('Recent History').

William of Newburgh (*c.*1135–?1198), historian. An Augustinian canon from Yorks., in the late 1190s he wrote the *Historia Rerum Anglicarum* ('History of English Affairs') covering the period from the NORMAN CONQUEST to his own day. His judicious approach – e.g. his cool treatment of BECKET – has won him many modern admirers. Although he liked a good story, his critical sense was affronted by tales of King ARTHUR and MERLIN; in his preface, he denounces GEOFFREY OF MONMOUTH as a writer of fiction masquerading as history.

William of Orange, *see* WILLIAM III

William of Wykeham (1324–1404), politician, prelate and patron of education. Having entered EDWARD III's service as EDINGTON's protégé, in 1356 he was appointed clerk of works at Windsor and turned it into the greatest CASTLE in England. He rapidly became Edward's most trusted minister – first, chief keeper and surveyor of the king's works, then royal SECRETARY (keeper of the secret seal) in 1361, keeper of the PRIVY SEAL in 1363 and chancellor (*see* LORD CHANCELLOR) in 1367. According to Froissart, 'Without him nothing was done.' In 1366, the king prevailed upon Pope Urban V to make him, despite his academic shortcomings, bishop of Winchester.

However, during the years of peace (1360–9), administration was allowed to become slack, and when the renewal of the HUNDRED YEARS WAR made this apparent,

William was dismissed at Parliament's insistence (1371). He joined in the GOOD PARLIAMENT's criticism of the court; as a result, JOHN OF GAUNT, who saw this as a betrayal, had him convicted of embezzlement in Nov. 1376. His estates were confiscated but, after a protest from the clergy, were restored in 1377. Two years later he founded New College, OXFORD, then Winchester School in 1382, both on a lavish scale. Between 1389 and 1391, in his new role as respected elder statesman, he served as RICHARD II's chancellor, but after 1394, he devoted most of his energy and money to rebuilding the nave of WINCHESTER Cathedral, where he now lies buried in a sumptuous CHANTRY chapel.

Wills These survive from the Anglo-Saxon period onwards and, after diocesan bureaucracies were established in the 13th–14th centuries, were recorded in probate registers (kept by church courts investigating and proving wills' genuineness). After 1066 'devising' (bequeathing) 'real property' (land) by will fell out of use until the 14th century, when the USE began to be employed to this end; the Statute of Wills (1540) legalized some devising of land. Henceforth, wills had two parts: the will, dealing with movable property (often specified in an accompanying inventory), and the testament, dealing with real property. Nuncupative wills are records of a dying person's wishes when no written will has been made; they are valid in default of any better will.

The Inheritance Act 1833 established modern procedure, although until 1858 the Church of England's courts retained control of probate. The historical value of wills is profound; often they are the only remotely personal documents that we possess about past individuals. *See also* INVENTORIES.

Wilson, Harold (Baron Wilson of Rievaulx) (1916–95), Labour politician and Prime Minister (1964–70, 1974–6). Born in Huddersfield and educated at Oxford, he became a LABOUR MP in 1945. He entered ATTLEE'S CABINET as president of the Board of Trade (1947–51), the youngest Cabinet minister since PITT THE YOUNGER. In 1963, on the sudden death of GAITSKELL, he was elected leader of the Labour Party, and became prime minister in 1964 with a majority of five. He increased the Labour majority to 97 in the election of 1966, but his government was increasingly beset by economic problems, forcing DEVALUATION in 1967. He proved unable to end the unilateral declaration of independence (UDI) in Rhodesia (*see* RHODESIA, SOUTHERN), and in 1969 was forced to withdraw *IN PLACE OF STRIFE*, a proposed Bill to curb unofficial STRIKES and limit TRADE UNION power. Important social reforms included the expansion of higher EDUCATION and the founding of the OPEN UNIVERSITY, as well as reforms of the laws on ABORTION, HOMOSEXUALITY and DIVORCE.

Defeated in 1970, Wilson was returned in Feb. 1974 with a minority government, which remained in power with an increased majority after a further election in Oct. By 1975, however, the government was faced with serious economic difficulties, so that when he resigned unexpectedly in March 1976, the country was on the verge of having to apply to the International Monetary Fund for a loan.

Wilson has attracted diverse criticism, not least for a perceived failure to improve the economy. The traditional Labour Left criticized his tendency to compromise at the expense of socialist commitments, while young left-wing activists denounced his support for the US in VIETNAM and maintenance of NUCLEAR WEAPONS. Persuasive counter-arguments point out that Wilson was faced with serious long-term difficulties in the British economy, and there was too high a level of expectation of what could be achieved. Even so, many of the social reforms of the Wilson era were of major significance in liberalizing British society.

Winchcombe, Glos., a town that enjoyed considerable importance in the Anglo-Saxon period. The centre of a territory controlled by the kings of the HWICCE, it was then taken over by MERCIA. Its monastery, which was a burial place for some members of the Mercian royal house, was subsequently refounded during the TENTH-CENTURY REFORM. It was dissolved in 1539. 'Winchcombeshire' existed until the 11th century, when it was absorbed into Glos.

Winchelsey, Robert (?–1313), Archbishop of Canterbury (1294–1313). Encouraged by Pope Boniface VIII, he led the English CHURCH'S opposition to EDWARD I's tax demands in 1296 and 1301. Further disputes followed and, in 1306, the king forced him into exile. EDWARD II invited him back, but Winchelsey's hostility to GAVESTON and the archbishop's appointment as an ORDAINER ensured that he maintained his reputation as a staunch opponent of an authoritarian crown – a 'second BECKET'.

Winchester, Hants. As the capital of one of the *CIVITATES* formed out of the kingdom of the ATREBATES, it was an important town in Roman times. However, excavations have shown that the street plan was almost completely reorganized as part of the creation of the *BURH* system by ALFRED THE GREAT. From the 9th to the 11th centuries, it was a focus of power, having quasi-capital-city status for the kings of WESSEX who carried out the conquest of England in the 10th century. It became a hub of MONASTICISM, and its BISHOPRIC, the wealthiest in England during the late Anglo-Saxon period, was one of the great centres of the TENTH-CENTURY REFORM during the time of St Ethelwold.

Winchester's cultural and political importance is attested by the survival of numerous splendid manuscripts from the so-called 'Winchester School' – such as the *Benedictional of St Ethelwold*, now in the British Library – and by the fact that several Anglo-Saxon kings are buried in the cathedral. It remained very important under the early Norman kings, but declined under the Angevins when basic institutions of government such as the TREASURY and EXCHEQUER were moved to London. The College, founded by WILLIAM OF WYKEHAM in 1382, is one of Britain's leading PUBLIC SCHOOLS.

'Wind of Change' Speech, Feb. 1960, speech made by Prime Minister Harold MACMILLAN to the South African Parliament in Cape Town during a tour of AFRICA, in which he described 'national consciousness' as a 'wind of change blowing through this continent'. It was intended to signal British government acceptance that the 1960s would be a decade of DECOLONIZATION in Africa, beginning with independence for KENYA.

Windscale Incident, Oct. 1957, the most serious nuclear accident in Britain to date, when a fire at the Windscale plutonium plant in Cumb. spread radiation over the surrounding area. The incident was played down by the Atomic Energy Authority and there were no direct injuries, although milk and other foodstuffs from the contaminated area had to be destroyed for some months thereafter. A number of fatalities caused by long-term exposure to radiation were later admitted and the name of the plant was changed for presentational reasons to Sellafield. *See also* ATOMIC ENERGY.

Windsor, Duke of, *see* EDWARD VIII

Windsor, Treaty of, 1175, treaty between RORY O'CONNOR and HENRY II. Henry recognized Rory as king of CONNACHT and overlord of all the Irish outside Henry's own acquisitions (DUBLIN and Waterford) and the 'English' LORDSHIPS of LEINSTER and Meath. To some extent, this implied acceptance of Rory's high-kingship, and indeed, Henry promised to help Rory against any Irish who would not obey him. In return, Rory agreed to pay Henry one HIDE from every ten rendered in tribute to him. However, given the fluctuations of native Irish politics and the rapaciousness of the English newcomers, no treaty could last for long.

Windward Islands Federation, colonial administration of smaller British possessions in the western Caribbean, which lasted from 1833 to 1958, when most began to run their own affairs and gradually attain independence. *See also* GRENADA; ST LUCIA; ST VINCENT AND THE GRENADINES.

Wine Trade Although wine has been produced in England at various times, notably in Roman Britain, the Middle Ages – VINEYARDS are specifically mentioned in *DOMESDAY BOOK*, for example – and in the past few decades, the prevailing climate has largely been inappropriate for viticulture. Hence, wine has usually had to be imported; and owing to the lack of native distilling traditions in England, to a sea-based international trading history, and to strong domestic demand, British influence on the wine trade has been important. During the Middle Ages, England imported wine from many European regions and was especially important in the development of the wines of south-west France; Bordeaux (until 1453 an English possession) was transformed into the most important wine region of France. In the 16th century the wine of Andalucia in southern Spain became immensely popular in England and laid the foundations for the sherry industry there.

With the arrival of a wider range of palatable beverages – TEA, coffee, chocolate, improved hopped beer, and later spirits – and the imposition of high rates of duty, the second half of the 17th century was a turning-point in the fortunes of the British wine trade. Wine consumption became more restricted to wealthier and frequently more discerning groups, and British tastes helped foster the development of the wines of the Bordeaux châteaux and of champagne. The difficulties in securing supplies in the frequent wars with France prompted the British to turn to the fortified red wines, port, of the Douro valley, Portugal; the survival of many British names and families in the port houses testifies to the continued traditions and link. The development of Sicily's Marsala wine was similarly an attempt, during the BLOCKADE imposed by Napoleon, to secure wine supplies. British influence upon the international wine trade has been immense, in developing new areas of production and supply (which in the 19th century included the New Worlds of the Americas and AUSTRALIA), as a major centre for the trade, and as the world's largest wine importer for domestic consumption.

Winstanley, Gerrard, *see* DIGGERS

'Winter of Discontent', 1978–9, a period of industrial unrest during the CALLAGHAN government, which played a decisive part in the victory of the CONSERVATIVES under THATCHER in May 1979. When the LABOUR government announced a 5 per cent pay limit in July 1978, a number of key TRADE UNIONS went on strike, their impact intensified, as the year wore on, by the worst winter weather since 1963. The events attained almost mythic dimensions in Conservative propaganda during the subsequent election campaign and throughout the 1980s, as evidence of uncontrolled union power.

Witchcraft The belief in witches – individuals with special powers to affect the world – was as common in Britain as elsewhere in Western Europe during the medieval period. Why then, in the late 15th century, did this suddenly turn into an active persecution that, up to the year 1700, may have destroyed *c.*40,000 people in Europe, most of them women?

The various explanations that have been put forward should probably be combined. An element may have been the growing professionalization of the practice of medicine, which meant virtual monopoly by men: traditional female medicine carried out by 'wise women' was regarded with increasing suspicion. In addition, the sudden interest in witchcraft on the part of a few influential churchmen – producing, for instance, the German textbook *Malleus Maleficarum* (1486) – fed a sense of religious disorientation caused by REFORMATION upheavals, which encouraged searches for enemies and scapegoats to destroy. Both Catholics and Protestants were affected.

In England, persecution was relatively mild, resulting in between 300 and 1,000 executions. English courts were less interested in devil worship than their continental counterparts, instead concentrating on the everyday harm (*maleficium*) inflicted by witches; it was no coincidence that English lawyers could not use TORTURE to extract sensational confessions. England produced a notable work of scepticism in *The Discoverie of Witchcraft* (1584) by the Kentish gentleman and NEO-PLATONIST scholar Reginald Scot (?1537–99). Ireland, with its own troubles, was relatively unaffected, but Scotland conformed more viciously to the continental model after a late start in 1590: by 1700, about 1,600 had died there.

The decline of the panic is equally puzzling, beginning as it did in the mid-17th century and predating the Enlightenment. The 20 executions that resulted from witch trials in Salem, MASSACHUSETTS in 1692 were a curiously late and isolated outbreak of the old paranoia. English and Scots witchcraft legislation was repealed in 1736. Early 20th-century views of witchcraft as a lineal survival of pagan religion have no foundation, but still command uninformed enthusiasm.

Witenagemot, the technical term used to describe the gatherings that took place with an Anglo-Saxon king, at which he took counsel and met with his nobles. The composition of the *witenagemot* was not set; it merely consisted of the men who happened to be with the king, although these were usually more numerous and prestigious at great religious festivals and when the king was resident in one of his palaces, than when he was on his travels. The gatherings were central to kingship and government because an Anglo-Saxon monarch was expected to listen to advice. A king who did not – e.g. ETHELRED II THE UNREADY, or *'Unraed'* ('No-Counsel') – was condemned by his contemporaries.

Wolfe, James (1727–59), soldier. A career soldier, he fought at DETTINGEN and CULLODEN. In the SEVEN YEARS WAR, he took part in successful attacks on Rochefort and Louisbourg; GEORGE II reputedly said, when told that Wolfe was mad, that he wished that this commander would bite some of the other generals. Promoted to major-general, Wolfe was put in charge of the expedition against QUEBEC; he was killed in the final battle, at which the French were defeated. The event was commemorated by Benjamin West in a renowned painting, exhibited at the ROYAL ACADEMY in 1770, which captured the public's imagination because of the artist's choice of recent history for his heroic subject matter.

Wolfenden Report, 1957. The moral preoccupations of the wartime and post-war world were addressed by the official Committee on Homosexual Offences and Prostitution under Sir John Wolfenden, which issued a major liberal statement that formed the basis of ensuing social reform. The committee was set up in the wake of a significant increase in the prosecution of street offences related to PROSTITUTION and in arrests and indictments for homosexual behaviour – some of them, embarrassingly, among the socially prominent. It found that the increase in offences was more the result of greater vigilance than greater activity, and incorporated the growing scientific and psychological sexual literature into its recommendations, which included making sexual behaviour private while tightening up the regulation of public behaviour. The government's response was the Street Offences Act 1959, which effectively drove prostitution off the streets and criminalized many of its aspects. Homosexual law reform had to wait until the privately moved Sexual Offences Act of 1967. *See also* HOMOSEXUALITY AND BRITISH LAW.

Wollstonecraft, Mary (1759–97), writer. Her career illustrates the limited range of opportunities open to – and the obligations hindering – literate and independent-minded women at the close of the 18th century. With scant formal education, she worked first as a paid companion for a widow, nursed her dying mother and sister, then with two friends started a school at Newington Green, London, and met Richard Price and other prominent DISSENTERS. After publishing *Thoughts on the Education of Daughters* in 1787, she was for a year governess to the children of Viscount Kingsborough in Ireland. She then worked on the *Analytical Review* and as a translator for the radical publisher Joseph Johnson. Her novel *Mary* (1788) was largely autobiographical. In 1790, she responded to BURKE's *Reflections on the Revolution in France* with *A Vindication of the Rights of Man*, followed in 1792 by *A Vindication of the Rights of Woman*, an exposure of the double standards of the time. While living in Paris, she wrote *An Historical and Moral View ... of the French Revolution* (1794). An unhappy affair resulted in an illegitimate daughter and an attempted suicide, and brought her personal notoriety: conservative critics linked her radical views with her 'disorderly' private life and censured both. She married William Godwin in 1797, but died after the birth of their daughter – the future Mary Shelley. She was a feminist polemicist, trenchant and persistent in the attention she drew to the inequalities between the sexes.

Wolsey, Thomas (?1472–1530), politician and Cardinal. The son of a prosperous Ipswich butcher, his undistinguished career as an Oxford don blossomed with a royal chaplaincy *c.*1507, and his rise was meteoric when HENRY VIII realized that here was the ideal man for the tedious work of government. In 1511, Wolsey became a royal councillor, and four years later, Henry obtained his elevation as cardinal and appointed him lord CHANCELLOR – uniquely, for life. He accumulated an astonishing array of Church offices, including the archbishopric of York, but because of William WARHAM's inconvenient longevity, Canterbury eluded him, and Henry twice failed to win his election as pope.

Meanwhile Wolsey dominated government, sidelining other councillors. He took particular interest in restructuring the equity and PREROGATIVE courts. His fitful use of his powers as LEGATE *a latere* (from 1518) for Church reform provoked conservative fury, and the aristocracy hated him. They were delighted to turn on him when he failed to secure annulment of Henry's marriage to CATHERINE OF ARAGON and the king's affection cooled.

Wolsey's ascendancy had already trembled in 1525, with the failure of his AMICABLE GRANT scheme, and he had then been forced to surrender his palace at Hampton Court for the king's use. Now, in 1529, he was dismissed as lord chancellor and lost his palace of York Place, WHITEHALL to the king. He was sent off to his archdiocese of York, desperate at the confiscation of his megalomaniac college foundations at Ipswich and OXFORD (Henry later revived the Oxford college as Christ Church). Arrested on treason charges arising from rather pathetic negotiations with French agents, he died on the way south.

Wolsey has had a bad press from history, being seen by Catholic historians as an embarrassment and by PROTESTANTS as a perfect symbol of a corrupt Church. Undoubtedly he squandered much of his great ability and his great powers in Church and state, but his overwhelming and understandable priority was to do Henry's bidding to keep royal favour. His reforms in the secular courts and his close attention to central intervention in LOCAL GOVERNMENT have been assessed by recent research as being of lasting significance (*see TUDOR REVOLUTION IN GOVERNMENT*).

Women, Legal Status of

19TH CENTURY

At the opening of the 19th century women were in almost all respects socially and legally inferior to men and generally regarded by them as objects rather than as agents of their own destiny. The preoccupation with equal rights, the hallmark of British feminism in this period, found expression in the campaign for women's SUFFRAGE and in the movement, inspired by Mary WOLLSTONECRAFT, for women's equality before the law. By the close of the century some progress had been made. The principal advance occurred in the status of married women, who were no longer deemed to be the mere possessions of their husbands.

CHRONOLOGY

1792 Mary Wollstonecraft publishes *A Vindication of the Rights of Women with Strictures on Moral and Political Subjects*, which makes the case for the application of the egalitarian ideas associated with Thomas PAINE and the FRENCH REVOLUTION to the situation of women in Britain.

1839 Custody of Infants Act, inspired by the writings of Caroline Norton, provides for mothers of 'unblemished character' to claim custody of children under the age of seven in the event of parental separation, with a claim for access in respect of older children taken by the husband.

1857 MATRIMONIAL CAUSES ACT abolishes the need for a private Act of Parliament to obtain a DIVORCE. A civil divorce court established in London with the authority to grant judicial separations and divorces, and women permitted to sue for divorce if they can prove two of three charges: cruelty, desertion or adultery. The husband, though, entitled to a divorce on proof of one charge.

1870 MARRIED WOMEN'S PROPERTY ACT allows women to retain £200 of their own earnings; process begun of enabling women to retain their money and property when they marry.

1873 Custody of Infants Act provides for extension of access to children for all women in the event of separation or divorce.

1878 Matrimonial Causes Act provides for a wife to secure a separation on the grounds of cruelty and to claim maintenance and custody of the children. Magistrates also authorized to grant protection orders to wives whose husbands have been convicted of aggravated assault.

1882 MARRIED WOMEN'S ACT allows wives to claim maintenance on the grounds of desertion.

1884 MARRIED WOMEN'S PROPERTY ACT ensures that a married woman should have the same rights over property as an unmarried woman and could carry on trades and business using their property.

1886 Guardianship of Infants Act makes women eligible as the sole guardian of children in the event of a husband's death.

1891 Test case makes it possible for a wife to quit the matrimonial home and live separately from her husband.

1895 SUMMARY JURISDICTION (MARRIED WOMEN) Act authorizes magistrates to grant protection orders to wives driven from the matrimonial home by cruelty or failure to maintain them or their children.

20TH CENTURY

The legal landmarks affecting women in the 20th century mainly concerned divorce legislation and, after WORLD WAR II, employment opportunities (*see below*). After the war – when more women were mobilized for the war effort than in any other country apart from the Soviet Union – demand centred on seeking to redress economic and social inequalities. The number of women working outside the home as well increased steadily throughout the consumer boom years of the 1950s: by 1966 over 5 million married women had a job, compared to less than a million in 1930.

In 1975, designated 'International Women's Year' by the UNITED NATIONS, there was a flurry of legislation in Britain (*see below*) and an EQUAL OPPORTUNITIES COMMISSION was set up with the statutory duty to enforce these laws.

Despite these promising developments, the implementation of many of the provisions showed that the Acts left wide areas of interpretation and judgement. Figures for the year after the Act until 1983 show that, of the cases brought to an industrial tribunal under the terms of the Sex Discrimination Act, only 27 per cent were successful, and in the same period (1976–83), of the cases brought to the Equal Pay tribunal only 20 per cent were successful. The WOMEN'S MOVEMENT which emerged in the late 1960s and 1970s had four basic demands: equal pay; equal education and job opportunities; free contraception, and abortion on demand; and 24-hour nurseries. None can be said to have been fully achieved.

CHRONOLOGY

1923 Matrimonial Causes Act allows that adultery alone is sufficient grounds for a woman to sue for divorce.

1937 Matrimonial Causes Act adds desertion and insanity as grounds for divorce.

1945 Family Allowance Act. Child benefit to be paid directly to mothers.

1949 Legal Aid Act makes divorce possible for those who had previously been deterred by expense.

1967 ABORTION Act allows termination of pregnancy on social as well as medical grounds.

1969 Divorce Reform Act (implemented in 1971), the most significant divorce legislation of the 20th century, makes irretrievable breakdown of a marriage the only grounds for divorce.

1970 EQUAL PAY ACT designed to prevent discrimination in pay between men and women. Due to a five-year 'phasing-in' period, Act came into force in 1975.

1975 Designated 'International Women's Year' by the United Nations. Social Security Pensions Act gives women the chance to earn a full pension of their own, with special provision for people spending some years out of work – such as bringing up a family. Employment Protection Act gives women statutory right to paid maternity leave, protection against unfair dismissal during pregnancy, and the right to go back to their jobs up to 29 weeks after the birth of their baby. SEX DISCRIMINATION ACT applied to discrimination in EDUCATION, employment, HOUSING and the provision to the public of goods, facilities and services; also intended to cover cases of indirect discrimination.

1984 Amendment to Sex Discrimination Act entitles women to the same pay as men when doing work which is the same, broadly similar or of equal value.

1987 Sex Discrimination Act, conforms to EEC (*see* EUROPEAN UNION) directives, including one that gives women the right to continue in paid employment until the same age as men.

1991 Child Support Act sets up agency to secure maintenance payment from errant fathers. House of LORDS decision declares that rape within marriage is a criminal offence. Case brought against the ROYAL AIR FORCE and the ARMY leads to changes in the law to protect the employment and conditions of members of the armed services who become pregnant.

1994 Employment legislation gives the same rights of protection against dismissal and redundancy payments to part-time as to full-time workers: part-time workers over 16 now total 6.8 million. Approximately 44 per cent of women work part time, as compared to 9 per cent of men.

1994 Employment Rights Act guarantees every working woman the right to maternity leave. Government announces the equalization of the state pension age by 2020.

By 1998 the gap between male and female earnings had been narrowing but women still earned around four-fifths of the average male hourly rate, and the pay gap increases with age. The National Minimum Wage Act (1998) which came into effect in April 1999 setting the minimum wage at £3.60 an hour for those aged 22 or above is estimated to have benefited 1.3 million women.

Women's Franchise Voting in Victorian Britain was a gendered process. Women, though excluded from the parliamentary FRANCHISE, gradually acquired the right to participate in local elections. With the Municipal Corporations Act 1869 single women received the right to vote in municipal elections, and, following the Elementary Education Act 1870 women rate-payers could be elected to, and vote in, School BOARD elections. From 1875 women could become elected POOR LAW Guardians; and under the provisions of the LOCAL GOVERNMENT ACT 1888 women could vote for the new county and county borough councils. The Parish Councils Act 1894 enabled women to serve on urban and district councils, and from 1900 married women were entitled to vote in elections for the LONDON COUNTY COUNCIL. The Qualification of Women (County and Borough Councils) Act 1907 made women eligible to become councillors. The 1918 REPRESENTATION OF THE PEOPLE ACT gave the vote to women over 30 (men had it at 21), and it was not until 1928 that the age was lowered and women were finally granted the vote on equal terms with men. *See also* WOMEN'S SUFFRAGE CAMPAIGN.

Women's Freedom League A breakaway group from the WOMEN'S SOCIAL AND POLITICAL UNION, it was formed in 1907 by Charlotte Despard and Teresa Billington-Greig in protest against the dictatorship of the PANKHURSTS and their militant tactics, and with the specific intention of refusing to pay taxes until women obtained the vote. It was symptomatic of the growing tension within the WOMEN'S SUFFRAGE MOVEMENT.

Women's History, an increasingly significant area of historical studies, which initially focused on women in early modern society and the industrial period, and which followed on from the WOMEN'S SUFFRAGE movement after 1920. Pioneering studies by Eileen Power, Alice Clark, and Ivy Pinchbeck, examining women's lives in the past, provided a basis for the development from the 1960s of a more radical, feminist history, reflecting the wider political concerns of a growing WOMEN'S MOVEMENT. The growth of women's history was complemented by the rise of cognate and sympathetic areas of historical enquiry, notably SOCIAL and labour history, demography, FAMILY HISTORY, and ORAL HISTORY. Women's history first took organizational shape in Britain with a conference dedicated to the area at Ruskin College, Oxford, in 1970 – an offshoot of HISTORY WORKSHOP. Since then a wide range of theoretical and detailed empirical studies in women's history has been produced, much of the work being devoted to recapturing the lives and experience of ordinary women. There is concern among some historians that women's history should continue to be contextualized in wider historical studies and seen as part of an understanding of the agency of gender in historical debate.

Women's Institute (WI), rural organization for women, founded on Anglesey in 1917 based upon a Canadian model. The WI became one of the most popular – and, frequently, gently mocked – institutions in the countryside, providing a forum for debate as well as an outlet for jam-making endeavours. It widened many women's horizons, especially since it was founded on the eve of female suffrage, while its usefulness was frequently demonstrated in wartime and beyond, in the social and environmental causes it has campaigned for.

Women's League of Health and Beauty, women's recreational and gymnastic organization founded by Mrs Baggot-Stack in 1930. It proved immensely popular, with over 100,000 members by 1939, capturing a public mood for healthy, outdoor exercise.

Women's Movement, a term used both to describe the campaigns of women seeking the vote up until 1918 (*see* WOMEN'S FRANCHISE; WOMEN'S FREEDOM LEAGUE; WOMEN'S SOCIAL AND POLITICAL UNION; WOMEN'S SUFFRAGE CAMPAIGN), and the Women's Liberation Movement which started in the 1960s, uniting the personal with the political in demands for equal pay, freedom from sexual discrimination, ABORTION law reform, improved state provision for children, and greater educational and workplace opportunities for women, as well as an end to stereotypical representations of women and unequal relationships between men and women in legal, economic, domestic and sexual matters. National conferences were held between 1970 and 1978, and throughout the following decade and beyond women's groups campaigned for legal, social and cultural recognition of their rights, and continue to do so both collectively and individually (*see* WOMEN, LEGAL STATUS OF).

Women's Social and Political Union (WSPU) The creation of Emmeline and Christabel PANKHURST, it was formed in Manchester in 1903 and later moved to London. It published a journal, *Votes for Women*, and by 1910 had an estimated membership of 36,000. The WSPU was distinguished from the NATIONAL UNION OF WOMEN'S SUFFRAGE SOCIETIES by its dynastic leadership and militant tactics. The term 'suffragettes' was first coined by the *Daily Mail* in 1906 to separate them from the more moderate suffragists of the NUWSS. Its increasingly militant campaign made WOMEN'S SUFFRAGE a political issue without noticeably affecting legislative resistance to votes for women, while the autocratic style of leadership promoted secession and the formation of splinter-groups, such as the WOMEN'S FREEDOM LEAGUE.

Women's Suffrage Campaign The long struggle for votes for women has been the subject of considerable controversy between those historians who believe that the militant methods of the WOMEN'S SOCIAL AND POLITICAL UNION did more harm than good, and those who maintain that the pre-war campaign was of secondary importance by comparison with the war-induced improvements in the situation of women between 1914 and 1918. Others point to the politicizing effect that the activities of the WSPU had on the consciousness of many who had not previously confronted the urgency with which women sought the vote and the reasons why this should be so. *See also* WOMEN'S FRANCHISE.

CHRONOLOGY

1851 Formation of Sheffield Women's Political Association indicative of political awareness among women.

1865 J. S. MILL publishes article on 'Representative Government' asserting equality of women and right to the FRANCHISE.

1867 London Society for Women's Suffrage formed following defeat of Mill's amendment to Second Reform Bill (*see* REFORM ACT 1867) in favour of votes for women. Comparable societies formed in Birmingham, Bristol, Manchester and Edinburgh.

1872 Central Committee for Women's Suffrage formed to co-ordinate campaign; 14-year-old Emmeline Goulden (later PANKHURST) attends suffrage meeting addressed by Lydia Becker.

1897 NATIONAL UNION OF WOMEN'S SUFFRAGE SOCIETIES formed.

1903 WOMEN'S SOCIAL AND POLITICAL UNION formed to press campaign with 'deeds not words'.

1905, 7 Feb. 'Mud March', so called because of the foul weather, held by NUWSS in London to publicize its cause.

1905, Oct. First imprisonment of SUFFRAGETTES: Annie Kenney and Christabel Pankhurst detained after disrupting Liberal rally in Manchester.

1907 Qualification of Name Act enables women to stand for county borough councils, and to be mayor and chairman.

1908, 21 June Huge pageant and demonstration in Hyde Park attended by an estimated 250,000.

1908, Oct. Christabel and Emmeline Pankhurst with Flora Drummond arrested for obstruction when trying to march on the Houses of Parliament and receive three months' imprisonment in Holloway.

1909, July Public outcry follows force-feeding of Marion Wallace Dunlop by prison authorities after she goes on hunger strike in protest at her treatment as a criminal rather than a political offender.

1910, 11 Nov. 'Black Friday', a violent confrontation between policemen and SUFFRAGETTES outside Parliament following the rejection of the First Conciliation Bill, an all-party measure which would have given female house-holders the vote.

1911 Truce called by WSPU while Second Conciliation Bill debated.

1912, 1 March Following the defeat of the Second Conciliation Bill, suffragettes riot in London smashing West End shop windows: Emmeline Pankhurst again arrested; Christabel flees to Paris.

1913, March WSPU resorts to arson and bombing following abandonment of

General Electoral Reform Bill. Emmeline Pankhurst receives three years' imprisonment for the burning of LLOYD GEORGE's private residence and tells the court she regards herself as a prisoner of war.
1913, April 'CAT AND MOUSE' (Prisoners' Temporary Discharge) Act introduced by LIBERAL government to enable any hunger striker to be released on licence and rearrested once she is fit enough to serve her sentence.
1913, 4 June Emily Davison dies after throwing herself under the king's horse at the Epsom Derby. Status of martyr conferred on her by WSPU.
1914, 4 Aug. War declared against Germany; militant campaign suspended for duration; after her release from prison Mrs Pankhurst becomes a super-patriot and encourages women's war service in industrial employment.
1917 Speaker's Conference on Electoral Reform recommends that a limited number of women be enfranchised.
1918, Feb. REPRESENTATION OF THE PEOPLE ACT passed giving women over 30 the vote.
1919 Nancy, Lady ASTOR, elected MP for Plymouth Sutton to become the first woman to take her seat in the House of Commons.
1928 Franchise extended to women over the age of 21 on the same terms as men.

Wood's Halfpence, 1722–5. The granting of a patent to William Wood to coin halfpence and farthings for Ireland in 1722 provoked stormy opposition there. Critics – including Jonathan SWIFT, who propagandized against it in *The Drapier's Letters* – claimed that Wood stood to make excessive profits from the difference between the intrinsic and the face value of the COINS and also that production of the new coins would disrupt the economy. WALPOLE was inclined to read Irish opposition as a challenge to Ireland's constitutional subordination. But senior members of the Irish administration failed to rally to the defence of the patent, and it was withdrawn in 1725.

Woodville, Elizabeth (?1437–92), Queen of England. Daughter of Richard Woodville, when she married EDWARD IV there were few precedents for a queen of England who was both English herself and had numerous English relatives. Edward IV married her for love and proceeded to make her family powerful.

Her first husband Sir John Grey was killed at ST ALBANS in 1461. By marrying her in May 1464, Edward IV took on responsibility for providing for her many brothers and sisters, as well as for her two sons by her previous marriage. The apparent WOODVILLE monopoly of royal patronage led to deep resentment.

When Edward was driven into exile in 1470, Elizabeth took SANCTUARY at Westminster Abbey, where she gave birth to their first son (the future EDWARD V). In April 1483, she was forced into sanctuary again by the coup that followed her husband's death, but in June she was persuaded to release her younger son to the care of the Archbishop of Canterbury. RICHARD III then seized the throne, claiming that Edward had already been married when he 'married' her and that their children were therefore bastards – although, hitherto, they had been universally accepted as legitimate. By the autumn of 1483, probably realizing that her sons were dead, she was contemplating a marriage between her daughter, Elizabeth of York, and Henry Tudor (*see* HENRY VII), but after the collapse of BUCKINGHAM'S REBELLION, she came to terms with Richard, leaving sanctuary in return for his promise to provide for her and her daughters. In 1486, following Richard's fall and with her daughter wed to the new king, she was granted all her rights as queen-dowager and, the next year, retired to the convent of Bermondsey.

Woodville Family From 1464, when EDWARD IV married Elizabeth WOODVILLE, to 1483 when their sons, the 'princes in the Tower' (*see* EDWARD V), disappeared from view, the Woodvilles were the most favoured and most resented group in the politics of the WARS OF THE ROSES.

The rise in the family fortunes began *c.*1436, when Richard Woodville married the widowed Duchess of Bedford. Elizabeth was one of their children, and when she became queen, she ensured that her husband provided for her five brothers and seven unmarried sisters. Inevitably, their apparent monopoly of the benefits of royal patronage caused jealousy: Warwick's (*see* NEVILLE, RICHARD) illegal execution of Richard and John Woodville in 1469 was one indication of the anger of the excluded; the widespread support enjoyed by Richard of Gloucester (the future RICHARD III) in 1483 in the weeks after the arrest of Anthony Woodville, Earl Rivers was another. When Richard seized the throne, the parvenus became the unjustly disinherited, but in 1486 HENRY VII married Elizabeth of York, the daughter of Edward IV and Elizabeth Woodville.

Wool Subsidy, a customs duty imposed on wool exported from England to the Continent. The first regular duty was imposed by EDWARD I in 1275 at the rate of 6s 8d a sack; from then on, the anticipated yield of this duty enabled the crown to borrow on an unprecedented scale. The issue of the right to consent to indirect taxation became acute when both Edward I and EDWARD III suddenly raised the rate to 40s or more (the *MALTOTE*) to finance their wars against France. In the mid-14th century, PARLIAMENT's right to give or withhold consent to indirect taxation was conceded by the crown. In return, the wool subsidy was granted virtually continuously and at a rate (usually 43 shillings 4 pence per sack) that made it the backbone of royal finance. During the next century, it regularly yielded between half and two-thirds of the crown's total annual revenue. *See also* STAPLE, COMPANY OF.

Wool Trade, *see* CLOTH INDUSTRY; WOOLLEN INDUSTRY

Woollen Industry Wool has been one of the most important of all industrial sectors in Britain since a very early date. The economic importance of sheep-farming and of wool manufacture was securely established from the period of the 11th and 12th centuries, and undoubtedly has much earlier origins. The CLOTH INDUSTRY of the medieval and early modern period was almost exclusively woollen-based (*see* BY-EMPLOYMENT; PROTO-INDUSTRIALIZATION). It was aided by the WATER-POWERED mills from the 13th century. By the 18th century, when COTTON production began to take off, wool and closely woven worsted fabrics were still dominant, and the industry was to be found throughout the British Isles, although concentrated in the West Country and the West Riding of Yorks. The traditional centres in East Anglia were in near-terminal decline. Cotton rapidly overtook woollen manufacture, both in terms of volume of production and technological innovation, in the course of the late 18th and early 19th centuries, but both industries grew massively in aggregate terms. Wool textile production became even more concentrated in West Yorks., aided there by the development of cheap mass-production of worsteds as well as woollens by cheap labour and by the growth of EXPORTS via Hull and, later, LIVERPOOL. The north and west of the Yorks. textile region, centred on Halifax, concentrated on worsted production, whilst woollens were the speciality of the LEEDS and Wakefield areas. The industry followed Lancs. cotton in the transition from hand spinning, HANDLOOM WEAVING and domestic production to FACTORY production. Technological change and innovation during the INDUSTRIAL REVOLUTION was much the same as with cotton, but woollen fibres were more of a problem for mechanical handling, so the major innovations in spinning and weaving followed two decades or so behind their innovation in the cotton sector. Many Som. and Glos. centres, as well as those in the remoter parts of the Scottish Highlands and Islands or in other traditional areas such as Northants., followed Norfolk and Suffolk into decline. The Victorian growth and prosperity of Leeds, Bradford and elsewhere as manufacturing and warehouse centres are testimony to the power of wool and to its regional concentration. Woollen and worsted manufacture continued their strong growth, for both home and export markets, although there were many small producers and relatively few large combines. In the 20th century, the wool industries suffered less than cotton with the fall in textile exports, since for them home demand was more important, but in the depressed inter-war years demand and production went into lengthy decline. In the war and post-war years many firms went out of business, as the increasing importance of man-made fibres – nylon and 'Terylene' as well as rayon – made considerable inroads. Since the 1960s the woollen industries have experienced further decline, with small, specialist firms the principal survivors.

Worcester Having existed in Roman times, it was important during the Anglo-Saxon period as the chief town of the kingdom of HWICCE and, for that reason, became a BISHOPRIC in the later 7th century in the time of

Archbishop THEODORE. It was subsequently absorbed into MERCIA and was fortified during the reign of ALFRED THE GREAT.

Worcester, Battle of, 3 Sept. 1651, defeat of CHARLES II's Scots army by Oliver CROMWELL during the CIVIL WARS. Charles was forced to flee abroad.

Worcester, William (1415–82), writer. After a lifetime devoted to the complex business interests of Sir John Fastolf, in 1478 he was finally free to indulge his passion for ANTIQUARIAN studies. As he rode about Britain, he recorded – on sheets of paper he kept in his saddle-bag – the curiosities and places of interest he encountered. The result was the *Itinerary*, the notebook of his travels between 1478 and 1480 and the earliest historical guidebook written in England. Earlier, while Fastolf's secretary, he had responded to the loss of Normandy by writing the *Boke of Noblesse* in the forlorn hope of persuading HENRY VI to carry on the fight.

Work, traditionally seen by economic and social historians as an important topic for study. The rhythms of work in both pre-industrial and modern times, and the affiliations, loyalties, disaffections and oppositions experienced within a work context, have been regarded as important influences on culture, motivations, expectations, social life and politics. E. P. Thompson, for example, has stressed the shift from task- to time-oriented work regimes which occurred with industrialization, forming an important element in the internalization of disciplined and time-conscious work habits; and many historians and sociologists, following MARX, have emphasized the importance of the advanced division of labour in modern mechanized industry in alienating workers from the product of their labours. Changes in work have often been viewed as important in the formation of social and political identities, especially in the analysis of the emergence of the making of the English working class in the INDUSTRIAL REVOLUTION period. Too often, however, work has been identified in a restricted sense with waged work outside the home, whereas much work also of course occurs in unpaid domestic forms of endeavour and in home-based working of various kinds. The latter less formal work is mostly associated with women, which is probably why much of the history of work has so far had so little to say about the formation of social consciousness and political identity amongst women. Today there is more interest in the social and cultural importance of activities outside work, seen in the rise of histories of leisure. And there has been a decline in labour history associated with the recognition that the history of work (and the term and idea of work itself) needs to be deconstructed. *See also* CLASS AND CLASS CONSCIOUSNESS; UNEMPLOYMENT.

Workers' Educational Association (WEA), adult educational organization formed in 1903. It called for a 'highway' of educational opportunity to avoid the exclusion of millions from the advantages education brings, and became identified with left-leaning ideals and with research into equality of opportunity. It and the UNIVERSITIES' extra-mural classes, later often organized into adult education departments, helped underwrite the expansion of vocational and recreational learning of the inter-war and post-war years. It continues its work today. *See also* MECHANICS' INSTITUTES.

Workhouses, houses of shelter for the poor in which they are given work to do. The first attempts to employ the unemployed poor in public workhouses date from the mid-16th century. Workhouses were sometimes penal: the HOUSE OF CORRECTION, developed in the late 16th century, was of this form. In some workhouses, the emphasis was on RELIEF. Not all early workhouses were residential (*see* HOUSE OF INDUSTRY). In 1696, BRISTOL obtained an Act of Parliament to sanction the establishment of a large workhouse; its example was followed by numerous other cities. PARISH workhouses spread in the 1720s and 1730s, some being converted almshouses; the SOCIETY FOR THE PROPAGATION OF CHRISTIAN KNOWLEDGE (SPCK) encouraged their foundation. An Act of 1723 (sometimes called Knatchbull's Act, from its promoter, or Marriott's Act, from one of its publicists) allowed parishes to band together to set up workhouses, and to make admission a condition of obtaining relief; however, although some parishes did apply the 'workhouse test', outdoor relief remained predominant. Returns to Parliament in 1776 listed some 2,000 workhouses, with a capacity of 90,000 places.

Legislative measures such as GILBERT'S ACT were intended to facilitate and promote the institution of workhouses as an 'indoor' alternative to the increasing financial and social burden of relieving the poor who were living in their own homes. Although the process of parishes banding together and establishing workhouses had increased in the first three decades of the 19th century, especially in some southern and eastern counties where the problem of pauperism was becoming ever more evident, these institutions were still in the minority. The 1834 POOR LAW AMENDMENT ACT, instituting the New POOR LAW, was based on the premises that the workhouse was the basic institution, providing both a deterrent to falling into destitution and a means of reducing the financial and administrative burden. The workhouse system was most readily implemented in rural areas, of the south and east; it was slow to spread to many northern industrial areas, partly because of the inappropriateness of the institution for their employment problems and partly because of long and implacable opposition to the New Poor Law. The ANDOVER SCANDAL showed how heartless the workhouse overseers could be, and was the catalyst for limited reform, although it was rare for the work done in workhouses to be economically useful or for the uniforms or food to be better than adequate.

The fear of the workhouse with its degrading conditions was one of the most potent for the infirm and elderly poor in the 19th century, and the dismantling of the workhouse system and the introduction of OLD AGE PENSIONS in the first decades of the 20th century was greeted with near-universal relief. The old, frequently solid – if grim – workhouse buildings in towns were commonly turned into hospitals; many still survive.

Workmen's Compensation Acts 1897, 1906 The Act of 1897, an example of TORY social reform, made employers in certain dangerous trades (including factories, mining, quarrying, railways and building) financially responsible for all accidents to workers arising in the ordinary course of their employment, whether such accidents were due to the employers' negligence or not, thereby ending 'the doctrine of common employment' which, since it was first elaborated in a legal decision of 1837, had denied workpeople protection from negligent employers. The Act of 1906 extended the principle embodied in the 1897 Act to practically all kinds of employment, and gave workmen suffering from certain industrial diseases the right to compensation. It marked a significant step towards a more comprehensive social insurance.

World War I, 1914–18. The immediate causes of 'The Great War' (also called 'The war to end wars' by the novelist H. G. Wells), arose from the assassination of the heir to the Austro-Hungarian throne, Archduke Franz Ferdinand, at Sarajevo on 28 June 1914 by a young Slav nationalist, Gavrilo Princip. Attempts by Austria-Hungary to exploit this by blaming Serbia produced a reaction across Europe resulting in mutual declarations of war from the major powers in July and Aug. The German attack on neutral Belgium was the catalyst for a British declaration of war on 4 Aug. Underlying causes and responsibility for the war remain much disputed.

The small BRITISH EXPEDITIONARY FORCE played an important role in halting the main German advance into northern France at MONS in Aug., then at the MARNE in Sept. The opposing forces then executed outflanking manoeuvres known as 'the race to the sea', which left them facing each other in a trench line stretching from the Channel coast at Nieuport to the Swiss frontier. Both in land and sea warfare, technological and tactical developments had produced a dominance of the defender over the attacker which would only be reversed by further innovations in the course of the war (*see* WARFARE, LAND; WARFARE, NAVAL). The principal Allies (France, Britain and Russia together with Japan in the Far East, joined by Italy in May 1915) and the opposing Central Powers (Germany and Austria-Hungary, joined by Ottoman Turkey in Nov. 1914) were broadly equal in military strength, producing a general stalemate.

In 1915, renewed French and much smaller British attacks on the Western Front failed to break the German line. An initial British government assumption of 'business as usual' was gradually replaced by command economy mobilizing industry for war and the creation of a HOME FRONT. Financial orthodoxy was also abandoned with the introduction of deficit financing and the acceptance of massive war debts by the Allies, mainly to the United States. In May the SHELLS SCANDAL, a complaint by Field Marshal FRENCH that government ineptitude had failed to provide his army with enough ammunition, forced Prime Minister ASQUITH into a coalition, so ending the last LIBERAL government of Britain. Asquith was replaced by a second coalition in Dec. 1916, headed by his former deputy LLOYD GEORGE but dominated by the CONSERVATIVES, which split the Liberal Party and permanently weakened it.

Occupying much of industrial northern France and all Belgium except for the Ypres salient, the Germans during 1915 could afford to sit on the defensive in the west except for a small attack at YPRES, while supporting Austria–Hungary with offensives against Russia and Serbia, the latter being overrun at the end of the year after Bulgaria joined the Central Powers. Britain found its land strategy largely dictated by French needs to reclaim their occupied territories. With the largest and most powerful NAVY in the world, British naval strategy was based on a BLOCKADE of supplies to Germany, which produced serious shortages and food RIOTS in Germany by the end of the war; British control of the North Sea approaches to Germany was seriously challenged only by the German battlefleet, at the inconclusive Battle of JUTLAND in May 1916. Early German attempts to blockade Britain by unrestricted submarine warfare were suspended in May 1915, partly, after the sinking of the passenger liner *LUSITANIA*, through fears of bringing America into the war. But attempts to exploit British seapower by maritime expeditions proved ineffective. An Anglo-French landing at Gallipoli (*see* DARDANELLES CAMPAIGN) to force Turkey out of the war produced the same stalemate as elsewhere, and the troops were finally withdrawn in Jan. 1916. A French-led landing at Salonika in northern Greece in Oct. 1915 also produced stalemate.

These failures led to an increasing British focus on the Western Front. For the first and only time in its history, Britain created a mass ARMY to fight the main enemy land power (Germany) on the main land front. Almost 5 million men served in the British armed forces during the war, half of them volunteering after appeals by the war minister, Kitchener, and the remainder by CONSCRIPTION after Jan. 1916, together with 3 million from the BRITISH EMPIRE (many of these first-generation British settlers). Almost a million British and Imperial troops were killed in the war, and more than 1.5 million wounded. These losses were in proportion to the size of the armies created and the terrible nature of industrialized mass warfare. All the other belligerents each lost more than a million dead. But for Britain, with no peacetime tradition of a mass conscript army, the Great War was a unique social and psychological trauma.

In Feb. 1916 the Germans attacked the French at Verdun, with the intention of 'bleeding France white' in a pure battle of attrition which lasted all year. HAIG, who had replaced French as British commander-in-chief on the Western Front in Dec. 1915, undertook to play the major role in the Anglo-French offensive on the SOMME, which began on 1 July. The first day was uniquely disastrous for the British, with 57,000 casualties for little gain. By the end of the battle in Nov. the British and French had advanced little more than 5 miles. Meanwhile, Germany overran Romania, which had joined the Allies that year, giving the Central Powers access to its grain harvest.

Despite their successes in the east, the impact of Verdun and the Somme on the Germans was critical. Rather than repeat the experience of 'Somme fighting', in Feb. 1917 they retreated on the Western Front to extensive prepared positions known to the British as the Hindenburg Line, and once more began unrestricted submarine warfare in an attempt to starve Britain into defeat. Although British supplies of food were reduced to an emergency reserve of six weeks by April, the campaign was defeated, largely by the CONVOY SYSTEM and the introduction of RATIONING.

On 6 April, after British intelligence had revealed German attempts to foster a Mexican invasion of American territory, America declared war on Germany. The immediate value of the American fleet and munitions production, and their immense potential for creating a land army, meant that the Central Powers could no longer win a long war, although American troops actually played only a small role in the final Allied victory.

Although the Western Front was the main British theatre of war, 'sideshows' and secondary fronts employed 3.5 million British and Imperial troops, and small conflicts took place around the globe, in places as remote as German South-West Africa (modern Namibia) and New Guinea. Britain's control of the sea was vital to these campaigns and to mobilizing the forces of the Empire. The war against Ottoman Turkey in particular was semi-colonial in nature. A campaign in Mesopotamia resulted at first in disaster with the surrender of much of the force at Kut-el-Amara in April 1916; but by the end of 1917 Baghdad and Jerusalem had been captured by British and Imperial forces under Allenby.

The bleakest year of the war for the Allies was 1917. After a failed offensive in April the French army experienced widespread mutinies. In Oct. the Italians suffered a disaster at the Battle of Caparetto and needed French and British reinforcements. Russia collapsed in two revolutions in March and Nov. (the Bolshevik 'October Revolution'), leading to an armistice with the Central Powers in Dec. The year 1917 also represents a major turning-point in world history with the emergence of America and the Soviet Union into world politics, and the end of Europe's domination both of its own fate and of the rest of the world. Haig launched a series of attacks on the Western Front in 1917, first at ARRAS in April in support of the French at Lloyd George's insistence, meeting limited success with the capture of Vimy Ridge, followed by a smaller successful attack at Messines in June. A small British attack at CAMBRAI in Nov. showed how far tactics and technology had advanced, particularly in using TANKS. But the main British offensive for the year, the Third Battle of YPRES (often known as 'Passchendaele'), which lasted from July to Nov., gained only a few miles for heavy casualties, and remains intensely controversial. Its effects were to damage the British army severely (although unlike most belligerents, British mutinies were on an insignificant scale), and to destroy what little understanding remained between Haig and Robertson on one side and Lloyd George on the other.

In March 1918 the Germans began a series of offensives on the Western Front using troops released from the east, where the punitive Peace of Brest-Litovsk had been signed with Russia, in the hope of winning the war before major American forces could arrive. Despite some initial successes and very hard fighting, by July the Germans had failed to break through. Allied counter-attacks began on the Marne under the French Marshal Foch, appointed in the emergency as overall commander of all forces on the Western Front. The decisive British victory at AMIENS on 8 Aug., which convinced Germany to seek peace, was followed by the 'Hundred Days', a sustained period of semi-mobile warfare in which the British and French drove the Germans back, breaking through the Hindenburg Line in Sept. and liberating most of occupied Belgium and France.

The rout of Turkish forces in Palestine by Allenby, supported by Arab forces accompanied by T. E. Lawrence, led to Turkey agreeing an armistice on 30 Oct., joined by Austria–Hungary on 3 Nov. Defeated on the battlefield and with its home front collapsing, Germany also sued for an armistice on 11 Nov. The Russian, Austro-Hungarian, Ottoman Turkish and German Empires all broke up or lost territory, leading to the creation or resurrection of many new states. Fighting associated with the war did not finally stop until 1923.

In Britain the war led to significant extensions in the role and power of government. By its end most of the major sectors of the British ECONOMY were under government control, with new ministries being created. The general democratizing effect of the war also led to major political and social changes. Women were employed as a reserve of labour in INDUSTRY and AGRICULTURE to free men for the armed forces, as well as serving as nurses and support workers in the theatres of the war. The war transformed the bargaining power of organized labour, raising the number of TRADE UNION members to 6 million by 1920 and the living standards of the unskilled and semi-skilled. The LABOUR PARTY took its first seats in CABINET during the war and emerged strengthened, fashioning a new constitution in 1918 and contesting the 1918 KHAKI ELECTION as a national party for the first time. The 1918 Representation of the People Act, which enfranchised all men still without the vote and all women over 30, more than doubled the electorate.

The mobilization of the Home Front and creation of the mass armies of World War I, and in particular the decisive victories of its last months, were undoubtedly the greatest military achievements in British history. By 1923 the British Empire stood at its largest extent, with no serious rivals in Europe despite the loss of part of IRELAND. However, in absolute terms Britain had been greatly weakened, particularly in its debts to America which dominated the PARIS PEACE CONFERENCE. The inability of successive British governments to deliver 'a land fit for heroes', a peace which left Germany weak but with a strong sense of grievance, and the impact of the DEPRESSION, all led by the 1930s to a belief that the losses suffered in World War I had been excessive and futile, contributing to the inter-war policy of APPEASEMENT.

World War II, 1939–45. The worst and only truly global war in history, it was actually a number of interlocking wars which began for different reasons but ended together in 1945. The war in Europe had its immediate origins in the attempts under Adolf Hitler to reverse Germany's defeat in WORLD WAR I (*see* PARIS PEACE CONFERENCE) and to establish a German empire over Europe (and possibly the world). Hitler's breach of the MUNICH AGREEMENT by occupying northern Czechoslovakia (the modern Czech Republic) in March 1939 marked the final failure of the policy of APPEASEMENT pursued by Britain and France. Both countries accelerated preparations for war with Germany, and Britain introduced peace-time CONSCRIPTION for the first time in its history. In Aug. Britain and France offered security guarantees to Poland as Germany's likely next victim. Germany signed a surprise Non-Aggression Pact (the Molotov–Ribbentrop Pact) with its arch-enemy the Soviet Union, agreeing secretly to partition Poland, and invaded on 1 Sept. Two days later Britain and France declared war on Germany. Although Hitler did not expect the Anglo-French declaration, Germany is widely accepted as being responsible for the outbreak of war.

Britain and France took no military action to defend Poland, which was overrun at the end of the month. Nor did they declare war on the Soviet Union when it joined in the attack on 17 Sept. French strategy was based chiefly on the defence of the Maginot Line along its common frontier with Germany, and British strategy on support of France, to which the small and ill-equipped BRITISH EXPEDITIONARY FORCE was sent. Germany's navy was no real match for Britain's, and its army was not much larger than those of France and Britain combined, but it had much larger air forces, together with a small but valuable lead in technology, and equally valuable recent experience of military operations in Spain, Austria, Czechoslovakia and Poland itself.

Winter 1939–40 was relatively quiet except at sea, giving rise to its description as the 'PHONEY WAR'. Except for Germany, France and Britain, the whole of Europe was neutral and (notionally) at peace. In April Hitler forestalled Anglo-French moves by occupying Denmark and Norway. A chaotic campaign to defend Norway resulted on 10 May in CHAMBERLAIN resigning as prime minister to be replaced by CHURCHILL at the head of a coalition government. Also on 10 May Germany invaded the Netherlands, which surrendered four days later, and Belgium, which resisted until 28 May. Anglo-French forces driving into Belgium to meet the German advance were cut off by a German attack through the Ardennes forest north of the Maginot Line which reached the English Channel on 22 May. Allied forces in the north were forced back to the coast at DUNKIRK, where 338,000 were evacuated by 4 June. Renewed German attacks southwards split the French forces and took Paris. On 10 June Italy declared war on both France and Britain, and on 22 June France signed an armistice, accepting German occupation of northern France and a puppet French regime at Vichy. Rather than allow the French Mediterranean fleet to fall under German control the British sank it at MERS-EL-KEBIR in July, and in June 1941 overran French forces in Lebanon and Syria.

Britain now faced a hostile Europe from Norway to the Pyrenees, with Italy and its North African colonies astride its route to INDIA and the Far East, where another war threatened with an increasingly hostile Japan, which since 1937 had been involved in the conquest of China. In July the German air forces engaged the RAF (*see* ROYAL AIR FORCE) in the Battle of BRITAIN, but by Sept. heavy German losses led to the planned invasion of Britain (*see* Operation SEALION) being cancelled, although the BLITZ on British cities continued. Early RAF attempts to raid Germany in daylight proved costly failures, and night bombing began. Churchill based his strategy on Britain's survival in the hope that America would enter the war. Although the US was a non-belligerent nation, President Franklin D. Roosevelt openly supported Churchill, and in March 1941 instituted LEND-LEASE, allowing Britain virtually unlimited access to American war matériels. In Aug. Roosevelt and Churchill met for the ATLANTIC CHARTER declaration, stating their common aims for future world peace.

Italian forces in Albania attacked Greece in Oct. 1940 but were repulsed; an offensive mounted under Wavell into Libya in Dec. routed the Italians at Sidi Barrani and threatened to drive them out of North Africa altogether; and in Nov. British carrier-borne aircraft sank half their main surface fleet at Taranto. These failures produced pressure on Germany to come to Italy's aid. On 6 April 1941 a German attack on Yugoslavia (which surrendered on 17 April) and on Greece forced Britain to divert troops from North Africa, only to be forced off the Greek mainland at the end of the month, following which German airborne troops seized Crete. Meanwhile in March German forces sent to North Africa under Field Marshal Erwin Rommel joined the Italians in a new offensive, laying siege to Tobruk in April.

Britain's main naval campaign for the next two years was the Battle of the ATLANTIC against unrestricted German submarine warfare, and its main land campaign was in North Africa to prevent Rommel capturing Suez. Its only effective way of attacking Germany was the BOMBING OFFENSIVE, which increased in scale under Harris although Britain also encouraged Resistance movements (*see* SPECIAL OPERATIONS EXECUTIVE). In 1941 conscription was extended, including the first wartime conscription of women in any country. As in WORLD WAR I, about 5 million British and 3 million Imperial citizens served in the armed forces during the war. Britain's HOME FRONT moved to a full command economy (*see* RATIONING), and from 1942 over half the national income was devoted to the war effort, something unequalled by any other belligerent. Britain began to outproduce Germany in munitions, while important scientific and military inventions began to redress the initial German advantage.

On 22 June 1941 Germany attacked the Soviet Union, taking its leader Josef Stalin by complete surprise, and reached Leningrad (St Petersburg) in the north. On 12 July Britain and the Soviet Union signed a Treaty of Mutual Assistance. The Eastern Front saw the heaviest and most barbaric land fighting of the war, occupying two-thirds of all the German armed forces. On 7 Dec. the Japanese, needing raw materials (rubber, tin, oil, etc.) for their war in China, attacked the American Pacific Fleet at Pearl Harbor in the Hawaiian Islands as a preliminary to the seizure of British, French and Dutch colonies in South-East Asia. Next day America and Britain declared war on Japan, and on 11 Dec., just as German forces were repulsed from the outskirts of Moscow, Germany and Italy declared war on America. Although the Soviet Union remained at peace with Japan, the linking of the European war with that in Asia transformed World War II into a genuinely global conflict.

Early 1942 saw the German–Italian–Japanese Axis at the height of its power. The fall of SINGAPORE on 15 Feb. was the largest single loss of troops in British imperial history and marked the eclipse of British power in Asia. With Leningrad still under siege, a new German offensive in the Soviet Union took its forces to Stalingrad (Volgograd) by Sept. With most of eastern Europe under occupation Germany began its 'final solution', the death camps in which 6 million European Jews were killed. Nevertheless, after three years of victories, the involvement of the United States and the Soviet Union together with Britain meant that the Axis, which was being outproduced in war materials by four to one, could not possibly win a long war.

The advantage now lay with the Allies. Churchill and Roosevelt agreed a policy of defeating Germany before Japan, and together with Stalin as the 'Big Three' co-ordinated strategy in a series of conferences throughout the war. Germany in Europe and Japan in the Far East had relatively short lines of communication by land and sea respectively but major shortages in essential raw materials for industrialized war. The Allies had almost unlimited access to raw materials but very long lines of communication. For the British and Americans the main war effort went into a global transport system, and much of their strategy was dictated by the availability of ships and craft for amphibious landings.

The defeat of Rommel at EL ALAMEIN, first by Auchinleck and then by MONTGOMERY in Oct. 1942 (the last major British battle fought without American troops), together with landings in French North Africa (*see* TORCH) a month later, marked the turning-point for Hitler in the west. Although Germany occupied Vichy France in Nov. 1942, the last Axis troops surrendered in Tunisia in May 1943. In July the British and Americans invaded Sicily, followed by southern Italy two months later. Italy surrendered on 8 Sept. and by the war's end had changed sides, fighting alongside the Allies. But German troops in Italy defended stubbornly and Rome was not liberated until June 1944.

The turning-point in the east came in Jan. 1943 with the surrender of German forces at Stalingrad. In July the last German offensive in the east failed at Kursk, the biggest TANK battle in history, and thereafter the Axis forces were driven steadily back. In Jan. 1944 the siege of Leningrad, the longest in modern history, was relieved. Meanwhile the Anglo-American bomber offensive continued against German cities and industry, and the Battle of the Atlantic had finally swung the Allies' way. Only by massive efforts and calls for 'Total War' did Germany survive.

On 6 June 1944 (*see* D-DAY) in Operation OVERLORD the Allies opened their long-awaited Second Front in Normandy, the start of the liberation of France. Fighting was bitter, but with overwhelming Allied command of the air and sea the German forces were destroyed. Paris was liberated on 25 Aug., followed by the rest of France and Belgium. In a controversial episode, Allied supply problems and Anglo-American friction led to the failure at ARNHEM and the Germans recovered from rout on their own frontier. In Dec. the last major German offensive of the war, mounted through the Ardennes (the 'Battle of the BULGE'), failed. Germany was now effectively alone, all the European Axis members having either signed armistices or been overrun by Soviet troops. In March 1945 the Allies forced the Rhine, and in April Soviet troops reached Berlin, linking with American troops at Torgau at the end of the month and cutting Germany in two. On 30 April Hitler killed himself in Berlin. German forces surrendered unconditionally to the Allies in Italy on 2 May and in Germany itself on 7 May, with the following day proclaimed as VE Day (Victory in Europe).

Britain and America still remained at war with Japan. The turning-point of the war in BURMA was the decisive Japanese defeat by SLIM at KOHIMA-IMPHAL in July 1944, assisted by the CHINDITS under Wingate. Rangoon was liberated in May 1945. Meanwhile the American 'island hopping' campaign of amphibious landings across the Pacific brought them within range of Japan after hard fighting and heavy losses. Mass bombing raids and naval blockade had rendered Japan's position hopeless when the dropping of atomic bombs on Hiroshima and Nagasaki on 6 and 9 Aug., together with a Soviet declaration of war and invasion of Manchuria on 8 Aug., led to Japan's surrender on 14 Aug. and VJ Day (Victory over Japan) next day.

Britain's experience of World War II was different from the long stalemate of World War I. The war swung like a pendulum, with Britain on the weaker and losing side up to the end of 1941, and thereafter one of the almost inevitable victors. Lacking a major land front until 1944, Britain also did not create a large land army. By the end of the war, of eight Allied armies in Germany five were American and only one British (plus one each Canadian and French), together with one British imperial army each in Italy and Burma. Total British and Imperial war dead were under half a million, of which only 144,000 were British soldiers. In contrast the Soviet Union, which ended the war with its massive armies dominating eastern Europe, lost 20 million dead (perhaps many more) and the total on all sides was nearly 60 million.

Other aspects of World War II were virtually identical to the earlier war, especially the creation of a home front and command economy and the acceptance of economic dependence on America. Bombing took place on a much greater scale, the Blitz and V-WEAPONS costing the lives of over 60,000 British civilians. Once more the war produced major social and democratizing changes. Hopes for a better post-war world found expression in the 1942 BEVERIDGE REPORT and in 1944 government plans for a WELFARE STATE, including proposals for full employment, a national health service, and free secondary education, all implemented after the 1945 general election by the first-ever majority LABOUR government under ATTLEE, who had served in Churchill's war CABINET during the war.

Britain (and the BRITISH EMPIRE, the countries of which also declared war without hesitation) was the only country to fight against Germany – and later Japan – from the war's start to its end, and without itself being attacked first. The British willingness to endure six years of total war with virtually no government coercion pointed to a country remarkably united behind a common cause. This unity was strengthened by overwhelming evidence of German and Japanese brutality in occupied countries. Justifiable moral qualms about many Allied actions, and claims of 'victors' justice' in the subsequent war crimes trials, have not overturned the verdict that Britain was right to fight.

Since the 17th century Britain has been preoccupied with the BALANCE OF POWER in Europe and with its Empire. It now faced an entirely new situation, a major turning-point in history as 1945 confirmed the judgement of 1918. Despite American attempts to create a 'Big Five' (including France and Nationalist China) to police the world as permanent members of the UNITED NATIONS Security Council, it was clear that even Britain was a junior partner in a world split between the two superpowers. Virtually bankrupt, it began its slow but steady retreat from Empire, granting independence and partition to INDIA in 1947 and increasingly surrendering its global responsibilities to America. Apart from this, with eastern and central Europe under Soviet control and the onset of the COLD WAR, Britain's new military and international commitments were increasingly dictated by the NATO alliance to defend western Europe.

Wreck (*wreccum maris*). The royal right of 'wreck' – comprising the right to take and protect a ship and its contents wrecked on the foreshore – goes back to Anglo-Saxon times. The term 'wreck' does not occur in any authentic document written before the NORMAN CONQUEST. However, CHARTERS show that kings had retained the profits of the foreshore from a much earlier date, and that this valuable right and the important protection it afforded goods and the persons of wrecked seafarers existed long before 1066. On occasion, the right was granted to great lords or to monasteries, who would therefore exercise local jurisdiction over this aspect of law and order. All such rights (together with the general royal right) remain to the present day unless resumed by the CROWN (*see* RESUMPTION); they are subject to the provision that the original owner may reclaim his property within a year and a day of the wreck. The development of underwater archaeology resulted in the passing of the Protection of Wrecks Act 1973. Attempts to protect wrecks of historical and archaeological interest are continuing especially because of the growing realization of the immense potential of shipwrecks for improving our knowledge of the past.

Writs The existence of writs is an indication of the precocity of pre-1066 English government, since nothing similar survives from contemporary western Europe. A writ conveying instructions to local officials was written on a small piece of parchment, which was given authority by the king's SEAL. The first specimens are from CNUT's reign, but writs only survive in significant numbers from the time of EDWARD THE CONFESSOR. Earlier seals and references to sealed letters suggest an established pattern of oral and written communication, which writs made more formal. Under WILLIAM I THE CONQUEROR, Latin replaced Anglo-Saxon as the language of writs. The COMMON LAW rule that royal judges would only hear cases initiated by writs led to a great increase in demand for them, which resulted in the standardization of routine forms known as 'writs *de cursu*' ('writs of course'). These were normally in the form of letters from the king to SHERIFFS requiring them to take some action. From HENRY II onwards, sheriffs had to endorse and return such writs – known as 'returnable writs' – to the judges as evidence that they had carried out the king's instructions. By such means, the use of writs extended royal authority as far as 'the king's writ ran'.

The multiplication of different types of writ by the royal court became confusing for litigants, and the PROVISIONS OF OXFORD (1258) forbade the creation of new categories of original writs without the permission of the KING'S COUNCIL. However, this was by no means so severe a constraint as often thought, for within the existing categories many new variants were developed thereafter. Thus, it is reckoned that, while early in HENRY III's reign there were only 50 to 60 writs, there were 890 by 1320 and over 2,500 appear in William Rastell's register of writs published in 1531. Further flexibility flowed from the evolution of LEGAL FICTIONS for the common law courts and the dispensation of remedies in equity by newer tribunals, especially the court of CHANCERY. The writs remained the basis of common law procedure until their abolition in 1832, when provision was made for a single form of writ in which the type of action in the traditional categories was stated; even this requirement was abolished in 1852.

Wroxeter (*Viroconium Cornoviorum*), Staffs. This was established as a Roman LEGIONARY FORTRESS within the territory of the CORNOVII in about AD 50 to support military campaigns into Wales. At the end of the 1st century, it was transferred from military to civilian use and became the capital of the *CIVITAS* of the Cornovii. Excavations have shown that urban development was slow, although the circumference of its walls suggests that it was one of the largest towns of Roman Britain.

Wulfhere, King of Mercia (658–75). The son of PENDA OF MERCIA, he reasserted Mercian domination over southern Britain after the short period of NORTHUMBRIAN supremacy that had followed his father's defeat and death at the battle of the Winwaed. Wulfhere's achievements therefore consolidated the Mercian kingdom and helped to lay the basis for the 8th-century achievements of kings ETHELBALD and OFFA.

Wulfstan, Archbishop of York (1002–23). One of the heirs to the literary and educational endeavours of the TENTH-CENTURY REFORM, Wulfstan produced a succession of tracts that culminated in his *INSTITUTES OF POLITY*, and he was also responsible for drafting many of the LAW CODES of kings ETHELRED II THE UNREADY and CNUT. His aim was to instruct kings, bishops and others on their Christian responsibilities, emphasizing the threat to society if Christian precepts were not followed and if the conventional medieval division of people into the three groupings of those who prayed, fought and worked was not sustained.

Wyatt's Rebellion, 1554. A Kentish rising against MARY I, it was led by the younger Sir Thomas Wyatt – one component of an attempted PROTESTANT comeback by members of Northumberland's (*see* DUDLEY, JOHN) regime. Elsewhere, risings were stillborn, and in Kent the attempt to win popular support by stirring opposition to Mary's planned marriage with PHILIP II of Spain lost momentum. Then the government's expeditionary force deserted to the rebels, and Wyatt's forces marched on London. Mary personally steadied the panicked residents of the capital, and the rebel army disintegrated. Wyatt was executed.

Wyclif, John (*c.*1330–84), theologian. An OXFORD radical philosopher, in the 1370s he questioned both papal authority and the clergy's right to property, views that made him useful – as ideologue and propagandist – to the regime headed by JOHN OF GAUNT. In 1377, Pope Gregory XI condemned his opinions on the grounds that they were subversive of all authority. Wyclif responded the following year with his treatise *On the Truth of Holy Writ*, in which he argued that only the Bible was a sure source of authority; then, in 1379, he produced *On the Eucharist*, in which he denied the doctrine of TRANSUBSTANTIATION.

The outbreak of the PEASANTS' REVOLT in 1381, and the role of some preachers in it, meant that the government, already disturbed by Wyclif's refusal to compromise, no longer protected him from ecclesiastical censure; nor did the University of Oxford. In 1382, he withdrew to Lutterworth in Leics., where he continued writing until his death. His followers, driven from Oxford, began to take his ideas to a wider audience – the origin of the LOLLARD movement. Wyclif's conviction that the only certain source of authority was the word of God as revealed in the Bible was the inspiration behind translations of the BIBLE into English. Naturally, early English Protestants looked upon him as 'the morning star of the REFORMATION'.

Wykeham, William of, *see* WILLIAM OF WYKEHAM

Wyntoun, Andrew of, *see* ANDREW OF WYNTOUN

Y

Yalta Conference, second of the 'Big Three' summits attended by CHURCHILL, US President Roosevelt and Soviet Leader Stalin during WORLD WAR II. Held from 4–12 Feb. 1945, it was crucial for deciding the shape of post-war Europe at a point when victory over Nazi Germany was virtually assured. The United States and Britain were forced to acquiesce in effective Soviet influence over much of eastern Europe, with only flimsy guarantees about the future restoration of sovereignty to individual states. Preliminary agreements were reached on German reparations and a French zone of occupation, but the future of Germany was left undecided. The Soviet Union agreed to join the UNITED NATIONS and to enter the war against Japan in return for territorial gains in Manchuria. Yalta was seen by many East Europeans and anti-Communists as a betrayal, with Roosevelt and Churchill failing to stand up to Stalin.

Year Books, unofficial and anonymous reports of pleadings in COMMON LAW cases, and a principal source of procedural authority for pleaders. They begin in the late 13th century and continue into the early 16th century. Their successors, the so-called 'reports', usually bearing the names of famous lawyers and judges, differ not only in that some were printed, but that for the most part they constitute reports of judicial opinions, rather than of pleaders' arguments. The Year Books were written in 'law French', and so too were the reports until the later 17th century. Together the Year Books and reports constitute the essential literature of the law until the treatise, a systematic analysis of a particular aspect of the law, began in the later 18th century to supplement them.

Yeavering, Northumb. One of the principal residences of the NORTHUMBRIAN kings, it is mentioned by BEDE as being important in the days of EDWIN and OSWALD, but was later abandoned. Recent excavations have revealed a remarkable complex of buildings, which included several large halls – one over 27 m (89 ft) long and 13 m (43 ft) wide – and a ceremonial 'grandstand'. It appears to have been unfortified. The whole site is one of the best testimonies to the grandeur of early Anglo-Saxon KINGSHIP.

Yellow Ford, Battle of, 14 Aug. 1598. At this ford on the River Blackwater, Armagh, Hugh O'NEILL achieved his greatest victory, killing the English commander – his own brother-in-law, Sir Henry Bagenal – and defeating his force.

Yelverton's Act, *see* POYNINGS' LAW

YMCA, *see* YOUNG MEN'S CHRISTIAN ASSOCIATION

York, archiepiscopal seat and formerly second city of England. A LEGIONARY FORTRESS from the time of the early conquests, it was made one of the two provincial capitals of Roman Britain in the early 3rd century, and after the reconstruction of its fortifications early in the 4th it became one of the finest towns in the Roman Empire. CONSTANTINE I THE GREAT was proclaimed emperor there. York's importance under the Romans probably explains why it was designated by Pope Gregory the Great as one of the two archbishoprics to be established in England, a privilege it gained in 735 and still enjoys. It was clearly an important ecclesiastical centre in WILFRID's time, and one of its 8th-century products, ALCUIN, became adviser to the Emperor Charlemagne.

The turbulent kingdom of York – created in the 870s by the settlement in northern England of the VIKING armies led by HALFDAN – lasted (with interruptions) until 954, when the last Scandinavian king, ERIC

BLOODAXE, was expelled. During the kingdom's history, there were periods of submission to the English kings of WESSEX, as well as fresh Viking incursions, often from DUBLIN, led by the likes of RAGNALL and OLAF GUTHRICSSON.

Little is known about the way in which the Viking kings ruled what they called 'Jorvik', but what the evidence suggests is that they tried to imitate their English contemporaries. COINS were minted in their names, and their co-operation with successive archbishops of York points to a serious attempt to accept Christianity. The Viking kings' rule also saw the start of the dramatic expansion of the town of York, the population of which has been estimated at around 10,000, making it the second largest in England. ARCHAEOLOGY has unearthed an extraordinary amount of Jorvik.

After the NORMAN CONQUEST, two CASTLES dominated the town and served to establish Norman control in an often hostile region, where the new rulers extended their hegemony only slowly. The great MINSTER, or CATHEDRAL, was founded in 627 by EDWIN, but the present building dates from 1230–1475, representing every phase of GOTHIC architecture. In the later Middle Ages York had a population of some 10,000, and along with NORWICH was one of the two largest cities after LONDON. It had massive town walls, many portions of which survive, numerous churches, and magnificent civic buildings. After the REFORMATION York became the seat of the new COUNCIL OF THE NORTH, and it remained the largest centre of population in the north until the end of the 16th century. Gradually the city slipped from its former position of size and power, and by the 18th century was of county rather than regional or national importance. It became a part of the RAILWAY age with the first of two grand stations, built in 1840, and one of the principal railway engineering works, for the LNER and subsequently British Rail. The survival of York's picturesque ancient streets and buildings has led to its modern revival as a principal centre of tourism.

York, Duke of, *see* JAMES VII AND II

York, Richard of, *see* RICHARD OF YORK

Yorke, Philip, *see* HARDWICKE'S MARRIAGE ACT

Yorkist, the term used to describe the monarchs EDWARD IV, EDWARD V, RICHARD III and their families, descended from Edward IV's father RICHARD OF YORK; it is also a description for their followers in the WARS OF THE ROSES. Members of the Yorkist family who survived after 1485 frequently suffered murderous suspicion from the Tudor dynasty because of their potential rivalry for the throne.

Yorktown, Battle of, 1781, a decisive British defeat in the War of AMERICAN INDEPENDENCE. CORNWALLIS' army, coming from a successful but expensive campaign further south, was trapped and besieged at Yorktown, VIRGINIA by co-ordinated moves by French and American armies. A British fleet failed to drive off the French fleet at the drawn battle of the Chesapeake, and had to withdraw, leaving Cornwallis to surrender unconditionally to General George Washington. This effectively brought the active land war on the North American continent to an end and made the British willing to negotiate recognition of American Independence.

Young England, a TORY 'new party' formed by younger CONSERVATIVE dissidents in the late 1830s and 1840s. This political grouping revolved around George Smythe (later 7th Viscount Strangford), Lord John Manners (later 7th Duke of Rutland), Alexander Baillie-Cochrane and Benjamin DISRAELI, and coalesced in opposition to PEEL's reforming tendencies, frequently speaking and voting against the prime minister and Conservative policies. Disraeli's biographer, Robert Blake, describes the importance of Young England as being symbolic rather than one of measurable achievements, the political equivalent to the OXFORD MOVEMENT in religion, harking back to a world of aristocratic, paternalistic and feudal influence which was lost – or rather had never really existed – and declaring that wealth and high birth had duties as well as privileges. This led the Young England movement into an uneasy coalition of landowners, intellectuals and discontented industrial workers, in opposition to industrialists, WHIGS and shopkeepers, over such issues as the harsh terms of the 1834 POOR LAW AMENDMENT ACT, the Young Englanders' support for extending the terms of the FACTORY Acts, and their sympathy with the IRISH QUESTION, which Disraeli characterized as 'a dense population in extreme distress [inhabiting] an island ... with an absentee aristocracy, and an alien Church and in addition, the weakest executive in the world'. Disraeli's novel *Coningsby* (1844), in which Manners figures as Lord Henry Sydney, well describes the movement's romantic idealism.

Young Ireland, nationalist movement of the 1840s. It attracted supporters of O'CONNELL and middle-class patriots who rejected his alliance with the WHIGS and acceptance of a federal solution to the IRISH QUESTION in lieu of independence. The outbreak of the POTATO FAMINE led to greater militancy and further division as Young Ireland contemplated physical force. The abortive rising organized by William Smith O'Brien in July 1848 led to the arrest or flight of Young Ireland's leaders and the movement's rapid disintegration.

Young Men's Christian Association (YMCA) George Williams (1821–1905) founded this association as an offshoot of his bible and prayer meetings in 1844. It was, and remains, a lay and inter-denominational organization. Its goal has always been to win young men to the service of Jesus Christ through a fellowship based upon a programme of activities designed to train the mind and the body. The YMCA gradually acquired or built premises for hostels and club amenities in most cities and towns of any size. During both World Wars it did sterling service among soldiers, prisoners of war and displaced persons. Its sister society, the Young Women's Christian Association (YWCA), was founded in 1855. It is now an international organization, and also does considerable work in national camps, holiday centres and training courses.

Young Pretender, *see* STUART, CHARLES EDWARD

Ypres, Battles of, Belgium, three battles of WORLD WAR I fought around the town of Ypres (or Ypern), Oct.–Nov. 1914, April–May 1915, and July–Nov. 1917.

The first battle (19 Oct.–11 Nov. 1914) was an Anglo-French defence of Ypres against repeated German attacks. Despite covering itself in glory, the BRITISH EXPEDITIONARY FORCE took such heavy losses that its pre-war character was largely destroyed. The Allies were left with a salient east of Ypres overlooked on three sides by the Germans.

The smaller second battle (22 April–24 May 1915) began with the first large use of poison gas on the western front by the Germans, producing a limited withdrawal by French, British and Canadian troops.

The third battle (31 July–6 Nov. 1917), known as Passchendaele from the village captured at its end, was a British and DOMINION offensive under HAIG on a much larger scale. Intended to break the German line and ultimately liberate Belgium, the attack began well and was on the verge of success by early Oct. Thereafter a combination of good German defence, confused British plans and torrential rainfall produced a final advance of just 8 miles.

As with the SOMME, Haig has been much criticized for his methods and for continuing the attacks into winter. Casualties on both sides were about 300,000 men.

Z

Zambia, *see* RHODESIA, NORTHERN

Zanzibar, large island and trading centre off the coast of east Africa. Unusual in having a predominantly Arab culture, it was the world centre of clove production and the springboard for trading with, and exploration of, the mainland. Britain coerced Zanzibar in 1822 into an agreement to end the east African SLAVE TRADE. Trade treaties with other European nations followed. During the 1880s, Britain gained control of Zanzibar, which became a British protectorate in 1890, and by 1913 Zanzibar was essentially a British colony. From 1925, a system of 'indirect rule' was established. Although the colony was unusually acquiescent, independence movements had grown up by the 1950s and Zanzibar was given internal self-government in June 1963, swiftly followed by independence in Dec. A coup soon after led to union with TANGANYIKA to form Tanzania in April 1964.

Zeppelins, German airships used to carry out the first large-scale aerial bombardment of civilians in raids on England during WORLD WAR I. From 1915 they carried out 51 raids, killing and wounding over 2,000 people.

Zimbabwe, *see* RHODESIA, SOUTHERN

Zinoviev Letter, 25 Oct. 1924, a fraudulent 'Red scare' letter published in British newspapers a few days before the general election called by Ramsay MACDONALD's minority LABOUR government. The government had recognized the Soviet Union and sought to normalize relations, making it vulnerable to charges of Communist sympathies. The letter – allegedly sent to British Communists by Grigori Zinoviev, head of the Communist International, urging revolutionary activity – was one of many forgeries circulating at the time, but was treated as genuine by the Conservative press. The letter's effect on the election is impossible to estimate, but it is widely held to have contributed to the CONSERVATIVE victory, and the episode is still cited as a classic example of the use of the Communist bogey against Labour.

Zulu War, 1879. The Zulu people, in the British colony of NATAL, were fearsome warriors and seemed to pose an increasing threat to the British. In 1878, to provoke a war, the British presented the Zulu king, Cetewayo, with the impossible ultimatum that the Zulu army should be disbanded: in reply the Zulus declared war. They annihilated a large part of the British army at Isandlhwana, an event which led to the events at Rorke's Drift, on 22 Jan. 1879, where a small band of British soldiers gallantly defended their station to the end; the incident became one of the great events of the imperial struggle, and 11 Victoria Crosses for valour were awarded. However, the Zulus were no match for the concerted firepower of the British troops: 2,000 warriors, and 18 British soldiers fell at Nkambule in March 1879, and the Zulu capital of Ulundi was overwhelmed on 4 July (although Cetewayo had begun to sue for peace). The Zulu threat had been eliminated, and the war was a definitive event in Britain's securing of control in southern Africa.

Kings & Queens of the English, England & Britain

Edward the Elder	899–924	Henry VI	1422–61, 1470–1
Athelstan	924–39	Edward IV	1461–70, 1471–83
Edmund	939–46	Edward V	1483
Eadred	946–55	Richard III	1483–5
Eadwig	955–59	Henry VII	1485–1509
Edgar	959–75	Henry VIII	1509–47
Edward the Martyr	975–78	Edward VI	1547–53
Ethelred II the Unready	978–1016	Lady Jane Grey	1553
Edmund Ironside	1016	Mary I	1553–8
Cnut	1016–35	Elizabeth I	1558–1603
Harold I Harefoot	1037–40	James I	1603–25
Harthacnut	1040–42	Charles I	1625–49
Edward the Confessor	1042–66	Charles II	1660–85
Harold II	1066	James II	1685–8
William I	1066–87	William III & Mary II	1688–94
William II	1087–1100	William III	1694–1702
Henry I	1100–35	Anne	1702–14
Stephen	1135–54	George I	1714–27
Henry II	1154–89	George II	1727–60
Richard I	1189–99	George III	1760–1820
John	1199–1216	George IV	1820–30
Henry III	1216–72	William IV	1830–7
Edward I	1272–1307	Victoria	1837–1901
Edward II	1307–27	Edward VII	1901–10
Edward III	1327–77	George V	1910–36
Richard II	1377–99	Edward VIII	1936
Henry IV	1399–1413	George VI	1936–52
Henry V	1413–22	Elizabeth II	1952–

British Prime Ministers

Robert Walpole, 2nd Earl of Orford	1721–42
Spencer Compton, 1st Earl of Wilmington	1742–3
Henry Pelham	1743–54
Thomas Pelham-Holles, 4th Duke of Newcastle	1754–6
William Cavendish, 4th Duke of Devonshire	1756–7
William Pitt the Elder	1757–61
Thomas Pelham-Holles, 4th Duke of Newcastle	1757–62
John Stuart, 3rd Earl of Bute	1762–3
George Grenville	1763–5
Charles Wentworth, 2nd Marquess of Rockingham	1765–6
William Pitt the Elder	1766–7
Augustus Fitzroy, 3rd Duke of Grafton	1767–70
Frederick North, 2nd Earl of Guildford	1770–82
Charles Wentworth, 2nd Marquess of Rockingham	1782
William Petty, Earl of Shelburne	1782–3
William Cavendish Bentinck, 3rd Duke of Portland	1783
William Pitt the Younger	1783–1801
Henry Addington	1801–4
William Pitt the Younger	1804–6
William Grenville, 1st Baron Grenville	1806–7

William Cavendish Bentinck, 3rd Duke of Portland	1807–9
Spencer Perceval	1809–12
Robert Jenkinson, 2nd Earl of Liverpool	1812–27
George Canning	1827
Frederick Robinson, Viscount Goderich, 1st Earl of Ripon	1827–8
Arthur Wellesley, 1st Duke of Wellington	1828–30
Charles Grey, 2nd Earl Grey	1830–4
William Lamb, 2nd Viscount Melbourne	1834
Robert Peel	1834–5
William Lamb, 2nd Viscount Melbourne	1835–41
Robert Peel	1841–6
Lord John Russell, 1st Earl Russell	1846–52
Edward Stanley, 23rd Earl of Derby	1852
George Gordon, 4th Earl of Aberdeen	1852–5
John Temple, 3rd Viscount Palmerston	1855–8
Edward Stanley, 23rd Earl of Derby	1858–9
John Temple, 3rd Viscount Palmerston	1859–65
Lord John Russell, 1st Earl Russell	1865–6
Edward Stanley, 23rd Earl of Derby	1866–8
Benjamin Disraeli, 1st Earl of Beaconsfield	1868
W. E. Gladstone	1868–74
Benjamin Disraeli, 1st Earl of Beaconsfield	1874–80
W. E. Gladstone	1880–5
Robert Cecil, 3rd Marquess of Salisbury	1885–6
W. E. Gladstone	1886
Robert Cecil, 3rd Marquess of Salisbury	1886–92
W. E. Gladstone	1892–4
Archibald Primrose, 5th Earl of Rosebery	1894–5
Robert Cecil, 3rd Marquess of Salisbury	1895–1902
A. J. Balfour	1902–5
Henry Campbell-Bannerman	1905–8
H. H. Asquith	1908–16
Andrew Bonar Law	1922–3
Stanley Baldwin	1923–4
Ramsay MacDonald	1924
Stanley Baldwin	1924–9
Ramsey MacDonald	1929–35
Stanley Baldwin	1935–7
Neville Chamberlain	1937–40
Winston Churchill	1940–5
Clement Attlee	1945–51
Winston Churchill	1951–5
Anthony Eden	1955–7
Harold Macmillan	1957–63
Alec Douglas-Home	1963–4
Harold Wilson	1964–70
Edward Heath	1970–4
Harold Wilson	1974–6
James Callaghan	1976–9
Margaret Thatcher	1979–90
John Major	1990–7
Tony Blair	1997–

READ MORE IN PENGUIN

READ MORE IN PENGUIN

HISTORY

A History of Twentieth-Century Russia Robert Service

'A remarkable work of scholarship and synthesis . . . [it] demands to be read' *Spectator*. 'A fine book . . . It is a dizzying tale and Service tells it well; he has none of the ideological baggage that has so often bedevilled Western histories of Russia . . . A balanced, dispassionate and painstaking account' *Sunday Times*

A Monarchy Transformed: Britain 1603–1714 Mark Kishlansky

'Kishlansky's century saw one king executed, another exiled, the House of Lords abolished, and the Church of England reconstructed along Presbyterian lines . . . A masterly narrative, shot through with the shrewdness that comes from profound scholarship' *Spectator*

American Frontiers Gregory H. Nobles

'At last someone has written a narrative of America's frontier experience with sensitivity and insight. This is a book which will appeal to both the specialist and the novice' James M. McPherson, Princeton University

The Pleasures of the Past David Cannadine

'This is almost everything you ever wanted to know about the past but were too scared to ask . . . A fascinating book and one to strike up arguments in the pub' *Daily Mail*. 'He is erudite and rigorous, yet always fun. I can imagine no better introduction to historical study than this collection' *Observer*

Prague in Black and Gold Peter Demetz

'A dramatic and compelling history of a city Demetz admits to loving and hating . . . He embraces myth, economics, sociology, linguistics and cultural history . . . His reflections on visiting Prague after almost a half-century are a moving elegy on a world lost through revolutions, velvet or otherwise' *Literary Review*

READ MORE IN PENGUIN

HISTORY

The Vikings Else Roesdahl

Far from being just 'wild, barbaric, axe-wielding pirates', the Vikings created complex social institutions, oversaw the coming of Christianity to Scandinavia and made a major impact on European history through trade, travel and far-flung colonization. This study is a rich and compelling picture of an extraordinary civilization.

A Short History of Byzantium John Julius Norwich

In this abridgement of his celebrated trilogy, John Julius Norwich has created a definitive overview of 'the strange, savage, yet endlessly fascinating world of Byzantium'. 'A real life epic of love and war, accessible to anyone' *Independent on Sunday*

The Eastern Front 1914–1917 Norman Stone

'Without question one of the classics of post-war historical scholarship' Niall Ferguson. 'Fills an enormous gap in our knowledge and understanding of the Great War' *Sunday Telegraph*

The Idea of India Sunil Khilnani

'Many books about India will be published this year; I doubt if any will be wiser and more illuminating about its modern condition than this' *Observer*. 'Sunil Khilnani's meditation on India since Independence is a *tour de force*' *Sunday Telegraph*

The Penguin History of Europe J. M. Roberts

'J. M. Roberts has managed to tell the rich and remarkable tale of European history in fewer than 700 fascinating, well-written pages . . . few would ever be able to match this achievement' *The New York Times Book Review*. 'The best single-volume history of Europe' *The Times Literary Supplement*

READ MORE IN PENGUIN

HISTORY

Hope and Glory: Britain 1900–1990 Peter Clarke

'Splendid ... If you want a text book for the century, this is it' *Independent*. 'Clarke has written one of the classic works of modern history. His erudition is encyclopaedic, yet lightly and wittily borne. He writes memorably, with an eye for the telling detail, an ear for aphorism, and an instinct for irony' *Sunday Telegraph*

Instruments of Darkness: Witchcraft in England 1550–1750
James Sharpe

'Learned and enthralling ... Time and again, as I read this scrupulously balanced work of scholarship, I was reminded of contemporary parallels' Jan Morris, *Independent*

A Social History of England Asa Briggs

Asa Briggs's magnificent exploration of English society has been totally revised and brought right up to the present day. 'A treasure house of scholarly knowledge ... beautifully written, and full of the author's love of his country, its people and its landscape' *Sunday Times*

Hatchepsut: The Female Pharaoh Joyce Tyldesley

Queen – or, as she would prefer to be remembered king – Hatchepsut was an astonishing woman. Defying tradition, she became the female embodiment of a male role, dressing in men's clothes and even wearing a false beard. Joyce Tyldesley's dazzling piece of detection strips away the myths and restores the female pharaoh to her rightful place.

Fifty Years of Europe: An Album Jan Morris

'A highly insightful kaleidoscopic encyclopedia of European life ... Jan Morris writes beautifully ... Like a good vintage wine [*Fifty Years*] has to be sipped and savoured rather than gulped. Then it will keep warming your soul for many years to come' *Observer*

READ MORE IN PENGUIN

REFERENCE

The Penguin Dictionary of the Third Reich
James Taylor and Warren Shaw

This dictionary provides a full background to the rise of Nazism and the role of Germany in the Second World War. Among the areas covered are the major figures from Nazi politics, arts and industry, the German Resistance, the politics of race and the Nuremberg trials.

The Penguin Biographical Dictionary of Women

This stimulating, informative and entirely new Penguin dictionary of women from all over the world, through the ages, contains over 1,600 clear and concise biographies on major figures from politicians, saints and scientists to poets, film stars and writers.

Roget's Thesaurus of English Words and Phrases
Edited by Betty Kirkpatrick

This new edition of Roget's classic work, now brought up to date for the nineties, will increase anyone's command of the English language. Fully cross-referenced, it includes synonyms of every kind (formal or colloquial, idiomatic and figurative) for almost 900 headings. It is a must for writers and utterly fascinating for any English speaker.

The Penguin Dictionary of International Relations
Graham Evans and Jeffrey Newnham

International relations have undergone a revolution since the end of the Cold War. This new world disorder is fully reflected in this new Penguin dictionary, which is extensively cross-referenced with a select bibliography to aid further study.

The Penguin Guide to Synonyms and Related Words
S. I. Hayakawa

'More helpful than a thesaurus, more humane than a dictionary, the *Guide to Synonyms and Related Words* maps linguistic boundaries with precision, sensitivity to nuance and, on occasion, dry wit' *The Times Literary Supplement*

READ MORE IN PENGUIN

DICTIONARIES

Abbreviations
Ancient History
Archaeology
Architecture
Art and Artists
Astronomy
Biographical Dictionary of Women
Biology
Botany
Building
Business
Challenging Words
Chemistry
Civil Engineering
Classical Mythology
Computers
Contemporary American History
Curious and Interesting Geometry
Curious and Interesting Numbers
Curious and Interesting Words
Design and Designers
Economics
Eighteenth-Century History
Electronics
English and European History
English Idioms
Foreign Terms and Phrases
French
Geography
Geology
German
Historical Slang
Human Geography
Information Technology
International Finance
International Relations
Literary Terms and Literary Theory
Mathematics
Modern History 1789–1945
Modern Quotations
Music
Musical Performers
Nineteenth-Century World History
Philosophy
Physical Geography
Physics
Politics
Proverbs
Psychology
Quotations
Quotations from Shakespeare
Religions
Rhyming Dictionary
Russian
Saints
Science
Sociology
Spanish
Surnames
Symbols
Synonyms and Antonyms
Telecommunications
Theatre
The Third Reich
Third World Terms
Troublesome Words
Twentieth-Century History
Twentieth-Century Quotations